PRINCE'S BIEBER DICTIONARY OF LEGAL CITATIONS

A Reference Guide for Attorneys, Legal Secretaries, Paralegals, and Law Students

Sixth Edition
by
Mary Miles Prince

William S. Hein & Co., Inc.
Buffalo, New York
2001

Library of Congress Cataloging-In-Publication Data

Prince, Mary Miles.
  Prince's Bieber dictionary of legal citations : a reference guide
for attorneys, legal secretaries, paralegals, and law students.—
6th ed. / by Mary Miles Prince.

  p.   cm.
  ISBN 1-57588-669-3 (cloth : alk. paper)
  1. Law—United States—Abbreviations. 2. Citation of legal
authorities—United States. I. Title: Dictionary of Legal Citations.
II. Bieber, Doris M. Current American legal citations. III. Title.
KF246.P73 2001
349.73'01'48—dc21   2001024375

Printed in the United States of America

This volume is printed on acid-free paper.

To
Raymond and Caroline

Table of Contents

Publisher's Note vii

Preface ix

Prince's Bieber Dictionary of Legal Citations 1

Tables:
    1. States' Highest Courts 485
    2. Discontinued State Reporters 487
    3. Year, Congress & Session, Volume Numbers 489
    4. Numbering Acts of Congress 493

Appendix: The Bluebook: A Uniform System of Citation,
Seventeenth Edition (2000) 495

Publisher's Note

William S. Hein & Co., Inc. extends special thanks to the Columbia Law Review Association et al. for its permission to include The Bluebook: A Uniform System of Citation, Seventeenth Edition, as an appendix to Prince's Bieber Dictionary of Legal Citations, Sixth Edition. The inclusion of this appendix allows users the convenience of examining the source for the rules demonstrated in Prince's Bieber Dictionary without ever having to put the book down.

Preface

Prince's Bieber Dictionary of Legal Citations, Sixth Edition, is intended to assist the legal professional in citing legal authorities according to the rules given in The Bluebook: A Uniform System of Citation, Seventeenth Edition (2000). The publisher is pleased to again have reprint rights to The Bluebook, and the two books are bound together for user convenience.

Prince's Bieber Dictionary is meant to be a companion to The Bluebook, not a replacement, applying Bluebook rules to a representative collection of common legal authorities, which rules may be readily consulted by turning to the Bluebook portion of this publication. The citations included in Prince's Bieber Dictionary are based on Bluebook rules, and the abbreviations are those found in The Bluebook or derived from its guidelines.

Although The Bluebook does establish uniformity in citation form for court documents, the practitioner should remember that the specific citation rules contained in local rules, state supreme court rules, rules of trial or appellate procedure, and statutes supersede Bluebook rules. For the first time, Prince's Bieber Dictionary includes references to state court rules along with examples of how to cite cases according to those rules.

In addition to state court rule references and examples, this edition has been updated to reflect 17th Edition Bluebook revisions, along with numerous edition and title changes for entries found in the previous edition and many altogether new or revised entries, including additional books and periodicals, revised signal information, examples for citing patents, forthcoming publications, appendices, state administrative compilations, and The Bluebook itself, and revised and expanded public domain, electronic media, and book review entries. Also new with this edition is information contributed by Bernard J. Sussman, Law Librarian, United States Court of Appeals for Veterans Claims, providing users with a table of the names used by each state for its highest court; discontinued state reporter information; a table of years, showing for each year the Congress and session number, the volume numbers for the Congressional Record, for the <u>Statutes at Large</u>, and for the <u>Federal Register</u> for that year; and information about the numbering systems for federal legislation. <u>See</u> Tables.

Typeface conventions used for the examples in this book are those prescribed by <u>The Bluebook</u> for practitioners composing briefs and court documents. Therefore, ordinary type and underscoring are used in this book rather than, as in the writing of law review articles, ordinary roman type, italics, and large and small caps. The running footnote information concerning typeface conventions for those writing law review articles has also been updated.

The user should bear in mind that some publications, particularly foreign, frequently provide only the authors' initials and not first names and, therefore, cannot be cited precisely by current <u>Bluebook</u> rules.

Please note that the legal abbreviations listed are those found in <u>The Bluebook</u> or derived from its guidelines. For extensive lists of general legal abbreviations, consult <u>Bieber's Dictionary of Legal Abbreviations</u>, Fifth Edition,[1] and <u>World Dictionary of Legal Abbreviations</u>.[2]

I wish to thank Pauline Aranas, Assistant Dean for Library and Information Technology, Vanderbilt University Law School, for her support; Bernard J. Sussman for his suggestions and contributions to this reference work; Sherry S. Willis and Stephen M. Jackson for the proficiency of their typing; and for their assistance with the overall production of the Sixth Edition: Raymond Graham Prince, Yanika C. Smith, Stephen M. Jackson, and Anita Keteku.

Mary Miles Prince

---

[1]Mary Miles Prince, *Bieber's Dictionary of Legal Abbreviations* (5th ed. 2001).
[2]Igor I. Kavass & Mary Miles Prince, *World Dictionary of Legal Abbreviations* (1991).

PRINCE'S BIEBER DICTIONARY OF LEGAL CITATIONS

A

ABA
See American Bar Association publications.

ABA Journal
See American Bar Association Journal.

ABF
See American Bar Foundation publications.

abridged
Ab.:   abr.

Accord

–" 'Accord' is commonly used when two or more cases state or clearly support the proposition but the text quotes or refers to only one; the others are then introduced by 'accord.' " Bluebook Rule 1.2(a).

Ex.:   Usery v. Kennecott Copper Corp., 577 F.2d 1113 (10th Cir. 1977); accord, Marshall v. Union Oil Co., 616 F.2d 1113 (9th Cir. 1980).

"Furthermore, conclusory allegations unsupported by any factual assertions will not withstand a motion to dismiss. Briscoe v. LaHue, 663 F.2d 713, 723 (7th Cir. 1981). Accord Hiland Dairy, Inc. v. Kroger Co., 402 F.2d 968, 973 (8th Cir. 1968), cert. denied, 395 U.S. 961, 89 S. Ct. 2096, 23 L. Ed. 2d 748 (1969) (In testing the legal sufficiency of the complaint, conclusions of law and unreasonable inference or unwarranted deductions of fact are not admitted.)" –Taken from 675 F.2d 881 (1982).

Accountancy Law Reports (Commerce Clearing House)
Ab.:   Accountancy L. Rep. (CCH)

Accounting Standards, Generally Accepted
Ex.:   Accounting for the Costs of Computer Software to be Sold, Leased or Otherwise Marketed, Statement of Financial Accounting Standards No. 86, § 16 (Financial Accounting Standards Bd. 1985).

Acts and Joint Resolutions of the State of Iowa
Ab.:   year Iowa Acts
Ex.:   Act of Mar. 4, 1998, ch. 1010, 1999 Iowa Acts 7 (relating to the creation of a dental hygiene committee). –Citation to an entire session law.

In law review footnotes, the titles of books and the names of cases, except for procedural phrases, are not underlined. See Bluebook Rule 2.1(a). Further, the following are in large and small capitals: codes, restatements, standards, constitutions, periodicals, authors of books, titles of books, the abbreviated names of codes, most legislative materials except for bills and resolutions, codified ordinances, model codes, court rules, and sentencing guidelines. Refer to The Bluebook.

Act of Mar. 4, 1998, ch. 1010, sec. 1, § 147.14, 1999 Iowa Acts 7, 7.
–Citation to a section of a session law amending a prior act.

Acts and Joint Resolutions of South Carolina
Ab.:   year S.C. Acts
Ex.:   South Carolina Bed and Breakfast Act, ch. 4, 1998 S.C. Acts 1929.
–Citation to an entire session law.
South Carolina Bed and Breakfast Act, ch. 4, sec. 45-4-30-(A), 1998
S.C. Acts 1929, 1930. –Citation to a section of a session law.
–Identifying information may be added parenthetically according to
Bluebook Rule 12.4(a).

Acts and Resolves of Massachusetts
Ab.:   year Mass. Acts no.
Ex.:   Act of Apr. 25, 1997, ch. 9, 1997 Mass. Acts 38. –Citation to an entire
session law.
Act of Apr. 25, 1997, ch. 9, sec. 1, 1997 Mass. Acts 38, 38. –Citation
to a section of a session law.
–Identifying information may be added parenthetically according to
Bluebook Rule 12.4(a).

Acts and Resolves of Rhode Island and Providence Plantations
Ab.:   year R.I. Acts & Resolves

Acts and Resolves of Vermont
Ab.:   year Vt. Acts and Resolves
Ex.:   Act of Jan. 24, 1996, No. 65, 1996 Vt. Acts and Resolves 2 (relating to
tracking and killing of injured wildlife). –Citation to an entire session
law.
Act of Feb. 1, 1996, No. 67 sec. 1, § 801(a), 1996 Vt. Acts and
Resolves 3 (relating to motor vehicle financial responsibility).
–Citation to a section of a session law amending a prior act.

Acts, Indiana
Ab.:   year Ind. Acts no.
Ex.:   Act of Mar. 11, 1996, Pub. L. No. 15-1996, 1996-2 Ind. Acts 1029.
–Citation to an entire session law.
Act of Mar. 11, 1996, Pub. L. No. 15-1996, § 2, 1996-2 Ind. Acts
1029, 1030-33. –Citation to a section of a session law.
–Identifying information may be added parenthetically according to
Bluebook Rule 12.4(a).

Acts of Alabama
Ab.:   year Ala. Acts no.

In citing cases in law review footnotes, abbreviate any word listed in Table T.6;
the names of "states, countries, and other geographical units" unless they are named parties;
and any other words of eight or more letters "if substantial space is thereby saved and the
result is unambiguous." Bluebook Rule 10.2.2. On the other hand, in citing cases in text,
abbreviate only widely known acronyms and the following words: "&," "Ass'n," "Bros.,"
"Co.," "Corp.," "Inc.," "Ltd.," and "No." Bluebook Rule 10.2.1(c).

Ex.:   Act of July 19, 1995, No. 95-364, 1995-1 Ala. Acts 734. –Citation to
          an entire session law.

          Act of July 19, 1995, No. 95-364, § 2, 1995-1 Ala. Acts 734.
          –Citation to a section of a session law.

          –Identifying information may be added parenthetically according to
          Bluebook Rule 12.4(a).

Acts of Congress
Ab.:   Pub. L.
Ex.:   Act of June 13, 1978, Pub. L. No. 95-292, 92 Stat. 307. –Act Citation.

          Act of June 13, 1978, Pub. L. No. 95-292, § 4, 92 Stat. 307, 315.
          –Section Citation.

Acts of the General Assembly of the Commonwealth of Virginia
Ab.:   year Va. Acts ch.
Ex.:   Act of Apr. 6, 1995, ch. 824, 1995 Va. Acts 1693 (relating to stalking).
          –Citation to an entire session law.

          Act of Apr. 6, 1995, ch. 824, sec. 1, § 18.2-60.3, 1995 Va. Acts 1693,
          1693 (penalty for stalking). –Citation to a section of a session law
          amending a prior act.

Acts of the Legislature of West Virginia
Ab.:   year W. Va. Acts no.

Ex.:   Act of Mar. 11, 1995, ch. 166, 1995 W. Va. Acts 1251. –Citation to an
          entire session law.

          Act of Mar. 11, 1995, ch. 166, art. 1 § 9-1-2, 1995 W. Va. Acts 1251,
          1152-54. –Citation to a section of a session law.
          –Identifying information may be added parenthetically according to
          Bluebook Rule 12.4(a).

Acts of the Parliaments of Scotland, The
Ab.:   Scot. Parl. Acts

Acts of the Parliament of Southern Australia
Ab.:   S. Austl. Acts

Acts, Resolves and Constitutional Resolutions of the State of Maine
Ab.:   year Me. Acts

addenda
          –Explained and illustrated in Bluebook Rule 3.5.

Adelaide Law Review
Ab.:   Adel. L. Rev.

In law review footnotes, the titles of books and the names of cases, except for procedural
phrases, are not underlined. See Bluebook Rule 2.1(a). Further, the following are in large
and small capitals: codes, restatements, standards, constitutions, periodicals, authors of
books, titles of books, the abbreviated names of codes, most legislative materials except for
bills and resolutions, codified ordinances, model codes, court rules, and sentencing guidelines.
Refer to The Bluebook.

Ex.:   Keith Bennetts, <u>Bankruptcy: Its Consequences for Family Property</u>,
         11 Adel. L. Rev. 413 (1988). –Article Citation.

         Keith Bennetts, <u>Bankruptcy: Its Consequences for Family Property</u>,
         11 Adel. L. Rev. 413, 426-27 (1988). –Page Citation.

Administrative Adjudications and Arbitrations
See <u>Bluebook</u> Rule 14.3

Administrative Decisions under Immigration and Nationality Laws
Ab.:   I. & N. Dec.

Ex.:   <u>TEE</u>, 20 I. & N. Dec. 949 (B.I.A. 1995).

         <u>Hector Ponce De Leon-Ruiz</u>, Interim Decision No. 3261 (B.I.A. Jan. 3,
         1996). –Citation to current unbound material.

Administrative Law, by Bernard Schwartz
–Do not abbreviate the title.

Ex.:   Bernard Schwartz, <u>Administrative Law</u> § 6.9 (3d ed. 1991). –Section
         Citation.

         Bernard Schwartz, <u>Administrative Law</u> § 6.9, at 317 (3d ed. 1991).
         –Page Citation.

         Bernard Schwartz, <u>Administrative Law</u> § 6.9, at 317 n.10 (3d ed.
         1991). –Footnote Citation.

Administrative Law Journal
Ab.: Admin. L.J.

Ex.:   Marshall Breger, <u>Comments on Bernard Schwartz' Essay</u>, 5 Admin.
         L.J. 347 (1991). –Article Citation.

         Marshall Breger, <u>Comments on Bernard Schwartz' Essay</u>, 5 Admin.
         L.J. 347, 351-52 (1991). –Page Citation.

Administrative Law Journal of American University
Ab.:   Admin. L. J. Am. U.

Administrative Law Judge
Ab.:   A.L.J.

Administrative Law Review
Ab.:   Admin. L. Rev.

Ex.:   Sidney A. Shapiro, <u>Reflections on Teaching Administrative Law: Time
         for a Sequel</u>, 43 Admin. L. Rev. 501 (1991). –Article Citation.

         Sidney A. Shapiro, <u>Reflections on Teaching Administrative Law: Time
         for a Sequel</u>, 43 Admin. L. Rev. 501, 503-504 (1991). –Page Citation.

Administrative Law Third (Pike & Fischer)
Ab.:   Admin. L.3d (P & F)

In citing cases in law review footnotes, abbreviate any word listed in Table T.6;
the names of "states, countries, and other geographical units" unless they are named parties;
and any other words of eight or more letters "if <u>substantial</u> space is thereby saved and the
result is unambiguous." <u>Bluebook</u> Rule 10.2.2. On the other hand, in citing cases in text,
abbreviate only widely known acronyms and the following words: "&," "Ass'n," "Bros.,"
"Co.," "Corp.," "Inc.," "Ltd.," and "No." <u>Bluebook</u> Rule 10.2.1(c).

Ex.:   <u>Vulcan Arber Hill Corp. v. Reich</u>, [Decisions 10] Admin. L.3d (P&F)
        306 (D.C. Cir. April 19, 1996). –Citation to looseleaf material.

        <u>United States v. White</u>, 67 Admin. L.3d (P&F) 376 (2d Cir. 1988).
        –Citation to bound material.

        –The above examples are proper if the case is not yet available in, or is
        not reported in, an official or West reporter, a public domain citation,
        or in a widely used computer database.

        <u>River Parishes Co. v. Ornet Primoy Aluminum Corp.</u>, [10 Decisions]
        Admin. L.3d (P&F) 944 (F.M.C. Aug. 15, 1996). –Citation to
        administrative looseleaf material.

Administrative Law Treatise, by Kenneth C. Davis and Richard S. Pierce, Sr.
        –Do not abbreviate the title.

Ex.:   2 Kenneth C. Davis & Richard S. Pierce, Sr., <u>Administrative Law
        Treatise</u> § 9.10 (3d ed. 1994).). –Section Citation.

        3 Kenneth C. Davis & Richard S. Pierce, Sr., <u>Administrative Law
        Treatise</u> § 9.10, at 103 (3d ed. 1994).). –Page Citation.

        Kenneth C. Davis & Richard S. Pierce, Sr., <u>Administrative Law
        Treatise</u> § 9.10 (3d ed. Supp. 2000). –Supplement citation.

Administrative Rules of Montana
Ab.:   Mont. Admin. R. (year).
Ex.:   Mont. Admin. R. 2.43.604 (2001).

Administrative Rules of South Dakota
Ab.:   S.D. Admin. R. (year)
Ex.:   S.D. Admin. R. 20:04:15:152 (2000).

Admiralty [Court, Division]
Ab.:   Adm.

Admiralty and Maritime Law
        –Do not abbreviate the title.

Ex.:   Thomas J. Schoenbaum, <u>Admiralty and Maritime Law</u> § 16-1 (3d ed.
        2001). –Section Citation.

        Thomas J. Schoenbaum, <u>Admiralty and Maritime Law</u> § 16-1, at 879
        (3d ed. 2001). –Page Citation.

Advance Legislative Service to the General Statutes of North Carolina
Ab.:   N.C. Adv. Legis. Serv.

In law review footnotes, the titles of books and the names of cases, except for procedural
phrases, are not underlined. <u>See</u> <u>Bluebook</u> Rule 2.1(a). Further, the following are in large
and small capitals: codes, restatements, standards, constitutions, periodicals, authors of
books, titles of books, the abbreviated names of codes, most legislative materials except for
bills and resolutions, codified ordinances, model codes, court rules, and sentencing guidelines.
Refer to <u>The Bluebook</u>.

Ex.:   Act of June 21, 1996, ch. 712, 1996 N.C. Adv. Legis. Serv. 437
         (concerning impersonating law-enforcement or other public officers).
         –Citation to an entire session law.

         Act of June 21, 1996, ch. 712, sec. 1, § 14-277, 1996 N.C. Adv. Legis.
         Serv. 437, 437 (concerning impersonating law-enforcement or other
         public officers). –Citation to a section of a session law.

         –"Cite to N.C. Sess. Laws if therein." Bluebook Table T.1, p. 206.

Advisory Opinions
See Bluebook Rule 14.4.

Advocacy
Ab.:   Advoc.

Affirmative Action Compliance Manual for Federal Contractors (Bureau of National Affairs)
Ab.:   Aff. Action Compl. Man. (BNA)

Ex.:   Causal Agents and Theories of Discrimination, 2 Aff. Action Compl.
         Man. (BNA) ¶ 7003 (March 1995).

affirmed
Ab.:   aff'd

Ex.:   Cuppy v. Ward, 187 A.D. 625, 176 N.Y.S. 233, aff'd, 227 N.Y. 603,
         125 N.E. 915 (1919).

         68th St. Apts., Inc. v. Lauricella, 142 N.J. Super. 546, 362 A.2d 78
         (Law Div. 1976), aff'd per curiam, 150 N.J. Super. 47, 374 A.2d 1222
         (App. Div. 1977).

See Bluebook Rule 10.7 and Table T.9.

Agriculture Decisions (U.S.) (1942-date)
Ab.:   Agric. Dec.

Ex.:   Berriman Live Poultry Corp., 1 Agric. Dec. 53 (1942).

         Victor Fruit Growers, Inc., 1 Agric. Dec. 108 (1942).

         George Blades, 40 Agric. Dec. 1725 (1981). –Citation to current
         unbound material.

Agriculture
Ab.:   Agric.

AIDS Law & Litigation Reporter
Ab.:   AIDS L. & Litig. Rep. (Univ. Pub. Group)

Ex.:   Weeks v. Scott, 3 AIDS L. & Litig. Rep. (Univ. Pub. Group) 416
         (5th Cir. June 23, 1995).

         –This example is proper if the case is not yet available in, or is not
          reported in, an official or West reporter, a public domain citation, or
          in a widely used computer database.

In citing cases in law review footnotes, abbreviate any word listed in Table T.6;
the names of "states, countries, and other geographical units" unless they are named parties;
and any other words of eight or more letters "if substantial space is thereby saved and the
result is unambiguous." Bluebook Rule 10.2.2. On the other hand, in citing cases in text,
abbreviate only widely known acronyms and the following words: "&," "Ass'n," "Bros.,"
"Co.," "Corp.," "Inc.," "Ltd.," and "No." Bluebook Rule 10.2.1(c).

Air and Space Lawyer
    Ab.:   Air & Space Law.
    Ex.:   Rudolph V. Pino, Jr. & Frank A. Silane, <u>Civil Liability in Commercial Space Ventures Under United States Law</u>, Air & Space Law., Fall 1991, at 5. —Article Citation.

            Rudolph V. Pino, Jr. & Frank A. Silane, <u>Civil Liability in Commercial Space Ventures Under United States Law</u>, Air & Space Law., Fall 1991, at 5, 6-7. —Page Citation.

Air Force Law Review
    Ab.:   A.F. L. Rev.
    Ex.:   Jessica W. Julian, <u>Noriega: The Capture of a State Leader and Its Implications on Domestic Law</u>, 34 A.F. L. Rev. 153 (1991). –Article Citation.

            Jessica W. Julian, <u>Noriega: The Capture of a State Leader and Its Implications on Domestic Law</u>, 34 A.F. L. Rev. 153, 155-58 (1991). –Page Citation.

Air Law
    Ab.:   Air L.
    Ex.:   Yi Lu, <u>Legal Issues on Aircraft Finance in China</u>, Air L., 1991, at 2. –Article Citation.

            Yi Lu, <u>Legal Issues on Aircraft Finance in China</u>, Air L., 1991, at 2, 7-8. –Page Citation.

            Note Air Law:

                1975 vol. 1 - 1982 vol. 7—Consecutively paginated.

                1983 vol. 8 - present—Nonconsecutively paginated.

Akron Law Review
    Ab.:   Akron L. Rev.
    Ex.:   Frank P. Darr, <u>Deregulation of Telephone Services in Ohio</u>, 24 Akron L. Rev. 229 (1990). –Article Citation.

            Frank P. Darr, <u>Deregulation of Telephone Services in Ohio</u>, 24 Akron L. Rev. 229, 250-51 (1990). –Page Citation.

Akron Tax Journal
    Ab.:   Akron Tax J.
    Ex.:   Nicola Preston, <u>The Interpretation of Taxing Statutes: The English Perspective</u>, 7 Akron Tax J. 43 (1990). –Article Citation.

            Nicola Preston, <u>The Interpretation of Taxing Statutes: The English Perspective</u>, 7 Akron Tax J. 43, 55-59 (1990). –Page Citation.

Alabama Acts
    <u>See</u> Acts of Alabama.

In law review footnotes, the titles of books and the names of cases, except for procedural phrases, are not underlined. <u>See</u> Bluebook Rule 2.1(a). Further, the following are in large and small capitals: codes, restatements, standards, constitutions, periodicals, authors of books, titles of books, the abbreviated names of codes, most legislative materials except for bills and resolutions, codified ordinances, model codes, court rules, and sentencing guidelines. Refer to <u>The Bluebook</u>.

Alabama Administrative Code
Ab.:   Ala. Admin. Code r. (Year)

Ex.:   Ala. Admin. Code r. 70-X-.01 (1992).

Alabama Appellate Court Reports
Ab.:   Ala. App.

–Discontinued after 57 Ala. App. 740 (1975).

–Cite to So. or So. 2d if therein; otherwise, cite to Ala. App.

–Give parallel citations only in documents submitted to Alabama state courts. (Note: In citing a state court case in a document submitted to a court of that same state, the 16th ed. of The Bluebook prescribed a parallel citation; the 17th ed. prescribes that local rules shall control, but Alabama has no known local rules concerning parallel citations. For the sake of continuity, we advise giving a parallel citation in documents submitted to Alabama state courts. See Bluebook Rule 10.3.1 and Practitioners' Note P.3.)

Ex.:

–Before 45 Ala. App. 1 (1969) cite as follows:

In documents submitted to Alabama state courts:

Rivers v. Johnston, 44 Ala. App. 398, 210 So. 2d 707 (1968). –Case citation.

Rivers v. Johnston, 44 Ala. App. 398, 400, 210 So. 2d 707, 709 (1968). –Page citation.

In all other documents:

Rivers v. Johnston, 210 So. 2d 707 (Ala. Ct. App. 1968). –Case Citation.

Rivers v. Johnston, 210 So. 2d 707, 709 (Ala. Ct. App. 1968). –Page Citation.

–After 45 Ala. App. 1 (1969) and through 57 Ala. App. 740 (1975), cite as follows:

In documents submitted to Alabama state courts:

Holsombeck v. Pate, 47 Ala. App. 39, 249 So. 2d 861 (Civ. App. 1971). –Case Citation.

Holsombeck v. Pate, 47 Ala. App. 39, 42, 249 So. 2d 861, 864 (Civ. App. 1971). –Page Citation.

Hood v. State, 47 Ala. App. 192, 252 So. 2d 117 (Crim. App. 1971). –Case Citation.

Hood v. State, 47 Ala. App. 192, 197, 252 So. 2d 117, 120 (Crim. App. 1971). –Page Citation.

In all other documents:

In citing cases in law review footnotes, abbreviate any word listed in Table T.6; the names of "states, countries, and other geographical units" unless they are named parties; and any other words of eight or more letters "if substantial space is thereby saved and the result is unambiguous." Bluebook Rule 10.2.2. On the other hand, in citing cases in text, abbreviate only widely known acronyms and the following words: "&," "Ass'n," "Bros.," "Co.," "Corp.," "Inc.," "Ltd.," and "No." Bluebook Rule 10.2.1(c).

Holsombeck v. Pate, 249 So. 2d 861 (Ala. Civ. App. 1971).
–Case Citation.

Holsombeck v. Pate, 249 So. 2d 861, 864 (Ala. Civ. App. 1971).
–Page Citation.

Hood v. State, 252 So. 2d 117 (Ala. Crim. App. 1971).
–Case Citation.

Hood v. State, 252 So. 2d 117, 120 (Ala. Crim. App. 1971). –Page
Citation.

After 57 Ala. App. 740 (1975), cite as follows:

In all documents:

Poole v. State, 667 So. 2d 740 (Ala. Crim. App. 1995).
–Case Citation.

Poole v. State, 667 So. 2d 740, 742 (Ala. Crim. App. 1995).
–Page Citation.

Williams v. Ward, 667 So. 2d 1375 (Ala. Civ. App. 1995).
–Case Citation.

Williams v. Ward, 667 So. 2d 1375, 1378 (Ala. Civ. App. 1995).
–Page Citation.

Alabama Code
See Code of Alabama.

Alabama Constitution
Ab.:   Ala. Const. art.   , §   .

Ex.:   Ala. Const. art. XVI, § 279. –"Cite constitutional provisions currently
in force without date." Bluebook Rule 11.

Ala. Const. amend. 55 (repealed 1955).
Ala. Const. amend. 55, repealed by Ala. Const. amend. 223. –"If the
cited provision has been repealed, either indicate parenthetically the
fact and date of repeal or cite the repealing provision in full."
Bluebook Rule 11.

Ala. Const. art. IV, § 74 (amended 1939)
Ala. Const. art. IV, § 74, amended by Ala. Const. amend. 40. –"When
citing a provision that has been subsequently amended, either indicate
parenthetically the fact and date of amendment or cite the amending
provision in full." Bluebook Rule 11.

Ala. Const. of 1875, art. I, § 5 (1901). –"Cite constitutions that have
been totally superseded by year of adoption; if the specific provision
cited was adopted in a different year, give that year parenthetically."
Bluebook Rule 11.

Alabama Law Review
Ab.:   Ala. L. Rev.

In law review footnotes, the titles of books and the names of cases, except for procedural
phrases, are not underlined. See Bluebook Rule 2.1(a). Further, the following are in large
and small capitals: codes, restatements, standards, constitutions, periodicals, authors of
books, titles of books, the abbreviated names of codes, most legislative materials except for
bills and resolutions, codified ordinances, model codes, court rules, and sentencing guidelines.
Refer to The Bluebook.

Ex.:   Fred H. Miller, <u>U.C.C. Articles 3, 4 and 4A: A Study in Process and Scope</u>, 42 Ala. L. Rev. 405 (1991). –Article Citation.

Fred H. Miller, <u>U.C.C. Articles 3, 4 and 4A: A Study in Process and Scope</u>, 42 Ala. L. Rev. 405, 410-11 (1991). –Page Citation.

Alabama Lawyer

Ab.:   Ala. Law.

Ex.:   Andrew P. Campbell, <u>Litigating Minority Shareholder Rights and the New Tort of Oppression</u>, 53 Ala. Law. 108 (1992). –Article Citation.

Andrew P. Campbell, <u>Litigating Minority Shareholder Rights and the New Tort of Oppression</u>, 53 Ala. Law. 108, 110 (1992). –Page Citation.

Alabama Reports

Ab.:   Ala.

–Discontinued after 295 Ala. 388 (1976).

–Cite to So. or So. 2d if therein; otherwise, cite to Ala.

–Give parallel citations only in documents submitted to Alabama state courts. (<u>Note</u>: In citing a state court case in a document submitted to a court of that same state, the 16th ed. of <u>The Bluebook</u> prescribed a parallel citation; the 17th ed. prescribes that local rules shall control, but Alabama has no known local rules concerning parallel citations. For the sake of continuity, we advise giving a parallel citation in documents submitted to Alabama state courts. <u>See</u> <u>Bluebook</u> Rule 10.3.1 and Practitioners' Note P.3.)

–Through 295 Ala. 388 (1976), cite as follows:

In documents submitted to Alabama state courts:

<u>Johnson v. Alabama Public Service Commission</u>, 287 Ala. 417, 252 So. 2d 75 (1971). –Case Citation.

<u>Johnson v. Alabama Public Service Commission</u>, 287 Ala. 417, 422, 252 So. 2d 75, 79 (1971). –Page Citation.

In all other documents:

<u>Johnson v. Alabama Public Service Commission</u>, 252 So. 2d 75 (Ala. 1971). –Case Citation.

<u>Johnson v. Alabama Public Service Commission</u>, 252 So. 2d 75, 79 (Ala. 1971). –Page Citation.

–After 295 Ala. 388 (1976), cite as follows:

In all documents:

<u>Pilcher Land Corp. v. Johns</u>, 677 So. 2d 746 (Ala. 1996). –Case Citation.

<u>Pilcher Land Corp. v. Johns</u>, 677 So. 2d 746, 747 (Ala. 1996). –Page Citation.

In citing cases in law review footnotes, abbreviate any word listed in Table T.6; the names of "states, countries, and other geographical units" unless they are named parties; and any other words of eight or more letters "if <u>substantial</u> space is thereby saved and the result is unambiguous." <u>Bluebook</u> Rule 10.2.2. On the other hand, in citing cases in text, abbreviate only widely known acronyms and the following words: "&," "Ass'n," "Bros.," "Co.," "Corp.," "Inc.," "Ltd.," and "No." <u>Bluebook</u> Rule 10.2.1(c).

Alabama Session Laws
　　See Acts of Alabama.

Alaska Administrative Code
　　Ab.:　　Alaska Admin. Code tit. x, § x (year)
　　Ex.:　　Alaska Admin. Code tit. 2, § 06.010 (1991).

Alaska Constitution
　　Ab.:　　Alaska Const. art.　, §　.
　　Ex.:　　Alaska Const. art. VIII, § 8. –"Cite constitutional provisions currently
　　　　　in force without date." Bluebook Rule 11.

　　　　　Alaska Const. art. IX, § 17 (amended 1990). –"When citing a
　　　　　provision that has been subsequently amended, either indicate
　　　　　parenthetically the fact and date of amendment or cite the amending
　　　　　provision in full." Bluebook Rule 11.

　　　　　"If the cited provision has been repealed, either indicate parenthetically
　　　　　the fact and date or cite the repealing provision in full. Cite
　　　　　constitutions that have been totally superseded by year of adoption; if
　　　　　the specific provision cited was adopted in a different year, give that
　　　　　year parenthetically." Bluebook Rule 11.

Alaska Law Review
　　Ab.:　　Alaska L. Rev.
　　Ex.:　　David C. Crosby, The Constitutionality of Sobriety Checkpoints in
　　　　　Alaska, 8 Alaska L. Rev. 227 (1991). –Article Citation.
　　　　　David C. Crosby, The Constitutionality of Sobriety Checkpoints in
　　　　　Alaska, 8 Alaska L. Rev. 227, 230-33 (1991). –Page Citation.

Alaska Reports
　　Ab.:　　Alaska
　　　　　–Discontinued after 17 Alaska 779 (1959). Thereafter, cite only to
　　　　　P.2d or P.3d.
　　　　　–District Court of Alaska had local jurisdiction from 1884-1959; cite to
　　　　　F. Supp., F., or F.2d if therein; otherwise, cite to Alaska.
　　Ex.　　O'Dey v. Matson, 17 Alaska 763 (D. Alaska 1958). –Case Citation.
　　　　　O'Dey v. Matson, 17 Alaska 763, 765 (D. Alaska 1958).
　　　　　–Page Citation.
　　　　　Boone v. Gipson, 920 P.2d 746 (Alaska 1996). –Case Citation.
　　　　　Boone v. Gipson, 920 P.2d 746, 749 (Alaska 1996). –Page Citation.

Alaska Session Laws
　　See Session Laws of Alaska

Alaska Statutes
　　Ab.:　　Alaska Stat. §　(Lexis year)

In law review footnotes, the titles of books and the names of cases, except for procedural
phrases, are not underlined. See Bluebook Rule 2.1(a). Further, the following are in large
and small capitals: codes, restatements, standards, constitutions, periodicals, authors of
books, titles of books, the abbreviated names of codes, most legislative materials except for
bills and resolutions, codified ordinances, model codes, court rules, and sentencing guidelines.
Refer to The Bluebook.

Ex.:   Alaska Stat. § 10.15.115 (Lexis 2000).

Alaska Stat. § 42.05.712 (Lexis Supp. 1999).

Albany Law Journal of Science & Technology
Ab.:   Alb. L.J. Sci. & Tech.

Ex.:   Kenneth R. Adamo, <u>Attorney Disqualification in Patent Litigation</u>, 1 Alb. L.J. Sci. & Tech. 177 (1991). –Article Citation.

Kenneth R. Adamo, <u>Attorney Disqualification in Patent Litigation</u>, 1 Alb. L.J. Sci. & Tech. 177, 196 (1991). –Page Citation.

Albany Law Review
Ab.:   Alb. L. Rev.

Ex.:   Robert A. Prentice, <u>Section 12(2): A Remedy for Wrongs in the Secondary Market?</u>, 55 Alb. L. Rev. 97 (1991). –Article Citation.

Robert A. Prentice, <u>Section 12(2): A Remedy for Wrongs in the Secondary Market?</u>, 55 Alb. L. Rev. 97, 122-24 (1991). –Page Citation.

Alberta Law Reports
See <u>Bluebook</u> Table T.2.

Ab.:   Alta. L.R. or Alta. L.R.2d.

Ex.:   <u>Whitney v. MacLean</u>, [1931] 26 Alta. L.R. 209 (App. Div. Can.). –Case Citation.

Alberta Law Review
Ab.:   Alta. L. Rev.

Ex.:   Jacob S. Ziegel, <u>The New Personal Property Security Regimes -- Have We Gone Too Far?</u>, 28 Alta. L. Rev. 739 (1990). –Article Citation.

Jacob S. Ziegel, <u>The New Personal Property Security Regimes -- Have We Gone Too Far?</u>, 28 Alta. L. Rev. 739, 752-59 (1990). –Page Citation.

ALI
<u>See</u> American Law Institute publications.

ALI-ABA Course Materials Journal
Ab.:   ALI-ABA Course Materials J.

Ex.:   David B. Farer, <u>Underground Storage Tank Law</u>, ALI-ABA Course Materials J., June 1991, at 19. –Article Citation.

David B. Farer, <u>Underground Storage Tank Law</u>, ALI-ABA Course Materials J., June 1991, at 19, 21-22. –Page Citation.

All England Law Reports (1936-date)
See <u>Bluebook</u> Table T.2.

Ab.:   All E.R.

In citing cases in law review footnotes, abbreviate any word listed in Table T.6; the names of "states, countries, and other geographical units" unless they are named parties; and any other words of eight or more letters "if <u>substantial</u> space is thereby saved and the result is unambiguous." <u>Bluebook</u> Rule 10.2.2. On the other hand, in citing cases in text, abbreviate only widely known acronyms and the following words: "&," "Ass'n," "Bros.," "Co.," "Corp.," "Inc.," "Ltd.," and "No." <u>Bluebook</u> Rule 10.2.1(c).

Ex.:   Davitt v. Titcumb, [1989] 3 All E.R. 417 (Eng. Ch.). –Case Citation.

All States Tax Guide (Research Institute of America)
Ab.:   All St. Tax Guide (R.I.A.)

Ex.:   Richard v. Jefferson County, All States Tax Guide (R.I.A.) ¶ 985.42
           (U.S. June 10, 1996). –Citation to looseleaf material.

           –This example is proper if the case is not yet available in, or is not
           reported in, an official or West reporter, a public domain citation, or
           in a widely used computer database.

ALR
See American Law Reports.

Alternative Dispute Resolution, by Nancy Atlas, Steven Huber, and Wendy Trachte-Huber
           –Do not abbreviate the title.

Ex.:   Nancy Atlas, et al., Alternative Dispute Resolution, 25 (2000).
           –Page Citation.

           Nancy Atlas, et al., Alternative Dispute Resolution, 25 n.2 (2000).
           –Footnote Citation.

Am. Jur. 2d
See American Jurisprudence, Second Edition.

amendment(s)
Ab.:   amend., amends.

American Bankruptcy Law Journal
Ab.:   Am. Bankr. L.J.

Ex.:   Margaret Howard, Stripping Down Liens: Section 506(d) and the
           Theory of Bankruptcy, 65 Am. Bankr. L.J. 373 (1991). –Article
           Citation.

           Margaret Howard, Stripping Down Liens: Section 506(d) and the
           Theory of Bankruptcy, 65 Am. Bankr. L.J. 373, 384-87 (1991).
           –Page Citation.

American Bar Association Code of Professional Responsibility
See American Bar Association Model Code of Professional Responsibility.

American Bar Association Committee on Ethics and Professional Responsibility, Formal Opinion
Ab.:   ABA Comm. on Ethics and Professional Responsibility, Formal Op.
           (year)

In law review footnotes, the titles of books and the names of cases, except for procedural phrases, are not underlined. See Bluebook Rule 2.1(a). Further, the following are in large and small capitals: codes, restatements, standards, constitutions, periodicals, authors of books, titles of books, the abbreviated names of codes, most legislative materials except for bills and resolutions, codified ordinances, model codes, court rules, and sentencing guidelines. Refer to The Bluebook.

Ex.:   ABA Comm. on Ethics and Professional Responsibility, Formal Op. 402 (1996).

ABA Comm. on Ethics and Professional Responsibility, Formal Op. 401 (1996) (lawyers practicing in limited liability partnerships).
–Citation with a parenthetical reference to subject matter.

American Bar Association Committee on Ethics and Professional Responsibility, Informal Opinion

Ab.:   ABA Comm. on Ethics and Professional Responsibility, Informal Op. (year)

Ex.:   ABA Comm. on Ethics and Professional Responsibility, Informal Op. E-94-6 (1995).

American Bar Association Journal

Ab.:   A.B.A. J.

Ex.:   John Gibeaut, Taking Aim, A.B.A. J., Nov. 1996, at 50.
–Article Citation.

John Gibeaut, Taking Aim, A.B.A. J., Nov. 1996, at 50, 53.
–Page Citation.

American Bar Association Model Code of Judicial Conduct

Ab.:   Model Code of Judicial Conduct [provision] (year)

Ex.:   Model Code of Judicial Conduct Canon 3 (2000)

American Bar Association Model Code of Professional Responsibility

Ab.:   Model Code of Professional Responsibility [provision] (year)

Ex.:   Model Code of Professional Responsibility Canon 9 (1980).

Model Code of Professional Responsibility DR 4-101 (1980).

Model Code of Professional Responsibility EC 2-20 (1980).

American Bar Association Model Rules of Professional Conduct

Ab.:   Model Rules of Professional Conduct Rule (status if necessary, year)

Ex.:   Model Rules of Professional Conduct Rule 3.4 (2000).

American Bar Association Reports

Ab.:   A.B.A. Rep.

Ex.:   Report of the Commission on Standards of Judicial Administration, 97 A.B.A. Rep. 345 (1972).

American Bar Association Revised Model Business Corporation Act

Ab.:   Revised Model Business Corp. Act

Ex.:   Revised Model Business Corp. Act § 3.02 (1984).

American Bar Foundation Code of Professional Responsibility, Annotated

Ab.:   Annot. Code of Professional Responsibility

In citing cases in law review footnotes, abbreviate any word listed in Table T.6; the names of "states, countries, and other geographical units" unless they are named parties; and any other words of eight or more letters "if substantial space is thereby saved and the result is unambiguous." Bluebook Rule 10.2.2. On the other hand, in citing cases in text, abbreviate only widely known acronyms and the following words: "&," "Ass'n," "Bros.," "Co.," "Corp.," "Inc.," "Ltd.," and "No." Bluebook Rule 10.2.1(c).

Ex.:   Annot. Code of Professional Responsibility DR 4-101(c)(4) cmt. at 182
         (Am. Bar Found. 1979).

American Bar Foundation Research Journal
Ab.:   Am. B. Found. Res. J.
Ex.:   Frederick Schauer, <u>Causation Theory and the Causes of Sexual</u>
         <u>Violence</u>, 4 Am. B. Found. Res. J. 737 (1987). –Article Citation.

         Frederick Schauer, <u>Causation Theory and the Causes of Sexual</u>
         <u>Violence</u>, 4 Am. B. Found. Res. J. 737, 742-46 (1987). –Page Citation.

American Business Law Journal
Ab.:   Am. Bus. L.J.
Ex.:   Michael J. Phillips, <u>The Substantive Due Process Rights of College and</u>
         <u>University Faculty</u>, 28 Am. Bus. L.J. 567 (1991). –Article Citation.

         Michael J. Phillips, <u>The Substantive Due Process Rights of College and</u>
         <u>University Faculty</u>, 28 Am. Bus. L.J. 567, 591-93 (1991). –Page
         Citation.

American Constitutional Law, 3d ed., by Louis Fisher
         Louis Fisher, <u>American Constitutional Law</u> 155 (3d. ed. 2000). –Page
         Citation.

American Constitutional Law, by Laurence H. Tribe
         –Do not abbreviate the title.
Ex.:   Laurence H. Tribe, <u>American Constitutional Law</u> § 5-4 (3d ed. 2000).
         –Section Citation.

         Laurence H. Tribe, <u>American Constitutional Law</u> § 5-4, at 819 (3d ed.
         2000). –Page Citation.

         Laurence H. Tribe, <u>American Constitutional Law</u> § 5-4, at 819 n.48 (3d
         ed. 2000). –Footnote Citation.

American Criminal Law Review
Ab.:   Am. Crim. L. Rev.
Ex.:   Donald J. Hall, <u>Victims' Voices in Criminal Court: The Need for</u>
         <u>Restraint</u>, 28 Am. Crim. L. Rev. 233 (1991). –Article Citation.

         Donald J. Hall, <u>Victims' Voices in Criminal Court: The Need for</u>
         <u>Restraint</u>, 28 Am. Crim. L. Rev. 233, 236-38 (1991). –Page Citation.

American Federal Tax Reports, second series (Research Institute of America)
Ab.:   A.F.T.R.2d (R.I.A.)
Ex.:   <u>United States v. Clements</u>, 77 A.F.T.R.2d (R.I.A.) 648 (5th Cir. 1996).

         –This example is proper if the case is not yet available in, or is not
         reported in, an official or West reporter, a public domain citation, or
         in a widely used computer database.

In law review footnotes, the titles of books and the names of cases, except for procedural
phrases, are not underlined. <u>See</u> <u>Bluebook</u> Rule 2.1(a). Further, the following are in large
and small capitals: codes, restatements, standards, constitutions, periodicals, authors of
books, titles of books, the abbreviated names of codes, most legislative materials except for
bills and resolutions, codified ordinances, model codes, court rules, and sentencing guidelines.
Refer to <u>The Bluebook</u>.

American Indian Law Review
Ab.: Am. Indian L. Rev.
Ex.: Dean B. Suagee, The Application of the National Environmental Policy Act to "Development" in Indian Country, 16 Am. Indian L. Rev. 377 (1991). –Article Citation.

Dean B. Suagee, The Application of the National Environmental Policy Act to "Development" in Indian Country, 16 Am. Indian L. Rev. 377, 380-81 (1991). –Page Citation.

American Institute for Certified Public Accountants -- Professional Standards (Commerce Clearing House)
Ab.: AICPA – Prof. Standards

American Journal of Comparative Law, The
Ab.: Am. J. Comp. L.
Ex.: John Quigley, The Soviet Presidency, 39 Am. J. Comp. L. 67 (1991). –Article Citation.

John Quigley, The Soviet Presidency, 39 Am. J. Comp. L. 67, 75-76 (1991). –Page Citation.

American Journal of Criminal Law
Ab.: Am. J. Crim. L.
Ex.: Henry Dahl, The Influence and Application of the Standard Penal Code for Latin America, 17 Am. J. Crim. L. 235 (1990). –Article Citation.

Henry Dahl, The Influence and Application of the Standard Penal Code for Latin America, 17 Am. J. Crim. L. 235, 258-59 (1990). –Page Citation.

American Journal of International Law
Ab.: Am. J. Int'l L.
Ex.: George H. Aldrich, Prospects for United States Ratification of Additional Protocol I to the Geneva Conventions, 85 Am. J. Int'l L. 1 (1991). –Article Citation.

George H. Aldrich, Prospects for United States Ratification of Additional Protocol I to the Geneva Conventions, 85 Am. J. Int'l L. 1, 5-7 (1991). –Page Citation.

American Journal of Jurisprudence, The
Ab.: Am. J. Juris.
Ex.: Troy Harris-Abbott, On Law and Theology, 35 Am. J. Juris. 105 (1990). –Article Citation.

Troy Harris-Abbott, On Law and Theology, 35 Am. J. Juris. 105, 114-15 (1990). –Page Citation.

In citing cases in law review footnotes, abbreviate any word listed in Table T.6; the names of "states, countries, and other geographical units" unless they are named parties; and any other words of eight or more letters "if substantial space is thereby saved and the result is unambiguous." Bluebook Rule 10.2.2. On the other hand, in citing cases in text, abbreviate only widely known acronyms and the following words: "&," "Ass'n," "Bros.," "Co.," "Corp.," "Inc.," "Ltd.," and "No." Bluebook Rule 10.2.1(c).

American Journal of Law & Medicine
Ab.:   Am. J.L. & Med.

Ex.:   Bernard Friedland & Richard W. Valachovic, The Regulation of Dental Licensing: The Dark Ages?, 17 Am. J.L. & Med. 249 (1991). –Article Citation.

Bernard Friedland & Richard W. Valachovic, The Regulation of Dental Licensing: The Dark Ages?, 17 Am. J.L. & Med. 249, 251-52 (1991). –Page Citation.

American Journal of Legal History
Ab.:   Am. J. Legal Hist.

Ex.:   Andrew J. King, The Law of Slander in Early Antebellum America, 35 Am. J. Legal Hist. 1 (1991). –Article Citation.

Andrew J. King, The Law of Slander in Early Antebellum America, 35 Am. J. Legal Hist. 1, 14-17 (1991). –Page Citation.

American Journal of Tax Policy, The
Ab.:   Am. J. Tax Pol'y

Ex.:   H. David Rosenbloom, Toward a New Tax Treaty Policy for a New Decade, 9 Am. J. Tax Pol'y 77 (1991). –Article Citation.

H. David Rosenbloom, Toward a New Tax Treaty Policy for a New Decade, 9 Am. J. Tax Pol'y 77, 85-89 (1991). –Page Citation.

American Journal of Trial Advocacy
Ab.:   Am. J. Trial Advoc.

Ex.:   Morton G. Rosen, RICO Claims by Celebrities Against the Tabloid Media for Publication of Purloined Material, 15 Am. J. Trial Advoc. 47 (1991). –Article Citation.

Morton G. Rosen, RICO Claims by Celebrities Against the Tabloid Media for Publication of Purloined Material, 15 Am. J. Trial Advoc. 47, 51-53 (1991). –Page Citation.

American Jurisprudence, Second Series
Ab.:   Am. Jur. 2d §   (year)

Ex.:   9 Am. Jur. 2d Bankruptcy § 417 (1999). –Section Citation .

1 Am. Jur. 2d Abduction and Kidnapping § 6 (Supp. 2000). –Supplement Citation.

20 Am. Jur. 2d Costs § 54, at 49 n.68 (1995). –Footnote Citation.

American Law Institute Complex Litigation Project
Ab.:   ALI Complex Litigation Project §   (status if necessary, year)

Ex.:   ALI Complex Litigation Project § 601 (Tentative Draft No. 3, 1992)

ALI Complex Litigation Project § 3.07 (Proposed Final Draft, 1993)

In law review footnotes, the titles of books and the names of cases, except for procedural phrases, are not underlined. See Bluebook Rule 2.1(a). Further, the following are in large and small capitals: codes, restatements, standards, constitutions, periodicals, authors of books, titles of books, the abbreviated names of codes, most legislative materials except for bills and resolutions, codified ordinances, model codes, court rules, and sentencing guidelines. Refer to The Bluebook.

American Law Institute Federal Estate and Gift Taxation
> Ab.:   ALI Federal Estate and Gift Taxation § (year)
>
> Ex.:   ALI Federal Estate and Gift Taxation § EX 10 (1968).

American Law Institute Federal Income Tax Project
> Ab.:   ALI Fed. Income Tax Project at (status if necessary, year)
>
> Ex.:   ALI Fed. Income Tax Project at 20 (Tent. Draft No. 16, 1991).

American Law Institute Federal Securities Code
> Ab.:   ALI Federal Securities Code § (year)
>
> Ex.:   ALI Federal Securities Code § 202 (1978).

American Law Institute Model Code of Evidence
> Ab.:   Model Code of Evidence Rule (year)
>
> Ex.:   Model Code of Evidence Rule 310 (1942).

American Law Institute Model Land Development Code
> Ab.:   Model Land Dev. Code § (status if necessary, year)
>
> Ex.:   Model Land Dev. Code § 4-101 (1975).

American Law Institute Model Penal Code
> Ab.:   Model Penal Code § (status if necessary, year)
>
> Ex.:   Model Penal Code § 210.2 (Proposed Official Draft 1962).
>
>   Model Penal Code § 210.2, note on status of section (Proposed Official Draft 1962). –Citation to auxiliary material.

American Law Institute Principles of Corporate Governance: Analysis and Recommendations
> Ab.:   ALI Principles of Corporate Governance: Analysis and Recommendations § (status if necessary, year)
>
> Ex.:   ALI Principles of Corporate Governance: Analysis and Recommendations § 7.11 (1992).
>
>   ALI Principles of Corporate Governance: Analysis and Recommendations § 7.17 cmt. g (1992).

American Law Institute Proceedings
> Ab.:   A.L.I. Proc.
>
> Ex.:   Bennett Boskey, <u>Report of the Treasurer</u>, 66 A.L.I. Proc. 15 (1989).

American Law Institute Restatements
> <u>See</u> Restatement ...

American Law of Torts, The, by Stuart M. Speiser, Charles F. Krause, and Alfred W. Gans
> –Do not abbreviate the title.

In citing cases in law review footnotes, abbreviate any word listed in Table T.6; the names of "states, countries, and other geographical units" unless they are named parties; and any other words of eight or more letters "if <u>substantial</u> space is thereby saved and the result is unambiguous." <u>Bluebook</u> Rule 10.2.2. On the other hand, in citing cases in text, abbreviate only widely known acronyms and the following words: "&," "Ass'n," "Bros.," "Co.," "Corp.," "Inc.," "Ltd.," and "No." <u>Bluebook</u> Rule 10.2.1(c).

Ex.:   8 Stuart M. Speiser et al., <u>The American Law of Torts</u> § 34:7 (1993).
         –Section Citation.

         8 Stuart M. Speiser et al., <u>The American Law of Torts</u> § 34:7, at 35
         (1993). –Page Citation.

         8 Stuart M. Speiser et al., <u>The American Law of Torts</u> § 34:7, at 35
         n.48 (1993). –Footnote Citation.

American Law of Zoning, by Robert M. Anderson
         –Do not abbreviate the title.

Ex.:   2 Robert M. Anderson, <u>American Law of Zoning</u> § 9.44 (3d ed. 1986).
         –Section Citation.

         2 Robert M. Anderson, <u>American Law of Zoning</u> § 9.44, at 237 (3d ed.
         1986). –Page Citation.

         2 Robert M. Anderson, <u>American Law of Zoning</u> § 9.44, at 237 n.40
         (3d ed. 1986). –Footnote Citation.

         2 Kenneth H. Young, <u>Anderson's American Law of Zoning</u> § 10.18
         (4th ed. 1996). –Citation to Fourth Edition.

         2 Kenneth H. Young, <u>Anderson's American Law of Zoning</u> § 10.18, at
         429 (4th ed. 1996). –Page Citation to Fourth Edition.

         2 Kenneth H. Young, <u>Anderson's American Law of Zoning</u> § 10.18, at
         429 n.11 (4th ed. 1996). –Footnote Citation to Fourth Edition.

American Law Reports
Ab.:   A.L.R., A.L.R.2d, A.L.R.3d, A.L.R.4th, A.L.R.5th
Ex.:   A.W. Gans, Annotation, <u>Fee Simple Conditional</u>, 114 A.L.R. 602
         (1938). –Citation to annotation.

         R.D. Hursh, Annotation, <u>Liability of Operator of Flight Training
         School for Injury or Death of Trainee</u>, 17 A.L.R.2d 557 (1951).
         –Citation to annotation.

         Alan R. Gilbert, Annotation, <u>Proceedings For Injunction or Restraining
         Order as Basis of Malicious Prosecution Action</u>, 70 A.L.R.3d 536
         (1976). –Citation to annotation.

         Joe E. Smith, Annotation, <u>Applicability of Double Jeopardy to Juvenile
         Court Proceedings</u>, 5 A.L.R.4th 234 (1981). –Citation to annotation.

         Linda A. Sharp, Annotation, <u>Medical Malpractice in Connection with
         Diagnosis, Care, or Treatment of Diabetes</u>, 43 A.L.R.5th 87 (1996).
         –Citation to annotation.

American Law Reports, Federal
Ab.:   A.L.R. Fed.
Ex.:   Martha M. Cleary, Annotation, <u>Conduct of Union Officer Which
         Violates § 501 (a) of Landrum-Griffin Act (29 USCS § 501 (a))</u>, 107
         A.L.R. Fed. 448 (1992). –Citation to annotation.

In law review footnotes, the titles of books and the names of cases, except for procedural
phrases, are not underlined. <u>See</u> <u>Bluebook</u> Rule 2.1(a). Further, the following are in large
and small capitals: codes, restatements, standards, constitutions, periodicals, authors of
books, titles of books, the abbreviated names of codes, most legislative materials except for
bills and resolutions, codified ordinances, model codes, court rules, and sentencing guidelines.
Refer to <u>The Bluebook</u>.

American Lawyer
>   Ab.:   Am. Law.
>   Ex.:   Roger Parloff, <u>Maybe the Jury Was Right</u>, Am. Law., June 1992, at 7.
>   –Article Citation.

American Planning Law, by Norman Williams, Jr. and John M. Taylor
>   <u>See</u> Williams' American Planning Law

American Review of International Arbitration, The
>   Ab.:   Am. Rev. Int'l Arb.
>   Ex.:   Hans Smit, <u>Provisional Relief in International Arbitration: The ICC and Other Proposed Rules</u>, 1 Am. Rev. Int'l Arb. 388 (1990).
>   –Article Citation.
>
>   Hans Smit, <u>Provisional Relief in International Arbitration: The ICC and Other Proposed Rules</u>, 1 Am. Rev. Int'l Arb. 388, 391-92 (1990).
>   –Page Citation.

American Samoa Administrative Code
>   Ab.:   Am. Samoa Admin. Code §   (year)
>   Ex.:   Am. Samoa Admin. Code § 4.1205 (1985).

American Samoa Code Annotated
>   Ab.:   Am. Samoa Code Ann. § (year)
>   Ex.:   Am. Samoa Code Ann. § 16.0101 (1981).

American Society of International Law Proceedings
>   Ab.:   Am. Soc'y Int'l L. Proc.
>   Ex.:   David A. Jones, <u>Diplomatic Immunity: Recent Developments in Law and Practice</u>, 1991 Am. Soc'y Int'l L. Proc. 261. –Article Citation.
>
>   David A. Jones, <u>Diplomatic Immunity: Recent Developments in Law and Practice</u>, 1991 Am. Soc'y Int'l L. Proc. 261, 265. –Page Citation.
>
>   –This periodical also contains many speeches delivered at the Annual Meeting of the American Society of International Law. Cite speeches according to <u>Bluebook</u> Rule 17.1.5.

American State Papers
>   Ab.:   Am. St. Papers

American Stock Exchange Guide (Commerce Clearing House)
>   Ab.:   Am. Stock Ex. Guide (CCH)

In citing cases in law review footnotes, abbreviate any word listed in Table T.6;
the names of "states, countries, and other geographical units" unless they are named parties;
and any other words of eight or more letters "if <u>substantial</u> space is thereby saved and the
result is unambiguous." <u>Bluebook</u> Rule 10.2.2. On the other hand, in citing cases in text,
abbreviate only widely known acronyms and the following words: "&," "Ass'n," "Bros.,"
"Co.," "Corp.," "Inc.," "Ltd.," and "No." <u>Bluebook</u> Rule 10.2.1(c).

Ex.: TradingHalts Due to Extraordinary Market Volatility Rule, 2 Am. Stock Ex. Guide (CCH) ¶ 9267 (1998). –Citation to a rule of the American Stock Exchange and American Stock Exchange Clearing Corporation.

American University Journal of Gender and the Law
Ab.: Am. U. J. Gender & L.

Ex.: Sherry Young, Getting to Yes: The Case Against Banning Consensual Relationships in Higher Education, 4 Am. U. J. Gender & L. 269 (1996). –Article Citation.

Sherry Young, Getting to Yes: The Case Against Banning Consensual Relationships in Higher Education, 4 Am. U. J. Gender & L. 269, 270 (1996). –Page Citation.

American University Journal of International Law and Policy, The
Ab.: Am. U. J. Int'l L. & Pol'y

Ex.: M.C. Jozana, Proposed South African Bill of Rights: A Prescription for Equality or Neo-Apartheid?, 7 Am. U. J. Int'l L. & Pol'y 45 (1991). –Article Citation.

M.C. Jozana, Proposed South African Bill of Rights: A Prescription for Equality or Neo-Apartheid?, 7 Am. U. J. Int'l L. & Pol'y 45, 49-51 (1991). –Page Citation.

American University Law Review
Ab.: Am. U. L. Rev.

Ex.: Daniel J. Meador, Origin of the Federal Circuit: A Personal Account, 41 Am. U. L. Rev. 581 (1992). –Article Citation.

Daniel J. Meador, Origin of the Federal Circuit: A Personal Account, 41 Am. U. L. Rev. 581, 596-604 (1992). –Page Citation.

Anderson's American Law of Zoning, by Kenneth H. Young
Ex.: 4 Kenneth H. Young, Anderson's American Law of Zoning § 22.19 (4th ed. 1997). –Section Citation.

4 Kenneth H. Young, Anderson's American Law of Zoning § 22.19, at 52 (4th ed. 1997). –Page Citation.

4 Kenneth H. Young, Anderson's American Law of Zoning § 22.19, at 52 n.29 (4th ed. 1997). –Footnote Citation.

Anglo-American Law Review
Ab.: Anglo-Am. L. Rev.

Ex.: Timothy H. Jones, Regulatory Policy and Rule-Making, 20 Anglo-Am. L. Rev. 131 (1991). –Article Citation.

Timothy H. Jones, Regulatory Policy and Rule-Making, 20 Anglo-Am. L. Rev. 131, 140-45 (1991). –Page Citation.

In law review footnotes, the titles of books and the names of cases, except for procedural phrases, are not underlined. See Bluebook Rule 2.1(a). Further, the following are in large and small capitals: codes, restatements, standards, constitutions, periodicals, authors of books, titles of books, the abbreviated names of codes, most legislative materials except for bills and resolutions, codified ordinances, model codes, court rules, and sentencing guidelines. Refer to The Bluebook.

Annals of the American Academy of Political and Social Science, The
   Ab.:   Annals Am. Acad. Pol. & Soc. Sci.
   Ex.:   Richard D. Lamm, The Future of the Environment, Annals Am. Acad. Pol. & Soc. Sci., July 1992, at 57. –Article Citation.
           Richard D. Lamm, The Future of the Environment, Annals Am. Acad. Pol. & Soc. Sci., July 1992, at 57, 62-64. –Page Citation.

Annotated Code of Maryland
   Ab.:   Md. Code Ann., [subject] §   (year)
   Ex.:   Md. Code Ann. Transp. I § 13-917 (1990)
           Md. Code Ann., Tax-Prop. § 6-301 (Supp. 2000)
  See Bluebook Table T.1, pp. 207-08 for the abbreviation of each subject.
           –To cite 1957 Annotated Codes of Maryland, use the following format: Md. Ann. Code art. , § (year). See Bluebook p. 208.

Annotated Code of Professional Responsibility (ABF)
  See American Bar Foundation Code of Professional Responsibility, Annotated.

Annotated Laws of Massachusetts
   Ab.:   Mass. Ann. Laws ch. , § (Lexis year)
   Ex.:   Mass. Ann. Laws ch. 68, § 5 (Lexis 1998).
           Mass. Ann. Laws ch. 66, § 18 (Lexis Supp. 1999).
           –Cite to General Laws of the Commonwealth of Massachusetts if therein. See Bluebook Table T.1, p. 209.

Annotated Model Rules of Professional Conduct (ABA)
   Ab.:   Ann. Model Rules of Professional Conduct Rule , page (date)
   Ex.:   Ann. Model Rules of Professional Conduct Rule 1.7, 110 (1991).
           –Citation to an annotation.
           –Citation to the Model Rules of Professional Conduct is preferred when citing Rules or Comments.

Annotated Tax Cases (Eng.)
   Ab.:   Ann. Tax Cas.

Annotation
   Ex.:   John L. Isham, Annotation, Parking Facility Proprietor's Liability for Criminal Attack on Patron, 49 A.L.R.4th 1257 (1986). –Annotation Citation.
           Sonja A. Soehnel, Annotation, Sex Discrimination in Employment Against Female Attorney in Violation of Federal Civil Rights Laws –Federal Cases, 81 L. Ed. 2d 894 (1986). –Annotation Citation.
           Sonja A. Soehnel, Annotation, Sex Discrimination in Employment Against Female Attorney in Violation of Federal Civil Rights Laws– Federal Cases, 81 L. Ed. 2d 894, 897 (1986). –Page Citation.

In citing cases in law review footnotes, abbreviate any word listed in Table T.6; the names of "states, countries, and other geographical units" unless they are named parties; and any other words of eight or more letters "if substantial space is thereby saved and the result is unambiguous." Bluebook Rule 10.2.2. On the other hand, in citing cases in text, abbreviate only widely known acronyms and the following words: "&," "Ass'n," "Bros.," "Co.," "Corp.," "Inc.," "Ltd.," and "No." Bluebook Rule 10.2.1(c).

Annuaire Français de Droit International
Ab.: Do not abbreviate title.
Ex.: Julio A. Barberis, <u>Reflexions Sur La Coutume Internationale</u>, Annuaire Français de Droit International, 1990, at 8. −Article Citation.

Julio A. Barberis, <u>Reflexions Sur La Coutume Internationale</u>, Annuaire Français de Droit International, 1990, at 8, 22-23. −Page Citation.

Annual Report and Official Opinions of the Attorney General of Indiana
Ab.: Ind. Att'y Gen. Ann. Rep. & Official Op.

Annual Report and Official Opinions of the Attorney General of Maryland
Ab.: Md. Att'y Gen. Ann. Rep. & Official Op.

Annual Report of the Attorney General for the State of South Carolina to the General Assembly
Ab.: S.C. Att'y Gen. Ann. Rep.

Annual Report of the Attorney General, State of Florida
Ab.: Fla. Att'y Gen. Ann. Rep.

Annual Review of Banking Law
Ab.: Ann. Rev. Banking L.
Ex.: Sarah Hane Hughes, <u>A Call for International Legal Standards for Emerging Retail Electronic Payment Systems</u>, 15 Ann. Rev. Banking L. 197 (1996). −Article Citation.

Sarah Hane Hughes, <u>A Call for International Legal Standards for Emerging Retail Electronic Payment Systems</u>, 15 Ann. Rev. Banking L. 197, 200 (1996). −Page Citation.

Annual Survey of American Law
Ab.: Ann. Surv. Am. L.
Ex.: George S. Tolley III, <u>The Freedom of Information Act: Competing Interests in the Supreme Court</u>, 1990 Ann. Surv. Am. L. 497. −Article Citation.

George S. Tolley III, <u>The Freedom of Information Act: Competing Interests in the Supreme Court</u>, 1990 Ann. Surv. Am. L. 497, 525-30. −Page Citation.

anonymous
Ab.: anon.

Antitrust Bulletin
Ab.: Antitrust Bull.
Ex.: Robert L. Steiner, <u>Intraband Competition−Stepchild of Antitrust</u>, 36 Antitrust Bull. 155 (1991). −Article Citation.

Robert L. Steiner, <u>Intraband Competition−Stepchild of Antitrust</u>, 36 Antitrust Bull. 155, 160-61 (1991). −Page Citation.

In law review footnotes, the titles of books and the names of cases, except for procedural phrases, are not underlined. <u>See</u> <u>Bluebook</u> Rule 2.1(a). Further, the following are in large and small capitals: codes, restatements, standards, constitutions, periodicals, authors of books, titles of books, the abbreviated names of codes, most legislative materials except for bills and resolutions, codified ordinances, model codes, court rules, and sentencing guidelines. Refer to <u>The Bluebook</u>.

Antitrust Law, by Phillip E. Areeda and Donald F. Turner
–Do not abbreviate the title.

Ex.:   5 Phillip E. Areeda & Donald F. Turner, <u>Antitrust Law</u> § 1120a (1980).
–Section Citation.

5 Phillip E. Areeda & Donald F. Turner, <u>Antitrust Law</u> § 1120a, at 91 (1980). –Page Citation.

6 Phillip E. Areeda, <u>Antitrust Law</u> § 1406f, at 28 (1986).
–Page Citation.

Antitrust Law Journal
Ab.:   Antitrust L.J.

Ex.:   Harry M. Reasoner, <u>The State of Antitrust</u>, 59 Antitrust L.J. 63 (1990).
–Article Citation.

Harry M. Reasoner, <u>The State of Antitrust</u>, 59 Antitrust L.J. 63, 69-70 (1990). –Page Citation.

Appeal Cases, District of Columbia (1893-1941)
Ab.:   App. D.C.
–Cite to F. or F.2d if therein; otherwise, cite to App. D.C.

Ex.:   <u>Army & Navy Club v. District of Columbia</u>, 8 App. D.C. 544 (1896).
–Case Citation.

<u>Army & Navy Club v. District of Columbia</u>, 8 App. D.C. 544, 550 (1896). –Page Citation.

Appellate Court Administration Review
Ab.:   App. Ct. Admin. Rev.

Appellate Department
Ab.:   App. Dep't

Appellate Division
Ab.:   App. Div.

appended materials
–Explained and illustrated in <u>Bluebook</u> Rule 3.5.

appendix; appendices
Ab.:   app., apps.

–Explained and illustrated in <u>Bluebook</u> Rule 3.5.

Ex.:   Robert J. Hopperton, <u>Teaching the Rule Against Perpetuities in First Year Property</u>, 31 U. Tol. L. Rev. 55 app. II, at 71 (1999).

Appleman on Insurance, 2d,
See <u>Holmes' Appleman on Insurance</u>, 2d, by Eric Mills Holmes and L. Anthony Sutin.

In citing cases in law review footnotes, abbreviate any word listed in Table T.6; the names of "states, countries, and other geographical units" unless they are named parties; and any other words of eight or more letters "if <u>substantial</u> space is thereby saved and the result is unambiguous." <u>Bluebook</u> Rule 10.2.2. On the other hand, in citing cases in text, abbreviate only widely known acronyms and the following words: "&," "Ass'n," "Bros.," "Co.," "Corp.," "Inc.," "Ltd.," and "No." <u>Bluebook</u> Rule 10.2.1(c).

Arbitration Journal
   Ab.:   Arb. J.
   Ex.:   Donald L. Carper, <u>Remedies in Business Arbitration</u>, Arb. J.,
           Sept. 1991, at 49. –Article Citation.
           Donald L. Carper, <u>Remedies in Business Arbitration</u>, Arb. J.,
           Sept. 1991, at 49, 50-52. –Page Citation.

Arbitration Materials
   Ab.:   Arb. Mat'l

Arbitrator
   Ab.:   Arb.

Areeda & Turner on Antitrust Law
   <u>See</u> Antitrust Law, by Phillip Areeda & Donald F. Turner.

Arizona Administrative Code
   Ab.:   Ariz. Admin. Code § (year)

Arizona Administrative Register
   Ab.:   Ariz. Admin. Reg.
   Ex.:   Ariz. Admin. Code § R2-2-102 (1998).

Arizona Appeals Reports
   Ab.:   Ariz. App.
           –Discontinued after 27 Ariz. App. 797 (1976); cases thereafter found in
           Arizona Reports.
           –Cite to P., P.2d, or P.3d if therein; otherwise, cite to Ariz. App. or
           Ariz.
           –Give parallel citations only in documents submitted to Arizona state
           courts. <u>See</u> <u>Bluebook</u> Rule 10.3.1 and Practitioners' Note P.3; <u>see</u>
           <u>also</u> Ariz. R. Civ. App. P.13(a)(6), which requires a parallel citation.
           –Through 27 Ariz. App. 797 (1976), cite as follows:
           In documents submitted to Arizona state courts:
                   <u>Committee for Neighborhood Preservation v. Graham</u>, 14 Ariz.
                   App. 457, 484 P.2d 226 (1971). –Case Citation.
                   <u>Committee for Neighborhood Preservation v. Graham</u>, 14 Ariz.
                   App. 457, 460, 484 P.2d 226, 228 (1971). –Page Citation.
           In all other documents:
                   <u>Committee for Neighborhood Preservation v. Graham</u>, 484 P.2d
                   226 (Ariz. Ct. App. 1971). –Case Citation.
                   <u>Committee for Neighborhood Preservation v. Graham</u>, 484 P.2d
                   226, 228 (Ariz. Ct. App. 1971). –Page Citation.
           –After 27 Ariz. App. 797 (1976), cite as follows:

In law review footnotes, the titles of books and the names of cases, except for procedural
phrases, are not underlined. <u>See</u> <u>Bluebook</u> Rule 2.1(a). Further, the following are in large
and small capitals: codes, restatements, standards, constitutions, periodicals, authors of
books, titles of books, the abbreviated names of codes, most legislative materials except for
bills and resolutions, codified ordinances, model codes, court rules, and sentencing guidelines.
Refer to <u>The Bluebook</u>.

In documents submitted to Arizona state courts:

> <u>State v. Valdez</u>, 182 Ariz. 165, 894 P.2d 708 (Ct. App. 1994).
> –Case Citation.
>
> <u>State v. Valdez</u>, 182 Ariz. 165, 166, 894 P.2d 708, 713
> (Ct. App. 1994). –Page Citation.

In all other documents:

> <u>State v. Valdez</u>, 894 P.2d 708 (Ariz. Ct. App. 1994).
> –Case Citation.
>
> <u>State v. Valdez</u>, 894 P.2d 708, 713 (Ariz. Ct. App. 1994).
> –Page Citation.

Arizona Attorney

Ab.: Ariz. Att'y

Ex.: Roxana Bacon, <u>Supreme Court Adopts Sweeping Changes in Attorney Discipline</u>, Ariz. Att'y, Feb. 1992, at 10. –Article Citation.

Roxana Bacon, <u>Supreme Court Adopts Sweeping Changes in Attorney Discipline</u>, Ariz. Att'y, Feb. 1992, at 10, 11. –Page Citation.

Arizona Constitution

Ab.: Ariz. Const. art.   , pt.   , §   .

–Not all articles are subdivided into parts.

Ex.: Ariz. Const. art. VIII, pt. 2, § 1.
Ariz. Const. art. II, § 4. –"Cite constitutional provisions currently in force without date." <u>Bluebook</u> Rule 11.

Ariz. Const. art. XXIV (repealed 1932). –"If the cited provision has been repealed, either indicate parenthetically the fact and date of repeal or cite the repealing provision in full." <u>Bluebook</u> Rule 11.

Ariz. Const. art. XXVIII, § 1 (amended 1988). –"When citing a provision that has been subsequently amended, either indicate parenthetically the fact and date of amendment or cite the amending provision in full." <u>Bluebook</u> Rule 11.

Arizona Law Review

Ab.: Ariz. L. Rev.

Ex.: Michael H. LeRoy, <u>Strike Crossovers and Striker Replacements: An Empirical Test of the NLRB's No-Presumption Policy</u>, 33 Ariz. L. Rev. 291 (1991). –Article Citation.

Michael H. LeRoy, <u>Strike Crossovers and Striker Replacements: An Empirical Test of the NLRB's No-Presumption Policy</u>, 33 Ariz. L. Rev. 291, 295-97 (1991). –Page Citation.

Arizona Legislative Service (West)

Ab.: year Ariz. Legis. Serv.   (West)

In citing cases in law review footnotes, abbreviate any word listed in Table T.6; the names of "states, countries, and other geographical units" unless they are named parties; and any other words of eight or more letters "if <u>substantial</u> space is thereby saved and the result is unambiguous." <u>Bluebook</u> Rule 10.2.2. On the other hand, in citing cases in text, abbreviate only widely known acronyms and the following words: "&," "Ass'n," "Bros.," "Co.," "Corp.," "Inc.," "Ltd.," and "No." <u>Bluebook</u> Rule 10.2.1(c).

Ex.:   Act of Apr. 23, 1996, ch. 250, 1996 Ariz. Legis. Serv. 1464 (West)
         (relating to emergency medical services). –Citation to an entire act.

         Act of Apr. 23, 1996, Sec. 1, § 36-2201, 1996 Ariz. Legis. Serv. 1464,
         1464-66 (West) (relating to emergency medical services). –Citation to
         a session law amending a prior act.

         –"Cite to Ariz. Sess. Laws if therein." Bluebook Table T.1, p. 190.

Arizona Reports

Ab.:   Ariz.

         –Cite to P., P.2d, or P.3d if therein; otherwise, cite to Ariz.

         –Give parallel citations only in documents submitted to Arizona state
         courts. See Bluebook Rule 10.3.1 and Practitioners' Note P.3; see
         also Ariz. R. Civ. App. P.13(a)(6), which requires a parallel citation.

         In documents submitted to Arizona state courts:

         Zamora v. Reinstein, 185 Ariz. 272, 915 P.2d 1227 (1996).
         –Case Citation.

         Zamora v. Reinstein, 185 Ariz. 272, 273, 915 P.2d 1227, 1228
         (1996). –Page Citation.

         In all other documents, cite as follows:

         Zamora v. Reinstein, 915 P.2d 1227 (Ariz. 1996). –Case Citation.

         Zamora v. Reinstein, 915 P.2d 1227, 1228 (Ariz. 1996). –Page
         Citation.

Arizona Revised Statutes Annotated

Ab.:   Ariz. Rev. Stat. Ann. § (West year)

Ex.:   Ariz. Rev. Stat. Ann. § 23-1382 (West 1995).

         Ariz. Rev. Stat. Ann. § 49-550 (West Supp. 1999).

Arizona Session Laws

See Session Laws of Arizona.

Arizona State Law Journal

Ab.:   Ariz. St. L.J.

Ex.:   Russell L. Weaver, Challenging Regulatory Interpretations, 23 Ariz. St.
         L.J. 109 (1991). –Article Citation.

         Russell L. Weaver, Challenging Regulatory Interpretations, 23 Ariz. St.
         L.J. 109, 144-48 (1991). –Page Citation.

Arkansas Appellate Reports

Ab.:   Ark. App.

         –Bound with Arkansas Reports.

         –Cite to S.W., S.W.2d, or S.W.3d if therein; otherwise, cite to Ark.
         App.

In law review footnotes, the titles of books and the names of cases, except for procedural
phrases, are not underlined. See Bluebook Rule 2.1(a). Further, the following are in large
and small capitals: codes, restatements, standards, constitutions, periodicals, authors of
books, titles of books, the abbreviated names of codes, most legislative materials except for
bills and resolutions, codified ordinances, model codes, court rules, and sentencing guidelines.
Refer to The Bluebook.

–Give parallel citations only in documents submitted to Arkansas state courts. See Bluebook Rule 10.3.1 and Practitioners' Note P.3; see also Ark. Sup. Ct. R. 4-2(a)(7), which requires a parallel citation.

In documents submitted to Arkansas state courts, cite as follows:

Jessie v. Jessie, 53 Ark. App. 188, 920 S.W. 2d 874 (1996).
–Case Citation.

Jessie v. Jessie, 53 Ark. App. 188, 189, 920 S.W. 2d 874, 875 (1996).
–Page Citation.

In all other documents, cite as follows:

Jessie v. Jessie, 920 S.W.2d 874 (Ark. Ct. App. 1996). –Case Citation.

Jessie v. Jessie, 920 S.W.2d 874, 875 (Ark. Ct. App. 1996).
–Page Citation.

Arkansas Code of 1987 Annotated

Ab.: Ark. Code Ann. § (Lexis year)

Ex.: Ark. Code Ann. § 19-4-1801 (Lexis 1998).

Ark. Code. Ann. § 28-70-401 (Lexis Supp. 1999).

Arkansas Constitution

Ab.: Ark. Const. art. , §   .

Ex.: Ark. Const. art. XIV, § 2.–"Cite constitutional provisions currently in force without date." Bluebook Rule 11.

Ark. Const. art. III, § 3 (repealed in part 1963).

Ark. Const. art. III, § 3, repealed by Ark. Const. amend. L, § 1. –"If the cited provision has been repealed, either indicate parenthetically the fact and date of repeal or cite the repealing provision in full." Bluebook Rule 11.

Ark. Const. art. XIV, § 3 (amended 1948).

Ark. Const. art. XIV, § 3, amended by Ark. Const. amend. XL. –"When citing a provision that has been subsequently amended, either indicate parenthetically the fact and date of amendment or cite the amending provision in full." Bluebook Rule 11.

Ark. Const. of 1868, art. III, § 2 (1873). –"Cite constitutions that have been totally superseded by year of adoption; if the specific provision cited was adopted in a different year, give that year parenthetically." Bluebook Rule 11.

Arkansas Law Notes

Ab.: Ark. L. Notes

Ex.: Howard W. Brill, Punitive Damages in Arkansas -- Expanded? Restricted?, 1990 Ark. L. Notes 25. –Article Citation.

Howard W. Brill, Punitive Damages in Arkansas -- Expanded? Restricted?, 1990 Ark. L. Notes 25, 27-28. –Page Citation.

In citing cases in law review footnotes, abbreviate any word listed in Table T.6; the names of "states, countries, and other geographical units" unless they are named parties; and any other words of eight or more letters "if substantial space is thereby saved and the result is unambiguous." Bluebook Rule 10.2.2. On the other hand, in citing cases in text, abbreviate only widely known acronyms and the following words: "&," "Ass'n," "Bros.," "Co.," "Corp.," "Inc.," "Ltd.," and "No." Bluebook Rule 10.2.1(c).

Arkansas Law Review
    Ab.:   Ark. L. Rev.
    Ex.:   Mark R. Gillett, <u>Perfecting the Special Use Election: Congress Giveth and the Service Taketh Away</u>, 45 Ark. L. Rev. 171 (1992). –Article Citation.
            Mark R. Gillett, <u>Perfecting the Special Use Election: Congress Giveth and the Service Taketh Away</u>, 45 Ark. L. Rev. 171, 185-89 (1992). –Page Citation.

Arkansas Lawyer, The
    Ab.:   Ark. Law.
    Ex.:   Richard F. Hatfield, <u>Significant Developments in Probate & Trusts in the Past 25 Years</u>, Ark. Law., Jan. 1992, at 29. –Article Citation.
            Richard F. Hatfield, <u>Significant Developments in Probate & Trusts in the Past 25 Years</u>, Ark. Law., Jan. 1992, at 29, 32. –Page Citation.

Arkansas Register
    Ab.:   [v.] Ark. Reg. [p.] (year)
    Ex.:   23 Ark. Reg. 12 (2000)

Arkansas Reports
    Ab.:   Ark.
    –Cite to S.W., S.W.2d, or S.W.3d if therein; otherwise, cite to Ark.
    –Give parallel citations only in documents submitted to Arkansas state courts. <u>See</u> <u>Bluebook</u> Rule 10.3.1 and Practitioners' Note P.3; <u>see also</u> Ark. Sup. Ct. R. 4-2(a)(7), which requires a parallel citation.
    In documents submitted to Arkansas state courts, cite as follows:
        <u>Pledger v. Halvorson</u>, 324 Ark. 302, 921 S.W. 2d 576 (1996). –Case Citation.
        <u>Pledger v. Halvorson</u>, 324 Ark. 302, 304, 921 S.W. 2d 576, 578 (1996). –Page Citation.
    In all other documents, cite as follows:
        <u>Pledger v. Halvorson</u>, 921 S.W.2d 576 (Ark. 1996). –Case Citation.
        <u>Pledger v. Halvorson</u>, 921 S.W.2d 576, 578 (Ark. 1996). –Page Citation.

Arkansas Session Laws
    <u>See</u> General Acts of Arkansas.

Arkansas Statutes Annotated
    <u>See</u> Arkansas Code of 1987 Annotated.

Army Lawyer, The
    Ab.:   Army Law.

In law review footnotes, the titles of books and the names of cases, except for procedural phrases, are not underlined. <u>See</u> <u>Bluebook</u> Rule 2.1(a). Further, the following are in large and small capitals: codes, restatements, standards, constitutions, periodicals, authors of books, titles of books, the abbreviated names of codes, most legislative materials except for bills and resolutions, codified ordinances, model codes, court rules, and sentencing guidelines. Refer to <u>The Bluebook</u>.

Ex.:   Thomas K. Emswiller, <u>Security Assistance and Operations Law</u>, Army
        Law., Nov. 1991, at 10. –Article Citation.
        Thomas K. Emswiller, <u>Security Assistance and Operations Law</u>, Army
        Law., Nov. 1991, at 10, 13-15. –Page Citation.

Arrêts du Tribunal Fédéral (Switzerland)
Ab.:   ATF
        Constitutional cases   ATF Ia
        Administrative cases   ATF Ib
        Civil cases   ATF II
        Bankruptcy cases   ATF III
        Criminal cases   ATF IV
        Social cases   ATF V

article(s)
Ab.:   art., arts.

ASILS International Law Journal
Ab.:   ASILS Int'l L.J.
Ex.:   Johanna M. Klema, Note, <u>Strategic Defense Initiative and the New
        Interpretation of the ABM Treaty</u>, 10 ASILS Int'l L.J. 149 (1986).
        –Note Citation.
        Johanna M. Klema, Note, <u>Strategic Defense Initiative and the New
        Interpretation of the ABM Treaty</u>, 10 ASILS Int'l L.J. 149, 161-63
        (1986). –Page Citation.
        –A designation of the piece should appear before the title of the work
        to indicate that it is student written. <u>See</u> <u>Bluebook</u> Rule 16.5.1(a).

Assembl[yman, ywoman]
Ab.:   Assemb.

Atlantic Reporter
        –Do not give a parallel citation unless required by local rule. <u>See</u> <u>Bluebook</u>
        Practitioners' Note P.3. and Rule 10.3.1. <u>See also</u> the various state court and
        state reporter entries herein for local rule parallel citation requirements.
Ab.:   A.
Ex.:
        Connecticut:
            <u>Valente v. Hopper</u>, 126 A. 706 (Conn. 1924). –Case Citation.
            <u>Valente v. Hopper</u>, 126 A. 706, 708 (Conn. 1924). –Page Citation.
        Delaware:
            <u>Charles Tire Co. v. Owens</u>, 186 A. 737 (Del. Super. Ct. 1936).
            –Case Citation.
            <u>Charles Tire Co. v. Owens</u>, 186 A. 737, 738 (Del. Super. Ct. 1936).
            –Page Citation.

In citing cases in law review footnotes, abbreviate any word listed in Table T.6;
the names of "states, countries, and other geographical units" unless they are named parties;
and any other words of eight or more letters "if <u>substantial</u> space is thereby saved and the
result is unambiguous." <u>Bluebook</u> Rule 10.2.2. On the other hand, in citing cases in text,
abbreviate only widely known acronyms and the following words: "&," "Ass'n," "Bros.,"
"Co.," "Corp.," "Inc.," "Ltd.," and "No." <u>Bluebook</u> Rule 10.2.1(c).

Maine:

Pelletier v. Central Maine Power Co., 126 A. 836 (Me. 1924).
–Case Citation.

Pelletier v. Central Maine Power Co., 126 A. 836, 838 (Me. 1924).
–Page Citation.

Maryland:

Frey & Son, Inc. v. Magness, 157 A. 400 (Md. 1931). –Case Citation.

Frey & Son, Inc. v. Magness, 157 A. 400, 402 (Md. 1931).
–Page Citation.

New Hampshire:

Sarkise v. Boston & M.R.R., 186 A. 332 (N.H. 1936). –Case Citation.

Sarkise v. Boston & M.R.R., 186 A. 332, 335 (N.H. 1936).
–Page Citation.

New Jersey:

Paletz v. Camden Safe Deposit & Trust Co., 157 A. 456 (N.J. Ch. 1931). –Case Citation.

Paletz v. Camden Safe Deposit & Trust Co., 157 A. 456, 458 (N.J. Ch. 1931). –Page Citation.

Pennsylvania:

Davis v. Hillman, 126 A. 246 (Pa. 1924). –Case Citation.

Davis v. Hillman, 126 A. 246, 247 (Pa. 1924). –Page Citation.

Rhode Island:

Gorham v. Robinson, 186 A. 832 (R.I. 1936). –Case Citation.

Gorham v. Robinson, 186 A. 832, 839 (R.I. 1936). –Page Citation.

Vermont:

Pennock v. Goodrich, 157 A. 922 (Vt. 1932). –Case Citation.

Pennock v. Goodrich, 157 A. 922, 924 (Vt. 1932). –Page Citation.

Atlantic Reporter, Second Series

–Do not give a parallel citation unless required by local rule or unless the particular state has a public domain format. See Bluebook Practitioners' Note P.3 and Rules 10.3.1 and 10.3.3. See also the various state court and state reporter entries herein for public domain information and local rule parallel citation requirements.

–With volume 532 (1988), Atlantic Reporter, Second Series, became West's Atlantic Reporter, Second Series. Citation form is not affected by this title change.

Ab.:   A.2d

Ex.:

Connecticut:

State v. Robinson, 676 A.2d 384 (Conn. 1996). –Case Citation.

State v. Robinson, 676 A.2d 384, 388 (Conn. 1996). –Page Citation.

In law review footnotes, the titles of books and the names of cases, except for procedural phrases, are not underlined. See Bluebook Rule 2.1(a). Further, the following are in large and small capitals: codes, restatements, standards, constitutions, periodicals, authors of books, titles of books, the abbreviated names of codes, most legislative materials except for bills and resolutions, codified ordinances, model codes, court rules, and sentencing guidelines. Refer to The Bluebook.

Delaware:
> Acierno v. Worthy Bros. Pipeline Corp., 656 A.2d 1085 (Del. Super. Ct. 1995). –Case Citation.
> Acierno v. Worthy Bros. Pipeline Corp., 656 A.2d 1085, 1090 (Del. Super. Ct. 1995). –Page Citation.

District of Columbia:
> Davis v. Henderson, 652 A.2d 634 (D.C. 1995). –Case Citation.
> Davis v. Henderson, 652 A.2d 634, 636 (D.C. 1995). –Page Citation.

Maine:
> Dutil v. Burns, 674 A.2d 910 (Me. 1996). –Case Citation.
> Dutil v. Burns, 674 A.2d 910, 911 (Me. 1996). –Page Citation.

Maryland:
> Mangrum v. State, 676 A.2d 80 (Md. 1996). –Case Citation.
> Mangrum v. State, 676 A.2d 80, 84 (Md. 1996). –Page Citation.

New Hampshire:
> State v. Vandebogart, 652 A.2d 671 (N.H. 1994). –Case Citation.
> State v. Vandebogart, 652 A.2d 671, 679 (N.H. 1994). –Page Citation.

New Jersey:
> Anderson v. Piccotti, 676 A.2d 127 (N.J. 1996). –Case Citation.
> Anderson v. Piccotti, 676 A.2d 127, 136 (N.J. 1996). –Page Citation.

Pennsylvania:
> Commonwealth v. Brown, 676 A.2d 1178 (Pa. 1996). –Case Citation.
> Commonwealth v. Brown, 676 A.2d 1178, 1183 (Pa. 1996). –Page Citation.

Rhode Island:
> Bruzzese v. Wood, 674 A.2d 390 (R.I. 1996). –Case Citation.
> Bruzzese v. Wood, 674 A.2d 390, 394 (R.I. 1996). –Page Citation.

Vermont:
> State v. Quinn, 675 A.2d 1336 (Vt. 1996). –Case Citation.
> State v. Quinn, 675 A.2d 1336, 1338 (Vt. 1996). –Page Citation.

Atomic Energy Commission Reports (U.S.) (1956-1975)
Ab.:   A.E.C.
Ex.:   Southern California Edison Co., 7 A.E.C. 410 (1974).
        T.V.A. (Watts Bar Nuclear Plant, Units 1 and 2), 6 A.E.C. 37 (1973).

Attorney General
Ab.:   Att'y Gen.

Attorney General's Annual Report
Ab.:   Att'y Gen. Ann. Rep.

In citing cases in law review footnotes, abbreviate any word listed in Table T.6; the names of "states, countries, and other geographical units" unless they are named parties; and any other words of eight or more letters "if substantial space is thereby saved and the result is unambiguous." Bluebook Rule 10.2.2. On the other hand, in citing cases in text, abbreviate only widely known acronyms and the following words: "&," "Ass'n," "Bros.," "Co.," "Corp.," "Inc.," "Ltd.," and "No." Bluebook Rule 10.2.1(c).

Ex.:   1956 Att'y Gen. Ann. Rep. 118.

Attorney General's Opinions, generally
See Bluebook Rule 14.4.

Attorney General's Opinions (State)
See Opinions of the Attorney General, as titled by the individual state.

Attorney General's Opinions (U.S.)
See Opinions of the Attorney General (U.S.) (1789-date).

Auckland University Law Review
Ab.:   Auckland U. L. Rev.
Ex.:   Ian Narev, Unjust Enrichment and De Facto Relationships, 6 Auckland
         U. L. Rev. 504 (1991). –Article Citation.

         Ian Narev, Unjust Enrichment and De Facto Relationships, 6 Auckland
         U. L. Rev. 504, 511-12 (1991). –Page Citation.

Audio Recordings
See electronic media and other nonprint source.

Auditing Standards, Generally Accepted
Ex.:   Report on Audited Financial Statements, Statement on Auditing
         Standards No. 2, § 509 (American Inst. of Certified Pub. Accountants
         1974).

Australia Treaty Series
Ab.:   year Austl. T.S. No. .
Ex.:   Treaty Between the Government of Australia and the Government of
         the United Kingdom of Great Britain and Northern Ireland Concerning
         the Investigation of Drug Trafficking and Confiscation of the Proceeds
         of Drug Trafficking, Aug. 3, 1988, Austl.- Gr. Brit.- N. Ir., art. 8, 1990
         Austl. T.S. No. 33.

Australian Argus Law Reports
Ab.:   A.A.L.R.
Ex.:   Morris v. Morris, (1972) 1972-73 A.A.L.R. 893 (Austl.).

Australian Business Law Review
Ab.:   Austl. Bus. L. Rev.
Ex.:   Andrew Keay, The Parameters of Bankruptcy Examinations, 22 Austl.
         Bus. L. Rev. 75 (1994). –Article Citation.

         Andrew Keay, The Parameters of Bankruptcy Examinations, 22 Austl.
         Bus. L. Rev. 75, 79-81 (1994). –Page Citation.

Australian Law Journal, The
Ab.:   Austl. L.J.

In law review footnotes, the titles of books and the names of cases, except for procedural phrases, are not underlined. See Bluebook Rule 2.1(a). Further, the following are in large and small capitals: codes, restatements, standards, constitutions, periodicals, authors of books, titles of books, the abbreviated names of codes, most legislative materials except for bills and resolutions, codified ordinances, model codes, court rules, and sentencing guidelines. Refer to The Bluebook.

Ex.:   Laurence Claus, <u>Implication and the Concept of a Constitution</u>, 69 Austl. L.J. 887 (1995). –Article Citation.

Laurence Claus, <u>Implication and the Concept of a Constitution</u>, 69 Austl. L.J. 887, 890-96 (1995). –Page Citation.

Australian Law Reports

Ab.:   A.L.R.

Ex.:   <u>Commonwealth of Australia and Another v. Esber</u>, (1991) 101 A.L.R. 35 (Fed. Ct.) (Austl.). –Case Citation.

<u>Commonwealth of Australia and Another v. Esber</u>, (1991) 101 A.L.R. 35, 38 (Fed. Ct.) (Austl.). –Page Citation.

Australian Yearbook of International Law, The

Ab.:   Austl. Y.B. Int'l L.

Ex.:   Yash Chai, <u>Human Rights and Governance: The Asia Debate</u>, 15 Austl. Y.B. Int'l L. 1 (1994). –Article Citation.

Yash Chai, <u>Human Rights and Governance: The Asia Debate</u>, 15 Austl. Y.B. Int'l L. 1, 11 (1994). –Page Citation.

author(s)

See various title entries in this work. <u>See also</u> <u>Bluebook</u> rules 15.1. and 16.1.

Ex.:   Jeffrey M. Hertzfeld, <u>Negotiating East-West Deals: Case Studies for Lawyers in Current Legal Aspects of Doing Business With Sino-Soviet Nations</u> 8 (James T. Haight ed., 1973).

authorities, order of authorities within each signal

<u>See</u> <u>Bluebook</u> Rule 1.4.

Automobile Liability Insurance, by Irvin E. Schermer

–Do not abbreviate the title.

Ex.:   1 Irvin F. Schermer, <u>Automobile Liability Insurance</u> § 4.01[1] (3d ed. 1995). –Section Citation.

1 Irvin F. Schermer, <u>Automobile Liability Insurance</u> § 4.01[1], at 4-4 (3d ed. 1995). –Page Citation.

1 Irvin F. Schermer, <u>Automobile Liability Insurance</u> § 4.01[1], at 4-4 n.15 (3d ed. 1995). –Footnote Citation.

Aviation Law Reports (Commerce Clearing House)

Ab.:   Av. L. Rep. (CCH)

Av. Cas. (CCH)

In citing cases in law review footnotes, abbreviate any word listed in Table T.6; the names of "states, countries, and other geographical units" unless they are named parties; and any other words of eight or more letters "if <u>substantial</u> space is thereby saved and the result is unambiguous." <u>Bluebook</u> Rule 10.2.2. On the other hand, in citing cases in text, abbreviate only widely known acronyms and the following words: "&," "Ass'n," "Bros.," "Co.," "Corp.," "Inc.," "Ltd.," and "No." <u>Bluebook</u> Rule 10.2.1(c).

B

Bail Court
    Ab.:   Bail Ct.

Baldwin's Official Edition, Kentucky Revised Statutes Annotated
    Ab.:   Ky. Rev. Stat. Ann. §   (West year)
    Ex.:   Ky. Rev. Stat. Ann. § 123.120 (West 1998).
             Ky. Rev. Stat. Ann. § 92.560 (West Supp. 1999).

Baldwin's Ohio Legislative Service (West)
    Ab.:   year Ohio Legis. Serv. (West)
    Ex.:   Act of Sept. 11, 1996, No. 351, 1996 Ohio Legis. Serv. 3343 (West)
             (concerning peace officer training council). –Citation to an entire
             session law.
             Act of Sept. 11, 1996, No. 351, sec. 1, §109.71, 1996 Ohio Legis. Serv.
             3343-44, (West) (concerning definition of peace officer).
             –Citation to a session law amending a prior act.

Baldwin's Ohio Revised Code Annotated (West)
    Ab.:   Ohio Rev. Code Ann. §   (West year)
    Ex.:   Ohio Rev. Code Ann. § 4511.452 (West 1999).
             Ohio Rev. Code Ann. § 3111.12 (West Supp. 2000).

Ballentine's Law Dictionary
    Ab.:   <u>Ballentine's Law Dictionary</u> page (ed. year)
    Ex.:   <u>Ballentine's Law Dictionary</u> 98 (3d ed. 1969).

Bank Regulation, by Michael P. Malloy
             –Do not abbreviate the title.
    Ex.:   Michael P. Malloy, Bank Regulation § 3.5 (1999). –Section Citation.
             Michael P. Malloy, Bank Regulation § 3.5, at 69 (1999). –Page
             Citation.
             Michael P. Malloy, Bank Regulation § 3.5, at 69 n.8 (1999).
             –Footnote Citation.

Banking Law Journal, The
    Ab.:   Banking L.J.
    Ex.:   Katrina Grider, <u>Employer Liability Under FIRREA</u>, 109 Banking L.J.
             129 (1992). –Article Citation.
             Katrina Grider, <u>Employer Liability Under FIRREA</u>, 109 Banking L.J.
             129, 131-36 (1992). –Page Citation.

In law review footnotes, the titles of books and the names of cases, except for procedural
phrases, are not underlined. See <u>Bluebook</u> Rule 2.1(a). Further, the following are in large
and small capitals: codes, restatements, standards, constitutions, periodicals, authors of
books, titles of books, the abbreviated names of codes, most legislative materials except for
bills and resolutions, codified ordinances, model codes, court rules, and sentencing guidelines.
Refer to <u>The Bluebook</u>.

Bankruptcy Appellate Panel
Ab.:   B.A.P.
Ex.:   Hal, Inc. v. United States (In re Hal, Inc.), 196 B.R. 159 (B.A.P. 9th Cir. 1996).

Bankruptcy Cases
Ex.:   Chase Lumber & Fuel Co. v. Koch (In re Koch), 197 B.R. 654 (Bankr. W.D. Wis. 1996)
        Nunez v. Nunez (In re Nunez), 196 B.R. 150 (B.A.P. 9th Cir. 1996).
        –If both the adversary and nonadversary name appear at the beginning of the opinion, cite as above, giving the adversary name first followed in parenthesis by the nonadversary name.
        –If only the nonadversary or adversary name appear at the beginning of the opinion, cite as follows:
                In re Calore Express Co., Inc., 199 B.R. 424 (Bankr. D. Mass. 1996).
                Bell v. Alden Owners, Inc., 199 B.R. 451 (S.D.N.Y. 1996).

Bankruptcy Court
Ab.:   Bankr.
Ex.:   In re Masegian, 134 B.R. 402, 403 (Bankr. E.D. Cal. 1991).

Bankruptcy Court Decisions
Ab.:   Bankr. Ct. Dec. (CRR)

Bankruptcy Court Rules
Ab.:   Bankr. R.
Ex.:   Bankr. R. 3002(c)(5).

Bankruptcy Law Reports (Commerce Clearing House) (formerly reporter)
Ab.:   Bankr. L. Rep. (CCH)
Ex.:   In re Fernandez, 3 Bankr. L. Rep. (CCH) ¶ 74,279 (Bankr. D. Kan. Sept. 30, 1991). –Citation to looseleaf material.
        In re Goodwin, [1985-1986 Transfer Binder] Bankr. L. Rep. (CCH) ¶ 71,025 (Bankr. D. Me. 1986).
        In re Citadel Properties, Inc., [1987-1989 Transfer Binder] Bankr. L. Rep. (CCH) ¶ 72,301 (Bankr. M.D. Fla. 1988). –Citations to transfer binder.
        –The above examples are proper if the case is not yet available in, or not reported in, an official or West reporter, a public domain citation, or in a widely used computer database.

Bankruptcy Law and Practice, by Daniel R. Cowans, Mark C. Ellenberg, Elizabeth Van Horn, & Russell W. Savory
        –Do not abbreviate the title.

In citing cases in law review footnotes, abbreviate any word listed in Table T.6; the names of "states, countries, and other geographical units" unless they are named parties; and any other words of eight or more letters "if substantial space is thereby saved and the result is unambiguous." Bluebook Rule 10.2.2. On the other hand, in citing cases in text, abbreviate only widely known acronyms and the following words: "&," "Ass'n," "Bros.," "Co.," "Corp.," "Inc.," "Ltd.," and "No." Bluebook Rule 10.2.1(c).

Ex.: 3 Daniel R. Cowans et al., <u>Bankruptcy Law and Practice</u> § 11.1 (7th ed. 1998). –Section Citation.

3 Daniel R. Cowans et al., <u>Bankruptcy Law and Practice</u> § 11.1, at 3 (7th ed. 1998). –Page Citation.

3 Daniel R. Cowans et al., <u>Bankruptcy Law and Practice</u> § 11.1, at 3 n.1 (7th ed. 1998). –Footnote citation.

Bankruptcy Reporter
Ab.: B.R.
Ex.: <u>In re Masegian</u>, 134 B.R. 402, 403 (Bankr. E.D. Cal. 1991).

Bar Bulletin: State Bar of New Mexico
Ab.: B. Bull. St. B. N.M.
Section A–nonconsecutively paginated
Ex.: Matthew E. Cohen, <u>Income Tax Aspects of Lawsuits</u>, B. Bull. St. B. N.M., Dec. 19, 1991, at 6. –Article Citation.

Matthew E. Cohen, <u>Income Tax Aspects of Lawsuits</u>, B. Bull. St. B. N.M., Dec. 19, 1991, at 6, 8. –Page Citation.

Section B–consecutively paginated
Ex.: <u>Proposed Amendments of Bar Commission Rules</u>, 30 B. Bull. St. B. N.M. 1055 (1991). –Article Citation.

Baron
Ab.: B.

Basic citation forms for briefs and legal memoranda.
<u>See</u> various title entries of this work. <u>See also</u> examples included on the last page and inside back cover of <u>The Bluebook</u>.

Basic Text on Labor Law, by Robert A. Gorman
–Do not abbreviate the title.
Ex.: Robert A. Gorman, <u>Basic Text on Labor Law, Unionization and Collective Bargaining</u> 670 (Jesse H. Choper, et al. eds., 1976). –Page Citation.

Baylor Law Review
Ab.: Baylor L. Rev.
Ex.: Kevin F. Risley, <u>Why Texas Courts Should Not Retain the Inherent Power to Impose Sanctions</u>, 44 Baylor L. Rev. 253 (1992). –Article Citation.

Kevin F. Risley, <u>Why Texas Courts Should Not Retain the Inherent Power to Impose Sanctions</u>, 44 Baylor L. Rev. 253, 262-65 (1992). –Page Citation.

Behavioral Sciences and the Law
Ab.: Behav. Sci. & L.

In law review footnotes, the titles of books and the names of cases, except for procedural phrases, are not underlined. <u>See</u> Bluebook Rule 2.1(a). Further, the following are in large and small capitals: codes, restatements, standards, constitutions, periodicals, authors of books, titles of books, the abbreviated names of codes, most legislative materials except for bills and resolutions, codified ordinances, model codes, court rules, and sentencing guidelines. Refer to <u>The Bluebook</u>.

Ex.:   Michael Perlin, <u>Dignity Was the First to Leave: Godinez v. Moran,</u>
            <u>Colin Ferguson, and the Trial of Mentally Disabled Criminal</u>
            <u>Defendants,</u> 14 Behav. Sci. & L. 81 (1996). –Article Citation.

            Michael Perlin, <u>Dignity Was the First to Leave: Godinez v. Moran,</u>
            <u>Colin Ferguson, and the Trial of Mentally Disabled Criminal</u>
            <u>Defendants,</u> 14 Behav. Sci. & L. 81, 86 (1996). –Page Citation.

Bench and Bar of Minnesota
Ab.:   Bench & B. Minn.
Ex.:   Marshall H. Tanick & Edwin Cheeseboro, <u>Football Law in Minnesota:</u>
            <u>From Antitrust to Zebras,</u> Bench & B. Minn., Jan. 1992, at 18. –Article
            Citation.

            Marshall H. Tanick & Edwin Cheeseboro, <u>Football Law in Minnesota:</u>
            <u>From Antitrust to Zebras,</u> Bench & B. Minn., Jan. 1992, at 18, 19.
            –Page Citation.

Benefits Law Journal
Ab.:   Benefits L.J.
Ex.:   Eric L. Smithback & Steven T. Idelson, <u>Municipal Retiree Benefits:</u>
            <u>Many Plans but No Prefunding –Yet,</u> 3 Benefits L.J. 477 (1990-91).
            –Article Citation.

            Eric L. Smithback & Steven T. Idelson, <u>Municipal Retiree Benefits:</u>
            <u>Many Plans but No Prefunding –Yet,</u> 3 Benefits L.J. 477, 478 (1990-
            91). –Page Citation.

Bergin on Estates in Land and Future Interests
See Preface to Estates in Land and Future Interests, by Thomas F. Bergin &
            Paul G. Haskell.

Berkeley Women's Law Journal
Ab.:   Berkeley Women's L.J.
Ex.:   Judy Scales-Trent, <u>Using Literature in Law School: The Importance of</u>
            <u>Reading and Telling Tales,</u> 7 Berkeley Women's L.J. 90 (1992).
            –Article Citation.

            Judy Scales-Trent, <u>Using Literature in Law School: The Importance of</u>
            <u>Reading and Telling Tales,</u> 7 Berkeley Women's L.J. 90, 98 (1992).
            –Page Citation.

Beverly Hills Bar Association Journal
Ab.:   Beverly Hills B. Ass'n. J.

In citing cases in law review footnotes, abbreviate any word listed in Table T.6;
the names of "states, countries, and other geographical units" unless they are named parties;
and any other words of eight or more letters "if <u>substantial</u> space is thereby saved and the
result is unambiguous." <u>Bluebook</u> Rule 10.2.2. On the other hand, in citing cases in text,
abbreviate only widely known acronyms and the following words: "&," "Ass'n," "Bros.,"
"Co.," "Corp.," "Inc.," "Ltd.," and "No." <u>Bluebook</u> Rule 10.2.1(c).

Ex.:   Michael A. Bertz, <u>Pattern of Racketeering Activity–A Jury Issue:
Opposing Views</u>, 26 Beverly Hills B. Ass'n. J. 24 (1992). –Article
Citation.

Michael A. Bertz, <u>Pattern of Racketeering Activity–A Jury Issue:
Opposing Views</u>, 26 Beverly Hills B. Ass'n. J. 24, 26 (1992). –Page
Citation.

**Biennial Report and Official Opinions of the Attorney General of the State of
West Virginia**
Ab.:   Op. W. Va. Att'y Gen.

<u>See</u> Opinions of the Attorney General of West Virginia.

Biennial Report of the Attorney General of the State of South Dakota
<u>See</u> Opinions of the Attorney General of South Dakota.

Biennial Report of the Attorney General of the State of Iowa
<u>See</u> Opinions of the Attorney General of Iowa.

Biennial Report of the Attorney General of the State of Michigan
<u>See</u> Opinions of the Attorney General of Michigan.

Bill of Rights Journal, The
Ab.:   Bill Rts. J.

Ex.:   David L. Sobel, <u>Free Speech and National Security</u>, Bill Rts. J., Dec.
1987, at 5. –Article Citation.

David L. Sobel, <u>Free Speech and National Security</u>, Bill Rts. J., Dec.
1987, at 5, 7. –Page Citation.

Bills, Congressional
<u>See</u> Congressional Bills.

**Bittker and Eustice on Federal Income Taxation of Corporations and
Shareholders**
<u>See</u> Federal Income Taxation of Corporations and Shareholders, by Boris I.
Bittker & James S. Eustice.

Black (United States Reports)
<u>See</u> United States Reports.

Black's Law Dictionary
Ab.:   Black's Law Dictionary (ed. year)

Ex.:   <u>Black's Law Dictionary</u> 1123 (7th ed. 1999).

Blashfield Automobile Law and Practice, by Patrick D. Kelly
    –Do not abbreviate the title.

Ex.:   11 Patrick D. Kelly, <u>Blashfield Automobile Law and Practice</u> § 421.2
(rev. 3d ed. 1977). –Section Citation.

In law review footnotes, the titles of books and the names of cases, except for procedural
phrases, are not underlined. <u>See</u> Bluebook Rule 2.1(a). Further, the following are in large
and small capitals: codes, restatements, standards, constitutions, periodicals, authors of
books, titles of books, the abbreviated names of codes, most legislative materials except for
bills and resolutions, codified ordinances, model codes, court rules, and sentencing guidelines.
Refer to <u>The Bluebook</u>.

11 Patrick D. Kelly, <u>Blashfield Automobile Law and Practice</u> § 421.2, at 279 (rev. 3d ed. 1977). –Page Citation.

11 Patrick D. Kelly, <u>Blashfield Automobile Law and Practice</u> § 421.2, at 101 n.26 (rev. 3d ed. Supp. 2000). –Footnote Citation to Supplement.

Blue Sky Law Reports (Commerce Clearing House)
> Ab.:   Blue Sky L. Rep. (CCH)

> Ex.:   <u>Carney v. Mantuano</u>, 3 Blue Sky L. Rep. (CCH) ¶ 74,122 (Wis. Ct. App. Sept. 25, 1996). –Citation to looseleaf material.

> <u>Gohler v. Wood</u>, [1993-1994 Decisions Tansfer Binder] Blue Sky L. Rep. (CCH) ¶ 73,269 (S.D. Utah April 29, 1994). –Citation to transfer binder material.

> –The above examples are proper if the case is not yet available in, or is not reported in, an official or West reporter, a public domain citation, or in a widely used computer database.

(The) Bluebook: A Uniform System of Citation, 17th ed.
> Ab.:   The Bluebook

>   Bluebook

> Ex.:   <u>The Bluebook: A Uniform System of Citation</u> R. 15.7(f), at 114 (Columbia Law Review Ass'n et al. eds., 17th ed. 2000).

> <u>The Bluebook: A Uniform System of Citation</u> 310 tbl. T.10 (Columbia Law Review Ass'n et al. eds., 17th ed. 2nd prtg. 2000).

Board of Contract Appeals
> <u>See</u> Contract Appeals Decisions.

Board of Tax Appeals
> <u>See</u> Reports of the United States Board of Tax Appeals.

Bogert on Trusts
> <u>See</u> Trusts, by George T. Bogert.

Book Review
> –Non-Student-Written Book Reviews. <u>See</u> <u>Bluebook</u> Rule 16.6.1.

In citing cases in law review footnotes, abbreviate any word listed in Table T.6; the names of "states, countries, and other geographical units" unless they are named parties; and any other words of eight or more letters "if <u>substantial</u> space is thereby saved and the result is unambiguous." <u>Bluebook</u> Rule 10.2.2. On the other hand, in citing cases in text, abbreviate only widely known acronyms and the following words: "&," "Ass'n," "Bros.," "Co.," "Corp.," "Inc.," "Ltd.," and "No." <u>Bluebook</u> Rule 10.2.1(c).

Ex.: Jason S. Johnston, <u>Not So Cold an Eye: Richard Posner's Pragmatism</u>, 44 Vand. L. Rev. 741 (1991) (reviewing Richard A. Posner, <u>The Problems of Jurisprudence</u> (1990)). –The citation should "include a second parenthetical after the date parenthetical indicating, if relevant to the purpose of the citation and not clear from the surrounding discussion, the author, title, and publication date of the book reviewed." <u>Bluebook</u> Rule 16.6.1

Jason S. Johnston, <u>Not So Cold an Eye: Richard Posner's Pragmatism</u>, 44 Vand. L. Rev. 741 (1991) (book review). –If it is unnecessary to identify the book under review, include the words "book review" in a second parenthetical. <u>Bluebook</u> Rule 16.6.1

–Student-Written Reviews. <u>See</u> <u>Bluebook</u> Rule 16.6.2(c).

Ex.: Thomas C. Grey, Book Note, 106 Yale L.J. 493 (1996) (reviewing Neil Duxbury, <u>Patterns of American Jurisprudence</u> (1995)). –Signed, student-written, untitled book review.

Geoffrey C. Rupp, Book Note, <u>DNA's Dark Side</u>, 110 Yale L. J. 163 (2000) (reviewing Jim Duyer, Peter Neufeld & Barry Scheck, <u>Actual Innocence: Five Days to Execution and Other Dispatches from the Wrongly Convicted</u> (2000)) –Signed, student-written, titled book review.

Book Note, <u>Translating Truth</u>, 114 Harv. L. Rev. 640 (2000) (reviewing Peter Brooks, <u>Troubling Confessions: Speaking Guilt in Law and Literature</u> (2000)). –Unsigned, student-written book review.

Boston Bar Journal
Ab.: Boston B.J.

Ex.: Paul J. Liacos, <u>The Origins of the Massachusetts Supreme Judicial Court</u>, Boston B.J., Mar.-Apr. 1992, at 4. –Article Citation.

Paul J. Liacos, <u>The Origins of the Massachusetts Supreme Judicial Court</u>, Boston B.J., Mar.-Apr. 1992, at 4, 6. –Page Citation.

Boston College Environmental Affairs Law Review
Ab.: B.C. Envtl. Aff. L. Rev.

Ex.: James P. Boggs, <u>NEPA in the Domain of Federal Indian Policy: Social Knowledge and the Negotiation of Meaning</u>, 19 B.C. Envtl. Aff. L. Rev. 31 (1991). –Article Citation.

James P. Boggs, <u>NEPA in the Domain of Federal Indian Policy: Social Knowledge and the Negotiation of Meaning</u>, 19 B.C. Envtl. Aff. L. Rev. 31, 35-39 (1991). –Page Citation.

Boston College International and Comparative Law Review
Ab.: B.C. Int'l & Comp. L. Rev.

In law review footnotes, the titles of books and the names of cases, except for procedural phrases, are not underlined. <u>See</u> <u>Bluebook</u> Rule 2.1(a). Further, the following are in large and small capitals: codes, restatements, standards, constitutions, periodicals, authors of books, titles of books, the abbreviated names of codes, most legislative materials except for bills and resolutions, codified ordinances, model codes, court rules, and sentencing guidelines. Refer to <u>The Bluebook</u>.

Ex.:   Clyde H. Crockett, <u>The Role of Federal Common Law in Alien Tort
Statute Cases</u>, 14 B.C. Int'l & Comp. L. Rev. 29 (1991). –Article
Citation.

Clyde H. Crockett, <u>The Role of Federal Common Law in Alien Tort
Statute Cases</u>, 14 B.C. Int'l & Comp. L. Rev. 29, 42-46 (1991). –Page
Citation.

Boston College Law Review
Ab.:   B.C. L. Rev.

Ex.:   Dean M. Hashimoto, <u>Justice Brennan's Use of Scientific and Empirical
Evidence in Constitutional and Administrative Law</u>, 32 B.C. L. Rev.
739 (1991). –Article Citation.

Dean M. Hashimoto, <u>Justice Brennan's Use of Scientific and Empirical
Evidence in Constitutional and Administrative Law</u>, 32 B.C. L. Rev.
739, 752-55 (1991). –Page Citation.

Boston College Third World Law Journal
Ab.:   B.C. Third World L.J.

Ex.:   Louis W. Sullivan & Ronald W. Roskens, <u>Child Survival and AIDS in
Sub-Saharan Africa: Findings and Recommendations of the
Presidential Mission to Africa</u>, 11 B.C. Third World L.J. 227 (1991).
–Article Citation.

Louis W. Sullivan & Ronald W. Roskens, <u>Child Survival and AIDS in
Sub-Saharan Africa: Findings and Recommendations of the
Presidential Mission to Africa</u>, 11 B.C. Third World L.J. 227, 240-41
(1991). –Page Citation.

Boston University International Law Journal
Ab.:   B.U. Int'l L.J.

Ex.:   Dennis S. Karjala, <u>The Closely Held Enterprise Under Japanese Law</u>,
7 B.U. Int'l L.J. 229 (1989). –Article Citation.

Dennis S. Karjala, <u>The Closely Held Enterprise Under Japanese Law</u>,
7 B.U. Int'l L.J. 229, 230 (1989). –Page Citation.

Boston University Journal of Tax Law
Ab.:   B.U. J. Tax L.

Ex.:   Stewart G. Thomsen, <u>Irrevocable Life Insurance Trust Planning Into
the Nineties</u>, 7 B.U. J. Tax L. 109 (1991). –Article Citation.

Stewart G. Thomsen, <u>Irrevocable Life Insurance Trust Planning Into
the Nineties</u>, 7 B.U. J. Tax L. 109, 119-20 (1991). –Page Citation.

In citing cases in law review footnotes, abbreviate any word listed in Table T.6;
the names of "states, countries, and other geographical units" unless they are named parties;
and any other words of eight or more letters "if <u>substantial</u> space is thereby saved and the
result is unambiguous." <u>Bluebook</u> Rule 10.2.2. On the other hand, in citing cases in text,
abbreviate only widely known acronyms and the following words: "&," "Ass'n," "Bros.,"
"Co.," "Corp.," "Inc.," "Ltd.," and "No." <u>Bluebook</u> Rule 10.2.1(c).

Boston University Law Review
Ab.:   B.U. L. Rev.
Ex.:   Erwin Chemerinsky, Ending the Parity Debate, 71 B.U. L. Rev. 593
        (1991). –Article Citation.

        Erwin Chemerinsky, Ending the Parity Debate, 71 B.U. L. Rev. 593,
        598-600 (1991). –Page Citation.

Boston University Public Interest Law Journal
Ab.:   B.U. Pub. Int. L.J.
Ex.:   Gerry Singsen, The Role of Competition in Making Grants for the
        Provision of Legal Services to the Poor, 1 B.U. Pub. Int. L.J. 57 (1991).
        –Article Citation.

        Gerry Singsen, The Role of Competition in Making Grants for the
        Provision of Legal Services to the Poor, 1 B.U. Pub. Int. L.J. 57, 69
        (1991). –Page Citation.

Bracton Law Journal
Ab.:   Bracton L.J.
Ex.:   Nicholas Grief, Legal Aspects of Nuclear Testing, 23 Bracton L.J. 25
        (1991). –Article Citation.

        Nicholas Grief, Legal Aspects of Nuclear Testing, 23 Bracton L.J. 25,
        33-35 (1991). –Page Citation.

brief, citation to
        –Explained and illustrated in Bluebook Rule 10.8.3.

briefs, basic citation forms
        See various title entries of this work. See also examples included on the last
        page and inside back cover of Bluebook.

briefs, typeface conventions for briefs
        See Bluebook Practitioners' Notes, pp. 11-19.

Brigham Young University Journal of Public Law
Ab.:   B.Y.U. J. Pub. L.
Ex.:   Robert E. Riggs & Michael R. Moss, Supreme Court Voting Behavior:
        1987 Term, 3 B.Y.U. J. Pub. L. 1 (1989). –Article Citation.

        Robert E. Riggs & Michael R. Moss, Supreme Court Voting Behavior:
        1987 Term, 3 B.Y.U. J. Pub. L. 1, 4-5 (1989). –Page Citation.

Brigham Young University Law Review
Ab.:   B.Y.U. L. Rev.
Ex.:   Arthur Austin, The Waste Land, 1991 B.Y.U. L. Rev. 1229. –Article
        Citation.

        Arthur Austin, The Waste Land, 1991 B.Y.U. L. Rev. 1229, 1233-35.
        –Page Citation.

In law review footnotes, the titles of books and the names of cases, except for procedural
phrases, are not underlined. See Bluebook Rule 2.1(a). Further, the following are in large
and small capitals: codes, restatements, standards, constitutions, periodicals, authors of
books, titles of books, the abbreviated names of codes, most legislative materials except for
bills and resolutions, codified ordinances, model codes, court rules, and sentencing guidelines.
Refer to The Bluebook.

British Columbia Statutes
    Ab.:   S.B.C.
    Ex.:   International Financial Business Act, ch. 16, 1988 S.B.C. 105 (Can.).
             –Citation to an entire act.
             International Financial Business Act, ch. 16, § 9, 1988 S.B.C. 105, 109
             (Can.). –Citation to a section of an act.

British Journal of Criminology
    Ab.:   Brit. J. Criminology
    Ex.:   Roy D. King & Kathleen McDermott, British Prisons 1970-1987, 29
             Brit. J. of Criminology 107 (1989). –Article Citation.
             Roy D. King & Kathleen McDermott, British Prisons 1970-1987, 29
             Brit. J. of Criminology 107, 114 (1989). –Page Citation.

British Tax Review
    Ab.:   Brit. Tax Rev.
    Ex.:   Peter Sundgren, Interpretation of Tax Treaties--A Case Study, 1990
             Brit. Tax Rev. 286. –Article Citation.
             Peter Sundgren, Interpretation of Tax Treaties--A Case Study, 1990
             Brit. Tax Rev. 286, 289-90. –Page Citation.

British Yearbook of International Law
    Ab.:   Brit. Y.B. Int'l L.
    Ex.:   Campbell McLachlan, Splitting the Proper Law in Private International
             Law, 61 Brit. Y.B. Int'l L. 311 (1990). –Article Citation.
             Campbell McLachlan, Splitting the Proper Law in Private International
             Law, 61 Brit. Y.B. Int'l L. 311, 315-17 (1990). –Page Citation.

Bromberg and Lowenfels on Securities Fraud & Commodities Fraud, by Alan R. Bromberg and Lewis D. Lowenfels
             –Do not abbreviate the title.
    Ex.:   4 Alan R. Bromberg & Lewis D. Lowenfels, Bromberg and Lowenfels
             on Securities Fraud & Commodities Fraud § 15.07 (230) (2d ed. 2000).
             –Section Citation.
             4 Alan R. Bromberg & Lewis D. Lowenfels, Bromberg and Lowenfels
             on Securities Fraud & Commodities Fraud § 15.07(230), at 15:169 (2d
             ed. 2000). –Page Citation.

Brooklyn Journal of International Law
    Ab.:   Brook. J. Int'l L.
    Ex.:   Jacob S. Ziegel, Canadian Perspectives on Transborder Insolvencies,
             17 Brook. J. Int'l L. 539 (1991). –Article Citation.
             Jacob S. Ziegel, Canadian Perspectives on Transborder Insolvencies,
             17 Brook. J. Int'l L. 539, 551-53 (1991). –Page Citation.

In citing cases in law review footnotes, abbreviate any word listed in Table T.6; the names of "states, countries, and other geographical units" unless they are named parties; and any other words of eight or more letters "if substantial space is thereby saved and the result is unambiguous." Bluebook Rule 10.2.2. On the other hand, in citing cases in text, abbreviate only widely known acronyms and the following words: "&," "Ass'n," "Bros.," "Co.," "Corp.," "Inc.," "Ltd.," and "No." Bluebook Rule 10.2.1(c).

Brooklyn Law Review
    Ab.:   Brook. L. Rev.

    Ex.:   Thomas J. Meskill, Caseload Growth: Struggling to Keep Pace, 57
             Brook. L. Rev. 299 (1991). −Article Citation.

             Thomas J. Meskill, Caseload Growth: Struggling to Keep Pace, 57
             Brook. L. Rev. 299, 299-301 (1991). −Page Citation.

Buffalo Law Review
    Ab.:   Buff. L. Rev.

    Ex.:   Michael Ariens, Evidence of Religion and the Religion of Evidence, 40
             Buff. L. Rev. 65 (1992). −Article Citation.

             Michael Ariens, Evidence of Religion and the Religion of Evidence, 40
             Buff. L. Rev. 65, 78-81 (1992). −Page Citation.

Bulletin Board Systems (BBS)
    See Internet Sources.

Bulletin of the European Communities
    Ab.:   Bull. Eur. Commmunities

    Ex.:   Role of the Community in the World, Bull. Eur. Communities, June
             1991, at 43. −Article Citation.

             Role of the Community in the World, Bull. Eur. Communities, June
             1991, at 43, 45-46. −Page Citation.

BundesGerichts Entscheidungen (Switzerland)
    Ab.:   BGE

Constitutional cases	BGE Ia
Administrative cases	BGE Ib
Civil cases	BGE II
Bankruptcy cases	BGE III
Criminal cases	BGE IV
Social cases	BGE V

Bureau of National Affairs
    Ab.:   BNA

Bürgerliches Gesetzbuch (F.R.G.)
    Ab.:   BGB

    See Bluebook Rule 20.1.3.

    Ex.:   Bürgerliches Gesetzbuch [BGB] § 2116 (F.R.G.).

             BGB § 2116. −Subsequent abbreviated citation.

Burns Indiana Statutes Annotated
    Ab.:   Ind. Code Ann. § (Lexis year)

In law review footnotes, the titles of books and the names of cases, except for procedural phrases, are not underlined. See Bluebook Rule 2.1(a). Further, the following are in large and small capitals: codes, restatements, standards, constitutions, periodicals, authors of books, titles of books, the abbreviated names of codes, most legislative materials except for bills and resolutions, codified ordinances, model codes, court rules, and sentencing guidelines. Refer to The Bluebook.

Ex.:   Ind. Code Ann. § 6-7-1-16 (Lexis 1999)

          Ind. Code Ann. § 6-1.1-12-285 (Lexis Supp. 2000)

          –"Cite to Indiana Code if therein." Bluebook Table T.1, p. 201.

Business America
Ab.:   Bus. Am.

Ex.:   Jean H. Grier, Legal Obligations to Remove Trade Barriers in New
          U.S. Trade Agreements With Japan, Bus. Am., Feb. 11, 1991, at 5.
          –Article Citation.

          Jean H. Grier, Legal Obligations to Remove Trade Barriers in New
          U.S. Trade Agreements With Japan, Bus. Am., Feb. 11, 1991, at 5, 7-9.
          –Page Citation.

Business Law Journal
Ab.:   Bus. L.J.

Ex.:   Daniel L. Goelzer & Susan Nash, Expanding Disclosure in Control
          Transactions: The Proposed Significant Equity Participant Regulations
          and the Co-Bidder Cases, 1 Bus. L.J. 1 (1990). –Article Citation.

          Daniel L. Goelzer & Susan Nash, Expanding Disclosure in Control
          Transactions: The Proposed Significant Equity Participant Regulations
          and the Co-Bidder Cases, 1 Bus. L.J. 1, 3-4 (1990). –Page Citation.

Business Lawyer
Ab.:   Bus. Law.

Ex.:   Victor Futter, An Answer to the Public Perception of Corporations: A
          Corporate Ombudsperson?, 46 Bus. Law. 29 (1990). –Article Citation.

          Victor Futter, An Answer to the Public Perception of Corporations: A
          Corporate Ombudsperson?, 46 Bus. Law. 29, 35-38 (1990). –Page
          Citation.

Business Week
Ab.:   Bus. Wk.

Ex.:   Christopher Farrell, The Recovery: Why So Slow?, Bus. Wk., July 20,
          1992, at 60. –Article Citation.

          Christopher Farrell, The Recovery: Why So Slow?, Bus. Wk., July 20,
          1992, at 60, 63. –Page Citation.

But cf.
          –"But cf." is used when the "cited authority supports a proposition
          analagous to the contrary of the main proposition." Bluebook Rule
          1.2(c).

In citing cases in law review footnotes, abbreviate any word listed in Table T.6;
the names of "states, countries, and other geographical units" unless they are named parties;
and any other words of eight or more letters "if substantial space is thereby saved and the
result is unambiguous." Bluebook Rule 10.2.2. On the other hand, in citing cases in text,
abbreviate only widely known acronyms and the following words: "&," "Ass'n," "Bros.,"
"Co.," "Corp.," "Inc.," "Ltd.," and "No." Bluebook Rule 10.2.1(c).

Ex.:   "In <u>Brown</u> there was evidence that the corporation's agents had misled the plaintiff about the name of the corporation they represented. <u>Id.</u> at 1409 n. 3. <u>But cf.</u> <u>Hofferman v. Westinghouse Elec. Corp.</u>, 653 F.Supp. 423, 429 (D.D.C. 1986) (holding Rule 15(c) relation back proper where defendants conduct partly responsible for plaintiff's mistake in naming wrong party)." –Taken from 952 F.2d 1008, 1012 (8th Cir. 1991).

But see

–"<u>But see</u>" is used when the "cited authority clearly supports a proposition contrary to the main proposition. '<u>But see</u>' is used where '<u>see</u>' would be used for support." <u>Bluebook</u> Rule 1.2(c).

Ex.:   "After <u>Hughey</u>, any other conclusion seems unsupportable. <u>But see</u> <u>United States v. Hurt</u>, 940 F.2d 130, 131 (5th Cir. 1991); <u>United States v. Duvall</u>, 926 F.2d 875, 876-77 (9th Cir. 1991)." –Taken from 952 F.2d 1262, 1264 n.3 (10th Cir. 1991).

In law review footnotes, the titles of books and the names of cases, except for procedural phrases, are not underlined. <u>See</u> <u>Bluebook</u> Rule 2.1(a). Further, the following are in large and small capitals: codes, restatements, standards, constitutions, periodicals, authors of books, titles of books, the abbreviated names of codes, most legislative materials except for bills and resolutions, codified ordinances, model codes, court rules, and sentencing guidelines. Refer to <u>The Bluebook</u>.

C

(Les) Cahiers de Droit
Ab.:   C. de D.
Ex.:   Dominique Goubau, L'adoption d'un enfant contre la volunté de ses parents, 35 C. de D. 151 (1994). –Article Citation.

Dominique Goubau, L'adoption d'un enfant contre la volunté de ses parents, 35 C. de D. 151, 155 (1994). –Page Citation.

–"If desired, the original language title may be followed by a translation or a shortened name in English in brackets in the same typeface as the original." Bluebook Rule 19.1.2.

Cahiers de Droit Fiscal International (International Fiscal Association)
Ab.:   C. de D. Fisc. Int'l
Ex.:   Dr. Guillermo H. Fernández, General Aspects of the Deduction of Interest and other Financing Expenses, 79 Cahiers de Droit Fiscal International [C. de D. Fisc. Int'l] 23 (1994). –Article Citation.

Dr. Guillermo H. Fernández, General Aspects of the Deduction of Interest and other Financing Expenses, 79 C. de D. Fisc. Int'l 23, 26 (1994). –Page Citation.

Calamari & Perillo on Contracts
See Law of Contracts, by John D. Calamari & Joseph M. Perillo.

California Advance Legislative Service (Deering)
Ab.:   year Cal. Adv. Legis. Serv. (Deering)
–Cite to Statutes of California if therein. See Bluebook Table T.1, p. 193.

California Annotated and Unannotated Code (Deering)
See Deering's Annotated and Unannotated California Code.

California Appellate Reports
Ab.:   Cal. App., Cal. App. 2d, Cal. App. 3d, Cal. App. 4th
–In documents submitted to California state courts, cite to Cal. App., Cal. App. 2d, Cal. App. 3d, or Cal. App. 4th, if therein. In all other documents, cite only to P. or P.2d (before 1960) or to Cal Rptr. or Cal. Rptr. 2d (after 1959) if therein; otherwise, cite

---

In law review footnotes, the titles of books and the names of cases, except for procedural phrases, are not underlined. See Bluebook Rule 2.1(a). Further, the following are in large and small capitals: codes, restatements, standards, constitutions, periodicals, authors of books, titles of books, the abbreviated names of codes, most legislative materials except for bills and resolutions, codified ordinances, model codes, court rules, and sentencing guidelines. Refer to The Bluebook.

to a California Appellate Report.

–Give parallel citations, if at all, only in documents submitted to California state courts. See Bluebook Rule 10.3.1 and Practitioners' Note P.3; see also Cal. R. Ct. 313(c), which requires citation only to Cal. App., Cal. App. 2d, Cal. App. 3d, or Cal. App. 4th.

In documents submitted to California state courts, cite as follows:

VanDerHoof v. Chambon, 121 Cal. App. 118, 8 P.2d 925 (1932). –Case Citation.

VanDerHoof v. Chambon, 121 Cal. App. 118, 131, 8 P.2d 925, 930 (1932). –Page Citation.

Brantley v. Pisaro, 42 Cal. App. 4th 1591, 50 Cal. Rptr. 2d 431 (1996). –Case Citation.

Brantley v. Pisaro, 42 Cal. App. 4th 1591, 1593, 50 Cal. Rptr. 2d 431, 433 (1996). –Page Citation.

In all other documents, cite as follows:

VanDerHoof v. Chambon, 8 P.2d 925 (Cal. Dist. Ct. App. 1932). –Case Citation.

VanDerHoof v. Chambon, 8 P.2d 925, 930 (Cal. Dist. Ct. App. 1932). –Page Citation.

Brantley v. Pisaro, 50 Cal. Rptr. 2d 431 (Ct. App. 1996). –Case Citation.

Brantley v. Pisaro, 50 Cal. Rptr. 2d 431, 433 (Ct. App. 1996). –Page Citation.

California Appellate Reports Supplement
Ab.:   Cal. App. Supp.

Cal. App. 2d Supp.

Cal. App. 3d Supp.

Cal. App. 4th Supp.

–In documents submitted to California state courts, cite to Cal. App. Supp., Cal. App. 2d Supp., Cal. App. 3d Supp., or Cal. App. 4th Supp., if therein. In all other documents, cite only to P. or P.2d (before 1960) or to Cal Rptr. or Cal. Rptr. 2d (after 1959), if therein; otherwise, cite to a California Appellate Report Supplement.

–Bound with Cal. App.

–Give parallel citations, if at all, only in documents submitted to California state courts. See Bluebook Rule 10.3.1 and Practitioners' Note P.3; see also Cal. R. Ct. 313(c), which requires citation only to Cal. App. Supp., Cal. App. 2d Supp., Cal. App. 3d Supp., or Cal. App. 4th Supp.

In documents submitted to California state courts, cite as follows:

In citing cases in law review footnotes, abbreviate any word listed in Table T.6; the names of "states, countries, and other geographical units" unless they are named parties; and any other words of eight or more letters "if substantial space is thereby saved and the result is unambiguous." Bluebook Rule 10.2.2. On the other hand, in citing cases in text, abbreviate only widely known acronyms and the following words: "&," "Ass'n," "Bros.," "Co.," "Corp.," "Inc.," "Ltd.," and "No." Bluebook Rule 10.2.1(c).

People v. Studley, 44 Cal. App. 4th Supp. 1, 52 Cal. Rptr. 2d 461 (App. Dep't Super. Ct. 1996). –Case Citation.

People v. Studley, 44 Cal. App. 4th Supp. 1, 5, 52 Cal. Rptr. 2d 461, 463 (App. Dep't Super. Ct. 1996). –Page Citation.

In all other documents, cite as follows:

People v. Studley, 52 Cal. Rptr. 2d 461 (App. Dep't Super. Ct. 1996). –Case Citation.

People v. Studley, 52 Cal. Rptr. 2d 461, 463 (App. Dep't Super. Ct. 1996). –Page Citation.

California Attorney General Opinions
See Opinions of the Attorney General of California.

California Bankruptcy Journal
Ab.:   Cal. Bankr. J.

California Code Annotated (West)
See West's Annotated California Code.

California Code of Regulations
Ab.:   Cal. Code Regs. tit. , § (year)
Ex.:   Cal. Code Regs. tit. 11, § 2 (1978)

California Constitution
Ab.:   Cal. Const. art. , § .
Ex.:   Cal. Const. art. I, § 6. –"Cite constitutional provisions currently in force without date." Bluebook Rule 11.

Cal. Const. art. IV, § 27 (repealed 1980). –"If the cited provision has been repealed, either indicate parenthetically the fact and date of repeal or cite the repealing provision in full." Bluebook Rule 11.

Cal. Const. art. IV, § 2 (amended 1990). –"When citing a provision that has been subsequently amended, either indicate parenthetically the fact and date of amendment or cite the amending provision in full." Bluebook Rule 11.

Cal. Const. of 1849, art. I, § 1 (1879). –"Cite constitutions that have been totally superseded by year of adoption; if the specific provision cited was adopted in a different year, give that year parenthetically." Bluebook Rule 11.

California Jurisprudence, third edition
Ab.:   Cal. Jur. 3d
Ex.:   58 Cal. Jur. 3d Specific Performance § 43 (1980).

California Law Review
Ab.:   Cal. L. Rev.

In law review footnotes, the titles of books and the names of cases, except for procedural phrases, are not underlined. See Bluebook Rule 2.1(a). Further, the following are in large and small capitals: codes, restatements, standards, constitutions, periodicals, authors of books, titles of books, the abbreviated names of codes, most legislative materials except for bills and resolutions, codified ordinances, model codes, court rules, and sentencing guidelines. Refer to The Bluebook.

Ex.: Richard L. Roe, <u>Valuing Student Speech: The Work of the Schools as Conceptual Development</u>, 79 Cal. L. Rev. 1269 (1991). –Article Citation.

Richard L. Roe, <u>Valuing Student Speech: The Work of the Schools as Conceptual Development</u>, 79 Cal. L. Rev. 1269, 1277-78 (1991). –Page Citation.

California Lawyer
Ab.: Cal. Law.
Ex.: Gregory Tordahl, <u>Making the Workplace Safe for Computer Users</u>, Cal. Law., Feb. 1992, at 51. –Article Citation.

Gregory Tordahl, <u>Making the Workplace Safe for Computer Users</u>, Cal. Law., Feb. 1992, at 51, 58. –Page Citation.

California Legislative Service (West)
Ab.: year Cal. Legis. Serv. (West)
Ex.: Act of September 11, 1996, ch. 418, 1996 Cal. Legis. Serv. 2228 (West) (relating to economic development). –Citation to an entire session law.

Act of Sept. 21, 1996, ch. 694 sec. 3, § 8020(a), 1996 Cal. Legis. Serv. 3125, 3125-26, (West) (relating to shorthand reporters). –Citation to a session law amending a prior act.

California Regulatory Law Reporter
Ab.: Cal. Reg. L. Rep.

California Regulatory Notice Register
Ab.: Cal. Regulatory Notice Reg.

California Reporter, West's
<u>See</u> West's California Reporter

California Reports
Ab.: Cal., Cal. 2d, Cal. 3d, Cal. 4th

–In documents submitted to California state courts, cite to Cal., Cal. 2d, Cal. 3d, or Cal. 4th if therein. In all other documents, cite to P., P.2d, or P.3d if therein; otherwise, cite to Cal., Cal. 2d, Cal. 3d, or Cal. 4th or to Cal. Rptr. or Cal. Rptr. 2d.

–Give parallel citations, if at all, only in documents submitted to California state courts. <u>See</u> <u>Bluebook</u> Rule 10.3.1 and Practitioners' Note P.3; <u>see also</u> Cal. R. Ct. 313(c), which requires citation only to Cal., Cal. 2d, Cal. 3d, or Cal. 4th.

In documents submitted to California state courts, cite as follows:

In citing cases in law review footnotes, abbreviate any word listed in Table T.6; the names of "states, countries, and other geographical units" unless they are named parties; and any other words of eight or more letters "if <u>substantial</u> space is thereby saved and the result is unambiguous." <u>Bluebook</u> Rule 10.2.2. On the other hand, in citing cases in text, abbreviate only widely known acronyms and the following words: "&," "Ass'n," "Bros.," "Co.," "Corp.," "Inc.," "Ltd.," and "No." <u>Bluebook</u> Rule 10.2.1(c).

Mangini v. Aerojet-General Corp., 12 Cal. 4th 1087, 912 P.2d 1220, 51 Cal. Rptr. 2d 272 (1996). –Case Citation.

Mangini v. Aerojet-General Corp., 12 Cal. 4th 1087, 1088, 912 P.2d 1220, 1222, 51 Cal. Rptr. 2d 272, 273 (1996). –Page Citation.

In all other documents, cite as follows:

Mangini v. Aerojet-General Corp., 912 P.2d 1220 (Cal. 1996). –Case Citation.

Mangini v. Aerojet-General Corp., 912 P.2d 1220, 1222 (Cal. 1996). –Page Citation.

California Session Laws
See California Legislative Service (West) and Statutes of California.

California Unreported Cases
Ab.:   Cal. Unrep.

Ex.:   Ganahl v. Soher, 2 Cal. Unrep. 415 (Super. Ct. 1884). –Case Citation.

Ganahl v. Soher, 2 Cal. Unrep. 415, 416 (Super Ct. 1884). –Page Citation.

California Western International Law Journal
Ab.:   Cal. W. Int'l L.J.

Ex.:   Mark Gibney, Compensation for Civilians Harmed in the Pursuit of Foreign Policy Goals: Recent Litigation in U.S. Courts, 22 Cal. W. Int'l L.J. 59 (1991). –Article Citation.

Mark Gibney, Compensation for Civilians Harmed in the Pursuit of Foreign Policy Goals: Recent Litigation in U.S. Courts, 22 Cal. W. Int'l L.J. 59, 72-74 (1991). –Page Citation.

California Western Law Review
Ab.:   Cal. W. L. Rev.

Ex.:   Michael Ariens, On the Road of Good Intentions: Justice Brennan and the Religion Clauses, 27 Cal. W. L. Rev. 311 (1991). –Article Citation.

Michael Ariens, On the Road of Good Intentions: Justice Brennan and the Religion Clauses, 27 Cal. W. L. Rev. 311, 314-17 (1991). –Page Citation.

Callaghan & Co.
Ab.:   Callaghan

Cambrian Law Review, The
Ab.:   Cambrian L. Rev.

In law review footnotes, the titles of books and the names of cases, except for procedural phrases, are not underlined. See Bluebook Rule 2.1(a). Further, the following are in large and small capitals: codes, restatements, standards, constitutions, periodicals, authors of books, titles of books, the abbreviated names of codes, most legislative materials except for bills and resolutions, codified ordinances, model codes, court rules, and sentencing guidelines. Refer to The Bluebook.

Ex.:   John Hughes, <u>Legal and Ethical Implications of Clinical Research on Human Subjects</u>, 22 Cambrian L. Rev. 5 (1991). –Article Citation.

John Hughes, <u>Legal and Ethical Implications of Clinical Research on Human Subjects</u>, 22 Cambrian L. Rev. 5, 22-24 (1991). –Page Citation.

Cambridge Law Journal
Ab.:   Cambridge L.J.
Ex.:   P.P. Craig, <u>The Common Law, Reasons and Administrative Justice</u>, 53 Cambridge L.J. 282 (1994). –Article Citation.

P.P. Craig, <u>The Common Law, Reasons and Administrative Justice</u>, 53 Cambridge L.J. 282, 285 (1994). –Page Citation.

Campaigns and the Court: The U.S. Supreme Court in Presidential Elections, by Donald Grier Stephenson, Jr.
          –Do not abbreviate the title.
Ex.:   Donald Grier Stephenson, Jr., <u>Campaigns and the Court: The U.S. Supreme Court in Presidential Elections</u> 185 (1999). –Page Citation.

Donald Grier Stephenson, Jr., <u>Campaigns and the Court: The U.S. Supreme Court in Presidential Elections</u> 185 n.124 (1999). Footnote Citation.

Campbell Law Review
Ab.:   Campbell L. Rev.
Ex.:   Anthony M. Brannon, <u>Successful Shadowboxing: The Art of Impeaching Hearsay Declarants</u>, 13 Campbell L. Rev. 157 (1991). –Article Citation.

Anthony M. Brannon, <u>Successful Shadowboxing: The Art of Impeaching Hearsay Declarants</u>, 13 Campbell L. Rev. 157, 160-67 (1991). –Page Citation.

Canada Gazette
Ab.:   C. Gaz.
Ex.:   <u>An Act to Implement the North American Free Trade Agreement</u>, 16 C. Gaz. Part III 374 (1994 Can.).

Canada: Supreme Court Reports (1876-date)
          –Cite to S.C.R. if therein; otherwise, cite to D.L.R. <u>See</u> Bluebook Table T.2.
Ab.:   S.C.R.
Ex.:   <u>Leiriao v. Town of Val-Bélair</u>, [1991] 3 S.C.R. 349 (Can.). –Case Citation.

Canada Treaty Series
Ab.:   year Can. T.S. No. .

In citing cases in law review footnotes, abbreviate any word listed in Table T.6; the names of "states, countries, and other geographical units" unless they are named parties; and any other words of eight or more letters "if <u>substantial</u> space is thereby saved and the result is unambiguous." <u>Bluebook</u> Rule 10.2.2. On the other hand, in citing cases in text, abbreviate only widely known acronyms and the following words: "&," "Ass'n," "Bros.," "Co.," "Corp.," "Inc.," "Ltd.," and "No." <u>Bluebook</u> Rule 10.2.1(c).

Canada-United States Law Journal
Ab.:   Can.-U.S. L.J.

Ex.:   Malcom E. Wheeler, Comparative Aspects of Dispute Resolution in Particular Subject Areas: Product Liability, 17 Can.-U.S. L.J. 359 (1991). –Article Citation.

       Malcom E. Wheeler, Comparative Aspects of Dispute Resolution in Particular Subject Areas: Product Liability, 17 Can.-U.S. L.J. 359, 360-61 (1991). –Page Citation.

Canada-U.S. Business Law Review
Ab.:   Can.-U.S. Bus. L. Rev.

Ex.:   Guy Dionne, Entering the EEC to Provide Services: The Case of Insurance, 4 Can.-U.S. Bus. L. Rev. 113 (1990-1991). –Article Citation.

       Guy Dionne, Entering the EEC to Provide Services: The Case of Insurance, 4 Can.-U.S. Bus. L. Rev. 113, 122 (1990-1991). –Page Citation.

Canadian-American Law Journal
Ab.:   Can.-Am. L.J.

Ex.:   Alan L. Schechter, United States - Canadian Bankruptcy Litigation: Is the Treaty the Way to Go?, 4 Can.-Am. L.J. 1 (1988). –Article Citation.

       Alan L. Schechter, United States - Canadian Bankruptcy Litigation: Is the Treaty the Way to Go?, 4 Can.-Am. L.J. 1, 21 (1988). –Page Citation.

Canadian Bar Review
Ab.:   Can. B. Rev.

Ex.:   John J. Chapman, Judicial Scrutiny of Domestic Commercial Arbitral Awards, 74 Can. B. Rev. 401 (1995). –Article Citation.

       John J. Chapman, Judicial Scrutiny of Domestic Commercial Arbitral Awards, 74 Can. B. Rev. 401, 410-411 (1995). –Page Citation.

Canadian Constitution
Ab.:   Can. Const.

Canadian Tax Journal
Ab.:   Can. Tax J.

Ex.:   Al Katiya, Proposed Changes to the SR and ED Program Under the Income Tax Act, 42 Can. Tax J. 309 (1994). –Article Citation.

       Al Katiya, Proposed Changes to the SR and ED Program Under the Income Tax Act, 42 Can. Tax J. 309, 311-12 (1994). –Page Citation.

Canadian Tax Reports (Commerce Clearing House)
Ab.:   Can. Tax Rep. (CCH)

In law review footnotes, the titles of books and the names of cases, except for procedural phrases, are not underlined. See Bluebook Rule 2.1(a). Further, the following are in large and small capitals: codes, restatements, standards, constitutions, periodicals, authors of books, titles of books, the abbreviated names of codes, most legislative materials except for bills and resolutions, codified ordinances, model codes, court rules, and sentencing guidelines. Refer to The Bluebook.

Canadian Yearbook of International Law
Ab.:   Can. Y.B. Int'l L.
Ex.:   William A. Schabas, <u>Reservations to Human Rights Treaties: Time for Innovation and Reform</u>, 32 Can. Y.B. Int'l L. 39 (1994). –Article Citation.

William A. Schabas, <u>Reservations to Human Rights Treaties: Time for Innovation and Reform</u>, 32 Can. Y.B. Int'l L. 39, 45-46 (1994). –Page Citation.

Canal Zone Code
Ab.:   C.Z. Code tit. , § (year)
Ex.:   C.Z. Code tit. 6, § 1191(b) (1963). –Section Citation.

Capital Defense Digest
Ab.:   Cap. Def. Dig.

Capital University Law Review
Ab.:   Cap. U. L. Rev.
Ex.:   Gregory M. Travalio, <u>Values and Schizophrenia in Intercollegiate Athletics</u>, 20 Cap. U. L. Rev. 587 (1991). –Article Citation.

Gregory M. Travalio, <u>Values and Schizophrenia in Intercollegiate Athletics</u>, 20 Cap. U. L. Rev. 587, 593-95 (1991). –Page Citation.

Cardozo Arts and Entertainment Law Journal
Ab.:   Cardozo Arts & Ent. L. J.
Ex.:   Sherri L. Burr, <u>Artistic Parody: A Theoretical Construct</u>, 14 Cardozo Arts & Ent. L.J. 65 (1996). –Article Citation.

Sherri L. Burr, <u>Artistic Parody: A Theoretical Construct</u>, 14 Cardozo Arts & Ent. L.J. 65, 67 (1996). –Page Citation.

Cardozo Law Review
Ab.:   Cardozo L. Rev.
Ex.:   Matthew P. Bergman, <u>Status, Contract, and History: A Dialectical View</u>, 13 Cardozo L. Rev. 171 (1991). –Article Citation.

Matthew P. Bergman, <u>Status, Contract, and History: A Dialectical View</u>, 13 Cardozo L. Rev. 171, 181-87 (1991). –Page Citation.

Case citations
See <u>Bluebook</u> Rule 10.1 for samples of basic case citations in law reviews, briefs, and legal memoranda. Sample citations are provided for each stage in the course of litigation and alternative citations are provided when the case is available in alternative sources (i.e., a final decision by a federal district court available in an electronic database, service, newspaper, or as a slip opinion.)

In citing cases in law review footnotes, abbreviate any word listed in Table T.6; the names of "states, countries, and other geographical units" unless they are named parties; and any other words of eight or more letters "if <u>substantial</u> space is thereby saved and the result is unambiguous." <u>Bluebook</u> Rule 10.2.2. On the other hand, in citing cases in text, abbreviate only widely known acronyms and the following words: "&," "Ass'n," "Bros.," "Co.," "Corp.," "Inc.," "Ltd.," and "No." <u>Bluebook</u> Rule 10.2.1(c).

case names

–In text: Give the last name of an individual and the full name of an institution, political entity, or corporation without abbreviation except as provided in <u>Bluebook</u> Rule 10.2.1.

–In citations: In addition to the rules for a case name in text, abbreviate according to Rule 10.2.2 and Table T.6.

–Basic citation forms: <u>See</u> various title entries in this work. See also <u>Bluebook</u> Rules 10.1, 10.2, 10.6 (parenthetical information regarding cases), 10.7 (prior and subsequent history), and 10.8 (special citation forms).

–In law review footnotes: <u>See</u> the guidelines and illustrations on pp. 56-73 of <u>The Bluebook</u>.

Case Western Reserve Journal of International Law

Ab.: Case W. Res. J. Int'l L.

Ex.: Michael I. Kraus, <u>The Perils of Rural Land Use Planning: The Case of Canada</u>, 23 Case W. Res. J. Int'l L. 65 (1991). –Article Citation.

Michael I. Kraus, <u>The Perils of Rural Land Use Planning: The Case of Canada</u>, 23 Case W. Res. J. Int'l L. 65, 71-74 (1991). –Page Citation.

Case Western Reserve Law Review

Ab.: Case W. Res. L. Rev.

Ex.: Michael P. Healy, <u>Direct Liability for Hazardous Substance Cleanups Under CERCLA: A Comprehensive Approach</u>, 42 Case W. Res. L. Rev. 65 (1992). –Article Citation.

Michael P. Healy, <u>Direct Liability for Hazardous Substance Cleanups Under CERCLA: A Comprehensive Approach</u>, 42 Case W. Res. L. Rev. 65, 77-80 (1992). –Page Citation.

cases, basic citation forms

<u>See</u> various title entries in this work. See also <u>Bluebook</u> Rule 10.

cases, subsequent citation to

<u>See</u> subsequent citations to cases, statutes, and prior citations.

Casner on Estate Planning

<u>See</u> Estate Planning, by A. James Casner and Jeffrey N. Pennell.

Catholic Lawyer, The

Ab.: Cath. Law.

Ex.: Angela C. Carmella, <u>Landmark Preservation of Church Property</u>, 34 Cath. Law. 41 (1991). –Article Citation.

Angela C. Carmella, <u>Landmark Preservation of Church Property</u>, 34 Cath. Law. 41, 50-53 (1991). –Page Citation.

In law review footnotes, the titles of books and the names of cases, except for procedural phrases, are not underlined. <u>See</u> <u>Bluebook</u> Rule 2.1(a). Further, the following are in large and small capitals: codes, restatements, standards, constitutions, periodicals, authors of books, titles of books, the abbreviated names of codes, most legislative materials except for bills and resolutions, codified ordinances, model codes, court rules, and sentencing guidelines. Refer to <u>The Bluebook</u>.

Catholic University Law Review
 Ab.: Cath. U. L. Rev.
 Ex.: David M. Cohen, <u>Claims for Money in the Claims Court</u>, 40 Cath. U. L. Rev. 533 (1991). –Article Citation.

   David M. Cohen, <u>Claims for Money in the Claims Court</u>, 40 Cath. U. L. Rev. 533, 534-38 (1991). –Page Citation.

CBA Record
 Ab.: CBA Rec.
 Ex.: Sherwin J. Malkin, <u>Beware the Lost Volume Seller</u>, CBA Rec., May 1992, at 20. –Article Citation.

   Sherwin J. Malkin, <u>Beware the Lost Volume Seller</u>, CBA Rec., May 1992, at 20, 23. –Page Citation.

CD-ROM
 "Information found on CD-ROM usually is available in print form, and citation to the print form is preferred where available. If the information is accessed on CD-ROM, it should be cited to CD-ROM. When citing cases on CD-ROM, the possibility exists that a case published near the date of the CD-ROM itself may have been included in slip opinion form, and (like a decision in an advance sheet) may have been edited or otherwise changed before the case was published in final form.

 When citing CD-ROM media, include the title of the material, the publisher of the CD-ROM, the version searched, and the date of the material, if available, or the date of the version searched. The information may be provided in a source-date parenthetical or, if the information is voluminous, as related authority (rule 1.6)." –<u>Bluebook</u> Rule 18.3.

 Ex. <u>Taylor v. Heldman</u>, No. M1999-00729-COA-R3-CV, (Tenn. Ct. App. 2000) (Tennessee Unpublished Decisions, 1985-2000, West CD-ROM Libraries, current through Nov. 1, 2000).

   5 C.F.R. § 630.101 (West LawDesk Code of Federal Regulations CD-ROM, current through Sept. 2000).

   1 Lee R. Russ and Thomas F. Segalla, <u>Couch on Insurance</u> §1.4 (Couch on Insurance West LawDesk CD-ROM, July 2000).

certiorari denied
 Ab.: cert. denied
 Ex.: <u>Bernhard v. Harrah's Club</u>, 16 Cal. 3d 313, 546 P.2d 719, 128 Cal. Rptr. 215, <u>cert. denied</u>, 429 U.S. 859 (1976).

certiorari granted
 Ab.: cert. granted

In citing cases in law review footnotes, abbreviate any word listed in Table T.6; the names of "states, countries, and other geographical units" unless they are named parties; and any other words of eight or more letters "if <u>substantial</u> space is thereby saved and the result is unambiguous." <u>Bluebook</u> Rule 10.2.2. On the other hand, in citing cases in text, abbreviate only widely known acronyms and the following words: "&," "Ass'n," "Bros.," "Co.," "Corp.," "Inc.," "Ltd.," and "No." <u>Bluebook</u> Rule 10.2.1(c).

Ex.:   Walker v. Armco Steel Corp., 592 F.2d 1133 (10th Cir. 1979), cert. granted, No. 78-1862, 48 U.S.L.W. 3186 (Oct. 1, 1979).

Cf.

–"Cf." is used when the "cited authority supports a proposition different from the main proposition but sufficiently analgous to lend support." Bluebook Rule 1.2(a).

Ex.:   "The St. John testimony was not so extremely inflammatory and repetitive that it could not be cured by an admonition to the jury. Cf. United States v. Gillespie, 852 F.2d 475, 479 (9th Cir. 1988) (extreme prejudice from admission of improper evidence of defendant's homosexuality could not be cured by admonition to jury)." –Taken from 941 F.2d 761, 765 (9th Cir. 1991).

Chancellor
Ab.:   C.

Chancery
Ab.:   Ch.

Chancery Court
Ab.:   Ch.

Chancery Division
Ab.:   Ch.

chapter(s)
Ab.:   ch., chs.

Charter of the United Nations
Ab.:   U.N. Charter
Ex.:   U.N. Charter art. 33, para. 1.

Chartered Life Underwriters
Ab.:   C.L.U.

Chemical Regulation Reporter (Bureau of National Affairs)
Ab.:   Chem. Reg. Rep. (BNA)

Chicago Board Options Exchange (Commerce Clearing House)
Ab.:   Chicago Bd. Options Ex. (CCH)

Chicago-Kent Law Review
Ab.:   Chi.-Kent L. Rev.

Ex.:   Gordon S. Wood, Classical Republicanism and the American Revolution, 66 Chi.-Kent L. Rev. 13 (1990). –Article Citation.
Gordon S. Wood, Classical Republicanism and the American Revolution, 66 Chi.-Kent L. Rev. 13, 14-15 (1990). –Page Citation.

In law review footnotes, the titles of books and the names of cases, except for procedural phrases, are not underlined. See Bluebook Rule 2.1(a). Further, the following are in large and small capitals: codes, restatements, standards, constitutions, periodicals, authors of books, titles of books, the abbreviated names of codes, most legislative materials except for bills and resolutions, codified ordinances, model codes, court rules, and sentencing guidelines. Refer to The Bluebook.

Chicago Tribune
    Ab.:   Chi. Trib.

Chicano Law Review
    Ab.:   Chicano L. Rev.
    Ex.:   Adela de la Torre & Refugio Rochin, Hispanic Poor and the Effects of Immigration Reform, 10 Chicano L. Rev. 1 (1990). –Article Citation.
            Adela de la Torre & Refugio Rochin, Hispanic Poor and the Effects of Immigration Reform, 10 Chicano L. Rev. 1, 3-6 (1990). –Page Citation.

Chief Baron
    Ab.:   C.B.

Chief Judge
    Ab.:   C.J.

Chief Justice
    Ab.:   C.J.

Children's Court
    Ab.:   Child. Ct.

Children's Legal Rights Journal
    Ab.:   Children's Legal Rts. J.
    Ex.:   David W. Lloyd, Ritual Child Abuse: Where Do We Go From Here?, Winter 1991, at 12. –Article Citation.
            David W. Lloyd, Ritual Child Abuse: Where Do We Go From Here?, Winter 1991, at 12, 13-15. –Page Citation.

China Law Reporter (ABA Section of International Law)
    Ab.:   P.R.C. L. Rep.
    Ex.:   Zhengdong Huang, Negotiation in China: Cultural and Practical Characteristics, 6 P.R.C. Law Rep. 139 (1990). –Article Citation.
            Zhengdong Huang, Negotiation in China: Cultural and Practical Characteristics, 6 P.R.C. Law Rep. 139, 142-43 (1990). –Page Citation.

Chommie on Federal Income Taxation
    See Law of Federal Income Taxation, by Michael D. Rose and John C. Chommie.

Chronicle
    Ab.:   Chron.

Cincinnati Bar Association Journal
    Ab.:   Cincinnati B.A. J.

In citing cases in law review footnotes, abbreviate any word listed in Table T.6; the names of "states, countries, and other geographical units" unless they are named parties; and any other words of eight or more letters "if substantial space is thereby saved and the result is unambiguous." Bluebook Rule 10.2.2. On the other hand, in citing cases in text, abbreviate only widely known acronyms and the following words: "&," "Ass'n," "Bros.," "Co.," "Corp.," "Inc.," "Ltd.," and "No." Bluebook Rule 10.2.1(c).

Circuit Court (old federal)
   Ab.:   C.C.

Circuit Court (state)
   Ab.:   Cir. Ct.

Circuit Court of Appeal(s) (state)
   Ab.:   Cir. Ct. App.

Circuit Court of Appeals (federal)
   See U.S. Court of Appeals ...

Cited in
   Ex.:   Unif. Probate Code §§ 2-102, 2-103 (1969), cited in Wellman, The Uniform Probate Code: A Possible Answer to Probate Avoidance, 44 Ind. L.J. 191, 200 (1969).
   See Bluebook Rule 1.6(d) for proper use of cited in.

City Court
   Ab.:   [name city] City Ct.

Civil Aeronautics Board Reports (U.S.) (1940-date) (vol. 1 by C.A.A.)
   Ab.:   C.A.B.
   Ex.:   Pandair Freight Ltd., Foreign Indirect Permit, 60 C.A.B. 205 (1972). Braniff Airways, 1 C.A.B. 291 (1939). –Citation to the first volume of the series, published by the Civil Aeronautics Authority.

Civil Appeals
   Ab.:   Civ. App.

Civil Court of Record
   Ab.:   Civ. Ct. Rec.

Civil Procedure, by Fleming James, Jr., Geoffrey C. Hazard, Jr., and John Leubsdorf
   –Do not abbreviate the title.
   Ex.:   Fleming James, Jr. et al., Civil Procedure § 9.4 (4th ed. 1992). – Section Citation.
   Fleming James, Jr. et al., Civil Procedure § 9.4, at 470 (4th ed. 1992). –Page Citation.
   Fleming James, Jr. et al., Civil Procedure § 9.4, at 470 n.1 (4th ed. 1992). –Footnote Citation.

Civil Procedure, by Jack H. Friedenthal, Mary Kay Kane, and Arthur R. Miller
   –Do not abbreviate the title.
   Ex.:   Jack H. Friedenthal et al., Civil Procedure § 14.10 (3d ed. 1999). –Section Citation.
   Jack H. Friedenthal et al., Civil Procedure § 14.10, at 679-89 (3d ed. 1999). –Page Citation.

In law review footnotes, the titles of books and the names of cases, except for procedural phrases, are not underlined. See Bluebook Rule 2.1(a). Further, the following are in large and small capitals: codes, restatements, standards, constitutions, periodicals, authors of books, titles of books, the abbreviated names of codes, most legislative materials except for bills and resolutions, codified ordinances, model codes, court rules, and sentencing guidelines. Refer to The Bluebook.

Jack H. Friedenthal et al., <u>Civil Procedure</u> § 14.10, at 679 n.2 (3d ed. 1999). –Footnote Citation.

Civil Rights Digest
> Ab.:   Civ. Rts. Dig.

C.J.S.
> <u>See</u> Corpus Juris Secundum.

Claims Court
> Ab.:   Cl. Ct.
> –Created 1982, successor to the Court of Claims (Ct. Cl.). In 1992, succeeded by the United States Court of Federal Claims (Fed. Cl.).
> –Cite to F. Supp. or F.2d, if therein; otherwise to United States Claims Court Reporter.

Claims Court Reporter
> Ab.:   Cl. Ct.
> –Cite to the Claims Court Reporter as follows:
> Ex.:   <u>Mobley v. United States</u>, 8 Cl. Ct. 767 (1985).

clause(s)
> Ab.:   cl., cls.

Clearinghouse Review
> Ab.:   Clearinghouse Rev.
> Ex.:   Paula Roberts, <u>Child Support Enforcement in 1991</u>, 25 Clearinghouse Rev. 1098 (1992). –Article Citation.
> Paula Roberts, <u>Child Support Enforcement in 1991</u>, 25 Clearinghouse Rev. 1098, 1102-03 (1992). –Page Citation.
> –If the author of the article is an institutional author, cite according to <u>Bluebook</u> Rule 15.1.3.

Cleveland State Law Review
> Ab.:   Clev. St. L. Rev.
> Ex.:   Himanshu S. Amin, <u>The Lack of Protection Afforded Software Under the Current Intellectual Property Laws</u>, 43 Clev. St. L. Rev. 19 (1995). –Article Citation.
> Himanshu S. Amin, <u>The Lack of Protection Afforded Software Under the Current Intellectual Property Laws</u>, 43 Clev. St. L. Rev. 19, 25 (1995). –Page Citation.

Close Corporations, by F. Hodge O'Neal & Robert B. Thompson
> <u>See</u> O'Neal's Close Corporations, by F. Hodge O'Neal & Robert B. Thompson.

Code administratif (France)
> <u>See</u> <u>Bluebook</u> Rule 20.1.3 and 20.5.2 and Table T.2.
> Ab.:   C. adm.

In citing cases in law review footnotes, abbreviate any word listed in Table T.6; the names of "states, countries, and other geographical units" unless they are named parties; and any other words of eight or more letters "if <u>substantial</u> space is thereby saved and the result is unambiguous." <u>Bluebook</u> Rule 10.2.2. On the other hand, in citing cases in text, abbreviate only widely known acronyms and the following words: "&," "Ass'n," "Bros.," "Co.," "Corp.," "Inc.," "Ltd.," and "No." <u>Bluebook</u> Rule 10.2.1(c).

Ex.:   Code administratif [C. adm.] art. 60 (Fr.).
          C. adm. art. 60. –Subsequent abbreviated citation.

Code civil (France)
See Bluebook Rules 20.1.3 and 19.5.2 and Table T.2.
Ab.:   C. civ.
Ex.:   Code civil [C. civ.] art. 1165 (Fr.).
          C. civ. art. 1165. –Subsequent abbreviated citation.

Code de commerce (France)
See Bluebook Rules 20.1.3 and 19.5.2 and Table T.2.
Ab.:   C. com.
Ex.:   Code de commerce [C. com.] art. 632 (Fr.).
          C. com. art. 632. –Subsequent abbreviated citation.

Code de procédure pénale
See Bluebook Rule 20.1.3 and 19.5.2 and Table T.2.
Ab.:   C. pr. pén.

Code du travail
See Bluebook Rule 20.1.3 and 19.5.2 and Table T.2.
Ab.:   C. trav.
Ex.:   Code du travail [C. trav.] art. L. 434-7 (Fr.).
          C. trav. art. L. 434-7. –Subsequent abbreviated citation.

Code of Alabama
Ab.:   Ala. Code §   (year)
Ex.:   Ala. Code § 35-5-221 (1999).
          Ala. Code § 40-14-40 (Supp. 1999).

Code of Colorado Regulations
Ab.:   [v] Colo. Code Regs. §   (year)
Ex.:   3 Colo. Code Regs. § 3-1-9, App. A (2000)

Code of Federal Regulations
Ab.:   C.F.R.
Ex.:   23 C.F.R. § 750.308 (1996).
          Regulation D, 12 C.F.R. § 204 (1996). –Cite to a regulation with a
          popular name.
          –For citations to the Federal Register, see the entry under Federal
          Register.

Code of Georgia Annotated (Harrison)
Ab.:   Ga. Code Ann. §   (Harrison year)
Ex.:   Ga. Code Ann. § 110-104 (Harrison 1973).
          Ga. Code Ann. § 67-2001 (Harrison Supp. 1984).

In law review footnotes, the titles of books and the names of cases, except for procedural phrases, are not underlined. See Bluebook Rule 2.1(a). Further, the following are in large and small capitals: codes, restatements, standards, constitutions, periodicals, authors of books, titles of books, the abbreviated names of codes, most legislative materials except for bills and resolutions, codified ordinances, model codes, court rules, and sentencing guidelines. Refer to The Bluebook.

–"Cite to the official version of Ga. Code Ann. (published by Michie) if therein." <u>Bluebook</u> Table T.1, p. 199.

Code of Georgia Annotated, Official (Michie)
<u>See</u> Official Code of Georgia Annotated (Michie).

Code of Iowa
Ab.:   Iowa Code §   (year)
Ex.:   Iowa Code § 633.273 (1979).

Code of Laws of South Carolina 1976 Annotated, Code of Regulations
Ab.:   S.C. Code Ann. Regs. (year)
Ex.:   S.C. Code Ann. Regs. 69-2 (2000).

Code of Laws of South Carolina 1976 Annotated (West)
Ab.:   S.C. Code Ann. § (West year)
Ex.:   S.C. Code Ann. § 40-5-20 (West 2000).

Code of Maine Rules
Ab.:   Code Me. R.
Ex.:   Code Me. R. 01-001-05 (2000).

Code of Maryland Regulations
Ab.:   Md. Regs. Code
Ex.:   Md. Regs. Code 17.05.01.01 (2000)

Code of Massachusetts Regulations
Ab.:   Mass. Regs. Code tit. , § (year)
Ex.:   Mass. Regs. Code tit. 104, § 29.15 (2000).

Code of Professional Responsibility ABA
<u>See</u> American Bar Association Model Code of Professional Responsibility.

Code of Professional Responsibility Annotated (ABF)
<u>See</u> American Bar Foundation Code of Professional Responsibility, Annotated.

Code of Rhode Island Rules
Ab.:   R.I. Code R.
Ex.:   R.I. Code R. CR92-01 (1993)

Code of Vermont Rules
Ab.:   Vt. Code R. (year)
Ex.:   Vt. Code R. 28 060 001 (1998).

Code of Virginia Annotated
Ab.:   Va. Code Ann. § (Michie year)
Ex.:   Va. Code Ann. § 19-2-325 (Michie 2000).
              Va. Code Ann. § 63-1-195 (Michie Supp. 2000).

Code pénal (Fr.)
<u>See</u> <u>Bluebook</u> Rule 20.1.3 and 20.5.2 and Table T.2.

In citing cases in law review footnotes, abbreviate any word listed in Table T.6; the names of "states, countries, and other geographical units" unless they are named parties; and any other words of eight or more letters "if <u>substantial</u> space is thereby saved and the result is unambiguous." <u>Bluebook</u> Rule 10.2.2. On the other hand, in citing cases in text, abbreviate only widely known acronyms and the following words: "&," "Ass'n," "Bros.," "Co.," "Corp.," "Inc.," "Ltd.," and "No." <u>Bluebook</u> Rule 10.2.1(c).

Ab.: C. pén.
Ex.: Code pénal [C. pén.] art. 418 (Fr.)
C. pén. art. 418. –Subsequent abbreviated citation.

codified statutes
Ab.: cod. st.

Código Civil para el Distrito Federal (Mexico)
Ab.: C.C.D.F.; See Bluebook Rule 20.1.3.
Ex.: Código Civil para el Distrito Federal [C.C.D.F.] art. 1118 (Mex.).
C.C.D.F. art. 1118. –Subsequent abbreviated citation.

Código de Comercio (Mexico)
Ab.: Cód.Com.; See Bluebook Rule 20.1.3.
Ex.: Código de Comercio [Cód.Com.] art. 94 (Mex.).
Cód.Com. art. 94. –Subsequent abbreviated citation.

Código Penal para el Distrito Federal (Mexico)
Ab.: C.P.D.F.; See Bluebook Rule 20.1.3.
Ex.: Código Penal para el Distrito Federal [C.P.D.F.] art. 387 (Mex.).
C.P.D.F. art. 387. –Subsequent abbreviated citation.

Collections of Decisions of the European Commission of Human Rights
Ab.: Eur. Comm'n H.R. Dec. & Rep. See Bluebook Rule 21.5.3 and Table T.3.
Ex.: Farragut v. France, App. No. 10103/82, 42 Eur. Comm'n H.R. Dec. & Rep. 77, 83 (1982). –Page Citation.

Collective Bargaining Negotiations & Contracts (Bureau of National Affairs)
Ab.: Collective Bargaining Negot. & Cont. (BNA)

College Law Digest
Ab.: College L. Dig. (Nat'l Ass'n College & Univ. Att'ys)

Collier Bankruptcy Manual
–Do not abbreviate the title.
Ex.: 2 Collier Bankruptcy Manual ¶ 523.05[2] (Lawrence P. King ed., 3d ed. 1990). –Paragraph Citation.
2 Collier Bankruptcy Manual ¶ 523.05[2], at 523-21 (Lawrence P. King ed., 3d ed. 1990). –Page Citation.
2 Collier Bankruptcy Manual ¶ 523.05[2], at 523-21 n.51b (Lawrence P. King ed., 3d ed. 1990). –Footnote Citation.

Collier Bankruptcy Practice Guide
–Do not abbreviate the title.

In law review footnotes, the titles of books and the names of cases, except for procedural phrases, are not underlined. See Bluebook Rule 2.1(a). Further, the following are in large and small capitals: codes, restatements, standards, constitutions, periodicals, authors of books, titles of books, the abbreviated names of codes, most legislative materials except for bills and resolutions, codified ordinances, model codes, court rules, and sentencing guidelines. Refer to The Bluebook.

Ex.:   5 <u>Collier Bankruptcy Practice Guide</u> ¶ 85.08 (Asa S. Herzog &
            Lawrence P. King eds., 2000). –Paragraph Citation.
            5 <u>Collier Bankruptcy Practice Guide</u> ¶ 85.08, at 85-18 (Asa S. Herzog
            & Lawrence P. King eds., 2000). –Page Citation.
            5 <u>Collier Bankruptcy Practice Guide</u> ¶ 88.08, at 85-18 n.1 (Asa S.
            Herzog & Lawrence P. King eds., 2000). –Footnote Citation.

Collier on Bankruptcy
            –Do not abbreviate the title.
Ex.:   5 <u>Collier on Bankruptcy</u> ¶ 544.08 (Lawrence P. King ed., 15th ed.
            2000). –Paragraph Citation.
            5 <u>Collier on Bankruptcy</u> ¶ 544.08, at 544-15 (Lawrence P. King ed.,
            15th ed. 2000). –Page Citation.
            5 <u>Collier on Bankruptcy</u> ¶ 544.08, at 544-15 n.3 (Lawrence P. King
            ed., 15th ed. 2000). –Footnote Citation.

Colonial Lawyer, The
Ab.:   Colonial Law.
Ex.:   Keith Finch, Note, <u>Virginia's New Rule 11 "Clone" -- An Empirical
            Study</u>, 19 Colonial Law. 1 (1990). –Article Citation.
            Keith Finch, Note, <u>Virginia's New Rule 11 "Clone" -- An Empirical
            Study</u>, 19 Colonial Law. 1, 9-12 (1990). –Page Citation.
            –A designation of the piece should appear before the title of the work
            to indicate that it is student written. <u>See</u> <u>Bluebook</u> Rule 16.6.2

Colorado
Ab.:   Colo.

Colorado Bar Association
Ab.:   Colo. B.A.

Colorado Code of Regulations
            <u>See</u> Code of Colorado Regulations.

Colorado Constitution
Ab.:   Colo. Const. art.   , §   .
Ex.:   Colo. Const. art. II, § 7. –"Cite constitutional provisions currently in
            force without date." <u>Bluebook</u> Rule 11.
            Colo. Const. art. V, § 37 (repealed 1974). –"If the cited provision has
            been repealed, either indicate parenthetically the fact and date of repeal
            or cite the repealing provision in full." <u>Bluebook</u> Rule 11.
            Colo. Const. art. IV, § 18 (amended 1990). –"When citing a provision
            that has been subsequently amended, either indicate parenthetically the
            fact and date of amendment or cite the amending provision in full."
            <u>Bluebook</u> Rule 11.

In citing cases in law review footnotes, abbreviate any word listed in Table T.6;
the names of "states, countries, and other geographical units" unless they are named parties;
and any other words of eight or more letters "if <u>substantial</u> space is thereby saved and the
result is unambiguous." <u>Bluebook</u> Rule 10.2.2. On the other hand, in citing cases in text,
abbreviate only widely known acronyms and the following words: "&," "Ass'n," "Bros.,"
"Co.," "Corp.," "Inc.," "Ltd.," and "No." <u>Bluebook</u> Rule 10.2.1(c).

Colorado Court of Appeals Reports

Ab.: Colo. App.

–Discontinued after 44 Colo. App. 561 (1980).

–Cite to P., P.2d, or P.3d if therein; otherwise, cite to Colo. App.

–Give parallel citations, if at all, only in documents submitted to Colorado state courts. See Bluebook Rule 10.3.1 and Practitioners' Note P.3; see also internal rules of the Colorado Supreme Court and Court of Appeals, which do not appear to require a parallel citation.

Through 44 Colo. App. 561 (1980), cite as follows:

In documents submitted to Colorado state courts, cite as follows:

> Alley v. Kal, 44 Colo. App. 561, 610 P.2d 191 (1980). –Case Citation.

> Alley v. Kal, 44 Colo. App. 561, 564, 610 P.2d 191, 193 (1980). –Page Citation.

In all other documents, cite as follows:

> Alley v. Kal, 610 P.2d 191 (Colo. Ct. App. 1980). –Case Citation.

> Alley v. Kal, 610 P.2d 191, 193 (Colo. Ct. App. 1980). –Page Citation.

–After 44 Colo. App. 561 (1980), cite as follows:

In all documents:

> Dewey v. Hardy, 917 P.2d 305 (Colo. Ct. App. 1996). –Case Citation.

> Dewey v. Hardy, 917 P.2d 305, 311 (Colo. Ct. App. 1996). –Page Citation.

Colorado Journal of International & Environmental Law and Policy

Ab.: Colo. J. Int'l Envtl. L. & Pol'y

Ex.: M. Wray Witten, Institutional Failure in the Water and Sanitation Decade, 2 Colo. J. Int'l Envtl. L. & Pol'y 277 (1991). –Article Citation.

M. Wray Witten, Institutional Failure in the Water and Sanitation Decade, 2 Colo. J. Int'l Envtl. L. & Pol'y 277, 293-294 (1991). –Page Citation.

Colorado Lawyer

Ab.: Colo. Law.

Ex.: Cassandra G. Sasso, Liability of Fiduciaries under ERISA, 21 Colo. Law. 197 (1991). –Article Citation.

Cassandra G. Sasso, Liability of Fiduciaries under ERISA, 21 Colo. Law. 197, 198 (1991). –Page Citation.

Colorado Legislative Service (West)

Ab.: year Colo. Legis Serv. (West)

In law review footnotes, the titles of books and the names of cases, except for procedural phrases, are not underlined. See Bluebook Rule 2.1(a). Further, the following are in large and small capitals: codes, restatements, standards, constitutions, periodicals, authors of books, titles of books, the abbreviated names of codes, most legislative materials except for bills and resolutions, codified ordinances, model codes, court rules, and sentencing guidelines. Refer to The Bluebook.

Ex.:   Act of Apr. 16, 1996, No. 97, Sec. 3, § 30-15-402(1), 1996 Colo. Legis. Serv. 403, 403 (West) (concerning ordinance violations punishable by fines). –Citation to a session law amending prior act.

Act of Apr. 16, 1996, No. 97, § 3, 1996 Colo. Legis. Serv. 403 (West) (concerning ordinance violations punishable by fines). –Citation to an entire session law.

Colorado Register
Ab.:   Colo. Reg.

Colorado Reports
Ab.:   Colo.

–Discontinued after 200 Colo. 549 (1980).

–Cite to P., P.2d or P.3d if therein; otherwise, cite to Colo.

–Give parallel citations, if at all, only in documents submitted to Colorado state courts. See Bluebook Rule 10.3.1 and Practitioners' Note P.3; see also internal rules of the Colorado Supreme Court and Court of Appeals, which do not appear to require a parallel citation.

–Through 200 Colo. 549 (1980), cite as follows:

In documents submitted to Colorado state courts:

Mishek v. Stanton, 200 Colo. 514, 616 P.2d 135 (1980). –Case Citation.

Mishek v. Stanton, 200 Colo. 514, 515, 616 P.2d 135, 136 (1980). –Page Citation.

In all other documents:

Mishek v. Stanton, 616 P.2d 135 (Colo. 1980). –Case Citation.

Mishek v. Stanton, 616 P.2d 135, 136 (Colo. 1980). –Page Citation.

–After 200 Colo. 549 (1980), cite as follows:

In all documents:

Boyer v. Karakehian, 915 P.2d 1295 (Colo. 1996). –Case Citation.

Boyer v. Karakehian, 915 P.2d 1295, 1296-97 (Colo. 1996). –Page Citation.

Colorado Revised Statutes Annotated (West)
Ab.:   Colo. Rev. Stat. Ann. §   (West year)

Ex.:   Colo. Rev. Stat. Ann. § 16-8-122 (West 1999).

Colo. Rev. Stat. § 39-22-508 (West Supp. 2000).

Colorado Session Laws
See Session Laws of Colorado and Colorado Legislative Service (West).

In citing cases in law review footnotes, abbreviate any word listed in Table T.6; the names of "states, countries, and other geographical units" unless they are named parties; and any other words of eight or more letters "if substantial space is thereby saved and the result is unambiguous." Bluebook Rule 10.2.2. On the other hand, in citing cases in text, abbreviate only widely known acronyms and the following words: "&," "Ass'n," "Bros.," "Co.," "Corp.," "Inc.," "Ltd.," and "No." Bluebook Rule 10.2.1(c).

Columbia Business Law Review
Ab.:   Colum. Bus. L. Rev.
Ex.:   Marc I. Steinberg, <u>Attorney Liability for Client Fraud</u>, 1991 Colum. Bus. L. Rev. 1. –Article Citation.

Marc I. Steinberg, <u>Attorney Liability for Client Fraud</u>, 1991 Colum. Bus. L. Rev. 1, 3-7. –Page Citation.

Columbia Human Rights Law Review
Ab.:   Colum. Hum. Rts. L. Rev.
Ex.:   Mark Parts, <u>The Eighth Amendment and the Requirement of Active Measures to Prevent the Spread of AIDS in Prison</u>, 22 Colum. Hum. Rts. L. Rev. 217 (1991). –Article Citation.

Mark Parts, <u>The Eighth Amendment and the Requirement of Active Measures to Prevent the Spread of AIDS in Prison</u>, 22 Colum. Hum. Rts. L. Rev. 217, 225-27 (1991). –Page Citation.

Columbia Journal of Asian Law
Ab.:   Colum. J. Asian L.
Ex.:   Richard Cullen & Pinky D. W. Choy, <u>The Internet in China</u>, 13 Colum. J. Asian L. 99 (1999). –Article Citation.

Columbia Journal of Environmental Law
Ab.:   Colum. J. Envtl. L.
Ex.:   Robert Abrams, <u>The Maturing Discipline of Environmental Prosecution</u>, 16 Colum. J. Envtl. L. 279 (1991). –Article Citation.

Robert Abrams, <u>The Maturing Discipline of Environmental Prosecution</u>, 16 Colum. J. Envtl. L. 279, 280-85 (1991). –Page Citation.

Columbia Journal of Gender & Law
Ab.:   Colum. J. Gender & L.
Ex.:   Angela L. Padilla & Jennifer J. Winrich, <u>Christianity, Feminism, and the Law</u>, 1 Colum. J. Gender & L. 67 (1991). –Article Citation.

Angela L. Padilla & Jennifer J. Winrich, <u>Christianity, Feminism, and the Law</u>, 1 Colum. J. Gender & L. 67, 73 (1991). –Page Citation.

Columbia Journal of Law and Social Problems
Ab.:   Colum. J.L. & Soc. Probs.
Ex.:   Matthew T. Golden, Note, <u>On Replacing the Replacement Worker Doctrine</u>, 25 Colum. J.L. & Soc. Probs. 51 (1991). –Article Citation.

Matthew T. Golden, Note, <u>On Replacing the Replacement Worker Doctrine</u>, 25 Colum. J.L. & Soc. Probs. 51, 58-60 (1991). –Page Citation.

–A designation of the piece should appear before the title of the work to indicate that it is student written. <u>See</u> Bluebook Rule 16.6.2

In law review footnotes, the titles of books and the names of cases, except for procedural phrases, are not underlined. <u>See</u> Bluebook Rule 2.1(a). Further, the following are in large and small capitals: codes, restatements, standards, constitutions, periodicals, authors of books, titles of books, the abbreviated names of codes, most legislative materials except for bills and resolutions, codified ordinances, model codes, court rules, and sentencing guidelines. Refer to <u>The Bluebook</u>.

Columbia Journal of Transnational Law
Ab.: Colum. J. Transnat'l L.
Ex.: Louis Henkin, The Invasion of Panama Under International Law: A Gross Violation, 29 Colum. J. Transnat'l L. 293 (1991). –Article Citation.
Louis Henkin, The Invasion of Panama Under International Law: A Gross Violation, 29 Colum. J. Transnat'l L. 293, 312-15 (1991). –Page Citation.

Columbia Journal of World Business
Ab.: Colum. J. World Bus.
Ex.: Roberto E. Batres, A Mexican View of the North American Free Trade Agreement, Colum. J. World Bus., Summer 1991, at 78. –Article Citation.
Roberto E. Batres, A Mexican View of the North American Free Trade Agreement, Colum. J. World Bus., Summer 1991, at 78, 81. –Page Citation.

Columbia Law Review
Ab.: Colum. L. Rev.
Ex.: David Yassky, Eras of the First Amendment, 91 Colum. L. Rev. 1699 (1991). –Article Citation.
David Yassky, Eras of the First Amendment, 91 Colum. L. Rev. 1699, 1717-20 (1991). –Page Citation.

Columbia-VLA Journal of Law & the Arts
Ab.: Colum.-VLA J.L. & Arts
Ex.: Leo J. Raskind, The Continuing Process of Refining and Adapting Copyright Principles, 14 Colum.-VLA J.L. & Arts 125 (1990). –Article Citation.
Leo J. Raskind, The Continuing Process of Refining and Adapting Copyright Principles, 14 Colum.-VLA J.L. & Arts 125, 126 (1990). –Page Citation.

COMM/ENT
See Hastings Communication and Entertainment Law Journal.

Commentaries, by William Blackstone
Ex.: 1 William Blackstone, Commentaries, *35. –The asterisk denotes the page number in the original edition. See Bluebook Rule 15.4(d).

Commerce Clearing House
Ab.: CCH

Commerce Court
Ab.: Comm. Ct.

Commercial Law Journal
Ab.: Com. L.J.

In citing cases in law review footnotes, abbreviate any word listed in Table T.6; the names of "states, countries, and other geographical units" unless they are named parties; and any other words of eight or more letters "if substantial space is thereby saved and the result is unambiguous." Bluebook Rule 10.2.2. On the other hand, in citing cases in text, abbreviate only widely known acronyms and the following words: "&," "Ass'n," "Bros.," "Co.," "Corp.," "Inc.," "Ltd.," and "No." Bluebook Rule 10.2.1(c).

Ex.:   Rhett Frimet, <u>The Birth of Bankruptcy in the United States</u>, 96 Com.
           L.J. 160 (1991). –Article Citation.

           Rhett Frimet, <u>The Birth of Bankruptcy in the United States</u>, 96 Com.
           L.J. 160, 164-66 (1991). –Page Citation.

Commissioner
Ab.:   Comm'r

Commissioner's Decisions, U.S. Patent Office
<u>See</u> Patents, Decisions of the Commissioner and of U.S. Courts (1869-date).

Committee prints, Congressional
<u>See</u> Congressional Committee Prints.

Commodity Futures Law Reports (Commerce Clearing House)
Ab.:   Comm. Fut. L. Rep. (CCH)

Ex.:   <u>Schroeder v. Indorsky</u>, 2 Comm. Fut. L. Rep. (CCH) ¶ 26,698
           (S.D.N.Y. Apr. 24, 1996). –Citation to looseleaf material.

           <u>Buckwalter v. Global Futures Holdings, Inc.</u>, 2 Comm. Fut. L. Rep.
           (CCH) ¶ 26,309 (Comm. Fut. Trading Comm'n Feb. 17, 1995).
           –Citation to looseleaf administative material.

           <u>Aamot v. Kassel</u>, [1993-1994 Decisions Transfer Binder] Comm. Fut.
           L. Rep. (CCH) ¶ 25,815 (6th Cir. Aug 6, 1993). –Citation to transfer
           binder material.

           –The above examples are proper if the case is not yet available in, or is
           not reported in, an official or West reporter, a public domain citation,
           or in a widely used computer database.

           <u>Bosley v. Cecil</u>, 2 Comm. Fut. L. Rep. (CCH) ¶ 25,128 (Comm. Fut.
           Trading Comm'n Sept. 10, 1991). –Citation to looseleaf administrative
           material.

           <u>Ferruggia v. Shearson Lehman Hutton, Inc.</u>, [1992-1994 Decisions
           Transfer Binder] Comm. Fut. L. Rep. (CCH) ¶ 25,653 (Comm. Fut.
           Trading Comm'n Jan. 26, 1993). –Citation to transfer binder
           administrative material.

Common Extravagants (Catholic Church) (1261-1484)
Ab.:   Extrav. Com.

Common Market Law Reports (European Community)
           –Cite the Court of Justice of the European Communities and the Court
           of First Instance to E.C.R., if therein. Otherwise, cite to C.M.L.R.,
           Common Mkt. Rep. (CCH) or CEC (CCH), if therein, in that order of
           preference. <u>See</u> <u>Bluebook</u> Rule 21.5.2 and Table T.3.
Ab.:   C.M.L.R.

In law review footnotes, the titles of books and the names of cases, except for procedural
phrases, are not underlined. <u>See</u> <u>Bluebook</u> Rule 2.1(a). Further, the following are in large
and small capitals: codes, restatements, standards, constitutions, periodicals, authors of
books, titles of books, the abbreviated names of codes, most legislative materials except for
bills and resolutions, codified ordinances, model codes, court rules, and sentencing guidelines.
Refer to <u>The Bluebook</u>.

Ex.:   Case 98/86, Ministere Public v. Mathot, 51 C.M.L.R. 411 (1987).

Common Market Law Review
Ab.:   Common Mkt. L. Rev.

Ex.:   Gaudencio Esteban, The Reform of Company Law in Spain, 28
         Common Mkt. L. Rev. 935 (1991). –Article Citation.

         Gaudencio Esteban, The Reform of Company Law in Spain, 28
         Common Mkt. L. Rev. 935, 938-41 (1991). –Page Citation.

Common Market Reports (Commerce Clearing House)
Ab.:   Common Mkt. Rep. (CCH)

Ex.:   Regina v. Kirk, [1983-1985 Transfer Binder] Common Mkt. Rep.
         (CCH) ¶ 14,070 (1984). –Citation to transfer binder.

Common Pleas
Ab.:   C.P. [When appropriate, name county or similar subdivision] See
         Bluebook Table T.7.

Commonwealth
Ab.:   Commw.

Commonwealth Court
Ab.:   Commw. Ct.

Commonwealth Law Reports (Austl.)
Ab.:   C.L.R.

Ex.:   Jago v. District Court (N.S.W.), (1990) 168 C.L.R. 23 (Austl.). –Case
         Citation.

Communication(s)
Ab.:   Comm.

Comparative Juridical Review
Ab.:   Comp. Jurid. Rev.

Ex.:   Lajos Schmidt, Legal Aspects of Doing Business With and In Hungary,
         26 Comp. Jurid. Rev. 127 (1989). –Article Citation.

         Lajos Schmidt, Legal Aspects of Doing Business With and In Hungary,
         26 Comp. Jurid. Rev. 127, 137-40 (1989). –Page Citation.

Comparative Labor Law Journal
Ab.:   Comp. Lab. L.J.

Ex.:   Manfred Weiss, The Transition of Labor Law and Industrial Relations:
         The Case of German Unification -- A Preliminary Perspective,
         13 Comp. Lab. L.J. 1 (1991). –Article Citation.

         Manfred Weiss, The Transition of Labor Law and Industrial Relations:
         The Case of German Unification -- A Preliminary Perspective,
         13 Comp. Lab. L.J. 1, 8-9 (1991). –Page Citation.

In citing cases in law review footnotes, abbreviate any word listed in Table T.6;
the names of "states, countries, and other geographical units" unless they are named parties;
and any other words of eight or more letters "if substantial space is thereby saved and the
result is unambiguous." Bluebook Rule 10.2.2. On the other hand, in citing cases in text,
abbreviate only widely known acronyms and the following words: "&," "Ass'n," "Bros.,"
"Co.," "Corp.," "Inc.," "Ltd.," and "No." Bluebook Rule 10.2.1(c).

Comparative Law
Ab.: Comp. L.
Ex.: Allan D. Smith, <u>Recruit Cosmos: The Viewpoint From U.S. Law</u>, 7 Comp. L. 67 (1990). –Article Citation.

Allan D. Smith, <u>Recruit Cosmos: The Viewpoint From U.S. Law</u>, 7 Comp. L. 67, 73-75 (1990). –Page Citation.

Compare [and] <u>with</u>
–"<u>Compare</u>" and "<u>with</u>" are used when a "comparison of the authorities cited will offer support for or illustrate the proposition." <u>Bluebook</u> Rule 1.2(b).

Ex.: "The district court's order of restitution in the amount of $23,208 exceeds its statutory authority and is therefore an abuse of discretion. <u>Compare</u> Jalilian, 896 F.2d at 448-49, <u>with</u> United States v. Jack, 868 F.2d 1186, 1188-89 (10th Cir.) (probation order of district court expressly authorized by FPA), <u>cert. denied</u>, 490 U.S. 1112, 109 S. Ct. 3171, 104 L. Ed. 2d 1032 (1989)." –Taken from 952 F.2d 1262, 1266 (10th Cir. 1991).

compilation
Ab.: comp.

compiled
Ab.: comp.

compiled statutes
Ab.: comp. stat.

Complex Criminal Litigation: Prosecuting Drug Enterprises and Organized Crime, 2d ed., by Jimmy Gurulé.
–Do not abbreviate the title

Ex.: Jimmy Gurulé, <u>Complex Criminal Litigation: Prosecuting Drug Enterprises and Organized Crime</u> §1-4 (2d ed. 2000). –Section Citation.

Comptroller General
Ab.: Comp. Gen.

Computer/Law Journal
Ab.: Computer/L.J.
Ex.: George S. Cole, <u>Tort Liability for Artificial Intelligence and Expert Systems</u>, 10 Computer/L.J. 127 (1990). –Article Citation.

George S. Cole, <u>Tort Liability for Artificial Intelligence and Expert Systems</u>, 10 Computer/L.J. 127, 145-49 (1990). –Page Citation.

Congress
Ab.: Cong.

In law review footnotes, the titles of books and the names of cases, except for procedural phrases, are not underlined. <u>See</u> <u>Bluebook</u> Rule 2.1(a). Further, the following are in large and small capitals: codes, restatements, standards, constitutions, periodicals, authors of books, titles of books, the abbreviated names of codes, most legislative materials except for bills and resolutions, codified ordinances, model codes, court rules, and sentencing guidelines. Refer to <u>The Bluebook</u>.

Congressional Bills
–Pre-enactment and post-enactment when used to document legislative history.

House of Representatives:

Ab.:   H.R.

Ex.:   H.R. 44, 101st Cong. (1990).

H.R. 44, 101st Cong., § 1 (1990). –Citation to a section of a bill.

H.R. 44, 101st Cong., 136 Cong. Rec. 9704 (1990).–Citation if the bill is printed in the Congressional Record.

H.R. 4111, 102d Cong. (1991) (enacted). –Citation to House Bill without parallel citation to Statutes at Large.

H.R. 4111, 102d Cong., 106 Stat. 986 (1991). –Citation with parallel reference to Statutes at Large.

Senate:

Ab.:   S.

Ex.:   S. 1045, 101st Cong. (1990).

S. 1045, 101st Cong., § 1 (1990). –Citation to a section of a bill.

S. 1045, 101st Cong., 136 Cong. Rec. 16438 (1990). –Citation if the bill is printed in the Congressional Record.

Congressional Committee Prints
Ab.:   Comm. Print

Ex.:   Subcomm. on Select Revenue Measures of the House Comm. on Ways and Means, 103d Cong., 1st Sess., Description of Miscellaneous Revenue Proposals 5 (Comm. Print 1993).

Congressional Debates
Ex.:   126 Cong. Rec. H2061 (daily ed. Mar. 24, 1980) (remark of Rep. Duncan). –Unbound.

122 Cong. Rec. 5447-48 (1976). –Bound.

Congressional Digest
Ab.:   Cong. Dig.

Congressional Documents
House Document:

Ab.:   H.R. Doc.

Ex.:   H.R. Doc. No. 104-159 (1996).

Board of Trustees, Federal Old-Age and Survivors Insurance and Disability Insurance Trust Funds, 1995 Annual Report of the Board of Trustees of the Federal Old Age and Survivors Insurance and Disability Insurance Trust Funds, H.R. Doc. No. 104-159, at 4 (1996). –Citation if the title and author are to be given.

In citing cases in law review footnotes, abbreviate any word listed in Table T.6; the names of "states, countries, and other geographical units" unless they are named parties; and any other words of eight or more letters "if substantial space is thereby saved and the result is unambiguous." Bluebook Rule 10.2.2. On the other hand, in citing cases in text, abbreviate only widely known acronyms and the following words: "&," "Ass'n," "Bros.," "Co.," "Corp.," "Inc.," "Ltd.," and "No." Bluebook Rule 10.2.1(c).

–Give parallel citation to the permanent edition of United States Code
Congressional and Administrative News. See Bluebook Rule 13.4(a).

Senate Document:

Ab.:   S. Doc.

Ex.:   S. Doc. No. 104-4 (1996).

Bipartisan Task Force on Funding Disaster Relief, Federal Disaster
Assistance: Report of the Senate Task Force on Funding Disaster
Relief, S. Doc. No. 104-4, at 15 (1995). –Citation if the title and
author are to be given.

–Give parallel citation to the permanent edition of United States Code
Congressional and Administrative News. See Bluebook Rule 13.4(a).

Congressional Hearings
–Use full title.

Ex.:   Reproductive Hazards and Miliary Service: What are the Risks of
Radiation, Agent Orange, and Gulf War Exposures?: Hearing Before
the Senate Comm. on Veterans' Affairs, 103d Cong. 140 (1994)
(statement of Jackie C. Maxwell, Director of Atomic Parents, National
Association of Radiation Survivors).

Evidence Against a Higher Minimum Wage: Hearing Before the Joint
Economic Committee, 104th Cong. 88 (1995) (statement of Sen.
Connie Mack).

Congressional Index (Commerce Clearing House)
Ab.:   Cong. Index (CCH)

Congressional Record (U.S.)
Ab.:   Cong. Rec.

Ex.:   95 Cong. Rec. 7441 (1949).

Debate: 130 Cong. Rec. H7758 (daily ed. July 25, 1984) (statement of
Rep. Dingell)

Statement: 130 Cong. Rec. S8955 (daily ed. June 29, 1984) (statement
of Sen. Cranston)

Congressional Reports
House of Representatives Reports:

Ab.:   H.R. Rep.

Ex.:   H.R. Rep. No. 103-403, at 21 (1994).

H.R. Rep. No. 103-403 (1994), reprinted in 1994 U.S.C.C.A.N. 3598,
3599. –Citation when a parallel citation to the permanent edition of
United States Code Congressional and Administrative News exists.

Senate Reports:

Ab.:   S. Rep.

In law review footnotes, the titles of books and the names of cases, except for procedural
phrases, are not underlined. See Bluebook Rule 2.1(a). Further, the following are in large
and small capitals: codes, restatements, standards, constitutions, periodicals, authors of
books, titles of books, the abbreviated names of codes, most legislative materials except for
bills and resolutions, codified ordinances, model codes, court rules, and sentencing guidelines.
Refer to The Bluebook.

Ex.:   S. Rep. No. 103-300, at 7 (1994).

          S. Rep. No. 103-300 (1994), reprinted in 1994 U.S.C.C.A.N. 3683,
          3687. –Citation when a parallel citation to the permanent edition of
          United States Code Congressional and Administrative News exists.

Congressional Resolutions

          House of Representatives Simple Resolutions:

          –A parallel citation to the Congressional Record may be provided if of
            assistance to the reader in locating an enacted resolution. See
            Bluebook Rule 13.2(b).

Ab.:   H.R. Res.

Ex.:   H.R. Res. 510, 104th Cong. (1996). –Unenacted.

          H.R. Res. 531, 104th Cong., 142 Cong. Rec. H10,971 (daily ed. Sept.
          24, 1996). –When the unenacted resolution is printed in the
          Congressional Record.

          H.R. Res. 525, 104th Cong., 142 Cong. Rec. H10,927 (daily ed. Sept.
          24, 1996) (enacted).

          –When the resolution has been enacted.

          House of Representatives Concurrent Resolutions:

          –A parallel citation to Statutes at Large may be provided if of
            assistance to the reader in locating an enacted concurrent resolution.
            No parenthetical noting enactment is necessary if parallel citation is
            given to Statutes at Large. See Bluebook Rule 13.2(b).

Ab.:   H.R. Con. Res.

Ex.:   H.R. Con. Res. 21, 104th Cong. (1996). –Unenacted.

          H.R. Con. Res. 230, 104th Cong. (1996) (enacted). –Enacted.

          H.R. Con. Res. 145, 104th Cong., 142 Cong. Rec. H11,239 (daily ed.
          Sept. 26, 1996).

          –When the unenacted resolution is printed in the Congressional
          Record.

          H.R. Con. Res. 237, 103d Cong., 108 Stat. 5075 (1994). –When the
          resolution has been enacted and appears in Statutes at Large (if it has
          yet to appear, cite to the Congressional Record with parenthetical
          noting enactment).

          House of Representatives Joint Resolutions:

Ab.:   H.R.J. Res.

Ex.:   H.R.J. Res. 70, 104th Cong. (1996). –Unenacted.

          H.R.J. Res. 191, 104th Cong. (1996) (enacted). –Enacted.

          H.R.J. Res. 197, 104th Cong., 121 Cong. Rec. H11,636 (daily ed. Sept.
          28, 1996) (enacted). –When the text of the enacted resolution can be
          found in the Congressional Record.

In citing cases in law review footnotes, abbreviate any word listed in Table T.6;
the names of "states, countries, and other geographical units" unless they are named parties;
and any other words of eight or more letters "if substantial space is thereby saved and the
result is unambiguous." Bluebook Rule 10.2.2. On the other hand, in citing cases in text,
abbreviate only widely known acronyms and the following words: "&," "Ass'n," "Bros.,"
"Co.," "Corp.," "Inc.," "Ltd.," and "No." Bluebook Rule 10.2.1(c).

–Cite enacted Joint Resolutions as statutes except when used to document legislative history, in which case the format for unenacted joint resolutions should be used. Only enacted resolutions appear in the Statutes at Large. See Bluebook Rule 13.2.

H.R.J. Res. 208, 92d Cong., 86 Stat. 1523 (1972).

Senate Simple Resolutions:

Ab.:   S. Res.

Ex.:   S. Res. 296, 104th Cong. (1996). –Unenacted.

S. Res. 301, 104th Cong., 142 Cong. Rec. S11,435 (daily ed. Sept. 26, 1996). –When the text of the unenacted resolution can be found in the Congressional Record.

S. Res. 275, 104th Cong., 142 Cong. Rec. S11,201 (daily ed. Sept. 24, 1996) (enacted).

–When the resolution has been enacted.

Senate Concurrent Resolutions:

Ab.:   S. Con. Res.

Ex.:   S. Con. Res. 74, 104th Cong. (1996). –Unenacted.

S. Con. Res. 47, 104th Cong., 142 Cong. Rec. S12,292 (Oct. 3, 1996) (enacted). –When a printing of the unenacted resolution can be found in the Congressional Record and has not yet appeared in Statutes at Large.

Senate Joint Resolutions:

Ab.:   S.J. Res.

Ex.:   S.J. Res. 60, 104th Cong. (1996). –Unenacted.

S.J. Res. 65, 104th Cong., 142 Cong. Rec. S11,999 (1994). –When a printing of the unenacted resolution can be found in the Congressional Record.

–Cite enacted Joint Resolutions as statutes except when used to document legislative history, in which case the format for unenacted joint resolutions should be used. Only enacted resolutions appear in the Statutes at Large. See Bluebook Rule 13.2.

Connecticut
Ab.:   Conn.

Connecticut Appellate Reports
Ab.:   Conn. App.
–Cite to A. or A.2d if therein; otherwise, cite to Conn. App.

In law review footnotes, the titles of books and the names of cases, except for procedural phrases, are not underlined. See Bluebook Rule 2.1(a). Further, the following are in large and small capitals: codes, restatements, standards, constitutions, periodicals, authors of books, titles of books, the abbreviated names of codes, most legislative materials except for bills and resolutions, codified ordinances, model codes, court rules, and sentencing guidelines. Refer to The Bluebook.

–Give parallel citations only in documents submitted to Connecticut
state courts. See Bluebook Rule 10.3.1 and Practitioners' Note P.3;
see also Conn. R. App. P. § 67-11, which requires in the table of
authorities, but not in the argument portion of a brief, a parallel
citation to the regional reporter.

In documents submitted to Connecticut state courts, cite as follows:

> Dunbar v. Lindbolm, 41 Conn. App. 903, 673 A.2d 1184 (1996).
> –Case Citation.

> Dunbar v. Lindbolm, 41 Conn. App. 903, 906, 673 A.2d 1184,
> 1187 (1996). –Page Citation.

In all other documents, cite as follows:

> Dunbar v. Lindbolm, 673 A.2d 1184 (Conn. App. Ct. 1996).
> –Case Citation.

> Dunbar v. Lindbolm, 673 A.2d 1184, 1187 (Conn. App. Ct.
> 1996). –Page Citation.

Connecticut Bar Journal
Ab.:   Conn. B.J.

Ex.:   Arthur E. Balbiner and Gaetano Ferro, Survey of 1991 Developments
in Connecticut Family Law, 66 Conn. B.J. 40 (1992). –Article
Citation.

Arthur E. Balbiner and Gaetano Ferro, Survey of 1991 Developments
in Connecticut Family Law, 66 Conn. B.J. 40, 44-45 (1992). –Page
Citation.

Connecticut Circuit Court Reports
Ab.:   Conn. Cir. Ct.

–Discontinued after 6 Conn. Cir. Ct. 751 (1974). Thereafter cite only to
A.2d.

–Give parallel citations only in documents submitted to Connecticut
state courts. See Bluebook Rule 10.3.1 and Practitioners' Note P.3;
see also Conn. R. App. P. § 67-11, which requires in the table of
authorities, but not in the argument portion of a brief, a parallel
citation to the regional reporter.

In documents submitted to Connecticut state courts, cite as follows:

> LeClair v. Woodward, 6 Conn. Cir. Ct. 727, 316 A.2d 791 (1970).
> –Case Citation.

> LeClair v. Woodward, 6 Conn. Cir. Ct. 727, 730, 316 A.2d 791,
> 793 (1970). –Page Citation.

In all other documents, cite as follows:

In citing cases in law review footnotes, abbreviate any word listed in Table T.6;
the names of "states, countries, and other geographical units" unless they are named parties;
and any other words of eight or more letters "if substantial space is thereby saved and the
result is unambiguous." Bluebook Rule 10.2.2. On the other hand, in citing cases in text,
abbreviate only widely known acronyms and the following words: "&," "Ass'n," "Bros.,"
"Co.," "Corp.," "Inc.," "Ltd.," and "No." Bluebook Rule 10.2.1(c).

LeClair v. Woodward, 316 A.2d 791 (Conn. Cir. Ct. 1970). –Case Citation.

LeClair v. Woodward, 316 A.2d 791, 793 (Conn. Cir. Ct. 1970). –Page Citation.

Connecticut Constitution
Ab.:   Conn. Const. art. , §   .

Ex.:   Conn. Const. art. IV, § 15. –"Cite constitutional provisions currently in force without date."   Bluebook Rule 11.

Conn. Const. art. VI, § 9 (repealed 1980).   Conn. Const. art. VI, § 9, repealed by Conn. Const. amend. XIII. –"If the cited provision has been repealed, either indicate parenthetically the fact and date of repeal or cite the repealing provision in full."   Bluebook Rule 1.

Conn. Const. art. I, § 8 (amended 1982).

Conn. Const. art. I, § 8, amended by Conn. Const. amend. XVII. –"When citing a provision that has been subsequently amended, either indicate parenthetically the fact and date of amendment or cite the amending provision in full."   Bluebook Rule 11.

Conn. Const. of 1818, art. VI, § 8. –"Cite constitutions that have been totally superseded by year of adoption; if the specific provision cited was adopted in a different year, give that year parenthetically." Bluebook Rule 11.

Connecticut General Statutes
See General Statutes of Connecticut.

Connecticut General Statutes Annotated (West)
Ab.:   Conn. Gen. Stat. Ann. §   (West year).

Ex.:   Conn. Gen. Stat. Ann. § 26-91 (West 1999).

Conn. Gen. Stat. Ann. § 54-82h (West Supp. 2000).

–"Cite to General Statutes of Connecticut if therein."   Bluebook Table T.1, p. 195.

Connecticut Journal of International Law
Ab.:   Conn. J. Int'l L.

Ex.:   Matthew Lippman, Nuremberg: Forty Five Years Later, 7 Conn. J. Int'l L. 1 (1991). –Article Citation.

Matthew Lippman, Nuremberg: Forty Five Years Later, 7 Conn. J. Int'l L. 1, 7 (1991). –Page Citation.

Connecticut Law Review
Ab.:   Conn. L. Rev.

Ex.:   Richard Briffault, The Role of Local Control in School Finance Reform, 24 Conn. L. Rev. 773 (1992). –Article Citation.

Richard Briffault, The Role of Local Control in School Finance Reform, 24 Conn. L. Rev. 773, 775 (1992). –Page Citation.

In law review footnotes, the titles of books and the names of cases, except for procedural phrases, are not underlined. See Bluebook Rule 2.1(a). Further, the following are in large and small capitals: codes, restatements, standards, constitutions, periodicals, authors of books, titles of books, the abbreviated names of codes, most legislative materials except for bills and resolutions, codified ordinances, model codes, court rules, and sentencing guidelines. Refer to The Bluebook.

Connecticut Legislative Service (West)

Ab.:   year Conn. Legis. Serv. (West)

Ex.:   Act of June 12, 1996, P.A. 92-266, 1996 Conn. Legis. Serv. 984 (West) (concerning local telephone service). –Citation to an entire session law.

Act of June 12, 1996, P.A. 92-266, sec. 2, § 16-256c, 1996 Conn. Legis. Serv. 984, 984 (West) (concerning local telephone service). –Citation to a session law amending prior act.

–"Cite to Conn. Acts, Conn. Pub. Acts, or Conn. Spec. Acts, if therein." Bluebook Table T.1, p. 195.

Connecticut Probate Law Journal, The

Ab.:   Conn. Prob. L.J.

Ex.:   Koreen Labrecque, Note, Grandparent Visitation After Stepparent Adoption, 6 Conn. Prob. L.J. 61 (1991). –Article Citation.

Koreen Labrecque, Note, Grandparent Visitation After Stepparent Adoption, 6 Conn. Prob. L.J. 61, 78-79 (1991). –Page Citation.

–These examples indicate the article was written by a student. See Bluebook Rule 16.6.2

Connecticut Public Acts

Ab.:   year Conn. Pub. Acts

–Used for years 1650-1971. See Bluebook Table T.1, p. 195.

Connecticut Public & Special Acts

Ab.:   year Conn. Acts (Reg. [Spec.] Sess.)

Ex.:   Act of July 6, 1995, No. 95-281, 1995-2 Conn. Acts (Reg. Sess.) 1317 (concerning hawkers and peddlers). –Citation to an entire session law.

Act of July 6, 1995, No. 95-281, sec. 2, § 21-38, 1995-2 Conn. Acts (Reg. Sess.) 1317, 1318. –Citation to a section of a session law amending a prior act.

–Used for years 1972-date. See Bluebook Table T.1, p. 195.

Connecticut Regulations of State Agencies

See Regulations of Connecticut State Agencies.

Connecticut Reports

Ab.:   Conn.

–Cite to A. or A.2d if therein; otherwise, cite to Conn.

–Give parallel citations only in documents submitted to Connecticut state courts. See Bluebook Rule 10.3.1 and Practitioners' Note P.3; see also Conn. R. App. P. § 67-11, which requires in the table of authorities, but not in the argument position of a brief, a parallel citation to the regional reporter.

In citing cases in law review footnotes, abbreviate any word listed in Table T.6; the names of "states, countries, and other geographical units" unless they are named parties; and any other words of eight or more letters "if substantial space is thereby saved and the result is unambiguous." Bluebook Rule 10.2.2. On the other hand, in citing cases in text, abbreviate only widely known acronyms and the following words: "&," "Ass'n," "Bros.," "Co.," "Corp.," "Inc.," "Ltd.," and "No." Bluebook Rule 10.2.1(c).

In documents submitted to Connecticut state courts, cite as follows:

> Westerson v. Coccoli, 237 Conn. 907, 674 A.2d 1334 (1996).
> –Case Citation.

> Westerson v. Coccoli, 237 Conn. 907, 908, 674 A.2d 1334, 1335 (1996). –Page Citation.

In all other documents, cite as follows:

> Westerson v. Coccoli, 674 A.2d 1334 (Conn. 1996). –Case Citation.

> Westerson v. Coccoli, 674 A.2d 1334, 1335 (Conn. 1996). –Page Citation.

Connecticut Session Laws

See Connecticut Public Acts, Connecticut Public and Special Acts, Connecticut Special Acts, and Connecticut Legislative Service (West).

Connecticut Special Acts

Ab.: year Conn. Spec. Acts

–Used for years 1789-1971. See Bluebook Table T.1, p. 195.

Connecticut Supplement

–Cite to A. or A.2d if therein; otherwise, cite to Conn. Supp.

–Give parallel citations only in documents submitted to Connecticut state courts. See Bluebook Rule 10.3.1 and Practitioners' Note P.3; see also Conn. R. App. P. § 67-11, which requires in the table of authorities, but not in the argument portion of a brief, a parallel citation to the regional reporter.

Ab.: Conn. Supp.

In documents submitted to Connecticut state courts, cite as follows:

> Brown v. Ellis, 40 Conn. Supp. 165, 484 A.2d 944 (Super Ct. 1984). –Case Citation.

> Brown v. Ellis, 40 Conn. Supp. 165, 170, 484 A.2d 944, 947 (Super Ct. 1984). –Page Citation.

> Gulash v. Stylarama, 33 Conn. Supp. 108, 364 A.2d 1221 (C.P. 1975). –Case Citation.

> Gulash v. Stylarama, 33 Conn. Supp. 108, 111, 364 A.2d 1221, 1222 (C.P. 1975). –Page Citation.

In all other documents, cite as follows:

> Brown v. Ellis, 484 A.2d 944 (Conn. Super Ct. 1984). –Case Citation.

> Brown v. Ellis, 484 A.2d 944, 947 (Conn. Super Ct. 1984). –Page Citation.

> Gulash v. Stylarama, 364 A.2d 1221 (Conn. C.P. 1975). –Case Citation.

In law review footnotes, the titles of books and the names of cases, except for procedural phrases, are not underlined. See Bluebook Rule 2.1(a). Further, the following are in large and small capitals: codes, restatements, standards, constitutions, periodicals, authors of books, titles of books, the abbreviated names of codes, most legislative materials except for bills and resolutions, codified ordinances, model codes, court rules, and sentencing guidelines. Refer to The Bluebook.

<u>Gulash v. Stylarama</u>, 364 A.2d 1221, 1222 (Conn. C.P. 1975).
–Page Citation.

Consolidated Laws Service (Statutory Compilation)
    Ab.:   N.Y. [subject] Law § (Consol. year)
    <u>See</u> <u>Bluebook</u> Table T.1, pp. 219-21 for the abbreviation of each subject.

Consolidated Laws Service (Uncompiled Laws) (New York)
    <u>See</u> <u>Bluebook</u> Table T.1, pp. 219-21 for abbreviation of Acts.

Consolidated Regulations of Canada
    Ab.:   C.R.C.

Consolidated Treaty Series (a.k.a. Parry's Consolidated Treaty Series)
    Ab.:   Consol. T.S.
    Ex.:   Exchange of Declarations for the Provisional Regulation of
          Commercial Relations, Nov. 5, 1876, Fr.–Rom., 151 Consol. T.S. 121.

constitution
    Ab.:   const.

Constitution of the United States
    <u>See</u> United States Constitution.

constitutional
    Ab.:   const.

Constitutional Commentary
    Ab.:   Const. Commentary
    Ex.:   Daniel O. Conkle, <u>Compromising on Abortion</u>, 8 Const. Commentary
          353 (1991). –Article Citation.
          Daniel O. Conkle, <u>Compromising on Abortion</u>, 8 Const. Commentary
          353, 354-55 (1991). –Page Citation.

Constitutional Law, by Gerald Gunther and Kathleen M. Sullivan
    –Do not abbreviate the title.
    Ex.:   Gerald Gunther & Kathleen M. Sullivan, <u>Constitutional Law</u> 25 (13th
          ed. 1997). –Page Citation.

Constitutional Law, by John E. Nowak and Ronald D. Rotunda
    –Do not abbreviate the title.
    Ex.:   John E. Nowak & Ronald D. Rotunda, <u>Constitutional Law</u> § 11.9 (6th
          ed. 2000). –Section Citation.
          John E. Nowak & Ronald D. Rotunda, <u>Constitutional Law</u> § 11.9, at
          420 (6th ed. 2000). –Page Citation.
          John E. Nowak & Ronald D. Rotunda, <u>Constitutional Law</u> § 11.9, at
          420 n.33 (6th ed. 2000). –Footnote Citation.

In citing cases in law review footnotes, abbreviate any word listed in Table T.6;
the names of "states, countries, and other geographical units" unless they are named parties;
and any other words of eight or more letters "if <u>substantial</u> space is thereby saved and the
result is unambiguous." <u>Bluebook</u> Rule 10.2.2. On the other hand, in citing cases in text,
abbreviate only widely known acronyms and the following words: "&," "Ass'n," "Bros.,"
"Co.," "Corp.," "Inc.," "Ltd.," and "No." <u>Bluebook</u> Rule 10.2.1(c).

Constitutional Law, by Norman Redlich, Bernard Schwartz, & John Attanasion
  –Do not abbreviate the title.
  Ex.:   Norman Redlich et al., <u>Constitutional Law</u> 618-22 (3d ed. 1996).
          –Page Citation.

          Norman Redlich et al., <u>Constitutional Law</u> 618-22, n.4 (3d ed. 1996).
          –Footnote Citation.

          Norman Redlich et al., <u>Constitutional Law</u> 42-26 (3d ed. 1996 & Supp.
          1998). –Supplement Citation.

Constitutional Law Journal (Seton Hall Law School)
  Ab.:   Const. L.J.
  Ex.:   Ronald K. Chen, <u>Once More Into the Breach: Fact Versus Opinion</u>
          <u>Revisited After Mikovich v. Lorain Journal Co.</u>, 1 Const. L.J. 331
          (1991).–Article Citation.

          Ronald K. Chen, <u>Once More Into the Breach: Fact Versus Opinion</u>
          <u>Revisited After Mikovich v. Lorain Journal Co.</u>, 1 Const. L.J. 331, 340
          (1991).–Page Citation.

<u>construed in</u>
  Ex.:   Congressional Budget and Impoundment Control Act § 402, 31 U.S.C.
          § 1352 (1974), <u>construed in</u> Muskie, <u>Sunset Legislation: Restoring</u>
          <u>Public Confidence in Government</u>, 4 J. Legis. 11, 13 (1977).
  <u>See</u> <u>Bluebook</u> Rule 1.6(d) for proper use of <u>construed in</u>.

Consumer Credit Guide (Commerce Clearing House)
  Ab.:   Consumer Cred. Guide (CCH)
  Ex.:   <u>Lee v. Nationwide Cassel, L.P.</u>, 6 Consumer Cred. Guide (CCH) ¶
          95,260 (Ill. App. Ct. Dec. 22, 1995). –Citation to looseleaf material.

          <u>Atkinson v. General Elec. Credit Corp.</u>, [1980-1989 Decisions Transfer
          Binder] Consumer Cred. Guide (CCH) ¶ 95,809 (11th Cir. Feb. 21,
          1989). –Citation to transfer binder material.

          –The above examples are proper if the case is not yet available in, or is
          not reported in, an official or West reporter, a public domain citation,
          or in a widely used computer database.

Consumer Product Safety Guide (Commerce Clearing House)
  Ab.:   Consumer Prod. Safety Guide (CCH)
  Ex.:   <u>United States v. ILLCO Toy Co.</u>, 3 Consumer Prod. Safety Guide
          (CCH) ¶ 75,455 (S.D.N.Y. Jan. 17, 1991). –Citation to looseleaf
          material.

          <u>United States v. Salem Carpet Mills, Inc.</u>, [1977-1979 Developments
          Transfer Binder] Consumer Prod. Safety Guide (CCH) ¶ 75,212 (N.D.
          Ga. 1978). –Citation to transfer binder material.

          –The above examples are proper if the case is not yet available in, or is

---

In law review footnotes, the titles of books and the names of cases, except for procedural
phrases, are not underlined. <u>See</u> <u>Bluebook</u> Rule 2.1(a). Further, the following are in large
and small capitals: codes, restatements, standards, constitutions, periodicals, authors of
books, titles of books, the abbreviated names of codes, most legislative materials except for
bills and resolutions, codified ordinances, model codes, court rules, and sentencing guidelines.
Refer to <u>The Bluebook</u>.

not reported in, an official or West reporter, a public domain citation, or in a widely used computer database.

contra

"'Contra' is used when the "cited authority directly states the contrary of the proposition. 'Contra' is used where [no signal] would be used for support. " Bluebook Rule 1.2(a).

Ex.: "... Harman v. United States, 199 F.2d 34, 36 (4th Cir. 1952) ("when the witness testified that the statement was true it became a part of his testimony, and not a mere matter of impeachment"). Contra United States v. Check, 582 F.2d 688, 680, 3 Fed. R. Evid. Serv. 685 (2d Cir. 1978) (the admission of prior consistent statements is error unless offered to rebut a charge of fabrication or improper motive)." –Taken from 946 F.2d 147, 153 (1st Cir. 1991).

Contract Appeals Decisions (bound as Board of Contract Appeals Decisions) (Commerce Clearing House)

Ab.: Cont. App. Dec. (CCH)

Ab.: B.C.A. (CCH) (bound)

Contracts, by E. Allan Farnsworth

–Do not abbreviate the title.

Ex.: E. Allan Farnsworth, Contracts § 4.13 (2d ed. 1990). –Section Citation.

E. Allan Farnsworth, Contracts § 4.13, at 261 (2d ed. 1990). –Page Citation.

E. Allan Farnsworth, Contracts § 4.13, at 261 n.7 (2d ed. 1990). –Footnote Citation.

Contracts and Conveyances of Real Property, by Milton R. Friedman

–Do not abbreviate the title.

Ex.: 1 Milton R. Friedman, Contracts and Conveyances of Real Property § 1.2(f) (6th ed. 1998). –Section Citation.

1 Milton R. Friedman, Contracts and Conveyances of Real Property § 1.2(f), at 108 (6th ed. 1998). –Page Citation.

1 Milton R. Friedman, Contracts and Conveyances of Real Property § 1.2(f), at 108 n.2 (6th ed. 1998). –Footnote Citation.

Contracts Cases, Federal

See Government Contracts Reports.

Conveyancer and Property Lawyer, The (new series)

Ab.: Conv. & Prop. Law. (n.s.)

In citing cases in law review footnotes, abbreviate any word listed in Table T.6; the names of "states, countries, and other geographical units" unless they are named parties; and any other words of eight or more letters "if substantial space is thereby saved and the result is unambiguous." Bluebook Rule 10.2.2. On the other hand, in citing cases in text, abbreviate only widely known acronyms and the following words: "&," "Ass'n," "Bros.," "Co.," "Corp.," "Inc.," "Ltd.," and "No." Bluebook Rule 10.2.1(c).

Ex.:   Alan Prichard, <u>New Jurisdictions for Rent Assessment Committees?</u>,
        1991 Conv. & Prop. Law. (n.s.) 447. –Article Citation.

        Alan Prichard, <u>New Jurisdictions for Rent Assessment Committees?</u>,
        1991 Conv. & Prop. Law. (n.s.) 447, 448-49. –Page Citation.

Cooley Law Review
Ab.:   Cooley L. Rev.

Ex.:   Timothy A. Boughman, <u>Michigan's "Uncommon Law"</u> of Homicide,
        7 Cooley L. Rev. 1 (1990). –Article Citation.

        Timothy A. Boughman, <u>Michigan's "Uncommon Law"</u> of Homicide,
        7 Cooley L. Rev. 1, 15-17 (1990). –Page Citation.

        –In 1991 this publication changed its name to Thomas M. Cooley Law
        Review.

Cooper's Tennessee Chancery Reports
Ab.:   Coop. Tenn. Ch.

Copyright, by Paul Goldstein
        –Do not abbreviate the title.

Ex.:   2 Paul Goldstein, <u>Copyright</u> § 11.4.2.2 (2d ed. 1996). –Section
        Citation.

        2 Paul Goldstein, <u>Copyright</u> § 11.4.2.2, at 11:61 (2d ed. 1996). –Page
        Citation.

        2 Paul Goldstein, <u>Copyright</u> § 11.4.2.2, at 11:61 n.58 (2d ed. 1996).
        –Footnote Citation.

Copyright Decisions (1909-date) (U.S.)
Ab.:   Copyright Dec.

Ex.:   <u>Jackson v. Stone and Simon Adver., Inc.</u>, 40 Copy. Dec. 693 (E.D.
        Mich. 1974).

Copyright Law Decisions (Commerce Clearing House)
Ab.:   Copyright L. Dec. (CCH)

Ex.:   <u>Rano v. Sipa Press, Inc.</u>, 1992-1994 Copyright L. Dec. (CCH) ¶ 27,067
        (9th Cir. Mar. 2, 1993). –Citation to Bound Material.

        –This example is proper if the case is not yet available in, or is not
        reported in, an official or West reporter, a public domain citation, or
        in a widely used computer database.

Copyright Law Reporter (Commerce Clearing House)
Ab.:   Copyright L. Rep. (CCH)

Ex.:   <u>Adler v. World Bazaars, Inc.</u>, 2 Copyright L. Rep. (CCH) ¶ 27,524
        (S.D.N.Y. Aug. 16, 1995). –Citation to looseleaf material.

        <u>Pillsbury Co. v. Milky Way Products</u>, 1978-1981 Copyright L. Dec.
        (CCH) ¶ 25,139 (N.D. Ga. 1978). –Citation to bound material.

In law review footnotes, the titles of books and the names of cases, except for procedural
phrases, are not underlined. <u>See</u> <u>Bluebook</u> Rule 2.1(a). Further, the following are in large
and small capitals: codes, restatements, standards, constitutions, periodicals, authors of
books, titles of books, the abbreviated names of codes, most legislative materials except for
bills and resolutions, codified ordinances, model codes, court rules, and sentencing guidelines.
Refer to <u>The Bluebook</u>.

–The above examples are proper if the case is not yet available in an official or West reporter, or is not reported in an official or West reporter.

Copyright Law Symposium (American Society of Composers, Authors, & Publishers)

Ab.:   Copyright L. Symp. (ASCAP)

Ex.:   Jack B. Hicks, Copyright and Computer Databases: Is Traditional Compilation Law Adequate?, 37 Copyright L. Symp. (ASCAP) 85 (1990). –Article Citation.

          Jack B. Hicks, Copyright and Computer Databases: Is Traditional Compilation Law Adequate?, 37 Copyright L. Symp. (ASCAP) 85, 87-89 (1990). –Page Citation.

Corbin on Contracts, by Arthur Linton Corbin

        –Do not abbreviate the title.

Ex.:   3A Arthur Linton Corbin, Corbin on Contracts § 644, at 81 (1960). –Page Citation.

          6A Arthur Linton Corbin, Corbin on Contracts § 1375 (1962). – Section Citation.

          3 Eric Mills Holmes, Corbin on Contracts § 9.20 (Joseph M. Perillo ed., rev. ed. 1996). –Section Citation to Revised Edition.

          3 Eric Mills Holmes, Corbin on Contracts § 9.20, at 299 (Joseph M. Perillo ed., rev. ed. 1996). –Page Citation to Revised Edition.

          5 Margaret N. Kniffen, Corbin on Contracts, § 24.5 (Joseph M. Perillo ed., rev. ed. 1998). –Section Citation.

          4 Lawrence A. Cunningham and Arthur J. Jacobson, Corbin on Contracts § 782, at 108 (Cum. Supp. Fall 2000). –Supplement Citation.

Cornell International Law Journal

Ab.:   Cornell Int'l L.J.

Ex.:   Michael E. Solimine, Forum-Selection Clauses and the Privatization of Procedure, 25 Cornell Int'l L.J. 51 (1992). –Article Citation.

          Michael E. Solimine, Forum-Selection Clauses and the Privatization of Procedure, 25 Cornell Int'l L.J. 51, 77 (1992). –Page Citation.

Cornell Law Review

Ab.:   Cornell L. Rev.

Ex.:   Dennis Patterson, Postmodernism/Feminism/Law, 77 Cornell L. Rev. 254 (1992). –Article Citation.

          Dennis Patterson, Postmodernism/Feminism/Law, 77 Cornell L. Rev. 254, 262-67 (1992). –Page Citation.

In citing cases in law review footnotes, abbreviate any word listed in Table T.6; the names of "states, countries, and other geographical units" unless they are named parties; and any other words of eight or more letters "if substantial space is thereby saved and the result is unambiguous." Bluebook Rule 10.2.2. On the other hand, in citing cases in text, abbreviate only widely known acronyms and the following words: "&," "Ass'n," "Bros.," "Co.," "Corp.," "Inc.," "Ltd.," and "No." Bluebook Rule 10.2.1(c).

Corporate Counsel Weekly (Bureau of National Affairs)
>   Ab.:   Corp. Couns. Wkly. (BNA)

Corporate Income Taxation, by Douglas A. Kahn and Jeffrey S. Lehman
>   –Do not abbreviate the title.
>   Ex.:   Douglas A. Kahn & Jeffrey S. Lehman, <u>Corporate Income Taxation</u> § 6.19.4 (5th ed. 2001). –Section Citation.
>
>   Douglas A. Kahn & Jeffrey S. Lehman, <u>Corporate Income Taxation</u> § 6.19.4, at 550 (5th ed. 2001). –Page Citation.

Corporate Law and Practice, by Larry D. Soderquist, Linda O. Smiddy, A.A. Sommer, Jr. and Pat K. Chew
>   –Do not abbreviate the title.
>   Ex.:   Larry Soderquist et. al, <u>Corporate Law and Practice</u> § 2.2.4 (2d ed. 1999). –Section Citation.
>
>   Larry Soderquist et. al, <u>Corporate Law and Practice</u> § 2.2.4, at 23 (2d ed. 1999). –Page Citation.
>
>   Larry Soderquist et. al, <u>Corporate Law and Practice</u> § 2.2.4, at 23 n.29 (2d ed. 1999). –Footnote Citation.

Corporate Law of Banks, The, by Michael P. Malloy
>   –Do not abbreviate the title.
>   Ex.:   2 Michael P. Malloy, <u>The Corporate Law of Banks</u> § 8.2.5 (1988). –Section Citation.
>
>   2 Michael P. Malloy, <u>The Corporate Law of Banks</u> § 8.2.5, at 741 (1988). –Page Citation.
>
>   2 Michael P. Malloy, <u>The Corporate Law of Banks</u> § 8.2.5, at 741 n.104 (1988). –Footnote Citation.

Corporate Practice Commentator
>   Ab.:   Corp. Prac. Commentator
>   Ex.:   Daniel R. Fischel, <u>The Economics of Lender Liability</u>, 33 Corp. Proc. Commentator 195 (1991). –Article Citation.
>
>   Daniel R. Fischel, <u>The Economics of Lender Liability</u>, 33 Corp. Proc. Commentator 195, 217-19 (1991). –Page Citation.
>
>   –This publication is a compilation of articles from other publications. If available, citations should be to the original publication.

Corporate Secretary's Guide (Commerce Clearing House)
>   Ab.:   Corp. Secretary's Guide (CCH)

In law review footnotes, the titles of books and the names of cases, except for procedural phrases, are not underlined. <u>See</u> <u>Bluebook</u> Rule 2.1(a). Further, the following are in large and small capitals: codes, restatements, standards, constitutions, periodicals, authors of books, titles of books, the abbreviated names of codes, most legislative materials except for bills and resolutions, codified ordinances, model codes, court rules, and sentencing guidelines. Refer to <u>The Bluebook</u>.

Ex.:   Study Paints Favorable Picture of Corporate Boards, 3 Corp.
        Secretary's Guide (CCH) ¶ 48,017 (May 1988). —Citation to unsigned
        looseleaf commentary.

Corpus Juris Secundum
Ab.:   C.J.S.
Ex.:   47A C.J.S. Internal Revenue § 68 (2000).
        44 C.J.S. Insurance § 9 (Supp. 2000). —Supplement Citation.
        77 C.J.S. Insurance § 33, at 104 n.34.5 (Supp. 2000). —Footnote
        Citation.

Cost Accounting Standards Guide (Commerce Clearing House)
Ab.:   Cost Accounting Stand. Guide (CCH)

Couch on Insurance, by Lee R. Russ & Thomas F. Segalla
        —Do not abbreviate the title.
Ex.:   14 Lee R. Russ & Thomas F. Segalla, Couch on Insurance § 199:4 (3d
        ed. 1999). —Section Citation.
        14 Lee R. Russ & Thomas F. Segalla, Couch on Insurance § 199:4, at
        199-13 (3d ed. 1999). —Page Citation.
        14 Lee R. Russ & Thomas F. Segalla, Couch on Insurance § 199:4, at
        199-13 n.14 (3d ed. 1999). —Footnote Citation.

County Court
Ab.:   [name of county] County Ct.

Court Administrative Orders
See Bluebook Rule 14.8

Court Management Journal
Ab.:   Ct. Mgmt. J.

Court Martial Reports (1951-1975) (U.S.)
Ab.:   C.M.R.
Ex.:   United States v. Burwell, 50 C.M.R. 192 (1975). —Case Citation.
        United States v. Burwell, 50 C.M.R. 192, 193 (1975). —Page Citation.

Court of Appeal (England)
Ab.:   C.A.

Court of Appeal(s) (state)
Ab.:   Ct. App.

Court of Appeal for East Africa Digest of Decisions of the Court
Ab.:   E. Afr. Ct. App. Dig.
See Bluebook Rule 21.55 and Table T.3.

In citing cases in law review footnotes, abbreviate any word listed in Table T.6;
the names of "states, countries, and other geographical units" unless they are named parties;
and any other words of eight or more letters "if substantial space is thereby saved and the
result is unambiguous." Bluebook Rule 10.2.2. On the other hand, in citing cases in text,
abbreviate only widely known acronyms and the following words: "&," "Ass'n," "Bros.,"
"Co.," "Corp.," "Inc.," "Ltd.," and "No." Bluebook Rule 10.2.1(c).

Court of Appeals (federal)
Ab.:   Cir.

Court of Claims
Ab.:   Ct. Cl.
–Succeeded in 1982 by the United States Claims Court (Cl. Ct.).
–Cite to Federal Reporter series or Federal Supplement series if therein; otherwise to Court of Claims Reports.

Court of Claims Reports
Ab.:   Ct. Cl.
–Cite to Federal Reporter series or Federal Supplement series if therein; otherwise, cite to the Reports as follows:
Ex.:   Kay Mfg. v. United States, 230 Ct. Cl. 83 (1982).
–After 231 Ct. Cl. 105 (1982), title became Claims Court Reporter (Cl. Ct.).

Court of Claims Rules (Rules of the Court of Claims of the United States)
Ab.:   Ct. Cl. R.
Ex.:   Ct. Cl. R. 176.

Court of Criminal Appeals
Ab.:   Crim. App.

Court of Customs and Patent Appeals Reports
Ab.:   C.C.P.A.
–Cite to Federal Reporter Series if therein; otherwise, cite as follows:
Ex.:   Krupp Int'l Inc. v. United States Int'l Trade Comm'n, 67 C.C.P.A. 166 (1980).

Court of Customs Appeals
Ab.:   Ct. Cust. App.

Court of Customs Appeals Reports
Ab.:   Ct. Cust.
–Cite to Federal Reporter Series if therein; otherwise, cite as follows:
Ex.:   Wells Fargo & Co. v. United States, 7 Ct. Cust. 346 (1916).
–Becomes C.C.P.A after volume 16.

Court of Errors and Appeals
Ab.:   Ct. Err. & App.

Court of Federal Claims
Ab.:   Fed. Cl.
–Created 1992, formerly United States Claims Court (Cl. Ct., created 1992) which was in turn successor to the Court of Claims (Ct. Cl.).
–Cite to Federal Claims Reporter.

In law review footnotes, the titles of books and the names of cases, except for procedural phrases, are not underlined. See Bluebook Rule 2.1(a). Further, the following are in large and small capitals: codes, restatements, standards, constitutions, periodicals, authors of books, titles of books, the abbreviated names of codes, most legislative materials except for bills and resolutions, codified ordinances, model codes, court rules, and sentencing guidelines. Refer to The Bluebook.

Court of International Trade Reports
Ab.:   Ct. Int'l Trade
Ex.:   <u>Torrington Co. v. United States</u>, 21 Ct. Int'l Trade 491 (1997).

**Court of Justice of the European Communities
(Common Market cases)**
Ab.:   E.C.J.; <u>see</u> <u>Bluebook</u> Rule 21.5.2 and Table T.3.

Court of Military Appeals
Ab.:   C.M.A.

Court of Military Review
Ab.:   C.M.R.

Court of [General, Special] Sessions
Ab.:   Ct. Gen. Sess.
Ct. Spec. Sess.

Court Rules (Federal and State)
<u>See</u> Rules of Evidence and Procedure.

Courtroom Evidence Handbook, by Steven Goode and Olin Guy Wellborn III
–Do not abbreviate the title.
Ex.:   Steven Goode & Olin Guy Wellborn III, <u>Courtroom Evidence Handbook</u> 246 (1997). –Page Citation.
Steven Goode & Olin Guy Wellborn III, <u>Courtroom Evidence Handbook</u> 246 n.17 (1997). –Footnote Citation.

Courts, Health Science and the Law
Ab.:   Cts. Health Sci. & L.
Ex.:   David Rosenberg, <u>Damage Scheduling in Mass Exposure Cases</u>, 1 Cts. Health Sci. & L. 335 (1991).–Article Citation.
David Rosenberg, <u>Damage Scheduling in Mass Exposure Cases</u>, 1 Cts. Health Sci. & L. 335, 343-45 (1991).–Page Citation.

Cowans Bankruptcy Law and Practice, by Daniel R. Cowans
–Do not abbreviate the title.
Ex.:   Daniel R. Cowans, <u>Cowans Bankruptcy Law and Practice</u> § 18.4 (6th ed. 1994). –Section Citation.
Daniel R. Cowans, <u>Cowans Bankruptcy Law and Practice</u> § 18.4, at 510 (6th ed. 1994). –Page Citation.
Daniel R. Cowans, <u>Cowans Bankruptcy Law and Practice</u> § 18.4, at 510 n.47 (6th ed. 1994). –Footnote Citation.

Cranch (United States Reports)
<u>See</u> United States Reports.

Creighton Law Review
Ab.:   Creighton L. Rev.

In citing cases in law review footnotes, abbreviate any word listed in Table T.6; the names of "states, countries, and other geographical units" unless they are named parties; and any other words of eight or more letters "if <u>substantial</u> space is thereby saved and the result is unambiguous." <u>Bluebook</u> Rule 10.2.2. On the other hand, in citing cases in text, abbreviate only widely known acronyms and the following words: "&," "Ass'n," "Bros.," "Co.," "Corp.," "Inc.," "Ltd.," and "No." <u>Bluebook</u> Rule 10.2.1(c).

Ex.:   Wayne A. Kalkwarf, <u>The Jurisdictional Dilemma in Reopening Social Security Decisions</u>, 23 Creighton L. Rev. 545 (1990). –Article Citation.

Wayne A. Kalkwarf, <u>The Jurisdictional Dilemma in Reopening Social Security Decisions</u>, 23 Creighton L. Rev. 545, 551-53 (1990). –Page Citation.

Crime and Delinquency
Ab.:   Crime & Delinq.

Ex.:   Barry C. Feld, <u>The Punitive Juvenile Court and the Quality of Procedural Justice: Distinctions Between Rhetoric and Reality</u>, 36 Crime & Delinq. 443 (1990). –Article Citation.

Barry C. Feld, <u>The Punitive Juvenile Court and the Quality of Procedural Justice: Distinctions Between Rhetoric and Reality</u>, 36 Crime & Delinq. 443, 459-62 (1990). –Page Citation.

Crime and Justice
Ab.:   Crime & Just.

Ex.:   Jack Katz, <u>The Motivation of the Persistent Robber</u>, Crime & Just., 1991, at 277. –Article Citation.

Jack Katz, <u>The Motivation of the Persistent Robber</u>, Crime & Just., 1991, at 277, 289-91. –Page Citation.

Criminal Appeals Reports (Eng.) (1908-date)
<u>See</u> <u>Bluebook</u> Table T.2.

Ab.:   Crim. App. R.

Ex.:   <u>Cruttenden</u>, 93 Crim. App. R. 119 (1991) (Eng.). –Case Citation.

Criminal Law, by Wayne R. LaFave
–Do not abbreviate the title.

Ex.:   Wayne R. LaFave, <u>Criminal Law</u> § 4.6(b) (3d Student ed. 2000). –Section Citation.

Wayne R. LaFave, <u>Criminal Law</u> § 4.6(b), at 385 (3d Student ed. 2000).   –Page Citation.

Wayne R. LaFave, <u>Criminal Law</u> § 4.6(b), at 385 n.27 (3d Student ed. 2000). –Footnote Citation.

Criminal Law Bulletin
Ab.:   Crim. L. Bull.

Ex.:   Richard A. Powers III, <u>Anticipatory Search Warrants: Future Probable Cause</u>, 28 Crim. L. Bull. 59 (1992). –Article Citation.

Richard A. Powers III, <u>Anticipatory Search Warrants: Future Probable Cause</u>, 28 Crim. L. Bull. 59, 61-63 (1992). –Page Citation.

In law review footnotes, the titles of books and the names of cases, except for procedural phrases, are not underlined. <u>See</u> <u>Bluebook</u> Rule 2.1(a). Further, the following are in large and small capitals: codes, restatements, standards, constitutions, periodicals, authors of books, titles of books, the abbreviated names of codes, most legislative materials except for bills and resolutions, codified ordinances, model codes, court rules, and sentencing guidelines. Refer to <u>The Bluebook</u>.

Criminal Law Forum
  Ab.: Crim. L.F.
  Ex.: Friedrich-Christian Schroeder, <u>The Rise and Fall of the Criminal Law of the German Democratic Republic</u>, 2 Crim. L.F. 217 (1991). –Article Citation.

  Friedrich-Christian Schroeder, <u>The Rise and Fall of the Criminal Law of the German Democratic Republic</u>, 2 Crim. L.F. 217, 222-24 (1991). –Page Citation.

Criminal Law Reporter (Bureau of National Affairs)
  Ab.: Crim. L. Rep. (BNA)
  Ex.: <u>Albernaz v. U.S.</u>, [General] Crim. L. Rep. (BNA) 1015 (U.S. Sept. 23, 1996). –Citation to looseleaf material.

  <u>Batson v. Kentucky</u>, 59 Crim. L. Rep. (BNA) 1007 (U.S. 1986). –Citation to bound material.

  –The above examples are proper if the case is not yet available in, or is not reported in, an official or West reporter, a public domain citation, or in a widely used computer database.

Criminal Law Review, The
  Ab.: Crim. L. Rev.
  Ex.: C.J. Miller, <u>Some Problems of Contempt</u>, 1992 Crim. L. Rev. 107. –Article Citation.

  C.J. Miller, <u>Some Problems of Contempt</u>, 1992 Crim. L. Rev. 107, 110-11. –Page Citation.

Criminal Procedure, by Wayne R. LaFave, Jerold H. Israel, and Nancy J. King
  –Do not abbreviate the title.
  Ex.: Wayne R. LaFave, Jerold H. Israel, & Nancy J. King, <u>Criminal Procedure</u> § 11.9 (3d ed. 2000). –Section Citation.

  Wayne R. LaFave, Jerold H. Israel, & Nancy J. King, <u>Criminal Procedure</u> § 11.9, at 624 (3d ed. 2000). –Page Citation.

  Wayne R. LaFave, Jerold H. Israel, & Nancy J. King, <u>Criminal Procedure</u> § 11.9, at 624 n.17 (3d ed. 2000). –Footnote Citation.

Cumberland Law Review
  Ab.: Cumb. L. Rev.
  Ex.: Andrew W. Austin, <u>Faith and the Constitutional Definition of Religion</u>, 22 Cumb. L. Rev. 1 (1991). –Article Citation.

  Andrew W. Austin, <u>Faith and the Constitutional Definition of Religion</u>, 22 Cumb. L. Rev. 1, 17-19 (1991). –Page Citation.

Cumulative Bulletin (U.S.)
  Ab.: C.B.

In citing cases in law review footnotes, abbreviate any word listed in Table T.6; the names of "states, countries, and other geographical units" unless they are named parties; and any other words of eight or more letters "if <u>substantial</u> space is thereby saved and the result is unambiguous." <u>Bluebook</u> Rule 10.2.2. On the other hand, in citing cases in text, abbreviate only widely known acronyms and the following words: "&," "Ass'n," "Bros.," "Co.," "Corp.," "Inc.," "Ltd.," and "No." <u>Bluebook</u> Rule 10.2.1(c).

Ex.:   (1919-1921) T.B.R. 39, 1 C.B. 45 (1919). –Citation to volumes of the Cumulative Bulletin from 1919-1921 are by volume number.

(1921-1936) I.T. 2258, 5-1 C.B. 10 (1926). –Citation to volumes of the Cumulative Bulletin from 1921-1936 are by volume and part numbers.

(1937-date) Rev. Rul. 95-44, 1995-1 C.B. 3. –Citation to volumes of the Cumulative Bulletin from 1937 to date are by year and part numbers.

Rev. Rul. 82-4, 1982-1 I.R.B. 14. –Citation to the material found in the Cumulative Bulletin before a bound volume is issued is to the Internal Revenue Bulletin.

Current Legal Forms With Tax Analysis, by Jacob Rabkin and Mark H. Johnson
    –Do not abbreviate the title.

Ex.:   8A Jacob Rabkin & Mark H. Johnson, Current Legal Forms With Tax Analysis Form 21.14 (1992).

8A Jacob Rabkin & Mark H. Johnson, Current Legal Forms With Tax Analysis Form 21.14, at 21-1521 (1992). –Page Citation.

Current Legal Problems
Ab.:   Current Legal Probs.

Ex.:   James J. Fawcett, The Interrelationship of Jurisdiction and Choice of Law in Private International Law, 1991 Current Legal Probs. 39. –Article Citation.

James J. Fawcett, The Interrelationship of Jurisdiction and Choice of Law in Private International Law, 1991 Current Legal Probs. 39, 49. –Page Citation.

Current Medicine for Attoneys
Ab.:   Current Med. for Att'ys

Customs Bulletin and Decisions (U.S.) (1967-date)
Ab.:   Cust. B. & Dec.

Ex.:   T.D. 67-1, 1 Cust. B. & Dec. 1 (1967).

C.S.D. 79-4, 13 Cust. B. & Dec. 998 (1978).

T.D. 96-64, 30 Cust. B. & Dec. No. 37/38, at 1 (Aug. 17, 1996). –Citation to current, unbound material.

Customs Court Reports (1938-1980)
Ab.:   Cust. Ct.

–Cite to Federal Reporter series or Federal Supplement series if therein, otherwise, cite to the Reports as follows:

In law review footnotes, the titles of books and the names of cases, except for procedural phrases, are not underlined. See Bluebook Rule 2.1(a). Further, the following are in large and small capitals: codes, restatements, standards, constitutions, periodicals, authors of books, titles of books, the abbreviated names of codes, most legislative materials except for bills and resolutions, codified ordinances, model codes, court rules, and sentencing guidelines. Refer to The Bluebook.

Ex.:   <u>T.D. Downing Co. v. United States</u>, 60 Cust. Ct. 345 (1968). –Case
Citation.

<u>T.D. Downing Co. v. United States</u>, 60 Cust. Ct. 345, 347 (1968).
–Page Citation.

Customs Court Rules (Rules of the United States Customs Court)

Ab.:   Cust. Ct. R.

Ex.:   Cust. Ct. R. 11.1.

Cyclopedia of Trial Practice, by Syndey C. Schweitzer
–Do not abbreviate the title.

Ex.:   4 Sydney C. Schweitzer, <u>Cyclopedia of Trial Practice</u> § 731 (3d ed.
1985). –Section Citation.

4 Sydney C. Schweitzer, <u>Cyclopedia of Trial Practice</u> § 731, at 499 (3d
ed. 1985). –Page Citation.

4 Sydney C. Schweitzer, <u>Cyclopedia of Trial Practice</u> § 731, at 499 n.2
(3d ed. 1985). –Footnote Citation.

4 Sydney C. Schweitzer, <u>Cyclopedia of Trial Practice</u> § 740 (3d ed.
Supp. 1995). –Section Citation to Supplement.

In citing cases in law review footnotes, abbreviate any word listed in Table T.6;
the names of "states, countries, and other geographical units" unless they are named parties;
and any other words of eight or more letters "if <u>substantial</u> space is thereby saved and the
result is unambiguous." <u>Bluebook</u> Rule 10.2.2. On the other hand, in citing cases in text,
abbreviate only widely known acronyms and the following words: "&," "Ass'n," "Bros.,"
"Co.," "Corp.," "Inc.," "Ltd.," and "No." <u>Bluebook</u> Rule 10.2.1(c).

D

Dalhousie Law Journal
Ab.: Dalhousie L.J.
Ex.: Dawn Russell, <u>Paedophilia: The Criminal Responsibility of Canada's Churches</u>, 15 Dalhousie L.J. 380 (1992). –Article Citation.

Dawn Russell, <u>Paedophilia: The Criminal Responsibility of Canada's Churches</u>, 15 Dalhousie L.J. 380, 389-93 (1992). –Page Citation.

Dallas (United States Reports)
<u>See</u> United States Reports

Dalloz (France)
<u>See</u> Recueil Dalloz

Damages in Tort Actions, by Marilyn Minzer et al.
–Do not abbreviate the title.
Ex.: 5 Marilyn Minzer et al., <u>Damages in Tort Actions</u> § 40.33[3] (1989). –Section Citation.

5 Marilyn Minzer et al., <u>Damages in Tort Actions</u> § 40.33[3], at 40-131 (1989). –Page Citation.

5 Marilyn Minzer et al., <u>Damages in Tort Actions</u> § 40.33[3], at 40-131 n.18 (1989). –Footnote Citation.

Debates, Congressional
<u>See</u> Congressional Debates

Decisiones de Puerto Rico
Ab.: P.R. Dec.

Decisioni del Tribunale Federale (Switzerland)
Ab.: DTF

Constitutional cases	DTF Ia
Administrative cases	DTF Ib
Civil cases	DTF II
Bankruptcy cases	DTF III
Criminal cases	DTF IV
Social cases	DTF V

In law review footnotes, the titles of books and the names of cases, except for procedural phrases, are not underlined. <u>See</u> <u>Bluebook</u> Rule 2.1(a). Further, the following are in large and small capitals: codes, restatements, standards, constitutions, periodicals, authors of books, titles of books, the abbreviated names of codes, most legislative materials except for bills and resolutions, codified ordinances, model codes, court rules, and sentencing guidelines. Refer to <u>The Bluebook</u>.

Decisions and Orders of the National Labor Relations Board (U.S.) (1935-date)

Ab.:   N.L.R.B.

Ex.:   <u>Maramount Corp.</u>, 317 N.L.R.B. 1035 (1995). –Citation to official reporter.

<u>Wisconsin Steel Indus., Inc.</u>, 321 N.L.R.B. No. 175 (Aug. 27, 1996). –Slip opinion.

<u>Alanis Airport Serv., Inc.</u>, 316 N.L.R.B. No 185, [5 Labor Relations] Lab. L. Rep. (CCH) (1995-1996 NLRB Dec.) ¶ 15,769 (April 14, 1995). –Slip opinion when reported in looseleaf unofficial case service.

<u>Inland Container Corp.</u>, 275 N.L.R.B. No. 60, 1985-1986 NLRB Dec. (CCH) ¶ 17,343 (May 7, 1985). –Slip opinion when reported in bound unofficial case service.

Decisions of the Commissioner of Patents

Ab.:   Dec. Comm'r Pat.

<u>See</u> Patents, Decisions of the Commissioner.

Decisions of the Comptroller General of the United States (1921-date)

Ab.:   Comp. Gen.

Ex.:   <u>In re Ostrom Painting & Sandblasting, Inc.</u>, 72 Comp. Gen. 207 (1993).

<u>Decision of the Comptroller General B-261166</u> (July 18, 1995). –Citation to unpublished decisions. (Note: Unpublished decisions in the Digest of the Comptroller General of the United States ceased publication July-Sept. 1995).

Decisions of the Employees' Compensation Appeals Board

Ab.:   Emp. Comp. App. Bd.

Ex.:   <u>In re Zerega</u>, 45 Empl. Comp. App. Bd. 860 (1994).

Decisions of the Federal Labor Relations Authority

Ab.:   F.L.R.A.

Ex.:   <u>Overseas Education Association</u>, 51 F.L.R.A. 1246 (1996). –Case Citation.

<u>Overseas Education Association</u>, 51 F.L.R.A. 1246, 1251 (1996). –Page Citation.

Decisions of the Federal Maritime Commission

Ab.:   F.M.C.

Ex.:   <u>Proctor & Schwartz, Inc.</u>, 24 F.M.C. 133 (1982). –Case Citation.

Decisions of the Judicial Committee of the Privy Council re the British North American Act, 1867, and the Canadian Constitution (Canada)

Ab.:   Olms.

In citing cases in law review footnotes, abbreviate any word listed in Table T.6; the names of "states, countries, and other geographical units" unless they are named parties; and any other words of eight or more letters "if <u>substantial</u> space is thereby saved and the result is unambiguous." <u>Bluebook</u> Rule 10.2.2. On the other hand, in citing cases in text, abbreviate only widely known acronyms and the following words: "&," "Ass'n," "Bros.," "Co.," "Corp.," "Inc.," "Ltd.," and "No." <u>Bluebook</u> Rule 10.2.1(c).

Decisions of the United States Department of the Interior (1881-date)
   Ab.:   Pub. Lands Dec. –Citation for vols. 1-52.
             Interior Dec. –Citation for vol. 53 onward.
   Ex.:   Union Pacific Ry. Co., 25 Pub. Lands Dec. 540 (1897).
             Amoco Production Co., 101 Interior Dec. 39 (1994).

Decisions of the United States Maritime Commission (U.S.) (1919-1947)
   Ab.:   Dec. U.S. Mar. Comm'n
   Ex.:   Acme Novelty Co., 2 Dec. U.S. Mar. Comm'n 412 (1940).

Deering's Annotated California Code
   Ab.:   Cal. [subject] Code §   (Deering year)
             See Bluebook Table T.1, pp. 192-93 for the abbreviation of each
             subject.
   Ex.:   Cal. Corp. Code § 317 (Deering Supp. 1979).
             –"Cite to either the West's or the Deering subject matter code if
             therein." Bluebook Table T.1, p. 192.

Defense Counsel Journal
   Ab.:   Def. Couns. J.
   Ex.:   Harry Downs, Strategic Management of Complex Litigation: Reaching
             Objectives, 59 Def. Couns. J. 86 (1992). –Article Citation.
             Harry Downs, Strategic Management of Complex Litigation: Reaching
             Objectives, 59 Def. Couns. J. 86, 90-91 (1992). –Page Citation.

Defense of Drunk Driving Cases, by Richard E. Erwin, Marilyn K. Minzer,
Leon A. Greenberg, Herbert M. Goldstein, and Arne K. Bergh
             –Do not abbreviate the title.
   Ex.:   3 Richard E. Erwin et al., Defense of Drunk Driving Cases § 24.19[c]
             (3d ed. 1990). –Section Citation.
             3 Richard E. Erwin et al., Defense of Drunk Driving Cases § 24.19[c],
             at 24-42.1 (3d ed. 1990). –Page Citation.
             3 Richard E. Erwin et al., Defense of Drunk Driving Cases § 24.19[c],
             at 24-42.1 n.5 (3d ed. 1990). –Footnote Citation.

Defense Law Journal
   Ab.:   Def. L.J.
   Ex.:   Kent D. Syverud, The Duty to Settle, 40 Def. L.J. 155 (1991).
             –Article Citation.
             Kent D. Syverud, The Duty to Settle, 40 Def. L.J. 155, 161-65 (1991).
             –Page Citation.

Delaware
   Ab.:   Del.

In law review footnotes, the titles of books and the names of cases, except for procedural phrases, are not underlined. See Bluebook Rule 2.1(a). Further, the following are in large and small capitals: codes, restatements, standards, constitutions, periodicals, authors of books, titles of books, the abbreviated names of codes, most legislative materials except for bills and resolutions, codified ordinances, model codes, court rules, and sentencing guidelines. Refer to The Bluebook.

Delaware Chancery Reports

Ab.:   Del. Ch.

–Discontinued after 43 Del. Ch. 534 (1968).

–Cite to A. or A.2d if therein; otherwise, cite to Del. Ch.

–Parallel citations are not required either in documents submitted to Delaware state courts or in any other documents. See Bluebook Rule 10.3.1 and Practitioners' Note P.3; see also Del. Ch. Ct. R. 171(g), Del. Sup. Ct. R. 14(g), Del. Super. Ct. Civ. R. 107(c)(4), Del. Ct. C.P. Civ. R. 107(c)(4), Del. Civ. Prac. L.R. 7.1.3(a)(5), and Del. Fam. Ct. Civ. R. 107(c)(5).

In documents submitted to Delaware state courts, cite as follows:

Mayer v. Mayer, Del. Ch., 132 A.2d 617 (1957). –Case Citation.

Mayer v. Mayer, Del. Ch., 132 A.2d 617, 619 (1957). –Page Citation.

In all other documents, cite as follows:

Mayer v. Mayer, 132 A.2d 617 (Del. Ch. 1957). –Case Citation.

Mayer v. Mayer, 132 A.2d 617, 619 (Del. Ch. 1957). –Page Citation.

Delaware Code Annotated

Ab.:   Del. Code Ann. tit.   , §   (year)

Ex.:   Del. Code Ann. tit. 18, § 314 (2001).

Delaware Constitution

Ab.:   Del. Const. art.   , §   .

Ex.:   Del. Const. art. II, § 3. –"Cite constitutional provisions currently in force without date." Bluebook Rule 11.

Del. Const. art. IV, § 25 repealed by 51 Del. Laws, c. 78. –"If the cited provision has been repealed, either indicate parenthetically the fact and date of repeal or cite the repealing provision in full." Bluebook Rule 11.

Del. Const. art. I, § 20 (amended 1986). –"When citing a provision that has been subsequently amended, either indicate parenthetically the fact and date of amendment or cite the amending provision in full." Bluebook Rule 11.

Del. Const. of 1792, art. I, § 19. –"Cite constitutions that have been totally superseded by year of adoption; if the specific provision cited was adopted in a different year, give that year parenthetically." Bluebook Rule 11.

Delaware Journal of Corporate Law

Ab.:   Del. J. Corp. L.

In citing cases in law review footnotes, abbreviate any word listed in Table T.6; the names of "states, countries, and other geographical units" unless they are named parties; and any other words of eight or more letters "if substantial space is thereby saved and the result is unambiguous." Bluebook Rule 10.2.2. On the other hand, in citing cases in text, abbreviate only widely known acronyms and the following words: "&," "Ass'n," "Bros.," "Co.," "Corp.," "Inc.," "Ltd.," and "No." Bluebook Rule 10.2.1(c).

Ex.:   Lyman Johnson, <u>Sovereignty Over Corporate Stock</u>, 16 Del. J. Corp. L. 485 (1991). –Article Citation.

Lyman Johnson, <u>Sovereignty Over Corporate Stock</u>, 16 Del. J. Corp. L. 485. 490 (1991). –Page Citation.

Delaware Lawyer
Ab.:   Del. Law.

Ex.:   William Pricket, <u>Scull & Heap</u>, Del. Law., Fall 1991, at 31. –Article Citation.

William Pricket, <u>Scull & Heap</u>, Del. Law., Fall 1991, at 31, 31-32. –Page Citation.

Delaware Register of Regulations
Ab.:   Del. Reg. of Regs.

Delaware Reports (1920-1966)
Ab.:   Del.

–Discontinued after 59 Del. 302 (1966).

–Cite to A. or A.2d if therein; otherwise, cite to Del.

–Parallel citations are not required either in documents submitted to Delaware state courts or in any other document. <u>See</u> Bluebook Rule 10.3.1 and Practitioners' Note P.3; <u>see also</u> Del. Ch. Ct. R. 171(g), Del. Sup. Ct. R. 14(g), Del. Super. Ct. Civ. R. 107(c)(4), Del. Ct. C.P. Civ. R. 107(c)(4), Del. Civ. Prac. L.R. 7.1.3(a)(5), and Del. Fam. Ct. Civ. R. 107(c)(5).

In documents submitted to Delaware state courts, cite as follows:

<u>Carey v. Bryan & Rollins</u>, Del. Supr., 105 A.2d 201 (1954). –Case Citation.

<u>Carey v. Bryan & Rollins</u>, Del. Supr., 105 A.2d 201, 202 (1954). –Page Citation.

In all other documents, cite as follows:

<u>Carey v. Bryan & Rollins</u>, 105 A.2d 201 (Del. 1954). –Case Citation.

<u>Carey v. Bryan & Rollins</u>, 105 A.2d 201, 202 (Del. 1954). –Page Citation.

Delaware Session Laws
<u>See</u> Laws of Delaware
Ab.:   vol. Del. Laws (year)

Denver Journal of International Law and Policy
Ab.:   Denv. J. Int'l L. & Pol'y

In law review footnotes, the titles of books and the names of cases, except for procedural phrases, are not underlined. <u>See</u> Bluebook Rule 2.1(a). Further, the following are in large and small capitals: codes, restatements, standards, constitutions, periodicals, authors of books, titles of books, the abbreviated names of codes, most legislative materials except for bills and resolutions, codified ordinances, model codes, court rules, and sentencing guidelines. Refer to <u>The Bluebook</u>.

Ex.:   Kevin Ryan, <u>Rights, Intervention, and Self-Determination</u>, 20 Denv. J.
        Int'l L. & Pol'y 55 (1991). –Article Citation.

        Kevin Ryan, <u>Rights, Intervention, and Self-Determination</u>, 20 Denv. J.
        Int'l L. & Pol'y 55, 61-66 (1991). –Page Citation.

Denver Law Journal
Ab.:   Denv. L.J.
Ex.:   John A. Martin & Elizabeth A. Prescott, <u>The Problem of Delay in the
        Colorado Court of Appeals</u>, 58 Denver L.J. 1 (1980). –Article Citation.

        John A. Martin & Elizabeth A. Prescott, <u>The Problem of Delay in the
        Colorado Court of Appeals</u>, 58 Denver L.J. 1, 2-6 (1980). –Page
        Citation.

        –In 1985, this publication changed its name to Denver University Law
        Review.

Denver University Law Review
Ab.:   Denv. U. L. Rev.
Ex.:   Ben A. Rich, <u>The Assault on Privacy in Healthcare Decisionmaking</u>,
        68 Denv. U. L. Rev. 1 (1991). –Article Citation.

        Ben A. Rich, <u>The Assault on Privacy in Healthcare Decisionmaking</u>,
        68 Denv. U. L. Rev. 1, 21-27 (1991). –Page Citation.

        –In 1985, Denver Law Journal changed its name to Denver University
        Law Review.

Department of State Bulletin
Ab.:   Dep't St. Bull.
Ex.:   James A. Baker, <u>Power for Good: American Foreign Policy in the New
        Era</u>, Address Before the American Society of Newspaper Editors
        (ASNE) (Apr. 14, 1989), in Dep't St. Bull., June 1989, at 8, 11.
        –Address Citation.

Department of State Dispatch
Ab.:   Dep't St. Dispatch
Ex.:   Alan Larson, <u>U.S. Perspective on the WTO Ministerial Meeting</u>, Dep't
        St. Dispatch, Dec. 1999, at 7, 8.

DePaul Business Law Journal
Ab.:   DePaul Bus. L.J.
Ex.:   David Ackerman, <u>Planning for Ownership Succession in the Closely
        Held Business</u>, 3 DePaul Bus. L.J. 245 (1991). –Article Citation.

        David Ackerman, <u>Planning for Ownership Succession in the Closely
        Held Business</u>, 3 DePaul Bus. L.J. 245, 254 (1991). –Page Citation.

DePaul Law Review
Ab.:   DePaul L. Rev.

In citing cases in law review footnotes, abbreviate any word listed in Table T.6;
the names of "states, countries, and other geographical units" unless they are named parties;
and any other words of eight or more letters "if <u>substantial</u> space is thereby saved and the
result is unambiguous." <u>Bluebook</u> Rule 10.2.2. On the other hand, in citing cases in text,
abbreviate only widely known acronyms and the following words: "&," "Ass'n," "Bros.,"
"Co.," "Corp.," "Inc.," "Ltd.," and "No." <u>Bluebook</u> Rule 10.2.1(c).

Ex.: Steven R. Greenberger, <u>Democracy and Congressional Tenure</u>, 41 DePaul L. Rev. 37 (1991). –Article Citation.

Steven R. Greenberger, <u>Democracy and Congressional Tenure</u>, 41 DePaul L. Rev. 37, 38-40 (1991). –Page Citation.

Detroit College of Law Review
Ab.: Det. C.L. Rev.

Ex.: John E. Sanchez, <u>Religious Affirmative Action in Employment: Fearful Symmetry</u>, 3 Det. C.L. Rev. 1019 (1991). –Article Citation.

John E. Sanchez, <u>Religious Affirmative Action in Employment: Fearful Symmetry</u>, 3 Det. C.L. Rev. 1019, 1019 (1991). –Page Citation.

Developing Labor Law, The
–Do not abbreviate the title.

Ex.: 2 <u>The Developing Labor Law</u> § 8(e) (Patrick Hardin ed., 3rd ed. 1992). –Section Citation.

2 <u>The Developing Labor Law</u> § 8(e), at 1359 (Patrick Hardin ed., 3rd ed. 1992). –Page Citation.

2 <u>The Developing Labor Law</u> § 8(e), at 1361 n.219 (Patrick Hardin ed., 3rd ed. 1992). –Footnote Citation.

Dickinson Journal of International Law
Ab.: Dick. J. Int'l L.

Ex.: John A. Maher, <u>National Cooperative Production Amendments of 1993: Limited Cartelism Invited!</u>, 12 Dick. J. Int'l L. 195 (1994). –Article Citation.

John A. Maher, <u>National Cooperative Production Amendments of 1993: Limited Cartelism Invited!</u>, 12 Dick. J. Int'l L. 195, 212-213 (1994). –Page Citation.

Dickinson Law Review
Ab.: Dick. L. Rev.

Ex.: Thomas Grexa, <u>Title VII Tenure Litigation in the Academy and Academic Freedom --A Current Appraisal</u>, 96 Dick. L. Rev. 11 (1991). –Article Citation.

Thomas Grexa, <u>Title VII Tenure Litigation in the Academy and Academic Freedom --A Current Appraisal</u>, 96 Dick. L. Rev. 11, 26-27 (1991). –Page Citation.

Digest and Decisions of the Employees' Compensation Appeals Board (U.S.) (1947-date)
(v. 1-35 titled Decisions of the Emplopyees' Compensation Appeals Board; v.36-present-current title)
Ab.: Empl. Comp. App. Bd.

In law review footnotes, the titles of books and the names of cases, except for procedural phrases, are not underlined. <u>See</u> Bluebook Rule 2.1(a). Further, the following are in large and small capitals: codes, restatements, standards, constitutions, periodicals, authors of books, titles of books, the abbreviated names of codes, most legislative materials except for bills and resolutions, codified ordinances, model codes, court rules, and sentencing guidelines. Refer to <u>The Bluebook</u>.

Ex.:   Gary L. Whitmore, 43 Empl. Comp. App. Bd. 441 (1992).

Digest of International Law, by Green Haywood Hackworth
Ab.:   Hackworth Digest
Ex.:   Prisoners of War, 6 Hackworth Digest § 576, at 274.
         –Include the title of the section, volume number, author's name and the
         word Digest, and section number. Page number should be included as
         necessary. See Bluebook Rule 21.10(b).

Digest of International Law, by John B. Moore
         –Do not abbreviate the title.
Ex.:   4 John B. Moore, A Digest of International Law § 590 (1906).
         –Section Citation.
         4 John B. Moore, A Digest of International Law § 590, at 272 (1906).
         –Page Citation.

Digest of International Law, by Marjorie M. Whiteman
Ab.:   Whiteman Digest
Ex.:   Capture, 11 Whiteman Digest § 7, at 55.
         –Include the title of the section, volume number, author's name and the
         word Digest, and section number. Page number should be included as
         necessary. See Bluebook Rule 21.10(b).

Digest of United States Practice in International Law
Ab.:   Digest
Ex.:   Sovereign Immunity: Foreign Sovereign Immunities Act: Assassination
         Within the United States, 1980 Digest § 7, at 546.

dissenting opinion
Ex.:   Roe v. Wade, 410 U.S. 113, 171 (1973) (Rehnquist, J., dissenting).
See Bluebook Rule 10.6.

District Court (federal)
Ab.:   D.

District Court (state)
Ab.:   Dist. Ct.

District Court of Appeal(s)
Ab.:   Dist. Ct. App.

District of Columbia Appeals Cases (1893-1941)
See Appeal Cases, District of Columbia (1893-1941)

District of Columbia Code Annotated (1981)
Ab.:   D.C. Code Ann. §   (year)
Ex.:   D.C. Code Ann. § 45-1624 (1996).
         D.C. Code Ann. § 1-602.2 (1992).

In citing cases in law review footnotes, abbreviate any word listed in Table T.6;
the names of "states, countries, and other geographical units" unless they are named parties;
and any other words of eight or more letters "if substantial space is thereby saved and the
result is unambiguous." Bluebook Rule 10.2.2. On the other hand, in citing cases in text,
abbreviate only widely known acronyms and the following words: "&," "Ass'n," "Bros.,"
"Co.," "Corp.," "Inc.," "Ltd.," and "No." Bluebook Rule 10.2.1(c).

D.C. Code Ann. § 1.2485.1 (Supp. 2000).

District of Columbia Code Encyclopedia
Ab.: D.C. Code Encycl. § (West year)

District of Columbia Court of Appeals
Ab.: D.C.
–1943-date, cite to A.2d.
Ex.: Sayyad v. Fawzi, 674 A.2d 905 (D.C. 1996). –Article Citation.
Sayyad v. Fawzi, 674 A.2d 905, 906 (D.C. 1996). –Page Citation.

District of Columbia, Laws in Statutes at Large relating to
Ab.: volume Stat. (year)

District of Columbia Law Review
Ab.: D.C. L. Rev.
Ex.: Margaret Beyer, Juvenile Detention to 'Protect' Children from Neglect,
3 D.C. L. Rev. 213 (1995). –Article Citation.
Margaret Beyer, Juvenile Detention to 'Protect' Children from Neglect,
3 D.C. L. Rev. 213, 215 (1995). –Page Citation.

District of Columbia Register
Ab.: D.C. Reg.

District of Columbia Session Laws
See District of Columbia Statutes at Large

District of Columbia Statutes at Large
Ab.: year D.C. Stat.
Ex.: Tax Amnesty Act of 1986, No. 6-209, 1986 D.C. Stat. 677. –Citation
to an entire session law.

Divisional Court
Ab.: Div. Ct.

Documents, Congressional
See Congressional Documents

Documents of the United Nations Conference on International Organization
Ab.: U.N.C.I.O. Docs.
See Bluebook Rule 21.7.6.

Domestic Relations Court
Ab.: Dom. Rel. Ct.

In law review footnotes, the titles of books and the names of cases, except for procedural
phrases, are not underlined. See Bluebook Rule 2.1(a). Further, the following are in large
and small capitals: codes, restatements, standards, constitutions, periodicals, authors of
books, titles of books, the abbreviated names of codes, most legislative materials except for
bills and resolutions, codified ordinances, model codes, court rules, and sentencing guidelines.
Refer to The Bluebook.

Dominion Law Reports (Canada) (1912-date)
  –Cite to Canada: Supreme Court Reports (S.C.R.), Federal Court
  Reports (F.C.R.) or Exchequer Court Reports (Ex. C.R.) if therein;
  otherwise cite to D.L.R. See Bluebook Table T.2.

Ab.:   D.L.R.

Ex.:   Bateman v. Toronto Dominion Bank, [1991] D.L.R.4th 354, 359
        (Can.). –Page Citation.

Drake Law Review
Ab.:   Drake L. Rev.

Ex.:   Frona M. Powell, Mistake of Fact in the Sale of Real Property,
        40 Drake L. Rev. 91 (1991). –Article Citation.

        Frona M. Powell, Mistake of Fact in the Sale of Real Property,
        40 Drake L. Rev. 91, 113-15 (1991). –Page Citation.

Duke Journal of Comparative & International Law
Ab.:   Duke J. Comp. & Int'l L.

Ex.:   Michael P. Scharf, The Jury is Still Out on the Need for an
        International Criminal Court, 1991 Duke J. Comp. & Int'l L. 135
        (1991). –Article Citation.

        Michael P. Scharf, The Jury is Still Out on the Need for an
        International Criminal Court, 1991 Duke J. Comp. & Int'l L. 135, 154-
        55 (1991). –Page Citation.

Duke Law Journal
Ab.:   Duke L.J.

Ex.:   Mark H. Grunewald, The NLRB's First Rulemaking: An Exercise in
        Pragmatism, 41 Duke L.J. 274 (1991). –Article Citation.

        Mark H. Grunewald, The NLRB's First Rulemaking: An Exercise in
        Pragmatism, 41 Duke L.J. 274, 281-82 (1991). –Page Citation.

Duquesne Law Review
Ab.:   Duq. L. Rev.

Ex.:   David E. Seidelson, The Appropriate Judicial Response to Evidence of
        the Violation of a Criminal Statute in a Negligence Action, 30 Duq. L.
        Rev. 1 (1991). –Article Citation.

        David E. Seidelson, The Appropriate Judicial Response to Evidence of
        the Violation of a Criminal Statute in a Negligence Action, 30 Duq. L.
        Rev. 1, 11-15 (1991). –Page Citation.

In citing cases in law review footnotes, abbreviate any word listed in Table T.6;
the names of "states, countries, and other geographical units" unless they are named parties;
and any other words of eight or more letters "if substantial space is thereby saved and the
result is unambiguous." Bluebook Rule 10.2.2. On the other hand, in citing cases in text,
abbreviate only widely known acronyms and the following words: "&," "Ass'n," "Bros.,"
"Co.," "Corp.," "Inc.," "Ltd.," and "No." Bluebook Rule 10.2.1(c).

E

EEOC Compliance Manual (Bureau of National Affairs)
  Ab.:   EEOC Compl. Man. (BNA)

EEOC Compliance Manual (Commerce Clearing House)
  Ab.:   EEOC Compl. Man. (CCH)
  Ex.:   St. Mary's Honor Ctr. v. Hicks, EEOC Compl. Man. (CCH) ¶ 2099
            (EEOC April 12, 1994). –Citation to looseleaf material.

Ecclesiastical
  Ab.:   Eccl.

Ecclesiastical Court
  Ab.:   Eccl. Ct.

Ecclesiastical Law Journal
  Ab.:   Ecclesiastical L.J.
  Ex.:   Rupert Bursell, The Parson's Freehold, 2 Ecclesiastical L.J. 259
            (1992). –Article Citation.

            Rupert Bursell, The Parson's Freehold, 2 Ecclesiastical L.J. 259, 264
            (1992). –Page Citation.

Ecology Law Quarterly
  Ab.:   Ecology L.Q.
  Ex.:   David J. Bederman, International Control of Marine "Pollution" by
            Exotic Species, 18 Ecology L.Q. 677 (1991). –Article Citation.

            David J. Bederman, International Control of Marine "Pollution" by
            Exotic Species, 18 Ecology L.Q. 677, 690-95 (1991). –Page Citation.

Economic Analysis of Law, by Richard A. Posner
            –Do not abbreviate the title.
  Ex.   Richard A. Posner, Economic Analysis of Law § 14.7 (4th ed. 1992).
            –Section Citation.

            Richard A. Posner, Economic Analysis of Law § 14.7, at 414 (4th ed.
            1992). –Page Citation.

edition
  Ab.:   ed.

editor
  Ab.:   ed.

In law review footnotes, the titles of books and the names of cases, except for procedural
phrases, are not underlined. See Bluebook Rule 2.1(a). Further, the following are in large
and small capitals: codes, restatements, standards, constitutions, periodicals, authors of
books, titles of books, the abbreviated names of codes, most legislative materials except for
bills and resolutions, codified ordinances, model codes, court rules, and sentencing guidelines.
Refer to The Bluebook.

Education Law Reporter (West)
   Ab.:   Educ. L. Rep.

E.g.

   –"E.g." is used when the "cited authority states the proposition; other authorities also state the proposition, but citation to them would not be helpful or is not necessary. 'E.g.' may also be used in combination with other signals, preceded by a comma ....." Bluebook Rule 1.2(a).

   Ex.:   "It is well settled that a speaker's rights are not lost merely because compensation is received; a speaker is no less a speaker because he or she is paid to speak. E.g., New York Times Co. v. Sullivan, 376 U.S. at 265-66." -- Taken from 487 U.S. 781, 801 (1987).

Electronic media and other nonprint sources
   –See Bluebook Rule 18.

   "Information should be cited in a manner that indicates clearly which source actually was used or accessed by the author. This rule requires the use and citation of traditional printed sources, except when the information is not available in a printed source, or if the traditional source is obscure or hard to find and when citation to an electronic source will substantially improve access to the same information contained in the traditional source. In the latter case, to the extent possible, the traditional source should be used and cited, and the electronic source may be given as a parallel citation using the explanatory phrase "available at"; no explanatory phrase should be included when the author accesses only the electronic source. For material found exclusively on the Internet, such as on-line journals, the explanatory phrase "at" should be used." –Bluebook Rule 18.

   Commercial Electronic Databases.

      –Cases.

      "When a case is unreported but available on a widely used electronic database, then it may be cited to that database. Provide the case name, docket number, database identifier, court name, and full date of the most recent major disposition of the case. The database identifier must contain enough information for a reader to identify the database and find the case. If the database has identifying codes or numbers that uniquely identify the case (as do LEXIS and Westlaw after 1986) these must be given. Screen or page numbers, if assigned, should be preceded by an asterisk; paragraph numbers, if assigned, should be preceded by a paragraph symbol." –Bluebook Rule 18.1.1.

In citing cases in law review footnotes, abbreviate any word listed in Table T.6; the names of "states, countries, and other geographical units" unless they are named parties; and any other words of eight or more letters "if substantial space is thereby saved and the result is unambiguous." Bluebook Rule 10.2.2. On the other hand, in citing cases in text, abbreviate only widely known acronyms and the following words: "&," "Ass'n," "Bros.," "Co.," "Corp.," "Inc.," "Ltd.," and "No." Bluebook Rule 10.2.1(c).

Ex.:

> Williams v. East Coast Truck Lines, No. 98-1903, 1999 U.S. App. LEXIS 16773, at *2 (4th Cir. July 19, 1999).

> Ashley v. ITT Hartford, No. C 97-3226 TEH, 1999 U.S. Dist. LEXIS 1228, at *3 (N.D. Cal. Jan. 20, 1998).

> Jackson v. Samedan Oil Corp., No. Civ.A.98-0472, 2000 WL 343361, at *6 (E.D. La. Mar. 31, 2000).

> Reed v. Hamilton, No. W1999-00440-COA-R3-CV, 2000 WL 558613, at *4 (Tenn. Ct. App. May 4, 2000).

> Hoffmann Elec. Co. v. Undlin, 2000 WL 1869556, at *4 (Minn. Ct. App. Dec. 26, 2000) (WESTLAW MN-CS). "Citation to cases that have not been assigned unique database identifiers should include all relevant information." –Bluebook Rule 18.1.1.
> "A public domain form (rule 10.3.3) may be used in place of an electronic database citation." –Bluebook Rule 18.1.1.

–Statutes

"Cite codes and session laws according to rules 12.3 and 12.4. In addition when citing a code contained in an electronic database, give parenthetically the name of the database and information regarding the currency of the database as provided by the database itself (rather than the year of the code according to rule 12.3.2). In accordance with rule 12.3.1(d), also give the name of the publisher, editor, or compiler unless the code is published, edited, compiled by, or under the supervision of, federal or state officials." –Bluebook Rule 18.1.2.
Ex.:

> Mich. Comp. Laws Ann. § 431.316 (West, WESTLAW through No. 225 of 2000 Reg. Sess.)

> Cal. Prob. Code § 6110 (Matthew Bender, LEXIS through 2000 Sess.)

–Legislative, Administrative and Executive Materials

"Cite legislative, administrative, and executive materials according to rules 13 and 14. In addition, when citing materials contained in a commercial electronic database, give the name of the database and any identifying codes or numbers that uniquely identify the material." –Bluebook Rule 18.1.3.

–federal bill (unenacted)
Ex.:

In law review footnotes, the titles of books and the names of cases, except for procedural phrases, are not underlined. See Bluebook Rule 2.1(a). Further, the following are in large and small capitals: codes, restatements, standards, constitutions, periodicals, authors of books, titles of books, the abbreviated names of codes, most legislative materials except for bills and resolutions, codified ordinances, model codes, court rules, and sentencing guidelines. Refer to The Bluebook.

H.R. 1390, 106th Cong. § 3(c) (1999), WL 1999 CONG US HR 1390.

–federal report

Ex.:

H.R. Rep. No. 106-556 (2000), 2000 WL 347371. –information accessed only through Westlaw.

H.R. Rep. No. 100-946(I) (1988), reprinted in 1988 U.S.C.C.A.N. 3636, 1988 WL 170033.

–congressional debate

Ex.:

147 Cong. Rec. S1105 (daily ed. Feb. 7, 2001) (statement of Sen. Sarbanes), LEXIS 147 Cong Rec S 1104 *S1105.

–federal regulation cited to Code of Federal Regulations

Ex.:

Regulation D, 12 C.F.R. § 204.1 (2000), WL 12 CFR s 204.1

–administrative adjudication

Ex.:

In re Tomy Corp., 99 F.T.C. 1 (1982), WL 99 F.T.C. 1.

–formal advisory opinion

Ex.:

41 Op. Att'y Gen. 88 (1951), 1951 US AG LEXIS 1.

–revenue ruling

Ex.:

Rev. Rul. 99-14, 1999-1 C.B. 835, 1999 IRB LEXIS 132.

–Secondary Materials

" When citing secondary materials to a database, provide a complete citation to the document using the rules applicable to that type of authority, and a citation to the database in accordance with rule 18 regarding the use of explanatory phrases to indicate the actual source used by the author. If the database assigns a unique identifier or code to each document within the database, include that identifier or code to assist the reader in locating the document cited.

When the traditional source is accessed, increased accessibility to the source may be provided in the form of a parallel citation to a commercial electronic database using 'available at.' " –Bluebook Rule 18.1.4.

In citing cases in law review footnotes, abbreviate any word listed in Table T.6; the names of "states, countries, and other geographical units" unless they are named parties; and any other words of eight or more letters "if substantial space is thereby saved and the result is unambiguous." Bluebook Rule 10.2.2. On the other hand, in citing cases in text, abbreviate only widely known acronyms and the following words: "&," "Ass'n," "Bros.," "Co.," "Corp.," "Inc.," "Ltd.," and "No." Bluebook Rule 10.2.1(c).

–newspaper

Ex.:

> Beth Daley, <u>Global Warming: What Lies Ahead?</u>, Boston Globe, Jan. 29, 2001, <u>available at</u> 2001 WL 3916574.

–newswire

Ex.:

> <u>Grant to Fund Water Pollution Studies, Education</u>, AP Newswires, Jan. 1, 2001, <u>available at</u> WL 1/1/01 APWIRES 14:58:00.

"If only the commercial database is accessed, provide the traditional and commercial database citations using no explanatory phrase."
–Bluebook Rule 18.1.4.

–periodical

Ex.:

> Jennifer Cannon and Michelle Haas, Recent Development, <u>The Human Cloning Prohibition Act: Did Congress Go Too Far?</u>, 35 Harv. J. Legis. 637 (1998), WL 35 HVJL 637.

–press release

Ex.:

> <u>Analysis: What's the Future of U.S. National Defense?</u>, UPI, Dec. 18, 2000, LEXIS, Nexis Library, UPI File.

The Internet

For a detailed discussion of basic citation principles, including elements of Internet citation, basic citation forms, the Uniform Resource Locator, changed or multiple URLs and multiple format options, date of Internet citations, parenthetical information, pinpoint citation, and preservation of information, <u>see</u> <u>Bluebook</u> Rule 18.2.1.

–Cases

"A case must be cited first to a traditional source (rule 10) or electronic database (rule 18.1), except that an Internet source may be cited instead where the information is not available in a traditional source or electronic database. An additional citation in the form of a parallel or related-authority citation (rule 1.6) may be provided where the Internet source will substantially improve access to the same information contained in the traditional source." –<u>Bluebook</u> Rule 18.2.2(a).

Ex.:

> <u>Kuwait Airways Corp. v. Iraqi Airways Co</u>. (H.L. Feb. 8, 2001), <u>available at</u> http://www.parliament.the-stationery-office.co.uk/pa/ldjudgmt/ldjudgmt.htm.

In law review footnotes, the titles of books and the names of cases, except for procedural phrases, are not underlined. <u>See</u> <u>Bluebook</u> Rule 2.1(a). Further, the following are in large and small capitals: codes, restatements, standards, constitutions, periodicals, authors of books, titles of books, the abbreviated names of codes, most legislative materials except for bills and resolutions, codified ordinances, model codes, court rules, and sentencing guidelines. Refer to <u>The Bluebook</u>.

State v. Hodge, No. E2000-00040-CCA-R3-CD (Tenn. Crim. App. Feb. 9, 2001), available at http://www.tsc.state.tn.us/PDF/tcca/011/HodgeTR.pdf at 3.

"Prior or subsequent history of the case (rule 10.7) should follow the Internet citation unless it also is contained at the same Internet address. When the Internet site offers the case in pdf format, the case should be cited to that format in order to allow for a more precise citation (rule 18.2.1(g))." –Bluebook Rules 18.2.2(b) & (c).

Ex.:

Troxel v. Granville, 530 U.S. 57 (2000), available at Cornell Legal Info. Inst., http://supct.law.cornell.edu/supct/pdf/99-138P.ZO, aff'g 940 P.2d 698 (Wash. 1997).

–Constitutions & Statutes

"Constitutions and statutes must be cited first to a traditional source (rules 11 and 12), or electronic database (rule 18.1), unless the information is not available in a traditional source or electronic database. An additional citation in the form of a parallel or related authority citation may be provided where the Internet source will substantially improve access to the same information contained in the traditional source." –Bluebook Rule 18.2.3.

Ex.:

Cal. Const. art. I, § 2(b), available at http://www.leginfo.ca.gov/.const/.article_1 (last visited Mar. 12, 2001).

Ky. Rev. Stat. § 5.031 (1996), State of Kentucky, available at http://162.114.4.13/KRS/005-00/031.PDF

Beaverton Code ch. 4.01.100 (1989), available at http://www.ci.beaverton.or.us/departments/attorney/docs/chapter4/ pdf

"Information concerning repeal, amendment, and prior history of a statute (rule 12.6) should precede the Internet citation." –Bluebook Rule 18.2.3(b)

–Legislative Material

"Legislative material must be cited first to a traditional source (rule 13) or electronic database (rule 18.1). An additional citation in the form of a parallel or related-authority citation may be provided where the Internet source will substantially improve access to the same information in the traditional source." –Bluebook Rule 18.2.4.

In citing cases in law review footnotes, abbreviate any word listed in Table T.6; the names of "states, countries, and other geographical units" unless they are named parties; and any other words of eight or more letters "if substantial space is thereby saved and the result is unambiguous." Bluebook Rule 10.2.2. On the other hand, in citing cases in text, abbreviate only widely known acronyms and the following words: "&," "Ass'n," "Bros.," "Co.," "Corp.," "Inc.," "Ltd.," and "No." Bluebook Rule 10.2.1(c).

–pending federal legislation

Ex.:

> Drug Importer Death Penalty Act, H.R. 213, 107th Cong. § 2
> (2001), <u>available at</u> http://thomas.loc.gov/cgi-
> bin/query/z?c107:H.R.213:

–congressional debate

Ex.:

> 147 Cong. Rec. S1206 (daily ed. Feb. 8, 2001) (statement of Sen.
> Wellstone), <u>available at</u> http://thomas.loc.gov/cgi-
> n/query/D?r107:27:./temp/~r1072bw484::

–recently enacted state public act

Ex.:

> Act of June 28, 2000, ch. 999, 2000 Tenn. Pub. Acts 3 (concerning
> Tennessee Millenium Trust), Public and Private Acts, State of
> Tenn. 102nd Gen. Assemb., <u>available at</u>
> http://www.state.tn.us/sos/acts/101pub/pc999/pdf

–pending state bill

Ex.:

> SB 2, 2001 Gen. Assemb., Reg. Sess. (Fla. 2001), <u>available at</u>
> http://www.leg.state.fl.us/data/session/2001/Senate/bills/billtext/pd
> f/s0020.pdf

–Administrative and Executive Materials

> <u>See</u> <u>Bluebook</u> Rule 18.2.5.

–final rules and regulations

Ex.:

> Or. Admin. R. ch. 177-010-0025 (2001), <u>available at</u>
> http://archweb.sos.state.or.us/rules/OARS_100?01R_177/177_010.
> html

–proposed federal regulations

Ex.:

> Airworthiness Directives: Pilatus Aircraft Ltd. Model PC-7
> Airplanes, 66 Fed. Reg. 57, 58 (proposed Dec. 21, 2000) (to be
> codified at 14 C.F.R. pt. 39), GPO Access, <u>available at</u>
> http://www.access.gpo.gov/su_docs/aces/aces140.html

–Books, Journals, and Magazines

In law review footnotes, the titles of books and the names of cases, except for procedural
phrases, are not underlined. <u>See</u> <u>Bluebook</u> Rule 2.1(a). Further, the following are in large
and small capitals: codes, restatements, standards, constitutions, periodicals, authors of
books, titles of books, the abbreviated names of codes, most legislative materials except for
bills and resolutions, codified ordinances, model codes, court rules, and sentencing guidelines.
Refer to <u>The Bluebook</u>.

"Books, journals and magazines should be cited first to a traditional source except that an Internet source may be cited where information is not available in a traditional source or electronic database. An additional citation in the form of a parallel or related authority citation (rule 1.6) may be provided where the Internet will substantially improve access to the same information contained in the traditional source." –<u>Bluebook</u> Rule 18.2.6.

–traditional print source

Ex.:

> George J. Edwards., Jr., <u>The Grand Jury</u> 12 (1906), <u>available at</u> http://www.constitution.org/gje/gj_01.htm

"An Internet site, in providing a printed work, may include corresponding information about the print format. Such information may be included in the citation for a more accurate pinpoint citation." –<u>Bluebook</u> Rule 18.2.6(a).

Ex.:

> Y. Daphne Coelho-Adam, Note, <u>Fishing for the Smoking Gun: The Need for British Courts to Grant American Style Extraterritorial Discovery Requests in U.S. Industry-Wide Tort Actions</u>, 33 Vand. J. Trans. L. 1225, 1238 (2000), <u>available at</u> http://www.vanderbilt.edu/Law/journal/33-5-3.htm

–on-line journals

"Citations to journals that appear only on the Internet should include the volume number, the title of the journal, the sequential article number, the explanatory phrase "<u>at</u>" to indicate an on-line journal (rule 18.2.1(b)), and the Internet address. Pinpoint citations should refer to the paragraph number, if available." –<u>Bluebook</u> Rule 18.2.6(b).

Ex.:

> Susan. W. Brenner, <u>State Cybercrime Legislation in the United States of America: A Survey</u>, 7 Rich. J.L. & Tech. 28, ¶ 14 (Winter 2001), <u>at</u> http://www.richmond.edu/jolt/v7:3/article2.html
> –pinpoint citation.

–Other Secondary Sources

In citing cases in law review footnotes, abbreviate any word listed in Table T.6; the names of "states, countries, and other geographical units" unless they are named parties; and any other words of eight or more letters "if <u>substantial</u> space is thereby saved and the result is unambiguous." <u>Bluebook</u> Rule 10.2.2. On the other hand, in citing cases in text, abbreviate only widely known acronyms and the following words: "&," "Ass'n," "Bros.," "Co.," "Corp.," "Inc.," "Ltd.," and "No." <u>Bluebook</u> Rule 10.2.1(c).

"Other secondary sources, such as news reports, newspapers, and other non-legal publications (rule 16.5), if not found on a commercial electronic database, may be cited to an Internet site, since such information is likely to be much more accessible on the Internet than in the traditional source. When citing such secondary sources, provide a complete citation to the document using the rules applicable to that type of authority. For material found exclusively on the Internet, the explanatory phrase "at" should be used. If the Internet site assigns a unique identifier or code to each document within the database, include that identifier or code to assist the reader in locating the document cited." –Bluebook Rule 18.2.7.

–speech

Ex.:

> Attorney General Janet Reno, Farewell Address to the Justice Dept. Staff (Jan. 11, 2001), available at http://www.usdoj.gov/archive/ag/speeches/2001/011101agfarewell.htm

–newspaper

Ex.:

> Richard W. Stevenson, Greenspan Hints Tax Cut Might Help Weak Economy, N.Y. Times, Jan. 25, 2001, http://www.nytimes.com/2001/01/25/business/25CND-GSPAN.html –article accessed only on the Internet.

–news release

Ex.:

> News Release, U.S. Dept. of Housing and Urban Dev., Mel Martinez to Head Department of Housing and Urban Development (Jan. 20, 2001), http://www.hud.gov/about/secretary/martinezanouncment.cfm –accessed only on the Internet.

–For additional examples, see Bluebook Rule 18.2.7.

–Other Information Sources

During the past year, most Gopher sites have ceased to exist because the information was moved to a Web server. Also, Telnet sites now appear to link to online catalogs rather than providing full text retrieval.

–FTP

Ex.:

In law review footnotes, the titles of books and the names of cases, except for procedural phrases, are not underlined. See Bluebook Rule 2.1(a). Further, the following are in large and small capitals: codes, restatements, standards, constitutions, periodicals, authors of books, titles of books, the abbreviated names of codes, most legislative materials except for bills and resolutions, codified ordinances, model codes, court rules, and sentencing guidelines. Refer to The Bluebook.

Cal. Penal Code § 502, ftp://ftp.sen.ca.gov/penal502.txt (as of Oct. 27, 1993) (on file with author). –accessed only on Internet.

–E-mail and Listserv postings

"In citing personal e-mail messages, analogize to unpublished letters (rule17.1.3).The date of the message and possibly the time-stamp may be needed for specific identification of the message. Archival information may be included parenthetically, and is recommended (rule 18.2.1(h). The e-mail addresses of the sender and recipient are not required or suggested, although they may be included if there is a reason for doing so." –<u>Bluebook</u> Rule 18.2.9.

Ex.:

E-mail from Andrew Morton, Bluebook Editor, University of Pennsylvania Law Review, to Kathleen Hartnett, Harvard Law Review (Sept. 1, 1999, 07.16:09 EST) (on file with author).

"Postings to listservs should follow a similar format, including the author's e-mail address and the address of the listserv." –<u>Bluebook</u> Rule 18.2.9.

Ex.:

Posting of Maitland Stewart, mstewart@paw.org, to Paramount-Fan@paramount.org (Feb. 16, 2001) (on file with author).

CD-ROM

"Information found on CD-ROM usually is available in print form, and citation to the print form is preferred where available. If the information is accessed on CD-ROM, it should be cited to CD-ROM. When citing cases on CD-ROM, the possibility exists that a case published near the date of the CD-ROM itself may have been included in slip opinion form, and (like a decision in an advance sheet) may have been edited or otherwise changed before the case was published in final form.

When citing CD-ROM media, include the title of the material, the publisher of the CD-ROM, the version searched, and the date of the material, if available, or the date of the version searched. The information may be provided in a source-date parenthetical or, if the information is voluminous, as related authority (rule 1.6)." –<u>Bluebook</u> Rule 18.3.

Ex.:

<u>Taylor v. Heldman</u>, No. M1999-00729-COA-R3-CV, (Tenn. Ct. App. 2000) (Tennessee Unpublished Decisions, 1985-2000, West CD-ROM Libraries, current through Nov. 1, 2000).

5 C.F.R. § 630.101 (West LawDesk Code of Federal Regulations CD-ROM, current through Sept. 2000).

In citing cases in law review footnotes, abbreviate any word listed in Table T.6; the names of "states, countries, and other geographical units" unless they are named parties; and any other words of eight or more letters "if <u>substantial</u> space is thereby saved and the result is unambiguous." <u>Bluebook</u> Rule 10.2.2. On the other hand, in citing cases in text, abbreviate only widely known acronyms and the following words: "&," "Ass'n," "Bros.," "Co.," "Corp.," "Inc.," "Ltd.," and "No." <u>Bluebook</u> Rule 10.2.1(c).

1 Lee R. Russ and Thomas F. Segalla, <u>Couch on Insurance</u> §1.4 (Couch on Insurance West LawDesk CD-ROM, July 2000).

Microform

"In general, when a document is reproduced in microform, it is not necessary to indicate this fact unless it would otherwise be difficult for a reader to identify and obtain the source. When citing material as "<u>microformed on</u>" a service, provide a complete citation to the original document and a citation to the microform in accordance with rule 1.6 regarding citations to related authority." –<u>Bluebook</u> Rule 18.4.1.

Ex.:

S.2626, 101st Cong. § 4 (1990), <u>microformed on</u> Sup. Docs. Y1.4/1:101-2351 (U.S. Gov't Printing Office).

<u>Turner v. Fouch</u>, 396 U.S. 346 (1969) (No. 71-3120) <u>microformed on</u> U.S. Supreme Court Records and Briefs (Microform, Inc.).

Films, Broadcasts, and Noncommercial Videotapes

–<u>See</u> entries herein for films, television broadcasts, and videotapes, and <u>Bluebook</u> Rule 18.5.

Audio Recordings

–<u>See</u> <u>Bluebook</u> Rule 18.6.1.

Ex.:

The Rolling Stones, <u>Emotional Rescue</u> (Atlantic Records 1980). –Citation to an entire audio recording.

Marvin Gaye, <u>I Heard It Through The Grapevine,</u> <u>on</u> <u>The Big Chill</u> (Motown Record Co. 1983). –Citation to a particular song on a recording.

Short Citation Forms

Commercial Electronic Databases

See <u>Bluebook</u> Rule 18.7(a).

Ex.:

<u>Reed v. Hamilton</u>, No. W1999-00440-COA-R3-CV, 2000 WL 558613, at *4 (Tenn. Ct. App. May 4, 2000)
becomes
<u>Reed</u>, 2000 WL 558613, at *3.

<u>Ashley v. ITT Hartford</u>, No. C 97-3226 TEH, 1998 U.S. Dist. LEXIS 1228, at *3 (N.D. Cal. Jan. 20, 1998)
becomes
<u>Ashley</u>, 1998 U.S. Dist. LEXIS 1228, at *5.

In law review footnotes, the titles of books and the names of cases, except for procedural phrases, are not underlined. See <u>Bluebook</u> Rule 2.1(a). Further, the following are in large and small capitals: codes, restatements, standards, constitutions, periodicals, authors of books, titles of books, the abbreviated names of codes, most legislative materials except for bills and resolutions, codified ordinances, model codes, court rules, and sentencing guidelines. Refer to <u>The Bluebook</u>.

H.R. 1390, 106th Cong. § 3(c) (1999), WL 1999 CONG US HR 1390

becomes

HR 1390 § 3(c), WL 1999 CONG US HR 1390.

Regulation D, 12 C.F.R. § 204.1 (2000), WL 12 CFR s 204.1

becomes

12 C.F.R. § 204.1, WL 12 CFR s 204.1 *or* WL 12 CFR s 204.1.

See <u>Bluebook</u> Rules 18.7(b), (c), and (d) for instruction on short citation forms for CD-ROM, microform, Internet, films, broadcasts, and audio recordings.

Electronic sources and databases
    –<u>See</u> electronic media and other nonprint sources.

E-mail messages
    "In citing personal e-mail messages, analogize to unpublished letters (rule17.1.3).The date of the message and possibly the time-stamp may be needed for specific identification of the message. Archival information may be included parenthetically, and is recommended (rule 18.2.1(h). The e-mail addresses of the sender and recipient are not required or suggested, although they may be included if there is a reason for doing so." –<u>Bluebook</u> Rule 18.2.9.

    Ex.

    E-mail from Andrew Morton, Bluebook Editor, University of Pennsylvania Law Review, to Kathleen Hartnett, Harvard Law Review (Sept. 1, 1999, 07.16:09 EST) (on file with author).

    "Postings to listservs should follow a similar format, including the author's e-mail address and the address of the listserv." –<u>Bluebook</u> Rule 18.2.9.

    Ex.

    Posting of Maitland Stewart, mstewart@paw.org, to Paramount-Fan@paramount.org (Feb. 16, 2001) (on file with author).

Emory International Law Review
    Ab.:   Emory Int'l L. Rev.

In citing cases in law review footnotes, abbreviate any word listed in Table T.6; the names of "states, countries, and other geographical units" unless they are named parties; and any other words of eight or more letters "if <u>substantial</u> space is thereby saved and the result is unambiguous." <u>Bluebook</u> Rule 10.2.2. On the other hand, in citing cases in text, abbreviate only widely known acronyms and the following words: "&," "Ass'n," "Bros.," "Co.," "Corp.," "Inc.," "Ltd.," and "No." <u>Bluebook</u> Rule 10.2.1(c).

Ex.:   Bruce Zagaris & Elizabeth Kingma, <u>Asset Forfeiture International and Foreign Law: An Emergency Regime</u>, 5 Emory Int'l L. Rev. 445 (1991). –Article Citation.

Bruce Zagaris & Elizabeth Kingma, <u>Asset Forfeiture International and Foreign Law: An Emergency Regime</u>, 5 Emory Int'l L. Rev. 445, 449-50 (1991). –Page Citation.

Emory Law Journal
Ab.:   Emory L.J.
Ex.:   Michael Corrado, <u>Automatism and the Theory of Action</u>, 39 Emory L.J. 1191 (1990). –Article Citation.

Michael Corrado, <u>Automatism and the Theory of Action</u>, 39 Emory L.J. 1191, 1193 (1990). –Page Citation.

Employee Benefits Cases (Bureau of National Affairs)
Ab.:   Employee Benefits Cas. (BNA)

Employee Relations Law Journal
Ab.:   Employee Rel. L.J.
Ex.:   Niall A. Paul, <u>The Civil Rights Act of 1991: What Does It Really Accomplish?</u>, 17 Employee Rel. L.J. 567 (1992). –Article Citation.

Niall A. Paul, <u>The Civil Rights Act of 1991: What Does It Really Accomplish?</u>, 17 Employee Rel. L.J. 567, 569-72 (1992). –Page Citation.

Employment and Training Reporter (Bureau of National Affairs)
Ab.:   Empl. & Training Rep. (BNA)

Employment Practices Guide (Commerce Clearing House)
         –Bound as Employment Practices Decisions (Commerce Clearing House)
Ab.:   Empl. Prac. Guide (CCH)
         –Bound as Empl. Prac. Dec. (CCH)
Ex.:   <u>Quaratino v. Wright</u>, 67 Empl. Prac. Dec. (CCH) ¶ 43,795 (2nd Cir. Nov. 20, 1995). –Citation to bound material.

<u>Cordova v. West</u>, 4 Empl. Prac. Guide (CCH) (69 Empl. Prac. Dec.) ¶ 44,309 (D. Colo. May 17, 1996). –Citation to looseleaf material.

–The above examples are proper if the case is not yet available in, or is not reported in, an official or West reporter, a public domain citation, or in a widely used computer database.

EEOC Discusses Liability of Labor Organizations under ADEA, [Sept. 1989 - Sept. 1991 New Developments Transfer Binder] ¶ 5271 (EEOC May 11, 1990) –Citation to bound administrative materials.

In law review footnotes, the titles of books and the names of cases, except for procedural phrases, are not underlined. See <u>Bluebook</u> Rule 2.1(a). Further, the following are in large and small capitals: codes, restatements, standards, constitutions, periodicals, authors of books, titles of books, the abbreviated names of codes, most legislative materials except for bills and resolutions, codified ordinances, model codes, court rules, and sentencing guidelines. Refer to <u>The Bluebook</u>.

EEOC Issues Guidance as Workers' Compensation and NADA, 2 Empl. Prac. Guide (CCH) ¶ 5426 (EEOC Sept. 3, 1996). –Citation to looseleaf administrative material.

Employment Safety and Health Guide (Commerce Clearing House)
  Ab.:   Empl. Safety & Health Guide (CCH)

en banc
          –Do not abbreviate
  Ex.:   United States v. Aguilar, 21 F.3d 1475 (9th Cir. 1994) (en banc).

Encyclopedia of European Community Law
  Ab.:   E.E.C.L.

Encyclopedia of Public International Law
          –Do not abbreviate the title.
  Ex.:   11 Encyclopedia of Public International Law 160 (1989).

Endnote(s)
          See Bluebook Rule 3.3(c) and (d).
          See footnotes.

Energy Law Journal
  Ab.:   Energy L.J.
  Ex.:   Philip M. Marston, Pipeline Restructuring: The Future of Open-Access Transportation, 12 Energy L.J. 53 (1991). –Article Citation.
          Philip M. Marston, Pipeline Restructuring: The Future of Open-Access Transportation, 12 Energy L.J. 53, 61-64 (1991). –Page Citation.

Energy Management (Commerce Clearing House)
  Ab.:   Energy Mgmt. (CCH)

English Law Reports and other materials
          –Explained and illustrated in Bluebook at Rule 20.3.1, and Table T.2.

English Reports–Full Reprint (U.K.)
          See Bluebook Table T.2 and Rule 20.3.1.
  Ab.:   Eng. Rep.
  Ex.:   Ridgway v. Wharton, 10 Eng. Rep. 1287 (1857). –Case Citation.
          Donegani v. Donegani, 12 Eng. Rep. 571 (P.C. 1835) (appeal taken from Lower Can.). –Case Citation.
          Leaf v. Coles, 42 Eng. Rep. 517 (Ch. 1851). –Case Citation.
          Marston v. Roe, 112 Eng. Rep. 742 (Q.B. 1838). –Case Citation.
          Milker v. Seagrave, 125 Eng. Rep. 935 (C.P. 1723). –Case Citation.

Entertainment and Sports Lawyer
  Ab.:   Ent. & Sports Law.

In citing cases in law review footnotes, abbreviate any word listed in Table T.6; the names of "states, countries, and other geographical units" unless they are named parties; and any other words of eight or more letters "if substantial space is thereby saved and the result is unambiguous." Bluebook Rule 10.2.2. On the other hand, in citing cases in text, abbreviate only widely known acronyms and the following words: "&," "Ass'n," "Bros.," "Co.," "Corp.," "Inc.," "Ltd.," and "No." Bluebook Rule 10.2.1(c).

Ex.:   Robert Acosta-Lewis, <u>A Basic Approach to Securing Event Sponsorship Rights</u>, Ent. & Sports Law., Spring 1991, at 1. –Article Citation.

Robert Acosta-Lewis, <u>A Basic Approach to Securing Event Sponsorship Rights</u>, Ent. & Sports Law., Spring 1991, at 1, 19. –Page Citation.

Entscheidungen des Bundegerichtshofes in Strafsachen (Germany)
Ab.:   BGHSt; <u>see</u> <u>Bluebook</u> Rule 20.3.2 and Table T.2.
Ex.:   Entscheidungen des Bundesgerichtshofes in Strasachen [BGHSt] 36, 124 (F.R.G.). –Case Citation.

BGHSt 36, 124. –Subsequent Abbreviated Case Citation.

BGHSt 36, 124 (125). –Subsequent Abbreviated Page Citation.

Entscheidungen des Bundegerichtshofes in Zivilsachen (Germany)
Ab.:   BGHZ, <u>see</u> <u>Bluebook</u> Rule 20.3.2 and Table T.2.
Ex.:   Entscheidungen des Bundesgerichtshofes in Zivilsachen [BGHZ] 114, 218 (F.R.G.). –Case Citation.

BGHZ 114, 218. –Subsequent Abbreviated Case Citation.

BGHZ 114, 218 (219). –Subsequent Abbreviated Page Citation.

Entscheidungen des Bundesverfassungsgerichts (Germany)
Ab.:   BVerfGE; <u>see</u> <u>Bluebook</u> Rule 20.3.2 and Table T.2.
Ex.:   Entscheidungen des Bundesverfassungsgerichts [BverfGE] 83, 82 (F.R.G.). –Case Citation.

BVerfGE 83, 82. –Subsequent Abbreviated Case Citation.

BVerfGE 83, 82 (82). –Subsequent Abbreviated Page Citation.

Entscheidungen des Bundesverwaltungsgericht (Germany)
Ab.:   BVerwGE; <u>see</u> <u>Bluebook</u> Rule 20.3.2 and Table T.2.
Ex.:   Entscheidungen des Bundesverwaltungsgericht [BVerwGE] 85, 108. –Case Citation.

BVerwG, 85, 108. –Subsequent Abbreviated Case Citation.

BVerwGE 85, 108 (108). –Subsequent Abbreviated Page Citation.

Environmental Law
Ab.:   Envtl. L.
Ex.:   Laksham Guruswamy, <u>Integrated Environmental Control: The Expanding Matrix</u>, 22 Envtl. L. 77 (1991). –Article Citation.

Laksham Guruswamy, <u>Integrated Environmental Control: The Expanding Matrix</u>, 22 Envtl. L. 77, 83-87 (1991). –Page Citation.

Environmental Law Reporter (Environmental Law Institute)
Ab.:   Envtl. L. Rep. (Envtl. L. Inst.)

In law review footnotes, the titles of books and the names of cases, except for procedural phrases, are not underlined. <u>See</u> <u>Bluebook</u> Rule 2.1(a). Further, the following are in large and small capitals: codes, restatements, standards, constitutions, periodicals, authors of books, titles of books, the abbreviated names of codes, most legislative materials except for bills and resolutions, codified ordinances, model codes, court rules, and sentencing guidelines. Refer to <u>The Bluebook</u>.

Ex.:   Alabama Power Co. v. Gorsuch, 12 Envtl. L. Rep. (Envtl. L. Inst.) 20218 (D.C. Cir. Feb. 5, 1982). –Citation to looseleaf material.

Committee for Charter Protection for Parks v. Brown, 10 Envtl. L. Rep. (Envtl. L. Inst.) 20,246 (S.D. Cal. 1980). –Citation to non-current looseleaf material.

Arizona v. Nucar Corp., 26 Envtl. L. Rep. (Envtl. L. Inst.) 20,061 (9th Cir. Sept. 15, 1995).

–The above examples are proper if the case is not yet available in an official or West reporter, or is not reported in an official or West reporter.

Trauberman, Dunwoody & Horne, Compensation for Toxic Substances Pollution: Michigan Case Study, 10 Envtl. L. Rep. (Envtl. L. Inst.) 50,021 (Sept. 1980).

–Citation to current or non-current looseleaf material. The citation is to an article or monograph written by the named contributors.

Nuclear Weapons and "Secret" Impact Statements: High Court Applies FOIA Exemptions to EIS Disclosure Rules, 12 Envtl. L. Rep. (Envtl. L. Inst.) 10,007 (Feb. 1982). –Citation to current or non-current looseleaf material; this citation is to an editorial comment written by the publisher's staff.

Environment Regulation Handbook
Ab.:   Env't Reg. Handbook (Env't Information Center)

Environment Reporter (Bureau of National Affairs)
–Bound as Environment Reporter Cases (Bureau of National Affairs)
Ab.:   Env't Rep. (BNA)
–Bound as Env't Rep. Cas. (BNA)
Ex.:   City of Albuquerque v. EPA, [Decisions] Env't Rep. (BNA) (43 Env't Rep. Cas.) 1276 (10th Cir. Oct. 7, 1996). –Citation to looseleaf material.

Papas v. Upjohn Co., 32 Env't Rep. Cas. (BNA) 1815 (11th Cir. 1991). –Citation to bound material.

–The above examples are proper if the case is not yet available in, or is not reported in, an official or West reporter, a public domain citation, or in a widely used computer database.

Statutes

Nuclear Regulatory Commission Standards for Protection Against Radiation, [8 Rederal Regulations] Env't Rep. (BNA) 151:0101 (June 17, 1996). –Citation to looseleaf statutes.

Equal Employment Compliance Manual
Ab.:   Eq. Empl. Compl. Man. (CBC)

In citing cases in law review footnotes, abbreviate any word listed in Table T.6; the names of "states, countries, and other geographical units" unless they are named parties; and any other words of eight or more letters "if substantial space is thereby saved and the result is unambiguous." Bluebook Rule 10.2.2. On the other hand, in citing cases in text, abbreviate only widely known acronyms and the following words: "&," "Ass'n," "Bros.," "Co.," "Corp.," "Inc.," "Ltd.," and "No." Bluebook Rule 10.2.1(c).

equity
   Ab.:   eq.

Equity Court or Division
   Ab.:   Eq.

Estate Planning, by A. James Casner & Jeffrey N. Pennell
   –Do not abbreviate the title.

   Ex.:   3 A. James Casner & Jeffrey N. Pennell, Estate Planning § 7.2.2.3 (6th ed. 1999). –Section Citation.

         3 A. James Casner & Jeffrey N. Pennell, Estate Planning § 7.2.2.3, at 7.2C4 (6th ed. 1999). –Page Citation.

         3 A. James Casner & Jeffrey N. Pennell, Estate Planning § 7.2.2.3, at 7.204 n.62 (6th ed. 1999). –Footnote Citation.

et al.
         –If a book, pamphlet or other nonperiodic material has more than two authors, use the first author's name followed by "et al." See Bluebook Rule 15.1.1.

         –Do not use "et al." to indicate multiple parties in cases, but use name of first party only. See Bluebook Rule 10.2.1(a).

et seq.
         –Should not be used when citing consecutive sections or subsections. Always use inclusive numbers. See Bluebook Rule 3.4(b).

European Community Cases (CCH) (Beginning 1989; Common Mkt. Rep. through 1988)
   Ab.:   CEC (CCH)

   Ex.:   Case 341/87, EMJ Electrola v. Patricia, 1990-1 CEC (CCH) 322, 333. –Page Citation.

European Consultative Assembly Debates
   Ab.:   Eur. Consult. Ass. Deb. See Bluebook Rule 21.8.3.

European Court of Human Rights
   Ab.:   Eur. Ct. H.R.

         –"Cite a case before the European Court to European Court of Human Rights, Reports of Judgments and Decisions (Eur. Ct. H.R.). For older decisions, the cases may also be cited to European Court of Human Rights, Series A or B (e.g., Eur. Ct. H.R. (ser. A)) or to Yearbook of the European Convention on Human Rights (Y.B. Eur. Conv. on H.R.)." - Bluebook Rule 21.5.3.

   Ex.:   Laino v. Italy, 1999-I Eur. Ct. H.R. 3611, 366.

         Fischer v. Austria, 312 Eur. Ct. H.R. (ser. A) at 23 (1995).

In law review footnotes, the titles of books and the names of cases, except for procedural phrases, are not underlined. See Bluebook Rule 2.1(a). Further, the following are in large and small capitals: codes, restatements, standards, constitutions, periodicals, authors of books, titles of books, the abbreviated names of codes, most legislative materials except for bills and resolutions, codified ordinances, model codes, court rules, and sentencing guidelines. Refer to The Bluebook.

European Human Rights Reports
Ab.:   Eur. H.R. Rep.
Ex.:   Cossey v. United Kingdom, App. No. 10843/84, 13 Eur. H.R. Rep. 662
          (1991). –Case Citation.
          –If case does not appear in Eur. Comm'n H.R. Dec. & Rep. or Y.B.
          Eur. Conv. on H.R., then it is permissible to use Eur. H.R. Rep. See
          Bluebook Rule 21.5.3.

European Law Review
Ab.:   Eur. L. Rev.
Ex.:   Scott Crosby, The Single Market and the Rule of Law, 16 Eur. L. Rev.
          451 (1991). –Article Citation.
          Scott Crosby, The Single Market and the Rule of Law, 16 Eur. L. Rev.
          451, 461-64 (1991). –Page Citation.

European Treaty Series (1948 - date)
Ab.:   Europ. T.S. No.
Ex.:   Convention on Insider Trading, May 1989, art. 7, Europ. T.S. No. 130.
See also Founding Treaties, Bluebook Rule 21.8.2.

European Yearbook
Ab.:   Eur. Y.B.
Ex.:   Daniel Tarschys, The Council of Europe Heading Towards the Year
          2000, 42 Eur. Y.B. 53 (1994). –Article Citation.

Executive Agreement Series (U.S. Dep't State) (1922-1945)
Ab.:   E.A.S. No.
Ex.:   Agreement Respecting a Committee of Inquiry into the Position of
          Jews in Europe and Palestine, Dec. 10, 1945, U.S.–U.K., 59 Stat. 1729.

Executive Document
Ab.:   Exec. Doc.

Executive Order
Ab.:   Exec. Order
Ex.:   Exec. Order No. 12, 893, 3 C.F.R. 867 (1995), reprinted as amended in
          31 U.S.C. § 501 (1996). –Page Citation.

Exempt Organizations Reports (Commerce Clearing House)
Ab.:   Exempt Org. Rep. (CCH)

Ex parte
          –Procedural phrases should always be italicized, regardless of whether
          the rest of the case name is italicized. See Bluebook Rule 10.2.1(b).

In citing cases in law review footnotes, abbreviate any word listed in Table T.6;
the names of "states, countries, and other geographical units" unless they are named parties;
and any other words of eight or more letters "if substantial space is thereby saved and the
result is unambiguous." Bluebook Rule 10.2.2. On the other hand, in citing cases in text,
abbreviate only widely known acronyms and the following words: "&," "Ass'n," "Bros.,"
"Co.," "Corp.," "Inc.," "Ltd.," and "No." Bluebook Rule 10.2.1(c).

ex rel.

–Expressions such as "on the relation of," "for the use of," and "on behalf of" should be abbreviated "<u>ex rel.</u>" <u>See</u> <u>Bluebook</u> Rule 10.2.1(b).

–Procedural phrases should always be italicized, or underlined, even if the rest of the case name may not be. <u>See</u> <u>Bluebook</u> Rule 10.2.1(b).

In law review footnotes, the titles of books and the names of cases, except for procedural phrases, are not underlined. <u>See</u> <u>Bluebook</u> Rule 2.1(a). Further, the following are in large and small capitals: codes, restatements, standards, constitutions, periodicals, authors of books, titles of books, the abbreviated names of codes, most legislative materials except for bills and resolutions, codified ordinances, model codes, court rules, and sentencing guidelines. Refer to <u>The Bluebook</u>.

F

Fair Employment Practice Cases (Bureau of National Affairs)
Ab.:   See Labor Relations Reporter

Family Court
Ab.:   Fam. Ct.

Family Division
Ab.:   Fam. Div.

Family Law Quarterly
Ab.:   Fam. L.Q.
Ex.:   Andrew Schepard, <u>Divorce, Interspousal Torts, and Res Judicata,</u> 24 Fam. L.Q. 127 (1990). –Article Citation.

Andrew Schepard, <u>Divorce, Interspousal Torts, and Res Judicata,</u> 24 Fam. L.Q. 127, 133-35 (1990). –Page Citation.

Family Law Reporter (Bureau of National Affairs)
Ab.:   Fam. L. Rep. (BNA)
Ex.:   <u>DuJack v. DuJack,</u> [Current Developments] Fam. L. Rep. (BNA) (22 Fam. L. Rep.) 1024 (N.Y. App. Div. Nov. 2, 1995). –Citation to looseleaf material.

<u>Speer v. Dealy,</u> 19 Fam. L. Rep. (BNA) 1222 (Neb. Feb. 26, 1993). –Citation to bound material.

–The above examples are proper if the case is not yet available in, or is not reported in, an official or West reporter, a public domain citation, or in a widely used computer database.

Angela Arkin Byne, <u>Using DNA Evidence to Prove Paternity: What the Attorney Needs to Know,</u> 19 Fam. L. Rep. (BNA) 3001 (Dec. 15, 1992). –Citation to bound article or monograph.

Family Law Tax Guide (Commerce Clearing House)
Ab.:   Fam. L. Tax Guide (CCH)

Federal Audit Guide (Commerce Clearing House)
Ab.:   Fed. Audit Guide (CCH)

In law review footnotes, the titles of books and the names of cases, except for procedural phrases, are not underlined. <u>See</u> Bluebook Rule 2.1(a). Further, the following are in large and small capitals: codes, restatements, standards, constitutions, periodicals, authors of books, titles of books, the abbreviated names of codes, most legislative materials except for bills and resolutions, codified ordinances, model codes, court rules, and sentencing guidelines. Refer to <u>The Bluebook</u>.

Federal Banking Law Reporter (Commerce Clearing House)

Ab.:   Fed. Banking L. Rep. (CCH)

Ex.:   Rivera v. Fair Chevrolet Geo Partnership, [Current] Fed. Banking L. Rep. (CCH) ¶ 100,101 (D.C. Conn. Mar. 25, 1996). –Citation to looseleaf material.

RTC v. City Fed., [1995-1996 Transfer Binder] Fed. Banking L. Rep. (CCH) ¶ 100,026 (3rd Cir. 1995). –Citation to transfer binder material.

–The above examples are proper if the case is not yet available in, or is not reported in, an official or West reporter, a public domain citation, or in a widely used computer database.

Federal Bar News & Journal

Ab.:   Fed. B. News & J.

Ex.:   A. Darby Dickerson, Contractual Jury Waiver Provisions, 39 Fed. B. News & J. 206 (1992). –Article Citation.

A. Darby Dickerson, Contractual Jury Waiver Provisions, 39 Fed. B. News & J. 206, 209-10 (1992). –Page Citation.

Federal Carriers Reports (Commerce Clearing House)

Ab.:   Fed. Carr. Rep. (CCH)

Fed. Carr. Cas. (CCH (bound))

Federal Cases

Ab.:   F. Cas.

See Bluebook Table T.1, p.184.

Ex.:   Corfield v. Coryell, 6 F. Cas. 546 (C.C.E.D Pa. 1825) (No. 3230). –Case Citation.

DeLovio v. Boit, 7 F. Cas. 418 (C.C.D. Mass. 1815) (No. 3776). –Case Citation.

Federal Claims Reporter

Ab.:   Fed. Cl.

Ex.:   Davis v. United States, 35 Fed. Cl. 392 (1996).

Federal Communications Commission Record

Ab.:   F.C.C.R.

Ex.:   In the Matter of KIDS-TV 6, 14 F.C.C.R. 13351 (1999).

Federal Communications Commission Reports (1934-1986)

Ab.:   F.C.C., F.C.C. 2d

Ex.:   Deregulation of Radio, 73 F.C.C.2d 457 (1979).

A.T. & T. Co., 88 F.C.C.2d 1656 (1982).

Federal Communications Law Journal

Ab.:   Fed. Comm. L.J.

In citing cases in law review footnotes, abbreviate any word listed in Table T.6; the names of "states, countries, and other geographical units" unless they are named parties; and any other words of eight or more letters "if substantial space is thereby saved and the result is unambiguous." Bluebook Rule 10.2.2. On the other hand, in citing cases in text, abbreviate only widely known acronyms and the following words: "&," "Ass'n," "Bros.," "Co.," "Corp.," "Inc.," "Ltd.," and "No." Bluebook Rule 10.2.1(c).

Ex.:   David R. Poe, <u>As the World Turns: Cable Television and the Cycle of Regulation</u>, 43 Fed. Comm. L.J. 141 (1991). –Article Citation.

David R. Poe, <u>As the World Turns: Cable Television and the Cycle of Regulation</u>, 43 Fed. Comm. L.J. 141, 153-55 (1991). –Page Citation.

Federal Contracts Report (Bureau of National Affairs)
Ab.:   Fed. Cont. Rep. (BNA)

Federal Court Reports (Canada) (1971-date)
–Cite to Federal Court Reports (F.C.) or Exchequer Court Reports (Ex. C.R.) if therein; otherwise, cite to Dominion Law Reports (D.L.R.). <u>See</u> <u>Bluebook</u> Table T.2., p. 254.
Ab.:   F.C.
Ex.:   <u>Mileva v. Canada</u>, [1991] 3 F.C. 398, 401 (Can.). –Page Citation.

Federal Election Campaign Financing Guide (Commerce Clearing House)
Ab.:   Fed. Election Camp. Fin. Guide (CCH)

Federal Energy Regulatory Commission Reports (Commerce Clearing House)
Ab.:   Fed. Energy Reg. Comm'n Rep. (CCH)

Federal Estate and Gift Tax Reporter (Commerce Clearing House)
Ab.:   Fed. Est. & Gift Tax Rep. (CCH)
          –Bound as U.S. Tax Cas. (CCH)
Ex.:   <u>Hall v. United States</u>, 3 Fed. Est. & Gift Tax Rep. (CCH) (92-1 U.S. Tax Cas.) ¶ 60,096 (M.D. Tenn. Nov. 22, 1991). –Citation to looseleaf material.

<u>Estate of Moran v. United States</u>, 96-1 U.S. Tax Cas. (CCH) ¶ 50,141 (9th Cir. 1996). –Citation to bound material.

–The above examples are proper if the case is not yet available in, or is not reported in, an official or West reporter, a public domain citation, or in a widely used computer database.

Priv. Ltr. Rul. 91-35-044, <u>reprinted in</u> 3 Fed. Est. & Gift Tax Rep. (CCH) ¶ 12,312 (June 3, 1991). –Proper citation to an IRS private letter ruling found in this service.

Federal Excise Tax Reports (Commerce Clearing House)
Ab.:   Fed. Ex. Tax Rep. (CCH)
          –Bound as U.S. Tax Cas. (CCH)
Ex.:   <u>Amax Coal Co. v. United States</u>, Fed. Ex. Tax Rep. (CCH) (96-1 U.S. Tax Cas.) ¶ 70,053 (S.D. Ind. Feb. 2, 1996). –Citation to looseleaf material.

<u>United States v. Miller</u>, 79-2 U.S. Tax Cas. (CCH) ¶ 16,318 (N.D. Tex. 1979). –Citation to bound material.

In law review footnotes, the titles of books and the names of cases, except for procedural phrases, are not underlined. <u>See</u> <u>Bluebook</u> Rule 2.1(a). Further, the following are in large and small capitals: codes, restatements, standards, constitutions, periodicals, authors of books, titles of books, the abbreviated names of codes, most legislative materials except for bills and resolutions, codified ordinances, model codes, court rules, and sentencing guidelines. Refer to <u>The Bluebook</u>.

–The above examples are proper if the case is not yet available in, or is not reported in, an official or West reporter, a public domain citation, or in a widely used computer database.

Federal Income Gift and Estate Taxation (Matthew Bender)
Ab.:   Fed. Inc. Gift & Est. Tax'n (MB)

Federal Income Taxation, by Michael D. Rose and John C. Chommie
–Do not abbreviate the title.

Ex.:   Michael D. Rose & John C. Chommie, Federal Income Taxation § 3.33 (3d ed. 1988). –Section Citation.

Michael D. Rose & John C. Chommie, Federal Income Taxation § 3.33, at 183 (3d ed. 1988). –Page Citation.

Michael D. Rose & John C. Chommie, Federal Income Taxation § 3.33, at 183 n.19 (3d ed. 1988). –Footnote Citation.

Federal Income Taxation of Corporations and Shareholders, by Boris I. Bittker and James S. Eustice
–Do not abbreviate the title.

Ex.:   Boris I. Bittker and James S. Eustice, Federal Income Taxation of Corporations and Shareholders § 357 (7th ed. 2000). –Section Citation.

Boris I. Bittker and James S. Eustice, Federal Income Taxation of Corporations and Shareholders § 357, at 12-202 (7th ed. 2000). –Page Citation.

Federal Income Taxation of Individuals, by Borris I. Bittker and Martin J. McMahan, Jr.
–Do not abbreviate the title.

Ex.:   Boris I. Bittker & Martin J. McMahan, Jr., Federal Income Taxation of Individuals § 29.12 (2d ed. 1995 & Supp. 1997). –Section Citation.

Boris I. Bittker & Martin J. McMahan, Jr., Federal Income Taxation of Individuals § 29.12, at 29-34 (2d ed. 1995 & Supp. 1997). –Page Citation.

Federal Law Reports (Austl.)
Ab.:   F.L.R.
Ex.:   Mougios v. Floros, (1989) 99 F.L.R. 121 (S.C. N.S.W.) (Austl.).

Federal Law Review
Ab.:   Fed. L. Rev.
Ex.:   Lee Aitken, Jurisdiction, Liability and "Double Function" Legislation, 19 Fed. L. Rev. 31 (1990). –Article Citation.

Lee Aitken, Jurisdiction, Liability and "Double Function" Legislation, 19 Fed. L. Rev. 31, 37-39 (1990). –Page Citation.

In citing cases in law review footnotes, abbreviate any word listed in Table T.6; the names of "states, countries, and other geographical units" unless they are named parties; and any other words of eight or more letters "if substantial space is thereby saved and the result is unambiguous." Bluebook Rule 10.2.2. On the other hand, in citing cases in text, abbreviate only widely known acronyms and the following words: "&," "Ass'n," "Bros.," "Co.," "Corp.," "Inc.," "Ltd.," and "No." Bluebook Rule 10.2.1(c).

Federal Maritime Commission Reports (U.S.) (1947-date)

Ab.: F.M.C.

Ex.: Universal Nolin UMC Industries, 19 F.M.C. 780 (1977).

Federal Mine Safety and Health Review Commission Decisions

Ab.: F.M.S.H.R.C.

Ex.: Local 2274, United Mine Workers, 8 F.M.S.H.R.C. 1310 (1986). —Case Citation.

Local 2274, United Mine Workers, 8 F.M.S.H.R.C. 1310, 1313 (1986). —Page Citation.

Federal Power Commission Reports (U.S.) (1931-1977)

Ab.: F.P.C.

Ex.: Northern Natural Gas Co., 58 F.P.C. 1744 (1977). —Case Citation.

Federal Practice and Procedure, by Charles Alan Wright, Arthur R. Miller, and others

—Do not abbreviate the title.

Ex.: 7A Charles A. Wright et al., Federal Practice and Procedure § 1753 (2d ed. 1986). —Section Citation.

7A Charles A. Wright et al., Federal Practice and Procedure § 1753, at 45 (2d ed. 1986). —Page Citation.

7A Charles A. Wright et al., Federal Practice and Procedure § 1753, at 3 (2d ed. Supp. 1999). —Supplement Citation.

Federal Probation

Ab.: Fed. Probation

Ex.: Thomas W. White, Corrections: Out of Balance, Fed. Probation, Dec. 1989, at 31. —Article Citation.

Thomas W. White, Corrections: Out of Balance, Fed. Probation, Dec. 1989, at 31, 34. —Page Citation.

Federal Register

Ab.: Fed. Reg.

Ex.: 61 Fed. Reg. 56,640 (Oct. 27, 1996).

61 Fed. Reg. 56,746 (Nov. 13, 1996) (to be codified at 29 C.F.R. pt.1910). —Where Fed. Reg. so indicates.

Comment Request, 61 Fed. Reg. 56,659 (Nov. 5, 1996). —When material is not of a permanent nature.

61 Fed. Reg. 56,656 (proposed Nov. 4, 1996) (to be codified at 49 C.F.R. pt. 1310). —Proposed rule.

Federal Reporter

—With volume 831 (1988), Federal Reporter, Second Series, became West's Federal Reporter, Second Series. Citation form is not affected by this title change.

In law review footnotes, the titles of books and the names of cases, except for procedural phrases, are not underlined. See Bluebook Rule 2.1(a). Further, the following are in large and small capitals: codes, restatements, standards, constitutions, periodicals, authors of books, titles of books, the abbreviated names of codes, most legislative materials except for bills and resolutions, codified ordinances, model codes, court rules, and sentencing guidelines. Refer to The Bluebook.

Ab.:   F., F.2d, F.3d

Ex.:   Pan-Am. Petroleum Transp. Co. v. Robins Dry Dock & Repair Co., 281 F. 97 (2d Cir. 1922). –Case Citation.

         Pan-Am. Petroleum Transp. Co. v. Robins Dry Dock & Repair Co., 281 F. 97, 98 (2d Cir. 1922). –Page Citation.

         Foy v. Donnelly, 959 F.2d. 1307 (7th Cir. 1990). –Case Citation.

         Foy v. Donnelly, 959 F.2d. 1307, 1309 (7th Cir. 1990). –Page Citation.

         Johnson v. Heffron, 88 F.3d 404 (6th Cir. 1996). –Case Citation.

         Johnson v. Heffron, 88 F.3d 404, 406 (6th Cir. 1996). –Page Citation.

Federal Reserve Bulletin (1915-date)

Ab.:   Fed. Res. Bull.

Ex.:   Alan Greenspan, Statement Before the Committee on Banking, Housing and Urban Affairs, U.S. Senate (Apr. 16, 1991), in 77 Fed. Res. Bull. 423 (1991). –Statement Citation.

Federal Rules Decisions

     –With volume 117 (1988), Federal Rules Decisions became West's Federal Rules Decisions. Citation form is not affected by this title change.

Ab.:   F.R.D.

Ex.:   Gonzales v. Wing, 167 F.R.D. 352 (N.D. N.Y. 1996).

Federal Rules of Appellate Procedure

Ab.:   Fed. R. App. P.

Ex.:   Fed. R. App. P. 34.

         See also Rules of Evidence and Procedure and Bluebook Rule 12.8.3.

Federal Rules of Civil Procedure

Ab.:   Fed. R. Civ. P.

Ex.:   Fed. R. Civ. P. 23.

         See also Rules of Evidence and Procedure and Bluebook Rule 12.8.3.

Federal Rules of Criminal Procedure

Ab.:   Fed. R. Crim. P.

Ex.:   Fed. R. Crim. P. 18.

         See also Rules of Evidence and Procedure and Bluebook Rule 12.8.3.

Federal Rules of Evidence

Ab.:   Fed. R. Evid.

Ex.:   Fed. R. Evid. 804(b)(4).

         See also Rules of Evidence and Procedure and Bluebook Rule 12.8.3.

In citing cases in law review footnotes, abbreviate any word listed in Table T.6; the names of "states, countries, and other geographical units" unless they are named parties; and any other words of eight or more letters "if substantial space is thereby saved and the result is unambiguous." Bluebook Rule 10.2.2. On the other hand, in citing cases in text, abbreviate only widely known acronyms and the following words: "&," "Ass'n," "Bros.," "Co.," "Corp.," "Inc.," "Ltd.," and "No." Bluebook Rule 10.2.1(c).

Federal Rules of Evidence Service
Ab.:   Fed. R. Evid. Serv. (West)

Federal Rules of Habeas Procedure
Ab.:   28 U.S.C. § 2254 R. ____ (person in state custody)
          28 U.S.C. § 2255 R. ____ (person in federal custody)
Ex.:   28 U.S.C. § 2254 R. 9(b).
          28 U.S.C. § 2255 R. 5.

Federal Rules Service, Third Series
Ab.:   Fed. R. Serv. 3d (West)
Ex.:   Gordon v. Gouline, 34 Fed. R. Serv. 3d 967 (West) (D.C. Cir. Apr. 19, 1996). –Citation to bound material.

          –The above example is proper if the case is not yet available in, or is not reported in, an official or West reporter, a public domain citation, or in a widely used computer database.

Federal Securities Code (ALI)
          See American Law Institute Federal Securities Code

Federal Securities Law Reports (Commerce Clearing House)
Ab.:   Fed. Sec. L. Rep. (CCH)
Ex.:   Energy Factors, Inc. v. Nueva Energy Co., [Current] Fed. Sec. L. Rep. (CCH) ¶ 96,446 (S.D.N.Y. Nov. 22, 1991). –Citation to looseleaf material.

          SEC v. Weil, [1980 Transfer Binder] Fed. Sec. L. Rep. (CCH) ¶ 97,541 (M.D. Fla. 1980). –Citation to transfer binder material.

          –The above examples are proper if the case is not yet available in, or is not reported in, an official or West reporter, a public domain citation, or in a widely used computer database.

          Funding Capital Corp., Exchange Act Release No. 29,425, [1991 Transfer Binder] Fed. Sec. L. Rep. (CCH) ¶ 84,836 (SEC July 10, 1991). –Citation to transfer binder administrative material.

Federal Supplement
          –With volume 671 (1988), Federal Supplement became West's Federal Supplement. Citation form is not affected by this title change.
Ab.:   F. Supp.
Ex.:   Marchwinski v. Oliver Tyrone Corp., 461 F. Supp. 160 (W.D. Pa. 1978). –Case Citation.
          Marchwinski v. Oliver Tyrone Corp., 461 F. Supp. 160, 162 (W.D. Pa. 1978). –Page Citation.

Federal Tax Coordinator Second (Research Institute of America)
Ab.:   Fed. Tax Coordinator 2d (R.I.A.)

In law review footnotes, the titles of books and the names of cases, except for procedural phrases, are not underlined. See Bluebook Rule 2.1(a). Further, the following are in large and small capitals: codes, restatements, standards, constitutions, periodicals, authors of books, titles of books, the abbreviated names of codes, most legislative materials except for bills and resolutions, codified ordinances, model codes, court rules, and sentencing guidelines. Refer to The Bluebook.

Ex.:   How the Estate Tax Works, 22A. Fed. Tax Coordinator 2d (R.I.A.)
        ¶ R-100M0, at 46,051 (Apr. 18, 1996). –Citation to section of
        publication.

Federal Taxation of Income, Estates and Gifts, by Boris I. Bittker and Lawrence Lokken
        –Do not abbreviate the title.
Ex.:   3 Boris I. Bittker & Lawrence Lokken, Federal Taxation of Income,
        Estates and Gifts § 75.2.6, at 75-29 (2d ed. 1991). –Page Citation.

        1 Boris I. Bittker & Lawrence Lokken, Federal Taxation of Income,
        Estates, and Gifts ¶ 22.2.2 (3d ed. 1999). –Section Citation.

Federal Trade Commission Decisions (U.S.) (1915-date)
Ab.:   F.T.C.
Ex.:   Mannesmann, A.G., 115 F.T.C. 412 (1980). –Case Citation.

Federalist, The
Ab.:   The Federalist No. (author)
Ex.:   The Federalist No. 15 (A. Hamilton).
        The Federalist No. 41, at 248 (J. Madison) (H. Lodge ed. 1888).

Films
Ex.:   To Catch a Thief (Paramount 1955).

Fire & Casualty Cases
        See Insurance Law Reports

Fleming and Hazard on Civil Procedure
        See Civil Procedure, by James Fleming, Jr. & Geoffrey C. Hazard, Jr.

Fletcher Forum of World Affairs, The
Ab.:   Fletcher F. World Aff.
Ex.:   Kent Jones, Selectivity and the Changing Structure of Trade Policy,
        16 Fletcher F. World Aff. 15 (1992). –Article Citation.

        Kent Jones, Selectivity and the Changing Structure of Trade Policy,
        16 Fletcher F. World Aff. 15, 16-20 (1992). –Page Citation.

Fletcher Cyclopedia of the Law of Private Corporations, by William Meade Fletcher
        –Do not abbreviate the title.
Ex.:   1 William Meade Fletcher et. al., Fletcher Cyclopedia of the Law of
        Private Corporations § 41.10 (perm ed., rev. vol. 1999 and Cum. Supp.
        2000). –Section Citation.

        3A James Solheim & Kenneth Elkins, Fletcher Cyclopedia of the Law
        of Private Corporations § 1117 (perm. ed., rev. vol. 1994 and Supp.
        2000). –Section Citation.

In citing cases in law review footnotes, abbreviate any word listed in Table T.6; the names of "states, countries, and other geographical units" unless they are named parties; and any other words of eight or more letters "if substantial space is thereby saved and the result is unambiguous." Bluebook Rule 10.2.2. On the other hand, in citing cases in text, abbreviate only widely known acronyms and the following words: "&," "Ass'n," "Bros.," "Co.," "Corp.," "Inc.," "Ltd.," and "No." Bluebook Rule 10.2.1(c).

3A James Solheim & Kenneth Elkins, <u>Fletcher Cyclopedia of the Law of Private Corporation</u> § 1117, at 218 (perm. ed., rev. vol. 1994 and Supp. 2000). –Page Citation.

Florida Administrative Code Annotated
Ab.:   Fla. Admin. Code Ann. r. (year)
Ex.:   Fla. Admin. Code Ann. r. 2-2.001 (1997)

Florida Administrative Weekly
Ab.:   Fla. Admin. Weekly

Florida, Annual Report of the Attorney General
See Annual Report of the Attorney General, State of Florida

Florida Bar Journal
Ab.:   Fla. B.J.
Ex.:   Nicholas J. Watkins & Joel Stewart, <u>Employer Sanctions and the Employer's Response</u>, Fla. B.J., May 1992, at 60. –Article Citation.
        Nicholas J. Watkins & Joel Stewart, <u>Employer Sanctions and the Employer's Response</u>, Fla. B.J., May 1992, at 60, 62-3. –Page Citation.

Florida Constitution
Ab.:   Fla. Const. art. , §   .
Ex.:   Fla. Const. art. III, § 5. –"Cite constitutional provisions currently in force without date." <u>Bluebook</u> Rule 11.
        Fla. Const. art. V (repealed 1973) . –"If the cited provision has been repealed, either indicate parenthetically the fact and date of repeal or cite the repealing provision in full." <u>Bluebook</u> Rule 11.
        Fla. Const. art. III , § 7 (amended 1980). –"When citing a provision that has been subsequently amended, either indicate parenthetically the fact and date of amendment or cite the amending provision in full." <u>Bluebook</u> Rule 11.
        Fla. Const. of 1868, art. XII , §§ 7, 8 (1968). –"Cite constitutions that have been totally superseded by year of adoption; if the specific provision cited was adopted in a different year, give that year parenthetically." <u>Bluebook</u> Rule 11.

Florida District Court of Appeals
Ab.:   Fla. Dist. Ct. App.
        –Cite to So. 2d. if therein; otherwise to Fla. L. Weekly.
        In documents submitted to Florida state courts, cite as follows:
        <u>Oakley v. State</u>, 677 So. 2d 879 (Fla. 2d DCA 1996). –Case Citation.
        <u>Oakley v. State</u>, 677 So. 2d 879, 880 (Fla. 2d DCA 1996). –Page Citation.
        In all other documents, cite as follows:

In law review footnotes, the titles of books and the names of cases, except for procedural phrases, are not underlined. See <u>Bluebook</u> Rule 2.1(a). Further, the following are in large and small capitals: codes, restatements, standards, constitutions, periodicals, authors of books, titles of books, the abbreviated names of codes, most legislative materials except for bills and resolutions, codified ordinances, model codes, court rules, and sentencing guidelines. Refer to <u>The Bluebook</u>.

Oakley v. State, 677 So. 2d 879 (Fla. Dist. Ct. App. 1996). –Case
Citation.

Oakley v. State, 677 So. 2d 879, 880 (Fla. Dist. Ct. App. 1996).
–Page Citation.

–See Bluebook Table T.1, p.198; see also Fla. R. App. P. 9.800.

Florida Journal of International Law
Ab.:   Fla. J. Int'l L.

Ex.:   Karen Y. Crabbs, The German Abortion Debate: Stumbling Block to
         Unity, 6 Fla. J. Int'l L. 213 (1991). –Article Citation.

         Karen Y. Crabbs, The German Abortion Debate: Stumbling Block to
         Unity, 6 Fla. J. Int'l L. 213, 217-19 (1991). –Page Citation.

Florida Law Review
Ab.:   Fla. L. Rev.

Ex.:   Michael L. Radelet & Glenn L. Pierce, Choosing Those Who Will Die:
         Race and the Death Penalty in Florida, 43 Fla. L. Rev. 1 (1991).
         –Article Citation.

         Michael L. Radelet & Glenn L. Pierce, Choosing Those Who Will Die:
         Race and the Death Penalty in Florida, 43 Fla. L. Rev. 1, 7 (1991).
         –Page Citation.

Florida Reports
Ab.:   Fla.

         –Discontinued after 160 Fla. 974 (1948).

         –Cite to So. or So. 2d if therein; otherwise, cite to Fla.

         –Give parallel citations only in documents submitted to Florida state
         courts. See Bluebook Rule 10.3.1 and Practitioners' Note P.3; see
         also Fla. R. App. P. 9.800, which requires a parallel citation.

         –Through 160 Fla. 974 (1948), cite as follows:

         In documents submitted to Florida state courts:

         Winfield v. Truitt, 71 Fla. 38, 70 So. 775 (1916). –Case Citation.

         Winfield v. Truitt, 71 Fla. 38, 48, 70 So. 775, 778-79 (1916).
         –Page Citation.

         In all other documents:

         Winfield v. Truitt, 70 So. 775 (Fla. 1916). –Case Citation.

         Winfield v. Truitt, 70 So. 775, 778-79 (Fla. 1916). –Page Citation.

         –After 160 Fla. 974 (1948), cite as follows:

         In all documents:

         Florida Bar v. McAtee, 674 So. 2d 734 (Fla. 1996). –Case Citation.

         Florida Bar v. McAtee, 674 So. 2d 734, 736 (Fla. 1996). –Page
         Citation.

In citing cases in law review footnotes, abbreviate any word listed in Table T.6;
the names of "states, countries, and other geographical units" unless they are named parties;
and any other words of eight or more letters "if substantial space is thereby saved and the
result is unambiguous." Bluebook Rule 10.2.2. On the other hand, in citing cases in text,
abbreviate only widely known acronyms and the following words: "&," "Ass'n," "Bros.,"
"Co.," "Corp.," "Inc.," "Ltd.," and "No." Bluebook Rule 10.2.1(c).

Florida Session Laws
See Florida Session Law Service and Laws of Florida

Florida Session Law Service (West)
Ab.:   year Fla. Sess. Law Serv.   (West)
Ex.:   Act of July 1, 1996, ch. 96-414, 1996 Fla. Sess. Law Serv. 2248 (West) (relating to driver's licenses). –Citation to an entire session law.

Act of July 1, 1996, ch. 96-414, sec. 4, § 322.16, 1996 Fla. Sess. Law Serv. 2248, 2250-51 (West) (relating to driver's license restrictions). –Citation to a session law amending a prior act.

"–Cite to Fla. Laws if therein ." Bluebook Table T.1, p. 198.

Florida State University Law Review
Ab.:   Fla. St. U. L. Rev.
Ex.:   Daniel E. Georges-Abeyie, Law Enforcement and Racial and Ethnic Bias, 19 Fla. St. U. L. Rev. 717 (1992). –Article Citation.

Daniel E. Georges-Abeyie, Law Enforcement and Racial and Ethnic Bias, 19 Fla. St. U. L. Rev. 717, 723-26 (1992). –Page Citation.

Florida Statutes
Ab.:   Fla. Stat.   (year)
Ex.:   Fla. Stat. ch. 236.012(1) (1977).

Florida Statutes Annotated (Harrison)
Ab.:   Fla. Stat. Ann. ch. (Harrison year)
Ex.:   Fla. Stat. Ann. ch. 921.07 (Harrison 1967).
         –"Cite to Florida Statutes if therein." Bluebook Table T.1, p. 198.

Florida Statutes Annotated (West)
Ab.:   Fla. Stat. Ann. § (West year)
Ex.:   Fla. Stat. Ann. § 794.011 (West 2000).

Fla. Stat. Ann. § 985.215 (West Supp. 2000).
–"Cite to Florida Statutes if therein." Bluebook Table T.1, p. 198.

Florida Supplement
Ab.:   Fla. Supp.

Fla. Supp. 2d

–Cite Florida Circuit Court (Fla. Cir. Ct.), County Court (e.g. Dade County Ct.), Public Service Commission (Fla. P.S.C.) and other lower courts of record to Fla. Supp. or Fla. Supp. 2d., if therein, otherwise to Fla. L. Weekly Supp. See Bluebook Table T.1, p. 198; see also Fla. R. App. P. 9.800.

In documents submitted to Florida state courts, cite as follows:

In law review footnotes, the titles of books and the names of cases, except for procedural phrases, are not underlined. See Bluebook Rule 2.1(a). Further, the following are in large and small capitals: codes, restatements, standards, constitutions, periodicals, authors of books, titles of books, the abbreviated names of codes, most legislative materials except for bills and resolutions, codified ordinances, model codes, court rules, and sentencing guidelines. Refer to The Bluebook.

Peavy v. Boyd, 48 Fla. Supp. 101 (Fla. 11ᵗʰ Cir. Ct. 1977). –Case Citation.

Garcia v. Ruiz, 50 Fla. Supp. 2d 176 (Fla. Dade County Ct. 1991). –Case Citation.

In all other documents, cite as follows:

Peavy v. Boyd, 48 Fla. Supp. 101 (Cir. Ct. 1977). –Case Citation.

Garcia v. Ruiz, 50 Fla. Supp. 2d 176 (County Ct. 1991). –Case Citation.

Food Drug Cosmetic Law Journal

Ab.:   Food Drug Cosm. L.J.

Ex.:   Hugh Latimer, Whither the FTC on Food Advertising?, 46 Food Drug Cosm. L.J. 503 (1991). –Article Citation.

Hugh Latimer, Whither the FTC on Food Advertising?, 46 Food Drug Cosm. L.J. 503, 511-12 (1991). –Page Citation.

Food Drug Cosmetic Law Reporter (Commerce Clearing House)

Ab.:   Food Drug Cosm. L. Rep. (CCH)

Ex.:   Moore v. Armour Pharm. Co., [New Matters] Food Drug Cosm. L. Rep. (CCH) ¶ 38,188 (M.D. Fla. Aug. 27, 1990). –Citation to looseleaf material.

DeVito v. HEM, Inc., [1988-1989 Developments Transfer Binder] Food Drug Cosm. L. Rep. (CCH) ¶ 38,108 (M.D. Pa. 1988). –Citation to transfer binder material.

–The above examples are proper if the case is not yet available in, or is not reported in, an official or West reporter, a public domain citation, or in a widely used computer database.

footnote(s)

Ab.:   note, notes

         n., nn.

Ex.:   supra note 211.

         J. William Futrell, The Hidden Crisis in Georgia Land Use, 10 Ga. L. Rev. 53, 88, n.124 (1975).

         J. William Futrell, The Hidden Crisis in Georgia Land Use, 10 Ga. L. Rev. 53, 89, nn.133-34 (1975).

         See Bluebook Rules 3.3(b), (c), and (d).

Fordham Environmental Law Journal

Ab.:   Fordham Envtl. L.J.

In citing cases in law review footnotes, abbreviate any word listed in Table T.6; the names of "states, countries, and other geographical units" unless they are named parties; and any other words of eight or more letters "if substantial space is thereby saved and the result is unambiguous." Bluebook Rule 10.2.2. On the other hand, in citing cases in text, abbreviate only widely known acronyms and the following words: "&," "Ass'n," "Bros.," "Co.," "Corp.," "Inc.," "Ltd.," and "No." Bluebook Rule 10.2.1(c).

Ex.:   Peter N. Ching & Brian M. Diglio, Note, <u>Staff Accounting Bulletin 92:</u>
<u>A Paradigmatic Shift in Disclosure Standards</u>, 7 Fordham Envtl. L.J. 75
(1995). –Article Citation.

Peter N. Ching & Brian M. Diglio, Note, <u>Staff Accounting Bulletin 92:</u>
<u>A Paradigmatic Shift in Disclosure Standards</u>, 7 Fordham Envtl. L.J. 75
(1995). –Page Citation.

Fordham International Law Journal
Ab.:   Fordham Int'l L.J.
Ex.:   Julian M. Joshua, <u>The Right to be Heard in EEC Competition</u>
<u>Procedures</u>, 15 Fordham Int'l L.J. 16 (1991-1992). –Article Citation.

Julian M. Joshua, <u>The Right to be Heard in EEC Competition</u>
<u>Procedures</u>, 15 Fordham Int'l L.J. 16, 29-35 (1991-1992). –Page
Citation.

Fordham Law Review
Ab.:   Fordham L. Rev.
Ex.:   William E. Kovacic, <u>Reagan's Judicial Appointees and Antitrust in the</u>
<u>1990's</u>, 60 Fordham L. Rev. 49 (1991). –Article Citation.

William E. Kovacic, <u>Reagan's Judicial Appointees and Antitrust in the</u>
<u>1990's</u>, 60 Fordham L. Rev. 49, 57-59 (1991). –Page Citation.

Fordham Urban Law Journal
Ab.:   Fordham Urb. L.J.
Ex.:   Cyrus Vance, <u>Foreword: Legal Ethics and Government Integrity</u>,
18 Fordham Urb. L.J. 153 (1990-1991). –Article Citation.

Cyrus Vance, <u>Foreword: Legal Ethics and Government Integrity</u>,
18 Fordham Urb. L.J. 153, 154-55 (1990-1991). –Page Citation.

Foreign Broadcast Information Service
Ab.:   F.B.I.S.

forewords, prefaces, and introductions
Ex.:   Norman Dorsen, Foreword to William L. Dwyer, <u>The Goldmark Case:</u>
<u>An American Libel Trial</u> at vii, xi (1984). –Citation for a preface,
foreword, introduction, or epilogue by someone other than the author.

Formal Advisory Opinions
<u>See</u> <u>Bluebook</u> Rule 14.4

Forthcoming Publications
<u>See</u> <u>Bluebook</u> Rule 17.2.

In law review footnotes, the titles of books and the names of cases, except for procedural
phrases, are not underlined. <u>See</u> <u>Bluebook</u> Rule 2.1(a). Further, the following are in large
and small capitals: codes, restatements, standards, constitutions, periodicals, authors of
books, titles of books, the abbreviated names of codes, most legislative materials except for
bills and resolutions, codified ordinances, model codes, court rules, and sentencing guidelines.
Refer to <u>The Bluebook</u>.

Ex.:   Brendan A. Thompson, Note, Final Exit: Should the Double Effect Rule Regarding the Legality of Euthenasia in the United Kingdom be Laid to Rest?, 33 Vand. J. Trans. L. (forthcoming Oct. 2000).

Mary Miles Prince, Prince's Bieber Dictionary of Legal Citations (6th ed. forthcoming 2001).

Franchise Law Journal

Ab.:   Franchise L.J.

Ex.:   Jay Conison, Restrictive Lease Covenants and the Law of Monopoly, Franchise L.J., Winter 1990, at 3. –Article Citation.

Jay Conison, Restrictive Lease Covenants and the Law of Monopoly, Franchise L.J., Winter 1990, at 3, 5. –Page Citation.

Fundamentals of Securities Regulation, by Louis Loss and Joel Seligman
–Do not abbreviate the title.

Ex.:   Louis Loss and Joel Seligman, Fundamentals of Securities Regulation 1121 (3d ed. 1995). –Page Citation.

Louis Loss and Joel Seligman, Fundamentals of Securities Regulation 1121 n.102 (3d ed. 1995). –Footnote Citation.

In citing cases in law review footnotes, abbreviate any word listed in Table T.6; the names of "states, countries, and other geographical units" unless they are named parties; and any other words of eight or more letters "if substantial space is thereby saved and the result is unambiguous." Bluebook Rule 10.2.2. On the other hand, in citing cases in text, abbreviate only widely known acronyms and the following words: "&," "Ass'n," "Bros.," "Co.," "Corp.," "Inc.," "Ltd.," and "No." Bluebook Rule 10.2.1(c).

G

GATT - Basic Instruments and Selected Documents
Ab.: B.I.S.D.
Ex.: Working Party on the Free Trade Agreement between EFTA and Turkey, Dec. 17, 1993, GATT B.I.S.D. (Supp. 40) at 48 (1995).

GATT - General Agreement on Tariffs and Trade Documents
Ab.: GATT Doc.
Ex.: Observers Status of Governments in the Council of Representatives, GATT Doc. L/7286 (July 21, 1993) (communication from the Committee on Trade and Development).

Gavel, The (Milwaukee Bar Association)
Ab.: Gavel
Ex.: Russell Eisenberg, Recent Developments in Sales and Secured Transactions Law, Gavel, Fall 1975, at 8. –Article Citation.
Russell Eisenberg, Recent Developments in Sales and Secured Transactions Law, Gavel, Fall 1975, at 8, 9. –Page Citation.

Gavel, The (State Bar Association of North Dakota)
Ab.: Gavel
Ex.: Beth Baumstark, U.C.C. Refiling Procedures, Gavel, Dec. 1991-1992, at 15. –Article Citation.
Beth Baumstark, U.C.C. Refiling Procedures, Gavel, Dec. 1991-1992, at 15, 16. –Page Citation.

General Acts of Arkansas
Ab.: year Ark. Acts
Ex.: Act of Aug. 26, 1994, No. 62, 1995-2 Ark. Acts 333. –Citation to an entire session law.
Act of Aug. 26, 1994, No. 62, Sec. 3, § 16-13-326, 1995-2 Ark. Acts 333, 340.
–Citation to a section of session law amending a prior act.
–Identifying information may be added parenthetically according to Bluebook Rule 12.4(a).

In law review footnotes, the titles of books and the names of cases, except for procedural phrases, are not underlined. See Bluebook Rule 2.1(a). Further, the following are in large and small capitals: codes, restatements, standards, constitutions, periodicals, authors of books, titles of books, the abbreviated names of codes, most legislative materials except for bills and resolutions, codified ordinances, model codes, court rules, and sentencing guidelines. Refer to The Bluebook.

General and Special Laws of the State of Texas
  A.:   year Tex. Gen. Laws
  Ex.:   Act of June 17, 1995, ch. 1013, 1995-5 Tex. Gen. Laws 5068 (relating
           to electric cooperative corporations). –Citation to an entire session
           law.
           Act of June 17, 1995, ch. 1013, sec. 1, § 2.2011, 1995-5 Tex. Gen.
           Laws 5068, 5068-71 (relating to electric cooperative corporations
           exemption from rate regulation). –Citation to a section of a session law
           amending a prior act.

General Laws of Mississippi
  Ab.:   year Miss. Laws
  Ex.:   Act of Apr. 7, 1995, ch. 570, 1995-2 Miss. Laws 874. –Citation to an
           entire session law.
           Act of Apr. 7, 1995, ch. 570, sec. 2, §37-13-107, 1995-2 Miss. Laws
           874, 881. –Citation to a section of a session law amending a prior act.
           –Identifying information may be added parenthetically according to
           Bluebook Rule 12.4(a).

General Laws of Rhode Island
  Ab.:   R.I. Gen. Laws. §   (year)
  Ex.:   R.I. Gen. Laws § 5-22-26 (1999).
           R.I. Gen. Laws § 4-12-8 (Supp. 1999).

General Laws of the Commonwealth of Massachusetts (Mass. Bar Assoc./West)
  Ab.:   Mass. Gen. Laws ch.   ,   §   (year)
  Ex.:   Mass. Gen. Laws ch. 6 § 6:12I (1994).

General Statutes of Connecticut
  Ab.:   Conn. Gen. Stat. §   (year)
  Ex.:   Conn. Gen. Stat. § 17a-112(b) (1995).

General Statutes of North Carolina
  Ab.:   N.C. Gen. Stat. §   (year)
  Ex.:   N.C. Gen. Stat. § 20-87.1 (1999).
           N.C. Gen. Stat. § 96-13 (Supp. 2000).

Generally Accepted Accounting Principles
  See Accounting Standards, Generally Accepted.

George Mason Law Review
  Ab.:   Geo. Mason L. Rev.

In citing cases in law review footnotes, abbreviate any word listed in Table T.6;
the names of "states, countries, and other geographical units" unless they are named parties;
and any other words of eight or more letters "if substantial space is thereby saved and the
result is unambiguous." Bluebook Rule 10.2.2. On the other hand, in citing cases in text,
abbreviate only widely known acronyms and the following words: "&," "Ass'n," "Bros.,"
"Co.," "Corp.," "Inc.," "Ltd.," and "No." Bluebook Rule 10.2.1(c).

Ex.: Michael J. Phillips, <u>Entry Restrictions in the Lochner Court</u>, 4 Geo. Mason L. Rev. 405 (1996). −Article Citation.

Michael J. Phillips, <u>Entry Restrictions in the Lochner Court</u>, 4 Geo. Mason L. Rev. 405, 410 (1996). −Page Citation.

George Mason University Civil Rights Law Journal
Ab.: Geo. Mason U. Civ. Rts. L.J.

Ex.: Peter E. Millspaugh, <u>When Self-Organization Includes Racial Harassment: Must the NLRA Yield to Title VII?</u>, 2 Geo. Mason U. Civ. Rts. L.J. 1 (1991). −Article Citation.

Peter E. Millspaugh, <u>When Self-Organization Includes Racial Harassment: Must the NLRA Yield to Title VII?</u>, 2 Geo. Mason U. Civ. Rts. L.J. 1, 1-2 (1991). −Page Citation.

George Mason University Law Review
Ab.: Geo. Mason U. L. Rev.

Ex.: Konrad Bonsack, <u>Damages Assessment, Janis Joplin's Yearbook, and the Pie-Powder Court</u>, 13 Geo. Mason U. L. Rev. 1 (1990). −Article Citation.

Konrad Bonsack, <u>Damages Assessment, Janis Joplin's Yearbook, and the Pie-Powder Court</u>, 13 Geo. Mason U. L. Rev. 1, 11-15 (1990). −Page Citation.

George Washington Journal of International Law and Economics, The
Ab.: Geo. Wash. J. Int'l L. & Econ.

Ex.: Charles Lister, <u>Two Cheers for Competition: Spain's New Antitrust and Unfair Competition Acts</u>, 24 Geo. Wash. J. Int'l L. & Econ. 587 (1991). −Article Citation.

Charles Lister, <u>Two Cheers for Competition: Spain's New Antitrust and Unfair Competition Acts</u>, 24 Geo. Wash. J. Int'l L. & Econ. 587, 587-88 (1991). −Page Citation.

George Washington Law Review, The
Ab.: Geo. Wash. L. Rev.

Ex.: Herbert Hovenkamp, <u>Rationality in Law & Economics</u>, 60 Geo. Wash. L. Rev. 293 (1992). −Article Citation.

Herbert Hovenkamp, <u>Rationality in Law & Economics</u>, 60 Geo. Wash. L. Rev. 293, 294-97 (1992). −Page Citation.

Georgetown Immigration Law Journal
Ab.: Geo. Immigr. L.J.

In law review footnotes, the titles of books and the names of cases, except for procedural phrases, are not underlined. <u>See</u> <u>Bluebook</u> Rule 2.1(a). Further, the following are in large and small capitals: codes, restatements, standards, constitutions, periodicals, authors of books, titles of books, the abbreviated names of codes, most legislative materials except for bills and resolutions, codified ordinances, model codes, court rules, and sentencing guidelines. Refer to <u>The Bluebook</u>.

Ex.:   Bruce A. Hake, <u>Dual Representation in Immigration Practice: The
         Simple Solution is the Wrong Solution</u>, 5 Geo. Immigr. L.J. 581
         (1991). –Article Citation.

         Bruce A. Hake, <u>Dual Representation in Immigration Practice: The
         Simple Solution is the Wrong Solution</u>, 5 Geo. Immigr. L.J. 581, 591-
         93 (1991). –Page Citation.

Georgetown International Environmental Law Review
Ab.:   Geo. Int'l Envtl. L. Rev.
Ex.:   William T. Burke, <u>Regulation of Driftnet Fishing on the High Seas and
         the New International Law of the Sea</u>, 3 Geo. Int'l Envtl. L. Rev. 265
         (1990). –Article Citation.

         William T. Burke, <u>Regulation of Driftnet Fishing on the High Seas and
         the New International Law of the Sea</u>, 3 Geo. Int'l Envtl. L. Rev. 265,
         281-82 (1990). –Page Citation.

Georgetown Journal of Legal Ethics, The
Ab.:   Geo. J. Legal Ethics
Ex.:   Roger C. Crampton, <u>The Lawyer as Whistleblower: Confidentiality and
         the Government Lawyer</u>, 5 Geo. J. Legal Ethics 291 (1991). –Article
         Citation.

         Roger C. Crampton, <u>The Lawyer as Whistleblower: Confidentiality and
         the Government Lawyer</u>, 5 Geo. J. Legal Ethics 291, 299-300 (1991).
         –Page Citation.

Georgetown Law Journal, The
Ab.:   Geo. L.J.
Ex.:   Edward L. Rubin, <u>Legislative Methodology: Some Lessons from the
         Truth-in-Lending Act</u>, 80 Geo. L.J. 233 (1991). –Article Citation.

         Edward L. Rubin, <u>Legislative Methodology: Some Lessons from the
         Truth-in-Lending Act</u>, 80 Geo. L.J. 233, 242-45 (1991). –Page
         Citation.

Georgia Appeals Reports
Ab.:   Ga. App.
         –Cite to S.E. or S.E.2d if therein; otherwise, cite to Ga. App.
         –Give parallel citations, if at all, only in documents submitted to
         Georgia state courts. <u>See</u> Bluebook Rule 10.3.1 and Practitioners'
         Note P.3; <u>see</u> <u>also</u> Ga. Sup. Ct. R. 22 and Ga. Ct. App. R. 23(c),
         which require only a citation to the official reporter.
         In documents submitted to Georgia state courts, cite as follows:
             <u>Harris v. State</u>, 222 Ga. App. 56, 473 S.E.2d 229 (1996). –Case
             Citation.
             <u>Harris v. State</u>, 222 Ga. App. 56, 59, 473 S.E.2d 229, 230 (1996).
             –Page Citation.

In citing cases in law review footnotes, abbreviate any word listed in Table T.6;
the names of "states, countries, and other geographical units" unless they are named parties;
and any other words of eight or more letters "if <u>substantial</u> space is thereby saved and the
result is unambiguous." Bluebook Rule 10.2.2. On the other hand, in citing cases in text,
abbreviate only widely known acronyms and the following words: "&," "Ass'n," "Bros.,"
"Co.," "Corp.," "Inc.," "Ltd.," and "No." Bluebook Rule 10.2.1(c).

In all other documents, cite as follows:

Harris v. State, 222 S.E.2d 56 (Ga. Ct. App. 1996). –Case Citation.

Harris v. State, 222 S.E.2d 56, 59 (Ga. Ct. App. 1996). –Page Citation.

Georgia Appellate Practice, by Christopher J. McFadden, Edward C. Brewer, III, and Charles R. Sheppard
–Do not abbreviate the title.

Ex.:   Christopher J. McFadden et al., Georgia Appellate Practice § 2-101 (1996). –Section Citation.

Christopher J. McFadden et al., Georgia Appellate Practice § 2-101, at 124 (1996). –Page Citation.

Christopher J. McFadden et al., Georgia Appellate Practice § 2-101, at 125 & n.16 (1996). –Footnote Citation.

Georgia Code
See Official Code of Georgia Annotated (Michie).

Georgia Code Annotated
See Code of Georgia Annotated (Harrison)

Georgia Constitution
Ab.:   Ga. Const. art.   , §   , ¶   .

Ex.:   Ga. Const. art. I, § I, ¶ XIII. –"Cite constitutional provisions currently in force without date." Bluebook Rule 11.

Ga. Const. art. III, § VIII, ¶ XII (1976, amended 1979). –"Cite provisions which have been repealed or amended by giving the date of the adoption of the particular provision and the date of repeal or amendment." Bluebook Rule 11.

Ga. Const. art. VIII , § 1 , ¶ I (amended 1990). –"When citing a provision that has been subsequently amended, either indicate parenthetically the fact and date of amendment or cite the amending provision in full." Bluebook Rule 11.

Ga. Const. art. I , § , ¶ 12 (1983). –"Cite constitutions that have been totally superseded by year of adoption; if the specific provision cited was adopted in a different year, give that year parenthetically." Bluebook Rule 11.

Georgia Journal of International and Comparative Law
Ab.:   Ga. J. Int'l & Comp. L.

In law review footnotes, the titles of books and the names of cases, except for procedural phrases, are not underlined. See Bluebook Rule 2.1(a). Further, the following are in large and small capitals: codes, restatements, standards, constitutions, periodicals, authors of books, titles of books, the abbreviated names of codes, most legislative materials except for bills and resolutions, codified ordinances, model codes, court rules, and sentencing guidelines. Refer to The Bluebook.

Ex.:   Charles Mwalimu, <u>Police, State Security Forces and Constitutionalism of Human Rights in Zambia</u>, 21 Ga. J. Int'l & Comp. L. 217 (1991). –Article Citation.

Charles Mwalimu, <u>Police, State Security Forces and Constitutionalism of Human Rights in Zambia</u>, 21 Ga. J. Int'l & Comp. L. 217, 223-24 (1991). –Page Citation.

Georgia Journal of Southern Legal History, The
Ab.:   Ga. J.S. Legal Hist.

Ex.:   Thomas D. Russell, <u>Historical Study of Personal Injury Litigation: A Comment on Method</u>, 1 Ga. J.S. Legal Hist. 109 (1991). –Article Citation.

Thomas D. Russell, <u>Historical Study of Personal Injury Litigation: A Comment on Method</u>, 1 Ga. J.S. Legal Hist. 109, 113-15 (1991). –Page Citation.

Georgia Law Review
Ab.:   Ga. L. Rev.

Ex.:   John A. Robertson, <u>Assessing Quality of Life: A Response to Professor Kamisar</u>, 25 Ga. L. Rev. 1243 (1991). –Article Citation.

John A. Robertson, <u>Assessing Quality of Life: A Response to Professor Kamisar</u>, 25 Ga. L. Rev. 1243, 1247-52 (1991). –Page Citation.

Georgia Laws
Ab.:   year Ga. Laws

Ex.:   Act of Apr. 12, 1995, No. 318, 1995-1 Ga. Laws 569. –Citation to an entire session law.

Act of Apr. 12, 1995, No. 318, sec. 1, § 31-21-44.1, 1995-1 Ga. Laws 569, 569. –Citation to a section of a session law amending a prior act.

–Identifying information may be added parenthetically according to <u>Bluebook</u> Rule 12.4(a).

Georgia Official Code
<u>See</u> Official Code of Georgia Annotated (Michie)

Georgia, Opinions of the Attorney General
<u>See</u> Opinions of the Attorney General of Georgia

Georgia Reports
Ab.:   Ga.

–Cite to S.E. or S.E.2d if therein; otherwise, cite to Ga.

–Give parallel citations, if at all, only in documents submitted to Georgia state courts. <u>See</u> <u>Bluebook</u> Rule 10.3.1 and Practitioners' Note P.3; <u>see</u> <u>also</u> Ga. Sup. Ct. R. 22 and Ga. Ct. App. R. 23(c), which require only a citation to the official reporter.

In citing cases in law review footnotes, abbreviate any word listed in Table T.6; the names of "states, countries, and other geographical units" unless they are named parties; and any other words of eight or more letters "if <u>substantial</u> space is thereby saved and the result is unambiguous." <u>Bluebook</u> Rule 10.2.2. On the other hand, in citing cases in text, abbreviate only widely known acronyms and the following words: "&," "Ass'n," "Bros.," "Co.," "Corp.," "Inc.," "Ltd.," and "No." <u>Bluebook</u> Rule 10.2.1(c).

In documents submitted to Georgia state courts, cite as follows:

Taylor v. Chitwood, 266 Ga. 793, 471 S.E.2d 511 (1996). –Case Citation.

Taylor v. Chitwood, 266 Ga. 793, 794, 471 S.E.2d 511, 512 (1996). –Page Citation.

In all other documents, cite as follows:

Taylor v. Chitwood, 266 S.E.2d 793 (Ga. 1996). –Case Citation.

Taylor v. Chitwood, 266 S.E.2d 793, 794 (Ga. 1996). –Page Citation.

Georgia Rules and Regulations
See Official Compilation Rules and Regulations of the State of Georgia

Georgia Session Laws
See Georgia Laws

Georgia State Bar Journal
Ab.:   Ga. St. B.J.

Ex.:   Marc Treadwell, An Analysis of Georgia's Proposed Rules of Evidence, 26 Ga. St. B.J. 173 (1990). –Article Citation.

Marc Treadwell, An Analysis of Georgia's Proposed Rules of Evidence, 26 Ga. St. B.J. 173, 174-75 (1990). –Page Citation.

Georgia State University Law Review
Ab.:   Ga. St. U. L. Rev.

Ex.:   Byard Q. Clemmans, Personal Liability of the Military Official, 7 Ga. St. U. L. Rev. 417 (1991). –Article Citation.

Byard Q. Clemmans, Personal Liability of the Military Official, 7 Ga. St. U. L. Rev. 417, 423 (1991). –Page Citation.

German Yearbook of International Law
Ab.:   German Y.B. Int'l L.

Ex.:   Albert Bleckmann, General Theory of Obligations Under Public International Law, 38 German Y.B. Int'l L. 26 (1995). –Article Citation.

Albert Bleckmann, General Theory of Obligations Under Public International Law, 38 German Y.B. Int'l L. 26, 28-30 (1995). –Page Citation.

Glendale Law Review
Ab.:   Glendale L. Rev.

Ex.:   Frederick Grab, Photo-Radar: What's Wrong with this Picture?, 10 Glendale L. Rev. 51 (1991). –Article Citation.

Frederick Grab, Photo-Radar: What's Wrong with this Picture?, 10 Glendale L. Rev. 51, 59-61 (1991). –Page Citation.

In law review footnotes, the titles of books and the names of cases, except for procedural phrases, are not underlined. See Bluebook Rule 2.1(a). Further, the following are in large and small capitals: codes, restatements, standards, constitutions, periodicals, authors of books, titles of books, the abbreviated names of codes, most legislative materials except for bills and resolutions, codified ordinances, model codes, court rules, and sentencing guidelines. Refer to The Bluebook.

Golden Gate University Law Review
Ab.:   Golden Gate U. L. Rev.
Ex.:   Allan E. Morgan, ADR: In Search of the Emperor's New Clothes, 21 Golden Gate U. L. Rev. 351 (1991). –Article Citation.

Allan E. Morgan, ADR: In Search of the Emperor's New Clothes, 21 Golden Gate U. L. Rev. 351, 353-55 (1991). –Page Citation.

Gonzaga Law Review
Ab.:   Gonz. L. Rev.
Ex.:   Charles H. Sheldon, "We Feel Constrained to Hold...." An Inquiry into the Basis for Decision in the Exercise of State Judicial Review, 27 Gonz. L. Rev. 73 (1991-92). –Article Citation.

Charles H. Sheldon, "We Feel Constrained to Hold...." An Inquiry into the Basis for Decision in the Exercise of State Judicial Review, 27 Gonz. L. Rev. 73, 79-80 (1991-92). –Page Citation.

Gorman on Labor Law
See Basic Text on Labor Law, by Robert A. Gorman

Government Contracts, by John Cosgrove McBride and Thomas J. Touhey
        –Do not abbreviate the title.
Ex.:   8 John C. McBride & Thomas J. Touhey, Government Contracts § 49.40[2] (1992). –Section Citation.

8 John C. McBride & Thomas J. Touhey, Government Contracts § 49.40[2], at 49-67 (1992). –Page Citation.

Government Contracts Reports (Commerce Clearing House)
        –Bound as Contracts Cases, Federal (Commerce Clearing House)-Cont. Cas. Fed. (CCH)
Ab.:   Gov't Cont. Rep. (CCH)
Ex.:   Kit-San-Azusa v. United States, 8 Gov't Cont. Rep. (CCH) (40 Cont. Cas. Fed.) ¶ 76,732 (Fed. Cl. Jan. 24, 1995). –Citation to looseleaf material.

Miller Elevator Co., Inc. v. United States, 39 Cont. Cas. Fed. (CCH) ¶ 76,635 (Fed. Cl. Feb. 24, 1994). –Citation to bound material.

–The above examples are proper if the case is not yet available in, or is not reported in, an official or West reporter, a public domain citation, or in a widely used computer database.

Government Employee Relations Report (Bureau of National Affairs)
Ab.:   Gov't Empl. Rel. Rep. (BNA)

In citing cases in law review footnotes, abbreviate any word listed in Table T.6; the names of "states, countries, and other geographical units" unless they are named parties; and any other words of eight or more letters "if substantial space is thereby saved and the result is unambiguous." Bluebook Rule 10.2.2. On the other hand, in citing cases in text, abbreviate only widely known acronyms and the following words: "&," "Ass'n," "Bros.," "Co.," "Corp.," "Inc.," "Ltd.," and "No." Bluebook Rule 10.2.1(c).

Ex.:   <u>EEOC v. AFSCME</u>, [Current Reports July-Dec.] Gov't Empl. Rel. Rep. (BNA) 939:34 (N.D.N.Y. June 14, 1996). –Citation to looseleaf material.

<u>EEOC v. Wyoming</u>, [Jan.-June 1981] Gov't Empl. Rel. Rep. (BNA) 916:37 (D. Wyo. 1981). –Citation to bound material.

–The above examples are proper if the case is not yet available in, or is not reported in, an official or West reporter, a public domain citation, or in a widely used computer database.

<u>United States Dep't of Agri., Meat Grading Branch Livestock Div. v. American Fed'n of Gov't Employees</u>, [July-Dec. 1978] Gov't Emp. Rel. Rep. (BNA) 780:45 (1978) (Doyle, Arb.). –Citation to bound administrative material.

Great Britain Treaty Series (1883-date)
Ab.:   year Gr. Brit. T.S. No. (Cmnd.)

Guam Civil Code
Ab.:   Guam Civ. Code § (year)
        –Guam Code Annotated will eventually replace this statutory compilation.

Guam Code Annotated
Ab.:   Guam Code Ann. § (year)
Ex.:   3 Guam Code Ann. § 4112 (1995).

Guam Code of Civil Procedure
Ab.:   Guam Civ. P. Code § (year)
        –Guam Code Annotated will eventually replace this statutory compilation.

Guam Government Code
Ab.:   Guam Gov't Code § (year)
        –Guam Code Annotated will eventually replace this statutory compilation.

Guam Session Law
Ab.:   year Guam Sess. Laws
Ex.:   Act of Aug. 19, 1994, No. 22-138, [1993-1994] 2 Guam Sess. Laws 620. –Citation to an entire session law.

Act of Aug. 19, 1994, No. 22-138, § 1, [1993-1994] 2 Guam Sess. Laws 620, 621-28. –Citation to a section of a session law.

–Identifying information may be added parenthetically according to <u>Bluebook</u> Rule 12.4(a).

Guild Practitioner
Ab.:   Guild Prac.

In law review footnotes, the titles of books and the names of cases, except for procedural phrases, are not underlined. <u>See</u> Bluebook Rule 2.1(a). Further, the following are in large and small capitals: codes, restatements, standards, constitutions, periodicals, authors of books, titles of books, the abbreviated names of codes, most legislative materials except for bills and resolutions, codified ordinances, model codes, court rules, and sentencing guidelines. Refer to <u>The Bluebook</u>.

H

Hackworth Digest
See Digest of International Law, by Green Haywood Hackworth.

Hague Court Reports
Ab.:   Hague Ct. Rep. (Scott) or Hague Ct. Rep. 2d (Scott)

Hague Yearbook of International Law
Ab.:   Hague Y.B. Int'l L.
Ex.:   P.K. Menon, Subjects of Modern International Law, 3 Hague Y.B. Int'l
        L. 30 (1990). –Article Citation.

        P.K. Menon, Subjects of Modern International Law, 3 Hague Y.B. Int'l
        L. 30, 33 (1990). –Page Citation.

Hamline Law Review
Ab.:   Hamline L. Rev.
Ex.:   Stephen E. Kalish, The Side-Switching Staff Person in a Law Firm:
        Uncomplimentary Assumptions and an Ethics Curtain, 15 Hamline L.
        Rev. 35 (1991). –Article Citation.

        Stephen E. Kalish, The Side-Switching Staff Person in a Law Firm:
        Uncomplimentary Assumptions and an Ethics Curtain, 15 Hamline L.
        Rev. 35, 41-45 (1991). –Page Citation.

Handbook of the Law of Antitrust, by Lawrence A. Sullivan
        –Do not abbreviate the title.
Ex.:   Lawrence A. Sullivan, Handbook of the Law of Antitrust § 184 (1977).
        –Section Citation.

        Lawrence A. Sullivan, Handbook of the Law of Antitrust § 184, at 529
        (1977). –Page Citation.

Harvard Blackletter Journal
Ab.:   Harv. Blackletter J.
Ex.:   Roy L. Brooks, The Ecology of Inequality: The Rise of African-
        American Underclass, 8 Harv. Blackletter J. 1 (1991). –Article
        Citation.

        Roy L. Brooks, The Ecology of Inequality: The Rise of African-
        American Underclass, 8 Harv. Blackletter J. 1, 2 (1991). –Page
        Citation.

Harvard Civil Rights–Civil Liberties Law Review
Ab.:   Harv. C.R.-C.L. L. Rev.

In law review footnotes, the titles of books and the names of cases, except for procedural
phrases, are not underlined. See Bluebook Rule 2.1(a). Further, the following are in large
and small capitals: codes, restatements, standards, constitutions, periodicals, authors of
books, titles of books, the abbreviated names of codes, most legislative materials except for
bills and resolutions, codified ordinances, model codes, court rules, and sentencing guidelines.
Refer to The Bluebook.

Ex.:   Larry Gastin, The Interconnected Epidemics of Drug Dependency and
         AIDS, 26 Harv. C.R.-C.L. L. Rev. 113 (1991). –Article Citation.
         Larry Gastin, The Interconnected Epidemics of Drug Dependency and
         AIDS, 26 Harv. C.R.-C.L. L. Rev. 113, 121-24 (1991). –Page Citation.

Harvard Environmental Law Review
Ab.:   Harv. Envtl. L. Rev.
Ex.:   Allson Rieser, Ecological Preservation as a Public Property Right: An
         Emerging Doctrine in Search of a Theory, 15 Harv. Envtl. L. Rev. 393
         (1991). –Article Citation.
         Allson Rieser, Ecological Preservation as a Public Property Right: An
         Emerging Doctrine in Search of a Theory, 15 Harv. Envtl. L. Rev. 393,
         411-12 (1991). –Page Citation.

Harvard Human Rights Journal
Ab.:   Harv. Hum. Rts. J.
Ex.:   Richard B. Lillich, The United States Constitution and International
         Human Rights Law, 3 Harv. Hum. Rts. J. 53 (1990). –Article Citation.
         Richard B. Lillich, The United States Constitution and International
         Human Rights Law, 3 Harv. Hum. Rts. J. 53, 54-58 (1990). –Page
         Citation.

Harvard International Law Journal
Ab.:   Harv. Int'l L.J.
Ex.:   Joel R. Paul, Comity in International Law, 32 Harv. Int'l L.J. 1 (1991).
         –Article Citation.
         Joel R. Paul, Comity in International Law, 32 Harv. Int'l L.J. 1, 15-23
         (1991). –Page Citation.

Harvard Journal of Law and Public Policy
Ab.:   Harv. J.L. & Pub. Pol'y
Ex.:   Herbert R. Northrup, The Railway Labor Act - Time for Repeat?,
         13 Harv. J.L. & Pub. Pol'y 441 (1990). –Article Citation.
         Herbert R. Northrup, The Railway Labor Act - Time for Repeat?,
         13 Harv. J.L. & Pub. Pol'y 441, 490-92 (1990). –Page Citation.

Harvard Journal of Law & Technology
Ab.:   Harv. J.L. & Tech.
Ex.:   Randolph N. Janakait, Forensic Science: The Need for Regulation,
         4 Harv. J.L. & Tech. 109 (1991). –Article Citation.
         Randolph N. Janakait, Forensic Science: The Need for Regulation,
         4 Harv. J.L. & Tech. 109, 116-17 (1991). –Page Citation.

Harvard Journal on Legislation
Ab.:   Harv. J. on Legis.

In citing cases in law review footnotes, abbreviate any word listed in Table T.6;
the names of "states, countries, and other geographical units" unless they are named parties;
and any other words of eight or more letters "if substantial space is thereby saved and the
result is unambiguous." Bluebook Rule 10.2.2. On the other hand, in citing cases in text,
abbreviate only widely known acronyms and the following words: "&," "Ass'n," "Bros.,"
"Co.," "Corp.," "Inc.," "Ltd.," and "No." Bluebook Rule 10.2.1(c).

Ex.:   Thomas E. Baker, <u>Why Congress Should Repeal the Federal
        Employers' Liability Act of 1908</u>, 29 Harv. J. on Legis. 79 (1992).
        –Article Citation.

        Thomas E. Baker, <u>Why Congress Should Repeal the Federal
        Employers' Liability Act of 1908</u>, 29 Harv. J. on Legis. 79, 109-10
        (1992). –Page Citation.

Harvard Law Review
Ab.:   Harv. L. Rev.
Ex.:   Elner R. Elhauge, <u>The Scope of Antitrust Process</u>, 104 Harv. L. Rev.
        667 (1991). –Article Citation.

        Elner R. Elhauge, <u>The Scope of Antitrust Process</u>, 104 Harv. L. Rev.
        667, 688-89 (1991). –Page Citation.

Harvard Negotiation Law Review
Ab.:   Harv. Negot. L. Rev.
Ex.:   John Lande, <u>Failing Faith in Litigation: A survey of Business Lawyers'
        and Executives' Opinions</u>, Harv. Negot. L. Rev., Spring 1998, at 1, 3.
        –Page Citation.

Harvard Women's Law Journal
Ab.:   Harv. Women's L.J.
Ex.:   Naomi R. Cahn, <u>Defining Feminist Litigation</u>, 14 Harv. Women's L.J.
        1 (1991). –Article Citation.

        Naomi R. Cahn, <u>Defining Feminist Litigation</u>, 14 Harv. Women's L.J.
        1, 16-17 (1991). –Page Citation.

Harvard World Tax Series
Ab.:   Harv. W. Tax Ser.

Hastings Communications and Entertainment Law Journal
Ab.:   Hastings Comm. & Ent. L.J.
Ex.:   Leonard D. Duboff, <u>What is Art? Toward a Legal Definition</u>,
        12 Hastings Comm. & Ent. L.J. 303 (1990). –Article Citation.

        Leonard D. Duboff, <u>What is Art? Toward a Legal Definition</u>,
        12 Hastings Comm. & Ent. L.J. 303, 346-49 (1990). –Page Citation.

Hastings Constitutional Law Quarterly
Ab.:   Hastings Const. L.Q.

In law review footnotes, the titles of books and the names of cases, except for procedural
phrases, are not underlined. <u>See</u> Bluebook Rule 2.1(a). Further, the following are in large
and small capitals: codes, restatements, standards, constitutions, periodicals, authors of
books, titles of books, the abbreviated names of codes, most legislative materials except for
bills and resolutions, codified ordinances, model codes, court rules, and sentencing guidelines.
Refer to <u>The Bluebook</u>.

Ex.: Steven A. Blum, <u>Public Executions: Understanding the "Cruel and Unusual Punishments" Clause</u>, 19 Hastings Const. L.Q. 413 (1992). –Article Citation.

Steven A. Blum, <u>Public Executions: Understanding the "Cruel and Unusual Punishments" Clause</u>, 19 Hastings Const. L.Q. 413, 418-20 (1992). –Page Citation.

Hastings International and Comparative Law Review

Ab.: Hastings Int'l & Comp. L. Rev.

Ex.: Lynn Berat, <u>The Future of Customary Law in Nambia: A Call for an Integration Model</u>, 15 Hastings Int'l & Comp. L. Rev. 1 (1991). –Article Citation.

Lynn Berat, <u>The Future of Customary Law in Nambia: A Call for an Integration Model</u>, 15 Hastings Int'l & Comp. L. Rev. 1, 29-30 (1991). –Page Citation.

Hastings Law Journal

Ab.: Hastings L.J.

Ex.: Andrew Kuu, <u>Mistake, Frustration, and the Windfall Principle of Contract Remedies</u>, 43 Hastings L.J. 1 (1991). –Article Citation.

Andrew Kuu, <u>Mistake, Frustration, and the Windfall Principle of Contract Remedies</u>, 43 Hastings L.J. 1, 19-20 (1991). –Page Citation.

Hawaii Administrative Rules Directory

Ab.: Haw. Admin. R. § (year).

Ex.: Haw. Admin. R. § 4-7-3 (1981).

Hawaii Appellate Reports

Ab.: Haw. App.

–Discontinued after 10 Haw. App. 631 (1994). Cases from the Intermediate Court of Appeals (Haw. Ct. App.) are now found in West's Hawaii Reports (Haw.) beginning with vol. 76.

–Cite to P.2d or P.3d if therein; otherwise, cite to Haw. App.

–Give parallel citations only in documents submitted to Hawaii state courts. <u>See</u> Bluebook Rule 10.3.1 and Practitioners' Note P.3; <u>see also</u> Haw. R. Ann. 28 and Haw. R. App. P. 28(b)(1), which require a parallel citation.

–Through 10 Haw. App. 631 (1994), cite as follows:

In documents submitted to Hawaii state courts:

Hong v. Kong, 5 Haw. App. 174, 683 P.2d 833 (Ct. App. 1984). –Case Citation.

Hong v. Kong, 5 Haw. App. 174, 177, 683 P.2d 833, 835 (Ct. App. 1984). –Page Citation.

In all other documents:

In citing cases in law review footnotes, abbreviate any word listed in Table T.6; the names of "states, countries, and other geographical units" unless they are named parties; and any other words of eight or more letters "if <u>substantial</u> space is thereby saved and the result is unambiguous." Bluebook Rule 10.2.2. On the other hand, in citing cases in text, abbreviate only widely known acronyms and the following words: "&," "Ass'n," "Bros.," "Co.," "Corp.," "Inc.," "Ltd.," and "No." Bluebook Rule 10.2.1(c).

Hong v. Kong, 683 P.2d 833 (Haw. Ct. App. 1984). –Case Citation.

Hong v. Kong, 683 P.2d 833, 835 (Haw. Ct. App. 1984). –Page Citation.

–After 10 Haw. App. 631 (1994), cite as follows:

In documents submitted to Hawaii state courts:

Baldonado v. Liberty Mutual Insurance Co., 81 Haw. 403, 917 P.2d 730 (Ct. App. 1996). –Case Citation.

Baldonado v. Liberty Mutual Insurance Co., 81 Haw. 403, 405, 917 P.2d 730, 732 (Ct. App. 1996). –Page Citation.

In all other documents:

Baldonado v. Liberty Mutual Insurance Co., 917 P.2d 730 (Haw. Ct. App. 1996). –Case Citation.

Baldonado v. Liberty Mutual Insurance Co., 917 P.2d 730, 732 (Haw. Ct. App. 1996). –Page Citation.

Hawaii Attorney General Report
Ab.:   See Opinions of the Attorney General of Hawaii.

Hawaii Bar Journal
Ab.:   Haw. B.J.

Ex.:   Dana B. Tasdina & Robin L. Filion, The Judicial Improvements Acts of 1990: Historic Changes in Federal Civil Procedure Aimed at Improving the Efficiency of Federal Courts and Reducing the Uncertainty and Cost Associated with Federal Litigation, 23 Haw. B.J. 41 (1991). –Article Citation.

Dana B. Tasdina & Robin L. Filion, The Judicial Improvements Acts of 1990: Historic Changes in Federal Civil Procedure Aimed at Improving the Efficiency of Federal Courts and Reducing the Uncertainty and Cost Associated with Federal Litigation, 23 Haw. B.J. 41, 43 (1991). –Page Citation.

Hawaii Constitution
Ab.:   Haw. Const. art.   , §   .

Ex.:   Haw. Const. art. I, § 1. –"Cite constitutional provisions currently in force without date." Bluebook Rule 11.

–"If the cited provision has been repealed, either indicate parenthetically the fact and date of repeal or cite the repealing provision in full." Bluebook Rule 11.

In law review footnotes, the titles of books and the names of cases, except for procedural phrases, are not underlined. See Bluebook Rule 2.1(a). Further, the following are in large and small capitals: codes, restatements, standards, constitutions, periodicals, authors of books, titles of books, the abbreviated names of codes, most legislative materials except for bills and resolutions, codified ordinances, model codes, court rules, and sentencing guidelines. Refer to The Bluebook.

Haw. Const. art. I, § 12 (amended 1978). –"When citing a provision that has been subsequently amended, either indicate parenthetically the fact and date of amendment or cite the amending provision in full." Bluebook Rule 11.

Haw. Const. art. XVII (formerly at art. XV). –Hawaii's constitution was renumbered in 1976; renumbered provisions may be parenthetically noted.

Hawaii Reports, West's
- Ab.: Haw.
  - –Cite to P.2d or P.3d if therein; otherwise, cite to Haw.
  - –Give parallel citations only in documents submitted to Hawaii state courts. See Bluebook Rule 10.3.1 and Practitioners' Note P.3; see also Haw. R. Ann. 28 and Haw. R. App. P. 28(b)(1), which require a parallel citation.
  - In documents submitted to Hawaii state courts, cite as follows:
    - Richard v. Metcalf, 82 Haw. 249, 921 P.2d 169 (1996). –Case Citation.
    - Richard v. Metcalf, 82 Haw. 249, 251, 921 P.2d 169, 171 (1996). –Page Citation.
  - In all other documents, cite as follows:
    - Richard v. Metcalf, 921 P.2d 169 (Haw. 1996). –Case Citation.
    - Richard v. Metcalf, 921 P.2d 169, 171 (Haw. 1996). –Page Citation.

Hawaii Revised Statutes
- Ab.: Haw. Rev. Stat. §   (year)
- Ex.: Haw. Rev. Stat. § 171-58 (1993).

Hawaii Revised Statutes Annotated
See Michie's Hawaii Revised Statutes Annotated

Hawaii Session Laws
See Session Laws of Hawaii

Hearings, Congressional
See Congressional hearings

Hein's United States Treaties and Other International Agreements
See Bluebook Rule 21.4.5(c).
- Ab.: Hein's No. KAV
- Ex.: Swap Agreement, Jan. 30, 1992, U.S.-Pan., Hein's No. KAV 3145.

In citing cases in law review footnotes, abbreviate any word listed in Table T.6; the names of "states, countries, and other geographical units" unless they are named parties; and any other words of eight or more letters "if substantial space is thereby saved and the result is unambiguous." Bluebook Rule 10.2.2. On the other hand, in citing cases in text, abbreviate only widely known acronyms and the following words: "&," "Ass'n," "Bros.," "Co.," "Corp.," "Inc.," "Ltd.," and "No." Bluebook Rule 10.2.1(c).

Hein's United States Treaties and Other International Agreements - Current Microfiche Service

Ex.: Convention for the Safety of Life at Sea, 1974, amendments concerning radiocommunications for the global maritime distress and safety system, Nov. 9, 1988, No. KAV 3200 (Temp. State Dept. No. 92-72), Hein's United States Treaties and Other International Agreements - Current Microfiche Service.

hereinafter

See Bluebook Rule 4.2(b).

High Technology Law Journal (Boalt Hall School of Law, University of California-Berkeley)

Ab.: High Tech. L.J.

Ex.: Lee B. Burgunder & Carey E. Heckman, An Emerging Theory of Computer Software Genericism, 1987 High Tech. L.J. 229. –Article Citation.

Lee B. Burgunder & Carey E. Heckman, An Emerging Theory of Computer Software Genericism, 1987 High Tech. L.J. 229, 230-31. –Page Citation.

Hofstra Labor Law Journal

Ab.: Hofstra Lab. L.J.

Ex.: Jeffrey J. Olsen, A Comprehensive Review of Private Sector Drug Testing Law, 8 Hofstra Lab. L.J. 223 (1991). –Article Citation.

Jeffrey J. Olsen, A Comprehensive Review of Private Sector Drug Testing Law, 8 Hofstra Lab. L.J. 223, 239-40 (1991). –Page Citation.

Hofstra Law Review

Ab.: Hofstra L. Rev.

Ex.: Ralph Nader, Leadership and the Law, 19 Hofstra L. Rev. 543 (1991). –Article Citation.

Ralph Nader, Leadership and the Law, 19 Hofstra L. Rev. 543, 559-60 (1991) –Page Citation.

Hofstra Property Law Journal

Ab.: Hofstra Prop. L.J.

Ex.: Anne M. Fealey, Privacy and Publicity, Then and Now, 3 Hofstra Prop. L.J. 15 (1989). –Article Citation.

Anne M. Fealey, Privacy and Publicity, Then and Now, 3 Hofstra Prop. L.J. 15, 19-20 (1989). –Page Citation.

Holmes' Appleman on Insurance, 2d., by Eric Mills Holmes and L. Anthony Sutin.

–Do not abbreviate title.

In law review footnotes, the titles of books and the names of cases, except for procedural phrases, are not underlined. See Bluebook Rule 2.1(a). Further, the following are in large and small capitals: codes, restatements, standards, constitutions, periodicals, authors of books, titles of books, the abbreviated names of codes, most legislative materials except for bills and resolutions, codified ordinances, model codes, court rules, and sentencing guidelines. Refer to The Bluebook.

Ex.: 14 Eric Mills Holmes and L. Anthony Sutin, <u>Holmes' Appleman on Insurance</u> ¶ 107.2 (2d ed. 2000). –Section Citation.
14 Eric Mills Holmes and L. Anthony Sutin, <u>Holmes' Appleman on Insurance</u> ¶ 107.2, at 553 (2d ed. 2000). –Page Citation.
14 Eric Mills Holmes and L. Anthony Sutin, <u>Holmes' Appleman on Insurance</u> ¶ 107.2, at 553 n.97 (2d ed. 2000). –Footnote Citation.

Hong Kong Law Journal
Ab.: H.K. L.J.
Ex.: Michael Wikinson, <u>Taking Other Offences Into Consideration in Hong Kong</u>, 21 H.K. L.J. 19 (1991). –Article Citation.
Michael Wikinson, <u>Taking Other Offences Into Consideration in Hong Kong</u>, 21 H.K. L.J. 19, 19-20 (1991). –Page Citation.

House Bills (U.S. Congress)
<u>See</u> Congressional Bills

House Concurrent Resolution
<u>See</u> Congressional Resolutions

House Conference Report
Ab.: H.R. Conf. Rep.
Ex.: H.R. Conf. Rep. No. 99-962, at 7 (1986).

House Joint Resolution
<u>See</u> Congressional Resolutions

House Resolution
<u>See</u> Congressional Resolutions

Houston Journal of International Law
Ab.: Hous. J. Int'l L.
Ex.: Dean C. Alexander, <u>The North American Free Trade Area: Potential Framework for an Agreement</u>, 14 Hous. J. Int'l L. 85 (1991). –Article Citation.
Dean C. Alexander, <u>The North American Free Trade Area: Potential Framework for an Agreement</u>, 14 Hous. J. Int'l L. 85, 89-90 (1991). –Page Citation.

Houston Law Review
Ab.: Hous. L. Rev.
Ex.: G. Sidney Buchanan, <u>Women in Combat: An Essay on Ultimate Rights and Responsibilities</u>, 28 Hous. L. Rev. 503 (1991). –Article Citation.
G. Sidney Buchanan, <u>Women in Combat: An Essay on Ultimate Rights and Responsibilities</u>, 28 Hous. L. Rev. 503, 546-47 (1991). –Page Citation.

In citing cases in law review footnotes, abbreviate any word listed in Table T.6; the names of "states, countries, and other geographical units" unless they are named parties; and any other words of eight or more letters "if <u>substantial</u> space is thereby saved and the result is unambiguous." <u>Bluebook</u> Rule 10.2.2. On the other hand, in citing cases in text, abbreviate only widely known acronyms and the following words: "&," "Ass'n," "Bros.," "Co.," "Corp.," "Inc.," "Ltd.," and "No." <u>Bluebook</u> Rule 10.2.1(c).

Howard (United States Reports)
See United States Reports

Howard Journal of Criminal Justice, The
Ab.: How. J. Crim. Just.
Ex.: Peter Raynor, Sentencing With and Without Reports: A Local Study, 30 How. J. Crim. Just. 293 (1991). –Article Citation.

Peter Raynor, Sentencing With and Without Reports: A Local Study, 30 How. J. Crim. Just. 293, 309-10 (1991). –Page Citation.

Howard Law Journal
Ab.: How. L.J.
Ex.: Victor Goode, Cultural Racism in Public Education: A Legal Tactic for Black Texans, 33 How. L.J. 321 (1990). –Article Citation.

Victor Goode, Cultural Racism in Public Education: A Legal Tactic for Black Texans, 33 How. L.J. 321, 329-30 (1990). –Page Citation.

Human Life Review, The
Ab.: Hum. Life Rev.
Ex.: Joseph Sobran, AIDS and the Tribe, 18 Hum. Life Rev. 18 (1992). –Article Citation.

Joseph Sobran, AIDS and the Tribe, 18 Hum. Life Rev. 18, 19-20 (1992). –Page Citation.

Human Rights
Ab.: Hum. Rts.

Human Rights Quarterly
Ab.: Hum. Rts. Q.
Ex.: Douglas Sanders, Collective Rights, 13 Hum. Rts. Q. 368 (1991). –Article Citation.

Douglas Sanders, Collective Rights, 13 Hum. Rts. Q. 368, 379-80 (1991). –Page Citation.

In law review footnotes, the titles of books and the names of cases, except for procedural phrases, are not underlined. See Bluebook Rule 2.1(a). Further, the following are in large and small capitals: codes, restatements, standards, constitutions, periodicals, authors of books, titles of books, the abbreviated names of codes, most legislative materials except for bills and resolutions, codified ordinances, model codes, court rules, and sentencing guidelines. Refer to The Bluebook.

I

ICC Practitioner's Journal
Ab.:   ICC Prac. J.

Ex.:   Charles L. Freed, <u>Current Status of the Keogh Doctrine</u>, 51 ICC Prac. J. 599 (1984). –Article Citation.

Charles L. Freed, <u>Current Status of the Keogh Doctrine</u>, 51 ICC Prac. J. 599, 604 (1984). –Article Citation.

<u>Id.</u>; <u>id.</u>

–"<u>Id.</u>" should be used when citing to the immediately preceding authority. <u>See</u> <u>Bluebook</u> Rule 4.1. <u>See also</u> Practitioners' Note P.4.

Text:

Ex.:   "Similarly, in <u>United States v. Nicholson</u>, 885 F.2d 481 (8th Cir. 1989), the court accepted the race-neutral reason for peremptorily challenging a juror who 'had a relative who was incarcerated.' <u>Id.</u> at 483. . . . On remand, the prosecutor recalled the fact that one juror had an incarcerated relative. <u>Id.</u>" –Taken from <u>United States v. Johnson</u>, 941 F.2d 1102, 1109 (10th Cir. 1991).

footnotes:

Ex.:   123. 414 A.2d 220 (Me. 1980).

124. <u>Id.</u> at 223.

125. <u>Id.</u> –Taken from 45 Vand. L. Rev. 161, 180 nn.123-25 (1992).

209. <u>See Grady</u>, 110 S. Ct. at 2104 (Scalia, J., dissenting).

210. <u>See id.</u> –Taken from 45 Vand. L. Rev. 273, 302 nn.209-210 (1992).

256. 445 U.S. 684 (1980).

257. <u>See id.</u> at 695. –Taken from 45 Vand. L. Rev. 273, 308 nn.256-57 (1992).

Idaho Administrative Code
Ab.:   Idaho Admin. Code r.   (year)

Ex.:   Idaho Admin. Code r. 02.02.07-103 (1993).

Idaho Attorney General's Annual Report
Ab.:   Idaho Att'y Gen. Ann. Rep.

<u>See</u> Opinions of the Attorney General of Idaho.

In law review footnotes, the titles of books and the names of cases, except for procedural phrases, are not underlined. <u>See</u> <u>Bluebook</u> Rule 2.1(a). Further, the following are in large and small capitals: codes, restatements, standards, constitutions, periodicals, authors of books, titles of books, the abbreviated names of codes, most legislative materials except for bills and resolutions, codified ordinances, model codes, court rules, and sentencing guidelines. Refer to <u>The Bluebook</u>.

Idaho Constitution

Ab.:   Idaho Const. art.   , §   .

Ex.:   Idaho Const. art. I, § 13. –"Cite constitutional provisions currently in force without date." Bluebook Rule 11.

Idaho Const. art. X, § 6 (repealed 1931). –"If the cited provision has been repealed, either indicate parenthetically the fact and date of repeal or cite the repealing provision in full." Bluebook Rule 11.

Idaho Const. art. XX, § 1 (amended 1974). –"When citing a provision that has been subsequently amended, either indicate parenthetically the fact and date of amendment or cite the amending provision in full." Bluebook Rule 11.

Idaho Const. of 1890, art. XIX, §§ 1, 2. –"Cite constitutions that have been totally superseded by year of adoption; if the specific provision cited was adopted in a different year, give that year parenthetically." Bluebook Rule 11.

Idaho Court of Appeals

Ab.:   Idaho Ct. App.

–Cite to P., P.2d, or P.3d if therein; otherwise, cite to Idaho

–Give parallel citations only in documents submitted to Idaho state courts. (Note: In citing a state court case in a document submitted to a court of that same state, the 16th ed. of The Bluebook prescribed a parallel citation; the 17th ed. prescribes that local rules shall control, but Idaho has no known local rules concerning parallel citations. For the sake of continuity, we advise giving a parallel citation in documents submitted to Idaho state courts. See Bluebook Rule 10.3.1 and Practitioners' Note P.3.)

In documents submitted to Idaho state courts, cite as follows:

Ohio v. Smith, 127 Idaho 771, 906 P.2d 141 (Ct. App. 1995). –Case Citation.

Ohio v. Smith, 127 Idaho 771, 773, 906 P.2d 141, 143 (Ct. App. 1995). –Page Citation.

In all other documents, cite as follows:

Hines v. Wells, 814 P.2d 437 (Idaho Ct. App. 1991). –Case Citation.

Hines v. Wells, 814 P.2d 437, 438 (Idaho Ct. App. 1991). –Page Citation.

Idaho Law Review

Ab.:   Idaho L. Rev.

In citing cases in law review footnotes, abbreviate any word listed in Table T.6; the names of "states, countries, and other geographical units" unless they are named parties; and any other words of eight or more letters "if substantial space is thereby saved and the result is unambiguous." Bluebook Rule 10.2.2. On the other hand, in citing cases in text, abbreviate only widely known acronyms and the following words: "&," "Ass'n," "Bros.," "Co.," "Corp.," "Inc.," "Ltd.," and "No." Bluebook Rule 10.2.1(c).

Ex.: Bruce J. Wilcox, The Constitutionality of Exclusive Cable Franchising, 28 Idaho L. Rev. 33 (1991-1992). –Article Citation.

Bruce J. Wilcox, The Constitutionality of Exclusive Cable Franchising, 28 Idaho L. Rev. 33, 39-40 (1991-1992). –Page Citation.

Idaho Official Code (Michie)
Ab.: Idaho Code § (Michie year)
Ex.: Idaho Code § 63-2565 (Michie 2000).
Idaho Code § 14-512 (Michie Supp. 2000).

Idaho Reports
Ab.: Idaho

–Cite to P., P.2d, or P.3d if therein; otherwise, cite to Idaho.

–Give parallel citations only in documents submitted to Idaho state courts. (Note: In citing a state court case in a document submitted to a court of that same state, the 16th ed. of The Bluebook prescribed a parallel citation; the 17th ed. prescribes that local rules shall control, but Idaho has no known local rules concerning parallel citations. For the sake of continuity, we advise giving a parallel citation in documents submitted to Idaho state courts. See Bluebook Rule 10.3.1 and Practitioners' Note P.3.)

In documents submitted to Idaho state courts, cite as follows:
Higginson v. Wadsworth, 128 Idaho 439, 915 P.2d 1 (1996). –Case Citation.

Higginson v. Wadsworth, 128 Idaho 439, 442, 915 P.2d 1, 4 (1996). –Page Citation.

In all other documents, cite as follows:
Higginson v. Wadsworth, 915 P.2d 1 (Idaho 1996). –Case Citation.

Higginson v. Wadsworth, 915 P.2d 1, 4 (Idaho 1996). –Page Citation.

Idaho Session Laws
See Session Laws, Idaho

IDEA: The Journal of Law and Technology
Ab.: IDEA
Ex.: Scott M. Alter, Trade Secrets and Telecommunications: The Problems with Local Area Networks, 31 IDEA 297 (1991). –Article Citation.

Scott M. Alter, Trade Secrets and Telecommunications: The Problems with Local Area Networks, 31 IDEA 297, 299-300 (1991).

Illinois
Ab.: Ill. Const. art. , § .

In law review footnotes, the titles of books and the names of cases, except for procedural phrases, are not underlined. See Bluebook Rule 2.1(a). Further, the following are in large and small capitals: codes, restatements, standards, constitutions, periodicals, authors of books, titles of books, the abbreviated names of codes, most legislative materials except for bills and resolutions, codified ordinances, model codes, court rules, and sentencing guidelines. Refer to The Bluebook.

Ex.:　Ill. Const. art. II, § 2. –"Cite constitutional provisions currently in force without date." Bluebook Rule 11.

–"If the cited provision has been repealed, either indicate parenthetically the fact and date of repeal or cite the repealing provision in full." Bluebook Rule 11.

Ill. Const. art. III, § 1 (amended 1988). –"When citing a provision that has been subsequently amended, either indicate parenthetically the fact and date of amendment or cite the amending provision in full." Bluebook Rule 11.

Ill. Const. of 1870, art. V, § 24. –"Cite constitutions that have been totally superseded by year of adoption; if the specific provision cited was adopted in a different year, give that year parenthetically." Bluebook Rule 11.

Illinois Administrative Code
Ab.:　Ill. Admin. Code tit. , § (year).

Ex.:　Ill. Admin. Code tit. 62, § 240.312 (2000).

Illinois Annotated Statutes, West's Smith-Hurd
See West's Smith-Hurd Illinois Compiled Statutes Annotated

Illinois Appellate Court Reports
Ab.:　Ill. App., Ill. App. 2d, Ill. App. 3d

–In documents submitted to Illinois state courts, cite to Ill. App., Ill. App. 2d, or Ill. App. if therein; otherwise, cite to N.E. or N.E.2d. In all other documents, cite to N.E. or N.E.2d if therein; otherwise, cite to Ill. App., Ill. App. 2d, or Ill. App. 3d.

–Give parallel citations only in documents submitted to Illinois state courts. See Bluebook Rule 10.3.1 and Practitioners' Note P.3; see also Ill. Sup. Ct. R.6, which requires citation to Ill., Ill. App. 2d, or Ill. App. 3d and permits a parallel citation to the regional reporter and/or to Ill. Dec.

In documents submitted to Illinois state courts, cite as follows:

First National Bank v. Strong, 278 Ill. App. 3d 762, 663 N.E.2d 432, 215 Ill. Dec. 421 (1996). –Case Citation.

First National Bank v. Strong, 278 Ill. App. 3d 762, 765, 663 N.E.2d 432, 434, 215 Ill. Dec. 421, 427 (1996). –Page Citation.

In all other documents, cite as follows:

First National Bank v. Strong, 663 N.E.2d 432 (Ill. App. Ct. 1996). –Case Citation.

First National Bank v. Strong, 663 N.E.2d 432, 434 (Ill. App. Ct. 1996). –Page Citation.

In citing cases in law review footnotes, abbreviate any word listed in Table T.6; the names of "states, countries, and other geographical units" unless they are named parties; and any other words of eight or more letters "if substantial space is thereby saved and the result is unambiguous." Bluebook Rule 10.2.2. On the other hand, in citing cases in text, abbreviate only widely known acronyms and the following words: "&," "Ass'n," "Bros.," "Co.," "Corp.," "Inc.," "Ltd.," and "No." Bluebook Rule 10.2.1(c).

Illinois Bar Journal
Ab.: Ill. B.J.
Ex.: John M. Ferguson, <u>Fees -- Their Judgment or Ours?</u>, Ill. B.J., Feb. 1979, at 348. –Article Citation.

John M. Ferguson, <u>Fees -- Their Judgment or Ours?</u>, Ill. B.J., Feb. 1979, at 348, 350. –Page Citation.

Illinois Compiled Statutes
Ab.: x Ill. Comp. Stat. x/x-x (West year)
Ex.: 720 Ill. Comp. Stat. 5/12-7.1 (West 1992).

Illinois Court of Claims Reports
Ab.: Ill. Ct. Cl.
Ex.: <u>Maier v. State</u>, 32 Ill. Ct. Cl. 924 (1979). –Case Citation.

<u>Maier v. State</u>, 32 Ill. Ct. Cl. 924, 926-27 (1979). –Page Citation.

Illinois Law Review (1906 - 1951)
Ab.: Ill. L.R.
Ex.: Frances A. Allen, The *Wolf* Case: Search and Seizure, Federalism, and the Civil Liberties. Ill. L.R., Mar.-Apr. 1950, at 1. –Article Citation.

Frances A. Allen, The *Wolf* Case: Search and Seizure, Federalism, and the Civil Liberties. Ill. L.R., Mar.-Apr. 1950, at 1, 25-29. –Page Citation.

–In 1952, this publication changed its name to Northwestern University Law Review.

<u>See</u> Northwestern University Law Review.

Illinois Legislative Service (West)
Ab.: year Ill. Legis. Serv. (West)
Ex.: Act of Aug. 9, 1996, P.A. 89-622, 1996 Ill. Legis. Serv. 2743 (West) (concerning the school code). –Citation to an entire session law.

Act of Aug. 9, 1996, P.A. 89-622, sec. 5, § 2-3.13a, 1996 Ill. Legis. Serv. 2743, 2743-44 (West) (concerning School Code regarding scholastic records of transferring students). –Citation to a session law amending prior act.

–"Cite to Ill. Laws if therein." <u>Bluebook</u> Table T.1, p. 201.

Illinois Register
Ab.: Ill. Reg.
Ex.: 6 Ill. Reg. 12.367 (1982).

Illinois Reports
Ab.: Ill., Ill. 2d

In law review footnotes, the titles of books and the names of cases, except for procedural phrases, are not underlined. <u>See</u> <u>Bluebook</u> Rule 2.1(a). Further, the following are in large and small capitals: codes, restatements, standards, constitutions, periodicals, authors of books, titles of books, the abbreviated names of codes, most legislative materials except for bills and resolutions, codified ordinances, model codes, court rules, and sentencing guidelines. Refer to <u>The Bluebook</u>.

–In documents submitted to Illinois state courts, cite to Ill. or Ill. 2d if
therein; otherwise, cite to N.E. or N.E.2d. In all other documents, cite
N.E. or N.E.2d. if therein; otherwise, cite to Ill. or Ill. 2d.

–Give parallel citations only in documents submitted to Illinois state
courts. See Bluebook Rule 10.3.1 and Practitioners' Note P.3; see
also Ill. Sup. Ct. R.6, which requires citation to Ill. or Ill. 2d and
permits a parallel citation to the regional reporter and/or to Ill. Dec.

In documents submitted to Illinois state courts, cite as follows:

People v. Bounds, 171 Ill. 2d 1, 662 N.E.2d 1168, 215 Ill. Dec. 28
(1995). –Case Citation.

People v. Bounds, 171 Ill. 2d 1, 5, 662 N.E.2d 1168, 1171, 215 Ill.
Dec. 28, 35 (1995). –Page Citation.

In all other documents, cite as follows:

People v. Bounds, 662 N.E.2d 1168 (Ill. 1995). –Case Citation.

People v. Bounds, 662 N.E.2d 1168, 1171 (Ill. 1995). –Page
Citation.

Illinois Session Laws
See Laws of Illinois and Illinois Legislative Service (West)

Immigration Journal
Ab.:   Immigr. J.
Ex.:   Roxana C. Bacon, Estopping the INS, Immigr. J., Jan.-Feb. 1982, at 8.
          –Article Citation.

          Roxana C. Bacon, Estopping the INS, Immigr. J., Jan.-Feb. 1982, at 8,
          9. –Page Citation.

in

          –Use for citation of shorter works in collection. Bluebook Rules 15.5.1
          and 1.6(a).
Ex.:   Uriel Gorney, American Precedent in the Supreme Court of Israel, in
          Comparative Law of Israel and the Middle East 93, 104-05 (Nicholas
          N. Kittrie 1971).

in banc
–Do not abbreviate
–See en banc

In the Public Interest
Ab.:   In Pub. Interest

In citing cases in law review footnotes, abbreviate any word listed in Table T.6;
the names of "states, countries, and other geographical units" unless they are named parties;
and any other words of eight or more letters "if substantial space is thereby saved and the
result is unambiguous." Bluebook Rule 10.2.2. On the other hand, in citing cases in text,
abbreviate only widely known acronyms and the following words: "&," "Ass'n," "Bros.,"
"Co.," "Corp.," "Inc.," "Ltd.," and "No." Bluebook Rule 10.2.1(c).

Ex.:   Brenna Mahoney, <u>Tracking: The End to Equal Educational</u>
         <u>Opportunity</u>, In Pub. Interest, Spring 1991, at 51. –Article Citation.
         Brenna Mahoney, <u>Tracking: The End to Equal Educational</u>
         <u>Opportunity</u>, In Pub. Interest, Spring 1991, at 51, 54-55. –Page
         Citation.

Indiana Administrative Code
Ab.:   Ind. Admin. Code tit. , r. (year)
Ex.:   Ind. Admin. Code tit. 846, r. 1-8-5 (1988).

Indiana, Annual Report and Official Opinions of the Attorney General
<u>See</u> Annual Report and Official Opinions of the Attorney General of
Indiana

Indiana Appellate Court Reports (1890-1971) (continued as Indiana Court of Appeals Reports)
Ab.:   Ind. App.

–Cite to N.E. or N.E.2d if therein; otherwise, cite to Ind. App.

–Give parallel citations only in documents submitted to Indiana state
courts. <u>See</u> <u>Bluebook</u> Rule 10.3.1 and Practitioners' Note P.3; <u>see</u>
<u>also</u> Ind. R. App. P. 8.2(B).

In documents submitted to Indiana state courts, cite as follows:

   <u>Evans v. Enoco Colleries, Inc.</u>, 137 Ind. App. 11, 202 N.E.2d 595
   (1964). –Case Citation.

   <u>Evans v. Enoco Colleries, Inc.</u>, 137 Ind. App. 11, 13, 202 N.E.2d
   595, 596 (1964). –Page Citation.

In all other documents, cite as follows:

   <u>Evans v. Enoco Colleries, Inc.</u>, 202 N.E.2d 595 (Ind. App. 1964).
   –Case Citation.

   <u>Evans v. Enoco Colleries, Inc.</u>, 202 N.E.2d 595, 596 (Ind. App.
   1964). –Page Citation.

Indiana Code
Ab.:   Ind. Code §   (year)
Ex.:   Ind. Code § 32-2-1-1 (1993).

Indiana Code Annotated
<u>See</u> West's Annotated Indiana Code

Indiana Constitution
Ab.:   Ind. Const. art.   , §   .

In law review footnotes, the titles of books and the names of cases, except for procedural
phrases, are not underlined. <u>See</u> <u>Bluebook</u> Rule 2.1(a). Further, the following are in large
and small capitals: codes, restatements, standards, constitutions, periodicals, authors of
books, titles of books, the abbreviated names of codes, most legislative materials except for
bills and resolutions, codified ordinances, model codes, court rules, and sentencing guidelines.
Refer to <u>The Bluebook</u>.

Ex.:   Ind. Const. art. I, § 19. –"Cite constitutional provisions currently in
        force without date." Bluebook Rule 11.

        Ind. Const. art. II, § 5 (repealed 1881). –"If the cited provision has
        been repealed, either indicate parenthetically the fact and date of repeal
        or cite the repealing provision in full." Bluebook Rule 11.

        Ind. Const. art. V, § 17 (amended 1984). –"When citing a provision
        that has been subsequently amended, either indicate parenthetically the
        fact and date of amendment or cite the amending provision in full."
        Bluebook Rule 11.

        Ind. Const. art. XII, § 4. –"Cite constitutions that have been totally
        superseded by year of adoption; if the specific provision cited was
        adopted in a different year, give that year parenthetically." Bluebook
        Rule 11.

Indiana Court of Appeals Reports
Ab.:   Ind. App.

        –Discontinued after 182 Ind. App. 697 (1979).

        –Cite to N.E. or N.E.2d if therein; otherwise, cite to Ind. App.

        –Give parallel citations only in documents submitted to Indiana state
         courts. See Bluebook Rule 10.3.1 and Practitioners' Note P.3; see
         also Ind. R. App. P. 8.2(B).

        –Through 182 Ind. App. 697 (1979), cite as follows:

        In documents submitted to Indiana state courts:

                Keck v. Kerbs, 182 Ind. App. 530, 395 N.E.2d 845 (1979). –Case
                Citation.

                Keck v. Kerbs, 182 Ind. App. 530, 530, 395 N.E.2d 845, 845
                (1979). –Page Citation.

        In all other documents:

                Keck v. Kerbs, 395 N.E.2d 845 (Ind. Ct. App. 1979). –Case
                Citation.

                Keck v. Kerbs, 395 N.E.2d 845, 845 (Ind. Ct. App. 1979). –Page
                Citation.

        –After 182 Ind. App. 697 (1979), cite as follows:

        In all documents:

                Cram v. Howell, 662 N.E.2d 678 (Ind. Ct. App. 1996). –Case
                Citation.

                Cram v. Howell, 662 N.E.2d 678, 680 (Ind. Ct. App. 1996). –Page
                Citation.

Indiana International & Comparative Law Review
Ab.:   Ind. Int'l & Comp. L. Rev.

In citing cases in law review footnotes, abbreviate any word listed in Table T.6;
the names of "states, countries, and other geographical units" unless they are named parties;
and any other words of eight or more letters "if substantial space is thereby saved and the
result is unambiguous." Bluebook Rule 10.2.2. On the other hand, in citing cases in text,
abbreviate only widely known acronyms and the following words: "&," "Ass'n," "Bros.,"
"Co.," "Corp.," "Inc.," "Ltd.," and "No." Bluebook Rule 10.2.1(c).

Ex.:   John Quigley, <u>Apartheid Outside Africa: The Case of Israel</u>, 2 Ind. Int'l & Comp. L. Rev. 221 (1991). –Article Citation.

John Quigley, <u>Apartheid Outside Africa: The Case of Israel</u>, 2 Ind. Int'l & Comp. L. Rev. 221, 239-40 (1991). –Page Citation.

Indiana Law Journal
Ab.:   Ind. L.J.
Ex.:   Timothy J. Moran, <u>Formal Restrictions on Televised Political Advertising: Elevating Political Debate Without Supressing Free Speech</u>, 67 Ind. L.J. 663 (1992). –Article Citation.

Timothy J. Moran, <u>Formal Restrictions on Televised Political Advertising: Elevating Political Debate Without Supressing Free Speech</u>, 67 Ind. L.J. 663, 669-70 (1992). –Page Citation.

Indiana Law Review
Ab.:   Ind. L. Rev.
Ex.:   Paul H. Brietzke, <u>Urban Development and Human Development</u>, 25 Ind. L. Rev. 741 (1992). –Article Citation.

Paul H. Brietzke, <u>Urban Development and Human Development</u>, 25 Ind. L. Rev. 741, 756-57 (1992). –Page Citation.

Indiana Register
Ab.:   Ind. Reg.

Indiana Reports
Ab.:   Ind.
–Discontinued after 275 Ind. 699 (1981).
–Cite to N.E. or N.E.2d if therein; otherwise, cite to Ind.
–Give parallel citations only in documents submitted to Indiana state courts. <u>See</u> <u>Bluebook</u> Rule 10.3.1 and Practitioners' Note P.3; <u>see also</u> Ind. R. App. P. 8.2(B).
–Through 275 Ind. 699 (1981), cite as follows:
In documents submitted to Indiana state courts:
   <u>Moon v. State</u>, 275 Ind. 651, 419 N.E.2d 740 (1981). –Case Citation.
   <u>Moon v. State</u>, 275 Ind. 651, 655, 419 N.E.2d 740, 743 (1981). –Page Citation.
In all other documents:
   <u>Moon v. State</u>, 419 N.E.2d 740 (Ind. 1981). –Case Citation.
   <u>Moon v. State</u>, 419 N.E.2d 740, 743 (Ind. 1981). –Page Citation.
–After 275 Ind. 699 (1981), cite as follows:
In all documents:

In law review footnotes, the titles of books and the names of cases, except for procedural phrases, are not underlined. <u>See</u> <u>Bluebook</u> Rule 2.1(a). Further, the following are in large and small capitals: codes, restatements, standards, constitutions, periodicals, authors of books, titles of books, the abbreviated names of codes, most legislative materials except for bills and resolutions, codified ordinances, model codes, court rules, and sentencing guidelines. Refer to <u>The Bluebook</u>.

Humbert v. Smith, 664 N.E.2d 356 (Ind. 1996). –Case Citation.
Humbert v. Smith, 664 N.E.2d 356, 357 (Ind. 1996). –Page
Citation.

Indiana Session Laws
See Acts, Indiana

Indiana Statutes Annotated
See Burns Indiana Statutes Annotated

Industrial and Labor Relations Review
Ab.:   Indus. & Lab. Rel. Rev.
Ex.:   Kevin J. Murphy, Determinants of Contract Duration in Collective
        Bargaining Agreements, 45 Indus. & Lab. Rel. Rev. 352 (1992).
        –Article Citation.

        Kevin J. Murphy, Determinants of Contract Duration in Collective
        Bargaining Agreements, 45 Indus. & Lab. Rel. Rev. 352, 355-56
        (1992). –Page Citation.

Industrial Law Journal
Ab.:   Indus. L.J.
Ex.:   Kenneth Miller, Piper Alpha and the Cullen Report, 20 Indus. L.J. 176
        (1991). –Article Citation.

        Kenneth Miller, Piper Alpha and the Cullen Report, 20 Indus. L.J. 176,
        179-80 (1991). –Page Citation.

Industrial Relations
Ab.:   Indus. Rel.
Ex.:   Joseph D. Reid, Jr., Future Unions, 31 Indus. Rel. 122 (1992). –Article
        Citation.

        Joseph D. Reid, Jr., Future Unions, 31 Indus. Rel. 122, 126-27 (1992).
        –Page Citation.

Industrial Relations Law Journal
Ab.:   Indus. Rel. L.J.
Ex.:   Mark Daniels, The Regulation of Severance Plans Under ERISA,
        12 Indus. Rel. L.J. 340 (1990). –Article Citation.

        Mark Daniels, The Regulation of Severance Plans Under ERISA,
        12 Indus. Rel. L.J. 340, 349-50 (1990). –Page Citation.

infra

        –"Portions of text, footnotes, and groups of authorities within the piece
        in which the citation is made may be cited through the use of 'supra'
        or 'infra'." See Bluebook Rule 3.6.
Ex.:   See infra notes 198-203 and accompanying text.

In citing cases in law review footnotes, abbreviate any word listed in Table T.6;
the names of "states, countries, and other geographical units" unless they are named parties;
and any other words of eight or more letters "if substantial space is thereby saved and the
result is unambiguous." Bluebook Rule 10.2.2. On the other hand, in citing cases in text,
abbreviate only widely known acronyms and the following words: "&," "Ass'n," "Bros.,"
"Co.," "Corp.," "Inc.," "Ltd.," and "No." Bluebook Rule 10.2.1(c).

Inheritance, Estate & Gift Tax Reports (Commerce Clearing House)
  Ab.:   Inher. Est. & Gift Tax Rep. (CCH) (jurisdiction and ¶)
  Ex.:   Offret v. DiDomenico, [State Current] Inher. Est. & Gift Tax Rep.
        (CCH) ¶ 21,426 (Ohio May 26, 1993). –Citation to looseleaf material.
        Cranley v. Schirmer, [1965-1973 All State New Matters Transfer
        Binder] Inher. Est. & Gift Tax Rep. (CCH) ¶ 93,913 (Conn. Super. Ct.
        1967). –Citation to transfer binder material.
        –The above examples are proper if the case is not yet available in, or is
        not reported in, an official or West reporter, a public domain citation,
        or in a widely used computer database.

In re
        –Expressions such as "in the matter of," "petition of," and
        "application of" should be abbreviated "In re". See Bluebook Rule
        10.2.1(b).
        –"Procedural phrases should always be italicized [or underlined],
        regardless of whether the rest of the case name is italicized." See
        Bluebook Rule 10.2.1(b).
  Ex.:   See In re T.J. Ronan Paint Corp., 98 A.D.2d 413, 419-20 (N.Y. App.
        Div. 1984).

Institute on Estate Planning (University of Miami Law Center)
  Ab.:   Inst. on Est. Plan.
  Ex.:   Jeffrey A. Schoenblum, Working With the Unified Credit, 1 Inst. on
        Est. Plan. ¶ 1400 (1981). –Article Citation.
        Jeffrey A. Schoenblum, Working With the Unified Credit, 1 Inst. on
        Est. Plan.¶ 1400, ¶ 1404.2 (1981). –Paragraph Citation.

Institute on Federal Taxation (New York University)
  Ab.:   Inst. on Fed. Tax'n
  Ex.:   C. Ellen McNeil, The Limitations on Interest Deductions, 48 Inst. on
        Fed. Tax'n § 5.00 (1990). –Article Citation.
        C. Ellen McNeil, The Limitations on Interest Deductions, 48 Inst. on
        Fed. Tax'n § 5.05[4], at 5-19 (1990). –Page Citation.

Institute on Mineral Law (Louisiana State University)
  Ab.:   Inst. on Min. L.
  Ex.:   Arthur R. Carmondy, Jr., Legal Problems in the Development and
        Mining of Lignite, 23 Inst. on Min. L. 39 (1977). –Article Citation.
        Arthur R. Carmondy, Jr., Legal Problems in the Development and
        Mining of Lignite, 23 Inst. on Min. L. 39, 48-51 (1977). –Page
        Citation.

Institute on Oil and Gas Law and Taxation (Southwestern Legal Foundation)
  Ab.:   Inst. on Oil & Gas L. & Tax'n

In law review footnotes, the titles of books and the names of cases, except for procedural
phrases, are not underlined. See Bluebook Rule 2.1(a). Further, the following are in large
and small capitals: codes, restatements, standards, constitutions, periodicals, authors of
books, titles of books, the abbreviated names of codes, most legislative materials except for
bills and resolutions, codified ordinances, model codes, court rules, and sentencing guidelines.
Refer to The Bluebook.

Ex.:	Bruce S. Marks, <u>Commercial Conflict Management and Alternative Dispute Resolution in the Oil and Gas Industry</u>, 41 Inst. on Oil & Gas L. & Tax'n § 9.03 (1990). –Article Citation.

Bruce S. Marks, <u>Commercial Conflict Management and Alternative Dispute Resolution in the Oil and Gas Industry</u>, 41 Inst. on Oil & Gas L. & Tax'n § 9.03, at 9-41 (1990). –Page Citation.

Institute on Planning, Zoning and Eminent Domain Proceedings (Southwestern Legal Foundation)
Ab.:	Inst. on Plan. Zoning & Eminent Domain
Ex.:	Christopher J. Caso, <u>Zoning and the First Amendment</u>, 1991 Inst. on Plan. Zoning & Eminent Domain § 5.0. –Article Citation.

Christopher J. Caso, <u>Zoning and the First Amendment</u>, 1991 Inst. on Plan. Zoning & Eminent Domain § 5.0, at 5.03[3]. –Page Citation.

Institute on Private Investments and Investors Abroad Proceedings
Ab.:	Inst. on Priv. Inv. & Inv. Abroad

Institute on Securities Regulation
Ab.:	Inst. on Sec. Reg.
Ex.:	Robert D. Rosenbaum, <u>Proxy Reform</u>, 22 Inst. on Sec. Reg. 77 (1991). –Article Citation.

Robert D. Rosenbaum, <u>Proxy Reform</u>, 22 Inst. on Sec. Reg. 77, 83 (1991). –Page Citation.

institutional authors
<u>See</u> authors

Insurance Counsel Journal
Ab.:	Ins. Couns. J.
Ex.:	Ronald Lee Gilman, <u>Dishonesty Alone Does Not Deck a Fidelity Insurer</u>, 51 Ins. Couns. J. 529 (1984). –Article Citation.

Ronald Lee Gilman, <u>Dishonesty Alone Does Not Deck a Fidelity Insurer</u>, 51 Ins. Couns. J. 529, 530-31 (1984). –Page Citation.

Insurance Law and Practice, by John A. Appleman and Jean Appleman
–Do not abbreviate the title.
Ex.:	19A John A. Appleman & Jean Appleman, <u>Insurance Law and Practice</u> § 10751 (1982). –Section Citation.

19A John A. Appleman & Jean Appleman, <u>Insurance Law and Practice</u> § 10751, at 269 (1982). –Page Citation.

19A John A. Appleman & Jean Appleman, <u>Insurance Law and Practice</u> § 10751, at 269 n. 12 (1982). –Footnote Citation.

<u>See</u> entry herein for <u>Appleman on Insurance</u>, 2d, by Eric Mills Holmes and Mark S. Rhodes.

In citing cases in law review footnotes, abbreviate any word listed in Table T.6; the names of "states, countries, and other geographical units" unless they are named parties; and any other words of eight or more letters "if <u>substantial</u> space is thereby saved and the result is unambiguous." <u>Bluebook</u> Rule 10.2.2. On the other hand, in citing cases in text, abbreviate only widely known acronyms and the following words: "&," "Ass'n," "Bros.," "Co.," "Corp.," "Inc.," "Ltd.," and "No." <u>Bluebook</u> Rule 10.2.1(c).

Insurance Law Reports (Commerce Clearing House)
(formerly Reporter)
Ab.: Ins. L. Rep. (CCH)

Intellectual Property Law
Ab.: Intell. Prop. L.
Ex.: Kyung Jae Park, Protection Against Counterfeiting in Korea, 1 Intell. Prop. L. 71 (1991). –Article Citation.
Kyung Jae Park, Protection Against Counterfeiting in Korea, 1 Intell. Prop. L. 71, 73-74 (1991). –Page Citation.

Intellectual Property Law Review
Ab.: Intell. Prop. L. Rev.
Ex.: Alan Lawrence, The Value of Copyright Law as a Deterrent to Discovery Abuse, 23 Intell. Prop. L. Rev. 605 (1991). –Article Citation.
Alan Lawrence, The Value of Copyright Law as a Deterrent to Discovery Abuse, 23 Intell. Prop. L. Rev. 605, 611 (1991). –Page Citation.

Inter-Alia, Journal of the Nevada State Bar
Ab.: Inter-Alia
Ex.: John C. Orenschall & C. Nicholas Pereos, A Primer in Nevada Water Law, Inter-Alia, April 1978, at 7. –Article Citation.
John C. Orenschall & C. Nicholas Pereos, A Primer in Nevada Water Law, Inter-Alia, April 1978, at 7, 9-10. –Page Citation.

Internal Revenue Code
Ab.: 26 U.S.C. § (year)
I.R.C. § (year).
–When citing to the Internal Revenue Code, "26 U.S.C." may be replaced with "I.R.C." See Bluebook Rule 12.8.1.
Ex.: 26 U.S.C. § 401 (1992).
I.R.C. § 401 (1992).
–When citing to the Internal Revenue Code as it appears in an unofficial code, identify the publisher in the date parenthetical.
Ex.: 26 U.S.C.A. § 401 (West 1996).
I.R.C. § 401 (West 1996).

Internal Revenue Regulations
See Treasury Regulations

Internal Revenue Rulings
See Revenue Rulings

In law review footnotes, the titles of books and the names of cases, except for procedural phrases, are not underlined. See Bluebook Rule 2.1(a). Further, the following are in large and small capitals: codes, restatements, standards, constitutions, periodicals, authors of books, titles of books, the abbreviated names of codes, most legislative materials except for bills and resolutions, codified ordinances, model codes, court rules, and sentencing guidelines. Refer to The Bluebook.

Internal Revenue Service Positions (Commerce Clearing House)
Ab.:   IRS Pos. (CCH)

International and Comparative Law Quarterly
Ab.:   Int'l & Comp. L.Q.
Ex.:   Geoff Gilbert, The Irish Interpretation of the Poltical Offence Exemption, 41 Int'l & Comp. L.Q. 66 (1991). –Article Citation.
      Geoff Gilbert, The Irish Interpretation of the Poltical Offence Exemption, 41 Int'l & Comp. L.Q. 66, 69-70 (1991). –Page Citation.

International Arbitral Awards
Ex.:   Argentine-Chile Frontier Case (Arg. v. Chile), 16 R.I.A.A. 109 (1969). See Bluebook Rule 20.6. and Table T.5 for frequently cited arbitration reporters.

International Atomic Energy Agency Documents
Ab.:   IAEA Doc.

International Business Lawyer
Ab.:   Int'l Bus. Law.
Ex.:   Peter Cameron, A Conference Overview, 20 Int'l Bus. Law. 50 (1992). –Article Citation.
      Peter Cameron, A Conference Overview, 20 Int'l Bus. Law. 50, 51-52 (1992). –Page Citation.

International Centre for Settlement of Investment Disputes (World Bank ICSID)
Ab.:   ICSID (W. Bank)

International Chamber of Commerce Arbitration
Ab.:   Int'l Comm. Arb.

International Civil Aviation Organization Documents
Ab.:   ICAO Doc.

International Court of Justice
Ab.:   I.C.J.
      –Cite decisions to I.C.J.; cite separately published pleadings to I.C.J. Pleadings; cite rules and acts to I.C.J. Acts & Docs. See Bluebook Table T.3.

International Court of Justice, Pleadings, Oral Arguments, Documents
Ab.:   I.C.J. Pleadings

In citing cases in law review footnotes, abbreviate any word listed in Table T.6; the names of "states, countries, and other geographical units" unless they are named parties; and any other words of eight or more letters "if substantial space is thereby saved and the result is unambiguous." Bluebook Rule 10.2.2. On the other hand, in citing cases in text, abbreviate only widely known acronyms and the following words: "&," "Ass'n," "Bros.," "Co.," "Corp.," "Inc.," "Ltd.," and "No." Bluebook Rule 10.2.1(c).

Ex.:   Canter-Memorial of Libya (Lib. v. Malta), 1991 I.C.J. Pleadings (2 Continental Shelf) 1 (May 23, 1976). See Bluebook Rule 21.5.1(f) and Table T.3.

International Court of Justice Reports of Judgments, Advisory Opinions, and Orders
Ab.:   I.C.J.

Ex.:   Border and Transborder Armed Actions (Nicar. v. Hond.), 1988 I.C.J. 68 (Dec. 20). –Case Citation.

Applicability of the Obligation to Arbitrate Under Section 21 of the United Nations Headquarters Agreement of 26 June 1947, 1988 I.C.J. 12 (Apr. 26). –Advisory Opinion Citation.

International Court of Justice, Rules and Acts
Ab.:   I.C.J. Acts & Docs.; see Bluebook Rule 21.5.1(g) and Table T.3.

International Court of Justice Yearbook
Ab.:   I.C.J.Y.B.

Ex.:   1988-1989 I.C.J.Y.B. 95 (1989).

International Digest of Health Legislation
Ab.:   Int'l Dig. Health Legis.

Ex.:   M. Bolis, First Subregional Meeting on Women, Health and Legislation. 42 Int'l Dig. Health Legis. 797 (1991). –Article Citation.

M. Bolis, First Subregional Meeting on Women, Health and Legislation. 42 Int'l Dig. Health Legis. 797, 798-799 (1991). –Page Citation.

International Environment Reporter (Bureau of National Affairs)
Ab.:   Int'l Envt. Rep. (BNA)

Ex.:   Parliament, Commission Inch Closer to Bar on Experts & Hazardous Waste, [Current Reports] Int'l Envt. Rep. (BNA) Vol. 19, at 47 (Jan. 24, 1996). –Cite to looseleaf monograph, article, or commentary.

International Financial Law Review
Ab: Int'l Fin. L. Rev.

Ex.:   Marcus Collins, Reviving Thailand's Securities Market, 11 Int'l Fin. L. Rev. 30 (1992). –Article Citation.

Marcus Collins, Reviving Thailand's Securities Market, 11 Int'l Fin. L. Rev. 30, 31-32 (1992). –Page Citation.

International Journal of Law and Psychiatry
Ab.:   Int'l J.L. & Psychiatry

In law review footnotes, the titles of books and the names of cases, except for procedural phrases, are not underlined. See Bluebook Rule 2.1(a). Further, the following are in large and small capitals: codes, restatements, standards, constitutions, periodicals, authors of books, titles of books, the abbreviated names of codes, most legislative materials except for bills and resolutions, codified ordinances, model codes, court rules, and sentencing guidelines. Refer to The Bluebook.

Ex.: Jeffrey Rubin, Economic Aspects of Law and Psychiatry, 14 Int'l J.L. & Psychiatry 299 (1991). –Article Citation.

Jeffrey Rubin, Economic Aspects of Law and Psychiatry, 14 Int'l J.L. & Psychiatry 299, 297-98 (1991). –Page Citation.

International Journal of Legal Information
Ab.: Int'l J. Legal Info.

Ex.: Ralph Lansky, Law Libraries in Germany: An Introduction, 19 Int'l J. Legal Info. 179 (1991). –Article Citation.

Ralph Lansky, Law Libraries in Germany: An Introduction, 19 Int'l J. Legal Info. 179, 189-90 (1991). –Page Citation.

International Labour Review
Ab.: Int'l Lab. Rev.

Ex.: George Psacharopoulos, From Manpower Planning to Labour Market Analysis, 130 Int'l Lab. Rev. 459 (1991). –Article Citation.

George Psacharopoulos, From Manpower Planning to Labour Market Analysis, 130 Int'l Lab. Rev. 459, 464-65 (1991). –Page Citation.

International Law Commission
Ab.: Int'l L. Comm'n

International Law Commission Yearbook
Ab.: Y.B. Int'l L. Comm'n

Ex.: Summary Records of the 1814th Meeting, [1984] 1 Y.B. Int'l L. Comm'n 2, U.N. Doc. A/CN.4/SER.A/1984.

International Law Reports
Ab.: I.L.R.
     Int'l L. Rep.

Ex.: S v. Mharapara, 84 I.L.R. 1 (Zimb. S. Ct. 1985). –Case Citation.

S v. Mharapara, 84 I.L.R. 1, 17 (Zimb. S. Ct. 1985). –Page Citation.

International Lawyer, The
Ab.: Int'l Law.

Ex.: Hiram E. Chodosh, Swap Centres in The People's Republic of China, 25 Int'l Law 415 (1991). –Article Citation.

Hiram E. Chodosh, Swap Centres in The People's Republic of China, 25 Int'l Law 415, 429-30 (1991). –Page Citation.

International Legal Materials
Ab.: Int'l Legal Materials

Ex.: International Court of Justice: Judgment in Case concerning the Arbitral Award of 31 July 1989 (Guinea Bissau v. Senegal), 31 Int'l Legal Materials 32 (1992) –Article Citation.

In citing cases in law review footnotes, abbreviate any word listed in Table T.6; the names of "states, countries, and other geographical units" unless they are named parties; and any other words of eight or more letters "if substantial space is thereby saved and the result is unambiguous." Bluebook Rule 10.2.2. On the other hand, in citing cases in text, abbreviate only widely known acronyms and the following words: "&," "Ass'n," "Bros.," "Co.," "Corp.," "Inc.," "Ltd.," and "No." Bluebook Rule 10.2.1(c).

International Court of Justice: Judgment in Case concerning the
Arbitral Award of 31 July 1989 (Guinea Bissau v. Senegal), 31 Int'l
Legal Materials 32, 33-35 (1992). –Page Citation.

International Legal Perspectives
Ab.: Int'l Leg. Persp.
Ex.: Todd Beard, The Tax Consequences of Conducting Operations Abroad,
Int'l Legal Persp., Spring 1992, at 65. –Article Citation.
Todd Beard, The Tax Consequences of Conducting Operations Abroad,
Int'l Legal Persp., Spring 1992, at 65, 71. –Page Citation.

International Maritime Organization Assembly Resolutions
Ab.: IMO Assembly Res.

International Organization
Ab.: Int'l Org.
Ex.: Raymond F. Hopkins, Reform in the International Food Aid Regime:
The Role of Consensual Knowledge, 46 Int'l Org. 225 (1992). –Article
Citation.
Raymond F. Hopkins, Reform in the International Food Aid Regime:
The Role of Consensual Knowledge, 46 Int'l Org. 225, 249-50 (1992).
–Page Citation.

International Social Security Review
Ab.: Int'l Soc. Sec. Rev.
Ex.: Alan Borowski, The Economics and Politics of Retirement Incomes
Policy in Australia, 44 Int'l Soc. Sec. Rev. 27 (1991). –Article
Citation.
Alan Borowski, The Economics and Politics of Retirement Incomes
Policy in Australia, 44 Int'l Soc. Sec. Rev. 27, 31-32 (1991). –Page
Citation.

International Symposium on Comparative Law
Ab.: Int'l Symp. on Comp. L.

International Tax & Business Lawyer
Ab.: Int'l Tax & Bus. Law.
Ex.: James J. Fisman, Enforcement of Securities Laws Violations in the
United Kingdom, Int'l Tax & Bus. Law., Summer 1991, at 131.
–Article Citation.
James J. Fisman, Enforcement of Securities Laws Violations in the
United Kingdom, Int'l Tax & Bus. Law., Summer 1991, at 131, 149-50.
–Page Citation.

International Tax Journal, The
Ab.: Int'l Tax J.

In law review footnotes, the titles of books and the names of cases, except for procedural
phrases, are not underlined. See Bluebook Rule 2.1(a). Further, the following are in large
and small capitals: codes, restatements, standards, constitutions, periodicals, authors of
books, titles of books, the abbreviated names of codes, most legislative materials except for
bills and resolutions, codified ordinances, model codes, court rules, and sentencing guidelines.
Refer to The Bluebook.

Ex.:   Walter T. Raineri, <u>Dual Consolidated Losses</u>, 16 Int'l Tax J. 167 (1990). –Article Citation.

Walter T. Raineri, <u>Dual Consolidated Losses</u>, 16 Int'l Tax J. 167, 170-71 (1990). –Page Citation.

International Tax Planning Manual (Commerce Clearing House)
Ab.:   Int'l Tax Planning Man. (CCH)

International Trade Law Journal
Ab.:   Int'l Trade L.J.
Ex.:   David L. Simon, <u>Legal Developments in U.S.-R.O.C. Trade Since Derecognition</u>, 7 Int'l Trade L.J. 203 (1983). –Article Citation.

David L. Simon, <u>Legal Developments in U.S.-R.O.C. Trade Since Derecognition</u>, 7 Int'l Trade L.J. 203, 228-29 (1983). –Page Citation.

International Trade Reporter (Bureau of National Affairs)
         –Bound as International Trade Reporter Decisions-Int'l Trade Rep. Dec. (BNA).
Ab.:   Int'l Trade Rep. (BNA)
Ex.:   <u>Timken Co. v. United States</u>, [Decisions] Int'l Trade Rep. (BNA) (18 Int'l Trade Rep. Dec.) 1065 (Ct. Int'l Trade Jan. 3, 1996). –Case Citation to looseleaf material.

<u>Sharp Corp. v. United States</u>, 12 Int'l Trade Rep. Dec. (BNA) 1340 (Ct. Int'l Trade 1990). –Citation to bound material.

–This example is proper if the case is not yet available in, or is not reported in, an official or West reporter, a public domain citation, or in a widely used computer database.

International Trade Reporter Decisions
Ab.:   I.T.R.D. (BNA)
Ex.:   <u>Torrington Co. v. United States</u>, 17 I.T.R.D. 1961 (Fed. Cir. 1996).
         –If possible, cite to official reporters.

Internet sources
         <u>See</u> Electronic media and other nonprint resources

Interstate Commerce Commission Reports, Motor Carrier Cases
Ab.:   M.C.C.
Ex.:   <u>In re Manufacturers Express, Inc.</u>, 126 M.C.C. 174 (1976).

Interstate Commerce Commission Reports, Second Series
Ab.:   I.C.C.2d

In citing cases in law review footnotes, abbreviate any word listed in Table T.6; the names of "states, countries, and other geographical units" unless they are named parties; and any other words of eight or more letters "if <u>substantial</u> space is thereby saved and the result is unambiguous." <u>Bluebook</u> Rule 10.2.2. On the other hand, in citing cases in text, abbreviate only widely known acronyms and the following words: "&," "Ass'n," "Bros.," "Co.," "Corp.," "Inc.," "Ltd.," and "No." <u>Bluebook</u> Rule 10.2.1(c).

Ex.:   Delaware & Hudson Ry. Co. v. Consolidated Rail Corp., 9 I.C.C.2d 989 (1993).

Interviews, unpublished
See Bluebook Rule 17.1.4

Ex.:   Interview with Pam Malone, President of the National Association for Legal Placement, in Nashville, Tenn. (Dec. 10, 1996). –author conducted interview.

Interview by Stephen Teel with Don Welch, Associate Dean, Vanderbilt University Law School, Nashville, Tenn. (Jan 2, 1997). – author did not conduct interview.

Iowa Administrative Bulletin
Ab.:   Iowa Admin. Bull.

Iowa Administrative Code
Ab.:   Iowa Admin. Code r. (year).

Ex.:   Iowa Admin. Code r. 27-6 (2000).

Iowa, Biennial Report of the Attorney General
See Biennial Report of the Attorney General, State of Iowa

Iowa Code
See Code of Iowa

Iowa Code Annotated (West)
Ab.:   Iowa Code Ann. §   (West year)

Ex.:   Iowa Code Ann. § 476.15 (West 1999)

Iowa Code Ann. § 809A.12 (West Supp. 2000).

–"Cite to Iowa Code if therein." Bluebook Table T.1, p. 202.

Iowa Constitution
Ab.:   Iowa Const. art.   , §   .

Ex.:   Iowa Const. art. I, § 6. –"Cite constitutional provisions currently in force without date." Bluebook Rule 11.

Iowa. Const. art. I, § 5 (repealed 1992). –"If the cited provision has been repealed, either indicate parenthetically the fact and date of repeal or cite the repealing provision in full." Bluebook Rule 11.

Iowa. Const. art. III, § 6 (amended 1968). –"When citing a provision that has been subsequently amended, either indicate parenthetically the fact and date of amendment or cite the amending provision in full." Bluebook Rule 11.

Iowa Const. of 1846, art. V, § 4. –"Cite constitutions that have been totally superseded by year of adoption; if the specific provision cited was adopted in a different year, give that year parenthetically." Bluebook Rule 11.

In law review footnotes, the titles of books and the names of cases, except for procedural phrases, are not underlined. See Bluebook Rule 2.1(a). Further, the following are in large and small capitals: codes, restatements, standards, constitutions, periodicals, authors of books, titles of books, the abbreviated names of codes, most legislative materials except for bills and resolutions, codified ordinances, model codes, court rules, and sentencing guidelines. Refer to The Bluebook.

Iowa Court of Appeals
   Ab.:   Iowa Ct. App.
           –Cite to N.W.2d
   Ex.:   Ames v. Poston, 551 N.W.2d 340 (Iowa Ct. App. 1996). –Case
           Citation.
           Ames v. Poston, 551 N.W.2d 340, 341 (Iowa Ct. App. 1996). –Page
           Citation.

Iowa Law Review
   Ab.:   Iowa L. Rev.
   Ex.:   Beryl R. Jones, Copyrights and State Liability, 76 Iowa L. Rev. 701
           (1991). –Article Citation.
           Beryl R. Jones, Copyrights and State Liability, 76 Iowa L. Rev. 701,
           719-20 (1991). –Page Citation.

Iowa Lawyer, The
   Ab.:   Iowa Law.
   Ex.:   Jennifer J. Rose, Walk Awhile in Your Client's Shoes, Iowa Law., Feb.
           1992, at 24. –Article Citation.
           Jennifer J. Rose, Walk Awhile in Your Client's Shoes, Iowa Law., Feb.
           1992, at 24, 25. –Page Citation.

Iowa Legislative Service (West)
   Ab.:   year Iowa Legis. Serv. (West).
   Ex.:   Act of May 16, 1996, No. 196, 1996 Iowa Legis. Serv. 526 (West)
           (speed limit increase). –Citation to an entire session law.
           Act of May 16, 1996, No. 196, sec. 1 § 321.285(6), 1996 Iowa Legis.
           Serv. 526, 527 (West) (speed limit for multi-laned highway). –Citation
           to a session law amending prior act.
           –"Cite to Iowa Acts if therein." Bluebook Table T.1, p. 202.

Iowa Reports
   Ab.:   Iowa
           –Discontinued after 261 Iowa 1395 (1968).
           –Cite to N.W. or N.W.2d if therein; otherwise, cited to Iowa.
           –Give parallel citations only in documents submitted to Iowa state
           courts. See Bluebook Rule 10.3.1 and Practitioners' Note P.3; see
           also Iowa R. App. P. 14(e), which requires a parallel citation.
           –Through 261 Iowa 1395 (1968), cite as follows:
           In documents submitted to Iowa state courts:
              Burlington & Summit Apartments v. Manolato, 233 Iowa 15, 7
              N.W.2d 26 (1943). –Case Citation.

In citing cases in law review footnotes, abbreviate any word listed in Table T.6;
the names of "states, countries, and other geographical units" unless they are named parties;
and any other words of eight or more letters "if substantial space is thereby saved and the
result is unambiguous." Bluebook Rule 10.2.2. On the other hand, in citing cases in text,
abbreviate only widely known acronyms and the following words: "&," "Ass'n," "Bros.,"
"Co.," "Corp.," "Inc.," "Ltd.," and "No." Bluebook Rule 10.2.1(c).

Burlington & Summit Apartments v. Manolato, 233 Iowa 15, 18, 7 N.W.2d 26, 28 (1943). –Page Citation.

In all other documents:

Burlington & Summit Apartments v. Manolato, 7 N.W.2d 26 (Iowa 1943). –Case Citation.

Burlington & Summit Apartments v. Manolato, 7 N.W.2d 26, 28 (Iowa 1943). –Page Citation.

–After 261 Iowa 1395 (1968), cite as follows:

In all documents:

Rokusek v. Jensen, 548 N.W.2d 570 (Iowa 1996). –Case Citation.

Rokusek v. Jensen, 548 N.W.2d 570, 573 (Iowa 1996). –Page Citation.

Iowa Session Laws
See Acts and Joint Resolutions of the State of Iowa and Iowa Legislative Service.

Iran-United States Claims Tribunal Reports
Ab.: Iran-U.S. Cl. Trib. Rep.

Ex.: Stewart v. Iran, 24 Iran-U.S. Cl. Trib. Rep. 116 (1991).

Irish Law Times Reports (1866-1980)
–Cite to Irish Reports (I.R.) if therein; otherwise, cite to I.L.T.R. See Bluebook Rule 20.3.1 and Table T.2.

Ab.: I.L.T.R.

Ex.: Elkinson v. Cassidy, [1975] 110 I.L.T.R. 27 (C.C.) (Ire.).

Irish Reports (1868 - date)
Ab.: I.R. See Bluebook Rule 20.3.1 and Table T.2.

Ex.: Roche v. Peilow, [1985] 1985 I.R. 232 (Ire.).

Israel Law Review
Ab.: Isr. L. Rev.

Ex.: Ruth Lapidoth, Jerusalem and the Peace Process, 28 Isr. L. Rev. 402 (1994). –Article Citation.

Ruth Lapidoth, Jerusalem and the Peace Process, 28 Isr. L. Rev. 402, 410-12 (1994). –Page Citation.

Israel Yearbook on Human Rights
Ab.: Isr. Y.B. on Hum. Rts.

Ex.: Tania Domb, The Gaza and Jericho Autonomy and Human Rights, 25 Isr. Y.B. on Hum. Rts. 21 (1995). –Article Citation.

Tania Domb, The Gaza and Jericho Autonomy and Human Rights, 25 Isr. Y.B. on Hum. Rts. 21, 23-24 (1995). –Page Citation.

In law review footnotes, the titles of books and the names of cases, except for procedural phrases, are not underlined. See Bluebook Rule 2.1(a). Further, the following are in large and small capitals: codes, restatements, standards, constitutions, periodicals, authors of books, titles of books, the abbreviated names of codes, most legislative materials except for bills and resolutions, codified ordinances, model codes, court rules, and sentencing guidelines. Refer to The Bluebook.

Italian Yearbook of International Law, The

Ab.:   Ital. Y.B. Int'l L.

Ex.:   Salvatore Vitale, New Cooperation Treaty Between Italy and
        Argentina, 1987 Ital. Y.B. Int'l L. 163. –Article Citation.

        Salvatore Vitale, New Cooperation Treaty Between Italy and
        Argentina, 1987 Ital. Y.B. Int'l L. 163, 167-68. –Page Citation.

In citing cases in law review footnotes, abbreviate any word listed in Table T.6;
the names of "states, countries, and other geographical units" unless they are named parties;
and any other words of eight or more letters "if substantial space is thereby saved and the
result is unambiguous." Bluebook Rule 10.2.2. On the other hand, in citing cases in text,
abbreviate only widely known acronyms and the following words: "&," "Ass'n," "Bros.,"
"Co.," "Corp.," "Inc.," "Ltd.," and "No." Bluebook Rule 10.2.1(c).

J

John Marshall Law Review, The
Ab.:   J. Marshall L. Rev.
Ex.:   James M. Smith, <u>Legal Issues Confronting Families Affected by HIV</u>, 24 J. Marshall L. Rev. 543 (1991). –Article Citation.
          James M. Smith, <u>Legal Issues Confronting Families Affected by HIV</u>, 24 J. Marshall L. Rev. 543, 559-60 (1991). –Page Citation.

Jones on Evidence, by Clifford S. Fishman
          –Do not abbreviate the title.
Ex.:   2 Clifford S. Fishman, <u>Jones on Evidence</u> § 9.19 (7th ed. 1994). –Section Citation.
          2 Clifford S. Fishman, <u>Jones on Evidence</u> § 9.19, at 111 (7th ed. 1994). –Page Citation.
          2 Clifford S. Fishman, <u>Jones on Evidence</u> § 9.19, at 111 n.80 (7th ed. 1994). –Footnote Citation.
          2 Clifford S. Fishman, <u>Jones on Evidence</u> § 9.19 (7th ed. Supp. 1995). –Citation to Supplement Section.

Journal of Accountancy
Ab.:   J. Acct.
Ex.:   Paul Caster, <u>The Role of Confirmations as Audit Evidence</u>, J. Acct., Feb. 1992, at 73. –Article Citation.
          Paul Caster, <u>The Role of Confirmations as Audit Evidence</u>, J. Acct., Feb. 1992, at 73, 75-76. –Page Citation.

Journal of African Law
Ab.:   J. Afr. L.
Ex.:   Bojosi Otlhogile, <u>Infanticide in Bechuanaland: A Footnote to Schapera</u>, 34 J. Afr. L. 159 (1990). –Article Citation.
          Bojosi Otlhogile, <u>Infanticide in Bechuanaland: A Footnote to Schapera</u>, 34 J. Afr. L. 159, 159-60 (1990). –Page Citation.

Journal of Agricultural Taxation & Law
Ab.:   J. Agric. Tax & L.
Ex.:   Gary L. Maydew, <u>Incorporating the Family Farm May Generally Be Done Tax-Free</u>, 14 J. Agric. Tax & L. 53 (1992). –Article Citation.

In law review footnotes, the titles of books and the names of cases, except for procedural phrases, are not underlined. <u>See</u> Bluebook Rule 2.1(a). Further, the following are in large and small capitals: codes, restatements, standards, constitutions, periodicals, authors of books, titles of books, the abbreviated names of codes, most legislative materials except for bills and resolutions, codified ordinances, model codes, court rules, and sentencing guidelines. Refer to <u>The Bluebook</u>.

Gary L. Maydew, <u>Incorporating the Family Farm May Generally Be Done Tax-Free</u>, 14 J. Agric. Tax & L. 53, 59-60 (1992). –Page Citation.

Journal of Air Law and Commerce
Ab.: J. Air L. & Com.

Ex.: Alan B. Rich, <u>Current Issues in Removal Jurisdiction</u>, 57 J. Air L. & Com. 395 (1991). –Article Citation.

Alan B. Rich, <u>Current Issues in Removal Jurisdiction</u>, 57 J. Air L. & Com. 395, 419-20 (1991). –Page Citation.

Journal of Arts Management and Law
Ab.: J. Arts Mgmt. & L.

Ex.: Harry H. Chartrand, <u>Context and Continuity: Philistines, Pharisees and Art in English Culture</u>, 21 J. Arts Mgmt. & L. 141 (1991). –Article Citation.

Harry H. Chartrand, <u>Context and Continuity: Philistines, Pharisees and Art in English Culture</u>, 21 J. Arts Mgmt. & L. 141, 149-50 (1991). –Page Citation.

Journal of Broadcasting & Electronic Media
Ab.: J. Broadcasting & Electronic Media

Ex.: Donald R. Browne, <u>Local Radio in Switzerland: The Limits of Localism</u>, 35 J. Broadcasting & Electronic Media 449 (1991). –Article Citation.

Donald R. Browne, <u>Local Radio in Switzerland: The Limits of Localism</u>, 35 J. Broadcasting & Electronic Media 449, 459-60 (1991). –Page Citation.

Journal of Business Law, The
Ab.: J. Bus. L.

Ex.: M. G. Bridge, <u>Form, Substance and Innovation in Personal Property Security Law</u>, 36 J. Bus. L. 1 (1992). –Article Citation.

M. G. Bridge, <u>Form, Substance and Innovation in Personal Property Security Law</u>, 36 J. Bus. L. 1, 19-20 (1992). –Page Citation.

Journal of Chinese Law
Ab.: J. Chinese L.

Ex.: Lester Ross, <u>Force Majeure and Related Doctrines of Excuse in Contract Law of the People's Republic of China</u>, 5 J. Chinese L. 1 (1991). –Article Citation.

Lester Ross, <u>Force Majeure and Related Doctrines of Excuse in Contract Law of the People's Republic of China</u>, 5 J. Chinese L. 1, 49-50 (1991). –Page Citation.

In citing cases in law review footnotes, abbreviate any word listed in Table T.6; the names of "states, countries, and other geographical units" unless they are named parties; and any other words of eight or more letters "if <u>substantial</u> space is thereby saved and the result is unambiguous." <u>Bluebook</u> Rule 10.2.2. On the other hand, in citing cases in text, abbreviate only widely known acronyms and the following words: "&," "Ass'n," "Bros.," "Co.," "Corp.," "Inc.," "Ltd.," and "No." <u>Bluebook</u> Rule 10.2.1(c).

Journal of Church and State
Ab.:   J. Church & St.
Ex.:   Walter Sawatsky, Truth Telling in Eastern Europe: The Liberation and the Burden, 33 J. Church & St. 701 (1991). –Article Citation.

Walter Sawatsky, Truth Telling in Eastern Europe: The Liberation and the Burden, 33 J. Church & St. 701, 715-16 (1991). –Page Citation.

Journal of Collective Negotiations in the Public Sector
Ab.:   J. Collective Negot. Pub. Sector
Ex.:   Clete Bulach, The Collective Bargaining Potpourri: Is There a Right Way?, 20 J. Collective Negot. Pub. Sector 281 (1991). –Article Citation.

Clete Bulach, The Collective Bargaining Potpourri: Is There a Right Way?, 20 J. Collective Negot. Pub. Sector 281, 289-90 (1991). –Page Citation.

Journal of College and University Law, The
Ab.:   J.C. & U.L.
Ex.:   Andrew H. Baida, Not All Minority Scholarships Are Created Equal: Why Some May Be More Constitutional Than Others, 18 J.C. & U.L. 333 (1992). –Article Citation.

Andrew H. Baida, Not All Minority Scholarships Are Created Equal: Why Some May Be More Constitutional Than Others, 18 J.C. & U.L. 333, 349-50 (1992). –Page Citation.

Journal of Common Market Studies
Ab.:   J. Common Mkt. Stud.
Ex.:   Alfred Tovias, EC-Eastern Europe: A Case Study of Hungary, 29 J. Common Mkt. Stud. 291 (1991). –Article Citation.

Alfred Tovias, EC-Eastern Europe: A Case Study of Hungary, 29 J. Common Mkt. Stud. 291, 298-99 (1991). –Page Citation.

Journal of Conflict Resolution, The
Ab.:   J. Conflict Resol.
Ex.:   Chae-han Kim, Third-Party Participation in Wars, 35 J. Conflict Resol. 659 (1991). –Article Citation.

Chae-han Kim, Third-Party Participation in Wars, 35 J. Conflict Resol. 659, 669-70 (1991). –Page Citation.

Journal of Consumer Affairs, The
Ab.:   J. Consumer Aff.

In law review footnotes, the titles of books and the names of cases, except for procedural phrases, are not underlined. See Bluebook Rule 2.1(a). Further, the following are in large and small capitals: codes, restatements, standards, constitutions, periodicals, authors of books, titles of books, the abbreviated names of codes, most legislative materials except for bills and resolutions, codified ordinances, model codes, court rules, and sentencing guidelines. Refer to The Bluebook.

Ex.:   James D. Reschovsky, <u>The Emergency Food Relief System: An Empirical Study</u>, 25 J. Consumer Aff. 258 (1991). –Article Citation.

James D. Reschovsky, <u>The Emergency Food Relief System: An Empirical Study</u>, 25 J. Consumer Aff. 258, 269-70 (1991). –Page Citation.

Journal of Contemporary Criminal Justice
Ab.:   J. Contemp. Crim. Just.

Ex.:   Charles H. Rogovin & Frederick T. Martens, <u>The Evil Men Do</u>, 8 J. Contemp. Crim. Just. 62 (1992). –Article Citation.

Charles H. Rogovin & Frederick T. Martens, <u>The Evil Men Do</u>, 8 J. Contemp. Crim. Just. 62, 74 (1992). –Page Citation.

Journal of Contemporary Health Law and Policy
Ab.:   J. Contemp. Health L. & Pol'y

Ex.:   Charles F. Rice, <u>The Coming Retreat from Roe v. Wade</u>, J. Contemp. Health L. & Pol'y, Spring 1988, at 1. –Article Citation.

Charles F. Rice, <u>The Coming Retreat from Roe v. Wade</u>, J. Contemp. Health L. & Pol'y, Spring 1988, at 1, 19-20. –Page Citation.

Journal of Contemporary Law
Ab.:   J. Contemp. L.

Ex.:   Edwin B. Firmage, <u>The War Power of Congress and Revision of the War Powers Resolution</u>, 17 J. Contemp. L. 237 (1991). –Article Citation.

Edwin B. Firmage, <u>The War Power of Congress and Revision of the War Powers Resolution</u>, 17 J. Contemp. L. 237, 249-50 (1991). –Page Citation.

Journal of Contemporary Legal Issues, The
Ab.:   J. Contemp. Legal Issues

Ex.:   David M. Star, <u>The Private-Facts Torts in California and Beyond: Is There Life After Florida Star?</u>, 3 J. Contemp. Legal Issues 199 (1989-1990). –Article Citation.

David M. Star, <u>The Private-Facts Torts in California and Beyond: Is There Life After Florida Star?</u>, 3 J. Contemp. Legal Issues 199, 204-05 (1989-1990). –Page Citation.

Journal of Corporate Taxation, The
Ab.:   J. Corp. Tax'n

Ex.:   Gilbert D. Bloom, <u>Private Letter Rulings</u>, 19 J. Corp. Tax'n 160 (1992). –Article Citation.

Gilbert D. Bloom, <u>Private Letter Rulings</u>, 19 J. Corp. Tax'n 160, 161-62 (1992). –Page Citation.

In citing cases in law review footnotes, abbreviate any word listed in Table T.6; the names of "states, countries, and other geographical units" unless they are named parties; and any other words of eight or more letters "if <u>substantial</u> space is thereby saved and the result is unambiguous." <u>Bluebook</u> Rule 10.2.2. On the other hand, in citing cases in text, abbreviate only widely known acronyms and the following words: "&," "Ass'n," "Bros.," "Co.," "Corp.," "Inc.," "Ltd.," and "No." <u>Bluebook</u> Rule 10.2.1(c).

Journal of Corporation Law, The
Ab.:   J. Corp. L.
Ex.:   Martin Riger, <u>The Trust Indenture as Bargained Contract: The Persistence of Myth</u>, 16 J. Corp. L. 211 (1991). –Article Citation.
Martin Riger, <u>The Trust Indenture as Bargained Contract: The Persistence of Myth</u>, 16 J. Corp. L. 211, 229-30 (1991). –Page Citation.

Journal of Criminal Law
Ab.:   J. Crim. L.
Ex.:   Jennifer A. James, <u>Cut-throat Defenses and Character Evidence</u>, 55 J. Crim. L. 103 (1991). –Article Citation.
Jennifer A. James, <u>Cut-throat Defenses and Character Evidence</u>, 55 J. Crim. L. 103, 115-16 (1991). –Page Citation.

Journal of Criminal Law and Criminology, The
Ab.:   J. Crim. L. & Criminology
Ex.:   Ellen H. Steury, <u>Specifying "Criminalization" of the Mentally Disordered Misdemeanant</u>, 82 J. Crim. L. & Criminology 334 (1991). –Article Citation.
Ellen H. Steury, <u>Specifying "Criminalization" of the Mentally Disordered Misdemeanant</u>, 82 J. Crim. L. & Criminology 334, 339-42 (1991). –Page Citation.

Journal of Dispute Resolution
Ab.:   J. Disp. Resol.
Ex.:   Jeffrey W. Stempel, <u>Reconsidering the Employment Contract Exclusion in Section 1 of the Federal Arbitration Act: Correcting the Judiciary's Failure of Statutory Vision</u>, 1991 J. Disp. Resol. 259 (1991). –Article Citation.
Jeffrey W. Stempel, <u>Reconsidering the Employment Contract Exclusion in Section 1 of the Federal Arbitration Act: Correcting the Judiciary's Failure of Statutory Vision</u>, 1991 J. Disp. Resol. 259, 270-71 (1991). –Page Citation.

Journal of Energy Law and Policy
Ab.:   J. Energy L. & Pol'y
Ex.:   Adrian J. Bradbrook, <u>The Role of the Courts in Advancing the Use of Solar Energy</u>, 9 J. Energy L. & Pol'y 135 (1989). –Article Citation.
Adrian J. Bradbrook, <u>The Role of the Courts in Advancing the Use of Solar Energy</u>, 9 J. Energy L. & Pol'y 135, 137 (1989). –Page Citation.

Journal of Energy, Natural Resources and Environmental Law
Ab.:   J. Energy Nat. Resources & Envtl. L.

In law review footnotes, the titles of books and the names of cases, except for procedural phrases, are not underlined. <u>See</u> Bluebook Rule 2.1(a). Further, the following are in large and small capitals: codes, restatements, standards, constitutions, periodicals, authors of books, titles of books, the abbreviated names of codes, most legislative materials except for bills and resolutions, codified ordinances, model codes, court rules, and sentencing guidelines. Refer to <u>The Bluebook</u>.

Ex.: Phillip W. Lear, <u>Accretion, Reliction, Erosion, and Avulsion: A Survey of Riparian and Littoral Title Problems</u>, 11 J. Energy Nat. Resources & Envtl. L. 265 (1991). –Article Citation.

Phillip W. Lear, <u>Accretion, Reliction, Erosion, and Avulsion: A Survey of Riparian and Littoral Title Problems</u>, 11 J. Energy Nat. Resources & Envtl. L. 265, 269-73 (1991). –Page Citation.

Journal of Environmental Law and Litigation
Ab.: J. Envtl. L. & Litig.

Ex.: Brian J. Preston, <u>Public Enforcement of Environmental Laws in Australia</u>, 6 J. Envtl. L. & Litig. 39 (1991). –Article Citation.

Brian J. Preston, <u>Public Enforcement of Environmental Laws in Australia</u>, 6 J. Envtl. L. & Litig. 39, 42-46 (1991). –Page Citation.

Journal of Family Law
Ab.: J. Fam. L.

Ex.: Elizabeth L. Gibson, <u>Artificial Insemination by Donor: Information, Communication and Regulation</u>, 30 J. Fam. L. 1 (1991-92). –Article Citation.

Elizabeth L. Gibson, <u>Artificial Insemination by Donor: Information, Communication and Regulation</u>, 30 J. Fam. L. 1, 20-25 (1991-92). –Page Citation.

Journal of Forensic Sciences
Ab.: J. Forensic Sci.

Ex.: Rena A. Merrill & Edward G. Bartick, <u>Analysis of Ballpoint Pen Inks by Diffuse Reflectance Infrared Spectometry</u>, 37 J. Forensic Sci. 528 (1992). –Article Citation.

Rena A. Merrill & Edward G. Bartick, <u>Analysis of Ballpoint Pen Inks by Diffuse Reflectance Infrared Spectometry</u>, 37 J. Forensic Sci. 528, 536-38 (1992). –Page Citation.

Journal of Health and Hospital Law
Ab.: J. Health & Hosp. L.

Ex.: Richard D. Raskin, <u>Laboratory Testing Under the Microscope: The Clinical Laboratory Improvement Amendments of 1988</u>, 25 J. Health & Hosp. L. 33 (1992). –Article Citation.

Richard D. Raskin, <u>Laboratory Testing Under the Microscope: The Clinical Laboratory Improvement Amendments of 1988</u>, 25 J. Health & Hosp. L. 33, 34-35 (1992). –Page Citation.

Journal of Health, Politics, Policy and Law
Ab.: J. Health Pol. Pol'y & L.

Ex.: Harvey M. Sapolsky, <u>Empire and the Business of Health Insurance</u>, 16 J. Health Pol. Pol'y & L. 747 (1991). –Article Citation.

In citing cases in law review footnotes, abbreviate any word listed in Table T.6; the names of "states, countries, and other geographical units" unless they are named parties; and any other words of eight or more letters "if <u>substantial</u> space is thereby saved and the result is unambiguous." <u>Bluebook</u> Rule 10.2.2. On the other hand, in citing cases in text, abbreviate only widely known acronyms and the following words: "&," "Ass'n," "Bros.," "Co.," "Corp.," "Inc.," "Ltd.," and "No." <u>Bluebook</u> Rule 10.2.1(c).

Harvey M. Sapolsky, <u>Empire and the Business of Health Insurance</u>, 16 J. Health Pol. Pol'y & L. 747, 757-58 (1991). –Page Citation.

Journal of Intellectual Property
Ab.:   J. Intell. Prop.

Ex.:   Alyson Lewis, <u>Playing Around with Barbie: Expanding Fair Use for Cultural Icons</u>, 1 J. Intell. Prop. 61 (1999). –Article Citation.

Alyson Lewis, <u>Playing Around with Barbie: Expanding Fair Use for Cultural Icons</u>, 1 J. Intell. Prop. 61, 75 (1999). –Page Citation.

Journal of International Arbitration
Ab.:   J. Int'l Arb.

Ex.:   Alexander C. Hoagland, <u>Modification of Mexican Arbitration Law</u>, J. Int'l Arb., Mar. 1990, at 91. –Article Citation.

Alexander C. Hoagland, <u>Modification of Mexican Arbitration Law</u>, J. Int'l Arb., Mar. 1990, at 91, 99-100. –Page Citation.

Journal of International Law and Practice
Ab.:   J. Int'l L. & Prac.

Ex.:   Alison Matsumoto, Comment, <u>A Place of Considerations of Culture in the American Criminal Justice System: Japanese Law and the Kimura Case</u>, 4 J. Int'l L. & Prac. 507 (1995). –Article Citation.

Alison Matsumoto, Comment, <u>A Place of Considerations of Culture in the American Criminal Justice System: Japanese Law and the Kimura Case</u>, 4 J. Int'l L. & Prac. 507, 511 (1995). –Page Citation.

Journal of International Money and Finance
Ab.:   J. Int'l Money & Fin.

Ex.:   Janet Ceglowski, <u>Intertemporal Substitution in Import Demand</u>, 10 J. Int'l Money & Fin. 118 (1991). –Article Citation.

Janet Ceglowski, <u>Intertemporal Substitution in Import Demand</u>, 10 J. Int'l Money & Fin. 118, 119-21 (1991). –Page Citation.

Journal of Juvenile Law
Ab.:   J. Juv. L.

Ex.:   Patricia A. Andreoni, <u>Juvenile Extradition: Denial of Due Process</u>, 1989 J. Juv. L. 193. –Article Citation.

Patricia A. Andreoni, <u>Juvenile Extradition: Denial of Due Process</u>, 1989 J. Juv. L. 193, 219-20. –Page Citation.

Journal of Labor Research
Ab.:   J. Lab. Res.

In law review footnotes, the titles of books and the names of cases, except for procedural phrases, are not underlined. <u>See</u> Bluebook Rule 2.1(a). Further, the following are in large and small capitals: codes, restatements, standards, constitutions, periodicals, authors of books, titles of books, the abbreviated names of codes, most legislative materials except for bills and resolutions, codified ordinances, model codes, court rules, and sentencing guidelines. Refer to <u>The Bluebook</u>.

Ex.:   Javed Ashraf, <u>Union Wage Premiums in an Instrumental Variables Framework</u>, 13 J. Lab. Res. 231 (1992). –Article Citation.

Javed Ashraf, <u>Union Wage Premiums in an Instrumental Variables Framework</u>, 13 J. Lab. Res. 231, 232-35 (1992). –Page Citation.

Journal of Land Use and Environmental Law
Ab.:   J. Land Use & Envtl. L.

Ex.:   William R. Mitchell, <u>CERCLA: The Problem of Lender Liability</u>, 7 J. Land Use & Envtl. L. 101 (1991). –Article Citation.

William R. Mitchell, <u>CERCLA: The Problem of Lender Liability</u>, 7 J. Land Use & Envtl. L. 101, 109-10 (1991). –Page Citation.

Journal of Law and Commerce, The
Ab.:   J.L. & Com.

Ex.:   Mark F. Nowak, <u>Occupational Noise Exposure of Railroad Workers – Which Regulation Applies?</u>, 11 J.L. & Com. 39 (1991). –Article Citation.

Mark F. Nowak, <u>Occupational Noise Exposure of Railroad Workers – Which Regulation Applies?</u>, 11 J.L. & Com. 39, 44-45 (1991). –Page Citation.

Journal of Law & Economics, The
Ab.:   J.L. & Econ.

Ex.:   Pauline M. Ippolito, <u>Resale Price Maintenance: Empirical Evidence from Litigation</u>, 34 J.L. & Econ. 263 (1991). –Article Citation.

Pauline M. Ippolito, <u>Resale Price Maintenance: Empirical Evidence from Litigation</u>, 34 J.L. & Econ. 263, 273-78 (1991). –Page Citation.

Journal of Law and Education
Ab.:   J.L. & Educ.

Ex.:   Gretchen Martin, <u>HIV/AIDS and Adolescents: Implications for School Policies</u>, 20 J.L. & Econ. 325 (1991). –Article Citation.

Gretchen Martin, <u>HIV/AIDS and Adolescents: Implications for School Policies</u>, 20 J.L. & Econ. 325, 333-34 (1991). –Page Citation.

Journal of Law and Health
Ab.:   J.L. & Health

Ex.:   James J. Nocon, <u>Physicians and Maternal - Fetal Conflicts: Duties, Rights and Responsibilities</u>, 5 J.L. & Health 1 (1990-91). –Article Citation.

James J. Nocon, <u>Physicians and Maternal - Fetal Conflicts: Duties, Rights and Responsibilities</u>, 5 J.L. & Health 1, 29-32 (1990-91). –Page Citation.

In citing cases in law review footnotes, abbreviate any word listed in Table T.6; the names of "states, countries, and other geographical units" unless they are named parties; and any other words of eight or more letters "if <u>substantial</u> space is thereby saved and the result is unambiguous." <u>Bluebook</u> Rule 10.2.2. On the other hand, in citing cases in text, abbreviate only widely known acronyms and the following words: "&," "Ass'n," "Bros.," "Co.," "Corp.," "Inc.," "Ltd.," and "No." <u>Bluebook</u> Rule 10.2.1(c).

Journal of Law and Policy
Ab.:   J.L. & Pol'y
Ex.:   George Smith & Gloria Dabiri, The Judicial Role in the Treatment of Juvenile Delinquents, 3 J.L. & Pol'y 347 (1995). –Article Citation.

George Smith & Gloria Dabiri, The Judicial Role in the Treatment of Juvenile Delinquents, 3 J.L. & Pol'y 347, 350 (1995). –Page Citation.

Journal of Law and Politics
Ab.:   J.L. & Pol.
Ex.:   Shiela B. Kamerman, Doing Better by Children: Focus on Families, 8 J.L. & Pol. 75 (1990). –Article Citation.

Shiela B. Kamerman, Doing Better by Children: Focus on Families, 8 J.L. & Pol. 75, 79-80 (1990). –Page Citation.

Journal of Law and Society
Ab.:   J.L. & Soc'y
Ex.:   Carol Smart, The Legal and Moral Ordering of Child Custody, 18 J.L. & Soc'y 485 (1991). –Article Citation.

Carol Smart, The Legal and Moral Ordering of Child Custody, 18 J.L. & Soc'y 485, 491-93 (1991). –Page Citation.

Journal of Law and Technology
Ab.:   J.L. & Tech.
Ex.:   S. Neil Hosenball, Financing Space Ventures, J.L. & Tech., Winter 1989, at 15. –Article Citation.

S. Neil Hosenball, Financing Space Ventures, J.L. & Tech., Winter 1989, at 15, 16. –Page Citation.

Journal of Law, Economics, and Organization, The
Ab.:   J. L. Econ. & Org.
Ex.:   Denis C. Mueller, Constitutional Rights, 7 J.L. Econ. & Org. 313 (1991). –Article Citation.

Denis C. Mueller, Constitutional Rights, 7 J.L. Econ. & Org. 313, 329-31 (1991). –Page Citation.

Journal of Legal Education
Ab.:   J. Legal Educ.
Ex.:   Judith S. Kaye, One Judge's View of Academic Law Review Writing, 1989 J. Legal Educ. 313. –Article Citation.

Judith S. Kaye, One Judge's View of Academic Law Review Writing, 1989 J. Legal Educ. 313, 315. –Page Citation.

Journal of Legal History
Ab.:   J. Legal Hist.
Ex.:   Peter Goodrich, Eating Law: Commons, Common Land, Common Law, 12 J. Legal Hist. 246 (1991). –Article Citation.

In law review footnotes, the titles of books and the names of cases, except for procedural phrases, are not underlined. See Bluebook Rule 2.1(a). Further, the following are in large and small capitals: codes, restatements, standards, constitutions, periodicals, authors of books, titles of books, the abbreviated names of codes, most legislative materials except for bills and resolutions, codified ordinances, model codes, court rules, and sentencing guidelines. Refer to The Bluebook.

Peter Goodrich, <u>Eating Law: Commons, Common Land, Common Law</u>, 12 J. Legal Hist. 246, 249-51 (1991). –Page Citation.

Journal of Legal Pluralism
Ab.:   J. Legal Pluralism
Ex.:   Koti E. Agorsah, <u>Women in African Traditional Politics</u>, 1990-91 J. Legal Pluralism 77. –Article Citation.
Koti E. Agorsah, <u>Women in African Traditional Politics</u>, 1990-91 J. Legal Pluralism 77, 79-80. –Page Citation.

Journal of Legal Studies, The
Ab.:   J. Legal Stud.
Ex.:   Lloyd Cohen, <u>Holdouts and Free Rides</u>, 20 J. Legal Stud. 351 (1991). –Article Citation.
Lloyd Cohen, <u>Holdouts and Free Rides</u>, 20 J. Legal Stud. 351, 359-60 (1991). –Page Citation.

Journal of Legislation
Ab.:   J. Legis.
Ex.:   W.H. Moore, <u>U.S. Energy Prospects: 1990's and Beyond</u>, 17 J. Legis. 193 (1991). –Article Citation.
W.H. Moore, <u>U.S. Energy Prospects: 1990's and Beyond</u>, 17 J. Legis. 193, 197-98 (1991). –Page Citation.

Journal of Maritime Law and Commerce
Ab.:   J. Mar. L. & Com.
Ex.:   David J. Sharpe, <u>Removal to Admiralty Revisited</u>, 22 J. Mar. L. & Com. 485 (1991). –Article Citation.
David J. Sharpe, <u>Removal to Admiralty Revisited</u>, 22 J. Mar. L. & Com. 485, 493-95 (1991). –Page Citation.

Journal of Medicine and Philosophy
Ab.:   J. Med. & Phil.
Ex.:   E. Haavi Morreim, <u>Access Without Excess</u>, 17 J. Med. & Phil. 1 (1992). –Article Citation.
E. Haavi Morreim, <u>Access Without Excess</u>, 17 J. Med. & Phil. 1, 6-7 (1992). –Page Citation.

Journal of Mineral Law and Policy
Ab.:   J. Min. L. & Pol'y
Ex.:   John S. Palmore, <u>Kentucky's New Nuisance Statute</u>, 7 J. Min. L. & Pol'y 1 (1991-1992). –Article Citation.
John S. Palmore, <u>Kentucky's New Nuisance Statute</u>, 7 J. Min. L. & Pol'y 1, 9-10 (1991-1992). –Page Citation.

In citing cases in law review footnotes, abbreviate any word listed in Table T.6; the names of "states, countries, and other geographical units" unless they are named parties; and any other words of eight or more letters "if substantial space is thereby saved and the result is unambiguous." Bluebook Rule 10.2.2. On the other hand, in citing cases in text, abbreviate only widely known acronyms and the following words: "&," "Ass'n," "Bros.," "Co.," "Corp.," "Inc.," "Ltd.," and "No." Bluebook Rule 10.2.1(c).

Journal of Pension Planning & Compliance
Ab.:   J. Pension Plan. & Compliance
Ex.:   Nicholas P. Damico, <u>Rollovers for AU: Simplification or Riff-OH?</u>, 18 J. Pension Plan. & Compliance 42 (1992). –Article Citation.

Nicholas P. Damico, <u>Rollovers for AU: Simplification or Riff-OH?</u>, 18 J. Pension Plan. & Compliance 42, 49-51 (1992). –Page Citation.

Journal of Police Science and Administration
Ab.:   J. Police Sci. & Admin.
Ex.:   Harvey L. McMurray, <u>Attitudes of Assaulted Police Officers and Their Policy Implications</u>, 17 J. Police Sci. & Admin. 44 (1990). –Article Citation.

Harvey L. McMurray, <u>Attitudes of Assaulted Police Officers and Their Policy Implications</u>, 17 J. Police Sci. & Admin. 44, 46-48 (1990). –Page Citation.

Journal of Products Liability
Ab.:   J. Prod. Liab.
Ex.:   William J. Warfel, <u>State-of-the-Art Evidence in Long-Tall Product Liability Litigation: The Transformation of the Tort System into a Compensation System</u>, 13 J. Prod. Liab. 183 (1991). –Article Citation.

William J. Warfel, <u>State-of-the-Art Evidence in Long-Tall Product Liability Litigation: The Transformation of the Tort System into a Compensation System</u>, 13 J. Prod. Liab. 183, 189-94 (1991). –Page Citation.

Journal of Psychiatry & Law
Ab.:   J. Psychiatry & L.
Ex.:   Sana Loue, <u>Homo-Sexuality and Immigration Law: A Reexamination</u>, 18 J. Psychiatry & L. 109 (1990). –Article Citation.

Sana Loue, <u>Homo-Sexuality and Immigration Law: A Reexamination</u>, 18 J. Psychiatry & L. 109, 110-19 (1990). –Page Citation.

Journal of Research in Crime and Delinquency
Ab.:   J. Res. Crime & Delinq.
Ex.:   Julie Horney & Tneke Haen-Marshall, <u>An Experimental Comparison of Two Self-Report Methods of Measuring Lambda</u>, 29 J. Res. Crime & Delinq. 102 (1992). –Article Citation.

Julie Horney & Tneke Haen-Marshall, <u>An Experimental Comparison of Two Self-Report Methods of Measuring Lambda</u>, 29 J. Res. Crime & Delinq. 102, 109-10 (1992). –Page Citation.

Journal of Space Law
Ab.:   J. Space L.

In law review footnotes, the titles of books and the names of cases, except for procedural phrases, are not underlined. <u>See</u> Bluebook Rule 2.1(a). Further, the following are in large and small capitals: codes, restatements, standards, constitutions, periodicals, authors of books, titles of books, the abbreviated names of codes, most legislative materials except for bills and resolutions, codified ordinances, model codes, court rules, and sentencing guidelines. Refer to <u>The Bluebook</u>.

Ex.:   Carl Q. Christol, <u>The Moon and Mars Missions: Can International Law Meet the Challenge?</u>, 19 J. Space L. 123 (1991). –Article Citation.

Carl Q. Christol, <u>The Moon and Mars Missions: Can International Law Meet the Challenge?</u>, 19 J. Space L. 123, 123 (1991). –Page Citation.

Journal of State Government, The
Ab.:   J. St. Gov't

Ex.:   William A. O'Neil, <u>Meeting the Challenge of Leadership</u>, 63 J. St. Gov't 3 (1990). –Article Citation.

William A. O'Neil, <u>Meeting the Challenge of Leadership</u>, 63 J. St. Gov't 3, 4 (1990). –Page Citation.

Journal of State Taxation
Ab.:   J. St. Tax'n

Ex.:   Jean Yingst-Sickles, <u>Corporate State Taxation of Federal Safe Harbour Leases</u>, J. St. Tax'n, Winter 1991, at 17. –Article Citation.

Jean Yingst-Sickles, <u>Corporate State Taxation of Federal Safe Harbour Leases</u>, J. St. Tax'n, Winter 1991, at 17, 20. –Page Citation.

Journal of Taxation, The
Ab.:   J. Tax'n

Ex.:   Jasper L. Cummings, Jr., & Samuel P. Staff, <u>The Impact of New S Corporation Revisions</u>, 85 J. Tax'n 197 (1996). –Article Citation.

Jasper L. Cummings, Jr., & Samuel P. Staff, <u>The Impact of New S Corporation Revisions</u>, 85 J. Tax'n 197, 198-99 (1996). –Page Citation.

Journal of the American Academy of Matrimonial Lawyers
Ab.:   J. Am. Acad. Matrim. Law.

Ex.:   Reba G. Rasor, <u>The Contingent Fee and Domestic Law</u>, 7 J. Am. Acad. Matrim. Law 43 (1991). –Article Citation.

Reba G. Rasor, <u>The Contingent Fee and Domestic Law</u>, 7 J. Am. Acad. Matrim. Law 43, 59-62 (1991).

Journal of the American Board of Trial Advocates
Ab.:   J. Am. Board Trial Advocates

Ex.:   Keith Evans, <u>The Jury and the Democratic Impulse</u>, 1 J. Am. Board Trial Advocates 87 (1991). –Article Citation.

Keith Evans, <u>The Jury and the Democratic Impulse</u>, 1 J. Am. Board Trial Advocates 87, 89-94 (1991). –Page Citation.

Journal of the American Medical Association
Ab.:   JAMA

In citing cases in law review footnotes, abbreviate any word listed in Table T.6; the names of "states, countries, and other geographical units" unless they are named parties; and any other words of eight or more letters "if <u>substantial</u> space is thereby saved and the result is unambiguous." <u>Bluebook</u> Rule 10.2.2. On the other hand, in citing cases in text, abbreviate only widely known acronyms and the following words: "&," "Ass'n," "Bros.," "Co.," "Corp.," "Inc.," "Ltd.," and "No." <u>Bluebook</u> Rule 10.2.1(c).

Ex.:   Warren S. Browner, et al., <u>In-Hospital and Long-term Mortality in Male Veterans Following Noncardiac Surgery</u>, 268 JAMA 228 (1992). –Article Citation.

Warren S. Browner, et al., <u>In-Hospital and Long-term Mortality in Male Veterans Following Noncardiac Surgery</u>, 268 JAMA 228, 231 (1992). –Page Citation.

Journal of the American Society of CLU & ChFC
Ab.:   J. Am. Soc'y CLU & ChFC

Ex.:   Robert W. Cooper & Garry L. Frank, <u>Business Ethics in the Insurance Industry</u>, J. Am. Soc'y CLU & ChFC, May 1991, at 74. –Article Citation.

Robert W. Cooper & Garry L. Frank, <u>Business Ethics in the Insurance Industry</u>, J. Am. Soc'y CLU & ChFC, May 1991, at 74, 76-77. –Page Citation.

Journal of the Copyright Society of the U.S.A.
Ab.:   J. Copyright Soc'y U.S.A.

Ex.:   David B. Wolf, <u>Is There Any Copyright Protection for Maps After Feist?</u>, 39 J. Copyright Soc'y U.S.A. 224 (1992). –Article Citation.

David B. Wolf, <u>Is There Any Copyright Protection for Maps After Feist?</u>, 39 J. Copyright Soc'y U.S.A. 224, 229-30 (1992). –Page Citation.

Journal of the Indian Law Institute
Ab.:   J. Indian L. Inst.

Ex.:   Chhatrapati Singh, <u>The Concept of Time in Law: Basis of Laws of Limitation and Prescription</u>, 32 J. Indian L. Inst. 328 (1990). –Article Citation.

Chhatrapati Singh, <u>The Concept of Time in Law: Basis of Laws of Limitation and Prescription</u>, 32 J. Indian L. Inst. 328, 329 (1990). –Page Citation.

Journal of the Kansas Bar Association
Ab.:   J. Kan. B.A.

Ex.:   Paul B. Rusor, <u>Commercial Transacting Under the New Bankruptcy Act</u>, J. Kan. B.A., Fall 1979, at 199. –Article Citation.

Paul B. Rusor, <u>Commercial Transacting Under the New Bankruptcy Act</u>, J. Kan. B.A., Fall 1979, at 199, 200-01. –Page Citation.

Journal of the Legal Profession, The
Ab.:   J. Legal Prof.

In law review footnotes, the titles of books and the names of cases, except for procedural phrases, are not underlined. <u>See</u> <u>Bluebook</u> Rule 2.1(a). Further, the following are in large and small capitals: codes, restatements, standards, constitutions, periodicals, authors of books, titles of books, the abbreviated names of codes, most legislative materials except for bills and resolutions, codified ordinances, model codes, court rules, and sentencing guidelines. Refer to <u>The Bluebook</u>.

Ex.:   Glenn S. Kaplan, Chinese Walls: A New Approach, 15 J. Legal Prof.
          63 (1990). –Article Citation.

          Glenn S. Kaplan, Chinese Walls: A New Approach, 15 J. Legal Prof.
          63, 72-74 (1990). –Page Citation.

Journal of the Missouri Bar
Ab.:   J. Mo. B.
Ex.:   Timothy E. Gammon, When Are Acts of an Insured Expected or
          Intended?, 48 J. Mo. B. 115 (1992). –Article Citation.

          Timothy E. Gammon, When Are Acts of an Insured Expected or
          Intended?, 48 J. Mo. B. 115, 116 (1992). –Page Citation.

Journal of the Patent [and Trademark] Office Society
Ab.:   J. Pat. [& Trademark] Off. Soc'y
Ex.:   Jerome Rosenstook, Appeals Practice, 73 J. Pat. [& Trademark] Off.
          Soc'y 565 (1991). –Article Citation.

          Jerome Rosenstook, Appeals Practice, 73 J. Pat. [& Trademark] Off.
          Soc'y 565, 569-72 (1991). –Page Citation.

Journal of World Trade
Ab.:   J. World Trade
Ex.:   Steven M. Hoffer, May Exchange Rate Volatility Cause Dumping
          Injury?, J. World Trade, June 1992, at 61. –Article Citation.

          Steven M. Hoffer, May Exchange Rate Volatility Cause Dumping
          Injury?, J. World Trade, June 1992, at 61, 68-70. –Page Citation.

          –Formerly J. of World Trade Law (vol. 1 1967 - vol. 21 1987).

          –Nonconsecutively paginated from 1987-date.

Journal Officiel Des Communautés Européenes
Ab.:   J.O.; refer to Bluebook Table T.3 and Rule 21.8.2.
See Official Journal of the European Community.

Judge
Ab.:   J.

Judges
Ab.:   JJ.

Judicial Panel on Multidistrict Litigation
Ab.:   J.P.M.L.

Judicature
Ab.:   Do not abbreviate title.

In citing cases in law review footnotes, abbreviate any word listed in Table T.6;
the names of "states, countries, and other geographical units" unless they are named parties;
and any other words of eight or more letters "if substantial space is thereby saved and the
result is unambiguous." Bluebook Rule 10.2.2. On the other hand, in citing cases in text,
abbreviate only widely known acronyms and the following words: "&," "Ass'n," "Bros.,"
"Co.," "Corp.," "Inc.," "Ltd.," and "No." Bluebook Rule 10.2.1(c).

Ex.:   Nancy J. King, Jury Research and Reform: An Introduction,
         79 Judicature 214 (1996). –Article Citation.

         Nancy J. King, Jury Research and Reform: An Introduction,
         79 Judicature 214, 214 (1996). –Page Citation.

Juridical Review
Ab.:   Jurid. Rev.

Ex.:   Paul Robertshaw, Regional Jury Verdicts in Scotland, Jurid. Rev., Oct.
         1991, at 222 . –Article Citation.

         Paul Robertshaw, Regional Jury Verdicts in Scotland, Jurid. Rev., Oct.
         1991, at 222, 224. –Page Citation.

Jurimetrics: Journal of Law, Science and Technology
Ab.:   Jurimetrics J.

Ex.:   Evan L. Rosenfield, The Strict Products Liability Crisis and Beyond: Is
         There Hope for an AIDS Vaccine?, 31 Jurimetrics J. 187 (1991).
         –Article Citation.

         Evan L. Rosenfield, The Strict Products Liability Crisis and Beyond: Is
         There Hope for an AIDS Vaccine?, 31 Jurimetrics J. 187, 192 (1991).
         –Page Citation.

Jurisprudencia de la Suprema Corte (Mexico)
Ab.:   J.S.C.; See Bluebook Table T.2.

Jurisprudencia del Tribunal Supremo (Spain)
Ab.:   J.T.S.; See Bluebook Table T.2.

Jurist, The
Ab.:   Jurist

Ex.:   James A. Coriden, The Canonical Doctrine of Reception, 50 Jurist 58
         (1990). –Article Citation.

         James A. Coriden, The Canonical Doctrine of Reception, 50 Jurist 58,
         59-62 (1990). –Page Citation.

Justice
Ab.:   J.

Justice of the Peace Reports (England) (1837-date)
Ab.:   J.P.

Ex.:   Vandyk v. Oliver, 140 J.P. 180 (H.L. 1976) (Eng.). –Case Citation.

Justice System Journal, The
Ab.:   Just. Sys. J.

Ex.:   Mark A. Zaflarano, A Call to Leadership, 15/2 Just. Sys. J. 628 (1991).
         –Article Citation.

         Mark A. Zaflarano, A Call to Leadership, 15/2 Just. Sys. J. 628, 635-38

In law review footnotes, the titles of books and the names of cases, except for procedural
phrases, are not underlined. See Bluebook Rule 2.1(a). Further, the following are in large
and small capitals: codes, restatements, standards, constitutions, periodicals, authors of
books, titles of books, the abbreviated names of codes, most legislative materials except for
bills and resolutions, codified ordinances, model codes, court rules, and sentencing guidelines.
Refer to The Bluebook.

(1991). –Page Citation.

Justices
    Ab.:   J.J.

Juvenile Court
    Ab.:   Juv. Ct.

In citing cases in law review footnotes, abbreviate any word listed in Table T.6; the names of "states, countries, and other geographical units" unless they are named parties; and any other words of eight or more letters "if substantial space is thereby saved and the result is unambiguous." Bluebook Rule 10.2.2. On the other hand, in citing cases in text, abbreviate only widely known acronyms and the following words: "&," "Ass'n," "Bros.," "Co.," "Corp.," "Inc.," "Ltd.," and "No." Bluebook Rule 10.2.1(c).

K

Kansas Administrative Regulations
Ab.:   Kan. Admin. Regs. (year)
Ex.:   Kan. Admin. Regs. r. 91-8-26 (1999).

Kansas Bar Association Journal
Ab.:   Kan. B. Ass'n. J.

Kansas City Law Review
See UMKC Law Review

Kansas Constitution
Ab.:   Kan. Const. art , §   .
Ex.:   Kan. Const. art. 11, § 2. –"Cite constitutional provisions currently in force without date." Bluebook Rule 11.

Kan. Const. art. 10, § 3 (repealed 1972). –"If the cited provision has been repealed, either indicate parenthetically the fact and date of repeal or cite the repealing provision in full." Bluebook Rule 11.

Kan. Const. art. 12, § 2 (amended 1906). –"When citing a provision that has been subsequently amended, either indicate parenthetically the fact and date of amendment or cite the amending provision in full." Bluebook Rule 11.

Kansas Court of Appeals Reports
Ab.:   Kan. App., Kan. App. 2d

–Cite to P., P.2d, or P.3d if therein; otherwise, cite to Kan. App. or Kan. App. 2d

–Give parallel citations only in documents submitted to Kansas state courts. See Bluebook Rule 10.3.1 and Practitioners' Note P.3; see also Kan. Sup. Ct. R. 6.08, which requires a parallel citation.

In documents submitted to Kansas state courts, cite as follows:

Lonning v. Anderson, 22 Kan. App. 2d 474, 921 P.2d 813 (1996). –Case Citation.

Lonning v. Anderson, 22 Kan. App. 2d 474, 476, 921 P.2d 813, 815 (1996). –Page Citation.

In all other documents, cite as follows:

Lonning v. Anderson, 921 P.2d 813 (Kan. Ct. App. 1996). –Case Citation.

In law review footnotes, the titles of books and the names of cases, except for procedural phrases, are not underlined. See Bluebook Rule 2.1(a). Further, the following are in large and small capitals: codes, restatements, standards, constitutions, periodicals, authors of books, titles of books, the abbreviated names of codes, most legislative materials except for bills and resolutions, codified ordinances, model codes, court rules, and sentencing guidelines. Refer to The Bluebook.

Lonning v. Anderson, 921 P.2d 813, 815 (Kan. Ct. App. 1996).
–Page Citation.

Kansas Journal of Law and Public Policy
Ab.:   Kan. J.L. & Pub. Pol'y

Kansas Law Review
See University of Kansas Law Review

Kansas, Opinions of the Attorney General
See Opinions of the Attorney General of Kansas

Kansas Register
Ab.:   Kan. Reg.

Kansas Reports
Ab.:   Kan.
–Cite to P., P.2d, or P.3d if therein; otherwise, cite to Kan.
–Give parallel citations only in documents submitted to Kansas state
courts. See Bluebook Rule 10.3.1 and Practitioners' Note P.3; see
also Kan. Sup. Ct. R. 6.08, which requires a parallel citation.
In documents submitted to Kansas state courts, cite as follows:
Degollado v. Gallegos, 260 Kan. 169, 917 P.2d 823 (1996). –Case
Citation.
Degollado v. Gallegos, 260 Kan. 169, 170, 917 P.2d 823, 824
(1996). –Page Citation.
In all other documents, cite as follows:
Degollado v. Gallegos, 917 P.2d 823 (Kan. 1996). –Case Citation.
Degollado v. Gallegos, 917 P.2d 823, 824 (Kan. 1996). –Page
Citation.

Kansas Session Laws
See Session Laws of Kansas

Kansas Statutes Annotated
Ab.:   Kan. Stat. Ann. §   (year)
Ex.:   Kan. Stat. Ann. § 79-1444 (1997).
          Kan. Stat. Ann. § 80-1903 (Supp. 1999).

Kansas Statutes Annotated, Vernon's
See Vernon's Kansas Statutes Annotated

Keio Law Review
Ab.:   Keio L. Rev.
Ex.:   Brian J. Arnold, The New Canadian General Anti-tax Avoidance Rule,
          6 Keio L. Rev. 49 (1990). –Article Citation.
          Brian J. Arnold, The New Canadian General Anti-tax Avoidance Rule,
          6 Keio L. Rev. 49, 59-63 (1990). –Page Citation.

In citing cases in law review footnotes, abbreviate any word listed in Table T.6;
the names of "states, countries, and other geographical units" unless they are named parties;
and any other words of eight or more letters "if substantial space is thereby saved and the
result is unambiguous." Bluebook Rule 10.2.2. On the other hand, in citing cases in text,
abbreviate only widely known acronyms and the following words: "&," "Ass'n," "Bros.,"
"Co.," "Corp.," "Inc.," "Ltd.," and "No." Bluebook Rule 10.2.1(c).

Kentucky Acts
Ab.:   year Ky. Acts
Ex.:   Act of Apr. 11, 1996, ch. 369, 1996-2 Ky. Acts 1787. –Citation to an entire session law.

Act of Apr. 11, 1996, ch. 369, sec. 2, § 42.066 1996-2 Ky. Acts 1787, 1788. –Citation to a section of a session law amending a prior act.
–Identifying information may be added parenthetically according to Bluebook Rule 12.4(a).

Kentucky Administrative Register
Ab.:   Ky. Admin. Reg.

Kentucky Administrative Regulations Service
Ab.:   [title] Ky. Admin. Regs.   (year)
Ex.:   30 Ky. Admin. Regs. 3:030 (1994).

Kentucky Bench and Bar
Ab.:   Ky. Bench & B.
Ex.:   Gerald R. Toner & Ellen Cox Call, Three Cases that Shaped Kentucky's History, Ky. Bench & B., Winter 1992, at 11. –Article Citation.

Gerald R. Toner & Ellen Cox Call, Three Cases that Shaped Kentucky's History, Ky. Bench & B., Winter 1992, at 11, 12. –Page Citation.

Kentucky Constitution
Ab.:   Ky. Const. §   .
Ex.:   Ky. Const. § 6. –"Cite constitutional provisions currently in force without date." Bluebook Rule 11.
Ky. Const. § 31 (repealed 1979). –"If the cited provision has been repealed, either indicate parenthetically the fact and date of repeal or cite the repealing provision in full." Bluebook Rule 11.
Ky. Const. § 147 (amended 1945). –"When citing a provision that has been subsequently amended, either indicate parenthetically the fact and date of amendment or cite the amending provision in full." Bluebook Rule 11.
Ky. Const. of 1850, art. 11, § 2 (1891). –"Cite constitutions that have been totally superseded by year of adoption; if the specific provision cited was adopted in a different year, give that year parenthetically." Bluebook Rule 11.

Kentucky Court of Appeals
Ab.:   Ky. Ct. App.
–Cite to S.W.2d or S.W.3d if therein; otherwise, cite to Ky. App. Rptr. or Ky. L. Summary. See Bluebook Table T.1 and Ky. R. Civ. P. 76.12(4)(g).

In law review footnotes, the titles of books and the names of cases, except for procedural phrases, are not underlined. See Bluebook Rule 2.1(a). Further, the following are in large and small capitals: codes, restatements, standards, constitutions, periodicals, authors of books, titles of books, the abbreviated names of codes, most legislative materials except for bills and resolutions, codified ordinances, model codes, court rules, and sentencing guidelines. Refer to The Bluebook.

In documents submitted to Kentucky state courts, cite as follows:

Leeco, Inc. v. Agner, Ky. App., 919 S.W.2d 227 (1996). –Case Citation.

Leeco, Inc. v. Agner, Ky. App., 919 S.W.2d 227, 228 (1996). –Page Citation.

In all other documetns, cite as follows:

Leeco, Inc. v. Agner, 919 S.W.2d 227 (Ky. Ct. App. 1996). –Case Citation.

Leeco, Inc. v. Agner, 919 S.W.2d 227, 228 (Ky. Ct. App. 1996). –Page Citation.

Kentucky Law Journal
Ab.:   Ky. L.J.
Ex.:   Henry H. Perritt, Jr., The Internet Is Changing the Public International Legal System, 88 Ky. L.J. 885 (1999-2000). –Article Citation.

Henry H. Perritt, Jr., The Internet Is Changing the Public International Legal System, 88 Ky. L.J. 885, 889 (1999-2000). –Page Citation.

Kentucky Reports
Ab.:   Ky.
–Discontinued after 314 Ky. 885 (1951).
–Cite to S.W., S.W.2d, or S.W.3d if therein; otherwise, cite to Ky.
–Give parallel citations only in documents submitted to Kentucky state courts. See Bluebook Rule 10.3.1 and Practitioners' Note P.3; see also Ky. R. Civ. P. 76.12(4)(g), which requires a parallel citation.
–Through 314 Ky. 885 (1951), cite as follows:
In documents submitted to Kentucky state courts:

Wagner v. Wagner's Administratrix, 188 Ky. 692, 223 S.W. 1011 (1920). –Case Citation.

Wagner v. Wagner's Administratrix, 188 Ky. 692, 693, 223 S.W. 1011, 1011-12 (1920). –Page Citation.

In all other documents:

Wagner v. Wagner's Administratrix, 223 S.W. 1011 (Ky. 1920). – Case Citation.

Wagner v. Wagner's Administratrix, 223 S.W. 1011, 1011-12 (Ky. 1920). –Page Citation.

–After 314 Ky. 885 (1951), cite as follows:
In documents submitted to Kentucky state courts:

Candler v. Blevins, Ky., 922 S.W.2d 376 (1996). –Case Citation.

Candler v. Blevins, Ky., 922 S.W.2d 376, 377 (1996). –Page Citation.

In all other documents:

Candler v. Blevins, 922 S.W.2d 376 (Ky. 1996). –Case Citation.

In citing cases in law review footnotes, abbreviate any word listed in Table T.6; the names of "states, countries, and other geographical units" unless they are named parties; and any other words of eight or more letters "if substantial space is thereby saved and the result is unambiguous." Bluebook Rule 10.2.2. On the other hand, in citing cases in text, abbreviate only widely known acronyms and the following words: "&," "Ass'n," "Bros.," "Co.," "Corp.," "Inc.," "Ltd.," and "No." Bluebook Rule 10.2.1(c).

<u>Candler v. Blevins</u>, 922 S.W.2d 376, 377 (Ky. 1996). –Page
Citation.

Kentucky Revised Statutes Annotated
<u>See</u> Baldwin's Official Edition, Kentucky Revised Statutes Annotated.

Kentucky Revised Statutes Annotated (Baldwin)
<u>See</u> Baldwin's Official Edition, Kentucky Revised Statutes Annotated

Kentucky Revised Statutes Annotated, Official Edition (Lexis)
   Ab.:   Ky. Rev. Stat. Ann. § (Lexis year)
   Ex.:   Ky. Rev. Stat. Ann. § 433-750 (Lexis 1999).
           Ky. Rev. Stat. Ann. § 288-430 (Lexis Supp. 1998).

Kentucky Session Laws
<u>See</u> Kentucky Acts.

Korea and World Affairs: A Quarterly Review
   Ab.:   Korea & World Aff.
   Ex.:   Yong-Sup Han, <u>China's Leverages Over North Korea</u>, 18 Korea &
           World Aff. 233 (1994). –Article Citation.
           Yong-Sup Han, <u>China's Leverages Over North Korea</u>, 18 Korea &
           World Aff. 233, 235-37 (1994). –Page Citation.

Korea Journal of Comparative Law
   Ab.:   Korea J. Comp. L.
   Ex.:   Seong-Ki Kim, <u>Patent Law of China</u>, 18 Korea J. Comp. L. 90 (1990).
           –Article Citation.
           Seong-Ki Kim, <u>Patent Law of China</u>, 18 Korea J. Comp. L. 90, 91-95
           (1990). –Page Citation.

In law review footnotes, the titles of books and the names of cases, except for procedural
phrases, are not underlined. <u>See</u> <u>Bluebook</u> Rule 2.1(a). Further, the following are in large
and small capitals: codes, restatements, standards, constitutions, periodicals, authors of
books, titles of books, the abbreviated names of codes, most legislative materials except for
bills and resolutions, codified ordinances, model codes, court rules, and sentencing guidelines.
Refer to <u>The Bluebook</u>.

L

Labor Arbitration Awards (Commerce Clearing House)
Ab.: Lab. Arb. Awards (CCH)
Ex.: <u>NACCO v. Independent Builders Union</u>, Lab. Arb. Awards (CCH) (96-2 Lab. Arb. Awards) ¶ 6312 (Mar. 25, 1996) (Belshaw, Arb.). –Citation to looseleaf administrative material.

<u>Beta Steel Corp. v. International Longshoremen's Ass'n, Local 2038</u>, 95-1 Lab. Arb. Awards (CCH) ¶ 5165 (1995) (Traynor, Arb.). –Citation to bound administrative material.

Labor Arbitration Reports (Bureau of National Affairs)
Ab.: Lab. Arb. Rep. (BNA)
<u>See</u> Labor Relations Reporter (Bureau of National Affairs).

Labor Law Journal
Ab.: Lab. L.J.
Ex.: John A. Gray, <u>Preferential Affirmative Action in Employment</u>, 43 Lab. L.J. 23 (1992). –Article Citation.

John A. Gray, <u>Preferential Affirmative Action in Employment</u>, 43 Lab. L.J. 23, 25-27 (1992). –Page Citation.

Labor Law Reporter (Commerce Clearing House)
–Bound as: Labor Cases; NLRB Decisions
Ab.: Lab. L. Rep. (CCH)
–Bound as: Lab. Cas (CCH); NLRB Dec. (CCH)
Ex.: <u>Cox v. Nashe</u>, [3 State Laws] Lab. L. Rep. (CCH) (131 Lab. Cas.) ¶ 58,034 (9th Cir. Aug. 23, 1995). –Citation to looseleaf material.

<u>Stanley v. McDaniel</u>, [2 Wage-Hour] Lab. L. Rep. (CCH) (131 Lab. Cas.) ¶ 33,349 (Ohio Ct. App. Feb. 27, 1996). –Citation to looseleaf material.

<u>United States v. Carson</u>, 130 Lab. Cas. (CCH) ¶ 11,313 (S.D.N.Y. 1995). –Citation to bound material.

–The above examples are proper if the case is not yet available in, or is not reported in, an official or West reporter, a public domain citation, or in a widely used computer database.

<u>Department of Labor v. New Way Laundry & Cleaning</u>, [2 Wage-Hour] Lab. L. Rep. (CCH) ¶ 32,425 (Wage Appeals Board Mar. 15, 1996). –Looseleaf administrative material.

In law review footnotes, the titles of books and the names of cases, except for procedural phrases, are not underlined. <u>See</u> Bluebook Rule 2.1(a). Further, the following are in large and small capitals: codes, restatements, standards, constitutions, periodicals, authors of books, titles of books, the abbreviated names of codes, most legislative materials except for bills and resolutions, codified ordinances, model codes, court rules, and sentencing guidelines. Refer to <u>The Bluebook</u>.

Opinion Letter of the Wage-Hour Administrator No. 1546 (WH 493) [Sept. 1978 - Jan. 1981 Transfer Binder, Wages-Hours Administrative Rulings] Lab. L. Rep. (CCH) ¶ 31,281 (Wage Appeals Board 1979). –Citation to transfer binder administrative material.

Checker Cab Co., 1981-82 NLRB Dec. (CCH) ¶ 18,827 (NLRB 1982). –Citation to bound administrative material.

Labor Lawyer
Ab.:   Lab. Law.

Ex.:   Steven H. Winterbauer, Sexual Harassment: The Reasonable Woman Standard, 7 Lab. Law. 811 (1991). –Article Citation.

Steven H. Winterbauer, Sexual Harassment: The Reasonable Woman Standard, 7 Lab. Law. 811, 813-816 (1991). –Page Citation.

Labor Relations Reference Manual (Bureau of National Affairs)
Ab.:   L.R.R.M. (BNA)

Labor Relations Reporter (Bureau of National Affairs)
–Bound as: Fair Employment Practices Cases; Labor Arbitration Reports; Labor Relations Reference Manual; Wage and Hour Cases

Ab.:   Lab. Rel. Rep. (BNA)
–Bound as: Fair Empl. Prac. Cas. (BNA); Lab. Arb. Rep. (BNA); L.R.R.M. (BNA); Wage & Hour Cas. (BNA)

Ex.:   Rich v. Delta Air Lines, 5 Lab. L. Rep. (BNA) (3 Wage & Hour Cas.) 1 (N.D. Ga. Feb. 7, 1996). –Citation to looseleaf material.

Miller v. Butcher, 7 Lab. L. Rep. (BNA) (71 Fair Empl. Prac. Cas.) 641 (5th Cir. July 29, 1996). –Citation to looseleaf material.

Providence and Mercy Hospitals v. NLRB, 2 Lab. L. Rep. (BNA) (153 L.R.R.M). 2097 (1st Cir. Aug. 28, 1996). –Citation to looseleaf material.

IAFF Local 2916 v. PERC, 152 L.R.R.M. (BNA) 2668 (Wash. 1995). –Citation to bound material.

Vega v. Gasper, 2 Wage & Hour Cas.2d (BNA) 614 (5th Cir. 1994). –Citation to bound material.

Jones v. Clinton, 70 Fair Empl. Prac. Cas. (BNA) 585 (8th Cir. 1996). –Citation to bound material.

–The above examples are proper if the case is not yet available in, or is not reported in, an official or West reporter, a public domain citation, or in a widely used computer database.

Tower Automotive, 2 Lab. Rel. Rep. (BNA) (153 L.R.R.M.) 1241 (NLRB Nov. 12, 1996).
–Citation to looseleaf administrative material.

In citing cases in law review footnotes, abbreviate any word listed in Table T.6; the names of "states, countries, and other geographical units" unless they are named parties; and any other words of eight or more letters "if substantial space is thereby saved and the result is unambiguous." Bluebook Rule 10.2.2. On the other hand, in citing cases in text, abbreviate only widely known acronyms and the following words: "&," "Ass'n," "Bros.," "Co.," "Corp.," "Inc.," "Ltd.," and "No." Bluebook Rule 10.2.1(c).

Dunlop Tire Corp., 3 Lab. Rel. Rep. (BNA) (107 Lab. Arb. Rep.) 97 (July 5, 1996) (Kindig, Arb.). –Citation to looseleaf administrative material.

Sanderson Plumbing Products, 106 Lab. Arb. Rep. (BNA) 535 (1996) (Howell, Arb.).
–Citation to bound administrative material.

LaFave & Scott on Criminal Law
See Criminal Law, by Wayne R. LaFave & Austin W. Scott, Jr.

Land and Water Law Review
Ab.: Land & Water L. Rev.

Ex.: Joseph R. Membrino, Indian Reserved Water, Rights, Federalism and the Trust Responsibility, 27 Land & Water L. Rev. 1 (1992). –Article Citation.

Joseph R. Membrino, Indian Reserved Water, Rights, Federalism and the Trust Responsibility, 27 Land & Water L. Rev. 1, 9 (1992). –Page Citation.

Land Use and Environment Law Review
Ab.: Land Use & Env't L. Rev.

Ex.: David L. Callies, Property Rights: Are There Any Left?, 21 Land Use & Env't L. Rev. 181 (1990). –Article Citation.

David L. Callies, Property Rights: Are There Any Left?, 21 Land Use & Env't L. Rev. 181, 189-92 (1990). –Page Citation.

Lane's Goldstein Trial Techniques, by Fred Lane
–Do not abbreviate the title.

Ex.: 2 Fred Lane, Lane's Goldstein Trial Techniques § 13.95 (3d ed. 1985 & Supp. 1991). –Section Citation.

2 Fred Lane, Lane's Goldstein Trial Techniques § 13.95, at 13-170 (3d ed. 1985 & Supp. 1991). –Page Citation.

2 Fred Lane, Lane's Goldstein Trial Techniques § 13.95, at 13-170 n.12 (3d ed. 1985 & Supp. 1991). –Footnote Citation.

Larson on Workmen's Compensation
See Law of Worker's Compensation, by Arthur Larson

Law & Anthropology
Ab.: Do not abbreviate title.

Ex.: Maureen Davies, International Developments in Indigenous Rights, 2 Law & Anthropology 29 (1987). –Article Citation.

Maureen Davies, International Developments in Indigenous Rights, 2 Law & Anthropology 29, 30-33 (1987). –Page Citation.

In law review footnotes, the titles of books and the names of cases, except for procedural phrases, are not underlined. See Bluebook Rule 2.1(a). Further, the following are in large and small capitals: codes, restatements, standards, constitutions, periodicals, authors of books, titles of books, the abbreviated names of codes, most legislative materials except for bills and resolutions, codified ordinances, model codes, court rules, and sentencing guidelines. Refer to The Bluebook.

Law and Contemporary Problems
Ab.:   Law & Contemp. Probs.

Ex.:   Peter Huber, <u>Medical Experts and the Ghost of Galileo</u>, Law &
Contemp. Probs., Summer 1991, at 119. –Article Citation.

Peter Huber, <u>Medical Experts and the Ghost of Galileo</u>, Law &
Contemp. Probs., Summer 1991, at 119, 130-34. –Page Citation.

Law and History Review
Ab.:   Law & Hist. Rev.

Ex.:   David C. Frederick, <u>John Quincy Adams, Slavery and the
Disappearance of the Right of Petition</u>, Law & Hist. Rev., Spring 1991,
at 113. –Article Citation.

David C. Frederick, <u>John Quincy Adams, Slavery and the
Disappearance of the Right of Petition</u>, Law & Hist. Rev., Spring 1991,
at 113, 120-22. –Page Citation.

Law and Human Behavior
Ab.:   Law & Hum. Behav.

Ex.:   Virginia Aldigé Hiday, <u>Dangerousness of Civil Commitment
Candidates: A Six-Month Follow-Up</u>, 14 Law & Hum. Behav. 551
(1990). –Article Citation.

Virginia Aldigé Hiday, <u>Dangerousness of Civil Commitment
Candidates: A Six-Month Follow-Up</u>, 14 Law & Hum. Behav. 551,
552 (1990). –Page Citation.

Law & Inequality Journal
Ab.:   Law & Ineq. J.

Ex.:   Eila Savela, <u>Homelessness and the Affordable Housing Shortage: What
Is to be Done?</u>, 9 Law & Ineq. J. 279 (1991). –Article Citation.

Eila Savela, <u>Homelessness and the Affordable Housing Shortage: What
Is to be Done?</u>, 9 Law & Ineq. J. 279, 281-82 (1991). –Page Citation.

Law and Philosophy
Ab.:   Law & Phil.

Ex.:   Daniel Brudney, <u>Hypothetical Consent and Moral Force</u>, 10 Law &
Phil. 235 (1991). –Article Citation.

Daniel Brudney, <u>Hypothetical Consent and Moral Force</u>, 10 Law &
Phil. 235, 240-42 (1991). –Page Citation.

Law and Policy
Ab.:   Law & Pol'y

In citing cases in law review footnotes, abbreviate any word listed in Table T.6;
the names of "states, countries, and other geographical units" unless they are named parties;
and any other words of eight or more letters "if <u>substantial</u> space is thereby saved and the
result is unambiguous." <u>Bluebook</u> Rule 10.2.2. On the other hand, in citing cases in text,
abbreviate only widely known acronyms and the following words: "&," "Ass'n," "Bros.,"
"Co.," "Corp.," "Inc.," "Ltd.," and "No." <u>Bluebook</u> Rule 10.2.1(c).

Ex.:   Frank Anechiarico & Stephen L. Lockwood, <u>The Responsibility of the Police Command for Street Level Actions</u>, 12 Law & Pol'y 331 (1990). –Article Citation.

Frank Anechiarico & Stephen L. Lockwood, <u>The Responsibility of the Police Command for Street Level Actions</u>, 12 Law & Pol'y 331, 333 (1990). –Page Citation.

Law and Policy in International Business
Ab.:   Law & Pol'y Int'l Bus.

Ex.:   John P. Simpson, <u>Rules of Origin in Transition: A Changing Environment and Prospects for Reform</u>, 22 Law & Pol'y Int'l Bus. 665 (1991). –Article Citation.

John P. Simpson, <u>Rules of Origin in Transition: A Changing Environment and Prospects for Reform</u>, 22 Law & Pol'y Int'l Bus. 665, 669-70 (1991). –Page Citation.

Law and Psychology Review
Ab.:   Law & Psychol. Rev.

Ex.:   William W. Patton, <u>Opening Student's Eyes: Visual Learning Theory in the Socratic Classroom</u>, 15 Law & Psychol. Rev. 1 (1991). –Article Citation.

William W. Patton, <u>Opening Student's Eyes: Visual Learning Theory in the Socratic Classroom</u>, 15 Law & Psychol. Rev. 1, 6-10 (1991). –Page Citation.

Law & Social Inquiry
Ab.:   Law & Soc. Inquiry

Ex.:   Stephen M. Griffin, <u>Bringing the State into Constitutional Theory: Public Authority and the Constitution</u>, 16 Law & Soc. Inquiry 659 (1991). –Article Citation.

Stephen M. Griffin, <u>Bringing the State into Constitutional Theory: Public Authority and the Constitution</u>, 16 Law & Soc. Inquiry 659, 663 (1991). –Page Citation.

Law & Society Review
Ab.:   Law & Soc'y Rev.

Ex.:   Janet A. Gilboy, <u>Deciding Who Gets In: Decisionmaking by Immigration Inspectors</u>, 25 Law & Soc'y Rev. 571 (1991). –Article Citation.

Janet A. Gilboy, <u>Deciding Who Gets In: Decisionmaking by Immigration Inspectors</u>, 25 Law & Soc'y Rev. 571, 577-78 (1991). –Page Citation.

Law and State
Ab.:   Law & St.

In law review footnotes, the titles of books and the names of cases, except for procedural phrases, are not underlined. <u>See</u> Bluebook Rule 2.1(a). Further, the following are in large and small capitals: codes, restatements, standards, constitutions, periodicals, authors of books, titles of books, the abbreviated names of codes, most legislative materials except for bills and resolutions, codified ordinances, model codes, court rules, and sentencing guidelines. Refer to <u>The Bluebook</u>.

Ex.:   Hugo J. Hahn, <u>International Loan and Guarantee Agreements</u>, 41 Law & St. 29 (1990). –Article Citation.

Hugo J. Hahn, <u>International Loan and Guarantee Agreements</u>, 41 Law & St. 29, 30-32 (1990). –Page Citation.

Law in Japan: An Annual
Ab.:   Law in Japan
Ex.:   Akio Takeuchi, <u>Legal Control of Commodity Fraud Transactions</u>, 22 Law in Japan 26 (1989). –Article Citation.

Akio Takeuchi, <u>Legal Control of Commodity Fraud Transactions</u>, 22 Law in Japan 26, 27-30 (1989). –Page Citation.

Law Journal Reports (U.K.)
<u>See</u> <u>Bluebook</u> Table T.2.
Ab.:   L.J.R.
Ex.:   <u>Lipshitz v. Valero</u>, 1948 L.J.R. 625 (P.C. 1947) (Eng.) (taken on appeal from Palestine). –Case Citation.

Law Journal Reports, King's Bench, New Series (U.K.)
<u>See</u> <u>Bluebook</u> Table T.2.
Ab.:   L.J.K.B.
Ex.:   <u>Price v. Webb</u>, 82 L.J.K.B. 720 (1913) (Eng.). –Case Citation.

Law Journal Reports, King's Bench, Old Series (U.K.)
<u>See</u> <u>Bluebook</u> Table T.2.
Ab.:   L.J.K.B.O.S.
Ex.:   <u>Marsden v. Stanfield</u>, 6 L.J.K.B.O.S. 159 (1828) (Eng.). –Case Citation.

Law Library Journal
Ab.:   Law Libr. J.
Ex.:   Marsha Trimble, <u>Archives and Manuscripts: New Collecting Areas for Law Libraries</u>, 83 Law Libr. J. 429 (1991). –Article Citation.

Marsha Trimble, <u>Archives and Manuscripts: New Collecting Areas for Law Libraries</u>, 83 Law Libr. J. 429, 431-32 (1991). –Page Citation.

Law, Medicine & Health Care
Ab.:   Law Med. & Health Care
Ex.:   Carol Levine, <u>Children in HIV/AIDS Clinical Trials: Still Vulnerable after All These Years</u>, 19 Law Med. & Health Care 231 (1991). –Article Citation.

Carol Levine, <u>Children in HIV/AIDS Clinical Trials: Still Vulnerable after All These Years</u>, 19 Law Med. & Health Care 231, 235-36 (1991). –Page Citation.

Law of Bankruptcy, The, by Charles Jordan Tabb
–Do not abbreviate the title.

In citing cases in law review footnotes, abbreviate any word listed in Table T.6; the names of "states, countries, and other geographical units" unless they are named parties; and any other words of eight or more letters "if <u>substantial</u> space is thereby saved and the result is unambiguous." <u>Bluebook</u> Rule 10.2.2. On the other hand, in citing cases in text, abbreviate only widely known acronyms and the following words: "&," "Ass'n," "Bros.," "Co.," "Corp.," "Inc.," "Ltd.," and "No." <u>Bluebook</u> Rule 10.2.1(c).

Ex.:   Charles Jordan Tabb, <u>The Law of Bankruptcy</u> § 8.1 (1997). –Section
Citation.

Charles Jordan Tabb, <u>The Law of Bankruptcy</u> § 8.1, at 575 (1997).
–Page Citation.

Charles Jordan Tabb, <u>The Law of Bankruptcy</u> § 8.1, at 575 n.2 (1997).
–Footnote Citation.

Law of Contracts, The, by John D. Calamari and Joseph M. Perillo
–Do not abbreviate the title.

Ex.:   John D. Calamari & Joseph M. Perillo, <u>The Law of Contracts</u> § 4.10
(4th ed. 1998). –Section Citation.

John D. Calamari & Joseph M. Perillo, <u>The Law of Contracts</u> § 4.10, at
188 (4th ed. 1998). –Page Citation.

John D. Calamari & Joseph M. Perillo, <u>The Law of Contracts</u> § 4.10, at
188 n.44 (4th ed. 1998). –Footnote Citation.

Law of Easements and Licenses in Land, The, by Jon W. Bruce and James W. Ely, Jr.
–Do not abbreviate the title.

Ex.:   Jon W. Bruce and James W. Ely, Jr., <u>The Law of Easements and
Licenses in Land</u> ¶ 1.04[4] (rev. ed. 1995). –Section Citation.

Jon W. Bruce and James W. Ely, Jr., <u>The Law of Easements and
Licenses in Land</u> ¶ 1.04[4], at 1-30 (rev. ed. 1995). –Page Citation.

Jon W. Bruce and James W. Ely, Jr., <u>The Law of Easements and
Licenses in Land</u> ¶ 1.04[4], at 4-35 n.157.1 (Supp. 2000). –Footnote
Citation in Supplement.

Law of Federal Courts, The, by Charles A. Wright
–Do not abbreviate the title.

Ex.:   Charles A. Wright, <u>The Law of Federal Courts</u> § 70 (5th ed. 1994).
–Section Citation.

Charles A. Wright, <u>The Law of Federal Courts</u> § 70, at 498 (5th ed.
1994). –Page Citation.

Charles A. Wright, <u>The Law of Federal Courts</u> § 70, at 498 n.49 (5th
ed. 1994). –Footnote Citation.

Law of Federal Income Taxation, Second Edition, by Michael D. Rose and John C. Chommie
–Do not abbreviate the title.

Ex.:   Michael D. Rose & John C. Chommie, <u>Law and Federal Income
Taxation</u> § 139 (2d ed. 1973).

Michael D. Rose & John C. Chommie, <u>Law of Federal Income
Taxation</u> § 139, at 431 (2d ed. 1973).

Law of Municipal Corporations, The, by Eugene McQuillin
–Do not abbreviate the title.

In law review footnotes, the titles of books and the names of cases, except for procedural
phrases, are not underlined. See <u>Bluebook</u> Rule 2.1(a). Further, the following are in large
and small capitals: codes, restatements, standards, constitutions, periodicals, authors of
books, titles of books, the abbreviated names of codes, most legislative materials except for
bills and resolutions, codified ordinances, model codes, court rules, and sentencing guidelines.
Refer to <u>The Bluebook</u>.

Ex.:   John H. Silvestri and Mark S. Nelson, 1 <u>Law of Municipal</u>
         <u>Corporations</u> § 3.28.30 (3d ed., rev. vol. 1999 & Cum. Supp. 2000).
         –Section Citation to vol. revised by named authors.

         Eugene McQuillan, 3 <u>Law of Municipal Corporations</u> § 12.59, at 329
         (3d ed., rev. vol. 2001). –Page Citation to vol. revised by editorial
         staff.

Law of Probation and Parole, The, by Neil P. Cohen
         –Do not abbreviate the title.

Ex.:   Neil P. Cohen, <u>The Law of Probation and Parole</u> § 7.30 (2d ed. 1999).
         –Section Citation.

         Neil P. Cohen, <u>The Law of Probation and Parole</u> § 7.30, at 7-57 (2d ed.
         1999). –Page Citation.

         Neil P. Cohen, <u>The Law of Probation and Parole</u> § 7.30, at 7-57 n.3 (2d
         ed. 1999). –Footnote Citation.

Law of Property, The, by Ralph E. Boyer, Herbert Hovenkamp, and Sheldon F.
  Kurtz
         –Do not abbreviate the title.

Ex.:   Ralph E. Boyer et al., <u>The Law of Property</u> § 10.21 (4th ed. 1991).
         –Section Citation.

         Ralph E. Boyer et al., <u>The Law of Property</u> § 10.21, at 321 (4th ed.
         1991). –Page Citation.

Law of Property, The, by William B. Stoebuck & Dale A. Whitman
         –Do not abbreviate the title.

Ex.:   William B. Stoebuck & Dale A. Whitman, <u>The Law of Property</u>
         § 10.21 (4th ed. 2000). –Section Citation.

         William B. Stoebuck & Dale A. Whitman, <u>The Law of Property</u>
         § 10.21, at 321 (4th ed. 2000). –Page Citation.

Law of Real Property, The, by Richard R. Powell
         –Do not abbreviate the title.

Ex.:   2 Richard R. Powell, <u>The Law of Real Property</u> § 15.04[1] (Michael
         Allan Wolf ed., 2000). –Section Citation.

         2 Richard R. Powell, <u>The Law of Real Property</u> § 15.04[1], at 15-61
         (Michael Allan Wolf ed., 2000). –Page Citation.

         2 Richard R. Powell, <u>The Law of Real Property</u> § 15.04[1], at 15-61
         n.20 (Michael Allan Wolf ed., 2000). –Footnote Citation.

Law of Remedies, by Dan B. Dobbs
         –Do not abbreviate the title.

In citing cases in law review footnotes, abbreviate any word listed in Table T.6;
the names of "states, countries, and other geographical units" unless they are named parties;
and any other words of eight or more letters "if <u>substantial</u> space is thereby saved and the
result is unambiguous." <u>Bluebook</u> Rule 10.2.2. On the other hand, in citing cases in text,
abbreviate only widely known acronyms and the following words: "&," "Ass'n," "Bros.,"
"Co.," "Corp.," "Inc.," "Ltd.," and "No." <u>Bluebook</u> Rule 10.2.1(c).

Ex.:   Dan B. Dobbs, <u>Law of Remedies</u> § 6.5(2) (2d ed. 1993). –Section Citation.

Dan B. Dobbs, <u>Law of Remedies</u> § 6.5(2), at 123 (2d ed. 1993). –Page Citation.

Dan B. Dobbs, <u>Law of Remedies</u> § 6.5(2), at 123 n.40 (2d ed. 1993). –Footnote Citation.

Law of Restitution, The, by George E. Palmer
–Do not abbreviate the title.

Ex.:   2 George E. Palmer, <u>The Law of Restitution</u> § 9.5 (1978). –Section Citation.

2 George E. Palmer, <u>The Law of Restitution</u> § 9.5, at 267 (1978). –Page Citation.

2 George E. Palmer, <u>The Law of Restitution</u> § 9.5, at 267 n.17 (1978). –Footnote Citation.

Lawrence Kaplan, <u>Palmer's Law of Restitution</u> § 2.2(a), at 50 (Supp. No. 2 1998). –Supplement Citation.

Law of Securities Regulation, The, by Thomas Lee Hazen
–Do not abbreviate the title.

Ex.:   Thomas L. Hazen, <u>The Law of Securities Regulation</u> § 4.27 (3d ed. 1996). –Section Citation.

Thomas L. Hazen, <u>The Law of Securities Regulation</u> § 4.27, at 306 (3d ed. 1996). –Page Citation.

Thomas L. Hazen, <u>The Law of Securities Regulation</u> § 4.27, at 306 n.14 (3d ed. 1996). –Footnote Citation.

Law of Torts, The, by Dan B. Dobbs
–Do not abbreviate the title.

Ex.:   1 Dan B. Dobbs, <u>The Law of Torts</u> § 7 (2001). –Section Citation

1 Dan B. Dobbs, <u>The Law of Torts</u> § 7, at 11 (2001). –Page Citation

1 Dan B. Dobbs, <u>The Law of Torts</u> § 19, at 37 n.3 (2001). –Footnote Citation

Law of Torts, The, by Fowler V. Harper, Fleming James, Jr., and Oscar S. Gray
–Do not abbreviate the title.

Ex.:   4 Fowler V. Harper et al., <u>The Law of Torts</u> § 22.6 (2d ed. 1986). –Section Citation to second edition.

4 Fowler V. Harper et al., <u>The Law of Torts</u> § 22.6, at 303 (2d ed. 1986). –Page Citation to second edition.

4 Fowler V. Harper et al., <u>The Law of Torts</u> § 22.6, at 303 n.19 (2d ed. 1986). –Footnote Citation to second edition.

In law review footnotes, the titles of books and the names of cases, except for procedural phrases, are not underlined. <u>See</u> Bluebook Rule 2.1(a). Further, the following are in large and small capitals: codes, restatements, standards, constitutions, periodicals, authors of books, titles of books, the abbreviated names of codes, most legislative materials except for bills and resolutions, codified ordinances, model codes, court rules, and sentencing guidelines. Refer to <u>The Bluebook</u>.

1 Fowler V. Harper et al., The Law of Torts § 1.1 (3d ed. 1996).
–Section Citation to third edition.

Law of Trusts and Trustees, The, by Amy Morris Hess, George Gleason Bogert, and George Taylor Bogert
   –Do not abbreviate the title.

Ex.   Amy Morris Hess et al., The Law of Trusts and Trustees § 646 (3d ed. 2000). – Section Citation.

      Amy Morris Hess et al., The Law of Trusts and Trustees § 646, at 442 (3d ed. 2000). – Page Citation.

      Amy Morris Hess et al., The Law of Trusts and Trustees § 646, at 442 n.2 (3d ed. 2000). – Footnote Citation

Law of Workers' Compensation, The, by Arthur Larson and Lex K. Larson
   –Do not abbreviate the title.

Ex.   2 Arthur Larson & Lex K. Larson, Larson's Workers' Compensation Law § 43.03 (2000). – Section Citation.

      2 Arthur Larson & Lex K. Larson, Larson's Workers' Compensation Law § 43.03, at 43-11 (2000). – Page Citation.

      2 Arthur Larson & Lex K. Larson, Larson's Workers' Compensation Law § 43.03, at 43-11 n.1 (2000). – Footnote Citation.

Law Office Economics and Management
Ab.:   Law Off. Econ. & Mgmt.

Ex.:   James G. Frierson, Does Your Law Office Meet the Requirements of the Americans With Disabilities Act?, 32 Law Off. Econ. & Mgmt. 397 (1992). –Article Citation.

      James G. Frierson, Does Your Law Office Meet the Requirements of the Americans With Disabilities Act?, 32 Law Off. Econ. & Mgmt. 397, 401 (1992). –Page Citation.

Law Practice Management
Ab.:   L. Prac. Mgmt.

Ex.:   Jack Kaufman, The Staff Lawyer, L. Prac. Mgmt., July-Aug. 1990, at 30. –Article Citation.

      Jack Kaufman, The Staff Lawyer, L. Prac. Mgmt., July-Aug. 1990, at 30, 31-2. –Page Citation.

Law Quarterly Review, The
Ab.:   L.Q. Rev.

Ex.:   Ruth Deech, Divorce Law and Empirical Studies, 106 L.Q. Rev. 229 (1990). –Article Citation.

      Ruth Deech, Divorce Law and Empirical Studies, 106 L.Q. Rev. 229, 239-43 (1990). –Page Citation.

In citing cases in law review footnotes, abbreviate any word listed in Table T.6; the names of "states, countries, and other geographical units" unless they are named parties; and any other words of eight or more letters "if substantial space is thereby saved and the result is unambiguous." Bluebook Rule 10.2.2. On the other hand, in citing cases in text, abbreviate only widely known acronyms and the following words: "&," "Ass'n," "Bros.," "Co.," "Corp.," "Inc.," "Ltd.," and "No." Bluebook Rule 10.2.1(c).

Law Reports: Admiralty and Ecclesiastical Cases (U.K.)
Ab.:   L.R.-Adm. & Eccl.
See Bluebook Table T.2.
Ex.:   Sheppard v. Bennett, 3 L.R.-Adm. & Eccl. 167 (Eccl. 1870) (Eng.).
          –Case Citation.
          The Waverly, 3 L.R.-Adm. & Eccl. 369 (Adm. 1871) (Eng.). –Case
          Citation.

Law Reports: Appeal Cases (U.K.) (1891-date)
See Bluebook Table T.2. Indicate the court only if it is the Privy Council.
          (P.C.).
Ab.:   A.C.
Ex.:   Beckford v. The Queen, [1988] A.C. 130 (P.C.) (Eng.) (appeal taken
          from Jam.). –Privy Council Case Citation.
          Polkey v. Dayton Ltd., [1988] A.C. 344 (Eng.). –House of Lords Case
          Citation.

Law Reports: Chancery Division (U.K.)
See Bluebook Table T.2.
Ab.:   1891-date: Ch.
          1875-1890: Ch. D.
          1865-1875: L.R. -Ch.
Ex.:   Briggs v. Upton, 7 L.R.-Ch. 376 (1871) (Eng.). –Case Citation.
          Doucet v. Geoghegan, 9 Ch. D. 441 (1877) (Eng.). –Case Citation.
          Rignoll Developments Ltd. v. Halil, 1988 Ch. 190 (1987) (Eng.).
          –Case Citation.

Law Reports: Common Pleas (England)
See Bluebook Table T.2.
Ab.:   1875-1880: C.P.D.
          1865-1875: L.R.-C.P.
Ex.:   Abel v. Lee, 6 L.R.-C.P. 365 (1871) (Eng.). –Case Citation.
          Pickard v. Baylis, 5 C.P.D. 235 (1879) (Eng.). –Case Citation.

Law Reports: English & Irish Appeal Cases (U.K.)
See Bluebook Table T.2.
Ab.:   L.R.-E. & I. App.
Ex.:   Allen v. Bishop of Gloucester, 6 L.R.-E. & I. App. 219 (1873) (Eng.).
          –Case Citation.

Law Reports: Exchequer (England)
See Bluebook Table T.2.
Ab.:   1875-1880: Ex. D.

In law review footnotes, the titles of books and the names of cases, except for procedural
phrases, are not underlined. See Bluebook Rule 2.1(a). Further, the following are in large
and small capitals: codes, restatements, standards, constitutions, periodicals, authors of
books, titles of books, the abbreviated names of codes, most legislative materials except for
bills and resolutions, codified ordinances, model codes, court rules, and sentencing guidelines.
Refer to The Bluebook.

1865-1875: L.R.-Ex.

Ex.:   Holker v. Poritt, 8 L.R.-Ex. 107 (1873) (Eng.). –Case Citation.
         Gilbertson v. Ferguson, 5 Ex. D. 57 (1879) (Eng.). –Case Citation.

Law Reports: Family (England)
See Bluebook Table T.2, p. 294, and Rule 20.3.1.
Ab.:   Fam.
Ex.:   McVeigh v. Beattie, 1988 Fam. 69 (1987) (Eng.). –Case Citation.

Law Reports: Privy Council (U.K.)
See Bluebook Table T.2.
Ab.:   L.R.–P.C.
Ex.:   Richer v. Voyer, 5 L.R.–P.C. 461 (1874) (U.K.). –Case Citation.

Law Reports: Probate and Divorce (England)
See Bluebook Table T.2.
Ab.:   L.R.-P. & D. (1865-75)
Ex.:   Davies v. Gregory, 3 L.R.-P. & D. 28 (1873) (Eng.). –Case Citation.

Law Reports: Probate Division (England)
See Bluebook Table T.2.
Ab.:   P.D. (1875-90)
Ex.:   Scott v. Sebright, 12 P.D. 21 (1886) (Eng.). –Case Citation.

Law Reports: Probate, Divorce & Admiralty Division (England)
See Bluebook Table T.2.
Ab.:   P. (1891-1971)
Ex.:   P. v. P., 1971 P. 217 (C.A.) (Eng.). –Court of Appeals–Case Citation.
         Adams v. Adams, 1971 P. 188 (1970) (Eng.). –Case Citation.

Law Reports: Queen's and King's Bench (England)
See Bluebook Table T.2. Indicate the court only if it is the Court of Appeals.
Ab.:   1952-date: Q.B.
         1901-1951: K.B.
         1891-1900: Q.B.
         1875-1890: Q.B.D.
         1865-1875: L.R.–Q.B.
Ex.:   Foster v. Robinson, [1951] 1 K.B. 149 (1950) (Eng. C.A.). –Court of
         Appeal–Case Citation.
         Longden-Griffiths v. Smith, [1951] 1 K.B. 295 (1950) (Eng.). –Case
         Citation.
         F.C. Shepherd & Co. Ltd. v. Jerrom, [1987] 1 Q.B. 301 (1986) (Eng.
         C.A.). –Court of Appeal–Case Citation.

In citing cases in law review footnotes, abbreviate any word listed in Table T.6;
the names of "states, countries, and other geographical units" unless they are named parties;
and any other words of eight or more letters "if substantial space is thereby saved and the
result is unambiguous." Bluebook Rule 10.2.2. On the other hand, in citing cases in text,
abbreviate only widely known acronyms and the following words: "&," "Ass'n," "Bros.,"
"Co.," "Corp.," "Inc.," "Ltd.," and "No." Bluebook Rule 10.2.1(c).

Coastplace Ltd. v. Hartley, [1987] 1 Q.B. 948 (Eng.). –Case Citation.

Law Reports: Scotch & Divorce Appeal Cases (U.K.)
See Bluebook Table T.2.
Ab.:   L.R.-S. & D. App.
Ex.:   Carlton v. Thompson, 1 L.R.-S. & D. App. 232 (1867) (Eng.). –Case
Citation.

law review
See periodicals

law review footnotes, typeface conventions for law review footnotes
See Bluebook Rules 2.1 and 7. See also the excellent examples on the inside
front cover and on the facing page next to the inside front cover of The
Bluebook.

law review texts, typeface conventions for law review texts
See Bluebook Rules 2.2 and 7.

Law Teacher, The
Ab.:   Law Tchr.
Ex.:   Stephen Migdal & Martin Cartwright, Student Based Learning - A
Polytechnic's Experience, 25 Law Tchr. 120 (1991). –Article Citation.
Stephen Migdal & Martin Cartwright, Student Based Learning - A
Polytechnic's Experience, 25 Law Tchr. 120, 122 (1991). –Page
Citation.

Law/Technology
Ab.:   Law/Tech.
Ex.:   Linda Maher, Environmental Concerns: In Domestic and International
Regulatory Frameworks for Biotechnology, 1991 Law/Tech. 1.
–Article Citation.
Linda Maher, Environmental Concerns: In Domestic and International
Regulatory Frameworks for Biotechnology, 1991 Law/Tech. 1, 5.
–Page Citation.

Law Times Reports (England) (1859-1947)
Ab.:   L.T.R. See Bluebook Table T.2.
Ex.:   Glanville v. Sulton and Co., 138 L.T.R. 336 (K.B. 1928) (Eng.). –Case
Citation.

Lawasia
Ab.:   Do not abbreviate title.

In law review footnotes, the titles of books and the names of cases, except for procedural
phrases, are not underlined. See Bluebook Rule 2.1(a). Further, the following are in large
and small capitals: codes, restatements, standards, constitutions, periodicals, authors of
books, titles of books, the abbreviated names of codes, most legislative materials except for
bills and resolutions, codified ordinances, model codes, court rules, and sentencing guidelines.
Refer to The Bluebook.

Ex.:   Stanley Yeo, <u>Reforming Duress Under Indian Penal Code</u>, 1987
         Lawasia 85. –Article Citation.

         Stanley Yeo, <u>Reforming Duress Under Indian Penal Code</u>, 1987
         Lawasia 85, 90-93. –Page Citation.

Laws of Delaware
Ab.:   vol. Del. Laws   (year)
Ex.:   Act of July 15, 1994, ch. 444, 69 Del. Laws 921 (1994). –Citation to
         an entire session law.

         Act of July 15, 1994, ch. 444, § 2, 69 Del. Laws 921, 922 (1994).
         –Citation to a section of a session law.

         –Identifying information may be added parenthetically according to
         <u>Bluebook</u> Rule 12.4(a).

Laws of Florida
Ab.:   year Fla. Laws ch.
Ex.:   Act of June 16, 1995, ch. 95-334, 1995-1 Fla. Laws 2987. –Citation to
         an entire session law.

         Act of June 16, 1995, ch. 95-334, sec. 1, § 295.101, 1995-1 Fla. Laws
         2987, 2987-88. –Citation to a section of a session law.

         –Identifying information may be added parenthetically according to
         <u>Bluebook</u> Rule 12.4(a).

Laws of Illinois
Ab.:   year Ill. Laws
Ex.:   Act of June 30, 1995, No. 89-71, 1995-1 Ill. Laws 1507. –Citation to
         an entire session law.

         Act of June 30, 1995, No. 89-71, sec. 5(a), § 6-106.1, 1995-1 Ill. Laws
         1507, 1507. –Citation to a section of a session law amending a prior
         act.

         –Identifying information may be added parenthetically according to
         <u>Bluebook</u> Rule 12.4(a).

Laws of Maryland
Ab.:   year Md. Laws
Ex.:   Act of Apr. 11, 1995, ch. 98, 1995-3 Md. Laws 1453 (radiation control
         - definition of a person). –Citation to an entire session law.

         Act of Apr. 11, 1995, ch. 98, § 1, 1995-3 Md. Laws 1453, 1453-54
         (radiation control - definition of a person). –Citation to a section of a
         session law.

Laws of Minnesota
Ab.:   year Minn. Laws

In citing cases in law review footnotes, abbreviate any word listed in Table T.6;
the names of "states, countries, and other geographical units" unless they are named parties;
and any other words of eight or more letters "if <u>substantial</u> space is thereby saved and the
result is unambiguous." <u>Bluebook</u> Rule 10.2.2. On the other hand, in citing cases in text,
abbreviate only widely known acronyms and the following words: "&," "Ass'n," "Bros.,"
"Co.," "Corp.," "Inc.," "Ltd.," and "No." <u>Bluebook</u> Rule 10.2.1(c).

Ex.: Act of Apr. 11, 1996, ch. 442, 1996-2 Minn. Laws 1176 (relating to driving while intoxicated). –Citation to an entire session law.

Act of Apr. 11, 1996, ch. 442, sec. 2, § 168.024, 1996-2 Minn. Laws 1176, 1178 (acquiring another vehicle during plate impounding). –Citation to a section of a session law.

Laws of Missouri

Ab.: year Mo. Laws

Ex.: Act of June 27, 1995, 1995 Mo. Laws 826 (concerning licensing of cosmetologists). –Citation to an entire session law.

Act of June 27, 1995, 1995 Mo. Laws 826, 826-27, sec. A(1-4), § 329.010 (licensing of cosmetologists - definitions). –Citation to a section of a session law amending a prior act.

Laws of Montana

Ab.: year Mont. Laws

Ex.: Act of Apr. 14, 1995, ch. 466, 1995-3 Mont. Laws 2244. –Citation to an entire session law.

Act of Apr. 14, 1995, ch. 466, sec. 3, § 41-5-521, 1995-3 Mont. Laws 2244, 2245. –Citation to a section of a session law amending a prior act.

Laws of Nebraska

Ab.: year Neb. Laws

Ex.: Act of Mar. 25, 1996, No. 1041, 1995-2 Neb. Laws 750. –Citation to an entire session law.

Act of Mar. 25, 1996, No. 1041, sec. 7, § 77-2708, 1995-2 Neb. Laws 750, 756-58. –Citation to a section of a session law amending a prior act.

–Identifying information may be added parenthetically according to Bluebook Rule 12.4(a).

Laws of New Jersey

Ab.: year N.J. Laws

Ex.: Act of Aug. 11, 1994, ch. 95, 1994-2 N.J. Laws 884 (concerning admissibility of evidence in prosecutions for sex crimes). –Citation to an entire session law.

Act of Aug. 11, 1994, ch. 95, sec. 1, § 2C:14-7, 1994-2 N.J. Laws 884, 884-85 (sex crimes - victim's previous sexual conduct). –Citation to a section of a session law amending a prior act.

Laws of New Mexico

Ab.: year N.M. Laws

In law review footnotes, the titles of books and the names of cases, except for procedural phrases, are not underlined. See Bluebook Rule 2.1(a). Further, the following are in large and small capitals: codes, restatements, standards, constitutions, periodicals, authors of books, titles of books, the abbreviated names of codes, most legislative materials except for bills and resolutions, codified ordinances, model codes, court rules, and sentencing guidelines. Refer to The Bluebook.

Ex.: Act of Feb. 15, 2000, ch. 3, 2000 N.M. Laws 24 (relating to unemployment compensation). –Citation to an entire session law.

Act of Feb. 15, 2000, ch. 3, sec. 1, § 51-1-4, 2000 N.M. Laws 24, 24. –Citation to a section of a session law.

–Identifying information may be added parenthetically according to Bluebook Rule 12.4(a).

Laws of New York
Ab.: year N.Y. Laws

Ex.: Act of Aug. 2, 1995, ch. 389, 1995-3 N.Y. Laws 3171 (regarding child custody and support). –Citation to an entire session law.

Act of Aug. 2, 1995, ch. 389, sec. 1, § 240(1), 1995-3 N.Y. Laws 3171, 3171 (orders for child custody and support). –Citation to a section of a session law amending a prior act.

Laws of North Dakota
Ab.: year N.D. Sess. Laws

Ex.: Act of Mar. 31, 1999, ch. 394, 1999-2 N.D. Sess. Laws 1524. –Citation to an entire session law.

Act of Mar. 31, 1999, ch. 394, Sec. 5, § 43-40-08, 1999-2 N.D. Sess. Laws 1524, 1527 (concerning occupational therapist licensing practice). –Citation to a section of a session law.

Laws of Pennsylvania
Ab.: year Pa. Laws

Ex.: Act of June 13, 1995, No. 1995-8, 1995-1 Pa. Laws 52. –Citation to an entire session law.

Act of June 13, 1995, No. 1995-8, sec. 1(a), § 910, 1995-1 Pa. Laws 52, 52-53 –Citation to a section of a session law amending a prior act.

–Identifying information may be added parenthetically according to Bluebook Rule 12.4(a).

Laws of Puerto Rico
Ab.: year P.R. Laws

Ex.: Act of Nov. 28, 1989, No. 5, 1989 P.R. Laws 549. –Citation to an entire session law.

Act of Nov. 28, 1989, No. 5, sec. 1, § 16-102A, 1989 P.R. Laws 549, 549-50. –Citation to a section of a session law amending a prior act.

–Identifying information may be added parenthetically according to Bluebook Rule 12.4(a).

Laws of Puerto Rico Annotated
Ab.: P.R. Laws Ann. tit. , § (year)

In citing cases in law review footnotes, abbreviate any word listed in Table T.6; the names of "states, countries, and other geographical units" unless they are named parties; and any other words of eight or more letters "if substantial space is thereby saved and the result is unambiguous." Bluebook Rule 10.2.2. On the other hand, in citing cases in text, abbreviate only widely known acronyms and the following words: "&," "Ass'n," "Bros.," "Co.," "Corp.," "Inc.," "Ltd.," and "No." Bluebook Rule 10.2.1(c).

Ex.:   P.R. Laws Ann. tit. 13, § 8684 (1996).

        P.R. Laws Ann. tit. 31, § 2456 (Supp. 1992).

Laws of South Dakota
Ab.:   year S.D. Sess. Laws

Ex.:   Act of Feb. 14, 1996, ch. 40, 1996 S.D. Laws 85. –Citation to an entire
        session law.

        Act of Feb. 14, 1996, ch. 40, sec. 1, § 5-14-23, 1996 S.D. Laws 85, 85.
        –Citation to a section of a session law amending a prior act.

        –Identifying information may be added parenthetically according to
        Bluebook Rule 12.4(a).

Laws of the State of Maine
Ab.:   year Me. Laws

Ex.:   Act of Mar. 11, 1999, ch. 7, 1999-1 Me. Laws 29. –Citation to an
        entire session law.

        Act of Mar. 11, 1999, ch. 7, sec. 7, § 6575, 1999-1 Me. Laws 29, 30.
        –Citation to a section of a session law.

        –Identifying information may be added parenthetically according to
        Bluebook Rule 12.4(a).

Laws of the State of New Hampshire
Ab.:   year N.H. Laws

Ex.:   Act of June 21, 1995, ch. 280, 1995 N.H. Laws 469. –Citation to an
        entire session law.

        Act of June 21, 1995, ch. 280, sec. 3, § 510-A8, II, 1995 N.H. Laws
        469, 469-70. –Citation to a section of a session law amending a prior
        act.

        –Identifying information may be added parenthetically according to
        Bluebook Rule 12.4(a).

Laws of Utah
Ab.:   year Utah Laws

Ex.:   Act of Feb. 17, 1995, ch. 286, 1995 Utah Laws 943. –Citation to an
        entire session law.

        Act of Feb. 17, 1995, ch. 286, sec. 2 § 77-18-15, 1995 Utah Laws 943,
        944-45. –Citation to a section of a session law amending a prior act.

        –Identifying information may be added parenthetically according to
        Bluebook Rule 12.4(a).

Laws of Washington
Ab.:   year Wash. Laws

Ex.:   Act of Feb. 18, 2000, ch. 3, 2000 Wash. Laws 19 (relating to jail

In law review footnotes, the titles of books and the names of cases, except for procedural
phrases, are not underlined. See Bluebook Rule 2.1(a). Further, the following are in large
and small capitals: codes, restatements, standards, constitutions, periodicals, authors of
books, titles of books, the abbreviated names of codes, most legislative materials except for
bills and resolutions, codified ordinances, model codes, court rules, and sentencing guidelines.
Refer to The Bluebook.

booking). –Citation to an entire session law.

Act of Feb. 18, 2000, ch. 3, sec. 1, § 36.28A, 2000 Wash. Laws 19, 20. –Citation to a section of a session law.

Laws of Wisconsin
Ab.:   year Wis. Laws

Ex.:   Act of Dec. 16, 1993, No. 120, 1993-1 Wis. Laws 781 (relating to snowmobile rail crossings). –Citation to an entire session law.

Act of Dec. 16, 1993, No. 120, sec. 2, 1993-1 Wis. Laws 781, 781-82 (relating to snowmobile rail crossings requiring permits). –Citation to a section of a session law.

Lawyer's Edition, United States Supreme Court Reports
See United States Supreme Court Reports, Lawyer's Edition.

Lawyer's Manual on Professional Conduct (ABA/BNA)
Ab.:   Laws. Man. on Prof. Conduct (ABA/BNA)

Ex.:   State Bar of New Mexico Opinion 1986-5 [1986-1990 Ethics Opinions] Laws. Man. on Prof. Conduct (ABA/BNA) 901:6003 (Oct. 24, 1985). –Citation to looseleaf material.

Leader's Product Liability Law and Strategy
Ab.:   Leader's Product Liability L. & Strategy

Ex.:   Mark Shayne, Defending Against Claims For Lost Wages & Profits, Leader's Product Liability L. & Strategy, Dec. 1991, at 1. –Article Citation.

Mark Shayne, Defending Against Claims For Lost Wages & Profits, Leader's Product Liability L. & Strategy, Dec. 1991, at 1, 1. –Page Citation.

League of Nations Covenant
See Bluebook Rule 21.8.1, and Table T.3.

   –Cite as a constitution.

Ex.:   League of Nations Covenant art. 18, para. 2.

League of Nations Offical Journal
See Bluebook Rule 21.8.1, and Table T.3.

Ab.:   League of Nations O. J.

League of Nations Treaty Series
See Bluebook Rule 21.8.1, and Table T.3.

Ab.:   L.N.T.S.

In citing cases in law review footnotes, abbreviate any word listed in Table T.6; the names of "states, countries, and other geographical units" unless they are named parties; and any other words of eight or more letters "if substantial space is thereby saved and the result is unambiguous." Bluebook Rule 10.2.2. On the other hand, in citing cases in text, abbreviate only widely known acronyms and the following words: "&," "Ass'n," "Bros.," "Co.," "Corp.," "Inc.," "Ltd.," and "No." Bluebook Rule 10.2.1(c).

Ex.:   International Convention for the Unification of Certain Rules Relating
        to the Immunity of State-Owned Vessels, 176 L.N.T.S. 199 (1926).

Legal Issues of European Integration
Ab.:   Legal Issues Eur. Integration
Ex.:   Nicholas J. Skaelatos, European Lawyers' Right to Transnational Legal
        Practice in The European Community, 1991 Legal Issues Eur.
        Integration, at 49. –Article Citation.
        Nicholas J. Skaelatos, European Lawyers' Right to Transnational Legal
        Practice in The European Community, 1991 Legal Issues Eur.
        Integration, at 49, 52. –Page Citation.

Legal Malpractice, by Ronald E. Mallen and Jeffrey M. Smith
        –Do not abbreviate the title.
Ex.:   1 Ronald E. Mallen & Jeffrey M. Smith, Legal Malpractice § 2.6 (5th
        ed. 2000). –Section Citation.
        1 Ronald E. Mallen & Jeffrey M. Smith, Legal Malpractice § 2.6, at 67
        (5th ed. 2000). –Page Citation.
        1 Ronald E. Mallen & Jeffrey M. Smith, Legal Malpractice § 2.6, at 67
        n.2 (5th ed. 2000). –Footnote Citation.

Legal Medicine
Ab.:   Legal Med.
Ex.:   Bernard J. Ficarra, Physicians' Legal and Moral Responsibility to Treat
        Contagious Disease, 1991 Legal Med. 93. –Article Citation.
        Bernard J. Ficarra, Physicians' Legal and Moral Responsibility to Treat
        Contagious Disease, 1991 Legal Med. 93, 94. –Page Citation.

legal memoranda, basic citation forms
        See various title entries of this work. See also examples included on the facing
        page next to the inside back cover and on the inside back cover of The
        Bluebook.

legal memoranda, typeface conventions for legal memoranda
        See Bluebook Practitioners' Notes, pp. 11-19.

Legal Studies
Ab.:   Legal Stud.
Ex.:   Andrew J. Cunningham, "To the Uttermost Ends of the Earth?" The
        War Crimes Act and International Law, 11 Legal Stud. 281 (1991).
        –Article Citation.
        Andrew J. Cunningham, "To the Uttermost Ends of the Earth?" The
        War Crimes Act and International Law, 11 Legal Stud. 281, 286-87
        (1991). –Page Citation.

Legal Times
Ab.:   Legal Times

In law review footnotes, the titles of books and the names of cases, except for procedural
phrases, are not underlined. See Bluebook Rule 2.1(a). Further, the following are in large
and small capitals: codes, restatements, standards, constitutions, periodicals, authors of
books, titles of books, the abbreviated names of codes, most legislative materials except for
bills and resolutions, codified ordinances, model codes, court rules, and sentencing guidelines.
Refer to The Bluebook.

Ex.:	John Murawski, <u>Law Faces Budget Ax-Again</u>, Legal Times, Feb. 24, 1992, at 2. –Article Citation.

John Murawski, <u>Law Faces Budget Ax-Again</u>, Legal Times, Feb. 24, 1992, at 2, 12. –Page Citation.

–"Give only the first page of the piece and do not indicate the location of specific material." <u>See</u> <u>Bluebook</u> Rule 16.5.

Legislative History (separately bound)
<u>See</u> <u>Bluebook</u> Rule 13.6

Ex.:	H.R. Rep. No. 901, 91st Cong., 2d Sess. 3 (1970), <u>reprinted in</u> 4 <u>Railway Labor Act of 1926: A Legislative History</u> § 5 (Michael H. Campbell & Edward C. Brewer, III eds. 1988).

H.R. Rep. No. 101-787, at 25 (1990), <u>reprinted in</u> 1 <u>Individuals with Disabilities Education Act: A Legislative History of Public Law 101-476 as Amended by Public Law 102-119, Doc. No. 4</u> (Bernard D. Reams, Jr., J.D., Ph.D. 1994).

Leiden Journal of International Law
Ab.:	Leiden J. Int'l L.

Ex.:	Sam Muller, <u>International Organizations and Their Officials: To Tax or Not to Tax?</u>, 6 Leiden J. Int'l L. 47 (1993). –Article Citation.

Sam Muller, <u>International Organizations and Their Officials: To Tax or Not to Tax?</u>, 6 Leiden J. Int'l L. 47, 57 (1993). –Page Citation.

Lesotho Law Journal
Ab.:	Lesotho L.J.

Ex.:	Kenneth Asamoa Acheampoug, <u>The African Charter and the Equalization of Human Rights</u>, 7 Lesotho L.J. 21 (1991). –Article Citation.

Kenneth Asamoa Acheampoug, <u>The African Charter and the Equalization of Human Rights</u>, 7 Lesotho L.J. 21, 29-31 (1991). –Page Citation.

Letters, unpublished
Ex.:	Letter from Kurt Grasinger, Film Critic, <u>The New Yorker</u>, to Jean Winter, Editor, <u>Vanderbilt Law School Brief</u> (Feb. 26, 1996) (on file with author).

Lex et Scientia
Ab.:	Lex et Scientia

Ex.:	Mark E. Kalmansohn, Note, <u>Law, Lawyers, and Literature</u>, 12 Lex et Scientia 92 (1976).

Mark E. Kalmansohn, Note, <u>Law, Lawyers, and Literature</u>, 12 Lex et Scientia 92, 105 (1976).

In citing cases in law review footnotes, abbreviate any word listed in Table T.6; the names of "states, countries, and other geographical units" unless they are named parties; and any other words of eight or more letters "if <u>substantial</u> space is thereby saved and the result is unambiguous." <u>Bluebook</u> Rule 10.2.2. On the other hand, in citing cases in text, abbreviate only widely known acronyms and the following words: "&," "Ass'n," "Bros.," "Co.," "Corp.," "Inc.," "Ltd.," and "No." <u>Bluebook</u> Rule 10.2.1(c).

LEXIS
See pending and unreported cases; see also electronic media and other nonprint
resources and Bluebook Rules 10.9(ii), 16.5(d), 18.1.1, 18.1.2, & 18.1.3

Licensing Law and Business Report
Ab.: Licensing L. & Bus. Rep.

Life, Health & Accident Insurance Cases
See Insurance Law Reports

Lincoln Law Review
Ab.: Lincoln L. Rev.
Ex.: Robert W. McGee, The "Essence of the Transaction" Test for
Computer Software Tangibility and Taxation, 20 Lincoln L. Rev. 21
(1991). –Article Citation.
Robert W. McGee, The "Essence of the Transaction" Test for
Computer Software Tangibility and Taxation, 20 Lincoln L. Rev. 21,
23 (1991). –Page Citation.

Lindey on Entertainment, Publishing, and the Arts, by Alexander Lindey
–Do not abbreviate the title.
Ex.: 3 Alexander Lindey, Lindey on Entertainment, Publishing, and the Arts
§ 17.02[2] (2d ed. 1992). –Section Citation.
3 Alexander Lindey, Lindey on Entertainment, Publishing, and the Arts
§ 17.02[2], at 17.112 (2d ed. 1992). –Page Citation.

Lindey and Parley on Separation Agreements and Ante-Nuptial Contracts, by Alexander Lindey & Louis I. Parley
–Do not abbreviate this title.
Ex.: 2 Alexander Lindey & Louis I. Parley, Lindey and Parley on
Separation Agreements and Ante-Nuptial Contracts § 61.35 (2d ed.
2000). –Section Citation.
2 Alexander Lindey & Louis I. Parley, Lindey and Parley on
Separation Agreements and Ante-Nuptial Contracts § 61.35, at 61-20
(2d ed. 2000). –Page Citation.
2 Alexander Lindey & Louis I. Parley, Lindey and Parley on
Separation Agreements and Ante-Nuptial Contracts § 61.35, at 61-20
n.1 (2d ed. 2000). –Footnote Citation.

Lipscomb's Walker on Patents, by Ernest Lipscomb III
–Do not abbreviate the title.
Ex.: 6 Ernest B. Lipscomb III, Lipscomb's Walker on Patents § 21:7 (3d ed.
1987). –Section Citation.
6 Ernest B. Lipscomb III, Lipscomb's Walker on Patents § 21:7, at 278
(3d ed. 1987). –Page Citation.
6 Ernest B. Lipscomb III, Lipscomb's Walker on Patents § 21:7, at 278
n.11 (3d ed. 1987). –Footnote Citation.

In law review footnotes, the titles of books and the names of cases, except for procedural
phrases, are not underlined. See Bluebook Rule 2.1(a). Further, the following are in large
and small capitals: codes, restatements, standards, constitutions, periodicals, authors of
books, titles of books, the abbreviated names of codes, most legislative materials except for
bills and resolutions, codified ordinances, model codes, court rules, and sentencing guidelines.
Refer to The Bluebook.

Liquor Control Law Reports (Commerc Clearing House)
> Ab.:   Liquor Cont. L. Rep. (CCH)

Listserv messages
> See Electronic media and other nonprint resources

Litigation
> Ab.:   Litig.
> Ex.:   Michael E. Tigar, Discovering Your Litigator's Voice, Litig., Summer 1990, at 1. –Article Citation.
> Michael E. Tigar, Discovering Your Litigator's Voice, Litig., Summer 1990, at 1, 3. –Page Citation.

Lloyd's Law Reports (U.K.) (1968-date)
> See Bluebook Table T.2.
> Ab.:   Lloyd's Rep.
> Ex.:   Vesta v. Butcher, [1989] 1 Lloyd's Rep. 331 (1988) (Eng.). –Case Citation.
> Haiti v. Duvalier, [1989] 1 Lloyd's Rep. 111 (C.A. 1988) (Eng.). –Case Citation.

Lloyd's List Law Reports (U.K.) (1919-1967)
> See Bluebook Table T.2.
> Ab.:   Lloyd's List L. Rep.
> Ex.:   The "Lucille Bloomfield", [1966] 2 Lloyd's List L. Rep. 239 (Adm. 1966) (Eng.). –Case Citation.
> Stoney Stanton Supplies, Ltd. v. Midland Bank, Ltd., [1966] 2 Lloyd's List L. Rep. 373 (C.A. 1966) (Eng.). –Case Citation.

Lloyd's Maritime and Commercial Law Quarterly
> Ab.:   Lloyd's Mar. & Com. L.Q.
> Ex.:   David Milman, The Courts and the Companies Acts: the Judicial Contribution to Company Law, 1990 Lloyd's Mar. & Com. L.Q. 401 (1990). –Article Citation.
> David Milman, The Courts and the Companies Acts: the Judicial Contribution to Company Law, 1990 Lloyd's Mar. & Com. L.Q. 401, 415 (1990). –Page Citation.

looseleaf services
> Ex.:
> current unbound:
> Standard Metals Corp. v. Tomlin, [Current] Fed. Sec. L. Rep. (CCH) ¶ 98,004 (S.D.N.Y. May 20, 1981). –Citation for a case.

In citing cases in law review footnotes, abbreviate any word listed in Table T.6; the names of "states, countries, and other geographical units" unless they are named parties; and any other words of eight or more letters "if substantial space is thereby saved and the result is unambiguous." Bluebook Rule 10.2.2. On the other hand, in citing cases in text, abbreviate only widely known acronyms and the following words: "&," "Ass'n," "Bros.," "Co.," "Corp.," "Inc.," "Ltd.," and "No." Bluebook Rule 10.2.1(c).

Sea-Land Service, Inc. v. Federal Maritime Commission [Current Materials] Admin. L.2d (P & F) (50 Admin. L.2d) 927 (D.C. Cir. Apr.14, 1981). –Citation for a case for which the bound volume number is known.

transfer binder:

SEC v. Wencke, [1980 Transfer Binder] Fed. Sec. L. Rep. (CCH) ¶ 97,533 (9th Cir. June 9, 1980). –Citation to transfer binder.

bound:

Bartell v. Cohen, 29 Admin. L. 2d (P & F) 342 (7th Cir. 1971).

–The above example is proper if the case is not yet available in, or is not reported in, an official or West reporter, a public domain citation, or a widely used computer database.

Lord Justice
Ab.: L.J.

Los Angeles Bar Bulletin
Ab.: L.A. B. Bull.
Ex.: Murray Projector, Valuation of Retirement Benefits in Marriage Dissoultions, 50 L.A. B. Bull. 229 (1975). –Article Citation.
Murray Projector, Valuation of Retirement Benefits in Marriage Dissoultions, 50 L.A. B. Bull. 229, 232 (1975). –Page Citation.

Los Angeles Lawyer
Ab.: L.A. Law.
Ex.: Randall L. Erickson, Mechanics' Lien Actions: New Standing Amendments and Future Trends, L.A. Law., Feb. 1992, at 22. –Article Citation.
Randall L. Erickson, Mechanics' Lien Actions: New Standing Amendments and Future Trends, L.A. Law., Feb. 1992, at 22, 23. –Page Citation.

Loss on Securities Regulation
See Securities Regulation, by Louis Loss and Joel Seligman.

Louisiana Administrative Code
Ab.: La. Admin. Code tit. , § (year)
Ex.: La. Admin. Code tit. 33, § 4301 (2000).

Louisiana Annual Reports
Ab.: La. Ann.

In law review footnotes, the titles of books and the names of cases, except for procedural phrases, are not underlined. See Bluebook Rule 2.1(a). Further, the following are in large and small capitals: codes, restatements, standards, constitutions, periodicals, authors of books, titles of books, the abbreviated names of codes, most legislative materials except for bills and resolutions, codified ordinances, model codes, court rules, and sentencing guidelines. Refer to The Bluebook.

Ex.:   State v. Edwards, 34 La. Ann. 1012 (1882). –Case Citation.
         State v. Edwards, 34 La. Ann. 1012, 1013 (1882). –Page Citation.

Louisiana Bar Journal
Ab.:   La. B.J.
Ex.:   William C. Swanson, Stress and the Practice of Law, 37 La. B.J. 7
         (1989). –Article Citation.
         William C. Swanson, Stress and the Practice of Law, 37 La. B.J. 7, 8
         (1989). –Page Citation.

Louisiana Children's Code Annotated
See West's Louisiana Children's Code Annotated

Louisiana Civil Code Annotated
See West's Louisiana Civil Code Annotated

Louisiana Code of Civil Procedure Annotated
See West's Louisiana Code of Civil Procedure Annotated

Louisiana Code of Criminal Procedure Annotated
See West's Louisiana Code of Criminal Procedure Annotated

Louisiana Code of Evidence Annotated
See West's Louisiana Code of Evidence Annotated

Louisiana Constitution
Ab.:   La. Const. art.   , pt.   , §   .
         –Not all articles are subdivided into parts.
Ex.:   La. Const. art. I, § 10. –"Cite constitutional provisions currently in
         force without date." Bluebook Rule 11.
         La. Const. art. XIV, § 29 (repealed 1986). –"If the cited provision has
         been repealed, either indicate parenthetically the fact and date of repeal
         or cite the repealing provision in full." Bluebook Rule 11.
         La. Const. art. XII, § 6 (amended 1990). –"When citing a provision
         that has been subsequently amended, either indicate parenthetically the
         fact and date of amendment or cite the amending provision in full."
         Bluebook Rule 11.
         La. Const. of 1921, art. I, § 7 (1974). –"Cite constitutions that have
         been totally superseded by year of adoption; if the specific provision
         cited was adopted in a different year, give that year parenthetically."
         Bluebook Rule 11.

Louisiana Court of Appeals
Ab.:   La. Ct. App.

In citing cases in law review footnotes, abbreviate any word listed in Table T.6;
the names of "states, countries, and other geographical units" unless they are named parties;
and any other words of eight or more letters "if substantial space is thereby saved and the
result is unambiguous." Bluebook Rule 10.2.2. On the other hand, in citing cases in text,
abbreviate only widely known acronyms and the following words: "&," "Ass'n," "Bros.,"
"Co.," "Corp.," "Inc.," "Ltd.," and "No." Bluebook Rule 10.2.1(c).

–Cite to So. or So. 2d if therein; in addition, give public domain citation if available.

–Prior to inclusion in So. in 1928, cite as follows:

In all documents:

Hirsch v. Ashford, 5 La. App. 290 (1927) –Case Citation.

Hirsch v. Ashford, 5 La. App. 290, 292 (1927) –Page Citation.

–From 1928 until January 1, 1994, when a public domain format was adopted, cite as follows:

In all documents:

Perry v. W.K. Henderson Iron Works & Supply Co., 133 So. 805 (La. Ct. App. 1931). –Case Citation.

Perry v. W.K. Henderson Iron Works & Supply Co., 133 So. 805, 806 (La. Ct. App. 1931). –Page Citation.

–After January 1, 1994, cite as follows:

In all documents:

Taylor v. Sider, 99-2521 (La. App. 4 Cir. 5/31/00), 765 So. 2d 416–Case Citation.

Taylor v. Sider, 99-2521, p. 4 (La. App. 4 Cir. 5/31/00), 765 So. 2d 416, 419 –Page Citation.

See Bluebook Rules 10.3.1 and 10.3.3, Table T.1, and Practitioners' Note P.3; see also La. Sup. Ct. Gen. Admin. R. § 8.

Louisiana Law Review
Ab.:   La. L. Rev.

Ex.:   Walter F. Murphy, Civil Law, Common Law, and Constitutional Democracy, 52 La. L. Rev. 91 (1991). –Article Citation.

Walter F. Murphy, Civil Law, Common Law, and Constitutional Democracy, 52 La. L. Rev. 91, 119 (1991). –Page Citation.

Louisiana, Opinions of the Attorney General
See Opinions of the Attorney General of Louisiana

Louisiana Register
Ab.:   La. Reg.

Louisiana Revised Statutes Annotated
See West's Louisiana Revised Statutes Annotated

Louisiana Session Laws
See State of Louisiana: Acts of the Legislature and Louisiana Session Law Service (West)

Louisiana Session Law Service (West).
Ab.:   year La. Sess. Law Serv. (West)

In law review footnotes, the titles of books and the names of cases, except for procedural phrases, are not underlined. See Bluebook Rule 2.1(a). Further, the following are in large and small capitals: codes, restatements, standards, constitutions, periodicals, authors of books, titles of books, the abbreviated names of codes, most legislative materials except for bills and resolutions, codified ordinances, model codes, court rules, and sentencing guidelines. Refer to The Bluebook.

Ex.:   Act of June 27, 1996, S.B. No. 76, 1996 La. Sess. Law Serv. 218
(West) (capital companies). –Citation to an entire session law.
Act of June 27, 1996, S.B. No. 76, sec. 1, § 22:1068, 1996 La. Sess.
Law Serv. 218, 218-19 (West) (capital companies tax reduction).
–Citation to a session law amending a prior act.
–"Cite to La. Acts if therein." Bluebook Table T.1, p. 206.

Louisiana Supreme Court
See public domain citations.

Ab.:   La.
–Cite to So. or So. 2d if therein; in addition, give public domain
citation if available.
–Through 263 La. 1111 (1972), when Louisiana Reports were
discontinued, cite as follows:

In documents submitted to Louisiana state courts:
Schmidt v. City of New Orleans, 164 La. 1006, 115 So. 63 (1927).
–Case Citation.
Schmidt v. City of New Orleans, 164 La. 1006, 1008-09, 115 So.
63, 64 (1927). –Page Citation.

In all other documents:
Schmidt v. City of New Orleans, 115 So. 63 (La. 1927). –Case
Citation.
Schmidt v. City of New Orleans, 115 So. 63, 64 (La. 1927). –Page
Citation.

–After 263 La. 1111 (1972) and until January 1, 1994, when a public
format was adopted, cite as follows:

In all documents:
Pendleton v. Barrett, 675 So. 2d 720 (La. 1996). –Case Citation.
Pendleton v. Barrett, 675 So. 2d 720, 722 (La. 1996). –Page
Citation.

–After January 1, 1994, cite as follows:

In all documents:
In re Carreras, 2000-1094 (La. 6/16/00), 765 So. 2d 321. –Case
Citation.
In re Carreras, 2000-1094, p. 4 (La. 6/16/00), 765 So. 2d 321, 323.
–Page Citation.

See Bluebook Rules 10.3.1 and 10.3.3, Table T.1, and Practitioners'
Note P.3; see also La. Sup. Ct. Gen. Admin. R. § 8.

Loyola Consumer Law Reporter
Ab.:   Loy. Consumer L. Rep.

In citing cases in law review footnotes, abbreviate any word listed in Table T.6;
the names of "states, countries, and other geographical units" unless they are named parties;
and any other words of eight or more letters "if substantial space is thereby saved and the
result is unambiguous." Bluebook Rule 10.2.2. On the other hand, in citing cases in text,
abbreviate only widely known acronyms and the following words: "&," "Ass'n," "Bros.,"
"Co.," "Corp.," "Inc.," "Ltd.," and "No." Bluebook Rule 10.2.1(c).

Ex.:   Michael N. Petkovich, <u>Consumer Rights Under the Americans With Disabilities Act</u>, 4 Loy. Consumer L. Rep. 44 (1992). –Article Citation.

Michael N. Petkovich, <u>Consumer Rights Under the Americans With Disabilities Act</u>, 4 Loy. Consumer L. Rep. 44, 46 (1992). –Page Citation.

Loyola Entertainment Law Journal
Ab.:   Loy. Ent. L.J.
Ex.:   Jill M. Eshman, <u>Bank Financing of a Motion Picture Production</u>, 12 Loy. Ent. L.J. 87 (1992). –Article Citation.

Jill M. Eshman, <u>Bank Financing of a Motion Picture Production</u>, 12 Loy. Ent. L.J. 87, 88-89 (1992). –Page Citation.

Loyola Law Review
Ab.:   Loy. L. Rev.
Ex.:   Robert J. Aravjo, <u>Legal Education and Jesuit Universities: Mission and Ministry of the Society of Jesus?</u>, 37 Loy. L. Rev. 245 (1991). –Article Citation.

Robert J. Aravjo, <u>Legal Education and Jesuit Universities: Mission and Ministry of the Society of Jesus?</u>, 37 Loy. L. Rev. 245, 249-51 (1991). –Page Citation.

Loyola of Los Angeles International and Comparative Law Journal
Ab.:   Loy. L.A. Int'l & Comp. L.J.
Ex.:   Anne Moebes, <u>Negotiating International Copyright Protection: The United States and European Community Positions</u>, 14 Loy. L.A. Int'l & Comp. L.J. 301 (1992). –Article Citation.

Anne Moebes, <u>Negotiating International Copyright Protection: The United States and European Community Positions</u>, 14 Loy. L.A. Int'l & Comp. L.J. 301, 310-12 (1992). –Page Citation.

Loyola of Los Angeles Law Review
Ab.:   Loy. L.A. L. Rev.
Ex.:   Richard L. Antognini, <u>When Will My Troubles End? The Loss in Progress Defense in Progressive Loss Insurance Cases</u>, 25 Loy. L.A. L. Rev. 419 (1992). –Article Citation.

Richard L. Antognini, <u>When Will My Troubles End? The Loss in Progress Defense in Progressive Loss Insurance Cases</u>, 25 Loy. L.A. L. Rev. 419, 431 (1992). –Page Citation.

Loyola University of Chicago Law Journal
Ab.:   Loy. U. Chi. L.J.

In law review footnotes, the titles of books and the names of cases, except for procedural phrases, are not underlined. <u>See</u> <u>Bluebook</u> Rule 2.1(a). Further, the following are in large and small capitals: codes, restatements, standards, constitutions, periodicals, authors of books, titles of books, the abbreviated names of codes, most legislative materials except for bills and resolutions, codified ordinances, model codes, court rules, and sentencing guidelines. Refer to <u>The Bluebook</u>.

Ex.:   Candace M. Zierdt, <u>Compensation for Birth Mothers: A Challenge to the Adoption Laws</u>, 23 Loy. U. Chi. L.J. 25 (1991). —Article Citation.

           Candace M. Zierdt, <u>Compensation for Birth Mothers: A Challenge to the Adoption Laws</u>, 23 Loy. U. Chi. L.J. 25, 27-31 (1991). —Page Citation.

In citing cases in law review footnotes, abbreviate any word listed in Table T.6; the names of "states, countries, and other geographical units" unless they are named parties; and any other words of eight or more letters "if <u>substantial</u> space is thereby saved and the result is unambiguous." <u>Bluebook</u> Rule 10.2.2. On the other hand, in citing cases in text, abbreviate only widely known acronyms and the following words: "&," "Ass'n," "Bros.," "Co.," "Corp.," "Inc.," "Ltd.," and "No." <u>Bluebook</u> Rule 10.2.1(c).

M

Madden & Owen on Products Liability, by David G. Owen, M. Stuart Madden, and Mary J. Davis
  –Do not abbreviate the title.

Ex.:   3 David G. Owen et al., Madden & Owen on Products Liability,
        § 2-301 (3d ed. 2000) –Section Citation.

        3 David G. Owen et al., Madden & Owen on Products Liability,
        § 2-301, at 170 (3d ed. 2000) –Page Citation.

Madras Law Journal
  Ab.:   Madras L.J.

Ex.:   R. Govindarajan, "Burden of Proof" Under the Tamil Nadu Debt
        Relief Acts, Madras L.J., July-Dec. 1983, at 28. –Article Citation.

        R. Govindarajan, "Burden of Proof" Under the Tamil Nadu Debt
        Relief Acts, Madras L.J., July-Dec. 1983, at 28, 29-30. –Page Citation.

Magistrate
  Ab.:   Mag.

Maine Bar Journal
  Ab.:   Me. B.J.

Ex.:   James H. Young, II, Medicaid Eligibility, 5 Me. B.J. 214 (1990).
        –Article Citation.

        James H. Young, II, Medicaid Eligibility, 5 Me. B.J. 214, 215 (1990).
        –Page Citation.

Maine Constitution
  Ab.:   Me. Const. art.   , pt.   , §   .
        –Not all articles are subdivided into parts.

Ex.:   Me. Const. art. I, § 4. –"Cite constitutional provisions currently in
        force without date." Bluebook Rule 11.

        Me. Const. art. XI, § 2 (amended 1988).

        Me. Const. art. XI, § 2, amended by Me. Const. Amend. CLVIII.
        –"When citing a provision that has been subsequently amended, either
        indicate parenthetically the fact and date of amendment or cite the
        amending provision in full." Bluebook Rule 11.

Maine Law Review
  Ab.:   Me. L. Rev.

In law review footnotes, the titles of books and the names of cases, except for procedural
phrases, are not underlined. See Bluebook Rule 2.1(a). Further, the following are in large
and small capitals: codes, restatements, standards, constitutions, periodicals, authors of
books, titles of books, the abbreviated names of codes, most legislative materials except for
bills and resolutions, codified ordinances, model codes, court rules, and sentencing guidelines.
Refer to The Bluebook.

Ex.:   Dennis M. Doiron, <u>A Better Interpretation of the Wrongful Death Act</u>, 43 Me. L. Rev. 449 (1991). –Article Citation.

Dennis M. Doiron, <u>A Better Interpretation of the Wrongful Death Act</u>, 43 Me. L. Rev. 449, 455-57 (1991). –Page Citation.

Maine Legislative Service (West)

Ab.:   year Me. Legis. Serv. (West)

Ex.:   Act of Mar. 25, 1996, ch. 565, 1996 Me. Legis. Serv. 380 (West) –Citation to an entire session law.

Act of Mar. 25, 1996, ch. 565, sec. 1, § 1603, 1996 Me. Legis Serv. 380, 380-81 (West) –Citation to a section of a session law amending prior act.

–"Cite to Me. Laws if therein." <u>Bluebook</u> Table T.1, p. 207.

Maine Revised Statutes Annotated (West)

Ab.:   Me. Rev. Stat. Ann. tit.   , § (West year)

Ex.:   Me. Rev. Stat. Ann. tit. 24, § 2332-B (West 2000).

Me. Rev. Stat. Ann. tit. 25, § 1547 (West Supp. 1999).

Maine Session Laws

<u>See</u> Acts, Resolves and Constitutional Resolutions of the State of Maine; Laws of the State of Maine; and Maine Legislative Service (West).

Maine Supreme Judicial Court

Ab.:   Me.

–Cite to A. or A.2d if therein; in addition, give public domain citation if available.

–Through 161 Me. 541 (1965), cite as follows:

In documents submitted to Maine state courts:

<u>Porter v. Porter</u>, 138 Me. 1, 20 A.2d 465 (1941). –Case Citation.

<u>Porter v. Porter</u>, 138 Me. 1, 8, 20 A.2d 465, 468 (1941). –Page Citation.

<u>See</u> Michal D. Seitzinger & Charles K. Leadbetter, <u>Uniform Maine Citations</u> (1992), which requires a parallel citation.

In all other documents:

<u>Porter v. Porter</u>, 20 A.2d 465 (Me. 1941). –Case Citation.

<u>Porter v. Porter</u>, 20 A.2d 465, 468 (Me. 1941). –Page Citation.

–After 161 Me. 541 (1965), and until January 1, 1997, when a public domain format was adopted, cite as follows:

In all documents:

<u>Feinerman v. Barrett</u>, 673 A.2d 1341 (Me. 1996). –Case Citation.

In citing cases in law review footnotes, abbreviate any word listed in Table T.6; the names of "states, countries, and other geographical units" unless they are named parties; and any other words of eight or more letters "if <u>substantial</u> space is thereby saved and the result is unambiguous." <u>Bluebook</u> Rule 10.2.2. On the other hand, in citing cases in text, abbreviate only widely known acronyms and the following words: "&," "Ass'n," "Bros.," "Co.," "Corp.," "Inc.," "Ltd.," and "No." <u>Bluebook</u> Rule 10.2.1(c).

Feinerman v. Barrett, 673 A.2d 1341, 1343 (Me. 1996). –Page
Citation.

–After January 1, 1997, cite as follows:
In all documents:
Holland v. Sebunya, 2000 ME 160, 759 A.2d 205. –Case Citation.

Holland v. Sebunya, 2000 ME 160, ¶ 24, 759 A.2d 205, 213.
–Pinpoint Citation.

See Bluebook Rules 10.3.1 and 10.3.3, Table T.1, and Practitioners'
Note P.3; see also Or. SJC-216 (Me. Aug. 20, 1996) and Michal D.
Seitzinger & Charles K. Leadbetter, Uniform Maine Citations (1992).

Major Tax Planning
 Ab.: Major Tax Plan.
 Ex.: William P. Wasserman & Terence F. Cuff, Helping the Kids Buy a
   House, 47 Major Tax Plan. ¶ 2202.2 (1995). –Section Citation.

   William P. Wasserman & Terence F. Cuff, Helping the Kids Buy a
   House, 47 Major Tax Plan. ¶ 2202.2, at 22-6 (1995). –Page Citation.

Malaya Law Review
 Ab.: Malaya L.R.
 Ex.: Tan C. Han, The General Exception of Necessity Under the Singapore
   Penal Code, 1990 Malaya L.R. 271. –Article Citation.

   Tan C. Han, The General Exception of Necessity Under the Singapore
   Penal Code, 1990 Malaya L.R. 271, 279-80. –Page Citation.

Malayan Law Journal
 Ab.: Malayan L.J.
 Ex.: Lee Wah Bank Ltd. v. National Union Bank of Employees, [1981] 1
   Malayan L.J. 169 (Sup. Ct. 1981).

Manitoba & Saskatchewan Tax Reporter (Commerce Clearing House)
 Ab.: Man. & Sask. Tax Rep. (CCH)

Manitoba Gazette
 Ab.: M. Gaz.

Manitoba Law Journal
 Ab.: Man. L.J.
 Ex.: Humar Foster, Forgotten Arguments: Aboriginal Title and Sovereignty
   in Canada Jurisdiction Act Cases, 21 Man. L.J. 343 (1992). –Article
   Citation.

   Humar Foster, Forgotten Arguments: Aboriginal Title and Sovereignty
   in Canada Jurisdiction Act Cases, 21 Man. L.J. 343, 346 (1992).
   –Page Citation.

In law review footnotes, the titles of books and the names of cases, except for procedural
phrases, are not underlined. See Bluebook Rule 2.1(a). Further, the following are in large
and small capitals: codes, restatements, standards, constitutions, periodicals, authors of
books, titles of books, the abbreviated names of codes, most legislative materials except for
bills and resolutions, codified ordinances, model codes, court rules, and sentencing guidelines.
Refer to The Bluebook.

Manitoba Law Reports (Canada) (1875-1883)
See Bluebook Table T.2.
Ab.: Man. L. R.
Ex.: Onofriechuk v. Burlacu, [1959] 67 Man. L. R. 223 (Ct. App.) (Can.).
–Case Citation.
Onofriechuk v. Burlacu, [1959] 67 Man. L. R. 223, 224 (Ct. App.)
(Can.). –Page Citation.

Manitoba Reports (Canada) (1883-1961)
See Bluebook Table T.2.
Ab.: Man. R.

Manitoba Reports (2d) (Canada) (1979 - Date)
See Bluebook Table T.2.
Ab.: Man. R.2d

manuscript
Ab.: ms.

Maritime Law Reporter (Commerce Clearing House)
Ab.: Maritime L. Rep. (CCH)

Maritime Lawyer, The
Ab.: Mar. Law.
Ex.: Curtis G. Pew et al., Maritime Courts in the Middle Kingdom: China's
Great Leap Seaward, 11 Mar. Law. 237 (1986). –Article Citation.
Curtis G. Pew et al., Maritime Courts in the Middle Kingdom: China's
Great Leap Seaward, 11 Mar. Law. 237, 249-53 (1986). –Page
Citation.

Marquette Law Review
Ab.: Marq. L. Rev.
Ex.: Ronald R. Hofer, Standards of Review - Looking Beyond the Labels,
74 Marq. L. Rev. 231 (1991). –Article Citation.
Ronald R. Hofer, Standards of Review - Looking Beyond the Labels,
74 Marq. L. Rev. 231, 233 (1991). –Page Citation.

Maryland, Annotated Code of the Public General Laws
See Annotated Code of Maryland

Maryland, Annual Report and Official Opinions of the Attorney General
See Annual Report and Official Opinions of the Attorney General of Maryland

Maryland Appellate Reports
Ab.: Md. App.
–Cite to A.2d if therein; otherwise, cite to Md. App.

In citing cases in law review footnotes, abbreviate any word listed in Table T.6;
the names of "states, countries, and other geographical units" unless they are named parties;
and any other words of eight or more letters "if substantial space is thereby saved and the
result is unambiguous." Bluebook Rule 10.2.2. On the other hand, in citing cases in text,
abbreviate only widely known acronyms and the following words: "&," "Ass'n," "Bros.,"
"Co.," "Corp.," "Inc.," "Ltd.," and "No." Bluebook Rule 10.2.1(c).

–Give parallel citations, if at all, only in documents submitted to Maryland state courts. See Bluebook Rule 10.3.1 and Practitioners' Note P.3; see also Md. R. App. Rev. 8-504(a), which requires only a citation to Md. App.

In documents submitted to Maryland state courts, cite as follows:

Lebac v. Lebac, 109 Md. App. 396, 675 A.2d 131 (1996). –Case Citation.

Lebac v. Lebac, 109 Md. App. 396, 397, 675 A.2d 131, 132 (1996). –Page Citation.

In all other documents, cite as follows:

Lebac v. Lebac, 675 A.2d 131 (Md. Ct. Spec. App. 1996). –Case Citation.

Lebac v. Lebac, 675 A.2d 131, 132 (Md. Ct. Spec. App. 1996). –Page Citation.

Maryland Bar Journal
Ab.:   Md. B.J.

Ex.:   Gary I. Strausberg, Punitive Damages: Another View, Md. B. J., Jan.-Feb. 1992, at 8. –Article Citation.

Gary I. Strausberg, Punitive Damages: Another View, Md. B. J., Jan.-Feb. 1992, at 8, 9. –Page Citation.

Maryland Code of Regulations
See Code of Maryland Regulations

Maryland Constitution
Ab.:   Md. Const. art.   , §   .

Ex.:   Md. Const. art. III, § 38. –"Cite constitutional provisions currently in force without date." Bluebook Rule 11.

Md. Const. art. XI, § 3 (repealed 1956). –"If the cited provision has been repealed, either indicate parenthetically the fact and date of repeal or cite the repealing provision in full." Bluebook Rule 11.

Md. Const. art. VIII, § 7 (amended 1982). –"When citing a provision that has been subsequently amended, either indicate parenthetically the fact and date of amendment or cite the amending provision in full." Bluebook Rule 11.

–The Declaration of Rights is listed separately from the body of the constitution. The form for the citation is that used by Maryland Law Review.

Maryland Journal of Contemporary Legal Issues
Ab.:   Md. J. Contemp. Legal Issues

In law review footnotes, the titles of books and the names of cases, except for procedural phrases, are not underlined. See Bluebook Rule 2.1(a). Further, the following are in large and small capitals: codes, restatements, standards, constitutions, periodicals, authors of books, titles of books, the abbreviated names of codes, most legislative materials except for bills and resolutions, codified ordinances, model codes, court rules, and sentencing guidelines. Refer to The Bluebook.

Ex.:   Edmund G. Howe, <u>Advanced Directives After <i>Cruzan:</i> Are More Too Many?</u>, 2 Md. J. Contemp. Legal Issues 299 (1991). –Article Citation.

Edmund G. Howe, <u>Advanced Directives After <i>Cruzan:</i> Are More Too Many?</u>, 2 Md. J. Contemp. Legal Issues 299, 316 (1991). –Page Citation.

Maryland Journal of International Law and Trade
Ab.:   Md. J. Int'l L. & Trade

Ex.:   Joseph P. Hornyak, <u>Treatment of Dumped Imports From Nonmarket Economy Countries</u>, 15 Md. J. Int'l L. & Trade 23 (1991). –Article Citation.

Joseph P. Hornyak, <u>Treatment of Dumped Imports From Nonmarket Economy Countries</u>, 15 Md. J. Int'l L. & Trade 23, 25 (1991). –Page Citation.

Maryland Law Review
Ab.:   Md. L. Rev.

Ex.:   Richard H. McNeer, <u>Nontidal Wetlands Protection in Maryland and Virginia</u>, 51 Md. L. Rev. 105 (1992). –Article Citation.

Richard H. McNeer, <u>Nontidal Wetlands Protection in Maryland and Virginia</u>, 51 Md. L. Rev. 105, 131 (1992). –Page Citation.

Maryland Register
Ab.:   Md. Reg.

Maryland Reports
Ab.:   Md.

–Cite to A. or A.2d if therein; otherwise, cite to Md.

–Give parallel citations, if at all, only in documents submitted to Maryland state courts. <u>See</u> <u>Bluebook</u> Rule 10.3.1 and Practitioners' Note P.3; <u>see also</u> Md. R. App. Rev. 8-504(a), which requires only a citation to Md.

In documents submitted to Maryland state courts, cite as follows:

<u>Manner v. Stephenson</u>, 342 Md. 461, 677 A.2d 560 (1996). –Case Citation.

<u>Manner v. Stephenson</u>, 342 Md. 461, 463, 677 A.2d 560, 561 (1996). –Page Citation.

In all other documents, cite as follows:

<u>Manner v. Stephenson</u>, 677 A.2d 560 (Md. 1996). –Case Citation.

<u>Manner v. Stephenson</u>, 677 A.2d 560, 561 (Md. 1996). –Page Citation.

Maryland Session Laws
<u>See</u> Laws of Maryland

In citing cases in law review footnotes, abbreviate any word listed in Table T.6; the names of "states, countries, and other geographical units" unless they are named parties; and any other words of eight or more letters "if <u>substantial</u> space is thereby saved and the result is unambiguous." <u>Bluebook</u> Rule 10.2.2. On the other hand, in citing cases in text, abbreviate only widely known acronyms and the following words: "&," "Ass'n," "Bros.," "Co.," "Corp.," "Inc.," "Ltd.," and "No." <u>Bluebook</u> Rule 10.2.1(c).

Massachusetts Annotated Laws
  See Annotated Laws of Massachusetts (Lexis)

Massachusetts Appeals Court Reports
  Ab.:   Mass. App. Ct.
  –Cite to N.E. or N.E.2d if therein; otherwise, cite to Mass. App. Ct.
  –Give parallel citations, if at all, only in documents submitted to Massachusetts state courts. See Bluebook Rule 10.3.1 and Practitioners' Note P.3; see also Mass. R. App. P. 16(g) and Mass. Dist. & Mun. App. Div. R. 16(g), which require only a citation to Mass. App. Ct.
  In documents submitted to Massachusetts state courts, cite as follows:
  Cournoyer v. Cournoyer, 40 Mass. App. Ct. 302, 663 N.E.2d 863 (1996). –Case Citation.
  Cournoyer v. Cournoyer, 40 Mass. App. Ct. 302, 304, 663 N.E.2d 863, 865 (1996). –Page Citation.
  In all other documents, cite as follows:
  Cournoyer v. Cournoyer, 663 N.E.2d 863 (Mass. App. Ct. 1996). –Case Citation.
  Cournoyer v. Cournoyer, 663 N.E.2d 863, 865 (Mass. App. Ct. 1996). –Page Citation.

Massachusetts Appellate Decisions (1941-1977)
  Ab.:   Mass. App. Dec.
  Ex.:   LaBonte v. Miller, 159 Mass. App. Dec. 128 (1976). –Case Citation.

Massachusetts Appellate Division, Advance Sheets
  Ab.:   year Mass. App. Div. Adv. Sh.

Massachusetts Appellate Division Reports
  Ab.:   Mass. App. Div.
  Ex.:   Oyegbola v. Desimone, 1995 Mass. App. Div. 91 (Dist. Ct.). –Case Citation.
  Oyegbola v. Desimone, 1995 Mass. App. Div. 91, 93 (Dist. Ct.). –Page Citation.

Massachusetts Code of Regulations
  See Code of Massachusetts Regulations

Massachusetts Constitution
  Ab.:   Mass. Const. pt. , ch. , § , art. .
  Mass. Const. amend. art. . –Citing to amendments.
  Ex.:   Mass. Const. pt. 2, ch. 1, § 1, art. IV. –"Cite constitutional provisions currently in force without date." Bluebook Rule 11.

In law review footnotes, the titles of books and the names of cases, except for procedural phrases, are not underlined. See Bluebook Rule 2.1(a). Further, the following are in large and small capitals: codes, restatements, standards, constitutions, periodicals, authors of books, titles of books, the abbreviated names of codes, most legislative materials except for bills and resolutions, codified ordinances, model codes, court rules, and sentencing guidelines. Refer to The Bluebook.

–"If the cited provision has been repealed, either indicate parenthetically the fact and date of repeal or cite the repealing provision in full." <u>Bluebook</u> Rule 11.

Mass. Const. pt. 1, art. XXVI (amended 1982).

Mass. Const. pt. 1, art. XXVI, <u>amended by</u> Mass. Const. amend. art. CXVI. –"When citing a provision that has been subsequently amended, either indicate parenthetically the fact and date of amendment or cite the amending provision in full." <u>Bluebook</u> Rule 11.

Massachusetts General Laws
<u>See</u> General Laws of the Commonwealth of Massachusetts. (Mass. Bar Assoc./West)

Massachusetts General Laws Annotated (West)
Ab.:   Mass. Gen. Laws Ann. ch. , § (West year)
Ex.:   Mass. Gen. Laws Ann. ch. 231, § 108 (West 2000).
       Mass. Gen. Laws Ann. ch. 244, § 14 (West Supp. 2000).
       –"Cite to Massachusetts General Laws if therein." <u>Bluebook</u> Table T.1, p. 209.

Massachusetts Law Review
Ab.:   Mass. L. Rev.
Ex.:   Michael D. Weisman & Ben T. Clements, <u>Protecting Reasonable Expectations: Proof of Lost Profits for New Businesses</u>, 76 Mass. L. Rev. 186 (1991). –Article Citation.
       Michael D. Weisman & Ben T. Clements, <u>Protecting Reasonable Expectations: Proof of Lost Profits for New Businesses</u>, 76 Mass. L. Rev. 186, 188 (1991). –Page Citation.

Massachusetts Legislative Service (West)
Ab.:   year Mass. Legis. Serv. (West)
Ex.:   Act of Aug. 9, 1995, ch. 296, 1996 Mass. Legis. Serv. 971 (West) (use of firearms during hunting season). –Citation to an entire session law.
       Act of Aug. 9, 1995, ch. 297, sec. 2, ch. 175 § 108, 1996 Mass. Legis. Serv. 972, 972 (West) (health insurance). –Citation to a session law amending prior act.

Massachusetts, Report of the Attorney General
<u>See</u> Report of the Attorney General, State of Massachusetts

Massachusetts Reports
Ab.:   Mass.
       –Cite to N.E. or N.E.2d if therein; otherwise, cite to Mass.

In citing cases in law review footnotes, abbreviate any word listed in Table T.6; the names of "states, countries, and other geographical units" unless they are named parties; and any other words of eight or more letters "if <u>substantial</u> space is thereby saved and the result is unambiguous." <u>Bluebook</u> Rule 10.2.2. On the other hand, in citing cases in text, abbreviate only widely known acronyms and the following words: "&," "Ass'n," "Bros.," "Co.," "Corp.," "Inc.," "Ltd.," and "No." <u>Bluebook</u> Rule 10.2.1(c).

–Give parallel citations, if at all, only in documents submitted to Massachusetts state courts. See Bluebook Rule 10.3.1 and Practitioners' Note P.3; see also Mass. R. App. P. 16(g) and Mass. Dist. & Mun. App. Div. R. 16(g), which require only a citation to Mass.

In documents submitted to Massachusetts state courts, cite as follows:

Moakley v. Eastwick, 423 Mass. 52, 666 N.E.2d 505 (1996). –Case Citation.

Moakley v. Eastwick, 423 Mass. 52, 54, 666 N.E.2d 505, 506 (1996). –Page Citation.

In all other documents, cite as follows:

Moakley v. Eastwick, 666 N.E.2d 505 (Mass. 1996). –Case Citation.

Moakley v. Eastwick, 666 N.E.2d 505, 506 (Mass. 1996). –Page Citation.

Massachusetts Session Laws
See Acts and Resolves of Massachusetts and Massachusetts Legislative Service. (West)

Massachusetts Supplement
Ab.:   Mass. Supp.

Master of the Rolls
Ab.:   M.R.

Matthew Bender
Ab.:   MB

McCormick on Evidence
–Do not abbreviate the title.

Ex.:   2 McCormick on Evidence § 217 (John W. Strong ed., 5th ed. 1999). –Section Citation.

2 McCormick on Evidence § 217, at 30 (John W. Strong ed., 5th ed. 1999). –Page Citation.

2 McCormick on Evidence § 217, at 30 n.8 (John W. Strong ed., 5th ed. 1999). –Footnote Citation.

McGill Law Journal
Ab.:   McGill L.J.

Ex.:   Brian R. Cheffins, European Community Company and Securities Law: A Canadian Perspective, 36 McGill L.J. 1282 (1991). –Article Citation.

Brian R. Cheffins, European Community Company and Securities Law: A Canadian Perspective, 36 McGill L.J. 1282, 1292 (1991). –Page Citation.

In law review footnotes, the titles of books and the names of cases, except for procedural phrases, are not underlined. See Bluebook Rule 2.1(a). Further, the following are in large and small capitals: codes, restatements, standards, constitutions, periodicals, authors of books, titles of books, the abbreviated names of codes, most legislative materials except for bills and resolutions, codified ordinances, model codes, court rules, and sentencing guidelines. Refer to The Bluebook.

McKinney's Consolidated Laws of New York Annotated
Ab.: N.Y. [subject] Law § (McKinney year)
See Bluebook Table T.1, pp. 219-20 for the abbreviation of each subject.
Ex.: N.Y. Educ. Law § 1718 (McKinney 2000).
N.Y. C.P.L.R. § 2310 (McKinney Supp. 2000).

Media Law Reporter (Bureau of National Affairs)
Ab.: Media L. Rep. (BNA)
Ex.: Cable News Network Inc. v. Video Monitoring Servs. of Am., [Decisions] Media L. Rep. (BNA) (19 Media L. Rep.) 1289 (11th Cir. Sept. 4, 1991). –Cite to looseleaf material.

Moffatt v. Brown, 15 Media L. Rep. (BNA) 1601 (Alaska 1988). –Cite to bound material.

–The above examples are proper if the case is not yet available in, or is not reported in, an official or West reporter, a public domain citation, or in a widely used computer database.

Mediator
Ab.: Med.

Medical Trial Technique Quarterly
Ab.: Med. Trial Tech. Q.
Ex.: Carol Docan, Risk & Responsibility: The Working Woman Makes the Choice, Not the Employer, 38 Med. Trial Tech. Q. 145 (1991). –Article Citation.
Carol Docan, Risk & Responsibility: The Working Woman Makes the Choice, Not the Employer, 38 Med. Trial Tech. Q. 145, 148 (1991). –Page Citation.

Medicare and Medicaid Guide (Commerce Clearing House)
Ab.: Medicare & Medicaid Guide (CCH)
Ex.: Sutphin Pharmacy, Inc. v. Rhodes, 5 Medicare & Medicaid Guide (CCH) ¶ 39,496 (S.D.N.Y. July, 26, 1991). –Cite to looseleaf material.
Westchester Gen. Hosp. v. HEW, [1979-1 Transfer Binder] Medicare & Medicaid Guide (CCH) ¶ 29,526 (M.D. Fla. 1979). –Cite to transfer binder material.

–The above examples are proper if the case is not yet available in, or is not reported in, an official or West reporter, a public domain citation, or in a widely used computer database.

Medicine and Law
Ab.: Med. & L.
Ex.: Arie Scholosberg, Issues in Psychiatric Prevention and Enforcement of Treatment, 10 Med. & L. 483 (1991). –Article Citation.

In citing cases in law review footnotes, abbreviate any word listed in Table T.6; the names of "states, countries, and other geographical units" unless they are named parties; and any other words of eight or more letters "if substantial space is thereby saved and the result is unambiguous." Bluebook Rule 10.2.2. On the other hand, in citing cases in text, abbreviate only widely known acronyms and the following words: "&," "Ass'n," "Bros.," "Co.," "Corp.," "Inc.," "Ltd.," and "No." Bluebook Rule 10.2.1(c).

Arie Scholosberg, Issues in Psychiatric Prevention and Enforcement of Treatment, 10 Med. & L. 483, 484 (1991). –Page Citation.

Medicine, Science, and the Law
Ab.:   Med. Sci. & L.
Ex.:   Alec Samuels, Informed Consent: The Law, 32 Med. Sci & L. 35 (1992). –Article Citation.
Alec Samuels, Informed Consent: The Law, 32 Med. Sci & L. 35, 38 (1992). –Page Citation.

Medico-Legal Journal
Ab.:   Medico-Legal J.
Ex.:   Michael Kirby, Aids and Prisons in Australia, 59 Medico-Legal J. 252 (1991). –Ariticle Citation.
Michael Kirby, Aids and Prisons in Australia, 59 Medico-Legal J. 252, 253 (1991). –Page Citation.

medium neutral citations
See public domain citations.

Melanesian Law Journal
Ab.:   Melanesian L.J.
Ex.:   Isikeli Mataitoga, Constitution-Making in Fiji: The Search for a Practical Solution, 19 Melanesian L.J. 43 (1991). –Article Citation.
Isikeli Mataitoga, Constitution-Making in Fiji: The Search for a Practical Solution, 19 Melanesian L.J. 43, 45-46 (1991). –Page Citation.

Melbourne University Law Review
Ab.:   Melb. U. L. Rev.
Ex.:   Richard G. Fox, The Meaning of Proportionality in Sentencing, 19 Melb. U. L. Rev. 489 (1994). –Article Citation.
Richard G. Fox, The Meaning of Proportionality in Sentencing, 19 Melb. U. L. Rev. 489, 497 (1994). –Page Citation.

memoranda, basic citation forms
See various title entries of this work. See also examples included on the facing page next to the inside back cover and on the inside back cover of The Bluebook.

memoranda, typeface conventions for legal memoranda
See Bluebook Practitioners' Notes, pp. 11-19.

memorandum decision
Ab.:   mem.

In law review footnotes, the titles of books and the names of cases, except for procedural phrases, are not underlined. See Bluebook Rule 2.1(a). Further, the following are in large and small capitals: codes, restatements, standards, constitutions, periodicals, authors of books, titles of books, the abbreviated names of codes, most legislative materials except for bills and resolutions, codified ordinances, model codes, court rules, and sentencing guidelines. Refer to The Bluebook.

Ex.:   <u>Farlow v. Hardin</u>, 61 F.3d 30 (11th Cir. 1995) (mem.).

Memphis State University Law Review
Ab.:   Mem. St. U. L. Rev.
Ex.:   Robert Banks, Jr. & Elizabeth T. Collins, <u>Judicial Notice in Tennessee</u>, 21 Mem. St. U. L. Rev. 431 (1991). –Article Citation.
           Robert Banks, Jr. & Elizabeth T. Collins, <u>Judicial Notice in Tennessee</u>, 21 Mem. St. U. L. Rev. 431, 435 (1991). –Page Citation.
<u>See</u> University of Memphis Law Review.

Mercer Law Review
Ab.:   Mercer L. Rev.
Ex.:   Robert M. Travis & Edward C. Brewer, III, <u>Products Liability Law in Georgia Including Recent Developments</u>, 43 Mercer L. Rev. 27 (1991). –Article Citation.
           Robert M. Travis & Edward C. Brewer, III, <u>Products Liability Law in Georgia Including Recent Developments</u>, 43 Mercer L. Rev. 27, 33-34 (1991). –Page Citation.

Merit Systems Protection Board Reporter (U.S.)
Ab.:   M.S.P.B.
Ex.:   <u>Gometz v. Office of Personnel Management</u>, 69 M.S.P.B. 115 (1995).

Michie's Hawaii Revised Statutes Annotated
Ab.:   Haw. Rev. Stat. Ann. §   (Lexis year)
Ex.:   Haw. Rev. Stat. Ann. § 334-31 (Lexis 2000).
           Haw. Rev. Stat. Ann. § 710-1077 (Lexis Supp. 1999).
           –"Cite to Hawaii Revised Statutes if therein." <u>Bluebook</u> Table T.1, p. 199.

Michie's Nevada Revised Statutes Annotated (Lexis)
<u>See</u> Nevada Revised Statutes Annotated

Michie's West Virginia Code Annotated (Lexis)
<u>See</u> West Virginia Code Annotated

Metropolitan
Ab.:   Metro.

Michigan Administrative Code
Ab.:   Mich. Admin. Code r.   (Year)
Ex.:   Mich. Admin. Code r. 259-801 (1982).

Michigan Appeals Reports
Ab.:   Mich. App.
           –Cite to N.W. or N.W.2d if therein; otherwise, cite to Mich. App.

In citing cases in law review footnotes, abbreviate any word listed in Table T.6; the names of "states, countries, and other geographical units" unless they are named parties; and any other words of eight or more letters "if <u>substantial</u> space is thereby saved and the result is unambiguous." <u>Bluebook</u> Rule 10.2.2. On the other hand, in citing cases in text, abbreviate only widely known acronyms and the following words: "&," "Ass'n," "Bros.," "Co.," "Corp.," "Inc.," "Ltd.," and "No." <u>Bluebook</u> Rule 10.2.1(c).

–Give parallel citations only in documents submitted to Michigan state courts. See Bluebook Rule 10.3.1 and Practitioners' Note P.3; see also Michigan Uniform System of Citation I (A)(5)(m), which requires a parallel citation.

In documents submitted to Michigan state courts, cite as follows:

People v. Sawyer, 215 Mich. App. 183, 545 N.W.2d 6 (1996). –Case Citation.

People v. Sawyer, 215 Mich. App. 183, 185, 545 N.W.2d 6, 8 (1996). –Page Citation.

In all other documents, cite as follows:

People v. Sawyer, 545 N.W.2d 6 (Mich. Ct. App. 1996). –Case Citation.

People v. Sawyer, 545 N.W.2d 6, 8 (Mich. Ct. App. 1996). –Page Citation.

Michigan Bar Journal
Ab.: Mich. B.J.

Ex.: Steven E. Goren, The Workers' Compensation Exclusive Remedy Rule and Its Exceptions, 71 Mich. Bar J. 59 (1992). –Article Citation.

Steven E. Goren, The Workers' Compensation Exclusive Remedy Rule and Its Exceptions, 71 Mich. Bar J. 59, 60 (1992). –Page Citation.

Michigan, Biennial Report of the Attorney General
See Opinions of the Attorney General of Michigan

Michigan Business Law Journal
Ab.: Mich. Bus. L.J.

Michigan Compiled Laws (1979)
Ab.: Mich. Comp. Laws § (year)

Michigan Compiled Laws Annotated (West)
Ab.: Mich. Comp. Laws Ann. § (West year)

Ex.: Mich. Comp. Laws Ann. § 331.1 (West 1999).

Mich. Comp. Laws Ann. § 333.5131 (West Supp. 2000).

–"Cite to Michigan Compiled Laws if therein." See Bluebook Table T.1, p. 210.

Michigan Constitution
Ab.: Mich. Const. art. , § .

Ex.: Mich. Const. art. I, § 23. –"Cite constitutional provisions currently in force without date." Bluebook Rule 11.

–"If the cited provision has been repealed, either indicate parenthetically the fact and date of repeal or cite the repealing provision in full." Bluebook Rule 11.

Mich. Const. art. I, § 15 (amended 1978). –"When citing a provision

In law review footnotes, the titles of books and the names of cases, except for procedural phrases, are not underlined. See Bluebook Rule 2.1(a). Further, the following are in large and small capitals: codes, restatements, standards, constitutions, periodicals, authors of books, titles of books, the abbreviated names of codes, most legislative materials except for bills and resolutions, codified ordinances, model codes, court rules, and sentencing guidelines. Refer to The Bluebook.

that has been subsequently amended, either indicate parenthetically the fact and date of amendment or cite the amending provision in full." Bluebook Rule 11.

Mich. Const. of 1908, art. II, § 22 (1963). –"Cite constitutions that have been totally superseded by year of adoption; if the specific provision cited was adopted in a different year, give that year parenthetically." Bluebook Rule 11.

Michigan Corporate Finance and Business Law Journal
Ab.:   Mich. Corp. Fin. & Bus. L.J.

Michigan Court of Claims Reports (1938-1942)
Ab.:   Mich. Ct. Cl.

Michigan Journal of International Law
Ab.:   Mich. J. Int'l L.

Ex.:   Gerald L. Neuman, "We Are the People": Alien Suffrage in German and American Perspective, 13 Mich. J. Int'l L. 259 (1992). –Article Citation.

        Gerald L. Neuman, "We Are the People": Alien Suffrage in German and American Perspective, 13 Mich. J. Int'l L. 259, 261 (1992). –Page Citation.

Michigan Law Review
Ab.:   Mich. L. Rev.

Ex.:   James A. Gardner, The Failed Discourse of State Constitutionalism, 90 Mich. L. Rev. 761 (1992). –Article Citation.

        James A. Gardner, The Failed Discourse of State Constitutionalism, 90 Mich. L. Rev. 761, 767-68 (1992). –Page Citation.

Michigan Legislative Service (West)
Ab.:   year Mich. Legis. Serv. (West).

Ex.:   Act of June 26, 1996, P.A. 335, 1996 Mich. Legis. Serv. 912 (West) (relating to education of children of veterans). –Citation to an entire session law.

        Act of Feb. 26, 1996, P.A. 63, sec. 1, § 287-261, 1996 Mich. Legis. Serv. 130, 130-31 (West) (relating to dogs and the protection of livestock and poultry from damage by dogs). –Citation to a session law amending prior act.

        –"Cite to Mich. Pub. Acts if therein." Bluebook Table T.1, p. 210.

Michigan Register
Ab.:   Mich. Reg. (month year)

Michigan Reports
Ab.:   Mich.

        –Cite to N.W. or N.W.2d if therein; otherwise, cite to Mich.

In citing cases in law review footnotes, abbreviate any word listed in Table T.6; the names of "states, countries, and other geographical units" unless they are named parties; and any other words of eight or more letters "if substantial space is thereby saved and the result is unambiguous." Bluebook Rule 10.2.2. On the other hand, in citing cases in text, abbreviate only widely known acronyms and the following words: "&," "Ass'n," "Bros.," "Co.," "Corp.," "Inc.," "Ltd.," and "No." Bluebook Rule 10.2.1(c).

–Give parallel citations only in documents submitted to Michigan state courts. See Bluebook Rule 10.3.1 and Practitioners' Note P.3; see also Michigan Uniform System of Citation I (A)(5)(m), which requires a parallel citation.

In documents submitted to Michigan state courts, cite as follows:

Meatte v. Meatte, 450 Mich. 987, 548 N.W.2d 638 (1996). –Case Citation.

Meatte v. Meatte, 450 Mich. 987, 988, 548 N.W.2d 638, 639 (1996). –Page Citation.

In all other documents, cite as follows:

Meatte v. Meatte, 548 N.W.2d 638 (Mich. 1996). –Case Citation.

Meatte v. Meatte, 548 N.W.2d 638, 639 (Mich. 1996). –Page Citation.

Michigan Session Laws
See Public and Local Acts of the Legislature of the State of Michigan and Michigan Legislative Service (West)

Michigan Statutes Annotated (Lexis)
Ab.:   Mich. Stat. Ann. §   (Lexis year).

–Cite to Michigan Compiled Laws if therein. Otherwise, cite to Michigan Compiled Laws Annotated. See Bluebook Table T.1, p. 211.

–"Cite to Michigan Statutes Annotated only under Bluebook Rule 12.3.1(h)." See Bluebook Table T.1, p. 211.

Milbank Quarterly, The
Ab.:   Milbank Q.

Ex.:   Robert A. Aronowitz, Lyme Disease: The Social Construction of a New Disease and Its Social Consequence, 69 Milbank Q. 79 (1991). –Article Citation.

Robert A. Aronowitz, Lyme Disease: The Social Construction of a New Disease and Its Social Consequence, 69 Milbank Q. 79, 82-83 (1991). –Page Citation.

Military Justice Reporter
Ab.:   M.J.

Ex.:   United States v. Dickens, 30 M.J. 986 (A.C.M.R. 1990). –Case Citation.

United States v. Dickens, 30 M.J. 986, 988 (A.C.M.R. 1990). –Page Citation.

United States v. Brown, 30 M.J. 839, 841 (N-M.C.M.R. 1990). –Page Citation.

In law review footnotes, the titles of books and the names of cases, except for procedural phrases, are not underlined. See Bluebook Rule 2.1(a). Further, the following are in large and small capitals: codes, restatements, standards, constitutions, periodicals, authors of books, titles of books, the abbreviated names of codes, most legislative materials except for bills and resolutions, codified ordinances, model codes, court rules, and sentencing guidelines. Refer to The Bluebook.

United States v. Givens, 30 M.J. 294, 297 (C.M.A. 1990). –Page Citation.

United States v. Smith, 30 M.J. 1022, 1026 (A.F.C.M.R. 1990). –Page Citation.

Military Law Reporter
Ab.:   Mil. L. Rep.

Military Law Review
Ab.:   Mil. L. Rev.
Ex.:   Major David S. Jones, Fraternization: Time for a Rational Department of Defense Standard, 135 Mil. L. Rev. 37 (1992). –Article Citation.

Major David S. Jones, Fraternization: Time for a Rational Department of Defense Standard, 135 Mil. L. Rev. 37, 41-43 (1992). –Page Citation.

Minnesota Constitution
Ab.:   Minn. Const. art.   , §   .
Ex.:   Minn. Const. art. XIII, § 5. –"Cite constitutional provisions currently in force without date." Bluebook Rule 11.

–"If the cited provision has been repealed, either indicate parenthetically the fact and date of repeal or cite the repealing provision in full." Bluebook Rule 11.

Minn. Const. art. VIII, § 14 (amended 1990). –"When citing a provision that has been subsequently amended, either indicate parenthetically the fact and date of amendment or cite the amending provision in full." Bluebook Rule 11.

Minn. Const. of 1857 art. IX, § 16 (1974). –"Cite constitutions that have been totally superseded by year of adoption; if the specific provision cited was adopted in a different year, give that year parenthetically." Bluebook Rule 11.

Minnesota Court of Appeals
         –Cite to N.W.2d
Ab.:   Minn. Ct. App.
Ex.:   Wenzel v. Mathies, 542 N.W.2d 634 (Minn. Ct. App. 1996). –Case Citation.

Wenzel v. Mathies, 542 N.W.2d 634, 638 (Minn. Ct. App. 1996). –Page Citation.

Minnesota Law Review
Ab.:   Minn. L. Rev.
Ex.:   Jay L. Westbrook, Two Thoughts About Insider Preferences, 76 Minn. L. Rev. 73 (1991). –Article Citation.

Jay L. Westbrook, Two Thoughts About Insider Preferences, 76 Minn. L. Rev. 73, 93 (1991). –Page Citation.

In citing cases in law review footnotes, abbreviate any word listed in Table T.6; the names of "states, countries, and other geographical units" unless they are named parties; and any other words of eight or more letters "if substantial space is thereby saved and the result is unambiguous." Bluebook Rule 10.2.2. On the other hand, in citing cases in text, abbreviate only widely known acronyms and the following words: "&," "Ass'n," "Bros.," "Co.," "Corp.," "Inc.," "Ltd.," and "No." Bluebook Rule 10.2.1(c).

Minnesota, Opinions of the Attorney General
  See Opinions of the Attorney General of Minnesota

Minnesota Reports
  Ab.:   Minn.
  –Discontinued after 312 Minn. 602 (1977).
  –Cite to N.W. or N.W.2d if therein; otherwise, cite to Minn.
  –Give parallel citations only in documents submitted to Minnesota state
    courts. (Note: In citing a state court case in a document submitted to
    a court of that same state, the 16th ed. of The Bluebook prescribed a
    parallel citation; the 17th ed. prescribes that local rules shall control,
    but Minnesota has no known local rules concerning parallel citations.
    For the sake of continuity, we advise giving a parallel citation in
    documents submitted to Minnesota state courts. See Bluebook Rule
    10.3.1 and Practitioners' Note P.3.)
  –Through 312 Minn. 602 (1977), cite as follows
  In documents submitted to Minnesota state courts:
      Tyra v. Cheney, 129 Minn. 428, 152 N.W. 835 (1915). –Case
      Citation.
      Tyra v. Cheney, 129 Minn. 428, 430, 152 N.W. 835, 838 (1915).
      –Page Citation.
  In all other documents:
      Tyra v. Cheney, 152 N.W. 835 (Minn. 1915). –Case Citation.
      Tyra v. Cheney, 152 N.W. 835, 838 (Minn. 1915). –Page Citation.
  –After 312 Minn. 602 (1977), cite as follows:
  In all documents:
      In re Jensen, 542 N.W.2d 627 (Minn. 1996). –Case Citation.
      In re Jensen, 542 N.W.2d 627, 628 (Minn. 1996). –Page Citation.

Minnesota Rules
  Ab.:   Minn. R. (year)
  Ex.:   Minn. R. 1205.0300 (1997).

Minnesota Session Laws
  See Laws of Minnesota and Minnesota Session Law Service (West)

Minnesota Session Law Service (West)
  Ab.:   year Minn. Sess. Law Serv. (West)
  Ex.:   Act effective Sept. 1, 2000, ch. 488 2000 Minn. Sess. Law Serv. 1236
          (West) (public safety). –Citation to an entire session law.
          Act effective Sept. 1, 2000, ch. 488, art. 6, sec. 5, § 169.2151, 2000
          Minn. Sess. Law Serv. 1236 (West) (public safety). –Citation to a
          session law amending a prior act.

In law review footnotes, the titles of books and the names of cases, except for procedural
phrases, are not underlined. See Bluebook Rule 2.1(a). Further, the following are in large
and small capitals: codes, restatements, standards, constitutions, periodicals, authors of
books, titles of books, the abbreviated names of codes, most legislative materials except for
bills and resolutions, codified ordinances, model codes, court rules, and sentencing guidelines.
Refer to The Bluebook.

–"Cite to Minn. Laws if therein." <u>Bluebook</u> Table T.1, p. 211.

Minnesota State Register
Ab.:   Minn. Reg.

Minnesota Statutes
Ab.:   Minn. Stat. § (year)
Ex.:   Minn. Stat. § 611.07 (1978).
         Minn. Stat. § 363.01 (Supp. 1979).
         –"Cite to Minnesota Statutes if therein." <u>Bluebook</u> Table T.1, p. 211.

Minnesota Statutes Annotated (West)
Ab.:   Minn. Stat. Ann. §   (West year)
Ex.:   Minn. Stat. Ann. § 273.13 (West 1999).
         Minn. Stat. Ann. § 363.02 (West Supp. 2000).

Mississippi Code Annotated
Ab.:   Miss. Code Ann. §   (year)
Ex.:   Miss. Code Ann. § 49-5-31 (1999).
         Miss. Code Ann. § 79-11-519 (Supp. 2000).

Mississippi College Law Review
Ab.:   Miss. C. L. Rev.
Ex.:   Stephen L. Mikochik, <u>Employment Discrimination Against Americans
         With Disabilities</u>, 11 Miss. C. L. Rev. 255 (1991). –Article Citation.
         Stephen L. Mikochik, <u>Employment Discrimination Against Americans
         With Disabilities</u>, 11 Miss. C. L. Rev. 255, 256-57 (1991). –Page
         Citation.

Mississippi Constitution
Ab.:   Miss. Const. art.   , §   .
Ex.:   Miss. Const. art. 8, § 201. –"Cite constitutional provisions currently in
         force without date." <u>Bluebook</u> Rule 11.
         Miss. Const. art. 2, § 3 (repealed 1990). –"If the cited provision has
         been repealed, either indicate parenthetically the fact and date of repeal
         or cite the repealing provision in full." <u>Bluebook</u> Rule 11.
         Miss. Const. art. 10, § 225 (amended 1990). –"When citing a
         provision that has been subsequently amended, either indicate
         parenthetically the fact and date of amendment or cite the amending
         provision in full." <u>Bluebook</u> Rule 11.

Mississippi Court of Appeals
Ab.: Miss. Ct. App.
         –Cite to So. or So. 2d if therein; in addition, give public domain
         citation if available.
         –Until July 1, 1997, when a public domain format was adopted, cite as
         follows:

In citing cases in law review footnotes, abbreviate any word listed in Table T.6;
the names of "states, countries, and other geographical units" unless they are named parties;
and any other words of eight or more letters "if <u>substantial</u> space is thereby saved and the
result is unambiguous." <u>Bluebook</u> Rule 10.2.2. On the other hand, in citing cases in text,
abbreviate only widely known acronyms and the following words: "&," "Ass'n," "Bros.,"
"Co.," "Corp.," "Inc.," "Ltd.," and "No." <u>Bluebook</u> Rule 10.2.1(c).

In all documents:

Church v. Massey, 697 So. 2d 407 (Miss. Ct. App. 1997). –Case
Citation.

Church v. Massey, 697 So. 2d 407, 413 (Miss. Ct. App. 1997).
–Page Citation.

–From July 1, 1997, cite as follows:

In all documents:

Woodard v. State, 98-KA-01768-COA, 765 So. 2d 573 (Miss. Ct.
App. 2000) –Case Citation.

Woodard v. State, 98-KA-01768-COA, ¶12, 765 So. 2d 573, 575
(Miss. Ct. App. 2000) –Pinpoint Citation.

See Bluebook Rules 10.3.1 and 10.3.3, Table T.1, and Practitioners'
Note P.3; see also Miss. R. App. P. 28(e).

Mississippi Law Journal
Ab.:   Miss. L.J.
Ex.:   George Cochran, Rule 11: The Road To Amendment, 61 Miss. L.J. 5
          (1991). –Article Citation.

          George Cochran, Rule 11: The Road To Amendment, 61 Miss. L.J. 5,
          19 (1991). –Page Citation.

Mississippi Session Laws
See General Laws of Mississippi

Mississippi Supreme Court
Ab.:   Miss.

          –Cite to So. or So. 2d if therein; in addition, give public domain
          citation if available.

          –Through 254 Miss. 944 (1966), cite as follows:

In documents submitted to Mississippi state courts:

          Carter v. Witherspoon, 156 Miss. 597, 126 So. 388 (1930). –Case
          Citation.

          Carter v. Witherspoon, 156 Miss. 597, 603, 126 So. 388, 389
          (1930). –Page Citation.

In all other documents:

          Carter v. Witherspoon, 126 So. 388 (Miss. 1930). –Case Citation.

          Carter v. Witherspoon, 126 So. 388, 389 (Miss. 1930). –Page
          Citation.

          –After 254 Miss. 944 (1966), and until July 1, 1997, when a public
          domain format was adopted, cite as follows:

In all documents:

In law review footnotes, the titles of books and the names of cases, except for procedural
phrases, are not underlined. See Bluebook Rule 2.1(a). Further, the following are in large
and small capitals: codes, restatements, standards, constitutions, periodicals, authors of
books, titles of books, the abbreviated names of codes, most legislative materials except for
bills and resolutions, codified ordinances, model codes, court rules, and sentencing guidelines.
Refer to The Bluebook.

Bumpers v. Carruth, 669 So. 2d 83 (Miss. 1996). –Case Citation.

Bumpers v. Carruth, 669 So. 2d 83, 84 (Miss. 1996). –Page Citation.

–From July 1, 1997, cite as follows:

In all documents:

Grant v. Grant, 99-CA-00736-SCT, 765 So. 2d 1263 (Miss. 2000). –Case Citation.

Grant v. Grant, 99-CA-00736-SCT, ¶ 6, 765 So. 2d 1263, 1266 (Miss. 2000). –Pinpoint Citation.

See Bluebook Rules 10.3.1 and 10.3.3, Table T.1, and Practitioners' Note P.3; see also Miss. R. App. P. 28(e).

Missouri Annotated Statutes, Vernon's
See Vernon's Annotated Missouri Statutes (West)

Missouri Appeals Reports
Ab.:   Mo. App.

–Discontinued after 241 Mo. App. 1244 (1952).

–Cite to S.W., S.W.2d, or S.W.3d if therein; otherwise, cite to Mo. App.

–Give parallel citations only in documents submitted to Missouri state courts. (Note: In citing a state court case in a document submitted to a court of that same state, the 16th ed. of The Bluebook prescribed a parallel citation; the 17th ed. prescribes that local rules shall control, but Missouri has no known local rules concerning parallel citations. For the sake of continuity, we advise giving a parallel citation in documents submitted to Missouri state courts. See Bluebook Rule 10.3.1 and Practitioners' Note P.3.)

–Through 241 Mo. App. 1244 (1952), cite as follows:

In documents submitted to Missouri state courts:

Williams v. Williams, 240 Mo. App. 336, 205 S.W.2d 949 (1947). –Case Citation.

Williams v. Williams, 240 Mo. App. 336, 342-43, 205 S.W.2d 949, 953-54 (1947). –Page Citation.

In all other documents:

Williams v. Williams, 205 S.W.2d 949 (Mo. Ct. App. 1947). –Case Citation.

Williams v. Williams, 205 S.W.2d 949, 953-54 (Mo. Ct. App. 1947). –Page Citation.

–After 241 Mo. 1244 (1952), cite as follows:

In all documents:

Rhodes v. Blair, 919 S.W.2d 561 (Mo. Ct. App. 1996). –Case Citation.

In citing cases in law review footnotes, abbreviate any word listed in Table T.6; the names of "states, countries, and other geographical units" unless they are named parties; and any other words of eight or more letters "if substantial space is thereby saved and the result is unambiguous." Bluebook Rule 10.2.2. On the other hand, in citing cases in text, abbreviate only widely known acronyms and the following words: "&," "Ass'n," "Bros.," "Co.," "Corp.," "Inc.," "Ltd.," and "No." Bluebook Rule 10.2.1(c).

Rhodes v. Blair, 919 S.W.2d 561, 562 (Mo. Ct. App. 1996).
–Page Citation.

Missouri Code of State Regulations Annotated
   Ab.:   Mo. Code Regs. Ann. tit. , § (year)
   Ex.:   Mo. Code Regs. Ann. tit. 1, § 15-1.204 (1995).

Missouri Constitution
   Ab.:   Mo. Const. art. , §   .
   Ex.:   Mo. Const. art. IX, § 1(a). –"Cite constitutional provisions currently in force without date." Bluebook Rule 11.

       Mo. Const. art. XI, § 5 (repealed 1988) –"If the cited provision has been repealed, either indicate parenthetically the fact and date of repeal or cite the repealing provision in full." Bluebook Rule 11.

       Mo. Const. art. IV, § 12 (amended 1990). –"When citing a provision that has been subsequently amended, either indicate parenthetically the fact and date of amendment or cite the amending provision in full." Bluebook Rule 11.

       Mo. Const. of 1875 art. V, § 25. –"Cite constitutions that have been totally superseded by year of adoption; if the specific provision cited was adopted in a different year, give that year parenthetically." Bluebook Rule 11.

Missouri Law Review
   Ab.:   Mo. L. Rev.
   Ex.:   Marvin Hill, Jr. & Emily Delacenserie, Procrustean Beds and Draconian Choices: Lifestyle Regulations and Officious Intermeddlers–Bosses, Workers, Courts and Labor Arbitrators, 57 Mo. L. Rev. 51 (1992). –Article Citation.

       Marvin Hill, Jr. & Emily Delacenserie, Procrustean Beds and Draconian Choices: Lifestyle Regulations and Officious Intermeddlers–Bosses, Workers, Courts and Labor Arbitrators, 57 Mo. L. Rev. 51, 55-56 (1992). –Page Citation.

Missouri Legislative Service (West)
   Ab.:   year Mo. Legis. Serv. (West)
   Ex.:   Act of July 10, 1996, No. 145, 1996 Mo. Legis. Serv. 704 (West) (unemployment compensation income tax). –Citation to an entire session law.

       Act of July 10, 1996, No. 145, Sec. A, ch. 288.379, 1996 Mo. Legis. Serv. 704, 704 (West) (unemployment compensation income tax). –Citation to a section of a session law amending prior act.

       –"Cite to Mo. Laws if therein." Bluebook Table T.1, p. 212.

In law review footnotes, the titles of books and the names of cases, except for procedural phrases, are not underlined. See Bluebook Rule 2.1(a). Further, the following are in large and small capitals: codes, restatements, standards, constitutions, periodicals, authors of books, titles of books, the abbreviated names of codes, most legislative materials except for bills and resolutions, codified ordinances, model codes, court rules, and sentencing guidelines. Refer to The Bluebook.

Missouri Register
Ab.:   Mo. Reg.

Missouri Reports
Ab.:   Mo.
–Discontinued after 365 Mo. 1238 (1956).
–Cite to S.W., S.W.2d, or S.W.3d if therein; otherwise, cite to Mo.
–Give parallel citations only in documents submitted to Missouri state courts. (Note: In citing a state court case in a document submitted to a court of that same state, the 16th ed. of The Bluebook prescribed a parallel citation; the 17th ed. prescribes that local rules shall control, but Missouri has no known local rules concerning parallel citations. For the sake of continuity, we advise giving a parallel citation in documents submitted to Missouri state courts. See Bluebook Rule 10.3.1 and Practitioners' Note P.3.)
–Through 365 Mo. 1238 (1956), cite as follows:
In documents submitted to Missouri state courts:

State v. Anderson, 252 Mo. 83, 158 S.W. 817 (1913). –Case Citation.

State v. Anderson, 252 Mo. 83, 87, 158 S.W. 817, 821 (1913). –Page Citation.

In all other documents:

State v. Anderson, 158 S.W. 817 (Mo. 1913). –Case Citation.

State v. Anderson, 158 S.W. 817, 821 (Mo. 1913). –Page Citation.

–After 365 Mo. 1238 (1956), cite as follows:
In all documents:

Hollis v. Blevins, 926 S.W.2d 683 (Mo. 1996). –Case Citation.

Hollis v. Blevins, 926 S.W.2d 683, 684 (Mo. 1996). –Page Citation.

Missouri Revised Statutes
Ab.:   Mo. Rev. Stat. §   (year)
Ex.:   Mo. Rev. Stat. § 506.500 (1978).

Missouri Session Laws
See Laws of Missouri and Missouri Legislative Service

Model Business Corporation Act Annotated
Ex.:   2 Model Bus. Corp. Act Ann. § 8.09 (1994). –Citation to a section of the act.

2 Model Bus. Corp. Act Ann. § 8.09, at 8-83 (1994). –Citation to a page within the act.

See Bluebook Rule 12.8.5.

In citing cases in law review footnotes, abbreviate any word listed in Table T.6; the names of "states, countries, and other geographical units" unless they are named parties; and any other words of eight or more letters "if substantial space is thereby saved and the result is unambiguous." Bluebook Rule 10.2.2. On the other hand, in citing cases in text, abbreviate only widely known acronyms and the following words: "&," "Ass'n," "Bros.," "Co.," "Corp.," "Inc.," "Ltd.," and "No." Bluebook Rule 10.2.1(c).

Model Code of Evidence
See American Law Institute Model Code of Evidence

Model Code of Professional Responsibility (ABA)
See American Bar Association Model Code of Professional Responsibility.

Model Land Development Code
See American Law Institute Model Land Development Code

Model Penal Code (ALI)
See American Law Institute Model Penal Code

Modern Child Custody Practice, 2d ed., by Jeff Atkinson
    –Do not abbreviate the title.
Ex.:   2 Jeff Atkinson, Child Custody Practice, § 10-8 (2d ed. 2000).
        –Section Citation.
        2 Jeff Atkinson, Child Custody Practice, § 10-8, at 10-17 (2d ed. 2000).
        –Page Citation.

Model Rules of Professional Conduct (ABA)
See American Bar Association Model Rules of Professional Conduct.

Modern Law Review
Ab.:   Mod. L. Rev.
Ex.:   Yves Dezalay, Territorial Battles and Tribal Disputes, 54 Mod. L. Rev.
        792 (1991). –Article Citation.
        Yves Dezalay, Territorial Battles and Tribal Disputes, 54 Mod. L. Rev.
        792, 794 (1991). –Page Citation.

Modern Legal Systems Cyclopedia, by Kenneth R. Redden
    –Do not abbreviate the title.
Ex.:   3 Kenneth R. Redden, Modern Legal Systems Cyclopedia 3.250.31
        (1994). –Page Citation.
        3 Kenneth R. Redden, Modern Legal Systems Cyclopedia 3.250.31
        n.106 (1994). –Footnote Citation.

Modern Trials, by Melvin M. Belli, Sr.
    –Do not abbreviate the title.
Ex.:   3 Melvin M. Belli, Sr., Modern Trials § 50.33 (2d ed. 1982). –Section
        Citation.
        3 Melvin M. Belli, Sr., Modern Trials § 50.33, at 316 (2d ed. 1982).
        –Page Citation.

modified
Ab.:   Do not abbreviate title.

In law review footnotes, the titles of books and the names of cases, except for procedural phrases, are not underlined. See Bluebook Rule 2.1(a). Further, the following are in large and small capitals: codes, restatements, standards, constitutions, periodicals, authors of books, titles of books, the abbreviated names of codes, most legislative materials except for bills and resolutions, codified ordinances, model codes, court rules, and sentencing guidelines. Refer to The Bluebook.

Ex.:   Bonner v. Coughlin, 517 F.2d 1311 (7th Cir. 1975), modified en banc, 545 F.2d 565 (7th Cir. 1976).

Monash University Law Review
Ab.:   Monash U. L. Rev.

Ex.:   Dennis Rose, Judicial Reasonings and Responsibilities in Constitutional Cases, 20 Monash U. L. Rev. 195 (1994). –Article Citation.

Dennis Rose, Judicial Reasonings and Responsibilities in Constitutional Cases, 20 Monash U. L. Rev. 195, 205 (1994). –Page Citation.

Montana Administrative Register
Ab.:   Mont. Admin. Reg.

Montana Administrative Rules
See Administrative Rules of Montana

Montana Code Annotated
Ab.:   Mont. Code Ann. §   (year)

Ex.:   Mont. Code Ann. § 16-11-101 (1999).

Montana Constitution
Ab.:   Mont. Const. art.   , §   .

Ex.:   Mont. Const. art. IX, § 1. –"Cite constitutional provisions currently in force without date." Bluebook Rule 11.

–"If the cited provision has been repealed, either indicate parenthetically the fact and date of repeal or cite the repealing provision in full." Bluebook Rule 11.

Mont. Const. art. XI, § 5 (amended 1978). –"When citing a provision that has been subsequently amended, either indicate parenthetically the fact and date of amendment or cite the amending provision in full." Bluebook Rule 11.

Montana Law Review
Ab.:   Mont. L. Rev.

Ex.:   Scot Schermerhorn, Efficiency vs. Equity in Close Corporations, 52 Mont. L. Rev. 73 (1991). –Article Citation.

Scot Schermerhorn, Efficiency vs. Equity in Close Corporations, 52 Mont. L. Rev. 73, 78-80 (1991). –Page Citation.

Montana Session Laws
See Laws of Montana

Montana Supreme Court
Ab.:   Mont.

–Cite to P., P.2d, or P.3d if therein; in addition, give public domain citation if available.

In citing cases in law review footnotes, abbreviate any word listed in Table T.6; the names of "states, countries, and other geographical units" unless they are named parties; and any other words of eight or more letters "if substantial space is thereby saved and the result is unambiguous." Bluebook Rule 10.2.2. On the other hand, in citing cases in text, abbreviate only widely known acronyms and the following words: "&," "Ass'n," "Bros.," "Co.," "Corp.," "Inc.," "Ltd.," and "No." Bluebook Rule 10.2.1(c).

–Until January 1, 1998, when a public domain format was adopted, cite as follows:

In all documents submitted to Montana state courts:

> Berlin v. Boedecker, 268 Mont. 444, 887 P.2d 1180 (1994). –Case Citation.

> Berlin v. Boedecker, 268 Mont. 444, 445, 887 P.2d 1180, 1181 (1994). –Page Citation.

In all other documents:

> Berlin v. Boedecker, 887 P.2d 1180 (Mont. 1994). –Case Citation.

> Berlin v. Boedecker, 887 P.2d 1180, 1181 (Mont. 1994). –Page Citation.

–After January 1, 1998, cite as follows:

In documents submitted to Montana state courts:

> Benjamin v. Torgerson, 1999 MT 216, 295 Mont. 528, 985 P.2d 734 –Case Citation.

> Benjamin v. Torgerson, 1999 MT 216, ¶ 15, 295 Mont. 528, ¶ 15, 985 P.2d 734, ¶ 15 –Pinpoint Citation.

In all other documents:

> Benjamin v. Torgerson, 1999 MT 216, 985 P.2d 734. –Case Citation.

> Benjamin v. Torgerson, 1999 MT 216, ¶ 15, 985 P.2d 734, 737. –Pinpoint Citation.

See Bluebook Rules 10.3.1 and 10.3.3, Table T.1, and Practitioners' Note P.3; see also In re Opinion Forms & Citation Standards of the Sup. Ct. of Mont. (Dec. 16, 1997).

Monthly Labor Review

Ab.:   Monthly Lab. Rev.

Ex.:   Craig Hukill, Labor and the Supreme Court: Significant Issues of 1991-92, Monthly Lab. Rev., January 1992, at 34. –Article Citation.

Craig Hukill, Labor and the Supreme Court: Significant Issues of 1991-92, Monthly Lab. Rev., January 1992, at 34, 35. –Page Citation.

Moore on International Law

See Digest of International Law, by John B. Moore

Moore's Federal Practice and Procedure, by James W. Moore, Allan D. Vestal and Philip B. Kurland

–Do not abbreviate the title.

In law review footnotes, the titles of books and the names of cases, except for procedural phrases, are not underlined. See Bluebook Rule 2.1(a). Further, the following are in large and small capitals: codes, restatements, standards, constitutions, periodicals, authors of books, titles of books, the abbreviated names of codes, most legislative materials except for bills and resolutions, codified ordinances, model codes, court rules, and sentencing guidelines. Refer to The Bluebook.

Ex.:   7 James W. Moore et al., <u>Moore's Federal Practice and Procedure</u>
§ 60.26[4] (2d ed. 1990). –Section Citation.

7 James W. Moore et al., <u>Moore's Federal Practice and Procedure</u>
§ 60.26[4], at 60-252 (2d ed. 1990). –Page Citation.

12 James W. Moore et al., <u>Moore's Federal Practice and Procedure</u>
§ 350.01[2], at 3-7 n.8 (2d ed. 1990). –Footnote Citation.

motion–citation to
    –Explained in <u>Bluebook</u> Rule 10.8.3.

Motor Carrier Cases Reports (1936-1986)
    <u>See</u> Interstate Commerce Commission Reports, Motor Carrier Cases

Multistate and Multinational Estate Planning, by Jeffrey A. Schoenblum.
    –Do not abbreviate the title

Ex.:   1 Jeffrey A. Schoenblum, <u>Multistate and Multination Estate Planning</u>
§ 9.06 (1999). –Section Citation.

1 Jeffrey A. Schoenblum, <u>Multistate and Multination Estate Planning</u>
§ 9.06, at 409 (1999). –Page Citation.

1 Jeffrey A. Schoenblum, <u>Multistate and Multination Estate Planning</u>
§ 9.06, at 409 n.185 (1999). –Footnote Citation.

1 Jeffrey A. Schoenblum, <u>Multistate and Multination Estate Planning</u>
§ 6.02[D], at 11 n.27 (Cum. Supp. 2001). –Footnote Citation in
Supplement.

Municipal Finance Journal
    Ab.:   Mun. Fin. J.
    Ex.:   Amy V. Puelz, <u>Call Provisions and the Cost Effectiveness of Bond</u>
    <u>Insurance</u>, 12 Mun. Fin. J., at 23 (1991). –Article Citation.

Amy V. Puelz, <u>Call Provisions and the Cost Effectiveness of Bond</u>
<u>Insurance</u>, 12 Mun. Fin. J., at 23, 25 (1991). –Page Citation.

Mutual Funds Guide (Commerce Clearing House)
    Ab.:   Mut. Funds Guide (CCH)

In citing cases in law review footnotes, abbreviate any word listed in Table T.6;
the names of "states, countries, and other geographical units" unless they are named parties;
and any other words of eight or more letters "if <u>substantial</u> space is thereby saved and the
result is unambiguous." <u>Bluebook</u> Rule 10.2.2. On the other hand, in citing cases in text,
abbreviate only widely known acronyms and the following words: "&," "Ass'n," "Bros.,"
"Co.," "Corp.," "Inc.," "Ltd.," and "No." <u>Bluebook</u> Rule 10.2.1(c).

N

NARAS Journal
Ab.:   NARAS J.
Ex.:   Stephen F. Rhode, The Power of Suggestion: Does the First
        Amendment Protect Subliminal Rock Lyrics?, NARAS J., Spring 1991,
        at 21. –Article Citation.

        Stephen F. Rhode, The Power of Suggestion: Does the First
        Amendment Protect Subliminal Rock Lyrics?, NARAS J., Spring 1991,
        at 21, 27. –Page Citation.

National Black Law Journal
Ab.:   Nat'l Black L.J.
Ex.:   Joseph E. Broadus, No Disparate Impact: Gunther's Significant But
        Ignored Limitation on Sex-Based Pay Disparity Claims Under Title
        VII, 12 Nat'l Black L.J. 10 (1990). –Article Citation.

        Joseph E. Broadus, No Disparate Impact: Gunther's Significant But
        Ignored Limitation on Sex-Based Pay Disparity Claims Under Title
        VII, 12 Nat'l Black L.J. 10, 14 (1990). –Page Citation.

National Civic Review
Ab.:   Nat'l Civic Rev.
Ex.:   Bruce H. Kirschner, Electronic Democracy in the 21st Century,
        80 Nat'l Civic Rev. 406 (1991). –Article Citation.

        Bruce H. Kirschner, Electronic Democracy in the 21st Century,
        80 Nat'l Civic Rev. 406, 408 (1991). –Page Citation.

National Jewish Law Review
Ab.:   Nat'l Jewish L. Rev.
Ex.:   Moshe Tendler, Confidentiality: A Biblical Perspective on Rights In
        Conflict, 4 Nat'l Jewish L. Rev. 1 (1989). –Article Citation.

        Moshe Tendler, Confidentiality: A Biblical Perspective on Rights In
        Conflict, 4 Nat'l Jewish L. Rev. 1, 4 (1989). –Page Citation.

National Labor Relations Board Annual Report
Ab.:   NLRB Ann. Rep. (year)
Ex.:   45 NLRB Ann. Rep. 20 (1980).

National Labor Relations Board, Decisions and Orders of the (U.S.) (1935-date)
Ab.:   N.L.R.B.

In law review footnotes, the titles of books and the names of cases, except for procedural
phrases, are not underlined. See Bluebook Rule 2.1(a). Further, the following are in large
and small capitals: codes, restatements, standards, constitutions, periodicals, authors of
books, titles of books, the abbreviated names of codes, most legislative materials except for
bills and resolutions, codified ordinances, model codes, court rules, and sentencing guidelines.
Refer to The Bluebook.

Ex.: <u>Transport America, Inc.</u>, 320 N.L.R.B. 882 (1996).

National Law Journal, The
Ab.: Nat'l L.J.
Ex.: Randall Samborn, <u>Case Holds Key to U.S. Competitiveness</u>, Nat'l L.J., Apr. 6, 1992, at 1. –Article Citation.
<u>Phone Records Are Held to be Not Privileged</u>, Nat'l L.J., Apr. 6, 1992, at 6. –News Report.

National Public Employment Reporter
Ab.: Nat'l Pub. Empl. Rep. (Labor Rel. Press)

National Railroad Adjustment Board 1st-4th Div. (U.S.) (1934-1972)
Ab.: N.R.A.B. (x Div.)
Ex.: <u>Order of Ry. Conductors</u>, 15 N.R.A.B. (1st Div.) 198 (1938).

National Tax Journal
Ab.: Nat'l Tax J.
Ex.: George R. Zodrow, <u>On the "Traditional" and "New" Views of Dividend Taxation</u>, 44 Nat'l Tax J. 497 (1991). –Article Citation.
George R. Zodrow, <u>On the "Traditional" and "New" Views of Dividend Taxation</u>, 44 Nat'l Tax J. 497, 498 (1991). –Page Citation.

National Transportation Safety Board Decisions (U.S.) (1967-date)
Ab.: N.T.S.B.
Ex.: <u>Metro Air Sys.</u>, 2 N.T.S.B. 285 (1973).

Natural Gas Lawyer's Journal, The
Ab.: Nat. Gas Law. J.
Ex.: Bernard J. Kennedy, <u>Utilities and Insurance</u>, Nat. Gas Law. J., Feb. 1987, at 39. –Article Citation.
Bernard J. Kennedy, <u>Utilities and Insurance</u>, Nat. Gas Law. J., Feb. 1987, at 39, 43. –Page Citation.

Natural Resources Journal
Ab.: Nat. Resources J.
Ex.: Uday Desai, <u>The Politics of Federal State Relations: The Case of Surface Mining Regulations</u>, 31 Nat. Resources J. 785 (1991). –Article Citation.
Uday Desai, <u>The Politics of Federal State Relations: The Case of Surface Mining Regulations</u>, 31 Nat. Resources J. 785, 791-94 (1991). –Page Citation.

Naval Law Review
Ab.: Naval L. Rev.

In citing cases in law review footnotes, abbreviate any word listed in Table T.6; the names of "states, countries, and other geographical units" unless they are named parties; and any other words of eight or more letters "if <u>substantial</u> space is thereby saved and the result is unambiguous." <u>Bluebook</u> Rule 10.2.2. On the other hand, in citing cases in text, abbreviate only widely known acronyms and the following words: "&," "Ass'n," "Bros.," "Co.," "Corp.," "Inc.," "Ltd.," and "No." <u>Bluebook</u> Rule 10.2.1(c).

Ex.:   Commander D. Michael Hinkley, <u>Protecting American Interests in Antarctica: The Territorial Claims Dilemma</u>, 39 Naval L. Rev. 43 (1990). –Article Citation.

Commander D. Michael Hinkley, <u>Protecting American Interests in Antarctica: The Territorial Claims Dilemma</u>, 39 Naval L. Rev. 43, 45 (1990). –Page Citation.

Naval War College Review
Ab.:   Naval War C. Rev.
Ex.:   James P. Terry, <u>The Environment and the Laws of War: The Impact of Desert Storm</u>, 1992 Naval War C. Rev. 61. –Article Citation.

James P. Terry, <u>The Environment and the Laws of War: The Impact of Desert Storm</u>, 1992 Naval War C. Rev. 61, 64-65. –Page Citation.

Navajo Nation Code (Equity)
Ab.:   Nation Code tit. , § (Equity year)

Nebraska Administrative Code
Ab.:   Neb. Admin. Code
Ex.:   Neb. Admin. Code tit. 23, § 2-002.03 (1999).

Nebraska Administrative Rules & Regulations
Ab.:   Neb. Admin. R. & Regs. (year)

Nebraska Constitution
Ab.:   Neb. Const. art. , § .
Ex.:   Neb. Const. art. I, § 4. –"Cite constitutional provisions currently in force without date." <u>Bluebook</u> Rule 11.

Neb. Const. art. IV, § 9 (repealed 1934). –"If the cited provision has been repealed, either indicate parenthetically the fact and date of repeal or cite the repealing provision in full." <u>Bluebook</u> Rule 11.

Neb. Const. art. I, § 6 (amended 1920). –"When citing a provision that has been subsequently amended, either indicate parenthetically the fact and date of amendment or cite the amending provision in full." <u>Bluebook</u> Rule 11.

Neb. Const. of 1866, art. I, § I. –"Cite constitutions that have been totally superseded by year of adoption; if the specific provision cited was adopted in a different year, give that year parenthetically." <u>Bluebook</u> Rule 11.

Nebraska Court of Appeals Reports
Ab.:   Neb. Ct. App.
–Cite to N.W. or N.W.2d if therein; otherwise, cite to Neb. Ct. App.

In law review footnotes, the titles of books and the names of cases, except for procedural phrases, are not underlined. <u>See</u> <u>Bluebook</u> Rule 2.1(a). Further, the following are in large and small capitals: codes, restatements, standards, constitutions, periodicals, authors of books, titles of books, the abbreviated names of codes, most legislative materials except for bills and resolutions, codified ordinances, model codes, court rules, and sentencing guidelines. Refer to <u>The Bluebook</u>.

–Give parallel citations only in documents submitted to Nebraska State Courts. See Bluebook Rule 10.3.1 and Practitioners' Note P.3; see also Neb. Unif. Dist. Ct. R. 5(C), which requires a citation to both Neb. Ct. App. and the regional reporter, and Neb. Sup. Ct. R. 9(C), which expressly permits a parallel citation.

In documents submitted to Nebraska state courts, cite as follows:

Emerson v. Zagurski, 3 Neb. Ct. App. 658, 531 N.W.2d 237 (1995). –Case Citation.

Emerson v. Zagurski, 3 Neb. Ct. App. 658, 665, 531 N.W.2d 237, 240 (1995). –Page Citation.

In all other documents, cite as follows:

Emerson v. Zagurski, 531 N.W.2d 237 (Neb. Ct. App. 1995). –Case Citation.

Emerson v. Zagurski, 531 N.W.2d 237, 240 (Neb. Ct. App. 1995). –Page Citation.

Nebraska Law Review
Ab.:　　Neb. L. Rev.

Ex.:　　Robert F. Schopp, The Psychotherapist's Duty to Protect the Public: The Appropriate Standard and the Foundation in Legal Theory and Empirical Premises, 70 Neb. L. Rev. 327 (1991). –Article Citation.

Robert F. Schopp, The Psychotherapist's Duty to Protect the Public: The Appropriate Standard and the Foundation in Legal Theory and Empirical Premises, 70 Neb. L. Rev. 327, 332-33 (1991). –Page Citation.

Nebraska Laws
See Laws of Nebraska

Nebraska, Report of the Attorney General
See Report of the Attorney General of the State of Nebraska

Nebraska Reports
Ab.:　　Neb.

–Cite to N.W. or N.W.2d if therein; otherwise, cite to Neb.

–Give parallel citations only in documents submitted to Nebraska state courts. See Bluebook Rule 10.3.1 and Practitioners' Note P.3; see also Neb. Unif. Dist. Ct. R. 5(C), which requires a citation to both Neb. and the regional reporter, and Neb. Sup. Ct. R. 9(C), which expressly permits a parallel citation.

In documents submitted to Nebraska state courts, cite as follows:

In citing cases in law review footnotes, abbreviate any word listed in Table T.6; the names of "states, countries, and other geographical units" unless they are named parties; and any other words of eight or more letters "if substantial space is thereby saved and the result is unambiguous." Bluebook Rule 10.2.2. On the other hand, in citing cases in text, abbreviate only widely known acronyms and the following words: "&," "Ass'n," "Bros.," "Co.," "Corp.," "Inc.," "Ltd.," and "No." Bluebook Rule 10.2.1(c).

Venter v. Venter, 249 Neb. 712, 545 N.W.2d 431 (1996). –Case Citation.

Venter v. Venter, 249 Neb. 712, 715, 545 N.W.2d 431, 433 (1996). –Page Citation.

In documents submitted to Nebraska state courts, cite as follows:

Venter v. Venter, 545 N.W.2d 431 (Neb. 1996). –Case Citation.

Venter v. Venter, 545 N.W.2d 431, 433 (Neb. 1996). –Page Citation.

Nebraska Revised Statutes
See Revised Statutes of Nebraska

Nebraska Session Laws
See Laws of Nebraska

Negotiation Journal
Ab.: Negotiation J.

Ex.: Michael Wheeler, Fighting the Wimp Image: Why Calls for Negotiation Often Fall on Deaf Ears, 8 Negotiation J. 25 (1992). –Article Citation.

Michael Wheeler, Fighting the Wimp Image: Why Calls for Negotiation Often Fall on Deaf Ears, 8 Negotiation J. 25, 28 (1992). –Page Citation.

Netherlands International Law Review
Ab.: Neth. Int'l L. Rev.

Ex.: Kofi Otengkufuor, Starvation as a Means of Warfare in the Liberian Conflict, 41 Neth. Int'l L. Rev. 313 (1994). –Article Citation.

Kofi Otengkufuor, Starvation as a Means of Warfare in the Liberian Conflict, 41 Neth. Int'l L. Rev. 313, 315 (1994). –Page Citation.

Nevada Administrative Code
Ab.: Nev. Admin. Code ch.   , §   (year).

Ex.: Nev. Admin. Code ch. 445B, § 310 (2000).

Nevada Constitution
Ab.: Nev. Const. art.   , §   .

Ex.: Nev. Const. art. 5, § 5. –"Cite constitutional provisions currently in force without date." Bluebook Rule 11.

Nev. Const. art. 2, § 7 (repealed 1966). –"If the cited provision has been repealed, either indicate parenthetically the fact and date of repeal or cite the repealing provision in full." Bluebook Rule 11.

In law review footnotes, the titles of books and the names of cases, except for procedural phrases, are not underlined. See Bluebook Rule 2.1(a). Further, the following are in large and small capitals: codes, restatements, standards, constitutions, periodicals, authors of books, titles of books, the abbreviated names of codes, most legislative materials except for bills and resolutions, codified ordinances, model codes, court rules, and sentencing guidelines. Refer to The Bluebook.

Nev. Const. art. 4, § 24 (amended 1990). –"When citing a provision that has been subsequently amended, either indicate parenthetically the fact and date of amendment or cite the amending provision in full." Bluebook Rule 11.

Nevada Reports
Ab.:   Nev.

–Cite to P., P.2d, or P.3d if therein; otherwise, cite to Nev.

–Give parallel citations only in documents submitted to Nevada state courts. (Note: In citing a state court case in a document submitted to a court of that same state, the 16th ed. of The Bluebook prescribed a parallel citation; the 17th ed. prescribes that local rules shall control, but Nevada has no known local rules concerning parallel citations. For the sake of continuity, we advise giving a parallel citation in documents submitted to Nevada state courts. See Bluebook Rule 10.3.1 and Practitioners' Note P.3.)

In documents submitted to Nevada state courts, cite as follows:

     Smimrak v. Garcia-Mendoza, 112 Nev. 246, 912 P.2d 822 (1996). –Case Citation.

     Smimrak v. Garcia-Mendoza, 112 Nev. 246, 247, 912 P.2d 822, 824 (1996). –Page Citation.

In all other documents, cite as follows:

     Smimrak v. Garcia-Mendoza, 912 P.2d 822 (Nev. 1996). –Case Citation.

     Smimrak v. Garcia-Mendoza, 912 P.2d 822, 824 (Nev. 1996). –Page Citation.

Nevada Revised Statutes
Ab.:   Nev. Rev. Stat. §   (year)

Ex.:   Nev. Rev. Stat. § 81.3435 (1999).

Nevada Revised Statutes Annotated, Michie's (Lexis)
Ab.:   Nev. Rev. Stat. Ann. §   (Lexis year)

Ex.:   Nev. Rev. Stat. Ann. § 393.280 (Lexis 2000).

        Nev. Rev. Stat. Ann. § 673.377 (Lexis Supp. 1999).

–"Cite to Nev. Rev. Stat. if therein." Bluebook Table T.1, p. 214.

See Nevada Revised Statutes

Nevada Session Laws
See Statutes of Nevada

Nevada State Bar Journal, The
Ab.:   Nev. St. B.J.

In citing cases in law review footnotes, abbreviate any word listed in Table T.6; the names of "states, countries, and other geographical units" unless they are named parties; and any other words of eight or more letters "if substantial space is thereby saved and the result is unambiguous." Bluebook Rule 10.2.2. On the other hand, in citing cases in text, abbreviate only widely known acronyms and the following words: "&," "Ass'n," "Bros.," "Co.," "Corp.," "Inc.," "Ltd.," and "No." Bluebook Rule 10.2.1(c).

Ex.:   Harvey Dickerson, <u>Governor's Power on Board of Pardons Limited by Consitution</u>, Nev. St. B.J., Oct. 1972, at 4. –Article Citation.

Harvey Dickerson, <u>Governor's Power on Board of Pardons Limited by Consitution</u>, Nev. St. B.J., Oct. 1972, at 4, 5-6. –Page Citation.

New Brunswick Reports (Canada)
Ab.:   N.B.R., N.B.R.2d

Ex.:   <u>Johnson v. Barrieau</u>, 54 N.B.R. 429 (1928) (Can.). –Case Citation.

<u>Baniuk v. Carpenter</u>, 112 N.B.R.2d 332 (1990) (Can.). –Case Citation.

New England Journal of Medicine
Ab.:   New Eng. J. Med.

Ex.:   George E. Thibault, <u>Failure to Resolve a Diagnostic Inconsistency</u>, New Eng. J. Med., July 2, 1992, at 36. –Article Citation.

George E. Thibault, <u>Failure to Resolve a Diagnostic Inconsistency</u>, New Eng. J. Med., July 2, 1992, at 36, 37. –Page Citation.

New England Journal on Criminal and Civil Confinement
Ab.:   New Eng. J. on Crim. & Civ. Confinement

Ex.:   Jim Thomas, <u>The "Reality" of Prisoner Litigation: Repacking the Data</u>, 15 New Eng. J. on Crim. & Civ. Confinement 27 (1989). –Article Citation.

Jim Thomas, <u>The "Reality" of Prisoner Litigation: Repacking the Data</u>, 15 New Eng. J. on Crim. & Civ. Confinement 27, 29 (1989). –Page Citation.

New England Law Review
Ab.:   New Eng. L. Rev.

Ex.:   Edward Greer, <u>Rule II: Substantive Bias in Formal Uniformity After the Supreme Court Trilogy</u>, 26 New Eng. L. Rev. 111 (1991). –Article Citation.

Edward Greer, <u>Rule II: Substantive Bias in Formal Uniformity After the Supreme Court Trilogy</u>, 26 New Eng. L. Rev. 111, 120 (1991). –Page Citation.

New Hampshire Bar Journal
Ab.:   N.H. B.J.

Ex.:   Maureen D. Smith, <u>The Fleet Factors Rule of Lender Liability for Hazardous Waste Contamination</u>, 32 N.H. B.J. 142 (1991). –Article Citation.

Maureen D. Smith, <u>The Fleet Factors Rule of Lender Liability for Hazardous Waste Contamination</u>, 32 N.H. B.J. 142, 144 (1991). –Page Citation.

In law review footnotes, the titles of books and the names of cases, except for procedural phrases, are not underlined. <u>See</u> Bluebook Rule 2.1(a). Further, the following are in large and small capitals: codes, restatements, standards, constitutions, periodicals, authors of books, titles of books, the abbreviated names of codes, most legislative materials except for bills and resolutions, codified ordinances, model codes, court rules, and sentencing guidelines. Refer to <u>The Bluebook</u>.

New Hampshire Code of Administrative Rules Annotated
Ab.:   N.H. Code Admin. R. Ann.   [department name as abbreviated in Rules] (year)

New Hampshire Constitution
Ab.:   N.H. Const. pt.   , art.   .
Ex.:   N.H. Const. pt. 2, art. 89. –"Cite constitutional provisions currently in force without date." Bluebook Rule 11.

N.H. Const. pt. 2, art. 99 (repealed 1980). –"If the cited provision has been repealed, either indicate parenthetically the fact and date of repeal or cite the repealing provision in full." Bluebook Rule 11.

N.H. Const. pt. 1, art. 6 (amended 1968). –"When citing a provision that has been subsequently amended, either indicate parenthetically the fact and date of amendment or cite the amending provision in full." Bluebook Rule 11.

New Hampshire Reports
Ab.:   N.H.
–Cite to A. or A.2d if therein; otherwise, cite to N.H.

–Give parallel citations, if at all, only in documents submitted to New Hampshire state courts. See Bluebook Rule 10.3.1 and Practitioners' Note P.3; see also N.H. Sup. Ct. R. 16(9), which requires a citation only to N.H.

In documents submitted to New Hampshire state courts, cite as follows:
Mason v. Smith, 140 N.H. 696, 672 A.2d 705 (1996). –Case Citation.
Mason v. Smith, 140 N.H. 696, 698, 672 A.2d 705, 707 (1996). –Page Citation.

In all other documents, cite as follows:
Mason v. Smith, 672 A.2d 705 (N.H. 1996). –Case Citation.
Mason v. Smith, 672 A.2d 705, 707 (N.H. 1996). –Page Citation.

New Hampshire Revised Statutes Annotated
Ab.:   N.H. Rev. Stat. Ann. §   (1999)
Ex.:   N.H. Rev. Stat. Ann. § 189:49 (1999).
         N.H. Rev. Stat. Ann. § 515:7 (Supp. 2000).

New Hampshire Rulemaking Register
Ab.:   N.H. Rulemaking Reg.

New Hampshire Session Laws
See Laws of the State of New Hampshire

New Jersey Administrative Code
Ab.:   N.J. Admin. Code tit.   , §   (year)

In citing cases in law review footnotes, abbreviate any word listed in Table T.6; the names of "states, countries, and other geographical units" unless they are named parties; and any other words of eight or more letters "if substantial space is thereby saved and the result is unambiguous." Bluebook Rule 10.2.2. On the other hand, in citing cases in text, abbreviate only widely known acronyms and the following words: "&," "Ass'n," "Bros.," "Co.," "Corp.," "Inc.," "Ltd.," and "No." Bluebook Rule 10.2.1(c).

Ex.:   N.J. Admin. Code tit. 7, § 5D-2.1 (2000).

New Jersey Administrative Reports (1982-date)
Ab.:   N.J. Admin., N.J. Admin. 2d

New Jersey Constitution
Ab.:   N.J. Const. art.   ,   ¶   .

Ex.:   N.J. Const. art. I, ¶ 19. –"Cite constitutional provisions currently in force without date." Bluebook Rule 11.

N.J. Const. art. IV, ¶¶ 1-5 (repealed 1978). –"If the cited provision has been repealed, either indicate parenthetically the fact and date of repeal or cite the repealing provision in full." Bluebook Rule 11.

N.J. Const. art. VII, ¶ 2 (amended 1984). –"When citing a provision that has been subsequently amended, either indicate parenthetically the fact and date of amendment or cite the amending provision in full." Bluebook Rule 11.

N.J. Const. of 1844, art. I, ¶ 5 (1947). –"Cite constitutions that have been totally superseded by year of adoption, giving parenthetically the year of adoption of the specific provision cited if different." Bluebook Rule 11.

New Jersey Equity Reports
Ab.:   N.J. Eq.

–Discontinued in 1948.

–Cite to A. or A.2d if therein; otherwise, cite to N.J. Eq.

–Give parallel citations, if at all, only in documents submitted to New Jersey state courts. See Bluebook Rule 10.3.1 and Practitioners' Note P.3; see also N.J. R. App. Prac. 2:6-2(a)(5), which requires only a citation to N.J. Eq.

In documents submitted to New Jersey state courts, cite as follows:

Temple v. Clinton Trust Co., 142 N.J. Eq. 285, 59 A.2d 590 (Ch. 1948). –Case Citation.

Temple v. Clinton Trust Co., 142 N.J. Eq. 285, 289, 59 A.2d 590, 592 (Ch. 1948). –Page Citation.

In all other documents, cite as follows:

Temple v. Clinton Trust Co., 59 A.2d 590 (N.J. Ch. 1948). –Case Citation.

Temple v. Clinton Trust Co., 59 A.2d 590, 592 (N.J. Ch. 1948). –Page Citation.

New Jersey Law Journal
Ab.:   N.J. L.J.

In law review footnotes, the titles of books and the names of cases, except for procedural phrases, are not underlined. See Bluebook Rule 2.1(a). Further, the following are in large and small capitals: codes, restatements, standards, constitutions, periodicals, authors of books, titles of books, the abbreviated names of codes, most legislative materials except for bills and resolutions, codified ordinances, model codes, court rules, and sentencing guidelines. Refer to The Bluebook.

Ex.:   Alan B. Handler, <u>Taking Better Aim at Judicial Evaluation</u>, N.J. L.J., Mar. 26, 1981, at 1. –Article Citation.

Alan B. Handler, <u>Taking Better Aim at Judicial Evaluation</u>, N.J. L.J., Mar. 26, 1981, at 1, 12. –Page Citation.

New Jersey Law Reports (1790-1948)
Ab.:   N.J.L. Rep.

Ex.:   <u>Trade Ins. Co. v. Barracliff</u>, 45 N.J.L. 543 (1883). –Case Citation.

<u>Trade Ins. Co. v. Barracliff</u>, 45 N.J.L. 543, 546 (1883). –Page Citation.

New Jersey Lawyer
Ab.:   N.J. Law.

Ex.:   Deanne M. Wilson, <u>Women in Private Law Firms: An Underdeveloped Asset</u>, N.J. Law., July/Aug. 1991, at 42. –Article Citation.

Deanne M. Wilson, <u>Women in Private Law Firms: An Underdeveloped Asset</u>, N.J. Law., July/Aug. 1991, at 42, 43. –Page Citation.

New Jersey Miscellaneous Reports
Ab.:   N.J. Misc.

–Discontinued in 1949.

–Cite to A. or A.2d if therein; otherwise, cite to N.J. Misc.

–Give parallel citations, if at all, only in documents submitted to New Jersey state courts. <u>See</u> Bluebook Rule 10.3.1 and Practitioners' Note P.3; <u>see also</u> N.J. R. App. Prac. 2:6-2(a)(5), which requires in the absence of official reporting that such fact be stated and unofficial citation made.

In documents submitted to New Jersey state courts, cite as follows:
<u>Cooper Lumber Co. v. Dammers</u>, 2 N.J. Misc. 289, 125 A. 325 (Sup. Ct. 1924). –Case Citation.

<u>Cooper Lumber Co. v. Dammers</u>, 2 N.J. Misc. 289, 292, 125 A. 325, 326-27 (Sup. Ct. 1924). –Page Citation.

In all other documents, cite as follows:
<u>Cooper Lumber Co. v. Dammers</u>, 125 A. 325 (N.J. Sup. Ct. 1924). –Case Citation.

<u>Cooper Lumber Co. v. Dammers</u>, 125 A. 325, 326-27 (N.J. Sup. Ct. 1924). –Page Citation.

New Jersey Register
Ab.:   N.J. Reg.

New Jersey Reports
Ab.:   N.J.

–Cite to A. or A.2d if therein; otherwise, cite to N.J.

In citing cases in law review footnotes, abbreviate any word listed in Table T.6; the names of "states, countries, and other geographical units" unless they are named parties; and any other words of eight or more letters "if <u>substantial</u> space is thereby saved and the result is unambiguous." <u>Bluebook</u> Rule 10.2.2. On the other hand, in citing cases in text, abbreviate only widely known acronyms and the following words: "&," "Ass'n," "Bros.," "Co.," "Corp.," "Inc.," "Ltd.," and "No." <u>Bluebook</u> Rule 10.2.1(c).

–Give parallel citations, if at all, only in documents submitted to New Jersey state courts. See Bluebook Rule 10.3.1 and Practitioners' Note P.3; see also N.J. R. App. Prac. 2:6-2(a)(5), which requires only a citation to N.J.

In documents submitted to New Jersey state courts, cite as follows:

State v. Fertig, 143 N.J. 115, 668 A.2d 1076 (1996). –Case Citation.

State v. Fertig, 143 N.J. 115, 118, 668 A.2d 1076, 1077 (1996). –Page Citation.

In all other documents, cite as follows:

State v. Fertig, 668 A.2d 1076 (N. J. 1996). –Case Citation.

State v. Fertig, 668 A.2d 1076, 1077 (N.J. 1996). –Page Citation.

New Jersey Revised Statutes (1937)
Ab.:   N.J. Rev. Stat. §   (year)

New Jersey Sessions Laws
See Laws of New Jersey and New Jersey Session Law Service (West).

New Jersey Session Law Service (West)
Ab.:   year N.J. Sess. Law Serv. (West)
Ex.:   Act of June 28, 1996, ch. 53, 1996 N.J. Sess. Law Serv. 177 (West) (concerning adoption of building construction codes). –Citation to an entire session law.

Act of June 28, 1996, ch. 53, § 1, 1996 N.J. Sess. Law Serv. 177, 177 (West) (concerning adoption of building construction codes). –Citation to a section of a session law.

–"Cite to N.J. Laws if therein." Bluebook Table T.1, p. 216.

New Jersey Statutes Annotated (West)
Ab.:   N.J. Stat. Ann. §   (West year)
Ex.:   N.J. Stat. Ann. § 19:14-20 (West 1999).

N.J. Stat. Ann. § 39:3-75.3 (West Supp. 2000).

New Jersey Superior Court Reports
Ab.:   N.J. Super.
–Cite to A. or A.2d if therein; otherwise, cite to N.J. Super.
–Give parallel citations, if at all, only in documents submitted to New Jersey state courts. See Bluebook Rule 10.3.1 and Practitioners' Note P.3; see also N.J. R. App. Prac. 2:6-2(a)(5), which requires only a citation to N.J. Super.

In documents submitted to New Jersey state courts, cite as follows:

Rogan Equities, Inc. v. Santini, 289 N.J. Super. 95, 672 A.2d 1281 (App. Div. 1996). –Case Citation.

In law review footnotes, the titles of books and the names of cases, except for procedural phrases, are not underlined. See Bluebook Rule 2.1(a). Further, the following are in large and small capitals: codes, restatements, standards, constitutions, periodicals, authors of books, titles of books, the abbreviated names of codes, most legislative materials except for bills and resolutions, codified ordinances, model codes, court rules, and sentencing guidelines. Refer to The Bluebook.

Rogan Equities, Inc. v. Santini, 289 N.J. Super. 95, 98, 672 A.2d 1281, 1283 (App. Div. 1996). –Page Citation.

In all other documents, cite as follows:

Rogan Equities, Inc. v. Santini, 672 A.2d 1281 (N.J. Super. Ct. App. Div. 1996). –Case Citation.

Rogan Equities, Inc. v. Santini, 672 A.2d 1281, 1283 (N.J. Super. Ct. App. Div. 1996). –Page Citation.

New Jersey Tax Court Reports
Ab.:   N.J. Tax

New Law Journal
Ab.:   New L.J.

Ex.:   Roger Leng, Imprisonment for Prostitutes, 142 New L.J. 270 (1992). –Article Citation.

Roger Leng, Imprisonment for Prostitutes, 142 New L.J. 270, 271 (1992). –Page Citation.

New Mexico Administrative Code
Ab.:   N.M. Admin. Code tit. , §   (year) .

Ex.:   N.M. Admin. Code tit. 7, § 26.2.10 (2000).

New Mexico Advance Legislative Service (Michie)
Ab.:   year N.M. Adv. Legis. Serv.

Ex.:   Act of Mar. 5, 1996, ch. 50, 1996 N.M. Adv. Legis. Serv. 679 (relating to financial transactions). –Citation to an entire session law.

Act of Mar. 5, 1996, ch. 50, sec. 1A, § 58-15-17, 1996 N.M. Adv. Legis. Serv. 679, 679-80 (relating to financial transactions). –Citation to a section of a session law amending a prior act.

New Mexico Bar Bulletin (Bar Bulletin: State of New Mexico)
See Bar Bulletin: State Bar of New Mexico.

New Mexico Constitution
Ab.:   N.M. Const. art. , § .

Ex.:   N.M. Const. art. XX, § 13. –"Cite constitutional provisions currently in force without date." Bluebook Rule 11.

N.M. Const. art. XX, § 17 (repealed 1971). –"If the cited provision has been repealed, either indicate parenthetically the fact and date of repeal or cite the repealing provision in full." Bluebook Rule 11.

N.M. Const. art. XII, § 7 (amended 1990). –"When citing a provision that has been subsequently amended, either indicate parenthetically the fact and date of amendment or cite the amending provision in full." Bluebook Rule 11.

In citing cases in law review footnotes, abbreviate any word listed in Table T.6; the names of "states, countries, and other geographical units" unless they are named parties; and any other words of eight or more letters "if substantial space is thereby saved and the result is unambiguous." Bluebook Rule 10.2.2. On the other hand, in citing cases in text, abbreviate only widely known acronyms and the following words: "&," "Ass'n," "Bros.," "Co.," "Corp.," "Inc.," "Ltd.," and "No." Bluebook Rule 10.2.1(c).

New Mexico Court of Appeals
    Ab.:   N.M. Ct. App.
    –Cite to P., P.2d, or P.3d if therein; in addition, give public domain citation, if available.
    –Until January 1, 1996, when a public domain format was adopted, cite as follows:
    In documents submitted to New Mexico state courts:
        Yount v. Johnson, 121 N.M. 585, 915 P.2d 341 (Ct. App. 1996). –Case Citation.
        Yount v. Johnson, 121 N.M. 585, 586, 915 P.2d 341, 342 (Ct. App. 1996). –Page Citation.
    In all other documents:
        Yount v. Johnson, 915 P.2d 341 (N. M. Ct. App. 1996). –Case Citation.
        Yount v. Johnson, 915 P.2d 341, 342 (N.M. Ct. App. 1996). –Page Citation.
    –From January 1, 1996, cite as follows:
    In documents submitted to New Mexico state courts:
        State v. Cleave, 2000-NMCA-071, 129 N.M. 355 –Case Citation.
        or
        State v. Cleave, 2000-NMCA-071, 8 P.3d 157 –Case Citation.

        State v. Cleave, 2000-NMCA-071, ¶ 7, 129 N.M. 355, 358. –Pinpoint Citation.
        or
        State v. Cleave, 2000-NMCA-071, ¶ 7, P.3d 157, 159. –Pinpoint Citation.
    In all other documents:
        State v. Cleave, 2000-NMCA-071, 8 P.3d 157 –Case Citation.
        State v. Cleave, 2000-NMCA-071, ¶ 7, 8 P.3d 157, 159. –Pinpoint Citation.
        See Bluebook Rules 10.3.1 and 10.3.3, Table T.1, and Practitioners' Note P.3; see also N.M.R. App. P. 12-213(E) and In re the Adoption of Vendor Neutral Citations (N.M. Jan. 12, 1998).

New Mexico Law Review
    Ab.:   N.M. L. Rev.

In law review footnotes, the titles of books and the names of cases, except for procedural phrases, are not underlined. See Bluebook Rule 2.1(a). Further, the following are in large and small capitals: codes, restatements, standards, constitutions, periodicals, authors of books, titles of books, the abbreviated names of codes, most legislative materials except for bills and resolutions, codified ordinances, model codes, court rules, and sentencing guidelines. Refer to The Bluebook.

Ex.:   Richard B. Collins, <u>Justice Scalia and the Elusive Idea of</u>
         <u>Discrimination Against Interstate Commerce</u>, 20 N.M. L. Rev. 555
         (1990). –Article Citation.

         Richard B. Collins, <u>Justice Scalia and the Elusive Idea of</u>
         <u>Discrimination Against Interstate Commerce</u>, 20 N.M. L. Rev. 555,
         559-60 (1990). –Page Citation.

New Mexico Session Laws
<u>See</u> Laws of New Mexico and New Mexico Advance Legislative Service
(Michie).

New Mexico Statutes Annotated (Michie)
Ab.:   N.M. Stat. Ann. §   (Michie year).

Ex.:   N.M. Stat. Ann. § 50-9-4 (Michie 2000).

         N.M. Stat. Ann. § 52-1-22 (Michie Supp. 2000).

New Mexico Supreme Court
Ab.:   N.M.

         –Cite to P., P. 2d, or P.3d if therein; in addition, give public domain
         citation if available.

         –Until January 1, 1996, when a public domain format was adopted, cite
         as follows:

         In documents submitted to New Mexico state courts:

             <u>Buffett v. Vargas</u>, 121 N.M. 507, 914 P.2d 1004 (1985). –Case
             Citation.

             <u>Buffett v. Vargas</u>, 121 N.M. 507, 508, 914 P.2d 1004, 1005
             (1985). –Page Citation.

         In all other documents:

             <u>Buffett v. Vargas</u>, 914 P.2d 1004 (N.M. 1985). –Case Citation.

             <u>Buffett v. Vargas</u>, 914 P.2d 1004, 1005 (N.M. 1985). –Page
                 Citation.

         –After January 1, 1996, cite as follows:

         In documents submitted to New Mexico state courts:

             <u>In re Dawson</u>, 2000-NMSC-024, 129 N.M. 369. –Case Citation.
             or
             <u>In re Dawson</u>, 2000-NMSC-024, 8 P.3d 856. –Case Citation.

             <u>In re Dawson</u>, 2000-NMSC-024, ¶ 11, 129 N.M. 369, 374. –
                 Pinpoint Citation.
             or

In citing cases in law review footnotes, abbreviate any word listed in Table T.6;
the names of "states, countries, and other geographical units" unless they are named parties;
and any other words of eight or more letters "if <u>substantial</u> space is thereby saved and the
result is unambiguous." <u>Bluebook</u> Rule 10.2.2. On the other hand, in citing cases in text,
abbreviate only widely known acronyms and the following words: "&," "Ass'n," "Bros.,"
"Co.," "Corp.," "Inc.," "Ltd.," and "No." <u>Bluebook</u> Rule 10.2.1(c).

In re Dawson, 2000-NMSC-024, ¶ 11, 8 P.3d 856, 859. –Pinpoint
Citation.

In all other documents,:

In re Dawson, 2000-NMSC-024, 8 P.3d 856. –Case Citation.

In re Dawson, 2000-NMSC-024, ¶ 11, 8 P.3d 856, 859. –Pinpoint
Citation.

See Bluebook Rules 10.3.1 and 10.3.3, Table T.1, and Practitioners'
Note P.3; see also N.M.R. App. P. 12-213(E) and In re the
Adoption of Vendor Neutral Citations (N.M. Jan. 12, 1998).

New South Wales Reports (1960-date)
Ab.:   N.S.W.R.

Ex.:   Austin v. Royal (1999) 47 N.S.W.R. 27. –Case Citation.

New York Appellate Division Reports
Ab.:   A.D., A.D.2d

–Cite to N.Y.S. or N.Y.S.2d if therein; otherwise, cite to A.D. or
A.D.2d.

–Give parallel citations, if at all, only in documents submitted to New
York state courts. See Bluebook Rule 10.3.1 and Practitioners' Note
P.3; see also N.Y. Ct. App. R. 500.1 and 500.5(d)(3) and N.Y. Sup.
Ct. App. Div. R. 600.10, which require only a citation to A.D. or
A.D.2d.

In documents submitted to New York state courts, cite as follows:

Ferrer v. Dinkins, 218 A.D.2d 89, 635 N.Y.S.2d 965 (1996).
–Case Citation.

Ferrer v. Dinkins, 218 A.D.2d 89, 90, 635 N.Y.S.2d 965, 966
(1996). –Page Citation.

In all other documents, cite as follows:

Ferrer v. Dinkins, 635 N.Y.S.2d 965 (App. Div. 1996). –Case
Citation.

Ferrer v. Dinkins, 635 N.Y.S.2d 965, 966 (App. Div. 1996).
–Page Citation.

New York Codes, Rules and Regulations
See Official Compilation of Codes, Rules and Regulations of the State of New
York

New York Constitution
Ab.:   N.Y. Const. art.   , §   .

In law review footnotes, the titles of books and the names of cases, except for procedural
phrases, are not underlined. See Bluebook Rule 2.1(a). Further, the following are in large
and small capitals: codes, restatements, standards, constitutions, periodicals, authors of
books, titles of books, the abbreviated names of codes, most legislative materials except for
bills and resolutions, codified ordinances, model codes, court rules, and sentencing guidelines.
Refer to The Bluebook.

Ex.:   N.Y. Const. art. I, § 17. –"Cite constitutional provisions currently in
force without date." Bluebook Rule 11.

N.Y. Const. art. I, § 10 (repealed 1963). –"If the cited provision has
been repealed, either indicate parenthetically the fact and date of repeal
or cite the repealing provision in full." Bluebook Rule 11.

N.Y. Const. art. XIV, § 1 (amended 1987). –"When citing a provision
that has been subsequently amended, either indicate parenthetically the
fact and date of amendment or cite the amending provision in full."
Bluebook Rule 11.

N.Y. Const. of 1894, art. I, § 3 (1938). –"Cite constitutions that have
been totally superseded by year of adoption; if the specific provision
cited was adopted in a different year–give that year parenthetically."
Bluebook Rule 11.

New York Law Journal
Ab.:   N.Y. L.J.
Ex.:   Cerisse Anderson, Goldman Widow Gets Disbursement Order, N.Y.
L.J., Dec. 31, 1991, at 1. –Article Citation.

Cerisse Anderson, Goldman Widow Gets Disbursement Order, N.Y.
L.J., Dec. 31, 1991, at 1, 2. –Page Citation.

New York Law School Journal of Human Rights
Ab.:   N.Y.L. Sch. J. Hum. Rts.
Ex.:   Robert F. Kane & Fred M. Blum, The International Year of Bible
Reading: The Unconstitutional Use of the Political Process to Endorse
Religion, 8 N.Y.L. Sch. J. Hum. Rts. 333 (1991). –Article Citation.

Robert F. Kane & Fred M. Blum, The International Year of Bible
Reading: The Unconstitutional Use of the Political Process to Endorse
Religion, 8 N.Y.L. Sch. J. Hum. Rts. 333, 336-37 (1991). –Page
Citation.

New York Law School Journal of International and Comparative Law
Ab.:   N.Y.L. Sch. J. Int'l & Comp. L.
Ex.:   Hilary House, The Border That Wouldn't Go Away: Irish Integration in
the EC, 11 N.Y.L. Sch. J. Int'l & Comp. L. 229 (1990). –Article
Citation.

Hilary House, The Border That Wouldn't Go Away: Irish Integration in
the EC, 11 N.Y.L. Sch. J. Int'l & Comp. L. 229, 239 (1990). –Page
Citation.

New York Law School Law Review
Ab.:   N.Y.L. Sch. L. Rev.

In citing cases in law review footnotes, abbreviate any word listed in Table T.6;
the names of "states, countries, and other geographical units" unless they are named parties;
and any other words of eight or more letters "if substantial space is thereby saved and the
result is unambiguous." Bluebook Rule 10.2.2. On the other hand, in citing cases in text,
abbreviate only widely known acronyms and the following words: "&," "Ass'n," "Bros.,"
"Co.," "Corp.," "Inc.," "Ltd.," and "No." Bluebook Rule 10.2.1(c).

Ex.:   Howard M. Metzenbaum, <u>Telecommunications Policy: Protecting Consumers by Promoting Diversity</u>, 35 N.Y.L. Sch. L. Rev. 593 (1990). –Article Citation.

Howard M. Metzenbaum, <u>Telecommunications Policy: Protecting Consumers by Promoting Diversity</u>, 35 N.Y.L. Sch. L. Rev. 593, 599 (1990). –Page Citation.

New York, McKinney's Consolidated Laws Annotated
<u>See</u> McKinney's Consolidated Laws of New York Annotated

New York Miscellaneous Reports
Ab.:   Misc., Misc. 2d

–Cite to N.Y.S. or N.Y.S.2d if therein; otherwise, cite to Misc. or Misc. 2d.

–Give parallel citations, if at all, only in documents submitted to New York state courts. <u>See</u> <u>Bluebook</u> Rule 10.3.1 and Practitioners' Note P.3; <u>see also</u> N.Y. Ct. App. R. 500.1 and 500.5(d)(3) and N.Y. Sup. Ct. App. Div. R. 600.10, which require only a citation to Misc. or Misc. 2d.

In documents submitted to New York state courts, cite as follows:

<u>Okebiyi v. Cortines</u>, 167 Misc. 2d 1008, 641 N.Y.S.2d 791 (Sup. Ct. 1984). –Case Citation.

<u>Okebiyi v. Cortines</u>, 167 Misc. 2d 1008, 1009, 641 N.Y.S.2d 791, 792 (Sup. Ct. 1984). –Page Citation.

In all other documents, cite as follows:

<u>Okebiyi v. Cortines</u>, 641 N.Y.S.2d 791 (Sup. Ct. 1996). –Case Citation.

<u>Okebiyi v. Cortines</u>, 641 N.Y.S.2d 791, 792 (Sup. Ct. 1996). –Page Citation.

New York Opinions of Attorney General
<u>See</u> Opinions of Attorney General of New York

New York Reports
Ab.:   N.Y., N.Y.2d

–Cite to N.E. or N.E.2d if therein; otherwise, cite to N.Y., N.Y.2d, or N.Y.S.2d.

–Give parallel citations only in documents submitted to New York state courts. <u>See</u> <u>Bluebook</u> Rule 10.3.1, Table T.1, and Practitioners' Note P.3; <u>see also</u> N.Y. Ct. App. R. 500.1 and 500.5(d)(3) and N.Y. Sup. Ct. App. Div. R. 600.10, which require only a citation to N.Y. or N.Y.2d.

In documents submitted to New York state courts, cite as follows:

In law review footnotes, the titles of books and the names of cases, except for procedural phrases, are not underlined. <u>See</u> <u>Bluebook</u> Rule 2.1(a). Further, the following are in large and small capitals: codes, restatements, standards, constitutions, periodicals, authors of books, titles of books, the abbreviated names of codes, most legislative materials except for bills and resolutions, codified ordinances, model codes, court rules, and sentencing guidelines. Refer to <u>The Bluebook</u>.

Beckman v. Greentree Securities, Inc., 87 N.Y.2d 566, 663 N.E.2d 886, 640 N.Y.S.2d 845 (1996). –Case Citation.

Beckman v. Greentree Securities, Inc., 87 N.Y.2d 566, 569, 663 N.E.2d 886, 887, 640 N.Y.S.2d 845, 847 (1996). –Page Citation.

In all other documents, cite as follows:

Beckman v. Greentree Securities, Inc., 663 N.E.2d 886 (N.Y. 1996). –Case Citation.

Beckman v. Greentree Securities, Inc., 663 N.E.2d 886, 887 (N.Y. 1996). –Page Citation.

New York Session Laws
See McKinney's Session Laws of New York

New York State Bar Association Antitrust Law Symposium
Ab.:   N.Y. St. B.A. Antitrust L. Symp.

New York State Bar Journal
Ab.:   N.Y. St. B.J.
Ex.:   Michael E. O'Connor, U.S. Savings Bonds in the Estate, N.Y. St. B.J., Feb. 1992, at 39. –Article Citation.

Michael E. O'Connor, U.S. Savings Bonds in the Estate, N.Y. St. B.J., Feb. 1992, at 39, 41. –Page Citation.

New York State Register
Ab.:   N.Y. St. Reg.

New York Stock Exchange Guide (Commerce Clearing House)
Ab.:   N.Y.S.E. Guide (CCH)

New York Supplement and New York Supplement, second series
See West's New York Supplement

New York Times
Ab.:   N.Y. Times
Ex.:   Seth Mydans, Gates Threatens to Delay Leaving, N.Y. Times, June 8, 1992, at A7. –Signed article.

Chicago Police Kill Boy, 12, Who Pointed a Gun, N.Y. Times, June 8, 1992, at A7. –Unsigned news report.

New York University Institute on Federal Taxation
Ab.:   Inst. on Fed. Tax'n
Ex.:   Michael F. Klein, Jr. & David K. Grevengoed, Individual Alternative Minimum Tax, 48 Inst. on Fed. Tax'n § 6.0, at 6-14 (1990).

New York University Journal of International Law and Politics
Ab.:   N.Y.U. J. Int'l L. & Pol.

In citing cases in law review footnotes, abbreviate any word listed in Table T.6; the names of "states, countries, and other geographical units" unless they are named parties; and any other words of eight or more letters "if substantial space is thereby saved and the result is unambiguous." Bluebook Rule 10.2.2. On the other hand, in citing cases in text, abbreviate only widely known acronyms and the following words: "&," "Ass'n," "Bros.," "Co.," "Corp.," "Inc.," "Ltd.," and "No." Bluebook Rule 10.2.1(c).

Ex.:   Timothy A. Gelatt, <u>Lawyers in China: The Past Decade and Beyond</u>, 23 N.Y.U. J. Int'l L. & Pol. 751 (1991). –Article Citation.

Timothy A. Gelatt, <u>Lawyers in China: The Past Decade and Beyond</u>, 23 N.Y.U. J. Int'l L. & Pol. 751, 756 (1991). –Page Citation.

New York University Law Review
Ab.:   N.Y.U. L. Rev.
Ex.:   Robert Cooter & Bradley J. Freedman, <u>The Fiduciary Relationship: Its Economic Character and Legal Consequences</u>, 66 N.Y.U. L. Rev. 1045 (1991). –Article Citation.

Robert Cooter & Bradley J. Freedman, <u>The Fiduciary Relationship: Its Economic Character and Legal Consequences</u>, 66 N.Y.U. L. Rev. 1045, 1050 (1991). –Page Citation.

New York University Review of Law and Social Change
Ab.:   N.Y.U. Rev. L. & Soc. Change
Ex.:   Allan H. Macurdy, <u>Classical Nostalgia: Racism, Contract Ideology and Formalist Legal Reasoning in *Patterson v. McLean Credit Union*</u>, 18 N.Y.U. Rev. L. & Soc. Change 987 (1990-91). –Article Citation.

Allan H. Macurdy, <u>Classical Nostalgia: Racism, Contract Ideology and Formalist Legal Reasoning in *Patterson v. McLean Credit Union*</u>, 18 N.Y.U. Rev. L. & Soc. Change 987, 991 (1990-91). –Page Citation.

New Zealand Law Journal, The
Ab.:   N.Z. L. J.
Ex.:   J.L. Caldwell, <u>Is Scandalizing the Court a Scandal?</u> 1994 N.Z. L. J. 442. –Article Citation.

J.L. Caldwell, <u>Is Scandalizing the Court a Scandal?</u> 1994 N.Z. L. J. 442, 445. –Page Citation.

New Zealand Law Reports (1883 - date)
See <u>Bluebook</u> Table T.2. and Rule 20.3.1
Ab.:   N.Z.L.R.
Ex.:   <u>R v. Walters</u>, [1989] 2 N.Z.L.R. 33. –Case Citation.

New Zealand Universities Law Review
Ab.:   N.Z.U. L. Rev.
Ex.:   Gordon R. Walker, <u>A Model of an Initial Public Offering</u>, 15 N.Z.U. L. Rev. 396 (1993). –Article Citation.

Gordon R. Walker, <u>A Model of an Initial Public Offering</u>, 15 N.Z.U. L. Rev. 396, 400 (1993). –Page Citation.

Newfoundland and Prince Edward Island Reports (Canada) (1970-date)
Ab.:   Nfld. & P.E.I.R.

In law review footnotes, the titles of books and the names of cases, except for procedural phrases, are not underlined. See <u>Bluebook</u> Rule 2.1(a). Further, the following are in large and small capitals: codes, restatements, standards, constitutions, periodicals, authors of books, titles of books, the abbreviated names of codes, most legislative materials except for bills and resolutions, codified ordinances, model codes, court rules, and sentencing guidelines. Refer to <u>The Bluebook</u>.

Ex.:   Ford Credit Canada Ltd. v. Crosbie Realty Ltd., 90 Nfld. & P.E.I.R.
        191 (1991) (Can.). –Case Citation.

newsletter
  Ab.:   newsl.

newspapers
  See Bluebook Rule 16.5.
  Ex.:   Ruth Marcus, Court Cuts Federal Desegregation Role, Wash. Post,
          Apr.1, 1992, at A1. –Article Citation.
          Judge Drops Juror from Gotti Trial, Wash. Post, Apr. 1, 1992, at A7.
          –News Report Citation.
          –This format also applies to weekly newspapers and magazines.

Nimmer on Copyright, by Melville B. Nimmer and David Nimmer
  –Do not abbreviate the title.
  Ex.:   2 Melville B. Nimmer & David Nimmer, Nimmer on Copyright
          § 7.16[C] (1991). –Section Citation.

          2 Melville B. Nimmer & David Nimmer, Nimmer on Copyright
          § 7.16[C], at 7-169 (1991). –Page Citation.

          2 Melville B. Nimmer & David Nimmer, Nimmer on Copyright
          § 7.16[C], at 17-169 n.135 (1991). –Footnote Citation.

NLRB Decisions
  See Labor Law Reporter.

no [introductory] signal
  –"Cited authority (i) directly states the proposition, (ii) identifies the
  source of a quotation, or (iii) identifies an authority referred to in the
  text." Bluebook Rule 1.2(a).

North Carolina Administrative Code
  Ab.:   N.C. Admin. Code tit. , r.   (month year).
  Ex.:   N.C. Admin. Code tit. 7, r. 7.0102 (June 1989).

North Carolina Advance Legislative Service
  See Advance Legislative Service to the General Statutes of North Carolina

North Carolina Attorney General Reports
  Ab.:   N.C. Att'y Gen. Rep.
  See Opinions of the Attorney General of North Carolina.

North Carolina Central Law Journal
  Ab.:   N.C. Cent. L.J.

In citing cases in law review footnotes, abbreviate any word listed in Table T.6;
the names of "states, countries, and other geographical units" unless they are named parties;
and any other words of eight or more letters "if substantial space is thereby saved and the
result is unambiguous." Bluebook Rule 10.2.2. On the other hand, in citing cases in text,
abbreviate only widely known acronyms and the following words: "&," "Ass'n," "Bros.,"
"Co.," "Corp.," "Inc.," "Ltd.," and "No." Bluebook Rule 10.2.1(c).

Ex.: Thomas L. Fowler, <u>Filling the Box: Responding to Jury Duty Avoidance</u>, 23 N.C. Cent. L.J. 1 (1997-1998). –Article Citation.

Thomas L. Fowler, <u>Filling the Box: Responding to Jury Duty Avoidance</u>, 23 N.C. Cent. L.J. 1, 13 (1997-1998). –Page Citation.

North Carolina Constitution

Ab.: N.C. Const. art.   , §   .

Ex.: N.C. Const. art. I, § 20. –"Cite constitutional provisions currently in force without date." <u>Bluebook</u> Rule 11.

N.C. Const. art. IV, § 12 (amended 1982). –"When citing a provision that has been subsequently amended, either indicate parenthetically the fact and date of amendment or cite the amending provision in full." <u>Bluebook</u> Rule 11.

N.C. Const. of 1868, art. I, § 15. –"Cite constitutions that have been totally superseded by year of adoption; if the specific provision cited was adopted in a different year, give that year parenthetically." <u>Bluebook</u> Rule 11.

North Carolina Court of Appeals Reports

Ab.: N.C. App.

–Cite to S.E. or S.E.2d if therein; otherwise, cite to N.C. App.

–Give parallel citations only in documents submitted to North Carolina state courts. <u>See</u> <u>Bluebook</u> Rule 10.3.1 and Practitioners' Note P.3; <u>see also</u> N.C. R. App. P. App. B, which requires a parallel citation.

In documents submitted to North Carolina state courts, cite as follows:

<u>Hill v. Hill</u>, 121 N.C. App. 510, 466 S.E.2d 322 (1996). –Case Citation.

<u>Hill v. Hill</u>, 121 N.C. App. 510, 511, 466 S.E.2d 322, 323 (1996). –Page Citation.

In all other documents, cite as follows:

<u>Hill v. Hill</u>, 466 S.E.2d 322 (N.C. Ct. App. 1996). –Case Citation.

<u>Hill v. Hill</u>, 466 S.E.2d 322, 323 (N.C. Ct. App. 1996). –Page Citation.

North Carolina General Statutes

<u>See</u> General Statutes of North Carolina.

North Carolina Journal of International Law and Commercial Regulation

Ab.: N.C. J. Int'l L. & Com. Reg.

In law review footnotes, the titles of books and the names of cases, except for procedural phrases, are not underlined. <u>See</u> <u>Bluebook</u> Rule 2.1(a). Further, the following are in large and small capitals: codes, restatements, standards, constitutions, periodicals, authors of books, titles of books, the abbreviated names of codes, most legislative materials except for bills and resolutions, codified ordinances, model codes, court rules, and sentencing guidelines. Refer to <u>The Bluebook</u>.

Ex.:   Ross D. Petty, The U.S. International Trade Commisssion: Import
Advertising Arbiter or Artifice?, 17 N.C. J. Int'l L. & Com. Reg. 45
(1992). –Article Citation.

Ross D. Petty, The U.S. International Trade Commisssion: Import
Advertising Arbiter or Artifice?, 17 N.C. J. Int'l L. & Com. Reg. 45, 48
(1992). –Page Citation.

North Carolina Law Review
Ab.:   N.C. L. Rev.

Ex.:   James P. Nehf, A Legislative Framework for Reducing Fraud in the
Credit Repair Industry, 70 N.C. L. Rev. 781 (1992). –Article Citation.

James P. Nehf, A Legislative Framework for Reducing Fraud in the
Credit Repair Industry, 70 N.C. L. Rev. 781, 786 (1992). –Page
Citation.

North Carolina Reports
Ab.:   N.C.

–Cite to S.E. or S.E.2d if therein; otherwise, cite to N.C.

–Give parallel citations only in documents submitted to North Carolina
state courts. See Bluebook Rule 10.3.1 and Practitioners' Note P.3;
see also N.C. R. App. P. App. B, which requires a parallel citation.

In documents submitted to North Carolina state courts, cite as follows:
Grimsley v. Nelson, 342 N.C. 542, 467 S.E.2d 92 (1996). –Case
Citation.

Grimsley v. Nelson, 342 N.C. 542, 543, 467 S.E.2d 92, 93 (1996).
–Page Citation.

In all other documents, cite as follows:
Grimsley v. Nelson, 467 S.E.2d 92 (N. C. 1996). –Case Citation.

Grimsley v. Nelson, 467 S.E.2d 92, 93 (N. C. 1996). –Page
Citation.

North Carolina Session Laws
See Session Laws of North Carolina and Advance Legislative Service to the
General Statutes of North Carolina

North Dakota Administrative Code
Ab.:   N.D. Admin. Code § (year).

Ex.:   N.D. Admin. Code § 43-02-07-06 (1999).

North Dakota Century Code
Ab.:   N.D. Cent. Code §   (year)

Ex.:   N.D. Cent. Code § 57-12-06 (2000).

N.D. Cent. Code § 61-08-01 (Supp. 1999).

In citing cases in law review footnotes, abbreviate any word listed in Table T.6;
the names of "states, countries, and other geographical units" unless they are named parties;
and any other words of eight or more letters "if substantial space is thereby saved and the
result is unambiguous." Bluebook Rule 10.2.2. On the other hand, in citing cases in text,
abbreviate only widely known acronyms and the following words: "&," "Ass'n," "Bros.,"
"Co.," "Corp.," "Inc.," "Ltd.," and "No." Bluebook Rule 10.2.1(c).

North Dakota Constitution

Ab.:   N.D. Const. art.   , §   .

Ex.:   N.D. Const. art. I, § 7. –"Cite constitutional provisions currently in force without date." Bluebook Rule 11.

N.D. Const. art. II, § 17 (repealed 1984). –"If the cited provision has been repealed, either indicate parenthetically the fact and date of repeal or cite the repealing provision in full." Bluebook Rule 11.

N.D. Const. art. IX, § 13 (amended 1982). –"When citing a provision that has been subsequently amended, either indicate parenthetically the fact and date of amendment or cite the amending provision in full." Bluebook Rule 11.

North Dakota Court of Appeals

Ab.:   N.D. Ct. App.

–Cite to N.W.2d, if therein; in addition, give public domain citation if available.

–Until January 1, 1997, when a public domain format was adopted, cite as follows:

In all documents:

State v. Hersch, 467 N.W.2d 463 (N.D. Ct. App. 1991). –Case Citation.

State v. Hersch, 467 N.W.2d 463, 465 (N.D. Ct. App. 1991). –Page Citation.

–From January 1, 1997, cite as follows:

In all documents:

City of Bismarck v. Glass, 1998 ND App 1, 581 N.W.2d 474. –Case Citation.

City of Bismarck v. Glass, 1998 ND App 1, ¶ 7, 581 N.W.2d 474, 475. –Pinpoint Citation.

See Bluebook Rules 10.3.1 and 10.3.3, Table T.1, and Practitioners' Note P.3; see also N.D.R. Ct. 11.6.

North Dakota Law Review

Ab.:   N.D. L. Rev.

Ex.:   Warren H. Albrecht, Jr., The Changing Face of Employment Law and the Practical Lawyer, 67 N.D. L. Rev. 469 (1992). –Article Citation.

Warren H. Albrecht, Jr., The Changing Face of Employment Law and the Practical Lawyer, 67 N.D. L. Rev. 469, 480 (1992). –Page Citation.

North Dakota, Opinions of the Attorney General

See Opinions of the Attorney General of North Dakota

In law review footnotes, the titles of books and the names of cases, except for procedural phrases, are not underlined. See Bluebook Rule 2.1(a). Further, the following are in large and small capitals: codes, restatements, standards, constitutions, periodicals, authors of books, titles of books, the abbreviated names of codes, most legislative materials except for bills and resolutions, codified ordinances, model codes, court rules, and sentencing guidelines. Refer to The Bluebook.

North Dakota Session Laws
See Laws of North Dakota

North Dakota Supreme Court
Ab.:   N.D.
–Cite to N.W. or N.W.2d if therein; in addition, give public domain citation if available.
–Through 79 N.D. 865 (1953), cite as follows:
In documents submitted to North Dakota state courts:
Gunder v. Feeland, 51 N.D. 784, 200 N.W. 909 (1924). –Case Citation.
Gunder v. Feeland, 51 N.D. 784, 787, 200 N.W. 909, 911 (1924). –Page Citation.
In all other documents:
Gunder v. Feeland, 200 N.W. 909 (N.D. 1924). –Case Citation.
Gunder v. Feeland, 200 N.W. 909, 911 (N.D. 1924). –Page Citation.
–After 79 N.D. 865 (1953), and until January 1, 1997, when a public domain format was adopted, cite as follows:
In all documents:
Helmer v. Sortino, 545 N.W.2d 796 (N.D. 1996). –Case Citation.
Helmer v. Sortino, 545 N.W.2d 796, 798 (N.D. 1996). –Page Citation.
–After January 1, 1997, cite as follows:
In all documents:
Olson v. Olson, 2000 ND 120, 611 N.W.2d 892. –Case Citation.
Olson v. Olson, 2000 ND 120, ¶ 7, 611 N.W.2d 892, 895.   –Pinpoint Citation.
See Bluebook Rules 10.3.1 and 10.3.3, Table T.1, and Practitioners' Note P.3; see also N.D.R. Ct. 11.6.

North Eastern Reporter
–Do not give a parallel citation unless required by local rule. See Bluebook Practitioners' Note P.3 and Rule 10.3.1. See also the various state court and state reporter entries herein for local rule parallel citation requirements.
Ab.: N.E.
Ex.:
Illinois:
Chance v. Kinsella, 142 N.E. 194 (Ill. 1923). –Case Citation.
Chance v. Kinsella, 142 N.E. 194, 195 (Ill. 1923). –Page Citation.

In citing cases in law review footnotes, abbreviate any word listed in Table T.6; the names of "states, countries, and other geographical units" unless they are named parties; and any other words of eight or more letters "if substantial space is thereby saved and the result is unambiguous." Bluebook Rule 10.2.2. On the other hand, in citing cases in text, abbreviate only widely known acronyms and the following words: "&," "Ass'n," "Bros.," "Co.," "Corp.," "Inc.," "Ltd.," and "No." Bluebook Rule 10.2.1(c).

Indiana:

Pottenger v. Bond, 142 N.E. 616 (Ind. Ct. App. 1924). –Case Citation.

Pottenger v. Bond, 142 N.E. 616, 619 (Ind. Ct. App. 1924). –Page Citation.

Massachusetts:

Bagnell v. Boston Elevated Railway Co., 142 N.E. 63 (Mass. 1924). –Case Citation.

Bagnell v. Boston Elevated Railway Co., 142 N.E. 63, 64 (Mass. 1924). –Page Citation.

New York:

Jacobs v. Newman, 172 N.E. 514 (N.Y. 1930). –Case Citation.

Jacobs v. Newman, 172 N.E. 514, 516 (N.Y. 1930). –Page Citation.

Ohio:

Morris v. Daiker, 172 N.E. 540 (Ohio Ct. App. 1929). –Case Citation.

Morris v. Daiker, 172 N.E. 540, 541 (Ohio Ct. App. 1929). –Page Citation.

North Eastern Reporter, Second Series

–Do not give a parallel citation unless required by local rule or unless the particular state has a public domain format. See Bluebook Practitioners' Note P.3 and Rules 10.3.1 and 10.3.3. See also the various state court and state reporter entries herein for public domain information and local rule parallel citation requirements.

–With volume 514 (1988), North Eastern Reporter, Second Series, became West's North Eastern Reporter, Second Series. Citation form is not affected by this title change.

Ab.: N.E.2d

Ex.:

Illinois:

Bianchi v. Mikhail, 640 N.E.2d 1370 (Ill. App. Ct. 1994). –Case Citation.

Bianchi v. Mikhail, 640 N.E.2d 1370, 1378 (Ill. App. Ct. 1994). –Page Citation.

Indiana:

Eyster v. S.A. Birnbaum Contracting, Inc., 662 N.E.2d 201 (Ind. Ct. App. 1996). –Case Citation.

Eyster v. S.A. Birnbaum Contracting, Inc., 662 N.E.2d 201, 203 (Ind. Ct. App. 1996). –Page Citation.

Massachusetts:

Delk v. Gonzalez, 658 N.E.2d 681 (Mass. 1995). –Case Citation.

In law review footnotes, the titles of books and the names of cases, except for procedural phrases, are not underlined. See Bluebook Rule 2.1(a). Further, the following are in large and small capitals: codes, restatements, standards, constitutions, periodicals, authors of books, titles of books, the abbreviated names of codes, most legislative materials except for bills and resolutions, codified ordinances, model codes, court rules, and sentencing guidelines. Refer to The Bluebook.

Delk v. Gonzalez, 658 N.E.2d 681, 684 (Mass. 1995). –Page Citation.

New York:

Bartoo v. Buell, 662 N.E.2d 1068 (N.Y. 1996). –Case Citation.

Bartoo v. Buell, 662 N.E.2d 1068, 1070 (N.Y. 1996). –Page Citation.

Ohio:

Cleveland Bar Ass'n v. Frye, 640 N.E.2d 808 (Ohio 1994). –Case Citation.

Cleveland Bar Ass'n v. Frye, 640 N.E.2d 808, 809 (Ohio 1994). –Page Citation.

North Western Reporter
–Do not give a parallel citation unless required by local rule. See Bluebook Practitioners' Note P.3 and Rule 10.3.1. See also the various state court and state reporter entries herein for local rule parallel citation requirements.

Ab.: N.W.

Ex.:

Iowa:

Farnsworth v. Hazelett, 199 N.W 410 (Iowa 1924). –Case Citation.

Farnsworth v. Hazelett, 199 N.W. 410, 414 (Iowa 1924). –Page Citation.

Michigan:

Garwood v. Burton, 264 N.W. 349 (Mich. 1936). –Case Citation.

Garwood v. Burton, 264 N.W. 349, 351 (Mich. 1936). –Page Citation.

Minnesota:

Steensland v. Western & Southern Life Insurance Co., 264 N.W. 440 (Minn. 1936). –Case Citation.

Steensland v. Western & Southern Life Insurance Co., 264 N.W. 440, 441 (Minn. 1936). –Page Citation.

Nebraska:

Hilton v. Clements, 291 N.W. 483 (Neb. 1940). –Case Citation.

Hilton v. Clements, 291 N.W. 483, 486 (Neb. 1940). –Page Citation.

North Dakota:

Patterson Land Co. v. Lynn, 199 N.W. 766 (N.D. 1924). –Case Citation.

Patterson Land Co. v. Lynn, 199 N.W. 766, 768 (N.D. 1924). –Page Citation.

South Dakota:

Platt v. Rapid City, 291 N.W. 600 (S.D. 1940). –Case Citation.

Platt v. Rapid City, 291 N.W. 600, 602 (S.D. 1940). –Page Citation.

In citing cases in law review footnotes, abbreviate any word listed in Table T.6; the names of "states, countries, and other geographical units" unless they are named parties; and any other words of eight or more letters "if substantial space is thereby saved and the result is unambiguous." Bluebook Rule 10.2.2. On the other hand, in citing cases in text, abbreviate only widely known acronyms and the following words: "&," "Ass'n," "Bros.," "Co.," "Corp.," "Inc.," "Ltd.," and "No." Bluebook Rule 10.2.1(c).

Wisconsin:

> Stenson v. Schumacher, 290 N.W. 285 (Wis. 1940). –Case Citation.
>
> Stenson v. Schumacher, 290 N.W. 285, 288 (Wis. 1940). –Page Citation.

North Western Reporter, Second Series

–Do not give a parallel citation unless required by local rule or unless the particular state has a public domain format. See Bluebook Practitioners' Note P.3 and Rules 10.3.1 and 10.3.3. See also the various state court and state reporter entries herein for public domain information and local rule parallel citation requirements.

–With volume 414 (1988), North Western Reporter, Second Series, becames West's North Western Reporter, Second Series. Citation form is not affected by this title change.

Ab.: N.W.2d

Ex.:

Iowa:

> Ahlers v. Emacasco Insurance Co., 548 N.W.2d 892 (Iowa 1996). – Case Citation.
>
> Ahlers v. Emacasco Insurance Co., 548 N.W.2d 892, 894 (Iowa 1996). –Page Citation.

Michigan:

> Halabu v. Behnke, 541 N.W.2d 285 (Mich. Ct. App. 1995). –Case Citation.
>
> Halabu v. Behnke, 541 N.W.2d 285, 288 (Mich. Ct. App. 1995). –Page Citation.

Minnesota:

> State v. Ecker, 524 N.W.2d 712 (Minn. Ct. App. 1994). –Case Citation.
>
> State v. Ecker, 524 N.W.2d 712, 716 (Minn. Ct. App. 1994). –Page Citation.

Nebraska:

> Shuck v. Jacob, 548 N.W.2d 332 (Neb. 1996). –Case Citation.
>
> Shuck v. Jacob, 548 N.W.2d 332, 337 (Neb. 1996). –Page Citation.

North Dakota:

> Bruner v. Hager, 547 N.W.2d 551 (N.D. 1996). –Case Citation.
>
> Bruner v. Hager, 547 N.W.2d 551, 554 (N.D. 1996). –Page Citation.

South Dakota:

> State v. Arguello, 548 N.W.2d 463 (S.D. 1996). –Case Citation.
>
> State v. Arguello, 548 N.W.2d 463, 464 (S.D. 1996). –Page Citation.

In law review footnotes, the titles of books and the names of cases, except for procedural phrases, are not underlined. See Bluebook Rule 2.1(a). Further, the following are in large and small capitals: codes, restatements, standards, constitutions, periodicals, authors of books, titles of books, the abbreviated names of codes, most legislative materials except for bills and resolutions, codified ordinances, model codes, court rules, and sentencing guidelines. Refer to The Bluebook.

Wisconsin:

> Byers v. Labor and Industry Review Commission, 547 N.W.2d 788 (Wis. Ct. App. 1996). –Case Citation.
>
> Byers v. Labor and Industry Review Commission, 547 N.W.2d 788, 791 (Wis. Ct. App. 1996). –Page Citation.

Northern Illinois University Law Review

Ab.:   N. Ill. U. L. Rev.

Ex.:   Richard S. Wilbur, AIDS and the Federal Bureau of Prisons: A Unique Challenge, 11 N. Ill. U. L. Rev. 275 (1991). –Article Citation.

          Richard S. Wilbur, AIDS and the Federal Bureau of Prisons: A Unique Challenge, 11 N. Ill. U. L. Rev. 275, 279 (1991). –Page Citation.

Northern Ireland Law Reports (1925-date)

See Bluebook Table T.2 and Rule 20.3.1

Ab.:   N. Ir. L.R.

Ex.:   Conway v. Hannaway, 1988 N. Ir. L.R. 269 (Q.B. 1988). –Case Citation.

Northern Ireland Legal Quarterly

Ab.:   N. Ir. Legal Q.

Ex.:   Soli J. Sorabjee, Freedom of Expression and Censorship: Some Aspects of the Indian Experience, 45 N. Ir. Legal Q. 327 (1994). –Article Citation.

          Soli J. Sorabjee, Freedom of Expression and Censorship: Some Aspects of the Indian Experience, 45 N. Ir. Legal Q. 327, 337 (1994). –Page Citation.

Northern Kentucky Law Review

Ab.:   N. Ky. L. Rev.

Ex.:   Michael J. Newman, United States Magistrate Judges: Suggestions to Increase the Efficiency of Their Civil Role, 19 N. Ky. L. Rev. 99 (1991). –Article Citation.

          Michael J. Newman, United States Magistrate Judges: Suggestions to Increase the Efficiency of Their Civil Role, 19 N. Ky. L. Rev. 99, 103 (1991). –Page Citation.

Northrop University Law Journal of Aerospace, Business and Taxation

Ab.:   Northrop U. L.J. Aerospace Bus. & Tax'n

Ex.:   Mark J. Phillips, History and the Law: Judicial Process and the King's Writ, 7 Northrop U. L.J. Aerospace Bus. & Tax'n 77 (1986). –Article Citation.

          Mark J. Phillips, History and the Law: Judicial Process and the King's Writ, 7 Northrop U. L.J. Aerospace Bus. & Tax'n 77, 80-83 (1986). – Page Citation.

In citing cases in law review footnotes, abbreviate any word listed in Table T.6; the names of "states, countries, and other geographical units" unless they are named parties; and any other words of eight or more letters "if substantial space is thereby saved and the result is unambiguous." Bluebook Rule 10.2.2. On the other hand, in citing cases in text, abbreviate only widely known acronyms and the following words: "&," "Ass'n," "Bros.," "Co.," "Corp.," "Inc.," "Ltd.," and "No." Bluebook Rule 10.2.1(c).

Northwest Territories Reports (Canada) (1983-date)
Ab.:   N.W.T.R.

Northwestern Journal of International Law & Business
Ab.:   Nw. J. Int'l L. & Bus.
Ex.:   Frank L. Fine, The Impact of EEC Competition Law on the Music
          Industry, 12 Nw. J. Int'l L. & Bus. 508 (1992). –Article Citation.
          Frank L. Fine, The Impact of EEC Competition Law on the Music
          Industry, 12 Nw. J. Int'l L. & Bus. 508, 511-12 (1992). –Page Citation.

Northwestern University Law Review
Ab.:   Nw. U. L. Rev.
Ex.:   Roger D. Blair & Jeffrey L. Harrison, Cooperative Buying Monopoly
          Power, and Antitrust Policy, 86 Nw. U. L. Rev. 331 (1992). –Article
          Citation.
          Roger D. Blair & Jeffrey L. Harrison, Cooperative Buying Monopoly
          Power, and Antitrust Policy, 86 Nw. U. L. Rev. 331, 342 (1992) –Page
          Citation.

Norton Bankruptcy Law and Practice 2d, by William L. Norton
          –Do not abbreviate the title.
Ex.:   2 William L. Norton, Jr., Norton Bankruptcy Law and Practice § 42.14
          (2d ed. 1994). –Section Citation.
          2 William L. Norton, Jr., Norton Bankruptcy Law and Practice § 42.14,
          at 42-76 (2d ed. 1994). –Page Citation.
          2 William L. Norton, Jr., Norton Bankruptcy Law and Practice § 42.14,
          at 42-76 n.14 (2d ed. 1994). –Footnote Citation.

Notre Dame Estate Planning Institute Proceedings
Ab.:   Notre Dame Est. Plan. Inst. Proc.
Ex.:   Tucker, Estate and Income Tax Planning for Real Property Ownership,
          4 Notre Dame Est. Plan. Inst. Proc. 159 (1979). –Article Citation.
          Tucker, Estate and Income Tax Planning for Real Property Ownership,
          4 Notre Dame Est. Plan. Inst. Proc. 159, 197-98 (1979). –Page
          Citation.

Notre Dame Institute on Charitable Giving Foundations and Trusts
Ab.:   Notre Dame Inst. on Char. Giving Found. & Tr.

Notre Dame Journal of Law, Ethics & Public Policy
Ab.:   Notre Dame J.L. Ethics & Pub. Pol'y

In law review footnotes, the titles of books and the names of cases, except for procedural
phrases, are not underlined. See Bluebook Rule 2.1(a). Further, the following are in large
and small capitals: codes, restatements, standards, constitutions, periodicals, authors of
books, titles of books, the abbreviated names of codes, most legislative materials except for
bills and resolutions, codified ordinances, model codes, court rules, and sentencing guidelines.
Refer to The Bluebook.

Ex.:   Shanto Iyengar, How Television News Affects Voters: From Setting Agendas to Defining Standards, 6 Notre Dame J.L. Ethics & Pub. Pol'y 33 (1992). –Article Citation.

Shanto Iyengar, How Television News Affects Voters: From Setting Agendas to Defining Standards, 6 Notre Dame J.L. Ethics & Pub. Pol'y 33, 41-45 (1992). –Page Citation.

Notre Dame Law Review
Ab.:   Notre Dame L. Rev.
Ex.:   Gregory S. Crespi, The Mid-Life Crisis of the Law and Economics Movement: Confronting the Problems of Nonfalsifiability and Normative Bias, 67 Notre Dame L. Rev. 231 (1991). –Article Citation.

Gregory S. Crespi, The Mid-Life Crisis of the Law and Economics Movement: Confronting the Problems of Nonfalsifiability and Normative Bias, 67 Notre Dame L. Rev. 231, 242 (1991). –Page Citation.

Nouveau code de procédure civile (France)
See Bluebook Rules 20.1.3, 20.5.2, and Table T.2.
Ab.:   N.C.P.C.

Nova Law Review
Ab.:   Nova L. Rev.
Ex.:   Gary A. Poliakoff, The Florida Condominium Act, 16 Nova L. Rev. 471 (1991). –Article Citation.

Gary A. Poliakoff, The Florida Condominium Act, 16 Nova L. Rev. 471, 477-79 (1991). –Page Citation.

Nova Scotia Reports (Canada)
Ab.:   N.S.R., N.S.R.2d
Ex.:   Nuttal v. Vaughan, [1928] 60 N.S.R. 84 (Can.). –Case Citation.

Roberts v. Roberts, [1991] 104 N.S.R.2d 27 (Can.). –Case Citation.

Nuclear Regulation Reports (Commerce Clearing House)
Ab.:   Nuclear Reg. Rep. (CCH)
Ex.:   Kerr-McGee Chem. Corp. v. City of West Chicago, 2 Nuclear Reg. Rep. (CCH) ¶ 20,515 (7th Cir. Sept. 20, 1990). –Cite to looseleaf material.

Ohio Edison Co. v. Zech, [1985-1989 New Developments Transfer Binder] Nuclear Reg. Rep. (CCH) ¶ 20,460 (D.D.C. 1988). –Cite to transfer binder material.

–The above examples are proper if the case is not yet available in, or is not reported in, an official or West reporter, a public domain citation, or in a widely used computer database.

In citing cases in law review footnotes, abbreviate any word listed in Table T.6; the names of "states, countries, and other geographical units" unless they are named parties; and any other words of eight or more letters "if substantial space is thereby saved and the result is unambiguous." Bluebook Rule 10.2.2. On the other hand, in citing cases in text, abbreviate only widely known acronyms and the following words: "&," "Ass'n," "Bros.," "Co.," "Corp.," "Inc.," "Ltd.," and "No." Bluebook Rule 10.2.1(c).

Sacramento Mun. Util. Dist., 2 Nuclear Reg. Rep. (CCH) ¶ 31,178 (NRC Feb. 6, 1992). –Cite to looseleaf administrative material.

Wrangler Laboratories, [1986-1991 NRC Decisions Transfer Binder] Nuclear Reg. Rep. (CCH) ¶ 33,224.01 (NRC 1991). –Cite to transfer binder administrative material.

Nuclear Regulatory Commission Issuances
Ab.:   N.R.C.

Ex.:   Metropolitan Edison Co. (Three Mile Island, Unit 2), 11 N.R.C. 519 (1980).

Pacific Gas and Electric Co. (Diablo Canyon Nuclear Power Plant, Unit 1), 14 N.R.C. 950 (1981). –Cite to current unbound material.

Numerals and Symbols
See Bluebook Rule 6.2.

In law review footnotes, the titles of books and the names of cases, except for procedural phrases, are not underlined. See Bluebook Rule 2.1(a). Further, the following are in large and small capitals: codes, restatements, standards, constitutions, periodicals, authors of books, titles of books, the abbreviated names of codes, most legislative materials except for bills and resolutions, codified ordinances, model codes, court rules, and sentencing guidelines. Refer to The Bluebook.

O

Occupational Safety & Health Reporter (Bureau of National Affairs)
    –Bound as Occupational Safety & Health Cases (Bureau of National
    Affairs)
Ab.:   O.S.H. Rep. (BNA)
    –Bound as O.S.H. Cas. (BNA).
Ex.:   Secretary of Labor v. Sea Sprite Boat Co., [Decisions] O.S.H. Rep.
    (BNA) (17 O.S.H. Cas.) 1331 (5th Cir. Mar. 17, 1995). –Citation to
    looseleaf material.

    United Crane and Shovel Co. v. Department of Labor, 15 O.S.H. Cas.
    (BNA) 1464 (3d Cir. 1991). –Citation to bound material.

    –The above examples are proper only if the case is not yet available in
    an official or West reporter, or is not reported in an official or West
    reporter.

    Secretary of Labor v. Newell Recycling Co., [Decisions] O.S.H. Rep.
    (BNA) (17 O.S.H. Cas.) 1519 (O.S.H. Rev. Comm'n Nov. 13, 1995).
    –Citation to looseleaf administrative material.

    Secretary of Labor v. Trinity Indus., Inc., 15 O.S.H. Cas. (BNA) 1985
    (O.S.H. Rev. Comm'n 1992). –Citation to bound administrative
    material.

Ocean Development and International Law
Ab.:   Ocean Dev. & Int'l L.
Ex.:   Ted L. McDorman, Canada and the North Pacific Ocean: Recent
    Issues, 22 Ocean Dev. & Int'l L. 365 (1991). –Article Citation.

    Ted L. McDorman, Canada and the North Pacific Ocean: Recent
    Issues, 22 Ocean Dev. & Int'l L. 365, 373 (1991). –Page Citation.

Office of Thrift Supervision Journal
Ab.:   Off. Thrift Supervision J.
Ex.:   Mark Wohar, Should You Abandon the Thrift Charter, Off. Thrift
    Supervision J., June 1990, at 6. –Article Citation.

    Mark Wohar, Should You Abandon the Thrift Charter, Off. Thrift
    Supervision J., June 1990, at 6, 9. –Page Citation.

Official Code of Georgia Annotated (Lexis)
Ab.:   Ga. Code Ann. §   (year)

In law review footnotes, the titles of books and the names of cases, except for procedural
phrases, are not underlined. See Bluebook Rule 2.1(a). Further, the following are in large
and small capitals: codes, restatements, standards, constitutions, periodicals, authors of
books, titles of books, the abbreviated names of codes, most legislative materials except for
bills and resolutions, codified ordinances, model codes, court rules, and sentencing guidelines.
Refer to The Bluebook.

Ex.:   Ga. Code Ann. § 36-5-21 (2000).

         Ga. Code Ann. § 50-13-18 (Supp. 2000).

Official Compilation of Codes, Rules & Regulations of the State of New York

Ab.:   N.Y. Comp. Codes R. & Regs. tit. , §   (year)

Ex.:   N.Y. Comp. Codes R. & Regs. Tit. 8, § 50.2 (2001).

Official Compilation Rules & Regulations of the State of Georgia

Ab.:   Ga. Comp. R. & Regs. r.   (year)

Ex.:   Ga. Comp. R. & Regs. R. 40-1-2-04 (1971)

Official Compilation Rules and Regulations of the State of Tennessee

Ab.:   Tenn. Comp. R. & Regs. (year)

Ex.:   Tenn. Comp. R. & Regs. 0030-1-9-.03 (2000).

Official Journal of the European Community

Ab.:   O.J., O.J. Spec. Ed.

Ex.:   Commission Regulation 1203/91, 1991 O.J. (L 116) 22, 23.

         Commission Proposal for a Council Regulation on Certificates of Specific Character for Foodstuffs, art. 2(2), 1991 O.J. (C 30) 4,5.

         –Cite publications of the Council and of the Commission published beginning January 1, 1974, to the O.J. Cite documents published before December 31, 1973, to the Special Edition of the O.J. (O.J. Spec. Ed.), if available. Otherwise, cite to Journal Officiel des Communautés Européennes (J.O.). Bluebook Rule 21.8.2. See Table T.3 for dates which correspond with the abbreviations.

    See also Journal Officiel des Communautés Européennes.

Official Opinions of the Solicitor for the Post Office Department (U.S.) (1878-1951)

Ab.:   Op. Solic. P.O. Dep't

Ex.:   1 Op. Solic. P.O. Dep't 671 (1881).

         9 Op. Solic. P.O. Dep't 655 (1949).

OHA Law Journal, The

Ab.:   OHA L.J.

Ex.:   Joyce K. Barlow, Contempt Powers of the Administrative Law Judge, OHA L.J., Fall 1991, at 31. –Article Citation.

         Joyce K. Barlow, Contempt Powers of the Administrative Law Judge, OHA L.J., Fall 1991, at 31, 34. –Page Citation.

Ohio Administrative Code

Ab.:   Ohio Admin. Code §   (year)

In citing cases in law review footnotes, abbreviate any word listed in Table T.6; the names of "states, countries, and other geographical units" unless they are named parties; and any other words of eight or more letters "if substantial space is thereby saved and the result is unambiguous." Bluebook Rule 10.2.2. On the other hand, in citing cases in text, abbreviate only widely known acronyms and the following words: "&," "Ass'n," "Bros.," "Co.," "Corp.," "Inc.," "Ltd.," and "No." Bluebook Rule 10.2.1(c).

Ex.:   Ohio Admin. Code § 109:5-1-01 (2000).

Ohio Appellate Reports
Ab.:   Ohio App., Ohio App. 2d, Ohio App. 3d.

–Cite to N.E. or N.E.2d if therein; otherwise, cite to Ohio App., Ohio App.2d, or Ohio App.3d.

–Give parallel citations only in documents submitted to Ohio state courts. See Bluebook Rule 10.3.1 and Practitioners' Note P.3; see also, Ohio 1st Dist. Ct. App. R. 6(d)(1) and Ohio 12th Dist. Ct. App. R. 11(c), which require parallel citation , and Ohio 9th Dist. Ct. App. R. 7(E), which requires only a citation to Ohio App., Ohio App. 2d, or Ohio App. 3d.

–Beginning with 1 Ohio App. 3d 1 (1980), bound with Ohio St. 3d and Ohio Misc. 2d in Ohio Official Reports.

In documents submitted to Ohio state courts, cite as follows:

State v. Brown, 107 Ohio App. 3d 194, 668 N.E.2d 514 (1995). –Case Citation.

State v. Brown, 107 Ohio App. 3d 194, 196, 668 N.E.2d 514, 515 (1995). –Page Citation.

In all other documents, cite as follows:

State v. Brown, 668 N.E.2d 514 (Ohio Ct. App. 1995). –Case Citation.

State v. Brown, 668 N.E.2d 514, 515 (Ohio Ct. App. 1995). –Page Citation.

Ohio Bar Reports
Ab.:   Ohio B.

Ohio Circuit Court Decisions
         –Discontinued in 1923.
Ab.:   Ohio C.C. Dec.

Ohio Circuit Court Reports
         –Discontinued in 1901.
Ab.:   Ohio C.C.

Ohio Circuit Court Reports, New Series
         –Discontinued in 1922.
Ab.:   Ohio C.C. (n.s.)

Ohio Circuit Decisions
         –Discontinued in 1901.
Ab.:   Ohio Cir. Dec.

In law review footnotes, the titles of books and the names of cases, except for procedural phrases, are not underlined. See Bluebook Rule 2.1(a). Further, the following are in large and small capitals: codes, restatements, standards, constitutions, periodicals, authors of books, titles of books, the abbreviated names of codes, most legislative materials except for bills and resolutions, codified ordinances, model codes, court rules, and sentencing guidelines. Refer to The Bluebook.

Ohio Constitution
Ab.: Ohio Const. art.   , §   .

Ex.: Ohio Const. art. I, § 7. –"Cite constitutional provisions currently in force without date." Bluebook Rule 11.

Ohio Const. art. XV, § 5 (repealed 1976). –"If the cited provision has been repealed, either indicate parenthetically the fact and date of repeal or cite the repealing provision in full." Bluebook Rule 11.

Ohio Const. art. III, § 17a (amended 1989). –"When citing a provision that has been subsequently amended, either indicate parenthetically the fact and date of amendment or cite the amending provision in full." Bluebook Rule 11.

Ohio Const. of 1802, art. VIII, § 3 (1851). –"Cite constitutions that have been totally superseded by year of adoption; if the specific provision cited was adopted in a different year, give that year parenthetically." Bluebook Rule 11.

Ohio Decisions
–Discontinued in 1920.
Ab.: Ohio Dec.

Ohio Decisions, Reprint
Ab.: Ohio Dec. Reprint

Ohio Legislative Bulletin (Anderson)
Ab.: Pages Ohio Legislative Bulletin (Anderson)

Ohio Legislative Service
See Baldwin's Ohio Legislative Service

Ohio Miscellaneous Reports
Ab.: Ohio Misc., Ohio Misc. 2d

–Cite to Ohio Misc. or Ohio Misc.2d if therein; otherwise, cite to other reporters in order of preference found in Bluebook Table T.1.

–Beginning with 1 Ohio Misc. 2d 1 (1982), bound with Ohio App. 3d and Ohio St. 3d in Ohio Official Reports.

Ex.: Travelers Insurance Co. v. Dayton Power and Light Co., 76 Ohio Misc. 17 (C.P. 1996). –Case Citation.

Travelers Insurance Co. v. Dayton Power and Light Co., 76 Ohio Misc. 17, 19 (C.P. 1996). –Page Citation.

In re Lee, 58 Ohio Misc. 2d 4 (C.P. 1989). –Case Citation.

In re Lee, 58 Ohio Misc. 2d 4, 5 (C.P. 1989). –Page Citation.

Ohio Monthly Record
Ab.: Ohio Monthly Rec.

In citing cases in law review footnotes, abbreviate any word listed in Table T.6; the names of "states, countries, and other geographical units" unless they are named parties; and any other words of eight or more letters "if substantial space is thereby saved and the result is unambiguous." Bluebook Rule 10.2.2. On the other hand, in citing cases in text, abbreviate only widely known acronyms and the following words: "&," "Ass'n," "Bros.," "Co.," "Corp.," "Inc.," "Ltd.," and "No." Bluebook Rule 10.2.1(c).

Ohio Nisu Prius Reports
    Ab.:   Ohio N.P., Ohio N.P. (n.s.)
           –Discontinued in 1934.
           –Cite to Ohio Misc. or Ohio Misc. 2d if therein; otherwise, cite to other reporters in order of preference found in Bluebook Table T.1.
    Ex.:   Ross v. City of Columbus, 8 Ohio N.P. 420 (C.P. 1892).
           –Case Citation.
           Ross v. City of Columbus, 8 Ohio N.P. 420, 422 (C.P. 1892).
           –Page Citation.
           Spencer v. Athletic Ass'n Co., 32 Ohio N.P. (n.s.) 369 (Mun. Ct. 1934).
           –Case Citation.
           Spencer v. Athletic Ass'n Co., 32 Ohio N.P. (n.s.) 369, 373 (Mun. Ct. 1934). –Page Citation.

Ohio Northern University Law Review
    Ab.:   Ohio N.U. L. Rev.
    Ex.:   Kenneth W. Thornicroft, The War on Drugs Goes to Work: Employee Drug Testing and the Law, 17 Ohio N.U. L. Rev. 771 (1991). –Article Citation.
           Kenneth W. Thornicroft, The War on Drugs Goes to Work: Employee Drug Testing and the Law, 17 Ohio N.U. L. Rev. 771, 778 (1991). –Page Citation.

Ohio Opinions
    Ab.:   Ohio Op., Ohio Op. 2d, Ohio Op. 3d
           –Discontinued in 1982.
           –Cite to Ohio Misc. or Ohio Misc.2d if therein; otherwise, cite to other reporters in order of preference found in Bluebook Table T.1.
    Ex.:   Ohio Edison Co. v. McElrath, 60 Ohio Op. 462 (C.P. 1955).
           –Case Citation.
           Ohio Edison Co. v. McElrath, 60 Ohio Op. 462, 464 (C.P. 1955).
           –Page Citation.
           Whiting v. Roxy Ltd., 66 Ohio Op. 2d 369 (C.P. 1973).
           –Case Citation.
           Whiting v. Roxy Ltd., 66 Ohio Op. 2d 369, 371 (C.P. 1973).
           –Page Citation.
           State v. Ackerman, 19 Ohio Op. 3d 347 (C.P. 1979). –Case Citation.
           State v. Ackerman, 19 Ohio Op. 3d 347, 348 (C.P. 1979). –Page Citation.

Ohio, Opinions of the Attorney General
    See Opinions of the Attorney General of Ohio

In law review footnotes, the titles of books and the names of cases, except for procedural phrases, are not underlined. See Bluebook Rule 2.1(a). Further, the following are in large and small capitals: codes, restatements, standards, constitutions, periodicals, authors of books, titles of books, the abbreviated names of codes, most legislative materials except for bills and resolutions, codified ordinances, model codes, court rules, and sentencing guidelines. Refer to The Bluebook.

Ohio Revised Code Annotated (Anderson)
Ab.:   Ohio Rev. Code Ann. § (Anderson year)
See Page's Ohio Revised Code Annotated.

Ohio Revised Code Annotated (Banks-Baldwin)
See Baldwin's Ohio Revised Code Annotated (Banks-Baldwin)

Ohio Session Laws
See State of Ohio: Legislative Acts Passed and Joint Resolutions Adopted and Page's Ohio Legislative Bulletin (Anderson).

Ohio State Journal on Dispute Resolution
Ab.:   Ohio St. J. on Disp. Resol.

Ex.:   Roger Richman, Dispute Processing in China During Reform, 7 Ohio St. J. on Disp. Resol. 83 (1991). –Article Citation.

Roger Richman, Dispute Processing in China During Reform, 7 Ohio St. J. on Disp. Resol. 83, 88-91 (1991). –Page Citation.

Ohio State Law Journal
Ab.:   Ohio St. L.J.

Ex.:   Mark A. Hall & John D. Colombo, The Donative Theory of the Charitable Tax Exemption, 52 Ohio St. L.J. 1379 (1991). –Article Citation.

Mark A. Hall & John D. Colombo, The Donative Theory of the Charitable Tax Exemption, 52 Ohio St. L.J. 1379, 1407 (1991). –Page Citation.

Ohio State Reports
Ab.:   Ohio St., Ohio St. 2d, Ohio St. 3d.

–Cite to N.E. or N.E.2d if therein; otherwise, cite to Ohio St., Ohio St. 2d, or Ohio St. 3d.

–Give parallel citations only in documents submitted to Ohio state courts. See Bluebook Rule 10.3.1 and Practitioners' Note P.3; see also, Ohio 1st Dist. Ct. App. R. 6(d)(1) and Ohio 12th Dist. Ct. App. R. 11(c), which require parallel citation, and Ohio 9th Dist. Ct. App. R. 7(E), which requires only a citation to Ohio St., Ohio St. 2d, or Ohio St. 3d.

–Beginning with 1 Ohio St. 3d 1 (1982), bound with Ohio App. 3d and Ohio Misc. 2d in Ohio Official Reports.

In documents submitted to Ohio state courts, cite as follows:

Columbus Bar Ass'n v. Ewing, 75 Ohio St. 3d 244, 661 N.E.2d 1109 (1996). –Case Citation.

Columbus Bar Ass'n v. Ewing, 75 Ohio St. 3d 244, 250, 661 N.E.2d 1109, 1114 (1996). –Page Citation.

In citing cases in law review footnotes, abbreviate any word listed in Table T.6; the names of "states, countries, and other geographical units" unless they are named parties; and any other words of eight or more letters "if substantial space is thereby saved and the result is unambiguous." Bluebook Rule 10.2.2. On the other hand, in citing cases in text, abbreviate only widely known acronyms and the following words: "&," "Ass'n," "Bros.," "Co.," "Corp.," "Inc.," "Ltd.," and "No." Bluebook Rule 10.2.1(c).

In all other documents, cite as follows:

Columbus Bar Ass'n v. Ewing, 661 N.E.2d 1109 (Ohio 1996).
–Case Citation.

Columbus Bar Ass'n v. Ewing, 661 N.E.2d 1109, 1114 (Ohio 1996). –Page Citation.

Oil & Gas Tax Quarterly
Ab.:   Oil & Gas Tax Q.

Ex.:   Mimi L. Alciatore, Empirical Evidence of the Demand for Reserve Value Disclosures: An Update, 40 Oil & Gas Tax Q. 537 (1992). –Article Citation.

Mimi L. Alciatore, Empirical Evidence of the Demand for Reserve Value Disclosures: An Update, 40 Oil & Gas Tax Q. 537, 541 (1992). –Page Citation.

Oklahoma Administrative Code
Ab.:   Okla Admin. Code

Ex.:   Ohio Admin. Code § 35:40-17-57 (2000).

Oklahoma City University Law Review
Ab.:   Okla. City U. L. Rev.

Ex.:   Richard E. Coulson, Is Contractual Arbitration an Unconstitutional Waiver of the Right to Trial by Jury in Oklahoma?, 16 Okla. City U. L. Rev. 1 (1991). –Article Citation.

Richard E. Coulson, Is Contractual Arbitration an Unconstitutional Waiver of the Right to Trial by Jury in Oklahoma?, 16 Okla. City U. L. Rev. 1, 59 (1991). –Page Citation.

Oklahoma Constitution
Ab.:   Okla. Const. art.   , §   .

Ex.:   Okla. Const. art. I, § 3. –"Cite constitutional provisions currently in force without date." Bluebook Rule 11.

Okla. Const. art. IX, § 14 (repealed 1991). –"If the cited provision has been repealed, either indicate parenthetically the fact and date of repeal or cite the repealing provision in full." Bluebook Rule 11.

Okla. Const. art. II, § 11 (amended 1914). –"When citing a provision that has been subsequently amended, either indicate parenthetically the fact and date of amendment or cite the amending provision in full." Bluebook Rule 11.

Oklahoma Court of Appeals
Ab.:   Okla. Ct. App.

–Effective November 1, 1996, Oklahoma Court of Appeals became known as Oklahoma Court of Civil Appeals. See Oklahoma Court of Civil Appeals.

In law review footnotes, the titles of books and the names of cases, except for procedural phrases, are not underlined. See Bluebook Rule 2.1(a). Further, the following are in large and small capitals: codes, restatements, standards, constitutions, periodicals, authors of books, titles of books, the abbreviated names of codes, most legislative materials except for bills and resolutions, codified ordinances, model codes, court rules, and sentencing guidelines. Refer to The Bluebook.

Oklahoma Court of Civil Appeals
Ab.:   Okla. Civ. App.

–Cite to P.2d or P.3d if therein; in addition, give public domain citation, if available.

–For cases promulgated after April 30, 1997:

In all documents, cite as follows:

Brown v. NCI, Inc., 2000 OK CIV APP 78, 8 P.3d 195. –Case citation.

Brown v. NCI, Inc., 2000 OK CIV APP 78, ¶ 5, 8 P.3d 195, 196. –Pinpoint Citation.

–For cases promulgated before May 1, 1997:

In documents submitted to Oklahoma state courts, citation to P.2d or P.3d is required and parallel public domain citation, found at the Oklahoma State Courts' Network Web site, http://www.oscn.net, is encouraged:

Elledge v. Staring, 1996 OK CIV APP 161, 939 P.2d 1163. –Case Citation.

Elledge v. Staring, 1996 OK CIV APP 161, ¶ 7, 939 P.2d 1163, 1165. –Pinpoint Citation.

In all other documents, cite as follows:

Elledge v. Staring, 939 P.2d 1163 (Okla. Civ. App. 1996). –Case Citation.

Elledge v. Staring, 939 P.2d 1163, 1165 (Okla. Civ. App. 1996). –Page Citation.

See Bluebook Rules 10.3.1 and 10.3.3, Table T.1, and Practitioners' Note P.3; see also Okla. Sup. Ct. R. 1.200(e).

Oklahoma Court of Criminal Appeals
Ab.:   Okla. Crim.

–Cite to P., P.2d, or P.3d if therein; in addition, give public domain citation, if available.

–Through 97 Okla. Crim. 415 (1953), cite as follows:

In documents submitted to Oklahoma state courts:

Simmons v. State, 68 Okla. Crim. 337, 98 P.2d 623 (1940). –Case Citation.

Simmons v. State, 68 Okla. Crim. 337, 340, 98 P.2d 623, 624 (1940). –Page Citation.

In all other documents:

Simmons v. State, 98 P.2d 623 (Okla. Crim. App. 1940). –Case Citation.

In citing cases in law review footnotes, abbreviate any word listed in Table T.6; the names of "states, countries, and other geographical units" unless they are named parties; and any other words of eight or more letters "if substantial space is thereby saved and the result is unambiguous." Bluebook Rule 10.2.2. On the other hand, in citing cases in text, abbreviate only widely known acronyms and the following words: "&," "Ass'n," "Bros.," "Co.," "Corp.," "Inc.," "Ltd.," and "No." Bluebook Rule 10.2.1(c).

Simmons v. State, 98 P.2d 623, 624 (Okla. Crim. App. 1940).
–Page Citation.

–After 97 Okla. Crim. 415 (1953), and until Jan. 1, 1998, cite as follows:

In documents submitted to Oklahoma state courts:

Long v. State, 1985 OK CR 119, 706 P.2d 915. –Case Citation.

Long v. State, 1985 OK CR 119, ¶ 6, 706 P.2d 915, 917.
–Pinpoint Citation.

In all other documents:

Long v. State, 706 P.2d 915 (Okla. Crim. App. 1985). –Case
Citation.

Long v. State, 706 P.2d 915, 917 (Okla. Crim. App. 1985). –Page
Citation.

–For cases promulgated on or after January 1, 1998, cite as follows:

In all documents:

State v. McNeal, 2000 OK CR 13, 6 P.3d 1055. –Case Citation

State v. McNeal, 2000 Ok CR 13, ¶ 10, 6 P.3d 1055, 1057.
–Pinpoint Citation.

See Bluebook Rules 10.3.1 and 10.3.3, Table T.1, and Practitioners'
Note P.3; see also, Okla. Crim. App. R. 3.5(c), which strongly
encourages a parallel public domain citation for all cases promulgated
after 1/1/54. See also, the Oklahoma State Courts network Web site,
http://www.oscn.net, for parallel public domain citations for cases
decided between 1954 and 1998.

Oklahoma Gazette
Ab.:   Okla. Gaz.

Ex.:   19 Okla. Gaz. 1199 (1981).

Oklahoma Law Review
Ab.:   Okla. L. Rev.

Ex.:   Lawrence Kalevitch, Lien Avoidance on Exemptions: The False
Controversy Over Opt-Out, 44 Okla. L. Rev. 443 (1991).
–Article Citation.

Lawrence Kalevitch, Lien Avoidance on Exemptions: The False
Controversy Over Opt-Out, 44 Okla. L. Rev. 443, 449 (1991).
–Page Citation.

Oklahoma Register
Ab.:   Okla. Reg.

Oklahoma Session Laws
Ab.:   year Okla. Sess. Laws

In law review footnotes, the titles of books and the names of cases, except for procedural
phrases, are not underlined. See Bluebook Rule 2.1(a). Further, the following are in large
and small capitals: codes, restatements, standards, constitutions, periodicals, authors of
books, titles of books, the abbreviated names of codes, most legislative materials except for
bills and resolutions, codified ordinances, model codes, court rules, and sentencing guidelines.
Refer to The Bluebook.

Ex.: Act of May 25, 1995, ch. 287, 1995-2 Okla. Sess. Laws 1340.
–Citation to an entire session law
Act of May 25, 1995, ch. 287, § 3, 1995-2 Okla. Sess. Laws 1340, 1343-44.
–Citation to a section of a session law.
–Identifying information may be added parenthetically according to Bluebook Rule 12.4(a).

Oklahoma Session Law Service (West)
Ab.: year Okla. Sess. Law Serv. (West)
Ex.: Act of May 28, 1996, ch. 243, 1996 Okla. Sess. Law Serv. 953 (West) (motor vehicles emission control equipment). –Citation to an entire session law.
Act of May 28, 1996, ch. 243, sec. 1, § 856.1, 1996 Okla. Sess. Law Serv. 953, 953 (West) (motor vehicles emission control equipment). –Citation to a session law amending a prior act.
–"Cite to Okla. Sess. Laws if therein." Bluebook Table T.1, p. 226.

Oklahoma Statutes
Ab.: Okla. Stat. tit.   , §   (year)
Ex.: Okla. Stat. tit. 42, § 141 (1979).

Oklahoma Statutes Annotated (West)
Ab.: Okla. Stat. Ann. tit.   , §   (West year)
Ex.: Okla. Stat. Ann. tit. 19, § 138.4 (West 2000).
Okla. Stat. Ann. tit. 15, § 567 (West Supp. 2000).
–"Cite to Okla. Sess. Laws if therein." Bluebook Table T.1, p. 226.

Oklahoma Supreme Court
Ab.: Okla.
–Cite to P., P.2d, or P.3d if therein; in addition, give public domain citation, if available.
–For cases promulgated after April 30, 1997:
In all documents, cite as follows:
Farrimond v. State ex rel. Fisher, 2000 OK 52, 8 P.3d 872. –Case Citation.
Farrimond v. State ex rel. Fisher, 2000 Ok 52, ¶14, 8 P.3d 872, 975.   – Pinpoint Citation.
–For cases promulgated before May 1, 1997:

In citing cases in law review footnotes, abbreviate any word listed in Table T.6; the names of "states, countries, and other geographical units" unless they are named parties; and any other words of eight or more letters "if substantial space is thereby saved and the result is unambiguous." Bluebook Rule 10.2.2. On the other hand, in citing cases in text, abbreviate only widely known acronyms and the following words: "&," "Ass'n," "Bros.," "Co.," "Corp.," "Inc.," "Ltd.," and "No." Bluebook Rule 10.2.1(c).

In documents provided to Oklahoma state courts, citation to P., P.2d, or P.3d is required and parallel public domain citation, found at the Oklahoma State Courts Network Web Site, http://www.oscn.net, is encouraged:

> Skinner v. Braum's Ice Cream Store, 1995 OK 11, 890 P.2d 922. –Case Citation.

> Skinner v. Braum's Ice Cream Store, 1995 OK 11, ¶ 9, 890 P.2d 922, 925. –Pinpoint Citation.

In all other documents, cite as follows:

> Skinner v. Braum's Ice Cream Store, 890 P.2d 922 (Okla. 1995). –Case Citation.

> Skinner v. Braum's Ice Cream Store, 890 P.2d 922, 925 (Okla. 1995). –Page Citation.

See Bluebook Rules 103.1 and 10.3.3, Table T.1, and Practitioners' Note P.3; see also, Okla. Sup. Ct. R. 1.2000(e).

O'Neal's Close Corporations, by F. Hodge O'Neal and Robert B. Thompson
–Do not abbreviate the title.

Ex.:   F. Hodge O'Neal & Robert B. Thompson, O'Neal's Close Corporations § 8.04 (3d ed. 1988). –Section Citation.

F. Hodge O'Neal & Robert B. Thompson, O'Neal's Close Corporations § 8.04, at 8-19 (3d ed. 1988). –Page Citation.

Online Commercial Services
See electronic media and other nonprint resources.

Ontario Law Reports
See Bluebook Table T.2.
Ab.:   O.L.R.
Ex.:   McLaughlin v. Ontario Iron and Steel Co., [1910] 20 O.L.R. 335, 338 (Can.). –Page Citation.

Ontario Reports
See Bluebook Table T.2.
Ab.:   O.R., O.R.2d, O.R.3d
Ex.:   Paramount Pictures Corp. v. Howley, [1991] 5 O.R.3d 573, 575 (Can.). –Page Citation.

Jaffe v. Miller, [1990] 75 O.R.2d 133, 137 (Can.). –Page Citation.

Goldex Mines Ltd. v. Revill, [1973] 3 O.R. 869, 872 (Can.). –Page Citation.

Opiniones del Secretario de Justicia de Puerto Rico
Ab.:   Op. P.R. Att'y Gen.
See Opinions of the Attorney General of Puerto Rico.

In law review footnotes, the titles of books and the names of cases, except for procedural phrases, are not underlined. See Bluebook Rule 2.1(a). Further, the following are in large and small capitals: codes, restatements, standards, constitutions, periodicals, authors of books, titles of books, the abbreviated names of codes, most legislative materials except for bills and resolutions, codified ordinances, model codes, court rules, and sentencing guidelines. Refer to The Bluebook.

–If the opinion has a name or title, it may be included before the
citation.

Opinions of the Attorney General (U.S.) (1789-date)

Ab.:   Op. Att'y Gen.

–The name of the opinion may be included in the citation.
See Bluebook Rule 14.4.

Ex.:   42 Op. Att'y Gen. 301 (1965). –Citation to bound material.

Carriage in United States Vessels of Exports Financed by a
Government Agency, 42 Op. Att'y Gen. 301 (1965). –Citation to
bound material.

Authority of the United States Olympic Committee to Send American
Teams to the 1980 Summer Olympics, 43 Op. Att'y Gen. No. 23 (April
10, 1980). –Citation to separately paginated slip opinion. See
Bluebook Rule 14.4.

Opinions of the Attorney General and Report to the Governor of Virginia

Ab.:   Op. Va. Att'y Gen.

See Opinions of the Attorney General of Virginia.

Opinions of the Attorney General of Alabama

Ab.:   Op. Ala. Att'y Gen.

Ex.:   Op. Ala. Att'y Gen. No. 94-00089 (Jan. 14, 1994). –Citation to slip
opinion.

237 Ala. Q. Rep. Atty. Gen. 43 (1994). –Citation to opinion compiled
in the Quarterly Report of the Attorney General.

–If the opinion has a name or title, it may be included before the
citation.

Opinions of the Attorney General of Alaska

Ab.:   Op. Alaska Att'y Gen.

Ex.:   Op. Alaska Att'y Gen. No. 4 (Nov. 8, 1985). –Citation to a formal slip
opinion.

Informal Op. Alaska Att'y Gen. No. 663-94-0185 (Jan. 1, 1994).
–Citation to an informal slip opinion.

–If the opinion has a name or title, it may be included before the
citation.

Opinions of the Attorney General of Arizona

Ab.:   Op. Ariz. Att'y Gen.

In citing cases in law review footnotes, abbreviate any word listed in Table T.6;
the names of "states, countries, and other geographical units" unless they are named parties;
and any other words of eight or more letters "if substantial space is thereby saved and the
result is unambiguous." Bluebook Rule 10.2.2. On the other hand, in citing cases in text,
abbreviate only widely known acronyms and the following words: "&," "Ass'n," "Bros.,"
"Co.," "Corp.," "Inc.," "Ltd.," and "No." Bluebook Rule 10.2.1(c).

Ex.:   Op. Ariz. Att'y Gen. No. I95-002 (Aug. 30, 1995). –Citation to slip opinion.

        –If the opinion has a name or title, it may be included before the citation.

Opinions of the Attorney General of Arkansas
Ab.:   Op. Ark. Att'y Gen.

Ex.:   Op. Ark. Att'y Gen. No. 94-376 (Jan. 3, 1995). –Citation to slip opinion.

        –If the opinion has a name or title, it may be included before the citation.

Opinions of the Attorney General of California
Ab.:   Op. Cal. Att'y Gen.

Ex.:   Op. Cal. Att'y Gen. No. 94-817 (Jan. 13, 1995). –Citation to slip opinion.

        64 Op. Cal. Att'y Gen. 676 (1981). –Citation to compiled opinion.

        –If the opinion has a name or title, it may be included before the citation.

Opinions of the Attorney General of Colorado
Ab.:   Op. Colo. Att'y Gen.

Ex.:   Op. Colo. Att'y Gen. No. 95-1 (Feb. 17, 1995). –Citation to slip opinion.

        –If the opinion has a name or title, it may be included before the citation.

Opinions of the Attorney General of Connecticut
Ab.:   Op. Conn. Att'y Gen.

Ex.:   1989 Op. Conn. Att'y Gen. No. 89-018. –Citation to compiled opinion.

        –If the opinion has a name or title, it may be included before the citation.

Opinions of the Attorney General of Delaware
Ab.:   Op. Del. Att'y Gen.

Ex.:   1982 Op. Del. Att'y Gen. No. 95-IB03 (Jan. 25, 1995). –Citation to slip opinion.

        –If the opinion has a name or title, it may be included before the citation.

Opinions of the Attorney General of Florida
Ab.:   Op. Fla. Att'y Gen.

In law review footnotes, the titles of books and the names of cases, except for procedural phrases, are not underlined. See Bluebook Rule 2.1(a). Further, the following are in large and small capitals: codes, restatements, standards, constitutions, periodicals, authors of books, titles of books, the abbreviated names of codes, most legislative materials except for bills and resolutions, codified ordinances, model codes, court rules, and sentencing guidelines. Refer to The Bluebook.

Ex.:   Fla. Att'y Gen. No. 94-21 (March 16, 1994). –Citation to slip opinion, not yet compiled in the Annual Report of the Florida Attorney General. 1994 Fla. Atty. Gen. Ann. Rep. 51. –Citation to opinion in the Annual Report of the Florida Attorney General.

–If the opinion has a name or title, it may be included before the citation.

Opinions of the Attorney General of Georgia

Ab.:   Op. Ga. Att'y Gen.

Ex.:   Op. Ga. Att'y Gen. No. 94-10 (Mar. 14, 1994). –Citation to slip opinion.

1994 Op. Ga. Att'y Gen. 12, No. 94-6. –Citation to compiled opinion.

–If the opinion has a name or title, it may be included before the citation.

Opinions of the Attorney General of Hawaii

Ab.:   Op. Haw. Att'y Gen.

Ex.:   Op. Haw. Att'y Gen. No. 94-2 (Oct. 17, 1994). –Citation to slip opinion.

–If the opinion has a name or title, it may be included before the citation.

Opinions of the Attorney General of Idaho

Ab.:   Op. Idaho Att'y Gen.

Ex.:   Op. Idaho Att'y Gen. No. 95-06 (Oct. 26, 1995). –Citation to slip opinion.

1995 Idaho Att'y Gen. Ann. Rep. 5, No. 95-01. –Citation to opinion compiled in the Idaho Attorney General's Annual Report.

–If the opinion has a name or title, it may be included before the citation.

Opinions of the Attorney General of Illinois

Ab.:   Op. Ill. Att'y Gen.

Ex.:   Op. Ill. Att'y Gen. No. 95-002 (May 25, 1995). –Citation to slip opinion.

–If the opinion has a name or title, it may be included before the citation.

Opinions of the Attorney General of Indiana

Ab.:   Op. Ind. Att'y Gen.

In citing cases in law review footnotes, abbreviate any word listed in Table T.6; the names of "states, countries, and other geographical units" unless they are named parties; and any other words of eight or more letters "if <u>substantial</u> space is thereby saved and the result is unambiguous." <u>Bluebook</u> Rule 10.2.2. On the other hand, in citing cases in text, abbreviate only widely known acronyms and the following words: "&," "Ass'n," "Bros.," "Co.," "Corp.," "Inc.," "Ltd.," and "No." <u>Bluebook</u> Rule 10.2.1(c).

Ex.: Op. Ind. Att'y Gen. No. 95-1 (Mar. 23, 1995). –Citation to slip opinion.

1987-1988 Op. Ind. Att'y Gen. 1, No. 87-1. –Citation to opinion compiled in Official Opinions of the Attorney General of Indiana.

–If the opinion has a name or title, it may be included before the citation.

Opinions of the Attorney General of Iowa

Ab.: Op. Iowa Att'y Gen.

Ex.: Op. Iowa Att'y Gen. No. 93-7-5 (Jul. 28, 1993). –Citation to slip opinion.

1993-1994 Iowa Att'y Gen. Biennial Rep. 26, No. 93-7-6 (1993). –Citation to opinion contained in a Biennial Report of the Iowa Attorney General.

–If the opinion has a name or title, it may be included before the citation.

Opinions of the Attorney General of Kansas

Ab.: Op. Kan. Att'y Gen.

Ex.: Op. Kan. Att'y Gen. No. 94-121 (Sept. 20, 1994). –Citation to slip opinion.

29 Op. Kan. Att'y Gen. 34, No. 94-90 (1994). –Citation to compiled opinion.

–If the opinion has a name or title, it may be included before the citation.

Opinions of the Attorney General of Kentucky

Ab.: Op. Ky. Att'y Gen.

Ex.: Op. Ky. Att'y Gen. No. 95-24 (June 16, 1995). –Citation to slip opinion.

1995 Op. Ky. Att'y Gen. 2-111, No. 95-29. –Citation to compiled opinion.

–If the opinion has a name or title, it may be included before the citation.

Opinions of the Attorney General of Louisiana

Ab.: Op. La. Att'y Gen.

Ex.: Op. La. Att'y Gen. No. 92-169 (Dec. 4, 1992). –Citation to slip opinion.

1992-1993 Op. La. Att'y Gen. 18, No. 92-232 (1992). –Citation to compiled opinion.

–If the opinion has a name or title, it may be included before the citation.

In law review footnotes, the titles of books and the names of cases, except for procedural phrases, are not underlined. See Bluebook Rule 2.1(a). Further, the following are in large and small capitals: codes, restatements, standards, constitutions, periodicals, authors of books, titles of books, the abbreviated names of codes, most legislative materials except for bills and resolutions, codified ordinances, model codes, court rules, and sentencing guidelines. Refer to The Bluebook.

Opinions of the Attorney General of Maine
Ab.: Op. Me. Att'y Gen.

Ex.: Op. Me. Att'y Gen. No. 95-12 (July 11, 1995). –Citation to slip opinion.

–If the opinion has a name or title, it may be included before the citation.

Opinions of the Attorney General of Maryland
Ab.: Op. Md. Att'y Gen.

Ex.: 74 Op. Md. Att'y Gen. 112 (1989). –Citation to compiled opinion.

–If the opinion has a name or title, it may be included before the citation.

Opinions of the Attorney General of Massachusetts
Ab.: Op. Mass. Att'y Gen.

Ex.: Op. Mass. Att'y Gen. No. 93/94-1 (Aug. 9, 1993). –Citation to slip opinion.

1994 Op. Mass. Att'y Gen. 197, No. 93/94-1 (1993). –Citation to compiled opinion.

–If the opinion has a name or title, it may be included before the citation.

Opinions of the Attorney General of Michigan
Ab.: Op. Mich. Att'y Gen.

Ex.: Op. Mich. Att'y Gen. No. 6750 (Mar. 3, 1993). –Citation to slip opinion.

1993-1994 Op. Mich. Att'y Gen. 12, No. 6750 (1993). –Citation to opinion compiled in the Biennial Report of the Attorney General of the State of Michigan.

–If the opinion has a name or title, it may be included before the citation.

Opinions of the Attorney General of Minnesota
Ab.: Op. Minn. Att'y Gen.

Ex.: Op. Minn. Att'y Gen. No. 627e (Aug. 1, 1994). –Citation to slip opinion.

Op. Minn. Atty. Gen., 27 Minn. Legal Reg. 3 (1994). –Citation to opinion compiled in the Minnesota Legal Register.

–If the opinion has a name or title, it may be included before the citation.

Opinions of the Attorney General of Mississippi
Ab.: Op. Miss. Att'y Gen.

In citing cases in law review footnotes, abbreviate any word listed in Table T.6; the names of "states, countries, and other geographical units" unless they are named parties; and any other words of eight or more letters "if substantial space is thereby saved and the result is unambiguous." Bluebook Rule 10.2.2. On the other hand, in citing cases in text, abbreviate only widely known acronyms and the following words: "&," "Ass'n," "Bros.," "Co.," "Corp.," "Inc.," "Ltd.," and "No." Bluebook Rule 10.2.1(c).

Ex.:   1991 Op. Miss. Att'y Gen. No. 237 (May 11, 1995). –Citation to slip opinion.

–If the opinion has a name or title, it may be included before the citation.

Opinions of the Attorney General of Missouri
Ab.:   Op. Mo. Att'y Gen. No.

Ex.:   Op. Mo. Att'y Gen. No. 54-95 (Mar. 6, 1995). –Citation to slip opinion.

–If the opinion has a name or title, it may be included before the citation.

Opinions of the Attorney General of Montana
Ab.:   Op. Mont. Att'y Gen.

Ex.:   43 Op. Mont. Att'y Gen. 288 (1989). –Citation to compiled opinion.

–If the opinion has a name or title, it may be included before the citation.

Opinions of the Attorney General of Nebraska
Ab.:   Op. Neb. Att'y Gen.

Ex.:   Op. Neb. Att'y Gen. No. 230 (Oct. 17, 1984). –Citation to a slip opinion.

–If the opinion has a name or title, it may be included before the citation.

Opinions of the Attorney General of Nevada
Ab.:   Op. Nev. Att'y Gen.

Ex.:   Op. Nev. Att'y Gen. No. 95-02 (Feb. 23, 1995). –Citation to slip opinion.

1995 Op. Nev. Att'y Gen. 3. –Citation to opinion compiled in Official Opinions of the Attorney General of Nevada.

–If the opinion has a name or title, it may be included before the citation.

Opinions of the Attorney General of New Jersey
Ab.:   Op. N.J. Att'y Gen.

Ex.:   Op. N.J. Att'y Gen. No. 1-1991 (Feb. 19, 1991). –Citation to slip opinion.

–If the opinion has a name or title, it may be included before the citation.

Opinions of the Attorney General of New Mexico
Ab.:   Op. N.M. Att'y Gen. No.

In law review footnotes, the titles of books and the names of cases, except for procedural phrases, are not underlined. See Bluebook Rule 2.1(a). Further, the following are in large and small capitals: codes, restatements, standards, constitutions, periodicals, authors of books, titles of books, the abbreviated names of codes, most legislative materials except for bills and resolutions, codified ordinances, model codes, court rules, and sentencing guidelines. Refer to The Bluebook.

Ex.:   Op. N.M. Att'y Gen. No. 93-1 (Jan. 5, 1993). –Citation to slip opinion.
        –If the opinion has a name or title, it may be included before the
        citation.

Opinions of the Attorney General of New York
Ab.:   Op. N.Y. Att'y Gen.
Ex.:   Op. N.Y. Att'y Gen. No. F 95-1 (Mar. 30, 1995). –Citation to formal
        slip opinion.
        Informal Op. N.Y. Att'y Gen. No. I 95-1 (Jan. 24, 1995). –Citation to
        informal slip opinion.
        1979 Op. N.Y. Att'y Gen. 31. –Citation to compiled formal opinion.
        –If the opinion has a name or title, it may be included before the
        citation.

Opinions of the Attorney General of North Carolina
Ab.:   Op. N.C. Att'y Gen.
Ex.:   60 N.C. Att'y Gen. Rep. 19 (1990). –Citation to opinion compiled in
        the North Carolina Attorney General Reports.
        –If the opinion has a name or title, it may be included before the
        citation.

Opinions of the Attorney General, State of North Dakota
Ab.:   Op. N.D. Att'y Gen.
Ex.:   Op. N.D. Att'y Gen. No. 95-03 (Feb. 13, 1995). –Citation to slip
        opinion.
        1995 Op. N.D. Att'y Gen. 7. –Citation to compiled opinion.
        –If the opinion has a name or title, it may be included before the
        citation.

Opinions of the Attorney General of Ohio
Ab.:   Op. Ohio Att'y Gen.
Ex.:   Op. Ohio Att'y Gen. No. 95-1 (Mar. 28, 1995). –Citation to slip
        opinion.
        1995 Op. Ohio Att'y Gen. 2-1. –Citation to compiled opinion.
        –If the opinion has a name or title, it may be included before the
        citation.

Opinions of the Attorney General of Oklahoma
Ab.:   Op. Okla. Att'y Gen.
Ex.:   Op. Okla. Att'y Gen. No. 92-22 (Feb. 3, 1993). –Citation to slip
        opinion.
        24 Op. Okla. Att'y Gen. 34 (1993). –Citation to compiled opinion.

In citing cases in law review footnotes, abbreviate any word listed in Table T.6;
the names of "states, countries, and other geographical units" unless they are named parties;
and any other words of eight or more letters "if substantial space is thereby saved and the
result is unambiguous." Bluebook Rule 10.2.2. On the other hand, in citing cases in text,
abbreviate only widely known acronyms and the following words: "&," "Ass'n," "Bros.,"
"Co.," "Corp.," "Inc.," "Ltd.," and "No." Bluebook Rule 10.2.1(c).

–If the opinion has a name or title, it may be included before the citation.

Opinions of the Attorney General of Oregon
Ab.:   Op. Or. Att'y Gen.

Ex.:   Op. Or. Att'y Gen. No. 8227 (Jan. 27, 1994). –Citation to slip opinion

Op. Or. Att'y Gen. 58 (1994). –Citation to compiled opinion.

–If the opinion has a name or title, it may be included before the citation.

Opinions of the Attorney General of Pennsylvania
Ab.:   Op. Pa. Att'y Gen.

Ex.:   Op. Pa. Att'y Gen. No. 94-1 (Feb. 4, 1994). –Citation to slip opinion.

1978 Op. Pa. Att'y Gen. 117. –Citation to compiled opinion

–If the opinion has a name or title, it may be included before the citation.

Opinions of the Attorney General of Puerto Rico
Ab.:   Op. P.R. Sec. Just.

Ex.:   Op. P.R. Sec. Just. Num. 1991-3 (Feb. 6, 1991). –Citation to slip opinion.

62 Op. P.R. Sec. Just. 8 (1991). –Citation to opinion compiled in the Opiniones del Secretario de Justicia.

–If the opinion has a name or title, it may be included before the citation.

Opinions of the Attorney General of Rhode Island
Ab.:   Op. R.I. Att'y Gen.

Ex.:   Op. R.I. Att'y Gen. No. 95-02 (Jan. 11, 1995). –Citation to slip opinion.

–If the opinion has a name or title, it may be included before the citation.

Opinions of the Attorney General of South Carolina
Ab.:   Op. S.C. Att'y Gen.

Ex.:   Op. S.C. Att'y Gen. No. 93-8 (Feb. 17, 1993). –Citation to slip opinion.

1993 Op. S.C. Att'y Gen. 31. –Citation to compiled opinion.

–If the opinion has a name or title, it may be included before the citation.

Opinions of the Attorney General of South Dakota
Ab.:   Op. S.D. Att'y Gen.

In law review footnotes, the titles of books and the names of cases, except for procedural phrases, are not underlined. See Bluebook Rule 2.1(a). Further, the following are in large and small capitals: codes, restatements, standards, constitutions, periodicals, authors of books, titles of books, the abbreviated names of codes, most legislative materials except for bills and resolutions, codified ordinances, model codes, court rules, and sentencing guidelines. Refer to The Bluebook.

Ex.:　　Op. S.D. Att'y Gen. No. 93-12 (Dec. 1, 1993). –Citation to slip opinion.

1993-1994 S.D. Att'y Gen. Biennial Rep. 40 (1993). –Citation to opinion compiled in the Biennial Report of the Attorney General of the State of South Dakota.

–If the opinion has a name or title, it may be included before the citation.

Opinions of the Attorney General of Tennessee

Ab.:　　Op. Tenn. Att'y Gen.

Ex.:　　10 Op. Tenn. Att'y Gen. 757 (1981). –Cite to bound material. Prior to 1982, opinions are bound in numbered volumes and not separately paginated. See Bluebook Rule 14.4.

1989 Op. Tenn. Att'y Gen. No. 89-110. –Cite to bound material. After 1981, opinions are bound in volumes numbered by the year of publication. Opinions are separately paginated. See Bluebook Rule 14.4.

Op. Tenn. Att'y Gen. No. 95-008 (Mar. 1, 1995). –Cite to slip opinion that will eventually be included in a volume numbered by the year of publication. See Bluebook Rule 14.4.

–If the opinion has a name or title, it may be included before the citation.

Op. Tenn. Att'y Gen. No. 01-021 (Feb. 8, 2001), www.attorneygeneral.state.tn.us/2001/OP/OP21.pdf. –Citation to recent decision found only online.

Opinions of the Attorney General of Texas

Ab.:　　Op. Tex. Att'y Gen.

Ex.:　　Op. Tex. Att'y Gen. DM-317 (June 19, 1995). –Citation to slip formal opinion. (DM are the initials of the Texas Attorney General).

Op. Tex. Att'y Gen. No. LO95-011 (Mar. 17, 1995). –Citation to slip letter opinion.

Op. Tex. Att'y Gen. No. ORD-632 (Mar. 10, 1995). –Citation to slip open records decision.

–If the opinion has a name or title, it may be included before the citation.

Opinions of the Attorney General of Utah

Ab.:　　Op. Utah Att'y Gen.

Ex.:　　Op. Utah Att'y Gen. 96-3 Utah Bull. 32 (1995). –Citation to opinion compiled in the Utah State Bulletin.

–If the opinion has a name or title, it may be included before the citation.

In citing cases in law review footnotes, abbreviate any word listed in Table T.6; the names of "states, countries, and other geographical units" unless they are named parties; and any other words of eight or more letters "if substantial space is thereby saved and the result is unambiguous." Bluebook Rule 10.2.2. On the other hand, in citing cases in text, abbreviate only widely known acronyms and the following words: "&," "Ass'n," "Bros.," "Co.," "Corp.," "Inc.," "Ltd.," and "No." Bluebook Rule 10.2.1(c).

Opinions of the Attorney General of Virgin Islands
Ab.: Op. V.I. Att'y Gen.

Ex.: Op. V.I. Att'y Gen. No. 1984-3 (Apr. 24, 1984). –Citation to slip opinion.

10 Op. V.I. Att'y Gen. 16 (1984). –Citation to compiled opinion.

–If the opinion has a name or title, it may be included before the citation.

Opinions of the Attorney General of Virginia
Ab.: Op. Va. Att'y Gen.

Ex.: 1995 Op. Va. Att'y Gen. 61. –Citation to opinion compiled in Opinions of the Attorney General and Report to the Governor of Virginia.

–If the opinion has a name or title, it may be included before the citation.

Opinions of the Attorney General of Washington
Ab.: Op. Wash. Att'y Gen.

Ex.: 1995 Op. Wash. Att'y Gen. No. 1. –Citation to compiled opinion.

–If the opinion has a name or title, it may be included before the citation.

Opinions of the Attorney General of West Virginia
Ab.: Op. W.Va. Att'y Gen.

Ex.: 1992-1993 Op. W.Va. Att'y Gen. (Feb. 24, 1992). –Citation to slip opinion.

61 Op. W.Va. Att'y Gen. 13 (1985). –Citation to opinion compiled in the Biennial Report and Official Opinions of the Attorney General of the State of West Virginia.

–If the opinion has a name or title, it may be included before the citation.

Opinions of the Attorney General of Wisconsin
Ab.: Op. Wis. Att'y Gen.

Ex.: Op. Wis. Att'y Gen. No. 1-95 (Feb. 24, 1995). –Citation to slip opinion.

79 Op. Wis. Att'y Gen. 14 (1990). –Citation to compiled opinion.

–If the opinion has a name or title, it may be included before the citation.

Opinions of the Attorney General of Wyoming
Ab.: Op. Wyo. Att'y Gen.

In law review footnotes, the titles of books and the names of cases, except for procedural phrases, are not underlined. See Bluebook Rule 2.1(a). Further, the following are in large and small capitals: codes, restatements, standards, constitutions, periodicals, authors of books, titles of books, the abbreviated names of codes, most legislative materials except for bills and resolutions, codified ordinances, model codes, court rules, and sentencing guidelines. Refer to The Bluebook.

Ex.:   Op. Wyo. Att'y Gen. No. 95-002 (May 22, 1995). –Citation to slip opinion.

1995 Op. Wyo. Att'y Gen. 4. –Citation to compiled opinion.

–If the opinion has a name or title, it may be included before the citation.

Opinions of the Office of Legal Counsel (U.S. Department of Justice)
Ab.:   Op. Off. Legal Counsel
Ex.:   19 Op. Off. Legal Counsel 67 (1992).

–If the opinion has a name or title, it may be included before the citation.

Order of authorities within each signal
See Bluebook Rule 1.4.

Order of signals
See Bluebook Rule 1.3.

Ordinals

–"Unless part of a citation, ordinal numbers appearing in text and footnotes are controlled by Rule 6.2(a). If part of a citation, figures are used for all ordinal numbers." Bluebook Rule 6.2(b).

Ex.:   92d Cong.

51st Leg.

17th ed.

ordinances
Ex.:

–Citation to uncodified ordinance:

Knoxville, Tenn., Ordinance 0-155-78 (Sept. 8, 1978).

–Citations to codified ordinances:

Santa Monica, Cal., Mun. Code § 4.16.040 (1964).

Indianapolis, Ind., Rev. Code § 101-4 (1988).

Minneapolis, Minn., Code ch. 2, § 17 (1983).

Nashville and Davidson County, Tenn., Metropolitan Code § 3.33.040 (1995).

–Unified city/county government.

See Bluebook Rule 12.8.2.

Oregon Administrative Rules
Ab.:   Or. Admin. R.

In citing cases in law review footnotes, abbreviate any word listed in Table T.6; the names of "states, countries, and other geographical units" unless they are named parties; and any other words of eight or more letters "if substantial space is thereby saved and the result is unambiguous." Bluebook Rule 10.2.2. On the other hand, in citing cases in text, abbreviate only widely known acronyms and the following words: "&," "Ass'n," "Bros.," "Co.," "Corp.," "Inc.," "Ltd.," and "No." Bluebook Rule 10.2.1(c).

Ex.:   Or. Admin. R. 806-001-005 (1997).

Oregon Bulletin
Ab.:   Or. Bull.

Oregon Attorney General Opinions
See Opinions of the Attorney General of Oregon

Oregon Constitution
Ab.:   Or. Const. art. , §   .
Ex.:   Or. Const. art. II, § 9. –"Cite constitutional provisions currently in force without date." Bluebook Rule 11.

Or. Const. art. IX, § 1 (amended 1917). –"When citing a provision that has been subsequently amended, either indicate parenthetically the fact and date of amendment or cite the amending provision in full." Bluebook Rule 11.

Oregon Law Review
Ab.:   Or. L. Rev.
Ex.:   Joel K. Jacobson, The Collateral Source Rule and the Role of the Jury, 70 Or. L. Rev. 523 (1991). –Article Citation.

Joel K. Jacobson, The Collateral Source Rule and the Role of the Jury, 70 Or. L. Rev. 523, 528 (1991). –Page Citation.

Oregon Laws and Resolutions
Ab.:   year Or. Laws.

year Or. Laws Spec. Sess.
year Or. Laws Adv. Sh. No.
Ex.:   Act of Sept. 9, 1995, ch. 616, 1995 Or. Laws 1686. –Citation to an entire session law.

Act of Sept. 9, 1995, ch. 616, § 2, 1995 Or. Laws 1686, 1687. –Citation to a section in a session law.

–Identifying information may be added parenthetically according to Bluebook Rule 12.4(a).

Oregon Reports
Ab.:   Or.

–Cite to P., P.2d , or P.3d if therein; otherwise, cite to Or.

–Give parallel citations only in documents submitted to Oregon state courts. See Bluebook Rule 10.3.1 and Practitioners' Note P.3; see also, Or. Unif. Trial Ct. R. 2.010(13), which requires a citation to Or. And expressly permits a parallel citation.

In documents submitted to Oregon state courts, cite as follows:

Adams v. Kulongoski, 322 Or. 637, 912 P.2d 902 (1996). –Case Citation.

In law review footnotes, the titles of books and the names of cases, except for procedural phrases, are not underlined. See Bluebook Rule 2.1(a). Further, the following are in large and small capitals: codes, restatements, standards, constitutions, periodicals, authors of books, titles of books, the abbreviated names of codes, most legislative materials except for bills and resolutions, codified ordinances, model codes, court rules, and sentencing guidelines. Refer to The Bluebook.

Adams v. Kulongoski, 322 Or. 637, 638, 912 P.2d 902, 903 (1996). –Page Citation.

In all other documents, cite as follows:

Adams v. Kulongoski, 912 P.2d 902 (Or. 1996). –Case Citation.

Adams v. Kulongoski, 912 P.2d 902, 903 (Or. 1996). –Page Citation.

Oregon Reports, Court of Appeals
Ab.:   Or. App.

–Cite to P.2d or P.3d if therein; otherwise, cite to Or. App.

–Give parallel citations only in documents submitted to Oregon state courts. See Bluebook Rule 10.3.1 and Practitioners' Note P.3; see also, Or. Unif. Trial Ct. R. 2.010(13), which requires a citation to Or. App. and expressly permits a parallel citation.

In documents submitted to Oregon state courts, cite as follows:

Zell v. Fellner, 140 Or. App. 35, 914 P.2d 23 (1996). –Case Citation.

Zell v. Fellner, 140 Or. App. 35, 37, 914 P.2d 23, 24 (1996). –Page Citation.

In all other documents, cite as follows:

Zell v. Fellner, 914 P.2d 23 (Or. Ct. App. 1996). –Case Citation.

Zell v. Fellner, 914 P.2d 23, 24 (Or. Ct. App. 1996). –Page Citation.

Oregon Revised Statutes
Ab.:   Or. Rev. Stat. §   (year)
Ex.:   Or. Rev. Stat. § 801.365 (1999).

Oregon Revised Statutes Annotated
Ab.:   Or. Rev. Stat. Ann. §   (Butterworths year)
Ex.:   Or. Rev. Stat. Ann. § 118.025 (Butterworths 1990).

Oregon Session Laws
See Oregon Laws and Resolutions

Oregon State Bar Bulletin
Ab.:   Or. St. B. Bull.
Ex.:   Philip Yates, ADA Promises Greater Access to Businesses, Or. St. B. Bull., Jan. 1992, at 19. –Article Citation.

Philip Yates, ADA Promises Greater Access to Businesses, Or. St. B. Bull., Jan. 1992, at 19, 20. –Page Citation.

In citing cases in law review footnotes, abbreviate any word listed in Table T.6; the names of "states, countries, and other geographical units" unless they are named parties; and any other words of eight or more letters "if substantial space is thereby saved and the result is unambiguous." Bluebook Rule 10.2.2. On the other hand, in citing cases in text, abbreviate only widely known acronyms and the following words: "&," "Ass'n," "Bros.," "Co.," "Corp.," "Inc.," "Ltd.," and "No." Bluebook Rule 10.2.1(c).

Oregon Tax Reports
   Ab.:   Or. Tax
   Ex.:   <u>Rogers v. Department of Revenue</u>, 6 Or. Tax. 139, 142 (1975).

Orfield's Criminal Procedure Under the Federal Rules, by Mark S. Rhodes
   –Do not abbreviate the title.
   Ex.:   5 Mark S. Rhodes, <u>Orfield's Criminal Procedure Under the Federal Rules</u> § 24:4 (2d ed. 1987). –Section Citation.

        5 Mark S. Rhodes, <u>Orfield's Criminal Procedure Under the Federal Rules</u> § 33:64, at 368 (2d ed. 1987). –Page Citation.

        5 Mark S. Rhodes, <u>Orfield's Criminal Procedure Under the Federal Rules</u> § 33:64, at 368 n.7 (2d ed. 1987). –Footnote Citation.

        3 Mark S. Rhodes, <u>Orfield's Criminal Procedure Under the Federal Rules</u> § 24:4 (2d ed. Supp. 2000). –Citation to Supplement Section.

Orphans' Court
   Ab.:   Orphans' Ct.

Osgoode Hall Law Journal
   Ab.:   Osgoode Hall L.J.
   Ex.:   David Vaver, <u>Copyright in Legal Documents</u>, 31 Osgoode Hall L.J. 661 (1993). –Article Citation.

        David Vaver, <u>Copyright in Legal Documents</u>, 31 Osgoode Hall L.J. 661, 670-73 (1993). –Page Citation.

Otago Law Review
   Ab.:   Otago L. Rev.
   Ex.:   Graeme Austin, <u>Righting a Child's Right to Refuse Medical Treatment</u>, 7 Otago L. Rev. 578 (1992). –Article Citation.

        Graeme Austin, <u>Righting a Child's Right to Refuse Medical Treatment</u>, 7 Otago L. Rev. 578, 583-87 (1992). –Page Citation.

Ottawa Law Review
   Ab.:   Ottawa L. Rev.
   Ex.:   Denis J.E. Scott, <u>Interception of a Hacker's Computer Communication</u>, 25 Ottawa L. Rev. 525 (1993). –Article Citation.

        Denis J.E. Scott, <u>Interception of a Hacker's Computer Communication</u>, 25 Ottawa L. Rev. 525, 529 (1993). –Page Citation.

Oxford Journal of Legal Studies
   Ab.:   Oxford J. Legal Stud.
   Ex.:   Paul Roberts, <u>Science in the Criminal Process</u>, 14 Oxford J. Legal Stud. 469 (1994). –Article Citation.

        Paul Roberts, <u>Science in the Criminal Process</u>, 14 Oxford J. Legal Stud. 469, 472-77 (1994). –Page Citation.

In law review footnotes, the titles of books and the names of cases, except for procedural phrases, are not underlined. <u>See</u> Bluebook Rule 2.1(a). Further, the following are in large and small capitals: codes, restatements, standards, constitutions, periodicals, authors of books, titles of books, the abbreviated names of codes, most legislative materials except for bills and resolutions, codified ordinances, model codes, court rules, and sentencing guidelines. Refer to <u>The Bluebook</u>.

P

Pace Environmental Law Review
Ab.:   Pace Envtl. L. Rev.
Ex.:   Ludwik A. Teclaff, The River Basin Concept and Global Climate Change, 8 Pace Envtl. L. Rev. 355 (1991). –Article Citation.

Ludwik A. Teclaff, The River Basin Concept and Global Climate Change, 8 Pace Envtl. L. Rev. 355, 369-72 (1991). –Page Citation.

Pace Law Review
Ab.:   Pace L. Rev.
Ex.:   Vincent M. Bonventre, Court of Appeals - State Constitutional Law Review, 1990, 12 Pace L. Rev. 1 (1992). –Article Citation.

Vincent M. Bonventre, Court of Appeals - State Constitutional Law Review, 1990, 12 Pace L. Rev. 1, 49-51 (1992). –Page Citation.

Pace Yearbook of International Law
Ab.:   Pace Y.B. Int'l L.
Ex.:   Mohammed Bedjaoui, The "Manufacture" of Judgments at the International Court of Justice, 3 Pace Y.B. Int'l L. 29 (1991). –Article Citation.

Mohammed Bedjaoui, The "Manufacture" of Judgments at the International Court of Justice, 3 Pace Y.B. Int'l L. 29, 49-50 (1991). –Page Citation.

Pacific Law Journal
Ab.:   Pac. L.J.
Ex.:   Jeff Brown, Origins and Impact - A Public Defender's Perspective, 23 Pac. L.J. 881 (1992). –Article Citation.

Jeff Brown, Origins and Impact - A Public Defender's Perspective, 23 Pac. L.J. 881, 899 (1992). –Page Citation.

Pacific Reporter
–Do not give a parallel citation unless required by local rule. See Bluebook Practitioners' Note P.3. and Rule 10.3.1. See also the various state court and state reporter entries herein for local rule parallel citation requirements.
Ab.:   P.

In law review footnotes, the titles of books and the names of cases, except for procedural phrases, are not underlined. See Bluebook Rule 2.1(a). Further, the following are in large and small capitals: codes, restatements, standards, constitutions, periodicals, authors of books, titles of books, the abbreviated names of codes, most legislative materials except for bills and resolutions, codified ordinances, model codes, court rules, and sentencing guidelines. Refer to The Bluebook.

Ex.:

Arizona:

> Abbey v. Green, 235 P. 150 (Ariz. 1925). –Case Citation.
> Abbey v. Green, 235 P. 150, 153 (Ariz. 1925). –Page Citation.

California:

> Avery v. Peirson, 241 P. 406 (Cal. Dist. Ct. App. 1925).
> –Case Citation.
> Avery v. Peirson, 241 P. 406, 407 (Cal. Dist. Ct. App. 1925).
> –Page Citation.

Colorado:

> Estes v. Crann, 216 P. 517 (Colo. 1923). –Case Citation.
> Estes v. Crann, 216 P. 517, 518 (Colo. 1923). –Page Citation.

Idaho:

> State v. Main, 216 P. 731 (Idaho 1923). –Case Citation.
> State v. Main, 216 P. 731, 734 (Idaho 1923). –Page Citation.

Kansas:

> Indihar v. Western Coal & Mining Co., 241 P. 448 (Kan. 1925).
> –Case Citation.
> Indihar v. Western Coal & Mining Co., 241 P. 448, 450 (Kan. 1925).
> –Page Citation.

Montana:

> Weber v. City of Helena, 297 P. 455 (Mont. 1931). –Case Citation.
> Weber v. City of Helena, 297 P. 455, 465 (Mont. 1931). –Page
> Citation.

Nevada:

> McCulloch v. Bianchini, 297 P. 503 (Nev. 1931). –Case Citation.
> McCulloch v. Bianchini, 297 P. 503, 504 (Nev. 1931). –Page Citation.

New Mexico:

> Epstein v. Waas, 216 P. 506 (N.M. 1923). –Case Citation.
> Epstein v. Waas, 216 P. 506, 508 (N.M. 1923). –Page Citation.

Oklahoma:

> Exchange Oil Co. v. Crews, 216 P. 674 (Okla. 1923). –Case Citation.
> Exchange Oil Co. v. Crews, 216 P. 674, 675 (Okla. 1923). –Page
> Citation.

Oregon:

> Noble v. Yancey, 241 P. 335 (Or. 1925). –Case Citation.
> Noble v. Yancey, 241 P. 335, 338 (Or. 1925). –Page Citation.

In citing cases in law review footnotes, abbreviate any word listed in Table T.6; the names of "states, countries, and other geographical units" unless they are named parties; and any other words of eight or more letters "if substantial space is thereby saved and the result is unambiguous." Bluebook Rule 10.2.2. On the other hand, in citing cases in text, abbreviate only widely known acronyms and the following words: "&," "Ass'n," "Bros.," "Co.," "Corp.," "Inc.," "Ltd.," and "No." Bluebook Rule 10.2.1(c).

Utah:

>Oldroyd v. McCrea, 235 P. 580 (Utah 1925). –Case Citation.
>Oldroyd v. McCrea, 235 P. 580, 587 (Utah 1925). –Page Citation.

Washington:

>Trunk v. Wilkes, 297 P. 1091 (Wash. 1931). –Case Citation.
>Trunk v. Wilkes, 297 P. 1091, 1092 (Wash. 1931). –Page Citation.

Wyoming:

>Yellowstone Sheep Co. v. Diamond Dot Live Stock Co., 297 P. 1107 (Wyo. 1931). –Case Citation.
>Yellowstone Sheep Co. v. Diamond Dot Live Stock Co., 297 P. 1107, 1114 (Wyo. 1931). –Page Citation.

Pacific Reporter, Second Series

–Do not give a parallel citation unless required by local rule or unless the particular state has a public domain format. See Bluebook Practitioners' Note P.3. and Rule 10.3.1. See also the various state court and state reporter entries herein for public domain information and local rule parallel citation requirements.

–With volume 744 (1988), Pacific Reporter, Second Series, became West's Pacific Reporter, Second Series. Citation form is not affected by this title change.

Ab.:   P.2d

Ex.:

Alaska:

>Acevedo v. Burley, 994 P.2d 389 (Alaska 1999). –Case Citation.
>Acevedo v. Burley, 994 P.2d 389, 392 (Alaska 1999). –Page Citation.

Arizona:

>Randolph v. Groscost, 989 P.2d 751 (Ariz. 1999). –Case Citation.
>Randolph v. Groscost, 989 P.2d 751, 753 (Ariz. 1999). –Page Citation.

California:

>Samuels v. Mix, 989 P.2d 701 (Cal. 1999). –Case Citation.
>Samuels v. Mix, 989 P.2d 701, 715 (Cal. 1999). –Page Citation.

Colorado:

>People v. Kyler, 991 P.2d 810 (Colo. 1999). –Case Citation.
>People v. Kyler, 991 P.2d 810, 818 (Colo. 1999). –Page Citation.

Hawaii:

>State v. White, 990 P.2d 90 (Haw. 1999). –Case Citation.
>State v. White, 990 P.2d 90, 95 (Haw. 1999). –Page Citation.

In law review footnotes, the titles of books and the names of cases, except for procedural phrases, are not underlined. See Bluebook Rule 2.1(a). Further, the following are in large and small capitals: codes, restatements, standards, constitutions, periodicals, authors of books, titles of books, the abbreviated names of codes, most legislative materials except for bills and resolutions, codified ordinances, model codes, court rules, and sentencing guidelines. Refer to The Bluebook.

Idaho:

Clark v. City of Lewiston, 992 P.2d 172 (Idaho 1999). –Case Citation.

Clark v. City of Lewiston, 992 P.2d 172, 174 (Idaho 1999). –Page Citation.

Kansas:

State v. Johnson, 970 P.2d 990 (Kan. 1998). –Case Citation.

State v. Johnson, 970 P.2d 990, 992 (Kan. 1998). –Page Citation.

Montana:

Benson v. Heritage Inn, Inc., 971 P.2d 1227 (Mont. 1998). –Case Citation.

Benson v. Heritage Inn, Inc., 971 P.2d 1227, 1231 (Mont. 1998). –Page Citation.

Nevada:

Goodson v. State, 992 P.2d 472 (Nev. 1999). –Case Citation.

Goodson v. State, 992 P.2d 472, 474 (Nev. 1999). –Page Citation.

New Mexico:

State v. Lopez, 993 P.2d 727 (N.M.1999). –Case Citation.

State v. Lopez, 993 P.2d 727, 731 (N.M.1999). –Page Citation.

Oklahoma:

Jackson v. Jackson, 995 P.2d 1109 (Okla. 1999). –Case Citation.

Jackson v. Jackson, 995 P.2d 1109, 1112 (Okla. 1999). –Page Citation.

Oregon:

Sizemore v. Myers, 994 P.2d 792 (Or. 1999). –Case Citation.

Sizemore v. Myers, 994 P.2d 792, 793 (Or. 1999). –Page Citation.

Utah:

DeBry v. Godbe, 992 P.2d 979 (Utah 1999). –Case Citation.

DeBry v. Godbe, 992 P.2d 979, 984 (Utah 1999). –Page Citation.

Washington:

Phillips v. King County, 968 P.2d 871 (Wash. 1998). –Case Citation.

Phillips v. King County, 968 P.2d 871, 876 (Wash. 1998). –Page Citation.

Wyoming:

Griswold v. State, 994 P.2d 920 (Wyo. 1999). –Case Citation.

Griswold v. State, 994 P.2d 920, 926 (Wyo. 1999). –Page Citation.

Pacific Reporter, Third Series
–Do not give a parallel citation unless required by local rule or unless the particular state has a public domain format. See Bluebook

In citing cases in law review footnotes, abbreviate any word listed in Table T.6; the names of "states, countries, and other geographical units" unless they are named parties; and any other words of eight or more letters "if substantial space is thereby saved and the result is unambiguous." Bluebook Rule 10.2.2. On the other hand, in citing cases in text, abbreviate only widely known acronyms and the following words: "&," "Ass'n," "Bros.," "Co.," "Corp.," "Inc.," "Ltd.," and "No." Bluebook Rule 10.2.1(c).

Practitioners' Note P.3. and Rule 10.3.1. See also the various state court and state reporter entries herein for public domain information and local rule parallel citation requirements.

Ab.:   P.3d

Ex.:

Alaska:

Northern Alaska Environmental Center v. State Department of Natural Resources, 2 P.3d 629 (Alaska 2000). –Case Citation.

Northern Alaska Environmental Center v. State Department of Natural Resources, 2 P.3d 629, 634 (Alaska 2000). –Page Citation.

Arizona:

State v. Bass, 12 P.3d 796 (Ariz. 2000). –Case Citation.

State v. Bass, 12 P.3d 796, 809 (Ariz. 2000). –Page Citation.

California:

People v. Robles, 3 P.3d 311 (Cal. 2000). –Case Citation.

People v. Robles, 3 P.3d 311, 312 (Cal. 2000). –Page Citation.

Colorado:

Corsentino v. Cordova, 4 P.3d 1082 (Colo. 2000). –Case Citation.

Corsentino v. Cordova, 4 P.3d 1082, 1086 (Colo. 2000). –Page Citation.

Hawaii:

State v. Crisostomo, 12 P.3d 873 (Haw. 2000). –Case Citation.

State v. Crisostomo, 12 P.3d 873, 878 (Haw. 2000). –Page Citation.

Idaho:

State v. Daniels, 11 P.3d 1114 (Idaho 2000). –Case Citation.

State v. Daniels, 11 P.3d 1114, 1116 (Idaho 2000). –Page Citation.

Kansas:

In re Kroger Co., 12 P.3d 889 (Kan. 2000). –Case Citation.

In re Kroger Co., 12 P.3d 889, 893 (Kan. 2000). –Page Citation.

Montana:

Kingston v. Ameritrade, Inc., 12 P.3d 929 (Mont. 2000). –Case Citation.

Kingston v. Ameritrade, Inc., 12 P.3d 929, 931 (Mont. 2000). –Page Citation.

Nevada:

Hughes v. State, 12 P.3d 948 (Nev. 2000). –Case Citation.

Hughes v. State, 12 P.3d 948, 953 (Nev. 2000). –Page Citation.

In law review footnotes, the titles of books and the names of cases, except for procedural phrases, are not underlined. See Bluebook Rule 2.1(a). Further, the following are in large and small capitals: codes, restatements, standards, constitutions, periodicals, authors of books, titles of books, the abbreviated names of codes, most legislative materials except for bills and resolutions, codified ordinances, model codes, court rules, and sentencing guidelines. Refer to The Bluebook.

New Mexico:

> State v. Antillon, 2 P.3d 315 (N.M. 1999). –Case Citation.
>
> State v. Antillon, 2 P.3d 315, 316 (N.M. 1999). –Page Citation.

Oklahoma:

> Dixon Property Co. v. Shaw, 2 P.3d 330 (Okla. 1999). –Case Citation.
>
> Dixon Property Co. v. Shaw, 2 P.3d 330, 333 (Okla. 1999). –Page Citation.

Oregon:

> Bruce & Bruce v. City of Hillsboro, 6 P.3d 1097 (Or. 1999). –Case Citation.
>
> Bruce & Bruce v. City of Hillsboro, 6 P.3d 1097, 1097 (Or. 1999). –Page Citation.

Utah:

> Desert Miriah, Inc. v. B & L Auto, Inc., 12 P.3d 580 (Utah 2000). –Case Citation.
>
> Desert Miriah, Inc. v. B & L Auto, Inc., 12 P.3d 580, 581 (Utah 2000). –Page Citation.

Washington:

> Haley v. Highland, 12 P.3d 119 (Wash. 2000). –Case Citation.
>
> Haley v. Highland, 12 P.3d 119, 121 (Wash. 2000). –Page Citation.

Wyoming:

> Heinemann v. State, 12 P.3d 692 (Wyo. 2000). –Case Citation.
>
> Heinemann v. State, 12 P.3d 692, 699 (Wyo. 2000). –Page Citation.

Pacific Rim Law and Policy Journal

Ab.: Pac. Rim L. & Pol'y J.

Ex.: Yuan Cheng, Legal Protection of Trade Secrets in the Peoples' Republic of China, 5 Pac. Rim L. & Pol'y J. 261 (1996). –Article Citation.

Yuan Cheng, Legal Protection of Trade Secrets in the Peoples' Republic of China, 5 Pac. Rim L. & Pol'y J. 261, 262 (1996). –Page Citation.

page

–Repeat page number when citing to material on the first page of an article or case.

Ex.: Rochelle C. Dryfuss & Dorothy Nelkin, The Jurisprudence of Genetics, 45 Vand L. Rev. 313, 313 (1992).

–"p" and "pp" are used only for internal cross-reference.

In citing cases in law review footnotes, abbreviate any word listed in Table T.6; the names of "states, countries, and other geographical units" unless they are named parties; and any other words of eight or more letters "if substantial space is thereby saved and the result is unambiguous." Bluebook Rule 10.2.2. On the other hand, in citing cases in text, abbreviate only widely known acronyms and the following words: "&," "Ass'n," "Bros.," "Co.," "Corp.," "Inc.," "Ltd.," and "No." Bluebook Rule 10.2.1(c).

Ex.: See infra p. 41 and note 62.

  –Generally, use "at" with page number only if the page number will be confused with other parts of the citation or after "id."

Ex.: H.R. Rep. No. 103-403, at 21 (1994).

Ex.: Id. at 15.

See Bluebook Rule 3.3.

Page on the Law of Wills, by William J. Bowe and Douglas H. Parker
  –Do not abbreviate the title.

Ex.: 7 William J. Bowe & Douglas H. Parker, Page on the Law of Wills § 63.28 (rev. 1969). –Section Citation.

  7 William J. Bowe & Douglas H. Parker, Page on the Law of Wills § 63.28, at 186 (rev. 1969). –Page Citation.

  7 William J. Bowe & Douglas H. Parker, Page on the Law of Wills § 63.28 (Supp. 1987). –Citation to Supplement Section.

Page's Ohio Legislative Bulletin (Anderson)
  Ab.: year Ohio Legis. Bull. (Anderson)

Ex.: Act of Sept. 17, 1996, No. 166, 1996 Ohio Legis. Bull. 792 (Anderson) (organizing the Dept. of Transportation). –Citation to an entire session law.

  Act of Sept. 17, 1996, No. 166, sec. 1, § 121.05, 1996 Ohio Legis. Bull. 792, 793 (Anderson) (organizing the Dept. of Transportation). –Citation to a section of a session law amending prior act.

Page's Ohio Revised Code Annotated (Anderson)
  Ab.: Ohio Rev. Code Ann. § (Anderson year)

Ex.: Ohio Rev. Code Ann. § 4701.3 (Anderson 1995).

Paine on Tennessee Law of Evidence
  See Tennessee Law of Evidence, by Donald F. Paine

Panama Canal Zone Code
  See Canal Zone Code

Pan-American Treaty Series
  Ab.: Pan-Am. T.S.

paragraph(s)
  Ab.: ¶, ¶¶ if so in source. Otherwise para., paras.

Ex.: 2A Richard R. Powell, Powell on Real Property (Patrick J. Rohan ed., 1992) ¶ 269.

  2A Richard R. Powell, Powell on Real Property (Patrick J. Rohan ed., 1992) ¶¶ 269-27.

  See Bluebook Rule 3.4.

In law review footnotes, the titles of books and the names of cases, except for procedural phrases, are not underlined. See Bluebook Rule 2.1(a). Further, the following are in large and small capitals: codes, restatements, standards, constitutions, periodicals, authors of books, titles of books, the abbreviated names of codes, most legislative materials except for bills and resolutions, codified ordinances, model codes, court rules, and sentencing guidelines. Refer to The Bluebook.

Parallel citation for state court case

In documents submitted to state courts, citations to cases decided by the courts of that state should include a parallel citation if there is a public domain citation and if otherewise required by local rule. See Bluebook Practitioners' Note P.3, Rules 10.3.1, and 10.3.3; see also the various state court and state reporter entries herein for public domain information and local rule parallel citation requirements.

parenthetical information and explanatory parenthetical phrases

See Bluebook Rules 1.5, 1.6, and 10.6.

Parry's Consolidated Treaty Series (1648-1919)

Ab.:   Consol. T.S.

Partnership, by Alan R. Bromberg

See Crane and Bromberg on Partnership, by Alan R.. Bromberg

Partnership Taxation, by Arthur B. Willis, John S. Pennell, and Phillip F. Postlewaite

–Do not abbreviate the title.

Ex.:   2 Arthur B Willis et al., Partnership Taxation § 15.06 (6th ed. 1999).
–Section Citation.

2 Arthur B Willis et al., Partnership Taxation § 15.06, at 15-45 (6th ed. 1999). –Page Citation.

2 Arthur B Willis et al., Partnership Taxation § 15.06, at 15-45 n.170 (6th ed. 1999).
–Footnote Citation.

Patent Law Annual

Ab.:   Pat. L. Ann.

Ex.:   Charles S. Cotropia, The Trademark Law Revision Act of 1988, 26 Pat. L. Ann. 2-1 (1988). –Proceedings Citation.

Charles S. Cotropia, The Trademark Law Revision Act of 1988, 26 Pat. L. Ann. 2-1, 2-13–2-15 (1988). –Page Citation.

Patents, by Donald S. Chisum

–Do not abbreviate the title.

Ex.:   6 Donald S. Chisum, Patents § 21.03[3] (1992). –Section Citation.

6 Donald S. Chisum, Patents § 21.03[3], at 21-169 (1992). –Page Citation.

6 Donald S. Chisum, Patents § 21.03[3], at 21-169 n.18 (1992). –Footnote Citation.

Patents, Trademark, & Copyright Journal (Bureau of National Affairs)

Ab.:   Pat. Trademark & Copyright J. (BNA)

In citing cases in law review footnotes, abbreviate any word listed in Table T.6; the names of "states, countries, and other geographical units" unless they are named parties; and any other words of eight or more letters "if substantial space is thereby saved and the result is unambiguous." Bluebook Rule 10.2.2. On the other hand, in citing cases in text, abbreviate only widely known acronyms and the following words: "&," "Ass'n," "Bros.," "Co.," "Corp.," "Inc.," "Ltd.," and "No." Bluebook Rule 10.2.1(c).

Ex.: Bernard v. Commerce Drug Co., [Nov.-Apr.] Pat. Trademark & Copyright J. (BNA) No. 1055, at 10 (E.D.N.Y. Sept 27, 1991).
–Citation to looseleaf material.

–The above examples are proper if the case is not yet available in, or is not reported in, an official or West reporter, a public domain citation, or in a widely used computer database.

Patents, United States
See Bluebook Rule 14.9.
Ex.: U.S. Patent No. 6,079,520 (issued June 27, 2000).

pending and unreported cases
See also electronic media and other nonprint resources.
Ex.: United States v. Chen, No. 90-10434 (9th Cir. argued March 11, 1991).
–Pending case. See Bluebook Rule 10.8.1(a).

United States v. Chen, No. 90-10434, slip op. 6509, 6514 (9th Cir. May 23, 1991).
–Unreported case available only in separately printed slip opinion. See Bluebook Rule 10.8.1(a).

–An unreported case that is available on a widely used electronic database may be cited to that database. See Bluebook rule 18.1.1.

United States v. Chen, No. 90-10434, 1991 U.S. App. LEXIS 14034, at *2 (9th Cir. May 23, 1991).

Tipton v. Ahmad, No. 03A01-9201-CV-16, 1992 WL 91509, at *3 (Tenn. Ct. App. May 6, 1992).

Pennsylvania Bar Association Quarterly
Ab.: Pa. B. Ass'n. Q.
Ex.: Joyce S. Meyers, A Modest Proposal to Unclog the Courts: The Need for Corrective Legislation to Control the Asbestos Explosion, 53 Pa. B. Ass'n. Q. 20 (1992).
–Article Citation.

Joyce S. Meyers, A Modest Proposal to Unclog the Courts: The Need for Corrective Legislation to Control the Asbestos Explosion, 53 Pa. B. Ass'n. Q. 20, 24 (1992).
–Page Citation.

Pennsylvania Bulletin
Ab.: Pa. Bull.

Pennsylvania Code
Ab.: [tit.] Pa. Code § (year)

In law review footnotes, the titles of books and the names of cases, except for procedural phrases, are not underlined. See Bluebook Rule 2.1(a). Further, the following are in large and small capitals: codes, restatements, standards, constitutions, periodicals, authors of books, titles of books, the abbreviated names of codes, most legislative materials except for bills and resolutions, codified ordinances, model codes, court rules, and sentencing guidelines. Refer to The Bluebook.

Ex.:   6 Pa. Code § 21.27 (2000).

Pennsylvania Commonwealth Court Reports

Ab.:   Pa. Commw.

–Discontinued after 168 Pa. Commw. 698 (1994).

–Cite to A. or A.2d if therein; otherwise, cite to Pa. Commw.

–Give parallel citations only in documents submitted to Pennsylvania state courts. See Bluebook Rule 10.3.1 and Practitioners' Note P.3; see also Pa. R. App. P. 2119(b), which requires a parallel citation.

–Through 168 Pa. Commw. 698 (1994), cite as follows:

In documents submitted to Pennsylvania state courts, cite as follows:

> Peak v. Petrovitch, 161 Pa. Commw. 261, 636 A.2d 1248 (1994). –Case Citation.

> Peak v. Petrovitch, 161 Pa. Commw. 261, 262, 636 A.2d 1248, 1249 (1994). –Page Citation.

In all other documents, cite as follows:

> Peak v. Petrovitch, 636 A.2d 1248 (Pa. Commw. Ct. 1994). –Case Citation.

> Peak v. Petrovitch, 636 A.2d 1248, 1249 (Pa. Commw. Ct. 1994). –Page Citation.

–After 168 Pa. Commw. 698 (1994), cite as follows:

> Gueson v. Reed, 679 A.2d 284 (Pa. Commw. Ct. 1996). –Case Citation.

> Gueson v. Reed, 679 A.2d 284, 290 (Pa. Commw. Ct. 1996). –Page Citation.

Pennsylvania Consolidated Statutes

Ab.:   title Pa. Cons. Stat. §   (year)

Ex.:   18 Pa. Cons. Stat. § 4304 (1973 & Supp. 1994).

42 Pa. Cons. Stat. §§ 5984-85 (Supp. 1994).

–At the publication date of this book, Pennsylvania is undertaking its first official codification, Pennsylvania Consolidated Statutes. The old, unofficial compilation is Purdon's Pennsylvania Statutes Annotated, which uses a different numbering system. Purdon is also reprinting the new, official codification as Purdon's Pennsylvania Consolidated Statutes Annotated, which is currently bound with Purdon's Pennsylvania Statutes Annotated. –Cite to Pennsylvania Consolidated Statutes or Purdon's Pennsylvania Consolidated Statutes Annotated, in that order of preference. If the statute is contained in neither source, cite to Purdon's Pennsylvania Statutes Annotated (See Bluebook Rule 12.3.1(h)). See Bluebook Table T.1, page 228.

In citing cases in law review footnotes, abbreviate any word listed in Table T.6; the names of "states, countries, and other geographical units" unless they are named parties; and any other words of eight or more letters "if substantial space is thereby saved and the result is unambiguous." Bluebook Rule 10.2.2. On the other hand, in citing cases in text, abbreviate only widely known acronyms and the following words: "&," "Ass'n," "Bros.," "Co.," "Corp.," "Inc.," "Ltd.," and "No." Bluebook Rule 10.2.1(c).

Pennsylvania Consolidated Statutes Annotated
<u>See</u> Purdon's Pennsylvania Consolidated Statutes Annotated

Pennsylvania Constitution
Ab.: Pa. Const. art. , §   .

Ex.: Pa. Const. art. II, § 15. –"Cite constitutional provisions currently in force without date." <u>Bluebook</u> Rule 11.

Pa. Const. art. IV, § 19 (repealed 1967). –"If the cited provision has been repealed, either indicate parenthetically the fact and date of repeal or cite the repealing provision in full." <u>Bluebook</u> Rule 11.

Pa. Const. art. I, § 6 (amended 1971). –"When citing a provision that has been subsequently amended, either indicate parenthetically the fact and date of amendment or cite the amending provision in full." <u>Bluebook</u> Rule 11.

Pa. Const. of 1838, art. II, § 10 (1874). –"Cite constitutions that have been totally superseded by year of adoption; if the specific provision cited was adopted in a different year, give that year parenthetically." <u>Bluebook</u> Rule 11.

Pennsylvania District and County Reports
Ab.: Pa. D. & C., Pa. D. & C.2d, Pa. D. & C.3d, or Pa. D. & C.4th.

–Cite to the legal reporter for the county, if available, and to Pa. D. & C., Pa. D. & C.2d, Pa. D. & C.3d, or Pa. D. & C.4th.

Ex.: <u>In re Grady's Estate</u>, 34 Pa. D. & C. 143 (Orphan's Ct. 1938). –Case Citation.

<u>In re Grady's Estate</u>, 34 Pa. D. & C. 143, 149 (Orphan's Ct. 1938). –Page Citation.

<u>Academy of Natural Sciences v. City of Philadelphia</u>, 6 Pa. D. & C.2d 145 (C.P. 1955). –Case Citation.

<u>Academy of Natural Sciences v. City of Philadelphia</u>, 6 Pa. D. & C.2d 145, 149 (C.P. 1955). –Page Citation.

<u>Hurley v. Inland Fin. Co.</u>, 34 Pa. D. & C.3d 336 (C.P. 1984). –Case Citation.

<u>Hurley v. Inland Fin. Co.</u>, 34 Pa. D. & C.3d 336, 337 (C.P. 1984). –Page Citation.

<u>Kryeski v. Schott Glass Technicians, Inc.</u>, 9 Pa. D. & C.4th 399 (C.P. 1991). –Case Citation.

<u>Kryeski v. Schott Glass Technicians, Inc.</u>, 9 Pa. D. & C.4th 399, 402 (C.P. 1991). –Page Citation.

Pennsylvania Fiduciary Reporter
Ab.: Pa. Fiduc., Pa. Fiduc. 2d

In law review footnotes, the titles of books and the names of cases, except for procedural phrases, are not underlined. <u>See</u> <u>Bluebook</u> Rule 2.1(a). Further, the following are in large and small capitals: codes, restatements, standards, constitutions, periodicals, authors of books, titles of books, the abbreviated names of codes, most legislative materials except for bills and resolutions, codified ordinances, model codes, court rules, and sentencing guidelines. Refer to <u>The Bluebook</u>.

Ex.:　In re Zappardino Estate, 14 Pa. Fiduc. 212 (Orphan's Ct. 1964). –Case Citation.

In re Zappardino Estate, 14 Pa. Fiduc. 212, 216 (Orphan's Ct. 1964). –Page Citation.

In re Dolinger Estate, 4 Pa. Fiduc. 2d 327 (Orphan's Ct. 1984). –Case Citation.

In re Dolinger Estate, 4 Pa. Fiduc. 2d 327, 330 (Orphan's Ct. 1984). –Page Citation.

–Above examples are correct if case not reported in Pa. D. & C.3d.

Pennsylvania Legislative Service
See Purdon's Pennsylvania Legislative Service

Pennsylvania Session Laws
See Laws of Pennsylvania and Purdon's Pennsylvania Legislative Service (West).

Pennsylvania State Reports
Ab.:　Pa.

–Cite to A. or A.2d if therein; otherwise, cite to Pa.

–Give parallel citations only in documents submitted to Pennsylvania state courts. See Bluebook Rule 10.3.1 and Practitioners' Note P.3; see also Pa. R. App. P. 2119(b), which requires a parallel citation.

In documents submitted to Pennsylvanis state courts, cite as follows:

Commonwealth v. Birdseye, 543 Pa. 251, 670 A.2d 1124 (1996). –Case Citation.

Commonwealth v. Birdseye, 543 Pa. 251, 254, 670 A.2d 1124, 1125 (1996). –Page Citation.

In all other documents, cite as follows:

Commonwealth v. Birdseye, 670 A.2d 1124 (Pa. 1996). –Case Citation.

Commonwealth v. Birdseye, 670 A.2d 1124, 1125 (Pa. 1996). –Page Citation.

Pennsylvania Statutes Annotated (Purdon's)
See Purdon's Pennsylvania Statutes Annotated

Pennsylvania Superior Court Reports
Ab.:　Pa. Super.

–Discontinued after 456 Pa. Super. 801 (1997).

–Cite to A. or A.2d if therein; in addition, give public domain citation if available.

In citing cases in law review footnotes, abbreviate any word listed in Table T.6; the names of "states, countries, and other geographical units" unless they are named parties; and any other words of eight or more letters "if substantial space is thereby saved and the result is unambiguous." Bluebook Rule 10.2.2. On the other hand, in citing cases in text, abbreviate only widely known acronyms and the following words: "&," "Ass'n," "Bros.," "Co.," "Corp.," "Inc.," "Ltd.," and "No." Bluebook Rule 10.2.1(c).

–Except for public domain citation from January 1, 1999, give parallel citations only in documents submitted to Pennsylvania state courts. See Bluebook Rule 10.3.1 and Practitioners Note P.3; see also Pa. R. App. P. 2119(b), which requires a parallel citation.

–Through 456 Pa. Super 801 (1997), cite as follows:

In documents submitted to Pennsylvania state courts:

> Marchetti v. Karpowick, 446 Pa. Super. 509, 667 A.2d 724 (1995). –Case Citation.
>
> Marchetti v. Karpowick, 446 Pa. Super. 509, 512, 667 A.2d 724, 725. –Page Citation.

In all other documents:

> Marchetti v. Karpowick, 667 A.2d 724 (Pa. Super. Ct. 1995). –Case Citation.
>
> Marchetti v. Karpowick, 667 A.2d 724, 725 (Pa. Super. Ct. 1995). –Page Citation.

–After 456 Pa. Super. 801 (1997) and until January 1, 1999, when a public domain format was adopted, cite as follows:

In all documents:

> Cole v. Czegan, 722 A.2d 686 (Pa. Super Ct. 1998). –Case Citation.
>
> Cole v. Czegan, 722 A.2d 686, 689 (Pa. Super. Ct. 1998) –Page Citation.

–After January 1, 1999, cite as follows:

In all documents:

> Taylor v. Solberg, 2000 PA Super 262, 740 A.2d 735. –Case Citation.
>
> Taylor v. Solberg, 2000 PA Super 262, ¶ 15, 740 A.2d 735, 737. –Pinpoint Citation.

Pension Plan Guide (Commerce Clearing House)
Ab.:	Pens. Plan Guide (CCH)
Ex.:	Epright v. Environmental Resources Mgmt., 6 Pens. Plan Guide (CCH) ¶ 23,919D (3d Cir. Feb. 16, 1996). –Citation to looseleaf material.

Delaye v. Agripal, Inc., [1993-1996 Transfer Binder] Pens. Plan Guide (CCH) ¶ 23,904P (9th Cir. 1994). –Citation to transfer binder material.

Pepperdine Law Review
Ab.:	Pepp. L. Rev.

In law review footnotes, the titles of books and the names of cases, except for procedural phrases, are not underlined. See Bluebook Rule 2.1(a). Further, the following are in large and small capitals: codes, restatements, standards, constitutions, periodicals, authors of books, titles of books, the abbreviated names of codes, most legislative materials except for bills and resolutions, codified ordinances, model codes, court rules, and sentencing guidelines. Refer to The Bluebook.

Ex.:   Jessica L. Darraby, Is Culture a Justiciable Issue?, 18 Pepp. L. Rev.
        463 (1991). –Article Citation.

        Jessica L. Darraby, Is Culture a Justiciable Issue?, 18 Pepp. L. Rev.
        463, 468 (1991). –Page Citation.

per curiam
        –Do not abbreviate.

Ex.:   Gibbons v. United States Dist. Court, 416 F.2d 14 (9th Cir. 1969) (per
        curiam).

        Anderson v. Gladden, 303 F. Supp. 1134 (D. Or. 1967), aff'd per
        curiam, 416 F.2d 447 (9th Cir. 1969).

        Kent v. Prasse, 385 F.2d 406 (3d Cir. 1967) (per curiam).

        See Bluebook Rule 10.6.

periodicals
        See generally Bluebook Rule 16.

NON STUDENT-WRITTEN MATERIALS:

        –single law review article

        Thomas R. McCoy, Current State Action Theories, the Jackson Nexus
        Requirement, and Employee Discharges by Semi-Public and State-
        Aided Institutions, 31 Vand. L. Rev. 785 (1978). –Article Citation.

        Thomas R. McCoy, Current State Action Theories, the Jackson Nexus
        Requirement, and Employee Discharges by Semi-Public and State-
        Aided Institutions, 31 Vand. L. Rev. 785, 809-13 (1978). –Page
        Citation.

        –multipart law review articles:

        Peter L. Costas & Daniel E. Harris, Patents, Trademarks and
        Copyrights – The Legal Monopolies (pts. 1-2) 36 Conn. B.J. 569, 37
        Conn. B.J. 420 (1963). –For the series.

        Peter L. Costas & Daniel E. Harris, Patents, Trademarks and
        Copyrights – The Legal Monopolies (pt. 2) 37 Conn. B.J. 420 (1963).
        –For a single part of the series.

        –symposium:

        Symposium, Transnational Technology Transfer: Current Problems
        and Solutions for the Corporate Practitioner, 14 Vand. J. Transnat'l L.
        249 (1981).   –Symposium as a unit.

        Gabriel M. Wilner, The Transfer of Technology to Latin America,
        14 Vand. J. Transnat'l L. 269 (1981). –Article within the symposium.

        –book review:

        Barbara A. Black, Book Review, 90 Yale L.J. 232 (1980). –Citation to
        untitled book review.

In citing cases in law review footnotes, abbreviate any word listed in Table T.6;
the names of "states, countries, and other geographical units" unless they are named parties;
and any other words of eight or more letters "if substantial space is thereby saved and the
result is unambiguous." Bluebook Rule 10.2.2. On the other hand, in citing cases in text,
abbreviate only widely known acronyms and the following words: "&," "Ass'n," "Bros.,"
"Co.," "Corp.," "Inc.," "Ltd.," and "No." Bluebook Rule 10.2.1(c).

Barbara A. Black, 90 Yale L.J. 232 (1980) (reviewing David T. Konig, Law and Society in Puritan Massachusetts (1979)). –Citation which includes the title of the book reviewed.

Barbara A. Black, Community and Law in Seventeenth Century Massachusetts 90 Yale L.J. 232 (1980) (book review). –Citation to a book review when it is not necessary to identify the book under review titled.

–article in separately paginated issue:

John J. Creedon, Lifetime Gifts of Life Insurance, Prac. Law., Oct. 1974, at 27. –Article Citation.

Creedon, Lifetime Gifts of Life Insurance, Prac. John J. Law., Oct. 1974, at 27, 31-33. –Page Citation.

–When a periodical is paginated only within each issue, the date or period of the issue must be included in the citation. See Bluebook Rule 16.4.

–year used as the volume number:

Frank S. Bloch, Cooperative Federalism and the Role of Litigation in the Development of Federal AFDC Eligibility Policy, 1979 Wis. L. Rev. 1. –Article Citation.

STUDENT-WRITTEN MATERIALS:

–Signed materials

L. Allyn Dixon, Jr., Note, Broadcasters' First Amendment Rights: A New Approach?, 39 Vand. L. Rev. 323 (1986). See Bluebook Rule 16.5.1.

Karen Schoen, Comment, Insider Trading: The "Possession Versus Use" Debate, 148 U. Pa. L. Rev. 239, 241 (1999).

Meredith B. Brinegar, Recent Development, Limiting the Application of the Exclusionary Rule: The Good Faith Exception, 34 Vand. L. Rev. 213, 215 n.14 (1981).

–Unsigned materials

Note, The Judicial Role in Attacking Racial Discrimination in Tax-Exempt Private Schools, 93 Harv. L. Rev. 378 (1979).

Case Comment, Antitrust Scrutiny of Monopolists' Innovations: Berkey Photo, Inc. v. Eastman Kodak Co., 93 Harv. L. Rev. 408, 415-17 (1979).

Recent Case, 25 Vand. L. Rev. 240, 244-45 (1972).

–Book review

In law review footnotes, the titles of books and the names of cases, except for procedural phrases, are not underlined. See Bluebook Rule 2.1(a). Further, the following are in large and small capitals: codes, restatements, standards, constitutions, periodicals, authors of books, titles of books, the abbreviated names of codes, most legislative materials except for bills and resolutions, codified ordinances, model codes, court rules, and sentencing guidelines. Refer to The Bluebook.

Geoffrey C. Rapp, Book Note, <u>DNA's Dark Side</u>, 110 Yale L.J. 163 (2000) (reviewing Jim Duyer, Peter Neufeld & Barry Scheck, <u>Actual Innocence: Five Days to Execution and Other Dispatches from the Wrongly Convicted</u> (2000)). –signed, student-written, titled book review.

Thomas C. Grey, Book Note, 106 Yale L.J. 493 (1996) (reviewing Neil Duxbury, <u>Patterns of American Jurisprudence</u> (1995). –signed, student-written, untitled book review.

Book Note, <u>Translating Truth</u>, 114 Harv. L. Rev. 640 (2000) (reviewing Peter Brooks, <u>Troubling Confessions: Speaking Guilt in Law and Literature</u> (2000)). –unsigned, student-written book review.

permanent
Ab.:   perm.

Permanent Court of International Justice Advisory Opinions, Cases, Judgments, Pronouncements
Ab.:   P.C.I.J.
Ex.:   <u>Legal Status of Eastern Greenland</u>, 1933 P.C.I.J. (ser. C) No. 64 (April 5, 1933). –Case Citation.

<u>Legal Status of Eastern Greenland</u>, 1933 P.C.I.J. (ser. C) No. 64, at 1708-09 (April 5, 1933). –Page Citation.

<u>Advisory Opinion No. 11, Polish Postal Service in Danzig</u>, 1925 P.C.I.J. (ser. B) No. 11, at 6.

<u>See</u> <u>Bluebook</u> Rule 21.5.2 and Table T.3.

Permanent Court of International Justice Annual Reports
Ab.:   P.C.I.J. Ann. Rep.
Ex.:   <u>Rules for Financial Administration</u>, 1929-1930 P.C.I.J. Ann. Rep. (ser. E) No.6, at 339 (1930).

<u>See</u> <u>Bluebook</u> Rule 21.9 and cite according to Rule 16 (periodicals).

–Note: Decisions and other documents of the P.C.I.J. were published in six series (A through F).

Personnel Management
Ab.:   Personnel Mgmt. (P-H)

Peters (United States Reports)
<u>See</u> United States Reports

petition for certiorari filed
Ab.:   petition for cert. filed

In citing cases in law review footnotes, abbreviate any word listed in Table T.6; the names of "states, countries, and other geographical units" unless they are named parties; and any other words of eight or more letters "if <u>substantial</u> space is thereby saved and the result is unambiguous." <u>Bluebook</u> Rule 10.2.2. On the other hand, in citing cases in text, abbreviate only widely known acronyms and the following words: "&," "Ass'n," "Bros.," "Co.," "Corp.," "Inc.," "Ltd.," and "No." <u>Bluebook</u> Rule 10.2.1(c).

Ex.:   Harbor Tug and Barge Co. v. Papai, 67 F.3d 203 (9th Cir. 1996), petition for cert. filed, 65 U.S.L.W. 3073 (U.S. Apr. 9, 1996) (No. 95-1621).

petition for certiorari granted
Ab.:   cert. granted
Ex.:   Harbor Tug and Barge Co. v. Papai, 67 F.3d 203 (9th Cir. 1996), cert. granted, 65 U.S.L.W. 3254 (U.S. Oct. 1, 1996) (No. 95-1621).

Philippine Law Journal
Ab.:   Philippine L.J.
Ex.:   Evalyn G. Ursua, The Lawyer As Policymaker: A Challenge to Philippine Legal Education, 63 Philippine L.J. 186 (1988). –Article Citation.

       Evalyn G. Ursua, The Lawyer As Policymaker: A Challenge to Philippine Legal Education, 63 Philippine L.J. 186, 192 (1988). –Page Citation.

Philosophy & Public Affairs
Ab.:   Phil. & Pub. Aff.
Ex.:   David O. Brink, Mill's Deliberative Utilitarianism, 21 Phil. & Pub. Aff. 67 (1992). –Article Citation.

       David O. Brink, Mill's Deliberative Utilitarianism, 21 Phil. & Pub. Aff. 67, 78-79 (1992). –Page Citation.

photoduplicated reprint
Ab.:   photo. reprint

Pike & Fischer
Ab.:   P & F

Police Justice's Court
Ab.:   Police J. Ct.

Political Science Quarterly
Ab.:   Pol. Sci. Q.
Ex.:   Athan Theoharis, FBI Wiretapping: A Case Study of Bureaucratic Autonomy, 107 Pol. Sci. Q. 101 (1992). –Article Citation.

       Athan Theoharis, FBI Wiretapping: A Case Study of Bureaucratic Autonomy, 107 Pol. Sci. Q. 101, 119 (1992). –Page Citation.

Powell on Real Property (multivolume edition)
See Law of Real Property, (The) by Richard R. Powell

Practical Lawyer, The
Ab.:   Prac. Law.

In law review footnotes, the titles of books and the names of cases, except for procedural phrases, are not underlined. See Bluebook Rule 2.1(a). Further, the following are in large and small capitals: codes, restatements, standards, constitutions, periodicals, authors of books, titles of books, the abbreviated names of codes, most legislative materials except for bills and resolutions, codified ordinances, model codes, court rules, and sentencing guidelines. Refer to The Bluebook.

Ex.:   Patricia K. Loop, <u>Accomodating HIV-Positive Employees</u>, Prac. Law.,
        April 1992, at 27. –Article Citation.

        Patricia K. Loop, <u>Accomodating HIV-Positive Employees</u>, Prac. Law.,
        April 1992, at 27, 30. –Page Citation.

        –When a periodical is paginated only within each issue, the date or
        period of the issue must be included in the citation (<u>Bluebook</u> Rule
        16.3).

Practical Real Estate Lawyer, The
Ab.:   Prac. Real Est. Law.

Ex.:   Anthony J. Buonicore, <u>A Guide to Cleanup Jargon</u>, Prac. Real Est.
        Law., March 1992, at 25. –Article Citation.

        Anthony J. Buonicore, <u>A Guide to Cleanup Jargon</u>, Prac. Real Est.
        Law., March 1992, at 25, 32-35. –Page Citation.

Practical Tax Lawyer, The
Ab.:   Prac. Tax Law.

Ex.:   Kenneth N. Sacks, <u>Choosing the Right Small Business Retirement
        Plan</u>, Prac. Tax Law., Fall 1991, at 69. –Article Citation.

        Kenneth N. Sacks, <u>Choosing the Right Small Business Retirement
        Plan</u>, Prac. Tax Law., Fall 1991, at 69, 72-75. –Page Citation.

Pravovedenie (Former Soviet Union)
Ab.:   –Do not abbreviate the title.

prefaces and forewords (to books)
See <u>Bluebook</u> Rule 15.6.

Preface to Estates in Land and Future Interests, by Thomas F. Bergin and Paul G. Haskell
        –Do not abbreviate the title.

Ex.:   Thomas F. Bergin & Paul G. Haskell, <u>Preface to Estates in Land and
        Future Interests</u> 33 (2d ed. 1984). –Page Citation.

        Thomas F. Bergin & Paul G. Haskell, <u>Preface to Estates in Land and
        Future Interests</u> 33 n.34 (2d ed. 1984). –Footnote Citation.

Prentice-Hall, Inc.
Ab.:   P-H

Presidential Papers
See <u>Bluebook</u> Rule 14.7.

        Executive Orders
Ab.:   Exec. Order No.

In citing cases in law review footnotes, abbreviate any word listed in Table T.6;
the names of "states, countries, and other geographical units" unless they are named parties;
and any other words of eight or more letters "if <u>substantial</u> space is thereby saved and the
result is unambiguous." <u>Bluebook</u> Rule 10.2.2. On the other hand, in citing cases in text,
abbreviate only widely known acronyms and the following words: "&," "Ass'n," "Bros.,"
"Co.," "Corp.," "Inc.," "Ltd.," and "No." <u>Bluebook</u> Rule 10.2.1(c).

Ex.:   Exec. Order No. 12,375, 47 Fed. Reg. 34,105 (1982). –Citation to material not yet available in the Code of Federal Regulations.

Exec. Order No. 12,261, 3 C.F.R. 83 (1982).

Exec. Order No. 11,574, 3 C.F.R. 188 (1970), reprinted in 33 U.S.C. § 407 app. at 115 (1976). –Citation if the order is reprinted in U.S.C., U.S.C.A., or U.S.C.S.

Proclamations

Ab.:   Proclamation No.

Ex.:   Proclamation No. 4957, 47 Fed. Reg. 34,105 (1982). –Citation to material not yet available in the Code of Federal Regulations.

Proclamation No. 4871, 3 C.F.R. 56 (1982).

Proclamation No. 4420, 3 C.F.R. 11 (1976), reprinted in 90 Stat. 3081 (1976).

–Citation with optional parallel reference to a printing in Statutes at Large.

–Reorganization Plans

See Reorganization Plans (U.S.)

Preview of the United States Supreme Court Cases

Ab.:   Preview U.S. Sup. Ct. Cases

Ex.:   Geoffrey P. Miller, Revisiting the Contingency Factor in Fee-Shifting Awards, 1991-92 Preview U.S. Sup. Ct. Cases 327 (1992). –Article Citation.

Geoffrey P. Miller, Revisiting the Contingency Factor in Fee-Shifting Awards, 1991-92 Preview U.S. Sup. Ct. Cases 327, 329 (1992). –Page Citation.

Prince's Bieber Dictionary of Legal Citations, by Mary Miles Prince
–Do not abbreviate the title.

Ex.:   Mary Miles Prince, Prince's Bieber Dictionary of Legal Citations 333 (6th ed. 2001).

Principles of Evidence, by Irving Younger, Michael Goldsmith, and David A. Sonensheim
–Do not abbreviate the title.

Ex.:   Irving Younger et al., Principles of Evidence 879 (3d ed. 1997). –Page Citation.

Irving Younger et al., Principles of Evidence 881 n.22 (3d ed. 1997). –Footnote Citation.

In law review footnotes, the titles of books and the names of cases, except for procedural phrases, are not underlined. See Bluebook Rule 2.1(a). Further, the following are in large and small capitals: codes, restatements, standards, constitutions, periodicals, authors of books, titles of books, the abbreviated names of codes, most legislative materials except for bills and resolutions, codified ordinances, model codes, court rules, and sentencing guidelines. Refer to The Bluebook.

Prior Case History
       –Give only if significant to the point for which the case is cited or if the
       disposition cited does not intelligibly describe the issues in the case,
       as in a Supreme Court "mem." Bluebook Rule 10.7.

Ex.:   Cornelius v. Nutt, 472 U.S. 648 (1985), rev'g Devine v. Nutt, 718 F.2d
       1048 (Fed. Cir. 1983).

**Pritchard on the Law of Wills and Administration of Estates Embracing the
    Law and Practice in Tennesse, by Jack W. Robinson, Sr. and Jeff Mobley**
       –Do not abbreviate the title.

Ex.   2 Jack W. Robinson, Sr., & Jeff Mobley, Pritchard on the Law of Wills
       and Administration of Estates Embracing the Law and Practice in
       Tennessee § 663 (5ᵗʰ ed. 1994). –Section Citation.

       2 Jack W. Robinson, Sr., & Jeff Mobley, Pritchard on the Law of Wills
       and Administration of Estates Embracing the Law and Practice in
       Tennessee § 663, at 220 (5ᵗʰ ed. 1994). –Page Citation.

Private Acts of the State of Tennessee
Ab.:   year Tenn. Priv. Acts.

Ex.:   Act of Mar. 8, 1995, ch. 18, 1995 Tenn. Priv. Acts 40 (to amend
       charter of Gordonsville relative to the sale of intoxicating liquors).
       –Citation to an entire session law.

       Act of Mar. 8, 1995, ch. 18, § 3, 1995 Tenn. Priv. Acts 40, 40
       (amending charter of Gordonsville relative to the sale of intoxicating
       liquors). –Citation to a section of a session law.

Private Laws (U.S. Statutes at Large)
Ab.:   Priv. L. No.   , Stat.   (year)

Ex.:   Priv. L. No. 92-23, 85 Stat. 842 (1971).

Probate Court
Ab.:   Prob. Ct.

**Probate Law Journal (National College of Probate Judges and Boston
    University School of Law)**
Ab.:   Prob. L.J.

Probate Lawyer, The
Ab.:   Prob. Law.

Ex.:   Richard B. Covey, Reflections on Tax Writing and the Regulatory
       Process as It Affects Trusts and Estates, Prob. Law, Summer 1991, at 1.
       –Article Citation.

       Richard B. Covey, Reflections on Tax Writing and the Regulatory
       Process as It Affects Trusts and Estates, Prob. Law, Summer 1991, at 1,
       8-10. –Page Citation.

In citing cases in law review footnotes, abbreviate any word listed in Table T.6;
the names of "states, countries, and other geographical units" unless they are named parties;
and any other words of eight or more letters "if substantial space is thereby saved and the
result is unambiguous." Bluebook Rule 10.2.2. On the other hand, in citing cases in text,
abbreviate only widely known acronyms and the following words: "&," "Ass'n," "Bros.,"
"Co.," "Corp.," "Inc.," "Ltd.," and "No." Bluebook Rule 10.2.1(c).

Problematics of Moral and Legal Theory, The, by Richard A. Posner
–Do not abbreviate the title.
Ex.:   Richard A. Posner, <u>The Problematics of Moral and Legal Theory</u> 145 (1999). –Page Citation.

Problems of Communism
Ab.:   Probs. Communism
Ex.:   Cole Blasier, <u>Moscow's Retreat From Cuba</u>, Probs. Communism, Nov.-Dec. 1991, at 91. –Article Citation.

Cole Blasier, <u>Moscow's Retreat From Cuba</u>, Probs. Communism, Nov.-Dec. 1991, at 91, 95 (1991). –Page Citation.

Proceedings of the American Society of International Law
Ab.:   Proc. Am. Soc'y Int'l L.
Ex.:   Jeffrey M. Lang, <u>Self-Help in International Trade Disputes</u>, 84 Proc. Am. Soc'y Int'l L. 32 (1990). –Proceedings Citation.

Jeffrey M. Lang, <u>Self-Help in International Trade Disputes</u>, 84 Proc. Am. Soc'y Int'l L. 32, 38-39 (1990). –Page Citation.

Product Safety & Liability Reporter (Bureau of National Affairs)
Ab.:   Prod. Safety & Liab. Rep. (BNA)

Products Liability, by M. Stuart Madden
<u>See</u> Madden & Owen on Products Liability

Products Liability Reports (Commerce Clearing House)
Ab.:   Prod. Liab. Rep. (CCH)
Ex.:   <u>Wood v. Morbank Indus., Inc.</u>, 2 Prod. Liab. Rep. (CCH) ¶ 14,457 (11th Cir. Dec. 18 1995). –Citation to looseleaf material.

<u>Sumner v. General Motors Corp.</u>, [Mar. 1995 - Jan. 1996 Transfer Binder] Prod. Liab. Rep. (CCH) ¶ 14,345 (Mich. Ct. App. Aug. 18, 1995). –Citation to transfer binder material.

–The above examples are proper if the case is not yet available in, or is not reported in, an official or West reporter, a public domain citation, or in a widely used computer database.

Professional Negligence
Ab.:   Prof. Neg.
Ex.:   Steven Fennell, <u>Liability for a Client's Fraud</u>, 7 Prof. Neg. 151 (1991). –Article Citation.

Steven Fennell, <u>Liability for a Client's Fraud</u>, 7 Prof. Neg. 151, 154-55 (1991). –Page Citation.

Prosser and Keeton on the Law of Torts
–Do not abbreviate the title.

In law review footnotes, the titles of books and the names of cases, except for procedural phrases, are not underlined. <u>See</u> <u>Bluebook</u> Rule 2.1(a). Further, the following are in large and small capitals: codes, restatements, standards, constitutions, periodicals, authors of books, titles of books, the abbreviated names of codes, most legislative materials except for bills and resolutions, codified ordinances, model codes, court rules, and sentencing guidelines. Refer to <u>The Bluebook</u>.

Ex.: W. Page Keeton, <u>Prosser and Keeton on the Law of Torts</u> § 72 (5th ed. 1984). –Section Citation.

W. Page Keeton, <u>Prosser and Keeton on the Law of Torts</u> § 72, at 521 (5th ed. 1984). –Page Citation.

W. Page Keeton, <u>Prosser and Keeton on the Law of Torts</u> § 72, at 521 n.47 (5th ed. 1984). –Footnote Citation.

Public Acts of the State of Tennessee
Ab.: year Tenn. Pub. Acts
Ex.: Act of May 22, 1995, ch. 401, 1995 Tenn. Pub. Acts 678 (relative to collection of delinquent business taxes). –Citation to an entire session law.

Act of May 22, 1995, ch. 401, sec. 1, § 67-4-719, 1995 Tenn. Pub. Acts 678, 678 (relative to methods to collect delinquent business taxes). –Citation to a section of a session law amending a prior act.

Public and Local Acts of the Legislature of the State of Michigan
Ab.: year Mich. Pub. Acts
Ex.: Act of Dec. 26, 1994, No. 372, 1994 Mich. Pub. Acts 1821 (relating to Michigan estate tax). –Citation to an entire session law.

Act of Dec. 26, 1994, No. 372, sec. 1 § 202.256, 1994 Mich. Pub. Acts. 1821, 1821-22 (Michigan estate tax additional definitions). –Citation to a section of a session law amending prior act.

Public Contract Law Journal
Ab.: Pub. Cont. L.J.
Ex.: Frank K. Peterson, <u>In-House Counsel and Protective Orders in Bid Protests</u>, 21 Pub. Cont. L.J. 53 (1991). –Article Citation.

Frank K. Peterson, <u>In-House Counsel and Protective Orders in Bid Protests</u>, 21 Pub. Cont. L.J. 53, 55 (1991). –Page Citation.

public domain citations
"When citing a decision available in public domain format, if the jurisdiction's format can be cited in the following form, provide the case name, the year of decision, the state's two character postal code, the court abbreviation (unless the court is the state's highest court), the sequential number of the decision, and, if the decision is unpublished, a capital "U" after the sequential number of the decision. When referencing specific material within the decision, a pinpoint citation should be made to the paragraph number at which the material appears. If available, a parallel citation to the appropriate regional reporter must be provided." –Bluebook Rule 10.3.3.

The following examples are from jurisdictions that have adopted a public domain format identical to The Bluebook's:

In citing cases in law review footnotes, abbreviate any word listed in Table T.6; the names of "states, countries, and other geographical units" unless they are named parties; and any other words of eight or more letters "if <u>substantial</u> space is thereby saved and the result is unambiguous." <u>Bluebook</u> Rule 10.2.2. On the other hand, in citing cases in text, abbreviate only widely known acronyms and the following words: "&," "Ass'n," "Bros.," "Co.," "Corp.," "Inc.," "Ltd.," and "No." <u>Bluebook</u> Rule 10.2.1(c).

Maine Supreme Court
   Holland v. Sebunya, 2000 ME 160, ¶ 24, 759 A.2d 205, 213.
   –Pinpoint Citation.
Montana Supreme Court
   Benjamin v. Torgerson, 1999 MT 215, ¶ 15, 985 P.2d 734, 737.
   –Pinpoint Citation.
North Dakota Supreme Court
   Olson v. Olson, 2000 ND 120, ¶ 7, 611 N.W.2d 892, 895.
   –Pinpoint Citation.
Oklahoma Supreme Court
   Farrimond v. State ex rel. Fisher, 2000 OK 52 ,¶ 14, 8 P.3d 872,
   875. –Pinpoint Citation.
South Dakota Supreme Court
   Price v. Price, 2000 SD 64, ¶ 12, 611 N.W.2d 425, 429. –Pinpoint
   Citation.
Utah Supreme Court
   State v. Reed, 2000 UT 68, ¶11, 8 P.3d 1025, 1027. –Pinpoint
   Citation.
Wisconsin Supreme Court
   Rumage v. Gullberg, 2000 WI 53, ¶ 8, 611 N.W.2d 458, 461.
   –Pinpoint Citation.
United States District Court for the District of South Dakota
   United States v. Swift Hawk, 2000 DSD 52, ¶ 17, 125 F. Supp. 2d
   384, 389. –Pinpoint citation

-When citing cases from a jurisdiction that has adopted a public
   domain format different from The Bluebook's, observe the
   jurisdiction's format. See Bluebook Rule 10.3.3.

The following examples are from jurisdictions that have adopted a
public domain format slightly different from The Bluebook's:

North Dakota Court of Appeals
   City of Bismark v. Glass, 1998 ND App 1, ¶ 7, 581 N.W.2d
   474,475. –Pinpoint Citation.
Oklahoma Court of Civil Appeals
   Brown v. NCI, Inc., 2000 OK CIV APP 78, ¶ 5, 8 P.3d 195, 196.
   –Pinpoint Citation.
Oklahoma Court of Criminal Appeals

In law review footnotes, the titles of books and the names of cases, except for procedural
phrases, are not underlined. See Bluebook Rule 2.1(a). Further, the following are in large
and small capitals: codes, restatements, standards, constitutions, periodicals, authors of
books, titles of books, the abbreviated names of codes, most legislative materials except for
bills and resolutions, codified ordinances, model codes, court rules, and sentencing guidelines.
Refer to The Bluebook.

State v. McNeal, 2000 OK CR 13, ¶ 10, 6 P.3d 1055,1057.
–Pinpoint Citation.

Pennsylvania Superior Court

Taylor v. Solberg, 2000 PA Super 262, ¶ 15, 740 A.2d 735, 737.
–Pinpoint Citation.

Utah Court of Appeals

State v. Tryba, 2000 UT App 230, ¶ 8, P.3d 274, 277. –Pinpoint
Citation.

Wisconsin Court of Appeals

State v. Phillips, 2000 WI App 184, ¶ 10, 617 N.W.2d 522, 525.
–Pinpoint Citation.

United States Court of Appeals for the Sixth Circuit

Dorris v. Absher, 1999 FED App. 0200P, at 6, 179 F.3d 420, 425
(6th Cir.). –Pinpoint Citation.

The following examples are from jurisdictions that have adopted a
public domain format markedly different from The Bluebook's:

Louisiana

Taylor v. Sider, 99-2521, p. 3 (La. App. 4 Cir. 5/31/00), 765 So.
2d 416, 419. –Page Citation.

In re Carreras, 2000-1094, p. 3 (La. 6/16/00), 765 So. 2d 321, 323.
–Page Citation.

Mississippi

Woodard v. State, 98-KA-01768-COA, ¶ 12, 765 So. 2d 573, 575
(Miss. Ct. App. 2000). –Pinpoint Citation.

Grant v. Grant, 99-CA-00736-SCT, ¶ 6, 765 So. 2d 1263,1266
(Miss. 2000). –Pinpoint Citation.

New Mexico

State v. Cleave, 2000-NMCA-071, ¶ 7, 8 P.3d 157, 159.
–Pinpoint Citation.

In re Dawson, 2000-NMSC-024, ¶ 11, 8 P.3d 856, 859. –Pinpoint
Citation.

–For additional information concerning public domain citation, consult
the ABA at http://www.abanet.org, the American Association of Law
Libraries Citation Format Committee at
http://www.aallnet.org/committee/citation, pertinent state and federal
court web sites, and The Bluebook at http://www.legalbluebook.com.

Public Interest, The
    Ab.:   Pub. Interest

In citing cases in law review footnotes, abbreviate any word listed in Table T.6;
the names of "states, countries, and other geographical units" unless they are named parties;
and any other words of eight or more letters "if substantial space is thereby saved and the
result is unambiguous." Bluebook Rule 10.2.2. On the other hand, in citing cases in text,
abbreviate only widely known acronyms and the following words: "&," "Ass'n," "Bros.,"
"Co.," "Corp.," "Inc.," "Ltd.," and "No." Bluebook Rule 10.2.1(c).

Ex.: Irwin M. Stelzer, <u>What Thatcher Wrought</u>, Pub. Interest, Spring 1992, at 18. –Article Citation.

Irwin M. Stelzer, <u>What Thatcher Wrought</u>, Pub. Interest, Spring 1992, at 18, 39-40. –Page Citation.

Public Land Law Review
Ab.: Pub. Land L. Rev.

Ex.: Matthew J. McKinney, <u>Instream Flow Policy in Montana: A History and Blueprint for the Future</u>, 11 Pub. Land L. Rev. 81 (1990). –Article Citation.

Matthew J. McKinney, <u>Instream Flow Policy in Montana: A History and Blueprint for the Future</u>, 11 Pub. Land L. Rev. 81, 98-99 (1990). –Page Citation.

Public Law
Ab.: Pub. L.

Ex.: Itzhak Zamir, <u>Courts and Politics in Israel</u>, Pub. L., 1991, at 523. –Article Citation.

Itzhak Zamir, <u>Courts and Politics in Israel</u>, Pub. L., 1991, at 523, 529-30. –Page Citation.

Public Laws (U.S.)
Ab.: Pub. L.

Ex.: Act of Jan. 23, 1995, Pub. L. No. 104-1, 109 Stat. 3. –Act Citation.

Act of Jan. 23, 1995, Pub. L. No. 104-1, § 101, 109 Stat. 3. –Section Citation.

Public Laws of Rhode Island and Providence Plantations
Ab.: year R.I. Pub. Laws

Ex.: Act of July 11, 1994, ch. 303, 1994-3 R.I. Pub. Laws 1247. –Citation to an entire session law.

Act of July 11, 1994, ch. 303, sec. 1, § 11-34-8.1, 1994-3 R.I. Pub. Laws 1247, 1247. –Citation to a section of a session law.

–Identifying information may be added parenthetically according to <u>Bluebook</u> Rule 12.4(a).

Public Utilities Fortnightly
Ab.: Pub. Util. Fort.

Ex.: Robert D. Rosenberg, <u>Reducing Coal Transportation Costs</u>, Pub. Util. Fort., Oct. 11, 1990, at 31. –Article Citation.

Robert D. Rosenberg, <u>Reducing Coal Transportation Costs</u>, Pub. Util. Fort., Oct. 11, 1990, at 31, 35. –Page Citation.

Public Utilities Reports (PUR)
Ab.: Pub. Util. Rep.

In law review footnotes, the titles of books and the names of cases, except for procedural phrases, are not underlined. <u>See</u> <u>Bluebook</u> Rule 2.1(a). Further, the following are in large and small capitals: codes, restatements, standards, constitutions, periodicals, authors of books, titles of books, the abbreviated names of codes, most legislative materials except for bills and resolutions, codified ordinances, model codes, court rules, and sentencing guidelines. Refer to <u>The Bluebook</u>.

Ex.:   Re Transition to Competition in the Local Exchange Market, 171 Pub.
        Util. Rep. 4th 30 (N.Y. Pub. Serv. Comm'n 1996).

Publishing, Entertainment, Advertising & Allied Fields Law Quarterly
Ab.:   Pub. Ent. Advert. & Allied Fields L.Q.
Ex.:   Andrew E. Clark, The Trouble With T-Shirts: Merchandise
        Bootlegging in the Music Industry, 21 Pub. Ent. Advert. & Allied
        Fields L.Q. 323 (1983). –Article Citation.

        Andrew E. Clark, The Trouble With T-Shirts: Merchandise
        Bootlegging in the Music Industry, 21 Pub. Ent. Advert. & Allied
        Fields L.Q. 323, 327-330 (1983). –Page Citation.

Puerto Rico Constitution
Ab.:   P.R. Const. art. , § .
Ex.:   P.R. Const. art. II, § 14. –"Cite constitutional provisions currently in
        force without date." Bluebook Rule 11.

        P.R. Const. art. VII, § 3 (amended 1953). –"When citing a provision
        that has been subsequently amended, either indicate parenthetically the
        fact and date of amendment or cite the amending provision in full."
        Bluebook Rule 11.

Puerto Rico Laws
        See Laws of Puerto Rico

Puerto Rico Supreme Court
Ab.:   P.R.
        –Cite to P.R.R. (to 1978) or P.R. Offic. Trans. (from 1978) if therein;
        cite also to P.R. Dec. or P.R. Sent., in that order of preference:
            Ortiz v. Valdejully, 20 P.R. Offic. Trans. 1, 120 P.R. Dec. 1
            (1987). –Case Citation.
            Ortiz v. Valdejully, 20 P.R. Offic. Trans. 1, 4, 120 P.R. Dec. 1, 4
            (1987). –Page Citation.
        –The Puerto Rico Supreme Court also began assigning a public domain
        citation for its decisions effective January 1, 1998, which is the proper
        citation of the case until published in P.R. Dec., Puerto Rico's official
        reporter.
            Reyes v. Estado Libre Asociado de P.R., 2000 TSPR 49. –Case
            Citation. (in Spanish)
            Reyes v. Estado Libre Asociado de P.R., 2000 PRSC 49. –Case
            Citation. (in English)
        See Bluebook Rule Table T.1, p.244; see also Res. of the P.R. Sup. Ct.,
        June 1, 1999.

Purdon's Pennsylvania Consolidated Statutes Annotated
Ab.:   x Pa. Cons. Stat. Ann. § (West year)

In citing cases in law review footnotes, abbreviate any word listed in Table T.6;
the names of "states, countries, and other geographical units" unless they are named parties;
and any other words of eight or more letters "if substantial space is thereby saved and the
result is unambiguous." Bluebook Rule 10.2.2. On the other hand, in citing cases in text,
abbreviate only widely known acronyms and the following words: "&," "Ass'n," "Bros.,"
"Co.," "Corp.," "Inc.," "Ltd.," and "No." Bluebook Rule 10.2.1(c).

Ex.: 35 Pa. Cons. Stat. Ann. § 7312 (West 1993).

35 Pa. Cons. Stat. Ann. § 7312 (West Supp. 1996).

–At the publication date of this book, Pennsylvania is undertaking its first official codification, Pennsylvania Consolidated Statutes. The old, unofficial compilation is Purdon's Pennsylvania Statutes Annotated, which uses a different numbering system. Purdon is also reprinting the new, official codification as Purdon's Pennsylvania Consolidated Statutes Annotated, which is currently bound with Purdon's Pennsylvania Statutes Annotated. Cite to Pennsylvania Consolidated Statutes or Purdon's Pennsylvania Consolidated Statutes Annotated, in that order of preference. If the statute is contained in neither source, cite to Purdon's Pennsylvania Statutes Annotated (See Bluebook Rule 12.3.1(h)). See Bluebook Table T.1, p. 228.

Purdon's Pennsylvania Legislative Service (West)
Ab.: year Pa. Legis. Serv. (West)

Ex.: Health Security Act, No. 1996-85, 1996 Pa. Legis. Serv. 366 (West) (providing for certain health insurance benefits following the birth of a child). –Citation to an entire session law with a popular name.

Health Security Act, No. 1996-85, 1996 Pa. Legis. Serv. sec. 2, 366 (West). –Citation to a section of a session law with a popular name.

Purdon's Pennsylvania Statutes Annotated
Form: Pa. Stat. Ann. tit. x, § (West year)

Ex.: Pa. Stat. Ann. tit. 40, § 72 (West 1999).

Pa. Stat. Ann. tit. 63, § 456.04 (West Supp. 2000).

– At the publication date of this book, Pennsylvania is undertaking its first official codification, Pennsylvania Consolidated Statutes, the old, unofficial compilation entitled Purdon's Pennsylvania Statutes Annotated, which uses a different numbering system. Purdon is also reprinting the new, official codification as Pennsylvania's Consolidated Statutes Annotated, which is currently bound with Pennsylvania Statutes Annotated. Cite to Pennsylvania Consolidated Statutes or Pennsylvania Statutes Annotated, in that order of preference. If the statute is contained in neither source, cit to Pennsylvania Statutes Annotated (See Bluebook Rule 12.3.1(h)). See Bluebook Table T.1, p. 228.

In law review footnotes, the titles of books and the names of cases, except for procedural phrases, are not underlined. See Bluebook Rule 2.1(a). Further, the following are in large and small capitals: codes, restatements, standards, constitutions, periodicals, authors of books, titles of books, the abbreviated names of codes, most legislative materials except for bills and resolutions, codified ordinances, model codes, court rules, and sentencing guidelines. Refer to The Bluebook.

Q

Quarterly Journal
    Ab.:   Q. J.
    Ex.:   Ballard C. Gilmore, <u>Recent Corporate Decisions</u>, 11 Q.J. 43 (1991).
          –Article Citation.
          Ballard C. Gilmore, <u>Recent Corporate Decisions</u>, 11 Q.J. 43, 44 (1991).
          –Page Citation.

Quarterly Report of the Attorney General (Alabama)
    Ab.:   Ala. Q. Rep. Att'y Gen.
    <u>See</u> Opinions of the Attorney General of Alabama.

Queen's Law Journal
    Ab.:   Queen's L.J.
    Ex.:   Nicholas Bala, <u>Double Victims: Child Sexual Abuse and the Canadian
          Criminal Justice System</u>, 15 Queen's L.J. 3 (1990). –Article Citation.
          Nicholas Bala, <u>Double Victims: Child Sexual Abuse and the Canadian
          Criminal Justice System</u>, 15 Queen's L.J. 3, 22 (1990). –Page Citation.

Queensland Lawyer (Australia) (1973-date)
    Ab.:   Q. Law.
    Ex.:   <u>Jameson v. Smith</u>, 11 Q. Law. 47, (1989).

Queensland Reports (Australia) (1958-date)
    Ab.:   Q.R.
    Ex.:   <u>Sprenger v. Sanderson</u>,[1992] 1 Q.R. 580, 581 (1991) (Austl.).

Queensland State Reports (Australia) (1902-1957)
    Ab.:   Q. St. R.
    Ex.:   <u>Horton v. Byrne</u>, 1957 Q. St. R. 1, 7-9 (Austl.).

Queensland Supreme Court Reports (Australia) (1860-date)
    Ab.:   Q.S. Ct. R.
    Ex.:   <u>Miskin v. Hutchinson</u>, 5 Q.S. Ct. R. 85, 89 (1868).

quotations
          –Details for quotations are explained and illustrated in <u>Bluebook</u>
          Rule 5.

In law review footnotes, the titles of books and the names of cases, except for procedural phrases, are not underlined. <u>See</u> <u>Bluebook</u> Rule 2.1(a). Further, the following are in large and small capitals: codes, restatements, standards, constitutions, periodicals, authors of books, titles of books, the abbreviated names of codes, most legislative materials except for bills and resolutions, codified ordinances, model codes, court rules, and sentencing guidelines. Refer to <u>The Bluebook</u>.

quoted in
  Ex.:

> "As Wigmore notes sequestration 'already had in English practice an
> independent and continuous existence, even in the time of those earlier
> modes of trial which preceded the jury and were a part of our
> inheritance of the common Germanic law.' VI <u>Wigmore on Evidence</u>
> § 1837 at 348 (3rd 1940), <u>quoted in</u> <u>Geders v. United States</u>, 425 U.S.
> 80, 87, 96 S. Ct. 1330, 1334, 47 L. Ed. 2d 592 (1976). The rule serves
> two salutary purposes: (1) it prevents witnesses from tailoring
> testimony . . ." –Taken from 675 F.2d 825, 835 (1982).

quoting
  Ex.:

Ted J. Fiflis, <u>Soft Information: The SEC's Former Exogeneous Zone</u>,
26 UCLA L. Rev. 95, 116, n.71 (1978) ("A fact is material if there is a
substantial likelihood that a reasonable shareholder would consider it
important in deciding how to vote.")
(quoting <u>TSC Indus. v. Northway</u>, 426 U.S. 438, 449 (1976)).

In citing cases in law review footnotes, abbreviate any word listed in Table T.6;
the names of "states, countries, and other geographical units" unless they are named parties;
and any other words of eight or more letters "if <u>substantial</u> space is thereby saved and the
result is unambiguous." <u>Bluebook</u> Rule 10.2.2. On the other hand, in citing cases in text,
abbreviate only widely known acronyms and the following words: "&," "Ass'n," "Bros.,"
"Co.," "Corp.," "Inc.," "Ltd.," and "No." <u>Bluebook</u> Rule 10.2.1(c).

R

Rabkin & Johnson's Current Legal Forms with Tax Analysis
See Current Legal Forms with Tax Analysis, by Jacob Rabkin & Mark H. Johnson

RAND Journal of Economics, The
Ab.: RAND J. Econ.
Ex.: E. Nosal, <u>Renegotiating Incomplete Contracts</u>, 23 RAND J. Econ. 20 (1992). –Article Citation.
E. Nosal, <u>Renegotiating Incomplete Contracts</u>, 23 RAND J. Econ. 20, 21 (1992). –Page Citation.

Real Estate Commission
Ab.: Real Est. Comm'n

Real Estate Law Journal
Ab.: Real Est. L.J.
Ex.: Harvey Boneparth, <u>Taking a Deed in Lieu of Foreclosure: Pitfalls for the Lender</u>, 19 Real Est. L.J. 338 (1991). –Article Citation.
Harvey Boneparth, <u>Taking a Deed in Lieu of Foreclosure: Pitfalls for the Lender</u>, 19 Real Est. L.J. 338, 340-41 (1991). –Page Citation.

Real Property, Probate and Trust Journal
Ab.: Real Prop. Prob. & Tr. J.
Ex.: Jean A. Mortland, <u>Attorneys as Real Estate Brokers: Ethical Considerations</u>, 25 Real Prop. Prob. & Tr. J. 755 (1991). –Article Citation.
Jean A. Mortland, <u>Attorneys as Real Estate Brokers: Ethical Considerations</u>, 25 Real Prop. Prob. & Tr. J. 755, 759-63 (1991). –Page Citation.

record (court)–citation to
See <u>Bluebook</u> Rule 10.8.3.

Recueil Dalloz, Jurisprudence (France) (1945-64)
Ab.: D. Jur.
Ex.: Cass. 2e civ. Mar. 6, 1961 Recueil Dalloz, Jurisprudence [D. Jur.], 1961, 322 (Fr.).
See <u>Bluebook</u> Rule 20.1.3 and Table T.2.

In law review footnotes, the titles of books and the names of cases, except for procedural phrases, are not underlined. See <u>Bluebook</u> Rule 2.1(a). Further, the following are in large and small capitals: codes, restatements, standards, constitutions, periodicals, authors of books, titles of books, the abbreviated names of codes, most legislative materials except for bills and resolutions, codified ordinances, model codes, court rules, and sentencing guidelines. Refer to <u>The Bluebook</u>.

Recueil Dalloz-Sirey, Jurisprudence (France)
Ab.: D.
Ex.: Cass. 3e civ., Apr. 17, 1984, Recueil Dalloz-Sirey, Jurisprudence [D.] 1985, 234, note Najjar (Fr.).
See Bluebook Rule 20.1.3 and Table T.2.

Referee
Ab.: Ref.

Regent University Law Review
Ab.: Regent U. L. Rev.
Ex.: Herbert W. Titus, Public School Chaplains: Constitutional Solution to the School Prayer Controversy, 1 Regent U. L. Rev. 19 (1991). —Article Citation.
Herbert W. Titus, Public School Chaplains: Constitutional Solution to the School Prayer Controversy, 1 Regent U. L. Rev. 19, 21-23 (1991). —Page Citation.

Regulations of Connecticut State Agencies
Ab.: Conn. Agencies Regs. § (year)
Ex.: Conn. Agencies Regs. § 21a-29-2 (1984)

related authority
See cited in
construed in
quoted in
quoting
reprinted in.

Reorganization Plans (U.S.)
Ab.: Reorg. Plan No. # of year
Ex.: Reorg. Plan No. 1 of 1978, 43 Fed. Reg. 19,807. —Citation to material not yet available in the Code of Federal Regulations.
Reorg. Plan No. 3 of 1970, 3 C.F.R. 199 (1970).

In citing cases in law review footnotes, abbreviate any word listed in Table T.6; the names of "states, countries, and other geographical units" unless they are named parties; and any other words of eight or more letters "if substantial space is thereby saved and the result is unambiguous." Bluebook Rule 10.2.2. On the other hand, in citing cases in text, abbreviate only widely known acronyms and the following words: "&," "Ass'n," "Bros.," "Co.," "Corp.," "Inc.," "Ltd.," and "No." Bluebook Rule 10.2.1(c).

Reorg. Plan No. 1 of 1967, 3 C.F.R. 220 (1969), reprinted in 5 U.S.C. app. at 822 (1976) (repealed 1978). –Citation if the plan is reprinted in U.S.C., U.S.C.A., or U.S.C.S. In this example, the repeal of the plan is noted parenthetically.

Reorg. Plan No. 4 of 1978, 3 C.F.R. 332 (1979), reprinted in 5 U.S.C. app. at 412 (Supp. IV 1980) and in 92 Stat. 3790 (1978). –Citation with optional parallel reference to a printing in Statutes at Large.

replacement
Ab.:   repl.

Report of Cases before the Court of Justice of the European Communities
Ab.:   E.C.R.
Ex.:   Case C-244/89, Commission v. France, 1991 E.C.R. I-163. –Case Citation. See Bluebook Rule 21.5.2 and Table T.3: Intergovernmental Organizations.

Reports, Congressional
See Congressional Reports

Reports of Patent Cases (England) (1884-1885)
See Bluebook Table T.2. See also Reports of Patent, Design and Trademark cases.
Ab.:   R.P.C.
Ex.:   Lister v. Norton Bros. & Co., 2 R.P.C. 68 (Ch. 1885) (Eng.).
          –Case Citation.

Reports of Patent, Design, and Trade Mark Cases (England) (1884-date)
See Bluebook Table T.2.
Ab.:   R.P.D.T.M.C./R.P.C.
Ex.:   Duracell International Inc. v. Ever Ready Ltd., 106 R.P.D.T.M.C./R.P.C. 731 (Ch. 1989) (Eng.).
          –Note: These reporters are still designated "Reports of Patent Cases" on the outside cover.

Reports of the United States Board of Tax Appeals
Ab.:   B.T.A.
Ex.:   Boeing v. Commissioner, 46 B.T.A. 492 (1942).

Reports of the United States Tax Court
Ab.:   T.C.
Ex.:   Miller v. Commissioner, 104 T.C. 330 (1995).

Representative
Ab.:   Rep.

In law review footnotes, the titles of books and the names of cases, except for procedural phrases, are not underlined. See Bluebook Rule 2.1(a). Further, the following are in large and small capitals: codes, restatements, standards, constitutions, periodicals, authors of books, titles of books, the abbreviated names of codes, most legislative materials except for bills and resolutions, codified ordinances, model codes, court rules, and sentencing guidelines. Refer to The Bluebook.

reprint
    Ex.:   1 William Blackstone, <u>Commentaries</u> *35 (photo reprint 1979) (1765-1769).

reprinted in
    Ex.:   <u>United States Policy on Nonrecognition of Communist China</u>, 39 Dep't St. Bull. 385 (1958), <u>reprinted in</u> William W. Bishop, <u>International Law Cases and Materials</u> 351-54 (3d ed. 1962).

           S. Rep. No. 368, 96th Cong., 1st Sess. 4-5, <u>reprinted in</u> 1980 U.S.C.C.A.N. 236, 239-41.

Res Gestae
    Ab.:   Do not abbreviate title.
    Ex.:   Donald P. Bogard & Kenneth R. Yahne, <u>Corporate Pro Bono: Models for Replication</u>, 35 Res Gestae 508 (1992). –Article Citation.

           Donald P. Bogard & Kenneth R. Yahne, <u>Corporate Pro Bono: Models for Replication</u>, 35 Res Gestae 508, 512 (1992). –Page Citation.

Research in Law and Economics
    Ab.:   Res. L. & Econ.
    Ex.:   Victor P. Goldberg, <u>The International Salt Puzzle</u>, 14 Res. L. & Econ. 31 (1991). –Article Citation.

           Victor P. Goldberg, <u>The International Salt Puzzle</u>, 14 Res. L. & Econ. 31, 45-47 (1991). –Page Citation.

Resolutions, Congressional
    <u>See</u> Congressional Resolutions

Restatement (Second) of Agency (ALI)
    Ab.:   Restatement (Second) of Agency § ___ (year)
    Ex.:   Restatement (Second) of Agency § 84 cmt. b & c (1957).
           –Citation for Comment.
           Restatement (Second) of Agency § 15 app. (2000).
           –Citation for Agency Appendix.

Restatement (Third) of Agency (ALI)
    Ab.:   Restatement (Third) of Agency § ___ (Tentative Draft No. ___, year)
    Ex.:   Restatement (Third) of Agency § 1.03 (Tentative Draft No. 1, 2000).

Restatement of Conflict of Laws (ALI)
    Ab.:   Restatement of Conflict of Laws § ___ (year)
    Ex.:   Restatement of Conflict of Laws § 168 (1934).
           Restatement of Conflict of Laws § 288 reporter's note (1971).
           Restatement of Conflict of Laws § 115 cmt. e, illus. 4 (1969).

In citing cases in law review footnotes, abbreviate any word listed in Table T.6; the names of "states, countries, and other geographical units" unless they are named parties; and any other words of eight or more letters "if <u>substantial</u> space is thereby saved and the result is unambiguous." <u>Bluebook</u> Rule 10.2.2. On the other hand, in citing cases in text, abbreviate only widely known acronyms and the following words: "&," "Ass'n," "Bros.," "Co.," "Corp.," "Inc.," "Ltd.," and "No." <u>Bluebook</u> Rule 10.2.1(c).

Restatement (Second) of Conflict of Laws (ALI)

Ab.: Restatement (Second) of Conflict of Laws § ___ (year)

Ex.: Restatement (Second) of Conflict of Laws § 103 (1969).

Restatement (Second) of Conflict of Laws § 288 reporter's note (1971).

Restatement (Second) of Conflict of Laws § 115 cmt. e, illus. 4 (1969).

Restatement of Contracts (ALI)

Ab.: Restatement of Contracts § ___ (year)

Ex.: Restatement of Contracts § 405(1) (1932).

Restatement (Second) of Contracts (ALI)

Ab.: Restatement (Second) of Contracts § ___ (year)

Ex.: Restatement (Second) of Contracts § 272(1) & cmt. a (1979).

Restatement (Second) of Contracts § 1 app. (1997).

Restatement of Foreign Relations Law of the United States (ALI)

Ab.: Restatement of Foreign Relations Law of the United States § ___ (year)

Restatement (Second) of Foreign Relations Law of the United States (ALI)

Ab.: Restatement (Second) of Foreign Relations Law of the United States § ___ (year)

Ex.: Restatement (Second) of Foreign Relations Law of the United States § 41 (1965).

Restatement (Third) of Foreign Relations Law of the United States (ALI)

Ab.: Restatement (Third) of Foreign Relations Law of the United States § ___ (year)

Ex.: Restatement (Third) of Foreign Relations Law of the United States § 210 (1986).

Restatement (Third) of Foreign Relations Law of the United States § 210 reporter's note 3 (1986).

Restatement (Third) of Foreign Relations Law of the United States § 223 (Supp. 2000).

Restatement (Second) of Judgments (ALI)

Ab.: Restatement (Second) of Judgments § ___ (year)

Ex.: Restatement (Second) of Judgments § 4 (1980).

Restatement (Second) of Judgments § 28 (Supp. 2000).

Restatement (Third) of The Law Governing Lawyers(ALI)

Ab.: Restatement (Third) of The Law Governing Lawyers § ___ (year)

Ex.: Restatement (Third) of The Law Governing Lawyers § 1 (1998).

Restatement (Third) of The Law Governing Lawyers § 1 cmt. h (1998).

In law review footnotes, the titles of books and the names of cases, except for procedural phrases, are not underlined. See Bluebook Rule 2.1(a). Further, the following are in large and small capitals: codes, restatements, standards, constitutions, periodicals, authors of books, titles of books, the abbreviated names of codes, most legislative materials except for bills and resolutions, codified ordinances, model codes, court rules, and sentencing guidelines. Refer to The Bluebook.

Restatement of Property (ALI)

Ab.:   Restatement of Property § ___ (year)

Ex.:   Restatement of Property § 154 cmt. dd (Supp. 1992).

Restatement (Second) of Property (ALI)

Ab.:   Restatement (Second) of Property: subdivision § ___ (year)

Ex.:   Restatement (Second) of Property: Donative Transfers § 25.2 (1987).
Restatement (Second) of Property: Donative Transfers § 34.7 (1991).
Restatement (Second) of Property: Landlord & Tenant § 4.4 (Supp. 2000).

Restatement (Third) of Property (ALI)

Ab.:   Restatement (Third) of Property: subdivision § ___ (year)

Ex.:   Restatement (Third) of Property: Donative Transfers § 2.2 (1996).

Restatement (Third) of Property (ALI, Tentative Draft)

Ab.:   Restatement (Third) of Property: subdivision § ___ (Tentative Draft No. __, year)

Ex.:   Restatement (Third) of Property: Mortgages § 1.6 (Tentative Draft No. 5, 1996).

Restatement of Restitution (ALI)

Ab.:   Restatement of Restitution § ___ (year)

Ex.:   Restatement of Restitution § 189 cmt. a (1936).

Restatement (Second) of Restitution (ALI)

Ab.:   Restatement (Second) of Restitution § ___ (year)

Ex.:   Restatement (Second) of Restitution § 3 (Supp. 2000).

Restatement (Second) of Restitution (ALI, Tentative Draft)

Ab.:   Restatement (Second) of Restitution § ___ (Tentative Draft No.___, year)

Ex.:   Restatement (Second) of Restitution § 31 (Tentative Draft No. 2, 1984).
Restatement (Second) of Restitution § 46 cmt. a (Preliminary Draft No. 4, 1985).

Restatement (Third) of Restitution and Unjust Enrichment (ALI, Discussion Draft)

Ab.:   Restatement (Third) of Restitution and Unjust Enrichment § ___ (Discussion Draft No.___, year)

Ex.:   Restatement (Third) of Restitution and Unjust Enrichment § 16 (Discussion Draft, 1988).

Restatement of Security (ALI)

Ab.:   Restatement of Security § ___ (year)

In citing cases in law review footnotes, abbreviate any word listed in Table T.6; the names of "states, countries, and other geographical units" unless they are named parties; and any other words of eight or more letters "if substantial space is thereby saved and the result is unambiguous." Bluebook Rule 10.2.2. On the other hand, in citing cases in text, abbreviate only widely known acronyms and the following words: "&," "Ass'n," "Bros.," "Co.," "Corp.," "Inc.," "Ltd.," and "No." Bluebook Rule 10.2.1(c).

Ex.:   Restatement of Security § 50 (1996).
         Restatement of Security § 25 (Supp. 2000).

Restatement (Third) of Suretyship (ALI, Tentative Draft)
Ab.:   Restatement (Third) of Suretyship and Guaranty § ___ (year)
Ex.:   Restatement (Third) of Suretyship and Guaranty § 24 (1995).
         Restatement (Third) of Suretyship and Guaranty § 65 reporter's note (1995).
         Restatement (Third) of Suretyship and Guaranty § 60 cmt. a, illus. 4 (1995).

Restatement of Torts (ALI)
Ab.:   Restatement of Torts § ___ (year)
Ex.:   Restatement of Torts § 282 (1934).

Restatement (Second) of Torts (ALI)
Ab.:   Restatement (Second) of Torts § _____ (year)
Ex.:   Restatement (Second) of Torts § 402 (Supp. 2000).
         Restatement (Second) of Torts § 481 app. (Supp. 1995)
         –Citation for Torts Appendix Supplement.

Restatement (Third) of Torts: Products Liability (ALI, Tentative Draft)
Ab.:   Restatement (Third) of Torts: Products Liability § ____ (Tentative Draft No. ___, year)
Ex.:   Restatement (Third) of Torts: Products Liability § 2 (Tentative Draft No. 1, 1994).
         Restatement (Third) of Torts: Products Liability § 4 cmt. a (Tentative Draft No. 1, 1994).

Restatement (Third) of Torts: Products Liability (ALI)
Ab.:   Restatement (Third) of Torts: Products Liability § ____ (year)
Ex.:   Restatement (Third) of Torts: Products Liability § 19 (1997).
         Restatement (Third) of Torts: Products Liability § 20 cmt. g (1997).

Restatement (Second) of Trusts (ALI)
Ab.:   Restatement (Second) of Trusts § ___ (year)
Ex.:   Restatement (Second) of Trusts § 158 (1957).
         Restatement (Second) of Trusts § 2 app. (1987). –Citation for Trusts Appendix.
         Restatement (Second) of Trusts § 1 app. (Supp. 2000). –Citation for Trusts Appendix Supplement.

Restatement (Third) of Trusts (Prudent Investor Rule) (ALI)
Ab.:   Restatement (Third) of Trusts, Prudent Investor Rule § ___ (year)

In law review footnotes, the titles of books and the names of cases, except for procedural phrases, are not underlined. See Bluebook Rule 2.1(a). Further, the following are in large and small capitals: codes, restatements, standards, constitutions, periodicals, authors of books, titles of books, the abbreviated names of codes, most legislative materials except for bills and resolutions, codified ordinances, model codes, court rules, and sentencing guidelines. Refer to The Bluebook.

Ex.:   Restatement (Third) of Trusts, Prudent Investor Rule § 227 (1992).

Restatement (Third) of Trusts (ALI, Tentative Draft)
Ab.:   Restatement (Third) of Trusts § ___ (Tentative Draft No. ____, year)
Ex.:   Restatement (Third) of Trusts § 12 (Tentative Draft No. 1, 1996).

Restatement (Third) of Unfair Competition (ALI)
Ab.:   Restatement (Third) of Unfair Competition § ____ (year)
Ex.:   Restatement (Third) of Unfair Competition § 36 (1995).
       Restatement (Third) of Unfair Competition § 27 cmt. c, illus. 1 (1995).
       Restatement (Third) of Unfair Competition § 742 (Supp. 2000).

Revenue Procedures
Ab.:   Rev. Proc.
Ex.:   Rev. Proc. 92-43, 1992-23 I.R.B. 23. –Citation to a Revenue
       Proceeding not yet available in bound form.
       Rev. Proc. 91-11, 1991-1 C.B. 470. –Bound.

Revenue Rulings
Ab.:   Rev. Rul.
Ex.:   Rev. Rul. 96-33, 1996-27 I.R.B. 4. –Citation to a Revenue Ruling not
       yet available in bound form.
       Rev. Rul. 95-45, 1995-1 C.B. 53. –Bound.

reversed
Ab.:   rev'd
Ex.:   Young v. Edgcomb Steel Co., 363 F. Supp. 961 (M.D.N.C. 1973),
       rev'd, 499 F.2d 97 (4th Cir. 1974).
       Griggs v. Duke Power Co., 420 F.2d 1225 (4th Cir. 1970), rev'd in part,
       401 U.S. 424 (1971).
       Karlen v. Harris, 590 F.2d 39 (2d Cir. 1978), rev'd sub nom. Stryker's
       Bay Neighborhood Council v. Karlen, 444 U.S. 223 (1980). –Citation
       if the case has a different name on appeal.

Review of Litigation, The
Ab.:   Rev. Litig.
Ex.:   Alan B. Rich, Certified Pleadings: Interpreting Texas Rule 13 in Light
       of Federal Rule 11, 11 Rev. Litig. 59 (1991). –Article Citation.
       Alan B. Rich, Certified Pleadings: Interpreting Texas Rule 13 in Light
       of Federal Rule 11, 11 Rev. Litig. 59, 69-72 (1991). –Page Citation.

Review of Socialist Law
Ab.:   Rev. Socialist L.

In citing cases in law review footnotes, abbreviate any word listed in Table T.6;
the names of "states, countries, and other geographical units" unless they are named parties;
and any other words of eight or more letters "if substantial space is thereby saved and the
result is unambiguous." Bluebook Rule 10.2.2. On the other hand, in citing cases in text,
abbreviate only widely known acronyms and the following words: "&," "Ass'n," "Bros.,"
"Co.," "Corp.," "Inc.," "Ltd.," and "No." Bluebook Rule 10.2.1(c).

Ex.: George Ginsburgs, <u>The USSR and the Socialist Model of International Cooperation in Criminal Matters</u>, 17 Rev. Socialist L. 199 (1991). –Article Citation.

George Ginsburgs, <u>The USSR and the Socialist Model of International Cooperation in Criminal Matters</u>, 17 Rev. Socialist L. 199, 250-54 (1991). –Page Citation.

Review of Taxation of Individuals, The
Ab.: Rev. Tax'n Individuals
Ex.: Rolf Auster, <u>Tax Accounting</u>, 16 Rev. Tax'n Individuals 274 (1992). –Article Citation.

Rolf Auster, <u>Tax Accounting</u>, 16 Rev. Tax'n Individuals 274, 275-77 (1992). –Page Citation.

revised
Ab.: rev.

Revised Code of Washington
Ab.: Wash. Rev. Code § (year)
Ex.: Wash. Rev. Code § 26.33.120(1) (1996).

Revised Code of Washington Annotated (West)
Ab.: Wash. Rev. Code Ann. § (West year)
Ex.: Wash. Rev. Code Ann. § 9A.52.070 (West 2000).
Wash. Rev. Code Ann. § 25.05.125 (West Supp. 2000).
–"Cite to Washington Revised Code if therein." <u>Bluebook</u> Table T.1, p. 239.

Revised Model Business Corporation Act (ABA)
<u>See</u> American Bar Association Revised Model Business Corporation Act

Revised Ordinances of the Northwest Territories (Canada)
See <u>Bluebook</u> Rule 20.5.1 and Table T.2.
Ab.: R.O.N.W.T.
Ex.: Sale of Goods Ordinance, 2 R.O.N.W.T. ch. S, § 45(1) (1974) (Can.).

Revised Reports (England) (1785-1866)
<u>See</u> <u>Bluebook</u> Table T.2.
–Cite to Eng. Rep. if therein; otherwise, cite to Rev. Rep.
Ab.: Rev. Rep.
Ex.: <u>Markwell v. Markwell</u>, 145 Rev. Rep. 417 (Ch. 1864) (Eng.). –Case Citation.
<u>Parker v. Tootal</u>, 145 Rev. Rep. 91 (1865) (Eng.). –Case Citation.

In law review footnotes, the titles of books and the names of cases, except for procedural phrases, are not underlined. <u>See</u> <u>Bluebook</u> Rule 2.1(a). Further, the following are in large and small capitals: codes, restatements, standards, constitutions, periodicals, authors of books, titles of books, the abbreviated names of codes, most legislative materials except for bills and resolutions, codified ordinances, model codes, court rules, and sentencing guidelines. Refer to <u>The Bluebook</u>.

Revised Statutes of Alberta (Canada)
See Bluebook Rule 20.5.1 and Table T.2.
Ab.:   R.S.A.
Ex.:   Notaries Public Act, 5 R.S.A. ch. N-11, § 8(2) (1980) (Can.).

Revised Statutes of British Columbia (Canada)
See Bluebook Rule 20.5.1 and Table T.2.
Ab.:   R.S.B.C.
Ex.:   Power of Attorney Act, 5 R.S.B.C. ch. 334 (1979) (Can.).

Revised Statutes of Canada
See Bluebook Rule 20.5.1 and Table T.2.
Ab.:   R.S.C.
Ex.:   Bank Act, 1 R.S.C. ch. B-1, § 21(b) (1989) (Can.).

Revised Statutes of Manitoba (Canada)
See Bluebook Rule 20.5.1 and Table T.2.
Ab.:   R.S.M.
Ex.:   The Condominium Act, 1 R.S.M. ch. C-170, § 5(1) (1987) (Can.).

Revised Statutes of Nebraska
Ab.:   Neb. Rev. Stat. §   (year)
Ex.:   Neb. Rev. Stat. § 81-3435 (1999).
        Neb. Rev. Stat. § 60-3002 (Supp. 1999).

Revised Statutes of New Brunswick (Canada)
See Bluebook Rule 20.5.1 and Table T.2.
Ab.:   R.S.N.B.
Ex.:   Marine Insurance Act, 3 R.S.N.B. ch. M-1, § 21(6) (1973) (Can.).

Revised Statutes of Newfoundland (Canada)
See Bluebook Rule 20.5.1 and Table T.2.
Ab.:   NFld. R.S.
Ex.:   Newfoundland Human Rights Code, 8 Nfld. R.S. ch. 262, § 17(2) (1970) (Can.).

Revised Statutes of Nova Scotia (Canada)
See Bluebook Rule 20.5.1 and Table T.2.
Ab.:   R.S.N.S.
Ex.:   Accountant General of the Supreme Court Act, 9 R.S.N.S. ch. 1, § 30(1) (1989) (Can.).

Revised Statutes of Ontario (Canada)
See Bluebook Rule 20.5.1 and Table T.2.

In citing cases in law review footnotes, abbreviate any word listed in Table T.6; the names of "states, countries, and other geographical units" unless they are named parties; and any other words of eight or more letters "if substantial space is thereby saved and the result is unambiguous." Bluebook Rule 10.2.2. On the other hand, in citing cases in text, abbreviate only widely known acronyms and the following words: "&," "Ass'n," "Bros.," "Co.," "Corp.," "Inc.," "Ltd.," and "No." Bluebook Rule 10.2.1(c).

Ab.:   R.S.O.

Ex.:   Ontario Place Corporation Act, 5 R.S.O. ch. 353, § 10(a) (1980) (Can.).

Revised Statutes of Prince Edward Island (Canada)
See Bluebook Rule 20.5.1 and Table T.2.

Ab.:   R.S.P.E.I.

Ex.:   Lotteries Commission Act, 2 R.S.P.E.I. ch. L-17, § 4(1) (1988) (Can.).

Revised Statutes of Québec (Canada)
See Bluebook Rule 20.5.1 and Table T.2.

Ab.:   R.S.Q.

Ex.:   Lightning Rods Act, R.S.Q. ch. P-6, § 21 (1977) (Can.).

Revised Statutes of Saskatchewan (Canada)
See Bluebook Rule 20.5.1 and Table T.2.

Ab.:   R.S.S.

Ex.:   Saskatchewan Embalmers Act, 7 R.S.S. ch. S-15, § 3 (1978) (Can.).

Revised Statutes of the Yukon Territory (Canada)
See Bluebook Rule 20.5.1 and Table T.2.

Ab.:   R.S.Y.T.

Ex.:   Occupational Health and Safety Act, 2 R.S.Y.T. ch. 123, § 43 (1)
           (1986) (Can.).

Revista de Derecho Puertorriqueño
Ab.:   Rev. D.P.

Ex.:   José A. Cuevas Segarra, La Ley de Ventas Condicionales de Puerto
           Rico, Jurisprudencia, 106 Revista de Derecho Puertorriqueño [Rev.
           D.P.] 185 (1989-90). –Article Citation.

           –If desired, the original language title may be followed by a translation
           or a shortened name in English in brackets in the same typeface as the
           original. Bluebook Rules 20.1.3 and 20.6.

           –The first time a non-English language periodical is cited, use the full
           name of the publication and the abbreviation in brackets. Thereafter,
           the abbreviation, without brackets, is sufficient. Bluebook Rule 20.6.

Revista del Colegio de Abogados de Puerto Rico
Ab.:   Rev. Col. Ab. P.R.

In law review footnotes, the titles of books and the names of cases, except for procedural
phrases, are not underlined. See Bluebook Rule 2.1(a). Further, the following are in large
and small capitals: codes, restatements, standards, constitutions, periodicals, authors of
books, titles of books, the abbreviated names of codes, most legislative materials except for
bills and resolutions, codified ordinances, model codes, court rules, and sentencing guidelines.
Refer to The Bluebook.

Ex.:   Fuster, La misión de la Universidad Católica de Puerto Rico y la situación actual del país, 21 Revista de Derecho del Colegio de Abogados de Puerto Rico [Rev. Col. Ab. P.R.] 147 (1981). –Article Citation.

–If desired, the original language title may be followed by a translation or a shortened name in English in brackets in the same typeface as the original. Bluebook Rules 20.1.3 and 20.6.

Revue Critique de Droit International Privé
Ab.:   R.C.D.I.P.
Ex.:   Pierre-Yves Gautier, Les couples internationaux de concubins, 80 Revue Critique de Droit International Privé [R.C.D.I.P.] 525 (1991). –Article Citation.

–If desired, the original language title may be followed by a translation or a shortened name in English in brackets in the same typeface as the original. Bluebook Rules 20.1.3 and 20.6.

–The first time a non-English language periodical is cited, use the full name of the publication and the abbreviation in brackets. Thereafter, the abbreviation, without brackets, is sufficient. Bluebook Rule 20.6.

Revue de Droit (Université de Sherbrooke)
Ab.:   R.D.U.S.
Ex.:   Pierre F. Mercure, Principes de droit international applicables au phénomène des pluies acides, 21 Revue de Droit (Université de Sherbrooke) [R.D.U.S.] 373 (1991). –Article Citation.

–If desired, the original language title may be followed by a translation or a shortened name in English in brackets in the same typeface as the original. Bluebook Rules 20.1.3 and 20.6

–The first time a non-English language periodical is cited, use the full name of the publication and the abbreviation in brackets. Thereafter, the abbreviation, without brackets, is sufficient. Bluebook Rule 20.6.

Revue de Droit International et de Droit Comparé
Ab.:   R.D. Int'l. & D. Comp.
Ex.:   D.H. Bliesener, La compétence du CIRDI dans la pratique arbitrale, 68 Revue de Droit International et de Droit Comparé [R.D. Int'l. & D. Comp.] 95 (1991). –Article Citation.

–If desired, the original language title may be followed by a translation or a shortened name in English in brackets in the same typeface as the original. Bluebook Rules 20.1.3 and 20.6

–The first time a non-English language periodical is cited, use the full name of the publication and the abbreviation in brackets. Thereafter, the abbreviation, without brackets, is sufficient. Bluebook Rule 20.6.

In citing cases in law review footnotes, abbreviate any word listed in Table T.6; the names of "states, countries, and other geographical units" unless they are named parties; and any other words of eight or more letters "if substantial space is thereby saved and the result is unambiguous." Bluebook Rule 10.2.2. On the other hand, in citing cases in text, abbreviate only widely known acronyms and the following words: "&," "Ass'n," "Bros.," "Co.," "Corp.," "Inc.," "Ltd.," and "No." Bluebook Rule 10.2.1(c).

Revue Francaise de Droit Adminstratif
Ab.:   R. Fr. D. Admin.

Revue Générale de Droit
Ab.:   Rev. Gén.
Ex.:   Gil Rémillard, <u>Présentation du projet de Code civil du Québec</u>, 22 Revue Générale de Droit [Rev. Gén.] 5 (1991). −Article Citation.
    −If desired, the original language title may be followed by a translation or a shortened name in English in brackets in the same typeface as the original. <u>Bluebook</u> Rules 20.1.3 and 20.6.
    −The first time a non-English language periodical is cited, use the full name of the publication and the abbreviation in brackets. Thereafter, the abbreviation, without brackets, is sufficient. <u>Bluebook</u> Rule 20.6.

Revue Internationale de Droit Comparé
Ab.:   R.I.D.C.
Ex.:   Francois Rigaux, <u>La liberté de la vie privée</u>, 43 Revue Internationale de Droit Comparé [R.I.D.C.] 539 (1991). −Article Citation.
    −If desired, the original language title may be followed by a translation or a shortened name in English in brackets in the same typeface as the original. <u>Bluebook</u> Rules 20.1.3 and 20.6.
    −The first time a non-English language periodical is cited, use the full name of the publication and the abbreviation in brackets. Thereafter, the abbreviation, without brackets, is sufficient. <u>Bluebook</u> Rule 20.6.

Revue Juridique Thémis
Ab.:   R.J.T.
Ex.:   Diane L. Demers, <u>Maladies professionnelles et plausibilité biologique</u>, 25 Revue Juridique Thémis [R.J.T.] 29 (1991). −Article Citation.
    −If desired, the original language title may be followed by a translation or a shortened name in English in brackets in the same typeface as the original. <u>Bluebook</u> Rules 20.1.3 and 20.6.
    −The first time a non-English language periodical is cited, use the full name of the publication and the abbreviation in brackets. Thereafter, the abbreviation, without brackets, is sufficient. <u>Bluebook</u> Rule 20.6.

RFE/RL Research Report
Ab.:   RFE/RL Res. Rep.
Ex.:   Jan Obrman, <u>Slovak Politician Accused of Secret Police Ties</u>, RFE/RL Res. Rep., April 10, 1992, at 13. −Article Citation.
    Jan Obrman, <u>Slovak Politician Accused of Secret Police Ties</u>, RFE/RL Res. Rep., April 10, 1992, at 13, 15-16. −Page Citation.

Rhode Island Bar Journal
Ab.:   R.I. B.J.

In law review footnotes, the titles of books and the names of cases, except for procedural phrases, are not underlined. <u>See</u> <u>Bluebook</u> Rule 2.1(a). Further, the following are in large and small capitals: codes, restatements, standards, constitutions, periodicals, authors of books, titles of books, the abbreviated names of codes, most legislative materials except for bills and resolutions, codified ordinances, model codes, court rules, and sentencing guidelines. Refer to <u>The Bluebook</u>.

Ex.:   Raymond A. Marcaccio, <u>Decisions from the First Circuit: A Crisis for Victims of Age Discrimination</u>, R.I. B.J., May 1992, at 7.
–Article Citation.

Raymond A. Marcaccio, <u>Decisions from the First Circuit: A Crisis for Victims of Age Discrimination</u>, R.I. B.J., May 1992, at 7, 9-10.
–Page Citation.

Rhode Island Constitution
Ab.:   R.I. Const. art.   , §   .
Ex.:   R.I. Const. art. XII, § 1. –"Cite constitutional provisions currently in force without date." <u>Bluebook</u> Rule 11.

R.I. Const. art. I, § 9 (amended 1988). –"When citing a provision that has been subsequently amended, either indicate parenthetically the fact and date of amendment or cite the amending provision in full."
<u>Bluebook</u> Rule 11.

Rhode Island General Laws
<u>See</u> General Laws of Rhode Island

Rhode Island Reports
Ab.:   R.I.
–Discontinued in 1980 after 122 R.I. 923 (1980).
–Cite to A. or A.2d if therein; otherwise, cite to R.I.
–Give parallel citations only in documents submitted to Rhode Island state courts. (<u>Note</u>: In citing a state court case in a document submitted to a court of that same state, the 16th ed. of <u>The Bluebook</u> prescribed a parallel citation; the 17th ed. prescribes that local rules shall control, but Rhode Island has no known local rules concerning parallel citations. For the sake of continuity, we advise giving a parallel citation in documents submitted to Rhode Island state courts. <u>See</u> <u>Bluebook</u> Rule 10.3.1, Table T.1, and Practitioners' Note P.3.)
–Through 122 R.I. 923 (1980) cite as follows:
In documents submitted to Rhode Island courts:
    <u>Morgan v. Thomas</u>, 98 R.I. 204, 200 A.2d 696 (1964).
    –Case Citation.
    <u>Morgan v. Thomas</u>, 98 R.I. 204, 210, 200 A.2d 696, 699 (1964).
    –Page Citation.
In all other documents:
    <u>Morgan v. Thomas</u>, 200 A.2d 696 (R.I. 1964). –Case Citation.
    <u>Morgan v. Thomas</u>, 200 A.2d 696, 699 (R.I. 1964).
    –Page Citation.
–After 122 R.I. 923 (1980) cite as follows:

In citing cases in law review footnotes, abbreviate any word listed in Table T.6; the names of "states, countries, and other geographical units" unless they are named parties; and any other words of eight or more letters "if <u>substantial</u> space is thereby saved and the result is unambiguous." <u>Bluebook</u> Rule 10.2.2. On the other hand, in citing cases in text, abbreviate only widely known acronyms and the following words: "&," "Ass'n," "Bros.," "Co.," "Corp.," "Inc.," "Ltd.," and "No." <u>Bluebook</u> Rule 10.2.1(c).

In all documents:

Gushlaw v. Rohrbaugh, 673 A.2d 63 (R.I. 1996). –Case Citation.

Gushlaw v. Rohrbaugh, 673 A.2d 63, 64 (R.I. 1996). –Page Citation.

Rhode Island Session Laws
See Public Laws of Rhode Island and Providence Plantations.

Rocky Mountain Mineral Law Institute
Ab.:   Rocky Mtn. Min. L. Inst.

Ex.:   Thomas F. Cope, Environmental Liabilities of Non-Operating Parties, 37 Rocky Mtn. Min. L. Inst. 1-1 (1991). –Article Citation.

Thomas F. Cope, Environmental Liabilities of Non-Operating Parties, 37 Rocky Mtn. Min. L. Inst. 1-1, 1-27 (1991). –Page Citation.

Rules of Evidence and Procedure
–Use abbreviations such as those listed in Bluebook Rule 12.8.3 or those abbreviations suggested by the rules themselves.

Ex.:   Fed. R. Evid. 403.

Fed. R. Civ. P. 11.

Fed. R. Crim. P. 6.

Sup. Ct. R. 5.

Fed. R. App. P. 3.

3d Cir. R. 7(1).

Tenn. R. App. P. 6.

Rules of Habeas Procedure
See Federal Rules of Habeas Procedure.

Rules of the Court of Claims of the United States
See Court of Claims Rules.

Rules of the Supreme Court of the United States
See Supreme Court Rules.

Rules of the United States Customs Court
See Customs Court Rules.

Rutgers Computer and Technology Law Journal
Ab.:   Rutgers Computer & Tech. L.J.

Ex.:   Richard H. Stern, Copyright in Computer Programming Languages, 17 Rutgers Computer & Tech. L.J. 321 (1991). –Article Citation.

Richard H. Stern, Copyright in Computer Programming Languages, 17 Rutgers Computer & Tech. L.J. 321, 349-53 (1991). –Page Citation.

In law review footnotes, the titles of books and the names of cases, except for procedural phrases, are not underlined. See Bluebook Rule 2.1(a). Further, the following are in large and small capitals: codes, restatements, standards, constitutions, periodicals, authors of books, titles of books, the abbreviated names of codes, most legislative materials except for bills and resolutions, codified ordinances, model codes, court rules, and sentencing guidelines. Refer to The Bluebook.

Rutgers Law Journal
    Ab.:   Rutgers L.J.
    Ex.:   Robert H.A. Ashford, The Binary Economics of Louis Kelso: The
           Promise of Universal Capitalism, 22 Rutgers L.J. 3 (1990).
           –Article Citation.

           Robert H.A. Ashford, The Binary Economics of Louis Kelso: The
           Promise of Universal Capitalism, 22 Rutgers L.J. 3, 5-7 (1990).
           –Page Citation.

Rutgers Law Review
    Ab.:   Rutgers L. Rev.
    Ex.:   William G. Ross, The Ethics of Hourly Billing by Attorneys,
           44 Rutgers L. Rev. 1 (1991). –Article Citation.

           William G. Ross, The Ethics of Hourly Billing by Attorneys,
           44 Rutgers L. Rev. 1, 59-62 (1991). –Page Citation.

In citing cases in law review footnotes, abbreviate any word listed in Table T.6;
the names of "states, countries, and other geographical units" unless they are named parties;
and any other words of eight or more letters "if substantial space is thereby saved and the
result is unambiguous." Bluebook Rule 10.2.2. On the other hand, in citing cases in text,
abbreviate only widely known acronyms and the following words: "&," "Ass'n," "Bros.,"
"Co.," "Corp.," "Inc.," "Ltd.," and "No." Bluebook Rule 10.2.1(c).

S

St. John's Journal of Legal Commentary
Ab.: St. John's J. Legal Comment.
Ex.: John A. Maher & Kathryn C. Hoefer, <u>Federal Superlien: An Alternative to Lender Liability Under CERCLA</u>, 6 St. John's J. Legal Comment. 41 (1990). –Article Citation.

John A. Maher & Kathryn C. Hoefer, <u>Federal Superlien: An Alternative to Lender Liability Under CERCLA</u>, 6 St. John's J. Legal Comment. 41, 49-50 (1990). –Page Citation.

St. John's Law Review
Ab.: St. John's L. Rev.
Ex.: Peter Linzer, <u>White Liberal Looks at Racist Speech</u>, 65 St. John's L. Rev. 187 (1991). –Article Citation.

Peter Linzer, <u>White Liberal Looks at Racist Speech</u>, 65 St. John's L. Rev. 187, 188 (1991). –Page Citation.

St. Louis Bar Journal
Ab.: St. Louis B.J.
Ex.: Stephen H. Ringkamp, <u>Uninsured and Underinsured Motor Vehicle Coverage</u>, St. Louis B.J., Spring 1992, at 26. –Article Citation.

Stephen H. Ringkamp, <u>Uninsured and Underinsured Motor Vehicle Coverage</u>, St. Louis B.J., Spring 1992, at 26, 29-31. –Page Citation.

Saint Louis University Law Journal
Ab.: St. Louis U. L.J.
Ex.: Michael I. Krauss, <u>Tort Law and Private Ordering</u>, 35 St. Louis U. L.J. 623 (1991). –Article Citation.

Michael I. Krauss, <u>Tort Law and Private Ordering</u>, 35 St. Louis U. L.J. 623, 645-47 (1991). –Page Citation.

Saint Louis University Public Law Review
Ab.: St. Louis U. Pub. L. Rev.
Ex.: Mathew Staver, <u>Injunctive Relief and the Madsen Test</u>, 140 St. Louis U. Pub. L. Rev. 465 (1995). –Article Citation.

Mathew Staver, <u>Injunctive Relief and the Madsen Test</u>, 140 St. Louis U. Pub. L. Rev. 465, 467 (1995). –Page Citation.

St. Mary's Law Journal
Ab.: St. Mary's L.J.

In law review footnotes, the titles of books and the names of cases, except for procedural phrases, are not underlined. <u>See</u> <u>Bluebook</u> Rule 2.1(a). Further, the following are in large and small capitals: codes, restatements, standards, constitutions, periodicals, authors of books, titles of books, the abbreviated names of codes, most legislative materials except for bills and resolutions, codified ordinances, model codes, court rules, and sentencing guidelines. Refer to <u>The Bluebook</u>.

Ex.: H.N. Cunningham III, <u>Transborder-Road Transportation</u>, 23 St. Mary's L.J. 801 (1992). –Article Citation.

H.N. Cunningham III, <u>Transborder-Road Transportation</u>, 23 St. Mary's L.J. 801, 810-11 (1992). –Page Citation.

St. Thomas Law Review
Ab.: St. Thomas L. Rev.

Ex.: Frank Nussbaum, <u>The Economic Loss Rule and Intentional Torts: A Shield or a Sword?</u>, 8 St. Thomas L. Rev. 473 (1996). –Article Citation.

Frank Nussbaum, <u>The Economic Loss Rule and Intentional Torts: A Shield or a Sword?</u>, 8 St. Thomas L. Rev. 473, 480 (1996). –Page Citation.

Samford University (Cumberland School of Law) Law Review
<u>See</u> Cumberland Law Review

San Diego Law Review
Ab.: San Diego L. Rev.

Ex.: Girard Fisher, <u>Design Immunity for Public Entities</u>, 28 San Diego L. Rev. 214 (1991). –Article Citation.

Girard Fisher, <u>Design Immunity for Public Entities</u>, 28 San Diego L. Rev. 214, 249-50 (1991). –Page Citation.

Santa Clara Computer and High Technology Law Journal
Ab.: Santa Clara Computer & High Tech. L.J.

Ex.: Evan Finkel, <u>Copyright Protection for Computer Software in the Nineties</u>, 7 Santa Clara Computer & High Tech. L.J. 201 (1991). –Article Citation.

Evan Finkel, <u>Copyright Protection for Computer Software in the Nineties</u>, 7 Santa Clara Computer & High Tech. L.J. 201, 203-05 (1991). –Page Citation.

Santa Clara Law Review
Ab.: Santa Clara L. Rev.

Ex.: Russell W. Galloway, <u>The Free Exercise Clause After *Smith* II</u>, 31 Santa Clara L. Rev. 597 (1991). –Article Citation.

Russell W. Galloway, <u>The Free Exercise Clause After *Smith* II</u>, 31 Santa Clara L. Rev. 597, 599 (1991). –Page Citation.

Saskatchewan Law Review
Ab.: Saskatchewan. L.R.

Ex.: Tim Quigley, <u>Battered Women and the Defence of Provocation</u>, 55 Saskatchewan L.R. 223 (1991). –Article Citation.

Tim Quigley, <u>Battered Women and the Defence of Provocation</u>, 55 Saskatchewan L.R. 223, 229-30 (1991). –Page Citation.

In citing cases in law review footnotes, abbreviate any word listed in Table T.6; the names of "states, countries, and other geographical units" unless they are named parties; and any other words of eight or more letters "if <u>substantial</u> space is thereby saved and the result is unambiguous." <u>Bluebook</u> Rule 10.2.2. On the other hand, in citing cases in text, abbreviate only widely known acronyms and the following words: "&," "Ass'n," "Bros.," "Co.," "Corp.," "Inc.," "Ltd.," and "No." <u>Bluebook</u> Rule 10.2.1(c).

School Law Reporter
Ab.:   Sch. L.R. (Nat'l Org. on Legal Probs. in Educ.)
Ex.:   Patricia F. First & Lawrence F. Rossow, <u>The Spring of Race Riots and the Retreat from School Desegregation</u>, Sch. L.R., June 1992, at 1. –Article Citation.

Patricia F. First & Lawrence F. Rossow, <u>The Spring of Race Riots and the Retreat from School Desegregation</u>, Sch. L.R., June 1992, at 1, 2-3. –Page Citation.

Scott on Trusts
<u>See</u> Law of Trusts, by Austin W. Scott and William F. Fatcher

Scribes Journal of Legal Writing, The
Ab.:   Scribes J. Legal Writing
Ex.:   Albert P. Blaustein, <u>Constitutional Drafting</u>, 2 Scribes J. Legal Writing 49 (1991). –Article Citation.

Albert P. Blaustein, <u>Constitutional Drafting</u>, 2 Scribes J. Legal Writing 49, 53 (1991). –Page Citation.

Search and Seizure, by Wayne L. LaFave
–Do not abbreviate the title.
Ex.:   2 Wayne L. LaFave, <u>Search and Seizure</u> § 3.7(c) (3d ed. 1996). –Section Citation.

2 Wayne L. LaFave, <u>Search and Seizure</u> § 3.7(c), at 365 (3d ed. 1996). –Page Citation.

2 Wayne L. LaFave, <u>Search and Seizure</u> § 3.7(c), at 365 n.92 (3d ed. 1996). –Footnote Citation.

Seattle University Law Review
Ab.:   Seattle U. L. Rev.
Ex.:   Sherman Joyce, <u>Product Liability Law in the Federal Arena</u>, 19 Seattle U. L. Rev. 421 (1996). –Article Citation.

Sherman Joyce, <u>Product Liability Law in the Federal Arena</u>, 19 Seattle U. L. Rev. 421, 430 (1996). –Page Citation.

SEC Accounting Rules (Commerce Clearing House)
Ab.:   SEC Accounting R. (CCH)

SEC Docket (Commerce Clearing House)
Ab.:   SEC Docket
Ex.:   <u>Michael N. Karp, Esq.</u>, 60 SEC Docket 2731 (1996).

section(s)
Ab.:   §
Ex.:   George G. Bogert, <u>Trusts</u> § 36 (6th ed. 1987).

George G. Bogert, <u>Trusts</u> §§ 106-108 (6th ed. 1987).

In law review footnotes, the titles of books and the names of cases, except for procedural phrases, are not underlined. <u>See</u> Bluebook Rule 2.1(a). Further, the following are in large and small capitals: codes, restatements, standards, constitutions, periodicals, authors of books, titles of books, the abbreviated names of codes, most legislative materials except for bills and resolutions, codified ordinances, model codes, court rules, and sentencing guidelines. Refer to <u>The Bluebook</u>.

See Bluebook Rules 3.4 and 6.2(c).

Secured Transactions Guide (Commerce Clearing House)
Ab.:   Secured Transactions Guide (CCH)
Ex.:   Havins v. First Nat'l Bank, 5 Secured Transactions Guide (CCH)
¶ 55,534 (Tex. Ct. App. Mar. 27, 1996). –Citation to looseleaf
material.

Hampton Bank v. River City Yachts, Inc., [1987-1996 Decisions
Transfer Binder] Secured Transactions Guide (CCH) ¶ 55,510 (Minn.
Ct. App. Feb. 28, 1995).
–Citation to bound material material.

–The above examples are proper if the case is not yet available in, or is
not reported in, an official or West reporter, a public domain citation,
or in a widely used computer database.

Securities and Exchange Commission Decisions and Reports (1934-date)
Ab.:   S.E.C.
Ex.:   First Independence Group, Inc., 51 S.E.C. 662 (1993).

Commonwealth Bond Corp., 1 S.E.C. 13 (FTC 1934). –Citation to an
early decision rendered by the FTC.

Lewis Airways, Inc., 1 S.E.C. 330 (1936).

Securities and Exchange Commission No-Action Letters
Ab.:   SEC No-Action Letter
Ex.:   SML Commercial Mortgage Trust 1994 C-1 SEC No-Action Letter,
[1995-1996 Transfer Binder] Fed. Sec. L. Rep. (CCH) ¶ 77,107 (July
21, 1995).

Securities and Exchange Commission Releases
Ab.:   (act) Release No.
Ex.:   Adoption of Form D. Amendments, Exchange Act Release No. 6663,
[1986-1987 Transfer Binder] Fed. Sec. L. Rep. (CCH) ¶ 84,032 (Oct.
2, 1986).). –Citation to a release.

Thomas v. Kocherhans, Exchange Act Release No. 36556, [1995-1996
Transfer Binder] Fed. Sec. L. Rep. (CCH) ¶ 85,728 (Dec. 6, 1995).
–Citation to a release that is an adjudication.
See Bluebook Rules 14.1 and 14.6(b).

Securities & Federal Corporate Law Report (West)
Ab.:   Sec. & Fed. Corp. L. Rep. (West)

Securities Law Review
Ab.:   Sec. L. Rev.

In citing cases in law review footnotes, abbreviate any word listed in Table T.6;
the names of "states, countries, and other geographical units" unless they are named parties;
and any other words of eight or more letters "if substantial space is thereby saved and the
result is unambiguous." Bluebook Rule 10.2.2. On the other hand, in citing cases in text,
abbreviate only widely known acronyms and the following words: "&," "Ass'n," "Bros.,"
"Co.," "Corp.," "Inc.," "Ltd.," and "No." Bluebook Rule 10.2.1(c).

Ex.:   James D. Gordon III, <u>Interplanetary Intelligence About Promissory Notes as Securities</u>, 1992 Sec. L. Rev. 3. –Article Citation.

James D. Gordon III, <u>Interplanetary Intelligence About Promissory Notes as Securities</u>, 1992 Sec. L. Rev. 3, 28-29. –Page Citation.

<u>See</u> <u>Bluebook</u> Rule 16.3.

Securities Regulation, by Louis Loss and Joel Seligman
–Do not abbreviate the title.

Ex.:   1 Louis Loss & Joel Seligman, <u>Securities Regulation</u> 432 (3d ed. 1989). –Page Citation.

1 Louis Loss & Joel Seligman, <u>Securities Regulation</u> 311 (3d ed. Supp. 1990) –Page Citation to Supplement.

4 Louis Loss & Joel Seligman, <u>Securities Regulation</u> 1725 n.48 (3d ed. 1990) –Footnote Citation.

Securities Regulation & Law Report (Bureau of National Affairs)
Ab.:   Sec. Reg. & L. Rep. (BNA)
Ex.:   <u>Armstrong v. CFTC</u>, [Jan.-June] Sec. Reg. & L. Rep. (BNA) (28 Sec. Reg. & L. Rep.) No. 24, at 769 (U.S. June 10, 1996). –Citation to looseleaf material.

<u>U.S. v. Daiwa Bank Ltd.</u>, 27 Sec. Reg. & L. Rep. 1767 (S.D.N.Y. Nov. 2, 1995). –Citation to bound material.

–The above examples are proper if the case is not yet available in, or is not reported in, an official or West reporter, a public domain citation, or in a widely used computer database.

Securities Regulation Law Journal
Ab.:   Sec. Reg. L.J.
Ex.:   Mark A. Sargent, <u>Blue Sky Law</u>, 20 Sec. Reg. L.J. 96 (1992). –Article Citation.

Mark A. Sargent, <u>Blue Sky Law</u>, 20 Sec. Reg. L.J. 96, 97-98 (1992). –Page Citation.

See

–"<u>See</u>" is used when the "cited authority clearly supports the proposition. '<u>See</u>' is used instead of '[no signal]' when the proposition is not directly stated by the cited authority but obviously follows from it; there is an inferential step between the authority cited and the proposition it supports." <u>Bluebook</u> Rule 1.2(a).

In law review footnotes, the titles of books and the names of cases, except for procedural phrases, are not underlined. <u>See</u> <u>Bluebook</u> Rule 2.1(a). Further, the following are in large and small capitals: codes, restatements, standards, constitutions, periodicals, authors of books, titles of books, the abbreviated names of codes, most legislative materials except for bills and resolutions, codified ordinances, model codes, court rules, and sentencing guidelines. Refer to <u>The Bluebook</u>.

Ex.:　　"Given the wide gap between the sentence imposed and the sentence available under other similar guidelines, and the absence of any other explanation or basis for the discrepancy, I conclude the sentence was unreasonable. See Pearson, 911 F.2d at 191; Landry, 903 F.2d at 341." –Taken from 941 F.2d 745, 753 (9th Cir. 1991).

See also

–"See also" is used when the "cited authority constitutes additional source material that supports the proposition. 'See also' is commonly used to cite an authority supporting a proposition when authorities that state or directly support the proposition already have been cited or discussed." See Bluebook Rule 1.2(a).

Ex.:　　"If the government granted Mr. Plummer use and derivative use immunity, it would be required to have derived all the information on which the subsequent prosecution was based from a source wholly independent of the statements made in the interview. See Katsinger, 406 U.S. at 453, 92 S. Ct. at 1661; see also 18 U.S.C. § 6002." –Taken from 941 F.2d 799, 803 (9th Cir. 1991).

See generally

–"See generally" is used when the "cited authority presents helpful background material related to the proposition." See Bluebook Rule 1.4(d).

Ex.:　　"When, however, a Rule 59(e) motion seeks reconsideration of a grant of summary judgment, we conduct a de novo review. See id. at 122-23 n.5. See generally Dole v. Elliott Travel & Tours, Inc., 942 F.2d 962, 965 (6th Cir. 1991) (explaining procedure for district court's determination of summary judgment motion)." –Taken from 951 F.2d 110, 112 (6th Cir. 1991).

Selections from Williston's Treatise on the Law of Contracts, by Samuel Williston and George J. Thompson

–Do not abbreviate the title.

Ex.:　　Samuel Williston & George J. Thompson, Selections from Williston's Treatise on the Law of Contracts § 102A (rev. ed. 1938). –Section Citation.

Samuel Williston & George J. Thompson, Selections from Williston's Treatise on the Law of Contracts § 102A, at 131 (rev. ed. 1938). –Page Citation.

Samuel Williston & George J. Thompson, Selections from Williston's Treatise on the Law of Contracts § 102A, at 131 n.15 (rev. ed. 1938). –Footnote Citation.

Senate Bill (U.S. Congress)
See Congressional Bills

Senate Concurrent Resolution
See Congressional Resolutions

In citing cases in law review footnotes, abbreviate any word listed in Table T.6; the names of "states, countries, and other geographical units" unless they are named parties; and any other words of eight or more letters "if substantial space is thereby saved and the result is unambiguous." Bluebook Rule 10.2.2. On the other hand, in citing cases in text, abbreviate only widely known acronyms and the following words: "&," "Ass'n," "Bros.," "Co.," "Corp.," "Inc.," "Ltd.," and "No." Bluebook Rule 10.2.1(c).

Senate Conference Report
    Ex.:   S. Conf. Rep. No. 99-302, at 97 (1986).

Senate Executive Documents Weekly
    Ab.:   S. Exec. Doc. W.

Senate Joint Resolution
    See Congressional Resolutions

Senate Resolution
    See Congressional Resolutions

Senate Treaty Documents
    Ab.:   S. Treaty Doc. No.

Senator
    Ab.:   Sen.

series, serial(s)
    Ab.:   ser.

Services
    See Looseleaf services

Session Cases (Scotland)
    See Bluebook Table T.2, p. 295.
    Court of Session:
    Ab.:   1906- date : Sess. Cas
              1898-1906: F.
              1873-1898: R.
              1862-1873: M.
              1838-1862: D.
              1821-1838: S.
    Ex.:   Sowman v. Glasgow Dist. Council, 1984 Sess. Cas. 91 (Scot.).
            –Case Citation.
            Killin v. Weir, [1904-05] 7 Fr. 526 (Sess. 1905) (Scot.).
            –Case Citation.
            Macpherson v. Brown, [1897-98] 25 R. 945 (Sess. 1898) (Scot.).
            –Case Citation.
            Cook v. North British Railway Co., [1871-72] 10 M. 513 (Sess. 1872)
            (Scot.). –Case Citation.
            Forrest v. Magistrates of Leith, [1860-61] 23 D. 592 (Sess. 1861)
            (Scot.). –Case Citation.
            Cameron v. Chapman, [1837-38] 16 S. 907 (Sess. 1838) (Scot.).
            –Case Citation.

In law review footnotes, the titles of books and the names of cases, except for procedural phrases, are not underlined. See Bluebook Rule 2.1(a). Further, the following are in large and small capitals: codes, restatements, standards, constitutions, periodicals, authors of books, titles of books, the abbreviated names of codes, most legislative materials except for bills and resolutions, codified ordinances, model codes, court rules, and sentencing guidelines. Refer to The Bluebook.

High Court of Justiciary:
Ab.:   1917-date: J.C.

       1906-1916: Sess. Cas. (J.)

       1898-1906: Fr. (J.)

       1873-1898: R. (J.)

Ex.:   Smith v. Macdonald, 1984 J.C. 73 (H.C.J. 1984) (Scot.).
–Case Citation.

       Pollok v. McCabe, [1909-10] 3B Sess. Cas. (J.) 23 (H.C.J. 1909)
(Scot.). –Case Citation.

       Peters v. Olson, [1904-1905] 7 Fr. (J.) 86 (H.C.J. 1905) (Scot.).
–Case Citation.

       Wildridge v. Anderson, [1897-98] 25 R. (J.) 27 (H.C.J. 1897) (Scot.).
–Case Citation.

Session Laws, Arizona
See Arizona Session Laws and Arizona Legislative Service (West)

Session Laws of Alaska
Ab.:   year Alaska Sess. Laws

Ex.:   Act effective Sept. 4, 1995, ch. 75, 1995-2 Alaska Sess. Laws 1
(relating to workers' compensation insurance rate filing). –Citation to
an entire session law.

       Act effective Sept. 4, 1995, ch. 75, sec. 3, § 23.30.017, 1995-2 Alaska
Sess. Laws 1, 3. –Citation to a section of a session law amending prior
act.

       –Identifying information may be added parenthetically according to
Bluebook Rule 12.4(a).

Session Laws of Arizona
Ab.:   year Ariz. Sess. Laws

Ex.:   Act of Apr. 19, 1995, ch. 186, 1995-2 Ariz. Sess. Laws 1328 (relating
to alcoholic beverages - driver's license suspensions). –Citation to an
entire session law.

       Act of Apr. 19, 1995, ch. 186, sec. 27, § 4-222, 1995-2 Ariz. Sess.
Laws 1328, 1331. –Citation to a section of a session law amending
prior act.

Session Laws, Idaho
Ab.:   year Idaho Sess. Laws

Ex.:   Act of Mar. 14, 1996, ch. 231, 1996-1 Idaho Sess. Laws 757 (relating
to the sale of securities). –Citation to an entire session law.

       Act of Mar. 14, 1996, ch. 231, sec. 1, § 30-1403A, 1996-1 Idaho Sess.
Laws 757, 757-58 (relating to the sale of securities). –Citation to a
section of a session law amending a prior act.

In citing cases in law review footnotes, abbreviate any word listed in Table T.6;
the names of "states, countries, and other geographical units" unless they are named parties;
and any other words of eight or more letters "if substantial space is thereby saved and the
result is unambiguous." Bluebook Rule 10.2.2. On the other hand, in citing cases in text,
abbreviate only widely known acronyms and the following words: "&," "Ass'n," "Bros.,"
"Co.," "Corp.," "Inc.," "Ltd.," and "No." Bluebook Rule 10.2.1(c).

Session Laws of Colorado
Ab.:   year Colo. Sess. Laws
Ex.:   Act of Apr. 8, 1996, ch. 54, 1996-1 Colo. Sess. Laws 174. –Citation to an entire session law.

Act of Apr. 8, 1996, ch. 54, sec. 1, § 10-3-541, 1996-1 Colo. Sess. Laws 174, 174-77. –Citation to a section of a session law amending prior act.

–Identifying information may be added parenthetically according to Bluebook Rule 12.4(a).

Session Laws of Hawaii
Ab.:   year Haw. Sess. Laws
Ex.:   Act of Apr. 25, 1995, No. 59, 1995 Haw. Sess. Laws 90. –Citation to an entire session law.

Act of Apr. 25, 1995, No. 59, sec. 1, § 309-1.5, 1995 Haw. Sess. Laws 90, 90-91.
–Citation to a section of a session law amending a prior act.

–Identifying information may be added parenthetically according to Bluebook Rule 12.4(a).

Session Laws of Kansas
Ab.:   year Kan. Sess. Laws
Ex.:   Act of Mar. 22, 1996, ch. 60, 1996 Kan. Sess. Laws 174. –Citation to a section of a session law.

Act of Mar. 22, 1996, ch. 60, sec. 2, § 76-12b11, 1996 Kan. Sess. Laws 174, 175-76. –Citation to a section of a session law amending a prior act.

–Identifying information may be added parenthetically according to Bluebook Rule 12.4(a).

Session Laws of North Carolina
Ab.:   year N.C. Sess. Laws
Ex.:   Act of Mar. 20, 1999, ch. 4, 1999-1, N.C. Sess. Laws 3 (relating to deer hunting in Wilson Cty). –Citation to an entire session law.

Act of Mar. 20, 1999, ch. 4, sec. 1, 1999-1, N.C. Sess. Laws 3.3.
–Citation to a section of a session law amending a prior act.

–Identifying information may be added parenthetically according to Bluebook Rule 12.4(a).

Session Laws of the Virgin Islands
Ab.:   year V.I. Sess. Laws
Ex.:   Act of May 2, 1994, No. 5972, 1994 V.I. Sess. Laws 53 (creating the crime of stalking). –Citation to an entire session law.

Act of May 2, 1994, No. 5972, § 1, 1994 V.I. Sess. Laws 53, 53-54 (creating the crime of stalking). –Citation to a section of a session law.

In law review footnotes, the titles of books and the names of cases, except for procedural phrases, are not underlined. See Bluebook Rule 2.1(a). Further, the following are in large and small capitals: codes, restatements, standards, constitutions, periodicals, authors of books, titles of books, the abbreviated names of codes, most legislative materials except for bills and resolutions, codified ordinances, model codes, court rules, and sentencing guidelines. Refer to The Bluebook.

Session Laws of Wyoming
Ab.:   year Wyo. Sess. Laws

Ex.:   Act of July 1, 1998, ch. 3, 1998 Wyo. Laws 4. –Citation to an entire session law.

Act of July 1, 1998, ch. 3, sec. 104, § 21-13-102, 1998 Wyo. Laws 4, 8 (an act relating to public schools). –Citation to a section of a session law.

Seton Hall Journal of Sport Law
Ab.:   Seton Hall J. Sport L.

Ex.:   Roger I. Abrams, The All Star Baseball Law Team, 1 Seton Hall J. Sport L. 201 (1991). –Article Citation.

Roger I. Abrams, The All Star Baseball Law Team, 1 Seton Hall J. Sport L. 201, 209-13 (1991). –Page Citation.

Seton Hall Law Review
Ab.:   Seton Hall L. Rev.

Ex.:   Channing E. Brackey, Choices of Capital: Reducing Their Impact on Taxpayers and the Government, 22 Seton Hall L. Rev. 320 (1992). –Article Citation.

Channing E. Brackey, Choices of Capital: Reducing Their Impact on Taxpayers and the Government, 22 Seton Hall L. Rev. 320, 335 (1992). –Page Citation.

Seton Hall Legislative Journal
Ab.:   Seton Hall Legis. J.

Ex.:   Robert J. Araujo, Suggestions for a Foundation Course in Legislation, 15 Seton Hall Legis. J. 17 (1991). –Article Citation.

Robert J. Araujo, Suggestions for a Foundation Course in Legislation, 15 Seton Hall Legis. J. 17, 19-20 (1991). –Page Citation.

Shipping Regulation
Ab.:   Shipping Reg. (P & F)

short forms
See subsequent citation to legal authority.

shorter works in collection
See Bluebook Rule 15.5.

Ex.:   Henry M. Hart, Jr. & Albert M. Sacks, The Legal Process: Basic Problems, in The Marking and Application of Law 1345-63 (William N. Eskridge, Jr. & Philip P. Frickey eds., 1994).

sic

–Use "[sic]" to indicate significant mistakes in the original text. See Bluebook Rule 5.2.

In citing cases in law review footnotes, abbreviate any word listed in Table T.6; the names of "states, countries, and other geographical units" unless they are named parties; and any other words of eight or more letters "if substantial space is thereby saved and the result is unambiguous." Bluebook Rule 10.2.2. On the other hand, in citing cases in text, abbreviate only widely known acronyms and the following words: "&," "Ass'n," "Bros.," "Co.," "Corp.," "Inc.," "Ltd.," and "No." Bluebook Rule 10.2.1(c).

Ex.:   "George Bush and Dan Quayle was [sic] the favorites to win the 1992 election."

signals
See Bluebook Rules 1.2, 1.3, & 1.4.

See, herein, entries for Accord, But cf., But see, Cf., Compare, Contra, E.g., no [introductory] signal, See, See also, and See generally.

The absence of a signal, according to Bluebook Rule 1.2(a), means that the "cited authority (i) directly states the proposition, (ii) identifies the source of a quotation, or (iii) identifies an authority referred to in the text."

signals, order of
See Bluebook Rule 1.3.

Singapore Law Review
Ab.:   Sing. L. Rev.

Ex.:   Chung Wei Han, Japanese and Western Attitudes Towards Law, 12 Sing. L. Rev. 69 (1991). –Article Citation.

Chung Wei Han, Japanese and Western Attitudes Towards Law, 12 Sing. L. Rev. 69, 72 (1991). –Page Citation.

slip opinions
Ab.:   slip op.

Ex.:   United States v. Cutler, No. 86-3058, slip op. at 3 (9th Cir. Dec. 19, 1986). –Separately paginated.

Freeman v. Rideout, No. 86-2153, slip op. 6801, 6812 (2d Cir. Dec. 20, 1986). –Not separately paginated.

Social Justice
Ab.:   Soc. Just.

Ex.:   Rosa del Olmo, The Hidden Face of Drugs, Soc. Just., Winter 1991, at 10. –Article Citation.

Rosa del Olmo, The Hidden Face of Drugs, Soc. Just., Winter 1991, at 10, 15-20. –Page Citation.

Social Responsibility: Business, Journalism, Law Medicine
Ab.:   Soc. Resp.

Ex.:   Robert P. Clark, The Founding Fathers and the Bottom Line, 17 Soc. Resp. 28 (1991). –Article Citation.

Robert P. Clark, The Founding Fathers and the Bottom Line, 17 Soc. Resp. 28, 29-32 (1991). –Page Citation.

Social Sciences
Ab.:   Soc. Sci.

In law review footnotes, the titles of books and the names of cases, except for procedural phrases, are not underlined. See Bluebook Rule 2.1(a). Further, the following are in large and small capitals: codes, restatements, standards, constitutions, periodicals, authors of books, titles of books, the abbreviated names of codes, most legislative materials except for bills and resolutions, codified ordinances, model codes, court rules, and sentencing guidelines. Refer to The Bluebook.

Ex.:   E. Batalov, <u>Unity in Multiformity</u>, Soc. Sci. 1991 No. 4, at 91.
         –Article Citation.

         E. Batalov, <u>Unity in Multiformity</u>, Soc. Sci. 1991 No. 4, at 91, 99-100.
         –Page Citation.

Social Security Bulletin
Ab.:   Soc. Security Bull.
Ex.:   Daniel B. Radner, <u>Changes in the Incomes of Age Groups</u>, Soc.
         Security Bull., Dec. 1991, at 2. –Article Citation.

         Daniel B. Radner, <u>Changes in the Incomes of Age Groups</u>, Soc.
         Security Bull., Dec. 1991, at 2, 16-18. –Page Citation.

Social Security Claims and Procedures, by Harvey L. McCormick
         –Do not abbreviate the title.
Ex.:   1 Harvey L. McCormick, <u>Social Security Claims and Procedures</u> § 4:53
         (5th ed. 1998). –Section Citation.

Social Security Rulings, Cumulative Edition
Ab.:   year S.S.R. (Cum. Ed.)
Ex.:   <u>Rahman v. Harris</u>, 49 S.S.R. (Cum. Ed. 1988)

Sociology of Health & Illness
Ab.:   Soc. Health & Illness
Ex.:   Els Bransen, <u>Has Menstruation Been Medicalised? Or Will it Never</u>
         <u>Happen?</u>, 14 Soc. Health & Illness 98 (1992). –Article Citation.

         Els Bransen, <u>Has Menstruation Been Medicalised? Or Will it Never</u>
         <u>Happen?</u>, 14 Soc. Health & Illness 98, 100 (1992). –Page Citation.

Software Law Journal
Ab.:   Software L.J.
Ex.:   Ann C. Keays, <u>Software Trade Secret Protection</u>, 4 Software L.J. 577
         (1991). –Article Citation.

         Ann C. Keays, <u>Software Trade Secret Protection</u>, 4 Software L.J. 577,
         589-90 (1991). –Page Citation.

South Australia State Reports (1922-date)
Ab.:   S.A. St. R.
Ex.:   <u>Tanner v. South Australia</u>, (1988) 53 S.A. St. R. 307 (Austl.). <u>See</u>
         <u>Bluebook</u> Table T.2.

South Carolina, administrative compilation
         <u>See</u> Code of Laws of South Carolina 1976 Annotated (West), Code of
         Regulations

South Carolina Code Annotated
         <u>See</u> Code of Laws of South Carolina 1976 Annotated

---

In citing cases in law review footnotes, abbreviate any word listed in Table T.6;
the names of "states, countries, and other geographical units" unless they are named parties;
and any other words of eight or more letters "if <u>substantial</u> space is thereby saved and the
result is unambiguous." <u>Bluebook</u> Rule 10.2.2. On the other hand, in citing cases in text,
abbreviate only widely known acronyms and the following words: "&," "Ass'n," "Bros.,"
"Co.," "Corp.," "Inc.," "Ltd.," and "No." <u>Bluebook</u> Rule 10.2.1(c).

South Carolina Constitution

Ab.:   S.C. Const. art. , § .

Ex.:   S.C. Const. art. III, § 33. –"Cite constitutional provisions currently in force without date." Bluebook Rule 11.

S.C. Const. art. III, § 24 (amended 1989). –"When citing a provision that has been subsequently amended, either indicate parenthetically the fact and date of amendment or cite the amending provision in full." Bluebook Rule 11.

S.C. Const. of 1868, art. I, § 4 (1895). –"Cite constitutions that have been totally superseded by year of adoption; if the specific provision cited was adopted in a different year, give that year parenthetically." Bluebook Rule 11.

South Carolina Court of Appeals

Ab.:   S.C. Ct. App.

–Cite to S.E. or S.E.2d if therein; otherwise, cite to S.C.

–Give parallel citations only in documents submitted to South Carolina state courts. See Bluebook Rule 10.3.1 and Practitioners' Note P.3; see also S.C. App. Ct. R. 239(d), which requires a parallel citation.

In documents submitted to South Carolina state courts, cite as follows:

Patterson v. Reid, 318 S.C. 183, 456 S.E.2d 436 (Ct. App. 1995). –Case Citation.

Patterson v. Reid, 318 S.C. 183, 184, 456 S.E.2d 436, 437 (Ct. App. 1995). –Page Citation.

In all other documents, cite as follows:

Patterson v. Reid, 456 S.E.2d 436 (S.C. Ct. App. 1995). –Case Citation.

Patterson v. Reid, 456 S.E.2d 436, 437 (S.C. Ct. App. 1995). –Page Citation.

South Carolina Law Review

Ab.:   S.C. L. Rev.

Ex.:   Ellen S. Podgor, Mail Fraud: Opening Letters, 43 S.C. L. Rev. 223 (1992). –Article Citation.

Ellen S. Podgor, Mail Fraud: Opening Letters, 43 S.C. L. Rev. 223, 249-54 (1992). –Page Citation.

South Carolina Lawyer

Ab.:   S.C. Law.

Ex.:   W. Keith Shannon, Tips for Lawyers on Dealing with the News Media, S.C. Law., Jan.-Feb. 1992, at 15. –Article Citation.

W. Keith Shannon, Tips for Lawyers on Dealing with the News Media, S.C. Law., Jan.-Feb. 1992, at 15, 16. –Page Citation.

In law review footnotes, the titles of books and the names of cases, except for procedural phrases, are not underlined. See Bluebook Rule 2.1(a). Further, the following are in large and small capitals: codes, restatements, standards, constitutions, periodicals, authors of books, titles of books, the abbreviated names of codes, most legislative materials except for bills and resolutions, codified ordinances, model codes, court rules, and sentencing guidelines. Refer to The Bluebook.

South Carolina Session Laws
See Acts and Joint Resolutions of South Carolina

South Carolina State Register
Ab.:   S.C. Reg.

South Carolina Supreme Court
Ab.:   S.C.

–Cite to S.E. or S.E.2d if therein; otherwise, cite to S.C.

–Give parallel citations only in documents submitted to South Carolina state courts. See Bluebook Rule 10.3.1 and Practitioners' Note P.3; see also S.C. App. Ct. R. 239(d), which requires a parallel citation.

In documents submitted to South Carolina state courts, cite as follows:

Thomas v. Grayson, 318 S.C. 82, 456 S.E.2d 377 (1995). –Case Citation.

Thomas v. Grayson, 318 S.C. 82, 84, 456 S.E.2d 377, 378 (1995). –Page Citation.

In all other documents, cite as follows:

Thomas v. Grayson, 456 S.E.2d 377 (S.C. 1995). –Case Citation.

Thomas v. Grayson, 456 S.E.2d 377, 378 (S.C. 1995). –Page Citation.

South Dakota Administrative Rules
See Administrative Rules of South Dakota

South Dakota, Biennial Report of the Attorney General
See Biennial Report of the Attorney General of the State of South Dakota

South Dakota Codified Laws (Lexis)
Ab.:   S.D. Codified Laws, §   (Lexis year)
Ex.:   S.D. Codified Laws § 36-15-29 (Lexis 2000).
         S.D. Codified Laws § 16-16-73 (Lexis Supp. 2000).

South Dakota Constitution
Ab.:   S.D. Const. art.   , §   .
Ex.:   S.D. Const. art. XXI, § 8. –"Cite constitutional provisions currently in force without date." Bluebook Rule 11.

         S.D. Const. art. XXIV (repealed 1934). "If the cited provision has been repealed, either indicate parenthetically the fact and date of repeal or cite the repealing provision in full." Bluebook Rule 11.

         S.D. Const. art. XIV, § 1 (amended 1988). –"When citing a provision that has been subsequently amended, either indicate parenthetically the fact and date of amendment or cite the amending provision in full." Bluebook Rule 11.

In citing cases in law review footnotes, abbreviate any word listed in Table T.6; the names of "states, countries, and other geographical units" unless they are named parties; and any other words of eight or more letters "if substantial space is thereby saved and the result is unambiguous." Bluebook Rule 10.2.2. On the other hand, in citing cases in text, abbreviate only widely known acronyms and the following words: "&," "Ass'n," "Bros.," "Co.," "Corp.," "Inc.," "Ltd.," and "No." Bluebook Rule 10.2.1(c).

South Dakota Law Review
    Ab.:   S.D. L. Rev.
    Ex.:   Randall P. Bezanson, The Future First Amendment, 37 S.D. L. Rev. 11 (1992). –Article Citation.

            Randall P. Bezanson, The Future First Amendment, 37 S.D. L. Rev. 11, 12-13 (1992). –Page Citation.

South Dakota Register
    Ab.:   S.D. Reg.

South Dakota Session Laws
    See Laws of South Dakota

South Dakota Supreme Court
    Ab.:   S.D.

    –Cite to N.W. or N.W.2d if therein; in addition, give public domain citation if available.

    –Through 90 S.D. 692 (1976), cite as follows:

    In documents submitted to South Dakota state courts:

        Dunham v. First National Bank, 86 S.D. 727 (1972). –Case Citation.

        Dunham v. First National Bank, 86 S.D. 727, 733 (1972). –Page Citation.

    Or:

        Dunham v. First National Bank, 201 N.W.2d 227 (1972). –Case Citation.

        Dunham v. First National Bank, 201 N.W.2d 227, 230 (1972). –Page Citation.

    In all other documents:

        Dunham v. First National Bank, 201 N.W.2d 227 (S.D. 1972). –Case Citation.

        Dunham v. First National Bank, 201 N.W.2d 227, 230 (S.D. 1972). –Page Citation.

    –After 90 S.D. 692 (1976) and until January 1, 1996, when a public domain format was adopted, cite as follows:

    In all documents:

        Swenson v. Swenson, 529 N.W.2d 901 (S.D. 1995). –Case Citation.

        Swenson v. Swenson, 529 N.W.2d 901, 903 (S.D. 1995). –Page Citation.

    –After January 1, 1996, cite as follows:

    In all documents:

        Price v. Price, 2000 SD 64, 611 N.W.2d 425. –Case Citation.

In law review footnotes, the titles of books and the names of cases, except for procedural phrases, are not underlined. See Bluebook Rule 2.1(a). Further, the following are in large and small capitals: codes, restatements, standards, constitutions, periodicals, authors of books, titles of books, the abbreviated names of codes, most legislative materials except for bills and resolutions, codified ordinances, model codes, court rules, and sentencing guidelines. Refer to The Bluebook.

Price v. Price, 2000 SD 64, ¶ 12, 611 N.W.2d 425, 429.   –
Pinpoint Citation.

See Bluebook Rules 10.3.1 and 10.3.3, Table T.1, and Practitioners'
Note P.3; see also S.D. R. App. P. § 15-26A-69.1.

South Eastern Reporter
–Do not give a parallel citation unless required by local rule. See
Bluebook Practitioners' Note P.3 and Rule 10.3.1. See also the
various state court and state reporter entries herein for local rule
parallel citation requirements.

Ab.: S.E.

Ex.:

Georgia:

Pollard v. Kent, 200 S.E. 542 (Ga. Ct. App. 1938). –Case Citation.

Pollard v. Kent, 200 S.E. 542, 545 (Ga. Ct. App. 1938). –Page
Citation.

North Carolina:

Wilson v. City of Charlotte, 175 S.E. 306 (N.C. 1934). –Case Citation.

Wilson v. City of Charlotte, 175 S.E. 306, 307 (N.C. 1934). –Page
Citation.

South Carolina:

Craig v. Clearwater Mfg., 200 S.E. 765 (S.C. 1938). –Case Citation.

Craig v. Clearwater Mfg., 200 S.E. 765, 769 (S.C. 1938). –Page
Citation.

Virginia:

Simpson v. Simpson, 175 S.E. 320 (Va. 1934). –Case Citation.

Simpson v. Simpson, 175 S.E. 320, 325 (Va. 1934). –Page Citation.

West Virginia:

Buckland v. State Compensation Commissioner, 175 S.E. 785 (W. Va.
1934). –Case Citation.

Buckland v. State Compensation Commissioner, 175 S.E. 785, 786 (W.
Va. 1934). –Page Citation.

South Eastern Reporter, second series
–Do not give a parallel citation unless required by local rule or unless
the particular state has a public domain format. See Bluebook
Practitioners' Note P.3 and Rules 10.3.1 and 10.3.3. See also the
various state court and state reporter entries herein for public domain
information and local rule parallel citation requirements.

–With volume 361 (1988), South Eastern Reporter, Second Series,
became West's South Eastern Reporter, Second Series. Citation form
is not affected by this title change.

Ab.: S.E.2d

In citing cases in law review footnotes, abbreviate any word listed in Table T.6;
the names of "states, countries, and other geographical units" unless they are named parties;
and any other words of eight or more letters "if substantial space is thereby saved and the
result is unambiguous." Bluebook Rule 10.2.2. On the other hand, in citing cases in text,
abbreviate only widely known acronyms and the following words: "&," "Ass'n," "Bros.,"
"Co.," "Corp.," "Inc.," "Ltd.," and "No." Bluebook Rule 10.2.1(c).

Ex.:
Georgia:

> King v. State, 509 S.E.2d 32 (Ga. 1998). –Case Citation.
> King v. State, 509 S.E.2d 32, 36 (Ga. 1998). –Page Citation.

North Carolina:

> Stafford v. Stafford, 520 S.E.2d 785 (N.C. 1999). –Case Citation.
> Stafford v. Stafford, 520 S.E.2d 785, 786 (N.C. 1999). –Page Citation.

South Carolina:

> State v. Kennerly, 524 S.E.2d 837 (S.C. 1999). –Case Citation.
> State v. Kennerly, 524 S.E.2d 837, 839 (S.C. 1999). –Page Citation.

Virginia:

> Rivera v. Nedrich, 529 S.E.2d 310 (Va. 1999). –Case Citation.
> Rivera v. Nedrich, 529 S.E.2d 310, 313 (Va. 1999). –Page Citation.

West Virginia:

> State v. Calloway, 528 S.E.2d 490 (W. Va. 1999). –Case Citation.
> State v. Calloway, 528 S.E.2d 490, 499 (W. Va. 1999). –Page Citation.

South Texas Law Review

Ab.:   S. Tex. L. Rev.

Ex.:   Kenneth G. Engerrand, Seaman Status Reconstructed, 32 S. Tex. L. Rev. 169 (1991). –Article Citation.

Kenneth G. Engerrand, Seaman Status Reconstructed, 32 S. Tex. L. Rev. 169, 170-72 (1991). –Page Citation.

South Texas Law Review

Ab.:   S. Tex. L. Rev.

Ex.:   Kenneth G. Engerrand, Seaman Status Reconstructed, 32 S. Tex. L. Rev. 169 (1991). –Article Citation.

Kenneth G. Engerrand, Seaman Status Reconstructed, 32 S. Tex. L. Rev. 169, 170-72 (1991). –Page Citation.

South Western Reporter

–Do not give a parallel citation unless required by local rule. See Bluebook Practitioners' Note P.3 and Rule 10.3.1. See also the various state court and state reporter entries herein for local rule parallel citation requirements.

Ab.: S.W.

In law review footnotes, the titles of books and the names of cases, except for procedural phrases, are not underlined. See Bluebook Rule 2.1(a). Further, the following are in large and small capitals: codes, restatements, standards, constitutions, periodicals, authors of books, titles of books, the abbreviated names of codes, most legislative materials except for bills and resolutions, codified ordinances, model codes, court rules, and sentencing guidelines. Refer to The Bluebook.

Ex.:
Arkansas:
> Hart v. State, 257 S.W. 354 (Ark. 1924). –Case Citation.
> Hart v. State, 257 S.W. 354, 356 (Ark. 1924). –Page Citation.

Kentucky:
> Varney v. Orinoco Mining Co., 257 S.W. 1016 (Ky. 1924). –Case Citation.
> Varney v. Orinoco Mining Co., 257 S.W. 1016, 1018 (Ky. 1924). –Page Citation.

Missouri:
> State v. Mullinix, 257 S.W. 121 (Mo. 1923). –Case Citation.
> State v. Mullinix, 257 S.W. 121, 123 (Mo. 1923). –Page Citation.

Tennessee:
> Edwards v. Davis, 244 S.W. 359 (Tenn. 1922). –Case Citation.
> Edwards v. Davis, 244 S.W. 359, 361 (Tenn. 1922). –Page Citation.

Texas:
> Empire Gas & Fuel Co. v. Pendar, 244 S.W. 184 (Tex. Civ. App. 1922). –Case Citation.
> Empire Gas & Fuel Co. v. Pendar, 244 S.W. 184, 187 (Tex. Civ. App. 1922). –Page Citation.

South Western Reporter, second series

> –Do not give a parallel citation unless required by local rule or unless the particular state has a public domain format. See Bluebook Practitioners' Note P.3 and Rules 10.3.1 and 10.3.3. See also the various state court and state reporter entries herein for public domain information and local rule parallel citation requirements.
>
> –With volume 738 (1988), South Western Reporter, Second Series, became West's South Western Reporter, Second Series. Citation form is not affected by this title change.

Ab.: S.W.2d
Ex.:
Arkansas:
> Huffman v. Alderson, 983 S.W.2d 899 (Ark. 1998). –Case Citation.
> Huffman v. Alderson, 983 S.W.2d 899, 900 (Ark. 1998). –Page Citation.

Kentucky:
> Cavender v. Miller, 984 S.W.2d 848 (Ky. 1998). –Case Citation.
> Cavender v. Miller, 984 S.W.2d 848, 849 (Ky. 1998). –Page Citation.

In citing cases in law review footnotes, abbreviate any word listed in Table T.6; the names of "states, countries, and other geographical units" unless they are named parties; and any other words of eight or more letters "if substantial space is thereby saved and the result is unambiguous." Bluebook Rule 10.2.2. On the other hand, in citing cases in text, abbreviate only widely known acronyms and the following words: "&," "Ass'n," "Bros.," "Co.," "Corp.," "Inc.," "Ltd.," and "No." Bluebook Rule 10.2.1(c).

Missouri:

> Spradlin v. City of Fulton, 982 S.W.2d 255 (Mo. 1998). –Case Citation.
>
> Spradlin v. City of Fulton, 982 S.W.2d 255, 265 (Mo. 1998). –Page Citation.

Tennessee:

> State v. Blackmon, 984 S.W.2d 589 (Tenn. 1998). –Case Citation.
>
> State v. Blackmon, 984 S.W.2d 589, 593 (Tenn. 1998). –Page Citation.

Texas:

> Boyette v. State, 982 S.W.2d 428 (Tex. Crim. App. 1998). –Case Citation.
>
> Boyette v. State, 982 S.W.2d 428, 429 (Tex. Crim. App. 1998). –Page Citation.

South Western Reporter, Third Series

–Do not give a parallel citation unless required by local rule or unless the particular state has a public domain format. See Bluebook Practitioners' Note P.3 and Rules 10.3.1 and 10.3.3. See also the various state court and state reporter entries herein for public domain information and local rule parallel citation requirements.

Ab.: S.W.3d

Ex.:

Arkansas:

> Thetford v. State, 5 S.W.3d 478 (Ark. 1999). –Case Citation.
>
> Thetford v. State, 5 S.W.3d 478, 479 (Ark. 1999). –Page Citation.

Kentucky:

> Commissioner v. Davis, 14 S.W.3d 9 (Ky. 1999). –Case Citation.
>
> Commissioner v. Davis, 14 S.W.3d 9, 14 (Ky. 1999). –Page Citation.

Missouri:

> State v. Armentrout, 8 S.W.3d 99 (Mo. 1999). –Case Citation.
>
> State v. Armentrout, 8 S.W.3d 99, 109 (Mo. 1999). –Page Citation.

Tennessee:

> Ashe v. Radiation Oncology Ass'n, 9 S.W.3d 119 (Tenn. 1999). –Case Citation.
>
> Ashe v. Radiation Oncology Ass'n, 9 S.W.3d 119, 123 (Tenn. 1999). –Page Citation.

Texas:

> Garza v. State, 7 S.W.3d 164 (Tex. Crim. App. 1999). –Case Citation.
>
> Garza v. State, 7 S.W.3d 164, 167 (Tex. Crim. App. 1999). –Page Citation.

In law review footnotes, the titles of books and the names of cases, except for procedural phrases, are not underlined. See Bluebook Rule 2.1(a). Further, the following are in large and small capitals: codes, restatements, standards, constitutions, periodicals, authors of books, titles of books, the abbreviated names of codes, most legislative materials except for bills and resolutions, codified ordinances, model codes, court rules, and sentencing guidelines. Refer to The Bluebook.

Southern California Law Review
　　Ab.:　　S. Cal. L. Rev.
　　Ex.:　　Marion Crain, <u>Feminism, Labor and Power</u>, 65 S. Cal. L. Rev. 1819
　　　　　　(1992). –Article Citation.
　　　　　　Marion Crain, <u>Feminism, Labor and Power</u>, 65 S. Cal. L. Rev. 1819,
　　　　　　1883-85 (1992). –Page Citation.

Southern California Review of Law & Women's Studies
　　Ab.:　　S. Cal. Rev. L. & Women's Stud.

Southern Illinois University Law Journal
　　Ab.:　　S. Ill. U. L.J.
　　Ex.:　　Daniel R. Gordon, <u>The Demise of American Constitutionalism: Death</u>
　　　　　　<u>by Legal Education</u>, 1991 S. Ill. U. L.J. 39. –Article Citation.
　　　　　　Daniel R. Gordon, <u>The Demise of American Constitutionalism: Death</u>
　　　　　　<u>by Legal Education</u>, 1991 S. Ill. U. L.J. 39, 95. –Page Citation.

Southern Methodist University Law Journal
　　<u>See</u> Southwestern Law Journal

Southern Reporter
　　　　　　–Do not give a parallel citation unless required by local rule. <u>See</u>
　　　　　　<u>Bluebook</u> Practitioners' Note P.3 and Rule 10.3.1. <u>See also</u> the
　　　　　　various state court and state reporter entries herein for local rule
　　　　　　parallel citation requirements.
　　Ab.: So.
　　Ex.:
　　Alabama:
　　　　　　<u>Slaughter v. Green</u>, 87 So. 358 (Ala. 1921). –Case Citation.
　　　　　　<u>Slaughter v. Green</u>, 87 So. 358, 361 (Ala. 1921). –Page Citation.
　　Florida:
　　　　　　<u>Kennerly v. Hennessy</u>, 66 So. 729 (Fla. 1914). –Case Citation.
　　　　　　<u>Kennerly v. Hennessy</u>, 66 So. 729, 730 (Fla. 1914). –Page Citation.
　　Louisiana:
　　　　　　<u>Reynaud v. C.J. Walton & Son, Inc.</u>, 66 So. 549 (La. 1914). –Case
　　　　　　Citation.
　　　　　　<u>Reynaud v. C.J. Walton & Son, Inc.</u>, 66 So. 549, 550 (La. 1914).
　　　　　　–Page Citation.
　　Mississippi:
　　　　　　<u>Dedeaux v. State</u>, 87 So. 664 (Miss. 1921). –Case Citation.
　　　　　　<u>Dedeaux v. State</u>, 87 So. 664, 666 (Miss. 1921). –Page Citation.

In citing cases in law review footnotes, abbreviate any word listed in Table T.6;
the names of "states, countries, and other geographical units" unless they are named parties;
and any other words of eight or more letters "if <u>substantial</u> space is thereby saved and the
result is unambiguous." <u>Bluebook</u> Rule 10.2.2. On the other hand, in citing cases in text,
abbreviate only widely known acronyms and the following words: "&," "Ass'n," "Bros.,"
"Co.," "Corp.," "Inc.," "Ltd.," and "No." <u>Bluebook</u> Rule 10.2.1(c).

Southern Reporter, second series

–Do not give a parallel citation unless required by local rule or unless the particular state has a public domain format. See Bluebook Practitioners' Note P.3 and Rules 10.3.1 and 10.3.3. See also the various state court and state reporter entries herein for public domain information and local rule parallel citation requirements.

–With volume 513 (1988), Southern Reporter, Second Series, became West's Southern Reporter, Second Series. Citation form is not affected by this title change.

Ab.: So. 2d

Ex.:

Alabama:

Ex parte Panell, 756 So. 2d 862 (Ala. 1999). –Case Citation.

Ex parte Panell, 756 So. 2d 862, 872 (Ala. 1999). –Page Citation.

Florida:

State v. Thompson, 750 So. 2d 643 (Fla. 1999). –Case Citation.

State v. Thompson, 750 So. 2d 643, 647 (Fla. 1999). –Page Citation.

Louisiana:

Tardiff v. Valley Forge Insurance Co., 751 So. 2d 867 (La. 1999). – Case Citation.

Tardiff v. Valley Forge Insurance Co., 751 So. 2d 867, 869 (La. 1999). –Page Citation.

Mississippi:

Theobald v. Nosser, 752 So. 2d 1036 (Miss. 1999). –Case Citation.

Theobald v. Nosser, 752 So. 2d 1036, 1038 (Miss. 1999). –Page Citation.

Southern University Law Review

Ab.:   S.U. L. Rev.

Ex.:   Evelyn L. Wilson, Federal Habeas Corpus: An Avenue of Relief for State Prisoners, 18 S.U. L. Rev. 1 (1991). –Article Citation.

Evelyn L. Wilson, Federal Habeas Corpus: An Avenue of Relief for State Prisoners, 18 S.U. L. Rev. 1, 18 (1991). –Page Citation.

Southwestern Law Journal

Ab.:   Sw. L.J.

Ex.:   Elizabeth E. Mack, Another Weapon: The RICO Statute and the Prosecution of Environmental Offenses, 45 Sw. L.J. 1145 (1991). –Article Citation.

Elizabeth E. Mack, Another Weapon: The RICO Statute and the Prosecution of Environmental Offenses, 45 Sw. L.J. 1145, 1150 (1991). –Page Citation.

In law review footnotes, the titles of books and the names of cases, except for procedural phrases, are not underlined. See Bluebook Rule 2.1(a). Further, the following are in large and small capitals: codes, restatements, standards, constitutions, periodicals, authors of books, titles of books, the abbreviated names of codes, most legislative materials except for bills and resolutions, codified ordinances, model codes, court rules, and sentencing guidelines. Refer to The Bluebook.

Southwestern Legal Foundation Institute on Oil and Gas Law and Taxation
    See Institute on Oil and Gas Law and Taxation

Southwestern University Law Review
    Ab.:   Sw. U. L. Rev.
    Ex.:   Timothy A. Tosta et al., Environmental Review After *Goleta*, 21 Sw. U. L. Rev. 1079 (1992). –Article Citation.

            Timothy A. Tosta et al., Environmental Review After *Goleta*, 21 Sw. U. L. Rev. 1079, 1080-81 (1992). –Page Citation.

Soviet Law and Government
    Ab.:   Soviet L. & Gov't
    Ex.:   B.M. Lazarev, President of the USSR, Soviet L. & Gov't, Summer 1991, at 7. –Article Citation.

            B.M. Lazarev, President of the USSR, Soviet L. & Gov't, Summer 1991, at 7, 19-20. –Page Citation.

special
    Ab.:   spec.

Standard Federal Tax Reports (Commerce Clearing House)
    –Bound as U.S. Tax Cases (Commerce Clearing House)
    Ab.:   Stand. Fed. Tax Rep. (CCH)
    –Bound as U.S. Tax Cas.(CCH)
    Ex.:   Dotson v. U.S., [U.S. Tax Cases Advance Sheets] Stand. Fed. Tax Rep. (CCH) (96-2 U.S. Tax Cas.) ¶ 50,359 (5th Cir. June 27, 1996). –Citation to looseleaf material.

            Black Hills Corp. v. Commissioner, 96-1 U.S. Tax Cas. (CCH) ¶ 50,036 (8th Cir. Jan. 10, 1996). –Citation to bound material.

            –The above examples are proper if the case is not yet available in, or is not reported in, an official or West reporter, a public domain citation, or in a widely used computer database.

Standards for Inmates Legal Rights
    Ab.:   Standards for Inmates Legal Rights (National Sheriffs' Ass'n)

Standards for Traffic Justice
    Ab.:   Standards for Traffic Justice § (year)
    Ex.:   Standards for Traffic Justice § 1.2 (1975).

            Standards for Traffic Justice § 3.1 commentary at 5 (1975).

Standards, Generally Accepted
    See Bluebook Rule 12.8.5.

In citing cases in law review footnotes, abbreviate any word listed in Table T.6; the names of "states, countries, and other geographical units" unless they are named parties; and any other words of eight or more letters "if substantial space is thereby saved and the result is unambiguous." Bluebook Rule 10.2.2. On the other hand, in citing cases in text, abbreviate only widely known acronyms and the following words: "&," "Ass'n," "Bros.," "Co.," "Corp.," "Inc.," "Ltd.," and "No." Bluebook Rule 10.2.1(c).

Ex.:   ABA Standards for Criminal Justice Prosecution Function and Defense
         Function, Standard 3-2.4 commentary at 30 (1993).

         Accounting for the Costs of Computer Software to be Sold, Leased or
         Otherwise Marketed, Statement of Financial Accounting Standards No.
         86, § 16 (Financial Accounting Standards Bd. 1985).

Standards Relating to Appellate Delay Reduction
Ex.:   Standards Relating to Appellate Delay Reduction § 3.53 (1988).

**Standards Relating to Court Organization and Administration (American Bar
Association)**
Ab.:   Standards Relating to Court Org. & Admin. § (year)
Ex.:   Standards Relating to Court Org. § 2.1 (1980).

Standards Relating to the Function of the Trial Judge
Ab.:   Standards Relating to the Function of the Trial Judge § (status if
         necessary year)
Ex.:   Standards Relating to the Function of the Trial Judge § 2.4 (Tentative
         Draft 1972).

Stanford Environmental Law Journal
Ab.:   Stan. Envtl. L.J.
Ex.:   Renee Stone, Wetlands Protection and Development: The Advantages
         of Retaining Federal Control, 10 Stan. Envtl. L.J. 137 (1991). –Article
         Citation.

         Renee Stone, Wetlands Protection and Development: The Advantages
         of Retaining Federal Control, 10 Stan. Envtl. L.J. 137, 149-52 (1991).
         –Page Citation.

Stanford Journal of International Law
Ab.:   Stan. J. Int'l L.
Ex.:   Robert E. Lutz, The World Court in a Changing World: An Agenda for
         Expanding the Court's Role from a U.S. Perspective, 27 Stan. J. Int'l L.
         247 (1990). –Article Citation.

         Robert E. Lutz, The World Court in a Changing World: An Agenda for
         Expanding the Court's Role from a U.S. Perspective, 27 Stan. J. Int'l L.
         247, 249-51 (1990). –Page Citation.

Stanford Journal of International Studies
Ab.:   Stan. J. Int'l Stud.
Ex.:   John H. Barton, Tacit Political Restraints as a Way to Control
         Conventional Arms, 14 Stan. J. Int'l Stud. 29 (1979). –Article Citation.

         John H. Barton, Tacit Political Restraints as a Way to Control
         Conventional Arms, 14 Stan. J. Int'l Stud. 29, 40-45 (1979). –Page
         Citation.

In law review footnotes, the titles of books and the names of cases, except for procedural
phrases, are not underlined. See Bluebook Rule 2.1(a). Further, the following are in large
and small capitals: codes, restatements, standards, constitutions, periodicals, authors of
books, titles of books, the abbreviated names of codes, most legislative materials except for
bills and resolutions, codified ordinances, model codes, court rules, and sentencing guidelines.
Refer to The Bluebook.

Stanford Law & Policy Review
Ab.: Stan. L. & Pol'y Rev.
Ex.: Doug Bandow, <u>War on Drugs or War on America?</u>, 3 Stan. L. & Pol'y Rev. 242 (1991). –Article Citation.
Doug Bandow, <u>War on Drugs or War on America?</u>, 3 Stan. L. & Pol'y Rev. 242, 244 (1991). –Page Citation.

Stanford Law Review
Ab.: Stan. L. Rev.
Ex.: James M. O'Fallon, <u>Marbury</u>, 44 Stan. L. Rev. 219 (1992). –Article Citation.
James M. O'Fallon, <u>Marbury</u>, 44 Stan. L. Rev. 219, 249-55 (1992). –Page Citation.

State and Local Tax Service (RIA)
Ab.: St. & Loc. Tax Serv. (RIA)

State Constitutional Commentaries and Notes
Ab.: State Const. Commentaries & Notes
Ex.: Anthony Champagne, <u>The Role of Personality in Judicial Reform</u>, 2 State Const. Commentaries & Notes, Winter 1991, at 5. –Article Citation.
Anthony Champagne, <u>The Role of Personality in Judicial Reform</u>, 2 State Const. Commentaries & Notes, Winter 1991, at 5, 6-7. –Page Citation.

State Court Journal
Ab.: State Ct. J.
Ex.: David Prager, <u>The Road to More Effective Judicial System: The Kansas Experience</u>, State Ct. J., Summer 1991, at 20. –Article Citation.
David Prager, <u>The Road to More Effective Judicial System: The Kansas Experience</u>, State Ct. J., Summer 1991, at 20, 25-26. –Page Citation.

State of Louisiana: Acts of the Legislature
Ab.: year La. Acts
Ex.: Act of July 19, 1995, No. 593, 1995-2 La. Acts 1532. –Citation to an entire session law.
Act of July 19, 1995, No. 593, § 1, 1995-2 La. Acts 1532, 1532-35. –Citation to a section of a session law.
–Identifying information may be added parenthetically according to <u>Bluebook</u> Rule 12.4(a).

State of Ohio: Legislative Acts Passed and Joint Resolutions Adopted
Ab.: year Ohio Laws

In citing cases in law review footnotes, abbreviate any word listed in Table T.6; the names of "states, countries, and other geographical units" unless they are named parties; and any other words of eight or more letters "if <u>substantial</u> space is thereby saved and the result is unambiguous." <u>Bluebook</u> Rule 10.2.2. On the other hand, in citing cases in text, abbreviate only widely known acronyms and the following words: "&," "Ass'n," "Bros.," "Co.," "Corp.," "Inc.," "Ltd.," and "No." <u>Bluebook</u> Rule 10.2.1(c).

Ex.:   Act of Apr. 12, 1994, 1993-1994 Ohio Laws 6546. –Citation to an
entire session law.

Act of Apr. 12, 1994, sec. 2, 1993-1994 Ohio Laws 6546, 6548-50.
–Citation to a section of a session law.

–Identifying information may be added parenthetically according to
<u>Bluebook</u> Rule 12.4(a).

State of Utah Bulletin
Ab.:   Utah Bull.

State Tax Reporter (Commerce Clearing House)
Ab.:   St. Tax Rep. (CCH)

State Tax Guide (Commerce Clearing House)
Ab.:   St. Tax Guide (CCH)

State Tax Reporter -- Tennessee (Commerce Clearing House)
Ab.:   St. Tax Rep. (CCH) (Designate volume by state in brackets preceding
service abbreviation)

Ex.:   <u>Lowe's Companies v. Cardwell</u>, [Tennessee] St. Tax Rep. (CCH)
¶ 400-263 (Tenn. July 22, 1991). –Cite to looseleaf material.

–The above example is proper if the case is not yet available in, or is
not reported in, an official or West reporter, a public domain citation,
or in a widely used computer database.

State University of New York at Buffalo Law Review
<u>See</u> Buffalo Law Review

statutes and legislative materials
<u>See</u> specific entries for examples. <u>See also</u> <u>Bluebook</u> Rules 12.1 to 12.9 and
13.1 to 13.7.

Statutes and Statutory Construction, by Norman J. Singer
–Do not abbreviate the title.

Ex.   Norman J. Singer, 1 <u>Statutes and Statutory Construction</u> § 4.14 (5th ed.
1994 & Supp. 2001). –Section Citation.

Norman J. Singer, 2 <u>Statutes and Statutory Construction</u> § 42.9, at 527
(6th ed. 2001). –Page Citation.

Statutes at Large
Ab.:   Stat.   (year)

Ex.:   Act of June 15, 1933, ch. 86, 48 Stat. 152. –Cite to pre-1957 session
law. The citation is to a chapter in Statutes at Large.

Act of May 24, 1982, Pub. L. No. 97-179, 96 Stat. 90. –Cite to a post-
1956 session law.

National Monument Act, ch. 3060, 34 Stat. 225 (1906) (codified at
16 U.S.C. §§ 431-433). –Cite to a pre-1957 session law with a popular
name. The citation is to a chapter in Statutes at Large.

In law review footnotes, the titles of books and the names of cases, except for procedural
phrases, are not underlined. <u>See</u> <u>Bluebook</u> Rule 2.1(a). Further, the following are in large
and small capitals: codes, restatements, standards, constitutions, periodicals, authors of
books, titles of books, the abbreviated names of codes, most legislative materials except for
bills and resolutions, codified ordinances, model codes, court rules, and sentencing guidelines.
Refer to <u>The Bluebook</u>.

Northern Pacific Halibut Act of 1982, Pub. L. No. 97-176, 97 Stat. 78 (to be codified at 16 U.S.C. §§ 773-773k). –Cite to a post-1956 session law with a popular name.

Economic Recovery Tax Act of 1981, Pub. L. No. 97-34, § 403, 95 Stat. 172, 301-05 (codified in scattered sections in the I.R.C.). –Cite to a section within a session law.

Tennessee Valley Authority Act, ch. 32, 48 Stat. 58 (1933) (codified as amended at 16 U.S.C. §§ 831a-831dd (1982)). –Illustration of a citation when a session law has been codified and the code location is known. Some of the examples above also illustrate this situation.

The Bankruptcy Act, ch. 541, 30 Stat. 544 (1898) (repealed 1978). –Cite to a repealed statute.

National Industrial Recovery Act, ch. 90, § 3, 48 Stat. 195, 196-97 (1933), repealed by Act of June 14, 1935, ch. 246, 49 Stat. 375. –Cite to a repealed statute with a complete citation to the repealing statute.

Securities Act of 1933, ch. 38, § 2, 48 Stat. 74, 74 (current version at 15 U.S.C. § 77(b) (1976 & Supp. IV 1980)). –Cite to a version of a statute no longer in force. The current version is indicated parenthetically.

Securities Act of 1933, 15 U.S.C. § 77(b) (1976 & Supp. IV 1980) (original version at ch. 38, § 2, 48 Stat. 74, 74 (1933)). –Cite to a code provision's prior history.

Treaty of Alliance, Feb. 6, 1778, U.S.-Fr., 8 Stat. 6, T.S. No. 82. –Cite to treaties dated prior to 1945 to which the U.S. is a party. See Bluebook Rule 20.4.5.

Agreement Respecting Mutual Aid, Apr. 17, 1945, U.S. - S. Afr., 60 Stat. 1576, T.I.A.S. No. 15ll. –Cite to treaties from 1945 to the present to which the U.S. is a party. See Bluebook Rule 20.4.5.

Statutes - citing to secondary sources
Act of Feb. 2, 1995, Pub. L. No. 113-95, 1995 U.S.C.C.A.N. (113 Stat.) 166. See Bluebook Rule 12.5(b).

Statutes - Electronic Databases
See electronic media and other nonprint resources.

Statutes of Alberta (Canada)
Ab.:   S.A.
Ex.:   Legal Profession Act, ch. 9.1, 1990 S.A. 205 (Can.).

Statutes of British Columbia
See British Columbia Statutes

Statutes of California
Ab.:   year Cal. Stat.

In citing cases in law review footnotes, abbreviate any word listed in Table T.6; the names of "states, countries, and other geographical units" unless they are named parties; and any other words of eight or more letters "if substantial space is thereby saved and the result is unambiguous." Bluebook Rule 10.2.2. On the other hand, in citing cases in text, abbreviate only widely known acronyms and the following words: "&," "Ass'n," "Bros.," "Co.," "Corp.," "Inc.," "Ltd.," and "No." Bluebook Rule 10.2.1(c).

Ex.:   Act of Sept. 29, 1990, ch. 1580, 1990-4 Cal. Stat. 7553. –Citation to an entire session law.

Act of Sept. 29, 1990, ch. 1580, sec. 2, § 4573, 1990-4 Cal. Stat 7553, 7554-55.

–Citation to a section of a session law amending prior act.

–Identifying information may be added parenthetically according to Bluebook Rule 12.4(a).

Statutes of Canada
Ab.:   S.C.

Canadian Space Agency Act, ch.13, 1990 S.C. 223 (Can.).

Statutes of Nevada
Ab.:   year Nev. Stat.

Ex.:   Act of July 1, 1999, ch. 355, 1999 Nev. Stat. 1557. –Citation to an entire session law.

Act of July 1, 1999, ch. 355, sec. 1, § 931.180, 1999 Nev. Stat. 1557, 1557 (act relating to education personnel). –Citation to a section of a session law.

Statutes of Newfoundland (Canada)
Ab.:   S. Nfld.

Ex.:   The International Trusts Act, ch. 28, 1989 S. Nfld. 264 (Can.).

Statutes of Nova Scotia (Canada)
Ab.:   S.N.S.

Ex.:   School Boards Act, ch. 6, 1991 S.N.S. 61 (Can.).

Statutes of Ontario (Canada)
Ab.:   S.O.

Ex.:   Ontario Loan Act of 1990, ch. 21, 1990 S.O. 380 (Can.).

Statutes of Québec (Canada)
Ab.:   S.Q.

Ex.:   Act of Sept. 4, 1990, ch. 34, 1990 S.Q. 761 (Can.).

Statutes of Saskatchewan (Canada)
Ab.:   S.S.

Ex.:   Saskatchewan Gaming Commission Act, ch. S-18.1, 1989-1990 S.S. 625 (Can.).

Statutes of the Yukon Territory (Canada)
Ab.:   S.Y.T.

Ex.:   Fifth Appropriation Act, 1984-85, ch. 1, 1985 S.Y.T. 1 (Can.).

statutes, subsequent citation to
See subsequent citation to cases, statutes, and prior citations

---

In law review footnotes, the titles of books and the names of cases, except for procedural phrases, are not underlined. See Bluebook Rule 2.1(a). Further, the following are in large and small capitals: codes, restatements, standards, constitutions, periodicals, authors of books, titles of books, the abbreviated names of codes, most legislative materials except for bills and resolutions, codified ordinances, model codes, court rules, and sentencing guidelines. Refer to The Bluebook.

Stetson Law Review

    Ab.:   Stetson L. Rev.

    Ex.:   Morey W. McDaniel, Stockholders and Stakeholders, 21 Stetson L. Rev. 121 (1991). –Article Citation.

            Morey W. McDaniel, Stockholders and Stakeholders, 21 Stetson L. Rev. 121, 135-37 (1991). –Page Citation.

sub nom.

    Ex.:   United Jewish Org. v. Wilson, 510 F.2d 512 (2d Cir. 1975), cert. granted sub nom. United Jewish Org. v. Carey, 430 U.S. 144 (1977).

            Graves v. Barnes, 378 F. Supp. 640 (W.D. Tex. 1974), vacated as moot sub nom. White v. Regester, 422 U.S. 935 (1975). See Bluebook Rule 10.7.2.

subsequent case history

    –"Whenever a decision is cited in full, give the entire subsequent history of the case, but omit denials of certiorari or denials of similar discretionary appeals, unless the decision is less than two years old or the denial is particularly relevant. Omit also the history on remand or any denial of a rehearing, unless relevant to the point for which the case is cited. Finally, omit any disposition withdrawn by the deciding authority, such as an affirmance followed by reversal or rehearsing." Bluebook Rule 10.7.

    Ex.:   Shultz v. Consolidation Coal Co., 475 S.E.2d 467 (W. Va. 1996), cert. denied, 65 U.S.L.W. 3505 (U.S. Jan. 21, 1997) (No. 96-731).

            Pacemaker Diagnostic Clinic of America, Inc. v. Instromedix, Inc., 725 F.2d 537 (9th Cir.), cert. denied, 469 U.S. 824 (1984).

            Devine v. Nutt, 718 F.2d 1048 (Fed. Cir. 1983), rev'd sub nom. Cornelius v. Nutt, 472 U.S. 648 (1985).

subsequent citation to legal authority

    Ex.:   DeFunis, 416 U.S. at 334. –Subsequent citation for DeFunis v. Odegaard, 416 U.S. 312 (1974).

            15 U.S.C. § 2 or § 2. –Subsequent citation for 15 U.S.C. § 2 (1994).

            Id. –citation for material in preceding footnote or text.

            Id. at 470. –citation for page 470 of material in preceding footnote or text.

Commercial Electronic Databases

    Ex.:   Reed v. Hamilton, No. W1999-00440-COA-R3-CV, 2000 WL 558613, at *4 (Tenn. Ct. App. May 4, 2000)

            becomes

            Reed, 2000 WL 558613, at *3.

In citing cases in law review footnotes, abbreviate any word listed in Table T.6; the names of "states, countries, and other geographical units" unless they are named parties; and any other words of eight or more letters "if substantial space is thereby saved and the result is unambiguous." Bluebook Rule 10.2.2. On the other hand, in citing cases in text, abbreviate only widely known acronyms and the following words: "&," "Ass'n," "Bros.," "Co.," "Corp.," "Inc.," "Ltd.," and "No." Bluebook Rule 10.2.1(c).

Ashley v. ITT Hartford, No. C 97-3226 TEH, 1998 U.S. Dist. LEXIS
1228, at *3 (N.D. Cal. Jan. 20, 1998)
becomes
Ashley, 1998 U.S. Dist. LEXIS 1228, at *5.

H.R. 1390, 106th Cong. § 3(c) (1999), WL 1999 CONG US HR 1390
becomes
HR 1390 § 3(c), WL 1999 CONG US HR 1390.

Regulation D, 12 C.F.R. § 204.1 (2000), WL 12 CRF s 204.1.
becomes
12 C.F.R. § 204.1, WL 12 CFR s 204.1 *or* WL 12 CFR s 204.1.

See Bluebook Rules 4.1, 10.9, 12.9, 13.7, 14.10, 15.8, 16.7, 18.7, and 19.2. See
also the rules for the particular authority.

Suffolk Transnational Law Journal
Ab.:   Suffolk Transnat'l L.J.
Ex.:   Claudia M. Pardinas, The Enigma of the Legal Liability of
          Transnational Corporations, 14 Suffolk Transnat'l L.J. 405 (1991).
          –Article Citation.
          Claudia M. Pardinas, The Enigma of the Legal Liability of
          Transnational Corporations, 14 Suffolk Transnat'l L.J. 405, 435-47
          (1991). –Page Citation.

Suffolk University Law Review
Ab.:   Suffolk U. L. Rev.
Ex.:   Mark D. Robins, The Resurgence and Limits of the Demurrer,
          27 Suffolk U. L. Rev. 637 (1993). –Article Citation.
          Mark D. Robins, The Resurgence and Limits of the Demurrer,
          27 Suffolk U. L. Rev. 637, 650-52 (1993). –Page Citation.

Sullivan on Antitrust
See Handbook of the Law of Antitrust, by Lawrence A. Sullivan

Superior Court
Ab.:   Super. Ct.

supplement
See the various title entries in this work and Bluebook Rule 3.2(c).

supra
          –"Portions of text, footnotes, and groups of authorities within the piece
          in which the citation is made may be cited through the use of supra or
          infra." See Bluebook Rule 3.6.

In law review footnotes, the titles of books and the names of cases, except for procedural
phrases, are not underlined. See Bluebook Rule 2.1(a). Further, the following are in large
and small capitals: codes, restatements, standards, constitutions, periodicals, authors of
books, titles of books, the abbreviated names of codes, most legislative materials except for
bills and resolutions, codified ordinances, model codes, court rules, and sentencing guidelines.
Refer to The Bluebook.

–"When an authority has been fully cited previously, the <u>supra</u> form may be used (unless "<u>id.</u>" is appropriate)." <u>See</u> <u>Bluebook</u> Rule 4.2. <u>See also</u> Practitioners' Note P.4.

Supreme Court (federal)
Ab.:   U.S.

Supreme Court (other)
Ab.:   Sup. Ct.

Supreme Court, Appellate Division
Ab.:   App. Div.

Supreme Court, Appellate Term
Ab.:   App. Term

Supreme Court Historical Society Yearbook
Ab.:   Sup. Ct. Hist. Soc'y Y.B.

Supreme Court Practice, by Robert L. Stern, Eugene Gressman, Stephen M. Shapiro, and Kenneth S. Geller
    –Do not abbreviate this title.
Ex.:   Robert L. Stein et al., <u>Supreme Court Practice</u> § 4.28, at 216 (7th ed. 1993). –Page Citation.

Supreme Court Reporter
    –With volume 106 (1985), Supreme Court Reporter became West's Supreme Court Reporter. Citation form is not affected by this title change.
    –Cite to U.S if therein; otherwise, cite to S. Ct., L. Ed., or U.S.L.W., in that order of preference. <u>See</u> <u>Bluebook</u>, Table T.1.
Ab.:   S. Ct.
Ex.:   <u>Bush v. Vera</u>, 116 S. Ct. 1941 (1996). –Case Citation.
           <u>Bush v. Vera</u>, 116 S. Ct. 1941, 1961 (1996). –Page Citation.

Supreme Court Reports (Canada)
Ab.:   S.C.R.
Ex.:   <u>Canson Enterprises v. Broughton & Co.</u>, [1991] 3 S.C.R. 534 (Can.).

Supreme Court Review
Ab.:   Sup. Ct. Rev.
Ex.:   John M. Langbein, <u>The Supreme Court Flunks Trusts</u>, 1990 Sup. Ct. Rev. 207. –Article Citation.
           John M. Langbein, <u>The Supreme Court Flunks Trusts</u>, 1990 Sup. Ct. Rev. 207, 210-12. –Page Citation.

Supreme Court Rules (Rules of the Supreme Court of the United States).
Ab.:   Sup. Ct. R.

In citing cases in law review footnotes, abbreviate any word listed in Table T.6; the names of "states, countries, and other geographical units" unless they are named parties; and any other words of eight or more letters "if <u>substantial</u> space is thereby saved and the result is unambiguous." <u>Bluebook</u> Rule 10.2.2. On the other hand, in citing cases in text, abbreviate only widely known acronyms and the following words: "&," "Ass'n," "Bros.," "Co.," "Corp.," "Inc.," "Ltd.," and "No." <u>Bluebook</u> Rule 10.2.1(c).

Ex.:   Sup. Ct. R. 5.
        See also Rules of Evidence and Procedure and Bluebook Rule 12.8.3.

Supreme Judicial Court
Ab.:   Sup. Jud. Ct.

Surrogate's Court
Ab.:   Sur. Ct.

Swedish and International Arbitration
Ab.:   Swed. & Int'l Arb.
Ex.:   Sigvard Jarvin, The Place of Arbitration, 1990 Swed. & Int'l Arb. 85.
        –Article Citation.

        Sigvard Jarvin, The Place of Arbitration, 1990 Swed. & Int'l Arb. 85,
        86. –Page Citation.

Sydney Law Review
Ab.:   Sydney L. Rev.
Ex.:   John Gava, Scholarship and Community, 16 Sydney L. Rev. 443
        (1994). –Article Citation.

        John Gava, Scholarship and Community, 16 Sydney L. Rev. 443,
        444-52 (1994). –Page Citation.

symposia
Ex.:   Symposium, A Reevaluation of the Canons of Statutory Interpretation,
        45 Vand. L. Rev. 529 (1992). –When citing a symposium as a unit,
        cite to the first page of the first piece. See Bluebook Rule 16.5.3.

        Jonathan R. Macey & Geoffrey P. Miller, The Canons of Statutory
        Construction and Judicial Preferences, 45 Vand. L. Rev. 647 (1992).
        –Individual articles within a symposium are cited in the same manner
        as any other article. See Bluebook Rule 16.6.3.

Syracuse Journal of International Law and Commerce
Ab.:   Syracuse J. Int'l L. & Com.
Ex.:   Eugene T. Rossides, Cyprus and the Rule of Law, 17 Syracuse J. Int'l
        L. & Com. 21 (1991). –Article Citation.

        Eugene T. Rossides, Cyprus and the Rule of Law, 17 Syracuse J. Int'l
        L. & Com. 21, 55-67 (1991). –Page Citation.

Syracuse Law Review
Ab.:   Syracuse L. Rev.
Ex.:   Daniel Kramer, Torts, 42 Syracuse L. Rev. 737 (1991). –Article
        Citation.

        Daniel Kramer, Torts, 42 Syracuse L. Rev. 737, 749-50 (1991). –Page
        Citation.

In law review footnotes, the titles of books and the names of cases, except for procedural
phrases, are not underlined. See Bluebook Rule 2.1(a). Further, the following are in large
and small capitals: codes, restatements, standards, constitutions, periodicals, authors of
books, titles of books, the abbreviated names of codes, most legislative materials except for
bills and resolutions, codified ordinances, model codes, court rules, and sentencing guidelines.
Refer to The Bluebook.

T

Tasmanian Reports (Australia)
Ab.:   T.R.
Ex.:   Regina v. Farrell, 1988 T.R. 152 (Austl.).

Tax Adviser, The
Ab.:   Tax Adviser
Ex.:   Lorin D. Luchs, New Rules for Estimated Tax Payments, 23 Tax
         Adviser 203 (1992). –Article Citation.

         Lorin D. Luchs, New Rules for Estimated Tax Payments, 23 Tax
         Adviser 203, 206 (1992). –Page Citation.

Tax Court
Ab.:   T.C.

Tax Court Memorandum Decisions (Commerce Clearing House)
Ab.:   T.C.M. (CCH)
Ex.:   Kosman v. Commissioner, 71 T.C.M. (CCH) ¶ 51, 219(M) (1995).
         –The above example is proper if the case is not yet available in the
         Reports of the United States Tax Court (TC).

Tax Court Memorandum Decisions (Research Institute of America)
Ab.:   T.C.M. (RIA)
Ex.:   Peterson v. Commissioner, 1997 T.C.M. (RIA) ¶ 97,018 (Jan. 8,
         1997). –Citation to looseleaf materials.

         Ballard v. Commissioner, 1996 T.C.M. (RIA) ¶ 96,068. –Citation to
         bound volume.

Tax Court of the United Reports
Ab.:   T.C.
Ex.:   Hager v. Commissioner, 76 T.C. 66 (1981).

Tax Court Reported Decisions (Research Institute of America)
Ab.:   Tax Ct. Rep. Dec. (RIA)
Ex.:   Brookes v. Commissioner, 108 Tax Ct. Rep. Dec. (RIA) ¶ 108.1 (Jan 2,
         1997). –Citation to looseleaf material.

         P&X Markets, Inc. v. Commissioner, 106 Tax. Ct. Rep. Dec. (RIA)
         ¶ 106.26 (1996). –Citation to bound volume.

In law review footnotes, the titles of books and the names of cases, except for procedural
phrases, are not underlined. See Bluebook Rule 2.1(a). Further, the following are in large
and small capitals: codes, restatements, standards, constitutions, periodicals, authors of
books, titles of books, the abbreviated names of codes, most legislative materials except for
bills and resolutions, codified ordinances, model codes, court rules, and sentencing guidelines.
Refer to The Bluebook.

Tax Court Reports (Commerce Clearing House)
Ab.: Tax Ct. Rep. (CCH)

Ex.: Thompson v. Commissioner, [Current Memo Decisions] Tax Ct. Rep. (CCH) (72 T.C.M.) Dec. 51,605(M) (Oct. 17, 1996). –Citation to looseleaf material.

Cochrane v. Commissioner, [Current Regular Decisions] Tax Ct. Rep. (CCH) Dec. 51,490 (Aug. 7, 1996). –Citation to looseleaf material.

Brotman v. Commissioner, [1995 Transfer Binder] Tax Ct. Rep. (CCH) Dec. 50,860 (Aug. 24, 1995). –Transfer binder material.

–The above examples are proper if the case is not yet available in, or is not reported in, an official or West reporter, a public domain citation, or in a widely used computer database.

Tax Executive, The
Ab.: Tax Executive

Ex.: Leonard F. Francis, IRS Offset Program: A Case Study, 43 Tax Executive 389 (1991). –Article Citation.

Leonard F. Francis, IRS Offset Program: A Case Study, 43 Tax Executive 389, 389-90 (1991). –Page Citation.

Tax Law Review
Ab.: Tax L. Rev.

Ex.: William A. Klein, Tax Effects of Nonpayment of Child Support, 45 Tax L. Rev. 177 (1990). –Article Citation.

William A. Klein, Tax Effects of Nonpayment of Child Support, 45 Tax L. Rev. 177, 180-85 (1990). –Page Citation.

Tax Lawyer, The
Ab.: Tax Law.

Ex.: David S. Hudson, The Tax Concept of Research or Experimentation, 45 Tax Law. 85 (1991). –Article Citation.

David S. Hudson, The Tax Concept of Research or Experimentation, 45 Tax Law. 85, 89-90(1991). –Page Citation.

Tax Management International Journal
Ab.: Tax Mgmt. Int'l J.

Ex.: Brian Hornsby, The United Kingdom Budget Statement 1991 - Some Implications for U.S. Investors, 20 Tax Mgmt. Int'l J. 302 (1991). –Article Citation.

Brian Hornsby, The United Kingdom Budget Statement 1991 - Some Implications for U.S. Investors, 20 Tax Mgmt. Int'l J. 302, 304-05 (1991). –Page Citation.

Tax Notes
Ab.: Tax Notes

In citing cases in law review footnotes, abbreviate any word listed in Table T.6; the names of "states, countries, and other geographical units" unless they are named parties; and any other words of eight or more letters "if substantial space is thereby saved and the result is unambiguous." Bluebook Rule 10.2.2. On the other hand, in citing cases in text, abbreviate only widely known acronyms and the following words: "&," "Ass'n," "Bros.," "Co.," "Corp.," "Inc.," "Ltd.," and "No." Bluebook Rule 10.2.1(c).

Ex.:   Donald W. Kiefer, Tax Policy: What Happened? What Next?, 55 Tax
          Notes 1675 (1992). –Article Citation.

          Donald W. Kiefer, Tax Policy: What Happened? What Next?, 55 Tax
          Notes 1675, 1679 (1992). –Page Citation.

Tax Treaties (Commerce Clearing House)
Ab.:   Tax Treaties (CCH)

Taxation for Accountants
Ab.:   Tax'n for Acct.
Ex.:   Jerome Mauer, Partners Can Control Tax Effects of Retirement
          Payouts, 49 Tax'n for Acct. 201 (1992). –Article Citation.

          Jerome Mauer, Partners Can Control Tax Effects of Retirement
          Payouts, 49 Tax'n for Acct. 201, 206-07 (1992). –Page Citation.

Taxation for Lawyers
Ab.:   Tax'n for Law.
Ex.:   Eric J. Selter, Leasing Employees May Ease Benefit Compliance,
          20 Tax'n for Law. 270 (1992). –Article Citation.

          Eric J. Selter, Leasing Employees May Ease Benefit Compliance,
          20 Tax'n for Law. 270, 272 (1992). –Page Citation.

Taxation of the Closely Held Corporation, by Theodore Ness and Eugene L.
Vogel
          –Do not abbreviate the title.
Ex.:   Theodore Ness & Eugene L. Vogel, Taxation of the Closely Held
          Corporation ¶ 8.14[2][f] (5th ed. 1991). –Section Citation.

          Theodore Ness & Eugene L. Vogel, Taxation of the Closely Held
          Corporation ¶ 8.14[2][f], at 8-40 (5th ed. 1991). –Page Citation.

          Theodore Ness & Eugene L. Vogel, Taxation of the Closely Held
          Corporation ¶ 8.14[2][f], at 8-40 n.62 (5th ed. 1991). –Footnote
          Citation.

Taxes–The Tax Magazine
Ab.:   Taxes
Ex.:   Orrin Tilevitz, "Condopping" A Co-op, 69 Taxes 558 (1991). –Article
          Citation.

          Orrin Tilevitz, "Condopping" A Co-op, 69 Taxes 558, 560-61 (1991).
          –Page Citation.

television broadcasts
Ex.:   ABC World News Tonight (ABC television broadcast, Dec. 9, 1996).

Temple Environmental Law & Technology Journal
Ab.:   Temp. Int'l & Comp. L.J.

In law review footnotes, the titles of books and the names of cases, except for procedural
phrases, are not underlined. See Bluebook Rule 2.1(a). Further, the following are in large
and small capitals: codes, restatements, standards, constitutions, periodicals, authors of
books, titles of books, the abbreviated names of codes, most legislative materials except for
bills and resolutions, codified ordinances, model codes, court rules, and sentencing guidelines.
Refer to The Bluebook.

Ex.:   Charles H. Montague, <u>Conserving Rail Corridors</u>, 10 Temp. Envtl L. & Tech. J. 139 (1991). –Article Citation.

Charles H. Montague, <u>Conserving Rail Corridors</u>, 10 Temp. Envtl L. & Tech. J. 139, 149-52 (1991). –Page Citation.

Temple International and Comparative Law Journal
Ab.:   Temp. Int'l & Comp. L.J.

Ex.:   Donna E. Arzt, <u>Soviet Anti-Semitism: Legal Responses in an Age of Glasnost</u>, 4 Temp. Int'l & Comp. L.J. 163 (1990). –Article Citation.

Donna E. Arzt, <u>Soviet Anti-Semitism: Legal Responses in an Age of Glasnost</u>, 4 Temp. Int'l & Comp. L.J. 163, 172-73 (1990). –Page Citation.

Temple Law Quarterly
Ab.:   Temp. L.Q.

Temple Law Review
Ab.:   Temp. L. Rev.

Ex.:   Laura E. Little, <u>An Excursion into the Uncharted Waters of the Seventeenth Amendment</u>, 64 Temp. L. Rev. 629 (1991). –Article Citation.

Laura E. Little, <u>An Excursion into the Uncharted Waters of the Seventeenth Amendment</u>, 64 Temp. L. Rev. 629, 630-35 (1991). –Page Citation.

temporary
Ab.:   temp.

Temporary Treasury Regulation (Federal)
Ab.:   Temp. Treas. Reg.

Ex.:   Temp. Treas. Reg. § 1.897-6T(a)(2) (1985).

Tennessee Administrative Code
See Official Compilation Rules and Regulations of the State of Tennessee.

Tennessee Administrative Register
Ab.:   Tenn. Admin. Reg. (month year)

Ex.:   15 Tenn. Admin. Reg. 12 (Dec. 1989).

Tennessee Appeals Reports
Ab.:   Tenn. App.

–Discontinued in 1972 after 63 Tenn. App. 732 (1972).

–Cite to S.W., S.W.2d, or S.W.3d if therein; otherwise, cite to Tenn. App.

In citing cases in law review footnotes, abbreviate any word listed in Table T.6; the names of "states, countries, and other geographical units" unless they are named parties; and any other words of eight or more letters "if <u>substantial</u> space is thereby saved and the result is unambiguous." <u>Bluebook</u> Rule 10.2.2. On the other hand, in citing cases in text, abbreviate only widely known acronyms and the following words: "&," "Ass'n," "Bros.," "Co.," "Corp.," "Inc.," "Ltd.," and "No." <u>Bluebook</u> Rule 10.2.1(c).

–Give parallel citations only in documents submitted to Tennessee state courts. See Bluebook Rule 10.3.1 and Practitioners' Note P.3; see also Tenn. R. App. P. 27(h), which permits citation to either the official or South Western Reporter or both.

–Through 63 Tenn. App. 732 (1972), cite as follows:

In documents submitted to Tennessee state courts:

> Stevens v. Moore, 24 Tenn. App. 61, 139 S.W.2d 710 (1940). –Case Citation.

> Stevens v. Moore, 24 Tenn. App. 61, 67, 139 S.W.2d 710, 713 (1940). –Page Citation.

In all other documents:

> Stevens v. Moore, 139 S.W.2d 710 (Tenn. Ct. App. 1940). –Case Citation.

> Stevens v. Moore, 139 S.W.2d 710, 713 (Tenn. Ct. App. 1940). –Page Citation.

–After 63 Tenn. App. 732 (1972), cite as follows:

In all documents:

> Peaver v. Hunt, 924 S.W.2d 114 (Tenn. Ct. App. 1996). –Case Citation.

> Peaver v. Hunt, 924 S.W.2d 114, 115 (Tenn. Ct. App. 1996). – Page Citation.

Tennessee Bar Journal
Ab.: Tenn. B.J.

Ex.: Lucian T. Pera, Rule 11 Comes to Tennessee: The Emerging State Law of Sanctions, Tenn. B.J., Jan.-Feb. 1992, at 24. –Article Citation.

Lucian T. Pera, Rule 11 Comes to Tennessee: The Emerging State Law of Sanctions, Tenn. B.J., Jan.-Feb. 1992, at 24, 26. –Article Citation.

Tennessee Circuit Court Practice, by Lawrence A. Pivnick
–Do not abbreviate this title.

Ex.: Lawrence A. Pivnick, Tennessee Circuit Court Practice § 3-16 (2000). –Section Citation.

Lawrence A. Pivnick, Tennessee Circuit Court Practice § 3-16, at 255 (2000). –Page Citation.

Tennessee Code Annotated
Ab.: Tenn. Code Ann. § (year)

Ex.: Tenn. Code Ann. § 13-21-107 (1999).

Tenn. Code Ann. § 47-8-105 (Supp. 1998).

In law review footnotes, the titles of books and the names of cases, except for procedural phrases, are not underlined. See Bluebook Rule 2.1(a). Further, the following are in large and small capitals: codes, restatements, standards, constitutions, periodicals, authors of books, titles of books, the abbreviated names of codes, most legislative materials except for bills and resolutions, codified ordinances, model codes, court rules, and sentencing guidelines. Refer to The Bluebook.

Tennessee Constitution
Ab.:   Tenn. Const. art. , §

Ex.:   Tenn. Const. art. IX, §§ 1,2. –"Cite constitutional provisions currently in force without date."   Bluebook Rule 11.

Tenn. Const. art. XI,. § 14 (repealed 1978). –"If the cited provision has been repealed, either indicate parenthetically the fact and date of repeal or cite the repealing provision in full."   Bluebook Rule 11.

Tenn. Const. art. XI, § 28 (amended 1982). –"When citing a provision that has been subsequently amended, either indicate parenthetically the fact and date of amendment or cite the amending provision in full." Bluebook Rule 11.

Tenn. Const. of 1834, art. I, § 29 (1870), –"Cite constitutions that have been totally superseded by year of adoption; if the specific provision cited was adopted in a different year, give that year parenthetically."   Bluebook Rule 11.

Tennessee Corporations, by Ronald L. Gilman
–Do not abbreviate this title.

Ex.:   Ronald L. Gilman, Tennessee Corporations Form 19, at 117 (1991). –Page Citation.

Ronald L. Gilman, Tennessee Corporations § 11.4, at 92 (1991). –Page Citation.

Tennessee Criminal Appeals Reports
Ab.:   Tenn. Crim. App.

–Discontinued after 4 Tenn. Crim. App. 723 (1971).

–Cite to S.W., S.W.2d, or S.W.3d if therein; otherwise, cite to Tenn. Crim. App.

–Give parallel citations only in documents submitted to Tennessee state courts. See Bluebook Rule 10.3.1 and Practitioners' Note P.3; see also Tenn. R. App. P. 27(h), which permits citation to either the official or South Western Reporter or both.

–From 1 Tenn. Crim. App. 1 through 4 Tenn. Crim. App. 723, cite as follows:

In documents submitted to Tennessee state courts:

Stokely v. State, 4 Tenn. Crim. App. 241, 470 S.W.2d 37 (1971). –Case Citation.

Stokely v. State, 4 Tenn. Crim. App. 241, 245, 470 S.W.2d 37, 39 (1971). –Page Citation.

In all other documents:

Stokely v. State, 470 S.W.2d 37 (Tenn. Crim. App. 1971). –Case Citation.

In citing cases in law review footnotes, abbreviate any word listed in Table T.6; the names of "states, countries, and other geographical units" unless they are named parties; and any other words of eight or more letters "if substantial space is thereby saved and the result is unambiguous." Bluebook Rule 10.2.2. On the other hand, in citing cases in text, abbreviate only widely known acronyms and the following words: "&," "Ass'n," "Bros.," "Co.," "Corp.," "Inc.," "Ltd.," and "No." Bluebook Rule 10.2.1(c).

Stokely v. State, 470 S.W.2d 37, 39 (Tenn.. Crim. App. 1971). –
Page Citation.

–After 4 Tenn. Crim. App. 723, cite as follows:
In all documents:

State v. Forbes, 918 S.W.2d 431 (Tenn. Crim. App. 1995). –Case
Citation.

State v. Forbes, 918 S.W.2d 431, 450 (Tenn.. Crim. App. 1995).
–Page Citation.

Tennessee Divorce, Alimony & Child Custody, by W. Walton Garrett
–Do not abbreviate the title.

Ex.: W. Walton Garrett, Tennessee Divorce, Alimony & Child Custody,
§ 21-8 (2000). –Section Citation.

W. Walton Garrett, Tennessee Divorce, Alimony & Child Custody,
§ 21-8, at 307 (2000). –Page Citation.

Tennessee Jurisprudence
Ab.: Tenn. Jur. article's name § (year)
Ex.: 26 Tenn. Jur. Working Contracts § 5 (1985).

Tennessee Law of Evidence, by Neil P. Cohen, Donald F. Paine & Sarah Y. Sheppeared
–Do not abbreviate the title.

Ex.: Neil P. Cohen et al., Tennessee Law of Evidence § 617.1, at 439 (3d
ed. 1995).

Tennessee Law Review
Ab.: Tenn. L. Rev.

Ex.: T. Maxfield Bahner, Tennessee Law of Evidence, 58 Tenn. L. Rev. 709
(1991). –Article Citation.

T. Maxfield Bahner, Tennessee Law of Evidence, 58 Tenn. L. Rev.
709, 710 (1991). –Page Citation.

Tennessee Practice
–Do not abbreviate the title.

Ex.: 6 Nancy F. MacLean & Bradley A. MacLean, Tennessee Practice:
Civil Procedure Forms § 58.28 (2d ed. 1987). –Section Citation.

6 Nancy F. MacLean & Bradley A. MacLean, Tennessee Practice:
Civil Procedure Forms § 58.28, at 69 (2d ed. 1987). –Page Citation.

10 David L. Raybin, Tennessee Practice: Criminal Practice and
Procedure § 23.50, at 140 n.6 (1985). –Footnote Citation.

Tennessee Private Acts
See Private Acts of the State of Tennessee.

In law review footnotes, the titles of books and the names of cases, except for procedural phrases, are not underlined. See Bluebook Rule 2.1(a). Further, the following are in large and small capitals: codes, restatements, standards, constitutions, periodicals, authors of books, titles of books, the abbreviated names of codes, most legislative materials except for bills and resolutions, codified ordinances, model codes, court rules, and sentencing guidelines. Refer to The Bluebook.

Tennessee Public Acts
See Public Acts of the State of Tennessee.

Tennessee Reports
Ab.:   Tenn.
–Discontinued in 1972 after 225 Tenn. 727 (1972).
–Cite to S.W., S.W.2d, or S.W.3d if therein; otherwise, cite to Tenn.
–Give parallel citations only in documents submitted to Tennessee state courts. See Bluebook Rule 10.3.1 and Practitioners' Note P.3; see also Tenn. R. App. P. 27(h), which permits citation to either the official or South Western Reporter or both.
–Through 225 Tenn. 727 (1972), cite as follows:
In documents submitted to Tennessee state courts:

Cultra v. Cultra, 188 Tenn. 506, 221 S.W.2d 533 (1959). –Case Citation.

Cultra v. Cultra, 188 Tenn. 506, 509, 221 S.W.2d 533, 535 (1959). –Page Citation.

In all other documents:

Cultra v. Cultra, 221 S.W.2d 533 (Tenn. 1959). –Case Citation.

Cultra v. Cultra, 221 S.W.2d 533, 535 (Tenn. 1959). –Page Citation.

–After 225 Tenn. 727 (1972), cite as follows:
In all documents:

State v. Ricci, 914 S.W.2d 475 (Tenn. 1996). –Case Citation.

State v. Ricci, 914 S.W.2d 475, 476 (Tenn. 1996). –Page Citation.

Tennessee Rules and Regulations
See Official Compilation Rules and Regulations of the State of Tennessee.

Tennessee Session Laws
See Public Acts and Resolutions of the State of Tennessee and Private Acts of the State of Tennessee.

Territorial Sea Journal
Ab.:   Terr. Sea J.

Territories Law Reports (Canada) (1885-1907)
Ab.:   Terr. L.R.

Texas Administrative Code
Ab.:   [tit.] Tex. Admin. Code § (year)

In citing cases in law review footnotes, abbreviate any word listed in Table T.6; the names of "states, countries, and other geographical units" unless they are named parties; and any other words of eight or more letters "if substantial space is thereby saved and the result is unambiguous." Bluebook Rule 10.2.2. On the other hand, in citing cases in text, abbreviate only widely known acronyms and the following words: "&," "Ass'n," "Bros.," "Co.," "Corp.," "Inc.," "Ltd.," and "No." Bluebook Rule 10.2.1(c).

Ex.:   37 Tex. Admin. Code § 81.1 (2000).

Texas Bar Journal
Ab.:   Tex. B.J.
Ex.:   Russell Weintraub, <u>The Need for Forum Non Conveniens Legislation in Texas</u>, 55 Tex. B.J. 346 (1992). –Article Citation.

Russell Weintraub, <u>The Need for Forum Non Conveniens Legislation in Texas</u>, 55 Tex. B.J. 346, 347 (1992). –Page Citation.

Texas Codes Annotated (Vernon)
<u>See</u> Vernon's Texas Codes Annotated.

Texas Constitution
Ab.:   Tex. Const. Art.   , §   .
Ex.:   Tex. Const. art. XVI, § 22. –"Cite constitutional provisions currently in force without date." <u>Bluebook</u> Rule 11.

Tex. Const. art. III, § 42 (repealed 1962). –"If the cited provision has been repealed, either indicate parenthetically the fact and date of repeal or cite the repealing provision in full." <u>Bluebook</u> Rule 11.

Tex. Const. art. XI, § 3 (amended 1989). –"When citing a provision that has been subsequently amended, either indicate parenthetically the fact and date of amendment or cite the amending provision in full." <u>Bluebook</u> Rule 11.

Tex. Const. of 1869, art. I, § 4 (1876). –"Cite constitutions that have been totally superseded by year of adoption; if the specific provision cited was adopted in a different year, give that year parenthetically." <u>Bluebook</u> Rule 11.

Texas Court of Civil Appeals
Ab.:   Tex. Civ. App.

<u>See</u> Texas Courts of Appeals

Texas Court of Criminal Appeals
Ab.:   Tex. Crim. App.
–Cite to S.W., S.W.2d, or S.W.3d if therein; otherwise, cite to Tex. Crim.

–Give parallel citations only in documents submitted to Texas state courts. <u>See</u> <u>Bluebook</u> Rule 10.3.1 and Practitioners' Note P.3; <u>see also</u> Texas Law Review Ass'n, <u>Texas Rules of Form</u> (9th ed. 1997), which may be obtained from the Texas Law Review Business Office.

–Through 172 Tex. Crim. 655 (1962), when Texas Criminal Reports were discontinued, cite as follows:

In documents submitted to Texas state courts:

<u>Ex parte Burnett</u>, 85 Tex. Crim. 315, 211 S.W. 934 (1919).

In law review footnotes, the titles of books and the names of cases, except for procedural phrases, are not underlined. <u>See</u> <u>Bluebook</u> Rule 2.1(a). Further, the following are in large and small capitals: codes, restatements, standards, constitutions, periodicals, authors of books, titles of books, the abbreviated names of codes, most legislative materials except for bills and resolutions, codified ordinances, model codes, court rules, and sentencing guidelines. Refer to <u>The Bluebook</u>.

–Case Citation.

Ex parte Burnett, 85 Tex. Crim. 315, 319, 211 S.W. 934, 935 (1919). –Page Citation.

In all other documents:

Ex parte Burnett, 211 S.W. 934 (Tex. Crim. App. 1919). –Case Citation.

Ex parte Burnett, 211 S.W. 934, 935 (Tex. Crim. App.1919). –Page Citation.

–After 172 Tex. Crim. 655 (1962), cite as follows:

In all documents:

Robbins v. State, 914 S.W.2d 582 (Tex. Crim. App. 1996). –Case Citation.

Robbins v. State, 914 S.W.2d 582, 584 (Tex. Crim. App. 1996). –Page Citation.

Texas Courts of Appeals

Ab.: Tex. App.

–In 1981, the Texas Courts of Appeals (Tex. App.) replaced the Texas Court of Civil Appeals (Tex. Civ. App.), appeal still lying to the Texas Supreme Court (Tex.). At the same time the Texas Courts of Appeals became the intermediate appellate court for criminal cases, from whence appeal lies to the Texas Court of Criminal Appeals (Tex. Crim. App.).

–Give parallel citations only in documents submitted to Texas state courts, for any cases reported in Tex. Civ. App. between 1892 and 1911. See Bluebook 10.3.1 and Practitioners' Note P.3; see also Texas Law Review Ass'n, Texas Rules of Form (9th ed. 1997), which may be obtained from the Texas Law Review Business Office.

–In documents submitted to Texas state courts, identify the particular court of appeals:

–Houston [1st Dist.] (formerly Galveston until June 1957), Fort Worth, Austin, San Antonio, Dallas, Texarkana, Amarillo, El Paso, Beaumont, Waco, Eastland, Tyler, Corpus Christi and Houston [14th Dist.].

In addition, Texas state courts also require writ history (for civil cases before September 1, 1997) or petition history (for civil cases on or after September 1, 1997, and for criminal cases), as follows:

–For civil cases before September 1, 1997:

In citing cases in law review footnotes, abbreviate any word listed in Table T.6; the names of "states, countries, and other geographical units" unless they are named parties; and any other words of eight or more letters "if substantial space is thereby saved and the result is unambiguous." Bluebook Rule 10.2.2. On the other hand, in citing cases in text, abbreviate only widely known acronyms and the following words: "&," "Ass'n," "Bros.," "Co.," "Corp.," "Inc.," "Ltd.," and "No." Bluebook Rule 10.2.1(c).

(1) n.w.h. [no writ history]; (2) no writ; (3) writ requested; (4) writ dism'd by agr; (5) writ dism'd; (6) writ dism'd w.o.j. [writ dismissed for want of jurisdiction]; (7) writ dism'd judgm't cor. [writ dismissed, judgment correct]; (8) writ ref'd w.o.m. [writ refused for want of merit; (9) writ ref'd n.r.e. [writ refused, no reversible error]; (10) writ denied; (11) writ ref'd; (12) writ granted w.r.m. [writ granted without reference to the merits]; (13) writ granted

–For civil cases on or after September 1, 1997:

(1) no pet. h. [no petition history]; (2) no pet.; (3) pet. filed; (4) pet. dism'd by agr.; (5) pet. withdrawn; (6) pet. dism'd w.o.j. [petition dismissed for want of jurisdiction]; (7) pet. denied; (8) pet. ref'd [petition refused]; (9) pet. granted, judgm't vacated w.r.m. [petition granted, judgment vacated without reference to the merits]; (10) pet. granted

–For criminal cases:

(1) no pet. h. [no petition history]; (2) no pet.; (3) pet. filed; (4) pet. dism'd; (5) pet. ref'd, untimely filed; (6)pet. ref'd [petition refused]; (7) pet. granted; (8) rev. granted, without pet. [review granted, without petititon]

See Texas Law Review Ass'n, Texas Rules of Form (9th ed. 1997).

–In documents submitted to Texas state courts, cite as follows:

Tate v. State Bar, 920 S.W.2d 727(Tex. App. - Houston [1st Dist.] 1996, writ denied). –Case citation.

Tate v. State Bar, 920 S.W.2d 727, 728 (Tex. App. - Houston [1st Dist.] 1996, writ denied). –Page citation.

Johnson v. State, 919 S.W.2d 473 (Tex. App. - Fort Worth 1996, pet. ref'd). –Case Citation.

Johnson v. State, 919 S.W.2d 473, 480 (Tex. App. - Fort Worth 1996, pet. ref'd). –Page Citation.

Brightwell v. Rabeck, 430 S.W.2d 252 (Tex. Civ. App. - Fort Worth 1968, writ ref'd n.r.e.). –Case Citation.

Brightwell v. Rabeck, 430 S.W.2d 252, 255 (Tex. Civ. App. - Fort Worth 1968, writ ref'd n.r.e.). –Page Citation.

Outlaw v. Mayor, 999 S.W.2d 252 (Tex. App.-Waco 1999, no pet.) –Case Citation.

Outlaw v. Mayor, 999 S.W.2d 252, 254 (Tex. App.-Waco 1999, no pet.) –Page Citation.

–In all other documents, cite as follows:

Tate v. State Bar, 920 S.W.2d 727 (Tex. App. 1996) –Case Citation.

In law review footnotes, the titles of books and the names of cases, except for procedural phrases, are not underlined. See Bluebook Rule 2.1(a). Further, the following are in large and small capitals: codes, restatements, standards, constitutions, periodicals, authors of books, titles of books, the abbreviated names of codes, most legislative materials except for bills and resolutions, codified ordinances, model codes, court rules, and sentencing guidelines. Refer to The Bluebook.

Tate v. State Bar, 920 S.W.2d 727, 728 (Tex. App. 1996) –Page Citation.

Johnson v. State, 919 S.W.2d 473 (Tex. App. 1996) –Case Citation.

Johnson v. State, 919 S.W.2d 473, 480 (Tex. App. 1996) –Page Citation.

Brightwell v. Rabeck, 430 S.W.2d 252 (Tex. Civ. App. 1968) –Case Citation.

Brightwell v. Rabeck, 430 S.W.2d 252, 254 (Tex. Civ. App. 1968) –Page Citation.

Outlaw v. Mayor, 999 S.W.2d 252 (Tex. App. 1999) –Case Citation.

Outlaw v. Mayor, 999 S.W.2d 252, 254 (Tex. App.1999) –Page Citation.

Texas Digest of Opinions of the Attorney General
See Opinions of the Attorney General of Texas.

Texas International Law Journal
Ab.:   Tex. Int'l L.J.

Texas Law Review
Ab.:   Tex. L. Rev.

Ex.:   Alex W. Albright, The Texas Discovery Privileges: A Fool's Game?, 70 Tex. L. Rev. 781 (1992). –Article Citation.

Alex W. Albright, The Texas Discovery Privileges: A Fool's Game?, 70 Tex. L. Rev. 781, 833-35 (1992). –Page Citation.

Texas Register
Ab.:   Tex. Reg.

Texas Revised Civil Statutes Annotated
See Vernon's Texas Revised Civil Statutes Annotated.

Texas Session Laws
See General and Special Laws of the State of Texas and Vernon's Texas Session Law Service (West).

Texas Supreme Court
Ab.:   Tex.

Ex.:   –Cite to S.W., S.W.2d, or S.W.3d if therein; otherwise, cite to Tex.

–Give parallel citations only in documents submitted to Texas state courts. See Bluebook Rule 10.3.1 and Practitioners' Note P.3; see also Texas Law Review Ass'n, Texas Rules of Form (9ᵗʰ ed. 1997), which may be obtained from the Texas Law Review Business Office.

–Through 163 Tex. 638 (1962), cite as follows:

In citing cases in law review footnotes, abbreviate any word listed in Table T.6; the names of "states, countries, and other geographical units" unless they are named parties; and any other words of eight or more letters "if substantial space is thereby saved and the result is unambiguous." Bluebook Rule 10.2.2. On the other hand, in citing cases in text, abbreviate only widely known acronyms and the following words: "&," "Ass'n," "Bros.," "Co.," "Corp.," "Inc.," "Ltd.," and "No." Bluebook Rule 10.2.1(c).

In documents submitted to Texas state courts:

Gleich v. Bongio, 128 Tex. 606, 99 S.W.2d 881 (1937). –Case Citation.

Gleich v. Bongio, 128 Tex. 606, 611-612, 99 S.W.2d 881, 884 (1937). –Page Citation.

In all other documents:

Gleich v. Bongio, 99 S.W.2d 881 (Tex. 1937). –Case Citation.

Gleich v. Bongio, 99 S.W.2d 881, 884 (Tex. 1937). –Page Citation.

–After 163 Tex. 638 (1962), cite as follows:

In all documents:

Felts v. Harris County, 915 S.W.2d 482 (Tex. 1996). –Case Citation.

Felts v. Harris County, 915 S.W.2d 482, 483 (Tex. 1996). –Page Citation.

Texas Tech Law Review
Ab.: Tex. Tech L. Rev.
Ex.: George Anastaplo, The Constitution at Two Hundred: Explorations, 22 Tex. Tech L. Rev. 967 (1991). –Article Citation.

George Anastaplo, The Constitution at Two Hundred: Explorations, 22 Tex. Tech L. Rev. 967, 969-75 (1991). –Page Citation.

Third World Legal Studies
Ab.: Third World Legal Stud.
Ex.: Beverly M. Carl, Peanuts, Law Professors and Third World Lawyers, 1986 Third World Legal Stud.1. –Article Citation.

Beverly M. Carl, Peanuts, Law Professors and Third World Lawyers, 1986 Third World Legal Stud. 1, 8-9. –Page Citation.

Thomas M. Cooley Law Review
Ab.: T. M. Cooley L. Rev.
Ex.: Joseph Kimble, Plain English: A Charter for Clear Writing, 9 T. M. Cooley L. Rev. 1 (1992). –Article Citation.

Joseph Kimble, Plain English: A Charter for Clear Writing, 9 T. M. Cooley L. Rev. 1, 25-26 (1992). –Page Citation.

Thurgood Marshall Law Review
Ab.: T. Marshall L. Rev.
Ex.: Placido G. Gomez, White People Think Differently, 16 T. Marshall L. Rev. 543 (1991). –Article Citation.

Placido G. Gomez, White People Think Differently, 16 T. Marshall L. Rev. 543, 543-44 (1991). –Page Citation.

In law review footnotes, the titles of books and the names of cases, except for procedural phrases, are not underlined. See Bluebook Rule 2.1(a). Further, the following are in large and small capitals: codes, restatements, standards, constitutions, periodicals, authors of books, titles of books, the abbreviated names of codes, most legislative materials except for bills and resolutions, codified ordinances, model codes, court rules, and sentencing guidelines. Refer to The Bluebook.

Times Law Reports, The (England)
See Bluebook Table T.2.
Ab.: T.L.R.
Ex.: Beck v. Newbold, [1952] 2 T.L.R. 332 (C.A.) (Eng.). –Case Citation.

title(s)
Ab.: tit., tits.

Title News
Ab.: Title News
Ex.: Burton J. Rain, The Changing Partnership, Title News, Dec. 1989, at 5. –Article Citation.
Burton J. Rain, The Changing Partnership, Title News, Dec. 1989, at 5, 6. –Page Citation.

Tort & Insurance Law Journal
Ab.: Tort & Ins. L.J.
Ex.: James M. Fischer, Enforcement of Settlements: A Survey, 27 Tort & Ins. L.J. 82 (1991). –Article Citation.
James M. Fischer, Enforcement of Settlements: A Survey, 27 Tort & Ins. L.J. 82, 98-99 (1991). –Page Citation.

Touro Journal of Transnational Law
Ab.: Touro J. Transnat'l L.
Ex.: Yoram Dinstein, The Parameters and Content of International Criminal Law, 1 Touro J. Transnat'l L. 315 (1990). –Article Citation.
Yoram Dinstein, The Parameters and Content of International Criminal Law, 1 Touro J. Transnat'l L. 315, 332-34 (1990). –Page Citation.

Touro Law Review
Ab.: Touro L. Rev.
Ex.: William M. Brooks, A Comparison of a Mentally Ill Individual's Right to Refuse Medication Under the United States and the New York State Constitutions, 8 Touro L. Rev. 1 (1991). –Article Citation.
William M. Brooks, A Comparison of a Mentally Ill Individual's Right to Refuse Medication Under the United States and the New York State Constitutions, 8 Touro L. Rev. 1, 45-46 (1991). –Page Citation.

Trade Regulation Reporter (Commerce Clearing House)
–Bound as Trade Cases (Commerce Clearing House)
Ab.: Trade Reg. Rep. (CCH)
–Bound as Trade Cas. (CCH)

In citing cases in law review footnotes, abbreviate any word listed in Table T.6; the names of "states, countries, and other geographical units" unless they are named parties; and any other words of eight or more letters "if substantial space is thereby saved and the result is unambiguous." Bluebook Rule 10.2.2. On the other hand, in citing cases in text, abbreviate only widely known acronyms and the following words: "&," "Ass'n," "Bros.," "Co.," "Corp.," "Inc.," "Ltd.," and "No." Bluebook Rule 10.2.1(c).

Ex.: United States v. Motorola, Inc., 7 Trade Reg. Rep. (CCH) (1996-1 Trade Cas.) ¶ 71,402 (D.D.C. July 25, 1995). –Citation to looseleaf material.

Florida Seed Co., Inc. v. Monsanto Co., 1995-2 Trade Cas. (CCH) ¶ 71,240 (N.D. Ala. 1995). –Citation to bound material.

–The above examples are proper if the case is not yet available in, or is not reported in, an official or West reporter, a public domain citation, or in a widely used computer database.

Trademark Protection and Practice, by Jerome Gilson & Jeffrey M. Samuels
–Do not abbreviate the title.

Ex.: Jerome Gilson & Jeffrey M. Samuels, Trademark Protection and Practice 400 (1997). –Page Citation.

Trademark Reporter, The
Ab.: Trademark Rep.
Ex.: J. Joseph Bainton, Reflections on the Trademark Counterfeiting Act of 1984: Score a Few for the Good Guys, 82 Trademark Rep. 1 (1992). –Article Citation.

J. Joseph Bainton, Reflections on the Trademark Counterfeiting Act of 1984: Score a Few for the Good Guys, 82 Trademark Rep. 1, 4-5 (1992). –Page Citation.

translation
Ab.: trans.

translator
Ab.: trans.

Transnational Law & Contemporary Problems
Ab.: Transnat'l L. & Contemp. Probs.
Ex.: Richard A. Falk, Making Foreign Policy Lawful: A Citizen's Imperative, 1 Transnat'l L. & Contemp. Probs. 225 (1991). –Article Citation.

Richard A. Falk, Making Foreign Policy Lawful: A Citizen's Imperative, 1 Transnat'l L. & Contemp. Probs. 225, 230-31 (1991). –Page Citation.

Transnational Lawyer, The
Ab.: Transnat'l Law.
Ex.: Medim P. Vogt, Defensive Measures Against Public Offers Under Swiss Law, 4 Transnat'l Law. 53 (1991). –Article Citation.

Medim P. Vogt, Defensive Measures Against Public Offers Under Swiss Law, 4 Transnat'l Law. 53, 69-73 (1991). –Page Citation.

In law review footnotes, the titles of books and the names of cases, except for procedural phrases, are not underlined. See Bluebook Rule 2.1(a). Further, the following are in large and small capitals: codes, restatements, standards, constitutions, periodicals, authors of books, titles of books, the abbreviated names of codes, most legislative materials except for bills and resolutions, codified ordinances, model codes, court rules, and sentencing guidelines. Refer to The Bluebook.

Transportation Journal
Ab.:   Transp. J.
Ex.:   Terence A. Brown, Property Brokers: A Pilot Study of Shippers Perspectives, Transp. J., Fall 1991, at 45. –Article Citation.

Terence A. Brown, Property Brokers: A Pilot Study of Shippers Perspectives, Transp. J., Fall 1991, at 45, 47. –Page Citation.

Transportation Law Journal
Ab.:   Transp. L.J.
Ex.:   Melanie B. Daly, America - On the Road to Mass Transit, 19 Transp. L.J. 357 (1991). –Article Citation.

Melanie B. Daly, America - On the Road to Mass Transit, 19 Transp. L.J. 357, 369-75 (1991). –Page Citation.

Transportation Practitioners Journal
Ab.:   Transp. Prac. J.
Ex.:   William B. Tye & A. Lawrence Kolbe, Optimal Time Structures for Rates in Regulated Industries, 59 Transp. Prac. J. 176 (1992). –Article Citation.

William B. Tye & A. Lawrence Kolbe, Optimal Time Structures for Rates in Regulated Industries, 59 Transp. Prac. J. 176, 179 (1992). –Page Citation.

Treasury Decision as published in Internal Revenue Bulletin and Cumulative Bulletin
Ab.:   T.D.
Ex.:   T.D. 8323, 1991-1 C.B. 199. –Citation to bound cases.

T.D. 8414, 1992-93 I.R.B. 18. –Citation to unbound cases.

Treasury Decisions Under Customs and Other Laws (1898-1965)
Ab.:   Treas. Dec.
Ex.:   T.D. 20,471, 1 Treas. Dec. 16 (1899).

T.C. 56,416, 100 Treas. Dec. 249 (1965).

Treasury Decisions Under Internal Revenue Laws (1898-1942)
Ab.:   Treas. Dec. Int. Rev.
Ex.:   T.D. 5072, 36 Treas. Dec. Int. Rev. 265 (1941).

T.D. 20,459, 1 Treas. Dec. Int. Rev. 7 (1898).

Treasury Delegation Orders
Ab.:   Deleg. Order
Ex.:   Deleg. Order No. 213, 1985-46 I.R.B. 35. –Unbound

Deleg. Order No. 11 (Rev. 15), 1985-1 C.B. 423. –Bound

In citing cases in law review footnotes, abbreviate any word listed in Table T.6; the names of "states, countries, and other geographical units" unless they are named parties; and any other words of eight or more letters "if substantial space is thereby saved and the result is unambiguous." Bluebook Rule 10.2.2. On the other hand, in citing cases in text, abbreviate only widely known acronyms and the following words: "&," "Ass'n," "Bros.," "Co.," "Corp.," "Inc.," "Ltd.," and "No." Bluebook Rule 10.2.1(c).

Treasury Department Orders
Ab.: Treas. Dep't Order
Ex.: Treas. Dep't Order 150-02, 1986-19 I.R.B. 12. –Unbound.
Treas. Dep't Order 150-106, 1985 C.B. 758. –Bound.

Treasury Regulations (Federal)
See Bluebook Rule 14.5.1
Ab.: Treas. Reg. § (year)
Ex.: Treas. Reg. § 1.401(m)-1 (1991). –Unamended regulation.
Treas. Reg. § 1.401(m)-1 (as amended in 1995). –Amended regulation.

treaties (specific treaties)
Ex.: Definitive Treaty of Peace, Sept. 3, 1783, U.S.-Gr. Brit., 8 Stat. 80, T.S. No. 104.
Treaty of Ghent, Dec. 24, 1814, U.S.-Gr. Brit., 8 Stat. 218, T.S. No. 109. –Citation to a treaty with a widely known popular name.
Treaty of Ghent, Dec. 24, 1814, U.S.-Gr. Brit., art. 10 at 7. –Citation to a subdivision of a treaty.
Moscow Agreement, 1945, U.S.-U.K.-U.S.S.R., 60 Stat. 1899, T.I.A.S. No. 1555. –Citation to a treat with three or more parties.
Convention Respecting Sanitary Aerial Navigation, opened for signature Dec. 15, 1944, 59 Stat. 991, T.S No. 992. –Citation to multilateral treaty which is not signed on a single date.
Instrument for the Amendment of the Constitution of the International Labor Organization, Apr. 20, 1948, 62 Stat. 3485, T.I.A.S. No. 1868, 15 U.N.T.S. 35. –Agreement among three or more parties to which the United States is a party.
Constitution of the United Nations Educational, Scientific and Cultural Organization, Nov. 16, 1945, 4 U.N.T.S. 275. –Agreement among three or more parties to which the United States is not a party. If only two parties, give their names.
See generally Bluebook Rule 21.4.

Treaties and Other International Acts Series (U.S.)
Ab.: T.I.A.S. No.
Ex.: Security of Military Information, July 12, 1985, U.S.-Ecuador, T.I.A.S. No. 11,257, at 2.

Treatise on Constitutional Law: Substance and Procedure, by Ronald D. Rotunda & John E. Nowak
–Do not abbreviate the title.

In law review footnotes, the titles of books and the names of cases, except for procedural phrases, are not underlined. See Bluebook Rule 2.1(a). Further, the following are in large and small capitals: codes, restatements, standards, constitutions, periodicals, authors of books, titles of books, the abbreviated names of codes, most legislative materials except for bills and resolutions, codified ordinances, model codes, court rules, and sentencing guidelines. Refer to The Bluebook.

Ex.:   3 Ronald D. Rotunda & John E. Nowak, Treatise on Consitutional
Law: Substance and Procedure § 18.3 (3d ed. 1999). –Section Citation.

3 Ronald D. Rotunda & John E. Nowak, Treatise on Consitutional
Law: Substance and Procedure § 18.3, at 217 (3d ed. 1999). –Page
Citation.

3 Ronald D. Rotunda & John E. Nowak, Treatise on Consitutional
Law: Substance and Procedure § 18.3, at 217 n.7 (3d ed. 1999).   –
Footnote Citation.

Treatise on Environmental Law, by Frank P. Grad
–Do not abbreviate the title.

Ex.:   2 Frank P. Grad, Treatise on Environmental Law § 9.01[c] (1990).
–Section Citation.

2 Frank P. Grad, Treatise on Environmental Law § 9.01[c], at 9-22
(1990). –Page Citation.

2 Frank P. Grad, Treatise on Environmental Law § 9.01[c], at 9-22
n.47 (1990).
–Footnote Citation.

Treatise on the Law of Contracts, by Samuel Williston
–Do not abbreviate the title.

Ex.:   8 Samuel Williston, Treatise on the Law of Contracts § 949C (Walter
H. Jaeger ed., 3d ed. 1964). –Section Citation to Third Edition.

8 Samuel Williston, Treatise on the Law of Contracts § 949C, at 175
(Walter H. Jaeger ed., 3d ed. 1964). –Page Citation to Third Edition.

8 Samuel Williston, Treatise on the Law of Contracts § 949C, at 175
n.8 (Walter H. Jaeger ed., 3d ed. 1964). –Footnote Citation to Third
Edition.

3 Samuel Williston, Treatise on the Law of Contracts § 7.24 (Richard
A. Lord ed., 4th ed. 1992). –Section Citation to Fourth Edition.

3 Samuel Williston, Treatise on the Law of Contracts § 7.24, at 449
(Richard A. Lord ed., 4th ed. 1992). –Page Citation to Fourth Edition.

3 Samuel Williston, Treatise on the Law of Contracts § 7.24, at 449
n.13 (Richard A. Lord ed., 4th ed. 1992). –Footnote Citation to Fourth
Edition.

Treatise on the Law of Securities Regulation, by Thomas L. Hazen
–Do not abbreviate the title.

Ex.:   1 Thomas L. Hazen, Treatise on the Law of Securities Regulation
§ 4.12 (3d Practitioner's ed. 1995). –Section Citation.

1 Thomas L. Hazen, Treatise on the Law of Securities Regulation
§ 4.12, at 205 (3d Practitioner's ed. 1995). –Page Citation.

In citing cases in law review footnotes, abbreviate any word listed in Table T.6;
the names of "states, countries, and other geographical units" unless they are named parties;
and any other words of eight or more letters "if substantial space is thereby saved and the
result is unambiguous." Bluebook Rule 10.2.2. On the other hand, in citing cases in text,
abbreviate only widely known acronyms and the following words: "&," "Ass'n," "Bros.,"
"Co.," "Corp.," "Inc.," "Ltd.," and "No." Bluebook Rule 10.2.1(c).

1 Thomas L. Hazen, <u>Treatise on the Law of Securities Regulation</u> § 4.12, at 205 n.10 (3d Practitioner's ed. 1995). –Footnote Citation.

treatises
Ex.:   5A A. James Corbin, <u>Corbin on Contracts</u> § 1157 (1964).

A. James Casner, <u>Estate Planning</u> § 6.8.10 (5th ed. Supp. 1987).

<u>See also</u> author(s).

Treaty Series (U.S.)
Ab.:   T.S. No.

Ex.:   Definitive Treaty of Peace, Sept. 3, 1783, U.S.-Gr. Brit., 8 Stat. 80 T.S. 80, No. 104.

<u>See</u> <u>Bluebook</u> Rule 21.4.5. Only use T.S. No. if U.S.T. or Stat. is unavailable.

Trent Law Journal
Ab.:   Trent L.J.

Ex.:   Peter Jones, <u>Equal Pay</u>, 11 Trent L.J. 37 (1987). –Article Citation.

Peter Jones, <u>Equal Pay</u>, 11 Trent L.J. 37, 38-39 (1987). –Page Citation.

Trial
Ab.:   Trial

Ex.:   Alba Conte, <u>Class Action: Remedy for the Hostile Environment</u>, Trial, July 1992, at 18. –Article Citation.

Alba Conte, <u>Class Action: Remedy for the Hostile Environment</u>, Trial, July 1992, at 18, 23. –Page Citation.

Trial Lawyer's Guide, The
Ab.:   Trial Law. Guide

Ex.:   Angel L. Rodriguez, <u>Attorney's Fees in Class Actions</u>, 35 Trial Law. Guide 76 (1991). –Article Citation.

Angel L. Rodriguez, <u>Attorney's Fees in Class Actions</u>, 35 Trial Law. Guide 76, 79-83 (1991). –Page Citation.

Trial Lawyers Quarterly
Ab.:   Trial Law. Q.

Ex.:   Michael P. Koskoff, <u>Forum Non Conveniens</u>, Trial Law. Q., Fall 1991, at 15. –Article Citation.

Michael P. Koskoff, <u>Forum Non Conveniens</u>, Trial Law. Q., Fall 1991, at 15, 19-20. –Page Citation.

Tribe on American Constitutional Law
<u>See</u> American Constitutional Law, by Laurence H. Tribe.

Tribunax Arbitraux Mixtes
Ab.:   Trib. Arb. Mixtes

In law review footnotes, the titles of books and the names of cases, except for procedural phrases, are not underlined. <u>See</u> <u>Bluebook</u> Rule 2.1(a). Further, the following are in large and small capitals: codes, restatements, standards, constitutions, periodicals, authors of books, titles of books, the abbreviated names of codes, most legislative materials except for bills and resolutions, codified ordinances, model codes, court rules, and sentencing guidelines. Refer to <u>The Bluebook</u>.

Trusts, by George T. Bogert
    –Do Not abbreviate the title.
Ex.:   George T. Bogert, <u>Trusts</u> § 56 (6th Practitioner's ed. 1987). –Section
           Citation.

           George T. Bogert, <u>Trusts</u> § 56, at 213 (6th Practitioner's ed. 1987).
           –Page Citation.

           George T. Bogert, <u>Trusts</u> § 56, at 213 n.6 (6th Practitioner's ed. 1987).
           –Footnote Citation.

Trusts and Estates
    Ab.:   Tr. & Est.
    Ex.:   Judith McCue, <u>The States Are Acting to Reform Their Guardianship</u>
           <u>Statutes</u>, Tr. & Est., July 1992, at 32. –Article Citation.

           Judith McCue, <u>The States Are Acting to Reform Their Guardianship</u>
           <u>Statutes</u>, Tr. & Est., July 1992, at 32, 37. –Page Citation.

Tulane Environmental Law Journal
    Ab.:   Tul. Envtl. L.J.
    Ex.:   Anthony R. Chase, <u>The Lender Liability Paradox: A Fresh Approach</u>,
           5 Tul. Envtl. L.J. 1 (1991). –Article Citation.

           Anthony R. Chase, <u>The Lender Liability Paradox: A Fresh Approach</u>,
           5 Tul. Envtl. L.J. 1, 10-11 (1991). –Page Citation.

Tulane Law Review
    Ab.:   Tul. L. Rev.
    Ex.:   Symeon C. Symeonides, <u>Louisiana's New Law of Choice of Law for</u>
           <u>Tort Conflicts: An Exegesis</u>, 66 Tul. L. Rev. 677 (1992). –Article
           Citation.

           Symeon C. Symeonides, <u>Louisiana's New Law of Choice of Law for</u>
           <u>Tort Conflicts: An Exegesis</u>, 66 Tul. L. Rev. 677, 683-94 (1992).
           –Page Citation.

Tulane Maritime Law Journal
    Ab.:   Tul. Mar. L.J.
    Ex.:   Geoffrey Brice, <u>Unexplained Losses in Maritime Insurance</u>, 16 Tul.
           Mar. L.J. 105 (1991). –Article Citation.

           Geoffrey Brice, <u>Unexplained Losses in Maritime Insurance</u>, 16 Tul.
           Mar. L.J. 105, 110-111 (1991). –Page Citation.

Tulsa Law Journal
    Ab.:   Tulsa L.J.

In citing cases in law review footnotes, abbreviate any word listed in Table T.6;
the names of "states, countries, and other geographical units" unless they are named parties;
and any other words of eight or more letters "if <u>substantial</u> space is thereby saved and the
result is unambiguous." <u>Bluebook</u> Rule 10.2.2. On the other hand, in citing cases in text,
abbreviate only widely known acronyms and the following words: "&," "Ass'n," "Bros.,"
"Co.," "Corp.," "Inc.," "Ltd.," and "No." <u>Bluebook</u> Rule 10.2.1(c).

Ex.: Richard J. Apolla, Jr., <u>A Practitioners Guide to Oklahoma Trade Secrets Law. Past, Present, and Future: The Uniform Trade Secrets Act</u>, 27 Tulsa L.J. 137 (1991). –Article Citation.

Richard J. Apolla, Jr., <u>A Practitioners Guide to Oklahoma Trade Secrets Law. Past, Present, and Future: The Uniform Trade Secrets Act</u>, 27 Tulsa L.J. 137, 139-50 (1991). –Page Citation.

typeface conventions for briefs
See <u>Bluebook</u> Practitioners' Notes P.1 and Rule 7. <u>See also</u> the examples on the facing pages on the inside back cover of <u>The Bluebook</u>.

typeface conventions for law review footnotes
See <u>Bluebook</u> Rules 2.1 and 7. <u>See also</u> the examples on the facing pages on the inside front cover of <u>The Bluebook</u>.

typeface conventions for law review texts
See <u>Bluebook</u> Rules 2.2. and 7.

typeface conventions for legal memoranda
See <u>Bluebook</u> Practitioners' Notes P.1 and Rule 7. <u>See also</u> the examples on the facing pages on the inside back cover of <u>The Bluebook</u>.

In law review footnotes, the titles of books and the names of cases, except for procedural phrases, are not underlined. <u>See Bluebook</u> Rule 2.1(a). Further, the following are in large and small capitals: codes, restatements, standards, constitutions, periodicals, authors of books, titles of books, the abbreviated names of codes, most legislative materials except for bills and resolutions, codified ordinances, model codes, court rules, and sentencing guidelines. Refer to <u>The Bluebook</u>.

U

U.C. Davis Law Review
Ab.: U.C. Davis L. Rev.

Ex.: Elyn R. Saks, Multiple Personality Disorder and Criminal Responsibility, 25 U.C. Davis L. Rev. 383 (1992). –Article Citation.

Elyn R. Saks, Multiple Personality Disorder and Criminal Responsibility, 25 U.C. Davis L. Rev. 383, 385-87 (1992). –Page Citation.

U.C.L.A. Journal of Environmental Law and Policy
Ab.: UCLA J. Envtl. L. & Pol'y

Ex.: Linda A. Malone, The Necessary Interrelationship Between Land Use and Preservation of Groundwater Resources, 9 UCLA J. Env't L. & Pol'y 1 (1990). –Article Citation.

Linda A. Malone, The Necessary Interrelationship Between Land Use and Preservation of Groundwater Resources, 9 UCLA J. Env't L. & Pol'y 1, 55-67 (1990). –Page Citation.

UCLA Law Review
Ab.: UCLA L. Rev.

Ex.: Marc M. Arkin, Rethinking the Constitutional Right to a Criminal Appeal, 39 UCLA L. Rev. 503 (1992). –Article Citation.

Marc M. Arkin, Rethinking the Constitutional Right to a Criminal Appeal, 39 UCLA L. Rev. 503, 505 (1992). –Page Citation.

U.C.L.A. Pacific Basin Law Journal
Ab.: UCLA Pac. Basin L.J.

Ex.: Edward G. Eurney, Protection of Computer Programs Under Japanese Copyright Law, 9 UCLA Pac. Basin L.J. 1 (1991). –Article Citation.

Edward G. Eurney, Protection of Computer Programs Under Japanese Copyright Law, 9 UCLA Pac. Basin L.J. 1, 11-12 (1991). –Page Citation.

UMKC Law Review
Ab.: UMKC L. Rev.

In law review footnotes, the titles of books and the names of cases, except for procedural phrases, are not underlined. See Bluebook Rule 2.1(a). Further, the following are in large and small capitals: codes, restatements, standards, constitutions, periodicals, authors of books, titles of books, the abbreviated names of codes, most legislative materials except for bills and resolutions, codified ordinances, model codes, court rules, and sentencing guidelines. Refer to The Bluebook.

Ex.:   Robert J. Gregory, <u>The Clearly Expressed Intent and the Doctrine of Congressional Acquiescence</u>, 60 UMKC L. Rev. 27 (1991). –Article Citation.

Robert J. Gregory, <u>The Clearly Expressed Intent and the Doctrine of Congressional Acquiescence</u>, 60 UMKC L. Rev. 27, 55-61 (1991). –Page Citation.

Unemployment Insurance Reports (Commerce Clearing House)
Ab.:   Unempl. Ins. Rep. (CCH)

uniform acts
<u>See</u> <u>Bluebook</u> Rule 12.8.4.
Ex.:   U.C.C. § 9-312(5)(b) (1994).

Unif. Partnership Act § 103 (1994).

Unif. Common Interest Ownership Act § 1-104 (1994).

Unif. Probate Code § 6-107 (1989).

Unif. R. of Crim. P. 432 (amended 1991).

Uniform Commercial Code
Ab.:   U.C.C. §   (year U.C.C. last amended)
Ex.:   U.C.C. § 9-312(5)(b) (1994).

Uniform Commercial Code, by James J. White and Robert S. Summers
–Do not abbreviate this title.
Ex.:   James J. White & Robert S. Summers, <u>Uniform Commercial Code</u> § 9-2 (5th ed. 2000). –Section Citation.

James J. White & Robert S. Summers, <u>Uniform Commercial Code</u> § 9-2, at 343 (5th ed. 2000). –Page Citation.

James J. White & Robert S. Summers, <u>Uniform Commercial Code</u> § 9-2, at 343 n.2 (5th ed. 2000). –Footnote Citation.

Uniform Commercial Code, by Ronald A. Anderson
–Do not abbreviate this title.
Ex.:   9A Ronald A. Anderson, <u>Uniform Commercial Code</u> § 9-504:157 (3d ed. 1994). –Section Citation.

9A Ronald A. Anderson, <u>Uniform Commercial Code</u> § 9-504:157, at 545 (3d ed. 1994). –Page Citation.

9A Ronald A. Anderson, <u>Uniform Commercial Code</u> § 9-504:157, at 545 n.1064 (3d ed. 1994). –Footnote Citation.

9A Ronald A. Anderson, <u>Uniform Commercial Code</u> § 9-504:157 (3d ed. Supp. 1996). –Section Citation to Supplement.

Uniform Commercial Code Law Journal
Ab.:   UCC L.J.

In citing cases in law review footnotes, abbreviate any word listed in Table T.6; the names of "states, countries, and other geographical units" unless they are named parties; and any other words of eight or more letters "if <u>substantial</u> space is thereby saved and the result is unambiguous." <u>Bluebook</u> Rule 10.2.2. On the other hand, in citing cases in text, abbreviate only widely known acronyms and the following words: "&," "Ass'n," "Bros.," "Co.," "Corp.," "Inc.," "Ltd.," and "No." <u>Bluebook</u> Rule 10.2.1(c).

Ex.:   John M. Norwood, <u>Punitive Damages for Wrongful Dishonour of a Check</u>, 64 UCC L.J. 64 (1991). –Article Citation.

John M. Norwood, <u>Punitive Damages for Wrongful Dishonour of a Check</u>, 64 UCC L.J. 64, 69-70 (1991). –Page Citation.

Uniform Commercial Code Reporting Service (CBC)
Ab.:   U.C.C. Rep. Serv. (CBC)
Ex.:   <u>All American Auto Salvage v. Camp's Auto Wreckers</u>, [Current Materials] U.C.C. Rep. Serv. 2d (CBC) (30 U.C.C. Rep. Serv. 2d) 1 (N.J. Super. Aug. 1, 1996). –Citation to looseleaf material.

<u>Kultura, Inc. v. Southern Leasing Corp.</u>, 29 U.C.C. Rep. Serv. 2d (CBC) 1046 (Tenn. Mar. 25, 1996). –Citation to bound material.

–The above examples are proper if the case is not yet available in, or is not reported in, an official or West reporter, a public domain citation, or in a widely used computer database.

Uniform Laws Annotated
<u>See</u> <u>Bluebook</u> Rule 12.8.4.
Ab.:   U.L.A. (year uniform act repealed or amended if any).
Ex.:   Unif. Partnership Act § 302, 6 U.L.A. 35-36 (1994).

Union Labor Report
Ab.:   Union Lab. Rep. (BNA)

United Kingdom Statutes
<u>See</u> <u>Bluebook</u> Rule 20.5.1 and Table T.2. p. 290.
Ex.:   Channel Tunnel Act, 1987, c. 53 (Eng.).

United Nations Charter
<u>See</u> Charter of the United Nations

United Nations Documents
Ab.:   U.N. Doc.
<u>See</u> <u>Bluebook</u> Rule 21.7.2.

United Nations Juridical Yearbook
Ab.:   U.N. Jurid. Y.B.
Ex.:   1991 U.N. Jurid. Y.B. 276, U.N. Doc. ST/LEG/SER.C.29.

United Nations Official Records:
Economic and Social Council Official Records:
Ab.:   U.N. ESCOR
<u>See</u> <u>Bluebook</u> Rule 21.7.1(b)(iii).
General Assembly Official Records:
Ab.:   U.N. GAOR

In law review footnotes, the titles of books and the names of cases, except for procedural phrases, are not underlined. <u>See</u> <u>Bluebook</u> Rule 2.1(a). Further, the following are in large and small capitals: codes, restatements, standards, constitutions, periodicals, authors of books, titles of books, the abbreviated names of codes, most legislative materials except for bills and resolutions, codified ordinances, model codes, court rules, and sentencing guidelines. Refer to <u>The Bluebook</u>.

See Bluebook Rule 21.7.1(b)(i).
    Security Council Official Records:
Ab.:   U.N. SCOR
See Bluebook Rule 21.7.1(b)(ii).
    Trusteeship Council Official Records:
Ab.:   U.N. TCOR
See Bluebook Rule 21.7.1(b)(iv).
    Trade and Development Board Official Records:
Ab.:   U.N. TDBOR
See Bluebook Rule 21.7.1(b)(v).
    Note: All of the aforementioned documents may have an Annex or
    Supplement.

United Nations Reports of International Arbitral Awards
Ab.:   R.I.A.A.
Ex.:   Revaluation of German Mark, 19 R.I.A.A. 67 (U.N. 1980).

United Nations Resolutions in General Assembly Official Records
Ab.:   G.A. Res.
Ex.:   G.A. Res. 1068, U.N. GAOR., 11th Sess., Supp. No. 17, at 32, U.N.
    Doc. A/3572 (1957).
    See Bluebook Rule 21.7.1(a)(i).

United Nations Treaty Series
Ab.:   U.N.T.S.
Ex.:   Agreement on the Abolition of the Visa Requirement, Feb. 4, 1983,
    Hung.-Malta, art. 5, 1351 U.N.T.S. 166.

United Nations Yearbook
Ab.:   U.N.Y.B.
Ex.:   Legal Aspects of International Political Relations, 1986 U.N.Y.B. 986,
    U.N. Sales No. E.90.I.1.

United States Agricultural Decisions
See Agriculture Decisions (U.S.) .

United States Atomic Energy Commission Reports
See Atomic Energy Commission Reports (U.S.).

United States Civil Aeronautics Board Reports (vol. 1 by C.A.A.)
See Civil Aeronautics Board Reports (U.S.).

United States Claims Court
See Claims Court

In citing cases in law review footnotes, abbreviate any word listed in Table T.6;
the names of "states, countries, and other geographical units" unless they are named parties;
and any other words of eight or more letters "if substantial space is thereby saved and the
result is unambiguous." Bluebook Rule 10.2.2. On the other hand, in citing cases in text,
abbreviate only widely known acronyms and the following words: "&," "Ass'n," "Bros.,"
"Co.," "Corp.," "Inc.," "Ltd.," and "No." Bluebook Rule 10.2.1(c).

United States Claims Court Reporter
<u>See</u> Claims Court Reporter

United States Code
Ab.:   U.S.C.

Ex.:   42 U.S.C. § 7706(a) (1994).

5 U.S.C. app. § 103(a) (1994). –Citation to appendix.

23 U.S.C. § 101 (1994 & Supp. I 1995). –Citation to both main volume and the supplement.

42 U.S.C. §§ 677(a) - 677(b) (1994).

42 U.S.C. § 1320a(8) - (10) (1994). –Citations to consecutive subsections.

Sherman Act § 2, 15 U.S.C. § 2 (1994). –Citation to a section which is part of an act known by a popular name.

37 U.S.C. § 312 (1982), <u>amended by</u> 37 U.S.C. § 312 (Supp. III 1985). –Citation to a non-current version of a code section with a complete citation to the amending statute.

37 U.S.C. § 312 (Supp. III 1985) (amending 37 U.S.C. 312 (1982)). –Citation to a statute giving prior history parenthetically.

1 U.S.C. § 108 (1994) (originally enacted as Act of July 30, 1947, ch. 388, § 108, 61 Stat. 634, 635). –Citation to a statute giving prior history parenthetically.

2 U.S.C. § 25 (1994) (corresponds to Act of June 1, 1789, ch. 1, § 2, 1 Stat. 23, 23). –Citation to a statute giving prior history parenthetically.

United States Code Annotated
Ab.:   U.S.C.A. §   (West year)

Ex.:   5 U.S.C.A. § 8332 (West 1996).

19 U.S.C.A. § 1673 (West Supp. 1995). –Citation to a statute found in a supplemental volume.

7 U.S.C.A. § 1309 (West Supp. 1996). –Citation to a statute found in a pocket part.

United States Code Congressional and Administrative News
Ab.:   U.S.C.C.A.N.

Ex.:   Personal Responsibility and Work Opportunity Act of 1996, Pub. L. No. 104-193, 1996 U.S.C.C.A.N. (110 Stat.) 2105.

H.R. Rep. No. 104-311, at 96 (1995), <u>reprinted in</u> 1995 U.S.C.C.A.N. 793, 808.

United States Code Service (Lexis)
Ab.:   U.S.C.S. §   (Lexis)

In law review footnotes, the titles of books and the names of cases, except for procedural phrases, are not underlined. <u>See</u> <u>Bluebook</u> Rule 2.1(a). Further, the following are in large and small capitals: codes, restatements, standards, constitutions, periodicals, authors of books, titles of books, the abbreviated names of codes, most legislative materials except for bills and resolutions, codified ordinances, model codes, court rules, and sentencing guidelines. Refer to <u>The Bluebook</u>.

Ex.:   49 U.S.C.S. § 506 (Lexis 1998).

49 U.S.C.S. § 5301 (Lexis 1998 & Supp. 2000). –Citation to a statute found in both the main body and supplement of the code.

United States Comptroller General's Opinions
See Decisions of the Comptroller General of the United States.

United States Comptroller Treasury Decisions
See Decisions of the Comptroller General of the United States.

United States Constitution
Ab.:   U.S. Const.

Ex.:   U.S. Const. art. II, § 2.

U.S. Const. amend. XIV, § 1.

See Bluebook Rule 11.

United States Copyright Decisions
See Copyright Decisions (U.S).

United States Court Martial Reports
See Court Martial Reports.

United States Court of Appeals for the Armed Forces
Ab.:   C.A.A.F.

Ex.:   United States v. Melanson, 53 M. J. 1 (C.A.A.F. 2000).

Court Rules:

Ab.:   C.A.A.F.

Ex.:   C.A.A.F. R. 43

United States Court of Appeals for the First Circuit
Cases:

Ab.:   (1st Cir. year)

Ex.:   Montilla Records, Inc. v. Morales, 575 F.2d 324 (1st Cir. 1978).

Court Rules:

Ab.:   1st Cir. R.

Ex.:   1st Cir. R. 11.

United States Court of Appeals for the Second Circuit
Cases:

Ab.:   (2d Cir. year)

Ex.:   Central Hanover Bank & Trust Co. v. Herbst, 93 F.2d 510 (2d Cir. 1937).

Court Rules:

Ab.:   2d Cir. R.

In citing cases in law review footnotes, abbreviate any word listed in Table T.6; the names of "states, countries, and other geographical units" unless they are named parties; and any other words of eight or more letters "if substantial space is thereby saved and the result is unambiguous." Bluebook Rule 10.2.2. On the other hand, in citing cases in text, abbreviate only widely known acronyms and the following words: "&," "Ass'n," "Bros.," "Co.," "Corp.," "Inc.," "Ltd.," and "No." Bluebook Rule 10.2.1(c).

Ex.:   2d Cir. R. 4(b).

United States Court of Appeals for the Third Circuit
    Cases:
Ab.:   (3d Cir. year)
Ex.:   United States v. Anderskow, 88 F.3d 245 (3rd Cir. 1996).
    Court Rules:
Ab.:   3d Cir. R.
Ex.:   3d Cir. R. 15.1.

United States Court of Appeals for the Fourth Circuit
    Cases:
Ab.:   (4th Cir. year)
Ex.:   Fennell v. Monongahela Power Co., 350 F.2d 867 (4th Cir. 1965).
    Court Rules:
Ab.:   4th Cir. R.
Ex.:   4th Cir. R. 11.

United States Court of Appeals for the Fifth Circuit
    Cases:
Ab.:   (5th Cir. year)
Ex.:   John P. McGuire Co. v. Herzog, 421 F.2d 419 (5th Cir. 1970).
    Court Rules:
Ab.:   5th Cir. R.
Ex.:   5th Cir. R. 8.2.

United States Court of Appeals for Fifth Circuit (Fifth Circuit split)
See Bluebook Rule 10.8.2.
    –Decisions rendered in 1981, labeled as "5th Cir.":
Ex.:   Lewis v. Reagan, 660 F.2d 124 (5th Cir. Oct. 1981).
    –Decisions with unit information:
Ex.:   United States v. Wright, 661 F.2d 60 (5th Cir. Unit A 1981).
    –Decisions rendered after September 30, 1981, labeled as Former Fifth
      Circuit judgment:
Ex.:   Helms v. Jones, 660 F.2d 120 (Former 5th Cir. 1981).

United States Court of Appeals for the Sixth Circuit
See public domain citations.
    Cases:
Ab.:   (6th Cir. year)

In law review footnotes, the titles of books and the names of cases, except for procedural phrases, are not underlined. See Bluebook Rule 2.1(a). Further, the following are in large and small capitals: codes, restatements, standards, constitutions, periodicals, authors of books, titles of books, the abbreviated names of codes, most legislative materials except for bills and resolutions, codified ordinances, model codes, court rules, and sentencing guidelines. Refer to The Bluebook.

Ex.:   Johnson v. Heffron, 88 F.3d 404 (6th Cir. 1996).

Court Rules:

Ab.:   6th Cir. R.

Ex.:   6th Cir. R. 6(a).

United States Court of Appeals for the Seventh Circuit

Cases:

Ab.:   (7th Cir. year)

Ex.:   Booker v. Ward, 94 F.3d 1052 (7th Cir. 1996).

Court Rules:

Ab.:   7th Cir. R.

Ex.:   7th Cir. R. 10(b).

United States Court of Appeals for the Eighth Circuit

Cases:

Ab.:   (8th Cir. year)

Ex.:   NLRB v. Skelly Oil Co., 473 F.2d 1079 (8th Cir. 1973).

Court Rules:

Ab.:   8th Cir. R.

Ex.:   8th Cir. R. 11A.

United States Court of Appeals for the Ninth Circuit

Cases:

Ab.:   (9th Cir. year)

Ex.:   United States v. Neff, 615 F.2d 1235 (9th Cir. 1980).

Court Rules:

Ab.:   9th Cir. R.

Ex.:   9th Cir. R. 6-1.

United States Court of Appeals for the Tenth Circuit

Cases:

Ab.:   (10th Cir. year)

Ex.:   United States Fidelity & Guaranty Co. v. Sidwell, 525 F.2d 472 (10th Cir. 1975).

Court Rules:

Ab.:   10th Cir. R.

Ex.:   10th Cir. R. 2.1.

United States Court of Appeals for the Eleventh Circuit

Cases:

Ab.:   (11th Cir. year)

In citing cases in law review footnotes, abbreviate any word listed in Table T.6; the names of "states, countries, and other geographical units" unless they are named parties; and any other words of eight or more letters "if substantial space is thereby saved and the result is unambiguous." Bluebook Rule 10.2.2. On the other hand, in citing cases in text, abbreviate only widely known acronyms and the following words: "&," "Ass'n," "Bros.," "Co.," "Corp.," "Inc.," "Ltd.," and "No." Bluebook Rule 10.2.1(c).

Ex.:   Profitt v. Wainwright, 685 F.2d 1227 (11th Cir. 1982).
          Court Rules:
Ab.:   11th Cir. R.
Ex.:   11th Cir. R. 11-2.

United States Court of Appeals for the District of Columbia Circuit
          Cases:
Ab.:   (D.C. Cir. year)
Ex.:   Mountain States Legal Foundation v. Glickman, 484 F.2d 820 (D.C.
          Cir. 1973).
          Court Rules:
Ab.:   D.C. Cir. R.
Ex.:   D.C. Cir. R. 9(a).

United States Court of Appeals for the Federal Circuit
          Cases:
Ab.:   (Fed. Cir. year)
Ex.:   Medtronic Inc. v. Intermedics, Inc., 799 F.2d 734 (Fed. Cir. 1986).
          Court Rules:
Ab.:   Fed. Cir. R.
Ex.:   Fed. Cir. R. 11(a).
          –Succeeded United States Court of Customs and Patent Appeals and
          the appellate jurisdiction of the Court of Claims.
          –If not in F., F.2d, or F.3d cite to the official reporter (Court of Claims
          Reports or Court of Customs and Patent Appeals Reports).

United States Court of Appeals for Veterans Claims
Ab.:   Vet. App.
Ex.:   Dillon v. Brown, 8 Vet. App. 165 (1955).
          Court Rules:
Ab.:   Vet. App. R.
Ex.:   Vet. App. R. 4(a)

United States Court of Claims
          See Court of Claims.

United States Court of Claims Reports
          See Court of Claims Reports.

United States Court of Customs and Patent Appeals Reports
          See Court of Customs and Patent Appeals Reports.

In law review footnotes, the titles of books and the names of cases, except for procedural phrases, are not underlined. See Bluebook Rule 2.1(a). Further, the following are in large and small capitals: codes, restatements, standards, constitutions, periodicals, authors of books, titles of books, the abbreviated names of codes, most legislative materials except for bills and resolutions, codified ordinances, model codes, court rules, and sentencing guidelines. Refer to The Bluebook.

United States Court of Federal Claims
See Court of Federal Claims.

United States Court of International Trade
Ab.:   Ct. Int'l Trade
–Created 1980, successor to the United States Customs Court (Cust. Ct.), which was created in 1926.
–Cite to Court of International Trade in the following order of preference: Reports (Ct. Int'l Trade) if therein, otherwise to F. Supp., F. Supp. 2d., Customs Bulletin and Decisions (Cust. B. & Dec.), or to International Trade Reporter Decisions (I.T.R.D. (BNA)).
Ex.:   S.I. Stud, Inc. v. United States, 17 Ct. Int'l Trade 661 (1993).

Federal-Mogul Corp. v. United States, 918 F. Supp. 386 (Ct. Int'l Trade 1996).

Wolfe Shoe Co. v. United States, 30 Cust B. & Dec. No. 36, at 118 (Ct. Int'l Trade 1996).

Item Co. v. United States, 18 I.T.R.D. 1769 (Ct. Int'l Trade 1996).

United States Court of Military Appeals
See Court of Military Appeals.

United States Cumulative Bulletin
See Cumulative Bulletin (U.S.).

United States Customs Bulletin and Decisions
See Customs Bulletin and Decisions (U.S.).

United States Customs Court
Ab.:   Cust. Ct.
–Created 1926 and succeeded in 1980 by the United States Court of International Trade (Ct. Int'l Trade).
–Cite to Customs Court Reports (Cust. Ct.) if therein.
Ex.:   Connors Steel Co. v. United States, 85 Cust. Ct. 132 (1980).

United States Decisions of the Comptroller General
See Decisions of the Comptroller General (U.S.).

United States Decisions of the Department of the Interior
See Decisions of the United States Department of the Interior (U.S.).

United States Decisions of the Employees' Compensation Appeals Board
See Decisions of the Employees' Compensation Appeals Board (U.S.).

United States Decisions of the Federal Maritime Commission
See Decisions of the Federal Maritime Commission (U.S).

In citing cases in law review footnotes, abbreviate any word listed in Table T.6; the names of "states, countries, and other geographical units" unless they are named parties; and any other words of eight or more letters "if substantial space is thereby saved and the result is unambiguous." Bluebook Rule 10.2.2. On the other hand, in citing cases in text, abbreviate only widely known acronyms and the following words: "&," "Ass'n," "Bros.," "Co.," "Corp.," "Inc.," "Ltd.," and "No." Bluebook Rule 10.2.1(c).

United States Decisions of the United States Maritime Commission
See Decisions of the United States Maritime Commission.

United States Department of Justice
Ab.:   U.S. Dep't of Justice
Ex.:   Bureau of Justice Statistics, U.S. Dep't of Justice, Tracking Offenders:
          The Child Victim 1-2 (1984).
          –For citations to works by institutional authors, See Bluebook Rule
          15.1.3(a).

United States Department of State
Ab.:   U.S. Dep't of State
Ex.:   U.S. Dep't of State, Documents on Germany 1944-1985, at 348 (1985).
          –For citations to works by institutional authors, See Bluebook Rule
          15.1.3(a).

United States Department of State Bulletin
See Department of State Bulletin (U.S.).

United States Department of State Dispatch
Ab.:   U.S. Dep't St. Dispatch

United States District Court for the Middle District of Alabama
Ab.:   (M.D. Ala. year)

United States District Court for the Northern District of Alabama
Ab.:   (N.D. Ala. year)

United States District Court for the Southern District of Alabama
Ab.:   (S.D. Ala. year)

United States District Court for the District of Alaska
Ab.:   (D. Alaska year)

United States District Court for the District of Arizona
Ab.:   (D. Ariz. year)

United States District Court for the Eastern District of Arkansas
Ab.:   (E.D. Ark. year)

United States District Court for the Western District of Arkansas
Ab.:   (W.D. Ark. year)

United States District Court for the Central District of California
Ab.:   (C.D. Cal. year)

United States District Court for the Eastern District of California
Ab.:   (E.D. Cal. year)

In law review footnotes, the titles of books and the names of cases, except for procedural
phrases, are not underlined. See Bluebook Rule 2.1(a). Further, the following are in large
and small capitals: codes, restatements, standards, constitutions, periodicals, authors of
books, titles of books, the abbreviated names of codes, most legislative materials except for
bills and resolutions, codified ordinances, model codes, court rules, and sentencing guidelines.
Refer to The Bluebook.

United States District Court for the Northern District of California
Ab.:   (N.D. Cal. year)

United States District Court for the Southern District of California
Ab.:   (S.D. Cal. year)

United States District Court for the District of Colorado
Ab.:   (D. Colo. year)

United States District Court for the District of Connecticut
Ab.:   (D. Conn. year)

United States District Court for the District of Delaware
Ab.:   (D. Del. year)

United States District Court for the District of Columbia
Ab.:   (D.D.C. year)

United States District Court for the Middle District of Florida
Ab.:   (M.D. Fla. year)

United States District Court for the Northern District of Florida
Ab.:   (N.D. Fla. year)

United States District Court for the Southern District of Florida
Ab.:   (S.D. Fla. year)

United States District Court for the Middle District of Georgia
Ab.:   (M.D. Ga. year)

United States District Court for the Northern District of Georgia
Ab.:   (N.D. Ga. year)

United States District Court for the Southern District of Georgia
Ab.:   (S.D. Ga. year)

United States District Court for the District of Guam
Ab.:   (D. Guam year)

United States District Court for the District of Hawaii
Ab.:   (D. Haw. year)

United States District Court for the District of Idaho
Ab.:   (D. Idaho year)

United States District Court for the Central District of Illinois
Ab.:   (C.D. Ill. year)

United States District Court for the Northern District of Illinois
Ab.:   (N.D. Ill. year)

In citing cases in law review footnotes, abbreviate any word listed in Table T.6; the names of "states, countries, and other geographical units" unless they are named parties; and any other words of eight or more letters "if substantial space is thereby saved and the result is unambiguous." Bluebook Rule 10.2.2. On the other hand, in citing cases in text, abbreviate only widely known acronyms and the following words: "&," "Ass'n," "Bros.," "Co.," "Corp.," "Inc.," "Ltd.," and "No." Bluebook Rule 10.2.1(c).

United States District Court for the Southern District of Illinois
Ab.:   (S.D. Ill. year)

United States District Court for the Northern District of Indiana
Ab.:   (N.D. Ind. year)

United States District Court for the Southern District of Indiana
Ab.:   (S.D. Ind. year)

United States District Court for the Northern District of Iowa
Ab.:   (N.D. Iowa year)

United States District Court for the Southern District of Iowa
Ab.:   (S.D. Iowa year)

United States District Court for the District of Kansas
Ab.:   (D. Kan. year)

United States District Court for the Eastern District of Kentucky
Ab.:   (E.D. Ky. year)

United States District Court for the Western District of Kentucky
Ab.:   (W.D. Ky. year)

United States District Court for the Eastern District of Louisiana
Ab.:   (E.D. La. year)

United States District Court for the Middle District of Louisiana
Ab.:   (M.D. La. year)

United States District Court for the Western District of Louisiana
Ab.:   (W.D. La. year)

United States District Court for the District of Maine
Ab.:   (D. Me. year)

United States District Court for the District of Maryland
Ab.:   (D. Md. year)

United States District Court for the District of Massachusetts
Ab.:   (D. Mass. year)

United States District Court for the Eastern District of Michigan
Ab.:   (E.D. Mich. year)

United States District Court for the Western District of Michigan
Ab.:   (W.D. Mich. year)

United States District Court for the District of Minnesota
Ab.:   (D. Minn. year)

In law review footnotes, the titles of books and the names of cases, except for procedural phrases, are not underlined. See Bluebook Rule 2.1(a). Further, the following are in large and small capitals: codes, restatements, standards, constitutions, periodicals, authors of books, titles of books, the abbreviated names of codes, most legislative materials except for bills and resolutions, codified ordinances, model codes, court rules, and sentencing guidelines. Refer to The Bluebook.

United States District Court for the Northern District of Mississippi
Ab.:   (N.D. Miss. year)

United States District Court for the Southern District of Mississippi
Ab.:   (S.D. Miss. year)

United States District Court for the Eastern District of Missouri
Ab.:   (E.D. Mo. year)

United States District Court for the Western District of Missouri
Ab.:   (W.D. Mo. year)

United States District Court for the District of Montana
Ab.:   (D. Mont. year)

United States District Court for the District of Nebraska
Ab.:   (D. Neb. year)

United States District Court for the District of Nevada
Ab.:   (D. Nev. year)

United States District Court for the District of New Hampshire
Ab.:   (D.N.H. year)

United States District Court for the District of New Jersey
Ab.:   (D.N.J. year)

United States District Court for the District of New Mexico
Ab.:   (D.N.M. year)

United States District Court for the Eastern District of New York
Ab.:   (E.D.N.Y. year)

United States District Court for the Northern District of New York
Ab.:   (N.D.N.Y. year)

United States District Court for the Southern District of New York
Ab.:   (S.D.N.Y. year)

United States District Court for the Western District of New York
Ab.:   (W.D.N.Y. year)

United States District Court for the Eastern District of North Carolina
Ab.:   (E.D.N.C. year)

United States District Court for the Middle District of North Carolina
Ab.:   (M.D.N.C. year)

United States District Court for the Western District of North Carolina
Ab.:   (W.D.N.C. year)

In citing cases in law review footnotes, abbreviate any word listed in Table T.6;
the names of "states, countries, and other geographical units" unless they are named parties;
and any other words of eight or more letters "if substantial space is thereby saved and the
result is unambiguous." Bluebook Rule 10.2.2. On the other hand, in citing cases in text,
abbreviate only widely known acronyms and the following words: "&," "Ass'n," "Bros.,"
"Co.," "Corp.," "Inc.," "Ltd.," and "No." Bluebook Rule 10.2.1(c).

United States District Court for the District of North Dakota
Ab.:   (D.N.D. year)

United States District Court for the Northern Mariana Islands
Ab.:   (D. N. Mar. I. year)

United States District Court for the Northern District of Ohio
Ab.:   (N.D. Ohio year)

United States District Court for the Southern District of Ohio
Ab.:   (S.D. Ohio year)

United States District Court for the Eastern District of Oklahoma
Ab.:   (E.D. Okla. year)

United States District Court for the Northern District of Oklahoma
Ab.:   (N.D. Okla. year)

United States District Court for the Western District of Oklahoma
Ab.:   (W.D. Okla. year)

United States District Court for the District of Oregon
Ab.:   (D. Or. year)

United States District Court for the Eastern District of Pennsylvania
Ab.:   (E.D. Pa. year)

United States District Court for the Middle District of Pennsylvania
Ab.:   (M.D. Pa. year)

United States District Court for the Western District of Pennsylvania
Ab.:   (W.D. Pa. year)

United States District Court for the District of Puerto Rico
Ab.:   (D.P.R. year)

United States District Court for the District of Rhode Island
Ab.:   (D.R.I. year)

United States District Court for the District of South Carolina
Ab.:   (D.S.C. year)

United States District Court for the District of South Dakota
See public domain citations.
Ab.:   (D.S.D. year)

United States District Court for the Eastern District of Tennessee
Ab.:   (E.D. Tenn. year)

United States District Court for the Middle District of Tennessee
Ab.:   (M.D. Tenn. year)

In law review footnotes, the titles of books and the names of cases, except for procedural phrases, are not underlined. See Bluebook Rule 2.1(a). Further, the following are in large and small capitals: codes, restatements, standards, constitutions, periodicals, authors of books, titles of books, the abbreviated names of codes, most legislative materials except for bills and resolutions, codified ordinances, model codes, court rules, and sentencing guidelines. Refer to The Bluebook.

United States District Court for the Western District of Tennessee
    Ab.:   (W.D. Tenn. year)

United States District Court for the Eastern District of Texas
    Ab.:   (E.D. Tex. year)

United States District Court for the Northern District of Texas
    Ab.:   (N.D. Tex. year)

United States District Court for the Southern District of Texas
    Ab.:   (S.D. Tex. year)

United States District Court for the Western District of Texas
    Ab.:   (W.D. Tex. year)

United States District Court for the District of Utah
    Ab.:   (D. Utah year)

United States District Court for the District of Vermont
    Ab.:   (D. Vt. year)

United States District Court for the District of the Virgin Islands
    Ab.:   (D. V.I. year)

United States District Court for the Eastern District of Virginia
    Ab.:   (E.D. Va. year)

United States District Court for the Western District of Virginia
    Ab.:   (W.D. Va. year)

United States District Court for the Eastern District of Washington
    Ab.:   (E.D. Wash. year)

United States District Court for the Western District of Washington
    Ab.:   (W.D. Wash. year)

United States District Court for the Northern District of West Virginia
    Ab.:   (N.D.W. Va. year)

United States District Court for the Southern District of West Virginia
    Ab.:   (S.D.W. Va. year)

United States District Court for the Eastern District of Wisconsin
    Ab.:   (E.D. Wis. year)

United States District Court for the Western District of Wisconsin
    Ab.:   (W.D. Wis. year)

United States District Court for the District of Wyoming
    Ab.:   (D. Wyo. year)

In citing cases in law review footnotes, abbreviate any word listed in Table T.6; the names of "states, countries, and other geographical units" unless they are named parties; and any other words of eight or more letters "if substantial space is thereby saved and the result is unambiguous." Bluebook Rule 10.2.2. On the other hand, in citing cases in text, abbreviate only widely known acronyms and the following words: "&," "Ass'n," "Bros.," "Co.," "Corp.," "Inc.," "Ltd.," and "No." Bluebook Rule 10.2.1(c).

United States Federal Communications Commission Reports
See Federal Communications Commission Reports.

United States Federal Power Commission Reports
See Federal Power Commission Reports.

United States Federal Reserve Bulletin
See Federal Reserve Bulletin.

United States Federal Trade Commission Decisions
See Federal Trade Commission Decisions.

United States Interstate Commerce Commission Reports, Second Series
See Interstate Commerce Commission Reports, Second Series.

United States Law Week (Bureau of National Affairs)
    Ab.:   U.S.L.W. (BNA - publisher need not be indicated.)
    Ex.:   Immigration and Naturalization Serv. v. Yueh-Shaio Yang,
            65 U.S.L.W. 4009 (U.S. Nov. 13, 1996). –Citation to looseleaf
            material.
           –Cite only until case is available in an official or unofficial reporter.

United States Merit Systems Protection Board
See Merit Systems Protection Board Reporter (U.S.)

United States Motor Carrier Cases
See Motor Carrier Cases (U.S.).

United States National Labor Relations Board Decisions and Orders
See National Labor Relations Board, Decisions and Orders of the (U.S.).

United States National Railroad Adjustment Board, 1st-4th Div.
See National Railroad Adjustment Board, 1st-4th Div. (U.S.) (1934-1972).

United States National Transportation Safety Board Decisions
See National Transportation Safety Board Decisions (U.S.) (1967-date).

United States Official Opinions of the Solicitor for the Post Office Department
See Official Opinions of the Solicitor for the Post Office Department (1878-
1951).

United States Opinions of the Attorney General
See Opinions of the Attorney General (U.S.) (1789-date).

**United States Patents, Decisions of the Commissioner and of United States
Courts**
See Patents, Decisions of the Commissioner and of U.S. Courts (1869-date).

United States Patents Quarterly, The (Bureau of National Affairs)
    Ab.:   U.S.P.Q. (BNA)

In law review footnotes, the titles of books and the names of cases, except for procedural
phrases, are not underlined. See Bluebook Rule 2.1(a). Further, the following are in large
and small capitals: codes, restatements, standards, constitutions, periodicals, authors of
books, titles of books, the abbreviated names of codes, most legislative materials except for
bills and resolutions, codified ordinances, model codes, court rules, and sentencing guidelines.
Refer to The Bluebook.

Ex.:   Henkel Corp. v. Coral Inc., [Advance Sheets] U.S.P.Q. (BNA) (21 U.S.P.Q. 2d) 1081 (N.D. Ill. Dec. 28, 1990). –Citation to looseleaf material.

Solomon v. Greco, 18 U.S.P.Q. 2d (BNA) 1917 (E.D.N.Y. Oct. 2, 1990). –Citation to bound material.

–The above examples are proper if the case is not yet available in, or is not reported in, an official or West reporter, a public domain citation, or in a widely used computer database.

United States Public Laws
See Public Laws (U.S.).

United States Reports
    (91 U.S., 1875 to date)

Ab.:   U.S.

Ex.:   Willy v. Coastal Corp., 503 U.S. 131 (1992). –Case Citation.

Willy v. Coastal Corp., 503 U.S. 131, 135 (1992). –Page Citation.

O'Hare Truck Service Inc. v City of Northlake, No. 95-191, slip op. at 3 (U.S. June 28, 1996). –Slip Opinion.

United States Reports
–Cite to U.S if therein; otherwise, cite to S. Ct., L. Ed., or U.S.L.W., in that order of preference. See Bluebook Table T.1.

    (1 U.S. - 90 U.S., pre-1875)

Dallas (1790-1800):

Ab.:   Dall.

Ex.:   The Eliza, 4 U.S. (4 Dall.) 32 (1800). –Case Citation.

The Eliza, 4 U.S. (4 Dall.) 32, 38-39 (1800). –Page Citation.

Cranch (1801-1815):

Ab.:   Cranch

Ex.:   Finley v. Williams, 13 U.S. (9 Cranch) 164 (1815). –Case Citation.

Finley v. Williams, 13 U.S. (9 Cranch) 164, 167 (1815). –Page Citation.

Wheaton (1816-1827):

Ab.:   Wheat.

Ex.:   Janney v. Columbian Ins. Co., 23 U.S. (10 Wheat.) 409 (1825). –Case Citation.

Janney v. Columbian Ins. Co., 23 U.S. (10 Wheat.) 409, 416 (1825). –Page Citation.

Peters (1828-1842):

Ab.:   Pet.

In citing cases in law review footnotes, abbreviate any word listed in Table T.6; the names of "states, countries, and other geographical units" unless they are named parties; and any other words of eight or more letters "if substantial space is thereby saved and the result is unambiguous." Bluebook Rule 10.2.2. On the other hand, in citing cases in text, abbreviate only widely known acronyms and the following words: "&," "Ass'n," "Bros.," "Co.," "Corp.," "Inc.," "Ltd.," and "No." Bluebook Rule 10.2.1(c).

Ex.:   United States v. One Hundred and Twelve Casks of Sugar, 33 U.S. (8 Pet.) 275 (1834). –Case Citation.

United States v. One Hundred and Twelve Casks of Sugar, 33 U.S. (8 Pet.) 275, 279-80 (1834). –Page Citation.

Howard (1843-1860):

Ab.:   How.

Ex.:   Taylor v. Doe, 54 U.S. (13 How.) 287 (1851). –Case Citation.

Taylor v. Doe, 54 U.S. (13 How.) 287, 291 (1851). –Page Citation.

Black (1861-1862):

Ab.:   Black

Ex.:   Chicago City v. Robbins, 67 U.S. (2 Black) 418 (1862). –Case Citation.

Chicago City v. Robbins, 67 U.S. (2 Black) 418, 423 (1862). –Page Citation.

Wallace (1863-1874):

Ab.:   Wall.

Ex.:   Gaines v. Thompson, 74 U.S. (7 Wall.) 347 (1868). –Case Citation.

Gaines v. Thompson, 74 U.S. (7 Wall.) 347, 353 (1868). –Page Citation.

United States Securities and Exchange Commission Decisions and Reports
See Securities and Exchange Commission Decisions and Reports.

United States Sentencing Guidelines Manual
Ab.:   U.S. Sentencing Guidelines Manual

Ex.:   U.S. Sentencing Guidelines Manual § 2K2.4 (1998).

See Bluebook Rule 12.8.5

United States Statutes at Large
See Statutes at Large.

United States Supreme Court Reports
See Supreme Court Reporter.

United States Supreme Court Reports, Lawyers' Edition
–Cite to U.S if therein; otherwise, cite to S. Ct., L. Ed., or U.S.L.W., in that order of preference. See Bluebook Table T.1.

Ab.:   L. Ed., L. Ed. 2d

Ex.:   United States v. Di Re, 92 L. Ed. 210 (1948). –Case Citation.

United States v. Di Re, 92 L. Ed. 210, 219 (1948). –Page Citation.

ICC v. Transcon Lines, 130 L. Ed. 2d 562 (1995). –Case Citation.

ICC v. Transcon Lines, 130 L. Ed. 2d 562, 567 (1995). –Page Citation.

In law review footnotes, the titles of books and the names of cases, except for procedural phrases, are not underlined. See Bluebook Rule 2.1(a). Further, the following are in large and small capitals: codes, restatements, standards, constitutions, periodicals, authors of books, titles of books, the abbreviated names of codes, most legislative materials except for bills and resolutions, codified ordinances, model codes, court rules, and sentencing guidelines. Refer to The Bluebook.

United States Supreme Court Rules
Ab.:   Sup. Ct. R.
Ex.:   Sup. Ct. R. 6.

United States Tax Cases (Commerce Clearing House)
Ab.:   U.S. Tax Cas. (CCH)
See Federal Estate and Gift Tax Reporter (Commerce Clearing House)

United States Tax Court Reports
Ab.:   T.C.
Ex.:   Estate of Young v. C.I.R., 110 T.C. 297 (1998).

United States Treasury Decisions Under Customs & Other Laws (1898-1965)
See Treasury Decisions Under Customs & Other Laws (1898-1965)

United States Treasury Decisions Under Internal Revenue Laws (1898-1942)
See Treasury Decisions Under Internal Revenue Laws (1898-1942).

United States Treasury Department, Comptroller General's Opinion
See Decisions of the Comptroller General of the United States.

United States Treasury Regulations
See Treasury Regulations (Federal)

United States Treaties and Other International Acts Series
See Treaties and Other International Acts Series (U.S.).

United States Treaties and Other International Agreements
Ab.:   U.S.T.
Ex.:   Convention on Psychotropic Substances, Feb. 21, 1971, art. 3, 32
       U.S.T. 545, 551.

United States Treaty Series
See Treaty Series (U.S.).

University of Akron Law Review
See Akron Law Review.

University of Alabama Law Review
See Alabama Law Review.

University of Arizona Law Review
See Arizona Law Review.

University of Arkansas Law Review
See Arkansas Law Review

University of Arkansas at Little Rock Law Journal
Ab.:   U. Ark. Little Rock L.J.

In citing cases in law review footnotes, abbreviate any word listed in Table T.6;
the names of "states, countries, and other geographical units" unless they are named parties;
and any other words of eight or more letters "if substantial space is thereby saved and the
result is unambiguous." Bluebook Rule 10.2.2. On the other hand, in citing cases in text,
abbreviate only widely known acronyms and the following words: "&," "Ass'n," "Bros.,"
"Co.," "Corp.," "Inc.," "Ltd.," and "No." Bluebook Rule 10.2.1(c).

Ex.:   Vincene Verdun, <u>Postdated Checks: An Old Problem with a New Solution in the Revised U.C.C.</u>, 14 U. Ark. Little Rock L.J. 37 (1991). –Article Citation.

Vincene Verdun, <u>Postdated Checks: An Old Problem with a New Solution in the Revised U.C.C.</u>, 14 U. Ark. Little Rock L.J. 37, 59-60 (1991). –Page Citation.

University of Arkansas at Little Rock Law Review
Ab.:   U. Ark. Little Rock L. Rev.

Ex.:   Honorable Terry Crabtree, <u>Abstracting the Record</u>, 21 U. Ark. Little Rock L. Rev. 1 (1998). –Article Citation.

Honorable Terry Crabtree, <u>Abstracting the Record</u>, 21 U. Ark. Little Rock L. Rev. 1, 7 n.27 (1998). –Footnote Citation.

University of Baltimore Journal of Environmental Law
Ab.:   U. Balt. J. Envt'l L.

Ex.:   John C. Buckley, <u>Considering Environmental Law</u>, 1 U. Balt. J. Envt'l L. 1 (1991). –Article Citation.

John C. Buckley, <u>Considering Environmental Law</u>, 1 U. Balt. J. Envt'l L. 1, 1 (1991). –Page Citation.

University of Baltimore Law Review
Ab.:   U. Balt. L. Rev.

Ex.:   Ralph S. Brown, <u>Copyright-Like Protection for Designs</u>, 19 U. Balt. L. Rev. 308 (1989-1990). –Article Citation.

Ralph S. Brown, <u>Copyright-Like Protection for Designs</u>, 19 U. Balt. L. Rev. 308, 319-20 (1989-1990). –Page Citation.

University of Bridgeport Law Review
Ab.:   U. Bridgeport L. Rev.

Ex.:   Steven M. Spaeth, <u>The Deregulation of Transportation and Natural Gas Production in the United States and its Relevance to the Soviet Union and Eastern Europe in the 1990's</u>, U. Bridgeport L. Rev. 43 (1991). –Article Citation.

Steven M. Spaeth, <u>The Deregulation of Transportation and Natural Gas Production in the United States and its Relevance to the Soviet Union and Eastern Europe in the 1990's</u>, U. Bridgeport L. Rev. 43, 89-91 (1991). –Page Citation.

University of British Columbia Law Review
Ab.:   U. Brit. Colum. L. Rev.

In law review footnotes, the titles of books and the names of cases, except for procedural phrases, are not underlined. <u>See</u> <u>Bluebook</u> Rule 2.1(a). Further, the following are in large and small capitals: codes, restatements, standards, constitutions, periodicals, authors of books, titles of books, the abbreviated names of codes, most legislative materials except for bills and resolutions, codified ordinances, model codes, court rules, and sentencing guidelines. Refer to <u>The Bluebook</u>.

Ex.:   Benjamin Van Primmeler, <u>The Missing Lynx: Trapping Logging and Compensation</u>, 25 U. Brit. Colum. L. Rev. 335 (1991). –Article Citation.

Benjamin Van Primmeler, <u>The Missing Lynx: Trapping Logging and Compensation</u>, 25 U. Brit. Colum. L. Rev. 335, 340 (1991). –Page Citation.

University of California Law Review
<u>See</u> California Law Review.

University of Chicago Law Review
Ab.:   U. Chi. L. Rev.

Ex.:   James Q. Whitman, <u>Why Did the Revolutionary Lawyers Confuse Custom and Reason?</u>, 58 U. Chi. L. Rev. 1321 (1991). –Article Citation.

James Q. Whitman, <u>Why Did the Revolutionary Lawyers Confuse Custom and Reason?</u>, 58 U. Chi. L. Rev. 1321, 1329-31 (1991). –Page Citation.

University of Chicago Legal Forum
Ab.:   U. Chi. Legal F.

Ex.:   Robert K. Fullinwider, <u>Multicultural Education</u>, 1991 U. Chi. Legal F. 75. –Article Citation.

Robert K. Fullinwider, <u>Multicultural Education</u>, 1991 U. Chi. Legal F. 75, 79-83. –Page Citation.

University of Cincinnati Law Review
Ab.:   U. Cin. L. Rev.

Ex.:   Nicholas Wolfson, <u>Free Speech Theory and Hateful Words</u>, 60 U. Cin. L. Rev. 1 (1991). –Article Citation.

Nicholas Wolfson, <u>Free Speech Theory and Hateful Words</u>, 60 U. Cin. L. Rev. 1, 2 (1991). –Page Citation.

University of Colorado Law Review
Ab.:   U. Colo. L. Rev.

Ex.:   Alessandra Lippucci, <u>Surprised by Fish</u>, 63 U. Colo. L. Rev. 1 (1992). –Article Citation.

Alessandra Lippucci, <u>Surprised by Fish</u>, 63 U. Colo. L. Rev. 1, 69-70 (1992). –Page Citation.

University of Connecticut Law Review
<u>See</u> Connecticut Law Review

University of Dayton Law Review
Ab.:   U. Dayton L. Rev.

In citing cases in law review footnotes, abbreviate any word listed in Table T.6; the names of "states, countries, and other geographical units" unless they are named parties; and any other words of eight or more letters "if <u>substantial</u> space is thereby saved and the result is unambiguous." <u>Bluebook</u> Rule 10.2.2. On the other hand, in citing cases in text, abbreviate only widely known acronyms and the following words: "&," "Ass'n," "Bros.," "Co.," "Corp.," "Inc.," "Ltd.," and "No." <u>Bluebook</u> Rule 10.2.1(c).

LEGAL CITATIONS# LEGAL CITATIONS 439

Ex.: Terry A. Bethel, <u>Recent Supreme Court Employment Law Decisions, 1990-91</u>, 17 U. Dayton L. Rev. 33 (1991). –Article Citation.

Terry A. Bethel, <u>Recent Supreme Court Employment Law Decisions, 1990-91</u>, 17 U. Dayton L. Rev. 33, 39-42 (1991). –Page Citation.

University of Detroit Law Review
Ab.: U. Det. L. Rev.
Ex.: Lawrence C. Mann, <u>Mediation of Civil Cases: Neither Panacea nor Anathema (A Prescription for Change in Procedural Rules)</u>, 67 U. Det. L. Rev. 531 (1990). –Article Citation.

Lawrence C. Mann, <u>Mediation of Civil Cases: Neither Panacea nor Anathema (A Prescription for Change in Procedural Rules)</u>, 67 U. Det. L. Rev. 531, 564-70 (1990). –Page Citation.

University of Detroit Mercy Law Review
Ab.: U. Det. Mercy L. Rev.
Ex.: Luis Kutner, <u>Jesus Before the Sanhedrin</u>, 69 U. Det. Mercy L. Rev. 1 (1991). –Article Citation.

Luis Kutner, <u>Jesus Before the Sanhedrin</u>, 69 U. Det. Mercy L. Rev. 1, 8-9 (1991). –Page Citation.

University of Florida Journal of Law and Public Policy
Ab.: U. Fla. J.L. & Pub. Pol'y
Ex.: Michael I. Meyerson, <u>Impending Legal Issues for Integrated Broadband Networks</u>, 3 U. Fla. J.L. & Pub. Pol'y 49 (1990). –Article Citation.

Michael I. Meyerson, <u>Impending Legal Issues for Integrated Broadband Networks</u>, 3 U. Fla. J.L. & Pub. Pol'y 49, 53-54 (1990). –Page Citation.

University of Florida Law Review
Ab.: U. Fla. L. Rev.
Ex.: Donna D. Adler, <u>Master Limited Partnerships</u>, 40 U. Fla. L. Rev. 755 (1988). –Article Citation.

Donna D. Adler, <u>Master Limited Partnerships</u>, 40 U. Fla. L. Rev. 755, 778-80 (1988). –Page Citation.

University of Georgia Law Review
<u>See</u> Georgia Law Review

University of Hawaii Law Review
Ab.: U. Haw. L. Rev.

In law review footnotes, the titles of books and the names of cases, except for procedural phrases, are not underlined. <u>See</u> Bluebook Rule 2.1(a). Further, the following are in large and small capitals: codes, restatements, standards, constitutions, periodicals, authors of books, titles of books, the abbreviated names of codes, most legislative materials except for bills and resolutions, codified ordinances, model codes, court rules, and sentencing guidelines. Refer to <u>The Bluebook</u>.

Ex.:   Stanley K. Laughlin, Jr., The Constitutional Structure of the Courts of the United States Territories: The Case of American Samoa, 13 U. Haw. L. Rev. 379 (1991). –Article Citation.

Stanley K. Laughlin, Jr., The Constitutional Structure of the Courts of the United States Territories: The Case of American Samoa, 13 U. Haw. L. Rev. 379, 440-42 (1991). –Page Citation.

University of Houston Law Review
See Houston Law Review

University of Idaho Law Review
See Idaho Law Review

University of Illinois Law Review
Ab.:   U. Ill. L. Rev.
Ex.:   Martha G. Duncan, "A Strange Liking": Our Admiration for Criminals, 1991 U. Ill. L. Rev. 1. –Article Citation.

Martha G. Duncan, "A Strange Liking": Our Admiration for Criminals, 1991 U. Ill. L. Rev. 1, 49-52. –Page Citation.

University of Iowa Law Review
See Iowa Law Review

University of Kansas Law Review, The
Ab.:   U. Kan. L. Rev.
Ex.:   Thomas E. Baker, The Impropriety of Expert Witness Testimony on the Law, 40 U. Kan. L. Rev. 325 (1992). –Article Citation.

Thomas E. Baker, The Impropriety of Expert Witness Testimony on the Law, 40 U. Kan. L. Rev. 325, 249-52 (1992). –Page Citation.

University of Kentucky Law Review
See Kentucky Law Journal

University of Louisville Journal of Family Law
See Journal of Family Law

University of Maine Law Review
See Maine Law Review

University of Maryland Law Review
See Maryland Law Review

University of Memphis Law Review
Ab.:   U. Mem. L. Rev.
Ex.:   Neil D. Hamilton, State Regulation of Agricultural Production Contracts, 25 U. Mem. L. Rev. 1051 (1995). –Article Citation.

Neil D. Hamilton, State Regulation of Agricultural Production Contracts, 25 U. Mem. L. Rev. 1051, 1055 (1995). –Page Citation.

In citing cases in law review footnotes, abbreviate any word listed in Table T.6; the names of "states, countries, and other geographical units" unless they are named parties; and any other words of eight or more letters "if substantial space is thereby saved and the result is unambiguous." Bluebook Rule 10.2.2. On the other hand, in citing cases in text, abbreviate only widely known acronyms and the following words: "&," "Ass'n," "Bros.," "Co.," "Corp.," "Inc.," "Ltd.," and "No." Bluebook Rule 10.2.1(c).

University of Miami Entertainment and Sports Law Review
Ab.:   U. Miami Ent. & Sports L. Rev.
Ex.:   Terrill L. Johnson, The Antitrust Implications of the Divisional Structure of the National Collegiate Athletic Association, 8 U. Miami Ent. & Sports L. Rev. 97 (1991). –Article Citation.

Terrill L. Johnson, The Antitrust Implications of the Divisional Structure of the National Collegiate Athletic Association, 8 U. Miami Ent. & Sports L. Rev. 97, 111-12 (1991). –Page Citation.

University of Miami Inter-American Law Review
Ab.:   U. Miami Inter-Am. L. Rev.
Ex.:   Rudy Sandoval, Mexico's Path Towards the Free Trade Agreement with the U.S., 23 U. Miami Inter-Am. L. Rev. 133 (1991). –Article Citation.

Rudy Sandoval, Mexico's Path Towards the Free Trade Agreement with the U.S., 23 U. Miami Inter-Am. L. Rev. 133, 149-52 (1991). –Page Citation.

University of Miami Law Review
Ab.:   U. Miami L. Rev.
Ex.:   Keith N. Hylton, Litigation Costs and the Economic Theory of Tort Law, 46 U. Miami L. Rev. 111 (1991). –Article Citation.

Keith N. Hylton, Litigation Costs and the Economic Theory of Tort Law, 46 U. Miami L. Rev. 111, 119-22 (1991). –Page Citation.

University of Michigan Journal of Law Reform
Ab.:   U. Mich. J.L. Reform
Ex.:   Mark R. Brown, Accountability in Government and Section 1983, 25 U. Mich. J.L. Reform 53 (1991). –Article Citation.

Mark R. Brown, Accountability in Government and Section 1983, 25 U. Mich. J.L. Reform 53, 99 (1991). –Page Citation.

University of Michigan Law Review
See Michigan Law Review.

University of Minnesota Law Review
See Minnesota Law Review.

University of Mississippi Law Journal
See Mississippi Law Journal.

University of Missouri-Kansas City Law Review
See UMKC Law Review.

University of Missouri Law Review
See Missouri Law Review.

In law review footnotes, the titles of books and the names of cases, except for procedural phrases, are not underlined. See Bluebook Rule 2.1(a). Further, the following are in large and small capitals: codes, restatements, standards, constitutions, periodicals, authors of books, titles of books, the abbreviated names of codes, most legislative materials except for bills and resolutions, codified ordinances, model codes, court rules, and sentencing guidelines. Refer to The Bluebook.

University of Montana Law Review
See Montana Law Review.

University of Nebraska Law Review
See Nebraska Law Review.

University of New Brunswick Law Journal
Ab.:   U.N.B. L.J.
Ex.:   Dale Gibson, Equality for Some, 40 U.N.B. L.J. 2 (1991). –Article
        Citation.
        Dale Gibson, Equality for Some, 40 U.N.B. L.J. 2, 15 (1991). –Page
        Citation.

University of New Mexico Law Review
See New Mexico Law Review.

University of New South Wales Law Journal, The
Ab.:   U.N.S.W. L.J.
Ex.:   Neil F. Douglas, Freedom of Expression Under The Australian
        Constitution, 16 U.N.S.W. L.J. 315 (1993). –Article Citation.
        Neil F. Douglas, Freedom of Expression Under The Australian
        Constitution, 16 U.N.S.W. L.J. 315, 318-21 (1993). –Page Citation.

University of North Carolina Law Review
See North Carolina Law Review.

University of North Dakota Law Review
See North Dakota Law Review.

University of Oklahoma Law Review
See Oklahoma Law Review.

University of Oregon Law Review
See Oregon Law Review.

University of Pennsylvania Journal of Constitutional Law
Ab.:   U. Pa. J. Const. L.
Ex.:   Mark Tushnet, Returning with Interest; Observations on Some Putative
        Benefits of Studying Comparative Constitutional Law, 1 U. Pa. J.
        Const. L. 325 (1998). –Article Citation.

University of Pennsylvania Journal of International Business Law
Ab.:   U. Pa. J. Int'l Bus. L.

In citing cases in law review footnotes, abbreviate any word listed in Table T.6;
the names of "states, countries, and other geographical units" unless they are named parties;
and any other words of eight or more letters "if substantial space is thereby saved and the
result is unambiguous." Bluebook Rule 10.2.2. On the other hand, in citing cases in text,
abbreviate only widely known acronyms and the following words: "&," "Ass'n," "Bros.,"
"Co.," "Corp.," "Inc.," "Ltd.," and "No." Bluebook Rule 10.2.1(c).

Ex.:   Zipora Cohen, <u>Fiduciary Duties of Controlling Shareholders: A Comparative View</u>, 12 U. Pa. J. Int'l Bus. L. 379 (1991). –Article Citation.

Zipora Cohen, <u>Fiduciary Duties of Controlling Shareholders: A Comparative View</u>, 12 U. Pa. J. Int'l Bus. L. 379, 389-92 (1991). –Page Citation.

University of Pennsylvania Journal of International Economic Law
Ab.:   U. Pa. J. Int'l Econ. L.
Ex.:   Christopher T. Curtis, <u>The Status of Foreign Deposits Under the Federal Depositor - Preference Law</u>, 21 U. Pa. J. Int'l Econ. L. 237 (2000). –Article Citation.

Christopher T. Curtis, <u>The Status of Foreign Deposits Under the Federal Depositor - Preference Law</u>, 21 U. Pa. J. Int'l Econ. L. 237, 241 n.19 (2000). –Footnote Citation.

University of Pennsylvania Journal of Labor and Employment Law
Ab.:   U. Pa. J. Lab. & Emp. L.
Ex.:   Clyde W. Summers, <u>Employment at Will in the United States: The Divine Right of Employers</u>, 3 U. Pa. J. Lab. & Emp. L. 65 (2000). –Article Citation.

Clyde W. Summers, <u>Employment at Will in the United States: The Divine Right of Employers</u>, 3 U. Pa. J. Lab. & Emp. L. 65, 65 (2000). –Page Citation.

University of Pennsylvania Law Review
Ab.:   U. Pa. L. Rev.
Ex.:   Harold S. Lewis, Jr. & Theodore Y. Blumoff, <u>Reshaping Section 1983's Asymmetry</u>, 140 U. Pa. L. Rev. 755 (1992). –Article Citation.

Harold S. Lewis, Jr. & Theodore Y. Blumoff, <u>Reshaping Section 1983's Asymmetry</u>, 140 U. Pa. L. Rev. 755, 793-96 (1992). –Page Citation.

University of Pittsburgh Law Review
Ab.:   U. Pitt. L. Rev.
Ex.:   Stephen A. Newman, <u>Euthanasia: Orchestrating "The Last Syallable of . . . Time"</u>, 53 U. Pitt. L. Rev. 153 (1991). –Article Citation.

Stephen A. Newman, <u>Euthanasia: Orchestrating "The Last Syallable of . . . Time"</u>, 53 U. Pitt. L. Rev. 153, 169-70 (1991). –Page Citation.

University of Puget Sound Law Review
Ab.:   U. Puget Sound L. Rev.

In law review footnotes, the titles of books and the names of cases, except for procedural phrases, are not underlined. <u>See</u> <u>Bluebook</u> Rule 2.1(a). Further, the following are in large and small capitals: codes, restatements, standards, constitutions, periodicals, authors of books, titles of books, the abbreviated names of codes, most legislative materials except for bills and resolutions, codified ordinances, model codes, court rules, and sentencing guidelines. Refer to <u>The Bluebook</u>.

Ex.:   Earle A. Partington, <u>RICO, Merger, and Double Jeopardy</u>, 15 U. Puget Sound L. Rev. 1 (1991). –Article Citation.

Earle A. Partington, <u>RICO, Merger, and Double Jeopardy</u>, 15 U. Puget Sound L. Rev. 1, 29-30 (1991). –Page Citation.

University of Queensland Law Journal
Ab.:   U.Q. L.J.
Ex.:   Peter McDermott, <u>External Affairs and Treaties - The Founding Fathers' Perspective</u>, 16 U.Q. L.J. 123 (1990). –Article Citation.

Peter McDermott, <u>External Affairs and Treaties - The Founding Fathers' Perspective</u>, 16 U.Q. L.J. 123, 129-31 (1990). –Page Citation.

University of Richmond Law Review
Ab.:   U. Rich. L. Rev.
Ex.:   Harriette H. Shivers, <u>Guardianship Laws: Reform Efforts in Virginia</u>, 26 U. Rich. L. Rev. 325 (1992). –Article Citation.

Harriette H. Shivers, <u>Guardianship Laws: Reform Efforts in Virginia</u>, 26 U. Rich. L. Rev. 325, 329-32 (1992). –Page Citation.

University of San Diego Law Review
<u>See</u> San Diego Law Review.

University of San Francisco Law Review
Ab.:   U.S.F. L. Rev.
Ex.:   John E. Rumel, <u>The Hourglass and Due Process: The Propriety of Time Limits on Civil Trials</u>, 26 U.S.F. L. Rev. 237 (1992). –Article Citation.

John E. Rumel, <u>The Hourglass and Due Process: The Propriety of Time Limits on Civil Trials</u>, 26 U.S.F. L. Rev. 237, 249-52 (1992). –Page Citation.

University of Santa Clara Law Review
<u>See</u> Santa Clara Law Review.

University of South Carolina Law Review
<u>See</u> South Carolina Law Review.

University of South Dakota Law Review
<u>See</u> South Dakota Law Review.

University of Southern California Annual Tax Institute
<u>See</u> Major Tax Planning.

University of Tasmania Law Review
Ab.:   U. Tas. L. Rev.

In citing cases in law review footnotes, abbreviate any word listed in Table T.6; the names of "states, countries, and other geographical units" unless they are named parties; and any other words of eight or more letters "if <u>substantial</u> space is thereby saved and the result is unambiguous." <u>Bluebook</u> Rule 10.2.2. On the other hand, in citing cases in text, abbreviate only widely known acronyms and the following words: "&," "Ass'n," "Bros.," "Co.," "Corp.," "Inc.," "Ltd.," and "No." <u>Bluebook</u> Rule 10.2.1(c).

Ex.:   George Winterton, <u>Reserve Powers in an Australian Republic</u>, 12 U. Tas. L. Rev. 249 (1993). –Article Citation.

George Winterton, <u>Reserve Powers in an Australian Republic</u>, 12 U. Tas. L. Rev. 249, 256 (1993). –Page Citation.

University of Tennessee Law Review
<u>See</u> Tennessee Law Review.

University of Texas Law Review
<u>See</u> Texas Law Review.

University of the Pacific Law Journal
<u>See</u> Pacific Law Journal.

University of Toledo Law Review
Ab.:   U. Tol. L. Rev.

Ex.:   Andrew C. Barrett, <u>The Telecommunications Infrastructure of the Future</u>, 23 U. Tol. L. Rev. 85 (1991). –Article Citation.

Andrew C. Barrett, <u>The Telecommunications Infrastructure of the Future</u>, 23 U. Tol. L. Rev. 85, 89-90 (1991). –Page Citation.

University of Toronto Faculty of Law Review
Ab.:   U. Toronto Fac. L. Rev.

Ex.:   Jacqueline R. Castel, <u>Women's Sexual Exploitation in Therapy</u>, 49 U. Toronto Fac. L. Rev. 42 (1991). –Article Citation.

Jacqueline R. Castel, <u>Women's Sexual Exploitation in Therapy</u>, 49 U. Toronto Fac. L. Rev. 42, 59-61 (1991). –Page Citation.

University of Toronto Law Journal
Ab.:   U. Toronto L.J.

Ex.:   Jamie Cameron, <u>The Charter and Remedial Choice</u>, 45 U. Toronto L.J. 525 (1995). –Article Citation.

Jamie Cameron, <u>The Charter and Remedial Choice</u>, 45 U. Toronto L.J. 525, 530 (1995). –Page Citation.

University of Tulsa Law Journal
<u>See</u> Tulsa Law Journal.

University of Utah Law Review
<u>See</u> Utah Law Review.

University of Virginia Law Review
<u>See</u> Virginia Law Review.

University of Washington Law Quarterly
<u>See</u> Washington University Law Quarterly.

In law review footnotes, the titles of books and the names of cases, except for procedural phrases, are not underlined. <u>See</u> <u>Bluebook</u> Rule 2.1(a). Further, the following are in large and small capitals: codes, restatements, standards, constitutions, periodicals, authors of books, titles of books, the abbreviated names of codes, most legislative materials except for bills and resolutions, codified ordinances, model codes, court rules, and sentencing guidelines. Refer to <u>The Bluebook</u>.

University of West Los Angeles Law Review
Ab.: UWLA L. Rev.
Ex.: Tyron J. Sheppard & Richard Nevirs, <u>Constitutional Equity - Reparations at Last</u>, 22 UWLA L. Rev. 105 (1991). –Article Citation.
Tyron J. Sheppard & Richard Nevirs, <u>Constitutional Equity - Reparations at Last</u>, 22 UWLA L. Rev. 105, 109-11 (1991).
–Page Citation.

University of Western Australia Law Review
Ab.: U. W. Austl. L. Rev.
Ex.: Lakshman Marasinghe, <u>Choice of Forum in International Litigation</u>, 23 U. West. Austl. L. Rev 264 (1993). –Article Citation.
Lakshman Marasinghe, <u>Choice of Forum in International Litigation</u>, 23 U. West. Austl. L. Rev 264, 267-71 (1993). –Page Citation.

University of Wisconsin Law Review
<u>See</u> Wisconsin Law Review.

University of Wyoming Law Review
<u>See</u> Land and Water Law Review.

unpublished materials
–Explained and illustrated in <u>Bluebook</u> Rule 17.1.
Ex.: Robert Smith, URESA and Mexican Family Law (November 17, 1996) (unpublished manuscript, on file with <u>Vanderbilt Journal of Transnational Law</u>). –unpublished manuscript.
Letter from Kurt Grasinger, Film Critic, <u>The New Yorker</u>, to Jean Winter, Editor, <u>Vanderbilt Law School Brief</u> (Feb. 26, 1996) (on file with author). –unpublished letter.
<u>See</u> <u>Bluebook</u> Rule 17.1.3.
Interview with Pam Malone, President of the National Association for Legal Placement, in Nashville, Tenn. (Dec. 10, 1996). –author conducted interview.
Interview by Stephen Teel with Don Welch, Associate Dean, Vanderbilt University Law School, Nashville, Tenn. (Jan 2, 1997). –author did not conduct interview.
–unpublished interviews

unreported cases
<u>See</u> pending and unreported cases.

unreported decisions
<u>See</u> pending and unreported cases.

Urban Lawyer
Ab.: Urb. Law.

In citing cases in law review footnotes, abbreviate any word listed in Table T.6; the names of "states, countries, and other geographical units" unless they are named parties; and any other words of eight or more letters "if <u>substantial</u> space is thereby saved and the result is unambiguous." <u>Bluebook</u> Rule 10.2.2. On the other hand, in citing cases in text, abbreviate only widely known acronyms and the following words: "&," "Ass'n," "Bros.," "Co.," "Corp.," "Inc.," "Ltd.," and "No." <u>Bluebook</u> Rule 10.2.1(c).

Ex.: Daniel R. Mandelker & A. Dan Tarlock, <u>Shifting the Presumption of Constitutionality in Landuse Law</u>, 24 Urb. Law. 1 (1992). –Article Citation.

Daniel R. Mandelker & A. Dan Tarlock, <u>Shifting the Presumption of Constitutionality in Landuse Law</u>, 24 Urb. Law. 1, 39-40 (1992). –Page Citation.

Utah Administrative Code
Ab.: Utah Admin. Code
Ex.: Utah Admin. Code R81-4A-1 (2000).

Utah Bar Journal
Ab.: Utah B.J.

Utah Code Annotated
Ab.: Utah Code Ann. § (year)
Ex.: Utah Code Ann. § 76-6-504 (1999).
Utah Code Ann. § 76-5a-3 (Supp. 2000).

Utah Constitution
Ab.: Utah Const. art. , § .
Ex.: Utah Const. art. XII, § 19. –"Cite constitutional provisions currently in force without date." <u>Bluebook</u> Rule 11.
Utah Const. art. VI, § 23 (repealed 1982). –"If the cited provision has been repealed, either indicate parenthetically the fact and date of repeal or cite the repealing provision in full ." <u>Bluebook</u> Rule 11.
Utah Const. art. I, § 8 (amended 1988). –"When citing a provision that has been subsequently amended, either indicate parenthetically the fact and date of amendment or cite the amending provision in full." <u>Bluebook</u> Rule 11.

Utah Court of Appeals
Ab.: Utah Ct. App.
–Cite to P.2d. or P.3d if therein; in addition, give public domain citation if available.
–Until January 1, 1999, when a public domain format was adopted, cite as follows:
In all documents:
<u>Eyring v. Fairbanks</u>, 918 P.2d 489 (Utah Ct. App. 1996). –Case Citation.
<u>Eyring v. Fairbanks</u>, 918 P.2d 489, 492 (Utah Ct. App. 1996). –Page Citation.
–From January 1, 1999, cite as follows:
In all documents:

In law review footnotes, the titles of books and the names of cases, except for procedural phrases, are not underlined. <u>See</u> <u>Bluebook</u> Rule 2.1(a). Further, the following are in large and small capitals: codes, restatements, standards, constitutions, periodicals, authors of books, titles of books, the abbreviated names of codes, most legislative materials except for bills and resolutions, codified ordinances, model codes, court rules, and sentencing guidelines. Refer to <u>The Bluebook</u>.

State v. Tryba, 2000 UT App 230, 8 P.3d 274. –Case Citation.

State v. Tryba, 2000 UT App 230, ¶ 8, 8 P.3d 274, 277. –Pinpoint Citation.

See Bluebook Rules 10.3.1 and 10.3.3., Table T.1, and Practitioners' Note P.3; see also 386 Utah Adv. Rep. 3.

Utah Law Review
Ab.:   Utah L. Rev.

Ex.:   Allan J. Samansky, Nonstandard Thoughts About the Standard Deduction, 1991 Utah L. Rev. 531. –Article Citation.

Allan J. Samansky, Nonstandard Thoughts About the Standard Deduction, 1991 Utah L. Rev. 531, 534. –Page Citation.

Utah Session Laws
See Laws of Utah.

Utah Supreme Court
–Cite to P., P.2d, or P.3d if therein; in addition, give public domain citation if available.

–Through 30 Utah 2d 462 (1974), cite as follows:

In documents submitted to Utah state courts:

Hobbs v. Fenton, 25 Utah 2d 206, 479 P.2d 472 (1971). –Case Citation.

Hobbs v. Fenton, 25 Utah 2d 206, 209, 479 P.2d 472, 473-74 (1971). –Page Citation.

In all other documents:

Hobbs v. Fenton, 479 P.2d 472 (Utah 1971). –Case Citation.

Hobbs v. Fenton, 479 P.2d 472, 473-74 (Utah 1971). –Page Citation.

(Note: In citing a state court case in a document submitted to a court of that same state, the 16th ed. of The Bluebook prescribed a parallel citation; the 17th ed. prescribes that local rules shall control, but Utah has no known local rules concerning parallel citations, prior to Utah's adoption of a public domain format. For the sake of continuity, we advise giving a parallel citation in documents submitted to Utah state courts. See Bluebook Rule 10.3.1,Table T.1, and Practitioners' Note P.3.)

–After 30 Utah 2d 462 (1974) and until January 1, 1996, when a public domain format was adopted, cite as follows:

In all documents:

Tucker v. Tucker, 910 P.2d 1209 (Utah 1996). –Case Citation.

Tucker v. Tucker, 910 P.2d 1209, 1210 (Utah 1996). –Page Citation.

In citing cases in law review footnotes, abbreviate any word listed in Table T.6; the names of "states, countries, and other geographical units" unless they are named parties; and any other words of eight or more letters "if substantial space is thereby saved and the result is unambiguous." Bluebook Rule 10.2.2. On the other hand, in citing cases in text, abbreviate only widely known acronyms and the following words: "&," "Ass'n," "Bros.," "Co.," "Corp.," "Inc.," "Ltd.," and "No." Bluebook Rule 10.2.1(c).

-After January 1, 1996, cite as follows:

In all documents:

State v. Reed, 2000 UT 68, 8 P.3d 1025. –Case Citation.

State v. Reed, 2000 UT 68, ¶ 11, 8 P.3d 1025, 1027. –Pinpoint Citation.

See Bluebook Rules 10.3.1 and 10.3.3, Table T.1, and Practitioners' Note P.3; see also 386 Utah Adv. Rep. 3.

Utah State Bulletin
Ab.: Utah Bull.

See also Opinions of the Attorney General of Utah.

Utilities Law Reports (Commerce Clearing House)
Ab.: Util. L. Rep. (CCH)

In law review footnotes, the titles of books and the names of cases, except for procedural phrases, are not underlined. See Bluebook Rule 2.1(a). Further, the following are in large and small capitals: codes, restatements, standards, constitutions, periodicals, authors of books, titles of books, the abbreviated names of codes, most legislative materials except for bills and resolutions, codified ordinances, model codes, court rules, and sentencing guidelines. Refer to The Bluebook.

V

Valparaiso University Law Review
Ab.:   Val. U. L. Rev.
Ex.:   Laura G. Dooley, <u>Sounds of Silence on the Civil Jury</u>, 26 Val. U. L. Rev. 405 (1991). −Article Citation.

Laura G. Dooley, <u>Sounds of Silence on the Civil Jury</u>, 26 Val. U. L. Rev. 405, 409-11 (1991). −Page Citation.

Vanderbilt Journal of Entertainment Law & Practice
Ab.:   Vand. J. Ent. L. & Prac.
Ex.:   S. E. Oross, <u>Fighting the Phantom Menace; The Motion Picture Industry's Struggle to Protect Itself Against Digital Piracy</u>, 2 Vand. J. Ent. L. & Prac. 149, 152 (2000). −Page Citation.

Vanderbilt Journal of Transnational Law
Ab.:   Vand. J. Transnat'l L.
Ex.:   James D. Harmon, Jr., <u>RICO Meets Keiretsu: A Response to Predatory Transfer Pricing</u>, 25 Vand. J. Transnat'l L. 3 (1992). −Article Citation.

James D. Harmon, Jr., <u>RICO Meets Keiretsu: A Response to Predatory Transfer Pricing</u>, 25 Vand. J. Transnat'l L. 3, 35-36 (1992). −Page Citation.

Vanderbilt Law Review
Ab.:   Vand. L. Rev.
Ex.:   Barry Friedman, <u>Habeas and Hubris</u>, 45 Vand. L. Rev. 797 (1992). −Article Citation.

Barry Friedman, <u>Habeas and Hubris</u>, 45 Vand. L. Rev. 797, 823-25 (1992). −Page Citation.

Vanderbilt Lawyer, The
Ab.:   Vand. Law.
Ex.:   Thomas R. McCoy, <u>A Doctrinal Dilemma</u>, Vand. Law., Spring 1991, at 20. −Article Citation.

Thomas R. McCoy, <u>A Doctrinal Dilemma</u>, Vand. Law., Spring 1991, at 20, 21-23. −Page Citation.

vendor neutral citations
<u>See</u> public domain citations.

In law review footnotes, the titles of books and the names of cases, except for procedural phrases, are not underlined. <u>See</u> <u>Bluebook</u> Rule 2.1(a). Further, the following are in large and small capitals: codes, restatements, standards, constitutions, periodicals, authors of books, titles of books, the abbreviated names of codes, most legislative materials except for bills and resolutions, codified ordinances, model codes, court rules, and sentencing guidelines. Refer to <u>The Bluebook</u>.

Vermont Bar Journal and Law Digest
Ab.: Vt. B.J. & L. Dig.

Ex.: John M. Hall, The Ethical Duty to Assure a Client's Competency When Preparing Powers of Attorney, Vt. B.J. & L. Dig., Feb. 1992, at 34. –Article Citation.

John M. Hall, The Ethical Duty to Assure a Client's Competency When Preparing Powers of Attorney, Vt. B.J. & L. Dig., Feb. 1992, at 34, 35. –Page Citation.

Vermont Constitution
Ab.: Vt. Const. ch.   , §   .

Ex.: Vt. Const. ch. II , art. 67. –"Cite constitutional provisions currently in force without date." Bluebook Rule 11.

–"If the cited provision has been repealed, either indicate parenthetically the fact and date of repeal or cite the repealing provision in full." Bluebook Rule 11.

Vt. Const. ch. II, art. 68 (amended 1964). –"When citing a provision that has been subsequently amended, either indicate parenthetically the fact and date of amendment or cite the amending provision in full." Bluebook Rule 11.

Vt. Const. of 1786, ch. I, art. 7 (1793). –"Cite constitutions that have been totally superseded by year of adoption; if the specific provision cited was adopted in a different year, give that year parenthetically." Bluebook Rule 11.

Vermont Government Register
Ab.: Vt. Gov't Reg.

Vermont Law Review
Ab.: Vt. L. Rev.

Ex.: Kevin J. Greene, Terrorism as Impermissible Political Violence: An International Law Framework, 16 Vt. L. Rev. 461 (1992). –Article Citation.

Kevin J. Greene, Terrorism as Impermissible Political Violence: An International Law Framework, 16 Vt. L. Rev. 461, 488 (1992). –Page Citation.

Vermont Reports
Ab.: Vt.

–Cite to A. or A.2d if therein; otherwise, cite to Vt.

In citing cases in law review footnotes, abbreviate any word listed in Table T.6; the names of "states, countries, and other geographical units" unless they are named parties; and any other words of eight or more letters "if substantial space is thereby saved and the result is unambiguous." Bluebook Rule 10.2.2. On the other hand, in citing cases in text, abbreviate only widely known acronyms and the following words: "&," "Ass'n," "Bros.," "Co.," "Corp.," "Inc.," "Ltd.," and "No." Bluebook Rule 10.2.1(c).

–Give parallel citations only in documents submitted to Vermont state courts. (Note: In citing a state court case in a document submitted to a court of that same state, the 16th ed. of The Bluebook prescribed a parallel citation; the 17th ed. prescribes that local rules shall control, but Vermont has no known local rules concerning parallel citations. For the sake of continuity, we advise giving a parallel citation in documents submitted to Vermont state courts. See Bluebook Rule 10.3.1,Table T.1, and Practitioners' Note P.3.)

In documents submitted to Vermont state courts, cite as follows:

> Godino v. Cleanthes, 163 Vt. 237, 656 A.2d 991 (1996). –Case Citation.

> Godino v. Cleanthes, 163 Vt. 237, 240, 656 A.2d 991, 993 (1996). –Page Citation.

In all other documents, cite as follows:

> Godino v. Cleanthes, 656 A.2d 991 (Vt. 1996). –Case Citation.

> Godino v. Cleanthes, 656 A.2d 991, 993 (Vt. 1996). –Page Citation.

Vermont Session Laws
See Acts and Resolves of Vermont.

Vermont Statutes Annotated
Ab.:   Vt. Stat. Ann. tit.   , §   (year)
Ex.:   Vt. Stat. Ann. tit. 30, § 112 (2000).
          Vt. Stat. Ann. tit. 32, § 10105 (Supp. 2000).

Vernon's Annotated Missouri Statutes (West)
Ab.:   Mo. Ann. Stat. §   (West year)
Ex.:   Mo. Ann. Stat. § 163.191 (West 2000).
          Mo. Ann. Stat. § 316.233 (West Supp. 2000).
          –"Cite to Missouri Revised Statutes if therein." Bluebook Table T.1, p. 212.

Vernon's Kansas Statutes Annotated
Ab.:   Kan. subject Ann. § (West)
          See Bluebook Table T.1, p. 203 for the abbreviation of each subject.
Ex.:   Kan. U.C.C. Ann. § 84-6-102 (West 1968).
          Kan. U.C.C. Ann. § 84-6-106 (West Supp. 1986).

Vernon's Texas Code of Criminal Procedure Annotated
Ab.:   Tex. Code Crim. P. Ann. art. (Vernon year)

In law review footnotes, the titles of books and the names of cases, except for procedural phrases, are not underlined. See Bluebook Rule 2.1(a). Further, the following are in large and small capitals: codes, restatements, standards, constitutions, periodicals, authors of books, titles of books, the abbreviated names of codes, most legislative materials except for bills and resolutions, codified ordinances, model codes, court rules, and sentencing guidelines. Refer to The Bluebook.

Ex.:   Tex. Code Crim. P. Ann. art. 21.03 (Vernon 1989).

Vernon's Texas Codes Annotated
Form: Tex. [subject] Code Ann. § (Vernon year)
Ex.:   Tex. Loc., Gov't Code Ann. § 153.003 (Vernon 1999).
         Tex. Util. Code Ann. § 121.505 (Vernon Supp. 2000).
See Bluebook Table T.1, pp. 235-36.

Vernon's Texas Revised Civil Statutes Annotated
Ab.:   Tex. Rev. Civ. Stat. Ann. art. (Vernon year)
Ex: Tex. Rev. Civ. Stat. Ann. art. 1433 (Vernon 1997).
         Tex. Rev. Civ. Stat. Ann. art. 21.80 (Vernon 2000).

Vernon's Texas Session Law Service (West)
Ab.:   year Tex. Sess. Law Serv. (West)
Ex.:   Act of April 8, 1992, ch. 1, 1992 Tex. Sess. Law Serv. 1 (West) (senatorial district boundaries). –Citation to an entire session law.
         Act of Apr. 8, 1992, ch. 1, § 2, 1992 Tex. Sess. Law Serv. 1, 2 (West) (senatorial district boundaries). –Citation to a section of a session law.

Verträge der Bundesrepublik Deutschland
Ab.:   Vol. Verträge der Bundesrepublik Deutschland (ser. A), No.
Ex.:   68 Verträge der Bundesrepublik Deutschland (ser. A), No. 847.

Veterans Appeals Reporter
See West's Veterans Appeals Reporter.

Vice Chancellor
Ab.:   V.C.

Victorian Reports
Ab.:   V.R.
Ex.:   Saunders v. Nash, [1991] 2 V.R. 63 (Austl.).

Victoria University of Wellington Law Review
Ab.:   Vict. U. Wellington L. Rev.
Ex.:   Malcolm Luey, Proprietary Remedies in Insurance Subrogation, 25 Vict. U. Wellington L. Rev. 449 (1995). –Article Citation.
         Malcolm Luey, Proprietary Remedies in Insurance Subrogation, 25 Vict. U. Wellington L. Rev. 449, 452-54 (1995). –Page Citation.

videotapes, noncommercial
See Bluebook Rule 18.5.

In citing cases in law review footnotes, abbreviate any word listed in Table T.6; the names of "states, countries, and other geographical units" unless they are named parties; and any other words of eight or more letters "if substantial space is thereby saved and the result is unambiguous." Bluebook Rule 10.2.2. On the other hand, in citing cases in text, abbreviate only widely known acronyms and the following words: "&," "Ass'n," "Bros.," "Co.," "Corp.," "Inc.," "Ltd.," and "No." Bluebook Rule 10.2.1(c).

ex.   Videotape: The Call to Practice (Shyster Enterprises, Inc. 2001) (on file
with the Vanderbilt Univ. Law School Library).

Villanova Environmental Law Journal
Ab.:   Vill. Envtl. L.J.
Ex.:   Jerome B. Simandle, <u>Resolving Multi-Party Hazardous Waste</u>
<u>Litigation</u>, 2 Vill. Envtl. L.J. 111 (1991). –Article Citation.
Jerome B. Simandle, <u>Resolving Multi-Party Hazardous Waste</u>
<u>Litigation</u>, 2 Vill. Envtl. L.J. 111, 115-16 (1991). –Page Citation.

Villanova Law Review
Ab.:   Vill. L. Rev.
Ex.:   David Chang, <u>A Critique of Judicial Supremacy</u>, 36 Vill. L. Rev. 281
(1991). –Article Citation.
David Chang, <u>A Critique of Judicial Supremacy</u>, 36 Vill. L. Rev. 281,
333-35 (1991). –Page Citation.

Virgin Islands Code Annotated
Ab.:   V.I. Code Ann. tit.   , §   (year)
Ex.:   V.I. Code Ann. tit. 31, § 236 (1996).
V.I. Code Ann. tit. 32, § 441 (Supp. 1996).

Virgin Islands Reports
Ab.:   V.I.
Ex.:   <u>Vidal v. Virgin Islands Hous. Auth.</u>, 20 V.I. 3 (Terr. Ct. 1983).
–Case Citation.
<u>Vidal v. Virgin Islands Hous. Auth.</u>, 20 V.I. 3, 5 (Terr. Ct. 1983).
–Page Citation.

Virginia Administrative Code
Ab.:   [tit.] Va. Admin. Code § (year).
Ex.:   8 Va. Admin. Code § 85-10-50 (2000).

Virginia Bar Association Journal
Ab.:   Va. B. Ass'n J.
Ex.:   J.R. Zepkin, <u>Increasing the Litigator's Risk</u>, Va. B. Ass'n J., Spring
1992 at 16. –Article Citation.
J.R. Zepkin, <u>Increasing the Litigator's Risk</u>, Va. B. Ass'n J., Spring
1992 at 16, 18. –Page Citation.

Virginia Code
<u>See</u> Code of Virginia Annotated.

Virginia Constitution
Ab.:   Va. Const. art.   , §   .

In law review footnotes, the titles of books and the names of cases, except for procedural phrases, are not underlined. <u>See</u> <u>Bluebook</u> Rule 2.1(a). Further, the following are in large and small capitals: codes, restatements, standards, constitutions, periodicals, authors of books, titles of books, the abbreviated names of codes, most legislative materials except for bills and resolutions, codified ordinances, model codes, court rules, and sentencing guidelines. Refer to <u>The Bluebook</u>.

Ex.: Va. Const. art. XI, § 3. –"Cite constitutional provisions currently in force without date." <u>Bluebook</u> Rule 11.

Va. Const. art. VIII, § 8 (amended 1990). –"When citing a provision that has been subsequently amended, either indicate parenthetically the fact and date of amendment or cite the amending provision in full." <u>Bluebook</u> Rule 11.

Virginia Court of Appeals Reports
Ab.: Va. App.

–Cite to S.E. or S.E.2d if therein; otherwise, cite to Va. App.

–Give parallel citations only in documents submitted to Virginia state courts. <u>See</u> <u>Bluebook</u> Rule 10.3.1 and Practitioners' Note P.3; <u>see also</u> Va. Sup. Ct. R. 5:17, which requires a parallel citation.

In documents submitted to Virginia state courts, cite as follows:

<u>Rocco Turkeys, Inc. v. Lemus</u>, 21 Va. App. 503, 465 S.E.2d 156 (1996). –Case Citation.

<u>Rocco Turkeys, Inc. v. Lemus</u>, 21 Va. App. 503, 504, 465 S.E.2d 156, 157 (1996). –Page Citation.

In all other documents, cite as follows:

<u>Rocco Turkeys, Inc. v. Lemus</u>, 465 S.E.2d 156 (Va. Ct. App. 1996). –Case Citation.

<u>Rocco Turkeys, Inc. v. Lemus</u>, 465 S.E.2d 156, 157 (Va. Ct. App. 1996). –Page Citation.

Virginia Environmental Law Journal
Ab.: Va. Envtl. L.J.

Ex.: Steven F. Ferrey, <u>Shaping American Power: Federal Preemption and Technological Change</u>, 11 Va. Envtl. L.J. 47 (1991). –Article Citation.

Steven F. Ferrey, <u>Shaping American Power: Federal Preemption and Technological Change</u>, 11 Va. Envtl. L.J. 47, 55-56 (1991). –Page Citation.

Virginia Journal of International Law
Ab.: Va. J. Int'l L.

Ex.: Lawrence R. Helfer, <u>Lesbian and Gay Rights as Human Rights: Strategies for a United Europe</u>, 32 Va. J. Int'l L. 157 (1991). –Article Citation.

Lawrence R. Helfer, <u>Lesbian and Gay Rights as Human Rights: Strategies for a United Europe</u>, 32 Va. J. Int'l L. 157, 158 (1991). –Page Citation.

Virginia Journal of Social Policy and the Law
Ab.: Va. J. Soc. Pol'y & L.

In citing cases in law review footnotes, abbreviate any word listed in Table T.6; the names of "states, countries, and other geographical units" unless they are named parties; and any other words of eight or more letters "if <u>substantial</u> space is thereby saved and the result is unambiguous." <u>Bluebook</u> Rule 10.2.2. On the other hand, in citing cases in text, abbreviate only widely known acronyms and the following words: "&," "Ass'n," "Bros.," "Co.," "Corp.," "Inc.," "Ltd.," and "No." <u>Bluebook</u> Rule 10.2.1(c).

Ex.:   James A. Armstrong, Jr., From the Inside, 3 Va. J. Soc. Pol'y & L. 331
        (1996). –Article Citation.

        James A. Armstrong, Jr., From the Inside, 3 Va. J. Soc. Pol'y & L. 331,
        333 (1996). –Page Citation.

Virginia Law Review
Ab.:   Va. L. Rev.
Ex.:   Paul G. Mahoney, Precaution Cost and the Law of Fraud in Impersonal
        Markets, 78 Va. L. Rev. 623 (1992). –Article Citation.

        Paul G. Mahoney, Precaution Cost and the Law of Fraud in Impersonal
        Markets, 78 Va. L. Rev. 623, 659-60 (1992). –Page Citation.

Virginia Lawyer
        -alternates with Virginia Lawyer Register
Ab.:   Va. Law.
Ex.:   Hon. Frank J. Ceresi, The Drug Crisis in Family Court, Va. Law., Jan.,
        1992, at 18. –Article Citation.

        Hon. Frank J. Ceresi, The Drug Crisis in Family Court, Va. Law., Jan.,
        1992, at 18, 19. –Page Citation.

Virginia Lawyer Register
        See Virginia Lawyer

Virginia Opinions of the Attorney General and Report to the Governor
        See Opinions of the Attorney General and Report to the Governor of Virginia

Virginia Register of Regulations
Ab.:   Va. Regs. Reg.

Virginia Reports
Ab.:   Va.
        –Cite to S.E. or S.E.2d if therein; otherwise, cite to Va.
        –Give parallel citations only in documents submitted to Virginia state
        courts. See Bluebook Rule 10.3.1 and Practitioners' Note P.3; see
        also Va. Sup. Ct. R. 5:17, which requires a parallel citation.
        In documents submitted to Virginia state courts, cite as follows:
            Ware v. Jensen, 251 Va. 116, 465 S.E.2d 809 (1996).
            –Case Citation.
            Ware v. Jensen, 251 Va. 116, 117, 465 S.E.2d 809, 810 (1996).
            –Page Citation.
        In all other documents, cite as follows:
            Ware v. Jensen, 465 S.E.2d 809 (Va. 1996). –Case Citation.
            Ware v. Jensen, 465 S.E.2d 809, 810 (Va. 1996). –Page Citation.

In law review footnotes, the titles of books and the names of cases, except for procedural
phrases, are not underlined. See Bluebook Rule 2.1(a). Further, the following are in large
and small capitals: codes, restatements, standards, constitutions, periodicals, authors of
books, titles of books, the abbreviated names of codes, most legislative materials except for
bills and resolutions, codified ordinances, model codes, court rules, and sentencing guidelines.
Refer to The Bluebook.

Virginia Session Laws
    <u>See</u> Acts of the General Assembly of the Commonwealth of Virginia.

Virginia Tax Review
    Ab.:   Va. Tax Rev.

    Ex.:   Walter D. Schwidetzky, <u>Is it Time to Give the S Corporation a Proper Burial?</u>, 15 Va. Tax Rev. 591 (1996). –Article Citation.

             Walter D. Schwidetzky, <u>Is it Time to Give the S Corporation a Proper Burial?</u>, 15 Va. Tax Rev. 591, 601 (1996). –Page Citation.

volume(s)
    Ab.:   vol., vols.

In citing cases in law review footnotes, abbreviate any word listed in Table T.6; the names of "states, countries, and other geographical units" unless they are named parties; and any other words of eight or more letters "if <u>substantial</u> space is thereby saved and the result is unambiguous." <u>Bluebook</u> Rule 10.2.2. On the other hand, in citing cases in text, abbreviate only widely known acronyms and the following words: "&," "Ass'n," "Bros.," "Co.," "Corp.," "Inc.," "Ltd.," and "No." <u>Bluebook</u> Rule 10.2.1(c).

W

Wage and Hour Cases (Bureau of National Affairs)
    Ab.:   See Lab. Relations Reporter (BNA).

Wage-Price Law and Economics Review
    Ab.:   Wage-Price L. & Econ. Rev.

Wake Forest Law Review
    Ab.:   Wake Forest L. Rev.
    Ex.:   John L. Douglas, Deposit Insurance Reform, 27 Wake Forest L. Rev. 11 (1992). –Article Citation.

           John L. Douglas, Deposit Insurance Reform, 27 Wake Forest L. Rev. 11, 19-20 (1992). –Page Citation.

Wallace (United States Reports)
    See United States Reports

Washburn Law Journal
    Ab.:   Washburn L.J.
    Ex.:   Paul B. Rasor, A Law Teacher Looks at the Good Samaritan Story, 31 Washburn L.J. 71 (1991). –Article Citation.

           Paul B. Rasor, A Law Teacher Looks at the Good Samaritan Story, 31 Washburn L.J. 71, 77 (1991). –Page Citation.

Washington Administrative Code
    Ab.:   Wash. Admin. Code § (year)
    Ex.:   Wash. Admin. Code § 60-12-005 (2000).

Washington and Lee Law Review
    Ab.:   Wash. & Lee L. Rev.
    Ex.:   Edward Dumbauld, Thomas Jefferson's Equity Commonplace Book, 48 Wash. & Lee L. Rev. 1257 (1991). –Article Citation.

           Edward Dumbauld, Thomas Jefferson's Equity Commonplace Book, 48 Wash. & Lee L. Rev. 1257, 1270 (1991). –Page Citation.

Washington Appellate Reports
    Ab.:   Wash. App.
           –Cite to P., P.2d, or P.3d if therein; otherwise, cite to Wash. App.
           –Give parallel citations only in documents submitted to Washington state courts. See Bluebook Rule 10.3.1 and Practitioners' Note P.3; see also Wash. R. App. P. 10.4(g), which requires a parallel citation.

In law review footnotes, the titles of books and the names of cases, except for procedural phrases, are not underlined. See Bluebook Rule 2.1(a). Further, the following are in large and small capitals: codes, restatements, standards, constitutions, periodicals, authors of books, titles of books, the abbreviated names of codes, most legislative materials except for bills and resolutions, codified ordinances, model codes, court rules, and sentencing guidelines. Refer to The Bluebook.

In documents submitted to Washington state courts, cite as follows:

Riss v. Angel, 80 Wash. App. 553, 912 P.2d 1028 (1996). –Case Citation.

Riss v. Angel, 80 Wash. App. 553, 556, 912 P.2d 1028, 1031 (1996). –Page Citation.

In all other documents, cite as follows:

Riss v. Angel, 912 P.2d 1028 (Wash. Ct. App. 1996). –Case Citation.

Riss v. Angel, 912 P.2d 1028, 1031 (Wash. Ct. App. 1996). –Page Citation.

Washington Constitution
- Ab.: Wash. Const. art.   , §   .
- Ex.: Wash. Const. art. X, § 1. –"Cite constitutional provisions currently in force without date." Bluebook Rule 11.

  Wash. Const. art. II, § 33 (repealed 1966).
  Wash. Const. art. II, § 33, repealed by Wash. Const. amend. 42. –"If the cited provision has been repealed, either indicate parenthetically the fact and date of repeal or cite the repealing provision in full." Bluebook Rule 11.

  Wash. Const. art. IV, § 31 (amended 1989).
  Wash. Const. art. IV, § 3, amended by Wash. Const. amend. 85. –"When citing a provision that has been subsequently amended, either indicate parenthetically the fact and date of amendment or cite the amending provision in full." Bluebook Rule 11.

Washington Law Review
- Ab.: Wash. L. Rev.
- Ex.: Jule A. Davies, Direct Actions for Emotional Harm: Is Compromise Possible?, 67 Wash. L. Rev. 1 (1992). –Article Citation.

  Jule A. Davies, Direct Actions for Emotional Harm: Is Compromise Possible?, 67 Wash. L. Rev. 1, 39-40 (1992). –Page Citation.

Washington Lawyer, The
- Ab.: Wash. Law.
- Ex.: Susan L. Crowley & Ann Charnley, Watchword for the '90s: Client Service, Wash. Law., Jan./Feb. 1992, at 22. –Article Citation.

  Susan L. Crowley & Ann Charnley, Watchword for the '90s: Client Service, Wash. Law., Jan./Feb. 1992, at 22, 23. –Page Citation.

Washington Legislative Service (West)
- Ab.: year Wash. Legis. Serv.   (West)

In citing cases in law review footnotes, abbreviate any word listed in Table T.6; the names of "states, countries, and other geographical units" unless they are named parties; and any other words of eight or more letters "if substantial space is thereby saved and the result is unambiguous." Bluebook Rule 10.2.2. On the other hand, in citing cases in text, abbreviate only widely known acronyms and the following words: "&," "Ass'n," "Bros.," "Co.," "Corp.," "Inc.," "Ltd.," and "No." Bluebook Rule 10.2.1(c).

Ex.:   Act of Mar. 29, 1996, ch. 277, 1996 Wash. Legis. Serv. 926 (West) (relating to offender debts, correctional facilities). –Citation to an entire session law.

Act of Mar. 29, 1996, ch. 277, sec. 1, § 72.109.450, 1996 Wash. Legis. Serv. 926, 926-27 (West) (relating to offender debts, correctional facilities). –Citation to a session law amending a prior act.

–"Cite to Wash. Laws if therein." <u>Bluebook</u> Table T.1, p. 239.

Washington Reports
Ab.:   Wash. or Wash. 2d

–Cite to P., P.2d, or P.3d if therein; otherwise, cite to Wash. or Wash. 2d

–Give parallel citations only in documents submitted to Washington state courts. <u>See</u> <u>Bluebook</u> Rule 10.3.1 and Practitioners' Note P.3; <u>see also</u> Wash. R. App. P. 10.4(g), which requires a parallel citation.

In documents submitted to Washington state courts, cite as follows:

<u>State v. Johnson</u>, 128 Wash. 2d 431, 909 P.2d 293 (1996). –Case Citation.

<u>State v. Johnson</u>, 128 Wash. 2d 431, 434, 909 P.2d 293, 296 (1996). –Page Citation.

In all other documents, cite as follows:

<u>State v. Johnson</u>, 909 P.2d 293 (Wash. 1996). –Case Citation.

<u>State v. Johnson</u>, 909 P.2d 293, 296 (Wash. 1996). –Page Citation.

Washington Revised Code Annotated
<u>See</u> Revised Code of Washington Annotated (West)

Washington Session Laws
<u>See</u> Laws of Washington and Washington Legislative Service (West)

Washington State Register
Ab.:   Wash. St. Reg.

Washington Territory Reports (1854-1888)
Ab.:   Wash. Terr.

Washington University Journal of Urban and Contemporary Law
Ab.:   Wash. U. J. Urb. & Contemp. L.

Ex.:   Marc R. Buljon, <u>Off-Site Mitigation and the EIS Threshold: NEPA is Faulty Framework</u>, 41 Wash. U. J. Urb. & Contemp. L. 101 (1992). – Article Citation.

Marc R. Buljon, <u>Off-Site Mitigation and the EIS Threshold: NEPA is Faulty Framework</u>, 41 Wash. U. J. Urb. & Contemp. L. 101, 105-06 (1992). –Page Citation.

In law review footnotes, the titles of books and the names of cases, except for procedural phrases, are not underlined. <u>See</u> <u>Bluebook</u> Rule 2.1(a). Further, the following are in large and small capitals: codes, restatements, standards, constitutions, periodicals, authors of books, titles of books, the abbreviated names of codes, most legislative materials except for bills and resolutions, codified ordinances, model codes, court rules, and sentencing guidelines. Refer to <u>The Bluebook</u>.

Washington University Law Quarterly
  Ab.:   Wash. U. L.Q.
  Ex.:   Andrew Kull, <u>Unilateral Mistake: The Baseball Card Case</u>, 70 Wash.
           U. L.Q. 57 (1992). –Article Citation.
           Andrew Kull, <u>Unilateral Mistake: The Baseball Card Case</u>, 70 Wash.
           U. L.Q. 57, 59-63 (1992). –Page Citation.

Wayne Law Review
  Ab.:   Wayne L. Rev.
  Ex.:   Kenneth R. Thomas, <u>Public Courts and Private Litigation: Proposed
           Changes to the Use of Confidentiality and Sealing Orders in Civil
           Cases</u>, 37 Wayne L. Rev. 1761 (1991). –Article Citation.
           Kenneth R. Thomas, <u>Public Courts and Private Litigation: Proposed
           Changes to the Use of Confidentiality and Sealing Orders in Civil
           Cases</u>, 37 Wayne L. Rev. 1761, 1764 (1991). –Page Citation.

Weekly Compilation of Presidential Documents
  Ab.:   Weekly Comp. Pres. Doc.
  Ex.:   Remarks at the 53rd Annual Academy Awards Presentation
           Ceremonies, 17 Weekly Comp. Pres. Doc. 377 (Mar. 31, 1981).

Weekly Law Reports (England) (1953-date)
  <u>See</u> <u>Bluebook</u> Table T.2.
  Ab.:   W.L.R.
  Ex.:   <u>Reed v. Madon</u>, [1989] 2 W.L.R. 553 (Ch. 1988). (Eng.).
           –Case Citation.

Weekly Notes (England) (1866-1952)
  <u>See</u> <u>Bluebook</u> Table T.2.
  Ab.:   W.N.
  Ex.:   <u>Westminster Bank, Ltd. v. Imperial Airways, Ltd.</u>, 1936 W.N. 238
           (K.B. 1936) (Eng.). –Case Citation.

Weil's Code of Wyoming Rules
  Ab.:   Weil's Code Wyo. R.
  Ex.:   Weil's Code Wyo. R. 005-000-024 § 4 (2000).

Weinstein's Evidence, by Jack B. Weinstein and Margaret A. Berger
           –Do not abbreviate the title.
  Ex.:   3 Jack B. Weinstein & Margaret A. Berger, <u>Weinstein's Evidence</u>
           ¶ 608[05] (1996). –Paragraph Citation.

West Indian Law Journal
  Ab.:   W. Indian L.J.

In citing cases in law review footnotes, abbreviate any word listed in Table T.6;
the names of "states, countries, and other geographical units" unless they are named parties;
and any other words of eight or more letters "if <u>substantial</u> space is thereby saved and the
result is unambiguous." <u>Bluebook</u> Rule 10.2.2. On the other hand, in citing cases in text,
abbreviate only widely known acronyms and the following words: "&," "Ass'n," "Bros.,"
"Co.," "Corp.," "Inc.," "Ltd.," and "No." <u>Bluebook</u> Rule 10.2.1(c).

Ex.:   M.C. Jozanna, <u>The Proposed South African Bill of Rights - A Prescription for Equality or Neo-Apartheid</u>, 15 W. Indian L.J. 1 (1991). –Article Citation.

M.C. Jozanna, <u>The Proposed South African Bill of Rights - A Prescription for Equality or Neo-Apartheid</u>, 15 W. Indian L.J. 1, 29-32 (1991). –Page Citation.

West Indian Reports
Ab.:   W.I.R.

West Virginia, Biennial Report & Official Opinions of the Attorney General
<u>See</u> Biennial Report & Official Opinions of the Attorney General of the State of West Virginia.

West Virginia Code
Ab.:   W. Va. Code §   (year)

Ex.:   W. Va. Code § 20-5-5 (1996).

W. Va. Code § 20-2-5d (Supp. 1996).

West Virginia Code Annotated, Michie's (Lexis)
Ab.:   W. Va. Code Ann. §   (Lexis year)

Ex.:   W. Va. Code Ann. § 61-10-11 (Lexis 2000).

W. Va. Code Ann. § 51-9-3 (Lexis Supp. 2000).

West Virginia Code of State Rules
Ab.:   W. Va. Code St. R. §   (year)

Ex.:   W. Va. Code St. R. § 47-10-4.1.b. (2000).

West Virginia Constitution
Ab.:   W. Va. Const. art. , § .

Ex.:   W. Va. Const. art. XII, § 1. –"Cite constitutional provisions currently in force without date." <u>Bluebook</u> Rule 11.

W. Va. Const. art. X, § 2 (repealed 1970). –"If the cited provision has been repealed, either indicate parenthetically the fact and date of repeal or cite the repealing provision in full." <u>Bluebook</u> Rule 11.

W. Va. Const. art. VI, § 36 (amended 1984). –"When citing a provision that has been subsequently amended, either indicate parenthetically the fact and date of amendment or cite the amending provision in full." <u>Bluebook</u> Rule 11.

West Virginia Criminal Justice Review
Ab.:   W. Va. Crim. Just. Rev.

West Virginia Law Review
Ab.:   W. Va. L. Rev.

In law review footnotes, the titles of books and the names of cases, except for procedural phrases, are not underlined. <u>See</u> <u>Bluebook</u> Rule 2.1(a). Further, the following are in large and small capitals: codes, restatements, standards, constitutions, periodicals, authors of books, titles of books, the abbreviated names of codes, most legislative materials except for bills and resolutions, codified ordinances, model codes, court rules, and sentencing guidelines. Refer to <u>The Bluebook</u>.

Ex.:   Archibald Cox, <u>Ethics in Government: The Cornerstone of Public Trust</u>, 94 W. Va. L. Rev. 281 (1991-92). –Article Citation.

Archibald Cox, <u>Ethics in Government: The Cornerstone of Public Trust</u>, 94 W. Va. L. Rev. 281, 297-98 (1991-92). –Page Citation.

West Virginia Reports
Ab.:   W. Va.

–Cite to S.E. or S.E.2d if therein; otherwise, cite to W. Va.

–Give parallel citations only in documents submitted to West Virginia state courts. (<u>Note</u>: In citing a state court case in a document submitted to a court of that same state, the 16th ed. of <u>The Bluebook</u> prescribed a parallel citation; the 17th ed. prescribes that local rules shall control, but West Virginia has no known local rules concerning parallel citations. For the sake of continuity, we advise giving a parallel citation in documents submitted to West Virginia state courts. See <u>Bluebook</u> Rule 10.3.1 and Practitioners' Note P.3.)

In documents submitted to West Virginia state courts, cite as follows:

<u>Buckler v. Buckler</u>, 195 W. Va. 705, 466 S.E.2d 556 (1995). –Case Citation.

<u>Buckler v. Buckler</u>, 195 W. Va. 705, 707, 466 S.E.2d 556, 558 (1995). –Page Citation.

In all other documents, cite as follows:

<u>Buckler v. Buckler</u>, 466 S.E.2d 556 (W.Va. 1995). –Case Citation.

<u>Buckler v. Buckler</u>, 466 S.E.2d 556, 558 (W.Va. 1995). –Page Citation.

West Virginia Session Laws
<u>See</u> Acts of the Legislature of West Virginia

Western Legal History
Ab.:   W. Legal Hist.

Ex.:   Kent D. Richards, <u>Historical Antecedents to the Boldt Decision</u>, 4 W. Legal Hist. 69 (1991). –Article Citation.

Kent D. Richards, <u>Historical Antecedents to the Boldt Decision</u>, 4 W. Legal Hist. 69, 79-81 (1991). –Page Citation.

Western New England Law Review
Ab.:   W. New Eng. L. Rev.

In citing cases in law review footnotes, abbreviate any word listed in Table T.6; the names of "states, countries, and other geographical units" unless they are named parties; and any other words of eight or more letters "if <u>substantial</u> space is thereby saved and the result is unambiguous." <u>Bluebook</u> Rule 10.2.2. On the other hand, in citing cases in text, abbreviate only widely known acronyms and the following words: "&," "Ass'n," "Bros.," "Co.," "Corp.," "Inc.," "Ltd.," and "No." <u>Bluebook</u> Rule 10.2.1(c).

Ex.:   Francis J. Mootz, <u>Principles of Insurance Coverage: A Guide for the Employment Lawyer</u>, 18 W. New Eng. L. Rev. 5 (1996). –Article Citation.

Francis J. Mootz, <u>Principles of Insurance Coverage: A Guide for the Employment Lawyer</u>, 18 W. New Eng. L. Rev. 5, 11 (1996). –Page Citation.

Western State University Law Review
Ab.:   W. St. U. L. Rev.

Ex.:   Bruce I. Shapiro, <u>The Heavy Burden of Establishing Weight as a Handicap Under Anti-Discrimination Statutes</u>, 18 W. St. U. L. Rev. 565 (1991). –Article Citation.

Bruce I. Shapiro, <u>The Heavy Burden of Establishing Weight as a Handicap Under Anti-Discrimination Statutes</u>, 18 W. St. U. L. Rev. 565, 569-72 (1991). –Page Citation.

Western Weekly Reports (Canada)
–Cite provincial reporters, if therein, in the order of preference shown in <u>Bluebook</u> Table T.2, pp. 255-56; otherwise, cite D.L.R., W.W.R., A.P.R., E.L.R., M.P.R., or W.L.R. <u>Bluebook</u> Table T.2.

Ab.:   W.W.R.

Ex.:   <u>Livaditis v. Calgary</u>, [1992] 1 W.W.R. 53 (Alta. C.A. 1991) (Can.).

Westlaw
<u>See</u> pending and unreported cases; <u>see also</u> electronic media and other nonprint recources, and <u>Bluebook</u> Rules 10.9(ii), 16.5(d), 18.1.1, 18.1.2, & 18.1.3.

West's Annotated California Code
Ab.:   Cal. [subject] Code § (West year)

<u>See</u> <u>Bluebook</u> Table T.1, pp. 192-93, for the abbreviation of each subject.

Ex.:   Cal. Welf. & Inst. Code § 4689.2 (West 1998).

Cal. Gov't Code § 21419 (West Supp. 2000).

–"Cite to either the West or the Deering subject matter code if therein." <u>Bluebook</u> Table T.1, p. 192.

West's Annotated Indiana Code
Ab.:   Ind. Code Ann. § (West year)

Ex.:   Ind. Code Ann. § 5-1-4-10 (West 2000)

Ind. Code Ann. § 6-1.1-18.5 (West Supp. 2000)

–"Cite to Indiana Code if therein." <u>Bluebook</u> Table T.1, p. 201.

West's Bankruptcy Reporter
<u>See</u> Bankruptcy Reporter

In law review footnotes, the titles of books and the names of cases, except for procedural phrases, are not underlined. <u>See</u> <u>Bluebook</u> Rule 2.1(a). Further, the following are in large and small capitals: codes, restatements, standards, constitutions, periodicals, authors of books, titles of books, the abbreviated names of codes, most legislative materials except for bills and resolutions, codified ordinances, model codes, court rules, and sentencing guidelines. Refer to <u>The Bluebook</u>.

West's California Reporter

   Ab.:   Cal. Rptr.

          -Give parallel citations, if at all, only in documents submitted to California state courts. See Bluebook Rule 10.3.1 and Practitioners' Note P.3. See also Cal. R. Ct. 313(c), which requires citation only to the official reporters, Cal., Cal. 2d, Cal. 3d, or Cal. 4th, Cal. App., Cal. App. 2d, Cal. App. 3d, or Cal. App. 4th, or Cal. App. Supp., Cal. App. 2d Supp., Cal. App. 3d Supp., or Cal. App. 4th Supp.

          In documents submitted to California state courts, cite as follows:

          Mangini v. Aerojet-Gen Corp., 12 Cal. 4th 1087, 912 P.2d 1220, 51 Cal. Rptr. 2d 272 (1996). –Case Citation.

          Mangini v. Aerojet-Gen Corp., 12 Cal. 4th 1087, 1088, 912 P.2d 1220, 1222, 51 Cal. Rptr. 2d 272, 273 (1996). –Page Citation.

          Brantley v. Pisaro, 42 Cal. App. 4th 1591, 50 Cal. Rptr. 2d 431 (Ct. App. 1996). –Case Citation.

          Brantley v. Pisaro, 42 Cal. App. 4th 1591, 1593, 50 Cal. Rptr. 2d 431, 433 (Ct. App. 1996). –Page Citation.

          People v. Studley, 44 Cal. App. 4th Supp. 1, 52 Cal. Rptr. 2d 461 (App. Dep't Super. Ct. 1996). –Case Citation.

          People v. Studley, 44 Cal. App. 4th Supp. 1, 5, 52 Cal. Rptr. 2d 461, 463 (App. Dep't Super. Ct.1996). –Page Citation.

          In all other documents, cite as follows:

          Mangini v. Aerojet-Gen Corp., 912 P.2d 1220 (Cal. 1996). –Case Citation.

          Mangini v. Aerojet-Gen Corp., 912 P.2d 1220, 1222 (Cal. 1996) –Page Citation.

          Brantley v. Pisaro, 50 Cal. Rptr. 2d 431 (Ct. App 1996). –Case Citation.

          Brantley v. Pisaro, 50 Cal. Rptr. 2d 431, 433 (Ct. App. 1996). –Page Citation.

          People v. Studley, 52 Cal. Rptr. 2d 461 (App. Dep't Super. Ct. 1996). –Case Citation.

          People v. Studley, 52 Cal. Rptr. 2d 461, 463 (App. Dep't Super. Ct. 1996). – Page Citation.

West's Colorado Revised Statutes Annotated

   Ab.:   Colo. Rev. Stat. Ann. §   (West year)

   Ex.:   Colo. Rev. Stat. Ann. § 39-22-621 (West 1990).

          Colo. Rev. Stat. Ann. § 16-15-101 (West 1992).

          Colo. Rev. Stat. Ann. § 16-15.7-101 (West Supp. 1995).

In citing cases in law review footnotes, abbreviate any word listed in Table T.6; the names of "states, countries, and other geographical units" unless they are named parties; and any other words of eight or more letters "if substantial space is thereby saved and the result is unambiguous." Bluebook Rule 10.2.2. On the other hand, in citing cases in text, abbreviate only widely known acronyms and the following words: "&," "Ass'n," "Bros.," "Co.," "Corp.," "Inc.," "Ltd.," and "No." Bluebook Rule 10.2.1(c).

West's Hawaii Reports
See Hawaii Reports, West's.

West's Indiana Legislative Service
Ab.:   year Ind. Legis. Serv. (West)

West's Louisiana Children's Code Annotated
Ab.:   La. Ch. Code Ann. art. (West year)
Ex.:   La. Ch. Code Ann. art. 114 (West 1995).
      La. Ch. Code Ann. art. 601 (West Supp. 2001).

West's Louisiana Civil Code Annotated
Ab.:   La. Civ. Code Ann. art. (West year)
Ex.:   La. Civ. Code Ann. art. 218 (West 1993).
      La. Civ. Code Ann. art. 245 (West Supp. 1996).

West's Louisiana Code of Civil Procedure Annotated
Ab.:   La. Code Civ. Proc. Ann. art. (West year)
Ex.:   La. Code Civ. Proc. Ann. art. 2122 (West 1961).

West's Louisiana Code of Criminal Procedure Annotated
Ab.:   La. Code Crim. Proc. Ann. art. (West year)
Ex.:   La. Code Crim. Proc. Ann. art. 404 (West 1991).
      La. Code Crim. Proc. Ann. art. 230.2 (West Supp. 1996).

West's Louisiana Code of Evidence Annotated
Ab.:   La. Code Evid. Ann. art. (West year)
Ex.:   La. Code Evid. Ann. art. 613 (West 1995).
      La. Code Evid. Ann. art. 608 (West Supp. 1996)

West's Louisiana Revised Statutes Annotated
Ab.:   La. Rev. Stat. Ann. § (West year)
Ex.:   La. Rev. Stat. Ann. § 30.2002 (West 2000).
      La. Rev. Stat. Ann. § 11.2258 (West Supp. 2000).

West's Military Justice Reporter
See Military Justice Reporter.

West's Mississippi Legislative Service
Ab.:   Miss. Legis. Serv.
Ex.:   Act of April 17, 2000, ch. 392, 2000 Miss. Legis. Serv. 191 (West) (garbage disposal). –Citation to an entire session law.
      Act of April 17, 2000, ch. 392, sec. 1, § 17-17-5, 2000 Miss. Legis. Serv. 191, 191 (West). –Citation to a section of a session law amending a prior act.

In law review footnotes, the titles of books and the names of cases, except for procedural phrases, are not underlined. See Bluebook Rule 2.1(a). Further, the following are in large and small capitals: codes, restatements, standards, constitutions, periodicals, authors of books, titles of books, the abbreviated names of codes, most legislative materials except for bills and resolutions, codified ordinances, model codes, court rules, and sentencing guidelines. Refer to The Bluebook.

West's New York Supplement

Ab.: N.Y.S., N.Y.S.2d

–Give parallel citations, if at all, only in documents submitted to New York state courts. See Bluebook Rule 10.3.1 and Practitioners' Note P.3; see also N.Y. Ct. App. R. 500.1 and 500.5(d)(3) and N.Y. Sup. Ct. App. Div. R. 600.10, which require citation only to the official reporters, A.D. or A.D.2d, Misc. or Misc. 2d, or N.Y. or N.Y.2d.

In documents submitted to New York state courts, cite as follows:

Ferrer v. Dinkins, 218 A.D.2d 89, 635 N.Y.S.2d 965 (1996). –Case Citation.

Ferrer v. Dinkins, 218 A.D.2d 89, 90, 635 N.Y.S.2d 965, 966 (1996). –Page Citation.

Okebivi v. Cortines, 167 Misc. 2d 1008, 641 N.Y.S.2d 791 (Sup. Ct.1984). –Case Citation.

Okebivi v. Cortines, 167 Misc. 2d 1008, 1009, 641 N.Y.S.2d 791, 792 (Sup. Ct.1984). –Page Citation.

Beckman v. Greentree Securities, Inc., 87 N.Y.2d 566, 663 N.E.2d 886, 640 N.Y.S.2d 845 (1996). –Case Citation.

Beckman v. Greentree Securities, Inc., 87 N.Y.2d 566, 569, 663 N.E.2d 886, 887, 640 N.Y.S.2d 845, 847 (1996). –Page Citation.

In all other documents cite as follows:

Ferrer v. Dinkins, 635 N.Y.S.2d 965 (App. Div. 1996). –Case Citation.

Ferrer v. Dinkins, 635 N.Y.S.2d 965, 966 (App. Div. 1996). –Page Citation.

Okebiyi v. Cortines, 641 N.Y.S.2d 791 (Sup. Ct.1996). –Case Citation.

Okebiyi v. Cortines, 641 N.Y.S.2d 791, 792 (Sup. Ct.1996). –Page Citation.

Beckman v. Greentree Securities, Inc., 663 N.E.2d 886 (N.Y. 1996). –Case Citation.

Beckman v. Greentree Securities, Inc., 663 N.E.2d 886, 887 (N.Y. 1996). –Page Citation.

West's Smith-Hurd Illinois Compiled Statutes Annotated

Ab.: x Ill. Comp. Stat. Ann. (West year)

Ex.: 815 Ill. Comp. Stat. Ann. 307/10-30.5 (West 1999).

815 Ill. Comp. Stat. Ann. 307/10-80 (West Supp. 2000).

"Cite to Illinois Compiled Statutes if therein." Bluebook Table T.1 p. 200.

In citing cases in law review footnotes, abbreviate any word listed in Table T.6; the names of "states, countries, and other geographical units" unless they are named parties; and any other words of eight or more letters "if substantial space is thereby saved and the result is unambiguous." Bluebook Rule 10.2.2. On the other hand, in citing cases in text, abbreviate only widely known acronyms and the following words: "&," "Ass'n," "Bros.," "Co.," "Corp.," "Inc.," "Ltd.," and "No." Bluebook Rule 10.2.1(c).

West's Veterans Appeals Reporter
  Ab.:   Vet. App.
  Ex.:   Dillon v. Brown, 8 Vet. App. 165 (1995).

West's Wisconsin Legislative Service
  Ab.:   Year Wis. Legis. Serv.   (West)
  Ex.:   Act of June 27, 1996, Act 460, 1996 Wis. Legis. Serv. 3706 (West)
          (fruit and vegetable produce security). –Citation to an entire session
          law.

          Act of June 27, 1996, Act 460, sec. 1, § 20.115, 1996 Wis. Legis. Serv.
          3706, 3706 (West) (fruit and vegetable produce security). –Citation to
          a section of a session law.

          –"Cite to Wis. Laws if therein." Bluebook Table T.1, p. 240.

West's Wisconsin Statutes Annotated
  Ab.:   Wis. Stat. Ann. §   (West year)
  Ex.:   Wis. Stat. Ann. § 81.15 (West 2000).

          Wis. Stat. Ann. § 442.12 (West Supp. 1999).

          –"Cite to Wisconsin Statutes if therein."Bluebook Table T.1, p. 240.

Wharton's Criminal Procedure, by Charles E. Torcia
          –Do not abbreviate the title.
  Ex.:   1 Charles E. Torcia, Wharton's Criminal Procedure § 144 (13th ed.
          1989). –Section Citation.

          1 Charles E. Torcia, Wharton's Criminal Procedure § 144, at 509 (13th
          ed. 1989). –Page Citation.

          1 Charles E. Torcia, Wharton's Criminal Procedure § 144, at 509 n.39
          (13th ed. 1989). –Footnote Citation.

Wheaton (United States Reports)
  See United States Reports.

White and Summers on the UCC
  See Uniform Commercial Code, by James J. White & Robert S. Summers.

Whiteman Digest
  See Digest of International Law, by Marjorie M. Whiteman.

Whittier Law Review
  Ab.:   Whittier L. Rev.
  Ex.:   Matthew Lippman, Civil Resistance: Revitalizing International Law in
          the Nuclear Age, 13 Whittier L. Rev. 17 (1992). –Article Citation.

          Matthew Lippman, Civil Resistance: Revitalizing International Law in
          the Nuclear Age, 13 Whittier L. Rev. 17, 33 (1992). –Page Citation.

In law review footnotes, the titles of books and the names of cases, except for procedural
phrases, are not underlined. See Bluebook Rule 2.1(a). Further, the following are in large
and small capitals: codes, restatements, standards, constitutions, periodicals, authors of
books, titles of books, the abbreviated names of codes, most legislative materials except for
bills and resolutions, codified ordinances, model codes, court rules, and sentencing guidelines.
Refer to The Bluebook.

Wigmore on Evidence
–Do not abbreviate the title.

Ex.: I John H. Wigmore, Evidence § 6.4 (Tillers rev. 1983). –Citation to Volume One.

IA John H. Wigmore, Evidence § 62.2 (Tillers rev. 1983). –Citation to Volume One A.

II John H. Wigmore, Evidence § 290 (Chadbourne rev. 1979). –Citation to Volume Two.

III John H. Wigmore, Evidence § 769 (Chadbourne rev. 1970). –Citation to Volume Three.

IIIA John H. Wigmore, Evidence § 982 (Chadbourne rev. 1970). –Citation to Volume Three A.

IV John H. Wigmore, Evidence § 1151 (Chadbourne rev. 1972). –Citation to Volume Four.

V John H. Wigmore, Evidence § 1484 (Chadbourne rev. 1974). –Citation to Volume Five.

VI John H. Wigmore, Evidence § 1773 (Chadbourne rev. 1976). –Citation to Volume Six.

VII John H. Wigmore, Evidence § 2042 (Chadbourne rev. 1978). –Citation to Volume Seven.

VIII John H. Wigmore, Evidence § 2251 (McNaughton rev. 1961). –Citation to Volume Eight.

IX John H. Wigmore, Evidence § 2501 (Chadbourne rev. 1981). –Citation to Volume Nine.

IX John H. Wigmore, Evidence § 2501 (Supp. 1999). –Citation to Supplement.

Willamette Law Review
Ab.: Willamette L. Rev.

Ex.: Alfred L. Brophy, Law and Indentured Servitude in Mid-Eighteenth Century Pennsylvania, 28 Willamette L. Rev. 69 (1991). –Article Citation.

Alfred L. Brophy, Law and Indentured Servitude in Mid-Eighteenth Century Pennsylvania, 28 Willamette L. Rev. 69, 81-83 (1991). –Page Citation.

William & Mary Law Review
Ab.: Wm. & Mary L. Rev.

Ex.: Frederick Schauer, The First Amendment as Ideology, 33 Wm. & Mary L. Rev. 853 (1992). –Article Citation.

Frederick Schauer, The First Amendment as Ideology, 33 Wm. & Mary L. Rev. 853, 859-63 (1992). –Page Citation.

In citing cases in law review footnotes, abbreviate any word listed in Table T.6; the names of "states, countries, and other geographical units" unless they are named parties; and any other words of eight or more letters "if substantial space is thereby saved and the result is unambiguous." Bluebook Rule 10.2.2. On the other hand, in citing cases in text, abbreviate only widely known acronyms and the following words: "&," "Ass'n," "Bros.," "Co.," "Corp.," "Inc.," "Ltd.," and "No." Bluebook Rule 10.2.1(c).

William Mitchell Law Review
Ab.: Wm. Mitchell L. Rev.
Ex.: Rita C. DeMeules, Minnesota's Variable Approach to State
Constitutional Claims, 17 Wm. Mitchell L. Rev. 163 (1991). –Article
Citation.

Rita C. DeMeules, Minnesota's Variable Approach to State
Constitutional Claims, 17 Wm. Mitchell L. Rev. 163, 178-81 (1991).
–Page Citation.

Williams American Planning Law, by Norman Williams, Jr. and John M. Taylor
–Do not abbreviate the title.
Ex.: 1 Norman Williams, Jr. & John M. Taylor, Williams American
Planning Law § 4.04 (rev. ed. 1988). –Section Citation.

1 Norman Williams, Jr. & John M. Taylor, Williams American
Planning Law § 4.04, at 95 (rev. ed. 1988). –Page Citation.

Williston on Contracts (multi-volume treatise)
See Treatise on the Law of Contracts, by Samuel Williston.

Williston on Contracts Student Edition
See Selections from Williston's Treatise on the Law of Contracts, by Samuel
Williston and George J. Thompson.

Wisconsin Administrative Code
Ab.: Wis. Admin. Code § (year)
Ex.: Wis. Admin. Code § 16-06-150 (2000).

Wisconsin Bar Bulletin
Ab.: Wis. B. Bull.
Ex.: William M. Gabler, Isn't That Motion Frivolous, Counsel?, Wis. B.
Bul., Dec. 1988, at 17. –Article Citation.

William M. Gabler, Isn't That Motion Frivolous, Counsel?, Wis. B.
Bul., Dec. 1988, at 17, 61-62. –Page Citation.

Wisconsin Board of Tax Appeals Reports
Ab.: Wis. B.T.A.

Wisconsin Constitution
Ab.: Wis. Const. art. , § .
Ex.: Wis. Const. art. I, § 22. –"Cite constitutional provisions currently in
force without date." Bluebook Rule 11.

Wis. Const. art. III, §§ 4-6 (repealed 1986). –"If the cited provision
has been repealed, either indicate parenthetically the fact and date of
repeal or cite the repealing provision in full." Bluebook Rule 11.

In law review footnotes, the titles of books and the names of cases, except for procedural
phrases, are not underlined. See Bluebook Rule 2.1(a). Further, the following are in large
and small capitals: codes, restatements, standards, constitutions, periodicals, authors of
books, titles of books, the abbreviated names of codes, most legislative materials except for
bills and resolutions, codified ordinances, model codes, court rules, and sentencing guidelines.
Refer to The Bluebook.

Wis. Const. art. V, § 1 (amended 1990). –"When citing a provision that has been subsequently amended, either indicate parenthetically the fact and date of amendment or cite the amending provision in full." Bluebook Rule 11.

Wisconsin Court of Appeals
Ab.:   Wis. Ct. App.

–Cite to N.W. or N.W.2d if therein; in addition, give public domain citation if available.

–Until January 1, 2000, when public domain format was adopted, cite as follows:

In documents submitted to Wisconsin state courts:

> Huffman v. Altec International, Inc., 200 Wis. 2d 78, 546 N.W.2d 162 (Ct. App. 1996). –Case Citation.

> Huffman v. Altec International, Inc., 200 Wis. 2d 78, 80, 546 N.W.2d 162, 164 (Ct. App. 1996). –Case Citation.

In all other documents:

> Huffman v. Altec International, Inc., 546 N.W.2d 162 (Wis. Ct. App. 1996). –Case Citation.

> Huffman v. Altec International, Inc., 546 N.W.2d 162, 164 (Wis. Ct. App. 1996). –Page Citation.

–After January 1, 2000, cite as follows:

In documents submitted to Wisconsin state courts:

> State v. Phillips, 2000 WI App 184, 238 Wis. 2d 279, 617 N.W.2d 522. –Case Citation.

> State v. Phillips, 2000 WI App 184, ¶ 10, 238 Wis. 2d 279, 284, 617 N.W.2d 522, 525. –Pinpoint Citation.

In all other documents:

> State v. Phillips, 2000 WI App 184, 617 N.W.2d 522. –Case Citation.

> State v. Phillips, 2000 WI App 184, ¶ 10, 617 N.W.2d 522, 525. –Pinpoint Citation.

See Bluebook Rules 10.3.1 and 10.3.3, Table T.1, and Practitioners' Note P.3; see also Wis. App. P.R. 809.19(1)(e) and Wis. Sup. Ct. R. 80.02.

Wisconsin International Law Journal
Ab.:   Wis. Int'l L.J.

In citing cases in law review footnotes, abbreviate any word listed in Table T.6; the names of "states, countries, and other geographical units" unless they are named parties; and any other words of eight or more letters "if substantial space is thereby saved and the result is unambiguous." Bluebook Rule 10.2.2. On the other hand, in citing cases in text, abbreviate only widely known acronyms and the following words: "&," "Ass'n," "Bros.," "Co.," "Corp.," "Inc.," "Ltd.," and "No." Bluebook Rule 10.2.1(c).

Ex.:   Donna E. Arzt, <u>Religious Freedom in a Religious State: The Case of Israel in Comparative Constitutional Perspective</u>, 9 Wis. Int'l L.J. 1 (1990). –Article Citation.

Donna E. Arzt, <u>Religious Freedom in a Religious State: The Case of Israel in Comparative Constitutional Perspective</u>, 9 Wis. Int'l L.J. 1, 49-53 (1990). –Page Citation.

Wisconsin Law Review
Ab.:   Wis. L. Rev.

Ex.:   Ann Althouse, <u>Saying What Rights Are - In and Out of Context</u>, 1991 Wis. L. Rev. 929. –Article Citation.

Ann Althouse, <u>Saying What Rights Are - In and Out of Context</u>, 1991 Wis. L. Rev. 929, 929. –Page Citation.

Wisconsin Lawyer
Ab.:   Wisc. Law.

Ex.:   Christopher J. Johnson, <u>The Civil Rights Act of 1991</u>, Wisc. Law., Feb. 1992, at 12. –Article Citation.

Christopher J. Johnson, <u>The Civil Rights Act of 1991</u>, Wisc. Law., Feb. 1992, at 12, 13. –Page Citation.

Wisconsin Legislative Service (West)
<u>See</u> West's Wisconsin Legislative Service

Wisconsin Session Laws
<u>See</u> Laws of Wisconsin and West's Wisconsin Legislative Service.

Wisconsin Statutes (1975 and biannually)
Ab.:   Wis. Stat. §   (year)

Ex.:   Wis. Stat. § 757.295 (1977).

Wis. Stat. § 939.62 (Supp. 1980).

Wisconsin Statutes Annotated, West's
<u>See</u> West's Wisconsin Statutes Annotated.

Wisconsin Supreme Court
Ab.:   Wis. or Wis. 2d

–Cite to N.W. or N.W.2d if therein; in addition, give public domain citation if available.

–Until January 1, 2000, when a public domain format was adopted, cite as follows:

In documents submitted to Wisconsin state courts:

<u>Nowatske v. Osterloh</u>, 198 Wis. 2d 419, 543 N.W.2d 265 (1996). –Case Citation.

In law review footnotes, the titles of books and the names of cases, except for procedural phrases, are not underlined. <u>See</u> <u>Bluebook</u> Rule 2.1(a). Further, the following are in large and small capitals: codes, restatements, standards, constitutions, periodicals, authors of books, titles of books, the abbreviated names of codes, most legislative materials except for bills and resolutions, codified ordinances, model codes, court rules, and sentencing guidelines. Refer to <u>The Bluebook</u>.

Nowatske v. Osterloh, 198 Wis. 2d 419, 421, 543 N.W.2d 265, 268 (1996). –Page Citation.

In all other documents:

Nowatske v. Osterloh, 543 N.W.2d 265 (Wis. 1996). –Case Citation.

Nowatske v. Osterloh, 543 N.W.2d 265, 268 (Wis. 1996). –Page Citation.

–After January 1, 2000, cite as follows:

In documents submitted to Wisconsin state courts:

Rumager v. Gullberg, 2000 WI 53, 235 Wis. 2d 279, 611 N.W.2d 458. –Case Citation.

Rumager v. Gullberg, 2000 WI 53, ¶ 8, 235 Wis. 2d 279, 285, 611 N.W.2d 458, 461. –Pinpoint Citation.

In all other documents:

Rumager v. Gullberg, 2000 WI 53, 611 N.W.2d 458. –Case Citation.

Rumager v. Gullberg, 2000 WI 53, ¶ 8, 611 N.W.2d 458, 461. – Pinpoint Citation.

See Bluebook Rules 10.3.1 and 10.3.3, Table T.1, and Practitioners' Note P.3; see also Wis. App. P.R. 809.19(1)(e) and Wis. Sup. Ct. R. 80.02.

Women Lawyers Journal
Ab.:   Women Law. J.

Ex.:   James R. Giddings, Mandatory Sentences: Why Can't We Trust Our Judges?, Women Law. J., Summer 1991, at 6. –Article Citation.

James R. Giddings, Mandatory Sentences: Why Can't We Trust Our Judges?, Women Law. J., Summer 1991, at 6, 7. –Page Citation.

Women's Rights Law Reporter
Ab.:   Women's Rts. L. Rep.

Ex.:   Norma J. Wikler & Lynn H. Schafran, Learning from the New Jersey Supreme Court Task Force on Women in the Courts: Evaluation, Recommendations and Implications for Other States, 12 Women's Rts. L. Rep. 313 (1991). –Article Citation.

Norma J. Wikler & Lynn H. Schafran, Learning from the New Jersey Supreme Court Task Force on Women in the Courts: Evaluation, Recommendations and Implications for Other States, 12 Women's Rts. L. Rep. 313, 351-55 (1991). –Page Citation.

worker's compensation
Ab.:   worker's comp.

World Arbitration Reporter
Ab.:   World Arb. Rep.

In citing cases in law review footnotes, abbreviate any word listed in Table T.6; the names of "states, countries, and other geographical units" unless they are named parties; and any other words of eight or more letters "if substantial space is thereby saved and the result is unambiguous." Bluebook Rule 10.2.2. On the other hand, in citing cases in text, abbreviate only widely known acronyms and the following words: "&," "Ass'n," "Bros.," "Co.," "Corp.," "Inc.," "Ltd.," and "No." Bluebook Rule 10.2.1(c).

World Competition, Law and Economics Review
    Ab.:   World Competition L. & Econ. Rev.
    Ex.:   Piet Eeckhout, <u>The External Dimension of the EC Internal Market - A Portrait</u>, World Competition L. & Econ. Rev., Dec. 1991, at 5. –Article Citation.

            Piet Eeckhout, <u>The External Dimension of the EC Internal Market - A Portrait</u>, World Competition L. & Econ. Rev., Dec. 1991, at 5, 19-21. –Page Citation.

World Wide Web (WWW) Sites
    <u>See</u> electronic media and other nonprint resources.

Wright & Miller on Federal Practice and Procedure
    <u>See</u> Federal Practice and Procedure, by Charles A. Wright & Arthur R. Miller.

Wyoming Constitution
    Ab.:   Wyo. Const. art. , §
    Ex.:   Wyo. Const. art. 7, § 16. –"Cite constitutional provisions currently in force without date." <u>Bluebook</u> Rule 11.

            Wyo. Const. art. 9, § 6 (repealed 1990). –"If the cited provision has been repealed, either indicate parenthetically the fact and date of repeal or cite the repealing provision in full." <u>Bluebook</u> Rule 11.

            Wyo. Const. art. 9, § 15 (amended 1990). –"When citing a provision that has been subsequently amended, either indicate parenthetically the fact and date of amendment or cite the amending provision in full." <u>Bluebook</u> Rule 11.

Wyoming Lawyer
    Ab.:   Wyo. Law.
    Ex.:   Doug Moench, <u>Litigation and Image Enhancement</u>, Wyo. Law., Aug. 1991, at 18. –Article Citation.

            Doug Moench, <u>Litigation and Image Enhancement</u>, Wyo. Law., Aug. 1991, at 18, 19. –Page Citation.

Wyoming Reports
    Ab.:   Wyo.
    –Discontinued in 1959 after 80 Wyo. 492 (1959).
    –Cite to P., P.2d, or P.3d if therein; otherwise, cite to Wyo.

In law review footnotes, the titles of books and the names of cases, except for procedural phrases, are not underlined. <u>See</u> <u>Bluebook</u> Rule 2.1(a). Further, the following are in large and small capitals: codes, restatements, standards, constitutions, periodicals, authors of books, titles of books, the abbreviated names of codes, most legislative materials except for bills and resolutions, codified ordinances, model codes, court rules, and sentencing guidelines. Refer to <u>The Bluebook</u>.

–Give parallel citations only in documents submitted to Wyoming state courts. (Note: In citing a state court case in a document submitted to a court of that same state, the 16th ed. of The Bluebook prescribed a parallel citation; the 17th ed. prescribes that local rules shall control, but Wyoming has no known local rules concerning parallel citations. For the sake of continuity, we advise giving a parallel citation in documents submitted to Wyoming state courts. See Bluebook Rule 10.3.1, Table T.1, and Practitioners' Note P.3.)

–Through 80 Wyo. 492 (1959), cite as follows

In documents submitted to Wyoming state courts:

> Lucksinger v. Salisbury, 72 Wyo. 164, 262 P.2d 396 (1953). –Case Citation.
>
> Lucksinger v. Salisbury, 72 Wyo. 164, 173, 262 P.2d 396, 398-99 (1953). –Page Citation.

In all other documents:

> Lucksinger v. Salisbury, 262 P.2d 396 (Wyo. 1953). –Case Citation.
>
> Lucksinger v. Salisbury, 262 P.2d 396, 398-99 (Wyo. 1953). –Page Citation.

–After 80 Wyo. 492 (1959), cite as follows:

In all documents:

> Carrar v. Bourke, 910 P.2d 572 (Wyo. 1996). –Case Citation.
>
> Carrar v. Bourke, 910 P.2d 572, 573 (Wyo. 1996). –Page Citation.

Wyoming Rules and Regulations

See also Weil's Code of Wyoming Rules.

Ab.:   Wyo. R. & Regs.

Ex.:   Wyo. R. & Regs. ch. 18 sec. 4(a) (2000).

Wyoming Session Laws

See Session Laws of Wyoming.

Wyoming Statutes Annotated

Ab.:   Wyo. Stat. Ann. §   (Lexis year)

Ex.:   Wyo. Stat. Ann. § 35-7-1404 (Lexis 1999).

Wyo. Stat. Ann. § 14-3-302 (Lexis Supp. 2000).

In citing cases in law review footnotes, abbreviate any word listed in Table T.6; the names of "states, countries, and other geographical units" unless they are named parties; and any other words of eight or more letters "if substantial space is thereby saved and the result is unambiguous." Bluebook Rule 10.2.2. On the other hand, in citing cases in text, abbreviate only widely known acronyms and the following words: "&," "Ass'n," "Bros.," "Co.," "Corp.," "Inc.," "Ltd.," and "No." Bluebook Rule 10.2.1(c).

Y

Yale Journal of International Law
   Ab.:   Yale J. Int'l L.
   Ex.:   Geoffrey R. Watson, <u>Offenders Abroad: The Case for Nationality-Based Criminal Jurisdiction</u>, 17 Yale J. Int'l L. 41 (1992). –Article Citation.

   Geoffrey R. Watson, <u>Offenders Abroad: The Case for Nationality-Based Criminal Jurisdiction</u>, 17 Yale J. Int'l L. 41, 57-64 (1992). –Page Citation.

Yale Journal of Law and Feminism
   Ab.:   Yale J.L. & Feminism
   Ex.:   Ruth Colker, <u>Marriage</u>, 3 Yale J.L. & Feminism 321 (1991). –Article Citation.

   Ruth Colker, <u>Marriage</u>, 3 Yale J.L. & Feminism 321, 325 (1991). –Page Citation.

Yale Journal of Law and the Humanities
   Ab.:   Yale J.L. & Human.
   Ex.:   John M. Fischer, <u>The Trolley and the Sorites</u>, 4 Yale J.L. & Human. 105 (1992). –Article Citation.

   John M. Fischer, <u>The Trolley and the Sorites</u>, 4 Yale J.L. & Human. 105, 109-15 (1992). –Page Citation.

Yale Journal of Law and Liberation
   Ab.:   Yale J.L. & Lib.

Yale Journal of World Public Order
   Ab.:   Yale J. World Pub. Ord.
   Ex.:   Siegfried Wiessner, <u>The Public Order of the Geostationary Orbit: Blueprints for the Future</u>, 9 Yale J. World Pub. Ord. 217 (1983). –Article Citation.

   Siegfried Wiessner, <u>The Public Order of the Geostationary Orbit: Blueprints for the Future</u>, 9 Yale J. World Pub. Ord. 217, 231-32 (1983). –Page Citation.

In law review footnotes, the titles of books and the names of cases, except for procedural phrases, are not underlined. See <u>Bluebook</u> Rule 2.1(a). Further, the following are in large and small capitals: codes, restatements, standards, constitutions, periodicals, authors of books, titles of books, the abbreviated names of codes, most legislative materials except for bills and resolutions, codified ordinances, model codes, court rules, and sentencing guidelines. Refer to <u>The Bluebook</u>.

Yale Journal on Regulation
Ab.:   Yale J. on Reg.
Ex.:   George L. Priest, <u>Can Absólute Manufacturer Liability be Defended?</u>,
          9 Yale J. on Reg. 237 (1992). −Article Citation.

          George L. Priest, <u>Can Absolute Manufacturer Liability be Defended?</u>,
          9 Yale J. on Reg. 237, 249-52 (1992). −Page Citation.

Yale Law and Policy Review
Ab.:   Yale L. & Pol'y Rev.
Ex.:   David Cole, <u>First Amendment Antitrust: The End of Laissez-Faire in
          Campaign Finance</u>, 9 Yale L. & Pol'y Rev. 236 (1991). −Article
          Citation.

          David Cole, <u>First Amendment Antitrust: The End of Laissez-Faire in
          Campaign Finance</u>, 9 Yale L. & Pol'y Rev. 236, 259-60 (1991). −Page
          Citation.

Yale Law Journal
Ab.:   Yale L.J.
Ex.:   Heidi M. Hurd, <u>Challenging Authority</u>, 100 Yale L.J. 1611 (1991).
          −Article Citation.

          Heidi M. Hurd, <u>Challenging Authority</u>, 100 Yale L.J. 1611, 1639-45
          (1991). −Page Citation.

Yearbook Commercial Arbitration
Ab.:   Y.B. Com. Arb.
Ex.:   Neil Kaplan, <u>Hong Kong</u>, 16 Y.B. Com. Arb. 391 (1991). −Article
          Citation.

          Neil Kaplan, <u>Hong Kong</u>, 16 Y.B. Com. Arb. 391, 392 (1991). −Page
          Citation.

Yearbook of the European Convention on Human Rights
Ab.:   Y.B. Eur. Conv. on H.R.
Ex.:   <u>Farrell v. United Kingdom</u>, 1982 Y.B. Eur. Conv. on H.R.124 (Eur.
          Comm'n on H.R.).

          −When citing, note in a parenthetical whether the case was before the
          Court or the Commission. See <u>Bluebook</u> Rule 21.5.3.

Yearbook of the International Law Commission
Ab.:   Y.B. Int'l L. Comm'n
Ex.:   <u>Summary Records of the Meetings of the Forty-Sixth Session 2 May --
          22 July 1994</u>, [1994] 1 Y.B. Int'l L. Comm'n 19, U.N. Doc.
          A/CN.4/SER.A/1994.

Yearbook of the United Nations
Ab.:   U.N.Y.B.

In citing cases in law review footnotes, abbreviate any word listed in Table T.6;
the names of "states, countries, and other geographical units" unless they are named parties;
and any other words of eight or more letters "if <u>substantial</u> space is thereby saved and the
result is unambiguous." <u>Bluebook</u> Rule 10.2.2. On the other hand, in citing cases in text,
abbreviate only widely known acronyms and the following words: "&," "Ass'n," "Bros.,"
"Co.," "Corp.," "Inc.," "Ltd.," and "No." <u>Bluebook</u> Rule 10.2.1(c).

Ex.:   1986 U.N.Y.B. 672, U.N. Sales No. E.90.I.1.
          See Bluebook Rule 21.7.4.

Yearbook (or Year Book)
     Ab.:   Y.B.

Youth Court
     Ab.:   Youth Ct.

In law review footnotes, the titles of books and the names of cases, except for procedural phrases, are not underlined. See Bluebook Rule 2.1(a). Further, the following are in large and small capitals: codes, restatements, standards, constitutions, periodicals, authors of books, titles of books, the abbreviated names of codes, most legislative materials except for bills and resolutions, codified ordinances, model codes, court rules, and sentencing guidelines. Refer to The Bluebook.

Z

Zoning and Planning Law Report

Ab.:   Zoning & Plan. L. Rep.

Ex.:   Edith M. Netter, <u>Using Medication to Resolve Land Use Disputes</u>, 15 Zoning & Plan. L. Rep. 25 (1992). –Article Citation.

Edith M. Netter, <u>Using Medication to Resolve Land Use Disputes</u>, 15 Zoning & Plan. L. Rep. 25, 27-28 (1992). –Page Citation.

In law review footnotes, the titles of books and the names of cases, except for procedural phrases, are not underlined. <u>See</u> <u>Bluebook</u> Rule 2.1(a). Further, the following are in large and small capitals: codes, restatements, standards, constitutions, periodicals, authors of books, titles of books, the abbreviated names of codes, most legislative materials except for bills and resolutions, codified ordinances, model codes, court rules, and sentencing guidelines. Refer to <u>The Bluebook</u>.

TABLES

All information provided in the Tables was contributed by
Bernard J. Sussman, J.D., M.L.S., C.P., Law Librarian,
United States Court of Appeals for Veterans Claims.

Table 1

States' Highest Courts

A state's highest court is called "the Supreme Court," except in the following instances:

Court of Appeals
> District of Columbia
> Maryland
> New York

Supreme Judicial Court
> Maine
> Massachusetts

Supreme Court of Appeals
> West Virginia

Court of Criminal Appeals (co-exists with non-criminal Supreme Court)
> Oklahoma
> Texas

TABLE 2

Discontinued State Reporters
(Since circa 1950)

Arranged by State, the volume number of the last state volume and the parallel West regional reporter, and the year.

last volume	West parallel	year
295 Ala.	329 So.2d	1976
57 Ala. App.	326 So.2d	1975
27 Ariz. App.	558 P.2d	1976
200 Colo.	618 P.2d	1980
44 Colo. App.	620 P.2d	1980
6 Conn. Cir. Ct.	360 A.2d	1974
59 Del. (9 Story)	219 A.2d	1966
43 Del. Ch.	240 A.2d	1968
160 Fla.	40 So.2d	1948
10 Haw. App.	880 P.2d	1994
275 Ind.	419 N.E.2d	1981
182 Ind. App.	396 N.E.2d	1979
261 Iowa	158 N.W.2d	1968
314 Ky.	238 S.W.2d	1951
263 La.	270 So.2d	1972
161 Maine	215 A.2d	1965
312 Minn.	253 N.W.2d	1977
254 Miss.	183 S.W.2d	1966
365 Mo.	295 S.W.2d	1956
241 Mo. App.	252 S.W.2d	1952
79 N. D.	60 N.W.2d	1953
208 Okla.	258 P.2d	1953
97 Okla. Crim.	266 P.2d	1953
168 Pa. Commw.	652 A.2d	1994
456 Pa. Super.	691 A.2d	1997
122 R.I.	413 A.2d	1980
90 S. D.	245 N.W.2d	1976
225 Tenn.	476 S.W.2d	1972
63 Tenn. App.	480 S.W.2d	1972
4 Tenn. Crim. App.	475 S.W.2d	1971
163 Tex.	359 S.W.2d	1962
172 Tex. Crim.	362 S.W.2d	1962
30 Utah 2d	519 P.2d	1974
80 Wyo	345 P.2d	1959

Fla. Supp. discontinued in 1992, and Ohio Op. discontinued in 1982.
–No West parallel for either reporter.

Table 3

Year, Congress & Session, Volume Number

Year	Congress	Session	Fed Reg.	Cong. Rec.	Statutes at Large
1940	76	3	5	86	54
1941	77	1	6	87	55 See note
1942	77	2	7	88	56
1943	78	1	8	89	57
1944	78	2	9	90	58
1945	79	1	10	91	59 See note
1946	79	2	11	92	60
1947	80	1	12	93	61
1948	80	2	13	94	62
1949	81	1	14	95	63 See note
1950	81	2	15	96	64
1951	82	1	16	97	65
1952	82	2	17	98	66
1953	83	1	18	99	67
1954	83	2	19	100	68
1955	84	1	20	101	69
1956	84	2	21	102	70 See note
1957	85	1	22	103	71 See note
1958	85	2	23	104	72
1959	86	1	24	105	73
1960	86	2	25	106	74
1961	87	1	26	107	75
1962	87	2	27	108	76
1963	88	1	28	109	77
1964	88	2	29	110	78 See note
1965	89	1	30	111	79
1966	89	2	31	112	80
1967	90	1	32	113	81
1968	90	2	33	114	82
1969	91	1	34	115	83

1970	91	2	35	116	84
1971	92	1	36	117	85
1972	92	2	37	118	86
1973	93	1	38	119	87
1974	93	2	39	120	88
1975	94	1	40	121	89 See note
1976	94	2	41	122	90
1977	95	1	42	123	91
1978	95	2	43	124	92
1979	96	1	44	125	93
1980	96	2	45	126	94
1981	97	1	46	127	95
1982	97	2	47	128	96
1983	98	1	48	129	97
1984	98	2	49	130	98
1985	99	1	50	131	99
1986	99	2	51	132	100
1987	100	1	52	133	101
1988	100	2	53	134	102
1989	101	1	54	135	103
1990	101	2	55	136	104
1991	102	1	56	137	105
1992	102	2	57	138	106
1993	103	1	58	139	107
1994	103	2	59	140	108
1995	104	1	60	141	109
1996	104	2	61	142	110
1997	105	1	62	143	111
1998	105	2	63	144	112
1999	106	1	64	145	113
2000	106	2	65	146	114
2001	107	1	66	147	115
2002	107	2	67	148	116
2003	108	1	68	149	117
2004	108	2	69	150	118

Notes:

1941: West's <u>United States Code Congressional and Administrative News</u> (U.S.C.C.A.N.), then titled <u>United States Code Congressional Service</u>, begins coverage, with the beginning of the 77th Congress, 1st Session, 1941, with its own typesetting of the public laws in 55 <u>Statutes at Large</u>.

1945: The National Archives' occasional volume of <u>Codification of Presidential Proclamations & Executive Orders</u> begins its coverage with President Truman's first day in office, April 13, 1945 (Executive Order 9538, Proclamation 648).

1949: The Second Edition of the <u>Code of Federal Regulations</u> (C.F.R.) is published. The first edition was published in 1939, as a series of hardcover volumes with annual supplementary hardcover volumes. The 1949 Second Edition was similarly hardcover volumes with supplementary volumes. The Revised Edition of 1956 was hardcover with pocket parts. In 1964, the annual paperback volumes format was begun.

1956: <u>Code of Federal Regulations</u> (C.F.R.) changes format slightly, from hardcover main volumes with hardcover supplement volumes to a "revised edition" of hardcover volumes with annual pocket parts.

1957: The number of the Acts of Congress changes. Previously, from 1901 through the end of 1956, both the chapter number (which began with each session) and the public law number (which began with each Congress) were assigned to Acts- although most citation manuals and the <u>United States Code</u> gave only the chapter numbers. Starting with the beginning of the 57th Congress, 1st session, 1957, 71 <u>Statutes at Large</u>, chapter numbers are no longer used, the number of the congress is added as a prefix to the public law numbers, and only public law numbers are used.

1964: <u>Code of Federal Regulations</u> (C.F.R.) adopts its present format of annual paperback volumes replaced annually.

1975: Congress changes the format of the slip editions of the new laws and of the <u>Statutes at Large</u>. Previously, new laws were published in separate booklets, called slip editions, with temporary and unofficial page numbers and page breaks, and the official and permanent pagination of <u>Statutes at Large</u> did not appear until the <u>Statues at Large</u> volumes were printed, as much as a year or two after enactment. Starting with the beginning of the 95th Congress, 1st session, 1975, 89 <u>Statutes at Large</u>, a printing format was adopted so that the slip editions could immediately show the page numbers and page breaks which would appear in the Statutes at Large volumes. West's <u>United States Code Congressional & Administrative News</u> thereupon ceased its own typesetting of the laws and began photographically reproducing the slip editions of the public laws with the <u>Statute at Large</u> page numbers.

Numbering Acts of Congress

CHAPTER numbers were used from the 1st Congress, 1789, 1 <u>Statutes at Large</u>, through the 84th Congress, 1956, 70 <u>Statutes at Large</u>. The chapter numbers began with a new series each *session* of Congress (there are at least two sessions per two-year Congress).

PUBLIC LAW numbers are in a single series for the entire two-year Congress. Public law numbers were used in two stages.

First, public law numbers without the number of the Congress, were used simultaneously with the chapter numbers, from the first session of the 56th Congress, 1901, 32 <u>Statutes at Large</u>, through the second session of the 84th Congress, 1956, 70 <u>Statutes at Large</u> (<u>United States Code</u> source notes, and many citation manuals for Acts during that period mention only the chapter number, but not the public law number).

Then, with the start of the 85th Congress, 1957, 71 <u>Statutes at Large</u>, chapter numbers ceased and public law numbers were used exclusively. Now the public law number included a prefix with the number of the Congress (e.g., Public Law 85-1).

Until 1975, it was the practice of <u>Statutes at Large</u> to try to conserve space by following the end of one statute with the beginning of another on the same page in <u>Statutes at Large</u> (this sometimes got even three or more statutes on one page). Shortly after laws were enacted, a copy of the text was available in an individual slip edition with its own unofficial page numbers, and a year might elapse before the final and official <u>Statutes at Large</u> page numbers became available. But starting with the first session of the 94th Congress in 1975, 89 <u>Statutes at Large</u>, each statute began at the top of a new page. This change enabled the slip edition of each statute to reflect the permanent and official <u>Statutes at Large</u> page numbers almost immediately. This change also enabled West's <u>United States Code Congressional and Administrative News</u>, which previously had reset the Acts of Congress in its own typeface with its own unofficial page breaks, to photographically reproduce the <u>Statute at Large</u> pages, with the official page numbering, for its advance sheets and its permanent volumes (starting with the U.S.C.C.A.N. for 1975).

West's <u>United States Code Congressional and Administrative News</u> began as the <u>United States Code Congressional Service</u>, 77th Congress, 1st Session, 1941 (55 <u>Statutes at Large</u>). It was renamed the <u>United States Code Congressional and Administrative Service</u>, 82nd Congress, 1st Session, 1951 (65 <u>Statutes at Large</u>). It was given its present name of the <u>United States Code Congressional and Administrative News</u>, 82d Congress, 2d Session, 1952 (66 <u>Statutes at Large</u>). Starting in 1975, 94th Congress, 1st Session (89 <u>Statutes at Large</u>), it began reproducing the official pages and page numbers of <u>Statutes at Large</u> photographically, instead of doing its own typesetting of the statutes into its own unofficial page numbers.

Appendix

The Bluebook: A Uniform System of Citation

Seventeenth Edition (2000)

The Bluebook

A Uniform System of Citation

Seventeenth Edition

Quick Reference: Law Review Footnotes

This table gives examples of commonly used citation forms printed in the type-faces used in law review footnotes (as explained in **rule 2**). The last page and inside back cover present these same examples in the typefaces used in court documents and legal memoranda (as explained in **practitioners' note P.1**).

cases (rule 10)

reporter (rule 10.3)
Jackson v. Metro. Edison Co., 348 F. Supp. 954, 956–58 (M.D. Pa. 1972), *aff'd*, 483 F.2d 754 (3d Cir. 1973), *aff'd*, 419 U.S. 345 (1974).

Herrick v. Lindley, 391 N.E.2d 729, 731 (Ohio 1979).

service (rule 19)
In re Looney, [1987–1989 Transfer Binder] Bankr. L. Rep. (CCH) ¶ 72,447, at 93,590 (Bankr. W.D. Va. Sept. 9, 1988).

pending and unreported cases (rule 10.8.1)
Albrecht v. Stanczek, No. 87-C9535, 1991 U.S. Dist. LEXIS 5088, at *1 n.1 (N.D. Ill. Apr. 18, 1991).

Jackson v. Virginia, No. 77-1205, slip op. at 3 (4th Cir. Aug. 3, 1978) (per curiam), *aff'd*, 443 U.S. 307 (1979).

Charlesworth v. Mack, No. 90-345 (D. Mass. filed Sept. 18, 1990).

Charlesworth v. Mack, 925 F.2d 314 (1st Cir. 1991), *petition for cert. filed*, 60 U.S.L.W. 3422 (U.S. Jan. 14, 1992) (No. 92-212).

constitutions (rule 11)
N.M. CONST. art. IV, § 7.

statutes (rule 12)

code (rule 12.3)
Administrative Procedure Act § 6, 5 U.S.C. § 555 (1994).

22 U.S.C. § 2567 (Supp. I 1983).

session laws (rule 12.4)
Department of Transportation Act, Pub. L. No. 89-670, § 9, 80 Stat. 931, 944–47 (1966).

legislative materials (rule 13)

unenacted bill (rule 13.2)
H.R. 3055, 94th Cong. § 2 (1976).

hearing (rule 13.3)
Toxic Substances Control Act: Hearings on S. 776 Before the Subcomm. on the Env't of the Senate Comm. on Commerce, 94th Cong. 343 (1975).

report (rule 13.4)
S. REP. NO. 89-910, at 4 (1965).

books (rule 15)
DEBORAH L. RHODE, JUSTICE AND GENDER 56 (1989).

CHARLES DICKENS, BLEAK HOUSE 49–55 (Norman Page ed., Penguin Books 1971) (1853).

21 CHARLES ALAN WRIGHT & ARTHUR R. MILLER, FEDERAL PRACTICE AND PROCEDURE § 1006 (2d ed. 1987).

pamphlets (rule 15)
WOMEN'S BUREAU, U.S. DEP'T OF LABOR, LEAFLET NO. 55, A WORKING WOMAN'S GUIDE TO HER JOB RIGHTS (1978).

shorter works in collection (rule 15.5)
Urvashi Vaid, *Prisons, in* AIDS AND THE LAW 235, 237–39 (Harlon L. Dalton et al. eds., 1987).

OLIVER WENDELL HOLMES, *Law in Science and Science in Law, in* COLLECTED LEGAL PAPERS 210, 210 (1920).

John Adams, Argument and Report, *in* 2 LEGAL PAPERS OF JOHN ADAMS 285, 322–35 (L. Kinvin Wroth & Hiller B. Zobel eds., 1965).

periodical materials
(rule 16)

consecutively paginated journals (rule 16.3)	Patricia J. Williams, *Alchemical Notes: Reconstructed Ideals from Deconstructed Rights*, 22 HARV. C.R.–C.L. L. REV. 401, 407 (1987).
	Thomas R. McCoy & Barry Friedman, *Conditional Spending: Federalism's Trojan Horse*, 1988 SUP. CT. REV. 85, 100.
student-written work (rule 16.6.2)	Mei-lan E. Wong, Note, *The Implications of School Choice for Children with Disabilities*, 103 YALE L.J. 827, 830 n.10 (1993).
	Note, *The Death of a Lawyer*, 56 COLUM. L. REV. 606 (1956).
book review (rule 16.6.1)	Bruce Ackerman, *Robert Bork's Grand Inquisition*, 99 YALE L.J. 1419, 1422–25 (1990) (book review).
nonconsecutively paginated journals (rule 16.4)	Lynn Hirschberg, *The Misfit*, VANITY FAIR, Apr. 1991, at 158.
newspapers (rule 16.5)	Andrew Rosenthal, *White House Tutors Kremlin in How a Presidency Works*, N.Y. TIMES, June 15, 1990, at A1.
	Cop Shoots Tire, Halts Stolen Car, S.F. CHRON., Oct. 10, 1975, at 43.
unpublished manuscripts (rule 17.1.1)	Adrienne D. Davis, African American Literature and the Law: Revising and Revisiting Freedom 12–15 (Dec. 1989) (unpublished manuscript, on file with The Yale Law Journal).
letters (rule 17.1.3)	Letter from Carrie Flaxman, Senior Editor, The Yale Law Journal, to Erik Bertin, Executive Editor, University of Pennsylvania Law Review 2 (Apr. 7, 1996) (on file with the University of Pennsylvania Law Review).
interviews (rule 17.1.4)	Telephone Interview with Michael Leiter, President, Harvard Law Review (Oct. 22, 1999).
forthcoming publications (rule 17.2)	Pierre Schlag, *Law and Phrenology*, 110 HARV. L. REV. (forthcoming Jan. 1997) (manuscript at 31, on file with author).
Internet sources (rule 18.2)	J.T. Westermeier, *Ethical Issues for Lawyers on the Internet and World Wide Web*, 6 RICH. J.L. & TECH. 5, ¶ 7 (1999), *at* http://www.richmond.edu/jolt/v6i1/westermeier.html.
foreign cases (rule 20.3)	
common law	The King v. Lockwood, 99 Eng. Rep. 379 (K.B. 1782).
civil law	Entscheidungen des Bundesgerichtshofes in Zivilsachen [BGHZ] [Supreme Court] 53, 125 (126) (F.R.G.).
foreign constitutions (rule 20.4)	GRUNDGESETZ [GG] [Constitution] art. 51 (F.R.G.).
foreign statutes (rule 20.5)	
common law	Emergency Powers Act, No. 3 (1976) (Ir.).
civil law	CODE CIVIL [C. CIV.] art. 1112 (Fr.).
treaties (rule 21.4)	Treaty of Friendship, Commerce and Navigation, Apr. 2, 1953, U.S.-Japan, art. X, 4 U.S.T. 2063, 2071.
United Nations official records (rule 21.7.1)	U.N. GAOR, 10th Sess., Supp. No. 6A, at 5, U.N. Doc. A/2905 (1955).

Published and Distributed by
The Harvard Law Review Association
Gannett House
1511 Massachusetts Avenue
Cambridge, Massachusetts 02138
U.S.A.

First Printing 2000
Second Printing 2000
Printings are updated as appropriate.

Coordinating Editor:
Mary Miles Prince, Associate Director
Vanderbilt University Law School Library

Type/Production by
Annette Carroll, Hopedale, Massachusetts

Printing by
Star Printing, Brockton, Massachusetts

The Bluebook

A Uniform System of Citation

Seventeenth Edition

Compiled by the editors of the *Columbia Law Review*, the *Harvard Law Review*, the *University of Pennsylvania Law Review*, and *The Yale Law Journal*.

Preface to the Seventeenth Edition

This edition of the *Bluebook* retains the same basic approach to legal citation established by its predecessors. Some citation forms have been expanded, elaborated upon, and in some cases, modified from previous editions to reflect the ever-expanding range of authorities used in legal writing and in response to suggestions from the legal community. Here are some of the more noteworthy changes:

In **Introduction I.4**, dots have been inserted in the diagrammed examples to indicate one space between the constituent parts of each citation format, or where confusion about spacing may exist. These examples have also been placed at the beginning of the corresponding rules throughout the book.

Practitioners' Note P.7 no longer requires commas around abbreviated citations to other court documents if the citation serves merely as a clause.

Rule 1.2 on the use of introductory signals has been modified. The 15th Edition's version of the rule has been reinstated. "*E.g.*" returns as a separate signal. "*Contra*" is revived to indicate authority contrary to the proposition.

The citation order for student-written law review materials has changed in **rule 1.4**. All student-written law review materials, including book reviews, are part of the same classification for determining the order of sources within the same signal. A classification for electronic sources has also been included in **rule 1.4**.

Rule 6.2(a) no longer distinguishes between numerals in text and numerals in footnotes. Numbers zero through ninety-nine are spelled out in both text and footnotes. A rule for ordinals has been added as **rule 6.2(b)**.

Rule 10.2.1(c) has been reworded to make clear that only in two narrow circumstances (widely known acronyms and eight specific words) are words abbreviated in case names in textual sentences. For case names in citations, **rule 10.2.2** has been modified to require abbreviation of the first word in a case name when the word appears in **table T.6**. The word is abbreviated even if it is the only word in the party's name.

Rule 10.3.1(b) now requires a parallel citation to a regional reporter, if available, when using a public domain citation.

Rule 10.3.3 has been added to provide a format for public domain citations. The format is similar to the format adopted by several jurisdictions that currently make cases available in the public domain. For those jurisdictions that have adopted a format that is different from the *Bluebook* format, use the format the jurisdiction requires. For each jurisdiction that currently requires public domain citation, **table T.1** indicates the jurisdiction's required format.

A citation format for U.S. patents is now **rule 14.9**.

Rule 15.1.1 has been modified to allow for the listing of all authors when the number of authors is greater than two. All authors may be listed when the names of the authors are relevant.

Rule 16 (Periodical Materials) has been reorganized. **Rule 16.2** (Title) is new. Consequently, subsequent rules within **rule 16** have been renumbered. Additionally, the student-written law review materials under **rule 16.6** (Special Citation Forms) have been regrouped.

Rule 17 has been split into two rules, creating a new **rule 18**. As a result, **rules 18**, **19** and **20** have been renumbered as **rules 19**, **20**, and **21**, respectively. **Rule 17** now focuses on unpublished and forthcoming sources. **Rule 18** focuses on electronic media and other nonprint resources.

Rule 18 (Electronic Media and Other Nonprint Resources) requires the use and citation of traditional printed sources, except when the information is not available in a printed source, or when the use and citation of the traditional printed source is particularly difficult. New citation formats for e-mail and CD-ROMs are included in **rules 18.2.9** and **18.3**, respectively.

The tables have been updated and expanded. **Table T.1** now includes references to state judicial websites and information on state-specific public domain formats. A two character postal code has been added next to each state name for use in public domain citations only.

Table T.6 (Case Names) includes additional words that should be abbreviated in case citations.

Table T.10 (Legislative Documents) has been added. As a result, **tables T.10** to **T.16** have been renumbered.

Table T.14 (Periodicals) has been greatly expanded to include many more journals.

The compilers wish to thank our Coordinating Editor Mary Miles Prince for working with us in revising, clarifying, updating, and improving the *Bluebook*. The compilers would also like to acknowledge the outside commentators who contributed their expertise to the Seventeenth Edition of the *Bluebook*. The following provided invaluable assistance in planning and revising this edition: Edward C. Brewer, III, Alan Diefenbach, Paul George, C. Edward Good, Tracy McGaugh, Kent McKeever, Douglas Robbins, Karen Tucker, and the AALL Citation Formats Committee. The compilers are grateful to the law journal editors, law librarians, and practitioners who responded to our call for suggestions with helpful advice and comments.

Finally, the compilers request that any errors or omissions be reported and that suggestions for revisions be sent to the Harvard Law Review, Gannett House, 1511 Massachusetts Ave., Cambridge, Massachusetts 02138.

Contents

Preface v

Introduction

I   Introduction to Legal Citation and the *Bluebook* 3
   I.1 Structure of the *Bluebook* 3
   I.2 General Principles of Citation 4
   I.3 Use of Citations Generally 4
   I.4 Typical Legal Citations Analyzed 5

Practitioners' Notes

P   Practitioners' Notes 11
   P.1 Typeface Conventions for Court Documents and Legal
        Memoranda 11
   P.2 Citation Sentences and Clauses in Court Documents and
        Legal Memoranda 13
   P.3 Parallel Citations for State Court Cases 14
   P.4 Short Forms in Court Documents and Legal Memoranda 15
   P.5 Special Citation Forms for Federal Taxation Materials 16
   P.6 Capitalization in Court Documents and Legal Memoranda 17
   P.7 Abbreviated Citations to Other Court Documents and Letters . . . 18

General Rules of Citation and Style

1   Structure and Use of Citations 21
   1.1 Citation Sentences and Clauses in Law Review Footnotes 21
   1.2 Introductory Signals 22
   1.3 Order of Signals 24
   1.4 Order of Authorities Within Each Signal 25
   1.5 Parenthetical Information 28
   1.6 Related Authority 29

2   Typefaces for Law Reviews 30
   2.1 Typeface Conventions for Citations 30
   2.2 Typeface Conventions for Textual Material 32

3   Subdivisions 33
   3.1 Abbreviations 33
   3.2 Volumes, Parts, and Supplements 33
   3.3 Pages, Footnotes, Endnotes, and Graphical Materials 34
   3.4 Sections and Paragraphs 37
   3.5 Appended Material 39
   3.6 Internal Cross-References 39

4   Short Citation Forms 40
   4.1 "*Id.*" 40
   4.2 "*Supra*" and "Hereinafter" 42

5 Quotations **43**
   5.1 Indentation, Quotation Marks, Citation, and Punctuation 43
   5.2 Alterations.. 44
   5.3 Omissions.. 45
   5.4 Paragraph Structure 47

6 Abbreviations, Numerals, and Symbols **47**
   6.1 Abbreviations 47
   6.2 Numerals and Symbols................................. 49

7 Italicization for Stylistic Purposes **50**

8 Capitalization **51**

9 References to Judges, Officials, and Terms of Court **53**

Cases

10 Cases **55**
   10.1 Basic Citation Forms................................ 55
   10.2 Case Names....................................... 56
      10.2.1 Case Names in Textual Sentences............... 57
      10.2.2 Case Names in Citations 62
   10.3 Reporters and Other Sources 62
      10.3.1 Parallel Citations and Which Source(s) to Cite 62
      10.3.2 Reporters 63
      10.3.3 Public Domain Format......................... 64
   10.4 Court and Jurisdiction 64
   10.5 Date or Year 66
   10.6 Parenthetical Information Regarding Cases............... 67
      10.6.1 Weight of Authority.......................... 67
      10.6.2 Order of Parentheticals 67
   10.7 Prior and Subsequent History 68
      10.7.1 Explanatory Phrases and Weight of Authority 68
      10.7.2 Different Case Name on Appeal................. 69
   10.8 Special Citation Forms 70
      10.8.1 Pending and Unreported Cases................. 70
      10.8.2 Fifth Circuit Split 71
      10.8.3 Briefs, Records, Motions, and Memoranda.......... 71
   10.9 Short Forms for Cases 71

Constitutions, Statutes, and Legislative, Administrative, and Executive Materials

11 Constitutions.. **75**

12 Statutes **76**
   12.1 Basic Citation Forms 76
   12.2 Choosing the Proper Citation Form.................... 77
      12.2.1 General Rule 77
      12.2.2 Exceptions 78

12.3 Current Official and Unofficial Codes   78
    12.3.1 Additional Information   79
    12.3.2 Year of Code.   80
12.4 Session Laws.   81
12.5 Secondary Sources   83
12.6 Repeal, Amendment, and Prior History.   84
    12.6.1 Repeal   84
    12.6.2 Amendment   84
    12.6.3 Prior History   84
12.7 Explanatory Parenthetical Phrases   84
12.8 Special Citation Forms   85
    12.8.1 Internal Revenue Code   85
    12.8.2 Ordinances.   85
    12.8.3 Rules of Evidence and Procedure   86
    12.8.4 Uniform Acts.   86
    12.8.5 Model Codes, Restatements, Standards, and
            Sentencing Guidelines   87
    12.8.6 ABA Code of Professional Responsibility and
            Opinions on Ethics   89
12.9 Short Forms for Statutes   89

13 **Legislative Materials**   91
13.1 Basic Citation Forms   91
13.2 Bills and Resolutions   92
13.3 Hearings   93
13.4 Reports, Documents, and Committee Prints   93
13.5 Debates.   95
13.6 Separately Bound Legislative Histories   95
13.7 Short Forms for Legislative Materials   95

14 **Administrative and Executive Materials**   96
14.1 Basic Citation Forms.   96
14.2 Rules, Regulations, and Other Publications   97
14.3 Administrative Adjudications and Arbitrations   98
    14.3.1 Names   99
    14.3.2 Which Sources to Cite.   99
    14.3.3 Issuing Agency 100
14.4 Advisory Opinions 100
14.5 Federal Taxation Materials 100
    14.5.1 Treasury Regulations 100
    14.5.2 Treasury Determinations 101
    14.5.3 Cases. 102
14.6 SEC Materials 102
14.7 Presidential Papers and Executive Orders 103
14.8 Court Administrative Orders 103
14.9 Patents. 103
14.10 Short Forms for Regulations. 104

Books, Periodical Materials, and Other Secondary Sources

15 Books, Pamphlets, and Other Nonperiodic Materials. **107**
   15.1 Author, Editor, and Translator 107
         15.1.1 Author. 107
         15.1.2 Editor or Translator 108
         15.1.3 Institutional Authors and Editors 108
   15.2 Title 109
   15.3 Serial Number 110
   15.4 Edition, Publisher, and Date 110
   15.5 Shorter Works in Collection 112
         15.5.1 Shorter Works in Collection Generally 112
         15.5.2 Collected Documents 112
   15.6 Prefaces, Forewords, Introductions, and Epilogues 113
   15.7 Special Citation Forms 113
   15.8 Short Citation Forms 114
         15.8.1 Short Forms for Books, Pamphlets, and Nonperiodic
                 Materials Generally. 115
         15.8.2 Short Forms for Shorter Works in Collection 116

16 Periodical Materials. **117**
   16.1 Author 118
   16.2 Title 118
   16.3 Consecutively Paginated Journals 119
   16.4 Nonconsecutively Paginated Journals and Magazines. 119
   16.5 Newspapers. 120
   16.6 Special Citation Forms 121
         16.6.1 Non-Student-Written Book Reviews. 121
         16.6.2 Student-Written Law Review Materials 121
         16.6.3 Symposia, Colloquia, and Surveys 123
         16.6.4 Multipart Articles. 123
         16.6.5 Annotations. 124
         16.6.6 Proceedings, Regular Publications by Institutes, and
                 ABA Section Reports 124
         16.6.7 Newsletters and Other Noncommercially Distributed
                 Periodicals 125
   16.7 Short Citation Forms 125

17 Unpublished and Forthcoming Sources. **126**
   17.1 Unpublished Materials 126
         17.1.1 Manuscripts 127
         17.1.2 Dissertations and Theses 127
         17.1.3 Letters, Memoranda, and Press Releases 127
         17.1.4 Interviews. 127
         17.1.5 Speeches and Addresses 128
   17.2 Forthcoming Publications 128
   17.3 Short Citation Forms. 129

18 Electronic Media and Other Nonprint Resources............. **129**
  18.1 Commercial Electronic Databases 130
    18.1.1 Cases 130
    18.1.2 Constitutions and Statutes 131
    18.1.3 Legislative, Administrative, and Executive Materials. ... 131
    18.1.4 Secondary Materials............................ 132
  18.2 The Internet 132
    18.2.1 Basic Citation Principles....................... 132
    18.2.2 Cases.. 137
    18.2.3 Constitutions and Statutes 138
    18.2.4 Legislative Material........................... 138
    18.2.5 Administrative and Executive Materials 139
    18.2.6 Books, Journals, and Magazines.................. 139
    18.2.7 Other Secondary Sources....................... 140
    18.2.8 Other Information Services 140
    18.2.9 E-Mail Correspondence and Postings to Listservs..... 141
  18.3 CD-ROM... 141
  18.4 Microform 142
    18.4.1 Microform Collections Reproducing Preexisting Materials 142
    18.4.2 Microform Collections Containing Original Materials ... 142
  18.5 Films, Broadcasts, and Noncommercial Videotapes......... 142
  18.6 Audio Recordings 143
    18.6.1 Commercial Recordings 143
    18.6.2 Noncommercial Recordings 143
  18.7 Short Citation Forms................................ 143

Services

19 Services..................................... **147**
  19.1 Citation Form for Services 147
  19.2 Short Citation Forms 148

Foreign Materials

20 Foreign Materials......................... **151**
  20.1 Non-English-Language Documents................... 151
    20.1.1 Documents Appearing in More Than One Language .. 151
    20.1.2 Titles and Names of Documents in Languages
        Other than English 151
    20.1.3 Abbreviations in Languages Other Than English 151
    20.1.4 Languages That Do Not Use the Roman Alphabet. ... 152
    20.1.5 Citations to Translations of Non-English-Language
        Documents 152
  20.2 Jurisdiction Not Evident from Context 152
  20.3 Cases 152
    20.3.1 Common Law Cases........................... 152
    20.3.2 Civil Law and Other Non-Common Law Cases 153

20.4 Constitutions 153
20.5 Statutes 154
    20.5.1 Common Law Statutes 154
    20.5.2 Civil Law and Other Non-Common Law Statutes 154
20.6 Periodicals with Non-English-Language Titles 154
20.7 Short Citation Forms 155

International Materials

21 International Materials 157
21.1 Basic Citation Forms 157
21.2 Non-English-Language Documents 158
21.3 Jurisdiction Not Evident from Context 158
21.4 Treaties and Other International Agreements 158
    21.4.1 Name of the Agreement 159
    21.4.2 Date of Signing 160
    21.4.3 Parties to the Agreement 160
    21.4.4 Subdivisions 161
    21.4.5 Treaty Sources 161
21.5 International Law Cases 162
    21.5.1 The International Court of Justice and the Permanent
           Court of International Justice (World Court) 163
    21.5.2 The Court of Justice of the European Communities . . . 164
    21.5.3 The European Court of Human Rights 166
    21.5.4 The Inter-American Commission on Human Rights . . . 166
    21.5.5 The East African Court of Appeal 167
    21.5.6 Other Multinational Courts 167
    21.5.7 International Cases in National Courts 167
21.6 International Arbitrations 167
21.7 United Nations Materials 168
    21.7.1 Official Records 168
    21.7.2 Sales Documents 172
    21.7.3 Mimeographed Documents 173
    21.7.4 Yearbooks and Periodicals 173
    21.7.5 United Nations Charter 174
    21.7.6 Founding Documents 174
21.8 Materials of Other Intergovernmental Organizations 174
    21.8.1 League of Nations Materials 174
    21.8.2 European Community Materials 174
    21.8.3 Council of Europe Materials 177
    21.8.4 World Trade Organization and GATT (General
           Agreement on Tariffs and Trade) 177
    21.8.5 Other Intergovernmental Organizations' Materials 178
21.9 Yearbooks 179
21.10 Digests 179
21.11 Short Citation Forms 180

Tables and Abbreviations

T Tables and Abbreviations 183

Tables

T.1 United States Jurisdictions 183
    Federal. 183
    States and the District of Columbia. 188
        Alabama. 188
        Alaska 189
        Arizona. 190
        Arkansas 191
        California 191
        Colorado. 193
        Connecticut. 194
        Delaware 195
        District of Columbia. 196
        Florida 197
        Georgia 198
        Hawaii. 199
        Idaho 200
        Illinois. 200
        Indiana 201
        Iowa 202
        Kansas 203
        Kentucky. 204
        Louisiana 205
        Maine. 206
        Maryland 207
        Massachusetts 208
        Michigan. 210
        Minnesota. 211
        Mississippi 211
        Missouri 212
        Montana 213
        Nebraska 213
        Nevada. 214
        New Hampshire 214
        New Jersey. 215
        New Mexico 216
        New York. 217
        North Carolina 222
        North Dakota 223
        Ohio. 224
        Oklahoma. 226
        Oregon. 227
        Pennsylvania. 227

Rhode Island 229
South Carolina 230
South Dakota 231
Tennessee 232
Texas 233
Utah 236
Vermont 237
Virginia 238
Washington 239
West Virginia 239
Wisconsin 240
Wyoming 241
Other United States Jurisdictions 241
American Samoa 241
Canal Zone (now part of Panama) 242
Guam 242
Navajo Nation 243
Northern Mariana Islands 243
Puerto Rico 244
Virgin Islands 244
T.2   Foreign Jurisdictions 245
Argentine Republic 245
Australia 246
Australian States and Territories 248
Austria, Republic of 250
Austrian Länder 252
Brazil, Federative Republic of 252
Canada 254
Canadian Provinces and Territories 255
Catholic Church 257
China, People's Republic of 257
Czech Republic 259
France, Republic of 259
Germany, Federal Republic of 262
German Länder 265
Hungary, Republic of 266
India 266
Ireland (Éire), Republic of 268
Israel 269
Italy, Republic of 270
Japan 272
Mexico, United States of 276
Netherlands, Kingdom of the (Holland) 277
New Zealand 279
Roman Law 280
Russian Federation 281
South Africa 283

Spain 285
Switzerland.................................. 287
   Swiss Cantons 288
United Kingdom 289
   England and Wales...................... 292
   Northern Ireland (and Ireland Until 1924) 295
   Scotland.............................. 295
T.3   Intergovernmental Organizations 297
United Nations 297
League of Nations............................ 297
European Communities........................ 297
European Court and Commission of Human Rights... 298
Inter-American Commission on Human Rights....... 299
East African Court of Appeal 299
Other Intergovernmental Organizations 299
T.4   Treaty Sources...................................... 300

Abbreviations

T.5   Arbitral Reporters................................ 301
T.6   Case Names 302
T.7   Court Names 304
T.8   Court Documents 307
T.9   Explanatory Phrases 309
T.10 Legislative Documents 310
T.11 Geographical Terms 311
T.12 Judges and Officials.............................. 315
T.13 Months.. 316
T.14 Periodicals...................................... 317
T.15 Publishing Terms 342
T.16 Services.. 343
T.17 Subdivisions..................................... 349

Index

X Index 351

The Bluebook

A
Uniform
System
of
Citation

Seventeenth Edition

I | Introduction

I: Introduction to Legal Citation and the *Bluebook*   3
   I.1: Structure of the *Bluebook*   3
   I.2: General Principles of Citation   4
   I.3: Use of Citations Generally   4
   I.4: Typical Legal Citations Analyzed   5

Introduction to Legal Citation and the *Bluebook*

This section provides an introduction to legal citation for those who are new to the *Bluebook*. It explains the basic principles of legal citation and analyzes a number of representative citations to the most frequently cited sources in legal writing.

Note that this introduction is not comprehensive; it merely seeks to familiarize new users with the basic principles of legal citation and a few of the most common citation forms. To ensure accurate citation, then, it is important to consult the applicable rule or rules in the body of the book and the tables found in the back of the book, because they offer more detailed guidance on the particulars of various citation forms.

Structure of the *Bluebook*   I.1

The *Bluebook* contains three major parts. The first part (**rules 1 to 9**) sets forth general standards of citation and style to be used throughout legal writing. The second part (**rules 10 to 21**) presents specific rules of citation for cases, statutes, books, periodicals, foreign materials, international materials, and so forth. A third part (**tables T.1 to T.17**),   T.1–T.17
printed on light blue stock at the end of the book, consists of a series of tables to be used in conjunction with the rules. The tables show, among other things, which authority to cite and how to abbreviate properly. When a rule calls for a particular table, the table is cross-referenced in the margin of the book for quick access.

In addition to this introduction and the basic rules and tables, Practitioners' Notes, a special section for practitioners printed on light blue stock immediately following this introduction, provides extra guidance for those working on court documents and legal memoranda, including how to adapt the examples found throughout the body of the *Bluebook* for these types of documents. Practitioners should be careful to note cross-references in the rules and tables to relevant practitioners' notes; these cross-references are located in the margins of the book. Such a cross-reference is a signal that the practitioner may need additional guidance in using a particular rule.

A quick reference guide with examples of the most common citation forms in law review style is found on the inside front cover and first page of the book, and a parallel listing using the typeface conventions for court documents and legal memoranda appears on the very last page and inside back cover. Finally, located at the back of the book is a detailed index to the different citation topics covered in the *Bluebook*.

I.2   General Principles of Citation

The basic purpose of a legal citation is to allow the reader to locate a cited source accurately and efficiently. Thus, the citation forms in the *Bluebook* seek to provide the minimum amount of information necessary to lead the reader directly to the specific items cited.

As you become more familiar with legal citation, you will find that the citation forms for some sources, such as U.S. Supreme Court cases, become second nature, and you will no longer need to consult the *Bluebook* each time you cite those authorities. Some sources, however, are less frequently cited or have more complex citation forms, and you may find yourself referring to the *Bluebook* rule each time such a source appears to ensure that you are citing it correctly. Regardless of how well you know the rules, you may often need to refer to the tables in the back of the book for technical guidance.

Because of the ever-increasing range of authorities cited in legal writing, neither the *Bluebook* nor any other system of citation can be complete. When citing material of a type not explicitly discussed in this book, try to locate an analogous sort of authority that is discussed and use that citation form as a model. You may find **rule 17**, which deals with unpublished and forthcoming sources, particularly helpful in this regard. Always be sure to provide sufficient information to allow a reader to find the authority quickly and reliably.

For additional guidance on punctuation, capitalization, compounding, and other matters of style, you may wish to consult the *U.S. Government Printing Office Style Manual* (1984) or *The Chicago Manual of Style* (14th rev. ed. 1993).

I.3   Use of Citations Generally

In all types of legal writing, whether by scholars or by practitioners, it is customary to cite an authority or authorities to show support for a legal or factual proposition or argument. An author may cite authority that directly states the author's legal or factual proposition; authority that does not specifically state the author's proposition but directly supports it; authority that less directly supports the author's proposition but from which one can infer the proposition; authority that contradicts the author's proposition; and authority that provides background material that the reader might find useful in considering the proposition.

Each of these categories of authority is introduced by a different *signal*—an italicized or underlined word or words such as "*see*," "*see, e.g.*," or "*compare*"—or, in the case of authority that directly states the proposition, by no signal at all. In law review articles, citations to supporting authority appear in footnotes appended directly after the propositions in the text that they support. Sometimes law review footnotes themselves include propositions that are followed directly by supporting citations. In court documents and legal memoranda, citations generally appear within the text of the document, as full sentences or as clauses within sentences, directly after the propositions they support.

Certain kinds of authorities are considered more useful—or authoritative—than other kinds. If more than one authority is cited in support of a proposition, these supporting authorities are usually listed so that the more authoritative ones appear first.

Finally, it is common to include a short parenthetical explanation of a particular authority after the citation to the authority if it will help the reader understand how the source supports or relates to the author's assertion.

Typical Legal Citations Analyzed   **I.4**

What follows are representative citations for cases, constitutions, statutes, rules, regulations, books, periodicals, treaties, and United Nations documents, with explanations of their constituent parts. Note that the typeface conventions used here conform to those for law review footnotes. For an explanation of typeface styles to be used in court documents and legal memoranda, see **practitioners' note P.1.**   **P.1**

Dots are inserted in the examples to indicate one space between the components of each citation format.

(a) Cases (rule 10).

Citation of a U.S. Supreme Court case:

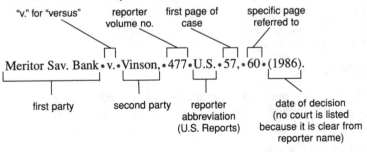

Citation of a case decided by the U.S. Court of Appeals for the Fourth Circuit, later reversed by the U.S. Supreme Court, with parenthetical information about the Fourth Circuit decision:

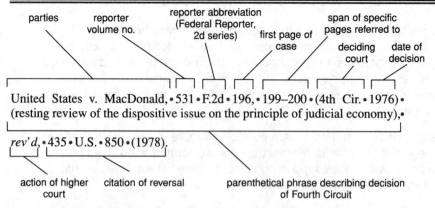

United States v. MacDonald, • 531 • F.2d • 196, • 199–200 • (4th Cir. • 1976) • (resting review of the dispositive issue on the principle of judicial economy), •

rev'd, • 435 • U.S. • 850 • (1978).

action of higher court   citation of reversal   parenthetical phrase describing decision of Fourth Circuit

Short form for the above case after it has been cited in full:

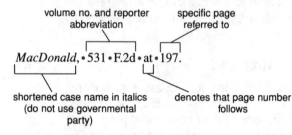

MacDonald, • 531 • F.2d • at • 197.

shortened case name in italics (do not use governmental party)   denotes that page number follows

(b) Constitutions (rule 11).

Citation of Section 2 of the Fourteenth Amendment to the U.S. Constitution:

abbreviation for "amendment"   no. of amendment cited

U.S. CONST. • amend. • XIV, • § • 2.

abbreviation of constitution cited   section symbol and specific section cited

(c) Statutes (rule 12).

Citation of an entire statute, the Comprehensive Environmental Response, Compensation, and Liability Act, as codified in the *United States Code*:

official name of act

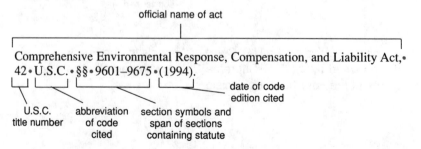

Comprehensive Environmental Response, Compensation, and Liability Act, • 42 • U.S.C. • §§ • 9601–9675 • (1994).

date of code edition cited

U.S.C. title number   abbreviation of code cited   section symbols and span of sections containing statute

Citation of an individual provision of the *United States Code*:

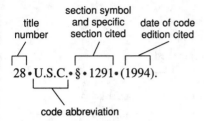

```
          section symbol
  title     and specific    date of code
  number    section cited    edition cited
   ┌─┐      ┌──────┐        ┌──────┐
  28 • U.S.C. • § • 1291 • (1994).
   └─────┘

     code abbreviation
```

(d) Rules (rule 12.8.3).

Citation of a Federal Rule of Civil Procedure:

```
            number of rule cited
                    ┌──┐
  FED. R. CIV. P. • 11.
  └────┬────┘

  abbreviation of set
    of rules cited
```

(e) Regulations (rule 14.2).

Citation of a particular provision of a regulation in the *Code of Federal Regulations*:

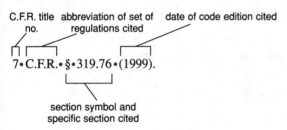

```
C.F.R. title  abbreviation of set of   date of code edition cited
   no.          regulations cited
  ┌┐ ┌──────┐              ┌──────┐
  7 • C.F.R. • § • 319.76 • (1999).
       └────────┘

       section symbol and
       specific section cited
```

(f) Books (rule 15).

Citation of a particular section of James and Hazard's treatise on civil procedure:

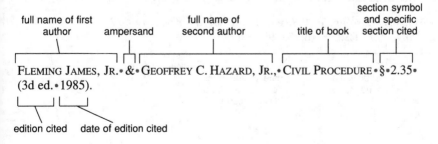

```
                                                      section symbol
  full name of first        full name of              and specific
     author      ampersand  second author  title of book  section cited
  ┌──────────┐    ┌┐┌─────────────┐      ┌──────────┐  ┌──┐
  FLEMING JAMES, JR. • & • GEOFFREY C. HAZARD, JR., • CIVIL PROCEDURE • § • 2.35 •
  (3d ed. • 1985).
  └───┘ └────┘

  edition cited   date of edition cited
```

Citation of a particular page within Charles Dickens's *Bleak House*:

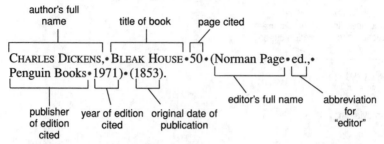

(g) Periodical materials (rule 16).

Citation of particular pages within a law review article with parenthetical information about what appears on those pages:

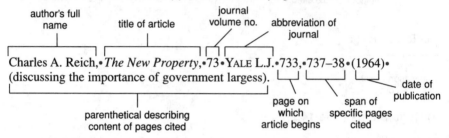

Citation of an entire magazine article:

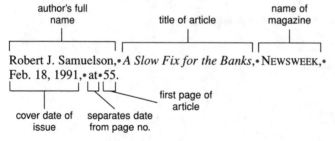

Citation of a signed newspaper article:

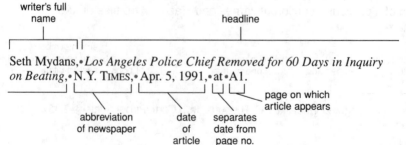

(h) Treaties (rule 21.4).

Citation of a treaty between the United States and one other party:

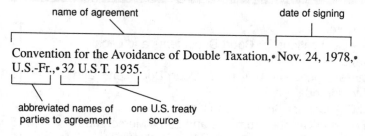

Citation of a treaty between the U.S. and two or more other parties:

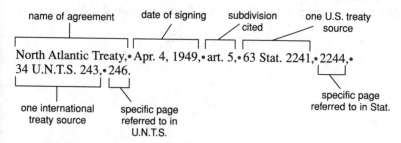

(i) United Nations materials (rule 21.7).

Citation of a resolution of the United Nations General Assembly:

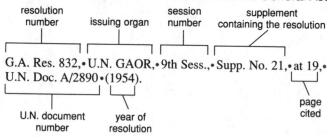

Practitioners' Notes

P Practitioners' Notes   **11**

P.1: Typeface Conventions for Court Documents and Legal   11
      Memoranda

P.2: Citation Sentences and Clauses in Court Documents and   13
      Legal Memoranda

P.3: Parallel Citations for State Court Cases   14

P.4: Short Forms in Court Documents and Legal Memoranda   15

P.5: Special Citation Forms for Federal Taxation Materials   16

P.6: Capitalization in Court Documents and Legal Memoranda   17

P.7: Abbreviated Citations to Other Court Documents and Letters 18

Practitioners' Notes

The rules and tables in the *Bluebook* are generally applicable to all types of legal writing, including court documents and legal memoranda. These practitioners' notes show how to adapt the examples in the *Bluebook*, which conform to the typeface conventions for law review footnotes, to the simpler style used in court documents and legal memoranda. They also provide some additional citation forms and further guidance of special interest to practitioners. Note that particular practitioners' notes are cross-referenced in the margins of the *Bluebook*; practitioners who are not yet familiar with the information contained in these notes should consult them as appropriate. In addition, the quick reference section on the very last page and inside back cover provides a list of representative citation forms as they would appear in practitioners' documents.

The practitioner should also be aware that many courts have their own rules of citation that may differ in some respects from the *Bluebook*. *Make sure that you are familiar with and abide by any additional or different citation requirements of the court to which the document is to be submitted.* If you are not certain about what a court requires, you should consult with the clerk of the court or with someone who is familiar with the court's rules.

Typeface Conventions for Court Documents and Legal Memoranda

Generally, only two typefaces are used in court documents and legal memoranda—ordinary type, such as courier, and italics (indicated in some materials by underscoring):

Ordinary type

Italics or underscoring

The examples in these practitioners' notes adhere to the typeface conventions for court documents and legal memoranda, using underscoring rather than italics because underscoring is more common in practice. The practitioner should substitute the simpler typeface conventions set forth in this section in place of the law review typeface style found in the examples in the rest of the book.

The following items should be underscored or italicized in practitioners' documents regardless of whether the material appears in the text of a document or in a footnote:

(a) Case names (rule 10.2). Underscore or italicize all case names, including the "v." and any procedural phrases such as "In re" and "Ex parte":

United States v. Reynolds, 449 F.2d 1347 (9th
Cir. 1971), cert. denied, 408 U.S. 924 (1972).

In re Winship, 397 U.S. 358 (1970).

(b) Names of publications (rules 15 and 16). In citations, always
underscore or italicize the title of a book or the title of an article
appearing in a periodical. Do not use large and small capitals. Authors'
names and periodical titles are not underscored or italicized. If an article or essay appears within a book, underscore or italicize the title of
the article or essay as well as that of the book:

Oliver Wendell Holmes, The Common Law 1
(1881).

Samuel D. Warren & Louis D. Brandeis, The
Right to Privacy, 4 Harv. L. Rev. 193, 195
(1890).

Vicki Hearne, Wise Men and Elephants, N.Y.
Times, Feb. 21, 1993, § 7, at 28.

Kay Deaux & Brenda Major, A Social-
Psychological Model of Gender, in Theoretical
Perspectives on Sexual Difference 89 (Deborah
L. Rhode ed., 1990).

Treat legislative materials (such as hearings, documents, and committee prints) (**rule 13**) as books; underscore or italicize their titles and
print the authors' names (if given) in ordinary type:

Corporate Rights and Responsibilities:
Hearings Before the Senate Comm. on Commerce,
94th Cong. 47 (1976).

Charles Davenport, Administrative Procedures
of the Internal Revenue Service, S. Doc. No.
94-266, at 619-726 (1975).

When reports or documents are cited without an author or title, do not
underscore or italicize them:

S. Rep. No. 89-1319 (1966).

When referring to a publication in a textual sentence rather than citing
it, underscore or italicize the name of the publication:

The library receives both The Yale Law Journal
and the Federal Reporter.

(c) Introductory signals (rule 1.2). Introductory signals are always
underscored or italicized when they appear in citation sentences or
clauses. When an introductory signal is part of a regular English sentence, however, it is not underscored or italicized:

See, e.g., Stringfellow v. Concerned Neighbors
in Action, 480 U.S. 370 (1987).

But see id.

> Compare Richardson-Merrell Inc. v. Koller, 472
> U.S. 424 (1985), with Firestone Tire & Rubber
> Co. v. Risjord, 449 U.S. 368 (1981), and
> Cobbledick v. United States, 309 U.S. 323
> (1940).

But:

> For a more pointed analysis of this issue, see
> United States v. Frady, 456 U.S. 152, 169
> (1982).

(d) Explanatory phrases introducing prior or subsequent history (rule 10.7.1). These should always be underscored or italicized:

> Kubrick v. United States, 581 F.2d 1092 (3d
> Cir. 1978), aff'g 435 F. Supp. 166 (E.D. Pa.
> 1977), rev'd, 444 U.S. 111 (1979).

(e) Words and phrases introducing related authority (rules 1.6, 15.5, 18.2, 18.4, 18.6, and 20.1.5). Underscore or italicize *"in,"* *"reprinted in,"* *"quoted in,"* *"available at,"* *"translated in,"* *"microformed on,"* and other similar words and phrases referring to related authority:

> Urvashi Vaid, Prisons, in AIDS and the Law
> 235, 237-39 (Harlon L. Dalton et al. eds.,
> 1987).

> H.R. Rep. No. 92-98, at 4 (1971), reprinted in
> 1971 U.S.C.C.A.N. 1017, 1017.

(f) Cross-references and short forms (rule 4). Always underscore or italicize *"supra,"* *"infra,"* and *"id."* (including the period), but not *"hereinafter."*

(g) Style (rules 5 and 7). Underscore or italicize words for emphasis, foreign words not commonly encountered in legal writing, and words italicized in the original of quoted matter.

(h) Everything else. Print everything else—including reporters, services, constitutions, statutory material, restatements, model codes, rules, executive orders, administrative materials, unpublished sources, and treaties—in ordinary roman type.

Citation Sentences and Clauses in Court Documents and Legal Memoranda

P.2

Citations in court documents and legal memoranda may be made in either of two ways: in citation sentences or in citation clauses. Authorities that support (or contradict) an *entire* sentence are given in separate citation sentences that begin with capital letters and end with periods. Authorities that support (or contradict) *only part* of a sentence are cited in clauses, set off by commas, that immediately follow the proposition they support (or contradict). In both citation sentences and clauses, multiple citations are separated with semicolons. Thus, a legal discussion in a court document or memorandum would appear:

> States have required defendants to prove both insanity, e.g., State v. Caryl, 543 P.2d 389, 397 (Mont. 1975); State v. Hinson, 172 S.E.2d 548, 554 (S.C. 1970), and self-defense, see, e.g., Quillen v. State, 110 A.2d 445, 449 (Del. 1955); State v. Skinner, 104 P. 223, 224 (Nev. 1909). See generally Wayne R. LaFave & Austin W. Scott, Jr., Handbook on Criminal Law § 8, at 46-51 (1972). In several jurisdictions, the defendant must even establish that a homicide was accidental. See, e.g., Chandle v. State, 198 S.E.2d 289, 291 (Ga. 1973); State v. Enlow, 536 S.W.2d 533, 535 (Mo. Ct. App. 1976).

P.7 See **practitioners' note P.7** for a sample factual discussion that cites court documents.

P.3 Parallel Citations for State Court Cases

T.1 In a document to be submitted to a state court, all citations to cases should be to the reporters preferred by local rules, including any parallel citations to the official state reporter, if required. If the decision is available through an official public domain citation, that citation may be required instead, as well as a citation to a traditional source provided in **table T.1**. See **rule 10.3.3** for general guidance on public domain citation (also known as medium neutral citation). Note, however, that local court rules may require a different format from that provided in **rule 10.3.3**.

T.1 Consult the relevant court rules and state listings in **table T.1** for guidance on the reporters of particular states. Note that when the state is clear from the official reporter title, it should be omitted from the date parenthetical (see **rule 10.4(b)**). Thus:

In a brief to a Georgia state court:

> Heard v. Neighbor Newspapers, 190 Ga. App. 756, 758, 380 S.E.2d 279, 281 (1989).

In a brief to a New York state court:

> People v. Taylor, 73 N.Y.2d 683, 690, 541 N.E.2d 386, 389, 543 N.Y.S.2d 357, 360 (1989).

In a brief to an Oklahoma state court:

> Calvey v. Daxon, 2000 OK 17, 997 P.2d 164.

For short forms and the use of "id." for cases for which a parallel citation is required, see **practitioners' note P.4.**

Short Forms in Court Documents and Legal Memoranda   P.4

Once a full citation is given, you may use a short form for cases, statutes, regulations, legislative materials, books, articles, periodical materials, and so forth so long as (i) it will be clear to the reader from the short form what is being referenced; (ii) the earlier full citation falls in the same general discussion; and (iii) the reader will have little trouble locating the full citation quickly. The short forms explained elsewhere in the book are generally applicable to court documents and memoranda, except that there is no note number referenced after a "supra" in a practitioner's document, and the typefaces should conform to **practitioners' note P.1.** Consult **rule 4** and the rules treating   P.1 particular materials for suggested short forms. See **practitioners' note P.7** for a discussion of abbreviated citation forms for court documents   P.7 and correspondence to be used within practitioners' documents.

(a) Cases. Citations to a case that has been cited in full in the same general discussion may be shortened to one of the following forms if the shortened citation clearly identifies the case. Note that the short forms listed below give only one or neither of the parties and do not give the first page of the case or the court or year of decision; they do, however, include the word "at" to indicate the page on which the specific material appears. In employing a short form, avoid using the name of a governmental or other common litigant to identify the case. Acceptable short forms for the citation "United States v. Calandra, 414 U.S. 338, 343 (1974)" are thus:

> Calandra, 414 U.S. at 343.
>
> 414 U.S. at 343.
>
> Id. at 343.
>
> **Not:** United States, 414 U.S. at 343.

For cases in which a parallel citation is required, shorter citation forms take a slightly different form. Thus,

> Chalfin v. Specter, 426 Pa. 464, 465, 233 A.2d 562, 563 (1967).

becomes one of the following short forms:

> Chalfin, 426 Pa. at 465, 233 A.2d at 563.
>
> 426 Pa. at 465, 233 A.2d at 563.

The id. form (see **rule 4.1**) for cases requiring parallel citations is as follows:

```
Id. at 465, 233 A.2d at 563.
```

(b) Statutes and regulations. In practitioners' documents, the first mention of a statute or regulation requires a full citation similar to the ones listed in the first column of the table appearing in **rule 12.9**. Subsequent citations to the statute or regulation in the same general discussion may employ any short form that clearly identifies the statute or regulation. See the table in **rule 12.9** for acceptable short forms for these sources.

(c) Constitutions. Do not use a short citation form other than "id." for constitutions.

(d) Books, pamphlets, and other nonperiodic materials; shorter works in collection; periodical materials; unpublished, forthcoming, and nonprint materials. Both "id." and "supra" may be used to refer to these materials after they have already been cited in full. Follow **rules 4, 15.8, 16.7, 17.3**, and **18.7**, omitting note number references in the "supra" form. Representative citations using "supra" would thus be:

```
Tribe, supra, § 15-1.

Heilbrun & Resnik, supra, at 1942 n.122.

Beneson et al., supra, at 3438.

Note, supra, at 1325.

Margolick, supra.

Indictment of Pregnant Woman for Drug Use
Dismissed, supra, at 5.

Andreas Huyssen, Mapping the Postmodern, in
Feminism/Postmodernism, supra, at 234, 234-35.
```

(e) Services. Follow **rule 19.2**.

P.5 Special Citation Forms for Federal Taxation Materials

In court documents and legal memoranda that discuss solely the current version of federal taxation laws, (i) citations to the Internal Revenue Code (**rule 12.8.1**) should omit the year and publisher; and (ii) citations to treasury regulations (**rule 14.5.1**) should omit the year of promulgation or last amendment:

```
I.R.C. § 61.

Treas. Reg. § 1.72-16(a).
```

In all other court documents and legal memoranda, use the citation forms provided in **rules 12.8.1** and **14.5**.

When citing Treasury determinations, the abbreviations contained in the introductory pages of each volume of the *Cumulative Bulletin* may be used. Hence, General Counsel Memoranda may be cited "G.C.M." instead of "Gen. Couns. Mem." In addition, when citing Private Letter Rulings in court documents and legal memoranda, the abbreviation "P.L.R." may be used instead of "Priv. Ltr. Rul." and the dashes may be removed from the ruling number.

Capitalization in Court Documents and Legal Memoranda   P.6

Practitioners generally should follow **rule 8** on matters of capitalization, with the following modifications and additions:

(a) Court. In addition to capitalizing "Court" when naming any court in full or when referring to the U.S. Supreme Court, practitioners should also capitalize "Court" in a court document when referring to the court that will be receiving that document:

> In <u>Brown v. Board of Education</u>, the Court relied heavily on social science data.

> The Court of Appeals for the Ninth Circuit held otherwise.

> This Court has already ruled on Defendant's Motion to Dismiss.

But:

> The court in <u>Watkins</u> clearly was trying to distinguish earlier precedent leading in the other direction.

(b) Party designations. Capitalize party designations such as "Plaintiff," "Defendant," "Appellant," "Appellee," and so forth when referring to parties in the matter that is the subject of the court document or memorandum:

> Plaintiff responds to Defendant's baseless allegations of misconduct.

> Appellees claim that this line of reasoning applies to the instant case as well.

But:

> In that case, which has since been seriously undermined, the plaintiffs alleged that the defendant acted in bad faith.

(c) Titles of court documents. In a court document or legal memorandum, capitalize the titles of court documents that have been filed in the matter that is the subject of the document. Do not, however, capitalize a reference to a court document by the generic name of the document rather than by its actual title or a shortened form of its actual title:

> In their Memorandum of Points and Authorities in Opposition to Defendants' Motion to Dismiss, Plaintiffs argue that Defendants are strictly liable for Plaintiffs' injuries. Plaintiffs further claim in their Memorandum in Opposition that there is ample case law on their side.

> For all the above reasons, Appellant's Petition for Rehearing ought to be granted.

> The Court's Order of May 7, 1990, directs Plaintiffs to cease widget production immediately.

But:

> Defendant's responses to the first set of interrogatories were filed on January 6, 1987.

> There is no doubt that the initial temporary restraining order was within the bounds of the Court's discretion.

P.7 Abbreviated Citations to Other Court Documents and Letters

It is common in practice, in citing other court filings in the same case, to abbreviate the titles of those documents and to cite a paragraph or a page within such a document using an "at" form. Such citations are generally enclosed in parentheses. If the citation serves as a full citation sentence, a period follows the paragraph or page cite inside the parentheses. If the citation serves merely as a clause, insert the parenthetical citation but do not include commas before and after the opening and closing parentheses. If the citation ends a sentence, the ending period comes outside the closing parenthesis. Multiple citations may be strung together using semicolons:

> Plaintiff was driving a blue, late-model sports car. (Michael Decl. ¶ 21.)

> The witness did not observe anything unusual on that day (R. at 101-05) and received no phone call until approximately 5:00 p.m. (R. at 106; Nunnelley Aff. ¶ 7).

Although shortened versions of document titles generally are permissible both in text and in citations, it is important to identify each document unambiguously so that a reader would have no trouble ascertaining which filing in the case is being referenced. **Table T.8** provides suggested abbreviations for the words most commonly found in the titles of court documents. A factual discussion in a legal brief or

T.8

memorandum using the suggested citation form and abbreviations would thus appear:

> In Defendant's Memorandum of Points and
> Authorities in Support of Defendant's Motion
> for Summary Judgment, Defendant asserts that
> the dangerous conditions giving rise to the
> accident resulted from someone else's negli-
> gence (Def.'s Mem. Supp. Summ. J. at 6, 9) and
> thus implies that Defendant was, indeed, aware
> of the risk. Yet in his Affidavit filed in
> support of the Motion, Defendant explicitly
> states he had no knowledge of the rising water
> level. (Branch Aff. ¶¶ 5-7; <u>see also</u> Roth Aff.
> Ex. A at 2.) This contradiction cannot ade-
> quately be resolved unless the Court allows
> further discovery.

See **practitioners' note P.2** for a sample discussion in a court docu-   P.2
ment or legal memorandum citing cases and outside authority.

To cite a letter in a court document or legal memorandum, the following form is suggested:

> (Letter from Berliner to Sellstrom of 7/20/90,
> at 3.)

Note that this form for letters differs from that used in law review footnotes (**rule 17.1.3**).

General Rules of Citation and Style

Rule 1: Structure and Use of Citations   21

Rule 2: Typefaces for Law Reviews   30

Rule 3: Subdivisions   33

Rule 4: Short Citation Forms   40

Rule 5: Quotations   43

Rule 6: Abbreviations, Numerals, and Symbols   47

Rule 7: Italicization for Stylistic Purposes   50

Rule 8: Capitalization   51

Rule 9: Titles of Judges, Officials, and Terms of Court   53

Structure and Use of Citations   1

Citations are made in citation sentences and clauses (**rule 1.1**) and are introduced by signals, which indicate the purposes of the citations and the degree of support the citations give (**rule 1.2**). Citation sentences and clauses may contain more than one signal. Signals are ordered according to **rule 1.3**. Individual citations following each signal are ordered according to **rule 1.4**. Additional information about an authority may be given parenthetically (**rule 1.5**), and related authority may be appended according to **rule 1.6**.

Citation Sentences and Clauses in Law Review   1.1
Footnotes

Citations may be made in one of two ways: in citation sentences or in citation clauses. In law review pieces, all citations appear in footnotes appended to the portions of the text to which they refer. If a footnote itself contains an assertion requiring support, a citation for the relevant authority should appear directly after the assertion. For an explanation of citation sentences and clauses in practitioners' documents, see **practitioners' note P.2**.   P.2

(a) Footnotes. For textual sentences within footnotes, citations appear either as citation sentences or citation clauses.

(i) Citation sentences. Authorities that support (or contradict) an entire sentence are given in a separate citation sentence immediately after the sentence they support (or contradict). The citation sentence starts with a capital letter and ends with a period.

(ii) Citation clauses. Authorities that support (or contradict) only part of a sentence within a footnote are cited in clauses, set off by commas, that immediately follow the proposition they support (or contradict).

(b) Text. Authorities that support (or contradict) a proposition made in text are placed in footnotes. The footnote call number should appear in the text at the end of a sentence if the source supports (or contradicts) the entire sentence. The call number should appear within the sentence next to the portion it supports if the source supports (or contradicts) only that part of the sentence. The call number comes after any punctuation mark, such as a comma, semicolon, or period, except for a dash. In any case, the citation in the footnote appears as a citation sentence, with a capital letter at the beginning and a period at the end.

(c) Example. In both citation sentences and clauses, introductory signals may precede citations (**rule 1.2**), and semicolons separate multiple citations (**rule 1.3**). Note that supportive and contradictory citations are to be listed in a certain order according to the signals that introduce them (**rule 1.3**). The following excerpt illustrates the use of citation sentences and clauses in a law review piece:

Some American jurisdictions place the burden of sustaining criminal defenses on the accused.[1] States have required defendants to prove both insanity[2] and self-defense.[3] In several jurisdictions the defendant must even establish that a homicide was accidental.[4]

---

[1] *See* John Calvin Jeffries, Jr. & Paul B. Stephan III, *Defenses, Presumptions, and the Burden of Proof in the Criminal Law*, 88 YALE L.J. 1325, 1329–30 (1979). The authors point out that the use of affirmative defenses may relieve the state of its duty to prove a sufficient factual basis for punishment, *id.* at 1357, and argue that the reasonable doubt standard should not be limited to those facts formally identified as elements of the offense charged, *id.* at 1327.

[2] *E.g.*, State v. Caryl, 543 P.2d 389, 390 (Mont. 1975); State v. Hinson, 172 S.E.2d 548, 551 (S.C. 1970).

[3] *See, e.g.*, Quillen v. State, 110 A.2d 445, 449 (Del. 1955); State v. Skinner, 104 P. 223, 224 (Nev. 1909). *See generally* WAYNE R. LAFAVE & AUSTIN W. SCOTT, JR., HANDBOOK ON CRIMINAL LAW § 8.1, at 704–06 (2d ed. 1986) (discussing the origin of embezzlement and false pretenses).

[4] *See, e.g.*, Chandle v. State, 198 S.E.2d 289, 290 (Ga. 1973); State v. Enlow, 536 S.W.2d 533, 541 (Mo. Ct. App. 1976).

1.2   Introductory Signals

(a) Signals that indicate support.

[no signal]	Cited authority (i) directly states the proposition, (ii) identifies the source of a quotation, or (iii) identifies an authority referred to in the text.
E.g.,	Cited authority states the proposition; other authorities also state the proposition, but citation to them would not be helpful or is not necessary. "*E.g.*" may also be used in combination with other signals, preceded by a comma: *See, e.g.*, *But see, e.g.*,
Accord	"*Accord*" is commonly used when two or more cases state or clearly support the proposition but the text quotes or refers to only one; the others are then introduced by "*accord*." Similarly, the law of one jurisdiction may be cited as being in accord with that of another.
See	Cited authority clearly supports the proposition. "*See*" is used instead of "[no signal]" when the proposition is

not directly stated by the cited authority but obviously follows from it; there is an inferential step between the authority cited and the proposition it supports.

See also   Cited authority constitutes additional source material that supports the proposition. *"See also"* is commonly used to cite an authority supporting a proposition when authorities that state or directly support the proposition already have been cited or discussed. The use of a parenthetical explanation of the source material's relevance (**rule 1.5**) following a citation introduced by *"see also"* is encouraged.

R
1–9

Cf.   Cited authority supports a proposition different from the main proposition but sufficiently analogous to lend support. Literally, *"cf."* means "compare." The citation's relevance will usually be clear to the reader only if it is explained. Parenthetical explanations (**rule 1.5**), however brief, are therefore strongly recommended.

(b) Signal that suggests a useful comparison.

Compare . . .   Comparison of the authorities cited will offer support
[and] . . .   for or illustrate the proposition. The relevance of the
with . . .   comparison will usually be clear to the reader only if
[and] . . .   it is explained. Parenthetical explanations (**rule 1.5**) following each authority are therefore strongly recommended.

> *Compare* Michael H. v. Gerald D., 491 U.S. 110, 121 (1989), *and* Catharine A. MacKinnon, Feminism Unmodified 49 (1987), *with* Loving v. Virginia, 388 U.S. 1, 12 (1967), Doe I v. McConn, 489 F. Supp. 76, 80 (S.D. Tex. 1980), *and* Kenneth L. Karst, *The Freedom of Intimate Association*, 89 Yale L.J. 624, 631 (1980).

(c) Signals that indicate contradiction.

Contra   Cited authority directly states the contrary of the proposition. *"Contra"* is used where "[no signal]" would be used for support.

But see   Cited authority clearly supports a proposition contrary to the main proposition. *"But see"* is used where *"see"* would be used for support.

But cf.   Cited authority supports a proposition analogous to the contrary of the main proposition. The use of a parenthetical explanation of the source material's relevance (**rule 1.5**) following a citation introduced by *"but cf."* is strongly recommended.

"But" should be omitted from *"but see"* and *"but cf."* whenever the signal follows another negative signal:

> *Contra* Blake v. Kline, 612 F.2d 718, 723–24 (3d Cir. 1979); *see* CHARLES ALAN WRIGHT, LAW OF FEDERAL COURTS § 48 (4th ed. 1983).

(d) Signal that indicates background material.

See generally   Cited authority presents helpful background material related to the proposition. The use of a parenthetical explanation of the source material's relevance (**rule 1.5**) following each authority introduced by *"see generally"* is encouraged.

(e) Signals as verbs. Signals may be used as the verbs of ordinary sentences, in which case they are not italicized (**rule 2.1(d)**). When signals are used as verbs, matter that would be included in a parenthetical explanation should be made part of the sentence itself.

Thus:

> *See* Louis Touton, Note, *The Property Power, Federalism, and the Equal Footing Doctrine*, 80 COLUM. L. REV. 817 (1980) (discussing the limits on the property power).

becomes:

> See Louis Touton, Note, *The Property Power, Federalism, and the Equal Footing Doctrine*, 80 COLUM. L. REV. 817 (1980), for a discussion of the limits on the property power.

"Cf." becomes "compare" and *"e.g."* becomes "for example" when used in this manner.

1.3   Order of Signals

When more than one signal is used, the signals (together with the authorities they introduce) should appear in the order in which they are listed in **rule 1.2**. Signals of the same basic type—supportive, comparative, contradictory, or background (**rule 1.2(a)–(d)**)—must be strung together within a single citation sentence and separated by semicolons. Signals of different types, however, must be grouped in different citation sentences. Thus:

> *See* Mass. Bd. of Ret. v. Murgia, 427 U.S. 307 (1976); *cf.* Palmer v. Ticcione, 433 F. Supp. 653 (E.D.N.Y. 1977) (upholding a mandatory retirement age for kindergarten teachers). *But see* Gault v. Garrison, 569 F.2d 993 (7th Cir. 1977) (holding that a classification of public school teachers based on age violated equal protection absent showing of justifiable and rational state purpose). *See generally* Comment, O'Neil v. Baine: *Application of Middle-Level*

Scrutiny to Old-Age Classifications, 127 U. PA. L. REV. 798 (1979) (advocating a new constitutional approach to old-age classifications).

Within a citation clause (**rule 1.1**), however, citation strings may contain signals of more than one type.

Order of Authorities Within Each Signal 1.4

Authorities within each signal are separated by semicolons.

If one authority is considerably more helpful or authoritative than the other authorities cited within a signal, it should precede the others.

Absent this or some other substance-related rationale for placing one authority before another, cite authorities in the order in which they are listed below. Citations listed in short form are ordered as though given in full.

(a) Constitutions and other foundational documents are cited in the following order:

    (1) federal
    (2) state (alphabetically by state)
    (3) foreign (alphabetically by jurisdiction)
    (4) foundational documents of the United Nations,
        the League of Nations, and the European Union,
        in that order

Constitutions of the same jurisdiction are cited in reverse chronological order.

(b) Statutes are cited according to jurisdiction in the following order:

Federal

    (1) statutes in U.S.C., U.S.C.A., or U.S.C.S. (by progressive order of U.S.C. title)
    (2) statutes currently in force but not in U.S.C., U.S.C.A., or U.S.C.S. (by reverse chronological order of enactment)
    (3) rules of evidence and procedure
    (4) repealed statutes (by reverse chronological order of enactment)

State
(alphabetically
by state)

    (5) statutes in the current codification (by order in the codification)
    (6) statutes currently in force but not in the current codification (by reverse chronological order of enactment)
    (7) rules of evidence and procedure
    (8) repealed statutes (by reverse chronological order of enactment)

Foreign
(alphabetically
by jurisdiction)

    (9) codes or statutes in the current codification (by order in the codification)
    (10) statutes currently in force but not in codes or the current codification (by reverse chronological order of enactment)
    (11) repealed statutes (by reverse chronological order of enactment)

(c) Treaties and other international agreements (other than the foundational documents of the United Nations, the League of Nations, and the European Union) are cited in reverse chronological order.

(d) Cases are arranged within a signal according to the courts issuing the cited opinions; subsequent and prior histories are irrelevant to the order of citation. Cases decided by the same court are arranged in reverse chronological order; for this purpose the numbered United States courts of appeals are treated as one court and all federal district courts are treated as one court. The ordering system is as follows:

Federal	(1) Supreme Court
	(2) courts of appeals, bankruptcy appellate panels, Emergency Court of Appeals, Temporary Emergency Court of Appeals, Court of Appeals for the Federal Circuit (previously the Court of Claims and the Court of Customs and Patent Appeals)
	(3) district courts, district bankruptcy courts, Court of International Trade (previously the Customs Court)
	(4) Judicial Panel on Multidistrict Litigation, Railroad Reorganization Court
	(5) Court of Federal Claims (previously the Claims Court), Court of Appeals for the Armed Forces (previously the Court of Military Appeals), Tax Court (previously the Board of Tax Appeals)
	(6) administrative agencies (alphabetically by agency)
State	(7) courts (alphabetically by state and then by rank within each state)
	(8) agencies (alphabetically by state and then alphabetically by agency within each state)
Foreign	(9) courts (alphabetically by jurisdiction and then by rank within each jurisdiction)
	(10) agencies (alphabetically by jurisdiction and then by agency within each jurisdiction)
International	(11) International Court of Justice, Permanent Court of International Justice, then other international tribunals and arbitral panels (alphabetically by name)

(e) Legislative materials are cited in the following order:

(1) bills and resolutions
(2) committee hearings
(3) reports, documents, and committee prints
(4) floor debates

Cite materials within each classification in reverse chronological order.

(f) Administrative and executive materials are cited in the following order:

Federal	(1) Executive Orders
	(2) current Treasury Regulations, proposed Treasury Regulations
	(3) all others currently in force (by progressive order of C.F.R. title)

(4) proposed rules not yet in force (by progressive order of future C.F.R. title, if any; otherwise by reverse chronological order of proposal)

(5) all materials repealed (by reverse chronological order of promulgation)

State

(6) state (alphabetically by state), currently in force, then repealed

Foreign

(7) foreign (alphabetically by jurisdiction), currently in force, then repealed

(g) Resolutions, decisions, and regulations of intergovernmental organizations are cited in the following order:

R
1-9

(1) United Nations and League of Nations, in reverse chronological order by issuing body (General Assembly, then Security Council, then other organs in alphabetical order)

(2) other organizations (alphabetically by name of organization)

(h) Records, briefs, and petitions are cited in that order, and within each classification by order of the court in which filed.

(i) Secondary materials are cited in the following order:

(1) model codes and restatements

(2) books, pamphlets, and shorter works in a collection of a single author's works (alphabetically by last name of author; if none, by first word of title)

(3) works in journals (not magazines or newspapers), including forthcoming works and shorter works in a collection of various authors' works (alphabetically by last name of author)

(4) book reviews not written by students (alphabetically by last name of reviewer)

(5) student-written law review materials including book reviews (alphabetically by last name of author; if none, by first word of title; if none, by periodical as abbreviated in citation)

(6) annotations (in reverse chronological order)

(7) magazine and newspaper articles (alphabetically by last name of author; if none, by first word of title)

(8) unpublished materials not forthcoming (alphabetically by last name of author; if none, by first word of title)

(9) electronic sources (alphabetically by last name of author; if none, by first word of title)

Within each classification, cite materials by the same author in alphabetical order by first word of title.

(j) Cross-references to the author's own textual material in text or footnotes.

1.5   Parenthetical Information

Information may be enclosed in parentheses and added to the basic citation. Parenthetical information is generally recommended when the relevance of a cited authority might not otherwise be clear to the reader (see **rule 1.2**). Explanatory parenthetical phrases begin with a present participle and should not begin with a capital letter:

> *See generally* Akhil Reed Amar, *Reports of My Death Are Greatly Exaggerated: A Reply*, 138 U. PA. L. REV. 1651 (1990) (arguing that the author and the two-tier theory of federal jurisdiction are still viable).

> *But see* Flanagan v. United States, 465 U.S. 259, 264 (1989) (explaining that the final judgment rule reduces the potential for parties to "clog the courts" with a succession of time-consuming appeals).

If, however, the parenthetical information quotes one or more full sentences or a portion of material that reads as a full sentence, it should begin with a capital letter and include appropriate closing punctuation:

> Mari J. Matsuda, *Public Response to Racist Speech: Considering the Victim's Story*, 87 MICH. L. REV. 2320, 2349 (1989) ("We are a legalized culture. If law is where racism is, then law is where we must confront it . . . . [L]et us present a competing ideology . . . .").

> 3 *Consequences of Changing U.S. Population: Hearings Before the House Select Comm. on Population*, 95th Cong. 11 (1978) (statement of Dr. David Birch) ("[T]here are more mayors of Rockville, Md., than there are mayors of Detroit.").

Where a complete participial phrase is unnecessary in context, a shorter parenthetical may be substituted:

> Such standards have been adopted to address a variety of environmental problems. *E.g.*, H.B. Jacobini, *The New International Sanitary Regulations*, 46 AM. J. INT'L L. 727, 727–28 (1952) (health-related water quality); Robert L. Meyer, Travaux Preparatoires *for the UNESCO World Heritage Convention*, 2 EARTH L.J. 45, 45–81 (1976) (conservation of protected areas).

Explanatory parenthetical phrases should precede any citation of subsequent history or other related authority (**rule 1.6**):

> Atl. Richfield Co. v. Fed. Energy Admin., 429 F. Supp. 1052, 1061–62 (N.D. Cal. 1976) ("[N]ot every person aggrieved by administrative action is necessarily entitled to due process."), *aff'd*, 556 F.2d 542 (Temp. Emer. Ct. App. 1977).

See also **rule 10.6** (parenthetical information for cases) and **rule 12.7** (parenthetical information for statutes).

Related Authority   1.6

Related authority or the volume in which a shorter work appears may be appended to a citation with an italicized explanatory phrase. The general format for such italicized explanatory phrases is to locate the specific material cited *"in"* a work *"at"* given pages or sections. Other prepositional phrases may be used as appropriate (e.g., *"available at"* (see **rule 18**), *"microformed on"* (see **rule 18.4**), or *"translated in"* (see **rule 20.1.5**)):

(a) *"In."* When citing a shorter work such as an article, essay, or speech originally published in a volume collecting such works, use *"in"* to introduce the collection as a whole (see **rule 15.5**):

> Kay Deaux & Brenda Major, *A Social-Psychological Model of Gender, in* THEORETICAL PERSPECTIVES ON SEXUAL DIFFERENCE 89, 93 (Deborah L. Rhode ed., 1990).

(b) *"Reprinted in."* A work that conveniently reprints a source originally published elsewhere may be introduced by *"reprinted in."* As far as possible, provide a complete citation for the original work, followed by *"reprinted in"* and the citation of the volume containing the reprint. See **rule 15.5**.

> Louis Loss, *The Conflict of Laws and the Blue Sky Laws*, 71 HARV. L. REV. 209 (1957), *reprinted in* LOUIS LOSS & EDWARD M. COWETT, BLUE SKY LAW 180 (1958).

> Thomas Jefferson, Kentucky Resolutions of 1798 and 1799, *reprinted in* 4 DEBATES ON THE ADOPTION OF THE FEDERAL CONSTITUTION 540 (Jonathan Elliot ed., 2d ed., Philadelphia, J.B. Lippincott 1888).

> S. REP. NO. 95-181, at 14 (1977), *reprinted in* 1977 U.S.C.C.A.N. 3401, 3414.

If the document appears in an appendix, note, or other addendum, see **rule 3.5** for appropriate citation forms.

(c) Relevant history. The prior or subsequent history of a case (**rule 10.7**) or of a statute (**rule 12.6**) may be appended to the main citation. See **rules 10.7** and **12.6** for circumstances in which the subsequent history of a case or statute *must* be indicated.

> Matthews v. Konieczny, 488 A.2d 5 (Pa. Super. Ct. 1985), *rev'd*, 527 A.2d 508 (Pa. 1987).

(d) Commentary. Works that discuss or quote the primary authority may also be appended to the citation without parentheses as related authorities. Use italicized phrases such as *"noted in," "construed in," "quoted in," "reviewed by," "cited with approval in,"* and *"questioned in."* Works that the primary authority discusses, cites, or otherwise mentions, however, should be indicated parenthetically. Thus:

R
1–9

Filled Milk Act § 1, 21 U.S.C. § 61 (1994), *construed in* Milnot
Co. v. Richardson, 350 F. Supp. 221 (S.D. Ill. 1972).

But:

Milnot Co. v. Richardson, 350 F. Supp. 221 (S.D. Ill. 1972)
(construing Filled Milk Act § 1, 21 U.S.C. § 61 (1994)).

Alexander Morgan Capron, *Tort Liability in Genetic Counseling*,
79 COLUM. L. REV. 618, 643 (1979) ("[I]n Judge Cardozo's classic
statement, 'The risk reasonably to be perceived defines the duty to
be obeyed'. . . ." (quoting Palsgraf v. Long Island R.R., 162 N.E.
99, 100 (N.Y. 1928))).

S. REP. No. 95-181, at 14 (1977) (citing Bituminous Coal
Operators' Ass'n v. Sec'y of the Interior, 547 F.2d 240 (4th Cir.
1977)), *reprinted in* 1977 U.S.C.C.A.N. 3401, 3414.

2   Typefaces for Law Reviews

Except as otherwise noted, the citation forms in this book are
designed for use in all types of legal writing. The typefaces in which
the forms are printed, however—except for those found in the practitioners' notes—correspond to the typeface conventions used in law
review footnotes. The typeface conventions for law review text (both
main text and footnote text) are less complex than those used in law
review citations and are explained in **rule 2.2**. **Rule 2.1** sets forth the
typeface conventions for citations in law reviews. For an explanation of
the typeface conventions commonly used in court documents and

P.1   legal memoranda, see **practitioners' note P.1**. The practitioner can
make ready use of the examples in the *Bluebook* by substituting the

P.1   typeface conventions outlined in **practitioners' note P.1** for those
found in the examples throughout the remainder of the book. Large
and small capitals do not appear in court documents and legal memoranda.

2.1   Typeface Conventions for Citations

Most law reviews use three different typefaces in citations:

Ordinary Roman, *Italics*, and LARGE AND SMALL CAPITALS

Some replace large and small capitals with ordinary roman type.
Thus:

Colin S. Diver, *The Optimal Precision of Administrative Rules*, 93
YALE L.J. 65 (1983).

becomes:

Colin S. Diver, *The Optimal Precision of Administrative Rules*, 93
Yale L.J. 65 (1983).

Other law reviews replace some italics, as well as all large and small capitals, with ordinary roman type:

Colin S. Diver, The Optimal Precision of Administrative Rules, 93 Yale L.J. 65 (1983).

The examples in this book follow the first convention, using all three typefaces. The following list explains the more important typeface conventions used in law review citations:

(a) Case names (rules 10.2, 14.3.1, 18.1.1, 18.2.2, 20.3, 21.5, and 21.6). Use ordinary roman type for case names in full citations, except for any procedural phrases, which are italicized:

State *ex rel.* Scott v. Zinn, 392 P.2d 417 (N.M. 1964).

When a case name appears within an article title in a citation, do not italicize it:

Thomas J. Madden & Nicholas W. Allard, *Bedtime for* Bivens*: Substituting the United States as Defendant in Constitutional Tort Suits*, 20 HARV. J. ON LEGIS. 470 (1983).

(b) Books (rule 15). Use large and small capitals for both author and title:

RICHARD KLUGER, SIMPLE JUSTICE (1976).

(c) Periodicals (rule 16). Italicize article titles and use large and small capitals for the name of the periodical. The author's name appears in roman type:

Katherine K. Baker, *Once a Rapist? Motivational Evidence and Relevancy in Rape Law*, 110 HARV. L. REV. 568 (1997).

(d) Introductory signals (rule 1.2). Italicize all introductory signals, including "*e.g.,*" when they appear within citation sentences or clauses:

See, e.g., Parker Drilling Co. v. Ferguson, 391 F.2d 581 (5th Cir. 1968).

Do not, however, italicize a signal word when it serves as the verb of an ordinary sentence:

For an analysis of risk allocation rules under the UCC, see Roger S. Goldman, Note, *Risk of Loss in Commercial Transactions: Efficiency Thrown into the Breach*, 65 VA. L. REV. 557, 563–72 (1979).

(e) Explanatory phrases (rules 1.6, 10.7, 12.6 and 18). Italicize all explanatory phrases:

Oreck Corp. v. Whirlpool Corp., 579 F.2d 126, 131 (2d Cir.), *cert. denied*, 439 U.S. 946 (1978).

(f) Punctuation. Italicize commas, semicolons, etc., only when they fall within italicized material, and not when they merely follow it:

> *See, e.g., id.*; Sabine Towing & Transp. Co. v. Zapata Upland Drilling, Inc., 553 F.2d 489 (5th Cir.), *cert. denied*, 434 U.S. 855 (1977).

2.2   Typeface Conventions for Textual Material

(a) Main text. The main text of law review pieces contains no citations. Only ordinary roman type and italics are used in the main text. Most material appears in ordinary roman type. Only the following are italicized:

(i) Case names. Italicize case names, including the *"v."* and all procedural phrases such as *"In re"* and *"ex rel."*:

> *Missouri ex rel. Gaines v. Canada*

(ii) Titles of publications, speeches, or articles. Thus:

> The library has a copy of *The Path of the Law*, which was published in the *Harvard Law Review*, a complete set of the *Federal Supplement*, and today's *Wall Street Journal*. It does not have a copy of *Hearings on S. 776* or *Alaska Statutes*.

(iii) Style. Italicize words for emphasis or other stylistic purposes (**rule 7**) and words that are emphasized in quoted matter (**rule 5.2**).

(b) Footnote text. Unlike the main text, a sentence in footnote text may include citations, which are contained in citation clauses embedded in the sentence (**rule 1.1(a)**).

(i) Case names. When a case name is grammatically part of the sentence in which it appears, it should be italicized:

> In *Loving v. Virginia*, the Court invalidated Virginia's miscegenation statute.

> In *Loving v. Virginia*, 388 U.S. 1 (1967), the Court invalidated Virginia's miscegenation statute.

When the case name is not grammatically part of the sentence, but rather used in a citation clause embedded in the footnote text, use the typeface conventions for citations (**rule 2.1(a)**):

> The Court has upheld race-specific statutes that disadvantage a racial minority, *e.g.*, Korematsu v. United States, 323 U.S. 214 (1944), but those decisions have been severely criticized.

> Justice Harlan quipped that "one man's vulgarity is another's lyric," Cohen v. California, 403 U.S. 15, 25 (1971), but failed to give further explanation.

(ii) All other authorities. When referring to any other type of authority, whether or not the reference is grammatically part of the sentence, use the typeface conventions for citations if the full citation or a citation shortened according to **rule 4** is given:

> A different view is expressed in LEARNED HAND, THE BILL OF RIGHTS (1958), and HOLMES, *supra* note 2.

If the reference appears without the full or shortened citation information, follow the typeface conventions for the main text of law reviews (**rule 2.2(a)(ii)**):

> Judge Hand explained his philosophy of judicial review in *The Bill of Rights.*

(c) Punctuation. Italicize commas, semicolons, etc., only when they fall within italicized material, and not when they merely follow it:

> When it decided *Sabine Towing*, the Fifth Circuit presented a somewhat different rationale for its holding.

Subdivisions 3

Abbreviations 3.1

Most subdivisions (such as columns or sections) in citations are abbreviated. See **table T.17** for a list of subdivision abbreviations. T.17

Volumes, Parts, and Supplements 3.2

A single work often appears in separately paginated (or sectioned or paragraphed) volumes, parts, or supplements. A citation to material that appears in one such volume, part, or supplement must identify the separately paginated subdivision in which the material appears.

(a) Volumes. When the volumes are numbered, cite the volume number in Arabic numerals. If the author of the entire volume is cited, the volume number precedes the author's name:

> 2 FREDERICK POLLOCK & FREDERIC WILLIAM MAITLAND, THE HISTORY OF ENGLISH LAW 205–06 (2d ed. 1911).

> 2 SUBCOMM. ON LABOR OF THE SENATE COMM. ON LABOR AND PUBLIC WELFARE, 92D CONG., LEGISLATIVE HISTORY OF THE EQUAL EMPLOYMENT OPPORTUNITY ACT OF 1972, at 1007 (1972).

Otherwise, the volume number precedes the volume's title:

> Donald H. Zeigler, *Young Adults as a Cognizable Group in Jury Selection*, 76 MICH. L. REV. 1045, 1047 (1978).

> Standard Oil Co. v. FTC, 1979-2 Trade Cas. (CCH) ¶ 62,776 (N.D. Ind. 1979).

If no volume number is given but the volume is readily identifiable by year, use the year of the volume instead:

> Thomas R. McCoy & Barry Friedman, *Conditional Spending: Federalism's Trojan Horse*, 1988 SUP. CT. REV. 85, 88.

> Donald A. Dripps, *Delegation and Due Process*, 1988 DUKE L.J. 657.

If the volume designation includes words, use brackets to avoid confusion:

> [1977–1978 Transfer Binder] Bankr. L. Rep. (CCH) ¶ 66,472

If volumes are numbered in a new series each year, give both the year and volume number, bracketing the year and placing it before the volume number to avoid confusion:

> [1943] 2 K.B. 154

(b) Separately paginated numbered parts. When works are divided into separately paginated (or sectioned or paragraphed) series, books, chapters, or other parts, include the relevant subdivisions in the citation:

> 26 CONG. REC. app. at 156 (1894) (statement of Rep. Hicks).

> ser. 14, pt. 2, at 150

> pt. 3, § 4, at 15

(c) Supplements. When citing a separately paginated, sectioned, or paragraphed supplement, identify the supplement and its date in parentheses:

> HAW. REV. STAT. § 296-46.1 (Supp. 1984).

> GEORGE GLEASON BOGERT, THE LAW OF TRUSTS AND TRUSTEES § 496 (rev. 2d ed. Supp. 1985).

To cite both the main volume and the supplement, use the form:

> 42 U.S.C. § 1397b (1982 & Supp. I 1983).

3.3   Pages, Footnotes, Endnotes, and Graphical Materials

(a) Pages. Give the page number or numbers before the date parenthetical, without any introductory abbreviation ("p." and "pp." are used only in internal cross-references (**rule 3.6**)):

> ARTHUR E. SUTHERLAND, CONSTITUTIONALISM IN AMERICA 45 (1965).

> H.R. REP. NO. 82-353, at 4–5 (1951).

Use "at" if the page number may be confused with another part of the citation; use a comma to set off "at" from preceding numerals:

> BIOGRAPHICAL DIRECTORY OF THE GOVERNORS OF THE UNITED STATES 1978–1983, at 257 (Robert Sobel & John W. Raimo eds., 1983).

> Thomas I. Emerson, *Foreword* to CATHARINE A. MACKINNON, SEXUAL HARASSMENT OF WORKING WOMEN, at vii, ix (1979).

If an article, case, or other source within a larger document is not separately paginated, cite the page on which the item begins:

> Bernard L. Diamond, *The Psychiatric Prediction of Dangerousness*, 123 U. PA. L. REV. 439 (1974).

> United States v. Bruno, 144 F. Supp. 593 (N.D. Ill. 1955).

> Government Employees Training Act, Pub. L. No. 85-507, 72 Stat. 507 (1958).

When referring to specific material within such a source, include both the page on which the source begins and the page on which the specific material appears, separated by a comma:

> Matthew Roskoski, Note, *A Case-by-Case Approach to Pleading Scienter Under the Private Securities Litigation Reform Act of 1995*, 97 MICH. L. REV. 2265, 2271–75 (1999).

> CATHARINE A. MACKINNON, *On Exceptionality: Women as Women in Law, in* FEMINISM UNMODIFIED 70, 76–77 (1987).

When referring specifically to the first page of a source, repeat the page number:

> Christina M. Fernández, Note, *Beyond* Marvin: *A Proposal for Quasi-Spousal Support*, 30 STAN. L. REV. 359, 359 (1978).

When citing material within a concurring or dissenting opinion, give only the initial page of the case and the page on which the specific material appears, not the initial page of the concurring or dissenting opinion:

> Baker v. Carr, 369 U.S. 186, 297 (1962) (Frankfurter, J., dissenting).

(b) Footnotes. To cite a footnote, give the page on which the footnote appears, "n.," and the footnote number, with no space between "n." and the number:

> Akhil Reed Amar, *The Two-Tiered Structure of the Judiciary Act of 1789*, 138 U. PA. L. REV. 1499, 1525 n.80 (1990).

To cite all of a footnote that spans more than one page, cite only the page on which the footnote begins, "n.," and the footnote number:

> Akhil Reed Amar, *The Two-Tiered Structure of the Judiciary Act of 1789*, 138 U. PA. L. REV. 1499, 1560 n.222 (1990).

R
1–9

When referring only to specific pages of a footnote that spans more than one page, cite only the specific pages, rather than the page on which the footnote begins:

> Akhil Reed Amar, *The Two-Tiered Structure of the Judiciary Act of 1789*, 138 U. PA. L. REV. 1499, 1561–62 n.222 (1990).

(c) Endnotes. To cite an endnote, give the page on which the endnote appears (not the page on which the call number appears), "n.," and the endnote number, with no space between "n." and the number:

> JOHN HART ELY, DEMOCRACY AND DISTRUST 215 n.85 (1980).

(d) Multiple pages, footnotes, and endnotes. When citing material that spans more than one page, give the inclusive page numbers, separated by a hyphen or dash. Always retain the last two digits, but drop other repetitious digits:

> Edward L. Rubin, Note, *Fairness, Flexibility, and the Waiver of Remedial Rights by Contract*, 87 YALE L.J. 1057, 1065–69 (1978).

If a hyphen or dash would be ambiguous because of the page numbering system, use the word "to":

> BORIS I. BITTKER & JAMES S. EUSTICE, FEDERAL INCOME TAXATION OF CORPORATIONS AND SHAREHOLDERS ¶ 5.06, at 5-31 to 5-32 (5th abr. ed. 1987).

Cite nonconsecutive pages by giving the individual page numbers separated by commas:

> Kleppe v. New Mexico, 426 U.S. 529, 531, 546 (1976).

When a point is often repeated throughout the entire source, use "*passim*":

> Mandel Corp., 47 B.T.A. 68 *passim* (1942).

Cite multiple footnotes and endnotes by using "nn.":

> 141 nn.180–86

Treat nonconsecutive footnotes and endnotes like nonconsecutive pages, but (except for internal cross-references) substitute an ampersand for the last comma:

> 291 nn.14 & 18, 316 nn.4, 6 & 8–9

To refer to a page in text as well as a footnote that begins on that page, use an ampersand between the page and the note number:

> Irene Merker Rosenberg, Winship *Redux: 1970 to 1990*, 69 TEX. L. REV. 109, 123 & n.90 (1990).

To refer to a page in text as well as an endnote whose call appears on that page, use an ampersand between the text page and the page on which the endnote appears. In the following example, the cited text is on p. 61 and the endnote is on p. 215:

JOHN HART ELY, DEMOCRACY AND DISTRUST 61 & 215 n.85 (1980).

(e) Graphical materials. When citing tables, figures, charts, graphs, or other graphical materials, give the page number on which the graphical material appears and the designation, if any, provided in the source. Use the abbreviations in **table T.17**:

T.17

Kevin M. Clermont & Theodore Eisenberg, *Xenophilia in American Courts*, 109 HARV. L. REV. 1120, 1131 tbl.2 (1996).

Jennifer Gerarda Brown & Ian Ayres, *Economic Rationales for Mediation*, 80 VA. L. REV. 323, 397 fig.6 (1994).

Sections and Paragraphs 3.4

If an authority is organized by section (§) or paragraph (¶), cite these. In addition, a page number may be provided if useful in locating specific matter within the section or paragraph:

15 U.S.C. § 18 (1982).

6 JAMES WM. MOORE ET AL., MOORE'S FEDERAL PRACTICE ¶ 56.07 (3d ed. 1997).

LAURENCE H. TRIBE, AMERICAN CONSTITUTIONAL LAW § 15-4, at 1314, § 15-6, at 1320 (2d ed. 1988).

If an authority is organized in part by indented paragraphs not introduced by paragraph symbols (¶), cite such paragraphs with the written abbreviation (para.), not the symbol:

THE DECLARATION OF INDEPENDENCE para. 2 (U.S. 1776).

Do not cite indented paragraphs if the authority is ordinarily cited by page:

Mandela Trial Scheduled Today, USA TODAY, Feb. 4, 1991, at A4.

Do not use "at" before a section or paragraph symbol:

Id. § 7.

MOORE ET AL., *supra* note 5, ¶ 56.07.

Not: *Id.* at § 7.

Not: MOORE ET AL., *supra* note 5, at ¶ 56.07.

Rule 6.2(c) discusses the use of section and paragraph symbols.

To cite session laws amending prior acts that are divided into sections within sections, see **rule 12.4(c)**.

(a) Subsections. Use the original punctuation separating sections from subsections unless the source contains no such separating punctuation, in which case place the subsection designation in parentheses. Thus, place "1." and "a)" in parentheses ("(1)" and "(a)"), but not ".01" or "-32":

> N.M. STAT. ANN. § 4-44-7(G) (Michie 1983).

> **Not:** N.M. STAT. ANN. § 4(44)(7)(G) (Michie 1983).

(b) Multiple sections and subsections. When citing consecutive sections or subsections, give inclusive numbers; do not use "*et seq.*" Identical digits or letters preceding a punctuation mark may be omitted, unless doing so would create confusion. Otherwise retain all digits.

> WASH. REV. CODE ANN. §§ 18.51.005–.52.900 (West 1989 & Supp. 1991).

> DEL. CODE ANN. tit. 9, §§ 817–819 (1989).

> **Not:** DEL. CODE ANN. tit. 9, §§ 817–19 (1989).

Note that letters are sometimes used to designate sections, rather than subsections, and that section designations may contain punctuation within them:

> 42 U.S.C. §§ 1396a–1396d (1994).

If a hyphen or dash would be ambiguous, use the word "to":

> 42 U.S.C. §§ 1973aa-2 to -4 (1994).

> MONT. CODE ANN. §§ 75-1-301 to -324 (1989).

When citing scattered sections, separate the sections with commas:

> N.J. STAT. ANN. §§ 18A:54-1, -3, -6 (West 1989).

Repeat digits if necessary to avoid confusion:

> N.J. STAT. ANN. §§ 18A:58-17, :58-25, :64A-22.1, :64A-22.6 (West 1989).

When citing multiple subsections within a single section, use only one section symbol:

> 28 U.S.C. § 105(a)(3)–(b)(1) (1994).

> 19 U.S.C. § 1485(a)(1)–(3) (1994).

> DEL. CODE ANN. tit. 9, § 6919(a)–(c) (1989).

> DEL. CODE ANN. tit. 9, § 6910(a), (c) (1989).

When citing multiple subsections within *different* sections, use two section symbols:

> 19 U.S.C. §§ 1485(a), 1486(b) (1994).

(c) Multiple paragraphs. Multiple paragraphs should be treated like multiple sections, following **rule 3.4(b)**:

> 1 Blue Sky L. Rep. (CCH) ¶¶ 4471–4474.
>
> MOORE ET AL., *supra* note 5, ¶¶ 54.32–.35.

Appended Material 3.5

Indicate an appendix or appended note or comment by placing the appropriate abbreviation (see **table T.17**) after the citation to the largest full subdivision to which the item is appended, whether page, section, paragraph, chapter, title, or volume:

T.17

> James Edwin Kee & Terrence A. Moan, *The Property Tax and Tenant Equality*, 89 HARV. L. REV. 531 app. (1976).
>
> RESTATEMENT (SECOND) OF TORTS § 623A cmt. a (1977).

Cite a particular page, section, or other subdivision in an appendix as follows:

> 50 U.S.C. app. § 454 (1988).
>
> Samuel Issacharoff & George Loewenstein, *Second Thoughts About Summary Judgment*, 100 YALE L.J. 73 app. at 124–25 (1990).

Other types of appended material that serve as commentary on the material to which they are appended, or that further discuss a point related to the textual discussion, should be cited as notes or appendices:

> FED. R. EVID. 702 advisory committee's note.
>
> RESTATEMENT (SECOND) OF PROPERTY § 2.1 cmt. c, illus. 2 (1977).

Further information necessary to identify which of several named notes is cited may be added parenthetically:

> 42 U.S.C. § 1862 note (1988) (Denial of Financial Assistance to Campus Disrupters).
>
> N.Y. BUS. CORP. LAW § 624 note (McKinney 1963) (Legislative Studies and Reports).

Appendices that reprint materials normally cited to another source should be cited according to **rule 1.6(b)**.

> An Act for the Prevention of Frauds and Perjuries, 29 Car. 2, c. 2, § 17 (1677) (Eng.), *reprinted in* JOHN P. DAWSON, WILLIAM BURNETT HARVEY & STANLEY D. HENDERSON, CASES AND COMMENTS ON CONTRACTS app. 1, at 942 (5th ed. 1988).

Internal Cross-References 3.6

Portions of text, footnotes, and groups of authorities within the piece in which the citation is made may be cited through the use of "*supra*" or *"infra."* "Note" and "part" are used to refer to footnotes and other parts within the same piece, respectively; "p." and "pp." are used to indicate other pages within the same piece. A variety of forms may be used. For example:

> *See supra* text accompanying notes 305–07.
>
> *See supra* notes 12–15, 92–97 and accompanying text.
>
> *See* cases cited *supra* note 22.
>
> *But see* sources cited *supra* note 24.
>
> *See* discussion *infra* Parts II.B.2, III.C.1.
>
> *See supra* Part IV.A–B.
>
> *See infra* pp. 106–07.
>
> *See infra* p. 50 and note 100.

4   Short Citation Forms

P.4 For additional guidance on the use of short forms in court documents and legal memoranda, see **practitioners' note P.4**. Consult the last section of the individual rules describing particular types of sources (**rules 10–21**) for additional information as to appropriate short forms.

4.1   *"Id."*

"Id." may be used in citation sentences and clauses for any kind of authority except internal cross-references as described in **rule 3.6**. In court documents and legal memoranda, use *"id."* when citing the immediately preceding authority. In law review footnotes, use *"id."* when citing the immediately preceding authority within the same foot-note or within the immediately preceding footnote *when the preceding footnote contains only one authority.* Indicate any particular in which the subsequent citation varies from the former. If the first citation refers to only one shorter work appearing within an authority, do not use *"id."* for a subsequent citation to the entire authority.

The following examples illustrate the use of *"id."* to refer to a variety of commonly cited materials:

> [1] Chalfin v. Specter, 233 A.2d 562 (Pa. 1967).
>
> [2] *Id.* at 563.
>
> [3] 42 U.S.C. § 1983 (1994).
>
> [4] *See id.* § 1981.
>
> [5] U.C.C. § 3-302(2) (1977); *see id.* § 3-303(a).
>
> [6] Dupey v. Dupey, [1977–1978 Transfer Binder] Fed. Sec. L. Rep. (CCH) ¶ 96,048, at 91,701 (5th Cir. May 9, 1977).

[7] *Id.* ¶ 96,052, at 91,705; *see also* U.S. CONST. art. I, § 8, cl. 10 (giving Congress the power to punish "Offenses against the Law of Nations").

[8] FLEMING JAMES, JR. & GEOFFREY C. HAZARD, JR., CIVIL PROCEDURE §§ 1.3–.5 (3d ed. 1985).

[9] *See id.* § 1.7.

[10] 3 WILLIAM HOLDSWORTH, A HISTORY OF ENGLISH LAW 255 (3d ed. 1927).

[11] 1 *id.* at 5–17 (2d ed. 1914).

[12] *See supra* text accompanying note 2.

[13] *See supra* text accompanying note 2.

[14] THOMAS C. SCHELLING, A PROCESS OF RESIDENTIAL SEGREGATION: NEIGHBORHOOD TIPPING 2, *reprinted in* ECONOMIC FOUNDATIONS OF PROPERTY LAW 307, 308 (Bruce A. Ackerman ed., 1975).

[15] *Id.* at 3, *reprinted in* ECONOMIC FOUNDATIONS OF PROPERTY LAW 307, 309 (Bruce A. Ackerman ed., 1975).

[16] JAMES & HAZARD, *supra* note 8, § 1.5.

[17] *See id.*

"Id." may not be used to refer to one authority in a preceding footnote if the preceding footnote cites more than one source:

[18] *See* Chalfin v. Specter, 233 A.2d 562 (Pa. 1967); Robert B. Reich, *Toward a New Consumer Protection*, 128 U. PA. L. REV. 1 (1979); Note, *Direct Loan Financing of Consumer Purchases*, 85 HARV. L. REV. 1409, 1415–17 (1972).

[19] *See Chalfin,* 233 A.2d at 570; CATHARINE A. MACKINNON, *On Exceptionality: Women as Women in Law, in* FEMINISM UNMODIFIED 70, 70 (1987).

Not:

[19] *See id.* at 570; CATHARINE A. MACKINNON, *On Exceptionality: Women as Women in Law, in* FEMINISM UNMODIFIED 70, 70 (1987).

Sources identified in explanatory parentheticals, explanatory phrases, or subsequent history, however, are ignored for the purposes of this rule. Thus, the following examples are **correct**:

[20] Tuten v. United States, 460 U.S. 660, 663 (1983) (quoting Ralston v. Robinson, 454 U.S. 201, 206 (1981)).

[21] *See id.* at 664.

[22] Dillon v. Gloss, 256 U.S. 368, 376 (1921), *quoted in* Nixon v. United States, 506 U.S. 224, 230 (1993).

[23] *See id.* at 374.

[24] Kohler v. Tugwell, 292 F. Supp. 978, 985 (E.D. La. 1968), *aff'd per curiam*, 393 U.S. 531 (1969).

[25] *See id.* at 980.

4.2   *"Supra"* and "Hereinafter"

"Supra" and "hereinafter" may be used to refer to legislative hearings; books; pamphlets; unpublished materials; nonprint resources; periodicals; services; treaties and international agreements; and regulations, directives, and decisions of intergovernmental organizations. *"Supra"* and "hereinafter" should not be used to refer to cases, statutes, constitutions, legislative materials (other than hearings), or regulations, except in extraordinary circumstances, such as when the name of the authority is extremely long:

> [26] *In re* Multidistrict Private Civil Treble Damage Antitrust Litig. Involving Motor Vehicle Air Pollution Control Equip., 52 F.R.D. 398 (C.D. Cal. 1970) [hereinafter *Air Pollution Control Antitrust Case*].

P.4   For an explanation of the use of *"supra"* in court documents and legal memoranda, see **practitioners' note P.4**. Appropriate short forms for cases, statutes, and legislative materials (other than hearings) are provided in the respective rules.

(a) *"Supra."* When an authority has been fully cited previously, the *"supra"* form may be used (unless *"id."* is appropriate). The *"supra"* form consists of the last name of the author of the work (unless the author is an institutional author, in which case the full institutional name should be used), followed by a comma and the word *"supra."* If no author is cited, use the title of the work; for unsigned student-written law review materials, use the appropriate designation (see **rule 16.6.2(b)**). Indicate the footnote in which the full citation can be found, unless the full citation is in the same footnote, in which case *"supra"* should be used without cross-reference. Volume, paragraph, section, or page numbers may be added to refer to specific material:

> [27] 2 HOLDSWORTH, *supra* note 10, at 6.

> [28] JAMES & HAZARD, *supra* note 8, § 7.21; W. PAGE KEETON ET AL., PROSSER AND KEETON ON THE LAW OF TORTS § 1, at 2 (5th ed. 1984).

> [29] Reich, *supra* note 18, at 5; *see also supra* text accompanying note 7.

> [30] KEETON ET AL., *supra* note 28, § 2, at 4; Note, *supra* note 18, at 1416.

> [31] *Cf.* SCHELLING, *supra* note 14, at 3, *reprinted in* ECONOMIC FOUNDATIONS OF PROPERTY LAW 307, 309 (Bruce A. Ackerman ed., 1975).

Note that citation of a second item or work found within a volume of collected materials already cited takes the form:

> [32] CATHARINE A. MACKINNON, *Desire and Power, in* FEMINISM UNMODIFIED, *supra* note 19, at 46, 47.

(b) "Hereinafter." For authority that would be cumbersome to cite with the usual *"supra"* form or for which the regular shortened form may confuse the reader, a special shortened form may be established. After the first citation of the authority, place the word "hereinafter" and the special shortened form in brackets. Thereafter, use the shortened form followed by a comma and the appropriate *"supra"* cross-reference **(rule 4.2(a))**. The shortened form should appear in the same typeface as it appears in the full citation. Thus:

> [33] *Proposed Amendments to the Federal Rules of Criminal Procedure: Hearings Before the Subcomm. on Criminal Justice of the House Comm. on the Judiciary*, 95th Cong. 92–93 (1977) [hereinafter *Hearings*] (testimony of Prof. Wayne LaFave).

> [34] PAUL M. BATOR ET AL., HART AND WECHSLER'S THE FEDERAL COURTS AND THE FEDERAL SYSTEM 330 (3d ed. 1988) [hereinafter HART & WECHSLER].

> [35] *Hearings, supra* note 33, at 33 (testimony of Hon. Edward Becker).

> [36] HART & WECHSLER, *supra* note 34, at 614.

Do not use the "hereinafter" form when a simple *"supra"* form is adequate:

> [37] 3 HOLDSWORTH, *supra* note 10, at 35.

The "hereinafter" form, however, should be used to distinguish two authorities appearing in the same footnote if the simple *"supra"* form would be confusing:

> [38] *See* Edward B. Rock, *The Logic and (Uncertain) Significance of Institutional Shareholder Activism*, 79 GEO. L.J. 445 (1991) [hereinafter Rock, *Shareholder Activism*]; Edward B. Rock, *Saints and Sinners: How Does Delaware Corporate Law Work?*, 44 UCLA L. REV. 1009, 1016–17 (1997) [hereinafter Rock, *Saints and Sinners*].

> [39] *See* Rock, *Saints and Sinners, supra* note 38, at 1019; Rock, *Shareholder Activism, supra* note 38, at 459–63.

Quotations   5

Indentation, Quotation Marks, Citation, and Punctuation   5.1

(a) Quotations of fifty or more words should be indented left and right, without quotation marks. Quotation marks *within* a block quotation should appear as they do in the original:

> [T]his presumptive privilege must be considered in light of
> our historic commitment to the rule of law. This is nowhere
> more profoundly manifest than in our view that "the twofold
> aim [of criminal justice] is that guilt shall not escape or
> innocence suffer." We have elected to employ an adversary
> system of criminal justice in which the parties contest all
> issues before a court of law. . . . The ends of criminal justice
> would be defeated if judgments were to be founded on a par-
> tial or speculative presentation of the facts. The very integri-
> ty of the judicial system and public confidence in the system
> depend on full disclosure of all the facts, within the frame-
> work of the rules of evidence. To ensure that justice is done,
> it is imperative to the function of courts that compulsory
> process be available for the production of evidence needed
> either by the prosecution or by the defense.

United States v. Nixon, 418 U.S. 683, 708–09 (1974) (citation
omitted). The Court then balanced this interest against the evils
of forced disclosure. *Id.* at 710.

In law review footnotes, court documents, and legal memoranda (in
which citations are permitted), the citation should not be indented but
should begin at the left margin on the line immediately following the
quotation, as shown above. In law review text (in which citations are
not permitted), the footnote number should appear after the final
punctuation of the quotation. See **rule 5.4** for rules of indentation to
show paragraph structure.

(b) Quotations of forty-nine or fewer words should be enclosed in
quotation marks but not otherwise set off from the rest of the text.
Quotation marks around material quoted inside another quote should
appear as single marks within the quotation in keeping with the standard convention. The footnote number or citation should follow immediately after the closing quotation mark unless it is more convenient to
place it elsewhere shortly before or after the quotation. Always place
commas and periods inside the quotation marks; place other punctuation marks inside the quotation marks only if they are part of the
matter quoted. When the material quoted would commonly be set off
from the text, such as lines of poetry or dialogue from a play, the
quotation may appear as a block quote per **rule 5.1(a)**, regardless of
its length.

5.2 Alterations

When a letter must be changed from upper to lower case, or vice
versa, enclose it in brackets. Substituted words or letters and other
inserted material should also be bracketed:

"[P]ublic confidence in the [adversary] system depend[s upon] full disclosure of all the facts, within the framework of the rules of evidence."

Indicate the omission of letters from a common root word with empty brackets ("judgment[]"). Significant mistakes in the original should be followed by "[sic]" and otherwise left as they appear in the original:

"This list of statutes are [sic] necessarily incomplete."

Indicate in a parenthetical clause after the citation any change of emphasis or omission of citations or footnote call numbers. Do not indicate the omission of a citation or footnote call number that follows the last word quoted:

> "The fact that individuals define themselves in a significant way through their sexual relationships suggests . . . that much of the richness of a relationship will come from the freedom to *choose* the form and nature of these *intensely personal bonds*." Bowers v. Hardwick, 478 U.S. 186, 205 (1986) (Blackmun, J., dissenting) (second emphasis added).

Do not indicate that emphasis in the quotation appears in the original. Do, however, note parenthetically when the source quoted contains material that has been altered from *its* original:

> The Court of Appeals recognized the city's substantial interest in limiting the sound emanating from the bandshell. The court concluded, however, that the city's sound-amplification guideline was not narrowly tailored to further this interest, because "it has not [been] shown . . . that the requirement of the use of the city's sound system and technician was the *least intrusive means* of regulating the volume."
>
> Ward v. Rock Against Racism, 491 U.S. 781, 797 (1989) (alteration in original) (citations omitted).

Whenever possible, a quotation within a quotation should be attributed to its original source:

> Chief Judge Wright noted that Congress's "*firm resolve* to insure that the CIA's 'power that flows from money and stealth' could not be turned loose in domestic investigations of Americans." Marks v. CIA, 590 F.2d 997, 1008 (D.C. Cir. 1978) (Wright, C.J., concurring in part and dissenting in part) (emphasis added) (quoting Weissman v. CIA, 565 F.2d 692, 695 (D.C. Cir. 1977)).

Omissions   5.3

Omission of a word or words is generally indicated by the insertion of an ellipsis, three periods separated by spaces and set off by a space before the first and after the last period (" . . . "), to take the place of the word or words omitted. These ellipses should *never* be used to begin a quotation; nor should they be used when individual words are merely altered (**rule 5.2**). Do not insert an ellipsis for an omitted footnote or citation; indicate such omission with the parenthetical phrase "(footnote omitted)" or "(citation omitted)" immediately following the citation to the quoted source.

(a) When using quoted language as a phrase or clause (rather than as a full sentence), do not indicate omission of matter before or after a quotation:

> Chief Justice Burger wrote that the availability of compulsory process is "imperative to the function of courts" and that "[t]he very integrity of the judicial system and public confidence in the system depend on full disclosure of all the facts."

Indicate omission of matter within such a phrase or clause thus:

> The Court warned that "judgments . . . founded on a partial or speculative presentation of the facts" would undermine the criminal justice system.

(b) When using quoted language as a full sentence:
(i) Where language *beginning* the original sentence has been deleted, capitalize the first letter and place it in brackets if it is not already capitalized. If the sentence begins the quotation, do not otherwise indicate any omission. Thus:

> "[I]t is imperative to the function of courts that compulsory process be available for the production of evidence needed either by the prosecution or by the defense."

(ii) Use an ellipsis where language *from the middle* of a quoted sentence is omitted:

> "The very integrity of the judicial system . . . depend[s] on full disclosure of all the facts, within the framework of the rules of evidence."

(iii) Omission of language *at the end* of a quoted sentence should be indicated by an ellipsis between the last word quoted and the final punctuation of the sentence quoted:

> "To ensure that justice is done, it is imperative to the function of courts that compulsory process be available . . . ."

(iv) Do not indicate the deletion of matter after the period or other final punctuation that concludes a final quoted sentence. If language *after the end* of a quoted sentence is deleted and the sentence is followed by further quotation, however, retain the punctuation at the end of the sentence and insert an ellipsis before the remainder of the quotation. Thus:

"The ends of criminal justice would be defeated if judgments were to be founded on a partial or speculative presentation of the facts. . . . [T]he judicial system and public confidence in the system depend on full disclosure of all the facts, within the framework of the rules of evidence."

(v) If language both *at the end and after the end* of a quoted sentence is deleted and followed by further quotation, use only one ellipsis to indicate both of the omissions:

"The ends of criminal justice would be defeated . . . . To ensure that justice is done, it is imperative to the function of the courts that compulsory process be available for the production of evidence needed either by the prosecution or by the defense."

R
1–9

Paragraph Structure   5.4

Do not indicate the original paragraph structure of quotations of *forty-nine or fewer words* enclosed in quotation marks according to **rule 5.1(b)**. The paragraph structure of an indented quotation of *fifty or more words* should be indicated by further indenting the first line of each paragraph. Indent the first sentence of the *first* quoted paragraph, however, only if the first word of the quoted passage is also the first word of the original paragraph; if language at the beginning of the first paragraph is omitted, do not indent the first line or use an ellipsis. To indicate omission at the beginning of *subsequent paragraphs*, insert and indent an ellipsis. Indicate the omission of one or more entire paragraphs by inserting and indenting four periods (". . . .") on a new line. Thus, **rules 5.1** and **5.2** might be quoted in part as follows:

> In law review footnotes, court documents, and legal memoranda (in which citations are permitted), the citation should not be indented but should begin at the left margin on the line immediately following the quotation . . . . In law review text (in which citations are not permitted), the footnote number should appear after the final punctuation . . . .
>
> . . . .
>
> . . . Substituted words or letters and other inserted material should also be bracketed.

Abbreviations, Numerals, and Symbols   6

Abbreviations   6.1

Abbreviations not listed in this book should be avoided unless substantial space will be saved and the resulting abbreviation is unambiguous. Tables at the end of this book contain lists of specific abbreviations. Note that in legal writing, the same word may be abbreviated differently for different uses.

(a) Spacing. In general, close up all adjacent single capitals.

    N.W.

    S.D.N.Y.

Do not close up single capitals with longer abbreviations:

    D. Mass.

    S. Ct.

T.14   In abbreviations of periodical names (see **table T.14**), close up all adjacent single capitals except when one or more of the capitals refers to the name of a geographic or institutional entity, in which case set the capital or capitals referring to the entity off from other adjacent single capitals with a space. Thus:

    Yale L.J.

    B.C. L. Rev.

    N.Y.U. L. Rev.

    S. Ill. U. L.J.

Individual numbers, including both numerals and ordinals, are treated as single capitals:

    F.3d

    S.E.2d

    A.L.R.4th

But:

    So. 2d

    Cal. App. 3d

    F. Supp. 2d

Close up initials in personal names:

    W.C. Fields

(b) Periods. Generally, every abbreviation should be followed by a period, except those in which the last letter of the original word is set off from the rest of the abbreviation by an apostrophe. Thus:

    Ave.

    Bldg.

But:

    Ass'n

    Dep't

Some entities with widely recognized initials, e.g.,

CBS, CIA, FCC, FDA, NAACP, NLRB

are commonly referred to in spoken language by their initials rather than by their full names; such abbreviations may be used without periods in text, in case names, and as institutional authors. Do not, however, omit the periods when the abbreviations are used as reporter names, in names of codes, or as names of courts of decision. Thus:

NLRB v. Baptist Hosp., 442 U.S. 773 (1979).

But:

East Belden Corp., 239 N.L.R.B. 776 (1978).

United States may be abbreviated to "U.S." when used as an adjective (do not omit the periods):

U.S. history

But:

history of the United States

In addition to the abbreviation "U.S.," always retain periods in abbreviations not commonly referred to in speech as initials (e.g., N.Y., S.D.).

Numerals and Symbols 6.2

(a) Numerals. In general, spell out the numbers zero to ninety-nine in both text and footnotes; for larger numbers use numerals. This general rule is subject, however, to the following exceptions:

(i) Any number that *begins a sentence* must be spelled out.

(ii) "Hundred," "thousand," and similar *round numbers* may be spelled out, if done so consistently.

(iii) When a *series* includes numbers both less than 100 and greater than or equal to 100, numerals should be used for the entire series:

They burned, respectively, 117, 3, and 15 homes.

(iv) Numerals should be used if the number includes a *decimal point*.

(v) Where material repeatedly refers to *percentages* or *dollar amounts*, numerals should be used for those percentages or amounts.

(vi) Numerals should be used for *section* or *other subdivision* numbers.

In numbers containing five or more digits, use commas to separate groups of three digits. Thus:

1,234,567

H17,326

But:

9876

(b) Ordinals. Unless part of a citation, ordinal numbers appearing in text and footnotes are controlled by **rule 6.2(a)**. If part of a citation, figures are used for all ordinal numbers.

82d Cong.

41st Leg.

4th ed.

(c) Section (§) and paragraph (¶) symbols. The first word of any sentence must be spelled out. In addition, spell out the words "section" and "paragraph" in the text (whether main text or footnote text) of law review pieces and other documents, except when referring to a provision in the U.S. Code (see **rule 12.9**) or a federal regulation (see **rule 14.10**). In citations, the symbols should be used (except when citing session laws amending prior acts as noted in **rule 12.4(c)**). When the symbols are used, there should be a space between "§" or "¶" and the numeral.

(d) Dollar ($) and percent (%) symbols. These symbols should be used wherever numerals are used, and the words should be spelled out wherever numbers are spelled out, but a symbol should never begin a sentence. There should not be a space between "$" or "%" and the numeral.

7   Italicization for Stylistic Purposes

Rules for the use of typefaces generally are discussed in **rule 2**. In addition, in all legal writing:

(a) Style. Italicize words or phrases for emphasis as a matter of style.

(b) Foreign words and phrases. Italicize foreign words or phrases that have not been incorporated into common English usage. There is a strong presumption that Latin words and phrases commonly used in legal writing have been incorporated into common usage and thus should not be italicized. Thus:

maison

aequam servare mentem

But:

gestalt

e.g.

i.e.

quid pro quo

res judicata

Note, however, that *"id."* is always italicized and "e.g." is italicized when used as a signal.

(c) Hypothetical parties or places. Italicize individual letters when used to represent the names of hypothetical parties or places:

A went to bank B in state X.

(d) The letter "l." Italicize the letter "l" when used as a subdivision:

§ 23*(l)*

(e) Equations. Italicize mathematical and other types of equations:

$E = mc^2$

$a > 2b$

R
1–9

Capitalization   8

In headings and titles, capitalize the initial word, the word immediately following a colon (if any), and all other words except articles, conjunctions of four or fewer letters, and prepositions of four or fewer letters.

The following listing indicates capitalization for words commonly used in legal writing. For other words, use the table of capitalizations found in the *Government Printing Office Style Manual*. Practitioners should also refer to **practitioners' note P.6** for further advice on capitalization.

P.6

Capitalize nouns referring to people or groups only when they identify specific persons, officials, groups, government offices, or government bodies:

the Social Security Administrator

the Administrator

the FDA

the Agency

Congress

the President

But:

the congressional hearings

the presidential veto

Capitalize:

Act	Only when referring to a specific act:
	The National Labor Relations Act
	the Act

Circuit	Only when used with a circuit number: the Fifth Circuit
Code	Only when referring to a specific code: the 1939 and 1954 Codes
Court **P.6**	Only when naming any court in full or when referring to the United States Supreme Court (with some exceptions for court documents and legal memoranda, see **practitioners' note P.6**): the California Supreme Court the supreme court (referring to a state supreme court) the Court (referring to the U.S. Supreme Court) the court of appeals the Court of Appeals for the Fifth Circuit
Commonwealth	Only if it is part of the full title of a state, if the word it modifies is capitalized, or when referring to a state as a governmental actor or party to litigation: the Commonwealth of Massachusetts the Commonwealth Commissioner the Commonwealth relitigated the issue
Constitution	Only when naming any constitution in full or when referring to the U.S. Constitution. Also, capitalize parts of the U.S. Constitution when referring to them in textual sentences, but not in citations: Fifth Amendment Preamble Supremacy Clause Bill of Rights Article I, Section 8, Clause 17 of the Constitution But: *see* U.S. CONST. art. I, § 8, cl. 17.
Federal	Only when the word it modifies is capitalized: the Federal Reserve federal spending
Judge, Justice	Only when giving the name of a specific judge or justice or when referring to a Justice of the United States Supreme Court: Judge Cedarbaum Justice Holmes the Justice (referring to a Justice of the United States Supreme Court)

State

Only if it is part of the full title of a state, if the word it modifies is capitalized, or when referring to a state as a governmental actor or party to litigation:

the State of Kansas

the State Commissioner

the State relitigated the issue

Term

Only when referring to a Term of the United States Supreme Court:

1978 Term

this Term

But:

Michaelmas term

References to Judges, Officials, and Terms of Court   9

Justices are referred to as "Justice Blank" and "Chief Justice Blank" or "the Chief Justice." Judges are referred to as "Judge Blank" and "Chief Judge Blank." Parenthetical references are to "Blank, J.," "Blank, C.J.," and "Blank & Space, JJ." Titles of judges and officials may be abbreviated as indicated in **table T.12**.

T.12

As a matter of etiquette, lists of judges should be in the order indicated at the beginning of each volume of the official reporter for the court. Justices of the United States Supreme Court are always listed with the Chief Justice first, and then in order of seniority.

A term of court currently in progress may be referred to as "this term." The immediately preceding term, no longer in progress at time of publication, should be referred to as "last term." Any term may be indicated by year:

the 1999 term

Capitalize "term" only when referring to a Term of the United States Supreme Court. See **rule 8**.

Cases

Rule 10: Cases   55
   10.1: Basic Citation Forms   55
   10.2: Case Names   56
   10.3: Reporters and Other Sources   62
   10.4: Court and Jurisdiction   64
   10.5: Date or Year   66
   10.6: Parenthetical Information Regarding Cases   67
   10.7: Prior and Subsequent History   68
   10.8: Special Citation Forms   70
   10.9: Short Forms for Cases   71

R
10

Cases   10

Citation of a U.S. Supreme Court case:

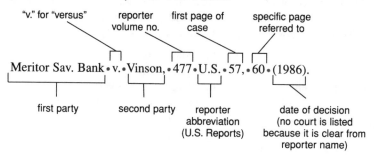

Citation of a case decided by the U.S. Court of Appeals for the Fourth Circuit, later reversed by the U.S. Supreme Court, with parenthetical information about the Fourth Circuit decision:

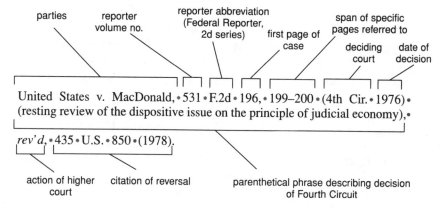

Short form for the above case after it has been cited in full:

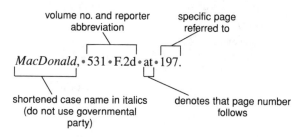

Basic Citation Forms   10.1

A full case citation includes the name of the case (**rule 10.2**); the published sources in which it may be found, if any (**rule 10.3**); a parenthetical that indicates the court and jurisdiction (**rule 10.4**) and the year or date of decision (**rule 10.5**); and the subsequent history of the case, if any (**rule 10.7**). It may also include additional parenthetical information (**rule 10.6**) and the prior history of the case (**rule 10.7**). Special citation forms for pending and unreported cases (**rule 10.8.1**) and for briefs, records, motions, and memoranda (**rule 10.8.3**) are discussed in **rule 10.8**. **Rule 14.3** provides citation forms for administrative adjudications and arbitrations.

filed but not decided	Charlesworth v. Mack, No. 90-345 (D. Mass. filed Sept. 18, 1990).
unpublished interim order	Charlesworth v. Mack, No. 90-345 (D. Mass. Oct. 25, 1990) (order granting preliminary injunction).
published interim order	Charlesworth v. Mack, 725 F. Supp. 1395 (D. Mass. 1990) (order granting preliminary injunction).
unpublished decision	Charlesworth v. Mack, No. 90-345, slip op. at 6 (D. Mass. Dec. 4, 1990).
decision published in service only	Charlesworth v. Mack, 1990 Fed. Sec. L. Rep. (CCH) ¶ 102,342 (D. Mass. Dec. 4, 1990).
decision published in newspaper only	Charlesworth v. Mack, N.Y. L.J., Dec. 5, 1990, at 1 (D. Mass. Dec. 4, 1990).
decision available in electronic database	Charlesworth v. Mack, No. 90-345, 1990 U.S. Dist. LEXIS 20837, at *6 (D. Mass. Dec. 4, 1990).
published decision	Charlesworth v. Mack, 727 F. Supp. 1407, 1412 (D. Mass. 1990).
appeal docketed	Charlesworth v. Mack, 727 F. Supp. 1407 (D. Mass. 1990), *appeal docketed*, No. 90-567 (1st Cir. Dec. 20, 1990).
brief, record, or appendix	Brief for Appellant at 7, Charlesworth v. Mack, 925 F.2d 314 (1st Cir. 1991) (No. 90-567).
disposition on appeal	Charlesworth v. Mack, 925 F.2d 314, 335 (1st Cir. 1991).
disposition in lower court showing subsequent history	Charlesworth v. Mack, 727 F. Supp. 1407, 1412 (D. Mass. 1990), *aff'd*, 925 F.2d 314 (1st Cir. 1991).
petition for certiorari filed	Charlesworth v. Mack, 925 F.2d 314 (1st Cir. 1991), *petition for cert. filed*, 60 U.S.L.W. 3422 (U.S. Jan. 14, 1992) (No. 92-212).
petition for certiorari granted	Charlesworth v. Mack, 925 F.2d 314 (1st Cir. 1991), *cert. granted*, 60 U.S.L.W. 3562 (U.S. Jan. 21, 1992) (No. 92-212).
disposition in Supreme Court published only in service	Charlesworth v. Mack, 60 U.S.L.W. 4420, 4421 (U.S. Feb. 4, 1992), *vacating as moot* 925 F.2d 314 (1st Cir. 1991).

10.2   Case Names

When a case name is used as part of a textual sentence, whether in the main text or in footnotes, it should conform to **rule 10.2.1**. When it appears as part of a citation, it should be further abbreviated according to **rule 10.2.2.** Thus:

> In *Southern Pacific Co. v. Jensen*, 244 U.S. 205 (1917), Justice McReynolds stressed the value of uniform laws.
>
> *Southern Pacific* also indicates the breadth of federal lawmaking power under the admiralty jurisdiction.

But:

> *See, e.g.*, S. Pac. Co. v. Jensen, 244 U.S. 205, 225–26 (1917) (Pitney, J., dissenting).

Note that the examples throughout **rule 10.2** employ the typeface conventions for law review citations. For an explanation of typeface conventions, see **rule 2.** For typeface conventions in court documents and legal memoranda, see **practitioners' note P.1.**   P.1

R
10

Case Names in Textual Sentences   10.2.1

In textual sentences, use the case name that appears at the beginning of the opinion in the cited reporter as modified by the paragraphs below. If no name appears in the cited reporter, use a popular name or cite as:

> Judgment of [full date]

To facilitate index location, always retain in full the first word in each party's name (including a relator) except as provided below. In extremely long case names, omit words not necessary for identification; the running head (at the top of each page of the case) may serve as a guide. In all case names, make the following modifications:

(a) Actions and parties cited. If the case is a consolidation of two or more actions, cite only the first listed:

> Shelley v. Kraemer
>
> **Not:** Shelley v. Kraemer, McGhee v. Sipes

Omit all parties other than the first listed on each side, but do not omit the first-listed relator or any portion of a partnership name:

> Fry v. Mayor of Sierra Vista
>
> **Not:** Fry v. Mayor & City Council of Sierra Vista

But:

> Massachusetts *ex rel.* Alison v. Pauly
>
> Eisen v. Spradlin, Lincoln & Amorosi

Omit words indicating multiple parties, such as "et al." Also omit alternative names given for the first-listed party on either side:

> Cheng v. Seinfeld
>
> **Not:** Cheng et al. v. Seinfeld d/b/a The Man, Inc.

Similarly, for in rem jurisdiction cases, omit all but the first-listed item or group of items:

> *In re* Three Pink Cadillacs
>
> **Not:** *In re* Three Pink Cadillacs, Two Turtle Doves, and a Partridge in a Pear Tree

Where real property is a party, use its common street address, if available:

> United States v. 6109 Grubb Road, 890 F.2d 659, 660 (3d Cir. 1989).
>
> **Not:** United States v. Real Property known as 6109 Grubb Road, Millcreek Township, Erie County, Pennsylvania, 890 F.2d 659, 660 (3d Cir. 1989).

Phrases or party names that would aid in identification of the case may be appended in parentheses after the formal case name:

> ILGWU v. NLRB (Bernhard-Altmann Texas Corp.)

In bankruptcy and similar cases, the case name might contain both an adversary and a nonadversary name. If both appear at the beginning of the opinion, cite the adversary name first, followed by the nonadversary name in parentheses. Include either a procedural phrase such as "*In re*" or "*ex rel.*" before the nonadversary name, followed by a descriptive or introductory phrase such as "estate of" or "interest of," if any. If only an adversary name or only a nonadversary name appears at the beginning of the opinion, cite the name supplied:

> Wallingford's, Inc. v. Waning (*In re* Waning), 120 B.R. 607, 611 (Bankr. D. Me. 1990).
>
> *In re* Drexel Burnham Lambert Group, Inc., 120 B.R. 724 (Bankr. S.D.N.Y. 1990).
>
> *In re* Estate of Benson, No. C7-95-2185, 1996 WL 118367 (Minn. Ct. App. Mar. 19, 1996).

(b) Procedural phrases. Abbreviate "on the relation of," "for the use of," "on behalf of," and similar expressions to "*ex rel.*" Abbreviate "in the matter of," "petition of," "application of," and similar expressions to "*In re.*" Omit all procedural phrases except the first. When adversary parties are named, omit all procedural phrases except "*ex rel.*":

> Gorman v. Bruh
>
> **Not:** *In re* Gorman v. Bruh

But:

> Massachusetts *ex rel.* Kennedy v. Armbruster
>
> *Ex parte* Young

Include any introductory or descriptive phrases such as "Accounting of," "Estate of," and "Will of." Thus:

> *In re* Will of Holt
>
> Estate of Haas v. Commissioner

Procedural phrases should always be italicized, regardless of whether the rest of the case name is italicized. Thus, in law review text:

> *Ex parte Young*

(c) Abbreviations. In textual sentences, whether in main text or in footnote text, abbreviate only widely known acronyms under **rule 6.1(b)** and these eight words: "&," "Ass'n," "Bros.," "Co.," "Corp.," "Inc.," "Ltd.," and "No." If one of these eight begins a party's name, however, do not abbreviate it.

> Philadelphia Electric Co. v. Hirsch
>
> **Not:** PECO v. Hirsch

But:

> NAACP v. Kaminski

In citations, further abbreviate case names, including the first words, according to **rule 10.2.2**.

> In *Penn Central Transportation Co. v. New York City*, 366 N.E.2d 1271 (N.Y. 1977), the court could have granted Penn Central a property interest.
>
> **Not:** In *Penn Cent. Transp. Co. v. New York City*, 366 N.E.2d 1271 (N.Y. 1977), the court could have granted Penn Central a property interest.

But in citations:

> *See, e.g.*, Penn Cent. Transp. Co. v. New York City, 366 N.E.2d 1271 (N.Y. 1977).

(d) "The." Omit "The" as the first word of a party's name, except as part of the name of the object of an in rem action or in cases in which "The King" or "The Queen" is a party. Thus:

> Miami Herald v. Sercus

But:

> Czervik v. The Flying Wasp
>
> The King v. Broadrup

Do not omit "The" in an established popular name, except when referring to the case textually. Thus:

> Neither of the *Civil Rights Cases* opinions was correct.
>
> **Not:** Neither of *The Civil Rights Cases* opinions was correct.

But:

> *See* The Civil Rights Cases, 109 U.S. 3 (1883).

(e) Descriptive terms. Omit terms such as "administrator," "appellee," "executor," "licensee," and "trustee" that describe a party already named:

> Burns v. McMillen
>
> **Not:** Burns v. McMillen, Administrator

But:

> Trustees of Dartmouth College v. Garodnick

(f) Geographical terms. Omit "State of," "Commonwealth of," and "People of," except when citing decisions of the courts of that state, in which case only "State," "Commonwealth," or "People" should be retained:

> Commonwealth v. Ferrone, 448 A.2d 637 (Pa. Super. Ct. 1982).
>
> **Not:** Commonwealth of Pennsylvania v. Ferrone, 448 A.2d 637 (Pa. Super. Ct. 1982).

But:

> Blystone v. Pennsylvania, 494 U.S. 299 (1990).

Omit "City of" and like expressions unless the expression begins a party name:

> Mayor of New York v. Clinton
>
> **Not:** Mayor of the City of New York v. Clinton

But:

> Butts v. City of Boston

Omit all prepositional phrases of location not following "City," or like expressions, unless the omission would leave only one word in the name of a party or the location is part of the name of a business:

> Surrick v. Board of Wardens
>
> **Not:** Surrick v. Board of Wardens of the Port of Philadelphia

But:

> Shapiro v. Bank of Harrisburg
>
> Eimers v. Mutual of Omaha

Include designations of national or larger geographical areas except in union names (**rule 10.2.1(i)(iv)**), but omit "of America" after "United States":

> United States v. Aluminum Co. of America

Retain all geographical designations not introduced by a preposition:

> Billman v. Indiana Department of Corrections

(g) Given names or initials. Generally, omit given names or initials of individuals, but not in names of business firms or where a party's surname is abbreviated:

> Meyer v. Gordon
>
> **Not:** Jennifer Cannon Meyer v. Daniel S. Gordon

But:

> Tanya Bartucz, Inc. v. Virginia J. Wise & Co.
>
> Linda R.S. v. Richard D.

Do not omit any part of a surname made up of more than one word:

> Van der Velt v. Standing Horse
>
> Abdul Ghani v. Subedar Shoedar Khan

Given names that follow a surname should be retained. Thus, retain the full name where the name is *entirely* in a language in which the surname is given first, such as Chinese, Korean, or Vietnamese:

> Yao Zhen Guang v. Yeh Zhi An
>
> Chow v. Ha Quang Jin
>
> **Not:** Timothy Chow v. Ha Quang Jin

Similarly, if a party's name is of Spanish or Portuguese derivation, cite the surname and all names following:

> Ortega y Gasset v. Alcala de Larosa

If in doubt, use the name under which the party appears in the index of the reporter cited.

(h) Business firm designations. Omit "Inc.," "Ltd.," "L.L.C.," "N.A.," "F.S.B.," and similar terms if the name also contains a word such as "Ass'n," "Bros.," "Co.," "Corp.," and "R.R.," clearly indicating that the party is a business firm:

> Wisconsin Packing Co. v. Indiana Refrigerator Lines, Inc.
>
> **Not:** Wisconsin Packing Co., Inc. v. Indiana Refrigerator Lines, Inc.

(i) Union and local union names. Cite a union name exactly as given in the official reporter. This general rule is subject, however, to the following exceptions:

(i) Only the smallest unit should be cited:

> NLRB v. Radio & Television Broadcast Engineers Local 1212
>
> **Not:** NLRB v. Radio & Television Broadcast Engineers Local 1212, IBEW, AFL-CIO

(ii) All craft or industry designations, except the first *full* such designation, should be omitted:

> Douds v. Local 294, International Brotherhood of Teamsters
>
> **Not:** Douds v. Local 294, International Brotherhood of Teamsters, Chauffeurs, Warehousemen & Helpers

But:

International Union of Doll & Toy Workers v. Local 379

(iii) A widely recognized abbreviation of the union's name (e.g., UAW) may be used in accordance with **rules 6.1(b)** and **10.2.1(c)**.

(iv) All prepositional phrases of location, including those of national or larger areas, should be omitted.

(j) Commissioner of Internal Revenue. Cite simply as "Commissioner."

10.2.2 Case Names in Citations

Cite case names in citations according to the rules given above, but with the following further modifications:

T.6   Always abbreviate any word listed in **table T.6**:

S. Consol. R.R. v. Consol. Transp. Co.

In re Consol. Transp. Co.

McGaugh v. Comm'r

T.11   Abbreviate states, countries, and other geographical units as indicated in **table T.11** unless the geographical unit is a named party:

In re W. Tex. Pepper Co.

LeBeau v. Univ. of Md.

But: Staub v. District of Columbia

Abbreviate other words of eight letters or more if *substantial* space is thereby saved and the result is unambiguous. Do not abbreviate "United States."

10.3 Reporters and Other Sources

10.3.1 Parallel Citations and Which Source(s) to Cite

T.1   The federal and state tables (**table T.1**) indicate which reporters to cite for the decisions of most courts. Note that many state court decisions are published in two or more sources.

(a) Parallel citations in state court documents. For citation of state court cases in documents submitted to courts of the state that originally decided them, refer to **practitioners' note P.3**.

P.3

(b) Case citations in all other documents. In all other documents, including *ordinary legal memoranda* and *law reviews*, cite the relevant regional reporter, if the decision is found therein:

Swedloff v. Phila. Transp. Co., 187 A.2d 152 (Pa. 1963).

If the decision is available as an official public domain citation (also referred to as medium neutral citation), that citation must be provided, as well as a parallel citation to the regional reporter, if available.

If the decision is not found in a regional reporter or available as a public domain citation, cite the other sources indicated in **table T.1**. Cite   T.1
decisions of unlisted courts analogously to those of courts listed in the tables. If a case is not available in an official or preferred unofficial reporter or as a public domain citation, cite another unofficial reporter, a widely used computer database (**rule 18.1.1**), a service (**rule 19**), a slip opinion (**rule 10.8.1(b)**), an Internet source (**rule 18.2.2**), or a newspaper (**rule 16.5**), in that order of preference:

> United States v. Carlisle, No. 90-2465SI, 1991 U.S. App. LEXIS 5863, at *3 (8th Cir. Apr. 10, 1991) (per curiam).

> *In re* Smithfield Estates, Inc., [1985–1986 Transfer Binder] Bankr. L. Rep. (CCH) ¶ 70,707 (Bankr. D.R.I. Aug. 9, 1985).

> Simmons v. Brothers, No. 90-627 (D. Mass. Dec. 19, 1990).

> Minnesota v. McArthur, No. C4-99-502 (Minn. Ct. App. Sept. 28, 1999), *available at* http://www.courts.state.mn.us/library/archive/ctapun/9909/ 502.htm.

> United States v. Palermo, N.Y. TIMES, Aug. 27, 1957, at 24 (S.D.N.Y. Aug. 26, 1957).

For citation to administrative reporters, see **rule 14.3.2**.

Reporters   10.3.2

Bound publications that print only cases (or cases and annotations) are considered reporters and are cited in roman type. A citation to a reporter consists of a volume designation (**rule 3.2**), the abbreviated name of the reporter (as shown in **table T.1**), and the page on which   T.1
the case report begins (**rule 3.3**):

> Envtl. Defense Fund v. EPA, 465 F.2d 528 (D.C. Cir. 1972).

Early American reporters were often named after their editors rather than after the courts whose cases they reported. Subsequently, official editor-named series have been combined into jurisdiction-named series with continuous volume numbering. Such reporters are now generally cited by the official series name and number only; the name of the reporter's editor is omitted:

> Cobb v. Davenport, 32 N.J.L. 369 (Sup. Ct. 1867).

> **Not:** 3 Vroom 369

But for United States Supreme Court reporters through 90 U.S. (23 Wall.) and a few early state reporters (see **table T.1**), give the name   T.1
of the reporter's editor and the volume of that series. If the pagination of the official jurisdiction-named reprints and the original reporters is the same, use the following form:

> Green v. Biddle, 21 U.S. (8 Wheat.) 1 (1823).

Hall v. Bell, 47 Mass. (6 Met.) 431 (1843).

If the pagination differs, give parallel citations to the reprints and the original reporters:

Wadsworth v. Ruggles, 23 Mass. 62, 6 Pick. 63 (1828).

10.3.3 Public Domain Format

T.1
T.7

When citing a decision available in public domain format (also referred to as medium neutral format), if the jurisdiction's format can be cited in the following form (see **table T.1**), provide the case name, the year of decision, the state's two character postal code, the **table T.7** court abbreviation (unless the court is the state's highest court), the sequential number of the decision, and, if the decision is unpublished, a capital "U" after the sequential number of the decision. When referencing specific material within the decision, a pinpoint citation should be made to the paragraph number at which the material appears. If available, a parallel citation to the appropriate regional reporter must be provided.

The following examples are representative of the recommended public domain citation format:

Beck v. Beck, 1999 ME 110, ¶ 6, 733 A.2d 981, 983.

Gregory v. Class, 1998 SD 106, ¶ 3, 584 N.W. 2d 873, 875.

Jones v. Fisher, 1998 OK Civ. App. 120U.

T.1

If a jurisdiction adopts a public domain format that differs from the above, the requirements of the jurisdiction's format should be observed (**table T.1**):

Cannon v. Am. Bowling Cong., 94-0647, p.1 (La. 4/29/94), 637 So. 2d 463.

Morton v. New Orleans Police Dep't, 96-1799 (La. App. 4 Cir. 2/5/97), 687 So. 2d 699.

Sullivan v. State, 98-KA-00521-SCT, ¶ 23 (Miss. 1999).

State v. Brennan, 1998-NMCA-176, ¶ 7, 970 P.2d 161, 164.

Information on jurisdictions adopting a public domain format since the publication of this edition may be found at http://www.legalbluebook.com.

10.4 Court and Jurisdiction

T.1/T.2
T.7/T.11

Every case citation must indicate which court decided the case. In American and other common law citations, give the name of the court and its geographical jurisdiction (abbreviated according to **tables T.1** or **T.2** if included therein and according to **tables T.7** and **T.11** in all other cases) in the parenthetical phrase that immediately follows the citation and includes the date or year of decision:

Commonwealth v. Virelli, 620 A.2d 543 (Pa. Super. Ct. 1992).

For citations to foreign cases, see **rule 20.3**.

A more detailed court designation than those specified by the following paragraphs may be given if necessary.

(a) Federal courts. In citations to *United States Law Week*, the United States Supreme Court is indicated: "U.S." Cite a decision by a Supreme Court Justice sitting alone in his or her capacity as a Circuit Justice:

Russo v. Byrne, 409 U.S. 1219 (Douglas, Circuit Justice 1972).

United States courts of appeals for numbered circuits, regardless of year, are indicated:

2d Cir.

Not: C.C.A.2d

Not: CA2

When citing the United States Court of Appeals for the District of Columbia Circuit and its predecessors, or when citing the Federal Circuit, use the following abbreviations:

D.C. Cir.

Fed. Cir.

For district court cases, give the district but not the division:

D.N.J.

D.D.C.

S.D. Cal.

Not: S.D. Cal. C.D.

Cite the old circuit courts (abolished 1912):

C.C.S.D.N.Y.

Cite the Judicial Panel on Multidistrict Litigation:

J.P.M.L.

Cite decisions of bankruptcy courts and bankruptcy appellate panels:

Bankr. E.D. Va.

B.A.P. 9th Cir.

(b) State courts. In general, indicate the state and court of decision. However, do not include the name of the court if the court of decision is the highest court of the state:

People v. Armour, 590 N.W.2d 61 (Mich. 1999).

Not: People v. Armour, 590 N.W.2d 61 (Mich. Sup. Ct. 1999).

Omit the jurisdiction if it is unambiguously conveyed by the reporter title:

Sigal v. Mandelker, 493 N.Y.S.2d 769 (App. Div. 1985).

Not: Sigal v. Mandelker, 493 N.Y.S.2d 769 (N.Y. App. Div. 1985).

Thus, when a decision is rendered by the highest court in a particular jurisdiction and the name of the reporter is the same as the name of that jurisdiction, neither the name of the court nor the name of the state need be given:

Bates v. Tappan, 99 Mass. 376 (1868).

Do not indicate the department or district in citing decisions of intermediate state courts unless that information is of particular relevance:

Schiffman v. Corsi, 50 N.Y.S.2d 897 (Sup. Ct. 1944).

When the department or district is of particular relevance, that information should be indicated as follows:

Schiffman v. Corsi, 50 N.Y.S.2d 897 (Sup. Ct. N.Y. County 1944).

10.5   Date or Year

(a) Decisions published in reporters. If possible, provide the year of decision; use the year of the term of court only if the year of decision is unavailable. In case of ambiguity, follow the year given in the running head (at the top of each page) in the reporter. Dates of United States Supreme Court cases, which usually are not given in the official reports before 108 U.S., may be found in *Lawyers' Edition* beginning with the December 1854 Term.

(b) Decisions published in other sources. Give the exact date for all unreported cases and for all cases cited to a looseleaf service, a slip opinion, an electronic database, or a newspaper.

(c) Pending cases. Use the date or year of the most recent major disposition. Indicate the significance of the date within a parenthetical phrase, unless its significance is explained elsewhere:

Charlesworth v. Mack, No. 90-567 (1st Cir. argued Jan. 10, 1991).

Otherwise no special notation is necessary:

Charlesworth v. Mack, 725 F. Supp. 1407 (D. Mass. 1990), *appeal docketed*, No. 90-567 (1st Cir. Dec. 20, 1990).

(d) Multiple decisions within a single year. When citing a case with several different decisions in the same year, include the year only with the last-cited decision in that year:

United States v. Eller, 114 F. Supp. 284 (M.D.N.C.), *rev'd*, 208 F.2d 716 (4th Cir. 1953).

However, if the exact date of decision is required in either case, include both dates:

DiNapoli v. Northeast Reg'l Parole Comm'n, 764 F.2d 143 (2d Cir. 1985), *petition for cert. filed*, 54 U.S.L.W. 3146 (U.S. Aug. 29, 1985) (No. 85-335).

Parenthetical Information Regarding Cases 10.6

Weight of Authority 10.6.1

(a) Generally. Information regarding the weight of the authority (e.g., en banc; in banc; 2-1 decision; mem.; per curiam; Brandeis, J.; unpublished table decision) may be added in a separate parenthetical phrase following the date of decision.

Webb v. Baxter Healthcare Corp., 57 F.3d 1067 (4th Cir. 1995) (unpublished table decision).

When a case is cited for a proposition that is not the single, clear holding of a majority of the court (e.g., alternative holding; by implication; dictum; dissenting opinion; plurality opinion; holding unclear), indicate that fact parenthetically:

Parker v. Randolph, 442 U.S. 62, 84 (1979) (Stevens, J., dissenting).

Garcia v. San Antonio Metro. Transit Auth., 469 U.S. 528, 570 (1985) (5-4 decision) (Powell, J., dissenting).

Information regarding related authority (**rule 1.6**) or prior or subsequent history (**rule 10.7**) that can properly be indicated with an explanatory phrase (**table T.9**) should not be given parenthetically. Thus:

T.9

Wersba v. Seiler, 393 F.2d 937 (3d Cir. 1968) (per curiam).

But:

Wersba v. Seiler, 263 F. Supp. 838, 843 (E.D. Pa. 1967), *aff'd per curiam*, 393 F.2d 937 (3d Cir. 1968).

(b) "Mem." and "Per curiam." The abbreviation "mem." stands for the word "memorandum" and designates a court disposition issued without an opinion. The phrase "per curiam" refers to a decision issued "by the court" as an institution as opposed to a decision issued by a particular judge. "Per curiam" may be used in a parenthetical to describe an opinion so denominated by the court.

Order of Parentheticals 10.6.2

Parenthetical phrases indicating the weight of the authority should precede explanatory parentheticals, which give other information (**rule 1.5**):

Green v. Georgia, 442 U.S. 95 (1979) (per curiam) (holding that exclusion of relevant evidence at a sentencing hearing constitutes a denial of due process).

Parenthetical information (weight of authority parentheticals as well as explanatory parentheticals) about a case should always directly follow the date of the cited case, before any citation of prior or subsequent history:

> Wolf v. Colorado, 338 U.S. 25, 47 (1949) (Rutledge, J., dissenting) (rejecting the Court's conception of the exclusionary rule), *aff'g* 187 P.2d 926 (Colo. 1947), *overruled by* Mapp v. Ohio, 367 U.S. 643 (1961).

10.7   Prior and Subsequent History

Whenever a decision is cited in full, give the entire *subsequent* history of the case, but omit denials of certiorari or denials of similar discretionary appeals, unless the decision is less than two years old or the denial is particularly relevant. Omit also the history on remand or any denial of a rehearing, unless relevant to the point for which the case is cited. Finally, omit any disposition withdrawn by the deciding authority, such as an affirmance followed by reversal on rehearing.

> Cent. Ill. Pub. Serv. Co. v. Westervelt, 342 N.E.2d 463 (Ill. App. Ct. 1976), *aff'd*, 367 N.E.2d 661 (Ill. 1977).

> **Not:** Cent. Ill. Pub. Serv. Co. v. Westervelt, 342 N.E.2d 463 (Ill. App. Ct. 1976), *aff'd*, 367 N.E.2d 661 (Ill. 1977), *cert. denied*, 434 U.S. 1070 (1978).

> Cheng v. GAF Corp., 631 F.2d 1052 (2d Cir. 1980), *vacated by* 450 U.S. 903 (1981).

> **Not:** Cheng v. GAF Corp., 631 F.2d 1052 (2d Cir. 1980), *vacated by* 450 U.S. 903, *remanded to* 659 F.2d 1058 (2d Cir. 1981).

Give *prior* history only if significant to the point for which the case is cited or if the disposition cited does not intelligibly describe the issues in the case, as in a Supreme Court "mem." Give separate decisions of other issues in the case with their prior and subsequent history only if relevant.

10.7.1   Explanatory Phrases and Weight of Authority

A partial list of explanatory phrases (as abbreviated) appears in **table T.9**.

T.9

(a) Prior or subsequent history. Append the prior or subsequent history of a case to the primary citation. Introduce and explain each decision with italicized words between each citation:

> Cooper v. Dupnik, 924 F.2d 1520, 1530 & n.20 (9th Cir. 1991), *rev'd en banc*, 963 F.2d 1220 (9th Cir. 1992).

If subsequent history itself has subsequent history, append the additional subsequent history with another explanatory phrase. For example, in the following case the Supreme Court reversed the Second Circuit:

Herbert v. Lando, 73 F.R.D. 387 (S.D.N.Y.), *rev'd*, 568 F.2d 974 (2d Cir. 1977), *rev'd*, 441 U.S. 153 (1979).

To show both prior and subsequent history, give the prior history first:

Kubrick v. United States, 581 F.2d 1092 (3d Cir. 1978), *aff'g* 435 F. Supp. 166 (E.D. Pa. 1977), *rev'd*, 444 U.S. 111 (1979).

Citations to prior or subsequent history should follow any parenthetical information given for the primary citation (**rule 10.6**).

(b) Significance of disposition. Give the reason for a disposition if the disposition does not carry the normal substantive significance:

vacated as moot,

appeal dismissed per stipulation,

(c) Overruled cases. Following **rule 1.6,** also note cases that have been overruled:

Nat'l League of Cities v. Usery, 426 U.S. 833 (1976), *overruled by* Garcia v. San Antonio Metro. Transit Auth., 469 U.S. 528 (1985).

(d) Multiple dispositions. Multiple dispositions following a primary case citation should be connected with the word "*and*" in italics:

United States v. Baxter, 492 F.2d 150 (9th Cir.), *cert. dismissed*, 414 U.S. 801 (1973), *and cert. denied*, 416 U.S. 940 (1974).

Different Case Name on Appeal   10.7.2

When the name of the case differs in prior or subsequent history, the new name must be given. To indicate a different name in *subsequent* history, use the phrase "sub nom." Thus:

Great W. United Corp. v. Kidwell, 577 F.2d 1256 (5th Cir. 1978), *rev'd sub nom.* Leroy v. Great W. United Corp., 443 U.S. 173 (1979).

To indicate a different name in *prior* history, use the following form:

Rederi v. Isbrandtsen Co., 342 U.S. 950 (1952) (per curiam), *aff'g by an equally divided Court* Isbrandtsen Co. v. United States, 96 F. Supp. 883 (S.D.N.Y. 1951).

Do not give a new name, however, (i) when the parties' names are merely reversed, (ii) when the citation in which the difference occurs is to a denial of certiorari or rehearing, or (iii) when, in the appeal of an administrative action, the name of the private party remains the same:

United Dairy Farmers Coop. Ass'n, 194 N.L.R.B. 1094, *enforced*, 465 F.2d 1401 (3d Cir. 1972).

But:

Perma Vinyl Corp., 164 N.L.R.B. 968 (1967), *enforced sub nom.* United States Pipe & Foundry Co. v. NLRB, 398 F.2d 544 (5th Cir. 1968).

10.8   Special Citation Forms

10.8.1 Pending and Unreported Cases

(a) Cases available on electronic media. See **rule 18**.

(b) Cases available in slip opinions. When a case is unreported but available in a separately printed slip opinion, give the docket number, the court, and the full date of the most recent major disposition of the case:

> Groucho Marx Prods. v. Playboy Enters., No. 77 Civ. 1782 (S.D.N.Y. Dec. 30, 1977).

Note any renumbering of the docket:

> United States v. Johnson, 425 F.2d 630 (9th Cir. 1970), *cert. granted*, 403 U.S. 956 (1971) (No. 577, 1970 Term; renumbered No. 70-8, 1971 Term).

Always give the full docket number:

> No. 75-31

> **Not:** No. 31

If the date given does not refer to the date of decision and the significance of the date is not indicated elsewhere, indicate that significance within the parenthetical phrase containing the date:

> Charlesworth v. Mack, No. 90-345 (D. Mass. filed Sept. 18, 1990).

To cite a particular page of a separately paginated slip opinion, use the form:

> Charlesworth v. Mack, No. 90-345, slip op. at 6 (D. Mass. Dec. 4, 1990).

If the case is not separately paginated, cite the page on which the case begins as well as the page on which any particular material appears:

> Charlesworth v. Mack, No. 90-567, slip op. 3458, 3465 (1st Cir. Jan. 19, 1991).

In pending or unreported adversary proceedings in bankruptcy, supply both the case number of the underlying nonadversary proceeding and the case number of the adversary proceeding:

> Brown v. Sachs (*In re* Brown), Ch. 7 Case No. 84-00170-G, Adv. No. 85-1190, slip op. at 5 (E.D. Mich. Jan. 24, 1986).

(c) Other pending and unreported cases. Cases that are not available in slip opinions or on electronic databases may be cited to services (**rule 19**), periodicals (**rule 16**), or the Internet (**rule 18.2.2**).

Fifth Circuit Split 10.8.2

On October 1, 1981, the Fifth Circuit of the United States Court of Appeals was divided to create the new Fifth and Eleventh Circuits. Cite cases decided during the transitional period leading to this reorganization according to the following rules: (i) cite decisions rendered in 1981 and labeled "5th Cir." by month; (ii) give unit information whenever available; (iii) designate as "Former 5th" any nonunit judgment labeled as a Former Fifth judgment and rendered after September 30, 1981:

> Birl v. Estelle, 660 F.2d 592 (5th Cir. Nov. 1981).
>
> Haitian Refugee Ctr. v. Smith, 676 F.2d 1023 (5th Cir. Unit B 1982).
>
> Trailways, Inc. v. ICC, 676 F.2d 1019 (5th Cir. Unit A Aug. 1981) (per curiam).
>
> McCormick v. United States, 680 F.2d 345 (Former 5th Cir. 1982).

Briefs, Records, Motions, and Memoranda 10.8.3

Use the designation given on the document itself, followed by a full citation to the case to which it relates. Indicate the docket number parenthetically:

> [1] Appellant's Opening Brief at 5, Rosenthal v. Carr, 614 F.2d 1219 (9th Cir. 1980) (No. 76-1917).
>
> [2] Brief for the National Labor Relations Board at 7, NLRB v. J.C. Penney Co., 620 F.2d 718 (9th Cir. 1980) (No. 78-3329); Record at 5, *J.C. Penney Co.* (No. 78-3329).
>
> [3] Brief of Amici Curiae Alabama Law Foundation, Inc. et al. at 5–6, Phillips v. Wash. Legal Found., 524 U.S. 156 (1998) (No. 96-1578).

A short form of the case name (**rule 10.9**) may be used, or the case name may be omitted, if the reference is unambiguous:

> [4] Respondents' Brief at 2, *Rosenthal* (No. 76-1917).
>
> [5] To support this contention, respondent referred to the physician's report. Record at 16.

In court documents, citations to briefs, records, motions, and memoranda should follow the forms provided in **practitioners' note P.7**.   P.7

Short Forms for Cases 10.9

(a) Footnotes. In law review footnotes, a short form for a case may be used if it clearly identifies a case that (1) is already cited in the *same* footnote, (2) is cited (in either full or short form, including "*id.*") in *a manner such that it can be readily found in one of the preceding five footnotes*, or (3) is named in the *same general textual discussion* to which the footnote is appended. Otherwise a full citation is required. Thus in the following example, the use of the short form in footnotes 4 and 7–9 is correct:

[1] United States v. Montoya de Hernandez, 473 U.S. 531 (1985).

[2] *Id.* at 537–38.

[3] *See* United States v. Martinez-Fuerte, 428 U.S. 543, 557 (1976); Cal. Bankers Ass'n v. Shultz, 416 U.S. 21, 62 (1974).

[4] *See Martinez-Fuerte*, 428 U.S. at 550.

[5] New York v. Belton, 453 U.S. 454, 457 (1981).

[6] *See id.* at 456.

[7] *See Montoya de Hernandez*, 473 U.S. at 540.

[8] *Cal. Bankers*, 416 U.S. at 55.

[9] *Martinez-Fuerte*, 428 U.S. at 550.

(i) Generally. Use of only one party's name in a short form citation is permissible if the reference is unambiguous. When only one party's name is used, it should be italicized. Acceptable short forms include:

United States v. Calandra, 414 U.S. at 343.

Calandra, 414 U.S. at 343.

414 U.S. at 343.

Id. at 343.

Omit the case name in the last two examples only if the reader will have no doubt about the case to which the citation refers.

When using only one party name in a short form citation, avoid using the name of a geographical or governmental unit, a governmental official, or other common litigant. Thus:

NAACP v. Alabama *ex rel.* Patterson, 357 U.S. 449 (1958).

becomes:

Patterson, 357 U.S. at 464.

Not: *NAACP*, 357 U.S. at 464.

Alabama, 357 U.S. at 464.

Reno v. Bossier Parish Sch. Bd., 520 U.S. 471 (1997).

becomes:

Bossier Parish Sch. Bd., 520 U.S. at 480.

Not: *Reno*, 520 U.S. at 480.

(ii) Commercial electronic databases. For cases that are available on an electronic database (**rule 18.1.1**), use a unique database identifier, if one has been assigned, in constructing a short form:

Clark v. Homrighous, No. CIV.A.90-1380-T, 1991 WL 55402, at *3 (D. Kan. Apr. 10, 1991).

becomes:

Clark, 1991 WL 55402, at *2.

Albrecht v. Stanczek, No. 87-C9535, 1991 U.S. Dist. LEXIS 5088, at *1 (N.D. Ill. Apr. 18, 1991).

becomes:

Albrecht, 1991 U.S. Dist. LEXIS 5088, at *2.

Lindquist v. Hart, 1 CA-CV 98-0323, at *2 (Ariz. Ct. App. July 15, 1999) (Loislaw.com, Ariz. Case Law).

becomes:

Lindquist, at *3 (Loislaw.com, Ariz. Case Law).

(b) Text. A case that has been cited in full in the same general discussion may be referred to (in main text or footnote text) by one of the parties' names without further citation:

The issue presented in *Bakke* has not been fully resolved.

Constitutions, Statutes, and Legislative, Administrative, and Executive Materials

Rule 11: Constitutions   75

Rule 12: Statutes   76
    12.1: Basic Citation Forms   76
    12.2: Choosing the Proper Citation Form   77
    12.3: Current Official and Unofficial Codes   78
    12.4: Session Laws   81
    12.5: Secondary Sources   83
    12.6: Repeal, Amendment, and Prior History   84
    12.7: Explanatory Parenthetical Phrases   84
    12.8: Special Citation Forms   85
    12.9: Short Forms for Statutes   89

Rule 13: Legislative Materials   91
    13.1: Basic Citation Forms   91
    13.2: Bills and Resolutions   92
    13.3: Hearings   93
    13.4: Reports, Documents, and Committee Prints   93
    13.5: Debates   95
    13.6: Separately Bound Legislative Histories   95
    13.7: Short Forms for Legislative Materials   95

Rule 14: Administrative and Executive Materials   96
    14.1: Basic Citation Forms   96
    14.2: Rules, Regulations, and Other Publications 97
    14.3: Administrative Adjudications and Arbitrations 98
    14.4: Advisory Opinions   100
    14.5: Federal Taxation Materials   100
    14.6: SEC Materials   102
    14.7: Presidential Papers and Executive Orders 103
    14.8: Court Administrative Orders   103
    14.9: Patents   103
    14.10: Short Forms for Regulations   104

Constitutions   11

Citation of Section 2 of the Fourteenth Amendment to the U.S. Constitution:

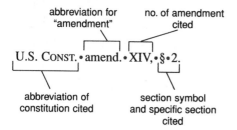

Cite the United States federal and state constitutions by "U.S." or the abbreviated name of the state and the word "CONST." Abbreviate the subdivisions of constitutions, such as article and clause, according to **table T.17**:

R

T.17   11–14

> U.S. CONST. art. I, § 9, cl. 2.

> U.S. CONST. amend. XIV, § 2.

> U.S. CONST. pmbl.

> N.M. CONST. art. IV, § 7.

Cite constitutional provisions currently in force without date. If the cited provision has been repealed, either indicate parenthetically the fact and date of repeal or cite the repealing provision in full:

> U.S. CONST. amend. XVIII (repealed 1933).

> U.S. CONST. amend. XVIII, *repealed by* U.S. CONST. amend. XXI.

When citing a provision that has been subsequently amended, either indicate parenthetically the fact and date of amendment or cite the amending provision in full:

> U.S. CONST. art. I, § 3, cl. 1 (amended 1913).

> U.S. CONST. art. I, § 3, cl. 1, *amended by* U.S. CONST. amend. XVII, § 1.

Cite constitutions that have been totally superseded by year of adoption; if the specific provision cited was adopted in a different year, give that year parenthetically:

> ARK. CONST. of 1868, art. III, § 2 (1873).

Do not use a short citation form (other than "*id.*") for constitutions.

12   Statutes

Citation of an entire statute, the Comprehensive Environmental Response, Compensation, and Liability Act, as codified in the *United States Code*:

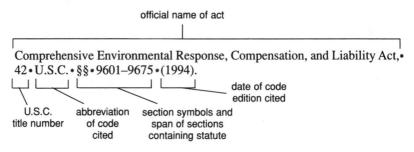

Citation of an individual provision of the *United States Code*:

```
         section symbol
  title   and specific   date of code
 number   section cited  edition cited
   /          /             /
 ┌─┐       ┌───┐         ┌────┐
 28 • U.S.C. • § • 1291 • (1994).
 └───┘
    \
     code abbreviation
```

12.1   Basic Citation Forms

Statutes may be cited to a current official or unofficial code (**rule 12.3**), official or privately published session laws (**rule 12.4**), or secondary sources (**rule 12.5**). Official and unofficial codes arrange statutes currently in force by subject matter. Official and privately published session laws report statutes in chronological order of enactment. Cite secondary sources—such as looseleaf services, the CIS microform service, periodicals, newspapers, or electronic databases—only when the above listed sources are not available.

Rule 12.2 explains when to use each of these basic citation forms. The next three rules discuss the citation forms for official and unofficial codes (**rule 12.3**), session laws (**rule 12.4**), and secondary sources (**rule 12.5**). **Rule 12.6** explains when the subsequent history of a statute must be cited, and **rule 12.7** discusses the use of explanatory parenthetical phrases with respect to statute citations. **Rule 12.8** outlines special citation forms for the Internal Revenue Code, ordinances, rules of evidence and procedure, uniform acts, model codes, restatements of the law, standards, sentencing guidelines, and the ABA Code of Professional Responsibility. **Rule 12.9** provides short forms for statutes.

Table T.1 lists citation forms for the codes and session laws of the federal and state governments, and other United States jurisdictions.

T.1

cited to current official code	42 U.S.C. § 1983 (1994). National Environmental Policy Act of 1969 § 102, 42 U.S.C. § 4332 (1994). Consumer Credit Code, Okla. Stat. tit. 14A, § 6-203 (Supp. 1990).
cited to current unofficial code	12 U.S.C.A. § 1426 (West Supp. 1991). Parking Authority Law, Pa. Stat. Ann. tit. 53, § 342 (West 1974 & Supp. 1990).
cited to official session laws	National Environmental Policy Act of 1969, Pub. L. No. 91-190, § 102, 83 Stat. 852, 853 (1970) (prior to 1975 amendment).
cited to privately published session laws	Health Care Facilities Act, Act No. 1979-48, 1979 Pa. Legis. Serv. 114 (to be codified at 35 Pa. Cons. Stat. §§ 448.101–.903).
cited to secondary source	Social Security Amendments of 1983, Pub. L. No. 98-21, 51 U.S.L.W. 203 (1983).

R
11–14

Choosing the Proper Citation Form 12.2

General Rule 12.2.1

(a) Statutes currently in force. If possible, cite statutes currently in force to the current official code or its supplement. Otherwise, cite a current unofficial code or its supplement, the official session laws, privately published session laws (e.g., *United States Code Congressional and Administrative News*), a widely used computer database, a looseleaf service, an Internet source, or a newspaper—in that order of preference.

> National Environmental Policy Act of 1969 § 102, 42 U.S.C. § 4332 (1994).

(b) Statutes no longer in force. Cite statutes no longer in force to the current official or unofficial code if they still appear therein. Otherwise, cite the last edition of the official or unofficial code in which the statute appeared or the session laws or a secondary source—in that order of preference. In any case, the fact of repeal or amendment *must* be noted parenthetically according to **rule 12.6.1** or **12.6.2**:

> Law of June 1, 1895, ch. 4322, § 23, 1895 Fla. Laws ch. 3, 20–21 (repealed 1969).
>
> Clayton Act, ch. 323, § 7, 38 Stat. 730, 731–32 (1914) (current version at 15 U.S.C. § 18 (1994)).

(c) Private laws. Cite private laws to the session laws if therein; otherwise cite a secondary source:

Priv. L. No. 94-75, 90 Stat. 2985 (1976).

12.2.2 Exceptions

(a) Scattered statutes. Cite the session laws if a statute appears in so many scattered sections or titles that no useful citation to the code is possible. Indicate parenthetically the general location of the codified sections. Thus:

Tax Reduction Act of 1975, Pub. L. No. 94-12, 89 Stat. 26 (codified as amended in scattered sections of 26 U.S.C.).

But:

Robinson-Patman Act, 15 U.S.C. §§ 13–13b, 21a (1994).

If the current version of a statute is split between the main body and the supplement of a code, it should be cited according to **rule 3.2(c)**:

42 U.S.C. § 3001 (1988 & Supp. V 1993).

If the current version of a statute can be determined only by reference to multiple sources (not just a code and its supplement), it should be cited according to **rule 12.6.2**:

31 U.S.C. § 3724 (1988), *amended by* Act of Dec. 7, 1989, 31 U.S.C.S. § 3724 (Law. Co-op. Supp. 1990).

(b) Historical fact. The historical fact of enactment, amendment, or repeal should be cited to the session laws. A parenthetical reference to the current version (see **rules 12.6.2** and **12.7**) may be added:

Two years later, Congress passed the Voting Rights Act of 1965, Pub. L. No. 89-110, 79 Stat. 445 (codified as amended at 42 U.S.C. §§ 1971, 1973 to 1973bb-1 (1994)).

(c) Materially different language. If the language in the current code (including its supplement) differs materially from the language in the session laws and the relevant title has not been enacted into positive law, cite the session laws. A parenthetical reference to the code version, introduced by the phrase "codified with some differences in language at" may be given. If differences in the language merely reflect subsequent amendments, however, cite the current code.

A current list of federal code titles that have been enacted into positive law appears in the preface to the latest edition or supplement of the *United States Code*. Similarly, state codes should indicate whether the titles contained therein have been enacted into positive law.

12.3   Current Official and Unofficial Codes

The official federal code is the *United States Code* (U.S.C.). Unofficial federal codes include the *United States Code Annotated* (U.S.C.A.)

and the *United States Code Service* (U.S.C.S.). Official and unofficial codes for each state (where they exist) are listed in **table T.1**. Cite the official code whenever possible.

All citations to codes contain the abbreviated name of the code found in **table T.1** printed in large and small capitals; the section, paragraph, or article number(s) of the statute; and the year of the code (determined according to **rule 12.3.2**):

> N.C. Gen. Stat. § 1-181 (1990).

Additional Information

12.3.1

Additional information may be required as follows:

(a) Name and original section number. Give the statute's name and original section number (as it appears in the appropriate session laws) only if the statute is commonly cited that way or the information would otherwise aid in identification. An official name, a popular name, or both may be used:

> Labor Management Relations (Taft-Hartley) Act § 301(a), 29 U.S.C. § 185(a) (1988).
>
> Occupational Safety and Health Act (OSHA) of 1970, 29 U.S.C. § 651 (1988 & Supp. V 1993).

(b) Title, chapter, or volume. If a code is divided into separately sectioned or paragraphed titles, chapters, or volumes, the title, chapter, or volume number must be indicated. When citing the federal code, give the title number before the name of the code:

> 42 U.S.C. § 1983 (1994).
>
> 12 U.S.C.S. § 1710 (Law. Co-op. 1978 & Supp. 1990).

The form for citation to state codes varies; **table T.1** indicates whether and in what manner to identify the title, chapter, or volume number of a state code. For example:

> Del. Code Ann. tit. 13, § 1301 (1981).
>
> Neb. Rev. Stat. § 28-501 (1989).

If each title, chapter, or volume of a code contains differently numbered sections or paragraphs, then the volume, chapter, or title number need not be given separately:

> Ga. Code Ann. § 96-1005 (Supp. 1988).

(c) Subject-matter codes. If a separately sectioned or paragraphed portion of a code is identified by subject matter rather than by a title, volume, or chapter number, give that subject-matter name as part of the code:

> Cal. Veh. Code § 11,506 (West 1987).
>
> Tex. Fam. Code Ann. § 5.01 (Vernon 1993).

R

11–14

T.1   **Table T.1** indicates which state codes require this treatment.

(d) Publisher, editor, or compiler. Unless a code is published, edited, or compiled by, or under the supervision of, federal or state officials, give the name of the publisher, editor, or compiler in the parenthetical phrase containing the year of the code:

> 42 U.S.C.A. § 300a-7 (West Supp. 1991).

> 18 U.S.C.S. § 1307 (Law. Co-op. 1979 & Supp. 1990).

> Cal. Veh. Code § 11,509 (West 1987 & Supp. 1991).

> N.Y. Bus. Corp. Law § 717 (McKinney 1983).

T.1   **Table T.1** indicates which federal and state codes require this information.

(e) Supplements. Cite material appearing in supplements (including pocket parts) according to **rule 3.2(c)**:

> 18 U.S.C. § 510(b) (Supp. I 1983).

> 12 U.S.C. § 1455 (1982 & Supp. I 1983).

(f) Compilations of uncodified laws. If a code contains uncodified laws printed in a separate compilation, cite in this manner:

> N.Y. Unconsol. Law § 751 (McKinney 1979).

(g) Appendices. If a statute appears in an appendix to a code, and the statute is numbered and otherwise printed as if it were part of that code, cite according to **rule 3.5**:

> 50 U.S.C. app. § 5 (1988).

If the statute is not printed as if it were part of a code, cite the session laws and add an explanatory phrase (see **rule 1.6(b)**) indicating that the statute is reprinted in the code's appendix:

> Act of Aug. 31, 1970, ch. 842, 1970 Mass. Acts 732, *reprinted in* Mass. Gen. Laws Ann. ch. 40 app. at 180 (West 1985).

(h) Differently numbered unofficial codes. If an unofficial code uses a numbering system that differs from the official code, cite the unofficial code only if the statute does not appear in the official code. Otherwise cite the official code. If the statute appears in both codes, the unofficial code section may be given parenthetically:

> Mich. Comp. Laws § 551.271 (1988) (Mich. Stat. Ann. § 25.15 (Michie 1984)).

12.3.2 Year of Code

When citing a bound volume of the current official or unofficial code, provide parenthetically the year that appears on the spine of the volume, the year that appears on the title page, or the latest copyright year—in that order of preference. If the date on the spine or title page spans more than one year, give all years covered. If the volume is a replacement of an earlier edition, use the year of the replacement volume, not the year of the original:

NEB. REV. STAT. § 33-114 (1989).

When citing a provision that appears in a supplement or pocket part, give the year that appears on the title page of the supplement or pocket part. If there is none, give the latest copyright year of the supplement or pocket part. In either case, if the date spans more than one year, give all years included:

IND. CODE ANN. § 36-7-1-22 (West Supp. 1990–1991).

To cite material that appears in both the main volume and a supplement or pocket part, give both years according to **rule 3.2(c)**:

VT. STAT. ANN. tit. 12, § 3087 (1973 & Supp. 1990).

If a code is published in looseleaf form, give the year that appears on the page on which the provision is printed or the year that appears on the first page of the subdivision in which the provision appears—in that order of preference—rather than the years indicated above:

ALASKA STAT. § 28-01-010 (Michie 1990).

R
11–14

Other dates (such as the date on which an act becomes effective) may also be given parenthetically according to **rule 12.7**:

OKLA. STAT. tit. 10, § 1102.1 (Supp. 1990) (effective Oct. 1, 1982).

Session Laws   12.4

(a) Name. When citing session laws, always give the name of the statute and the public law or chapter number. An official name, a popular name, or both may be used:

White-Slave Traffic (Mann) Act, ch. 395, 36 Stat. 825 (1910) (codified as amended at 18 U.S.C. §§ 2421–2424 (1994)).

Health Professions Education Extension Amendments of 1992, Pub. L. No. 102-408, 106 Stat. 1992.

If the statute has no official or popular name, identify the act with a full date. Use the form "Act of [date of enactment]," or, if that information is unavailable, "Act effective [date of effectiveness]." Other identifying information may be added parenthetically:

Act of Aug. 21, 1974, ch. 85, 1974 N.J. Laws 385 (providing unemployment compensation for jurors).

Not: An Act concerning unemployment compensation for persons serving on jury duty, and amending R.S. 43:21-4, ch. 85, 1974 N.J. Laws 385.

(b) Volume. Give the volume number (or, if none, the year) of the session laws, followed by the abbreviated name of the session laws in ordinary roman type. The official federal session laws, *Statutes at Large*, are abbreviated "Stat." Abbreviations for official and privately published state session laws appear in **table T.1**. When citing state session laws, begin the abbreviated title of the session laws with the name of the state abbreviated according to **table T.11**, even if the state name is not part of the official title; omit words in the official title not necessary for identification:

T.1

T.11

> 1978 Ark. Acts
>
> 1935–1936 Ill. Laws 4th Spec. Sess.
>
> 1878 Minn. Laws
>
> **Not:** 1878 Laws of Minn.

When citing an entire act, give the page of the session laws on which the act begins:

> National Environmental Policy Act of 1969, Pub. L. No. 91-190, 83 Stat. 852 (1970).

When citing only part of an act, give the section(s) or subsection(s) cited, the page on which the act begins, and the page(s) on which the relevant section(s) or subsection(s) appear(s):

> National Environmental Policy Act of 1969, Pub. L. No. 91-190, § 102, 83 Stat. 852, 853–54 (1970).
>
> Act of June 15, 1995, No. 302, § 3602(11), 1995 La. Sess. Law Serv. 344, 344 (West).

(c) Session laws amending prior acts. Session laws amending prior acts are often divided into sections within sections; that is, the session law is divided into primary sections, and these sections, in turn, contain sections of the amended act. Cite the *bill's* sections by abbreviation (sec.) and the *amended act's* sections by symbol (§):

> Labor-Management Relations Act, ch. 120, sec. 101, § 8(a)(3), 61 Stat. 136, 140–41 (1947).

(d) Year or date. Give parenthetically the year in which the statute was passed by the legislature. If no date of enactment is identified, give the date on which the statute became effective:

> McCarran-Ferguson Act, ch. 20, 59 Stat. 33 (1945) (codified as amended at 15 U.S.C. §§ 1011–1015 (1994)).

Omit the year of the statute's passage if the same year is part of the name of the statute or of the session laws:

> Securities Act of 1933, ch. 38, 48 Stat. 74 (codified as amended at 15 U.S.C. §§ 77a–77aa (1994)).
>
> Act of Apr. 25, 1978, No. 515, § 3, 1978 Ala. Acts 569, 569 (codified as amended at ALA. CODE § 9-3-12 (1987)).

(e) Codification information. If a statute has been or will ultimately be codified and the code location is known, give that information parenthetically:

> Act of July 12, 1985, ch. 223, § 3, 1985 Cal. Legis. Serv. 239, 241 (West) (to be codified at CAL. INS. CODE § 11589.5).

Secondary Sources   12.5

(a) Electronic media. See **rule 18**.

(b) Other Secondary Sources. When citing a statute to any source other than a code, session laws, or electronic database, give the name of the act and public law or chapter number as if citing to session laws (**rule 12.4**). When referring to a particular provision, give the section or subsection number after the public law or chapter number. If possible, cite federal statutes (particularly those enacted after 1974) to the *United States Code Congressional and Administrative News,* indicating the volume number (and page number, if known) of the *Statutes at Large* where the statute will appear (note: the page numbers in these two sources often differ):

R
11–14

> Act of July 19, 1985, Pub. L. No. 99-68, 1985 U.S.C.C.A.N. (99 Stat.) 166.

> Act of Aug. 13, 1954, ch. 731, 1954 U.S.C.C.A.N. (68 Stat. 717) 833.

When citing an entire act, give the page on which the act begins. When citing part of an act, give both the page on which the act begins and the pages on which the cited material appears. If the future code location of the statute is known, give that information parenthetically:

> Act of July 9, 1985, Pub. L. No. 99-61, § 110, 1985 U.S.C.C.A.N. (99 Stat.) 113, 115 (to be codified at 31 U.S.C. § 5112).

Cite other secondary sources according to **rule 19** (services) or **16** (periodicals) in that order of preference. Give the date or year appropriate for the cited source. If the name of a statute cited to a service includes the year, and the service was published in that year, the year of the service may be omitted. If the future location of the act in either a code or session laws is known, give that information parenthetically according to **rule 12.7**:

> Soil and Water Resources Conservation Act of 1977, Pub. L. No. 95-192, [Federal Laws] Env't Rep. (BNA) 71:8401 (to be codified at 16 U.S.C. §§ 2001–2009).

> Presidential and Executive Office Accountability Act of 1996, Pub. L. No. 104-331, [1 Lab. Rel.] Lab. L. Rep. (CCH) ¶ 660 (1997).

If a recent statute has not yet been published in any source, give only the name of the act; the public law or chapter number; the section or subsection number if referring to only part of the statute; the full date of enactment or, if none, the date of approval by the executive or effective date; and the future location, if known, in a code or session laws:

> Alabama Corporate Income Tax Reform Act, No. 85-515 (May 8, 1985).

12.6 Repeal, Amendment, and Prior History

12.6.1 Repeal

When citing a statute no longer in force, indicate the fact and date of repeal parenthetically. Include a full citation to the repealing statute when particularly relevant:

> Law of June 1, 1895, ch. 4322, § 23, 1895 Fla. Laws ch. 3, 20–21 (repealed 1969).

> Act of Jan. 24, 1923, ch. 42, 42 Stat. 1174, 1208, *repealed by* Budget and Accounting Procedures Act of 1950, ch. 946, §301(97), 64 Stat. 832, 844.

12.6.2 Amendment

When citing a version of a statute that has since been amended, indicate the fact and date of amendment parenthetically, cite the amending statute in full, or cite the current amended version parenthetically:

> Supplemental Appropriation Act of 1955, Pub. L. No. 663, § 1311, 68 Stat. 800, 830 (1954) (amended 1959).

> 33 U.S.C. § 1232 (1982), *amended by* 33 U.S.C. § 1232(f) (Supp. I 1983).

> Clayton Act, ch. 323, § 7, 38 Stat. 730, 731–32 (1914) (current version at 15 U.S.C. § 18 (1994)).

12.6.3 Prior History

When citing the current version of a statute, prior history may be given parenthetically according to **rule 12.7** if relevant:

> 33 U.S.C. § 1232(f) (Supp. I 1983) (amending 33 U.S.C. § 1232 (1982)).

> 28 U.S.C. § 1652 (1994) (originally enacted as Act of June 25, 1948, ch. 646, § 1652, 62 Stat. 869, 944).

> 28 U.S.C. § 1652 (1994) (corresponds to the Judiciary Act of 1789, ch. 20, § 34, 1 Stat. 73, 92).

> Clayton Act § 7, 15 U.S.C. § 18 (1994) (original version at ch. 323, § 7, 38 Stat. 730, 731–32 (1914)).

12.7 Explanatory Parenthetical Phrases

Explanatory parenthetical phrases are used to show the code location of statutes cited to session laws (**rules 12.2.2** and **12.4**) or secondary sources (**rule 12.5**); to give the unofficial code section when an unofficial code is numbered differently from an official code (**rule 12.3.1(h)**); to identify useful dates, such as the effective date of a statute (**rules 12.3.2** and **12.4(d)**); and to indicate the repeal (**rule 12.6.1**), amendment (**rule 12.6.2**), or prior history (**rule 12.6.3**) of a statute. In addition, explanatory parenthetical phrases may be used to give any other relevant information about a statute:

> 5 U.S.C. § 553(b) (1994) (requiring agencies to publish notice of proposed rulemaking in the *Federal Register*).

See generally **rule 1.5** (parenthetical information).

Special Citation Forms 12.8

Internal Revenue Code 12.8.1

In citations to the Internal Revenue Code, "26 U.S.C." may be replaced with "I.R.C." Thus:

> 26 U.S.C. § 61 (1994).

becomes:

> I.R.C. § 61 (1994).

In law review citations, the year of the current United States Code or its supplement (as appropriate) should always be given (**rule 12.3.2**). Citations to the Internal Revenue Code as it appears in an unofficial code should identify the unofficial code by placing the publisher's name in the parenthetical phrase containing the year of the version cited. Thus, citations to U.S.C.A. could appear:

> I.R.C. § 1371 (West Supp. 1991).

> I.R.C. § 1247 (West 1988).

See also **rule 12.9** regarding short form citation of statutes. For special citation forms for federal taxation materials in court documents and legal memoranda, see **practitioners' note P.5**.

P.5

Ordinances 12.8.2

Cite ordinances analogously to statutes. Always give the name of the political subdivision (such as a city or county) and the abbreviated state name at the beginning of the citation. Do not abbreviate the name of the political subdivision unless it is abbreviated in **table T.11**. If the ordinance is codified, give the name of the code (abbreviated according to **table T.1**), the section or other subdivision, and the year of the code (determined according to **rule 12.3.2**). Print the political subdivision, state, and code names in large and small capitals:

T.11

T.1

> Montgomery, Ala., Code § 3A-11 (1971).

> Portland, Or., Police Code art. 30 (1933).

> Fort Worth, Tex., Rev. Ordinances ch. 34, art. I, § 15 (1950).

If the ordinance is uncodified, give its number (or, if none, its name) and, in a parenthetical, the exact date of adoption. Print the political subdivision, state, and ordinance name in ordinary roman type:

> San Jose, Cal., Ordinance 16,043 (Jan. 17, 1972).

> Halifax County, Va., Ordinance to Regulate the Solicitation of Membership in Organizations (Aug. 6, 1956).

12.8.3 Rules of Evidence and Procedure

Citation of a Federal Rule of Civil Procedure:

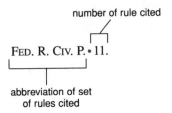

Cite current or uniform rules of evidence or procedure in large and small capitals, without any date. Use abbreviations such as the following or abbreviations suggested by the rules themselves:

> FED. R. CIV. P. 12(b)(6).

> FED. R. CRIM. P. 42(a).

> FED. R. APP. P. 2.

> 1ST CIR. R. 6(a).

> DEL. CT. C.P.R. 8(f).

> FED. R. EVID. 410.

> UNIF. R. EVID. 404(b).

> SUP. CT. R. 17.

When citing rules no longer in force, give the most recent official source in which they appear and indicate the date of repeal parenthetically:

> SUP. CT. R. 8, 306 U.S. 690 (1912) (repealed 1954).

12.8.4 Uniform Acts

When citing a uniform act as the law of a particular state, cite as a state statute:

> OKLA. STAT. tit. 12A, § 2-314 (1981).

When not citing to the law of a particular state, cite as a separate code:

> U.C.C. § 2-314 (1977).

When citing a uniform act to the *Uniform Laws Annotated* (U.L.A.), provide the title of the act using abbreviations in **table T.6**, the section number, the year of amendment or repeal (if any), the appropriate volume of the U.L.A., the page number on which the relevant section appears, and the year of publication:

T.6

> UNIF. ADOPTION ACT § 10, 9 U.L.A. 45 (1988).

Give the year in which the uniform act was last amended, even if the section referred to was not amended at that time. If a uniform act or section has been withdrawn, superseded, or amended, indicate that fact parenthetically according to **rule 12.6.1 or 12.6.2**:

> UNIF. PROBATE CODE § 2-706 (amended 1993), 8 U.L.A. 171 (Supp. 1995).

Model Codes, Restatements, Standards, and Sentencing Guidelines

12.8.5

Cite model codes, restatements, standards, sentencing guidelines, and similar materials in large and small capitals, by section, rule, or other relevant subdivision. For restatements, give the year in which the restatement was published. For model codes, standards, and sentencing guidelines, give the year in which the code, set of standards, or guidelines manual was adopted, unless the version cited indicates that it incorporates subsequent amendments. In that case, give the year of the last amendment, even when citing a portion not amended at that time. Usually the cover or title page of the source will indicate the date of the most recent amendments incorporated. When naming the code, restatement, or set of standards, use abbreviations listed in **table T.6** (abbreviation of case names) or suggested by the source itself.

T.6

> MODEL BUS. CORP. ACT § 57 (1979).
>
> RESTATEMENT (THIRD) OF UNFAIR COMPETITION § 3 (1995).
>
> STANDARDS RELATING TO APP. CTS. § 3.12 (1977).
>
> U.S. SENTENCING GUIDELINES MANUAL § 2D1.1(c) (1998).

If a code, restatement, set of standards, or sentencing guidelines manual is a tentative or proposed draft, indicate that fact parenthetically and give the year of the draft:

> MODEL LAND DEV. CODE § 2-402(2) (Proposed Official Draft 1975).
>
> RESTATEMENT (SECOND) OF TORTS § 847A (Tentative Draft No. 17, 1974).

If a restatement contains a subtitle, retain the subtitle in the citation:

RESTATEMENT (THIRD) OF PROP.: DONATIVE TRANSFERS § 2 (Tentative Draft No. 1, 1995).

Indicate the author's name parenthetically, unless the work was authored by the American Bar Association, the American Law Institute, the National Conference of Commissioners on Uniform State Laws, or a federal or state sentencing commission. Abbreviate the author's name according to **rule 15.1.3** (institutional authors).

MODEL CHILDREN'S CODE § 3.9B(2) (American Indian Law Ctr. 1976).

STANDARDS FOR INMATES' LEGAL RIGHTS Right 18 (National Sheriffs' Ass'n, Tentative Draft 1974).

Cite Generally Accepted Auditing Standards and Generally Accepted Accounting Principles as follows:

CODIFICATION OF ACCOUNTING STANDARDS AND PROCEDURES, Statement on Auditing Standards No. 1, § 150 (American Inst. of Certified Pub. Accountants 1972).

RESEARCH AND DEV. ARRANGEMENTS, Statement of Financial Accounting Standards No. 68, § 32 (Financial Accounting Standards Bd. 1982).

Comments, notes, and other addenda should be cited according to **rule 3.5**:

MODEL PENAL CODE § 223.6 note on status of section (Proposed Official Draft 1962).

RESTATEMENT (SECOND) OF CONFLICT OF LAWS § 305 cmt. b, illus. 1 (1971).

STANDARDS FOR TRAFFIC JUSTICE § 4.2 cmt. at 9 (1975).

Cite application notes, background commentary, introductory commentary, and appendices to sentencing guidelines as follows:

U.S. SENTENCING GUIDELINES MANUAL § 2F1.1, cmt. n.1 (1998).

U.S. SENTENCING GUIDELINES MANUAL § 2F1.1, cmt. background (1998).

U.S. SENTENCING GUIDELINES MANUAL ch. 3, pt. D, introductory cmt. (1998).

U.S. SENTENCING GUIDELINES MANUAL app. C (1998).

When citing a version of a code, restatement, or set of standards that has been withdrawn or amended, indicate that fact according to **rule 12.6.1 or 12.6.2**:

MODEL BUS. CORP. ACT § 2(f) (1969) (amended 1973).

ABA Code of Professional Responsibility and Opinions on Ethics 12.8.6

Cite the old *Model Code of Professional Responsibility* and the new *Model Rules of Professional Conduct* according to **rule 12.8.5**:

MODEL CODE OF PROF'L RESPONSIBILITY Canon 2 (1980).

MODEL RULES OF PROF'L CONDUCT R. 3.12 (Discussion Draft 1983).

Cite ethical considerations and disciplinary rules as follows:

MODEL CODE OF PROF'L RESPONSIBILITY EC 7-36 (1980).

MODEL CODE OF PROF'L RESPONSIBILITY DR 8-101 (1980).

Cite notes or other commentary according to **rule 3.5**:

MODEL RULES OF PROF'L CONDUCT R. 1.15 cmt. (1983).

Cite formal and informal opinions of the Committee on Ethics and Professional Responsibility (or the older Committees on Professional Ethics (1958–1971) and on Professional Ethics and Grievances (1919–1958)) by issuing body, opinion number, and year:

ABA Comm. on Prof'l Ethics and Grievances, Formal Op. 35 (1931).

ABA Comm. on Ethics and Prof'l Responsibility, Informal Op. 1414 (1978).

The subject of the opinion may be given parenthetically:

ABA Comm. on Ethics and Prof'l Responsibility, Formal Op. 338 (1974) (discussing the use of credit cards for the payment of legal services and expenses).

Short Forms for Statutes 12.9

(a) Main text. In law review text, use the forms listed in the "Text" column of the table below to refer to statutes. Provide a citation (in full or short form according to **rule 12.9(c)**) in an accompanying footnote when appropriate.

(b) Footnote text. Similarly, when referring to statutes in law review footnote text, use the forms listed in the "Text" column of the table below. Provide a citation (in full or short form according to **rule 12.9(c)**) in an accompanying citation clause or sentence when appropriate.

(c) Citations. In law review citations, use any of the forms listed in the "Short citation" column of the table below that clearly identifies a statute if the statute is already cited (in full or short form) in either the *same footnote* or in a manner such that it can be readily found in *one of the preceding five footnotes*. Otherwise, use the "Full citation" form.

	Full citation	Text	Short citation
named statutes	Administrative Procedure Act § 1, 5 U.S.C. § 551 (1994)	section 1 of the Administrative Procedure Act or section 1	§ 1 or 5 U.S.C. § 551 or Administrative Procedure Act § 1
U.S. Code provisions	42 U.S.C. § 1983 (1994)	42 U.S.C. § 1983 or § 1983	42 U.S.C. § 1983 or § 1983
state code provisions	DEL. CODE ANN. tit. 28, § 1701 (Supp. 1990)	title 28, section 1701 of the Delaware Code or section 1701	tit. 28, § 1701 or § 1701
session laws	National Environmental Policy Act of 1969, Pub. L. No. 91-190, § 102, 83 Stat. 852, 853–54 (1970)	section 102 of the National Environmental Policy Act or section 102	§ 102 or National Environmental Policy Act § 102 or § 102, 83 Stat. at 853–54

Note that except when referring to the U.S. Code provisions, the word "section" should be spelled out in law review text and footnote text, although the symbol "§" may be used in citations. See **rule 6.2(c)**.

(d) Electronic sources. See **rule 18.7**.

Legislative Materials   13

Besides statutes (**rule 12**), the legislative process generates bills and resolutions (**rule 13.2**); committee hearings (**rule 13.3**); reports, documents, and committee prints (**rule 13.4**); floor debates (**rule 13.5**); and, sometimes, separately bound legislative histories (**rule 13.6**). When citing any United States legislative material except debates, include the title (if relevant), abbreviated name of the house, the number of the Congress, the number assigned to the material, and the year of publication. State legislative materials are cited similarly except when indicated otherwise. Abbreviations for commonly used words in legislative materials are listed in **table T.10**.   T.10

In addition, include parenthetically the session number for House and Senate documents published before the 60th Congress (1907), House Reports published before the 47th Congress (1881), and Senate Reports published before the 40th Congress (1867). For House and Senate materials published after these dates, the session number can be inferred from the year of publication: first sessions always fall in odd-numbered years, while second sessions always fall in even-numbered years. On rare occasions, Congress holds a third session. When citing materials produced during a third session, provide this information parenthetically.

R
11–14

Basic Citation Forms   13.1

federal bill (unenacted)	Privacy Protection Act of 1998, H.R. 3224, 105th Cong. § 2(a) (1998).
	H.R. 11879, 55th Cong. (3d Sess. 1899).
federal resolution (unenacted)	H.R.J. Res. 79, 106th Cong. (1999).
state bill	H.R. 124, 179th Leg., 1st Spec. Sess. (Pa. 1995).
state resolution	S.J. Res. 836, 118th Leg., 3d Spec. Sess. (Me. 1999).
committee hearing	*Background and History of Impeachment: Hearing Before the Subcomm. on the Constitution of the House Comm. on the Judiciary*, 105th Cong. 22–23 (1998) (statement of Rep. Hutchinson, Member, House Comm. on the Judiciary).
federal report	H.R. REP. NO. 101-524, at 10 (1990), *reprinted in* 1990 U.S.C.C.A.N. 1448, 1451.
federal document	H.R. DOC. NO. 102-399, at 3 (1992).
committee print	STAFF OF HOUSE COMM. ON THE JUDICIARY, 93D CONG., CONSTITUTIONAL GROUNDS FOR PRESIDENTIAL IMPEACHMENT 38 (Comm. Print 1974).
congressional debate	145 CONG. REC. H1817 (daily ed. Apr. 12, 1999) (statement of Rep. Pease).

source reprinted in separately bound legislative history	SENATE COMM. ON LABOR AND PUBLIC WELFARE, LABOR-MANAGEMENT REPORTING AND DISCLOSURE ACT OF 1959, S. REP. NO. 86-187, at 4 (1959), *reprinted in* 1959 U.S.C.C.A.N. 2318, 2320, *and in* 1 NLRB, LEGISLATIVE HISTORY OF THE LABOR-MANAGEMENT REPORTING AND DISCLOSURE ACT OF 1959, at 397, 400 (1959).

13.2 Bills and Resolutions

(a) Unenacted federal bills and resolutions. When citing federal bills, include the name of the bill (if relevant), the abbreviated name of the house, the number of the bill, the number of the Congress, the section (if any), and the year of publication:

> S. 516, 105th Cong. § 2 (1997).

> H.R. 422, 106th Cong. (1999).

> Protection from Personal Intrusion Act, H.R. 2448, 105th Cong. § 2(a) (1997).

Cite resolutions analogously, using the following abbreviations:

> H.R. Res.

> S. Res.

> H.R. Con. Res.

> S. Con. Res.

> H.R.J. Res.

> S.J. Res.

> S. Exec. Res.

Thus:

> H.R.J. Res. 648, 105th Cong. (1998).

A parallel citation to either a published committee hearing or a legislative report may also be provided if it would assist the reader in locating the bill (**rules 13.3** and **13.4**).

(b) Enacted federal bills and resolutions. Enacted bills and joint resolutions are statutes (**rule 12**). They are cited as statutes except when used to document legislative history, in which case they are cited as unenacted bills.

Enacted simple and concurrent resolutions, which bind either one or both houses of Congress, should be cited as unenacted bills. Unless otherwise clear in context, the fact of enactment should be noted parenthetically:

> S. Res. 141, 106th Cong. (1999) (enacted).

> H.R. Con. Res. 196, 106th Cong. (1999) (enacted).

A parallel citation to the *Congressional Record* (for simple resolutions) or to the *Statutes at Large* (for concurrent resolutions) may be provided if it would assist the reader in locating the enacted resolution. Because only enacted resolutions are printed in Stat., a parenthetical noting enactment is not necessary when a parallel citation to Stat. is given:

> S. Res. 218, 83d Cong., 100 Cong. Rec. 2972 (1954) (enacted).

> S. Con. Res. 97, 94th Cong., 90 Stat. 3024 (1976).

(c) State bills and resolutions. When citing state bills and resolutions, include the abbreviated name of the legislative body, the number of the bill or resolution, the number of the legislative body (or, if not numbered, the year of same), and the number or designation of the legislative session. Provide the name of the state, abbreviated according to **table T.11,** and the year of enactment parenthetically.   T.11

> H.D. 636, 1999 Leg., 413th Sess. (Md. 1999).

> H.R. 189, 145th Gen. Assem., Reg. Sess. (Ga. 1999).

R
11–14

A parallel citation to state session laws may be provided if it would assist the reader in locating an enacted resolution.

> H.R.J. Res. 1, 40th Leg., 2d Spec. Sess., 1974 Utah Laws 7.

Hearings   13.3

When citing federal committee hearings, always include the entire subject-matter title as it appears on the cover, the bill number (if any), the subcommittee name (if any), the committee name, the number of the Congress, the page number of the particular material being cited (if any), and the year of publication. Subcommittee and committee names may be abbreviated according to **tables T.6, T.10,**   T.6/T.10
and **T.11**. Cite as follows: T.11

> *Protection from Personal Intrusion Act and Privacy Protection Act of 1998: Hearing on H.R. 2448 and H.R. 3224 Before the House Comm. on the Judiciary*, 105th Cong. 56–57 (1998) (statement of Richard Masur, President, Screen Actors Guild).

When citing state committee hearings, follow the same form, but also include the number of the legislative session:

> *Tax Credit for Cost of Providing Commuter Benefits to Employees: Hearing on H.D. 636 Before the House Comm. on Ways and Means*, 1999 Leg., 413th Sess. 5–8 (Md. 1999) (statement of Del. Paul Carlson, Member, House Comm. on Ways and Means).

Reports, Documents, and Committee Prints   13.4

(a) Numbered federal reports and documents. Citations to numbered federal reports should include the name of the house, the number of the Congress connected by a hyphen to the number of the report, the part or page number on which material being cited appears, and the year of publication. Use large and small caps:

> H.R. Rep. No. 99-253, pt. 1, at 54 (1985).
>
> S. Rep. No. 84-2, at 7 (1955).
>
> H.R. Conf. Rep. No. 98-1037, at 3 (1984).

Cite numbered federal documents analogously, using the following abbreviations:

> H.R. Doc. No.
>
> S. Doc. No.
>
> S. Exec. Doc. No.
>
> H.R. Misc. Doc. No.

When possible (and particularly for documents after 1974), give a parallel citation to the permanent edition of *United States Code Congressional and Administrative News* (**rule 12.5(b)**):

> S. Rep. No. 95-797, at 4 (1978), *reprinted in* 1978 U.S.C.C.A.N. 9260, 9263.

(b) Titles and authors. Titles of numbered reports or documents may be indicated; if the title is given, the author should also be named (see **rule 15.1.3** regarding institutional authors):

> Carlton Koepge, The Road to Industrial Peace, H.R. Doc. No. 82-563, at 29–30 (1952).
>
> U.S. Immigration Comm'n, Immigration Legislation, S. Doc. No. 61-758, at 613 (3d Sess. 1911).

(c) Unnumbered federal documents and committee prints. Committee prints and unnumbered documents must be cited as works of institutional authors (**rule 15.1.3**). Note that the number of the Congress is part of the author's name:

> Staff of Senate Comm. on the Judiciary, 81st Cong., Report on Antitrust Law 17 (Comm. Print 1950).

If the document or committee print is primarily the work of specific persons, that fact may be noted parenthetically.

(d) State materials. Citations to state legislative reports, documents, and similar materials must include the abbreviated name of the legislative body, the number of the legislative body connected by a hyphen to the number of the report or document, the number of the legislative session, the part or page number on which the material being cited appears, and the year of publication. Unless it is clear from the title or author information appearing in the citation, provide the name of the state abbreviated according to **table T.11** parenthetically:

T.11

> S. 178-247, 1st Sess., at 4 (Pa. 1994).

Titles of numbered reports or documents may be indicated; if the title is given, the author should also be named (see **rule 15.1.3** regarding institutional authors):

COMMONWEALTH OF PA. DEP'T OF AGRIC., ANNUAL REPORT OF THE STATE FOOD PURCHASE PROGRAM, S. 178-247, 1st. Sess., at 4 (1994).

Debates 13.5

Cite congressional debates after 1873 to the *Congressional Record*; use the daily edition only for matter not yet appearing in the bound edition:

123 CONG. REC. 17,147 (1977).

131 CONG. REC. S11,465–66 (daily ed. Sept. 13, 1985) (statement of Sen. Wallop).

Cite congressional debates through 1873 according to the following models:

1833–1873 CONG. GLOBE, 36th Cong., 1st Sess. 1672 (1860).

1824–1837 10 REG. DEB. 3472 (1834).

1789–1824 38 ANNALS OF CONG. 624 (1822).
For vol. 1, however, give the name(s) of the editor(s) in parentheses:
1 ANNALS OF CONG. 486 (Joseph Gales ed., 1789).

Separately Bound Legislative Histories 13.6

The legislative histories of several important acts are published separately (e.g., the Administrative Procedure Act; titles VII and IX of the Civil Rights Act of 1964; the Clean Air Act Amendments of 1970; the Equal Employment Opportunity Act; the Internal Revenue Acts; the National Labor Relations Act; the Occupational Safety and Health Act of 1970; and the Securities Exchange Act of 1934). If it would aid the reader in locating the source, a parallel citation may be given to such a separate publication. Cite these publications according to **rule 15** (books, pamphlets, and other nonperiodic materials):

H.R. REP. No. 80-245, at 6 (1947), *reprinted in* 1 NLRB, LEGISLATIVE HISTORY OF THE LABOR-MANAGEMENT RELATIONS ACT, 1947, at 292, 297 (1948).

Internal Revenue Amendments, Pub. L. No. 87-834, § 15(a), 76 Stat. 960, 1041–42 (1962) (codified at I.R.C. § 1248(a) (1994)), *reprinted in* JOINT COMM. ON INT. REV. TAX., 90TH CONG., LEGISLATIVE HISTORY OF THE INTERNAL REVENUE CODE OF 1954, at 473–74 (1967).

Short Forms for Legislative Materials 13.7

(a) Main text. In law review text, use the forms listed in the "Text" column of the table below to refer to legislative materials. Provide a citation (in full or short form according to **rule 13.7(c)**) in an accompanying footnote when appropriate.

(b) Footnote text. Similarly, when referring to legislative materials in law review footnote text, use the forms listed in the "Text" column of the table below. Provide a citation (in full or short form according to **rule 13.7(c)**) in an accompanying citation clause or sentence when appropriate.

(c) Citations. In law review citations, use any of the forms listed in the "Short citation" column of the table below that clearly identifies the legislative material if the legislative material is already cited (in full or short form) in either the *same footnote* or in a manner such that it can be readily found in *one of the preceding five footnotes*. Otherwise, use the "Full citation" form. See **rule 4.2** regarding the use of *"supra"* with legislative hearings.

	Full citation	Text	Short citation
federal bill (unenacted)	H.R. 3055, 94th Cong. (1976)	House Bill 3055	H.R. 3055
state resolution	S. Res. 20, 37th Leg., 2d Sess. (Okla. 1979)	Oklahoma Senate Resolution 20	Okla. S. Res. 20
federal report	H.R. REP. No. 92-98 (1971)	House Report 98	H.R. REP. No. 92-98
federal document	H.R. Doc. No. 94-208 (1975)	House Document 208	H.R. Doc. No. 94-208

(d) Electronic sources. See **rule 18.7**.

14 Administrative and Executive Materials

Administrative and executive materials include federal rules and regulations (**rule 14.2**), except those of the Treasury Department (**rule 14.5**); adjudications and arbitrations (**rule 14.3**); advisory opinions (**rule 14.4**); federal taxation materials (**rule 14.5**); SEC materials (**rule 14.6**); presidential papers and executive orders (**rule 14.7**); court administrative orders (**rule 14.8**); and patents (**rule 14.9**).

Cite state materials by analogy to the federal examples given in this rule. For additional information regarding citation of the administrative and executive materials of the various states, see **table T.1**.

T.1

14.1 Basic Citation Forms

federal regulation cited to the *Code of Federal Regulations*   FTC Credit Practices Rule, 16 C.F.R. § 444 (1999).

federal regulation cited to the *Federal Register*   Importation of Fruits and Vegetables, 60 Fed. Reg. 50,379 (Sept. 29, 1995) (to be codified at 7 C.F.R. pt. 300).

administrative adjudication	Reichhold Chems., Inc., 91 F.T.C. 246 (1978).
arbitration	Charles P. Ortmeyer, 23 Indus. Arb. 272 (1980) (Stern, Arb.).
formal advisory opinion	39 Op. Att'y Gen. 484 (1940).
Treasury regulation	Treas. Reg. § 1.302-2(b) (1955).
revenue ruling	Rev. Rul. 83-137, 1983-2 C.B. 41 (1983).
private letter ruling	Priv. Ltr. Rul. 86-01-012 (Sept. 30, 1985).
SEC no-action letter	Union Carbide Corp., SEC No-Action Letter, [1994–1995 Transfer Binder] Fed. Sec. L. Rep. (CCH) ¶ 76,911, at 78,641 (Apr. 15, 1994).
SEC release	Customer Limit Orders, Exchange Act Release No. 34,753, [1994–1995 Transfer Binder] Fed. Sec. L. Rep. (CCH) ¶ 85,434, at 85,748 (Sept. 29, 1994).
executive order	Exec. Order No. 11,609, 3 C.F.R. 586 (1971–1975), *reprinted as amended in* 3 U.S.C. § 301 app. at 404–07 (1994).

R

11–14

Rules, Regulations, and Other Publications   14.2

Citation of a particular provision of a regulation in the *Code of Federal Regulations*:

C.F.R. title   abbreviation of set of   date of code edition cited
   no.   regulations cited

7 • C.F.R. • § • 319.76 • (1999).

section symbol and
specific section cited

(a) Final rules and regulations. Whenever possible, cite all federal rules and regulations except Treasury materials (**rule 14.5**) to the *Code of Federal Regulations* (C.F.R.) by title, section or part (or, in certain circumstances, by page, as in **rule 14.7(a)**), and year:

FCC Broadcast Radio Services, 47 C.F.R. § 73.609 (1999).

Each title of C.F.R. is revised at least once a year; cite the most recent edition. If a rule or regulation is commonly known by name, its name should be given:

FTC Credit Practices Rule, 16 C.F.R. § 444 (1999).

The *Federal Register* (Fed. Reg.) publishes rules and regulations before they are entered into the C.F.R. Citations to rules or regulations in the *Federal Register* should give any commonly used name of the

rule or regulation, the volume and page on which the rule or regulation (or any preceding discussion thereof) begins, and the date. When
citing a part of a rule or regulation, give both the page on which the
rule or regulation (or preceding discussion) begins and the page(s) on
which the cited material appears. When the *Federal Register* indicates
where the rule or regulation will appear in C.F.R., give that information
parenthetically:

> Importation of Fruits and Vegetables, 60 Fed. Reg. 50,379, 50,381
> (Sept. 29, 1995) (to be codified at 7 C.F.R. pt. 300).

> Federal Acquisition Regulations for National Aeronautics and Space
> Administration, 55 Fed. Reg. 52,782 (Dec. 21, 1990) (to be codified
> at 48 C.F.R. pt. 1).

(b) Proposed rules and other notices. Administrative notices (which
are not transferred to C.F.R.) should be cited to the *Federal Register*.
When citing notices of proposed rules and regulations, follow the form
for final rules, but add the status to the date parenthetical:

> Control of Air Pollution from New Motor Vehicles and New Motor
> Vehicle Engines, 56 Fed. Reg. 9754 (proposed March 7, 1991) (to be
> codified at 40 C.F.R. pt. 86).

Cite notices pertaining to administrative adjudications according to
rule 14.3. Cite other administrative notices by volume, page, and
date. The citation may begin with a description or a commonly used
name:

> Meeting Notice, 65 Fed. Reg. 3415 (Jan. 21, 2000).

For rules and announcements not appearing in C.F.R. or Fed. Reg., cite
a service (**rule 19**) or the original form of issuance—in that order of
preference.

(c) Regular reports. Cite in the same manner as periodicals (**rule
16**). Always give the abbreviated agency name first and then use the
abbreviations for periodical names given in **table T.14**:

> 4 NLRB ANN. REP. 93 (1939).

> 1942 ATT'Y GEN. ANN. REP. 22.

> 1955–1956 MICH. ATT'Y GEN. BIENNIAL REP. pt. 1, at 621.

(d) Other publications. Cite as works by institutional authors (**rule
15.1.3**), including a serial number, if any (**rule 15.3**), unless issued as
congressional documents (**rule 13.4**).

14.3   Administrative Adjudications and Arbitrations

Citations to administrative cases and arbitrations should conform to
rule 10, except as follows:

Names   14.3.1

(a) Administrative adjudications. Cite by the full reported name of the first-listed private party or by the official subject-matter title. Omit all procedural phrases.

> Trojan Transp., Inc., 249 N.L.R.B. 642 (1980).
>
> Great Lakes Area Case, 8 C.A.B. 360 (1947).

Subject-matter titles may sometimes indicate the nature and stage of an adjudicatory proceeding. It is permissible to shorten such titles, and, if the nature and stage of the proceeding is not clear from the context, such information may be included in a parenthetical phrase at the end of the citation. The parenthetical phrase may consist of terms such as "initiation," "prelim. neg.," or "determination," or may be more elaborate. Thus:

> **Bottled Green Olives from Spain, 50 Fed. Reg. 28,237 (Dep't Commerce July 11, 1985) (final admin. review).**
>
> **Not:** Bottled Green Olives from Spain; Final Results of Administrative Review of Countervailing Duty Order, 50 Fed. Reg. 28,237 (Dep't Commerce July 11, 1985).

Cite the names of Tax Court and Board of Tax Appeals decisions (**rule 14.5.3**) as those of a court (**rule 10.2**), not as those of an agency:

> Hartung v. Comm'r, 55 T.C. 1 (1970).

(b) Arbitrations. Cite as court cases if adversary parties are named and as administrative adjudications if they are not. The arbitrator's name should be indicated parenthetically. Thus:

> Kroger Co. v. Amalgamated Meat Cutters, Local 539, 74 Lab. Arb. Rep. (BNA) 785, 787 (1980) (Doering, Arb.).
>
> Charles P. Ortmeyer, 23 Indus. Arb. 272 (1980) (Stern, Arb.).

Which Sources to Cite   14.3.2

(a) Official reporters. Cite the official reporter of the agency if the opinion appears therein:

> Tennessee Intrastate Rates & Charges, 286 I.C.C. 41 (1952).
>
> Deformed Steel Concrete Reinforcing Bar from Peru, 50 Fed. Reg. 28,230 (Dep't Commerce July 11, 1985).

For a list of official federal administrative reporters, see **table T.1**.   T.1

(b) Official releases and slip opinions. If the opinion does not appear in an official reporter, cite the official release or slip opinion. Provide the full date, any helpful publication number, and the number of the case or investigation:

> Iron Construction Castings from Brazil, Canada, India, and the People's Republic of China, USITC Pub. 1720, Inv. No. 701-TA-249 (June 1985).

R
11–14

If the opinion will later be published in an official bound volume, provide, if available, the volume number and the initial page number; if the initial page is not available, retain the case number:

> Rosenberg Library Ass'n, 269 N.L.R.B. No. 197 (Apr. 24, 1984).

Whenever possible, append a parallel citation to an unofficial reporter, service, or other source—in that order of preference:

> Rosenberg Library Ass'n, 269 N.L.R.B. No. 197, 1983–1984 NLRB Dec. (CCH) ¶ 16,238 (Apr. 24, 1984).

Once the official reporter is issued, however, cite only to that reporter:

> Rosenberg Library Ass'n, 269 N.L.R.B. 1173 (1984).

T.16 For a list of services and service abbreviations, see **table T.16**.

14.3.3 Issuing Agency

If the name of the issuing agency is not apparent from the name of the source, include the name of the agency abbreviated according to **rule 15.1.3(c)** in the parenthetical containing the date:

> General Dynamics Corp., 50 Fed. Reg. 45,949 (Dep't of Labor Nov. 5, 1985).

14.4 Advisory Opinions

Cite formal advisory opinions by volume, type of opinion (including issuing agency), page, and year:

> 42 Op. Att'y Gen. 111 (1962).

The name of the opinion may be included:

> Legality of Revised Phila. Plan, 42 Op. Att'y Gen. 405 (1969).

To refer to a specific page or pages, use a pinpoint cite:

> 1 Op. Off. Legal Counsel 168, 173–74 (1977).

If an opinion appears only in unpaginated or separately paginated slip opinions, but will eventually be included in a volume, cite according to the examples given in **rule 14.3.2**:

> Rights-of-Way Across Nat'l Forests, 43 Op. Att'y Gen. No. 26 (June 23, 1980).

14.5 Federal Taxation Materials

14.5.1 Treasury Regulations

If the regulation cited has never been amended, give the year of promulgation and cite without the source. If the regulation cited is a temporary regulation, that fact must be indicated:

> Treas. Reg. § 1.72-16(a) (1963).
>
> Treas. Reg. § 39.23(p)-3 (1953).

Temp. Treas. Reg. § 1.338-4T(k) (1985).

If any subsection of the regulation has been amended or for some other reason the regulation has appeared in substantially different versions, give the year of the last amendment and cite without the source. This form should be followed even if the particular subsection cited has never been amended:

Treas. Reg. § 1.61-2(c) (as amended in 1995).

When the fact that the regulation has been amended is relevant to the discussion, include the source of the amendment:

Treas. Reg. § 1.61-2(c) (as amended by T.D. 8607, 1995-36 I.R.B. 8).

Cite proposed Treasury regulations to the *Federal Register:*

Prop. Treas. Reg. § 1.704-1, 48 Fed. Reg. 9871 (Mar. 9, 1983).

For special citation forms for federal taxation materials in court documents and legal memoranda, see **practitioners' note P.5.**

P.5

Treasury Determinations

14.5.2 11–14

(a) Revenue Rulings, Revenue Procedures, Treasury Decisions. Cite to the *Cumulative Bulletin* (C.B.) or its advance sheet, the *Internal Revenue Bulletin* (I.R.B.), or to *Treasury Decisions Under Internal Revenue Laws* (Treas. Dec. Int. Rev.)—in that order of preference:

Rev. Rul. 83-137, 1983-2 C.B. 41.

Rev. Proc. 85-47, 1985-37 I.R.B. 10.

T.D. 2747, 20 Treas. Dec. Int. Rev. 457 (1918).

The *Cumulative Bulletin* has been numbered in three series: 1919 to 1921, by volume number; 1921 to 1936, by volume number and part number; and 1937 to date, by year and part number:

T.B.R. 29, 1 C.B. 230 (1919).

I.T. 2624, 11-1 C.B. 122 (1932).

T.D. 7522, 1978-1 C.B. 59.

The abbreviations used in the above examples and other abbreviations are explained in the introductory pages of each volume of the *Cumulative Bulletin.*

(b) Private Letter Rulings. Cite by number and the date issued, if available:

Priv. Ltr. Rul. 86-01-012 (Sept. 30, 1985).

(c) Technical Advice Memoranda. Cite by number and the date issued, if available:

Tech. Adv. Mem. 85-04-005 (Sept. 28, 1984).

(d) General Counsel Memoranda. Cite by number and the date on which the memorandum was approved:

> Gen. Couns. Mem. 39,417 (Sept. 30, 1985).

(e) Other Treasury determinations. Cite all other Treasury materials, including Technical Memoranda (Tech. Mem.), Office Memoranda (Off. Mem.), Technical Information Releases (Tech. Info. Rel.), Delegation Orders (Deleg. Order), Executive Orders (Exec. Order), Treasury Department Orders (Treas. Dep't Order), Notices, Announcements, and News Releases to the *Cumulative Bulletin* or the *Internal Revenue Bulletin* if therein. Otherwise cite by number and date issued:

> Deleg. Order No. 4 (Rev. 14), 1983-2 C.B. 405.
>
> I.R.S. Notice 84-9, 1984-1 C.B. 341.
>
> Tech. Mem. 1984-524 (June 14, 1984).
>
> I.R.S. News Release IR-84-111 (Oct. 19, 1984).

P.5   For special citation forms for Treasury materials in court documents and legal memoranda, see **practitioners' note P.5.**

14.5.3 Cases

Cite the names of Tax Court and Board of Tax Appeals decisions as those of a court (**rule 10.2**), not as those of an agency (**rule 14.3.1**):

> Benson v. Commissioner, 80 T.C. 789 (1983).
>
> Price v. Commissioner, 46 T.C.M. (CCH) 657 (1983).

If the Commissioner of the Internal Revenue Service has published an acquiescence (*acq.*), acquiescence in result only (*acq. in result*), or nonacquiescence (*nonacq.*) in a decision of the Tax Court or Board of Tax Appeals, that fact may be indicated in the citation of the case:

> New Mexico Bancorp. v. Commissioner, 74 T.C. 1342 (1980), *acq. in result*, 1983-2 C.B. 1.

Similarly, an action on decision (*action on dec.*) may be cited as subsequent history by appending its identifying number, if any, and its full date:

> Keller v. Commissioner, 79 T.C. 7 (1982), *action on dec.*, 1984-037 (Apr. 23, 1984).

See generally **rule 10.7** (prior and subsequent history of cases).

14.6 SEC Materials

(a) No-action letters. Cite the *Federal Register* or a service (**rule 19**). Include the full name of the correspondent and the full date on which the letter became publicly available:

> Union Carbide Corp., SEC No-Action Letter, [1994–1995 Transfer Binder] Fed. Sec. L. Rep. (CCH) ¶ 76,911, at 78,641 (Apr. 15, 1994).

(b) Releases. Cite the *Federal Register*, SEC Docket, or a service **(rule 19)**. If the release is an adjudication, abbreviate the parties' names according to **rule 14.3.1(a)**. If the release has a subject-matter title, it may be presented in a shortened form. Include the act under which the release was issued, the release number, and the full date:

> Customer Limit Orders, Exchange Act Release No. 34,753, [1994–1995 Transfer Binder] Fed. Sec. L. Rep. (CCH) ¶ 85,434, at 85,748 (Sept. 29, 1994).

Presidential Papers and Executive Orders   14.7

(a) Executive orders, presidential proclamations, and reorganization plans. Cite by page number to 3 C.F.R. **(rule 14.2)**, with a parallel citation to U.S.C. (or, if that is unavailable, U.S.C.A. or U.S.C.S.) whenever possible:

> Exec. Order No. 11,609, 3 C.F.R. 586 (1971–1975), *reprinted as amended in* 3 U.S.C. § 301 app. at 404–07 (1988).
>
> Exec. Order No. 11,732, 3 C.F.R. 791 (1971–1975), *reprinted in* 3 U.S.C. § 301 (1988).

R
11–14

Cite the *Federal Register* if the material is not in C.F.R.:

> Exec. Order No. 12,531, 50 Fed. Reg. 36,033 (Aug. 30, 1985).
>
> Proclamation No. 5366, 50 Fed. Reg. 37,635 (Sept. 14, 1985).

A parallel citation to the *Statutes at Large* may also be given:

> Reorg. Plan No. 1 of 1978, 3 C.F.R. 321 (1978), *reprinted in* 5 U.S.C. app. at 1366 (1988), *and in* 92 Stat. 3781 (1978).

(b) Other presidential papers. Presidential papers, speeches, and documents have been published in the *Public Papers of the Presidents* (PUB. PAPERS) since 1945. For material not yet recorded in the *Public Papers*, cite the *Weekly Compilation of Presidential Documents* (WEEKLY COMP. PRES. DOC.), since 1965, or the *U.S. Code Congressional and Administrative News* (U.S.C.C.A.N.) **(rule 12.5(b))**:

> President's Message to Congress Transmitting Rescissions and Deferrals, 11 WEEKLY COMP. PRES. DOC. 1334 (Dec. 1, 1975).

Court Administrative Orders   14.8

Cite the official reporter if therein; give the title of the order, if any:

> Order Discharging the Advisory Committee, 352 U.S. 803 (1956).

Patents   14.9

Cite the patent number and the date the patent was issued:

> U.S. Patent No. 4,405,829 (issued Sept. 20, 1983).

14.10   Short Forms for Regulations

(a) Main text. In law review text, use the forms listed in the "Text" column of the table below to refer to regulations. Provide a citation (in full or short form according to **rule 14.10(c)**) in an accompanying footnote when appropriate.

(b) Footnote text. Similarly, when referring to regulations in law review footnote text, use the forms listed in the "Text" column of the table below. Provide a citation (in full or short form according to **rule 14.10(c)**) in an accompanying citation clause or sentence when appropriate.

(c) Citations. In law review citations, use any of the forms listed in the "Short citation" column of the table below that clearly identifies the regulation if the regulation is already cited (in full or short form) in either the *same footnote* or in a manner such that it can be readily found in *one of the preceding five footnotes*. Otherwise, use the "Full citation" form.

	Full citation	Text	Short citation
Code of Federal Regulations	FTC Credit Practices Rule, 16 C.F.R. § 444 (1995)	16 C.F.R. § 444	16 C.F.R. § 444 or § 444
Federal Register	Importation of Fruits and Vegetables, 60 Fed. Reg. 50,379, 50,381 (Sept. 29, 1995) (to be codified at C.F.R. pt. 300)	Importation of Fruits and Vegetables	Importation of Fruits and Vegetables, 60 Fed. Reg. at 50,381

(d) Electronic sources. See **rule 18.7**.

Books, Periodical Materials, and Other Secondary Sources

Rule 15: Books, Pamphlets, and Other Nonperiodic Materials   107
     15.1: Author, Editor, and Translator   107
     15.2: Title   109
     15.3: Serial Number   110
     15.4: Edition, Publisher, and Date   110
     15.5: Shorter Works in Collection   112
     15.6: Prefaces, Forewords, Introductions, and Epilogues   113
     15.7: Special Citation Forms   113
     15.8: Short Citation Forms   114

Rule 16: Periodical Materials   117
     16.1: Author   118
     16.2: Title   118
     16.3: Consecutively Paginated Journals   119
     16.4: Nonconsecutively Paginated Journals and Magazines   119
     16.5: Newspapers   120
     16.6: Special Citation Forms   121
     16.7: Short Citation Forms   125

Rule 17: Unpublished and Forthcoming Sources   126
     17.1: Unpublished Materials   126
     17.2: Forthcoming Publications   128
     17.3: Short Citation Forms   129

Rule 18: Electronic Media and Other Nonprint Resources   129
     18.1: Commercial Electronic Databases   130
     18.2: The Internet   132
     18.3: CD-ROM   141
     18.4: Microform   142
     18.5: Films, Broadcasts, and Noncommercial Videotapes   142
     18.6: Audio Recordings   143
     18.7: Short Citation Forms   143

R
15–18

Books, Pamphlets, and Other Nonperiodic Materials   15

Citation of a particular section of James and Hazard's treatise on civil procedure:

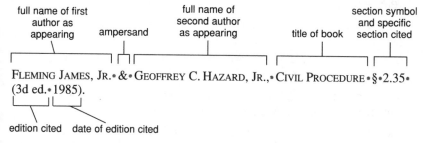

full name of first author as appearing | ampersand | full name of second author as appearing | title of book | section symbol and specific section cited

FLEMING JAMES, JR. • & • GEOFFREY C. HAZARD, JR., • CIVIL PROCEDURE • § • 2.35 • (3d ed. • 1985).

edition cited   date of edition cited

Citation of a particular page within Charles Dickens's *Bleak House*:

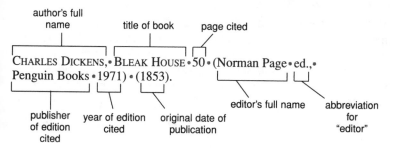

author's full name | title of book | page cited

CHARLES DICKENS, • BLEAK HOUSE • 50 • (Norman Page • ed., • Penguin Books • 1971) • (1853).

publisher of edition cited | year of edition cited | original date of publication | editor's full name | abbreviation for "editor"

R
15–18

Cite books, pamphlets, and other nonperiodic materials by volume, if more than one (**rule 3.2(a)**); author, editor, and/or translator (**rule 15.1**); title (**rule 15.2**); serial number, if any (**rule 15.3**); page, section, or paragraph (**rules 3.3** and **3.4**), if only part of a volume is cited; edition, if more than one has appeared; publisher, if not the original one; and date (**rule 15.4**). Cite prefaces or forewords according to **rule 15.6**, supplements according to **rule 3.2(c)**, and appendices according to **rule 3.5**.

Author, Editor, and Translator   15.1

Author   15.1.1

The first time a work is cited, always give the author's full name as it appears on the publication, including any designation such as "Jr." or "III" (inserting a comma before the designation only if the author does).

Two authors should appear separated by an ampersand in the order in which they are listed on the publication. Use large and small capitals:

MANCUR OLSON, THE LOGIC OF COLLECTIVE ACTION 53–65 (1965).

HAROLD W. FUSON, JR., TELLING IT ALL: A LEGAL GUIDE TO THE EXERCISE OF FREE SPEECH 57–58 (1995).

> A. LEO LEVIN & MEYER KRAMER, NEW PROVISIONS IN THE KETUBAH: A LEGAL OPINION 3–4 (1955).

If a work has more than two authors, use the first author's name followed by "ET AL." unless the inclusion of other authors is particularly relevant:

> A. LEO LEVIN ET AL., DISPUTE RESOLUTION DEVICES IN A DEMOCRATIC SOCIETY 77 (1985).

> TERESA A. SULLIVAN, ELIZABETH WARREN & JAY LAWRENCE WESTBROOK, AS WE FORGIVE OUR DEBTORS 121–42 (1989).

When citing a single volume of a multivolume work, give only the author(s) of the volume cited:

> 4 CHARLES ALAN WRIGHT & ARTHUR R. MILLER, FEDERAL PRACTICE AND PROCEDURE § 1006 (2d ed. 1987).

15.1.2 Editor or Translator

Regardless of whether a work has an author, always give the full name of an editor and/or translator according to **rule 15.1.1**, followed by "ed." or "trans.," in the parenthetical containing information about the edition, publisher, and date (see **rule 15.4**). A comma should separate the designation of an editor or translator from other publication information:

> MICHEL FOUCAULT, DISCIPLINE AND PUNISH 30–31 (Alan Sheridan trans., Vintage Books 2d ed. 1995) (1978).

> ETHICS OF CONSUMPTION: THE GOOD LIFE, JUSTICE, AND GLOBAL STEWARDSHIP 118–19 (David A. Crocker & Toby Linden eds., 1998).

> ALLEN SCHICK, THE CHANGING ROLE OF THE CENTRAL BUDGET OFFICE (Jon Blondal ed., 1997).

If a work has more than two editors or translators, use the first name followed by "et al.":

> AIDS AND THE LAW (Harlon L. Dalton et al. eds., 1987).

> THE BLUEBOOK: A UNIFORM SYSTEM OF CITATION (Columbia Law Review Ass'n et al. eds., 17th ed. 2000).

If a work has no named author, editor, or translator, it may be necessary to designate an edition by the name of the publisher (**rule 15.4**).

15.1.3 Institutional Authors and Editors

(a) Institutional authors. Citations to works by institutional authors begin with the author's complete name. Abbreviate according to **rule 15.1.3(c)**:

> EASTERN AIRLINES, INC., 1978 ANNUAL REPORT 5 (1979).

> CITY OF NEW HAVEN, RECYCLE NOW NEW HAVEN (1991).

Name first the smallest subdivision that prepared the work, then the overall body of which the subdivision is a part. Do not list any intermediate divisions:

> STATISTICAL ANALYSIS CTR., STATE CRIME COMM'N, CRIME IN GEORGIA 41 (1980).

If an individual has authored a work on behalf of an institution and the individual is credited on the cover or title page along with the institution, give the individual author first, followed by the institution. Cite only the largest institutional division listed; do not indicate any subdivisions:

> JUDITH A. LHAMON, NATIONAL ASS'N FOR LAW PLACEMENT, A FAIR SHAKE: LAWFUL AND EFFECTIVE INTERVIEWING 3 (1987).

> CAROLINE W. HARLOW, U.S. DEP'T OF JUSTICE, FEMALE VICTIMS OF VIOLENT CRIME 13 (1991).

(b) Institutional editors. Follow **rule 15.1.2**, substituting the name of the institution for the name of the individual editor:

> THE ROLE OF MEDIATION IN DIVORCE PROCEEDINGS 33 (Vt. Law Sch. Dispute Resolution Project ed., 1987).

(c) Abbreviations. Abbreviate the name of an institutional author or editor only if the result will be completely unambiguous. When abbreviating, use the abbreviations for case names in footnotes according to **table T.6**, and the geographical abbreviations listed in **table T.11**. "United States" should be abbreviated to "U.S." Omit "Inc.," "Ltd.," and similar terms if the name also contains words such as "Co.," "Bros.," "Corp.," and "Ass'n" clearly indicating that the institution is a business firm:

T.6
T.11

> CONSUMER DEPUTY PROGRAM, U.S. CONSUMER PROD. SAFETY COMM'N, CHILDREN'S SLEEPWEAR (1975).

> NAT'L MUN. LEAGUE, A MODEL ELECTION SYSTEM (1973).

Title   15.2

Cite the full main title as it appears on the title page, but capitalize according to **rule 8** (unless the title is not in English, in which case follow **rule 20.1.2(b)**). Give a subtitle only if it is particularly relevant. Do not abbreviate words or omit articles in the title. Use large and small capitals:

> CAPITAL FLOWS IN THE APEC REGION (Moshin S. Kahn & Carmen M. Reinhart eds., 1995).

> 6 JAMES WM. MOORE ET AL., MOORE'S FEDERAL PRACTICE ¶ 56.10 (3d ed. 1999).

When citing a single volume of a multivolume work, give the main title of the volume cited. If the title of a work ends with a numeral, the page number must be set off by a comma and the word "at" (**rule 3.3(a)**):

J.A.S. GRENVILLE, THE MAJOR INTERNATIONAL TREATIES, 1914–1973, at 114–15 (1974).

15.3   Serial Number

(a) Series issued by the author. When citing a publication that is one of a series issued by the author (other than U.N. documents (**rule 21.7**)), include the serial number as part of the title:

BUREAU OF INTELLIGENCE & RESEARCH, U.S. DEP'T OF STATE, PUB. NO. 8732, WORLD STRENGTH OF THE COMMUNIST PARTY ORGANIZATIONS 65 (1973).

WOMEN'S BUREAU, U.S. DEP'T OF LABOR, LEAFLET NO. 55, A WORKING WOMAN'S GUIDE TO HER JOB RIGHTS 4 (1978).

(b) Series issued by one other than the author. To cite a publication that is one of a series issued by someone other than the author, indicate the series and number parenthetically, abbreviating institutional entities according to **rule 15.1.3(c)**:

ALAN J. AUERBACH & LAURENCE J. KOTLIKOFF, NATIONAL SAVINGS, ECONOMIC WELFARE, AND THE STRUCTURE OF TAXATION 24–33 (Nat'l Bureau of Econ. Research, Working Paper No. 729, 1981).

Anne C. Vladek, *Counseling a Plaintiff During Litigation, in* EMPLOYMENT LITIGATION 1990, at 77, 80–82 (PLI Litig. & Admin. Practice Course, Handbook Series No. 386, 1990).

15.4   Edition, Publisher, and Date

(a) Editions. Always cite the latest edition of a work that supports the point under discussion.

(i) Single edition. When citing a work that has been published in only one edition, indicate the year of publication in parentheses. In general, cite by the date of the edition rather than the date of a particular printing:

DEBORAH L. RHODE, JUSTICE AND GENDER 56 (1989).

AIDS AND THE LAW (Harlon L. Dalton et al. eds., 1987).

If a printing differs in a respect relevant to the purposes of the citation, however, give the printing designation and the date of printing instead:

(6th prtg. 1980)

(ii) Multiple editions by the same publisher. When citing a work that has been published by the same publisher in more than one edition, indicate the edition and the year the edition was published. Follow the publisher's terminology when designating an edition (see **table T.15** for a list of publishing abbreviations):

T.15

FLEMING JAMES, JR. ET AL., CIVIL PROCEDURE § 2.3 (4th ed. 1992).

1 WILLIAM MEADE FLETCHER ET AL., FLETCHER CYCLOPEDIA OF THE LAW OF PRIVATE CORPORATIONS § 7.05 (perm. ed., rev. vol. 1999).

(iii) Editions by other than the original publisher. When citing a work that has been published by someone other than the original publisher, indicate the editor and/or translator if any (**rule 15.1.2**), the edition cited if not the first, and the publisher and date of publication of the edition cited. Abbreviate the publisher's name according to **rule 15.1.3(c)**. Unless the work is one that is regularly updated or revised, add a second parenthetical indicating the date of publication of the original edition:

> CHARLES DICKENS, BLEAK HOUSE 49–55 (Norman Page ed., Penguin Books 1971) (1853).

> JOHN C.H. WU, THE GOLDEN AGE OF ZEN 214–15 (Image Books 1996) (1975).

> SIMONE DE BEAUVOIR, THE SECOND SEX, at xvi–xvii (H.M. Parshley ed. & trans., Bantam Books 1961) (1949).

(b) Photoduplicated reprints. Cite photoduplicated reprints to the original, indicating in parentheses the existence of a reprint and the date of the reprint, followed by the publication date of the original in separate parentheses:

> PAUL W. GATES, HISTORY OF PUBLIC LAND LAW DEVELOPMENT 1 (photo. reprint 1979) (1968).

(c) Pre-1900 works. Cite works published before 1900 to a scholarly modern edition, according to **rule 15.4(a)**:

> JOHN LOCKE, TWO TREATISES OF GOVERNMENT 137–39 (Peter Laslett ed., Cambridge Univ. Press 1988) (1690).

If there is no modern edition, cite the first edition whenever possible. When citing a pre-1900 edition, indicate the place of publication and the publisher, separated by a comma:

> 1 JAMES F. STEPHEN, A HISTORY OF THE CRIMINAL LAW OF ENGLAND 156–57 (London, MacMillan 1883).

If the date or place of publication is not available, use the abbreviation "n.p." for "no place" or "n.d." for "no date."

(d) Star edition. In a very few well-known works, the page of the original edition (star page) is indicated, usually by an asterisk (*), in either the margin or the text of all recent editions. In such cases the date and edition may be omitted and the citation made to the star page, unless the material cited was inserted by the editor of a special edition. There is no space between the asterisk and the page number:

> 2 WILLIAM BLACKSTONE, COMMENTARIES *152.

(e) Supplements. Cite pocket parts and bound supplements according to **rule 3.2(c)**:

> 4 SYDNEY C. SCHWEITZER & JOSEPH RASCH, CYCLOPEDIA OF TRIAL PRACTICE § 895 (2d ed. Supp. 1984).

> 5 SAMUEL WILLISTON & RICHARD A. LORD, A TREATISE ON THE LAW
> OF CONTRACTS § 11:8 (4th ed. 1993 & Supp. 1999).

15.5   Shorter Works in Collection

Cite essays and articles in collection according to **rule 15.5.1**. Cite collections of other materials, such as letters, speeches, manuscripts, diaries, debates, newspaper articles, tracts, etc., according to **rule 15.5.2**.

15.5.1 Shorter Works in Collection Generally

(a) Shorter works by various authors. To cite an individual shorter work within a volume of collected works by various authors, list the author's full name according to **rule 15.1** in ordinary type followed by the title of the shorter work in italics, the word *"in,"* the volume number, if any (**rule 3.2(a)**), and the name of the volume as a whole in large and small capitals. Always note the page on which the shorter work begins as well as any pages on which specific material appears (**rule 3.3(a)**). Editors, translators, edition, publisher, and date should be noted parenthetically according to **rules 15.1** and **15.4**:

> Andrew G. Ferguson, *Continuing Seizure: Fourth Amendment Seizure in Section 1983 Malicious Prosecution Cases, in* 15 NAT'L LAWYERS GUILD, CIVIL RIGHTS LITIGATION AND ATTORNEY FEES ANNUAL HANDBOOK 54-1 (Steven Saltzman ed., 1999).
>
> Kay Deaux & Brenda Major, *A Social-Psychological Model of Gender, in* THEORETICAL PERSPECTIVES ON SEXUAL DIFFERENCE 89 (Deborah L. Rhode ed., 1990).

(b) Shorter works by the same author. If all the shorter works within a volume are by the same author, use the same form except print the author's name in large and small capitals and place the volume number, if any, before the author's name (**rule 3.2**):

> OLIVER WENDELL HOLMES, *Law in Science and Science in Law, in* COLLECTED LEGAL PAPERS 210, 210 (1920).
>
> ADRIENNE RICH, *Transcendental Etude, in* THE FACT OF A DOORFRAME 264, 267–68 (1984).

15.5.2 Collected Documents

(a) Documents originally unpublished. Cite letters, diaries, manuscripts, speeches, and other similar works that have never been published except in collection as you would any other shorter work in collection (**rule 15.5.1**), but print the name or description of the document in ordinary roman type. The date of the particular document or other identifying information, if available, may be included in a parenthetical following the document title:

> Letter from Virginia Woolf to Vita Sackville-West (Dec. 22, 1925), *in* 3 THE LETTERS OF VIRGINIA WOOLF, 1923–1928, at 224 (Nigel Nicolson & Joanne Trautmann eds., 1st Am. ed. 1978) (1977).

John Adams, Argument and Report, *in* 2 Legal Papers of John Adams 285, 322–35 (L. Kinvin Wroth & Hiller B. Zobel eds., 1965).

(b) Documents originally published. Use the *"reprinted in"* form (**rule 1.6(b)**) to cite collected materials that previously were published. As far as possible, provide a complete citation for the original work followed by *"reprinted in"* and the citation of the volume containing the reprint:

David Ramsay, An Address to the Freemen of South Carolina, on the Subject of the Federal Constitution (1788), *reprinted in* Pamphlets on the Constitution of the United States, Published During Its Discussion by the People, 1787–1788, at 376 (Paul L. Ford ed., B. Franklin 1971) (1888).

Prefaces, Forewords, Introductions, and Epilogues 15.6

Cite a preface, foreword, introduction, or epilogue by someone other than the author as follows:

L. Maria Child, *Introduction* to Harriet A. Jacobs, Incidents in the Life of a Slave Girl 3, 3–4 (L. Maria Child & Jean F. Yellin eds., Harvard Univ. Press 1987) (1861).

Henry M. Hart & Herbert Wechsler, *Preface to the First Edition* of Paul M. Bator et al., Hart and Wechsler's The Federal Courts and the Federal System, at xxvii, xxx (3d ed. 1988).

R
15–18

Cite to prefatory or other similar material by the author of the work without special designation:

John Hart Ely, Democracy and Distrust, at vii (1980).

Special Citation Forms 15.7

(a) Frequently cited works. A few frequently cited works require special citation forms:

Ballentine's Law Dictionary 1190 (3d ed. 1969).

Black's Law Dictionary 712 (7th ed. 1999).

88 C.J.S. *Trial* § 192 (1955).

17 Am. Jur. 2d *Contracts* § 74 (1964).

Cite proceedings, regular publications by institutes, and reports of sections of the American Bar Association according to **rule 16.6.6**. Cite the ABA Code and Rules of Professional Responsibility and opinions of the ABA Committee on Ethics and Professional Responsibility according to **rule 12.8.6**. Cite model codes or statutes and restatements according to **rule 12.8.5**.

(b) *The Federalist*. Cite an entire *Federalist* paper without indicating a specific edition, and include the author's name parenthetically:

The Federalist No. 23 (Alexander Hamilton).

Group together papers written by the same author:

THE FEDERALIST NOS. 23, 78 (Alexander Hamilton), NOS. 10, 51 (James Madison).

When citing particular material within a paper, however, list the usual publication information for the edition cited:

THE FEDERALIST NO. 5, at 53 (John Jay) (Clinton Rossiter ed., 1961).

(c) *Manual for Complex Litigation.* Citations to the *Manual for Complex Litigation* prepared by the Federal Judicial Center are as follows:

MANUAL FOR COMPLEX LITIGATION (THIRD) § 33.2 (1995).

MANUAL FOR COMPLEX LITIGATION § 2.10 (5th ed. 1982).

However, when citing an edition other than the edition prepared by the Federal Judicial Center, identify the source and publication date of the edition cited:

MANUAL FOR COMPLEX LITIGATION § 4.52 (1982) (supplement to CHARLES ALAN WRIGHT & ARTHUR R. MILLER, FEDERAL PRACTICE AND PROCEDURE (1969–1985)).

(d) *The Bible.* The *Bible* is cited as follows:

2 *Kings* 12:19.

The version may be indicated parenthetically if relevant:

Mark 9:21 (King James).

(e) Shakespeare. A Shakespearean play may be cited as follows:

WILLIAM SHAKESPEARE, THE SECOND PART OF KING HENRY THE SIXTH act 4, sc. 2.

To cite particular lines, a specific edition should be indicated as provided by **rule 15.4**.

(f) *The Bluebook.* The *Bluebook* is cited as follows:

THE BLUEBOOK: A UNIFORM SYSTEM OF CITATION R. 1.2(e), at 24 (Columbia Law Review Ass'n et al. eds., 17th ed. 2000).

THE BLUEBOOK: A UNIFORM SYSTEM OF CITATION 293 tbl. T.10 (Columbia Law Review Ass'n et al. eds., 16th ed. 9th prtg. 1999).

15.8   Short Citation Forms

Once a book, pamphlet, or other nonperiodic material has been cited in full in a law review footnote, a short form employing either "*id.*" or "*supra*" may be used to refer to the work in subsequent citations. Never use "*infra*" to refer to these materials. To refer to shorter works in a collection that have already been cited in full, consult **rule 15.8.2**. For further guidance on the use of short forms for books, pamphlets, and other nonperiodic materials in court documents and legal memoranda, see **practitioners' note P.4(d)**.

Short Forms for Books, Pamphlets, and Nonperiodic Materials Generally

15.8.1

(a) *Id.* If the work was cited as the immediately preceding authority within the same footnote or as the sole authority in the immediately preceding footnote, use *"id."* to refer to the work, indicating any difference in page, section, or paragraph number. If citing the same page(s) or subdivision(s), simply use *"id."* without indicating a page or subdivision. For a multivolume work, always indicate the volume number cited regardless whether it has changed. Note that "at" should precede any page number in a shortened citation (but not a section or paragraph number):

¹ ROBERT M. COVER, JUSTICE ACCUSED 19 (1975).

² *Id.* Cover goes on to discuss this concept in more detail. *Id.* at 22–30.

³ *See id.* at 207.

⁴ LAURENCE H. TRIBE, AMERICAN CONSTITUTIONAL LAW § 15-1, at 1303 (2d ed. 1988).

⁵ *Id.* §§ 15-9 to -10, at 1336–38.

⁶ 4 RICHARD R. POWELL, POWELL ON REAL PROPERTY ¶ 513[3], at 41-142 (Patrick J. Rohan ed., 1995).

⁷ 2 *id.* ¶ 203, at 20–17.

⁸ 1 *id.* ¶ 25, at 9–41.

R
15–18

(b) *Supra.* If the publication has been cited in full but not as the immediately preceding authority in the same footnote or as the sole authority in the immediately preceding footnote, use the author's last name or the name of the institutional author followed by *"supra"* to refer to the work. If there is no author, give the title instead; and if the first citation to the work gives a hereinafter form (**rule 4.2(b)**), use the hereinafter form in place of the author or title. Give the footnote in which the full citation appears unless the full citation is in the same footnote, in which case *"supra"* without a footnote reference may be used. Always indicate the page, section, or paragraph number cited except when citing the work in its entirety. Note that "at" should precede any page number in a *"supra"* citation (but not a section or paragraph number):

⁹ CITY OF NEW HAVEN, RECYCLE NOW NEW HAVEN (1991); *see also* THOMAS C. SCHELLING, A PROCESS OF RESIDENTIAL SEGREGATION: NEIGHBORHOOD TIPPING, *reprinted in* ECONOMIC FOUNDATIONS OF PROPERTY LAW 307, 308 (Bruce A. Ackerman ed., 1975); TRIBE, *supra* note 4, § 9-4, at 596. The recycling pamphlet explains the city's new program. CITY OF NEW HAVEN, *supra.*

¹⁰ COVER, *supra* note 1, at 148; 2 POWELL, *supra* note 6, ¶ 203, at 20-17.

[11] For an overview of how the American judiciary dealt with the issue, see generally COVER, *supra* note 1.

[12] *See, e.g.*, THE ROLE OF MEDIATION IN DIVORCE PROCEEDINGS (Vt. Law Sch. Dispute Resolution Project ed., 1987); WOMEN'S BUREAU, U.S. DEP'T OF LABOR, LEAFLET NO. 55, A WORKING WOMAN'S GUIDE TO HER JOB RIGHTS (1978) [hereinafter WORKING WOMAN'S GUIDE].

[13] See, for example, the research collected in THE ROLE OF MEDIATION IN DIVORCE PROCEEDINGS, *supra* note 12.

[14] *See, e.g.*, FEMINISM/POSTMODERNISM (Linda J. Nicholson ed., 1990); WORKING WOMAN'S GUIDE, *supra* note 12.

[15] *See* CITY OF NEW HAVEN, *supra* note 9 (noting that recycling helps the environment).

15.8.2 Short Forms for Shorter Works in Collection

To cite an essay, article, or document found within a volume of collected shorter works when the shorter work has already been cited in full, you may use "*id.*" to refer to the shorter work if it was cited as the immediately preceding authority within the same footnote or as the sole authority within the immediately preceding footnote. Do not use "*id.*" to refer to the collection as a whole when citing another shorter work within the collection. Use a "*supra*" form to refer to the collection as a whole. If the shorter work was not cited as the immediately preceding authority in the same footnote or as the sole authority in the immediately preceding footnote, use a "*supra*" form when citing the individual work and/or the collection as a whole. The "*supra*" form for the individual work should include the last name of the author or authors, or, if none, the title of the shorter work. The "*supra*" form for the entire volume should include the title of the collection (rather than an author) regardless whether the collected pieces have a single author or multiple authors. For further guidance on the use of short forms for shorter works in collection in court documents and legal

P.4   memoranda, see **practitioners' note P.4(d)**:

[16] Letter from Virginia Woolf to Vita Sackville-West (Dec. 22, 1925), *in* 3 THE LETTERS OF VIRGINIA WOOLF, 1923–1928, at 224 (N. Nicolson & Joanne Trautmann eds., 1st Am. ed. 1978); *cf.* Judith Butler, *Gender Trouble, Feminist Theory, and Psychoanalytic Discourse*, *in* FEMINISM/POSTMODERNISM, *supra* note 14, at 324, 324–25; Andreas Huyssen, *Mapping the Postmodern*, *in* FEMINISM/POSTMODERNISM, *supra* note 14, at 234, 234–35. Butler does not think "woman" can be adequately defined, Butler, *supra*, at 325, but Woolf's observations are especially compelling, Letter from Virginia Woolf to Vita Sackville-West, *supra*.

[17] A wholly different perspective is presented in AYN RAND, *The Cashing-In: The Student "Rebellion,"* *in* THE NEW LEFT 13, 20–24 (1971). *But see* Huyssen, *supra* note 16, at 234–35 (questioning whether postmodern transformation has generated genuinely new forms).

[18] *E.g.,* SCHELLING, *supra* note 9, at 310.

[19] *Id. But see* AYN RAND, *The Comprachicos, in* THE NEW LEFT, *supra* note 17, at 152, 203 (arguing that the educational establishment teaches ideas that destroy children's minds).

[20] *See* RAND, *supra* note 17, at 99; RAND, *supra* note 19, at 201.

Periodical Materials   16

Citation of particular pages within a law review article with parenthetical information about what appears on those pages:

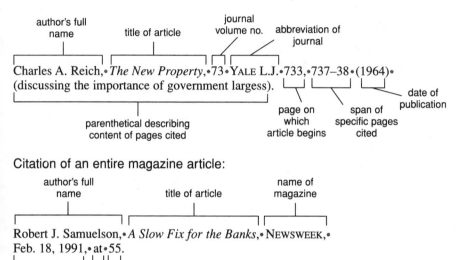

Citation of an entire magazine article:

Citation of a signed newspaper article:

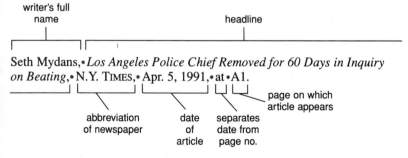

Follow **rule 16.3** to cite articles, essays, and other materials contained within periodicals that are consecutively paginated within volumes. The basic form is altered somewhat for nonconsecutively paginated periodicals (**rule 16.4**) and newspapers (**rule 16.5**). Special citation forms for student-written works, book reviews, symposia, colloquia, surveys, multipart articles, annotations, and noncommercially distributed periodicals such as newsletters are given in **rule 16.6**. Capitalize the titles of works cited according to **rule 8**. The name of the periodical should appear in large and small capitals whether it is a journal, magazine, or newspaper, and should be abbreviated T.14/T.11 according to **tables T.14** (periodical abbreviations) and **T.11** (geographic abbreviations). For purposes of this rule, the date of publication is the cover date of the periodical.

To cite journals and other periodical materials that appear only on the Internet, see **rule 18.2.6(b)**.

16.1   Author

For signed materials appearing in periodicals (including student-written materials), follow **rule 15.1.1**, but print in ordinary roman type. Thus:

> Kim Lane Scheppele, *Foreword: Telling Stories*, 87 MICH. L. REV. 2073, 2082 (1989).

> Robert P. Inman & Michael A. Fitts, *Political Institutions and Fiscal Policy: Evidence from the U.S. Historical Record*, 6 J.L. ECON. & ORG. 79, 79–82 (1990).

> Paul Butler et al., *Race, Law and Justice: The Rehnquist Court and the American Dilemma*, 45 AM. U. L. REV. 567, 569 (1996).

> Georgette C. Poindexter, LizabethAnn Rogovoy & Susan Wachter, *Selling Municipal Property Tax Receivables: Economics, Privatization, and Public Policy in an Era of Urban Distress*, 30 CONN. L. REV. 157 (1997).

> R. Gregory Cochran, Comment, *Is the Shrink's Role Shrinking? The Ambiguity of Federal Rule of Criminal Procedure 12.2 Concerning Government Psychiatric Testimony in Negativing Cases*, 147 U. PA. L. REV. 1403 (1999).

> Leslie A. Brueckner & Arthur H. Bryant, *End the Abuse of Class Action Suits*, USA TODAY MAG., Sept. 1, 1999, *available at* 1999 WL 3675682.

16.2   Title

Cite the full periodical title as it appears on the title page, but capitalize according to **rule 8** (unless the title is not in English, as described in **rule 20.1.2(b)**). Do not abbreviate words or omit articles in the title. Use italics:

> Edward B. Rock, *The Logic and (Uncertain) Significance of Institutional Shareholder Activism*, 79 GEO. L.J. 445 (1991).

> Cecilia Lacey O'Connell, Comment, *The Role of the Objector and the Current Circuit Court Confusion Regarding Federal Rule of Civil Procedure 23.1: Should Non-Named Shareholders Be Permitted To Appeal Adverse Judgements?*, 48 CATH. U. L. REV. 939, 943–46 (1999).

When the title contains a reference to material that would be italicized when appearing in the main text according to **rule 2.2(a)**, such materials should appear in ordinary roman type:

> Nathaniel A. Vitan, Book Note, *Grounded Paratroopers: On Collins and Skover's* The Death of Discourse, 13 J.L. & POL. 207, 210 (1997).

> Seth F. Kreimer, *Does Pro-Choice Mean Pro-Kevorkian? An Essay on Roe,* Casey, *and the Right To Die,* 44 AM. U. L. REV. 803, 812 (1995).

> Robert F. Housman & Barry I. Pershkow, *In the Wake of* Lucas v. South Carolina Coastal Council*: A Critical Look at Six Questions Practitioners Should Be Asking*, 23 ENVTL. L. REP. 10,008 (1993).

Consecutively Paginated Journals 16.3

Cite works found within periodicals that are consecutively paginated throughout an entire volume by author, title of work, volume number, periodical name, first page of the work and page or pages on which specific material appears (**rule 3.3(a)**), and year enclosed in parentheses at the end of the citation. Consult **tables T.11** and **T.14** to T.11/T.14 abbreviate the names of periodicals:

> David Rudovsky, *Police Abuse: Can the Violence Be Contained?*, 27 HARV. C.R.-C.L. L. REV. 465, 500 (1992).

> Kenneth R. Feinberg, *Mediation—A Preferred Method of Dispute Resolution*, 16 PEPP. L. REV. 5, 14 n.19 (1989).

> Richard A. Epstein, *The Supreme Court, 1987 Term—Foreword: Unconstitutional Conditions, State Power, and the Limits of Consent*, 102 HARV. L. REV. 4, 44 (1988).

R
15–18

If the periodical has no volume number but is nonetheless consecutively paginated throughout each volume, use the year of publication as the volume number and omit the parenthetical reference to the year:

> Thomas R. McCoy & Barry Friedman, *Conditional Spending: Federalism's Trojan Horse*, 1988 SUP. CT. REV. 85, 100.

> Stephen D. Sugarman, *Using Private Schools To Promote Public Values*, 1991 U. CHI. LEGAL F. 171.

Nonconsecutively Paginated Journals and Magazines 16.4

Works appearing within periodicals that are separately paginated within each issue should be cited by author, if any (**rule 16.1**); title of work; periodical name; date of issue as it appears on the cover; and first page of work and page or pages on which specific material appears following the word "at" (**rule 3.3(a)**). If there is no author listed, begin the citation with the title of the piece. Consult **tables T.11** T.11 and **T.14** to abbreviate the names of periodicals: T.14

Barbara Ward, *Progress for a Small Planet*, HARV. BUS. REV., Sept.–Oct. 1979, at 89, 90.

Andrew D. Irwin, *Ethics in Government Procurement/Edition III*, in BRIEFING PAPERS 2D No. 99–8, at 4–7 (Fed. Pub'ns 1999).

Joan B. Kelly, *Mediated and Adversarial Divorce: Respondents' Perceptions of Their Processes and Outcomes*, MEDIATION Q., Summer 1989, at 71.

Barbara Ehrenreich, *Iranscam: The Real Meaning of Oliver North*, MS., May 1987, at 24, 24.

Damages for a Deadly Cloud: The Bhopal Tragedy Will Cost Union Carbide $470 Million, TIME, Feb. 27, 1989, at 53.

16.5   Newspapers

(a) In general. Materials appearing in newspapers are generally cited in the same manner as those found in nonconsecutively paginated periodicals (**rule 16.4**) except that (i) after the date, give the designation of the section in which the piece is found if necessary to identify the page unambiguously, and (ii) give only the first page of the piece and do not indicate the location of specific material. Citations to signed articles should include the author's full name (**rule 16.1**); citations to unsigned pieces should begin with the title of the piece:

Ari L. Goldman, *O'Connor Warns Politicians Risk Excommunication over Abortion*, N.Y. TIMES, June 15, 1990, at A1.

Susan C. Schwab, Editorial, *UM Is Model for Ohio State, Not the Other Way Around*, BALT. SUN, Feb. 21, 1998, at 11A.

Cop Shoots Tire, Halts Stolen Car, S.F. CHRON., Oct. 10, 1975, at 43.

Jane Gross, *Silent Right: Lawyer Defends Principles from Her Jail Cell*, CHI. TRIB., Mar. 3, 1991, § 6, at 6.

Nancy Reagan, Editorial, *Just Say "Whoa,"* WALL ST. J., Jan. 23, 1996, at A14.

Michael Harwood, *The Ordeal: Life as a Medical Resident*, N.Y. TIMES, June 3, 1984, § 6 (Magazine), at 38.

(b) Place of publication. Include the place of publication in ordinary roman type in parentheses following the name of the newspaper if not clear from the name:

Trial Judge Will Not Give Enquiry Evidence, TIMES (London), June 13, 1990, at 3.

(c) Consecutively paginated newspapers. Cite an article in a newspaper paginated consecutively by volume according to **rule 16.3**:

New York County Lawyers Association: Edwin M. Otterbourg To Represent the Association in House of Delegates of American Bar Association, 124 N.Y. L.J. 1221 (1950).

(d) Commercial electronic databases. News reports published in electronic databases may be cited according to **rule 18.1.4**. If the article has been assigned a unique database identifier, include that identifier in the citation:

> Usha Lee McFarling, *Dying Frogs Called the "Canaries" of Ozone Loss*, BOSTON GLOBE, Mar. 8, 1994, at 1, *available at* LEXIS, News Library, Bglobe File.

> Usha Lee McFarling, *Dying Frogs Called the "Canaries" of Ozone Loss*, BOSTON GLOBE, Mar. 8, 1994, at 1, *available at* 1994 WL 5978840.

If the electronic database does not indicate the first page of the article, the page number need not be indicated:

> T.R. Fehrenbach, *TV's Alamo Tale Fairly Accurate*, SAN ANTONIO EXPRESS-NEWS, Mar. 17, 1996, *available at* 1996 WL 2824823.

Special Citation Forms 16.6

Non-Student-Written Book Reviews 16.6.1

Give the full name of the reviewer according to **rule 16.1** and the title of the review in italics. Include a second parenthetical after the date parenthetical indicating, if relevant to the purpose of the citation and not clear from the surrounding discussion, the author, title, and publication date of the book reviewed. If it is unnecessary to identify the book under review, simply include the words "book review" in the second parenthetical:

R
15–18

> Colin S. Diver, *Second Governance and Sound Law*, 89 MICH L. REV. 1436 (1991) (reviewing CHRISTOPHER F. EDLEY, JR., ADMINISTRATIVE LAW: RETHINKING JUDICIAL CONTROL OF BUREAUCRACY (1990)).

> Bruce Ackerman, *Robert Bork's Grand Inquisition*, 99 YALE L.J. 1419, 1422–25 (1990) (book review).

If a non-student-written review is untitled, cite it by the designation "Book Review"; it is unnecessary to include a second parenthetical unless there is a need to identify the book under review:

> Howard C. Westwood, Book Review, 45 U. CHI. L. REV. 255 (1977).

Student-Written Law Review Materials 16.6.2

(a) Signed, student-written materials. Signed and titled notes, comments, projects, etc. are cited in the same manner as any other signed article in a law review (**rule 16.3**), with the author's full name in ordinary roman type at the beginning of the citation (**rule 16.1**), except that the designation of the piece should appear before the title of the work (**rule 16.2**) to indicate that it is student-written. Cite student-written book reviews according to **rule 16.6.2(c)**.

A student work is considered signed if a student or students are credited with writing or contributing to the piece anywhere within the issue in which the work appears—on the first page of the piece, at the end of the piece, or in the table of contents. If a student work is signed only with initials, it is considered unsigned:

> Andrew D. Morton, Comment, *Much Ado About Newsgathering: Personal Privacy, Law Enforcement, and the Law of Unintended Consequences for Anti-Paparazzi Legislation*, 147 U. PA. L. REV. 1435, 1448–54 (1999).

> B. George Ballman, Jr., Note, *Amended Rule 6.1: Another Move Towards Mandatory Pro Bono? Is That What We Want?*, 7 GEO. J. LEGAL ETHICS 1139, 1162 n.155 (1994).

> Barry I. Pershkow, Recent Development, Maryland v. Craig: *A Child Witness Need Not View the Defendant During Testimony in Child Abuse Cases*, 65 TUL. L. REV. 935, 938, 941 (1991).

Signed, student-written commentary that is shorter, that falls under a designation such as Recent Case, Recent Statute, Recent Decision, Case Note, Recent Development, or Abstract, and that carries no title or merely a digest-like heading should be cited by author followed by the designation of the piece as given by the periodical, both in ordinary roman type. When appearing in the title, a case or statute citation should be included according to **rule 16.2** typeface and conventions. Thus:

> Catherine Hauber, Note, 30 U. KAN. L. REV. 611 (1982).

> Sally Anne Moore, Recent Case, H.L. v. Matheson, *101 S. Ct. 1164 (1981)*, 50 U. CIN. L. REV. 867, 868 (1981).

> **Not:** Sally Anne Moore, Recent Case, *Constitutional Law—Right of Privacy—Abortion—Family Law—Parent and Child—Standing—As Applied to Immature, Unemancipated and Dependent Minors, a State Statute Requiring a Physician To Notify a Pregnant Minor's Parents Prior to the Performing of an Abortion Is Constitutional*—H.L. v. Matheson, *101 S. Ct. 1164 (1981)*, 50 U. CIN. L. REV. 867, 868 (1981).

(b) Unsigned, student-written materials. Cite unsigned notes, comments, and shorter commentary by the designation given by the periodical, such as Note, Comment, Case Comment, Project, Recent Case, Case Note, etc., in ordinary roman type, followed by the title of the piece, if any, in italics:

> Note, *The Death of a Lawyer*, 56 COLUM. L. REV. 606 (1956).

> Case Comment, *Evidentiary Use of a Criminal Defendant's Reading Habits and Political Conversations:* United States v. Giese, 93 HARV. L. REV. 419, 425–27 (1979).

> Recent Case, 24 VAND. L. REV. 148, 151–52 (1970).

When there is no separable designation, italicize the entire title:

> *Developments in the Law—The Law of Cyberspace*, 112 HARV. L. REV. 1577, 1624 n.95 (1999).

> *The Supreme Court, 1998 Term—Leading Cases*, 113 HARV. L. REV. 368, 378 n.60 (1999).

(c) Student-written book reviews. If a review is written and signed by a student, include the author's name and the designation "Book Note" (regardless of the journal's designation) to indicate that it is student-written, followed by the title, if any. Add a parenthetical indicating the work under review if relevant to the purpose of the citation and not clear from the surrounding discussion:

> William Dubinsky, Book Note, 90 MICH. L. REV. 1512 (1992) (reviewing DANIEL A. FARBER & PHILIP P. FRICKEY, LAW AND PUBLIC CHOICE (1991)).

> Nathaniel A. Vitan, Book Note, *Irons vs. Rehnquist: A Critical Review of Peter Irons'* Brennan vs. Rehnquist, 12 J.L. & POL. 141 (1995).

An unsigned, student-written book review should be cited in the same manner as other unsigned student works, with a parenthetical citing the work under review if relevant:

> Book Note, *Let Us Reason Together*, 112 HARV. L. REV. 958 (1999) (reviewing PIERRE SCHLAG, THE ENCHANTMENT OF REASON (1998)).

Symposia, Colloquia, and Surveys   16.6.3

When citing a symposium or colloquium as a unit, do not give any author, but include "Symposium" or "Colloquium" in roman type before the title unless made clear by the title. Cite the first page of the first piece:

> Symposium, *Changing Images of the State*, 107 HARV. L. REV. 1179 (1994).

> Colloquium, *Legal Education Then and Now: Changing Patterns in Legal Training and in the Relationship of Law Schools to the World Around Them*, 47 AM. U. L. REV. 747 (1998).

> *The Brennan Center Symposium on Constitutional Law*, 87 CAL. L. REV. 1059 (1999).

If an article is part of a survey of the law of one jurisdiction, the title of the article should incorporate the title of the survey as follows:

> Alain A. Levasseur, *Sales, The Work of the Louisiana Appellate Courts for the 1977–1978 Term*, 39 LA. L. REV. 705 (1979).

Cite an individual article within a symposium, colloquium, or survey in the same manner as any other article:

> Eric A. Posner, *Law, Economics, and Inefficient Norms*, 144 U. PA. L. REV. 1697 (1996).

> Kevin R. Vodak, Comment, *A Plainly Obvious Need for New-Fashioned Municipal Liability: The Deliberate Indifference Standard and* Board of County Commissioners of Bryan County v. Brown, 48 DEPAUL L. REV. 785 (1999).

Multipart Articles   16.6.4

To cite an entire article that appears in more than one part, identify the numbers of the parts in parentheses after the article's main title and give the volume number, first page, and publication year for each part:

R
15–18

> Harlan F. Stone, *The Equitable Rights and Liabilities of Strangers to a Contract* (pts. 1 & 2), 18 COLUM. L. REV. 291 (1918), 19 COLUM. L. REV. 177 (1919).

If all of the parts appear in one volume, use the shortened form:

> L.L. Fuller, *Legal Fictions* (pts. 1–3), 25 ILL. L. REV. 363, 513, 877 (1930–1931).

To cite only some parts of a multipart article, indicate which part or parts are cited and give only the volume number(s), page number(s), and publication year(s) of the part(s) cited:

> L.L. Fuller, *Legal Fictions* (pt. 2), 25 ILL. L. REV. 513, 514 (1931).

16.6.5 Annotations

Cite discussions in selective case reporters (such as *American Law Reports* and *Lawyer's Reports Annotated*) by the author's full name, followed by the designation "Annotation" in ordinary roman type and the title of the work in italics:

> William B. Johnson, Annotation, *Use of Plea Bargain or Grant of Immunity as Improper Vouching for Credibility of Witness in Federal Cases*, 76 A.L.R. FED. 409 (1986).

16.6.6 Proceedings, Regular Publications by Institutes, and ABA Section Reports

T.11/T.14   Cite as periodicals, abbreviating according to **tables T.11** and **T.14**:

> Herbert F. Goodrich, *Annual Report of Adviser on Professional Relations*, 16 A.L.I. PROC. 48 (1939).

> George Vranesh, *Water Planning for Municipalities*, 24 ROCKY MTN. MIN. L. INST. 865 (1978).

If the volumes are unnumbered, use either the number of the institute (or proceedings) or the year of publication as a volume number; in the latter case omit the parenthetical reference to the year:

> David J. Beck, *Crude Oil Issues*, 30 INST. ON OIL & GAS L. & TAX'N 1 (1979).

> Julius L. Sackman, *Landmark Cases on Landmark Law*, 1979 INST. ON PLAN. ZONING & EMINENT DOMAIN 241.

> William J. Curtin, *Reverse Discrimination and Affirmative Action: Practical Considerations for the Utilities Industry*, 1978 A.B.A. SEC. PUB. UTIL. L. REP. 26.

If the publication is organized by paragraph or section numbers, use those numbers in citations:

> Max Gutierrez, Jr., *Estate Planning for the Unmarried Cohabitant*, 13 INST. ON EST. PLAN. ¶ 1600 (1979).

To cite part of an article identified by paragraph or section number, cite both the first paragraph or section number of the article and the paragraph or section number(s) where the relevant material appears. Add a page citation if necessary for further identification (see **rule 3.4**):

Walter F. O'Connor, *Taxation of Foreign Investors*, 38 INST. ON FED. TAX'N § 22.01, § 22.04, at 22-10 (1980).

Newsletters and Other Noncommercially Distributed Periodicals

16.6.7

Materials appearing in newsletters and other similar periodicals not commercially distributed should be cited in the same manner as non-consecutively paginated journals and magazines (**rule 16.4**), except that a parenthetical should follow the title of the publication indicating the issuing group or organization and its location. Abbreviate the name of the periodical according to **tables T.11** and **T.14** and the name of the issuing institution according to **rule 15.1.3(c)**:

T.11/T.14

Indictment of Pregnant Woman for Drug Use Dismissed, REPROD. RTS. UPDATE (ACLU/Reprod. Freedom Project, New York, N.Y.), Oct. 26, 1990, at 5.

Recent Grants, FCD UPDATE (Found. for Child Dev., New York, N.Y.), Dec. 1990, at 1, 7.

Short Citation Forms

16.7 R
15–18

Once a work in a periodical has been cited in full, use "*id.*" or "*supra*" to refer to it in subsequent citations.

(a) *Id.* If the work was cited as the immediately preceding authority within the same footnote or as the sole authority within the immediately preceding footnote, use "*id.*" to refer to the work, indicating any difference in page number:

[1] Lynn Hirschberg, *The Misfit*, VANITY FAIR, Apr. 1991, at 158.

[2] *See id.*; Recent Case, 24 VAND. L. REV. 148, 148 (1970).

[3] *See generally* Abram S. Benenson et al., *Reporting the Results of Human Immunodeficiency Virus Testing*, 262 JAMA 3435 (1989) (stating that actual laboratory results are often obscured by incorrect information).

[4] *Id.* at 3437.

[5] *See, e.g.*, Bruce Ackerman, *Robert Bork's Grand Inquisition*, 99 YALE L.J. 1419 (1990) (book review). *Compare id.* (arguing against constitutional transformation by judicial appointment), *with* Book Note, *Manual Labor, Chicago Style*, 101 HARV. L. REV. 1323 (1988) (arguing against stylistic transformation by self-appointment).

(b) *Supra.* Include the author's last name before "*supra*"; when there is no author, use the title of the piece, or, if listed before or instead of a title, the designation of the piece. However, if the first citation to the work gives a hereinafter form (**rule 4.2(b)**), use the hereinafter form in place of the author's name, title, or designation. Give the footnote in which the full citation appears unless the full citation is in the same footnote, in which case *"supra"* without a footnote reference may be used. In using a *"supra"* form, always indicate the page or pages cited except when citing the work in its entirety:

> 6 Ackerman, *supra* note 5, at 1425; *see also New York County Lawyers Association: Edwin M. Otterbourg To Represent the Association in House of Delegates of American Bar Association,* 124 N.Y. L.J. 1221 (1950) [hereinafter *Otterbourg To Represent*] (describing internal politics); Note, *The Death of a Lawyer,* 56 COLUM. L. REV. 606, 607 (1956) (in memoriam).

> 7 Recent Case, *supra* note 2, at 150. *But see* Randy E. Barnett, *A Consent Theory of Contract,* 86 COLUM. L. REV. 269, 275 (1986) (noting circularity of reliance theory of contract); Jennifer Roback, *Southern Labor Law in the Jim Crow Era: Exploitative or Competitive?,* 51 U. CHI. L. REV. 1161, 1164–65 (1984) (describing the importance of interaction between a competitive market and racially biased government).

> 8 *Cf.* David Margolick, *At the Bar: Elitist Yale Breaks Precedent and Invites a Symbol of Populism To Preside at a Legal Rite,* N.Y. TIMES, Apr. 12, 1991, at B16 (describing the reaction to students' decision to invite Judge Wapner to preside over a mock-trial competition at Yale). *See generally* Roback, *supra* note 7, at 1163 (outlining four basic types of legislation that aided enforcement of the labor-market cartel under Jim Crow laws).

> 9 See Book Note, *supra* note 5, for a cogent analysis of the more significant flaws in the competing theory.

> 10 *Otterbourg To Represent, supra* note 6; *see also* Note, *supra* note 6 (discussing problems that arise upon the death of a lawyer). *But see Cop Shoots Tire, Halts Stolen Car,* S.F. CHRON., Oct. 10, 1975, at 43 (discussing the legal ramifications of the officer's action).

> 11 This statement is quoted in Margolick, *supra* note 8.

> 12 *See, e.g., Cop Shoots Tire, Halts Stolen Car, supra* note 10.

17 Unpublished and Forthcoming Sources

17.1 Unpublished Materials

In general, cite unpublished materials not scheduled for publication by author; title or description; page or pages, if applicable; the most precise writing date available; and, if possible, information as to where the work can be located. Use ordinary roman type. See **rule 10.8.1** for how to cite pending and unreported cases and **rule 12.5** for how to cite statutes too recent to appear in any published source.

If materials that were originally unpublished are later collected and published, cite according to **rule 15.5.1**.

Manuscripts   17.1.1

Cite unpublished (or not formally published) manuscripts not scheduled for publication in ordinary roman type, beginning the citation with
the author's full name as explained in **rule 16.1**. The date of the
manuscript should be enclosed in parentheses after the title of the
work or the page cite. A second parenthetical should also be appended indicating that the work is unpublished and describing where it can
be found:

> Anatoliy Bizhko, Capitalism and Democracy 25 (Feb. 29, 2000)
> (unpublished manuscript, on file with The Yale Law Journal).

Dissertations and Theses   17.1.2

Cite unpublished dissertations and theses in the same manner as
other unpublished manuscripts, but add a parenthetical after the date
to indicate the type of work and the institution that awarded the degree:

> Karen Rubinstein Morton, Cognitive Complexity and Multicultural
> Assessment (2000) (unpublished Ph.D. dissertation, Indiana
> University) (on file with author).

> David S. Friedman, Specialization and Professionalization: The
> Increasing Division of Labor Within the American Legal Profession
> 32 (1993) (unpublished A.B. thesis, Harvard University) (on file with
> the Harvard University Library).

R
15–18

Letters, Memoranda, and Press Releases   17.1.3

When citing unpublished letters, memoranda, and press releases,
identify the writer and addressee (if any) by name, title, and institutional affiliation in the description of the document:

> Letter from Renee Chenault, News Anchor, NBC 10 Philadelphia, to
> Robert Toll, President, Toll Brothers, Inc. 3 (Feb. 23, 2000) (on file
> with the University of Pennsylvania Law Review).

> Memorandum from the Ad Hoc Committee on Women and
> Clerkships, to the Faculty of Yale Law School 14 (Feb. 13, 1991) (on
> file with author).

> Press Release, Screen Actors Guild, Screen Actors Guild Hails
> Passage of California Privacy Law (Sept. 30, 1998) (on file with
> author).

Within a court document or legal memorandum, to cite a letter that
relates to a pending case, see **practitioners' note P.7**.   P.7

To cite e-mail correspondence and postings to listservs, see **rule
18.2.9**.

Interviews   17.1.4

When citing an in-person or telephone interview, include the title and
institutional affiliation (if any) of the interviewee, and, for an in-person

interview, the location of the interview:

> Interview with Patricia Keane, Editor-in-Chief, UCLA Law Review, in Los Angeles, Cal. (Mar. 2, 2000).

> Telephone Interview with John J. Farrell, Senior Partner, Hildebrand, McLeod & Nelson (Nov. 11, 1999).

When the author has not personally conducted the interview, provide the name of the interviewer:

> Interview by Lauren Brook Eisen with Shane Spradlin, CEO, Nextel Communications, Potomac, Md. (Mar. 1, 2000).

17.1.5 Speeches and Addresses

Cite a speech or address as follows:

> Senator Hubert Humphrey, Address at the Harvard Law Review Annual Banquet (Mar. 29, 1958).

If the address has been transcribed but not published, include the location of the transcript in a second parenthetical:

> Herbert Wechsler, Remarks at the Meeting of the Bar of the Supreme Court of the United States in Memory of Chief Justice Stone 5 (Nov. 12, 1947) (transcript available in the Columbia Law School Library).

If the address has been published, cite using an *"in"* form according to **rules 1.6(a)** and **15.5.2**:

> James A. Baker, Principles and Pragmatism: American Policy Toward the Arab-Israeli Conflict, Address Before the American-Israeli Public Affairs Committee (May 22, 1989), *in* DEP'T ST. BULL., July 1989, at 24–25.

17.2   Forthcoming Publications

Cite a book, article, or other work scheduled for publication in the same manner as the published piece would be cited, with the same typefaces, except: (i) there is no page cite following the title of the journal or book; (ii) the designation "forthcoming" is included in the date parenthetical; and (iii) the month of publication, if available, should be included in the date parenthetical in addition to the year:

> Daniel R. Garodnick, Comment, *What's the BID Deal: Can the Grand Central Business Improvement District Serve a Special Limited Purpose?*, 148 U. PA. L. REV. (forthcoming May 2000).

> SARAH BARRINGER GORDON, THE TWIN RELICS OF BARBERISM (forthcoming 2001).

To cite a particular page of a forthcoming publication, add a second parenthetical with the manuscript page cite:

> F. Brandon Baer & James M. Feldman, *We're Low on Vermouth: The Trials and Tribulations of Two Summer Associates*, 1 J.L. & OPPRESSION (forthcoming 2001) (manuscript at 3, on file with authors).

Short Citation Forms   17.3

Use the *"id."* and *"supra"* forms in the same manner as they are employed for materials appearing in periodicals (**rule 16.7**), substituting the name of the source in place of an author when no author is listed, and enclosing a page citation to the manuscript version of a forthcoming publication in parentheses:

[1] Interview with Frank Van Dusen, President, Van Dusen Industries, Inc., in Rye, N.Y. (Feb. 15, 2000).

[2] *Id.*; *see also* J. Paul Oetken, Note, *Form and Substance in Critical Legal Studies*, 100 YALE L.J. (forthcoming May 2001) (manuscript at 17, on file with author). Oetken points out inherent contradictions in CLS rhetoric. *See id.* (manuscript at 10–12); *see also* Adrienne D. Davis, African American Literature and the Law: Revising and Revisiting Freedom 3–4 (Dec. 1989) (unpublished manuscript, on file with The Yale Law Journal) (describing depiction of the law in slave literature).

[3] *See* Oetken, *supra* note 2 (manuscript at 15); Davis, *supra* note 2, at 12.

[4] Interview with Frank Van Dusen, *supra* note 1; *see* Letter from Asma Hasan to Michael Cannon 2 (Mar. 15, 2000) (on file with author).

[5] *See* Letter from Asma Hasan to Michael Cannon, *supra* note 4.

R
15–18

Electronic Media and Other Nonprint Resources   18

Introduction. This rule covers citation of information found in electronic and other nonprint resources: widely used commercial electronic databases such as Westlaw and LEXIS (**rule 18.1**); the Internet (**rule 18.2**); CD-ROM (**rule 18.3**); microform (**rule 18.4**); films, broadcasts, and noncommercial videotapes (**rule 18.5**); and audio recordings (**rule 18.6**). Information contained in these sources varies considerably in authoritativeness, availability, convenience, and permanence. Due to the characteristics of and attitudes toward electronic and nonprint sources, this rule offers guidelines for citation to these sources while leaving room for change.

Information should be cited in a manner that indicates clearly which source actually was used or accessed by the author. This rule requires the use and citation of traditional printed sources, except when the information is not available in a printed source, or if the traditional source is obscure or hard to find and when citation to an electronic source will substantially improve access to the same information contained in the traditional source. In the latter case, to the extent possible, the traditional source should be used and cited, and the electronic source may be given as a parallel citation using the explanatory phrase "*available at*"; no explanatory phrase should be included when the author accesses only the electronic source. For material found exclusively on the Internet, such as on-line journals, the explanatory phrase "*at*" should be used.

Among electronic sources, this rule prefers the use and citation of the source that best satisfies the foregoing criteria for cite-worthiness as they affect the citing work (the author or editor may prefer, for example, an electronic database or governmental Internet site for authoritativeness, an Internet site for availability, or a CD-ROM for convenience). This rule also counsels the preservation of a record of information obtained during on-line research where there is doubt about the source's permanence.

18.1　Commercial Electronic Databases

Because of the reliability and authoritativeness of LEXIS and Westlaw, and other selected commercial electronic databases such as Dialog, cite such sources, if available, in preference to the other sources covered by **rule 18**. Citations to these electronic databases should be consistent with the present rule regardless of whether the databases are accessed through proprietary software or through a Web site such as http://www.westlaw.com or http://www. lexis.com.

18.1.1　Cases

Cases available on commercial electronic databases. When a case is unreported but available on a widely used electronic database, then it may be cited to that database. Provide the case name, docket number, database identifier, court name, and full date of the most recent major disposition of the case. The database identifier must contain enough information for a reader to identify the database and find the case. If the database has identifying codes or numbers that uniquely identify the case (as do LEXIS and Westlaw after 1986), these must be given. Screen or page numbers, if assigned, should be preceded by an asterisk; paragraph numbers, if assigned, should be preceded by a paragraph symbol.

United States v. Carlisle, No. 90-2465SI, 1991 U.S. App. LEXIS 5863, at *3 (8th Cir. Apr. 10, 1991) (per curiam).

Albrecht v. Stanczek, No. 87-C9535, 1991 U.S. Dist. LEXIS 5088, at *1 n.1 (N.D. Ill. Apr. 18, 1991).

Clark v. Homrighous, No. CIV.A.90-1380-T, 1991 WL 55402, at *3 (D. Kan. Apr. 10, 1991).

Kvaas Constr. Co. v. United States, No. 90-266C, 1991 WL 47632, at *1 (Cl. Ct. Apr. 8, 1991).

Staats v. Brown, No. 65681-9, 2000 WA 0042007, ¶ 25 (Wash. Jan. 6, 2000) (VersusLaw).

Citation to cases that have not been assigned unique database identifiers should include all relevant information:

> Frankel v. Banco Nacional de Mex., S.A., No. 82 Civ. 6547 (S.D.N.Y. May 31, 1983) (LEXIS, Genfed Library, Dist File).
>
> Lindquist v. Hart, 1 CA-CV 98-0323 (Ariz. Ct. App. July 15, 1999) (Loislaw.com, Ariz. Case Law).

A public domain form (**rule 10.3.3**) may be used in place of an electronic database citation.

Constitutions and Statutes   18.1.2

Materials available on commercial electronic databases. Cite codes and session laws according to **rules 12.3** and **12.4**. In addition, when citing a code contained in an electronic database, give parenthetically the name of the database and information regarding the currency of the database as provided by the database itself (rather than the year of the code according to **rule 12.3.2**). In accordance with **rule 12.3.1(d)**, also give the name of the publisher, editor, or compiler unless the code is published, edited, compiled by, or under the supervision of, federal or state officials:

> CAL. BUS. & PROF. CODE § 1670 (Deering, LEXIS through 1995 Sess.).
>
> CAL. BUS. & PROF. CODE § 1670 (West, WESTLAW through 1995 portion of 1995–96 Legis. Sess.).
>
> WIS. STAT. § 19.43 (LEXIS through 1994 legislation).
>
> WIS. STAT. § 19.43 (Loislaw.com through 1997-98 Legis. Sess.).
>
> WIS. STAT. ANN. § 19.43 (West, WESTLAW through 1995 Act 26).
>
> WASH. REV. CODE § 13.64.060 (VersusLaw through 1999 legislation).

R
15–18

Legislative, Administrative, and Executive Materials   18.1.3

Cite legislative, administrative, and executive materials according to **rules 13** and **14**. In addition, when citing materials contained in a commercial electronic database, give the name of the database and any identifying codes or numbers that uniquely identify the material.

federal bill (unenacted)	H.R. 3781, 104th Cong. § 2(b) (1976), WL 1996 CONG US HR 3781.
federal report	H.R. Rep. No. 92-98 (1971), *reprinted in* 1971 U.S.C.C.A.N. 1071, 1971 WL 11312.
congressional debate	142 Cong. Rec. H11460 (daily ed. Sept. 27, 1996) (statement of Rep. Tanner), LEXIS 142 Cong Rec H11452p*11460.

federal regulation cited to *Code of Federal Regulations*	FTC Credit Practices Rule, 16 C.F.R. § 444.1 (2000), WL 16 CFR s 444.1.
administrative adjudication	Reichold Chems., Inc., 91 F.T.C. 246 (1978), WL 91 F.T.C. 246.
formal advisory opinion	39 Op. Att'y Gen. 484 (1940), 1940 US AG LEXIS 16.
revenue ruling	Rev. Rul. 86-71, 1986-1 C.B. 102, 1986 IRB LEXIS 189.

18.1.4 Secondary Materials

When citing secondary materials to a database, provide a complete citation to the document using the rules applicable to that type of authority, and a citation to the database in accordance with **rule 18** regarding the use of explanatory phrases to indicate the actual source used by the author. If the database assigns a unique identifier or code to each document within the database, include that identifier or code to assist the reader in locating the document cited.

When the traditional source is accessed, increased accessibility to the source may be provided in the form of a parallel citation to a commercial electronic database using "*available at*":

> T.R. Fehrenbach, *TV's Alamo Tale Fairly Accurate*, SAN ANTONIO EXPRESS-NEWS, Mar. 17, 1996, *available at* 1996 WL 2824823.

> *Justice Minister Calls for Solving Int'l Legal Conflicts*, JAPAN ECON. NEWSWIRE PLUS, Apr. 22, 1991, *available at* DIALOG, File No. 612.

If only the commercial database is accessed, provide the traditional and commercial database citations using no explanatory phrase:

> Alan C. Michaels, *Constitutional Innocence*, 112 HARV. L. REV. 828 (1999), WL 112 HVLR 828.

> *Future of Space Station in Peril*, UPI, Oct. 31, 1989, LEXIS, Nexis Library, UPI File.

18.2 The Internet

18.2.1 Basic Citation Principles

Although the term "Internet" often can refer to a variety of on-line sources, including e-mail, Gopher, FTP, and Usenet, hereinafter "Internet" implies direct access via the World Wide Web unless explicitly stated to the contrary. Information should be cited in a manner that indicates clearly which source actually was used or accessed by the author. This rule requires the use and citation of traditional printed sources, except when the information is not available in a printed source, or if the traditional source is obscure or hard to find and when the citation to an Internet source will substantially improve access to the same information contained in the traditional source. In the latter case, to the extent possible, the traditional source should be used and cited. In such cases, the Internet source may be given as a parallel citation using the explanatory phrase *"available at"*; no explanatory phrase should be included when the author accesses only the Internet source (**rule 18**). For material found exclusively on the Internet, such as on-line journals, the explanatory phrase *"at"* should be used. The principles of Internet citation (other than the requirement of citing the source actually used or accessed by the author) are intended to be flexible guidelines applied in light of the nature of the information being cited, the state of the Internet as it develops over time, the standards or requirements applicable to the citing work, and the uses to which the citing work are to be put.

Both official and proprietary sources of federal and state law exist on the Internet, some permanent and comprehensive (such as Westlaw or LEXIS, **rule 18.1**), others permanent but not comprehensive (such as http://www.nlrb.gov, the National Labor Relations Board Web site), and still others transient and limited (such as some state supreme court and legislative Web sites). Other, usually non-proprietary sources of information, whether legal or factual in nature, are useful because they often contain information not available anywhere else. Many Internet sources, however, do not consistently satisfy traditional criteria for cite-worthiness. For that reason, it is necessary to indicate that such information was so accessed, and it may be desirable to create an archival record of information whose permanence is in question (**rule 18.2.1(h)**).

R
15–18

(a) Elements of Internet Citation. The elements of Internet citation are: the available information about the authority being cited (**rule 18.2.1(b)**); the appropriate explanatory phrase (if any) to indicate which source actually was used by the author (**rule 18.2.1**); the provider responsible for the Internet site, where not apparent from the Uniform Resource Locator (URL) (**rule 18.2.1(c)-(d)**); the URL (**rule 18.2.1(c)**); a date parenthetical (**rule 18.2.1(e)**); and any explanatory parenthetical (**rule 18.2.1(f)**). The problems of pinpoint citations to Internet sources are addressed in **rule 18.2.1(g)**.

(b) Basic Citation Forms.

Generally. The citation of information to Internet sources should indicate clearly and unambiguously the source actually used or accessed by the author of the citing work (**rule 18.2.1**).

Subject to such variations as are made necessary by the Internet source or the information itself, the general rules of citation and style contained in **rules 1** to **9** apply to such citations. Information other than the URL (**rule 18.2.1(c)**) should be provided in the form (**rules 10** to **21**) and typeface (**practitioners' note P.1, rule 2**) applicable to that other source or to its closest analogue, according to the most preferred method of citation that the available information permits.

When the traditional source is accessed, increased accessibility to the source may be provided in the form of a parallel citation to the Internet using *"available at"*:

> Am. Mining Cong. v. U.S. Army Corps of Eng'rs, No. CIV.A.93-1754-SSH (D.D.C. Jan. 23, 1997), *available at* http://www.wetlands.com/fed/tulloch1.htm.

If only the Internet is accessed, provide the traditional and Internet citations using no explanatory phrase:

> Minnesota v. McArthur, No. C4-99-502 (Minn. Ct. App. Sept. 28, 1999), http://www.courts.state.mn.us/library/archive/ctapun/9909/502.htm.

If the material is found exclusively on the Internet, use the explanatory phrase *"at"*:

> J.T. Westermeier, *Ethical Issues for Lawyers on the Internet and World Wide Web*, 6 RICH. J.L. & TECH. 5, ¶ 7 (1999), *at* http://www.richmond.edu/jolt/v6i1/westermeier.html.

(c) The Uniform Resource Locator. An accurate URL, the electronic address of the information, or portion thereof, is necessary for citation of Internet information. The URL also may provide information, such as the source or author of the information, that may not be available on the site itself. The URL should appear in regular roman typeface, without angled brackets.

The following is a typical breakdown of a URL for an Internet source:

> http://www.edf.org/pubs/EDF-Letter/1999/Jun/a_air.html

http	protocol (Hypertext Transfer Protocol), followed by "://" (colon, double slash)
www	World Wide Web server, followed by a period
edf	the organization presenting the information (here Environmental Defense Fund), followed by a period
org	designation that the provider is an organization, followed by a slash where other information is provided. Other provider designators include "com" for commercial providers, "edu" for educational institutions, and "gov" for governmental organizations.

The last two elements above are the "domain name," which may be divided into subdomains, as in law.yale.edu. Following the domain name, the rest of the URL defines a path to the document located on the server. The path may consisit of directories, subdirectories, and document designators within the actual Web page itself, the punctuation of which varies among Internet sites. For example:

pubs	directory within EDF's web site that deals with publications
EDF-Letter	subdirectory in reference to the type of EDF publication being accessed
1999/Jun/	year and month of the publication being accessed
a_air	article being accessed
html	or *htm*, document being accessed is in a format known as Hypertext Markup Language. Sometimes documents are made available in other formats, such as *pdf* (portable document format), *rtf* (rich text format), or *sgml* (standard generalized markup language). Graphics and photographic files are found in *gif, jpeg, mpeg,* and *vrml* formats.

When providing a URL for a document in html format, provide the complete URL if such address links directly to the document cited. The URL reference in any citation should always identify the protocol, server, and full domain name. A complete directory or subdirectory path to the document cited should be omitted if the URL provides sufficient information to locate the document being cited. Since pdf files provide the information in the original document format, it is recommended that Internet information be cited to a pdf file where available.

The following examples illustrate the proper syntax of a URL pointing to an html or pdf file. The House bill displayed in html format and cited as:

> H.R. 66, 106th Cong. (1999), *available at* http://thomas.loc.gov/ bss/d106/d106laws.html

displays the following URL, which should not be included in the citation, in the location or address window when the text of the bill is visible:

> http://frwebgate.access.gpo.gov/cgi-bin/getdoc.cgi?dbname=106_ cong_public_laws&docid=f:publ045.106.

The public law for the above bill appears in pdf format and is cited as:

> Route 66 Corridor Historic Preservation Act, Pub. L. No. 106-45, 113 Stat. 224 (1999), *available at* http://thomas.loc.gov/bss/d106/ d106laws.html.

The following URL, which should not be included in the citation, appears in the location or address window when the public law is visible:

> http://thomas.loc.gov/cgi-bin/toGPO/http://frwebgate.access.gpo.gov/ cgi-bin/getdoc.cgi?dbname+106_cong_public_laws&docid_ f:pub 1045.106.pdf.

(d) Changed or Multiple URLs and Multiple Format Options. URLs can change over time or be available in more than one version. The address of a site as stated in the URL may change between the date of first access and the date of later use of the citation. If the cited materials are moved to another directory on a site, or migrate to another Internet server, the manager of the Internet site will usually provide forwarding links to the new location. The Internet provider's name should be provided where it is not apparent from the URL so that the new Internet site may be found where no forwarding link is provided. The published citation to the information should contain the most recent URL available. If multiple URLs exist for high-traffic sites, the most general URL should be given. Finally, multiple URLs may exist where the same document is placed on the Internet site in multiple document formats.

For an example of a changed URL, a former citation to:

www2.nscu.edu/unity/lockers/project/aquatic_botany/pfiest.html# CYCLE

would be forwarded by the Internet browser to the "new" address:

www.pfiesteria.org/pfiest.html#CYCLE.

For an example of multiple URLs, a citation accessed by the author as

www1.yahoo.com

should be cited as

www.yahoo.com.

(e) Date of Internet Citations. A citation that includes both a traditional source and a parallel Internet source should provide the date for the former according to the rule applicable to the traditional source; the date for the Internet source may be included whenever such information will assist the reader. If the citation is only to an Internet source, a date must be provided, before the URL in the case of an online journal and after the URL in all other cases. The date provided should be one of the following, in order of preference: the date of the case, statute, article, or other material as specified in the information itself; the date the Internet site was last modified, using the terminology chosen by the Internet provider; or the date the Internet site was last visited to confirm the presence and location of the information. The nature of the date provided should be stated in the date parenthetical. If there is no date indicated anywhere in the information, that should be indicated in a parenthetical. Examples are as follows:

Randall R. Smith, *The Axel-Lute Uniqueness Principle and Internet Citation Form*, Personal Law Publishers, *at* http://www.plp.smith-book.com (Mar. 12, 1999).

TENN. COMP. R. & REGS. ch. 1200-1-2 (1999), *available at* http://www.state.tn.us/sos/rules/1200/1200-01/1200-01-02.pdf (last modified Sept. 15, 1999).

Randall R. Smith, *Jones on the Internet: Confusion and Confabulation*, Citation Debate Forum, *at* http://www.citations.org (last visited Jan. 20, 2000).

William D. Jones, Excerpts from Complaint in *Jones v. Smith* Defamation Litigation, Citation Litigation Forum, *at* http://www. citelitigation.com (n.d.).

Michael Guth, *An Expert System for Curtailing Electric Power*, 3 W. VA. J.L. & TECH. 2, ¶ 14 (Mar. 15, 1999), *at* http://www.wvjolt.wvu. edu/v3i2/guth.html.

(f) Parenthetical Information. Explanatory and other parentheticals (**rules 1.5, 10.6, 12.7**) should be placed after the date information for that aspect of the citation to which the parenthetical pertains. For example, a traditional explanatory parenthetical would be placed after the date of the case, followed by the URL and then any explanatory parenthetical for the URL:

> Wyoming v. Houghton, 119 S. Ct. 1297 (1999) (holding that police officers with probable cause to search a car may inspect the passengers' belongings), *available at* http://laws.findlaw.com/us/000/98-184.html.

(g) Pinpoint Citations. A pdf file displays the information in the same form as the original, as a "virtual" document. Where the information is in the same format as a traditional source, the pinpoint citation rules for that source should be used. For example:

> NEW YORK STATE COMM'N OF CORR., JAIL TIME MANUAL: A HANDBOOK FOR LOCAL CORRECTIONAL ADMINISTRATORS 2 (May 1998), *available at* http://www.scoc.state.ny.us/manuals.htm.

R
15–18

The html format usually cannot accommodate pinpoint citations unless there is a table of contents or other internal reference that permits relative specificity in the citation. "Screen page" or similar citations should be avoided since the length of a screen page can vary according to the user's software and monitor specifications.

(h) Preservation of Information. An accurate URL does not guarantee that the information can be readily accessed by the user. The information may be moved within the Internet site or to a different site, be removed entirely from the Internet, or be temporarily unavailable for technical reasons. Information about the provider derived from the URL or other citation elements may not enable the researcher to contact the provider or obtain the original information. Downloading, printing, or otherwise preserving the information as it exists at the time of access is therefore encouraged. The location of the archival copy should be indicated by a parenthetical as in the examples under **rule 17.1**:

> www.pfiesteria.org/pfiest.html#CYCLE (on file with the Harvard Law Review).

Cases   **18.2.2**

(a) A case must be cited first to a traditional source (**rule 10**) or electronic database (**rule 18.1**), except that an Internet source may be cited instead where the information is not available in a traditional source or electronic database. An additional citation in the form of a parallel or related-authority citation (**rule 1.6**) may be provided where the Internet source will substantially improve access to the same information contained in the traditional source.

> Hollins v. Dep't of Corr., No. 98-5777 (11th Cir. Oct. 5, 1999) (per curiam), *available at* http://www.law.emory.edu/11circuit/oct99/98-5777.ord.html.

> Regina v. Bow St. Magistrates Court (H.L. Aug. 5, 1999), *available at* http://www.parliament.thestationeryoffice.co.uk/pa/ld199899/ldjudgmt/jd990805/bow.htm.

(b) Prior or subsequent history of the case (**rule 10.7**) should follow the Internet citation unless it also is contained at the same Internet address. For example:

> Alden v. Maine, 527 U.S. 706 (1999), *available at* Cornell Legal Info. Inst., http://supct.law.cornell.edu/supct/html/98-436.ZS.html, *aff'g* 715 A.2d 182 (Me. 1998).

(c) When the Internet site offers the case in a pdf format, the case should be cited to that format in order to allow for a more precise citation (**rule 18.2.1(g)**).

18.2.3 Constitutions and Statutes

(a) Constitutions and statutes must be cited first to a traditional source (**rules 11** and **12**), or electronic database (**rule 18.1**), unless the information is not available in a traditional source or electronic database. An additional citation in the form of a parallel or related-authority citation may be provided where the Internet source will substantially improve access to the same information contained in the traditional source.

> 11 U.S.C. § 703 (1998), Cornell Legal Info. Inst., *available at* http://www.law.cornell.edu/uscode/11/703.html (as of Jan. 26, 1998).

> IOWA CODE § 230.12 (1997), State of Iowa, *available at* http://www.legis.state.ia.us/Indices/IACODE-1997.html.

> SANTA MONICA, CAL., MUN. CODE ch. 3.20 (1976), Seattle Pub. Library, *available at* http://www.spl.org/govpubs/municode.html.

(b) Information concerning repeal, amendment, and prior history of a statute (**rule 12.6**) should precede the Internet citation.

18.2.4 Legislative Material

Legislative material must be cited first to a traditional source (**rule 13**) or electronic database (**rule 18.1**). An additional citation in the form of a parallel or related-authority citation may be provided where the Internet source will substantially improve access to the same information contained in the traditional source.

Pending federal legislation:

H.R. 2762, 105th Cong. § 2 (1997), *available at* http://www.wetlands. com/pdf/hr2762ec.pdf (revised Nov. 5, 1997).

Congressional debate:

145 CONG. REC. H8876 (daily ed. Sept. 28, 1999) (statement of Rep. Gibbons), *available at* http://thomas.loc.gov.

Recently enacted state public act:

Act of Apr. 7, 1999, ch. 73, 1999 Tenn. Pub. Acts 147 (relative to underground utility damage prevention), Public and Private Acts, State of Tenn., 101st Gen. Assem., *available at* http://www.state.tn. us/sos/acts/acts.htm.

Pending state bill:

S. 56, 1999 145th Gen. Assem., Reg. Sess. (Ga. 1999), *available at* http://www.state.ga.us.

Administrative and Executive Materials   18.2.5

Administrative and executive materials must be cited first to a traditional source (**rule 14**) or electronic database (**rule 18.1**), unless the information is not available in a traditional source or electronic database. A parallel or related-authority citation may be provided where the Internet source will substantially improve access to the same information contained in the traditional source.

R
15–18

(a) Final rules and regulations.

33 C.F.R. § 402.4 (1999), GPO Access, *available at* http://www. access.gpo.gov/nara/cfr/cfr-table-search.html.

TENN. COMP. R. & REGS. ch. 1200-1-2 (1999), *available at* http://www.state.tn.us/sos/rules/1200/1200-01/1200-01-02.pdf (last modified Sept. 15, 1999).

(b) Proposed federal regulations.

Air Quality: Revision to Definition of Volatile Organic Compounds— Exclusion of t-Butyl Acetate, 64 Fed. Reg. 52,731, 52,732 (proposed Sept. 30, 1999) (to be codified at 40 C.F.R. pt. 51), GPO Access, *available at* http://www.access.gpo.gov/su-docs/aces/fr-cont.html.

Books, Journals and Magazines   18.2.6

Books, journals, and magazines should be cited first to a traditional source except that an Internet source may be cited where information is not available in a traditional source or electronic database. An additional citation in the form of a parallel or related authority citation (**rule 1.6**) may be provided where the Internet will substantially improve access to the same information contained in the traditional source.

(a) Traditional print source. An Internet site, in providing a printed work, may include corresponding information about the print format.

Such information may be included in the citation for a more accurate pinpoint citation.

Nancy Jean King, *The American Criminal Jury*, 62 LAW & CONTEMP. PROBS. 41, 57 (1999), *available at* http://www.law.duke.edu/ journals/lcp/articles/lcp62dSpring1999p41.htm.

WILLIAM BLACKSTONE, COMMENTARIES *1:38, *available at* http://www.lawmart.com/library/bla-102.shtml.

(b) On-line journals. Citations to journals that appear only on the Internet should include the volume number, the title of the journal, the sequential article number, the explanatory phrase "*at*" to indicate an on-line journal (**rule 18.2.1(b)**), and the Internet address. Pinpoint citations should refer to the paragraph number, if available.

Michael Guth, *An Expert System for Curtailing Electric Power*, 3 W. VA. J.L. & TECH. 2, ¶ 14 (Mar. 15, 1999), *at* http://www.wvjolt.wvu. edu/v3i2/guth.html.

18.2.7 Other Secondary Sources

Other secondary sources, such as news reports, newspapers, and other non-legal publications (**rule 16.5**), if not found on a commercial electronic database, may be cited to an Internet site, since such information is likely to be much more accessible on the Internet than in the traditional source. When citing such secondary sources, provide a complete citation to the document using the rules applicable to that type of authority. For material found exclusively on the Internet, the explanatory phrase "*at*" should be used. If the Internet site assigns a unique identifier or code to each document within the database, include that identifier or code to assist the reader in locating the document cited:

Associated Press, *Visitation Rights To Be Decided* (Sept. 28, 1999), *available at* AOL:Home/WebCenters/Legal/NewsHome/ LatestNewsStories/ Washington/SupremeCourt.

If the Internet site uses a headline or other entry to describe material (such as a letter) that ordinarily would be cited in a different form, organize the citation in a manner that will best facilitate finding the information on the Internet site:

State of New York Banking Department, The New York State Banking Department Comments on the FFIEC's Proposed Revisions to the Uniform Retail Credit Classification Policy (Sept. 16, 1998) (letter from Elizabeth McCaul, Acting Superintendent of Banks, to Keith Todd, Acting Executive Secretary, FFIEC), *available at* http://www.banking.state.ny/us/prlt0916.htm (last modified Aug. 3, 1999).

18.2.8 Other Information Services

With the emerging presence of HTTP as the dominant protocol on the Internet, other protocols such as FTP, Telnet, and Gopher, although still in use, largely have been subsumed by the World Wide Web. Today, both Internet Explorer and Netscape Navigator, the browsers most widely used on the Internet, provide the necessary means to access a variety of legal sites that formerly required individual stand-alone programs. With the evolution in browser technology, it is no longer useful or necessary to cite to each individual protocol. As far as the user is concerned, Internet browsers are indifferent to the particular protocol in use. Thus, instead of needing separate rules that apply to data obtained from a Gopher site or through a Telnet connection, correct citation form merely requires providing the address displayed in the browser window at the time of access. If, however, the connection to an alternative service, for example, Gopher or Telnet, is not made through a Web link, or if providing a Web address to the source is not feasible, sufficient instructions must be provided to guide others to the source being cited.

Telnet:

> Joe Lockhart, *The Briefing Room*, (June 28, 1999), *available at* NTIS Treasury Electronic Library, telnet://FedWorld.gov (on file with author).

E-Mail Correspondence and Postings to Listservs 18.2.9

In citing personal e-mail messages, analogize to unpublished letters (**rule 17.1.3**). The date of the message and possibly the time-stamp may be needed for specific identification of the message. Archival information may be included parenthetically, and is recommended (**rule 18.2.1(h)**). The e-mail addresses of the sender and recipient are not required or suggested, although they may be included if there is a reason for doing so.

> E-mail from Mary Miles Prince, Associate Director, Vanderbilt Law Library, to Edward C. Brewer, III, Assistant Professor of Law, Salmon P. Chase College of Law (Sept. 26, 1999, 06:15:08 CST) (on file with author).

Postings to listservs should follow a similar format, including the author's e-mail address and the address of the listserv.

> Posting of Archie Leach, aleach@act.org, to Art-Law@zealot.org (Apr. 14, 2000) (copy on file with author).

CD-ROM 18.3

(a) Information found on CD-ROM usually is available in print form, and citation to the print form is preferred where available. If the information is accessed on CD-ROM, it should be cited to CD-ROM. When citing cases on CD-ROM, the possibility exists that a case published near the date of the CD-ROM itself may have been included in slip opinion form, and (like a decision in an advance sheet) may have been edited or otherwise changed before the case was published in final form.

(b) When citing CD-ROM media, include the title of the material, the publisher of the CD-ROM, the version searched, and the date of the material, if available, or the date of the version searched. The information may be provided in a source-date parenthetical or, if the information is voluminous, as related authority (**rule 1.6**).

> 46 C.F.R. § 57.105(a) (West LawDesk Code of Federal Regulations CD-ROM, current through July 1, 1999).

> 7 LAWRENCE P. KING, COLLIER ON BANKRUPTCY ¶ 700.02 (Matthew Bender Authority Bankruptcy Law CD-ROM, rel. 13, Aug. 1999).

18.4   Microform

18.4.1 Microform Collections Reproducing Preexisting Materials

In general, when a document is reproduced in microform, it is not necessary to indicate this fact unless it would otherwise be difficult for a reader to identify and obtain the source. When citing material as "*microformed on*" a service, provide a complete citation to the original document and a citation to the microform in accordance with **rule 1.6** regarding citations to related authority. If the microform service assigns a unique identifier or code to each document reproduced, include that identifier to assist the reader in locating the document cited. Include the name of the publisher of the microform series in parentheses, abbreviated according to **rule 15.1.3(c)**:

> Petition for Writ of Certiorari for Defendant-Appellant, Cosman v. United States, 471 U.S. 1102 (1985) (No. 84-1585), *microformed on* U.S. Supreme Court Records and Briefs (Microform, Inc.).

> CAL. CODE REGS., tit. 26, § 23-2631(g) (Barclay's 1990), *microformed on* Cal. Code of Reg. 1990 Revised Format, Fiche 143 (Univ. Microforms Int'l).

> APPLICATION OF EMPLOYER SANCTIONS TO LONGSHORE WORK, H.R. REP. NO. 101-208 (1989), *microformed on* CIS No. 89-H523-17 (Cong. Info. Serv.).

> S. 1237, 99th Cong. § 505 (1985), *microformed on* Sup. Docs. No. Y 1.4/1:99-1237 (U.S. Gov't Printing Office).

18.4.2 Microform Collections Containing Original Materials

When a microform collection contains materials original to that collection, identify the microform set and its publisher, and use the publisher's system for identifying individual forms within the set. Use **rule 18.4.1** as a guide.

18.5   Films, Broadcasts, and Noncommercial Videotapes

Cite films in large and small capitals, and television or radio broadcasts in italics, by exact date (if available). Include the name of the company or network that produced or aired the film or broadcast:

> AIRPLANE! (Paramount Pictures 1980).
>
> *Law & Order: Tabula Rasa* (NBC television broadcast, Apr. 21, 1999).

Cite videotapes containing images that have not been commercially displayed or broadcast by the title of the tape (if any), the name of the person or institution that produced the video, and the year of production:

> Videotape: Installing Your OX-56z (Daniel J. Libenson Electronics Co. 1995) (on file with the Boston Public Library).
>
> Videotape: Raiders of the Lost Hark (Harvard Law School Drama Society 1996) (on file with the Harvard Law School Library).

Audio Recordings   18.6

Commercial Recordings   18.6.1

Cite commercial recordings by artist and title, providing the name of the recording company and the date of release (if available):

> COWBOY MOUTH, ARE YOU WITH ME? (MCA Records 1996).
>
> THE BEATLES, SONGS, PICTURES AND STORIES OF THE FABULOUS BEATLES (Vee-Jay Records).

R
15–18

If a particular song or musical work is referred to, cite it by analogy to **rule 15.5.1**:

> U2, *With or Without You, on* THE JOSHUA TREE (Island Records 1987).

Noncommercial Recordings   18.6.2

If the recording referred to is not commercially available, use ordinary roman type and indicate where a copy may be obtained:

> Audio tape: Conference on Business Opportunities in Space, held by the Center for Space Policy, Inc. and the Commonwealth of Massachusetts (Mar. 3–5, 1986) (on file with author).

Short Citation Forms   18.7

(a) Commercial electronic databases. For materials available on an electronic database, use a unique database identifier, if one has been assigned, in constructing a short form:

> Clark v. Homrighous, No. CIV.A.90-1380-T, 1991 WL 55402, at *3 (D. Kan. Apr. 10, 1991)

becomes: *Clark*, 1991 WL 55402, at *2.

> Albrecht v. Stanczek, No. 87-C9535, 1991 U.S. Dist. LEXIS 5088, at *1 (N.D. Ill. Apr. 18, 1991)

becomes: *Albrecht*, 1991 U.S. Dist. LEXIS 5088, at *2.

Lindquist v. Hart, 1 CA-CV 98-0323 (Ariz. Ct. App. July 15, 1999) (Loislaw.com, Ariz. Case Law)

becomes: *Lindquist*, at *3 (Loislaw.com, Ariz. Case Law).

H.R. 3781, 104th Cong. § 1 (1976), WL 1996 Cong US HR 3781

becomes: H.R. 3781 § 1, WL 1996 Cong US HR 3781.

FTC Credit Practices Rule, 16 C.F.R. § 444.1 (2000), WL 16 CFR s 444.1

becomes: 16 C.F.R. § 444.1, WL 16 CFR s 444.1 *or* WL 16 CFR s 444.1.

(b) CD-ROM and microform. When citing a separately published document available in CD-ROM or on microform, use the short form appropriate for the original document; it is not necessary to indicate the source once it has been given in the first full citation.

(c) Internet. If the document is separately published, use the short form appropriate for the original document. In addition, because of the potential lack of sufficient reliability and authoritativeness in Internet information sources, include the URL or Internet address.

(d) Films, broadcasts, and audio recordings. When citing films, broadcasts, and audio recordings, *"id."* and *"supra"* may be used according to **rule 4**:

[1] *Nightline: Microsoft Monopoly* (ABC television broadcast, Apr. 3, 2000) (transcript on file with the Columbia Law Review) [hereinafter *Nightline*].

[2] *Id.*

[3] *See id.*; MEAT LOAF, *For Crying Out Loud, on* BAT OUT OF HELL (Epic Records 1977).

[4] MEAT LOAF, *supra* note 3; *see also Nightline*, *supra* note 1 (describing Microsoft's response to the court ruling).

R
15–18

Services

Rule 19: Services   147
    19.1: Citation Form for Services   147
    19.2: Short Citation Forms   148

R
19

Services   19

Cases, administrative materials, and brief commentaries are often published unofficially in topical compilations called "services," which appear in looseleaf form initially and sometimes are published later as bound volumes. Consult *Legal Looseleafs in Print*, which is updated annually, for a comprehensive listing of services. **Rule 19.1** provides rules for citing services.

Citation Form for Services   19.1

Cite services by volume, abbreviated title in ordinary roman type, publisher, subdivision, and date. Consult **table T.16** for service and publisher abbreviations; if a service is not listed, refer to **table T.14** to abbreviate the words that make up its title:

T.16
T.14

> *In re* Smithfield Estates, Inc., [1985–1986 Transfer Binder] Bankr. L. Rep. (CCH) ¶ 70,707 (Bankr. D.R.I. Aug. 9, 1985).

> SEC v. Tex. Int'l Airlines, 29 Fed. R. Serv. 2d (CBC) 408 (D.D.C. 1979).

> Kovacs v. Comm'r, 74 A.F.T.R.2d (RIA) 354 (6th Cir. 1994).

When citing looseleaf material that will eventually be bound, add the name of the bound form in parentheses if it is different from the name of the looseleaf form; include the volume of the bound form if available:

> Marietta Concrete Co., 3 Lab. Rel. Rep. (BNA) (84 Lab. Arb. Rep.) 1158 (May 7, 1985) (Dworkin, Arb.).

(a) Volume. The volume designation of a service may be a number, a year, a descriptive subtitle from the volume's spine, or a combination of these:

> 5 Trade Reg. Rep.

> 1979-1 Trade Cas.

> [Current Developments] Hous. & Dev. Rep.

> [1979] 8 Stand. Fed. Tax Rep.

> [2 Wages-Hours] Lab. L. Rep.

> [1 Estate & Gift] U.S. Tax Rep.

In citing a transfer binder, the volume designation should indicate the years of material included in that binder:

> [1994–1995 Transfer Binder] Fed. Sec. L. Rep.

See generally **rule 3.2(a)** (designation of volumes and use of brackets).

(b) Publisher. Every citation to a service, whether looseleaf or bound, must indicate the publisher. Enclose an abbreviation of the publisher's name in parentheses following the service's title. Consult **table T.16**

R
19

T.16

for a list of service publisher abbreviations; if a publisher is not listed, abbreviate according to **rule 15.1.3(c)**.

4 Lab. L. Rep. (CCH) ¶ 9046

1980-1 Trade Cas. (CCH) ¶ 63,053

(c) Subdivision. Cite services by paragraph or section number if possible, otherwise by page number. See generally **rule 3.3** (pages and footnotes) and **rule 3.4** (sections and paragraphs). A report number may be given if it will assist the reader in locating the cited material:

> *Rhode Island Insurance Agents Agree Not To Rig Bids*, [Jan.–June] Antitrust & Trade Reg. Rep. (BNA) No. 967, at D-11 (June 5, 1980).

(d) Date. When citing a case reported in a service, give the exact date (for looseleaf services) or year (for bound services) of the case (**rule 10.5**):

> Defenders of Wildlife, Inc. v. Watt, [1982] 12 Envtl. L. Rep. (Envtl. L. Inst.) 20,210 (D.D.C. May 28, 1981).

When citing a statute or regulation, give the exact date of its enactment or promulgation unless the exact date is indicated elsewhere in the citation:

> Act of Sept. 26, 1980, Food Drug Cosm. L. Rep. (CCH) ¶ 653.

Citations to other material (such as articles or commentary) should give the exact date, if available. When citing otherwise undated material in a looseleaf service, give the date of the page on which the material is printed or the date of the subsection in which it is printed:

> *ERISA Preemption Bills Draw Praise from Labor and Criticism from Business*, [Aug. 1991–June 1993] Pens. Plan Guide (CCH) ¶ 26,263, at 27,037-10 (Aug. 2, 1991).

19.2   Short Citation Forms

(a) Cases. For cases, use short citation forms as provided by **rule 10.9**. Be sure to include the complete volume designation for the service binder and substitute paragraph or section numbers for page numbers where appropriate. If a case has both a paragraph or section number and page numbers, you may cite individual pages instead of the paragraph or section number in the short form to identify specific material. To cite the entire case in short form, give the paragraph or section number of the case or the first page number of the case, without using "at":

> [1] *In re* Looney, [1987–1989 Transfer Binder] Bankr. L. Rep. (CCH) ¶ 72,447, at 93,590 (Bankr. W.D. Va. Sept. 9, 1988).
>
> [2] *Id.*
>
> [3] *Id.* at 93,591.

⁴ Defenders of Wildlife, Inc. v. Watt, [1982] 12 Envtl. L. Rep. (Envtl. L. Inst.) 20,210, 20,211 (D.D.C. May 28, 1981).

⁵ *In re* Looney, [1987–1989 Transfer Binder] Bankr. L. Rep. (CCH) at 93,591.

⁶ *Defenders of Wildlife*, [1982] 12 Envtl. L. Rep. (Envtl. L. Inst.) at 20,212.

⁷ This was the approach taken in *Looney. See* [1987–1989 Transfer Binder] Bankr. L. Rep. (CCH) ¶ 72,447.

(b) Other materials. The short forms for other materials found in services, such as statutes, regulations, articles, and commentary, should conform to those for the same or analogous materials as they are described elsewhere in the *Bluebook.*

Foreign Materials

Rule 20: Foreign Materials   151
    20.1: Non-English-Language Documents   151
    20.2: Jurisdiction Not Evident from Context   152
    20.3: Cases   152
    20.4: Constitutions   153
    20.5: Statutes   154
    20.6: Periodicals with Non-English-Language Titles   154
    20.7: Short Citation Forms   155

Foreign Materials 20

Citation of foreign materials should conform as closely as possible to local citation practice, as modified by **rule 20**. Citation rules for specific countries are located in **table T.2**. The tables are arranged in alphabetical order by the name of the jurisdiction. **Rule 20** should be used along with the rules in **table T.2**.

T.2

T.2

Non-English-Language Documents 20.1

Documents Appearing in More than One Language 20.1.1

When citing a document that appears in equally authoritative versions in several languages including English, always use the English-language version of the document unless the purpose served by the citation requires otherwise.

Titles and Names of Documents in Languages Other than English 20.1.2

(a) Original language and translation. When citing a document in a language other than English, always give the document's full title or name in the original language the first time the document is cited. If desired, the original language title may be followed by a translation or shortened name in English in brackets in the same typeface as the original:

> Verdrag tot het Vermijden van Dubbele Belasting [Agreement for the Avoidance of Double Taxation]

Further references to the document may use this translated name or a shortened English name as a hereinafter reference (**rule 4.2(b)**):

> I. Demchenko, Val'utnyi Kurs i Val'utnyi Dolg [Hard Currency Exchange Rates and Hard Currency Obligations], IZVESTIIA, Nov. 6, 1990, at 1 [hereinafter Exchange Rates].

(b) Capitalization. Capitalize names and titles in languages other than English as they appear on the page. Capitalize translations according to **rule 8**.

R
20

Abbreviations in Languages Other than English 20.1.3

The abbreviations of reporters, codes, statutes, statutory collections, constitutions, and periodicals in languages other than English may be unfamiliar to the American reader. Therefore, the full form should be given the first time the source is cited, and the abbreviation should be given in brackets. Thereafter, the abbreviated form may be used without cross-reference.

Abbreviations for many legal materials in languages other than English are given in **table T.2**; for periodicals see **rule 20.6**. When abbreviating foreign legal materials for which an abbreviation is not provided, follow the usage of the source.

[1] BÜRGERLICHES GESETZBUCH [BGB] art. 13 (F.R.G.).

[2] BGB art. 12.

20.1.4 Languages That Do Not Use the Roman Alphabet

Transliterate all titles, names, or words cited that are not in the Roman alphabet, using a standard transliteration system.

20.1.5 Citations to Translations of Non-English-Language Documents

If desired, a work that conveniently reprints the primary authority in translation may be cited when referring to a foreign-language source that is not widely available to researchers in the United States. In such cases, provide the citation to the original source in accordance with **rules 20** and **21**, and provide a parallel citation to the translated version, according to **rule 1.6**, introduced by *"translated in"*:

BGHZ 54, 366 (F.R.G.), *translated in* 34 I.L.M. 975 (1995).

"Ley Federal de derechos de autor," D.O., 21 de diciembre de 1963 (Mex.), *translated in* COPYRIGHT LAWS AND TREATIES OF THE WORLD 521 (1992).

20.2 Jurisdiction Not Evident from Context

When citing any non-U.S. source, whether in English or in another language, indicate parenthetically the jurisdiction issuing the source, abbreviated according to **table T.11**, unless the jurisdiction is otherwise clear from the context or the other elements of the citation:

The Labor Procedure Act (R.C.L. 1990, 922) (Spain).

Weed v. Powell [1978] S.C.R. 354 (Can.).

Berry v. Dorsey (1955) 101 A.L.R. 35 (Austl.).

But:

Guthrie v. Huff [1980] 2 N.Z.L.R. 40.

20.3 Cases

Cite foreign cases according to **rule 10** as modified by the following instructions.

20.3.1 Common Law Cases

If the report does not clearly indicate the court deciding the case, indicate the court parenthetically:

The King v. Lockwood, 99 Eng. Rep. 379 (K.B. 1782).

MacBayne v. Patience, 1940 Sess. Cas. 221 (Scot. 1st Div.).

But if the court involved is the highest court in the jurisdiction, only the jurisdiction need be identified:

Weed v. Powell [1978] S.C.R. 354 (Can.).

Guthrie v. Huff [1980] 2 N.Z.L.R. 40.

Civil Law and Other Non-Common Law Cases 20.3.2

Cite cases from non-common law countries according to **table T.2** as modified by the following instructions. T.2

(a) Name of the court. Identify courts as indicated in **table T.2**. If not otherwise clear from the context, add a parenthetical English translation of the court designation: T.2

Entscheidungen des Bundesgerichtshofes in Zivilsachen [BGHZ] [Supreme Court] 53, 125 (126) (F.R.G.).

(b) Source. Cite the sources listed, with their abbreviations, in **table T.2**. As required by **rule 20.1.3**, give the full form the first time a source is cited, indicating in brackets the abbreviation that will be used subsequently. T.2

Many civil-law decisions do not appear in official reporters. If a case cited does not appear in an official source, cite a journal or periodical, issued within the jurisdiction if possible, or a reprint or translation of the decision according to **rule 1.6(b)** or **20.1.5** respectively.

(c) Jurisdiction. If the national jurisdiction is not evident from the citation or the context, include the jurisdiction, abbreviated according to **table T.11**, in parentheses at the end of the citation, as required by **rule 20.2**. T.11

(d) Annotations. Annotations to civil-law cases are cited according to **rule 3.5**:

Cass. le civ., Dec. 14, 1982, D. 1983, p. 416, note Aynès (Fr.).

Constitutions 20.4

Cite foreign constitutions according to **rule 11** as modified by the following instructions.

(a) Foreign constitutions in English. Cite English-language constitutions by country, abbreviated according to **table T.11**, and the word "CONST.," as provided by **rule 11**. Add explanatory parenthetical phrases as necessary: T.11

CAN. CONST. (Constitution Act, 1982) pt. I (Canadian Charter of Rights and Freedoms), § 2.

AUSTL. CONST. ch. I, pt. II, § 7.

(b) Foreign constitutions not in English. Cite constitutions not in English by name. If the nature of the document is not otherwise clear from the context, include "Constitution" in brackets following the document name in the first citation. Successive citations may exclude this translation.

> GRUNDGESETZ [GG] [Constitution] art. 51 (F.R.G.).

20.5 Statutes

20.5.1 Common Law Statutes

T.2

Cite like United States statutes (**rule 12**) if the jurisdiction's statutes appear in a codification or other compilation. Otherwise cite like English statutes (**table T.2**), noting the jurisdiction parenthetically at the end of the citation if not otherwise clear from the context:

> Emergency Powers Act, No. 3 (1976) (Ir.).

20.5.2 Civil Law and Other Non-Common Law Statutes

T.2

Cite generally according to rules found in **table T.2**. When citing a code, do not indicate the year of the code unless citing a version no longer in force. In accordance with **rule 20.1.3**, use the full publication name the first time the publication is cited, indicating in brackets the abbreviation that will be used subsequently. Thereafter, the abbreviated form may be used:

> CODE CIVIL [C. CIV.] art. 1112 (Fr.).

Give the publisher or editor and date of privately published sources only when citing an annotation rather than to the code itself:

> CODE CIVIL [C. CIV.] art. 1097(2) (64th ed. Petits Codes Dalloz 1965) (Fr.).

20.6 Periodicals with Non-English-Language Titles

In general, cite foreign-language periodicals according to **rule 16**, as modified by **rule 20.1**. Give the author; the title in the original language, capitalized according to **rule 20.1.2(b)**, followed by a translation or shortened name in English, if desired (**rule 20.1.2(a)**); the volume number of the periodical if appropriate (**rule 16.3**); the full name of the periodical, if it is being cited for the first time, followed by the abbreviation in brackets (**rule 20.1.3**); the page number(s); and the year (**rules 16.3** and **16.4**). A hereinafter form may be given, if desired, using the translated or shortened title (**rule 20.1.2(a)**).

> [1] Catherine Labrusse-Riou, *La filiation et la médecine moderne*, 38 REVUE INTERNATIONALE DE DROIT COMPARÉ [R.I.D.C.] 419 (1986).

[2]Marie-Thérèse Meulders-Klein, *L'enseignement du droit comparé en Belgique* [*Teaching Comparative Law in Belgium*], 40 R.I.D.C. 715, 720–21 (1988) [hereinafter *Teaching Comparative Law*]; Marie-Thérèse Meulders-Klein, *Le droit de l'enfant face au droit à l'enfant et les procréations médicalement assistées* [*The Right of a Child Versus the Right To Have a Child and Medically Assisted Procreation*], 87 Revue Trimestrielle de Droit Civil [R. Trim. D. Civ.] 645, 657 (1988) [hereinafter *The Right of a Child*].

[3] Labrusse-Riou, *supra* note 1, at 421.

[4]*The Right of a Child*, *supra* note 2, at 669.

Due to the wide variety of languages in foreign periodical titles, it is impossible to promulgate a general rule for periodical abbreviations. Therefore, include as much information as is necessary to identify uniquely the source.

Short Citation Forms 20.7

(a) Cases. For common law citations, use short forms analogous to those provided in **rule 10.9** when permitted by **rule 10.9**. For civil-law citation forms, because of the variety of foreign citation forms, it is impractical to promulgate a specific short form rule. Therefore, it is suggested that the short form should include information sufficient to identify the original citation.

(b) Constitutions. Do not use a short form (other than "*id.*") for constitutions. However, the jurisdiction may be omitted if clear from the particular context, even if it was required in a previous citation.

(c) Statutes. Use short forms analogous to those provided in **rule 12.9** when permitted by **rule 12.9**.

(d) Periodicals. Use short forms analogous to those provided in **rule 16.7**.

R
20

[1] Law No. 85-669 of July 11, 1985, J.O., July 12, 1985, p. 7885; JCP 1985, III, 57447 (Fr.).

[2] *Guthrie* [1980] 2 N.Z.L.R. at 45.

[3] Law No. 85-669 of July 11, 1985.

[4] *Id.*

International Materials

Rule 21: International Materials 157
    21.1: Basic Citation Forms 157
    21.2: Non-English-Language Documents 158
    21.3: Jurisdiction Not Evident from Context 158
    21.4: Treaties and Other International Agreements ... 158
    21.5: International Law Cases 162
    21.6: International Arbitrations 167
    21.7: United Nations Materials 168
    21.8: Materials of Other Intergovernmental Organizations 174
    21.9: Yearbooks 179
    21.10: Digests 179
    21.11: Short Citation Forms 180

International Materials   21

Basic Citation Forms   21.1

(a) Treaties and other international agreements (rule 21.4).

bilateral, U.S. a party   Treaty of Friendship, Commerce and Navigation, Apr. 2, 1953, U.S.-Japan, art. X, 4 U.S.T. 2063, 2071.

multilateral, U.S. a party   Agreement on International Classification of Trademarked Goods and Services, June 15, 1957, 23 U.S.T. 1336, 550 U.N.T.S. 45.

Treaty on the Non-Proliferation of Nuclear Weapons, *opened for signature* July 1, 1968, 21 U.S.T. 483, 729 U.N.T.S. 161.

U.S. not a party   Treaty of Neutrality, Jan. 5, 1929, Hung.-Turk., 100 L.N.T.S. 137.

Police Convention, Feb. 29, 1920, 127 L.N.T.S. 433.

(b) International law cases (rule 21.5).

World Court   Fisheries Jurisdiction (U.K. v. Ice.), 1972 I.C.J. 12 (Interim Protection Order of Aug. 17).

Court of Justice of the European Communities   Case C-213/89, The Queen v. Secretary of State for Transport *ex parte* Factortame Ltd., 1990 E.C.R. I-2433, [1990] 3 C.M.L.R. 1 (1990).

European Court of Human Rights   Ireland v. United Kingdom, 23 Eur. Ct. H.R. (ser. B) at 3 (1976).

Inter-American Commission on Human Rights   Case 68, Inter-Am. C.H.R. 61, OEA/ser. I./R./19.23, doc. 25 rev. 3 (1969).

East African Court of Appeal   Iden v. Haddad, 1968 E. Afr. L. Rep. 12 (appeal taken from Uganda).

(c) International arbitrations (rule 21.6).

Savarkar Case (Fr. v. Gr. Brit.), Hague Ct. Rep. (Scott) 275 (Perm. Ct. Arb. 1911).

(d) United Nations materials (rule 21.7).

official record   U.N. GAOR, 10th Sess., Supp. No. 6A, at 5, U.N. Doc. A/2905 (1955).

U.N. charter   U.N. CHARTER art. 2, para. 4.

| sales document | U.N. Dep't of Int'l Economic & Social Affairs, World Economic Survey, 1977, at I-19, U.N. Doc. ST/ESA/82, U.N. Sales No. E.78.II.C.1 (1977). |
| yearbook | *Summary Records of the 1447th Meeting*, [1977] 1 Y.B. Int'l L. Comm'n 175, U.N. Doc. A/CN.4/SER.A/1977. |

(e) European Union.

| European Community (**rule 21.8.2**) | Council Directive 90/313/EEC, 1990 O.J. (L 15) 561. |
| | Case 22/70, Commission v. Council, 1971 E.C.R. 263. |

(f) Council of Europe (rule 21.8.3).

Eur. Consult. Ass. Deb. 10th Sess. 639 (Oct. 16, 1958).
Reply of the Comm. of Ministers, Eur. Consult. Ass., 12th Sess., Doc. No. 1126 (1960).

(g) World Trade Organization and GATT (rule 21.8.4).

Swedish Anti-Dumping Duties, GATT B.I.S.D. (3d Supp.) at 81 (1955).

(h) Yearbooks (rule 21.9).

Revised Staff Regulations, 1922–1925 P.C.I.J. Ann. Rep. (ser. E) No. 1, at 81 (1925).

(i) Digests (rule 21.10).

Diplomatic Relations and Recognition, 1975 Digest § 3, at 36.

Access to Courts, 8 Whiteman Digest § 7, at 408.

21.2   Non-English-Language Documents

See **rule 20.1** regarding non-English-language documents.

21.3   Jurisdiction Not Evident from Context

T.3/T.11   When citing any non-U.S. source, whether in English or in a foreign language, indicate parenthetically the jurisdiction issuing the source, abbreviated according to **tables T.3** and **T.11**, unless the jurisdiction is otherwise clear from the context or the other elements of the citation:

Council Directive No. 66/45, art. 15, 1965–1966 O.J. Spec. Ed. 265, 268 (Euratom).

21.4   Treaties and Other International Agreements

Citation of a treaty between the United States and one other party:

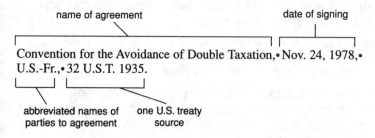

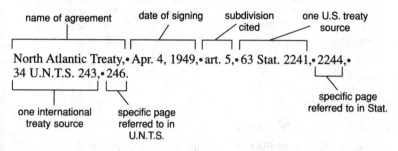

A citation to a treaty or other international agreement should include the agreement's name (**rule 21.4.1**); date of signing (**rule 21.4.2**); parties (**rule 21.4.3**); the subdivision referred to, if applicable (**rule 21.4.4**); and the source(s) in which the treaty can be found (**rule 21.4.5**).

Name of the Agreement 21.4.1

See **rule 20.1.2** regarding treatment of treaties whose names are not in English or that appear in several languages.

(a) First citation. The first time a treaty is cited, give its form (**rule 21.4.1(a)(i)**) and its subject matter (**rule 21.4.1(a)(ii)**), in either order. For example:

Agreement on Aerospace Disturbances

Consular Convention

(i) Form of agreement. The form designation indicates the type of agreement (e.g., Convention, Treaty, Understanding, Memorandum of Agreement). Use only the first form designation that appears on the title page. Omit all others. Thus:

Convention

Not: Convention & Supplementary Protocol

Cite lesser-included documents as subdivisions (**rule 21.4.4**).

(ii) Subject matter. Use the subject-matter description that appears as part of the title of the agreement.

> Protocol to the 1979 Convention on Long-Range Transboundary Air Pollution Concerning the Control of Emission of Volatile Organic Compounds or Their Transboundary Fluxes.

(b) Subsequent citations. If a treaty's name is very long, or if the treaty is commonly known by a popular name, subsequent citations to the treaty may use a shorter or popular name as a "hereinafter" short-form citation (**rule 4.2(b)**):

> [1] Protocol for the Prohibition of the Use in War of Asphyxiating, Poisonous or Other Gases, and of Bacteriological Methods of Warfare, June 17, 1925, 26 U.S.T. 571, 94 L.N.T.S. 65 [hereinafter Geneva Protocol]; *see also* U.S. CONST. art. I, § 9, cl. 2.

> [2] Geneva Protocol, *supra* note 1, art. VII, 26 U.S.T. at 577, 94 L.N.T.S. at 69.

21.4.2 Date of Signing

Give the exact date of signing:

> Protocol To Amend the Convention for the Suppression of the Traffic in Women and Children, Nov. 12, 1947.

When dates of signing are given for an agreement or exchange of notes between two parties, give the first and last dates of signing:

> Agreement on Weather Stations, Apr. 27-May 13, 1964, U.S.-Colom., 15 U.S.T. 1355.

If a treaty among three or more parties is not signed on a single date, use the date on which the treaty is opened for signature, done, approved, or adopted, and indicate the significance of the date:

> Constitution of the World Health Organization, *opened for signature* July 22, 1946, 62 Stat. 2679, 14 U.N.T.S. 185.

The date of entry into force or other date may be added parenthetically at the end of the citation if of particular relevance.

21.4.3 Parties to the Agreement

When citing an agreement between two parties, indicate both parties, T.11 abbreviating their names according to **table T.11**:

> U.S.-Japan

> Fr.-F.R.G.

Names of parties may but need not be given if there are three or more parties:

> U.S.-U.S.S.R.-U.K.-P.R.C.

Subdivisions 21.4.4

When citing only part of an agreement, or when citing an appended document, give the subdivision or appended document:

> Treaty on Commerce and Navigation, Dec. 3, 1938, U.S.-Iraq, art. III, para. 2, 54 Stat. 1790, 1792.

> Declaration on the Neutrality of Laos, July 23, 1962, Protocol, 14 U.S.T. 1104, 1129, 456 U.N.T.S. 301, 324.

For a discussion of citations to subdivisions and appendices, see **rules 3.4** and **3.5**.

Treaty Sources 21.4.5

See **table T.4** for a listing of international treaty sources. Treaty   **T.4**
sources of some foreign states are listed with the other materials of
those states in **table T.2**. Dates in the tables refer to the years of the   **T.2**
treaties contained in the source, not to the years in which the source
was published.

(a) Agreements to which the United States is a party.

(i) Two parties. For agreements between the United States and one other party, cite *one* of the following sources, listed in the following order of preference: U.S.T. or Stat.; T.I.A.S. or T.S. or E.A.S.; Senate Treaty Documents or Senate Executive Documents; the Department of State Dispatch; or Department of State Press Releases. If the agreement has not appeared in one of these official sources, cite an unofficial source (**rule 21.4.5(c)**):

> Treaty on the Limitation of Anti-Ballistic Missile Systems, May 26, 1972, U.S.-U.S.S.R., 23 U.S.T. 3435 [hereinafter ABM Treaty].

> Agreement on Defense and Economic Cooperation, Sept. 8, 1983, U.S.-Greece, T.I.A.S. No. 10,814, at 4.

> Memorandum of Understanding Regarding Bilateral Verification Experiment and Data Exchange Related to Prohibition of Chemical Weapons, Sept. 23, 1989, U.S.-U.S.S.R., art. V(1), DEP'T ST. BULL., Nov. 1989, at 18, 19 [hereinafter Chemical Weapons MOU].

Senate Treaty Documents, formerly called Senate Executive Documents, are legislative materials cited according to **rule 13.4**:

> Tax Convention, Sept. 21, 1989, U.S.-Finland, S. TREATY DOC. NO. 101-11 (1990).

Citations to Senate Executive Documents, which were issued prior to the 97th Congress, should include similar information. Thus, Executive W, 96-2 would be cited as:

> Migratory Birds Protection Agreement, Jan. 30, 1979, U.S.-Can., S. EXEC. DOC. W, 96-2, at 3 (1980).

(ii) Three or more parties. For agreements among three or more parties, cite *one* of the sources listed in **rule 21.4.5(a)(i)**, if therein. Cite *also* one source published by an intergovernmental organization (e.g., U.N.T.S., L.N.T.S., Pan-Am. T.S., or Europ. T.S.), if therein. If either of these official citations cannot be obtained, provide a citation to *one* unofficial treaty source (**rule 21.4.5(c)**):

> North Atlantic Treaty, Apr. 4, 1949, art. 5, 63 Stat. 2241, 2244, 34 U.N.T.S. 243, 246.

(b) Agreements to which the United States is not a party. Cite *one* source published by an intergovernmental organization, if therein. If not, cite the official source of one signatory, if therein, indicating parenthetically the jurisdiction whose source is cited according to **rule 20.2**, if not otherwise obvious from the context. If the treaty is not found in a signatory's treaty source, cite an unofficial treaty source (**rule 21.4.5(c)**):

> Agreement for the Avoidance of Double Taxation, Apr. 25, 1952, Neth.-Swed., art. 4, 163 U.N.T.S. 131, 136.
>
> Treaty of Neutrality, Jan. 25, 1929, Hung.-Turk., 100 L.N.T.S. 137.
>
> Agreement on Trade and Technical Co-Operation, Oct. 20, 1981, Austl.-Oman, 1982 Austl. T.S. No. 4.

(c) Unofficial treaty sources. When a treaty does not appear in the required sources listed under **rule 21.4.5(a)** or **21.4.5(b)**, provide a citation to International Legal Materials (I.L.M.), if therein:

> Convention on the Prohibition of Military or Any Other Hostile Use of Environmental Modification Techniques, May 18, 1977, 31 U.S.T. 333, 16 I.L.M. 88 [hereinafter Environmental Modification Convention].
>
> Montreal Protocol on Substances That Deplete the Ozone Layer, Sept. 16, 1987, 26 I.L.M. 1550 (entered into force Jan. 1, 1989).

If such a treaty is not found in I.L.M., cite one of the other unofficial treaty sources available. These include the official websites of governmental and intergovernmental organizations, as well as sources such as Consol. T.S. or Hein's microfiche treaty service in the United States, or to Martens Nouveau Recueil:

> Constitution of the International Labour Organization, June 28, 1919, art. 405, 49 Stat. 2712, 2722–24, 225 Consol. T.S. 378–79.
>
> Express Mail Agreement, July 9–23, 1990, U.S.-Mozam., Hein's No. KAV 2757, Temp. State Dep't No. 90-208, at 2.

If no other citation is available, cite a book (**rule 15**) or periodical (**rule 16**).

21.5   International Law Cases

Cite according to **rule 10** as modified by the following instructions.

The International Court of Justice and the Permanent Court of International Justice (World Court)

Cite a case before the International Court of Justice (I.C.J.) or the Permanent Court of International Justice (P.C.I.J.) by the case name (**rule 21.5.1(a)**); the names of the parties, if any (**rule 21.5.1(b)**); the volume and name of the publication in which the decision is found (**rule 21.5.1(c)**); the page on which the case begins or the number of the case (**rule 21.5.1(d)**); and the date (**rule 21.5.1(e)**). See **table T.3** for abbreviations for these materials.

> Military and Paramilitary Activities (Nicar. v. U.S.), 1986 I.C.J. 14 (June 27) (separate opinion of Judge Ago).
>
> Diversion of Water from the Meuse (Neth. v. Belg.), 1937 P.C.I.J. (ser. A/B) No. 70, at 7 (June 28).
>
> Pajzs, Czáky, and Esterházy Case (Hung. v. Yugo.), 1936 P.C.I.J. (ser. A/B) No. 68 (Dec. 16).

Cite pleadings and court rules and acts according to **rule 21.5.1(f)** and **21.5.1(g)**. Cite yearbooks and annual reports of the World Court according to **rule 21.9**.

(a) Case name. Give the case name as found on the first pages of the report, but omit introductory articles such as "The." Also omit the word "Case," unless the case name is a person's name. Do not otherwise abbreviate case names.

> Nuclear Tests
>
> **Not:** Nuclear Tests Case

(b) Parties' names. The names of the parties involved should be given in a parenthetical phrase immediately following the case name. Abbreviate the names of parties according to **rule 10.2.2** and **table T.11**, even in textual sentences. "United States" should be abbreviated to "U.S." in this parenthetical (but not in case names):

> (Nicar. v. U.S.)

In advisory opinions, no parties are listed:

> Interpretation of Peace Treaties with Bulgaria, Hungary and Romania, 1950 I.C.J. 65 (Mar. 30).
>
> Advisory Opinion No. 11, Polish Postal Service in Danzig, 1925 P.C.I.J. (ser. B) No. 11, at 6.

(c) Volume number and name of publication. Identify the volume by the date on its spine, as required by **rule 3.2(a)**. The International Court of Justice publishes its opinions in *Report of Judgments, Advisory Opinions and Orders* (abbreviated I.C.J.):

> 1972 I.C.J. 12

Decisions and other documents of the P.C.I.J. were published in six series (A through F). The series must be indicated in any citation to P.C.I.J. documents:

> 1937 P.C.I.J. (ser. A/B) No. 70

(d) Page or case number. Cite I.C.J. cases to the page on which they begin. Cite cases of the Permanent Court of International Justice by number:

> 1937 P.C.I.J. (ser. A/B) No. 70.

Use pinpoint cites to refer to specific pages:

> 1933 P.C.I.J. (ser. C) No. 62, at 12.

(e) Date. Provide the exact date, where available:

> Nuclear Tests (N.Z. v. Fr.), 1973 I.C.J. 135 (Interim Protection Order of June 22).

(f) Separately published pleadings. Cite separately published pleadings by the designation given on the document itself, followed by the names of the parties in a parenthetical phrase **(rule 21.5.1(b))**; the volume number and name of the publication **(rule 21.5.1(c))**; for cases before the I.C.J., the name of the case in parentheses (preceded by the volume number, if any); and the exact date. Separately published pleadings before the I.C.J. are published in *Pleadings, Oral Arguments, Documents* (abbreviated I.C.J. Pleadings), while those before the P.C.I.J. were published in P.C.I.J.:

> Memorial of the United Kingdom (U.K. v. Alb.), 1949 I.C.J. Pleadings (1 Corfu Channel) 17 (Sept. 30, 1947).
>
> Memorial of Denmark, Legal Status of Eastern Greenland (Den. v. Nor.), 1933 P.C.I.J. (ser. C) No. 62, at 12 (Oct. 31, 1931).

(g) Court rules and acts. Cite rules and acts of the World Court by title, volume number and name of publication **(rule 21.5.1(c))**, and page or document number **(rule 21.5.1(d))**:

> Travel and Subsistence Regulations of the International Court of Justice, 1947 I.C.J. Acts & Docs. 94.
>
> Revised Rules of the Court, 1926 P.C.I.J. 33 (ser. D) No. 1.

(h) Recent Materials. I.C.J. materials that have not yet been published may be cited to International Legal Materials (I.L.M.) **(rule 21.4.5(c))** or to the I.C.J. website (http://www.icj-cij.org) **(rule 18.2)**.

21.5.2 The Court of Justice of the European Communities

Cite a case before the Court of Justice of the European Communities by case number; the names of the parties, abbreviated according to **rule 10.2**; a citation to the official reports of the Court, including the year of decision **(rule 21.5.2(a))**; and a parallel citation to a private service, if possible **(rule 21.5.2(b))**.

Where the Commission, Council, or Parliament of the European

Communities is one of the parties, give its name as Commission, Council, or Parliament only, as appropriate:

> Case 58/69, Elz v. Commission, 16 E.C.R. 507 (1970).

> Case 48/69, Imperial Chem. Indus. v. Commission, 18 E.C.R. 619, [1971–1973 Transfer Binder] Common Mkt. Rep. (CCH) ¶ 8161 (1972).

Cases on European Community law are often decided in the courts of member states. These cases may be cited to the reporters of the particular member state and/or to one of the unofficial reporters collecting materials regarding the European Community (see **rule 21.5.7**). When citing such a case to European Community materials, always indicate the court, as well as the jurisdiction if not clear from context, as provided by **rule 20.2**:

> Leverton v. Clwyd County Council, 1 C.M.L.R. 574 (H.L. 1989) (U.K.).

(a) Official reports. For pre-1990 cases, cite the *Report of Cases Before the Court of Justice of the European Communities* (abbreviated E.C.R.); post-1990 cases are cited to the *Report of Cases Before the Court of Justice and the Court of First Instance.* Place the year designation before the reporter abbreviation. If an official report is not yet available, cite the official European Union website (http://europa. eu.int) **(rule 18.2)** or a private service **(rule 21.5.2(b))**.

> Case 111/79, Caterpillar Overseas v. Belgium, 1980 E.C.R. 773.

> Case 30/79, Land Berlin v. Wigei, 1980 E.C.R. 151.

> Joined Cases 56 & 58/64, Etablissements Consten, S.A.R.L. v. Commission, 1966 E.C.R. 299.

Beginning with Part I, 1990, page numbers in the E.C.R. begin with a "I" or "II" before the number:

> Case C-213/89, The Queen v. Secretary of State for Transport *ex parte* Factortame Ltd., 1990 E.C.R. I-2433, [1990] 3 C.M.L.R. 1 (1990).

(b) Private services. Whenever possible, provide a parallel citation to one of the private services providing selected reports of the court's opinions, in the following order of preference: *Common Market Law Reports* (C.M.L.R.) (when citing to volumes through 1973, include overall volume number after the year in brackets; when citing to volumes for 1974 and after, include the issue number after the year in brackets to reflect cessation of continuous issue numbering), *Common Market Reporter* (Common Mkt. Rep. (CCH)) (through 1988), or *European Community Cases* (CEC (CCH)) (beginning 1989). See **rule 19** for treatment of CCH looseleaf services:

> Case 148/78, Pubblico Ministero v. Ratti, 1979 E.C.R. 1629, 1 C.M.L.R. 96 (1980).

Case 4/69, Alfons Lütticke GmbH v. Commission, 1971 E.C.R. 325, [1971-1973 Transfer Binder] Common Mkt. Rep. (CCH) ¶ 8136 (1971).

21.5.3 The European Court of Human Rights

Cite a case before the European Court to *European Court of Human Rights, Reports of Judgements and Decisions* (Eur. Ct. H.R.). For older decisions, the cases may also be cited to *European Court of Human Rights, Series A or B* (e.g., Eur. Ct. H.R. (ser. A)) or to *Yearbook of the European Convention on Human Rights* (Y.B. Eur. Conv. on H.R.). More recent volumes contain several cases, but some earlier volumes contain only one case. Where a volume contains only one case, citation to a beginning page is unnecessary, and all page numbers may be indicated directly by "at." Cite cases before the European Court by case name, volume number, reporter, page number where applicable, and year:

Kampanis v. Greece, 318 Eur. Ct. H.R. 29, 35 (1995).

Ireland v. United Kingdom, 23 Eur. Ct. H.R. (ser. B) at 23 (1976).

If the volume number and year are the same, citations should drop the separate reference to the year.

Ergi v. Turkey, 1998-IV Eur. Ct. H.R. 1751, 1759.

Until 1999, cases were also heard before the now-defunct European Commission on Human Rights. These cases should be cited to *Collections of Decisions of the European Commission of Human Rights* (Eur. Comm'n H.R. Dec. & Rep.) or Y.B. Eur. Conv. on H.R., if therein. If not, cite *European Human Rights Reports* (Eur. H.R. Rep.). When citing Y.B. Eur. Conv. on H.R., indicate parenthetically whether the case was before the Commission or the Court. Indicate both the parties and the application number for the case.

Y. v. The Netherlands, App. No. 7245/32, 32 Eur. Comm'n H.R. Dec. & Rep. 345, 358 (1982).

Smith v. Belgium, App. No. 3324/76, 8 Eur. H.R. Rep. 445, 478 (1982) (Commission report).

Iversen v. Norway, 1963 Y.B. Eur. Conv. on H.R. 278 (Eur. Comm'n on H.R.).

If an official report of a recent case before the European Court is not available, materials may be cited to the Court's official website (http://www.ehcr.coe.int/eng) (**rule 18.2**).

21.5.4 The Inter-American Commission on Human Rights

Cite cases before the Inter-American Commission on Human Rights to the *Annual Report of the Inter-American Commission on Human Rights* (Inter-Am. C.H.R.). The citation should include the case number, the page on which the case begins, and the series and docket numbers:

Case 68, Inter-Am. C.H.R. 61, OEA/ser. I./R./20.23, doc. 25 rev. 3 (1969).

If an official report is not yet available, cite the Commission's official website (available via http://www.oas.org).

The East African Court of Appeal 21.5.5

Cite the *Law Reports of the Court of Appeal for Eastern Africa* (E. Afr. Ct. App.) for cases decided between 1934 and 1956. For cases decided after 1956, cite to *East Africa Law Reports* (E. Afr. L. Rep.) or to *Court of Appeal for East Africa Digest of Decisions of the Court* (E. Afr. Ct. App. Dig.). Indicate the country of origin parenthetically:

Iden v. Haddad, 1968 E. Afr. L. Rep. 12 (appeal taken from Uganda).

Other Multinational Courts 21.5.6

Cite *International Law Reports* (I.L.R.) (1950–date) or *Annual Digest and Reports of Public International Law Cases* (Ann. Dig.) (1919–1950). Volume numbers, rather than years, should be used; early issues of *Annual Digest* have been renumbered according to tables appearing in all volumes after volume 25. Include the name of the court and the year of the decision in a parenthetical:

Loomba v. Food & Agric. Org. of the United Nations, 47 I.L.R. 382 (Int'l Lab. Org. Admin. Trib. 1970).

Mayras v. Secretary-General of the League of Nations, 13 Ann. Dig. 199 (Admin. Trib. of the League of Nations 1946).

International Cases in National Courts 21.5.7

If an international case is decided by a national court whose reporter is not indicated in **table T.2**, cite I.L.R., Ann. Dig., C.M.L.R., or Common Mkt. Rep. (CCH) **(rule 21.5.2(b))**, or to a yearbook **(rule 21.9)**:

T.2

Ko Maung Tin v. U Gon Man, 14 Ann. Dig. 233 (High Ct. 1947) (Burma).

Abdul Ghani v. Subedar Shoedar Khan, 38 I.L.R. 3 (W. Pak. High Ct. 1964).

Even if the reporter of the deciding court appears in **table T.2**, a parallel citation to one of the above international reporters should be added in law review citations, although such a parallel citation is unnecessary in other contexts:

T.2

Blackburn v. Attorney Gen., [1971] 1 W.L.R. 1037, [1971] 10 C.M.L.R. 784 (Eng. C.A.).

International Arbitrations 21.6

Cite arbitral decisions by analogy to **rule 21.5**, modified as follows. If adversary parties are named, give the name as if it were a court case:

Massaut v. Stupp

Otherwise cite by the name of the first party plaintiff or by the subject matter if no name is given. Indicate parenthetically the nations involved, if not otherwise evident:

> Dillon Case (U.S. v. Mex.)
>
> The Montijo (U.S. v. Colom.)

T.5   Cite arbitration awards to the official source (unless that source is a pamphlet containing only a single judgment), if possible. Consult **table T.5** for frequently cited arbitration reporters. Unless the court or tribunal is identified unambiguously in the name of the reporter, it should be indicated parenthetically:

> Massaut v. Stupp, 9 Trib. Arb. Mixtes 316 (Ger.-Bel. 1929).
>
> Savarkar Case (Fr. v. Gr. Brit.), Hague Ct. Rep. (Scott) 275 (Perm. Ct. Arb. 1911).
>
> Austin Co. v. Machine Suzi Arak, 12 Iran-U.S. Cl. Trib. Rep. 288 (1986).

21.7   United Nations Materials

Citation of a resolution of the United Nations General Assembly:

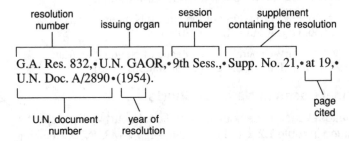

In general, materials published by the various organs of the United Nations fall into four categories: official records (**rule 21.7.1**), sales documents (**rule 21.7.2**), mimeographed documents (**rule 21.7.3**), and yearbooks or periodicals (**rule 21.7.4**).

21.7.1 Official Records

Official records are published by several of the principal U.N. organs. Each organ's official records ordinarily appear in three parts each session: (1) meeting records, which contain verbatim or summary reports of the body's plenary or committee meetings; (2) annexes, which contain committee reports and other materials gathered for consideration as part of the principal organ's agenda; and (3) supplements, which contain resolutions and other documents. Each part may occupy several volumes.

Researchers should note that these records are often revised in later editions by corrigenda and other supplements. Such revisions should be cited where relevant:

> *Report of the West African Industrial Co-Ordination Mission,*
> U.N. Economic Commission for Africa, 6th Sess., Agenda Item 5,
> at 1, U.N. Doc. E/CN.14/246 (1964), *revised by* U.N. Doc.
> E/CN.14/246/Corr. 1 (1964).

(a) Basic citation form for official records. Except as specified in **rule 21.7.1(b),** every citation to an official record should include the resolution number or author and/or title, as appropriate **(rule 21.7.1(a)(i))**; the United Nations organ that published the record and the committee, if any **(rule 21.7.1(a)(ii))**; the session number and the part, if any **(rule 21.7.1(a)(iii))**; the type of record cited, if appropriate **(rule 21.7.1(a)(iv))**; the subdivision **(rule 21.7.1(a)(v))**; the page(s) or paragraph(s) **(rule 21.7.1(a)(vi))**; the U.N. document number **(rule 21.7.1(a)(vii))**; the provisional status of the record, if appropriate, and the year of publication **(rule 21.7.1(a)(viii))**. For example:

> U.N. GAOR Special Political Comm., 27th Sess., 806th mtg.
> at 5, U.N. Doc. A/SPC/SR.806 (1972).

(i) Resolution number, author, and title. When citing a resolution, include the resolution number before the name of the organ whose record is being cited:

> G.A. Res. 832, U.N. GAOR, 9th Sess., Supp. No. 21, at 19,
> U.N. Doc. A/2890 (1954).

If the document has an author and/or title, that information may be included. Include the name of the author (according to **rule 16.1**) only if it is not apparent from the title:

> *Permanent Missions to the U.N.: Report of the Secretary-General,*
> U.N. GAOR 6th Comm., 4th Sess., Annex, Agenda Item 50, at 16,
> U.N. Doc. A/C.6/Annexes (1949).

The name of a speaker may be indicated parenthetically at the end of the citation **(rule 1.5)**.

(ii) Organs and committees. Indicate the organ whose official record contains the cited material, using the abbreviation given in **table T.3,** followed by the name of the committee, if any:

T.3

> U.N. GAOR 3d Comm.

(iii) Session number and part. Cite the session number as follows:

> 27th Sess.

If the session was divided into parts, note as follows:

> 27th Sess., pt. 1

(iv) Type of record. If a record is an Annex or Supplement, indicate that fact with its number:

> 27th Sess., pt. 1, Annex 1

9th Sess., Supp. No. 21

(v) Subdivisions. Because volumes of official records generally are not continuously paginated, the separately paginated subdivision must be indicated, set off by commas, after the session and part or type of record. Meeting records are ordinarily divided by meeting:

U.N. GAOR, 8th Sess., 462d plen. mtg.

U.N. GAOR Special Political Comm., 27th Sess., 806th mtg.

U.N. SCOR, 22d Sess., 1360th mtg.

Annexes ordinarily are divided by agenda item:

U.N. GAOR, 22d Sess., Annex 1, Agenda Item 23, addendum pt. 1

U.N. GAOR, 24th Sess., Annex 2, Agenda Item 72

Supplement volumes are divided by supplement number or other designation:

U.N. GAOR, 8th Sess., Supp. No. 19

U.N. SCOR, 17th Sess., Supp. for Jan.–Mar. 1962

(vi) Page(s) or paragraph(s). The volume and subdivision designations should be followed by the page(s) or paragraph(s) to which reference is intended. Introduce page number(s) with the word "at":

U.N. GAOR, 8th Sess., 462d plen. mtg. at 345

U.N. GAOR, Hum. Rts. Comm., 30th Sess., 739th mtg. at 1, U.N. Doc. CCPR/C/SR.739 (1987).

Because pagination may vary between versions in different languages, when citing to pages of a non-English version, that fact must be indicated parenthetically:

U.N. TCOR, 27th Sess., 1150th mtg. at 82, U.N. Doc. T/SR.1150 (1961) (French version).

Paragraph numbers, if available, may be used in lieu of page numbers:

U.N. GAOR 3d Comm., 29th Sess., 2058th mtg. ¶ 9, U.N. Doc. A/C.3/SR.2058 (1974).

If paragraph numbers are used, it is unnecessary to specify which lingual version has been used.

(vii) United Nations document number. Because microformed U.N. documents are catalogued by document number, every citation to an official record must include the U.N. document number, if available:

U.N. Doc. A/SPC/SR.806

If the cited official record is also available as a sales publication, the sales number (**rule 21.7.2(d)**) may be included following the document number.

(viii) Year. Give the year that appears on the document itself. If the version of the record cited is a provisional edition, insert the abbreviation "prov. ed." before the year in the date parenthetical.

(b) Specific types of official records. Except as otherwise specified below, cite according to **rule 21.7.1(a)**.

(i) General Assembly official records. Verbatim records generally are kept only for plenary meetings and meetings of the main committee; citations thus may refer to summary records:

> U.N. GAOR 4th Comm., 5th Sess., 187th mtg. at 285, U.N. Doc. A/C.4/SR.187 (1950).

Resolutions of the fifth and subsequent sessions (1950–date) have been published in the supplements:

> G.A. Res. 832, U.N. GAOR, 9th Sess., Supp. No. 21, at 19, U.N. Doc. A/2890 (1954).

Resolutions of the first four sessions (before 1950) are cited by resolution number, U.N. document number, page, and date:

> G.A. Res. 133, U.N. Doc. A/519, at 43 (1947).

(ii) Security Council official records. Verbatim records of plenary meetings are kept. Records of meetings after 1950 are cited:

> U.N. SCOR, 22d Sess., 1360th mtg. at 1, U.N. Doc. S/PV.1360 (1967).

Records of debates before 1951 do not have document numbers:

> U.N. SCOR, 1st Sess., 1st series, 3d mtg. at 22 (1946).

The Security Council does not publish annexes; since 1948 its supplements have been denominated by the time periods they cover:

> U.N. SCOR, 17th Sess., Supp. 4, Jan.–Mar. 1962, at 63, U.N. Doc. S/Supplements (1962).

(iii) Economic and Social Council official records. Session numbers do not correspond to those of the General Assembly or Security Council. Verbatim records of meetings are not kept:

> U.N. ESCOR, 32d Sess., 1156th mtg. at 29, U.N. Doc. E/SR.1156 (1961).

> E.S.C. Res. 337, U.N. ESCOR, 11th Sess., Supp. No. 1A, at 91, U.N. Doc. E/1849/Add.1 (1950).

Annexes were published only through the 55th session (1974). Summary records and supplements have been published annually since 1977 (rather than at the end of each session).

(iv) Trusteeship Council official records. Session numbers do not correspond to those of the General Assembly or Security Council. Verbatim records of plenary meetings are kept:

U.N. TCOR, 33d Sess., 1273d mtg. at 15, U.N. Doc. T/SR.1273 (1966).

T.C. Res. 1909, U.N. TCOR, 22d Sess., Supp. No. 1, at 3, U.N. Doc. T/1403 (1958).

(v) Trade and Development Board official records. Session numbers do not correspond to those of the General Assembly or Security Council. Verbatim records of meetings are not kept. Official records are commonly bound into a single volume for each session or a number of sessions:

U.N. TDBOR, 23d Sess., 566th mtg. at 3, U.N. Doc. TD/B/SR.566 (1981).

Committee reports appear in the supplements.

(vi) Official records of other principal and subsidiary organs. Cite materials published by the Development Programme, the U.N. Special Fund, and other subsidiary organs according to **rule 21.7.1(a)**:

United Nations Regular Programme of Technical Cooperation, Report by the Secretary-General, U.N. Development Programme, 9th Sess., Agenda Item 11, at 1, 3, U.N. Doc. DP/RP/8 (1969).

Decisions of the Administrative Tribunal should be cited to *Judgements of the U.N. Administrative Tribunal* (Judgements U.N. Admin. Trib.) by judgement (retaining the "e" in "judgement") number:

Eldridge v. Secretary-General of the United Nations, Judgements U.N. Admin. Trib. No. 32, at 144, U.N. Doc. AT/DEC/32 (1953).

21.7.2 Sales Documents

Numerous United Nations agencies publish, for sale to the public, documents other than official records. These sales documents may take many forms, such as reports, studies, or proceedings. Every citation to a sales document must include the author and/or title (**rule 21.7.2(a)**); the page(s) or paragraph(s) (**rule 21.7.2(b)**); the U.N. document number, if available (**rule 21.7.2(c)**); the sales number (**rule 21.7.2(d)**); and the year (**rule 21.7.2(e)**).

(a) Author and title. Give the author and/or title according to **rules 15.1** and **15.2**. Give the name of the author only if it is not apparent from the title of the document:

U.N. DEP'T OF INT'L ECONOMICS & SOCIAL AFFAIRS, U.N. MODEL DOUBLE TAXATION CONVENTION BETWEEN DEVELOPED AND DEVELOPING COUNTRIES at 243, U.N. Doc. ST/ESA/102, U.N. Sales No. E.80.XVI.3 (1980).

(b) Page(s) or paragraph(s). Cite according to **rule 21.7.1(a)(vi)**.

(c) United Nations document number. Include the U.N. document number (**rule 21.7.1(a)(vii)**), if available.

(d) United Nations sales number. Include the U.N. sales number:

U.N. DEP'T OF INT'L ECONOMIC & SOCIAL AFFAIRS, WORLD ECONOMIC SURVEY, 1977, at I-19, U.N. Doc. ST/ESA/82, U.N. Sales No. E.78.II.C.1 (1977).

(e) Year. Give the year of publication.

Mimeographed Documents   21.7.3

If a mimeographed document is reprinted as an official record or sales document, always cite to the official record or sales document instead of the mimeographed version of a document, if possible. Mimeographed documents should be cited by the name of the institutional author (**rule 21.7.3(a)**), the title of the document (**rule 21.7.3(b)**), the document number (**rule 21.7.3(c)**), and the year of publication.

(a) Institutional author. Give the name of the committee that produced the mimeographed document, as listed on the cover page of the document:

UNITED NATIONS, ECONOMIC AND SOCIAL COUNCIL, COMMITTEE ON ARRANGEMENTS FOR CONSULTATION WITH NON-GOVERNMENTAL ORGANIZATIONS, DEVELOPMENT OF TOURISM ON THE AFRICAN CONTINENT; STATEMENT SUBMITTED BY THE INTERNATIONAL UNION OF OFFICIAL TRAVEL ORGANIZATIONS, U.N. Doc. E/C.2/562 (1960).

(b) Title. Capitalize the title in accordance with **rule 8**.

(c) United Nations document number. Include the U.N. document number (**rule 21.7.1(a)(vii)**), if available.

Yearbooks and Periodicals   21.7.4

United Nations yearbooks and periodicals collect summaries of the work of subsidiary organizations and related documents. Citations should include the author and/or title of the document or separately designated article (if any); the name of the yearbook or periodical (abbreviated according to **rule 16.2**); and the U.N. document number (**rule 21.7.1(a)(vii)**) or, if none, the U.N. sales number (**rule 21.7.2(d)**). For example:

R
21

Summary Records of the 1447th Meeting, [1977] 1 Y.B. Int'l L. Comm'n 175, U.N. Doc. A/CN.4/SER.A/1977.

Human Rights in the Union of Burma in 1953, 1953 Y.B. on H.R. 31, U.N. Sales No. 1955.XIV.1.

1981 U.N. Jurid. Y.B. 41, U.N. Doc. ST/LEG/SER.C/19.

1985 U.N.Y.B. 1391, U.N. Sales No. E.84.I.1.

Material reprinted in yearbooks from other U.N. documents should be cited to the original source or to the official records of a U.N. organ:

Report of the International Law Commission to the General Assembly, 19 U.N. GAOR Supp. (No. 9) at 1, U.N. Doc. A/5509 (1963), *reprinted in* [1963] 2 Y.B. Int'l L. Comm'n 187, U.N. Doc. A/CN.4/SER.A/1963/Add.1.

21.7.5 United Nations Charter

Cite as a constitution (**rule 11**). Give only the appropriate article and paragraph:

U.N. CHARTER art. 2, para. 4.

21.7.6 Founding Documents

Cite documents of the initial conferences at San Francisco to *Documents of the United Nations Conference on International Organization* (U.N.C.I.O. Docs.). Include the document number, series symbol, volume, page(s), and year:

Doc. 463, II/3/19, 10 U.N.C.I.O. Docs. 51 (1945).

21.8 Materials of Other Intergovernmental Organizations

21.8.1 League of Nations Materials

Cite the League of Nations Covenant as a constitution (**rule 11**):

LEAGUE OF NATIONS COVENANT art. 15, para. 6.

Cite the official journal:

12 LEAGUE OF NATIONS O.J. 56 (1931).

LEAGUE OF NATIONS O.J. Spec. Supp. 154, at 11 (1936).

Cite other League of Nations materials by document number, followed by the year of issuance in parentheses; the title may be included:

Report Presented by the Comm. of Technical Experts on Double Taxation and Tax Evasion, League of Nations Doc. C.216 M.85 1927 II (1927).

21.8.2 European Community Materials

(a) Acts of the Council and Commission.

(i) Sources. Cite publications of the Council and of the Commission published beginning January 1, 1974 to the *Official Journal of the European Communities* (O.J.). Cite documents published before January 1, 1974, to the Special Edition of the *Official Journal of the European Communities* (O.J. SPEC. ED.), if available; otherwise cite to *Journal Officiel des Communautés Européennes* (J.O.).

Cite volumes of O.J. and J.O. by year. J.O. volumes published prior to 1968 were numbered in a single series. Since 1968, O.J. and J.O. have been published in parallel series, paginated separately by issue. Legislative acts appear in the "L" series, while other documents appear in the "C" series. Citations to O.J. and J.O. since 1968 must include the series and issue number; citations to J.O. before 1967 must include the issue number:

1971 J.O. (L 20) 1

1975 O.J. (L 337) 7

1964 J.O. (234) 5

Citations to O.J. Spec. Ed. must indicate the period covered by the issue:

1965–1966 O.J. Spec. Ed. 265

(ii) Legislative acts of the Council and Commission. Cite Regulations, Directives, and Decisions of the Council and Commission by the issuing institution, type of legislation, number, and any subdivision cited. If the act was not issued under the EC Treaty, indicate the authority for the promulgation of the act:

Council Directive 90/476, art. 5, 1990 O.J. (L 266) 1, 2.

Council Directive 66/45, art. 15, 1965–1966 O.J. Spec. Ed. 265, 268 (Euratom).

Commission Regulation 725/67, 1967 J.O. (253) 1.

If desired, all or part of the full name of the legislation may be given, with or without the date:

Commission Regulation 2751/90 of 26 September 1990 Fixing the Import Levies on Compound Feeding Stuffs, Annex, 1990 O.J. (L 264) 37, 38.

Council Regulation 2684/90 on Interim Measures Applicable After the Unification of Germany, art. 4, 1990 O.J. (L 263) 1, 2.

(iii) Other publications of the Council and Commission. Cite proposed Regulations, Directives, and Decisions and other notices of the Council and Commission, by issuing institution and title, as given at the beginning of the item:

Commission Proposal for a Council Regulation Amending Regulation 1785/81 EEC on the Common Organization of the Markets in the Sugar Sector, art. 1(12), 1985 O.J. (C 219) 4, 6.

Amended Commission Proposal for an Eleventh Council Directive on Company Law Concerning Disclosure Requirements in Respect of Branches Opened in a Member State by Certain Types of Companies Governed by the Law of Another State, 1988 O.J. (C 105) 6 [hereinafter Proposed Eleventh Directive].

Court of Justice, Codified Versions of the Rules of Procedure, art. 76, 1982 O.J. (C 39) 16, 18.

(iv) COM documents. Cite "COM" documents by title; the "COM" number, which consists of the word "COM," the last two digits of the year of publication in parentheses, and the running number assigned to the document; the word "final," unless the version cited is not final; and the page number cited:

Completing the Internal Market: White Paper from the Commission
to the European Council, COM(85)310 final at 7 [hereinafter
Completing the Internal Market].

If the document is later reprinted in the *Official Journal*, cite according
to **rule 21.8.2(a)(iii)**.

(b) Documents of the European Parliament.

(i) Debates. Debates of the European Parliamentary Assembly are
cited:

EUR. PARL. DEB. (38) 5 (Mar. 7, 1961).

Before debates are bound, cite them by *Journal* annex number:

Remarks of President Ortoli, 1975 O.J. (Annex 193) 123 (July
9, 1975) (Debates of European Parliament).

(ii) Documents. Cite documents to *European Parliament Session
Documents* (EUR. PARL. DOC.) (entitled *European Parliament Working
Documents* prior to 1988), if therein; otherwise cite to *Parlement
Européen Documents de Séance* (PARL. EUR. DOC.). Include the document number:

EUR. PARL. DOC. (COM 258) 5 (1973).

PARL. EUR. DOC. (SEC 64) 6 (1963).

If desired, the name may be included as well:

Commission Proposal for a Council Directive Relating to the
Supervision of Credit Institutions on a Consolidated Basis,
EUR. PARL. DOC. (COM 451 final—SYN 306) 1 (1990)
[hereinafter Consolidated Supervision Proposal].

(c) Founding treaties. Except for the initial citation, cite the treaties
creating the European Communities as constitutions (see **rule 11**).
The first citation to a founding treaty should give the full name, followed by the appropriate abbreviation in brackets. Cite sources as
indicated in **rule 21.4.5**:

TREATY OF AMSTERDAM AMENDING THE TREATY ON EUROPEAN UNION,
THE TREATIES ESTABLISHING THE EUROPEAN COMMUNITIES AND
CERTAIN RELATED ACTS, Oct. 2, 1997, O.J. (C 340) 1 (1997) [hereinafter TREATY OF AMSTERDAM].

TREATY ESTABLISHING THE EUROPEAN COMMUNITY, Nov. 10, 1997,
O.J. (C 340) 3 (1997) [hereinafter EC TREATY].

Subsequent citations should use the appropriate short form alone:

EC TREATY art. 177.

EEC TREATY arts. 85–86.

ECSC TREATY art. 57.

EURATOM TREATY art. 4.

Cite the EC Treaty for current references to the founding treaty, incorporating amendments to the 1957 EEC Treaty by the 1987 Single European Act ("SEA"), the 1992 Treaty on European Union ("TEU"), and the Treaty of Amsterdam.

The Treaty of Amsterdam significantly amended the EC Treaty, the TEU and certain other documents, resulting in the renumbering of the articles. Current citations should be to the article number as amended by the Treaty of Amsterdam. To cite to previous versions of the EC Treaty or the TEU, indicate the date of the version cited, and state in parentheses the current number of the article:

> EC TREATY art. 85 (as in effect 1985) (now article 81).
>
> TREATY ON EUROPEAN UNION arts. J–J.11 (as in effect 1996) (now articles 11–28).
>
> EC TREATY art. 53 (as in effect 1994) (repealed by the Treaty of Amsterdam).

(d) International treaties and agreements. Cite treaties among EC member countries or between the EC and nonmember states according to **rule 21.4.5(b)**.

(e) Recent Material. Documents not yet published in official sources may be available at the European Union's official website (http://europa.eu.int) **(rule 18.2)**.

Council of Europe Materials   21.8.3

Cite debates of the Parliamentary Assembly, formerly the Consultative Assembly, to the official reports:

> EUR. CONSULT. ASS. DEB. 10th Sess. 639 (Oct. 16, 1958).
>
> EUR. PARL. ASS. DEB. 23d Sess. 499 (Sept. 30, 1980).

Documents should be cited:

> *Reply of the Comm. of Ministers*, Eur. Consult. Ass., 12th Sess., Doc. No. 1126 (1960).

World Trade Organization and GATT   21.8.4
(General Agreement on Tariffs and Trade)

(a) Panel decisions, rulings, and reports. Cite to *Basic Instruments and Selected Documents* (B.I.S.D.), if therein. Include the title, document date, ordinal number of the supplement (annual volume), page, and year of publication.

> Netherlands Measure of Suspension of Obligations to the United States, Nov. 8, 1952, GATT B.I.S.D. (1st Supp.) at 32 (1953).
>
> GATT Secretariat, *An Analysis of the Proposed Uruguay Round Agreement, with Particular Emphasis on Aspects of Interest to Developing Countries*, MTN.TNC/W/122 (Nov. 29, 1993).

Because the texts of dispute panel reports are slow to appear in B.I.S.D., cite texts that have not yet been published to the official WTO website (http://www.wto.org), to *International Legal Materials* (I.L.M.) or another unofficial source known to be widely available:

> GATT Dispute Panel Report on U.S. Complaint Concerning E.C. Subsidies to Wheat Farmers, 18 Int'l Trade Rep. (BNA), No. 22, at 899–916 (Mar. 8, 1983).

(b) Founding agreements and side agreements. Except for initial citation, cite the agreement creating the GATT or, currently, the WTO, as constitutions (**rule 11**). The first citation to a founding agreement should give the full name, followed by the appropriate abbreviation in brackets. Cite initially to sources as indicated in **rule 21.4.5**, but include a standard unofficial source, as indicated below:

> Final Act Embodying the Results of the Uruguay Round of Multilateral Trade Negotiations, Apr. 15, 1994, LEGAL INSTRU-MENTS—RESULTS OF THE URUGUAY ROUND vol. 1 (1994), 33 I.L.M. 1125 (1994) [hereinafter Final Act].

The Uruguay Round resulted in a set of agreements and appended annexes, some of which constitute agreements on separate trade issues. Indicate to which other part of the agreements they attach, if any:

> Agreement on Trade-Related Aspects of Intellectual Property Rights, Apr. 15, 1994, Marrakesh Agreement Establishing the World Trade Organization [hereinafter WTO Agreement], Annex 1C, LEGAL INSTRUMENTS—RESULTS OF THE URUGUAY ROUND vol. 31, 33 I.L.M. 81 (1994) [hereinafter TRIPS Agreement].

> General Agreement on Tariffs and Trade, Oct. 30, 1947, 61 Stat. A-11, T.I.A.S. 1700, 55 U.N.T.S. 194 [hereinafter GATT].

Subsequent citations should use the appropriate short form alone, citing only to articles or paragraphs:

> Final Act para. 5.

> WTO Agreement art. III.

21.8.5   Other Intergovernmental Organizations' Materials

T.3

Generally, cite by analogy to United Nations materials (**rule 21.7**) and to the forms in **rule 21.8**. See **rule 20.1** regarding citation of materials in languages other than English. Citations should include the title; the resolution number, if any; the particular page(s) or paragraph(s) cited, if longer than one page; the name of the organization (abbreviated according to **table T.3**); the organization's document number, if any; and the most precise date available. Indicate parenthetically any other relevant information. Always provide enough information for the source to be located with a minimum of effort:

> *Supply Agreement for a Research Reactor in Romania* 3, IAEA Doc. INFCIRC/206 (June 12, 1974).

Assessment of Members' Contributions to the Regular Budget, Gen. Conf. Res. 434, IAEA Doc. GC(XXVIII)/RES/434 (Sept. 28, 1984).

Manual of All-Weather Operations, at 2-2, ICAO Doc. 9365-AN/910 (1st ed. 1982).

Condemnation of the Policies of Apartheid and Racial Discrimination of South Africa, Ass. Res. A15-7 (1964), *compiled in Assembly Resolutions in Force*, at I-21, ICAO Doc. 9509 (Oct. 10, 1986).

Geographical Distribution of ITU Staff, ITU Admin. Council Res. No. 580 (1981), *compiled in* RESOLUTIONS AND DECISIONS OF THE ADMINISTRATIVE COUNCIL OF THE INTERNATIONAL TELECOMMUNICATION UNION 2.1.1 (gen. rev. 1979 plus supps.).

A citation to a source that is particularly difficult to locate should include a parenthetical explaining its availability:

Provision of Facilities in Ports for the Reception of Oily Wastes from Ships, IMO Assembly Res. A. 585(14) (Nov. 20, 1985) (photocopy on file with author).

Yearbooks   21.9

Cite United Nations yearbooks according to **rule 21.7.4**. Cite other international yearbooks or annual reports as periodicals (**rule 16**). Italicize article titles, but do not italicize the names of materials not ordinarily italicized (such as case names in footnotes). Give the yearbook title in the original language (abbreviated according to **table T.14** and **rule 20.1.3**) and, if not obvious, the name of the issuing organization. For example:

Ronald Graveson, *The Inequality of the Applicable Law*, 1980 BRIT. Y.B. INT'L L. 231, 233.

Revised Staff Regulations, 1922–1925 P.C.I.J. ANN. REP. (ser. E) No. 1, at 81 (1925).

X. v. Belgium, 1961 Y.B. EUR. CONV. ON H.R. (Eur. Comm'n on H.R.) 224.

Jean Boulouis, *Cour de Justice des Communautés Européennes*, 1965 ANNUAIRE FRANÇAIS DE DROIT INTERNATIONAL (Centre National de la Recherche Scientifique) 333.

Recommendations of the Customs Co-Operation Council on the Customs Treatment of Products Imported for Testing, 1972 EUR. Y.B. (Council of Eur.) 429.

Digests   21.10

(a) Annual digests. Since 1973, the United States Department of State has published an annual *Digest of United States Practice in International Law.* These volumes are organized by topic and contain analysis and excerpts of documents in the field. In general, each section contains many subdivisions with individual subtitles. Provide the title for the entire section, the year of the *Digest*, the section number, and the page(s), if citing to particular pages within the section:

> Diplomatic Relations and Recognition, 1975 DIGEST § 3, at 36.

Provide subdivision titles, separated by colons, only if particularly relevant:

> Extradition: Double Criminality: Bigamy, 1980 DIGEST § 5, at 226 (when divorce in United States is valid, no crime of bigamy has been committed under U.S. law and double criminality is absent).

(b) Named digests. Earlier digests were multiple volume sets edited by a single editor and known by that person's name. For these digests, provide the title of the section (including subtitles only if particularly relevant, as under **rule 15.2**), the volume cited, the author's name followed by the word DIGEST, the section number, and the page reference, if any:

> Source: Custom, 1 Hackworth DIGEST § 3, at 16.

> Access to Courts, 8 Whiteman DIGEST § 7, at 408.

(c) Digests of another country. When citing the digests of another country, cite analogously to those published in the United States. If the digest is published as an annual series, cite as under **rule 21.10(a)**; if it is identified by its editor's name, cite as under **rule 21.10(b)**. The first time the digest is cited, always provide the complete name, followed by the abbreviation in brackets, as required by **rule 20.1.3**.

(d) Digests published as periodical sections. When a digest appears as an annual or periodical section of a journal, cite as a periodical under **rule 16**:

> Arthur W. Rovine, *Contemporary Practice of the United States Relating to International Law*, 67 AM. J. INT'L L. 760, 767 (1973) (describing discussions of terrorism in the U.N. Security Council).

21.11 Short Citation Forms

(a) Treaties and other international agreements. Subsequent citations to treaties and other international agreements may use both *"id."* and *"supra."* Provide the full name of the treaty, followed by *"supra,"* and the pages on which the cited material appears:

> Convention for the Avoidance of Double Taxation, *supra* note 6, at 25.

> Treaty on the Non-Proliferation of Nuclear Weapons, *supra* note 1, 21 U.S.T. at 486, 729 U.N.T.S. at 167.

If the original citation provided a "hereinafter" short title, use that title in a subsequent *"supra"* reference, as provided by **rule 21.4.1(b)**.

(b) International law cases and arbitrations. Use short forms analogous to those provided in **rule 10.9**, when permitted by **rule 10.9**.

(c) United Nations and other intergovernmental organization materials. Subsequent citations to materials of intergovernmental organizations may use both "*id.*" and "*supra*":

> G.A. Res. 832, *supra* note 4, at 22.
>
> *Permanent Missions to the U.N.: Report of the Secretary-General, supra* note 6, at 18.

If the first citation to the document included a "hereinafter" reference, use that form for subsequent "*supra*" cites:

> *Completing the Internal Market, supra* note 12, at 9.

(d) Yearbooks and digests. Subsequent citations to articles in yearbooks and digests should follow the short forms for periodicals (**rule 16.7**). Subsequent citations may be made using both "*id.*" and "*supra.*"

R
21

Tables and Abbreviations

Tables
    T.1   United States Jurisdictions   183
    T.2   Foreign Jurisdictions   245
    T.3   Intergovernmental Organizations   297
    T.4   Treaty Sources   300

Abbreviations
    T.5   Arbitral Reporters   301
    T.6   Case Names   302
    T.7   Court Names   304
    T.8   Court Documents   307
    T.9   Explanatory Phrases   309
    T.10 Legislative Documents   310
    T.11 Geographical Terms   311
    T.12 Judges and Officials   315
    T.13 Months   316
    T.14 Periodicals   317
    T.15 Publishing Terms   342
    T.16 Services   343
    T.17 Subdivisions   349

United States Jurisdictions

Federal

For more information about the federal court system, including a list of the district courts and the territorial jurisdiction of the courts of appeals, access http://www.uscourts.gov.

Supreme Court (U.S.): Cite to U.S., if therein; otherwise cite to S. Ct., L. Ed., or U.S.L.W. in that order of preference.

United States Reports

91 U.S. to date	1875–date U.S.
Wallace	1863–1874 e.g., 68 U.S. (1 Wall.)
Black	1861–1862 e.g., 66 U.S. (1 Black)
Howard	1843–1860 e.g., 42 U.S. (1 How.)
Peters	1828–1842 e.g., 26 U.S. (1 Pet.)
Wheaton	1816–1827 e.g., 14 U.S. (1 Wheat.)
Cranch	1801–1815 e.g., 5 U.S. (1 Cranch)
Dallas	1790–1800 e.g., 1 U.S. (1 Dall.)
Supreme Court Reporter	1882–date S. Ct.
Lawyer's Edition	1790–date L. Ed., L. Ed. 2d
United States Law Week	1933–date U.S.L.W.

Circuit Justices (e.g., Rehnquist, Circuit Justice): Cite to U.S., if therein; otherwise cite to S.Ct., L.Ed., or U.S.L.W., if therein, in that order of preference.

United States Reports	1893–date U.S.
Supreme Court Reporter	1893–date S. Ct.
Lawyer's Edition	1790–date L. Ed., L. Ed. 2d
United States Law Week	1933–date U.S.L.W.

(A few other opinions are reported in other reporters. E.g., United States v. Motlow, 10 F.2d 657 (Butler, Circuit Justice 1926).)

Courts of Appeals (e.g., 2d Cir., D.C. Cir.), previously **Circuit Courts of Appeals** (e.g., 2d Cir.), and **Court of Appeals of/for the District of Columbia** (D.C. Cir.): Cite to F., F.2d, or F.3d.

Federal Reporter	1891–date F., F.2d, F.3d

The Sixth Circuit has adopted a public domain format for cases after December 31, 1993. The format is:

Equality Fund v. City of Cincinnati, 1997 FED App. 0318P (6th Cir.).

Circuit Courts (e.g., C.C.S.D.N.Y., C.C.D. Cal.) (abolished 1912): Cite to F. or F. Cas.

Federal Reporter	1880–1912 F.

Federal Cases   1789–1880   F. Cas.
(Citations to F. Cas. should give the case num-
ber parenthetically. E.g., Oelrich v. Pittsburgh,
18 F. Cas. 598 (C.C.W.D. Pa. 1859) (No. 10,444).)

Temporary Emergency Court of Appeals (Temp. Emer. Ct. App.) (created 1971, abolished 1993), **Emergency Court of Appeals** (Emer. Ct. App.) (created 1942, abolished 1961), and **Commerce Court** (Comm. Ct.) (created 1910, abolished 1913): Cite to F. or F.2d.

Federal Reporter   1910–1993   F., F.2d

United States Court of Appeals for the Federal Circuit (Fed. Cir.) (created 1982), successor to the **United States Court of Customs and Patent Appeals** (C.C.P.A.) (previously the **Court of Customs Appeals** (Ct. Cust. App.)) and the appellate jurisdiction of the **Court of Claims** (Ct. Cl.): Cite to F., F.2d, or F.3d, if therein; otherwise cite to the respective official reporter.

Federal Reporter	1910–date	F., F.2d, F.3d
Court of Claims Reports	1956–1982	Ct. Cl.
Court of Customs and Patent Appeals Reports	1929–1982	C.C.P.A.
Court of Customs Appeals Reports	1910–1929	Ct. Cust.

United States Court of Federal Claims (Fed. Cl.) (created 1992), formerly **United States Claims Court** (Cl. Ct.) (created 1982), and successor to the original jurisdiction of the **Court of Claims** (Ct. Cl.): Cite to one of the following reporters:

Federal Claims Reporter	1992–date	Fed. Cl.
United States Claims Court Reporter	1982–1992	Cl. Ct.
Federal Reporter	1930–1932	F.2d
	1960–1982	F.2d
Federal Supplement	1932–1960	F. Supp.
Court of Claims Reports	1863–1982	Ct. Cl.

United States Court of International Trade (Ct. Int'l Trade) (created 1980), formerly **United States Customs Court** (Cust. Ct.) (created 1926): Cite to the official reporters if possible; if unavailable, cite to F. Supp. or F. Supp. 2d., to Cust. B. & Dec. (an official publication), or to I.T.R.D. (BNA) in that order of preference.

Court of International Trade Reports	1980–date	Ct. Int'l Trade
Customs Court Reports	1938–1980	Cust. Ct.
Federal Supplement	1980–date	F. Supp., F. Supp. 2d
Customs Bulletin and Decisions	1967–date	Cust. B. & Dec.

International Trade Reporter Decisions 1980–date I.T.R.D. (BNA)

District Courts (e.g., D. Mass., S.D.N.Y.): For cases after 1932, cite to F. Supp., F. Supp. 2d, F.R.D., or B.R., if therein; otherwise, cite to Fed. R. Serv., Fed. R. Serv. 2d, or Fed. R. Serv. 3d. For prior cases, cite to F., F.2d, or F. Cas. if therein.

Federal Supplement	1932–date	F. Supp., F. Supp. 2d
Federal Rules Decisions	1938–date	F.R.D.
Bankruptcy Reporter	1979–date	B.R.
Federal Rules Service	1938–date	Fed. R. Serv. (Callaghan), Fed. R. Serv. 2d (Callaghan), Fed. R. Serv. 3d (West)
Federal Reporter	1880–1932	F., F.2d
Federal Cases	1789–1880	F. Cas.

    (Citations to F. Cas. should give the case number parenthetically. E.g., *Ex parte* McKean, 16 F. Cas. 186 (E.D. Va. 1878) (No. 8848).)

The District of South Dakota has adopted a public domain format for cases after December 31, 1997. The format is:

Cain v. Apfel, 1998 DSD 35.

Bankruptcy Courts (e.g., Bankr. N.D. Cal.) and **Bankruptcy Appellate Panels** (e.g., B.A.P. 1st Cir.): Cite to B.R., if therein; otherwise cite to a service (**rule 19**).

Bankruptcy Reporter	1979–date	B.R.

The Bankruptcy Court for the District of South Dakota has adopted a public domain format for cases after December 31, 1997. The format is:

In re Dreps, 1999 Bk DSD 22.

Judicial Panel on Multidistrict Litigation (J.P.M.L.) (created 1968) and **Special Court, Regional Rail Reorganization Act** (Regional Rail Reorg. Ct.) (created 1973): Cite to F. Supp. or F. Supp. 2d.

Federal Supplement	1968–date	F. Supp., F. Supp. 2d

Tax Court (T.C.) (created 1942), previously **Board of Tax Appeals** (B.T.A.): Cite to T.C. or B.T.A., if therein; otherwise cite to T.C.M. (CCH), T.C.M. (P-H), T.C.M. (RIA), or B.T.A.M. (P-H).

United States Tax Court Reports	1942–date	T.C.
Reports of the United States Board of Tax Appeals	1924–1942	B.T.A.

T
T.1

Tax Court Memorandum Decisions	1942–date	T.C.M. (CCH)
	1942–1991	T.C.M. (P-H)
	1991–date	T.C.M. (RIA)
Board of Tax Appeals Memorandum Decisions	1928–1942	B.T.A.M. (P-H)

United States Court of Appeals for Veterans Claims (Vet. App.), previously **United States Court of Veterans Appeals** (Vet. App.) (created 1988): Cite to Vet. App. if therein.

| Veterans Appeals Reporter | 1990–date | Vet. App. |

United States Court of Appeals for the Armed Forces (C.A.A.F.), previously **United States Court of Military Appeals** (C.M.A.): Cite to C.M.A., if therein; otherwise, cite to M.J. or C.M.R.

Decisions of the United States Court of Military Appeals	1951–1975	C.M.A.
Military Justice Reporter	1978–date	M.J.
Court Martial Reports	1951–1975	C.M.R.

Military Service Courts of Criminal Appeals (A. Ct. Crim. App., A.F. Ct. Crim. App., C.G. Ct. Crim. App., N-M. Ct. Crim. App.), previously **Courts of Military Review** (e.g., A.C.M.R.), previously **Boards of Review** (e.g., A.B.R.): For cases after 1950, cite to M.J. or C.M.R. For earlier cases, cite to the official reporter.

| Military Justice Reporter | 1975–date | M.J. |
| Court Martial Reports | 1951–1975 | C.M.R. |

Statutory compilations: Cite to U.S.C. if therein.

United States Code	x U.S.C. § x (year)
(26 U.S.C. may be abbreviated as I.R.C.)	
United States Code Annotated	x U.S.C.A. § x (West year)
United States Code Service	x U.S.C.S. § x (Law. Co-op. year)
United States Code Unannotated	x U.S.C.U. § x (Gould year)

Session laws

| United States Statutes at Large | x Stat. xxx (year) |
| (Cite public laws before 1957 by chapter number; cite subsequent acts by public law number.) | |

Administrative compilation

| Code of Federal Regulations | 1938–date | x C.F.R. § x (year) |

Administrative register

| Federal Register | 1936–date | Fed. Reg. |

United States official administrative publications

Administrative Decisions Under Immigration and Nationality Laws	1940–date	I. & N. Dec.
Agriculture Decisions	1942–date	Agric. Dec.
Atomic Energy Commission Reports	1956–1975	A.E.C.
Civil Aeronautics Board Reports (vol. 1 by C.A.A.)	1940–1979	C.A.B.
Copyright Decisions	1909–date	Copy. Dec.
Cumulative Bulletin	1919–date	C.B.
Customs Bulletin and Decisions	1967–date	Cust. B. & Dec.
Decisions and Orders of the National Labor Relations Board	1935–date	N.L.R.B.
Decisions of the Commissioner of Patents	1869–date	Dec. Comm'r Pat.
Decisions of the Comptroller General	1922–date	Comp. Gen.
Decisions of the Department of the Interior and General Land Office in Cases Relating to Public Lands (vols. 1-52)	1881–1929	Pub. Lands Dec.
Decisions of the Department of the Interior (from vol. 53)	1930–date	Interior Dec.
Decisions of the Employees' Compensation Appeals Board	1946–date	Empl. Comp. App. Bd.
Decisions of the Federal Labor Relations Authority	1979–date	F.L.R.A.
Decisions of the United States Maritime Commission	1919–1986	Dec. U.S. Mar. Comm'n
Decisions of the United States Merit Systems Protection Board	1979–date	M.S.P.B.
Determinations of the National Mediation Board	1934–date	N.M.B.
Digest and Decisions of the Employees' Compensation Appeals Board	1946–date	Dig. & Dec. Empl. Comp. App. Bd.
Federal Communications Commission Record	1986–date	F.C.C.R.
Federal Communications Commission Reports	1934–1993	F.C.C., F.C.C.2d
Federal Energy Guidelines: FERC Reports	1977–date	F.E.R.C.
Federal Maritime Commission Reports	1947–date	F.M.C.
Federal Mine Safety and Health Review Commission Decisions	1979–date	F.M.S.H.R.C.
Federal Power Commission Reports	1931–1977	F.P.C.

Federal Reserve Bulletin	1915–date	Fed. Res. Bull.
Federal Service Impasses Panel Releases	1985–date	Fed. Serv. Imp. Pan. Rels.
Federal Trade Commission Decisions	1915–date	F.T.C.
Interstate Commerce Commission Reports	1887–date	I.C.C., I.C.C.2d
Interstate Commerce Commission Reports, Motor Carrier Cases	1936–1986	M.C.C.
Interstate Commerce Commission, Valuation Reports	1929–1964	I.C.C. Valuation Rep.
National Railroad Adjustment Board, 1st–4th Div.	1934–1972	e.g., N.R.A.B. (1st Div.)
National Transportation Safety Board Decisions	1967–date	N.T.S.B.
Nuclear Regulatory Commission Issuances	1975–date	N.R.C.
Official Gazette of the United States Patent Office	1872–date	Off. Gaz. Pat. Office
Official Opinions of the Solicitor for the Post Office Department	1873–1951	Op. Solic. P.O. Dep't
Opinions of the Attorneys General	1789–date	Op. Att'y Gen.
Opinions of Office of Legal Counsel of the Department of Justice	1977–date	Op. Off. Legal Counsel
Securities and Exchange Commission Decisions and Reports	1934–date	S.E.C.
Social Security Rulings, Cumulative Edition	1960–date	S.S.R. (Cum. Ed. year)
Treasury Decisions Under Customs and Other Laws	1898–1966	Treas. Dec.
Treasury Decisions Under Internal Revenue Laws	1898–1942	Treas. Dec. Int. Rev.

States and the District of Columbia

Note that in-state abbreviation and citation conventions may differ from those listed in this table. The abbreviations and citation conventions listed here are primarily intended to serve a national audience and to indicate clearly the source being cited. Practitioners should adhere to the local court rules.

Alabama (AL)
http://www.judicial.state.al.us

Supreme Court (Ala.): Cite to So. or So. 2d, if therein; otherwise, cite to one of the other reporters listed below.

Southern Reporter	1886–date	So., So. 2d
Alabama Reports	1840–1976	Ala.
Porter	1834–1839	Port.
Stewart and Porter	1831–1834	Stew. & P.
Stewart	1827–1831	Stew.
Minor	1820–1826	Minor

Court of Civil Appeals (Ala. Civ. App.) and **Court of Criminal Appeals** (Ala. Crim. App.), before 1969 **Court of Appeals** (Ala. Ct. App.): Cite to So. or So. 2d, if therein; otherwise, cite to Ala. App.

| Southern Reporter | 1911–date | So., So. 2d |
| Alabama Appellate Courts Reports | 1910–1976 | Ala. App. |

Statutory compilation

| Code of Alabama | ALA. CODE § x (year) |

Session laws

| Acts of Alabama | year Ala. Acts xxx |

Administrative compilation

| Alabama Administrative Code | ALA. ADMIN. CODE r. x (year) |

Alaska (AK)
http://www.alaska.net/~akctlib/homepage.htm

Supreme Court (Alaska): Cite to P.2d. or P.3d.

| Pacific Reporter | 1960–date | P.2d, P.3d |

Court of Appeals (Alaska Ct. App.): Cite to P.2d. or P.3d.

| Pacific Reporter | 1980–date | P.2d, P.3d |

District Courts of Alaska (D. Alaska): These courts had local jurisdiction from 1884 to 1959. Cite to F. Supp., F., or F.2d, if therein; otherwise cite to Alaska or Alaska Fed., in that order of preference.

Federal Supplement	1932–1959	F. Supp.
Federal Reporter	1884–1932	F., F.2d
Alaska Reports	1884–1959	Alaska
Alaska Federal Reports	1869–1937	Alaska Fed.

United States District Courts for California and Oregon, and **District Courts of Washington** (D. Cal., D. Or., D. Wash.): These courts had local jurisdiction in Alaska until 1884. Cite to F. or F. Cas., if therein; otherwise cite to Alaska Fed.

Federal Reporter   1880–1884 F.

Federal Cases   1867–1880 F. Cas.
  (Citations to F. Cas. should give the case number parenthetically. E.g.,
  The Ocean Spray, 18 F. Cas. 558 (D. Or. 1876) (No. 10,412)).

Alaska Federal Reports   1869–1937 Alaska Fed.

Statutory compilation

Alaska Statutes   ALASKA STAT. § x (Michie year)

Session laws

Session Laws of Alaska   year Alaska Sess. Laws
                                          xxx

Administrative compilation

Alaska Administrative Code   ALASKA ADMIN. CODE
                                          tit. x, § x (year)

Arizona (AZ)
http://www.supreme.state.az.us

Supreme Court (Ariz.): Cite to P., P.2d, or P.3d, if therein; otherwise,
cite to Ariz.

Pacific Reporter   1883–date P., P.2d, P.3d
Arizona Reports   1866–date Ariz.

Court of Appeals (Ariz. Ct. App.): Cite to P.2d or P.3d, if therein; otherwise, cite to one of the other reporters listed below.

Pacific Reporter   1965–date P.2d, P.3d
Arizona Reports   1976–date Ariz.
Arizona Appeals Reports   1965–1976 Ariz. App.

Statutory compilation: Cite to Ariz. Rev. Stat. if therein.

Arizona Revised Statutes   ARIZ. REV. STAT.
                                          § x (year)
Arizona Revised Statutes Annotated   ARIZ. REV. STAT. ANN.
                                          § x (West year)

Session laws: Cite to Ariz. Sess. Laws if therein.

Session Laws, Arizona   year Ariz. Sess. Laws xxx
Arizona Legislative Service   year Ariz. Legis. Serv.
(West)   xxx (West)

Administrative compilation

Arizona Administrative Code   ARIZ. ADMIN. CODE x (year)

Administrative register

Arizona Administrative Register   Ariz. Admin. Reg.

Arkansas (AR)
http://courts.state.ar.us

Supreme Court (Ark.): Cite to S.W., S.W.2d, or S.W.3d, if therein; otherwise, cite to Ark.

South Western Reporter	1886–date	S.W., S.W.2d, or S.W.3d
Arkansas Reports	1837–date	Ark.

Court of Appeals (Ark. Ct. App.): Cite to S.W.2d or S.W.3d, if therein; otherwise, cite to Ark. or Ark. App.

South Western Reporter	1979–date	S.W.2d, S.W.3d
Arkansas Appellate Reports	1981–date	Ark. App.
Arkansas Reports	1979–1981	Ark.

Statutory compilation

Arkansas Code of 1987 Annotated	ARK. CODE ANN. § x (Michie year)

Session laws

General Acts of Arkansas	year Ark. Acts xxx
Arkansas Advance Legislative Service (Michie)	year Ark. Adv. Legis. Serv. xxx (Michie)

Administrative register

Arkansas Register   Ark. Reg.

California (CA)
http://www.courtinfo.ca.gov

Supreme Court (Cal.): Cite to P., P.2d, or P.3d, if therein; otherwise, cite to one of the other reporters listed below.

Pacific Reporter	1883–date	P., P.2d, P.3d
California Reports	1850–date	Cal., Cal. 2d, Cal. 3d, Cal. 4th
West's California Reporter	1959–date	Cal. Rptr., Cal. Rptr. 2d
California Unreported Cases	1855–1910	Cal. Unrep.

Court of Appeal (Cal. Ct. App.), previously **District Court of Appeal** (Cal. Dist. Ct. App.): Cite to P. or P.2d (before 1960) or Cal. Rptr. or Cal.

Rptr. 2d (after 1959), if therein; otherwise, cite to a California Appellate Report.

West's California Reporter	1959–date	Cal. Rptr., Cal. Rptr. 2d
Pacific Reporter	1905–1959	P., P.2d
California Appellate Reports	1905–date	Cal. App., Cal. App. 2d, Cal. App. 3d, Cal. App. 4th

Appellate Departments of the Superior Court (Cal. App. Dep't Super. Ct.): Cite to P. or P.2d (before 1960) or to Cal. Rptr. or Cal. Rptr. 2d (after 1959), if therein; otherwise, cite to a California Appellate Report Supplement.

West's California Reporter	1959–date	Cal. Rptr., Cal. Rptr. 2d
Pacific Reporter	1929–1959	P., P.2d
California Appellate Reports Supplement (bound with Cal. App.)	1929–date	Cal. App. Supp., Cal. App. 2d Supp., Cal. App. 3d Supp., Cal. App. 4th Supp.

Statutory compilations: Cite to either the West or the Deering subject-matter code if therein.

West's Annotated California Code	CAL. [subject] CODE § x (West year)
Deering's Annotated California Code	CAL. [subject] CODE § x (Deering year)
Agricultural (renamed "Food and Agricultural" in 1972)	AGRIC.
Business and Professions	BUS. & PROF.
Civil	CIV.
Civil Procedure	CIV. PROC.
Commercial	COM.
Corporations	CORP.
Education	EDUC.
Elections	ELEC.
Evidence	EVID.
Family	FAM.
Financial	FIN.
Fish and Game	FISH & GAME
Food and Agricultural (formerly "Agricultural")	FOOD & AGRIC.
Government	GOV'T
Harbors and Navigation	HARB. & NAV.
Health and Safety	HEALTH & SAFETY
Insurance	INS.
Labor	LAB.

Military and Veterans	MIL. & VET.
Penal	PENAL
Probate	PROB.
Public Contract	PUB. CONT.
Public Resources	PUB. RES.
Public Utilities	PUB. UTIL.
Revenue and Taxation	REV. & TAX.
Streets and Highways	STS. & HIGH.
Unemployment Insurance	UNEMP. INS.
Vehicle	VEH.
Water	WATER
Welfare and Institutions	WELF. & INST.

Session laws:

Statutes of California	year Cal. Stat. xxx
California Legislative Service (West)	year Cal. Legis. Serv. xxx (West)
California Advance Legislative Service (Deering)	year Cal. Adv. Legis. Serv. xxx (Deering)

Administrative compilation

California Code of Regulations	CAL. CODE REGS. tit. x, § x (year)

Administrative register

California Regulatory Notice Register	Cal. Regulatory Notice Reg.

Colorado (CO)
http://www.courts.state.co.us

Supreme Court (Colo.): Cite to P., P.2d, or P.3d, if therein; otherwise, cite to Colo. if therein, or to Colo. Law. or Brief Times Rptr.

Pacific Reporter	1883–date	P., P.2d, P.3d
Colorado Reports	1864–1980.	Colo.
Colorado Lawyer		Colo. Law.
Brief Times Reporter		Brief Times Rptr.

Court of Appeals (Colo. Ct. App.): Cite to P., P.2d, or P.3d, if therein; otherwise, cite to Colo. App. if therein, or to Colo. Law. or Brief Times Rptr.

Pacific Reporter	1970–date	P.2d, P.3d
	1912–1915	P.
	1891–1905	P.

Colorado Court of Appeals Reports	1891–1905	Colo. App.
	1912–1915	Colo. App.
	1970–1980	Colo. App.

| Colorado Lawyer | Colo. Law. |
| Brief Times Reporter | Brief Times Rptr. |

Statutory compilation

| Colorado Revised Statutes | COLO. REV. STAT. § x (year) |
| West's Colorado Revised Statutes Annotated | COLO. REV. STAT. ANN. § x (West year) |

Session laws

| Session Laws of Colorado | year Colo. Sess. Laws xxx |
| Colorado Legislative Service (West) | year Colo. Legis. Serv. xxx (West) |

Administrative compilation

| Code of Colorado Regulations (by volume number) | x COLO. CODE REGS. § x (year) |

Administrative register

| Colorado Register | Colo. Reg. |

Connecticut (CT)

http://www.jud.state.ct.us

Supreme Court (Conn.), previously **Supreme Court of Errors** (Conn.): Cite to A. or A.2d, if therein; otherwise, cite to another reporter listed below.

Atlantic Reporter	1885–date	A., A.2d
Connecticut Reports	1814–date	Conn.
Day	1802–1813	Day
Root	1789–1798	Root
Kirby	1785–1789	Kirby

Appellate Court (Conn. App. Ct.): Cite to A.2d, if therein; otherwise, cite to Conn. App.

| Atlantic Reporter | 1983–date | A.2d |
| Connecticut Appellate Reports | 1983–date | Conn. App. |

Superior Court (Conn. Super. Ct.) and **Court of Common Pleas** (Conn. C.P.): Cite to A.2d, if therein; otherwise, cite to Conn. Supp. if therein, or to Conn. L. Rptr. or Conn. Super. Ct.

Atlantic Reporter	1954–date	A.2d
Connecticut Supplement	1935–date	Conn. Supp.
Connecticut Law Reporter		Conn. L. Rptr.
Connecticut Superior Court Reports		Conn. Super. Ct.

Circuit Court (Conn. Cir. Ct.): Cite to A.2d, if therein; otherwise, cite to Conn. Cir. Ct.

Atlantic Reporter	1961–1974	A.2d
Connecticut Circuit Court Reports	1961–1974	Conn. Cir. Ct.

Statutory compilations: Cite to CONN. GEN. STAT. if therein.

General Statutes of Connecticut	CONN. GEN. STAT. § x (year)
Connecticut General Statutes Annotated (West)	CONN. GEN. STAT. ANN. § x (West year)

Session laws: Cite to Conn. Acts, Conn. Pub. Acts, or Conn. Spec. Acts, if therein.

Connecticut Public & Special Acts	1972–date	year Conn. Acts xxx (Reg. [Spec.] Sess.)
Connecticut Public Acts	1650–1971	year Conn. Pub. Acts xxx
Connecticut Special Acts (published under various titles—i.e., Resolves & Private Laws, Private & Special Laws, Special Laws, Resolves & Private Acts, Resolutions & Private Acts, Private Acts & Resolutions, and Special Acts & Resolutions—and with various volume designations— i.e., by year or volume number)	1789–1971	year Conn. Spec. Acts xxx
Connecticut Legislative Service (West)		year Conn. Legis. Serv. xxx (West)

Administrative compilation

Regulations of Connecticut State Agencies	CONN. AGENCIES REGS. § x (year)

Administrative register

Connecticut Law Journal	Conn. L.J.

Delaware (DE)

http://courts.state.de.us

Supreme Court (Del.), previously **Court of Errors and Appeals** (Del.): Cite to A. or A.2d, if therein; otherwise, cite to Del. or Del. Cas.

Atlantic Reporter	1886–date	A., A.2d
Delaware Reports		
31 Del. to 59 Del.	1920–1966	Del.
Boyce	1909–1920	e.g., 24 Del. (1 Boyce)
Pennewill	1897–1909	e.g., 17 Del. (1 Penne.)
Marvel	1893–1897	e.g., 15 Del. (1 Marv.)
Houston	1855–1893	e.g., 6 Del. (1 Houst.)
Harrington	1832–1855	e.g., 1 Del. (1 Harr.)
Delaware Cases	1792–1830	Del. Cas.

Court of Chancery (Del. Ch.): Cite to A. or A.2d, if therein; otherwise, cite to Del. Ch. or Del. Cas.

Atlantic Reporter	1886–date	A., A.2d
Delaware Chancery Reports	1814–1968	Del. Ch.
Delaware Cases	1792–1830	Del. Cas.

Superior Court (Del. Super. Ct.), previously **Superior Court and Orphans' Court** (Del. Super. Ct. & Orphans' Ct.): Cite to A.2d, if therein; otherwise, cite to one of the official reporters listed under **Supreme Court.**

Atlantic Reporter	1951–date	A.2d

Family Court (Del. Fam. Ct.): Cite to A.2d.

Atlantic Reporter	1977–date	A.2d

Statutory compilation

Delaware Code Annotated	DEL. CODE ANN. tit. x, § x (year)

Session laws

Laws of Delaware (by volume number)	x Del. Laws xxx (year)

District of Columbia (DC)
http://www.dcca.state.dc.us

Court of Appeals (D.C.), previously **Municipal Court of Appeals** (D.C.): Cite to A.2d.

Atlantic Reporter	1943–date	A.2d

United States Court of Appeals for the District of Columbia Circuit (D.C. Cir.), previously **Court of Appeals of/for the District of Columbia** (D.C. Cir.), previously **Supreme Court of the District of**

Columbia (D.C.): Cite to F., F.2d, or F.3d if therein; otherwise, cite to U.S. App. D.C., App. D.C., or D.C.

Federal Reporter	1919–date	F., F.2d, F.3d
United States Court of Appeals Reports	1941–date	U.S. App. D.C.
Appeal Cases, District of Columbia	1893–1941	App. D.C.
District of Columbia Reports		
Tucker and Clephane	1892–1893	21 D.C. (Tuck. & Cl.)
Mackey	1880–1892	e.g., 12 D.C. (1 Mackey)
MacArthur and Mackey	1879–1880	11 D.C. (MacArth. & M.)
MacArthur	1873–1879	e.g., 8 D.C. (1 MacArth.)
Mackey	1863–1872	e.g., 6 D.C. (1 Mackey)
Hayward & Hazleton	1840–1863	5 D.C. (Hay. & Haz.)
Cranch	1801–1841	e.g., 1 D.C. (1 Cranch)

Statutory compilation

District of Columbia Code Annotated (1981)	D.C. CODE ANN. § x (year)

Session laws: Cite to Stat. or D.C. Stat. if therein; otherwise, cite to D.C. Reg.

United States Statutes at Large	x Stat. xxx (year)
District of Columbia Statutes at Large	year D.C. Stat. xxx
District of Columbia Register	x D.C. Reg. xxx (year)

Municipal regulations

D.C. Municipal Regulations	D.C. MUN. REGS. tit. x, § x (year)

Administrative register

District of Columbia Register	D.C. Reg.

Florida (FL)
http://www.flcourts.org

Supreme Court (Fla.): Cite to So. or So. 2d, if therein; otherwise, cite to Fla. if therein or to Fla. L. Weekly.

Southern Reporter	1886–date	So., So. 2d
Florida Reports	1846–1948	Fla.
Florida Law Weekly		Fla. L. Weekly

District Court of Appeal (Fla. Dist. Ct. App.): Cite to So. 2d., if therein; otherwise, cite to Fla. L. Weekly.

Southern Reporter	1957–date	So. 2d
Florida Law Weekly		Fla. L. Weekly

Circuit Court (Fla. Cir. Ct.), **County Court** (e.g., Fla. Orange County Ct.), **Public Service Commission** (Fla. P.S.C.), and other lower courts of record: Cite to Fla. Supp. or Fla. Supp. 2d., if therein; otherwise, cite to Fla. L. Weekly Supp.

Florida Supplement	1948–1992	Fla. Supp., Fla. Supp. 2d
Florida Law Weekly Supplement		Fla. L. Weekly Supp.

Statutory compilations: Cite to FLA. STAT. if therein.

Florida Statutes	FLA. STAT. ch. x.xxx (year)
Florida Statutes Annotated (West)	FLA. STAT. ANN. § x (West year)
Florida Statutes Annotated (Harrison)	FLA. STAT. ANN. ch. x.xxx (Harrison year)

Session laws: Cite to Fla. Laws if therein.

Laws of Florida	year Fla. Laws ch. xxx
Florida Session Law Service (West)	year Fla. Sess. Law Serv. xxx (West)

Administrative compilation

Florida Administrative Code Annotated	FLA. ADMIN. CODE ANN. r. x (year)

Administrative register

Florida Administrative Weekly	Fla. Admin. Weekly

Georgia (GA)
http://www.doas.state.ga.us/courts/supreme

Supreme Court (Ga.): Cite to S.E. or S.E.2d, if therein; otherwise, cite to Ga.

South Eastern Reporter	1887–date	S.E., S.E.2d
Georgia Reports	1846–date	Ga.

Court of Appeals (Ga. Ct. App.): Cite to S.E. or S.E.2d, if therein; otherwise, cite to Ga. App.

| South Eastern Reporter | 1907–date | S.E., S.E.2d |
| Georgia Appeals Reports | 1907–date | Ga. App. |

Statutory compilations: Cite to the official version of GA. CODE ANN. (published by Michie) if therein.

| Official Code of Georgia Annotated (Michie) | GA. CODE ANN. § x (year) |
| Code of Georgia Annotated (Harrison) | GA. CODE ANN. § x (Harrison year) |

Session laws

| Georgia Laws | year Ga. Laws xxx |

Administrative compilation

| Official Compilation Rules and Regulations of the State of Georgia | GA. COMP. R. & REGS. r. x (year) |

Hawaii (HI)
http://www.hawaii.gov/jud

Supreme Court (Haw.): Cite to P.2d or P.3d, if therein; otherwise, cite to Haw.

Pacific Reporter	1959–date	P.2d, P.3d
West's Hawaii Reports (begins with vol. 76)	1994–date	Haw.
Hawaii Reports (ends with vol. 75)	1847–1994	Haw.

Intermediate Court of Appeals (Haw. Ct. App.): Cite to P.2d or P.3d, if therein; otherwise, cite to Haw. App. or Haw.

Pacific Reporter	1980–date	P.2d, P.3d
West's Hawaii Reports (begins with vol. 76)	1994–date	Haw.
Hawaii Appellate Reports	1980–1994	Haw. App.

Statutory compilations: Cite to HAW. REV. STAT. if therein.

| Hawaii Revised Statutes | HAW. REV. STAT. § x (year) |
| Hawaii Revised Statutes Annotated | HAW. REV. STAT. ANN. § x (Michie year) |

Session laws

| Session Laws of Hawaii | year Haw. Sess. Laws xxx |

Idaho (ID)
http://www.state.id.us/judicial

Supreme Court (Idaho): Cite to P., P.2d, or P.3d, if therein; otherwise, cite to Idaho.

Pacific Reporter	1883–date	P., P.2d, P.3d
Idaho Reports	1866–date	Idaho

Court of Appeals (Idaho Ct. App.): Cite to P.2d or P.3d, if therein; otherwise, cite to Idaho.

Pacific Reporter	1982–date	P.2d, P.3d
Idaho Reports	1982–date	Idaho

Statutory compilation

Idaho Official Code (Michie)	IDAHO CODE § x (Michie year)

Session laws

Session Laws, Idaho	year Idaho Sess. Laws xxx

Illinois (IL)
http://www.state.il.us/court

Supreme Court (Ill.): Cite to N.E. or N.E.2d, if therein; otherwise, cite to one of the Illinois Reports listed below.

North Eastern Reporter	1886–date	N.E., N.E.2d
Illinois Reports		
11 Ill. to date	1849–date	Ill., Ill. 2d
Gilman	1844–1849	e.g., 6 Ill. (1 Gilm.)
Scammon	1832–1843	e.g., 2 Ill. (1 Scam.)
Breese	1819–1831	1 Ill. (Breese)
Illinois Decisions	1976–date	Ill. Dec.

Appellate Court (Ill. App. Ct.): Cite to N.E.2d, if therein; otherwise, cite to an Illinois Appellate Court Report.

North Eastern Reporter	1936–date	N.E.2d
Illinois Appellate Court Reports	1877–date	Ill. App., Ill. App. 2d, Ill. App. 3d
Illinois Decisions	1976–date	Ill. Dec.

Court of Claims (Ill. Ct. Cl.): Cite to Ill. Ct. Cl.

Illinois Court of Claims Reports	1889–date	Ill. Ct. Cl.

Statutory compilations: Cite to ILL. COMP. STAT. if therein.

Illinois Compiled Statutes	x ILL. COMP. STAT. x/x-x (year)
West's Smith-Hurd Illinois Compiled Statutes Annotated	x ILL. COMP. STAT. ANN. x/x-x (West year)

Session laws: Cite to Ill. Laws if therein.

Laws of Illinois	year Ill. Laws xxx
Illinois Legislative Service (West)	year Ill. Legis. Serv. xxx (West)

Administrative compilation

Illinois Administrative Code	ILL. ADMIN. CODE tit. x, § x (year)

Administrative register

Illinois Register	Ill. Reg.

Indiana (IN)
http://www.state.in.us/judiciary

Supreme Court (Ind.): Cite to N.E. or N.E.2d, if therein; otherwise, cite to Ind. or Blackf.

North Eastern Reporter	1885–date	N.E., N.E.2d
Indiana Reports	1848–1981	Ind.
Blackford	1817–1847	Blackf.

Court of Appeals (Ind. Ct. App.), previously **Appellate Court** (Ind. App.): Cite to N.E. or N.E.2d, if therein; otherwise, cite to Ind. App.

North Eastern Reporter	1891–date	N.E., N.E.2d
Indiana Court of Appeals Reports (prior to 1972, Indiana Appellate Court Reports)	1890–1979	Ind. App.

Statutory compilations: Cite to IND. CODE if therein.

Indiana Code	IND. CODE § x (year)
Burns Indiana Statutes Annotated	IND. CODE ANN. § x (Michie year)
West's Annotated Indiana Code	IND. CODE ANN. § x (West year)

Session laws: Cite to Ind. Acts if therein.

Acts, Indiana	year Ind. Acts xxx
West's Indiana Legislative Service	year Ind. Legis. Serv. xxx (West)

Burns Indiana Advance Legislative   year Ind. Adv. Legis. Serv.
Service (Michie)   xxx (Michie)

Administrative compilation

Indiana Administrative Code   IND. ADMIN. CODE tit. x,
                                               r. x (year)

Administrative register

Indiana Register   Ind. Reg.

Iowa (IA)
http://www.judicial.state.ia.us

Supreme Court (Iowa): Cite to N.W. or N.W.2d, if therein; otherwise, cite to another reporter listed below.

North Western Reporter	1879–date	N.W., N.W.2d
Iowa Reports (Cite to edition published by Clarke for volumes 1 through 8.)	1855–1968	Iowa
Greene	1847–1854	Greene
Morris	1839–1846	Morris
Bradford	1838–1841	Bradf.

Court of Appeals (Iowa Ct. App.): Cite to N.W.2d.

North Western Reporter	1977–date	N.W.2d

Statutory compilations: Cite to IOWA CODE if therein.

Code of Iowa   IOWA CODE § x (year)
Iowa Code Annotated (West)   IOWA CODE ANN. § x
                                               (West year)

Session laws: Cite to Iowa Acts if therein.

Acts and Joint Resolutions of the   year Iowa Acts xxx
State of Iowa

Iowa Legislative Service (West)   year Iowa Legis. Serv.
                                               xxx (West)

Administrative compilation

Iowa Administrative Code   IOWA ADMIN. CODE
                                               r. x–x.x (year)

Administrative register

Iowa Administrative Bulletin   Iowa Admin. Bull.

Kansas (KS)
http://www.kscourts.org

Supreme Court (Kan.): Cite to P., P.2d, or P.3d, if therein; otherwise, cite to Kan. or McCahon.

Pacific Reporter	1883–date	P., P.2d, P.3d
Kansas Reports	1862–date	Kan.
McCahon	1858–1868	McCahon

Court of Appeals (Kan. Ct. App.): Cite to P., P.2d, or P.3d, if therein; otherwise, cite to Kan. App. or Kan. App. 2d.

Pacific Reporter	1895–1901	P.
	1977–date	P.2d, P.3d
Kansas Court of Appeals Reports	1895–1901	Kan. App.
	1977–date	Kan. App. 2d

Statutory compilations: Cite to one of the following codes.

Kansas Statutes Annotated	KAN. STAT. ANN. § x (year)
Vernon's Kansas Statutes Annotated	
Uniform Commercial Code	KAN. U.C.C. ANN. § x (West year)
Code of Civil Procedure	KAN. CIV. PROC. CODE ANN. § x (West year)
Criminal Code	KAN. CRIM. CODE ANN. § x (West year)
Code of Criminal Procedure	KAN. CRIM. PROC. CODE ANN. § x (West year)
General Corporation Code	KAN. CORP. CODE ANN. § x (West year)
Probate Code	KAN. PROB. CODE ANN. § x (West year)

Session laws

Session Laws of Kansas	year Kan. Sess. Laws xxx

Administrative compilation

Kansas Administrative Regulations (updated by supplements)	KAN. ADMIN. REGS. x

Administrative register

Kansas Register	Kan. Reg.

Kentucky (KY)
http://www.aoc.state.ky.us

Supreme Court (Ky.): Before 1976 the **Court of Appeals** (Ky.) was the highest state court. Cite to S.W., S.W.2d, or S.W.3d, if therein; otherwise, cite to one of the Kentucky Reports listed below, if therein, or to Ky. Op., Ky. L. Rptr., Ky. App. Rptr., or Ky. L. Summary.

South Western Reporter	1886–date	S.W., S.W.2d, S.W.3d
Kentucky Reports		
78 Ky. to 314 Ky.	1879–1951	Ky.
Bush	1866–1879	e.g., 64 Ky. (1 Bush)
Duvall	1863–1866	e.g., 62 Ky. (1 Duv.)
Metcalf	1858–1863	e.g., 58 Ky. (1 Met.)
Monroe, Ben	1840–1857	e.g., 40 Ky. (1 B. Mon.)
Dana	1833–1840	e.g., 31 Ky. (1 Dana)
Marshall, J.J.	1829–1832	e.g., 24 Ky. (1 J.J. Marsh.)
Monroe, T.B.	1824–1828	e.g., 17 Ky. (1 T.B. Mon.)
Littell	1822–1824	e.g., 11 Ky. (1 Litt.)
Littell's Selected Cases	1795–1821	e.g., 16 Ky (1 Litt. Sel. Cas.)
Marshall, A.K.	1817–1821	e.g., 8 Ky. (1 A.K. Marsh.)
Bibb	1808–1817	e.g., 4 Ky. (1 Bibb)
Hardin	1805–1808	3 Ky. (Hard.)
Sneed	1801–1805	2 Ky. (Sneed)
Hughes	1785–1801	1 Ky. (Hughes)
Kentucky Opinions	1864–1886	Ky. Op.
Kentucky Law Reporter	1880–1908	Ky. L. Rptr.
Kentucky Appellate Reporter		Ky. App. Rptr.
Kentucky Law Summary		Ky. L. Summary

Court of Appeals (Ky. Ct. App.) (for decisions before 1976, see **Kentucky Supreme Court**): Cite to S.W.2d or S.W.3d, if therein; otherwise, cite to Ky. App. Rptr. or Ky. L. Summary.

South Western Reporter	1976–date	S.W.2d, S.W.3d
Kentucky Appellate Reporter		Ky. App. Rptr.
Kentucky Law Summary		Ky. L. Summary

Statutory compilations: Cite to one of the following official codes.

Baldwin's Official Edition, Kentucky Revised Statutes Annotated	KY. REV. STAT. ANN. § x (Banks-Baldwin year)
Kentucky Revised Statutes Annotated, Official Edition (Michie)	KY. REV. STAT. ANN. § x (Michie year)

Session laws: Cite to Ky. Acts if therein.

Kentucky Acts	year Ky. Acts xxx
Baldwin's Official Edition, Kentucky Revised Statutes and Rules Service (Banks-Baldwin)	year Ky. Rev. Stat. & R. Serv. xxx (Banks-Baldwin)

Administrative compilation

Kentucky Administrative Regulations Service (by title)	x KY. ADMIN. REGS. x:x (year)

Administrative register

Administrative Register of Kentucky	Ky. Admin. Reg.

Louisiana (LA)
http://www.state.la.us/state/judicial.htm

Public domain citation format: Louisiana has adopted a public domain citation format for cases after December 31, 1993. The format is:

> Sierra Club v. Givens, 97-0959 (La. App. 4 Cir. 9/26/97), *writ denied*, 97-2661 (La. 1/9/98).

Supreme Court (La.), before 1813 the **Superior Court of Louisiana** (La.) and the **Superior Court of the Territory of Orleans** (Orleans): Cite to So. or So. 2d, if therein; otherwise, cite to another reporter listed below.

Southern Reporter	1886–date	So., So. 2d
Louisiana Reports	1901–1972	La.
Louisiana Annual Reports	1846–1900	La. Ann.
Robinson	1841–1846	Rob.
Louisiana Reports	1830–1841	La.
Martin (Louisiana Term Reports)	1809–1830	Mart. (o.s.), Mart. (n.s.)

Court of Appeal (La. Ct. App.): Cite to So. or So. 2d, if therein; otherwise, cite to another of the reporters listed below.

Southern Reporter	1928–date	So., So. 2d
Louisiana Court of Appeals Reports	1924–1932	La. App.
Peltier's Decisions, Parish at Orleans	1917–1924	Pelt.
Teissier, Orleans Court of Appeals	1903–1917	Teiss.
Gunby's Reports	1885	Gunby
McGloin	1881–1884	McGl.

Statutory compilations: Cite to one of the following codes.

West's Louisiana Revised Statutes Annotated	LA. REV. STAT. ANN. § x (West year)
West's Louisiana Civil Code Annotated	LA. CIV. CODE ANN. art. x (West year)
West's Louisiana Code of Civil Procedure Annotated	LA. CODE CIV. PROC. ANN. art. x (West year)
West's Louisiana Code of Criminal Procedure Annotated	LA. CODE CRIM. PROC. ANN. art. x (West year)
West's Louisiana Code of Evidence Annotated	LA. CODE EVID. ANN. art. x (West year)
West's Louisiana Code of Juvenile Procedure Annotated	LA. CODE JUV. PROC. ANN. art. x (West year)

Session laws: Cite to La. Acts if therein.

State of Louisiana: Acts of the Legislature	year La. Acts xxx
Louisiana Session Law Service (West)	year La. Sess. Law Serv. xxx (West)

Administrative compilation

Louisiana Administrative Code	LA. ADMIN. CODE tit. x, § x (year)

Administrative register

Louisiana Register	La. Reg.

Maine (ME)
http://www.courts.state.me.us

Public domain citation format: Maine has adopted a public domain citation format for cases after December 31, 1996. The format is:

Bangor Publ'g Co. v. Union St. Mkt., 1998 ME 37.

Supreme Judicial Court (Me.): Cite to A. or A.2d, if therein; otherwise, cite to Me.

Atlantic Reporter	1885–date	A., A.2d
Maine Reports	1820–1965	Me.

Statutory compilation

Maine Revised Statutes Annotated (West)	ME. REV. STAT. ANN. tit. x, § x (West year)

Session laws: Cite to Me. Laws if therein.

Laws of the State of Maine	year Me. Laws xxx
Acts, Resolves and Constitutional Resolutions of the State of Maine	year Me. Acts xxx
Maine Legislative Service (West)	year Me. Legis. Serv. xxx (West)

Administrative Compilation

Code of Maine Rules	CODE ME. R. § x (year)

Maryland (MD)
http://www.courts.state.md.us

Court of Appeals (Md.): Cite to A. or A.2d, if therein; otherwise, cite to one of the other reporters listed below.

Atlantic Reporter	1885–date	A., A.2d
Maryland Reports	1851–date	Md.
Gill	1843–1851	Gill
Gill and Johnson	1829–1842	G. & J.
Harris and Gill	1826–1829	H. & G.
Harris and Johnson	1800–1826	H. & J.
Harris and McHenry	1770–1774 1780–1799	H. & McH.

Court of Special Appeals (Md. Ct. Spec. App.): Cite to A.2d, if therein; otherwise, cite to Md. App.

Atlantic Reporter	1967–date	A.2d
Maryland Appellate Reports	1967–date	Md. App.

Statutory compilations: Cite to MD. CODE ANN. by subject, if therein; otherwise, cite to MD. ANN. CODE of 1957.

Annotated Code of Maryland	MD. CODE ANN., [subject] § x (year)
Agriculture	AGRIC.
Business Occupations and Professions	BUS. OCC. & PROF.
Business Regulation	BUS. REG.
Commercial Law I	COM. LAW I
Commercial Law II	COM. LAW II
Constitutions	CONST.
Corporations and Associations	CORPS. & ASS'NS
Courts and Judicial Proceedings	CTS. & JUD. PROC.

T
T.1

Education	EDUC.
Environment	ENVIR.
Estates and Trusts	EST. & TRUSTS
Family Law	FAM. LAW
Financial Institutions	FIN. INST.
Health–General I	HEALTH–GEN. I
Health–General II	HEALTH–GEN. II
Health Occupations	HEALTH OCC.
Insurance	INS.
Labor and Employment	LAB. & EMPL.
Natural Resources I	NAT. RES. I
Natural Resources II	NAT. RES. II
Real Property	REAL PROP.
State Finance and Procurement	STATE FIN. & PROC.
State Government	STATE GOV'T
State Personnel and Pensions	STATE PERS. & PENS.
Tax–General	TAX–GEN.
Tax–Property	TAX–PROP.
Transportation I	TRANSP. I
Transportation II	TRANSP. II
Annotated Code of Maryland (1957)	MD. ANN. CODE art. x, § x (year)

Session laws

Laws of Maryland	year Md. Laws xxx

Administrative compilation

Code of Maryland Regulations	MD. REGS. CODE tit. x, § x (year)

Administrative register

Maryland Register	Md. Reg.

Massachusetts (MA)
http://www.state.ma.us/courts

Supreme Judicial Court (Mass.): Cite to N.E. or N.E.2d, if therein; otherwise, cite to Mass.

North Eastern Reporter	1885-date	N.E., N.E.2d
Massachusetts Reports		
97 Mass. to date	1867–date	Mass.
Allen	1861–1867	e.g., 83 Mass. (1 Allen)

Gray	1854–1860	e.g., 67 Mass. (1 Gray)
Cushing	1848–1853	e.g., 55 Mass. (1 Cush.)
Metcalf	1840–1844	e.g., 42 Mass. (1 Met.)
Pickering	1822–1839	e.g., 18 Mass. (1 Pick.)
Tyng	1806–1822	e.g., 2 Mass. (1 Tyng)
Williams	1804–1805	1 Mass. (1 Will.)

Appeals Court (Mass. App. Ct.): Cite to N.E.2d, if therein; otherwise, cite to Mass. App. Ct.

| North Eastern Reporter | 1972–date | N.E.2d |
| Massachusetts Appeals Court Reports | 1972–date | Mass. App. Ct. |

District Court (Mass. Dist. Ct.): Cite to Mass. App. Div., if therein; otherwise cite to Mass. Supp. or Mass. App. Dec. if therein; otherwise, cite to Mass. App. Div. Adv. Sh.

Appellate Division Reports	1936–1950 1980–date	Mass. App. Div.
Massachusetts Reports Supplement	1980–1983	Mass. Supp.
Appellate Decisions	1941–1977	Mass. App. Dec.
Appellate Division Advance Sheets	1975–1979	19xx Mass. App. Div. Adv. Sh. xxx

Statutory compilations: Cite to MASS. GEN. LAWS if therein.

General Laws of the Commonwealth of Massachusetts (Mass. Bar Ass'n/West)	MASS. GEN. LAWS ch. x, § x (year)
Massachusetts General Laws Annotated (West)	MASS. GEN. LAWS ANN. ch. x, § x (West year)
Annotated Laws of Massachusetts (Law. Co-op.)	MASS. ANN. LAWS ch. x, § x (Law. Co-op. year)

Session laws: Cite to Mass. Acts if therein.

Acts and Resolves of Massachusetts	year Mass. Acts xxx
Massachusetts Advance Legislative Serv. (Law. Co-op.)	year Mass. Adv. Legis. Serv. xxx (Law. Co-op.)
Massachusetts Legislative Service (West)	year Mass. Legis. Serv. xxx (West)

Administrative compilation

| Code of Massachusetts Regulations | MASS. REGS. CODE tit. x, § x (year) |

T T.1

Administrative register

Massachusetts Register   Mass. Reg.

Michigan (MI)
http://www.supremecourt.state.mi.us

Supreme Court (Mich.): Cite to N.W. or N.W.2d, if therein; otherwise, cite to another of the reporters listed below.

North Western Reporter	1879–date	N.W., N.W.2d
Michigan Reports	1847–date	Mich.
Douglass	1843–1847	Doug.
Blume, Unreported Opinions	1836–1843	Blume Unrep. Op.
Blume, Supreme Court Transactions	1805–1836	Blume Sup. Ct. Trans.

Court of Appeals (Mich. Ct. App.): Cite to N.W.2d, if therein; otherwise, cite to Mich. App.

North Western Reporter	1965–date	N.W.2d
Michigan Appeals Reports	1965–date	Mich. App.

Court of Claims (Mich. Ct. Cl.): Cite to Mich. Ct. Cl.

Michigan Court of Claims Reports	1939–1942	Mich. Ct. Cl.

Statutory compilations: Cite to MICH. COMP. LAWS if therein; otherwise cite to MICH. COMP. LAWS ANN. Cite to MICH. STAT. ANN. only under **rule 12.3.1(h)**.

Michigan Compiled Laws (1979)	MICH. COMP. LAWS § x (year)
Michigan Compiled Laws Annotated (West)	MICH. COMP. LAWS ANN. § x (West year)
Michigan Statutes Annotated (Michie)	MICH. STAT. ANN. § x (Michie year)

Session laws: Cite to Mich. Pub. Acts if therein.

Public and Local Acts of the Legislature of the State of Michigan	year Mich. Pub. Acts xxx
Michigan Legislative Service (West)	year Mich. Legis. Serv. xxx (West)

Administrative compilation

Michigan Administrative Code (1979) (updated by supplements)	MICH. ADMIN. CODE r. x (year)

Administrative register

Michigan Register   Mich. Reg. (month year)

Minnesota (MN)
http://www.courts.state.mn.us

Supreme Court (Minn.): Cite to N.W. or N.W.2d, if therein; otherwise, cite to Minn.

North Western Reporter	1879–date	N.W., N.W.2d
Minnesota Reports	1851–1977	Minn.

Court of Appeals (Minn. Ct. App.): Cite to N.W.2d, if therein.

North Western Reporter	1983–date	N.W.2d

Statutory compilations: Cite to MINN. STAT. if therein.

Minnesota Statutes	MINN. STAT. § x (year)
Minnesota Statutes Annotated (West)	MINN. STAT. ANN. § x (West year)

Session laws: Cite to Minn. Laws if therein.

Laws of Minnesota	year Minn. Laws xxx
Minnesota Session Law Service (West)	year Minn. Sess. Law Serv. xxx (West)

Administrative compilation

Minnesota Rules (replaces Minnesota Code of Agency Rules)	MINN. R. x.x (year)

Administrative register

Minnesota State Register   Minn. Reg.

Mississippi (MS)
http://www.mssc.state.ms.us

Public domain citation format: Mississippi has adopted a public domain citation format for cases after July 1, 1997. The format is:

Pro-Choice Miss. v. Fordice, 95-CA-00960-SCT (Miss. 1998).

Supreme Court (Miss.): Cite to So. or So. 2d, if therein; otherwise, cite to Miss. or Miss. Dec.

Southern Reporter	1886–date	So., So. 2d
Mississippi Reports		
23 Miss. to 254 Miss.	1851–1966	Miss.

Smedes and Marshall	1843–1850	e.g., 9 Miss. (1 S. & M.)
Howard	1834–1843	e.g., 2 Miss. (1 Howard)
Walker	1818–1832	1 Miss. (1 Walker)
Mississippi Decisions	1820–1885	Miss. Dec.

Court of Appeals (Miss. Ct. App.): Cite to So. 2d, if therein.

Southern Reporter	1995–date	So. 2d

Statutory compilation

Mississippi Code Annotated	MISS. CODE ANN. § x (year)

Session laws

General Laws of Mississippi	year Miss. Laws xxx

Administrative Register

Mississippi Official and Statistical Register	Miss. Reg.

Missouri (MO)
http://www.osca.state.mo.us

Supreme Court (Mo.): Cite to S.W., S.W.2d, or S.W.3d, if therein; otherwise, cite to Mo.

South Western Reporter	1886–date	S.W., S.W.2d, S.W.3d
Missouri Reports	1821–1956	Mo.

Court of Appeals (Mo. Ct. App.): Cite to S.W., S.W.2d, or S.W.3d, if therein; otherwise, cite to Mo. App.

South Western Reporter	1902–date	S.W., S.W.2d, S.W.3d
Missouri Appeals Reports	1876–1954	Mo. App.

Statutory compilations: Cite to MO. REV. STAT. if therein.

Missouri Revised Statutes	MO. REV. STAT. § x (year)
Vernon's Annotated Missouri Statutes (West)	MO. ANN. STAT. § x (West year)

Session laws: Cite to Mo. Laws if therein.

Laws of Missouri	year Mo. Laws xxx
Missouri Legislative Service (West)	year Mo. Legis. Serv. xxx (West)

Administrative compilation

Missouri Code of State Regulations
Annotated

M O. C ODE R EGS. A NN. tit. x,
§ x–x.x (year)

Administrative register

Missouri Register

Mo. Reg.

Montana (MT)
http://www.lawlibrary.state.mt.us/mtlegal.htm

Public domain citation format: Montana has adopted a public
domain citation format for cases after January 1, 1998. The format is:

Mont. Envtl. Info. Ctr. v. Dep't of Envtl. Quality, 1999 MT 248.

Supreme Court (Mont.): Cite to P., P.2d, or P.3d, if therein; otherwise,
cite to Mont. or to State Rptr.

Pacific Reporter	1883–date	P., P.2d, P.3d
Montana Reports	1868–date	Mont.
State Reporter		State Rptr.

Statutory compilations: Cite to M ONT. C ODE A NN. if therein.

Montana Code Annotated	M ONT. C ODE A NN. § x (year)
Revised Codes of Montana Annotated (Allen Smith Co.)	M ONT. R EV. C ODE A NN. § x (Smith year)

Session laws

Laws of Montana

year Mont. Laws xxx

Administrative compilation

Administrative Rules of Montana

M ONT. A DMIN. R. x (year)

Administrative register

Montana Administrative Register

Mont. Admin. Reg.

Nebraska (NE)
http://court.nol.org

Supreme Court (Neb.): Cite to N.W. or N.W.2d, if therein; otherwise,
cite to Neb.

North Western Reporter	1879–date	N.W., N.W.2d
Nebraska Reports	1860–date	Neb.

Court of Appeals (Neb. Ct. App.): Cite to N.W.2d, if therein.

| North Western Reporter | 1992–date | N.W.2d |
| Nebraska Court of Appeals Reports | 1992–date | Neb. Ct. App. |

Statutory compilations: Cite to NEB. REV. STAT. if therein.

| Revised Statutes of Nebraska | NEB. REV. STAT. § x
(year) |
| Revised Statutes of Nebraska
Annotated (Michie) | NEB. REV. STAT. ANN. § x
(Michie year) |

Session laws

| Laws of Nebraska | year Neb. Laws xxx |

Administrative compilation

| Nebraska Administrative Code | NEB. ADMIN. CODE
x (year) |

Nevada (NV)
http://test.state.nv.us/elec_judicial.html

Supreme Court (Nev.): Cite to P., P.2d, or P.3d, if therein; otherwise, cite to Nev.

| Pacific Reporter | 1883–date | P., P.2d, P.3d |
| Nevada Reports | 1865–date | Nev. |

Statutory compilation: Cite to NEV. REV. STAT. if therein.

| Nevada Revised Statutes | NEV. REV. STAT. x.x
(year) |
| Nevada Revised Statutes
Annotated (Michie) | NEV. REV. STAT. ANN.
x.x (Michie year) |

Session laws

| Statutes of Nevada | year Nev. Stat. xxx |

Administrative compilation

| Nevada Administrative Code | NEV. ADMIN. CODE ch. x,
§ x (year) |

New Hampshire (NH)
http://www.state.nh.us/courts/home.htm

Supreme Court (N.H.): Cite to A. or A.2d, if therein; otherwise, cite to N.H.

| Atlantic Reporter | 1885–date | A., A.2d |
| New Hampshire Reports | 1816–date | N.H. |

Statutory compilation

New Hampshire Revised Statutes
Annotated

N.H. Rev. Stat. Ann. § x
(year)

Session laws

Laws of the State of New Hampshire

year N.H. Laws xxx

Administrative compilation

New Hampshire Code of
Administrative Rules Annotated

N.H. Code Admin. R. Ann.
[department name as
abbreviated in Rules] x.x
(year)

Administrative register

New Hampshire Rulemaking Register

N.H. Rulemaking Reg.

New Jersey (NJ)
http://www.judiciary.state.nj.us

Supreme Court (N.J.), previously **Court of Errors and Appeals**
(N.J.): Cite to A. or A.2d, if therein; otherwise, cite to one of the other
reporters listed below.

Atlantic Reporter	1885–date	A., A.2d
New Jersey Reports	1948–date	N.J.
New Jersey Law Reports	1790–1948	N.J.L.
New Jersey Equity Reports	1847–1948	N.J. Eq.
New Jersey Miscellaneous Reports	1923–1948	N.J. Misc.

Superior Court (N.J. Super. Ct. App. Div., N.J. Super. Ct. Ch. Div., N.J.
Super. Ct. Law Div.), previously **Court of Chancery** (N.J. Ch.),
Supreme Court (N.J. Sup. Ct.), and **Prerogative Court** (N.J. Prerog.
Ct.): Cite to A. or A.2d, if therein; otherwise, cite to one of the other
reporters listed below.

Atlantic Reporter	1885–date	A., A.2d
New Jersey Superior Court Reports	1948–date	N.J. Super.
New Jersey Law Reports	1790–1948	N.J.L.
New Jersey Equity Reports	1830–1948	N.J. Eq.
New Jersey Miscellaneous Reports	1923–1948	N.J. Misc.

County Court (e.g., Essex County Ct.) and other lower courts: Cite to
A.2d, if therein; otherwise, cite to another of the reporters.

Tax Court (N.J. Tax Ct.): Cite to N.J. Tax if therein.

New Jersey Tax Court Reports	1979–date	N.J. Tax

T
T.1

Statutory compilations: Cite to N.J. STAT. ANN. if therein.

New Jersey Statutes Annotated (West)	N.J. STAT. ANN. § x (West year)
New Jersey Revised Statutes (1937)	N.J. REV. STAT. § x (year)

Session laws: Cite to N.J. Laws if therein.

Laws of New Jersey	year N.J. Laws xxx
New Jersey Session Law Service (West)	year N.J. Sess. Law Serv. xxx (West)

Administrative compilation

New Jersey Administrative Code	N.J. ADMIN. CODE tit. x, § x (year)

Administrative register

New Jersey Register	N.J. Reg.

Administrative reports

New Jersey Administrative Reports	1982–date	N.J. Admin., N.J. Admin. 2d

New Mexico (NM)
http://www.nmcourts.com

Public domain citation format: New Mexico has adopted a public domain citation format for cases after December 31, 1995. The format is:

> Atlixco Coalition v. Maggiore, 1998-NMCA-134.

Supreme Court (N.M.): Cite to P., P.2d, or P.3d if therein; otherwise, cite to N.M.

Pacific Reporter	1883–date	P., P.2d, P.3d
New Mexico Reports		
5 N.M. to date	1890–date	N.M.
Gildersleeve Reports (Gild., B.-W. ed. and John. are unofficial reports and are not preferred)	1883–1889	e.g., 3 N.M. (Gild., E.W.S. ed.)

Court of Appeals (N.M. Ct. App.): Cite to P.2d or P.3d, if therein; otherwise, cite to N.M.

Pacific Reporter	1967–date	P.2d, P.3d
New Mexico Reports	1967–date	N.M.

Statutory compilation

New Mexico Statutes Annotated
(Michie)

N.M. Stat. Ann. § x
(Michie year)

Session laws

Laws of New Mexico

year N.M. Laws xxx

New Mexico Advance Legislative
Service (Michie)

year N.M. Adv. Legis. Serv. xxx

Administrative compilation

New Mexico Administrative Code

N.M. Admin. Code tit. x, § x
(year)

Administrative register

New Mexico Register

N.M. Reg.

New York (NY)
http://www.courts.state.ny.us

Court of Appeals (N.Y.) after 1847: Cite to N.E. or N.E.2d, if therein;
otherwise, cite to N.Y., N.Y.2d, or N.Y.S.2d.

North Eastern Reporter	1885–date	N.E., N.E.2d
New York Reports	1847–date	N.Y., N.Y.2d
West's New York Supplement	1956–date	N.Y.S.2d

(The first series of N.Y. is reprinted in N.Y.S. and
N.Y.S.2d without separate pagination. Do not
include a parallel cite to N.Y.S. or N.Y.S.2d in
citations to the first series of N.Y.)

Court for the Correction of Errors (N.Y.) and **Supreme Court of
Judicature** (N.Y. Sup. Ct.) (highest state courts of law before 1848):
Cite to one of the following reporters.

Lockwood's Reversed Cases	1799–1847	Lock. Rev. Cas.
Denio's Reports	1845–1848	Denio
Hill and Denio Supplement (Lalor)	1842–1844	Hill & Den.
Hill's Reports	1841–1844	Hill
Edmond's Select Cases	1834–1853	Edm. Sel. Cas.
Yates' Select Cases	1809	Yates Sel. Cas.
Anthon's Nisi Prius Cases	1808–1851	Ant. N.P. Cas.
Wendell's Reports	1828–1841	Wend.
Cowen's Reports	1823–1829	Cow.
Johnson's Reports	1806–1823	Johns.
Caines' Reports	1796–1805	Cai. R.

T
T.1

Caines' Cases	1796–1805	Cai. Cas.
Coleman & Caines' Cases	1794–1805	Cole. & Cai. Cas.
Johnson's Cases	1799–1803	Johns. Cas.
Coleman's Cases	1791–1800	Cole. Cas.

Court of Chancery (N.Y. Ch.) (highest state court of equity before 1848): Cite to one of the following reporters.

Edwards' Chancery Reports	1831–1850	Edw. Ch.
Barbour's Chancery Reports	1845–1848	Barb. Ch.
Sandford's Chancery Reports	1843–1847	Sand. Ch.
Saratoga Chancery Sentinel	1841–1847	Sarat. Ch. Sent.
Paige's Chancery Reports	1828–1845	Paige Ch.
Clarke's Chancery Reports	1839–1841	Cl. Ch.
Hoffman's Chancery Reports	1839–1840	Hoff. Ch.
Hopkins' Chancery Reports	1823–1826	Hopk. Ch.
Lansing's Chancery Reports	1824–1826	Lans. Ch.
Johnson's Chancery Reports	1814–1823	Johns. Ch.
New York Chancery Reports Annotated	1814–1847	N.Y. Ch. Ann.

Supreme Court, Appellate Division (N.Y. App. Div.), previously **Supreme Court, General Term** (N.Y. Gen. Term): Cite to N.Y.S. or N.Y.S.2d, if therein; otherwise, cite to one of the other reporters listed below.

West's New York Supplement	1888–date	N.Y.S., N.Y.S.2d
Appellate Division Reports	1896–date	A.D., A.D.2d
Supreme Court Reports	1868–1896	N.Y. Sup. Ct.
Lansing's Reports	1869–1873	Lans.
Barbour's Supreme Court Reports	1847–1877	Barb.

Other lower courts (e.g., N.Y. App. Term., N.Y. Sup. Ct., N.Y. Ct. Cl., N.Y. Civ. Ct., N.Y. Crim. Ct., N.Y. Fam. Ct.): Cite to N.Y.S. or N.Y.S.2d, if therein; otherwise, cite to Misc. or Misc. 2d.

West's New York Supplement	1888–date	N.Y.S., N.Y.S.2d
New York Miscellaneous Reports	1892–date	Misc., Misc. 2d

Other lower courts before 1888: Cite to Abb. N. Cas., Abb. Pr., or How. Pr.

Abbott's New Cases	1876–1894	Abb. N. Cas.
Abbott's Practice Reports	1854–1875	Abb. Pr., Abb. Pr. (n.s.)
Howard's Practice Reports	1844–1886	How. Pr., How. Pr. (n.s.)

Statutory compilations: Cite to one of the following sources if therein.

McKinney's Consolidated Laws of New York Annotated	N.Y. [subject] LAW § x (McKinney year)
Consolidated Laws Service	N.Y. [subject] LAW § x (Consol. year)
Gould's New York Consolidated Laws Unannotated	N.Y. [subject] LAW § x (Gould year)
Abandoned Property	ABAND. PROP.
Agricultural Conservation and Adjustment	AGRIC. CONSERV. & ADJ.
Agriculture and Markets	AGRIC. & MKTS.
Alcoholic Beverage Control	ALCO. BEV. CONT.
Alternative County Government	ALT. COUNTY GOV'T
Arts and Cultural Affairs	ARTS & CULT. AFF.
Banking	BANKING
Benevolent Orders	BEN. ORD.
Business Corporation	BUS. CORP.
Canal	CANAL
City Home Rule	CITY HOME RULE
Civil Practice Law and Rules (Citations need not include additional designation as a section or rule.)	N.Y. C.P.L.R. x (McKinney year) or: N.Y. C.P.L.R. x (Consol. year)
Civil Rights	CIV. RIGHTS
Civil Service	CIV. SERV.
Commerce	COM.
Condemnation	CONDEMN.
Conservation	CONSERV.
Cooperative Corporations	COOP. CORP.
Correction	CORRECT.
County	COUNTY
Criminal Procedure	CRIM. PROC.
Debtor and Creditor	DEBT. & CRED.
Domestic Relations	DOM. REL.
Economic Development	ECON. DEV.
Education	EDUC.
Election	ELEC.
Eminent Domain Procedure	EM. DOM. PROC.
Employers' Liability	EMPL'RS LIAB.
Energy	ENERGY

T.1

Environmental Conservation	ENVTL. CONSERV.
Estates, Powers and Trusts	EST. POWERS & TRUSTS
Executive	EXEC.
General Associations	GEN. ASS'NS
General Business	GEN. BUS.
General City	GEN. CITY
General Construction	GEN. CONSTR.
General Municipal	GEN. MUN.
General Obligations	GEN. OBLIG.
Highway	HIGH.
Indian	INDIAN
Insurance	INS.
Judiciary Court Acts	JUD. CT. ACTS
Labor	LAB.
Legislative	LEGIS.
Lien	LIEN
Limited Liability Company	LTD. LIAB. CO.
Local Finance	LOCAL FIN.
Mental Hygiene	MENTAL HYG.
Military	MIL.
Multiple Dwelling	MULT. DWELL.
Multiple Residence	MULT. RESID.
Municipal Home Rule and Statute of Local Governments	MUN. HOME RULE
Navigation	NAV.
Not-for-Profit Corporation	NOT-FOR-PROFIT CORP.
Optional County Government	OPT. CTY. GOV'T.
Parks, Recreation and Historic Preservation	PARKS REC. & HIST. PRESERV.
Partnership	PARTNERSHIP
Penal	PENAL
Personal Property	PERS. PROP.
Private Housing Finance	PRIV. HOUS. FIN.
Public Authorities	PUB. AUTH.
Public Buildings	PUB. BLDGS.
Public Health	PUB. HEALTH
Public Housing	PUB. HOUS.
Public Lands	PUB. LANDS
Public Officers	PUB. OFF.
Public Service	PUB. SERV.

Racing, Pari-Mutuel Wagering and Breeding	RAC. PARI-MUT. WAG. & BREED.
Railroad	R.R.
Rapid Transit	RAPID TRANS.
Real Property	REAL PROP.
Real Property Actions and Proceedings	REAL PROP. ACTS.
Real Property Tax	REAL PROP. TAX
Religious Corporations	RELIG. CORP.
Retirement and Social Security	RETIRE. & SOC. SEC.
Rural Electric Cooperative	RURAL ELEC. COOP.
Second Class Cities	SECOND CLASS CITIES
Social Services	SOC. SERV.
Soil and Water Conservation Districts	SOIL & WATER CONSERV. DIST.
State	STATE
State Administrative Procedure Act	A.P.A.
State Finance	STATE FIN.
State Printing and Public Documents	STATE PRINT. & PUB. DOCS.
Statutes	STAT.
Surrogate's Court Procedure Act	SURR. CT. PROC. ACT
Tax	TAX
Town	TOWN
Transportation	TRANSP.
Transportation Corporations	TRANSP. CORP.
Unconsolidated	UNCONSOL.
Uniform Commercial Code	U.C.C.
Vehicle and Traffic	VEH. & TRAF.
Village	VILLAGE
Volunteer Ambulance Workers' Benefit	VOL. AMBUL. WORKERS' BEN.
Volunteer Firefighters' Benefit	VOL. FIRE. BEN.
Workers' Compensation	WORKERS' COMP.

Uncompiled laws: Cite to one of the following sources if therein. For the user's convenience, the McKinney's volume in which the law appears is indicated parenthetically below.

McKinney's Consolidated Laws	N.Y. [law] § x (McKinney year)

Consolidated Laws Service	N.Y. [law] § x (Consol. year)
Gould's New York Consolidated Laws Unannotated	N.Y. [law] § x (Gould year)
New York City Civil Court Act (29A)	CITY CIV. CT. ACT
New York City Criminal Court Act (29A)	CITY CRIM. CT. ACT
Code of Criminal Procedure (66)	CODE CRIM. PROC.
Court of Claims Act (29A)	CT. CL. ACT
Family Court Act (29A)	FAM. CT. ACT
Uniform City Court Act (29A)	UNIFORM CITY CT. ACT
Uniform City District Court Act (29A)	UNIFORM DIST. CT.
Uniform Justice Court Act (29A)	UNIFORM JUST. CT. ACT

Session laws

| Makinney's Session Laws of New York | year N.Y. Laws xxx |

Administrative compilation

| Official Compilation of Codes, Rules & Regulations of the State of New York | N.Y. COMP. CODES R. & REGS. tit. x, § x (year) |

Administrative register

| New York State Register | N.Y. St. Reg. |

North Carolina (NC)
http://www.aoc.state.nc.us

Supreme Court (N.C.): Cite to S.E. or S.E.2d, if therein; otherwise, cite to N.C.

South Eastern Reporter	1887–date	S.E., S.E.2d
North Carolina Reports		
63 N.C. to date	1868–date	N.C.
Phillips' Equity	1866–1868	62 N.C. (Phil. Eq.)
Phillips' Law	1866–1868	61 N.C. (Phil. Law)
Winston	1863–1864	60 N.C. (Win.)
Jones' Equity (54–59)	1853–1863	e.g., 54 N.C. (1 Jones Eq.)
Jones' Law (46–53)	1853–1862	e.g., 46 N.C. (1 Jones)
Busbee's Equity	1852–1853	45 N.C. (Busb. Eq.)
Busbee's Law	1852–1853	44 N.C. (Busb.)
Iredell's Equity (36–43)	1840–1852	e.g., 36 N.C. (1 Ired. Eq.)
Iredell's Law (23–35)	1840–1852	e.g., 23 N.C. (1 Ired.)

Devereux & Battle's Equity (21–22)	1834–1839	e.g., 21 N.C. (1 Dev. & Bat. Eq.)
Devereux & Battle's Law (18–20)	1834–1839	e.g., 20 N.C. (3 & 4 Dev. & Bat.)
Devereux's Equity (16–17)	1826–1834	e.g., 16 N.C. (1 Dev. Eq.)
Devereux's Law (12–15)	1826–1834	e.g., 12 N.C. (1 Dev.)
Hawks (8–11)	1820–1826	e.g., 8 N.C. (1 Hawks)
Murphey (5–7)	1804–1813 1818–1819	e.g., 5 N.C. (1 Mur.)
Taylor's North Carolina Term Reports	1816–1818	4 N.C. (Taylor)
Carolina Law Repository	1811–1816	4 N.C. (Car. L. Rep.)
Haywood (2–3)	1789–1806	e.g., 2 N.C. (1 Hayw.)
Conference by Cameron & Norwood	1800–1804	1 N.C. (Cam. & Nor.)
Taylor	1798–1802	1 N.C. (Tay.)
Martin	1778–1797	1 N.C. (Mart.)

Court of Appeals (N.C. Ct. App.): Cite to S.E.2d, if therein; otherwise, cite to N.C. App.

South Eastern Reporter	1968–date	S.E.2d
North Carolina Court of Appeals Reports	1968–date	N.C. App.

Statutory compilation

General Statutes of North Carolina	N.C. Gen. Stat. § x (year)

Session laws: Cite to N.C. Sess. Laws if therein.

Session Laws of North Carolina	year N.C. Sess. Laws xxx
Advance Legislative Service to the General Statutes of North Carolina	year N.C. Adv. Legis. Serv. xxx

Administrative compilation

North Carolina Administrative Code	N.C. Admin. Code tit. x, r. xx.xxxx (month year)

Administrative Register

North Carolina Register	N.C. Reg.

North Dakota (ND)
http://www.court.state.nd.us

Public Domain Citation Format: North Dakota has adopted a public domain citation format for cases after January 1, 1997. The format is:

Kjonaas v. Kjonaas, 1999 ND 50.

Supreme Court (N.D.): Cite to N.W. or N.W.2d, if therein.

North Western Reporter	1890–date	N.W., N.W.2d
North Dakota Reports	1890–1953	N.D.

Supreme Court of Dakota (Dakota): Cite to N.W., if therein.

North Western Reporter	1867–1889	N.W.
Dakota Reports	1867–1889	Dakota

Court of Appeals of North Dakota (N.D. Ct. App.): Cite to N.W.2d.

North Western Reporter	1987–date	N.W.2d

Statutory compilation

North Dakota Century Code	N.D. CENT. CODE § x (year)

Session Laws

Laws of North Dakota	year N.D. Laws xx

Administrative compilation

North Dakota Administrative Code	N.D. ADMIN. CODE § x (year)

Ohio (OH)
http://www.sconet.state.oh.us

Supreme Court (Ohio): Cite to N.E. or N.E.2d, if therein; otherwise, cite to another reporter listed below.

North Eastern Reporter	1885–date	N.E., N.E.2d
Ohio State Reports	1852–date	Ohio St., Ohio St. 2d, Ohio St. 3d
Ohio Reports	1821–1851	Ohio
Wilcox's Condensed Reports	1821–1836	Wilc. Cond. Rep.
Wright	1831–1834	Wright
Ohio Unreported Cases	1809–1899	Ohio Unrep. Cas.

Court of Appeals (Ohio Ct. App.): Cite to N.E. or N.E.2d, if therein; otherwise, cite to another reporter listed below.

North Eastern Reporter	1925–date	N.E., N.E.2d
Ohio Appellate Reports	1913–date	Ohio App., Ohio App. 2d, Ohio App. 3d
Ohio Courts of Appeals Reports	1906–1923	Ohio Ct. App.

Other law courts: Cite to Ohio Misc. or Ohio Misc. 2d, if therein; otherwise, cite to another reporter in the following order of preference.

Ohio Miscellaneous	1962–date	Ohio Misc., Ohio Misc. 2d
Ohio Bar Reports	1982–1987	Ohio B.
Ohio Opinions	1934–1982	Ohio Op., Ohio Op. 2d, Ohio Op. 3d
Ohio Law Abstract	1922–1964	Ohio Law Abs.
Ohio Nisi Prius Reports	1894–1934	Ohio N.P., Ohio N.P. (n.s.)
Ohio Decisions	1900–1922	Ohio Dec.
Ohio Decisions, Reprint	1840–1873	Ohio Dec. Reprint
Ohio Circuit Decisions	1885–1917	Ohio Cir. Dec.
Ohio Circuit Court Decisions	1901–1923	e.g., 13-23 Ohio C.C. Dec.
Ohio Circuit Court Reports	1885–1901	Ohio C.C.
Ohio Circuit Court Reports, New Series	1903–1917	Ohio C.C. (n.s.)
Ohio Law Reporter	1899–1934	Ohio L.R.
Unreported Ohio Appellate Cases (Anderson)	1990	Ohio App. Unrep.

Statutory compilations: Cite to one of the following codes.

Page's Ohio Revised Code Annotated (Anderson)	OHIO REV. CODE ANN. § x (Anderson year)
Baldwin's Ohio Revised Code Annotated (West)	OHIO REV. CODE ANN. § x (West year)

Session laws: Cite to Ohio Laws if therein.

State of Ohio: Legislative Acts Passed and Joint Resolutions Adopted	year Ohio Laws xx
Page's Ohio Legislative Bulletin (Anderson)	year Ohio Legis. Bull. xxx (Anderson)
Baldwin's Ohio Legislative Service (Banks-Baldwin)	year Ohio Legis. Serv. xxx (Banks-Baldwin)

Administrative compilation

Ohio Administrative Code (official compilation published by Banks-Baldwin)	OHIO ADMIN. CODE § x (year)

Administrative and executive registers

Ohio Monthly Record (Banks-Baldwin)	1977–date	Ohio Monthly Rec.
Ohio Government Reports	1965–1976	Ohio Gov't
Ohio Department Reports	1914–1964	Ohio Dep't

T.1

Oklahoma (OK)
http://www.oscn.net

Public domain citation format: Oklahoma has adopted a public domain citation format for cases after May 1, 1997. The format is:

> Herbert v. Okla. Christian Coalition, 1999 OK 90.

Supreme Court (Okla.): Cite to P., P.2d, or P.3d, if therein.

Pacific Reporter	1890–date	P., P.2d, P.3d
Oklahoma Reports	1893–1953	Okla.

Court of Appeals of Indian Territory (Indian Terr.): Cite to S.W., if therein; otherwise, cite to Indian Terr.

South Western Reporter	1896–1907	S.W.
Indian Territory Reports	1896–1907	Indian Terr.

Court of Criminal Appeals (Okla. Crim. App.), before 1959 **Criminal Court of Appeals** (Okla. Crim. App.): Cite to P., P.2d, or P.3d, if therein; otherwise, cite to Okla. Crim.

Pacific Reporter	1908–date	P., P.2d, P.3d
Oklahoma Criminal Reports	1908–1953	Okla. Crim.

Court of Civil Appeals (Okla. Civ. App.), before 1996 **Court of Appeals** (Okla. Ct. App.): Cite to P.2d or P.3d.

Pacific Reporter	1971–date	P.2d, P.3d

Statutory compilations: Cite to OKLA. STAT. if therein.

Oklahoma Statutes	OKLA. STAT. tit. x, § x (year)
Oklahoma Statutes Annotated (West)	OKLA. STAT. ANN. tit. x, § x (West year)

Session laws: Cite to Okla. Sess. Laws if therein.

Oklahoma Session Laws	year Okla. Sess. Laws xxx
Oklahoma Session Law Service (West)	year Okla. Sess. Law Serv. xxx (West)

Administrative compilation

Oklahoma Administrative Code	OKLA. ADMIN. CODE § x-x.x (year)

Administrative register

Oklahoma Register	1983–date	Okla. Reg.
Oklahoma Gazette	1962–1983	Okla. Gaz.

Oregon (OR)
http://www.ojd.state.or.us

Supreme Court (Or.): Cite to P., P.2d, or P.3d, if therein; otherwise, cite to Or.

Pacific Reporter	1883–date	P., P.2d, P.3d
Oregon Reports	1853–date	Or.

Court of Appeals (Or. Ct. App.): Cite to P.2d or P.3d, if therein; otherwise, cite to Or. App.

Pacific Reporter	1969–date	P.2d, P.3d
Oregon Reports, Court of Appeals	1969–date	Or. App.

Tax Court (Or. T.C.): Cite to Or. Tax.

Oregon Tax Reports	1962–date	Or. Tax

Statutory compilation

Oregon Revised Statutes	OR. REV. STAT. § x (year)

Session laws: Cite to Or. Laws. When citing statutes repealed during or after 1953, indicate parenthetically the former OR. REV. STAT. sections.

Oregon Laws and Resolutions	year Or. Laws xxx year Or. Laws Spec. Sess. xxx year Or. Laws Adv. Sh. No. xxx

Administrative compilation

Oregon Administrative Rules	OR. ADMIN. R. x (year)

Administrative register

Oregon Bulletin	Or. Bull.

Pennsylvania (PA)
http://www.aopc.org

Supreme Court (Pa.): Cite to A. or A.2d, if therein; otherwise, cite to a reporter listed below.

Atlantic Reporter	1885–date	A., A.2d
Pennsylvania State Reports	1845–date	Pa.
Monaghan	1888–1890	Monag.
Sadler	1885–1889	Sadler
Walker	1855–1885	Walk.

Pennypacker	1881–1884	Pennyp.
Grant	1814–1863	Grant
Watts and Sergeant	1841–1845	Watts & Serg.
Wharton	1835–1841	Whart.
Watts	1832–1840	Watts
Rawle	1828–1835	Rawle
Penrose and Watts	1829–1832	Pen. & W.
Sergeant and Rawle	1814–1828	Serg. & Rawle
Binney	1799–1814	Binn.
Yeates	1791–1808	Yeates
Addison	1791–1799	Add.
Dallas	1754–1806	Dall.
Alden	1754–1814	Ald.

Superior Court (Pa. Super. Ct.): Cite to A. or A.2d, if therein; otherwise, cite to Pa. Super. For cases decided after January 1, 1999, use the following public domain citation format:

Rapagnani v. Judas Co., 1999 PA Super. 203.

| Atlantic Reporter | 1931–date | A., A.2d |
| Pennsylvania Superior Court Reports | 1895–1997 | Pa. Super. |

Commonwealth Court (Pa. Commw. Ct.): Cite to A.2d, if therein; otherwise, cite to Pa. Commw.

| Atlantic Reporter | 1970–date | A.2d |
| Pennsylvania Commonwealth Court Reports | 1970–1994 | Pa. Commw. |

Other lower courts: Cite to the legal reporter for the county, if available, and to Pa. D. & C., Pa. D. & C.2d, Pa. D. & C.3d, or Pa. D. & C.4th, if therein. Otherwise cite to Pa. D. or Pa. C.

Pennsylvania District and County Reports	1921–date	Pa. D. & C., Pa. D. & C.2d, Pa. D. & C.3d, Pa. D. & C.4th
Pennsylvania District Reports	1892–1921	Pa. D.
Pennsylvania County Court Reports	1870–1921	Pa. C.

Statutory compilations: Pennsylvania is undertaking its first official codification, PA. CONS. STAT.; the old, unofficial compilation is Purdon's PA. STAT. ANN., which uses a different numbering system. Purdon is also reprinting the new, official codification as PA. CONS. STAT. ANN., which is currently bound with PA. STAT. ANN. Cite to PA. CONS. STAT. or PA. CONS. STAT. ANN., in that order of preference. If the statute is contained in neither source, cite to PA. STAT. ANN. (see **rule 12.3.1(h)**).

These publications should not be confused with PA. CODE, which is a code of regulations, not of legislation.

Pennsylvania Consolidated Statutes (by title)	x PA. CONS. STAT. § x (year)
Purdon's Pennsylvania Consolidated Statutes Annotated (by title) (West)	x PA. CONS. STAT. ANN. § x (West year)
Purdon's Pennsylvania Statutes Annotated (West)	PA. STAT. ANN. tit. x, § x (West year)

Session laws

Laws of Pennsylvania	year Pa. Laws xxx
Purdon's Pennsylvania Legislative Service (West)	year Pa. Legis. Serv. xxx (West)

Administrative compilation

Pennsylvania Code (by title)	x PA. CODE § x (year)

Administrative register

Pennsylvania Bulletin	Pa. Bull.

Rhode Island (RI)
http://www.courts.state.ri.us

Supreme Court (R.I.): Cite to A. or A.2d, if therein; otherwise, cite to R.I.

Atlantic Reporter	1885–date	A., A.2d
Rhode Island Reports	1828–1980	R.I.

Statutory compilation

General Laws of Rhode Island	R.I. GEN. LAWS § x (year)

Session laws: Cite to R.I. Pub. Laws if therein.

Public Laws of Rhode Island and Providence Plantations	year R.I. Pub. Laws xxx
Acts and Resolves of Rhode Island and Providence Plantations	year R.I. Acts & Resolves xxx

Administrative compilation

Code of Rhode Island Rules	R.I. CODE R. xx xxx xxx (year)

Administrative register

Rhode Island Government Register	R.I. Gov't Reg. (month year)

South Carolina (SC)
http://www.state.sc.us/judicial/jud.html

Supreme Court after 1868 (S.C.): Cite to S.E. or S.E.2d, if therein; otherwise, cite to S.C.

South Eastern Reporter	1887–date	S.E., S.E.2d
South Carolina Reports	1868–date	S.C.

Court of Appeals (S.C. Ct. App.): Cite to S.E.2d, if therein; otherwise, cite to S.C.

South Eastern Reporter	1983–date	S.E.2d
South Carolina Reports	1983–date	S.C.

Courts of law before 1868: Cite to S.C.L.

South Carolina Law Reports

Richardson (37–49)	1850–1868	e.g., 37 S.C.L. (3 Rich.)
Strobhart (32–36)	1846–1850	e.g., 32 S.C.L. (1 Strob.)
Richardson (30–31)	1844–1846	e.g., 30 S.C.L. (1 Rich.)
Speers (28–29)	1842–1844	e.g., 28 S.C.L. (1 Speers)
McMullan (26–27)	1840–1842	e.g., 26 S.C.L. (1 McMul.)
Cheves	1839–1840	25 S.C.L. (Chev.)
Rice	1838–1839	24 S.C.L. (Rice)
Dudley	1837–1838	23 S.C.L. (Dud.)
Riley	1836–1837	22 S.C.L. (Ril.)
Hill (19–21)	1833–1837	e.g., 19 S.C.L. (1 Hill)
Bailey (17–18)	1828–1832	e.g., 17 S.C.L. (1 Bail.)
Harper	1823–1824	16 S.C.L. (Harp.)
McCord (12–15)	1821–1828	e.g., 12 S.C.L. (1 McCord)
Nott and McCord (10–11)	1819–1820	e.g., 10 S.C.L. (1 Nott & McC.)
Mill (Constitutional) (8–9)	1817–1818	e.g., 8 S.C.L. (1 Mill)
Treadway (6–7)	1812–1816	e.g., 6 S.C.L. (1 Tread.)
Brevard (3–5)	1793–1816	e.g., 3 S.C.L. (1 Brev.)
Bay (1–2)	1783–1804	e.g., 1 S.C.L. (1 Bay)

Courts of equity before 1868: Cite to S.C. Eq.

South Carolina Equity Reports

Richardson's Equity (24–35)	1850–1868	e.g., 24 S.C. Eq. (3 Rich. Eq.)
Strobhart's Equity (20–23)	1846–1850	e.g., 20 S.C. Eq. (1 Strob. Eq.)
Richardson's Equity (18–19)	1844–1846	e.g., 18 S.C. Eq. (1 Rich. Eq.)

Speers' Equity	1842–1844	17 S.C. Eq. (Speers Eq.)
McMullan's Equity	1840–1842	16 S.C. Eq. (McMul. Eq.)
Cheves' Equity	1839–1840	15 S.C. Eq. (Chev. Eq.)
Rice's Equity	1838–1839	14 S.C. Eq. (Rice Eq.)
Dudley's Equity	1837–1838	13 S.C. Eq. (Dud. Eq.)
Riley's Chancery	1836–1837	12 S.C. Eq. (Ril. Eq.)
Hill's Chancery (10–11)	1833–1837	e.g., 10 S.C. Eq. (1 Hill Eq.)
Richardson's Cases	1831–1832	9 S.C. Eq. (Rich. Cas.)
Bailey's Equity	1830–1831	8 S.C. Eq. (Bail. Eq.)
McCord's Chancery (6–7)	1825–1827	e.g., 6 S.C. Eq. (1 McCord Eq.)
Harper's Equity	1824	5 S.C. Eq. (Harp. Eq.)
Desaussure's Equity (1–4)	1784–1817	e.g., 1 S.C. Eq. (1 Des.)

Statutory compilation

Code of Laws of South Carolina 1976 Annotated (Law. Co-op.)	S.C. CODE ANN. § x (Law. Co-op. year)

Session laws

Acts and Joint Resolutions, South Carolina	year S.C. Acts xxx

Administrative compilation: Administrative regulations appear in volumes 23–27 of S.C. CODE ANN.

Code of Laws of South Carolina 1976 Annotated (Law. Co-op.), Code of Regulations	x S.C. CODE ANN. REGS. x (year)

Administrative register

South Carolina State Register	S.C. Reg.

South Dakota (SD)
http://www.state.sd.us/state/judicial

Public domain citation format: South Dakota has adopted a public domain citation format for cases after December 31, 1996. The format is:

Fast Horse v. Weber, 1999 SD 97.

Supreme Court (S.D.): Cite to N.W. or N.W.2d, if therein; otherwise, cite to S.D.

North Western Reporter	1890–date	N.W., N.W.2d
South Dakota Reports	1890–1976	S.D.

Supreme Court of Dakota (Dakota): Cite to N.W., if therein; otherwise, cite to Dakota.

| North Western Reporter | 1879–1889 | N.W. |
| Dakota Reports | 1867–1889 | Dakota |

Statutory compilations

| South Dakota Codified Laws (Michie) | S.D. CODIFIED LAWS § x (Michie year) |

Session laws

| Laws of South Dakota | year S.D. Laws xxx |
| South Dakota Advance Code Service (Michie Butterworth) | year S.D. Adv. Code Serv. xxx (Michie Butterworth) |

Administrative compilation

| Administrative Rules of South Dakota | S.D. ADMIN. R. x (year) |

Administrative register

| South Dakota Register | S.D. Reg. |

Tennessee (TN)
http://www.tsc.state.tn.us

Supreme Court (Tenn.): Cite to S.W., S.W.2d, or S.W.3d, if therein; otherwise, cite to Tenn.

South Western Reporter	1886–date	S.W., S.W.2d, S.W.3d
Tennessee Reports		
60 Tenn. to 225 Tenn.	1872–1971	Tenn.
Heiskell	1870–1874	e.g., 48 Tenn. (1 Heisk.)
Coldwell	1860–1870	e.g., 41 Tenn. (1 Cold.)
Head	1858–1860	e.g., 38 Tenn. (1 Head)
Sneed	1853–1858	e.g., 33 Tenn. (1 Sneed)
Swan	1851–1853	e.g., 31 Tenn. (1 Swan)
Humphreys	1839–1851	e.g., 20 Tenn. (1 Hum.)
Meigs	1838–1839	19 Tenn. (Meigs)
Yerger	1818–1837	e.g., 9 Tenn. (1 Yer.)
Martin & Yerger	1825–1828	8 Tenn. (Mart. & Yer.)
Peck	1821–1824	7 Tenn. (Peck)
Haywood	1816–1818	e.g., 4 Tenn. (1 Hayw.)
Cooke	1811–1814	3 Tenn. (Cooke)
Overton	1791–1816	e.g., 1 Tenn. (1 Overt.)

Court of Appeals (Tenn. Ct. App.): Cite to S.W.2d or S.W.3d, if therein; otherwise, cite to Tenn. App.

South Western Reporter	1932–date	S.W.2d
Tennessee Appeals Reports	1925–1971	Tenn. App.

Court of Criminal Appeals (Tenn. Crim. App.): Cite to S.W.2d, if therein; otherwise, cite to Tenn. Crim. App.

South Western Reporter	1967–date	S.W.2d
Tennessee Criminal Appeals Reports	1967–1971	Tenn. Crim. App.

Statutory compilation

Tennessee Code Annotated	TENN. CODE ANN. § x (year)

Session laws

Public Acts of the State of Tennessee	year Tenn. Pub. Acts xxx
Private Acts of the State of Tennessee	year Tenn. Priv. Acts xxx

Administrative compilation

Official Compilation Rules & Regulations of the State of Tennessee	TENN. COMP. R. & REGS. x (year)

Administrative register

Tennessee Administrative Register	Tenn. Admin. Reg. (month year)

Texas (TX)
http://www.courts.state.tx.us

Supreme Court (Tex.): Cite to S.W., S.W.2d, or S.W.3d, if therein; otherwise, cite to one of the other reporters listed below.

South Western Reporter	1886–date	S.W., S.W.2d, S.W.3d
Texas Reports	1846–1962	Tex.
Synopses of the Decisions of the Supreme Court of Texas Arising from Restraints by Conscript and Other Military Authorities (Robards)	1862–1865	Robards (no volume number)
Texas Law Review (containing previously unpublished cases from the 1845 term)	1845–1846	65 TEX. L. REV. [e.g., Lamar v. Houston (Tex. 1845), 65 TEX. L. REV. 382 (Paulsen rep. 1986)]

Digest of the Laws of Texas (Dallam's Opinions)	1840–1844	Dallam (no volume number)
Texas Supreme Court Journal		Tex. Sup. Ct. J.

Court of Criminal Appeals (Tex. Crim. App.), previously **Court of Appeals** (Tex. Ct. App.): Cite to S.W., S.W.2d, or S.W.3d, if therein; otherwise, cite to one of the other reporters listed below.

South Western Reporter	1892–date	S.W., S.W.2d, S.W.3d
Texas Criminal Reports	1892–1962	Tex. Crim.
Texas Court of Appeals Reports	1876–1892	Tex. Ct. App.
Condensed Reports of Decisions in Civil Causes in the Court of Appeals (White & Willson vol. 1) (Willson vols. 2–4)	1876–1883 1883–1892	White & W. Willson

Commission of Appeals (Tex. Comm'n App.): Cite to S.W. or S.W.2d, if therein; otherwise, cite to Tex.

South Western Reporter	1886–1892 1918–1945	S.W. S.W.2d
Texas Reports	1879–1892 1918–1945	Tex.
Texas Unreported Cases (Posey)	1879–1884	Posey
Condensed Reports of Decisions in Civil Causes in the Court of Appeals (White & Willson)	1879–1883	White & W.

Officially published opinions of the commission of appeals from 1879 to 1892 were adopted by the supreme court and should be cited as opinions of the supreme court. Opinions of the commission of appeals from 1918 to 1945 have a notation from the supreme court that usually appears in the final paragraph of the opinion, i.e., opinion adopted, holding approved, or judgment adopted. Commission opinions that were adopted by the supreme court should be cited as opinions of the supreme court. "Holding approved" and "judgment adopted" opinions are cited by using "holding approved" or "judgm't adopted," e.g., Savage v. Cowen, 33 S.W.2d 433 (Tex. Comm'n App. 1930, judgm't adopted).

Courts of Appeals (Tex. App.), previously **Courts of Civil Appeals** (Tex. Civ. App.): Cite to S.W., S.W.2d, or S.W.3d, if therein.

South Western Reporter	1892–date	S.W., S.W.2d, S.W.3d
Texas Civil Appeals Reports	1892–1911	Tex. Civ. App.

For additional information on the history and structure of Texas courts and on the local citation rules, the following sources are suggested: TEXAS LAW REVIEW ASS'N, TEXAS RULES OF FORM (9th ed. 1997); LYDIA M.V. BRANDT, TEXAS LEGAL RESEARCH (1995); and A REFERENCE GUIDE TO TEXAS LAW AND LEGAL HISTORY (Karl T. Gruben & James E. Hambleton eds., 2d ed. 1987).

Statutory compilations: Texas is nearing the completion of a recodification of its laws. Cite to the new subject-matter TEX. CODE ANN. if therein; otherwise, cite to TEX. REV. CIV. STAT. ANN. or to one of the independent codes contained in the series *Vernon's Texas Civil Statutes* or *Vernon's Texas Statutes Annotated*. Note that the independent codes are not part of the new subject-matter TEX. CODE ANN.

Vernon's Texas Codes Annotated	TEX. [subject] CODE ANN. § x (Vernon year)
Agriculture	AGRIC.
Alcoholic Beverage	ALCO. BEV.
Business and Commerce	BUS. & COM.
Civil Practice and Remedies	CIV. PRAC. & REM.
Corporations and Associations	CORPS. & ASS'NS
Criminal Procedure	CRIM. PROC.
Education	EDUC.
Election	ELEC.
Family	FAM.
Financial	FIN.
Government	GOV'T
Health and Safety	HEALTH & SAFETY
Human Resources	HUM. RES.
Insurance	INS.
Labor	LAB.
Local Government	LOC. GOV'T
Natural Resources	NAT. RES.
Occupations	OCC.
Parks and Wildlife	PARKS & WILD.
Penal	PENAL
Probate	PROB.
Property	PROP.
Tax	TAX
Transportation	TRANSP.
Utilities	UTIL.
Water	WATER

T

T.1

Vernon's Texas Revised Civil Statutes Annotated	Tex. Rev. Civ. Stat. Ann. art. x, § x (Vernon year)
Vernon's Texas Business Corporation Act Annotated	Tex. Bus. Corp. Act Ann. art. x (Vernon year)
Vernon's Texas Code of Criminal Procedure Annotated	Tex. Code Crim. Proc. Ann. art. x (Vernon year)
Vernon's Texas Insurance Code Annotated	Tex. Ins. Code Ann. art. x (Vernon year)
Vernon's Texas Probate Code Annotated	Tex. Prob. Code Ann. § x (Vernon year)

Session laws: Cite to Tex. Gen. Laws if therein.

General and Special Laws of the State of Texas	year Tex. Gen. Laws xxx
Vernon's Texas Session Law Service	year Tex. Sess. Law Serv. xxx (Vernon)
Laws of the Republic of Texas	18xx Repub. Tex. Laws xxx

Session laws passed before 1941 must be cited according to the exact title, e.g., Tex. Loc. & Spec. Laws, Tex. Gen. & Spec. Laws, and Tex. Gen. Laws. The Revised Statutes were enacted and published separately in 1879, 1895, 1911, and 1925 and should be cited 1xxx Tex. Rev. Civ. Stat. xxx. The Code of Criminal Procedure and Penal Code were enacted and published separately in 1856, 1879, 1895, 1911, and 1925 and should be cited 1xxx Tex. Crim. Stat. xxx.

Administrative compilation

| Texas Administrative Code | x Tex. Admin. Code § x (West year) |

Administrative register

| Texas Register | Tex. Reg. |

Utah (UT)
http://courtlink.utcourts.gov

Public domain citation format: Utah has adopted a public domain citation format for cases after December 31, 1998. The format is:

Roundy v. Staley, 1999 UT App. 229.

Supreme Court (Utah): Cite to P., P.2d, or P.3d, if therein; otherwise, cite to Utah or Utah 2d.

| Pacific Reporter | 1881–date | P., P.2d, P.3d |
| Utah Reports | 1851–1974 | Utah, Utah 2d |

Court of Appeals (Utah Ct. App.): Cite to P.2d or P.3d.

Pacific Reporter	1987–date	P.2d, P.3d

Statutory compilation

Utah Code Annotated	UTAH CODE ANN. § x (year)

Session laws

Laws of Utah	year Utah Laws xxx

Administrative compilation

Utah Administrative Code	UTAH ADMIN. CODE x (year)

Administrative register

Utah State Bulletin	Utah Bull.

Vermont (VT)
http://www.state.vt.us/courts

Supreme Court (Vt.): Cite to A. or A.2d, if therein; otherwise, cite to another reporter listed below.

Atlantic Reporter	1885–date	A., A.2d
Vermont Reports	1826–date	Vt.
Aikens	1825–1828	Aik.
Chipman, D.	1789–1824	D. Chip.
Brayton	1815–1819	Brayt.
Tyler	1800–1803	Tyl.
Chipman, N.	1789–1791	N. Chip.

Statutory compilation

Vermont Statutes Annotated	VT. STAT. ANN. tit. x, § x (year)

Session laws

Acts and Resolves of Vermont	year Vt. Acts & Resolves xxx

Administrative compilation

Code of Vermont Rules	VT. CODE R. x (year)

Administrative and executive register

Vermont Government Register	Vt. Gov't Reg.

Virginia (VA)
http://www.courts.state.va.us

Supreme Court (Va.), previously **Supreme Court of Appeals** (Va.): Cite to S.E. or S.E.2d, if therein; otherwise, cite to Va.

South Eastern Reporter	1887–date	S.E., S.E.2d
Virginia Reports		
75 Va. to date	1880–date	Va.
Grattan	1844–1880	e.g., 42 Va. (1 Gratt.)
Robinson	1842–1844	e.g., 40 Va. (1 Rob.)
Leigh	1829–1842	e.g., 28 Va. (1 Leigh)
Randolph	1821–1828	e.g., 22 Va. (1 Rand.)
Gilmer	1820–1821	21 Va. (Gilmer)
Munford	1810–1820	e.g., 15 Va. (1 Munf.)
Hening & Munford	1806–1810	e.g., 11 Va. (1 Hen. & M.)
Call	1779–1825	e.g., 5 Va. (1 Call)
Virginia Cases, Criminal	1789–1826	e.g., 3 Va. (1 Va. Cas.)
Washington	1790–1796	e.g., 1 Va. (1 Wash.)

Court of Appeals (Va. Ct. App.): Cite to S.E.2d, if therein; otherwise, cite to Va. App.

South Eastern Reporter	1985–date	S.E.2d
Virginia Court of Appeals Reports	1985–date	Va. App.

Circuit Court (Va. Cir. Ct.): Cite to Va. Cir., if therein.

Virginia Circuit Court Opinions	1985–date	Va. Cir.

Statutory compilation

Code of Virginia Annotated	VA. CODE ANN. § x (Michie year)

Session laws

Acts of the General Assembly of the Commonwealth of Virginia	year Va. Acts ch. xxx

Administrative compilation

Virginia Administrative Code	x VA. ADMIN. CODE § x (West year)

Administrative register

Virginia Register of Regulations	Va. Regs. Reg.

Washington (WA)
http://www.courts.wa.gov

Supreme Court (Wash.): Cite to P., P.2d, or P.3d, if therein; otherwise, cite to one of the other reporters listed below.

Pacific Reporter	1880–date	P., P.2d, P.3d
Washington Reports	1889–date	Wash., Wash. 2d
Washington Territory Reports	1854–1888	Wash. Terr.

Court of Appeals (Wash. Ct. App.): Cite to P.2d or P.3d, if therein; otherwise, cite to Wash. App.

Pacific Reporter	1969–date	P.2d, P.3d
Washington Appellate Reports	1969–date	Wash. App.

Statutory compilations: Cite to WASH. REV. CODE if therein.

Revised Code of Washington	WASH. REV. CODE § x (year)
Revised Code of Washington Annotated (West)	WASH. REV. CODE ANN. § x (West year)

Session laws: Cite to Wash. Laws if therein.

Laws of Washington	year Wash. Laws xxx
Washington Legislative Service (West)	year Wash. Legis. Serv. xxx (West)

Administrative compilation

Washington Administrative Code	WASH. ADMIN. CODE § x (year)

Administrative register

Washington State Register	Wash. St. Reg.

West Virginia (WV)
http://www.state.wv.us/wvsca

Supreme Court of Appeals (W. Va.): Cite to S.E. or S.E.2d, if therein; otherwise, cite to W. Va.

South Eastern Reporter	1886–date	S.E., S.E.2d
West Virginia Reports	1864–date	W. Va.

Statutory compilation

West Virginia Code	W. VA. CODE § x (year)
West Virginia Code Annotated (Michie)	W. VA. CODE ANN. § x (Michie year)

Session laws

Acts of the Legislature of West
Virginia

year W. Va. Acts xxx

Administrative compilation

West Virginia Code of State Rules

W. VA. CODE ST. R. § x
(year)

Wisconsin (WI)

www.courts.state.wi.us

Public domain citation format: Wisconsin has adopted a public
domain citation format for cases after January 1, 2000. The format is:

> Bd. of Attorneys Prof'l Responsibility v. Wells (*In re* Disciplinary
> Proceedings Against Wells), 2000 WI 1 (per curiam).

Supreme Court (Wis.): Cite to N.W. or N.W.2d, if therein; otherwise,
cite to one of the other reporters listed below.

North Western Reporter	1879–date	N.W., N.W.2d
Wisconsin Reports	1853–date	Wis., Wis. 2d
Pinney	1839–1852	Pin.
Chandler	1849–1852	Chand.
Burnett	1842–1843	Bur.
Burnett (bound with session laws for Dec. 1841)	1841	Bur.

Court of Appeals (Wis. Ct. App.): Cite to N.W.2d, if therein; otherwise,
cite to Wis. 2d.

North Western Reporter	1978–date	N.W.2d
Wisconsin Reports	1978–date	Wis. 2d

Statutory compilations: Cite to WIS. STAT. if therein.

Wisconsin Statutes (1975 and biannually)	WIS. STAT. § x (year)
West's Wisconsin Statutes Annotated	WIS. STAT. ANN. § x (West year)

Session laws: Cite to WIS. Laws if therein.

Laws of Wisconsin	year Wis. Laws xxx
West's Wisconsin Legislative Service	year Wis. Legis. Serv. xxx (West)

Administrative compilation

Wisconsin Administrative Code   WIS. ADMIN. CODE § x (year)

Administrative register

Wisconsin Administrative Register   Wis. Admin. Reg.

Wyoming (WY)
http://courts.state.wy.us

Supreme Court (Wyo.): Cite to P., P.2d, or P.3d, if therein; otherwise, cite to Wyo.

Pacific Reporter	1883–date	P., P.2d, P.3d
Wyoming Reports	1870–1959	Wyo.

Statutory compilation

Wyoming Statutes Annotated   WYO. STAT. ANN. § x (Michie year)

Session laws

Session Laws of Wyoming   year Wyo. Sess. Laws xxx

Other United States Jurisdictions

American Samoa
http://www.samoanet.com/asg/asghcas97.html

High Court of American Samoa (Am. Samoa): Cite to Am. Samoa or Am. Samoa 2d, if therein.

American Samoa Reports   1900–date   Am. Samoa, Am. Samoa 2d

Statutory compilation

American Samoa Code Annotated   AM. SAMOA CODE ANN. § x (year)

Administrative compilation

American Samoa Administrative Code   AM. SAMOA ADMIN. CODE § x (year)

T.1

Canal Zone (CZ)
(now part of Panama)

United States District Court for the Eastern District of Louisiana
(E.D. La.): This court has jurisdiction over litigation pending as of Apr. 1, 1982, in the United States District Court for the District of the Canal Zone. Cite to F. Supp.

Federal Supplement   1982–date   F. Supp.

United States District Court for the District of the Canal Zone
(D.C.Z.): This court ceased to exist on Mar. 31, 1982. Cite to F. Supp.

Federal Supplement   1946–1982   F. Supp.

Statutory compilation

Panama Canal Code   C.Z. CODE tit. x, § x (19xx)
(enacted as Canal Zone Code,
Pub. L. No. 87-845, 76A
Stat. 1 (1962), and redesignated
and continued partially in force
by the Panama Canal Act of 1979,
Pub. L. No. 96-70, § 3303(b),
93 Stat. 452, 499)

Guam (GU)
http://www.justice.gov.gu

Supreme Court of the Territory of Guam (Guam): Cite using the following public domain format:

Adams v. Duenas, 1998 Guam 15.

District Court of Guam, Appellate Division (D. Guam App. Div.): This division ceased to exist on July 26, 1996. Cite to F. Supp., if therein; otherwise, cite to Guam.

Federal Supplement   1951–date   F. Supp.
Guam Reports   1955–date   Guam

Statutory compilations: Cite to GUAM CODE ANN. if therein.

Guam Code Annotated   x GUAM CODE ANN. § x (year)
(will eventually replace all
other statutory compilations)
Guam Civil Code   GUAM CIV. CODE § x (year)
Guam Code of Civil Procedure   GUAM CIV. P. CODE § x (year)
Guam Government Code   GUAM GOV'T CODE § x (year)

Session laws

Guam Session Laws

year Guam Sess. Laws xxx

Administrative compilation

Administrative Rules & Regulations
of the Government of Guam

GUAM ADMIN. R. & REGS.

Navajo Nation

Supreme Court (Navajo), previously **Court of Appeals** (Navajo): Cite to Navajo Rptr., if therein.

Navajo Reporter

1969–date   Navajo Rptr.

District Court (Navajo D. Ct.): Cite to Navajo Rptr. if therein.

Navajo Reporter

1969–date   Navajo Rptr.

Statutory compilation

Navajo Nation Code (Equity)

NATION CODE tit. x,
§ x (Equity year)

Northern Mariana Islands
http://www.cnmilaw.org

Supreme Court (N. Mar. I.): Cite to N. Mar. I., if therein.

Northern Mariana Islands Reports   1991–date   N. Mar. I.

District Court for the Northern Mariana Islands, Trial and Appellate Divisions (D. N. Mar. I. and D. N. Mar. I. App. Div.), and **Commonwealth Superior Court** (N. Mar. I. Commw. Super. Ct.), previously **Commonwealth Trial Court** (N. Mar. I. Commw. Trial Ct.): Cite to F. Supp., if therein; otherwise, cite to N. Mar. I. Commw. Rptr.

Federal Supplement   1979–date   F. Supp.

Northern Mariana Islands
Commonwealth Reporter   1979–date   N. Mar. I. Commw. Rptr.

Statutory compilation

Northern Mariana Islands
Commonwealth Code

x N. MAR. I. CODE § x (year)

Administrative register

Northern Mariana Islands Commonwealth
Register

N. Mar. I. Reg.

Puerto Rico (PR)

Public domain citation format: Puerto Rico has adopted a public domain citation format for cases after January 1, 1998. The format is:

Spanish: Guzman Rosario v. Departamento de Hacienda, 98 TSPR 148.

English: Guzman Rosario v. Departamento de Hacienda, 98 PRSC 148.

Supreme Court (P.R.): Cite to P.R.R. or P.R. Offic. Trans., if therein, and to P.R. Dec. or P.R. Sent., in that order of preference.

Puerto Rico Reports	1899–1978	P.R.R.
Official Translations of the Opinions of the Supreme Court of Puerto Rico	1978–date	P.R. Offic. Trans.
Decisiones de Puerto Rico	1899–date	P.R. Dec.
Sentencias del Tribunal Supremo de Puerto Rico	1899–1902	P.R. Sent.

Statutory compilation

Laws of Puerto Rico Annotated	x P.R. LAWS ANN. § x (year)

Session laws

Laws of Puerto Rico	year P.R. Laws xxx

Virgin Islands (VI)

All courts

Virgin Islands Reports	1917–date	V.I.

Statutory compilation

Virgin Islands Code Annotated	1962–date	x V.I. CODE ANN. § x (year)

Session laws

Session Laws of the Virgin Islands	year V.I. Sess. Laws xxx

Administrative compilation

Virgin Islands Rules and Regulations	x V.I. R. & REGS. § x (year)

Foreign Jurisdictions   T.2

Argentine Republic
(Civil Law)

Cases

Citation format: "<petitioner>," <court> <volume> <reporter> <page> (<year>). If the volume number contains the year, omit the last parenthetical.

> "Montenegro," CNEspecial Civ. y Com. [1982-D] L.L. 256.

Federal Jurisdiction: Corte Suprema de Justicia de la Nación (CSJN) (highest court on constitutional and federal matters): Cite to Fallos, if therein; otherwise cite to L.L., E.D., or J.A.; **Cámara Nacional de Casacion Penal** (C.N.C.P.) (highest federal court on criminal matters); **Cámara Federal de Apelaciones** (CFed.) (federal court of appeals) and **Juzgado Federal** (Juzg. Fed.) (lower federal courts): Cite to L.L., E.D., or J.A.

Colección Oficial de Fallos de la Corte Suprema de Justicia de la Nación	1863–date	e.g., 299 Fallos 142 (1977)
Revista Jurídica Argentina—La Ley	1936–date	e.g., [1985-E] L.L. 292
El Derecho	1962–date	e.g., 42 E.D. 934 (1972)
Jurisprudencia Argentina	1918–date	e.g., [1961-VI] J.A. 332

Ordinary Jurisdiction: Courts with jurisdiction over the federal district of Buenos Aires: Cámara Nacional de Apelaciones en lo Civil de la Capital Federal (CNCiv.) (court of appeals in civil matters, divided in sections A, B, C, etc.); **Cámara Nacional de Apelaciones en lo Comercial de la Capital Federal** (CNCom.) (court of appeals in commercial matters, divided in sections A, B, C, etc.); **Cámara Nacional de Apelaciones Especial Civil y Comercial de la Capital Federal** (CNEspecial Civ. y Com.) (court of appeals in civil and commercial matters); **Cámara Nacional de Apelaciones en lo Penal Económico de la Capital Federal** (CNPenal Económico) (court of appeals in criminal-economic matters); **Cámara Nacional de Apelaciones del Trabajo de la Capital Federal** (CNTrab.) (court of appeals in labor matters); **Cámara Nacional de Apelaciones en lo Federal y Contenciosoadministrativo de la Capital Federal** (CNFed.) (court of appeals in administrative matters); **Juzgado Nacional de Primera Instancia** (1a Inst.) (lower courts of ordinary jurisdiction): Cite to L.L., E.D., or J.A.

Provincial courts: Corte de Justicia (CJ), **Suprema Corte** (SC), **Tribunal Superior** (TS), **Tribunal Superior de Justicia** (Trib. Sup.), **Superior Tribunal** (ST) (highest state courts); **Cámara de Apelaciones en lo Civil y Comercial** (CApel.CC) (state court of appeals in civil and commercial matters); **Cámara de Apelaciones en lo Penal** (CApel. Penal) (state court of appeals in criminal matters); **Cámara del Trabajo** (CTrab.) (state court of appeals in labor matters); **Juzgado de Primera Instancia** (1a Inst.) (state lower courts of ordinary jurisdiction): Cite to L.L., E.D., or J.A., adding the name of the province.

Constitution

Constitución Argentina	CONST. ARG.

Codes

Código Civil	CÓD. CIV.
Código de Comercio	CÓD. COM.
Código Penal	CÓD. PEN.
Código Procesal Civil y Comercial de la Nación	CÓD. PROC. CIV. Y COM.
Código Procesal Penal de la Nación	CÓD. PROC. PEN.

Statutes and decrees
Citation format: <number of law>, <promulgation date>, [<volume>] <reporter> <page>.

> Law No. 23098, Oct. 19, 1984, [XLIV-D] A.D.L.A. 3733.

Cite to one of the following:

Boletín Oficial	B.O.
Anales de Legislación Argentina	A.D.L.A.
El Derecho — Legislación Argentina	E.D.L.A.
Anuario de Legislación	A.L.J.A.

Australia
(Common Law)

Cases
Citation format: <case name> (<year>) <volume> <reporter> <page>.

> Mabo v. Queensland [No 2] (1992) 175 CLR 1.

High Court of Australia (Austl.) and **Privy Council** (P.C.): For decisions of the High Court (highest appeals court), cite to an official Australian report series in the following order of preference. For Privy

Council decisions, cite to a report listed under United Kingdom if therein; otherwise cite to an official Australian report.

Commonwealth Law Reports	1903–date	C.L.R.
Federal Court Reports	1984–date	F.C.R.
Australian Argus Law Reports	1895–1973	A.A.L.R.

Other federal courts: Cite to one report below, in the following order of preference.

Federal Court Reports	1984–date	F.C.R.
Australian Law Reports	1973–date	A.L.R.
Federal Law Reports	1956–date	F.L.R.
Australian Law Journal Reports	1927–date	A.L.J.R.
Administrative Law Decisions	1976–date	A.L.D.
Australian Criminal Reports	1979–date	A. Crim. R.
Commonwealth Arbitration Reports	1906–1994	C.A.R.
Commonwealth Public Service Arbitration Reports	1921–1984	C.P.S.A.R.
Australian Company Law Reports	1974–1989	A.C.L.R.
Australian Corporations and Securities Reports	1989–date	A.C.S.R.
Australian Bankruptcy Cases	1928–1964	A.B.C.
Family Law Reports	1976–date	Fam. L. R.
Intellectual Property Reports	1982–date	I.P.R.
Australasian Tax Reports	1970–1990	A.T.R.
Australian Tax Reports	1990–date	A.T.R.
Australian and New Zealand Income Tax Reports	1940–1969	A.I.T.R.
Australian Tax Cases (CCH)	1969–date	A.T.C. (CCH)
Taxation Board of Review Decisions (New series after 1950)	1927–1968	T.B.R.D. (n.s.)
Commonwealth Taxation Board of Review Decisions, (New Series after 1950)	1927–1986	C.T.B.R. (n.s.)

Statutes, session laws, and regulations

Cite acts, rules, and regulations using the English statutory form, noting the jurisdiction parenthetically at the end of the citation if not otherwise clear from the context.

Trade Practices Act, 1974, c. 2 (Austl.)

Digests

Australian Digest	1825–1986	Austl. D.
Australian Digest, Second Edition	1963–1994	Austl. D.2d

Australian Digest, Third Edition	1987–date	Austl. D.3d
Australian Legal Monthly Digest	1947–date	Austl. L.M.D.
Australian Annual Digest	1860–1939	Austl. A.D.

Treaties Series

Australian Treaty Series	1947–date	year Austl. T.S. No. x

Australian States and Territories

Courts: Cite to a report below, in the following order of preference; otherwise cite to an Argus report.

New South Wales Law Reports	1960–date	N.S.W.L.R.
New South Wales State Reports	1901–date	N.S.W. St. R.
New South Wales Supreme Court Reports	1862–1880	N.S.W.S. Ct. R.
New South Wales Supreme Court Cases	1825–1862	N.S.W.S. Ct. Cas.
New South Wales Weekly Notes	1884–1970	N.S.W.W.N.
New South Wales Reports	1960–date	N.S.W.R.
New South Wales Industrial Arbitration Reports	1931–date	N.S.W. Indus. Arb. R.
New South Wales Arbitration Reports	1902–1930	N.S.W. Arb. R.
New South Wales Industrial Gazette	1912–1957	N.S.W. Indus. Gaz.
New South Wales Local Government Reports	1911–1956	N.S.W. Local Gov't R.
New South Wales Land Appeal Court Cases	1890–1921	N.S.W. Land App.
New South Wales Land and Valuations Court Reports	1922–1970	N.S.W.L.V.R.
New South Wales Worker's Compensation Reports	1926–date	N.S.W. Worker's Comp. R.
Queensland Reports	1958–date	Q.R.
Queensland State Reports	1902–1957	Q. St. R.
Queensland Law Journal and Reports	1879–1901	Q.L.J. & R.
Queensland Law Reports	1876–1878	Q.L.R.
Queensland Supreme Court Reports	1860–date	Q.S. Ct. R.
Queensland Lawyer	1973–date	Q. Law.
Queensland Justice of the Peace and Local Authorities Reports	1907–1972	Q.J.P.R.
Queensland Land Court Reports	1974–1987	Q. Land Ct. R.
Crown Lands Law Report— Queensland	1859–1973	Q. Cr. Lands L.R.
South Australian State Reports	1922–date	S.A. St. R.
South Australian Law Reports	1867–1921	S.A.L.R.
South Australian Industrial Reports	1916–date	S.A. Indus. R.

Tasmanian Reports	1979–date	T.R.
Tasmanian State Reports	1941–1978	T. St. R.
Tasmanian Law Reports	1897–1940	T.L.R.
Victorian Reports	1957–date	V.R.
Victorian Law Reports	1961–1969	V.L.R.
	1875–1956	V.L.R.
	1870–1872	V.L.R.
Australian Jurist Reports	1870–1874	A.J.R.
Reports of Cases, Supreme Court of Victoria	1861–1869	V.S. Ct.
Western Australian Law Reports	1899–1959	W.A.L.R.
Western Australian Reports	1960–date	W.A.R.
State Reports (Western Australia)	1979–date	
Western Australia Law Journal	1899–1959	W.A.L.J.

Statutory compilations

Laws of the Australian Capital Territory	1911–date	AUSTL. CAP. TERR. LAWS
New South Wales Acts (Reprints)	1924–date	N.S.W. ACTS
Public Acts of Queensland (Reprint)	1828–1936	QUEENSL. PUB. ACTS
South Australian Statutes	1837–date	S. AUSTL. STAT.
Tasmanian Statutes (Reprint)	1826–1959	TAS. STAT.
Victorian Statutes	1890–1958	VICT. STAT.
Victorian Reprints	1958–date	VICT. REPR. STAT.
Western Australian Reprinted Acts	1939–1969	W. AUSTL. REPR. ACTS

Session laws

Laws of the Australian Capital Territory		Austl. Cap. Terr. Laws
Statutes of New South Wales	1838–date	N.S.W. Stat.
New South Wales Rules, Regulations, and By-Laws	1917–date	N.S.W.R. Regs. & B.
Northern Territorial Ordinances	1911–1960	N. Terr. Austl. Ord.
Northern Territory of Australia Laws	1961–date	N. Terr. Austl. Laws
Queensland Statutes	1837–date	Queensl. Stat.
Queensland Subordinate Legislation	1991–date	Queensl. Sub. Leg.
Acts of the Parliament of South Australia	1848–1936	S. Austl. Acts
Acts and Ordinances of South Australia	1837–1866	S. Austl. Acts & Ord.
South Australian Statutory Instruments	1981–date	S. Austl. Stat. Inst.
Tasmanian Statutes	1926–date	Tas. Sess. Stat.
Tasmania Acts of Parliament	1899–1959	Tas. Acts
Tasmanian Statutory Rules		Tas. Stat. R.
Victoria Acts of Parliament	1856–date	Vict. Acts
Victoria Statutory Rules, Regulations, and By-Laws	1914–date	Vict. Stat. R. Regs. & B.
Statutes of Western Australia	1832–date	W. Austl. Stat.

T

T.2

Sources not provided above can be found in the comprehensive
Australian Guide to Legal Citation (1998).

Austria, Republic of
(Civil Law)

Cases
Citation format: <periodical> <volume number>/<case number>.

SZ 65/129.

Ordinary jurisdiction: Oberster Gerichtshof (OGH) (supreme
court): Cite to SZ for civil matters or SSt for criminal matters if therein; otherwise cite to a periodical; **Oberlandesgericht** (e.g., OLG
Wien) (court of appeals from a Landesgericht or Kreisgericht),
Landesgericht (e.g., LG Salzburg) (trial court and court of appeals
from Bezirksgericht, located in Länder capitals), **Kreisgericht** (e.g.,
KG Korneuburg) (same as Landesgericht, located in major cities other
than capitals): Cite to a periodical.

Entscheidungen des österreichischen Obersten Gerichtshofes in Zivilsachen	SZ
Entscheidungen des österreichischen Obersten Gerichtshofes in Strafsachen	SSt

Special jurisdiction: Arbeits- und Sozialgericht (ASG) (trial court
for labor and social insurance matters): Cite to ArbSlg for labor
matters, and SVSlg for social insurance matters, if therein;
Handelsgericht (HG) (trial court and court of appeals for commercial
matters): Cite to HS if therein; **Kartellobergericht** (KOG) (supreme
court for cartel law matters) and **Kartellgericht** (KartG) (trial court for
cartel law matters): Cite to periodicals.

Sammlung Arbeitsrechtlicher Entscheidungen	ArbSlg
Sozialversicherungsrechtliche Entscheidungen	SVSlg
Handelsrechtliche Entscheidungen	HS

Constitutional jurisdiction: Verfassungsgerichtshof (VfGH) (sole
court for constitutional matters): Cite to VfSlg if therein.

Erkenntnisse und Beschlüsse des Verfassungsgerichtshofes	VfSlg

Administrative jurisdiction: Verwaltungsgerichtshof (VwGH)
(sole court for administrative and tax matters): Cite to VwSlgNF-A for
administrative matters and to VwSlgNF-F for tax matters, or to VwSlg,
if therein.

Erkenntnisse und Beschlüsse des Verwaltungsgerichtshofes, Neue Folge	1945–date	VwSlgNF-A, VwSlgNF-F
Erkenntnisse und Beschlüsse des Verwaltungsgerichtshofes	1919–1945	VwSlg

Constitution

Bundes-Verfassungsgesetz (codification)	B-VG
Menschenrechtskonvention (European Convention on Human Rights)	MRK
Staatsgrundgesetz über die allgemeinen Rechte der Staatsbürger (federal "Bill of Rights")	STGG

Codes

Citation format: \<section> \<part> \<code>.

§ 364 Abs 2 ABGB.

Allgemeines Bürgerliches Gesetzbuch (Civil Code)	ABGB
Handelsgesetzbuch (Commercial Code)	HGB
Strafgesetzbuch (Penal Code)	StGB
Strafprozessordnung (Criminal Procedure Statute)	StPO
Zivilprozessordnung (Civil Procedure Statute)	ZPO

Statutes and regulations

Citation format: \<section> \<statute> \<compilation> \<statute number>/\<year>.

§ 2 RAO BGBL 556/1985.

Cite a Bundesverfassungsgesetz (BVG) (federal constitutional statute), Bundesgesetz (BG) (federal statute), or Verordnung (V or VO) (administrative regulation) to BGBl. Cite their predecessors, a Reichsgesetz (RG) or Gesetz (G) to RGBl or dRGBl, or a Staatsgesetz (StG) or Gesetz (G) to StGBl.

Bundesgesetzblatt	1945–date 1920–1938	BGBl
deutsches Reichsgesetzblatt	1938–1945	dRGBl
Staatsgesetzblatt	1918–1920	StGBl
Reichsgesetzblatt	1849–1918	RGBl

Periodicals

Juristische Blätter	JBL
Österreichische Juristen-Zeitung	ÖJZ
Evidenzblatt der Rechtsmittelentscheidungen	EvBL

Österreichisches Recht der Wirtschaft	RDW
Österreichisches Bank-Archiv	ÖBA
Österreichische Blätter für gewerblichen Rechtsschutz und Urheberrecht	ÖBL
ecolex	ECOLEX
Der Gesellschafter	GESRZ

Austrian Länder

Courts: All courts are federal courts, listed above.

Constitutions

Landes-Verfassungsgesetz (state constitution)	L-VG

Statutes and regulations: Cite a Landesverfassungsgesetz (LVG) (state constitutional statute), Landesgesetz (LG) (state statute), or Verordnung (V or VO) (administrative regulation) to LGBl:

Landesgesetzblatt	LGBl

Brazil, Federative Republic of
(Civil Law)

Cases

Citation format: <court>, <docket number>, <name of court reporter>, <judgment date>, <reporter> <publication date>, <page>.

> TRF-1, REO No. 0100985, Relator: Juiz Alves de Lima, 08.09.1992, D.J.U. O1.10.1992, p. 30,786.

Supremo Tribunal Federal (STF) (highest court of appeals on constitutional matters): Cite to R.T.J. or R.S.T.F.

Revista Trimestral de Jurisprudência	1956–date	e.g., R.T.J. 50/101
Revista do Supremo Tribunal Federal	1914–1956	R.S.T.F.

Higher Federal Courts: Superior Tribunal de Justiça (STJ) (highest court of appeals on all non-constitutional matters); **Tribunal Regional Federal** (indicate region 1 to 5, e.g., TRF-1) (regional federal court of appeals (matters of federal interest)); **Tribunal Superior Eleitoral** (TSE) (highest court of appeals on electoral law); **Tribunal Superior do Trabalho** (TST) (highest court of appeals on labor law); **Superior Tribunal Militar** (STM) (highest court of appeals on military law); **Vara da Justiça Federal** (JF) (federal district court (matters of federal interest)) (indicate number and city): Cite to Revista do Superior Tribunal de Justiça (R.S.T.J.), Revista do Tribunal Regional Federal (R.T.R.F.), Revista do Tribunal Superior do Trabalho

(R.T.S.T.), or Diário de Justiça da União (D.J.U.).

State Courts: Tribunal de Justiça (TJ followed by state initials, e.g., TJMG for Minas Gerais) (higher state court of appeals); **Tribunal de Alçada** (TA followed by state initials, e.g., TAMG for Minas Gerais, or by type of court and state initials, e.g., TACivSP for civil appeals in São Paulo) (auxiliary state court of appeals, for certain types of suits): Cite to Federal Judiciary Gazette (Diário de Justiça da União (D.J.U.)) or to State's Judiciary Gazette (Diário do Judiciário, <state name>), or to Revista Forense (R.F.) or Revista Dos Tribunais (R.T.).

Constitution

Constituição Federal	C.F.

Codes

Código Civil	C.C.
Código Comercial	C. Co.
Código Eleitoral	C.E.
Código Florestal	C. Flor.
Código de Mineração	C. Min.
Consolidação das Leis do Trabalho	C.L.T.
Código Penal	C.P.
Código Penal Militar	C.P.M.
Consolidação das Leis da Previdência Social	C.L.P.S.
Código de Processo Civil	C.P.C.
Código de Processo Penal	C.P.P.
Código de Propriedade Industrial	C.P.I.
Código de Proteçao e Defesa do Consumidor	C.D.C.
Código Tributário Nacional	C.T.N.

Statutes and decrees

Citation format: <statute/decree number>, <date of promulgation>, <official gazette>, <date of publication>.

Decreto No. 70.391, de 12 de abril de 1972, D.O. de 14.04.1972.

Diário Oficial da União (federal law)	D.O.U.
Diário Oficial, state name (state law)	D.O.E., e.g., D.O.E.S.P.
Revista Lex	Lex

Treaties and conventions

Coleção de Atos Internacionais	1927–1964	Col. Atos Internacionais, No. x

T

T.2

Canada
(Common Law)

Cases

Citation format: <case name>, [<year>] <reporter> <page number>.

Mann v. The Queen, [1962] S.C.R. 469.

Privy Council (P.C.) (criminal appeals until 1935, civil appeals until 1949): Cite to reports listed under **United Kingdom** if therein; otherwise cite to Olms.

Decisions of the Judicial Committee of the Privy Council re the British North American Act, 1867, and the Canadian Constitution	Olms.

Supreme Court of Canada (Can.): Cite to S.C.R. if therein; otherwise cite to D.L.R.

Canada: Supreme Court Reports	1876–date	S.C.R.
Dominion Law Reports	1912–date	D.L.R.

Federal Court (Fed. Ct.) (formerly the Exchequer Court): Cite to F.C. or Ex. C.R. if therein; otherwise cite to D.L.R.

Federal Court Reports	1971–date	F.C.
Exchequer Court Reports	1875–1971	Ex. C.R.

Tax Court of Canada (Can. Tax Ct.): Cite to C.T.C. or Tax A.B.C. if therein; otherwise cite to D.T.C. or D.L.R.

Canada Tax Cases	1985–date	C.T.C.
Canada Tax Appeal Board Cases	1945–1972	Tax A.B.C.
Dominion Tax Cases	1920–date	D.T.C.

Statutes

Citation format: Cite statutes appearing in the current national or provincial *Revision* (alphabetical consolidation of acts in force) analogously to codified United States statutes:

Juvenile Delinquents Act, R.S.C., ch. J-3, § 3(2) (1970) (Can.).

Cite subsequent statutes to the annual *Statutes of Canada* in a manner similar to that used for United States session laws (**rule 12.4**):

Act of Dec. 23, 1971, ch. 63, 1970-1972 S.C. 1311 (Can.).

When citing an act appearing in the current *Revision* as well as the act's subsequent amendment, the name of the amendment need not be given:

Securities Act, R.S.Q. ch. V-1 (1977), amended by ch. 79, 1979 S.Q. 1227 (Can.).

Statutory and regulatory compilations

Revised Statutes of Canada	R.S.C.
Consolidated Regulations of Canada	C.R.C.

Session laws and regulations

Statutes of Canada	S.C.
Statutes of the Province of Canada	S. Prov. C.
Canada Gazette	C. Gaz.

Treaties Service

Canada Treaty Series	1925–date	year Can. T.S. No. x

Canadian Provinces and Territories

Courts: Cite to provincial reporters, if therein, in the order of preference shown below; otherwise cite to D.L.R., W.W.R., A.P.R., E.L.R., M.P.R., or W.L.R.

Alberta Reports	1976–date	A.R.
Alberta Law Reports	1907–1932	Alta. L.R.
Alberta Law Reports (2d)	1976–1991	Alta. L.R.2d
Alberta Law Reports (3d)	1992–date	Alta. L.R.3d
British Columbia Reports	1867–1947	B.C.R.
British Columbia Law Reports	1976–1986	B.C.L.R.
British Columbia Law Reports (2d)	1986–date	B.C.L.R.2d
Manitoba Reports	1883–1961	Man. R.
Manitoba Reports (2d)	1979–date	Man. R.2d
Manitoba Law Reports	1875–1883	Man. L.R.
New Brunswick Reports	1825–1929	N.B.R.
New Brunswick Reports (2d)	1968–date	N.B.R.2d
Newfoundland and Prince Edward Island Reports	1970–date	Nfld. & P.E.I.R.
Newfoundland Law Reports	1817–1946	Nfld. L.R.
Northwest Territories Reports	1983–date	N.W.T.R.
Territories Law Reports	1885–1907	Terr. L.R.
Nova Scotia Reports	1965–1969 1834–1929	N.S.R.
Nova Scotia Reports (2d)	1969–date	N.S.R.2d
Ontario Law Reports	1900–1931	O.L.R.
Ontario Reports	1882–1900 1931–1973	O.R.
Ontario Reports (2d)	1973–1991	O.R.2d
Ontario Reports (3d)	1991–date	O.R.3d
Ontario Appeal Cases	1983–date	O.A.C.
Ontario Appeal Reports	1876–1900	O.A.R.

Recueils de jurisprudence du Québec, Cour d'appel	1870–1985	C.A.
Recueils de jurisprudence du Québec	1986–date	R.J.Q.
Recueils de jurisprudence/Rapports Judiciaires du Québec, Cour du Banc de la Reine/du Roi	1892–1969	B.R.
Recueils/Rapports de jurisprudence du Québec, Cour supérieure	1967–1985 1944–1966 1892–1941	C.S.
Recueils de jurisprudence du Québec, Cour provinciale, Cour des Sessions de la paix, Cour du bien-être social	1975–1985	C.P./C.S.P./C.B.E.S.
Saskatchewan Law Reports	1907-1931	Sask. L.R.
Saskatchewan Reports	1979-date	Sask. R.
Dominion Law Reports	1912-date	D.L.R.
Western Weekly Reports	1911-date	W.W.R.
Atlantic Provinces Reports	1975-date	A.P.R.
Eastern Law Reporter	1906-1914	E.L.R.
Maritime Provinces Reports	1929-1968	M.P.R.
Western Law Reporter	1905-1916	W.L.R.

Statutory compilations

Revised Statutes of Alberta	R.S.A.
Revised Statutes of British Columbia	R.S.B.C.
Revised Statutes of Manitoba	R.S.M.
Revised Statutes of New Brunswick	R.S.N.B.
Revised Statutes of Newfoundland	NFLD. R.S.
Revised Ordinances of the Northwest Territories	R.O.N.W.T.
Revised Statutes of Nova Scotia	R.S.N.S.
Revised Statutes of Ontario	R.S.O.
Revised Regulations of Ontario	R.R.O.
Revised Statutes of Prince Edward Island	R.S.P.E.I.
Revised Regulations of Prince Edward Island	R.R.P.E.I.
Revised Statutes of Québec	R.S.Q.
Revised Regulations of Quebéc	R.R.Q.
Statutes of Saskatchewan	S.S.
Statutes of the Yukon Territory	S.Y.T.

Session laws

Statutes of Alberta	S.A.
Alberta Gazette	A. Gaz.
British Columbia Statutes	S.B.C.
British Columbia Gazette	B.C. Gaz.

Manitoba Gazette	M. Gaz.
Statutes of Newfoundland	S. Nfld.
Ordinances of the Northwest Territories	O.N.W.T.
Statutes of Nova Scotia	S.N.S.
Statutes of Ontario	S.O.
Ontario Regulations	R.O.
Statutes of Québec	S.Q.
Statutes of Saskatchewan	S.S.
Saskatchewan Gazette	S. Gaz.
Statutes of the Yukon Territory	S.Y.T.

Sources not provided above can be found in the comprehensive *Canadian Guide to Uniform Legal Citation* (4th ed. 1998).

Catholic Church

Codes before 1917: Cite by the name of the individual document or fragment, as in the examples below, not by the title of a collection that includes the material. For other examples, see the *Bulletin of Medieval Canon Law.*

Gratian (c. 1140)
Part 1	e.g., D.33 c.1 (d.a.)
Part 2	e.g., C.9 q.3 c.1
Part 3	e.g., DE CONS. D.2 c.84
Decretals of Gregory IX (1234)	e.g., X 3.24.2
Decretals of Boniface VIII (1298)	e.g., VI 1.11.1
Constitutions of Clement V (1317)	e.g., CLEM. 3.5.7
Extravagants of John XXII (1316-1334)	e.g., EXTRAV. JO. 14.3
Common Extravagants (1261-1484)	e.g., EXTRAV. COM. 2.1.1

Codes after 1917: Cite to either the 1917 or 1983 *Codex Iuris Canonici.*

Codex Iuris Canonici (1917)	1917–1983	e.g., 1917 CODE c.430, § 1
Codex Iuris Canonici (1983)	1983–date	e.g., 1983 CODE c.515, § 3

China, People's Republic of (Civil Law)

Cases

Citation format: <case name>, <source>, <date of publication>, <page> (<court>, <date of decision>).

China National Technical Import/Export Corp. v. Industrial Resources Co. Inc., China L. & Prac., Aug. 22, 1988, at 26 (Shanghai Intermediate People's Court, May 11, 1988).

Courts: Zuigao Renmin Fayuan (Supreme People's Court) (court of first instance and last appeal in all matters): Cite to Zuigao Renmin Fayuan Gongbao; **Gaoji Renmin Fayuan** (High People's Court) (court of first instance and court of appeal in the provinces, autonomous regions, and municipalities directly under the central government subject to special leave to Zuigao Renmin Fayuan), **Zhongji Renmin Fayuan** (Intermediate People's Court) (court of first instance and court of appeal), **Difang Renmin Fayuan** (Basic People's Court) (court of first instance): Cite to one of the following sources:

Zuigao Renmin Fayuan Gongbao	Zuigao Renmin Fayuan Gongbao
Zhongguo Fazhibao	Fazhibao
Minzhu yu Fazhi	Minzhu yu Fazhi
Anli Xuanbian	Anli Xuanbian

Constitution: Give the promulgation year of the version cited.

Zhonghua Renmin Gongheguo Xianfa	e.g., XIANFA art. 35, sec. 1 (1982)

Statutes, regulations, and decrees: For laws, regulations, and official decrees of the PRC, cite to Fagui Huibian, Falü Huibian, Fagui Huibian, or Faling Huibian, if therein; otherwise cite to a secondary compilation such as Shewai Jingji Fagui, Zuixin Jingji Fagui, Jingji Ziliao, or Fagui Xuanbian.

Zhonghua Renmin Gongheguo Fagui Huibian	1979–date	Fagui Huibian
Zhonghua Renmin Gongheguo Falü Huibian	1979–1984	Falü Huibian
Zhonghua Renmin Gongheguo Fagui Huibian	1954–1963	Fagui Huibian
Zhongyang Renmin Zhengfu Faling Huibian	1949–1953	Faling Huibian
Zhongguo Shewai Jingji Fagui Huibian		Shewai Jingji Fagui
Zuixin Jingji Fagui		Zuixin Jingji Fagui
Jingji Ziliao Xuanbian		Jingji Ziliao
Fagui Xuanbian		Fagui Xuanbian

Treaties and conventions

Zhonghua Renmin Gongheguo Tiaoyue Ji	1955-date	year Zhonghua Renmin Gongheguo Tiaoyue Ji xxx

Czech Republic
(Civil Law)

Courts: Nejvyšší soud (supreme court), **Vyšší soud** (high court), **Krajský soud** (KS) (regional court of appeals): Cite to Sbírka soudních rozhodnutí a stanovisek, by case number (č.) and year:

Sbírka soudních
rozhodnutí a stanovisek

Sbírka soudních
rozhodnuti a
stanovisek, č. xx/19xx

Constitution

Ústavní zákon České republiky
(Constitution of the Czech Republic)

ÚSTAVA ČR

Statutes, regulations, and decisions of the Constitutional Court: Cite a statute (zákon) or constitutional statute (ústavní zákon) to Sb. Cite a regulation (vyhláska) to Sb. Cite a decision of the Constitutional Court (nález Ústavního soudu) to Sb.

Sbírka zákonů

Sb. (e.g., zákon
č. 1/1995 Sb.)

France, Republic of
(Civil Law)

Cases

Citation format: <court>, <region if applicable>, <date of decision>, <reporter or journal>, <year of publication>, <section of journal if applicable>, <page on which decision appears or decision number>, <author of case note>.

> T.G.I. Nice, May 30, 1990, D. 1991, Somm. 113, obs. F. Derrida.
>
> CA Paris, 1e ch., Dec. 20, 1994, J.C.P. 1994, II, 22250, note Neirinck.

Ordinary jurisdiction: Cour de cassation, the highest court of ordinary jurisdiction, ordinarily sits in chambers (previously sections), which are abbreviated as follows:

Assemblée plénière	1978–date	Cass. ass. plén.
Chambres réunies	to 1978	Cass. ch. réuns.
Chambre mixte		Cass. ch. mixte
Première chambre civile		Cass. 1e civ.
Deuxième chambre civile		Cass. 2e civ.
Troisième chambre civile		Cass. 3e civ.
Chambre criminelle		Cass. crim.
Chambre commerciale et financière		Cass. com.
Chambre sociale		Cass. soc.
Chambre des requêtes	to 1947	Cass. req.

| Chambres temporaires des expropriations | 1964–1967 | Cass. chs. exprops. |

Cite to Bull. civ. or Bull. crim., as appropriate, if therein, indicating part and case number. Otherwise, cite to one of the other reporters listed below.

| Bulletin des arrêts de la Cour de cassation, chambres civiles | 1792–date | e.g., year Bull. Civ. I, No. xx |
| Bulletin des arrêts de la Cour de cassation, chambres criminelles | 1798–date | e.g., year Bull. Crim., No. xx |

Also **Cours d'appel** (CA) (regional courts of appeal); **Tribunaux de grande instance** (T.G.I.), prior to 1958 **Tribunaux de première instance** (T.P.I.) (ordinary courts of original jurisdiction); **Cours d'assises** (criminal courts of original and appellate jurisdiction; do not abbreviate); and **Tribunaux d'instance** (Trib. inst.), prior to 1958 **Juges de paix** (J.P.) (courts of petty jurisdiction). All cites to a Cour d'appel or any tribunal should include the city or region, and the chamber if any. E.g., CA Paris, le ch.; or Trib. adm. Nantes (3e ch.). Cite to one of the following reporters:

Recueil Dalloz

Dalloz-Sirey,	1965–date,1956	
Jurisprudence		e.g., D. [year]
Informations Rapides		e.g., D. [year] inf. rap.
Sommaires Commentés		e.g., D. [year] somm.
Dalloz, *Jurisprudence*	1945–1964	D. Jur.
Analytique, *Jurisprudence*	1941–1944	D.A. Jur.
Critique, *Jurisprudence*	1941–1944	D.C. Jur.
Périodique et critique	1825–1940	
Cour de cassation		D.P. I
Cours royales, cours impériales, cours d'appel		D.P. II
Conseil d'Etat		D.P. III

Recueil Sirey (entitled *Recueil Général des Lois et des Arrêts* until 1950)

Sirey, *Jurisprudence*	1956–1964	S. Jur.
Sirey, *Jurisprudence*	1791–1955	
Cour de cassation		S. Jur. I
Other courts		S. Jur. II
Jurisprudence administrative		S. Jur. III
Gazette du Palais	1881–date	
Panorama de jurisprudence		e.g., Gaz. Pal. [year], 2, pan. jurispr.
Panorama de droit administratif		e.g., Gaz. Pal. [year], 2, pan. admin.

Panorama de jurisprudence fiscale		e.g., Gaz. Pal. [year], 2, pan. juris. fisc.
Sommaires des cours et tribunaux		e.g., Gaz. Pal. [year], 2, somm.
Juris-Classeur Périodique		
Edition Général (La Semaine Juridique)	1942–date	
Jurisprudence		e.g., JCP [year] II [no.]
Textes		e.g., JCP [year] III [no.]
Tableaux de Jurisprudence		e.g., JCP [year] IV [no.]
Informations		e.g., JCP [year] V [no.]
Bulletin Joly		e.g., Bull. Joly [year] [page]
Juris-Classeur Périodique		
Edition entreprise		e.g., JCP [year] éd. E. [year], [no.]
Edition avoués		e.g., JCP [year] éd. av. [year], [no.]
Edition commerce et industrie		e.g., JCP [year] éd. com. [year], [no.]
Edition notariale		e.g., JCP [year] éd. not. [year], [no.]
Gazette des Tribunaux	1825–1955	e.g., Gaz. Trib. [date]
Juris-Data		e.g., Juris-Data [no.]

Administrative jurisdiction: Tribunal des conflits (Trib. conflits) (reconciles disputes between the Conseil d'Etat and the Cour de cassation); **Conseil d'Etat** (do not abbreviate) (highest administrative court; and **Tribunaux administratifs** (Trib. adm.) (regional administrative courts of first instance): Cite to Lebon if therein; otherwise cite to Dalloz or Sirey.

Recueil des décisions [arrêts] du Conseil d'Etat	1821–date	Lebon

Constitutional jurisdiction: Conseil constitutionnel (Cons. const.) (constitutional court): Cite to Dalloz or Sirey.

Constitution

La Constitution	CONST.

Codes

Code administratif	C. ADM.
Code civil	C. CIV.
Code de commerce	C. COM.
Code pénal	C. PÉN.
Code de procédure pénale	C. PR. PÉN.
Code du travail	C. TRAV.
Nouveau code de procédure civile	N.C.P.C.

Statutes and decrees

Citation format: <law or decree number>, <date of law or decree>, J.O., <date of publication in J.O.>, <page>, <one other source (including date, section of journal, and page or item number)>.

> Law No. 85-669 of July 11, 1985, J.O., July 12, 1985, p. 7865; JCP 1985, III, 57447.

Cite to the J.O. and one other source.

Journal Officiel de la République Française		J.O.
Recueil Dalloz		
Dalloz-Sirey, *Législation*	1965–date 1956	D.S.L.
Dalloz, *Législation*	1945–1964	D.L.
Analytique, *Législation*	1941–1944	D.A.L.
Critique, *Législation*	1941–1944	D.C.L.
Périodique et critique	1848–1940 1825–1847	D.P. IV D.P. III
Bulletin législatif Dalloz	1918–1982	B.L.D.
Actualité législative Dalloz	1983–date	A.L.D.
La Semaine Juridique (Juris-Classeur Périodique)	1942–date 1927–date	e.g., J.C.P. III, No. x e.g., J.C.P., No. x
Collection complète, décrets, ordonnances, règlements et avis du Conseil d'Etat (Duvergier & Bocquet)	1788–1949	Duv. & Boc.

Treaties and conventions

Citation format: <title>, <date>, <countries>, J.O., <date of publication in J.O.>, <page>; <one other source>.

> Tourism Accord, Oct. 26, 1979, Fr.-Mex., J.O., June 15, 1980, p. 1478; 1980 Recueil des traités, No. 28.

Cite treaties to the Journal Officiel and to one of the following:

Recueil des traités et accords de la France	1961–date	year Recueil des traités, No. x
Recueil des traités de la France	1713–1906	x Recueil des traités xxx

Germany, Federal Republic of
(Civil Law)

Cases

Ordinary jurisdiction:

Citation format: <name of collection> <volume>, <page> (<pinpoint>).

BGHZ 54, 366 (367).

Supreme civil and criminal court: The **Bundesgerichtshof** (BGH) (supreme court), previously **Reichsgericht** (RG), sits in chambers, or **Senate**: **Bundesgerichtshof, Vereinigte Große Senate** (BGH Ver. Gr. Sen.); **Bundesgerichtshof, Großer Senat für Zivilsachen** (BGH Gr. Sen. Z.) (en banc panels to resolve conflicts among the Senate for civil cases); **Bundesgerichtshof, Großer Senat für Strafsachen** (BGH Gr. Sen. St.) (en banc panels to resolve conflicts among the Senate for criminal cases); and **Bundesgerichtshof, Senate** (BGH) (ordinary panels of the highest court): Cite civil matters to BGHZ or RGZ, and criminal matters to BGHSt or RGSt, if therein.

Entscheidungen des Bundesgerichtshofes in Zivilsachen	1951–date	BGHZ
Entscheidungen des Reichsgerichts in Zivilsachen	1880–1945	RGZ
Entscheidungen des Bundesgerichtshofes in Strafsachen	1951–date	BGHSt
Entscheidungen des Reichsgerichts in Strafsachen	1880–1945	RGSt

Lower civil and criminal courts:
Citation format: <court> <location>, <legal periodical>, <volume> (<year>), <page> (<pinpoint>).

OLG Hamburg, Recht der Internationalen Wirtschaft [RIW], 38 (1992), 941 (942).

Oberlandesgericht (OLG) (trial court for selected criminal matters and court of appeals): Cite civil matters to OLGZ, and criminal matters to OLGSt, if therein; **Bayerisches Oberstes Landesgericht** (BayObLG) (court of appeals for selected matters in Bavaria): Cite civil matters to BayObLGZ and criminal matters to BayObLGSt, if therein; **Landgericht** (LG) (trial court): Cite to periodicals.

Rechtsprechung der Oberlandesgerichte in Zivilsachen	OLGZ
Rechtsprechung der Oberlandesgerichte in Strafsachen	OLGSt
Entscheidungen des Bayerischen Obersten Landesgerichts in Zivilsachen	BayObLGZ
Entscheidungen des Bayerischen Obersten Landesgerichts in Strafsachen	BayObLGSt

Constitutional jurisdiction: Bundesverfassungsgericht (BVerfG) (federal constitutional court): Cite to BVerfGE, if therein.

Entscheidungen des Bundesverfassungsgerichts	1956–date	BVerfGE

Administrative jurisdiction: Bundesverwaltungsgericht (BVerwG) (highest administrative court): Cite to BVerwGE; **Oberverwaltungsgericht** (OVG) or **Verwaltungsgerichtshof** (VGH) (court of appeals): Cite to the Entscheidungen of the court; **Verwaltungsgericht** (VG) (trial court): Cite to periodicals.

Entscheidungen des Bundesverwaltungsgericht	1954–date	BVerwGE

Special jurisdiction: Bundesfinanzhof (BFH) (supreme tax court): Cite to BFHE, if therein; **Finanzgericht** (FG) (tax trial court): Cite to EFG, if therein; **Bundesarbeitsgericht** (BAG) (supreme labor court): Cite to BAGE, if therein; **Landesarbeitsgerichte** (LAG) (labor court of appeals): Cite to periodicals; **Bundessozialgericht** (BSG) (supreme social insurance court): Cite to BSGE, if therein; **Landessozialgericht** (LSG) (social insurance court of appeals): Cite to periodicals; **Bundespatentgericht** (BPatG) (federal court for patent matters): Cite to BPatGE, if therein:

Sammlung der Entscheidungen und Gutachten des Bundesfinanzhofs	1952–date	BFHE
Entscheidungen der Finanzgerichte		EFG
Entscheidungen des Bundesarbeitsgerichts	1954–date	BAGE
Entscheidungen des Bundessozialgerichts	1955–date	BSGE
Entscheidungen des Bundespatentgerichts	1962–date	BPatGE

Constitution

Grundgesetz (federal constitution)	GG

Codes
Citation format: <section or article> <paragraph or number> <code>.

§ 191 Nr. 5 ZPO.

Bürgerliches Gesetzbuch (Civil Code)	BGB
Gerichtsverfassungsgesetz (Court organizational statute)	GVG
Grundgesetz (Basic Law)	GG
Handelsgesetzbuch (Commercial Code)	HGB
Sozialgesetzbuch (Social Insurance Code)	SGB
Strafgesetzbuch (Penal Code)	StGB
Strafprozeßordnung (criminal procedure statute)	StPO
Verwaltungsverfahrensgesetz (Administrative Law Code)	VwVfG
Verwaltungsgerichtsordnung (Code of Administrative Procedure)	VwGO

Zivilprozeßordnung (civil   ZPO
procedure statute)

Statutes and decrees
Citation format: <full title> (<short title>), v. <day.month.year> (<legal gazette> S.<page>).

> Gesetz über eine Rentenversicherung der Handwerker
> (Handwerkerversicherungsgesetz), v. 8.9.1960 (BGBl. I S.737).

Cite a Bundesgesetz (federal statute) or Verordnung (VO) to BGBl or RGBl; a parallel citation to Bundesanzeiger may be added.

Bundesgesetzblatt, Teil I	1951–date	BGBl. I
Bundesgesetzblatt, Teil II	1951–date	BGBl. II
Reichsgesetzblatt	1871–1921	RGBl.
Reichsgesetzblatt, Teil I	1922–1945	RGBl. I
Reichsgesetzblatt, Teil II	1922–1945	RGBl. II
Bundesanzeiger	1949–date	BAnz.

Treaties and conventions: Cite treaties and conventions to BGBl. II if therein and use the citation format of statutes. Otherwise cite to:

Verträge der Bundesrepublik Deutschland	1955–date	x Verträge der Bundesrepublik Deutschland (ser. A), No. x

German Länder

The courts of ordinary and administrative jurisdiction are those of the federal system.

Constitutional jurisdiction: Staatsgerichtshof (StGH) or **Verfassungsgerichtshof** (e.g., VerfGH Bayern) (constitutional court of the Land): Cite to the official reporter of the court:

Verfassungsgerichtshof   e.g., VerfGH Bayern

Constitutions: Add the name of the Land.

Verfassung   e.g., VERF. BAYERN

Statutes and decrees: Cite a Landesgesetz (LG) (state statute) or Landesverordnung (LVO) (state administrative regulation) to the GVBl. of the individual Land.

Gesetz- und Verordnungsblatt   e.g., GVBl. Bayern

Hungary, Republic of
(Civil Law)

Constitutional and civil law courts: Alkotmánybíróság (constitutional law court): cite to MK., if therein. **Legfelsőbb Bíróság** (Supreme Court: court of appeal in civil and criminal matters of major importance and in commercial law suits); **Megyei bíróságok és Budapest főváros Bírósága** (county courts and the court of Budapest); **Helyi, városi,** or **kerületi bíróságok** (local, town, or district courts): cite to BH., if therein.

Magyar Közlöny (Hungarian Gazette)	MK.
Bírósági Határozatok	BH.

Constitution

A Magyar Köztársaság Alkotmánya	A MAGYAR KÖZTÁRSASÁG ALKOTMÁNYA

Codes

Polgári Törvénykönyv (Civil Code)	PTK.
Büntető Törvénykönyv (Penal Code)	BTK.
Polgári peres eljárás (Code of Civil Procedure)	PP.
Büntető eljárás (Code of Penal Procedure)	BE.
Gazdasági Társasági Törvény (Company Law)	GT. TV.
Törvény a külföldiek magyarországi beruházásáról (Law on Investments of Foreigners in Hungary)	TÖR. KÜL. MAGY. BERU.
Törvény a bíróságokról (Law on the Organization of the Courts)	BÍRÓSÁGI TV.

India
(Common Law)

Privy Council (P.C.) until 1949: Cite to reports listed under India Privy Council to I.A., Ind. App. or I. App., or to A.I.R. or Ind. Cas., in that order of preference.

Law Reports, Privy Council, Indian Appeals	1836–1872	I. App.
	1873–1950	I.A. or Ind. App.
All India Reporter	1914–date	e.g., A.I.R. year P.C. page
Indian Cases	1909–1947	Ind. Cas.

Supreme Court (India) and **Federal Court** (India Fed.), 1937–1950: Cite to S.C.R. if therein; otherwise cite to one of the other reporters listed below in the following order of preference:

Supreme Court Reports	1950–date	e.g., (year) volume S.C.R. page
All India Reporter	1914–date	e.g., A.I.R. year S.C. page
Supreme Court Journal	1936–date	S.C.J.
Supreme Court Cases	1969–date	e.g., (year) volume S.C.C. page
Unreported Judgments	1969–date	e.g., Unreported Judgments year page
Supreme Court Almanac	1979–date	e.g., year S.C.A.L.E. page
Federal Court Reports	1939–1950	F.C.R.
Federal Law Journal	1937–1949	F.L.J.
Indian Cases	1909–1947	Indian Cas.

High Court (e.g., Madras H.C.), **Supreme Court** (e.g., Calcutta S.C.) until 1860, **Court of the Judicial Commissioner** (e.g., C.J.C. Manipur), **Sadar Dewani Adalats** (e.g., S.D.A. Agra) until 1860: Cite to A.I.R., Indian Dec., or I.L.R., in that order of preference. When citing to A.I.R. or to I.L.R., give the state or regional jurisdiction parenthetically.

All India Reporter (different series for each state)	1914–date	e.g., 1954 A.I.R. 74 (Del.) 45
Indian Decisions	1774–date	Indian Dec.
Indian Law Reports (different series for each region)	1876–date	e.g., I.L.R. 53 (Cal.) 182

Statutory and regulatory compilations: Cite to A.I.R. only if material does not appear in one of the other compilations listed below.

India Code	INDIA CODE
Code of Civil Procedure	INDIA CODE CIV. PROC.
Code of Criminal Procedure	INDIA CODE CRIM. PROC.
Hindu Code	HINDU CODE
Indian Penal Code	INDIA PEN. CODE
General Statutory Rules and Orders	INDIA GEN. R. & O.
A.I.R. Manual: Unrepealed Central Acts (2d ed.)	INDIA A.I.R. MANUAL

T
T.2

Session laws and regulations

Citation format: <compilation> <part> (<year>), <name of law and issuing authority>, <place>, <date>.

C.I.S. Part I (1984), Order under Sec. 5 of the XYZ Ministry of ABC, New Delhi, 28 Jan. 1984.

Central Acts	India Cen. Acts
Subsidiary Legislation	India Subs. Leg.
Current Indian Statutes	C.I.S.

Ireland (Éire), Republic of
(Common Law)

Cases
Citation format: [<year>] <volume> <reporter> <page>.

> [1985] 1 I.R. 234.

Supreme Court of Éire (Ir. S.C.), **High Court** (Ir. H. Ct.), and **Court of Criminal Appeal** (Ir. C.C.A.): Cite to I.R. if therein; otherwise cite to I.L.T.R., I.L.R.M., I.L.R., Ir. Jur. Rep., or Frewen.

Employment Law Reports	1990–date	E.L.R.	e.g., [1990] E.L.R. 155
Irish Company Law Reports	1963–1993	I.C.L.R.	
Irish Reports	1868–date	I.R.	e.g., KSK Enter. Ltd. v. An Bord Pleanala, [1994] 2 I.R. 128, 135 (Ire.)
Irish Law Times Reports	1866–1980	I.L.T.R.	
Irish Law Reports Monthly	1976–date	I.L.R.M.	e.g., Director of Public Prosecutions v. Carolan, [1998] 2 I.L.R.M. 212 (Ir. H. Ct.)
Irish Law Reports	1838–1912	I.L.R.	
Irish Jurist Reports	1935–1966 1849–1866	Ir. Jur. Rep.	
Irish Tax Reports	1922–1927	I.T.R.	
Frewen	1924–1989	Frewen	e.g., 2 Frewen 57

Constitution: Cite by article, name of constitution, and year.

Irish Constitution (Bunreacht nah Eireann)	e.g., Art. 2, Constitution of Ireland, 1937
Constitution of the Irish Free State (Saorstat Eireann)	e.g., Art. 5, Constitution of the Irish Free State, 1922

Statutory compilations and session laws: Cite by title of act, number, and year.

Acts of the Oireachtas	1937–date e.g., Emergency Powers Act
Acts of the Oireachtas (Saorstát Éireann)	1922–1937

Administrative materials

Statutory Instruments	1947–date	S.I.
Statutory Rules and Orders	1922–1947	S.R. & O.

Parliamentary debates: Cite by volume, column, and full date.

| Dáil Debates | 1922–date | e.g., 83 DÁIL DEB. col. 556 (Feb. 17, 1979) |
| Seanad Debates | 1922–date | e.g., 87 SEANAD DEB. col. 970 (Mar. 21, 1977) |

Committee or commission reports

| White Papers (cite by title, parliament number, and date) | e.g., REPORT TO THE COMMITTEE TO RECOMMEND CERTAIN SAFEGUARDS FOR PERSONS IN CUSTODY AND FOR MEMBERS OF AN GARDA SIOCHANA, Prl. 3632 (1974) |

Treaty Series

| Ireland Treaty Series | 1930-date | year Ir. T.S. No. x |

Israel
(Common Law)

Supreme Court (S. Ct.): functions both as a **Court of Appeal**, hearing civil appeals (C.A.) and criminal appeals (Cr.A.) from the district courts; and a **High Court of Justice** (H.C.), sitting as court of first instance in constitutional and administrative cases. Cite to Piskei Din (P.D.), reports of decisions of the Supreme Court of Israel, 1948–date. Citation format: type of procedure, procedure number, parties' names, reporter volume, reporter abbreviation, first page of case, specific page referred to:

C.A. 579/83, Zonnenstein v. Gabasso, 42(2) P.D. 278, 289.

District Courts (D.C.): five district courts, hearing civil appeals (C.A.) and criminal appeals (Cr.A.) from the magistrate courts, and major civil claims (C.C.) and severe criminal cases (Cr.C.). Cite to Psakim Mehoziim (P.M.), reports of decisions of the district courts of Israel, 1948–date. Citation format: type of procedure, abbreviation of the district court's name (in parentheses), procedure number, parties' names, reporter volume, reporter abbreviation, first page of case, specific page referred to. The district court's names are: Jerusalem (Jm.), Tel-Aviv (T.A.), Haifa (Hi.), Be'er-Sheva (B.S.), and Nazareth (Nz.).

Cr.C. (Hi.) 181/85, The State of Israel v. Edri, 1988(1) P.M. 419, 425.

Statutes: Cite to Laws of the State of Israel (L.S.I.), authorized English translation of legislative enactment, 1949–date. Citation format: statute's name, year of legislation, code volume, abbreviation of code cited, first page of the statute, year of volume's publication.

The Contracts (General Part) Law, 1973, 27 L.S.I. 117, (1972–73).

If citation to the L.S.I. is impossible (the translation is partial), cite Sefer HaHukim (S.H.), legislative enactment of the Knesset (Israel legislator), 1949–date. Citation format: statute's name, year of legislation, abbreviation of code cited, specific page referred to.

The Contracts (General Part) Law, 1973, S.H. 118.

Legislative history: for legislative draft bills, cite to Hatza'ot Hok (H.H.), 1949–date. Citation format: suggested statute's name, year in which the draft was submitted, series' abbreviations, first page of the suggested legislation.

Draft bill amending the Income Tax Order (no. 21), 1974 H.H., 142.

For protocols of Knesset proceedings, cite to Divrei HaKnesset (D.K.), 1949–date. Citation format: series' abbreviations, the year in parentheses, first page of the records.

D.K. (1966) 2085.

Subsidiary legislation and regulation: cite to Kovetz HaTakanot (K.T.), regulation of the State of Israel, 1949–date. Citation format: subsidiary legislation name, year of legislation, series' abbreviation, volume number, first page of the subsidiary legislation.

Knesset Election ordinances, 1970, K.T. 2454, 42.

Treaties and conventions: cite to Kitvei Amana (K.A.), treaty and convention authorized by Israel. Citation format: treaty's name, series' abbreviation, volume number, first page of treaty.

Universal Copyrights Convention, K.A. 5, 1.

Italy, Republic of
(Civil Law)

Cases
Citation format: <court name>, <court session>, <date>, <case number>, <reporter or journal>, <section number>, <page or column number>.

Cass., sez. un., 17 nov. 1975, n.3852, Giur. It. 1977, I, 1, 132.

Ordinary jurisdiction: Corte di cassazione (Cass.) (court of last appeal in civil and criminal matters), **Corte d'appello** (Corte app.) (regional court of appeal), **Tribunale** (Trib.) (ordinary court of first instance), **Corte d'assise** (Corte ass.) (court of original jurisdiction for very serious crimes), and **Pretore** (Pret.) and **Conciliatore** (Concil.) (courts of petty jurisdiction): Cite to Foro It. or Giur. It. if therein.

Foro Italiano	1876–date	
Corte cost., cass.		Foro It. I
Criminal cases		Foro It. II
Administrative courts		Foro It. III
EEC and foreign cases		Foro It. IV
Miscellaneous		Foro It. V
Giurisprudenza Italiana (indicate section)	1849–date	e.g., Giur. It. II
Giurisprudenza completa della Corte suprema di cassazione	1944–1955	Giur. Compl. Cass. Civ., Giur. Compl. Cass. Crim.
Giurisprudenza delle imposte Dirette di registro e di negoziazione	1928–date	Giur. Imp. Reg. Negoz.
Giustizia civile (indicate section)	1951–date	e.g., Giust. Civ. II
Giustizia penale (indicate section)	1895–date	e.g., Giust. Pen. I

Administrative jurisdiction: Consiglio di stato (Cons. stato) (court of last appeal in administrative matters), **Tribunale amministrativo regionale** (Trib. ammin. reg.) (regional administrative court of first instance), **Corte dei conti** (Corte cont.) (high court for fiscal matters), and **Giunta provinciale amministrativa** (Giun. pro. ammin.) (formerly, the administrative court of first instance), **Consiglio di giustizia amministrativa per la Regione siciliana** (Cons. gius. ammin. reg. sic.) (administrative judicial body for the region of Sicily): Cite to Foro Amm. or Giur. It. if therein.

Foro Amministrativo	1925–date	e.g., Foro Amm. III
Giurisprudenza Italiana	1849–date	e.g., Giur. It. II

Constitutional jurisdiction: Corte costituzionale (Corte cost.) (highest court for constitutional matters): Cite to Racc. uff. corte cost. and to either Foro It. or Giur. It.

Raccolta ufficiale delle sentenze e ordinanze delle Corte costituzionale	1956–date	Racc. uff. corte cost.

Constitution

Costituzione	Cost.

Codes

Codice civile	C.C.
Codice di commercio (merged with Codice civile in 1942)	C. comm.
Codice della navigazione	C. nav.
Codice penale	C.P.
Codice di procedura civile	C.P.C.
Codice di procedura penale	C.P.P.

Statutes and decrees: Cite to Racc. Uff. or Gazz. Uff., or, if appropriate, to the official reporter for an autonomous region; give a parallel citation to Lex, Le Leggi, or Legisl. Ital. Cite by designation (e.g., Law, Royal Decree, Royal Decree-Law, Presidential Decree, Decree-Law, or Ministerial Decree), and give the exact dates of both the law's passage and its publication in Gazz. Uff., and its law number.

Gazzetta Ufficiale della Repubblica Italiana		Gazz. Uff.
Raccolta Ufficiale degli Atti Normativi della Repubblica Italiana	1987–date	Racc. Uff.
Raccolta Ufficiale delle Leggi e dei Decreti della Repubblica Italiana	–1987	Racc. Uff.
Bollettino Ufficiale della Sardegna		Boll. Uff. della Sardegna
Gazzetta Ufficiale della Sicilia		Gazz. Uff. della Sicilia
Lex—Legislazione Italiana (Utet) (indicate part)		Lex
Le Leggi (Sefi)		Le Leggi
La Legislazione Italiana (Giuffrè)		
National legislation		Legisl. Ital. I
Parliamentary reports		Legisl. Ital. II
Regional legislation		Legisl. Ital. III

Treaties and conventions

Trattati e Convenzioni fra L'Italia e gli Altri Stati	1861–1945	x Trattati e Convenzioni xxx

Current treaties are printed in Gazzeta Ufficiale and Raccolta Ufficiale when they are promulgated in the form of a law incorporating the text of the treaty. Cite current treaties according to **rule 21.4.5(b)** followed by a cite to either Gazz. Uff. or Racc. Uff., using the format given above.

Japan
(Civil Law)

Cases

Citation format: <plaintiff> v. <defendant>, <volume> <reporter or periodical> <page(s)> (<court>, <date>); or <defendant>, <volume> <reporter> <page(s)> (<agency>, <date>).

> Hayashi v. Uchiyama, 23 MINSHŪ 441, 444–45 (Sup. Ct., Feb. 27, 1969); K.K. Kyōeisha, 32 SHINKĒTSUSHŪ 3 (FTC, Apr. 18, 1985).

A. Cases under the Constitution of 1946.

Saikō Saibansho (Supreme Court: court of last appeal in all matters): Cite to reporters such as MINSHŪ or KEISHŪ if therein; otherwise cite to either reporters below, or topical reporters or periodicals. (See **"Topical Reporters"** and **"Periodicals"** sections.)

Saikō Saibansho minji hanreishū	1947–date	MINSHŪ
Saikō Saibansho keiji hanreishū	1947–date	KEISHŪ
Saikō Saibansho saibanshū minji	1947–date	SAIBANSHŪ MINJI
Saikō Saibansho saibanshū keiji	1947–date	SAIBANSHŪ KEIJI
Saibansho jihō	1948–date	SAIBANSHO JIHŌ
Saikō Saibansho minji hanrei tokuhō	1947–1950	SAIMIN HANTOKU
Saikō Saibansho keiji hanrei tokuhō	1947–1950	SAIKEI HANTOKU

Kōtō Saibansho (High Court: regional court of appeal for appeals from District, Family and Summary Courts); **Chihō Saibansho** (District Court: court of original jurisdiction in general civil and criminal cases; hears appeals from Summary Court); **Katei Saibansho** (Family Court: court of original jurisdiction in domestic relations and juvenile delinquency cases); **Kan`i Saibansho** (Summary Court: court of petty jurisdiction in minor civil and criminal cases): Cite to either reporters below, or topical reporters or periodicals (See **"Topical Reporters"** and **"Periodicals"** sections.).

Dai-Isshin keiji saiban reishū	1958	ISSHIN KEISHŪ
Kakyū saibansho minji saiban reishū	1950–1984	KAMINSHŪ
Kakyū saibansho keiji saiban reishū	1959–1968	KAKEISHŪ
Katei saiban geppō	1949–date	KASAI GEPPŌ
Keiji saiban geppō	1969–1988	KEISAI GEPPŌ
Kōtō saibansho keiji hanreishū	1947–date	KŌKEISHŪ
Kōtō saibansho keiji hanketsu tokuhō	1949–1954	KŌKEI HANTOKU
Kōtō saibansho keiji hanketsu sokuhōshū	1981–date	KŌKEI HANSOKUSHŪ
Kōtō saibansho keiji saiban tokuhō	1954–1958	KŌKEI SAITOKU
Kōtō saibansho minji hanreishū	1947–date	KŌMINSHŪ
Shōmu geppō	1955–date	SHŌMU GEPPŌ
Tōkyō Kōtō Saibansho minji hanketsu jihō	1953–date	TŌKŌMIN JIHŌ
Tōkyō Kōtō Saibansho keiji hanketsu jihō	1951–date	TŌKŌKEI JIHŌ

Topical Reporters

Chiteki zaisanken kankei minji gyōsei saiban reishū	1991–date	CHITEKI SAISHŪ
Gyōsei saiban geppō	1947–1950	GYŌSAI GEPPŌ
Gyōsei jiken saiban reishū	1950–date	GYŌSAISHŪ
Mutai zaisanken kankei minji gyōsei saiban reishū	1969–1990	MUTAI REISHŪ

Rōdō kankei minji gyōsei saiban shiryō	1948–1950	Rōsai shiryō
Rōdō kankei minji saiban reishū	1950–date	Rōminshū

Periodicals

Hanrei jihō	1953–date	Hanrei jihō
Hanrei taimuzu	1948–date	Hanrei taimuzu
Hōsō shinbun	1946–1964	Hōsō shinbun
Jurisuto	1952–date	Jurisuto
Junkan kin`yū hōmu jijō	1953–date	Kin`yū hōmu
Junkan shōji hōmu	1955–date	Shōji hōmu
Kin`yū shōji hanrei	1966–date	Kin`yū shōji
Kōtsū jiko minji saiban reishū	1968–date	Kōtsū minshū
Rōdō hanrei	1967–date	Rōdō hanrei
Rōdō hōritsu junpō	1949–date	Rōdō junpō

Kōsei Torihiki Iinkai (Fair Trade Commission: administers the enforcement of antitrust laws):

Kōsei Torihiki Iinkai shinketsushū	1975–date	Shinketsushū
Kōsei Torihiki Iinkai haijo meireishū	1962–date	Haijo meirei

B. Cases under the Constitution of 1889.

Daishin`in** or **Taishin`in (Great Court of Judicature: court of last appeal for civil and criminal matters, and the only court concerning matters of the imperial household and insurrection against the state): Cite to either reporters below, or newspapers or periodicals. (See "**Newspapers and Periodicals**" section.)

Taishin`in minji hanreishū	1922–1946	Taihan minshū
Taishin`in keiji hanreishū	1922–1947	Taihan keishū
Taishin`in minji hanketsuroku	1875–1887 1891–1921	Taihan minroku
Taishin`in keiji hanketsuroku	1875–1884 1886–1887 1891–1921	Taihan keiroku
Taishin`in minji hanketsu shōroku	1898–1921	Minshōroku
Taishin`in keiji hanketsu shōroku	1891–1921	Keishōroku
Meiji zenki Taishin`in miniji hanketsuroku	1875–1886	Meiji taihan minroku

Gyōsei Saibansho (Administrative Court: court for all administrative cases):

Gyōsei Saibansho hanketsuroku	1890–1947	Gyōroku

Newspapers and Periodicals: Cases from **Daishin`in** (Great Court of Judicature), **Kōsoin** (Court of Appeal), **Chihō Saibansho** (District Court), and **Ku Saibansho** (Ward Court).

Hōritsu shinbun	1900–1944	SHINBUN
Hōsō kiji	1891–1923	HŌSŌ KIJI
Hōsōkai zasshi	1924–1944	HŌSŌKAI ZASSHI
Hōgaku shirin	1899–1934*	SHIRIN
Taishin`in saibanrei	1926–1937	SAIBANREI
Hōritsu hyōron minpō, keihō, etc.	1912–1944	HŌRITSU HYŌRON MINPŌ, HŌRITSU HYŌRON KEIHŌ, etc.
Hōritsu shinpō	1924–1952	SHINPŌ
Taishin`in hanketsu zenshū	1934–1944	HANKETSU ZENSHŪ
Hōgaku	1932–1944*	HŌGAKU

*Publications continue to date, but cases are included through the years described above.

C. Legislative Materials

Constitutions

| Nihonkoku Kenpō (1946) | e.g., KENPŌ, art. 9, para. 2. |
| Dai Nihon Teikoku Kenpō (1889) | MEIJI KENPŌ |

Codes

Minpō (Civil code)	e.g., MINPŌ, art. 398-20, para 1, no. 1.
Shōhō (Commercial code)	SHŌHŌ
Minji soshōhō (Code of civil procedure)	MINSOHŌ
Keihō (Penal code)	KEIHŌ
Keiji soshōhō (Code of criminal procedure)	KEISOHŌ

Statutes (hōritsu): Cite statutes by name, number and year from authoritative sources such as Hōrei zensho, Kanpō, Genkō hōki sōran, Nihon genkō hōki, and Roppō zensho. Append translation, if desired.

Kenchiku kijunhō [Building standard law], Law No. 201 of 1950, art. 2, no. 9-2.

Rules and regulations (kisoku), cabinet orders (seirei), Prime Minister's Office orders (furei), ministry ordinances (shōrei), instructions (kunrei), notifications (kokuji), circulars (tsūtatsu): Cite from authoritative sources such as Hōrei zensho, Kanpō, Genkō hōki sōran, Nihon genkō hōki, Roppō zensho, and various tsūtatsushū. Append translation, if desired.

Shōnen shinpan kisoku [Rules of juvenile proceedings], Sup. Ct. Rule No. 33 of 1948, art. 26.

Treaties and conventions

Cite to treaty sets published by the Ministry of Foreign Affairs, Treaties Bureau, if therein; otherwise cite to Hōrei zensho or Kanpō. Append translation, if desired.

Jōyakushū: nikokukan jōyaku	1964–date	Nɪᴋᴏᴋᴜᴋᴀɴ ᴊōʏᴀᴋᴜsʜū
Jōyakushū: tasūkokukan jōyaku	1964–date	Tᴀsūᴋᴏᴋᴜᴋᴀɴ ᴊōʏᴀᴋᴜsʜū

> Nihonkoku to Chōka Jinmin Kyōwakoku to no aida no heiwa yōkō jōyaku [Treaty of peace and friendship between Japan and the People's Republic of China], Oct. 23, 1988, Japan-P.R.C. (Treaty No. 19), art. 2, Nɪᴋᴏᴋᴜᴋᴀɴ ᴊōʏᴀᴋᴜsʜū, 323, 327.

Mexico, United States of
(Civil Law)

Cases
Citation format: "<name of petitioner>", <volume> <reporter> <page> (<series> <year>).

> "Aragón, Raymundo," 14 S.J.F. 1109 (5a época 1924).

Federal courts: Suprema Corte de Justicia de la Nación (S.C.J.N.), the highest court of constitutional and federal jurisdiction, sits as a full court (pleno) and in chambers: First Chamber (civil and criminal), Second Chamber (administrative and labor). For decisions in the sixth and seventh *épocas*, cite to S.J.F., if therein; for decisions beginning with the eighth *época*, cite to either S.J.F. or Gaceta. If not found in S.J.F., cite to J.S.C. **Tribunales Colegiados de Circuito** (do not abbreviate): Cite to S.J.F., Bol. Info. Jud., or Gaceta Informativa de Legislación y Jurisprudencia.

Semanario Judicial de la Federación		S.J.F.
Gaceta		Gaceta
Jurisprudencia de la Suprema Corte		J.S.C.
Semanario Judicial de la Federación	1870–date	Semanario
Boletín de Información Judicial	1945–1965	Bol. Info. Jud.
Gaceta Informativa de Legislación y Jurisprudencia	–1984	Gaceta Informativa de Legislación y Jurisprudencia

Constitution

Constitución Política de los Estados Unidos Mexicanos	Cᴏɴsᴛ.

Codes

Código Civil para el Distrito Federal	C.C.D.F.
Código Civil (for each state)	e.g., C.C.Aɢᴜᴀsᴄᴀʟɪᴇɴᴛᴇs
Código de Comercio	Cóᴅ.Cᴏᴍ.
Código Penal para el Distrito Federal	C.P.D.F.

Código Penal (for each state)	e.g., C.P.Mexico
Código Federal de Procedimientos Civiles	C.F.P.C.
Código de Procedimientos Civiles para el Distrito Federal	C.P.C.D.F.
Código de Procedimientos Civiles (for each state)	e.g., C.P.C.Guerrero
Código Federal de Procedimientos Penales	C.F.P.P.
Código de Procedimientos Penales para el Distrito Federal	C.P.P.D.F.
Código de Procedimientos Penales (for each state)	e.g., C.P.P.Sonora
Código Fiscal de la Federación	C.F.F.
Ley de Competencia Económica	L.C.E.
Ley General del Equilibrio Ecológico y de Protección al Ambiente	L.G.E.E.
Ley del Impuesto Sobre la Renta	L.I.S.R.
Ley de Inversión Extranjera	L.I.E.
Ley Orgánica de la Administración Pública Federal	L.O.A.P.F.
Ley Orgánica del Poder Judicial Federal	L.O.P.J.F.
Ley Federal de Protección al Consumidor	L.F.P.C.
Ley de Quiebras y Suspensión de Pagos	L.Q.S.P.
Ley de Sociedades Mercantiles	L.S.M.
Ley de Títulos y Operaciones de Crédito	L.T.O.C.
Ley Federal del Trabajo	L.F.T.

Statutes and decrees

Citation format: "<subject matter>", <official gazette>, <date of publication>.

> "Decreto por el que se reforman y adicionan diversas disposiciones del Código de Comercio y del Código Federal de Procedimientos Civiles," D.O., 22 de julio de 1993.

Cite to D.O. for all federal legislation.

Diario Oficial de la Federación	D.O.

Netherlands, Kingdom of the (Holland)
(Civil Law)

Cases

Citation format: <plaintiff>/<defendant>, <court>, <city (except when citing HR)>, <date>, <reporter>, <publication number> (<initials of annotator>).

> Quint/Te Poel, HR 30 januari 1959, NJ 548 (ann. DJV).

Ordinary Courts: Hoge Raad der Nederlanden (HR) (highest court), **Gerechtshof** (Hof) (ordinary court of appeal), **Arrondissementsrechtbank** (Rb.) (ordinary court of first instance and court of appeal to the Kantongerecht), **Kantongerecht** (Ktg.) (court of first instance for labor, rent, and misdemeanor cases), **Hoog Militair Gerechtshof** (HMG) (military court of appeal), **Krijgsraad** (Kr.) (court martial): Cite to NJ or W.v.h.R. if therein; otherwise cite to a newspaper or periodical. When citing a decision by Hof, Rb., or Ktg., include the name of the place where the court sits immediately after the court's abbreviation.

Nederlandse Jurisprudentie	1913–date	NJ
Weekblad van het Recht (by issue number)	1839–1943	W.v.h.R.
Kort Geding	–date	KG
Kort Geding Kort		KGK

(when citing KG or KGK, name the sitting judge in lieu of party names)

Special Jurisdiction: Afdeling Rechtspraak van de Raad van State (Afd. Rechtspr.) (administrative court of highest instance), **Centrale Raad van Beroep** (CRvB) (court of appeal for Raad van Beroep and for Ambtenarengerecht), **Raad van Beroep (voor de Sociale Verzekering)** (RvB) (social security court), **Ambtenarengerecht** (Ambt.) (civil service court), **College van Beroep voor het Bedrijfsleven** (CBB) (court of appeal from decisions of public trade organizations): Cite to NJ, ARB, or RvdW.

Nederlandse Jurisprudentie	1971–date	NJ
Administratiefrechtelijke Beslissingen	1916–date	ARB
Rechtspraak van de Week	1939–date	RvdW

Tax Court: Tariefcommisie (Tar. Comm.) (court of appeal from tax decisions of administrative organs): Cite to BNB or B.

Beslissingen Nederlandse	1953–date	BNB
Belastingrechtspraak	1910–1952	B.

Constitutions

Statuut voor het Koninkrijk der Nederlanden (constitution of the federation, superior to the constitution of the Kingdom)	Statuut Ned.
Grondwet (constitution of the Kingdom)	Grw. Ned.

Codes

Burgerlijk Wetboek	BW
Nieuw Burgerlijk Wetboek	NBW

Wetboek van Burgerlijke Rechtsvordering	Rv.
Wetboek van Koophandel	WvK
Wetboek van Strafrecht	WvS
Wetboek van Strafvordering	Sv.
Faillissementswet	F.
Wet op de Rechterlijke Organisatie	R.O.

Statutes and decrees: Cite to Stb. or Hand.; a parallel citation to Alg. Med., Schuurman & Jordens, Cremers, or Fruin may be given.

Staatsblad van het Koninkrijk der Nederlanden	Stb.
Handelingen der Staten-Generaal	Hand.
Algemene Mededelingen	Alg. Med.
Nederlandse Staatswetten, editie Schuurman & Jordens	Schuurman & Jordens
Nederlandse Wetgeving, editie Cremers	Cremers
Nederlandsche Wetboeken, Fruinseries	Fruin

Treaties and conventions

Tractatenblad van het Koninkrijk der Nederlanden	1950–date	Tractatenblad

Periodicals

Nederlands Juristenblad	1926–date	NJB
Ars Aequi	1951–date	AA
Weekblad voor Privaatrecht, Notariaat en Registratie	1870–date	WPNR
Rechtsgeleerd Magazijn Themis	1839–date	RM THEMIS
Informatierecht/AMI	–date	AMI

New Zealand
(Common Law)

Cases
Citation format: <party> v. <party> [<year>] <volume> <reporter> <page>.

Anderson v. Gardner [1979] 1 N.Z.L.R. 415.

Judicial Committee of the Privy Council (P.C.): Cite to N.Z.L.R. or N.Z.P.C.C. if therein; otherwise cite to reporters listed under **United Kingdom**.

New Zealand Law Reports	1883–date	N.Z.L.R.
New Zealand Privy Council Cases	1840–1932	N.Z.P.C.C.

T
T.2

Court of Appeal (C.A.) and **High Court** (H.C.) (formerly the Supreme Court): Cite to N.Z.L.R. if therein; otherwise cite to G.L.R.

Gazette Law Reports   1898–1953   G.L.R.

Arbitration Court (Arb. Ct.): Cite to N.Z.L.R. if therein; otherwise cite to B.A.

Book of Awards   1894–date   B.A.

District Court (D.C.) (formerly the Magistrates' Court): Cite to D.C.R., M.C.D., or M.C.R.

District Court Reports   1980–date   D.C.R.
Magistrates' Court Decisions   1939–1980   M.C.D.
Magistrates' Court Reports   1906–1952   M.C.R.

Statutes, session laws, and regulations

Cite statutes, session laws, and regulations using the English statutory form, noting the jurisdiction parenthetically at the end of the citation if not otherwise clear from the context.

> Misuse of Drugs Act, 1975 (N.Z.)

Treaty Series

New Zealand Treaty Series   1950–date   year N.Z.T.S. No. x

Roman Law
(Civil Law)

Cite all Roman legal materials by the name of the individual document or fragment, as in the examples below, not by the title of a collection that includes the material. Citations to a particular English translation may be included parenthetically.

Institutes of Justinian
>   Citation format: work, book, title, section
>   e.g., J. INST. 2.23.pr.

Digest of Justinian
>   Citation format: work, book, section, item, author, work of author
>   e.g., DIG. 9.2.23.8 (Ulpian, Ad Edictum 18)

Code of Justinian
>   Citation format: work, book, title, section, emperors, date
>   e.g., CODE JUST. 2.45.3 (Diocletian & Maximian 290/293)

Novels
>   Citation format: work, number, section, date
>   e.g., NOV. 15.pr. (535)

Institutes of Gaius
>   Citation format: work, book, title
>   e.g., G. INST. 1.144 (F. de Zuleta trans.)

Code of Theodosius
    Citation format: work, book, title, section
        e.g., CODE THEOD. 8.4.14

Russian Federation
(Civil Law)

Courts: Verkhovnyi Sud RF (Verkh. Sud RF) (RF Supreme Court)
and **Plenum Verkhovnogo Suda RF** (Plenum Verkh. Suda RF)
(Plenum of the RF Supreme Court): Cite guiding explanations, directives, and decisions to Biull. Verkh. Suda RF, if therein; otherwise, cite
to a description of the case in a Russian periodical.

Biulleten' Verkhovnogo Suda RF   Biull. Verkh. Suda RF

Constitutional Court: Konstitutsionnyi Sud RF (Constitutional
Court of the RF): Cite decisions and decrees to Ross. Gazeta, Sobr.
Zakonod. RF, or Vestn. Konst. Suda RF.

Rossiiskaya Gazeta   e.g., Ross. Gazeta, 15
                                       May, 1995

Sobranie Zakonodatel'stva RF   e.g., Sobr. Zakonod.
                                       RF, 1995, No. 15
                                       [weekly], Art. No. 934

Vestnik Konstitutsionnogo Suda RF   e.g., Vestn. Konst.
                                       Suda RF, 1995, No. 9
                                       [monthly], case re:_

Arbitration Court: Vysshii Arbitrazhnyi Sud RF (the Highest
Arbitration Court of the RF): Cite decisions to Vestn. Vyssh. Arb. Suda
RF, if therein; otherwise, cite to a description of the case in a Russian
periodical.

Vestnik Vysshego Arbitrazhnogo Suda RF   e.g., Vestn. Vyssh. Arb.
                                           Suda RF, 1995, No. 9
                                           [monthly], p. 13

Other courts: Cite to a description of the case in a Russian periodical.

Constitution: Indicate the date of last amendment to the article
cited.

Konstitutsiia RF   KONST. RF (year)

Codes

Grazhdanskii Kodeks RF (Civil Code)   GK RF
Grazhdanskii Protsessual'nyi Kodeks   GPK RF
RF (Code of Civil Procedure)
Ugolovnyi Kodeks RF (Criminal Code)   UK RF

T
T.2

Ugolovno-Protsessual'nyi Kodeks RF (Code of Criminal Procedure)	UPK RF
Kodeks Zakonov o Brake, Seme i Opeke RF (Code of laws on marriage, family, and guardianship)	KZoBSO RF
Kodeks Zakonov o Trude RF (Labor Code)	KZoT RF

Statutes and decrees: Cite a federal law (federal'nyi zakon), constitutional law (federal'nyi konstitutsionnyi zakon), or decree (postanovlenie) adopted by the Federal Assembly of the Russian Federation to Sobr. Zakonod. RF, Vedomosti Fed. Sobr. RF or Ross. Gazeta. Cite an edict (ukaz) or decision (rasporiazhenie) of the President of the Russian Federation to Sobr. Zakonod. RF or Ross. Gazeta. Cite a decree (postanovlenie) or decision (rasporiazhenie) of the Government of the Russian Federation to Sobr. Zakonod. RF or Ross. Gazeta. Cite regulations of the ministries and other agencies of the Russian Federation to Biull. Norm. Akt. RF or Ross. Gazeta.

Sobranie Zakonodatel'stva RF	e.g., Sobr. Zakonod. RF, 1995, No. 10, Item 777
Vedomosti Federal'nogo Sobrania RF	Vedomosti Fed. Sobr. RF
Biulletin' Normativnykh Ministerstv i Vedomstv RF	e.g., Biull. Norm. Akt. RF, 1995, Aktov No. 9 [monthly], p. 56
Rossiiskaya Gazeta	Ross. Gazeta

Administrative regulations: For the regulations (polozhenie), instructions (instruktsiya), and clarifications (raz'yasneniya) of ministries and state agencies, cite to Biull. Norm. Akt. RF or to the publication in a Russian periodical.

Treaties and conventions

Biulletin' Mezhdunarodnykh Dogovorov RF	1993–date	x Biulletin' Mezhdunarodnykh Dogovorov RF No. x
Sbornik Mezhdunarodnykh Dogovorov SSSR	1980–1992	x Sbornik Mezhdunarodnykh Dogovorov SSSR No. x
Sbornik Deistvuiushchikh Dogovorov, Soglashenii i Konventsii, Zakliuchennykh s Inostrannymi Gosudarstvami	1924–1979	x Sbornik Deistvuiushchikh Dogovorov No. x

Periodicals

Newspapers:

Rossiiskaya Gazeta	Ross. Gazeta
Rossiiskie Vesti	Ross. Vesti
Ekonomika i Zhizn'	Ekon. i Zh.
Iuridicheskii Vestnik	Iur. Vestnik
Kommersant-Daily	Kommers.

Izvestiia	IZVESTIIA
Segodnya	SEGODNYA
Nezavisimaya	NEZAVISIMAYA

Magazines:

Zakonodatel'stvo i Ekonomika	ZAKONOD. I EKON.
Khoziaistvo i Pravo	KHOZ. I PRAVO
Gosudarstvo i Pravo	GOS. I PRAVO
Rossiiskaya Iustitsiya	ROSS. IUST.
Zakonnost'	ZAKONNOST'
Bankovskoye Delo	BANK. DELO
Financy	FINANCY
Dengi	DENGI
Kommersant	KOMMERSANT

South Africa
(Mixed jurisdiction - common & civil law)

Cases

Citation format: <year> (<volume>) <reporter> <page> (<court>).

1995 (2) SA 43 (CC).

1994 to date:

Constitutional Court (highest appellate court and occasionally court of first instance for all constitutional questions) (CC), **Appellate Division** (highest appellate court for all non-constitutional matters) (A), **Provincial & Local Divisions of Supreme Court** (original and appellate jurisdiction for all matters): Cite to SALR or BCLR if therein:

South African Law Reports	1947–date	e.g., 1995 (2) SALR 43 (CC)
Butterworths Constitutional Law Reports	1994–date	e.g., 1995 (4) BCLR 401 (SA)
South African Criminal Law Reports	1990–date	e.g., 1995 (1) SACR 45 (CC)
All South African Law Reports	1996–date	e.g., 1996 (1) AllSA 43 (CC)

1910–1994:

Judicial Committee of Privy Council (until 1950) (cite to Eng. Reports); **Appellate Division** (highest appellate court from Prov. and Local Divs. in all matters from 1950; highest domestic appellate court in all matters to 1950), **Provincial & Local Divisions of Supreme Court**, **Supreme Court (Appellate Division & Supreme Court) of Transkei** (1976–1994), **Supreme Court (Appellate Division & General Division) of Bophuthatswana** (1977–1994), **Supreme**

Court of Venda (1979–1994), **Supreme Court (Appellate Division & General Division) of Ciskei** (1981–1994): Cite to SALR if therein:

South African Law Reports	1947–date	e.g., 1994 (2) SA 434 (A)
South African Criminal Law Reports	1990–date	e.g., 1990 (1) SACR 42 (A)
Prentice-Hall Weekly Legal Series	1923–date	e.g., 1965 (1) PH, A148 (C)
Bophuthatswana Law Reports (6 vols.)	1977–1990	e.g., 4 BSC 346
Appellate Division Reports	1910–1946	e.g., 1943 A.D. 65
Cape Provincial Division Reports	1910–1946	e.g., 1943 C.P.D. 65
Eastern Districts Local Division Reports	1910–1946	e.g., 1943 E.P.D. 65
Griqualand West Local Division Reports	1910–1945	e.g., 1943 G.W.L. 65
Orange Free State Provincial Division Reports	1910–1946	e.g., 1943 O.P.D. 45
Transvaal Provincial Division Reports	1910–1946	e.g., 1910 T.P.D. 45
Witwatersrand Local Division Reports	1910–1946	e.g., 1932 W.L.D. 45
Natal Provincial Division Reports	1933–1946	e.g., 1943 N.P.D. 45
Natal Law Reports (New Series)	1879–1932	e.g., (1929) 50 N.L.R. 50
Industrial Law Reports (in I.L.J.)	1980–date	e.g., (1995) 16 I.L.J. 823 (LAC)
South African Tax Cases	1926–date	e.g., ITC No. 1328, 43 SATC 56
Bantu Appeal Court Reports	1961–date	e.g., 1963 B.A.C. 231 (S)
Native Appeal Court Reports	1952–1961	e.g., 1951 N.A.C. 231 (S)

Pre-1910:

Cape Supreme Court Reports	1880–1910	e.g., (1887) 5 S.C. 269
Reports of the Eastern Districts of the Cape of Good Hope	1891–1909	e.g., (1883) 3 E.D.C. 204
Orange River Colony Reports	1903–1909	e.g., 1905 O.R.C. 45
Transvaal Supreme Court Reports	1902–1909	e.g., 1908 T.S. 43
Witwatersrand High Court Reports	1902–1909	e.g., 1908 T.H. 18

Statutory compilations

Citation format: § 1 of Interpretation Act 33 of 1957

Butterworths Statutes of the Republic of South Africa	1910–date	BSRSA
Jutas Statutes of the Republic of South Africa	1991–date	JSRSA

Other legislation

Provincial Ordinances (collected by province by year) (1910–1994): e.g., Road Traffic Ordinance 21 of 1966 (Cape Province).

Laws of provincial legislatures (1994–date): e.g., Western Cape Colleges law 12 of 1994.

Citation format for bills, Proclamations, Regulations and other government notices (collected in Government Gazettes) (GG):

Bills: e.g., Prevention of Family Violence Bill, 1993, Bill 144-93 (GA).

Regulations: e.g., Government Notice (GN) R3/1981 *or* GN R3 of 2 January 1981.

Proclamations: e.g., Proc R255/1977 *or* Proc R255 in GG5766 of 7 October 1971.

Parliamentary debates

Hansard's Parliamentary Reports   e.g., House of Assembly
                                      Hansard 9 Dec 1993
                                      Col 14768

Spain
(Civil Law)

Cases
Citation format: S<abbreviation of the court>, <date> (<reporter>, <decision number>, <page (sometimes omitted)>).

   STS, Feb. 5, 1993 (R.J., No. 876, p. 1135).

Constitutional courts: Tribunal Constitucional (TC) (highest court on constitutional matters, divided into two chambers): Cite to B.J.C. or R.T.C., if therein; otherwise, cite to S.T.C.:

Boletín de Jurisprudencia Constitucional	B.J.C.
Repertorio Aranzadi del Tribunal Constitucional	R.T.C.
Sentencias del Tribunal Constitucional Sistematizadas y Comentadas	S.T.C.

Ordinary courts: Tribunal Supremo (TS) (highest court of ordinary jurisdiction, divided into four chambers: civil, criminal, administrative, and labor); **Audiencia Nacional** (national appellate courts of ordinary jurisdiction, divided into three chambers); **Audiencia Provincial** (provincial appellate courts in criminal and civil matters sitting in the capital of each province); **Tribunal Superior de Justicia** (TSJ) (highest court in the autonomous regions, divided into four chambers, with jurisdiction over cases arising from regional law); **Juzgado de Primera Instancia** (single-judge body sitting in the major town of each judicial district); **Juzgado de lo Contencioso Administrativo** (administrative cases); **Juzgado de lo Social** (social security); **Juzgado de Menores** (juvenile courts); **Juzgado de Vigilancia** (prison administration); **Juzgado de Paz** (justice of the peace with jurisdiction over minor civil and criminal matters). Cite to J.T.S. or R.A.J., if therein; otherwise cite to R.G.D.

Jurisprudencia del Tribunal Supremo	J.T.S.
Repertorio Aranzadi de Jurisprudencia	R.J.
Revista General de Derecho	R.G.D.

Constitution

Constitución	C.E.

Codes

Código Civil	C.C.
Código de Comercio	C.Com.
Código Penal	C.P.
Ley de Enjuiciamiento Civil	L.E.Civ.
Ley de Enjuiciamiento Criminal	L.E.Crim.
Ley de Procedimiento Administrativo	L.P.A.
Ley de Procedimiento Laboral	L.P.L.
Ley Orgánica del Poder Judicial	L.O.P.J.
Ley de la Jurisdicción Contencioso-Administrativa	L.J.C.A.
Ley Orgánica del Régimen Electoral General	L.O.R.E.G.
Ley Orgánica del Tribunal Constitucional	L.O.T.C.

Statutes and decrees

Citation format: <full title of statute>, (<compilation abbreviation> <year>, <marginal number assigned to statute>). Note: the rank of the statute (L.O., R.D.L., R.D.-Ley) is not included in the citation.

Art. X of the Labor Procedure Act (R.C.L. 1990, 922).

Cite a Ley Ordinaria (L.O.), Real Decreto (R.D.), Real Decreto Legislativo (R.D.L.), or Real Decreto Ley (R.D.-Ley) to B.O.E. or R.C.L.:

Boletín Oficial del Estado (Official Gazette)	B.O.E. (e.g., B.O.E., 1985, 166)
Repertorio Aranzadi Cronológico de Legislación	R.C.L. (e.g., R.C.L., 1985, 1463)

Switzerland
(Civil Law)

For federal legislative materials, give parallel German, French, and Italian citations, or give all citations in the language most relevant to the discussion in which the materials are cited. Cite cases in the language in which the decision is issued.

Cases

Citation format: <publication> <volume> <part> <page>.

> BGE 101 Ia 235.

Ordinary jurisdiction: Schweizerisches Bundesgericht, Tribunal fédéral suisse, Tribunale federale svizzero (federal court, highest court in Switzerland): Cite to the official publication, BGE, ATF, or DTF, if therein; otherwise cite to Pra. or JT. There are no lower federal courts; the lower courts are those of the cantons.

BundesGerichts Entscheidungen	BGE
Arrêts du Tribunal Fédéral	ATF
Decisioni del Tribunale Federale	DTF
Constitutional Cases	BGE (or ATF or DTF) Ia (I until 1972)
Administrative cases	BGE (or ATF or DTF) Ib (I until 1972)
Civil cases	BGE (or ATF or DTF) II
Bankruptcy cases	BGE (or ATF or DTF) III
Criminal cases	BGE (or ATF or DTF) IV
Social security cases	BGE (or ATF or DTF) V
Die Praxis des Bundesgerichts (Basel)	Pra.
Journal des Tribunaux	JT

Administrative: Cite administrative decisions of the federal agencies to VPB, JAAC, or GAAC:

Verwaltungspraxis der Bundesbehorden	VPB
Jurisprudence des autorités administratives de la Confédération	JAAC
Giurisprudenza della autorità amministrative della Confederazione	GAAC

Constitution

Bundesverfassung, Constitution fédérale, Costituzione federale	BV, Cst., Cost. Fed.

T.2

Codes

Schweizerisches Zivilgesetzbuch, Code civil suisse, Codice civile svizzero	ZGB, Cc, Cc
Schweizerisches Obligationenrecht, Code des obligations, Codice delle obligazioni	OR, Co, Co
Schweizerisches Strafgesetzbuch, Code pénal suisse, Codice penale svizzero	StGB, Cp, Cp

Statutes and decrees: Cite statutes, decrees, and codes to SR, RS, and RS if therein; otherwise cite to AS, RO, and RU or to BBl, FF, and FF. Some draft laws and decrees may be found in BBl, FF, and FF.

Systematische Sammlung des Bundesrechts, Recueil systématique du droit fédéral, Raccolta sistematica del diritto federale (cite by law number)		SR, RS, RS e.g., SR 210
Sammlung der Eidgenössischen Gesetze (entitled *Eidgenössische Gesetzessammlung*, 1927–1948; entitled *Amtliche Sammlung der Bundesgesetze und Verordnungen der schweizerischen Eidgenossssenschaft*, 1848–1926), Recueil officiel des lois et ordonnances de la Confédération suisse, Raccolta ufficiale delle leggi, decreti e regolamente della Confederazione svizzera (cite by year and page)	1848–date	AS, RO, RU e.g., AS 1995 90
Bundesblatt, Feuille fédérale suisse, Foglio federale svizzero (cite by year and page)		BBl, FF, FF e.g., BBl 1978 I 1493

Swiss Cantons

Cite cantonal material and give court names in the official language or languages of the canton.

Ordinary jurisdiction: Obergericht, Cour d'Appel, Corte d'Appello (cantonal court of appeal); **Bezirksgericht, Tribunal de district, Tribunale di Prima Istanza** (ordinary court of first instance); **Friedensrichter, Justice de Paix, Giudice di Pace** (court of petty jurisdiction): Cite to the official publication, if any, of the courts of that canton, if the case is found therein; otherwise, cite to one of the following sources:

Aktuelle Juristische Praxis	AJP
Basler Juristische Mitteilungen	BJM
Blätter für Zürcherische Rechtsprechung	ZR
Journal des Tribunaux, Cantonal	JT III

Schweizerische Juristenzeitung	SJZ
La Semaine Judicaire	SJ
Zeitschrift des Bernischen Juristenvereins	ZBJV
Zeitschrift für Schweizerisches Recht	ZSR
Repertorio di Giurisprudenza Patria	Rep.
Zentralblatt für Staats– und Gemeindeverwaltung	ZBl

Administrative jurisdiction: Verwaltungsgericht, Tribunal administratif, Tribunale amministrativo (administrative court): Cite to one of the sources listed above for courts of ordinary jurisdiction.

Statutes and decrees: Cite to the official compilation of the canton if therein; otherwise cite to the official gazette.

United Kingdom
(Common Law)

Cases
Citation format: <case name>, <volume> <reporter> <page> (<court if not clearly indicated by reporter> <year>).

> The King v. Lockwood, 99 Eng. Rep. 379 (K.B. 1782).

When citing to the K.B., Q.B., Ch., and P. reports (*Law Report* series), indicate the court of decision only if it is the Court of Appeal:

> Hastings v. Perkins, 1930 P. 217 (Eng. C.A.).

For the App. Cas. reports, indicate the court only if it is the Privy Council (P.C.). When citing decisions of the Privy Council, House of Lords, or other court that hears appeals from more than one jurisdiction, indicate parenthetically the jurisdiction from which the appeal was taken:

> British Columbia Elec. Ry. v. Loach, [1916] 1 App. Cas. 719 (P.C. 1915) (appeal taken from B.C.).
> Donoghue v. Stevenson, 1932 App. Cas. 562 (appeal taken from Scot.).

Judicial Committee of the Privy Council (P.C.) (matters referred by the Crown; appeals concerning certain constitutional questions from Northern Ireland; and appeals from the English Ecclesiastical Courts on certain matters, from the Probate, Divorce, and Admiralty Division in prize cases, and from the courts of the Channel Islands, the Isle of Man, the colonies, and those dominions that permit appeals from their highest courts): Cite to the Law Reports or to Eng. Rep.

Law Reports

Appeal Cases	1891–date	A.C.
	1876–1890	App. Cas.
Privy Council	1866–1875	L.R.-P.C.
English Reports—Full Reprint	1094–1873	Eng. Rep.

House of Lords (H.L.) (appeals from the English Court of Appeals, from the Scottish Court of Session, Inner House, in civil cases, from the Scottish Court-Martial Appeal Court, and from the Northern Ireland Court of Appeal): Cite to the Law Reports, to Eng. Rep., or to House of Lords section of Session Cases, listed under Scotland, in that order of preference.

Law Reports

Appeal Cases	1891–date	A.C.
	1875–1890	App. Cas.
English and Irish Appeals	1866–1875	L.R.-E. & I. App.
Scotch and Divorce Appeals	1866–1875	L.R.-S. & D. App.

Statutes

Citation format: Cite English statutes enacted before 1963 by name (often including the year), if any, regnal year(s), chapter, section, and schedule, if any:

> Supreme Court of Judicature Act, 1925, 15 & 16 Geo. 5, c. 49, § 226, sched. 6 (Eng.).

Indicate regnal years by year(s) of reign, abbreviated name of the monarch, and numeric designation of the monarch in arabic numerals; if the monarch was the first of that name, omit the numeric designation. Thus:

> 11 Hen. 7

But:

> 13 Eliz.

Abbreviate monarchs' names as follows:

Anne	Ann.	James	Jam.
Charles	Car.	Philip & Mary	Phil. & M.
Edward	Edw.	Richard	Rich.
Elizabeth	Eliz.	Victoria	Vict.
George	Geo.	William	Will.
Henry	Hen.	William & Mary	W. & M.

If a short title has been established by the Short Titles Act or the Statute Law Revision Act, it may be indicated parenthetically:

> Lord Campbell's Act (Fatal Accidents Act), 1846, 9 & 10 Vict., c. 93 (Eng.).

If the name is omitted or does not include the date or year, give the year parenthetically at the end of the citation, but before the jurisdiction:

> Hypnotism Act, 15 & 16 Geo. 6 & 1 Eliz. 2, c. 44, § 117 (1952) (Eng.).

For statutes enacted since 1962, omit the regnal year:

> Airports Authority Act, 1965, c. 16 (Eng.).

Statutory compilations and session laws: The compilation listed below includes statutes of the Commonwealth (Interregnum).

Acts and Ordinances of the Interregnum	1642–1660	ACTS & ORDS. INTERREGNUM

Administrative materials: Cite by title, year, and instrument number.

Statutory Instruments	1947–date	e.g., Patent Rules, (1958) SI 1958/73
Statutory Rules and Orders	1890–1947	Stat. R. & O.

Parliamentary debates

House of Lords, 5th series	1909–date	e.g., 218 PARL. DEB., H.L. (5th ser.) (1959) 260
House of Commons, 5th series	1909–1981	e.g., 525 PARL. DEB., H.C. (5th ser.) (1954) 300
House of Commons, 6th series	1981–date	
Parliamentary Debates, 1st to 4th series	1803–1908	e.g., 14 PARL. DEB. (2d ser.) (1826) 20
Parliamentary History of England	pre-1803	e.g., 13 PARL. HIST. ENG. 417 (1644)
Journal		H.L. JOUR., H.C. JOUR.

Committee or commission reports:
Citation format for Command Papers: title, year, [command number], page.

> LAW REFORM COMMITTEE, FIRST REPORT, 1953, Cmnd. 8809, at 4.

Abbreviate "Command" as follows:

1st series	1833–1869	[ ]
2d series	1870–1899	[C.]
3d series	1900–1918	[Cd.]
4th series	1919–1956	[Cmd.]
5th series	1957–1986	Cmnd.
6th series	1986–date	Cm.

Treaty Series: Include the Command number parenthetically:

Great Britain Treaty Series   1883–date   year Gr. Brit. T.S. No. x
(Cmnd. x)

England and Wales

Cases before 1865: Cite to Eng. Rep. if therein; otherwise cite to Rev. Rep. A preceding parallel citation to the original report may be given. In citing the Year Books, include regnal year, folio, term in which the plea was heard, and plea number; include a parallel citation to a nineteenth or twentieth century reprint if possible.

English Reports—Full Reprint	1220-1867	Eng. Rep.
Revised Reports	1785-1866	Rev. Rep.
Year Books	Y.B.	

    e.g., Y.B. 17 Edw. 4, fol. 2a, Pasch, pl. 3 (1477).

Year Books in reprint	Y.B.

    e.g., Y.B. 10 Edw. 2, Hil. 20 (1317), *reprinted in* 54 SELDEN SOCIETY 53 (1935).

Cases after 1864: Cite to Law Reports if therein. (Series and abbreviations of Law Reports are given under the separate court listings below.) Otherwise cite to W.L.R., All E.R., L.T.R., L.J.R., T.L.R., W.N., or another reporter, in that order of preference.

Law Reports—*see* listings under separate court designations below		
Weekly Law Reports	1953–date	W.L.R.
All England Law Reports	1936–date	All E.R.
Law Times Reports	1859–1947	L.T.R.
Law Times Reports, Old Series	1843–1859	L.T.O.S.
Law Journal Reports	1947–1949	L.J.R.
L.J.R., King's Bench, New Series	1831–1946	L.J.K.B.
L.J.R., King's Bench, Old Series	1822–1831	L.J.K.B.O.S.
Times Law Reports	1884–1952	T.L.R.
Weekly Notes	1866–1952	W.N.
Annotated Tax Cases	1922–date	Ann. Tax Cas.
Commercial Cases	1896–1941	Com. Cas.
De-Rating Appeals	1930–date	D.R.A.
Industrial Cases Reports (formerly Industrial Court Reports)	1975–date	I.C.R.
Justice of the Peace and Local Government Review Reports	1837–date	J.P.R.
Knight's Local Government Reports	1903–date	Knight's Local Gov't R.
Lloyd's List Law Reports	1951–date	Lloyd's Rep.
Lloyd's List Law Reports	1919–1950	Lloyd's List L. Rep.
Magisterial Cases	1896–1946	Mag. Cas.

Property Planning and Compensation Reports	1986–date	P.P. & C.R.
Property and Compensation Reports (formerly Planning and Compensation Reports)	1949–1985	P. & C.R.
Rating and Valuation Reporter	1960–date	R. & V.R.
Rating Appeals	1962–date	R.A.
Reports of Patent, Design, and Trade Mark Cases	1884–date	R.P.D.T.M.C. /R.P.C.
Reports of Patent Cases	1884–1885	R.P.C.
Reports of Tax Cases	1875–date	T.C.
Road Haulage Cases	1950–date	R.H.C.
Road Traffic Reports	1970–date	R.T.R.
Simon's Tax Cases	1973–date	S.T.C.
Solicitor's Journal	1857–date	Sol. J.
Taxation Reports	1939–date	T.R.

Supreme Court of Judicature (consists of the **Court of Appeal** and the **High Court of Justice** listed below).

Court of Appeal, Civil Division (C.A.) (civil appeals from divisions and divisional courts of the High Court, and from the county courts), prior to 1875 **Court of Exchequer Chamber** (Ex. Ch.): There is no Court of Appeal series of reports; cases are reported in the series of the courts below. Thus, for example, cite an appeal from Queen's Bench to Queen's Bench reports.

Court of Appeal, Criminal Division (C.A.), 1907–1966 **Court of Criminal Appeal** (Crim. App.), previously **Court of Crown Cases Reserved** (Cr. Cas. Res.) (appeals from Assizes and Quarter Sessions): Cite to Queen's (King's) Bench, listed below, or to L.R.-Cr. Cas. Res. if therein; otherwise cite to Crim. App. if therein.

Law Reports

Crown Cases Reserved	1865–1875	L.R.-C.C.R.
Criminal Appeal Reports	1908–date	Crim. App. R.

High Court of Justice (consisting of three parts, which sit both as courts of first instance, in which case they are known as the **Queen's (King's) Bench Division,** the **Chancery Division,** and the **Family Division,** and as courts of limited appellate jurisdiction, in which case they are known as divisional courts (e.g., the Queen's Bench Divisional Court)).

Queen's (King's) Bench Division (Q.B., K.B.) (trials in tort and contract and other commercial claims) and **Queen's (King's) Bench Divisional Court** (Q.B. Div'l Ct., K.B. Div'l Ct.) (appeals from magistrate's courts and Quarter Sessions), prior to 1875 **Court of Queen's**

(King's) Bench (Q.B., K.B.); incorporated in 1880 **Common Pleas Division** (C.P.D.) 1875–1880, previously **Court of Common Pleas** (C.P.) and **Exchequer Division** (Ex. D.) 1875–1880, previously **Court of Exchequer** (Ex.); also incorporated all nonfamily jurisdiction of Probate, Divorce, and Admiralty Division in 1971: Cite to Q.B., K.B., C.P., or Ex. if therein.

Law Reports

Queen's and King's Bench	1952–date	Q.B.
	1901–1951	K.B.
	1891–1900	Q.B.
	1875–1890	Q.B.D.
	1865–1875	L.R.-Q.B.
Common Pleas	1875–1880	C.P.D.
	1865–1875	L.R.-C.P.
Exchequer	1875–1880	Ex. D.
	1865–1875	L.R.-Ex.

Chancery Division (Ch.) (original equity jurisdiction: e.g., trusts, estates, wardship, mortgages, tax, partnership, and company law) and **Chancery Divisional Court** (Ch. Div'l Ct.) (appeals from, e.g., county court in bankruptcy, Industrial Injuries Commissioner, Chief Land Registrar), prior to 1875 the **Chancellor's Court** (Ch.), **Rolls Court** (M.R.), **Vice-Chancellors' Courts** (V.C.), and **Court of Appeal in Chancery** (Ch. App.): Cite to L.R.-Ch. or L.R.-Eq. if therein.

Law Reports

Chancery	1891–date	Ch.
	1875–1890	Ch. D.
	1866–1875	L.R.-Ch.
Equity	1866–1875	L.R.-Eq.

Family Division (Fam.) and **Family Divisional Court** (Fam. Div'l Ct.); 1875–1971 **Probate, Divorce, and Admiralty Division** (P.) and **Probate Divisional Court** (P. Div'l Ct.); previously **Court of Probate** (P.), **Court of Divorce and Matrimonial Causes** (D.), and **High Court of Admiralty** (Adm.); all nonfamily jurisdiction was removed to Queen's Bench in 1971: Cite to Fam., P., or L.R. Adm. & Eccl. if therein.

Law Reports

Family	1972–date	Fam.
Probate	1891–1971	P
	1875–1890	P.D.
	1865–1875	L.R.-P. & D.
Admiralty and	1865–1875	L.R.-Adm. & Eccl.
Ecclesiastical Cases		

Ecclesiastical courts: Cite to P. or L.R.-Adm. & Eccl., listed above, if therein.

County Courts (sixty-four circuits geographically unrelated to the counties; original jurisdiction of most civil cases under a specified amount in controversy): Cite according to **Cases after 1864** above.

Assizes (seven circuits), **Crown Courts** (Liverpool and Manchester), and the **Central Criminal Court,** previously **Old Bailey** (London) (original jurisdiction of most serious indictable offenses); **Quarter Sessions** (original jurisdiction of most indictable offenses; de novo review of magistrates' courts); **Magistrates' courts,** previously **Justices of the Peace** (trials of minor offenses): Cite according to **Cases after 1864** above.

Northern Ireland
(and Ireland Until 1924)

All courts (The court structure is similar to the English): Cite to N. Ir., Ir. R., L.R. Ir., Ir. R.-C.L., or Ir. Jur., if therein; otherwise cite to Ir. L.T.R.

Northern Ireland Law Reports	1925–date	N. Ir. L.R.
Irish Reports	1894–date	Ir. R.
Law Reports, Ireland	1878–1893	L.R. Ir.
Irish Reports, Common Law Series	1867–1878	Ir. R.-C.L.
Irish Jurist Reports	1849–1867	Ir. Jur.
Irish Law Times Reports	1867–date	Ir. L.T.R.

Statutory compilations and session laws

Northern Ireland Statutes	1972–date	N. Ir. Stat.
Northern Ireland Public General Acts	1947–1971	N. Ir. Pub. Gen. Acts
Northern Ireland Public General Statutes	1921–1946	N. Ir. Pub. Gen. Stat.
Statutes Revised, Northern Ireland		N. Ir. Rev. Stat.

Regulations

Statutory Rules and Orders of Northern Ireland	1922–date	Stat. R. & O.N. Ir.

Scotland

Court of Session (Sess.) (general original and appellate jurisdiction of civil cases): Cite to Sess. Cas.

Session Cases, Court of Session section	1906–date	Sess. Cas.
Fifth Series (edited by Fraser)	1898–1906	F.
Fourth Series (edited by Rettie)	1873–1898	R.
Third Series (edited by MacPherson)	1862–1873	M.

T
T.2

Second Series (edited by Dunlop)   1838–1862 D.
  First Series (edited by Shaw)   1821–1838 S.

High Court of Justiciary (H.C.J.) (criminal appeals and trials of the most serious crimes): Cite to J.C. or to Sess. Cas. (J.).

Justiciary Cases (sometimes bound with Session Cases)	1917–date	J.C.
Session Cases, High Court of Justiciary section	1906–1916	Sess. Cas. (J.)
Fifth Series (edited by Fraser)	1898–1906	F. (J.)
Fourth Series (edited by Rettie)	1873–1898	R. (J.)

Statutes

The Acts of the Parliaments of Scotland	1814–1875 1124–1707	Scot. Parl. Acts

Intergovernmental Organizations   T.3

United Nations

Principal Organs: In citations to official records, abbreviate the records of the principal organs of the United Nations as follows:

General Assembly	GAOR
Security Council	SCOR
Economic and Social Council	ESCOR
Trusteeship Council	TCOR
Trade and Development Board of the Conference on Trade and Development	TDBOR

Courts: International Court of Justice (I.C.J.): Cite decisions to I.C.J.; cite separately published pleadings to I.C.J. Pleadings; cite rules and acts to I.C.J. Acts & Docs.

Report of Judgments, Advisory Advisory Opinions, and Orders	1946–date	year I.C.J. xx
Pleadings, Oral Arguments, Documents	1946–date	year I.C.J. Pleadings xx
Acts and Documents	1946–date	year I.C.J. Acts & Docs. xx

Treaties and international agreements: Cite to U.N.T.S.

United Nations Treaty Series	1946–date	x U.N.T.S. xxx

League of Nations

Courts: Permanent Court of International Justice (P.C.I.J.): Cite decisions, separately published pleadings, and rules and acts to P.C.I.J., indicating the series and the case or document number:

Report of Judgments, Advisory Opinions, and Orders	1920–1945	19xx P.C.I.J. (ser. X) No. x

Treaties and international agreements: Cite to L.N.T.S.

League of Nations Treaty Series	1920–1945	x L.N.T.S. xxx (19xx)

European Communities

Courts: Cite cases before the **Court of Justice of the European Communities** (E.C.J.) and the **Court of First Instance** (Ct. First Instance) to E.C.R., if therein. If not, cite to C.M.L.R., or to Common Mkt. Rep. (CCH) or CEC (CCH), if therein, in that order of preference. Always provide a parallel citation to C.M.L.R., if possible; otherwise provide a parallel citation to Common Mkt. Rep. (CCH), or CEC (CCH), if possible.

Report of Cases Before the Court of Justice of the European Communities	1973–date	year E.C.R. xxx
Common Market Law Reports	–date	C.M.L.R.
European Community Cases	1989–date	CEC (CCH)
Common Market Reports	–1988	Common Mkt. Rep. (CCH)

Legislative acts: Cite acts of the **Council** and **Commission** to O.J., if therein; otherwise cite to O.J. SPEC. ED., if therein; otherwise cite to J.O. For issues of J.O. before 1967, always indicate the issue number. For issues of O.J. and J.O. dating from 1967 and later, always indicate the series and issue number.

Official Journal of the European Community	1973–date	e.g., 1973 O.J. (L 337) 7
Official Journal of the European Community, Special Edition	Covering the years before 1973	e.g., 1965–1966 O.J. SPEC. ED. 265
Journal Officiel des Communautés Européennes	1958–date	e.g.,1971 J.O. (L 20) 1

Parliamentary documents: Cite as follows:

European Parliamentary Debates	EUR. PARL. DEB. (XX) x
European Parliament Working Session or Session Documents	EUR. PARL. DOC. (COM xx) x
Parlement Européen Documents de Séance	PARL. EUR. DOC. (SEC xx) x

European Court and Commission of Human Rights

European Court of Human Rights: Cite to Eur. Ct. H.R. or to Y.B. Eur. Conv. on H.R.:

European Court of Human Rights	xx Eur. Ct. H.R. (xxxx)
Yearbook of the European Convention on Human Rights	Y.B. Eur. Conv. on H.R.

European Commission of Human Rights: Cite to Eur. Comm'n H.R. Dec. & Rep., Y.B. Eur. Conv. on Human Rights, or Eur. H.R. Rep., in that order of preference:

Collections of Decisions of the European Commission of Human Rights	xx Eur. Comm'n H.R. Dec. & Rep. xxx

European Human Rights Reports   xx Eur. H.R. Rep. xxx

Inter-American Commission on Human Rights

Cite to Inter-Am. C.H.R.:

Annual Report of the Inter-American   Case No. xx, Inter-Am.
Commission on Human Rights   C.H.R. xx

East African Court of Appeal

Cite to E. Afr. L. Rep., E. Afr. Ct. App. Dig., or to E. Afr. Ct. App.:

East Africa Law Reports   1956–date E. Afr. L. Rep.

Court of Appeal for East Africa   1956–date E. Afr. Ct. App. Dig.
Digest of Decisions of the Court

Law Reports of the Court of   1934–1956 E. Afr. Ct. App.
Appeal for Eastern Africa

Other Intergovernmental Organizations

International Labour Organisation   ILO

International Civil Aviation Organization   ICAO

World Health Organization   WHO

International Telecommunication Union   ITU

International Maritime Organization   IMO
(until May 1982 known as the Intergovernmental Maritime Consultative
Organization)

International Atomic Energy Agency   IAEA

General Agreement on Tariffs and Trade   GATT

World Trade Organization   WTO

World Meteorological Organization   WMO

Names of other organizations should be written out the first time they
are used with a parenthetical in brackets indicating the abbreviation
to be used in subsequent citations.

T
T.3

T.4   Treaty Sources

Dates refer to the years of the treaties contained in the source, not to the years
in which the source was published.

Official U.S. sources

United States Treaties and Other International Agreements	1950–date	x U.S.T. xxx
Statutes at Large	1778–1949 (indexed at 64 Stat. B1107)	x Stat. xxx
Treaties and Other International Acts Series	1945–date	T.I.A.S. No. x
Treaty Series	1778–1945	T.S. No. x
Executive Agreement Series	1922–1945	E.A.S. No. x
Senate Treaty Documents	1981–date	S. TREATY DOC. NO. x
Senate Executive Documents	1778–1980	S. EXEC. DOC. x

Intergovernmental treaty sources

United Nations Treaty Series	1946–date	x U.N.T.S. xxx
League of Nations Treaty Series	1920–1945	x L.N.T.S. xxx
Pan-American Treaty Series	1949–date	x Pan-Am. T.S. xxx
European Treaty Series	1948–date	Europ. T.S. No. x

Unofficial treaty sources

International Legal Materials	1962–date	x I.L.M. xxx
Nouveau recueil général des traités	1494–1943	x Martens Nouveau Recueil (ser. x) xxx
Parry's Consolidated Treaty Series	1648–1919	x Consol. T.S. xxx
Hein's United States Treaties and Other International Agreements	1984–date	Hein's No. KAV xxxx
Bevans	1776–1949	x Bevans xxx

Arbitral Reporters T.5

The following list gives abbreviations for frequently cited arbitration reporters. See **rule 21.6** for guidance on citing international arbitrations.

Arbitration Materials	Arb. Mat'l
Hague Court Reports, First Series	Hague Ct. Rep. (Scott)
Hague Court Reports, Second Series	Hague Ct. Rep. 2d (Scott)
International Centre for Settlement of Investment Disputes (World Bank ICSID)	ICSID (W. Bank)
International Chamber of Commerce Arbitration	Int'l Comm. Arb.
Iran-United States Claims Tribunal Reports	Iran-U.S. Cl. Trib. Rep.
Tribunaux Arbitraux Mixtes	Trib. Arb. Mixtes
United Nations Reports of International Arbitral Awards	R.I.A.A.
World Arbitration Reporter	World Arb. Rep. (issue number)

T
T.5

T.6   Case Names

Abbreviate case names in citations by abbreviating any word listed below (**rule 10.2.2**). It is permissible to abbreviate other words of eight letters or more if *substantial* space is thereby saved and the result is unambiguous. Unless otherwise indicated, plurals are formed by adding the letter "s".

Academy	Acad.	Cooperative	Coop.
Administrat[ive, ion]	Admin.	Corporation	Corp.
Administrat[or, rix]	Adm'[r, x]	Correction [s, al]	Corr.
Advertising	Adver.	Defense	Def.
Agricultur[e, al]	Agric.	Department	Dep't
America [n]	Am.	Detention	Det.
and	&	Development	Dev.
Associate	Assoc.	Director	Dir.
Association	Ass'n	Discount	Disc.
Atlantic	Atl.	Distribut[or, ing]	Distrib.
Authority	Auth.	District	Dist.
Automo[bile, tive]	Auto.	Division	Div.
Avenue	Ave.	East [ern]	E.
Bankruptcy	Bankr.	Econom[ic, ics, ical, y]	Econ.
Board	Bd.	Education [al]	Educ.
Broadcast [ing]	Broad.	Electric [al, ity]	Elec.
Brotherhood	Bhd.	Electronic	Elec.
Brothers	Bros.	Engineer	Eng'r
Building	Bldg.	Engineering	Eng'g
Business	Bus.	Enterprise	Enter.
Casualty	Cas.	Entertainment	Entm't
Cent[er, re]	Ctr.	Environment	Env't
Central	Cent.	Environmental	Envtl.
Chemical	Chem.	Equality	Equal.
College	Coll.	Equipment	Equip.
Commission	Comm'n	Examiner	Exam'r
Commissioner	Comm'r	Exchange	Exch.
Committee	Comm.	Execut[or, rix]	Ex'[r, x]
Community	Cmty.	Export [er, ation]	Exp.
Company	Co.	Federal	Fed.
Compensation	Comp.	Federation	Fed'n
Condominium	Condo.	Fidelity	Fid.
Congress [ional]	Cong.	Financ[e, ial, ing]	Fin.
Consolidated	Consol.	Foundation	Found.
Construction	Constr.	General	Gen.
Continental	Cont'l	Government	Gov't

Guaranty	Guar.	Property	Prop.
Hospital	Hosp.	Protection	Prot.
Housing	Hous.	Public	Pub.
Import [er, ation]	Imp.	Publication	Publ'n
Incorporated	Inc.	Publishing	Publ'g
Indemnity	Indem.	Railroad	R.R.
Independent	Indep.	Railway	Ry.
Industr[y, ies, ial]	Indus.	Refining	Ref.
Information	Info.	Regional	Reg'l
Institut[e, ion]	Inst.	Rehabilitation	Rehab.
Insurance	Ins.	Reproduct[ion, ive]	Reprod.
International	Int'l	Resource [s]	Res.
Investment	Inv.	Restaurant	Rest.
Laboratory	Lab.	Retirement	Ret.
Liability	Liab.	Road	Rd.
Limited	Ltd.	Savings	Sav.
Litigation	Litig.	School [s]	Sch.
Machine [ry]	Mach.	Science	Sci.
Maintenance	Maint.	Secretary	Sec'y
Management	Mgmt.	Securit[y, ies]	Sec.
Manufacturer	Mfr.	Service	Serv.
Manufacturing	Mfg.	Shareholder	S'holder
Maritime	Mar.	Social	Soc.
Market	Mkt.	Society	Soc'y
Marketing	Mktg.	South [ern]	S.
Mechanic [al]	Mech.	Steamship [s]	S.S.
Medic[al, ine]	Med.	Street	St.
Memorial	Mem'l	Subcommittee	Subcomm.
Merchan[t, dise, dising]	Merch.	Surety	Sur.
Metropolitan	Metro.	System [s]	Sys.
Municipal	Mun.	Technology	Tech.
Mutual	Mut.	Telecommunication	Telecomm.
National	Nat'l	Tele[phone, graph]	Tel.
North [ern]	N.	Temporary	Temp.
Organiz[ation, ing]	Org.	Transcontinental	Transcon.
Pacific	Pac.	Transport [ation]	Transp.
Partnership	P'ship	Trustee	Tr.
Person [al, nel]	Pers.	Turnpike	Tpk.
Pharmaceutic[s, al]	Pharm.	Uniform	Unif.
Preserv[e, ation]	Pres.	University	Univ.
Probation	Prob.	Utility	Util.
Product [ion]	Prod.	Village	Vill.
Professional	Prof'l	West [ern]	W.

T.7   Court Names

The following alphabetical list provides abbreviations for court names to be used in citing cases according to **rule 10.4**.

Administrative Court	Admin. Ct.
Admiralty [Court, Division]	Adm.
Aldermen's Court	Alder. Ct.
Appeals Court	App. Ct.
Appellate Court	App. Ct.
Appellate Department	App. Dep't
Appellate Division	App. Div.
Armed Services Board of Contract Appeals	A.S.B.C.A.
Bankruptcy Appellate Panel	B.A.P.
Bankruptcy [Court, Judge]	Bankr.
Board of Contract Appeals	B.C.A.
Board of Immigration Appeals	B.I.A.
Board of Tax Appeals	B.T.A
Borough Court	[name] Bor. Ct.
Central District	C.D.
Chancery [Court, Division]	Ch.
Children's Court	Child. Ct.
Circuit Court (old federal)	C.C.
Circuit Court (state)	Cir. Ct.
Circuit Court of Appeals (federal)	Cir.
Circuit Court of Appeals (state)	Cir. Ct. App.
City Court	[name] City Ct.
Civil Appeals	Civ. App.
Civil Court of Record	Civ. Ct. Rec.
Civil District Court	Civ. Dist. Ct.
Claims Court	Cl. Ct.
Commerce Court	Comm. Ct.
Commission	Comm'n
Common Pleas	C.P. [when appropriate, name county or similar subdivision]
Commonwealth Court	Commw. Ct.
Conciliation Court	Concil. Ct.
County Court	[name] County Ct.
County Judge's Court	County J. Ct.
Court	Ct.
Court of Appeal (English)	C.A.

Court of Appeals (federal)	Cir.
Court of Appeal [s] (state)	Ct. App.
Court of Appeals for the Armed Forces	C.A.A.F.
Court of Civil Appeals	Civ. App.
Court of Claims	Ct. Cl.
Court of Common Pleas	Ct. Com. Pl.
Court of Criminal Appeals	Crim. App.
Court of Customs and Patent Appeals	C.C.P.A.
Court of Customs Appeals	Ct. Cust. App.
Court of Errors	Ct. Err.
Court of Errors and Appeals	Ct. Err. & App.
Court of Federal Claims	Ct. Fed. Cl.
Court of [General, Special] Sessions	Ct. [Gen., Spec.] Sess.
Court of International Trade	Ct. Int'l Trade
Court of Military Appeals	C.M.A.
Court of Military Review	C.M.R.
Court of Special Appeals	Ct. Spec. App.
Court of Veterans Appeals	Ct. Vet. App.
Criminal Appeals	Crim. App.
Criminal District Court	Crim. Dist. Ct.
Customs Court	Cust. Ct.
District Court (federal)	D.
District Court (state)	Dist. Ct.
District Court of Appeal [s]	Dist. Ct. App.
Division	Div.
Domestic Relations Court	Dom. Rel. Ct.
Eastern District	E.D.
Emergency Court of Appeals	Emer. Ct. App.
Equity [Court, Division]	Eq.
Family Court	Fam. Ct.
High Court	High Ct.
Judicial District	Jud. Dist.
Judicial Division	Jud. Div.
Judicial Panel on Multidistrict Litigation	J.P.M.L.
Justice of the Peace's Court	J.P. Ct.

T

T.7

Juvenile Court	Juv. Ct.
Land Court	Land Ct.
Law Court	Law Ct.
Law Division	Law Div.
Magistrate Division	Magis. Div.
Magistrate's Court	Magis. Ct.
Middle District	M.D.
Municipal Court	[name] Mun. Ct.
Northern District	N.D.
Orphans' Court	Orphans' Ct.
Parish Court	[name] Parish Ct.
Police Justice's Court	Police J. Ct.
Prerogative Court	Prerog. Ct.
Probate Court	Prob. Ct.
Public Utilities Commission	P.U.C.
Real Estate Commission	Real Est. Comm'n
Recorder's Court	Rec's Ct.
Southern District	S.D.
Special Court Regional Rail Reorganization Act	Reg'l Rail Reorg. Ct.
Superior Court	Super. Ct.
Supreme Court (federal)	U.S.
Supreme Court (other)	Sup. Ct.
Supreme Court, Appellate Division	App. Div.
Supreme Court, Appellate Term	App. Term
Supreme Court of Errors	Sup. Ct. Err.
Supreme Judicial Court	Sup. Jud. Ct.
Surrogate's Court	Sur. Ct.
Tax Appeal Court	Tax App. Ct.
Tax Court	T.C.
Teen Court	Teen Ct.
Temporary Emergency Court of Appeals	Temp. Emer. Ct. App.
Territor[ial, y]	Terr.
Traffic Court	Traffic Ct.
Tribal Court	[name] Tribal Ct.
Tribunal	Trib.
Water Court	Water Ct.
Western District	W.D.
Workmen's Compensation Division	Workmen's Comp. Div.
Youth Court	Youth Ct.

Court Documents T.8

This table gives suggested abbreviations for citations of court documents and legal memoranda (not in other forms of legal writing) for the words most commonly found in the titles of court documents. In some cases, it indicates that a word should not be abbreviated. Words of more than six letters not appearing on the list may also be abbreviated if the abbreviation selected is unambiguous. Unless it would be confusing to the reader, omit all articles and prepositions from any abbreviated title. Practitioners may also want to leave out additional words in a document title if the document can be unambiguously identified without them (see **practitioners' note P.7**). Be sure to abbreviate documents consistently throughout a particular court document or legal memorandum.

Admission	Admis.
Admit	Admit
Affidavit	Aff.
Affirm	Affirm
Amended	Am.
Answer	Answer
Appeal	Appeal
Appellant	Appellant
Appellee	Appellee
Appendix	App. (except when citing to Joint Appendix—see below)
Attach	Attach
Attachment	Attach.
Attorney [s]	Att'y [s]
Brief	Br.
Certiorari	Cert.
Compel	Compel
Complaint	Compl.
Counterclaim	Countercl.
Court	Ct.
Cross-claim	Cross-cl.
Declaration	Decl.
Defendant ['s]	Def. ['s]
Defendants [']	Defs. [']
Demurrer	Dem.
Deny [ing]	Den.
Deposition	Dep.
Discovery	Disc.
Dismiss	Dismiss
Document [s]	Doc., Docs.
Exhibit	Ex.

Grant	Grant
Hearing	Hr'g
Injunction	Inj.
Interrogator[y, ies]	Interrog., Interrogs.
Joint Appendix	J.A.
Judgment	J.
Memorandum	Mem.
Minutes	Mins.
Motion	Mot.
Opinion	Op.
Opposition	Opp'n
Order	Order
Petition	Pet.
Petitioner	Pet'r
Plaintiff ['s]	Pl. ['s]
Plaintiffs [']	Pls. [']
Points and Authorities	P. & A.
Preliminary	Prelim.
Produc[e, tion]	Produc.
Quash	Quash
Reconsideration	Recons.
Record	R.
Rehearing	Reh'g
Reply	Reply
Reporter	Rep.
Request	Req.
Respondent	Resp't
Response	Resp.
Stay	Stay
Subpoena	Subpoena
Summary	Summ.
Support	Supp.
Suppress	Suppress
Temporary Restraining Order	T.R.O.
Testimony	Test.
Transcript	Tr.
Verified Statement	V.S.

Explanatory Phrases   T.9

The following table lists a number of explanatory phrases (some of which contain abbreviations) commonly used in indicating prior or subsequent history and weight of authority of judicial decisions. As indicated below, those phrases (such as "*aff'g*" or "*overruled by*") that are followed by a case citation as their direct object are *not* followed by commas. Those phrases (such as "*cert. denied,*") introducing a case citation for the action indicated by the explanatory phrase *are* followed by commas (which are *not* italicized, see **rule 2.1(f)**). See **rule 10.7** for guidance in using explanatory phrases.

acq.	*dismissing appeal from*
acq. in result	*enforced,*
aff'd,	*enforcing*
aff'd by an equally divided court,	*mandamus denied,*
aff'd mem.,	*modified,*
aff'd on other grounds,	*modifying*
aff'd on reh'g,	*nonacq.*
aff'g	*overruled by*
amended by	*petition for cert. filed,*
appeal denied,	*prob. juris. noted,*
appeal dismissed,	*reh'g granted [denied],*
appeal docketed,	*rev'd,*
appeal filed,	*rev'd on other grounds,*
argued,	*rev'd per curiam,*
cert. denied,	*rev'g*
cert. dismissed,	*vacated,*
cert. granted,	*vacating as moot*
certifying questions to	*withdrawn,*
denying cert. to	

T

T.10   Legislative Documents

This table gives suggested abbreviations for citation of the words most commonly found in legislative documents. In some cases, it indicates that a word should not be abbreviated. Words of more than six letters not appearing on the list may also be abbreviated if the abbreviation selected is unambiguous. Omit all articles and prepositions from any abbreviated title if the document can be identified unambiguously without them.

Annals	Annals
Annual	Ann.
Assembl[y, yman, ywoman]	Assemb.
Bill	B.
Committee	Comm.
Concurrent	Con.
Conference	Conf.
Congress [ional]	Cong.
Debate	Deb.
Delegate	Del.
Document [s]	Doc.
Executive	Exec.
Federal	Fed.
House of Delegates	H.D.
House of Representatives	H.R.
Joint	J.
Legislat[ion, ive]	Legis.
Legislature	Leg.
Miscellaneous	Misc.
Number	No.
Order	Order
Record	Rec.
Register	Reg.
Regular	Reg.
Report	Rep.
Representative	Rep.
Resolution	Res.
Senate	S.
Senator	Sen.
Service	Serv.
Session	Sess.
Special	Spec.
Subcommittee	Subcomm.

Geographical Terms   T.11

The following list provides abbreviations for geographical locations for use in case citations (**rules 10.2.2** and **10.4**), names of institutional authors (**rule 15.1.3**), periodical abbreviations (**rule 16** and **table T.14**), foreign materials (**rule 20.2**), and treaty citations (**rule 21.4.3**).

States, cities, and territories of the United States

Ala.	Haw.	Mont.	R.I.
Alaska	Idaho	Neb.	S.C.
Am. Sam.	Ill.	Nev.	S.D.
Ariz.	Ind.	N.H.	S.F.
Ark.	Iowa	N.J.	Tenn.
Balt.	Kan.	N.M.	Tex.
Cal.	Ky.	N.Y.	Utah
C.Z.	L.A.	N.C.	Vt.
Chi.	La.	N.D.	V.I.
Colo.	Me.	N. Mar. I.	Va.
Conn.	Md.	Ohio	Wash.
Del.	Mass.	Okla.	W. Va.
D.C.	Mich.	Or.	Wis.
Fla.	Minn.	Pa.	Wyo.
Ga.	Miss.	Phila.	
Guam	Mo.	P.R.	

Australian states and Canadian provinces and territories

Australia		Canada	
New South Wales	N.S.W.	Alberta	Alta.
		British Columbia	B.C.
Queensland	Queensl.	Manitoba	Man.
South Australia	S. Austl.	New Brunswick	N.B.
Tasmania	Tas.	Newfoundland	Nfld.
Victoria	Vict.	Northwest Territories	N.W.T.
West Australia	W. Austl.	Nova Scotia	N.S.
		Nunavut	Nun.
		Ontario	Ont.
		Prince Edward Island	P.E.I.
		Québec	Que.
		Saskatchewan	Sask.
		Yukon	Yukon

Foreign countries and regions

Afghanistan	Afg.	Australia	Austl.
Africa	Afr.	Austria	Aus.
Albania	Alb.	Azerbaijan	Azer.
Algeria	Alg.	Bahamas	Bah.
Andorra	Andorra	Bahrain	Bahr.
Angola	Angl.	Bangladesh	Bangl.
Anguilla	Anguilla	Barbados	Barb.
Antigua & Barbuda	Ant. & Barb.	Belarus	Belr.
Argentina	Arg.	Belgium	Belg.
Armenia	Arm.	Belize	Belize

Benin	Benin	Europe	Eur.
Bermuda	Berm.	Falkland Islands	Falkland Is.
Bhutan	Bhutan	Fiji	Fiji
Bolivia	Bol.	Finland	Fin.
Bosnia & Herzegovina	Bosn. & Herz.	France	Fr.
		Gabon	Gabon
Botswana	Bots.	Gambia	Gam.
Brazil	Braz.	Georgia	Geor.
Brunei	Brunei	Germany, Federal Republic of	F.R.G.
Bulgaria	Bulg.		
Burkina Faso	Burk. Faso	Ghana	Ghana
Burundi	Burundi	Gibraltar	Gib.
Cambodia	Cambodia	Great Britain	Gr. Brit.
Cameroon	Cameroon	Greece	Greece
Canada	Can.	Greenland	Green.
Cape Verde	Cape Verde	Grenada	Gren.
Cayman Islands	Cayman Is.	Guadeloupe	Guad.
		Guatemala	Guat.
Central African Republic	Cent. Afr. Rep.	Guinea	Guinea
Chad	Chad	Guinea-Bissau	Guinea-Bissau
Chile	Chile		
China, People's Republic of	P.R.C.	Guyana	Guy.
Colombia	Colom.	Haiti	Haiti
Comoros	Comoros	Honduras	Hond.
Congo	Congo	Hong Kong	H.K.
Costa Rica	Costa Rica	Hungary	Hung.
Côte d'Ivoire	Côte d'Ivoire	Iceland	Ice.
Croatia	Croat.	India	India
Cuba	Cuba	Indonesia	Indon.
Cyprus	Cyprus	Iran	Iran
Czech Republic	Czech Rep.	Iraq	Iraq
Denmark	Den.	Ireland	Ir.
Djibouti	Djib.	Israel	Isr.
Dominica	Dominica	Italy	Italy
Dominican Republic	Dom. Rep.	Jamaica	Jam.
Ecuador	Ecuador	Japan	Japan
Egypt	Egypt	Jordan	Jordan
El Salvador	El Sal.	Kazakhstan	Kaz.
England	Eng.	Kenya	Kenya
Equatorial Guinea	Eq. Guinea	Kiribati	Kiribati
Eritrea	Eri.	Korea, North	N. Korea
Estonia	Est.	Korea, South	S. Korea
Ethiopia	Eth.	Kuwait	Kuwait
		Kyrgyzstan	Kyrg.

Laos	Laos	Palau	Palau
Latvia	Lat.	Panama	Pan.
Lebanon	Leb.	Papua New Guinea	Papua N.G.
Lesotho	Lesotho	Paraguay	Para.
Liberia	Liber.	Peru	Peru
Libya	Libya	Philippines	Phil.
Liechtenstein	Liech.	Pitcairn Island	Pitcairn Is.
Lithuania	Lith.	Poland	Pol.
Luxembourg	Lux.	Portugal	Port.
Macau	Mac.	Qatar	Qatar
Macedonia	Maced.	Réunion	Réunion
Madagascar	Madag.	Romania	Rom.
Malawi	Malawi	Russia	Russ.
Malaysia	Malay.	Rwanda	Rwanda
Maldives	Maldives	St. Helena	St. Helena
Mali	Mali	St. Kitts & Nevis	St. Kitts & Nevis
Malta	Malta	St. Lucia	St. Lucia
Marshall Islands	Marsh. Is.	St. Vincent & the Grenadines	St. Vincent
Martinique	Mart.		
Mauritania	Mauritania	San Marino	San Marino
Mauritius	Mauritius	São Tomé and Príncipe	São Tomé & Príncipe
Mexico	Mex.		
Micronesia	Micr.	Saudi Arabia	Saudi Arabia
Moldova	Mold.		
Monaco	Monaco	Scotland	Scot.
Mongolia	Mong.	Senegal	Sen.
Montserrat	Montserrat	Serbia & Montenegro	Serb. & Mont.
Morocco	Morocco		
Mozambique	Mozam.	Seychelles	Sey.
Myanmar	Myan.	Sierra Leone	Sierra Leone
Namibia	Namib.		
Nauru	Nauru	Singapore	Sing.
Nepal	Nepal	Slovakia	Slovk.
Netherlands	Neth.	Slovenia	Slovn.
New Zealand	N.Z.	Solomon Islands	Solom. Is.
Nicaragua	Nicar.	Somalia	Somal.
Niger	Niger	South Africa	S. Afr.
Nigeria	Nig.	South America	S. Am.
North America	N. Am.	Spain	Spain
Northern Ireland	N. Ir.	Sri Lanka	Sri Lanka
Norway	Nor.	Sudan	Sudan
Oman	Oman	Suriname	Surin.
Pakistan	Pak.	Swaziland	Swaz.

Sweden	Swed.	Ukraine	Ukr.
Switzerland	Switz.	United Arab Emirates	U.A.E.
Syria	Syria	United Kingdom	U.K.
Taiwan	Taiwan	United States of	U.S.
Tajikistan	Taj.	America	
Tanzania	Tanz.	Uruguay	Uru.
Thailand	Thail.	Uzbekistan	Uzb.
Togo	Togo	Vanuatu	Vanuatu
Tonga	Tonga	Vatican City	Vatican
Trinidad and Tobago	Trin. &	Venezuela	Venez.
	Tobago	Vietnam	Vietnam
Tunisia	Tunis.	Virgin Islands, British	Virgin Is.
Turkey	Turk.	Wales	Wales
Turkmenistan	Turkm.	Western Samoa	W. Samoa
Turks and Caicos Islands	Turks &	Yemen	Yemen
	Caicos Is.	Zambia	Zambia
Tuvalu	Tuvalu	Zimbabwe	Zimb.
Uganda	Uganda		

Judges and Officials T.12

Abbreviate titles of judges and other officials according to the following table. See **rule 9** for further guidance in using abbreviated titles.

Administrative Law Judge	A.L.J.
Arbitrator	Arb.
Assembl[yman, ywoman]	Assemb.
Attorney General	Att'y Gen.
Baron	B.
Chancellor	C.
Chief Baron	C.B.
Chief Judge, Chief Justice	C.J.
Commissioner	Comm'r
Delegate	Del.
Judge, Justice	J.
Judges, Justices	JJ.
Lord Justics	L.J.
Magistrate	Mag.
Master of the Rolls	M.R.
Mediator	Med.
Referee	Ref.
Representative	Rep.
Senator	Sen.
Vice Chancellor	V.C.

T.13   Months

In citations, abbreviate the names of months as follows:

January	Jan.	July	July
February	Feb.	August	Aug.
March	Mar.	September	Sept.
April	Apr.	October	Oct.
May	May	November	Nov.
June	June	December	Dec.

Periodicals

The following alphabetical list gives abbreviations for the names of English language periodicals that are commonly cited or difficult to abbreviate, and for many words commonly found in periodical titles. In some cases, the list indicates that a word should not be abbreviated.

To use this list, first ascertain the correct name of the periodical you wish to cite. *Always use the title of the periodical that appears on the title page of the issue you are citing.* If the title of the periodical has changed over time, do not use an older or newer form of the title. Check to see if the periodical title you wish to cite is listed in the left-hand column of this list. If it is, you will find the full abbreviation for that periodical in the right-hand column.

Note that preferred abbreviation conventions for individual journals may differ from those listed in this table. The abbreviation conventions listed here are primarily intended to serve a national audience and to indicate clearly the source being cited.

If the periodical you wish to cite is not in the left-hand column of the list, you may determine the proper abbreviation by looking up each word of the periodical's title in this table and in the list of geographical abbreviations found in **table T.11**. Put together the abbreviations for each word to form the full abbreviated title. Omit the words "a," "at," "in," "of," and "the" from all abbreviated titles (but retain the word "on"). If any other word is listed neither here nor in **table T.11**, use the full word in the abbreviated title. If a periodical title consists of only one word after the words "a," "at," "in," "of," and "the" have been omitted, do not abbreviate the word. **Rule 6.1(a)** explains the spacing of abbreviations.

If a periodical title itself contains an abbreviation, use that abbreviation in the abbreviated title:

 IMF SURV.

Omit commas from periodical title abbreviations, but retain other punctuation:

 Peter H. Huang & Ho-Mou Wu, *More Order Without More Law: A Theory of Social Norms and Organizational Cultures*, 10 J.L. ECON. & ORG. 390 (1994).

 Nineteen States Adopt Code of Judicial Conduct, OYEZ! OYEZ!, Feb. 1974, at 11.

If a periodical has been renumbered in a new series, indicate that fact:

> Jill Martin, *The Statutory Sub-Tenancy: A Right Against the World?*, 41 CONV. & PROP. LAW. (n.s.) 96 (1977).

For periodical abbreviations in languages other than English, see **rules 20.1.3** and **20.6**.

ABA Journal	A.B.A. J.
Academ[ic, y]	ACAD.
Account [ant, ants, ing, ancy]	ACCT.
Adelaide Law Review	ADEL. L. REV.
Administrat[ive, or, ion]	ADMIN.
Administrative Law Journal	ADMIN. L.J.
Administrative Law Journal of American University	ADMIN. L.J. AM. U.
Administrative Law Review	ADMIN. L. REV.
Advoca[te, cy]	ADVOC.
Affairs	AFF.
Africa [n]	AFR.
African-American Law & Policy Report	AFR.-AM. L. & POL'Y REP.
Agricultur[e, al]	AGRIC.
Air	AIR
Air Force Law Review	A.F. L. REV.
Akron Law Review	AKRON L. REV.
Akron Tax Journal	AKRON TAX J.
Alabama Law Review	ALA. L. REV.
Alaska Law Review	ALASKA L. REV.
Albany Law Journal of Science & Technology	ALB. L.J. SCI. & TECH.
Albany Law Review	ALB. L. REV.
America [n, s]	AM.
American Bankruptcy Institute Law Review	AM. BANKR. INST. L. REV.
American Bankruptcy Law Journal	AM. BANKR. L.J.
American Bar Association	A.B.A.
American Bar Foundation Research Journal	AM. B. FOUND. RES. J.
American Criminal Law Review	AM. CRIM. L. REV.
American Indian Law Review	AM. INDIAN L. REV.
American Journal of Comparative Law	AM. J. COMP. L.
American Journal of Criminal Law	AM. J. CRIM. L.

American Journal of International Arbitration	Am. J. Int'l Arb.
American Journal of International Law	Am. J. Int'l L.
American Journal of Jurisprudence	Am. J. Juris.
American Journal of Law & Medicine	Am. J.L. & Med.
American Journal of Legal History	Am. J. Legal Hist.
American Journal of Trial Advocacy	Am. J. Trial Advoc.
American Law Institute	A.L.I.
American Law Reports	A.L.R.
American Review of International Arbitration	Am. Rev. Int'l Arb.
American University International Law Review	Am. U. Int'l L. Rev.
American University Journal of Gender, Social Policy & the Law	Am. U. J. Gender Soc. Pol'y & L.
American University Law Review	Am. U. L. Rev.
and	&
Anglo-American Law Review	Anglo-Am. L. Rev.
Animal Law	Animal L.
Annals	Annals
Annals of the American Academy of Political and Social Science	Annals Am. Acad. Pol. & Soc. Sci.
Annals of Health Law	Annals Health L.
Annual	Ann.
Annual Review of Banking Law	Ann. Rev. Banking L.
Annual Survey of American Law	Ann. Surv. Am. L.
Annual Survey of International and Comparative Law	Ann. Surv. Int'l & Comp. L.
Antitrust	Antitrust
Appellate	App.
Arbitrat[ion, ors]	Arb.
Arizona Journal of International and Comparative Law	Ariz. J. Int'l & Comp. L.
Arizona Law Review	Ariz. L. Rev.
Arizona State Law Journal	Ariz. St. L.J.
Arkansas Law Notes	Ark. L. Notes
Arkansas Law Review	Ark. L. Rev.
Army Lawyer	Army Law.
Art [s]	Art [s]
Asian Law Journal	Asian L.J.
Asian Pacific American Law Journal	Asian Pac. Am. L.J.
Asian-Pacific Law & Policy Journal	Asian-Pac. L. & Pol'y J.
Association	Ass'n
Atomic Energy Law Journal	Atom. Energy L.J.
Attorney [s]	Att'y [s]

Auckland University Law Review	AUCKLAND U. L. REV.
Banking Law Journal	BANKING L.J.
Bankruptcy	BANKR.
Bankruptcy Developments Journal	BANKR. DEV. J.
Bar	B.
Baylor Law Review	BAYLOR L. REV.
Behavior [al]	BEHAV.
Behavioral Sciences and the Law	BEHAV. SCI. & L.
Berkeley Journal of Employment and Labor Law	BERKELEY J. EMP. & LAB. L.
Berkeley Journal of Health Care Law	BERKELEY J. HEALTH CARE L.
Berkeley Journal of International Law	BERKELEY J. INT'L L.
Berkeley Technology Law Journal	BERKELEY TECH. L.J.
Berkeley Women's Law Journal	BERKELEY WOMEN'S L.J.
Black Law Journal	BLACK L.J.
Boston College Environmental Affairs Law Review	B.C. ENVTL. AFF. L. REV.
Boston College International and Comparative Law Review	B.C. INT'L & COMP. L. REV.
Boston College Law Review	B.C. L. REV.
Boston College Third World Law Journal	B.C. THIRD WORLD L.J.
Boston University International Law Journal	B.U. INT'L L.J.
Boston University Journal of Science & Technology Law	B.U. J. SCI. & TECH. L.
Boston University Journal of Tax Law	B.U. J. TAX L.
Boston University Law Review	B.U. L. REV.
Boston University Public Interest Law Journal	B.U. PUB. INT. L.J.
Brandeis Law Journal	BRANDEIS L.J.
Briefcase	BRIEFCASE
Brigham Young University Education and Law Journal	BYU EDUC. & L.J.
Brigham Young University Journal of Public Law	BYU J. PUB. L.
Brigham Young University Law Review	BYU L. REV.
British	BRIT.
Brooklyn Journal of International Law	BROOK. J. INT'L L.
Brooklyn Law Review	BROOK. L. REV.
Buffalo Criminal Law Review	BUFF. CRIM. L. REV.
Buffalo Environmental Law Journal	BUFF. ENVTL. L.J.
Buffalo Human Rights Law Review	BUFF. HUM. RTS. L. REV.
Buffalo Law Review	BUFF. L. REV.
Buffalo Public Interest Law Journal	BUFF. PUB. INT. L.J.

Buffalo Women's Law Journal	BUFF. WOMEN'S L.J.
Bulletin	BULL.
Business	BUS.
Business Law Journal	BUS. L.J.
Business Lawyer	BUS. LAW.
Business Week	BUS. WK.
California Bankruptcy Journal	CAL. BANKR. J.
California Criminal Law Review	CAL. CRIM. L. REV.
California Law Review	CAL. L. REV.
California Regulatory Law Reporter	CAL. REG. L. REP.
California State Bar Journal	CAL. ST. B.J.
California Western International Law Journal	CAL. W. INT'L L.J.
California Western Law Review	CAL. W. L. REV.
Cambridge Law Journal	CAMBRIDGE L.J.
Campbell Law Review	CAMPBELL L. REV.
Canada-United States Law Journal	CAN.-U.S. L.J.
Capital Defense Digest	CAP. DEF. DIG.
Capital University Law Review	CAP. U. L. REV.
Cardozo Arts & Entertainment Law Journal	CARDOZO ARTS & ENT. L.J.
Cardozo Law Review	CARDOZO L. REV.
Cardozo Online Journal of Conflict Resolution	CARDOZO ONLINE J. CONFLICT RESOL.
Cardozo Women's Law Journal	CARDOZO WOMEN'S L.J.
Case & Comment	CASE & COMMENT
Case Western Reserve Journal of International Law	CASE W. RES. J. INT'L L.
Case Western Reserve Law Review	CASE W. RES. L. REV.
Catholic Lawyer	CATH. LAW.
Catholic University Law Review	CATH. U. L. REV.
Central	CENT.
Chapman Law Review	CHAP. L. REV.
Chartered Life Underwriters	C.L.U.
Chicago Tribune	CHI. TRIB.
Chicago-Kent Law Review	CHI.-KENT L. REV.
Chicano Law Review	CHICANO L. REV.
Chicano-Latino Law Review	CHICANO-LATINO L. REV.
Child[ren, ren's]	CHILD.
Children's Legal Rights Journal	CHILD. LEGAL RTS. J.
Chronicle	CHRON.
Civil	CIV.
Civil Libert[y, ies]	C.L.
Civil Rights	C.R.

Clearinghouse Review	CLEARINGHOUSE REV.
Cleveland State Law Review	CLEV. ST. L. REV.
Cleveland-Marshall Law Review	CLEV.-MARSHALL L. REV.
Clinical Law Review	CLINICAL L. REV.
College	C.
Colorado Journal of International Environmental Law and Policy	COLO. J. INT'L ENVTL. L. & POL'Y
Colorado Lawyer	COLO. LAW.
Columbia Business Law Review	COLUM. BUS. L. REV.
Columbia Human Rights Law Review	COLUM. HUM. RTS. L. REV.
Columbia Journal of Asian Law	COLUM. J. ASIAN L.
Columbia Journal of East European Law	COLUM. J. E. EUR. L.
Columbia Journal of Environmental Law	COLUM. J. ENVTL. L.
Columbia Journal of European Law	COLUM. J. EUR. L.
Columbia Journal of Gender and Law	COLUM. J. GENDER & L.
Columbia Journal of Law and Social Problems	COLUM. J.L. & SOC. PROBS.
Columbia Journal of Transnational Law	COLUM. J. TRANSNAT'L L.
Columbia Law Review	COLUM. L. REV.
Columbia Science and Technology Law Review	COLUM. SCI. & TECH. L. REV.
Columbia-VLA Journal of Law & the Arts	COLUM.-VLA J.L. & ARTS
Commentary	COMMENT.
Commerc[e, ial]	COM.
Common Market Law Review	COMMON MKT. L. REV.
Communication [s]	COMM.
Comparative	COMP.
Comparative Labor Law Journal	COMP. LAB. L.J.
Comparative Labor Law & Policy Journal	COMP. LAB. L. & POL'Y J.
Computer	COMPUTER
Computer/Law Journal	COMPUTER/L.J.
Conference	CONF.
Congressional	CONG.
Congressional Digest	CONG. DIG.
Connecticut Journal of International Law	CONN. J. INT'L L.
Connecticut Law Review	CONN. L. REV.
Connecticut Probate Law Journal	CONN. PROB. L.J.
Constitution [al]	CONST.
Consumer	CONSUMER

Contemporary	CONTEMP.
Contract [s]	CONT.
Conveyancer and Property Lawyer (new series)	CONV. & PROP. LAW. (n.s.)
Cooley Law Review	COOLEY L. REV.
Copyright Law Symposium (American Society of Composers, Authors, & Publishers)	COPYRIGHT L. SYMP. (ASCAP)
Cornell International Law Journal	CORNELL INT'L L.J.
Cornell Journal of Law and Public Policy	CORNELL J.L. & PUB. POL'Y
Cornell Law Review	CORNELL L. REV.
Corporat[e, ion]	CORP.
Counsel [or, ors, or's]	COUNS.
Court [s]	CT[S].
Creighton Law Review	CREIGHTON L. REV.
Crime	CRIME
Criminal	CRIM.
Criminal Law Forum	CRIM. L.F.
Criminal Law Review	CRIM. L. REV.
Criminology	CRIMINOLOGY
Cumberland Law Review	CUMB. L. REV.
Current Medicine for Attorneys	CURRENT MED. FOR ATT'YS
Currents: The International Trade Law Journal	CURRENTS: INT'L TRADE L.J.
Dalhousie Law Journal	DALHOUSIE L.J.
DePaul Business Law Journal	DEPAUL BUS. L.J.
DePaul Journal of Health Care Law	DEPAUL J. HEALTH CARE L.
DePaul Law Review	DEPAUL L. REV.
DePaul-LCA Journal of Art and Entertainment Law and Policy	DEPAUL-LCA J. ART & ENT. L. & POL'Y
Defense	DEF.
Delaware Journal of Corporate Law	DEL. J. CORP. L.
Delinquency	DELINQ.
Denver Journal of International Law and Policy	DENV. J. INT'L L. & POL'Y
Denver University Law Review	DENV. U. L. REV.
Department of State Bulletin	DEP'T ST. BULL.
Development [s]	DEV.
Dickinson Journal of Environmental Law & Policy	DICK. J. ENVTL. L. & POL'Y
Dickinson Journal of International Law	DICK. J. INT'L L.
Dickinson Law Review	DICK. L. REV.
Digest	DIG.
The Digest: The National Italian-American Bar Assn. Law Journal	DIGEST

T
T.14

Diplomacy	DIPL.
Dispute	DISP.
District of Columbia Law Review	D.C. L. REV.
Drake Journal of Agricultural Law	DRAKE J. AGRIC. L.
Drake Law Review	DRAKE L. REV.
Duke Environmental Law & Policy Forum	DUKE ENVTL. L. & POL'Y F.
Duke Journal of Comparative & International Law	DUKE J. COMP. & INT'L L.
Duke Journal of Gender Law & Policy	DUKE J. GENDER L. & POL'Y
Duke Law Journal	DUKE L.J.
Duquesne Business Law Journal	DUQ. BUS. L.J.
Duquesne Law Review	DUQ. L. REV.
East [ern]	E.
Ecology Law Quarterly	ECOLOGY L.Q.
Econom [ic, ics, y]	ECON.
Economist	ECONOMIST
Education [al]	EDUC.
Elder Law Journal	ELDER L.J.
Elder's Advisor: The Journal of Elder Law and Post-Retirement Planning	ELDER'S ADVISOR
Emory International Law Review	EMORY INT'L L. REV.
Emory Law Journal	EMORY L.J.
Employment	EMP.
Energy	ENERGY
English	ENG.
Entertainment	ENT.
Environment	ENV'T
Environmental	ENVTL.
Environmental Law	ENVTL. L.
Environmental Lawyer	ENVTL. LAW.
Estate [s]	EST.
Ethics	ETHICS
Europe [an]	EUR.
Faculty	FAC.
Family	FAM.
Family and Conciliation Courts Review	FAM. & CONCILIATION CTS. REV.
Family Law Quarterly	FAM. L.Q.
Federal	FED.
Federal Circuit Bar Journal	FED. CIR. B.J.
Federal Communications Law Journal	FED. COMM. L.J.
Federal Probation	FED. PROBATION
Federation	FED'N
Financ[e, ial]	FIN.

Florida Journal of International Law	FLA. J. INT'L L.
Florida Law Review	FLA. L. REV.
Florida State Journal of Transnational Law & Policy	FLA. ST. J. TRANSNAT'L L. & POL'Y
Florida State University Journal of Land Use & Environmental Law	FLA. ST. U. J. LAND USE & ENVTL. L.
Florida State University Law Review	FLA. ST. U. L. REV.
Food Drug Cosmetic Law Journal	FOOD DRUG COSM. L.J.
For	FOR
Fordham Environmental Law Journal	FORDHAM ENVTL. L.J.
Fordham Intellectual Property, Media & Entertainment Law Journal	FORDHAM INTELL. PROP. MEDIA & ENT. L.J.
Fordham International Law Journal	FORDHAM INT'L L.J.
Fordham Law Review	FORDHAM L. REV.
Fordham Urban Law Journal	FORDHAM URB. L.J.
Foreign	FOREIGN
Foreign Broadcast Information Service	F.B.I.S.
Forensic	FORENSIC
Fortnightly	FORT.
Fortune	FORTUNE
Forum	F.
The Forum	FORUM
Foundation [s]	FOUND.
Gender	GENDER
General	GEN.
George Mason Law Review	GEO. MASON L. REV.
George Mason University Civil Rights Law Journal	GEO. MASON U. CIV. RTS. L.J.
George Washington Journal of International Law and Economics	GEO. WASH. J. INT'L L. & ECON.
George Washington Law Review	GEO. WASH. L. REV.
Georgetown Immigration Law Journal	GEO. IMMIGR. L.J.
Georgetown International Environmental Law Review	GEO. INT'L ENVTL. L. REV.
Georgetown Journal of Gender and the Law	GEO. J. GENDER & L.
Georgetown Journal of Legal Ethics	GEO. J. LEGAL ETHICS
Georgetown Journal on Poverty Law and Policy	GEO. J. ON POVERTY L. & POL'Y
Georgetown Law Journal	GEO. L.J.
Georgia Journal of International and Comparative Law	GA. J. INT'L & COMP. L.
Georgia Law Review	GA. L. REV.

Georgia State University Law Review	GA. ST. U. L. REV.
Glendale Law Review	GLENDALE L. REV.
Golden Gate University Law Review	GOLDEN GATE U. L. REV.
Gonzaga Law Review	GONZ. L. REV.
Government	GOV'T
Great Plains Natural Resources Journal	GREAT PLAINS NAT. RESOURCES J.
Guild Practitioner	GUILD PRAC.
Hamline Journal of Public Law and Policy	HAMLINE J. PUB. L. & POL'Y
Hamline Law Review	HAMLINE L. REV.
Harvard BlackLetter Law Journal	HARV. BLACKLETTER L.J.
Harvard Civil Rights-Civil Liberties Law Review	HARV. C.R.-C.L. L. REV.
Harvard Environmental Law Review	HARV. ENVTL. L. REV.
Harvard Human Rights Journal	HARV. HUM. RTS. J.
Harvard International Law Journal	HARV. INT'L L.J.
Harvard Journal of Law and Public Policy	HARV. J.L. & PUB. POL'Y
Harvard Journal of Law & Technology	HARV. J.L. & TECH.
Harvard Journal on Legislation	HARV. J. ON LEGIS.
Harvard Law Review	HARV. L. REV.
Harvard Negotiation Law Review	HARV. NEGOT. L. REV.
Harvard Women's Law Journal	HARV. WOMEN'S L.J.
Hastings Communications and Entertainment Law Journal	HASTINGS COMM. & ENT. L.J.
Hastings Constitutional Law Quarterly	HASTINGS CONST. L.Q.
Hastings International and Comparative Law Review	HASTINGS INT'L & COMP. L. REV.
Hastings Law Journal	HASTINGS L.J.
Hastings West-Northwest Journal of Environmental Law and Policy	HASTINGS W.-NW. J. ENVTL. L. & POL'Y
Hastings Women's Law Journal	HASTINGS WOMEN'S L.J.
Health	HEALTH
Health Matrix	HEALTH MATRIX
Herald	HERALD
High Technology Law Journal	HIGH TECH. L.J.
Hispanic	HISP.
Histor[ical, y]	HIST.
Hofstra Labor & Employment Law Journal	HOFSTRA LAB. & EMP. L.J.
Hofstra Law Review	HOFSTRA L. REV.
Hofstra Property Law Journal	HOFSTRA PROP. L.J.
Hospital	HOSP.
Houston Journal of International Law	HOUS. J. INT'L L.

Houston Law Review	Hous. L. Rev.
Howard Law Journal	How. L.J.
Human	Hum.
Human Rights Quarterly	Hum. Rts. Q.
Humanit[y, ies]	Human.
Idaho Law Review	Idaho L. Rev.
IDEA: The Journal of Law and Technology	IDEA
Illinois Bar Journal	Ill. B.J.
ILSA Journal of International & Comparative Law	ILSA J. Int'l & Comp. L.
Immigration	Immigr.
Immigration and Nationality Law Review	Immigr. & Nat'lity L. Rev.
In the Public Interest	In Pub. Interest
Independent	Indep.
Indian	Indian
Indiana International & Comparative Law Review	Ind. Int'l & Comp. L. Rev.
Indiana Journal of Global Legal Studies	Ind. J. Global Legal Stud.
Indiana Law Journal	Ind. L.J.
Indiana Law Review	Ind. L. Rev.
Industrial	Indus.
Industrial and Labor Relations Review	Indus. & Lab. Rel. Rev.
Information	Info.
Injury	Inj.
Institute	Inst.
Institute on Estate Planning	Inst. on Est. Plan.
Institute on Federal Taxation	Inst. on Fed. Tax'n
Institute on Oil and Gas Law and Taxation	Inst. on Oil & Gas L. & Tax'n
Institute on Planning, Zoning, and Eminent Domain	Inst. on Plan. Zoning & Eminent Domain
Institute on Private Investments and Investors Abroad	Inst. on Priv. Inv. & Inv. Abroad
Institute on Securities Regulation	Inst. on Sec. Reg.
Insurance	Ins.
Intellectual	Intell.
Interdisciplinary	Interdisc.
Interest	Int.
International	Int'l
International and Comparative Law Quarterly	Int'l & Comp. L.Q.

T
T.14

International Journal of Law and Psychiatry	INT'L J.L. & PSYCHIATRY
International Lawyer	INT'L LAW.
International Legal Perspectives	INT'L LEGAL PERSP.
International Organization	INT'L ORG.
Iowa Law Review	IOWA L. REV.
JAG Journal	JAG J.
John Marshall Journal of Computer & Information Law	J. MARSHALL J. COMPUTER & INFO. L.
John Marshall Law Review	J. MARSHALL L. REV.
Journal	J.
Journal of Agricultural Law	J. AGRIC. L.
Journal of Air Law and Commerce	J. AIR L. & COM.
Journal of Business Law	J. BUS. L.
Journal of Chinese Law	J. CHINESE L.
Journal of College and University Law	J.C. & U.L.
Journal of Contemporary Health Law and Policy	J. CONTEMP. HEALTH L. & POL'Y
Journal of Contemporary Law	J. CONTEMP. L.
Journal of Contemporary Legal Issues	J. CONTEMP. LEGAL ISSUES
Journal of Corporate Taxation	J. CORP. TAX'N
Journal of Corporation Law	J. CORP. L.
Journal of Criminal Law and Criminology	J. CRIM. L. & CRIMINOLOGY
Journal of Dispute Resolution	J. DISP. RESOL.
Journal of Energy Law and Policy	J. ENERGY L. & POL'Y
Journal of Energy, Natural Resources & Environmental Law	J. ENERGY NAT. RESOURCES & ENVTL. L.
Journal of Environmental Law and Litigation	J. ENVTL. L. & LITIG.
Journal of Family Law	J. FAM. L.
Journal of Gender, Race and Justice	J. GENDER RACE & JUST.
Journal of Health and Hospital Law	J. HEALTH & HOSP. L.
Journal of Health Care Law & Policy	J. HEALTH CARE L. & POL'Y
Journal of Health Law	J. HEALTH L.
Journal of Intellectual Property	J. INTELL. PROP.
Journal of Intellectual Property Law	J. INTELL. PROP. L.
Journal of International Arbitration	J. INT'L ARB.
Journal of International Legal Studies	J. INT'L LEGAL STUD.
Journal of International Wildlife Law and Policy	J. INT'L WILDLIFE L. & POL'Y
Journal of Land, Resources & Environmental Law	J. LAND RESOURCES & ENVTL. L.
Journal of Land Use and Environmental Law	J. LAND USE & ENVTL. L.

Journal of Law and Commerce	J.L. & COM.
Journal of Law and Economics	J.L. & ECON.
Journal of Law and Education	J.L. & EDUC.
Journal of Law and Health	J.L. & HEALTH
Journal of Law and Policy	J.L. & POL'Y
Journal of Law & Politics	J.L. & POL.
Journal of Law, Economics & Organization	J.L. ECON. & ORG.
Journal of Law in Society	J.L. SOC'Y
Journal of Legal Education	J. LEGAL EDUC.
Journal of Legislation	J. LEGIS.
Journal of Maritime Law and Commerce	J. MAR. L. & COM.
Journal of Medicine and Law	J. MED. & L.
Journal of Mineral Law & Policy	J. MIN. L. & POL'Y
Journal of Products Liability	J. PROD. LIAB.
Journal of Science & Technology Law	J. SCI. & TECH. L.
Journal of Small and Emerging Business Law	J. SMALL & EMERGING BUS. L.
Journal of Southern Legal History	J. S. LEGAL HIST.
Journal of Space Law	J. SPACE L.
Journal of Taxation	J. TAX'N
Journal of Technology Law & Policy	J. TECH. L. & POL'Y
Journal of the American Academy of Matrimonial Lawyers	J. AM. ACAD. MATRIM. LAW.
Journal of the American Medical Association	JAMA
Journal of the Legal Profession	J. LEGAL PROF.
Journal of the Patent and Trademark Office Society	J. PAT. & TRADEMARK OFF. SOC'Y
Journal of the Suffolk Academy of Law	J. SUFFOLK ACAD. L.
Judge [s]	JUDGE [S]
Judicature	JUDICATURE
Judicial	JUD.
Juridical Review	JURID. REV.
Jurimetrics: The Journal of Law, Science, and Technology	JURIMETRICS J.
Juris Doctor	JURIS DR.
Juris Magazine	JURIS MAG.
Jurist	JURIST
Justice	JUST.
Justice System Journal	JUST. SYS. J.
Juvenile	JUV.

T
T.14

Kansas Journal of Law and Public Policy	Kan. J.L. & Pub. Pol'y
Kentucky Law Journal	Ky. L.J.
Labo[r, ur]	Lab.
Labor Law Journal	Lab. L.J.
Labor Lawyer	Lab. Law.
Land	Land
Land and Water Law Review	Land & Water L. Rev.
La Raza Law Journal	La Raza L.J.
Law (first word)	Law
Law	L.
Law and Contemporary Problems	Law & Contemp. Probs.
Law and Human Behavior	Law & Hum. Behav.
Law and Inequality	Law & Ineq.
Law and Policy in International Business	Law & Pol'y Int'l Bus.
Law & Psychology Review	Law & Psychol. Rev.
Law & Social Inquiry	Law & Soc. Inquiry
Law & Society Review	Law & Soc'y Rev.
Law Library Journal	Law Libr. J.
Lawyer [s, s', 's]	Law.
Lawyer's Reports Annotated	L.R.A.
Legal	Legal
Legislat[ion, ive]	Legis.
Librar[y, ian, ies]	Libr.
Lincoln Law Review	Lincoln L. Rev.
Litigation	Litig.
Local	Loc.
Louisiana Law Review	La. L. Rev.
Loyola Consumer Law Review	Loy. Consumer L. Rev.
Loyola Law Review (New Orleans)	Loy. L. Rev.
Loyola of Los Angeles Entertainment Law Review	Loy. L.A. Ent. L. Rev.
Loyola of Los Angeles International & Comparative Law Review	Loy. L.A. Int'l & Comp. L. Rev.
Loyola of Los Angeles Law Review	Loy. L.A. L. Rev.
Loyola University of Chicago Law Journal	Loy. U. Chi. L.J.
Magazine	Mag.
Maine Law Review	Me. L. Rev.
Major Tax Planning	Major Tax Plan.
Management	Mgmt.
Maritime	Mar.
Marquette Intellectual Property Law Review	Marq. Intell. Prop. L. Rev.

Marquette Law Review	MARQ. L. REV.
Marquette Sports Law Journal	MARQ. SPORTS L.J.
Maryland Journal of Contemporary Legal Issues	MD. J. CONTEMP. LEGAL ISSUES
Maryland Journal of International Law and Trade	MD. J. INT'L L. & TRADE
Maryland Law Review	MD. L. REV.
Massachusetts Law Review	MASS. L. REV.
McGeorge Law Review	MCGEORGE L. REV.
McGill Law Journal	MCGILL L.J.
Media	MEDIA
Mediation	MEDIATION
Medic[al, ine]	MED.
Melbourne University Law Review	MELB. U. L. REV.
Mercer Law Review	MERCER L. REV.
Michigan Business Law Journal	MICH. BUS. L.J.
Michigan Journal of Gender & Law	MICH. J. GENDER & L.
Michigan Journal of International Law	MICH. J. INT'L L.
Michigan Journal of Race & Law	MICH. J. RACE & L.
Michigan Law Review	MICH. L. REV.
Michigan Telecommunications and Technology Law Review	MICH. TELECOMM. & TECH. L. REV.
Military Law Review	MIL. L. REV.
Mineral	MIN.
Minnesota Intellectual Property Review	MINN. INTELL. PROP. REV.
Minnesota Journal of Global Trade	MINN. J. GLOBAL TRADE
Minnesota Law Review	MINN. L. REV.
Mississippi College Law Review	MISS. C. L. REV.
Mississippi Law Journal	MISS. L.J.
Missouri Environmental Law and Policy Review	MO. ENVTL. L. & POL'Y REV.
Missouri Law Review	MO. L. REV.
Modern Law Review	MOD. L. REV.
Monash University Law Review	MONASH U. L. REV.
Montana Law Review	MONT. L. REV.
Monthly	MONTHLY
Monthly Labor Review	MONTHLY LAB. REV.
Municipal	MUN.
National	NAT'L
National Black Law Journal	NAT'L BLACK L.J.
Natural	NAT.
Natural Resources Journal	NAT. RESOURCES J.
Nebraska Law Review	NEB. L. REV.

Negligence	NEGL.
New England International and Comparative Law Annual	NEW. ENG. INT'L & COMP. L. ANN.
New England Journal of Medicine	NEW ENG. J. MED.
New England Journal on Criminal and Civil Confinement	NEW ENG. J. ON CRIM. & CIV. CONFINEMENT
New England Law Review	NEW ENG. L. REV.
New Law Journal	NEW L.J.
New Mexico Law Review	N.M. L. REV.
new series	(n.s.)
New York City Law Review	N.Y. CITY L. REV.
New York International Law Review	N.Y. INT'L L. REV.
New York Law School Journal of Human Rights	N.Y.L. SCH. J. HUM. RTS.
New York Law School Journal of International and Comparative Law	N.Y.L. SCH. J. INT'L & COMP. L.
New York Law School Law Review	N.Y.L. SCH. L. REV.
New York State Bar Association Antitrust Law Symposium	N.Y. ST. B.A. ANTITRUST L. SYMP.
New York University Environmental Law Journal	N.Y.U. ENVTL. L.J.
New York University Journal of International Law and Politics	N.Y.U. J. INT'L L. & POL.
New York University Journal of Legislation and Public Policy	N.Y.U. J. LEGIS. & PUB. POL'Y
New York University Law Review	N.Y.U. L. REV.
New York University Review of Law and Social Change	N.Y.U. REV. L. & SOC. CHANGE
New York University School of Law Moot Court Casebook	N.Y.U. MOOT CT. CASEBOOK
Newsletter	NEWSL.
NEXUS: A Journal of Opinion	NEXUS
North [ern]	N.
North Carolina Banking Institute	N.C. BANKING INST.
North Carolina Central Law Journal	N.C. CENT. L.J.
North Carolina Journal of International Law and Commercial Regulation	N.C. J. INT'L L. & COM. REG.
North Carolina Law Review	N.C. L. REV.
North Dakota Law Review	N.D. L. REV.
Northern Illinois University Law Review	N. ILL. U. L. REV.
Northern Kentucky Law Review	N. KY. L. REV.
Northwestern Journal of International Law & Business	NW. J. INT'L L. & BUS.
Northwestern University Law Review	NW. U. L. REV.
Nota Bene	NOTA BENE

Notre Dame Journal of Law, Ethics & Public Policy	Notre Dame J.L. Ethics & Pub. Pol'y
Notre Dame Law Review	Notre Dame L. Rev.
Nova Law Review	Nova L. Rev.
Ocean and Coastal Law Journal	Ocean & Coastal L.J.
Office	Off.
Ohio Northern University Law Review	Ohio N.U. L. Rev.
Ohio State Journal on Dispute Resolution	Ohio St. J. on Disp. Resol.
Ohio State Law Journal	Ohio St. L.J.
Oil and Gas Tax Quarterly	Oil & Gas Tax Q.
Oklahoma City University Law Review	Okla. City U. L. Rev.
Oklahoma Law Review	Okla. L. Rev.
on	on
Order	Ord.
Oregon Law Review	Or. L. Rev.
Organization	Org.
Osgoode Hall Law Journal	Osgoode Hall L.J.
Otago Law Review	Otago L. Rev.
Ottawa Law Review	Ottawa L. Rev.
Pace Environmental Law Review	Pace Envtl. L. Rev.
Pace Law Review	Pace L. Rev.
Pacific	Pac.
Pacific Law Journal	Pac. L.J.
Pacific Rim Law & Policy Journal	Pac. Rim L. & Pol'y J.
Patent	Pat.
Patent Law Annual	Pat. L. Ann.
Pepperdine Law Review	Pepp. L. Rev.
Performing Arts Review	Perf. Arts Rev.
Personal	Pers.
Perspective [s]	Persp.
Philosoph[ical, y]	Phil.
Planning	Plan.
Police	Police
Policy	Pol'y
Politic[al, s]	Pol.
Potomac Law Review	Potomac L. Rev.
Practi[cal, ce, tioners]	Prac.
Practical Lawyer	Prac. Law.
Preventive Law Reporter	Preventive L. Rep.
Preview of United States Supreme Court Cases	Preview U.S. Sup. Ct. Cas.
Probate	Prob.

Probate Law Journal (National College of Probate Judges and Boston University School of Law)	PROB. L.J.
Probation	PROBATION
Problems	PROBS.
Proce[edings, dure]	PROC.
Profession [al]	PROF.
Property	PROP.
Psychiatry	PSYCHIATRY
Psycholog[ical, y]	PSYCHOL.
Public	PUB.
Public Interest Law Reporter	PUB. INT. L. REP.
Public Land Law Review	PUB. LAND L. REV.
Public Land and Resources Law Review	PUB. LAND & RESOURCES L. REV.
Publishing, Entertainment, Advertising and Allied Fields Law Quarterly	PUB. ENT. ADVERT. & ALLIED FIELDS L.Q.
Quarterly	Q.
Quinnipiac Health Law Journal	QUINNIPIAC HEALTH L.J.
Quinnipiac Law Review	QUINNIPIAC L. REV.
Quinnipiac Probate Law Journal	QUINNIPIAC PROB. L.J.
Race and Ethnic Ancestry Law Journal	RACE & ETHNIC ANC. L.J.
Real	REAL
Real Property, Probate and Trust Journal	REAL PROP. PROB. & TR. J.
Record	REC.
Referees	REF.
Reform	REFORM
Regent University Law Review	REGENT U. L. REV.
Register	REG.
Regulat[ion, ory]	REG.
Relations	REL.
Report [s, er]	REP.
Reproduct[ion, ive]	REPROD.
Research	RES.
Reserve	RES.
Resolution	RESOL.
Resources	RESOURCES
Responsibility	RESP.
Review	REV.
Review of Litigation	REV. LITIG.
Revista de Derecho Puertorriqueno	REV. DER. P.R.

Revista Juridica Universidad de Puerto Rico	Rev. Jur. U.P.R.
Richmond Journal of Global Law & Business	Rich. J. Global L. & Bus.
Richmond Journal of Law and the Public Interest	Rich. J.L. & Pub. Int.
Richmond Journal of Law & Technology	Rich. J.L. & Tech.
Rights	Rts.
Risk	Risk
RISK: Health, Safety & Environment	RISK
Rocky Mountain Mineral Law Institute	Rocky Mtn. Min. L. Inst.
Roger Williams University Law Review	Roger Williams U. L. Rev.
Rutgers-Camden Law Journal	Rutgers-Cam. L.J.
Rutgers Computer and Technology Law Journal	Rutgers Computer & Tech. L.J.
Rutgers Law Journal	Rutgers L.J.
Rutgers Law Record	Rutgers L. Rec.
Rutgers Law Review	Rutgers L. Rev.
Rutgers Race and the Law Review	Rutgers Race & L. Rev.
St. John's Journal of Legal Commentary	St. John's J. Legal Comment.
St. John's Law Review	St. John's L. Rev.
Saint Louis University Law Journal	St. Louis U. L.J.
Saint Louis University Public Law Review	St. Louis U. Pub. L. Rev.
Saint Louis-Warsaw Transatlantic Law Journal	St. Louis-Warsaw Transatlantic L.J.
St. Mary's Law Journal	St. Mary's L.J.
St. Thomas Law Review	St. Thomas L. Rev.
San Diego Law Review	San Diego L. Rev.
San Fernando Valley Law Review	San Fern. V. L. Rev.
Santa Clara Computer and High Technology Law Journal	Santa Clara Computer & High Tech. L.J.
Santa Clara Law Review	Santa Clara L. Rev.
The Scholar: St. Mary's Law Review on Minority Issues	Scholar
School	Sch.
Scien[ce, ces, tific]	Sci.
Scientific American	Sci. Am.
Scottish	Scot.
Seattle University Law Review	Seattle U. L. Rev.
Section	Sec.
Securities	Sec.
Seton Hall Constitutional Law Journal	Seton Hall Const. L.J.

T

Seton Hall Journal of Sport Law	SETON HALL J. SPORT L.
Seton Hall Law Review	SETON HALL L. REV.
Seton Hall Legislative Journal	SETON HALL LEGIS. J.
Signs	SIGNS
Social	SOC.
Social Service Review	SOC. SERV. REV.
Socialist	SOCIALIST
Society	SOC'Y
Sociolog[ical, y]	SOC.
Software Law Journal	SOFTWARE L.J.
Solicitor [s, s', 's]	SOLIC.
South [ern]	S.
South Carolina Environmental Law Journal	S.C. ENVTL. L.J.
South Carolina Law Review	S.C. L. REV.
South Dakota Law Review	S.D. L. REV.
South Texas Law Review	S. TEX. L. REV.
Southern California Interdisciplinary Law Journal	S. CAL. INTERDISC. L.J.
Southern California Law Review	S. CAL. L. REV.
Southern California Review of Law & Women's Studies	S. CAL. REV. L. & WOMEN'S STUD.
Southern Illinois University Law Journal	S. ILL. U. L.J.
Southern Methodist University Law Review	SMU L. REV.
Southern University Law Review	S.U. L. REV.
Southwestern Journal of Law and Trade in the Americas	SW. J. L. & TRADE AM.
Southwestern Law Journal	SW. L.J.
Southwestern University Law Review	SW. U. L. REV.
Sports Lawyers Journal	SPORTS LAW. J.
Stanford Environmental Law Journal	STAN. ENVTL. L.J.
Stanford Journal of International Law	STAN. J. INT'L L.
Stanford Law & Policy Review	STAN. L. & POL'Y REV.
Stanford Law Review	STAN. L. REV.
State	ST.
State Bar of Texas Environmental Law Journal	ST. B. TEX. ENVTL. L.J.
Statistic[s, al]	STAT.
Stetson Law Forum	STETSON L.F.
Stetson Law Review	STETSON L. REV.
Studies	STUD.
Suffolk Journal of Trial & Appellate Advocacy	SUFFOLK J. TRIAL & APP. ADVOC.

Suffolk Transnational Law Review	SUFFOLK TRANSNAT'L L. REV.
Suffolk University Law Review	SUFFOLK U. L. REV.
Supreme Court Review	SUP. CT. REV.
Survey	SURV.
Sydney Law Review	SYDNEY L. REV.
Symposium	SYMP.
Syracuse Journal of International Law and Commerce	SYRACUSE J. INT'L L. & COM.
Syracuse Law Review	SYRACUSE L. REV.
System	SYS.
Tax	TAX
Tax Adviser	TAX ADVISER
Tax Law Review	TAX L. REV.
Tax Lawyer	TAX LAW.
Tax Management International Journal	TAX MGM'T INT'L J.
Tax Notes	TAX NOTES
Taxation	TAX'N
Taxes — The Tax Magazine	TAXES
Teacher [s]	TCHR[S].
Techn[ique, ology]	TECH.
Telecommunication [s]	TELECOMM.
Temple Environmental Law & Technology Journal	TEMP. ENVTL. L. & TECH. J.
Temple International and Comparative Law Journal	TEMP. INT'L & COMP. L.J.
Temple Law Review	TEMP. L. REV.
Temple Political and Civil Rights Law Review	TEMP. POL. & CIV. RTS. L. REV.
Tennessee Journal of Practice & Procedure	TENN. J. PRAC. & PROC.
Tennessee Law Review	TENN. L. REV.
Texas Forum on Civil Liberties and Civil Rights	TEX. F. ON C.L. & C.R.
Texas Hispanic Journal of Law and Policy	TEX. HISP. J.L. & POL'Y
Texas Intellectual Property Law Journal	TEX. INTELL. PROP. L.J.
Texas International Law Journal	TEX. INT'L L.J.
Texas Journal of Business Law	TEX. J. BUS. L.
Texas Journal of Women and the Law	TEX. J. WOMEN & L.
Texas Law Review	TEX. L. REV.
Texas Review of Law and Politics	TEX. REV. L. & POL.
Texas Tech Law Review	TEX. TECH L. REV.
Texas Wesleyan Law Review	TEX. WESLEYAN L. REV.
Third World Legal Studies	THIRD WORLD LEGAL STUD.
Thomas Jefferson Law Review	T. JEFFERSON L. REV.

Thomas M. Cooley Journal of Practical and Clinical Law	T.M. COOLEY J. PRAC. & CLINICAL L.
Thomas M. Cooley Law Review	T.M. COOLEY L. REV.
Thurgood Marshall Law Review	T. MARSHALL L. REV.
Toledo Journal of Great Lakes' Law, Science & Policy	TOL. J. GREAT LAKES' L. SCI. & POL'Y
Touro Journal of Transnational Law	TOURO J. TRANSNAT'L L.
Touro Law Review	TOURO L. REV.
Trade	TRADE
Trademark	TRADEMARK
Trademark Reporter	TRADEMARK REP.
Transnational	TRANSNAT'L
Transnational Law & Contemporary Problems	TRANSNAT'L L. & CONTEMP. PROBS.
The Transnational Lawyer	TRANSNAT'L LAW.
Transportation	TRANSP.
Transportation Law Journal	TRANSP. L.J.
Transportation Practitioners Journal	TRANSP. PRAC. J.
Trial	TRIAL
Trial Lawyer's Guide	TRIAL LAW. GUIDE
Tribune	TRIB.
Trust [s]	TR.
Tulane Environmental Law Journal	TUL. ENVTL. L.J.
Tulane European & Civil Law Forum	TUL. EUR. & CIV. L.F.
Tulane Journal of International and Comparative Law	TUL. J. INT'L & COMP. L.
Tulane Journal of Law and Sexuality	TUL. J.L. & SEXUALITY
Tulane Law Review	TUL. L. REV.
Tulane Maritime Law Journal	TUL. MAR. L.J.
Tulsa Journal of Comparative & International Law	TULSA J. COMP. & INT'L L.
Tulsa Law Journal	TULSA L.J.
UCLA Bulletin of Law and Technology	UCLA BULL. L. & TECH.
UCLA Entertainment Law Review	UCLA ENT. L. REV.
UCLA Journal of Environmental Law and Policy	UCLA J. ENVTL. L. & POL'Y
UCLA Journal of International Law and Foreign Affairs	UCLA J. INT'L L. & FOREIGN AFF.
UCLA Law Review	UCLA L. REV.
UCLA Pacific Basin Law Journal	UCLA PAC. BASIN L.J.
UCLA Women's Law Journal	UCLA WOMEN'S L.J.
UMKC Law Review	UMKC L. REV.
UN Monthly Chronicle	UN MONTHLY CHRON.
Uniform Commercial Code Law Journal	UCC L.J.

Uniform Commercial Code Reporter-Digest	UCC Rep.-Dig.
United States	U.S.
United States-Mexico Law Journal	U.S.-Mex. L.J.
Universit[ies, y]	U.
University of Arkansas at Little Rock Law Review	U. Ark. Little Rock L. Rev.
University of Baltimore Intellectual Property Law Journal	U. Balt. Intell. Prop. L.J.
University of Baltimore Journal of Environmental Law	U. Balt. J. Envtl. L.
University of Baltimore Law Forum	U. Balt. L.F.
University of Baltimore Law Review	U. Balt. L. Rev.
University of California at Davis Law Review	U.C. Davis L. Rev.
University of Chicago Law Review	U. Chi. L. Rev.
University of Chicago Legal Forum	U. Chi. Legal F.
University of Cincinnati Law Review	U. Cin. L. Rev.
University of Colorado Law Review	U. Colo. L. Rev.
University of Dayton Law Review	U. Dayton L. Rev.
University of Denver Water Law Review	U. Denv. Water L. Rev.
University of Detroit Mercy Law Review	U. Det. Mercy L. Rev.
University of the District of Columbia David Clarke School of Law Law Review	UDC/DCSL L. Rev.
University of Florida Journal of Law and Public Policy	U. Fla. J.L. & Pub. Pol'y
University of Florida Law Review	U. Fla. L. Rev.
University of Hawaii Law Review	U. Haw. L. Rev.
University of Illinois Journal of Law, Technology and Policy	U. Ill. J.L. Tech. & Pol'y
University of Illinois Law Review	U. Ill. L. Rev.
University of Kansas Law Review	U. Kan. L. Rev.
University of Memphis Law Review	U. Mem. L. Rev.
University of Miami Business Law Review	U. Miami Bus. L. Rev.
University of Miami Entertainment and Sports Law Review	U. Miami Ent. & Sports L. Rev.
University of Miami Inter-American Law Review	U. Miami Inter-Am. L. Rev.
University of Miami Law Review	U. Miami L. Rev.
University of Miami Yearbook of International Law	U. Miami Y.B. Int'l L.
University of Michigan Journal of Law Reform	U. Mich. J.L. Reform

T
T.14

University of Pennsylvania Journal of Constitutional Law	U. PA. J. CONST. L.
University of Pennsylvania Journal of International Economic Law	U. PA. J. INT'L ECON. L.
University of Pennsylvania Journal of Labor and Employment Law	U. PA. J. LAB. & EMP. L.
University of Pennsylvania Law Review	U. PA. L. REV.
University of Pittsburgh Law Review	U. PITT. L. REV.
University of Puget Sound Law Review	U. PUGET SOUND L. REV.
University of Richmond Law Review	U. RICH. L. REV.
University of San Francisco Law Review	U.S.F. L. REV.
University of San Francisco Maritime Law Journal	U.S.F. MAR. L.J.
University of Seattle Law Review	U. SEATTLE L. REV.
University of Toledo Law Review	U. TOL. L. REV.
University of Toronto Faculty of Law Review	U. TORONTO FAC. L. REV.
University of Toronto Law Journal	U. TORONTO L.J.
University of West Los Angeles Law Review	UWLA L. REV.
Urban	URB.
Urban Lawyer	URB. LAW.
Utah Law Review	UTAH L. REV.
Utilit[ies, y]	UTIL.
Valparaiso University Law Review	VAL. U. L. REV.
Vanderbilt Journal of Entertainment Law & Practice	VAND. J. ENT. L. & PRAC.
Vanderbilt Journal of Transnational Law	VAND. J. TRANSNAT'L L.
Vanderbilt Law Review	VAND. L. REV.
Vermont Law Review	VT. L. REV.
Villanova Environmental Law Journal	VILL. ENVTL. L.J.
Villanova Law Review	VILL. L. REV.
Villanova Sports & Entertainment Law Journal	VILL. SPORTS & ENT. L.J.
Virginia Environmental Law Journal	VA. ENVTL. L.J.
Virginia Journal of International Law	VA. J. INT'L L.
Virginia Journal of Law & Technology	VA. J.L. & TECH.
Virginia Journal of Social Policy and the Law	VA. J. SOC. POL'Y & L.
Virginia Journal of Sports and the Law	VA. J. SPORTS & L.
Virginia Law Review	VA. L. REV.
Virginia Tax Review	VA. TAX REV.
Wake Forest Law Review	WAKE FOREST L. REV.
Wall Street Journal	WALL ST. J.

Washburn Law Journal	WASHBURN L.J.
Washington & Lee Law Review	WASH. & LEE L. REV.
Washington Law Review	WASH. L. REV.
Washington Monthly	WASH. MONTHLY
Washington University Journal of Law and Policy	WASH. U. J.L. & POL'Y
Washington University Journal of Urban and Contemporary Law	WASH. U. J. URB. & CONTEMP. L.
Washington University Law Quarterly	WASH. U. L.Q.
Wayne Law Review	WAYNE L. REV.
Week	WK.
Weekly	WKLY.
Welfare	WELFARE
West [ern]	W.
West Virginia Law Review	W. VA. L. REV.
Western New England Law Review	W. NEW ENG. L. REV.
Western State University Law Review	W. ST. U. L. REV.
Whittier Law Review	WHITTIER L. REV.
Widener Journal of Public Law	WIDENER J. PUB. L.
Widener Law Symposium Journal	WIDENER L. SYMP. J.
Willamette Law Review	WILLAMETTE L. REV.
William and Mary Bill of Rights Journal	WM. & MARY BILL RTS. J.
William and Mary Journal of Women and the Law	WM. & MARY J. WOMEN & L.
William and Mary Law Review	WM. & MARY L. REV.
William Mitchell Law Review	WM. MITCHELL L. REV.
Wisconsin Environmental Law Journal	WIS. ENVTL. L.J.
Wisconsin International Law Journal	WIS. INT'L L.J.
Wisconsin Law Review	WIS. L. REV.
Wisconsin Women's Law Journal	WIS. WOMEN'S L.J.
Women ['s]	WOMEN['S]
Women's Rights Law Reporter	WOMEN'S RTS. L. REP.
World	WORLD
Yale Human Rights and Development Law Journal	YALE HUM. RTS. & DEV. L.J.
Yale Journal of International Law	YALE J. INT'L L.
Yale Journal of Law and Feminism	YALE J.L. & FEMINISM
Yale Journal of Law and the Humanities	YALE J.L. & HUMAN.
Yale Journal of World Public Order	YALE J. WORLD PUB. ORD.
Yale Journal on Regulation	YALE J. ON REG.
Yale Law and Policy Review	YALE L. & POL'Y REV.
Yale Law Journal	YALE L.J.
Yearbook (or Year Book)	Y.B.

T.15   Publishing Terms

Abbreviate publishing terms in citations according to **rule 15.4** and the following table:

abridge[d, ment]	abr.
annotated	ann.
anonymous	anon.
compil[ation, ed]	comp.
edit[ion, or]	ed.
manuscript	ms.
new series	n.s.
no date	n.d.
no place	n.p.
permanent	perm.
photoduplicated reprint	photo. reprint
printing	prtg.
replacement	repl.
revis[ed, ion]	rev.
special	spec.
temporary	temp.
translat[ion, or]	trans.
volume	vol.

Services   T.16

Abbreviations commonly used in referring to service publishers include:

Bureau of National Affairs	BNA
Clark Boardman Callaghan	CBC
Commerce Clearing House	CCH
Matthew Bender	MB
Pike & Fischer	P & F
Research Institute of America	RIA

Abbreviations for some of the most frequently cited services are listed below. Following each looseleaf service title, the list indicates the appropriate abbreviation of the service, the publisher, and corresponding bound services. Names of bound services that differ markedly from their looseleaf forms are printed in italics and cross-referenced to the looseleaf forms. See **rule 19** for further guidance on citation to services.

Accountancy Law Reports	Accountancy L. Rep. (CCH)
Administrative Law Third Series bound in same name	Admin. L.3d (P & F)
Affirmative Action Compliance Manual for Federal Contractors	Aff. Action Compl. Man. (BNA)
AIDS Law & Litigation Reporter	AIDS L. & Litig. Rep. (Univ. Pub. Group)
All States Tax Guide	All St. Tax Guide (RIA)
American Federal Tax Reports, Second Series	A.F.T.R.2d (RIA)
American Stock Exchange Guide	Am. Stock Ex. Guide (CCH)
Antitrust & Trade Regulation Report	Antitrust & Trade Reg. Rep. (BNA)
Aviation Law Reports bound as Aviation Cases	Av. L. Rep. (CCH) Av. Cas. (CCH)
Banking Reporter	Banking Rep. (BNA)
Bankruptcy Court Decisions	Bankr. Ct. Dec. (LRP)
Bankruptcy Law Reports	Bankr. L. Rep. (CCH)
Benefits Review Board Service	Ben. Rev. Bd. Serv. (MB)
BioLaw	BioLaw (Univ. Pub. Am.)
Blue Sky Law Reports	Blue Sky L. Rep. (CCH)
Board of Contract Appeals Decisions—see Contract Appeals Decisions	
Business Franchise Guide	Bus. Franchise Guide (CCH)

Canadian Commercial Law Guide	Can. Com. L. Guide (CCH)
Canadian Tax Reports	Can. Tax Rep. (CCH)
Chemical Regulation Reporter	Chem. Reg. Rep. (BNA)
Chicago Board Options Exchange	Chicago Bd. Options Ex. (CCH)
Collective Bargaining Negotiations & Contracts	Collective Bargaining Negot. & Cont. (BNA)
College Law Digest	College L. Dig. (Nat'l Ass'n College & Univ. Att'ys)
Collier Bankruptcy Cases, Second Series	Collier Bankr. Cas. 2d (MB)
Commodity Futures Law Reports	Comm. Fut. L. Rep. (CCH)
Common Market Reports	Common Mkt. Rep. (CCH)
Communications Regulations	Communications Reg. (P & F)
Congressional Index	Cong. Index (CCH)
Consumer Credit Guide	Consumer Cred. Guide (CCH)
Consumer Product Safety Guide	Consumer Prod. Safety Guide (CCH)
Contract Appeals Decisions bound as Board of Contract Appeals Decisions	Cont. App. Dec. (CCH) B.C.A. (CCH)
Contracts Cases, Federal —see Government Contracts Reports	
Copyright Law Decisions	Copyright L. Dec. (CCH)
Copyright Law Reporter	Copyright L. Rep. (CCH)
Corporation Guide	Corp. Guide (Aspen Law & Bus.)
Cost Accounting Standards Guide	Cost Accounting Stand. Guide (CCH)
Criminal Law Reporter	Crim. L. Rep. (BNA)
Daily Labor Report	Daily Lab. Rep. (BNA)
Dominion Tax Cases	Dominion Tax Cas. (CCH)
EEOC Compliance Manual	EEOC Compl. Man. (BNA)
EEOC Compliance Manual	EEOC Compl. Man. (CCH)
Employee Benefits Cases bound in same name	Employee Benefits Cas. (BNA)
Employee Benefits Compliance Coordinator	Empl. Coordinator (RIA)
Employment Practices Guide bound as Employment Practices Decisions—See also Labor Law Reports	Empl. Prac. Guide (CCH) Empl. Prac. Dec. (CCH)

Employment Safety and Health Guide	Empl. Safety & Health Guide (CCH)
bound as Occupational Safety and Health Decisions	O.S.H. Dec. (CCH)
Employment Testing: Law & Policy Reporter	Empl. Testing (Univ. Pub. Am.)
Energy Management & Federal Energy Guidelines	Energy Mgmt. (CCH)
Environment Reporter bound as Environment Reporter Cases	Env't Rep. (BNA) Env't Rep. Cas. (BNA)
Environmental Law Reporter	Envtl. L. Rep. (Envtl. L. Inst.)
Equal Employment Compliance Manual	Eq. Empl. Compl. Man. (CBC)
European Community Cases bound in same name	CEC (CCH)
Exempt Organizations Reports	Exempt Org. Rep. (CCH)
Fair Employment Practice Cases —see Labor Relations Reporter	
Family Law Reporter bound in same name	Fam. L. Rep. (BNA)
Family Law Tax Guide	Fam. L. Tax Guide (CCH)
Federal Audit Guides	Fed. Audit Guide (CCH)
Federal Banking Law Reporter	Fed. Banking L. Rep. (CCH)
Federal Carriers Reports bound as Federal Carriers Cases	Fed. Carr. Rep (CCH) Fed. Carr. Cas. (CCH)
Federal Contracts Report	Fed. Cont. Rep. (BNA)
Federal Election Campaign Financing Guide	Fed. Election Camp. Fin. Guide (CCH)
Federal Energy Regulatory Commission Reports	Fed. Energy Reg. Comm'n Rep. (CCH)
Federal Estate and Gift Tax Reporter bound as U.S. Tax Cases	Fed. Est. & Gift Tax Rep. (CCH) U.S. Tax Cas. (CCH)
Federal Excise Tax Reports	Fed. Ex. Tax Rep. (CCH)
Federal Income, Gift and Estate Taxation	Fed. Inc. Gift & Est. Tax'n (MB)
Federal Rules of Evidence Service bound in same name	Fed. R. Evid. Serv. (West)
Federal Rules Service, Second Series bound in same name	Fed. R. Serv. 2d (West)

T
T.16

Federal Securities Law Reports bound in same name	Fed. Sec. L. Rep. (CCH)
Federal Tax Coordinator Second	Fed. Tax. Coordinator 2d (RIA)
Federal Tax Guide Reports	Fed. Tax Guide Rep. (CCH)
Fire & Casualty Cases —see Insurance Law Reports	
Food Drug Cosmetic Law Reports	Food Drug Cosm. L. Rep. (CCH)
Government Contracts Reporter bound as Contracts Cases, Federal	Gov't Cont. Rep. (CCH) Cont. Cas. Fed. (CCH)
Government Employee Relations Report	Gov't Empl. Rel. Rep (BNA)
Housing & Development Reporter	Hous. & Dev. Rep. (West)
Human Resources Management OSHA Compliance Guide	OSHA Comp. Guide (CCH)
Inheritance, Estate and Gift Tax Reports	Inher. Est. & Gift Tax Rep. (CCH)
Insurance Law Reports bound as:	Ins. L. Rep. (CCH)
Fire & Casualty Cases	Fire & Casualty Cas. (CCH)
Life, Health & Accident Insurance Cases 2d	Life Health & Accid. Ins. Cas. 2d (CCH)
IRS Positions	IRS Pos. (CCH)
International Environment Reporter	Int'l Env't Rep. (BNA)
International Trade Reporter	Int'l Trade Rep. (BNA)
Labor Arbitration Awards bound in same name	Lab. Arb. Awards (CCH)
Labor Law Reporter bound as:	Lab. L. Rep. (CCH)
Labor Cases	Lab. Cas. (CCH)
NLRB Decisions See also Employment Practices Guide	NLRB Dec. (CCH)
Labor Relations Reporter bound as:	Lab. Rel. Rep. (BNA)
Fair Employment Practice Cases	Fair Empl. Prac. Cas. (BNA)
Labor Arbitration Reports	Lab. Arb. Rep. (BNA)
Labor Relations Reference Manual	L.R.R.M. (BNA)
Wage and Hour Cases	Wage & Hour Cas. (BNA)
Lawyers' Manual on Professional Conduct	Laws. Man. on Prof. Conduct (ABA/BNA)
Life, Health & Accident Insurance Cases —see Insurance Law Reports	

Liquor Control Law Reports	Liquor Cont. L. Rep. (CCH)
Media Law Reporter bound in same name	Media L. Rep. (BNA)
Medical Devices Reports	Med. Devices Rep. (CCH)
Medicare and Medicaid Guide	Medicare & Medicaid Guide (CCH)
Mutual Funds Guide	Mut. Funds Guide (CCH)
National Reporter on Legal Ethics & Professional Responsibility	Nat'l Rep. Legal Ethics (Univ. Pub. Am.)
New York Stock Exchange Guide	N.Y.S.E. Guide (CCH)
NLRB Decisions —see Labor Law Reports	
Noise Regulation Report	Noise Reg. Rep. (Bus. Pub.)
Nuclear Regulation Reports	Nuclear Reg. Rep. (CCH)
Occupational Safety & Health Reporter	O.S.H. Rep. (BNA)
bound as Occupational Safety & Health Cases	O.S.H. Cas. (BNA)

OFCCP Federal Contract
  Compliance Manual
	OFCCP Fed. Cont. Compl. Man.
	  (CCH)

Patent, Trademark & Copyright
  Journal
	Pat. Trademark & Copyright J.
	  (BNA)

Pension & Benefits Reporter	Pens. & Ben. Rep. (BNA)
Pension Plan Guide	Pens. Plan Guide (CCH)
Pension & Profit Sharing Second	Pens. & Profit Sharing 2d (RIA)
Personnel Management	Personnel Mgmt. (BNA)
Product Safety & Liability Reporter	Prod. Safety & Liab. Rep. (BNA)
Products Liability Reports	Prod. Liab. Rep. (CCH)
Public Utilities Reports bound in same name	Pub. Util. Rep. (PUR)
Radio Regulation Second	Rad. Reg. 2d (P & F)

Reporter on Human Reproduction
  and the Law
	Human Reprod. & L. Rep.
	  (Legal-Medical Studies)

School Law Reporter	School L. Rep. (Nat'l Org. on Legal Probs. in Educ.)
Search & Seizure Bulletin	Search & Seizure Bull. (Quinlan)
Secured Transactions Guide	Secured Transactions Guide (CCH)
SEC Accounting Rules	SEC Accounting R. (CCH)
Securities and Federal Corporate Law Report	Sec. & Fed. Corp. L. Rep. (West)
Securities Regulation & Law Report	Sec. Reg. & L. Rep. (BNA)

T.16

Shipping Regulation	Shipping Reg. (P & F)
Standard Federal Tax Reports bound as U.S. Tax Cases	Stand. Fed. Tax Rep. (CCH) U.S. Tax Cas. (CCH)
State and Local Tax Service	St. & Loc. Tax Serv. (RIA)
State and Local Taxes —see All States Tax Guide	
State Tax Guide	St. Tax Guide (CCH)
State Tax Reporter	St. Tax. Rep. (CCH)
Tax Court Memorandum Decisions bound in same name	T.C.M. (RIA) T.C.M. (CCH) [or (RIA)]
Tax Court Reported Decisions	Tax Ct. Rep. Dec. (RIA)
Tax Court Reports	Tax Ct. Rep. (CCH)
Tax-Exempt Organizations	Tax-Exempt Org. (RIA)
Tax Management	Tax Mgmt. (BNA)
Tax Treaties	Tax Treaties (CCH)
Trade Regulation Reporter bound as Trade Cases	Trade Reg. Rep. (CCH) Trade Cas. (CCH)
Unemployment Insurance Reports	Unempl. Ins. Rep. (CCH)
Uniform Commercial Code Reporting Service bound in same name	U.C.C. Rep. Serv. (CBC)
Union Labor Report	Union Lab. Rep. (BNA)
United States Law Week	U.S.L.W. (BNA—publisher need not be indicated)
United States Patents Quarterly bound in same name	U.S.P.Q. (BNA)
U.S. Supreme Court Bulletin	S. Ct. Bull. (CCH)
U.S. Tax Cases —see Federal Estate and Gift Tax Reporter; Standard Federal Tax Reports	
U.S. Tax Reporter	U.S. Tax Rep. (RIA)
Utilities Law Reports	Util. L. Rep. (CCH)
Wage and Hour Cases —see Labor Relations Reporter	
Workers' Compensation Business Management Guide	Workers' Comp. Bus. Mgmt. Guide (CCH)

Subdivisions

T.17

The following list provides abbreviations for names of document subdivisions frequently used in legal citations. See **rule 3** for further guidance in using these abbreviations.

Subdivision	Abbreviation
amendment [s]	amend., amends.
annotation [s]	annot., annots.
appendi[x, ces]	app., apps.
article [s]	art., arts.
book [s]	bk., bks.
chapter [s]	ch., chs.
clause [s]	cl., cls.
column [s]	col., cols.
commentary, comment [s]	cmt., cmts.
decision [s]	dec., decs.
example [s]	ex., exs.
figure [s]	fig., figs.
folio [s]	fol., fols.
footnote [s]	
in cross-references	note, notes
other references	n., nn.
illustration [s]	illus.
line [s]	l., ll.
number [s]	No., Nos.
page [s]	
in cross-references	p., pp.
other references	[at]
paragraph [s]	
if so in source	¶, ¶¶
otherwise	para., paras.
part [s]	pt., pts.
preamble	pmbl.
principle [s]	princ., princs.
rule	R.
schedule [s]	sched., scheds.
section [s]	
in amending act	sec., secs.
all other contexts	§, §§
series, serial [s]	ser.
table [s]	tbl., tbls.
title [s]	tit., tits.
volume [s]	vol., vols.

T
T.17

Index

Page references in regular type are to INSTRUCTIONS; page references in *Italics* are to EXAMPLES

Abbreviations
adjacent, spacing, 48
administrative reporters, *49,* 187–88
administrative reports, 98
agencies, *49,* 96–97
American reporters, 63–64, 183–244
"and," in case names, 59
arbitral reporters, 167–68, 301
Argentinian materials, 245–46
Australian materials, 246–50
Austrian materials, 250–52
authors, 107–09
bound services, 343–48
Brazilian materials, 252–53
business firms, 61, 109
Canadian materials, 254–57
Catholic Church materials, 257
case history, 68–69
case names, 56–62
case names, in citations, 62
case names, international, 162–67
Chinese materials, 257–58
citations, repeating, 40–43
closing up of, 48
codes, 49, 151–52 (see also name of
  jurisdiction)
codes, statutory, 78–81
commissions, 187–88
commonly abbreviated names, 49, 59
  62, 302–03
congressional reports and documents, 91–96, 310
corporate authors, 108–09
countries, 160, 311–14
court documents, 18–19, 307–08
court of decision, 64–66, 304–06
Czech Republic materials, 259
dollar symbol, 50
East African Court of Appeal
  materials, 167, 299
editions of books, 110–12, 342
English *Law Report* series, 292–93
English materials, 292–95
English-language periodicals, 48,
  317–41
English monarchs, 290
English statutes, 154, 290–91
European Communities materials,
  164–66, 174–77
European Court and Commission of
  Human Rights materials, 166
explanatory phrases, 68–69, 309
foreign countries, 311–14

foreign courts, 151–53 (see also
  name of jurisdiction)
foreign materials, 151–52, 245–96
foreign periodicals, 154–55
French materials, 259–62
generally, 47–50
German materials, 262–65
government reports, 93–95
"hereinafter," use of, 43
history of cases, 68–69
Hungarian materials, 266
Indian materials, 266–68
initials, commonly recognized, 49, 59,
  62
institutional authors, 108–09
Inter-American Commission on
  Human Rights materials, 166–67,
  299
intergovernmental organizations,
  297–99
international and world organization
  materials, 157–81
Ireland, Republic of, materials,
  268–69
Israeli materials, 269–70
Italian materials, 270–72
Japanese materials, 272–76
judges, titles, 53, 315
law journals and reviews, 317–41
League of Nations materials, 297
looseleaf services, 343–48
Mexican materials, 276–77
model codes, 87–88
months, 316
multiple citations of same work,
  40–43
multiple editions and printings,
  110–12
municipal ordinances, 85–86
names, commonly abbreviated, 49,
  59, 62
Netherlands materials, 277–79
New Zealand materials, 279–80
Northern Ireland materials, 295
new series, 318, 332
newsletters, 125
newspapers, 120–21
no date, 111
no place, 111
officials, titles, 53, 315
ordinances, 85–86
paragraph symbols, 37, 39, 50
parliamentary materials, British, 291

parties to treaties, 160
percent symbols, 50
periodicals, 48, 118, 317–41
periodicals, English-language,
   317–41
periodicals, foreign-language, 154–55
periods, 48–49
pluralization of, 302
prepositions in periodical names, 317
prior case history, 68–69
publishers of services, 343
publishing terms, 342
punctuation of, 48–49
repeating citations, 40–43
reporters, United States, 63–64,
   183–244
reporters, foreign, 153, 245–96
restatements, 87–88
Roman materials, 280–81
Russian Federation materials,
   281–83
Scottish materials, 295–96
section symbols, 37–38, 50
services, 343–48
session laws, 81–83 (see also name
   of jurisdiction)
South African materials, 283–85
spacing of, 48
Spanish materials, 285–86
standards, 87–88
statutes, 76–90 (see also name of
   jurisdiction)
subdivisions (e.g., section, article,
   chapter), 33–40, 349
subsequent case history, 68–69
Swiss materials, 287–89
taxation materials, 16–17, 100–02
titles of books and pamphlets,
   109–10
titles of individuals, 53
treaty series, 300
unions, 61–62
United Kingdom materials, 289–96
United Nations materials, 168–74, 297
"United States," 49, 60, 62, 109
use of abbreviations not listed in this
   book, 47
Welsh materials, 292–95
Abstracts, in law reviews, 122
"*Accord*," as signal, 22
Acquiescence, in tax cases, 102, 309
"Act," capitalization of, 51
Action on decision, 102

Accounting standards, 88
**Acts (see Codes, Session laws,
   Statutes)**
Addenda, 39
Addresses (speeches), 32, 128
Administrative agencies
  abbreviation of, 96–97
  adjudications, 98–100
  arbitrations, 98–100
  official releases, 99–100
  reporters, 187–88
  reports, 98–99
Administrative cases
  citation of, 98–100, 187–88
  exact date, when required, 99–100
  number of case, when required,
    99–100
  omission of procedural phrases,
    58–59
  parallel citation, 100
  recent, 99–100
  services, when cited, 100
  "*sub nom.*," use on appeal, 69
Administrative law judges, 53, 315
Administrative materials
  adjudications, *97*, 98–100, 102
  agency publications, *109*
  basic citation forms, 96–97
  cases, 69, 97, 98–100, 102
  citation order, 26–27
  Code of Federal Regulations, 96–97
  compilations of regulations, 97–98
  court administrative orders, 103
  executive orders, *97*, 103
  Federal Register, 96, 97–98
  federal rules and regulations, 96–98
  foreign (see name of country)
  generally, 96–104
  Internal Revenue Service, 16–17, *97,*
    100–102
  Internet sources, 139
  names of rules and regulations, 97–98
  notices, 98
  official releases, 99–100
  opinions, formal advisory, *97,* 100
  order within signal, 26–27
  popular names of rules and regula-
    tions, 97–98
  presidential orders, *97,* 103
  presidential papers, 103
  presidential proclamations, 103
  proposed rules and regulations, 98
  regulations, *96–97,* 97–98

Page references in regular type are to Instructions; page references in *Italics* are to Examples

reorganization plans, 103
revenue materials, 16–17, *97,*
 100–02
revenue rulings, 101–02
rules, *96–97,* 97–98
slip opinions, 99
state, 96–97, 188–241
tax materials, 16–17, *97,* 100–02
Treasury decisions, 101
Treasury materials, *97,* 100–02
Treasury regulations, *97,* 100–02
U.N. Administrative Tribunal, 172
United Kingdom, 289–96
United States Code, 103
varieties of, 96–97
Administrative Procedure Act, *90,* 95
Advance sheets, 101
Advisory committee notes, *39*
"*Affirmed***" and "***affirming***," in case**
 history, *68–69,* 309
Affidavits, 18–19, 307
Agencies, administrative (see
 Administrative agencies)
Agreements, international, 157,
 158–62
Alabama
sources of law, *82, 84,* 188–89
Alaska
sources of law, *81,* 189–90
Alberta
sources of law, 255–56
All England Law Reports, 292
Alphabets, foreign, 152
Alterations in quotations, 44–45
Alternative holding, indication of, 67
"*Amended by***"**
in constitution citation, *75*
in statute citation, *84*
Amended constitution, 75
Amended statutes, 77, 82, 84
Amendments
Canadian statutes, 254
constitutional, 75
model codes, 87–88
restatements, 87–88
standards, 87–88
statutes, 77, 82, 84
Treasury regulations, 16–17, 100–01
uniform acts, 87
"Amendment(s)," abbreviation of, 349
American Bar Association
publications, *89, 124*
section reports, 124–25

American Jurisprudence (Am. Jur.),
 113
American Law Institute
generally, 87–88
proceedings, *124*
publications, 88
American Law Reports (A.L.R.), 124
American Samoa
sources of law, 241
Ampersand
authors' names, *107, 108*
books and pamphlets, *107, 108*
case names, 59
editor's names, *108*
footnote citation, 36
Annals of Congress, 95
Annexes
generally, 39
U.N. records, 169, 170
Annotations
A.L.R., L.R.A., 124
generally, 39
Annual Digest and Reports of
 Public International Law
 Cases, 167
Annual reports
corporations, *108*
government agencies, 98
Permanent Court of International
 Justice, 163, 179
"*Appeal dismissed***," in case history,** 69
Appeal docketed, *56, 66*
Appeals, *56, 66,* 68–69
Appendices
codes, 80
generally, 39
statutes reprinted in codes, 80
"Appendi[x, ces]," abbreviation of,
 349
Arabic numerals
monarchs, 290
volumes, 33–34
Arbitrations
administrative, 98–100
international, *157,* 167–68
"Arbitrator," abbreviation of, 315
Arbitrators, indicated parenthetically,
 99
Argentina
sources of national law, 245–46
Arizona
sources of law, 190–91
Arkansas
sources of law, *82,* 191

Page references in regular type are to INSTRUCTIONS; page references in *Italics* are to EXAMPLES

Article (part of speech), capitalization of, 51
Articles
  appearing in two or more parts, 123–24
  basic citation forms, 117–18
  capitalization in titles, 51
  citation analyzed, 8
  citation order, 27
  collected essays, printed in, 112–13
  essays in collection, 112
  foreign periodicals, *151,* 154–55
  forthcoming publications, 128
  law reviews and journals, 117–20
  magazines, 119–20
  multipart, 123–24
  newspapers, 120–21
  no author given in source, 119–20, 122–23
  order within signal, 27
  page citation, 34–37
  periodicals, 117–26
  titles, capitalization, 51
  typeface in court documents and legal memoranda, 12
  typeface in law review citations, 31
  typeface in law review text, 32–33
"Article(s)," abbreviation of, 349
"Ass'n," in case names, 59, 61
"At," used in citation of pages or sections, *29,* 34–35, 37, 109–10, 170
"At," used in electronic media, 130, 133, 134, 140
"Attorney General," abbreviation of, 315
Attorney General, opinions, *98,* 100
Audio recordings, 143
Auditing standards, 88
Australia
  sources of national law, 246–50
  treaty source, 248
Austria
  sources of national law, 250–52
Authorities in text, identification of, 21
Authorities previously cited, 40–43
Authors
  annotation, 124
  articles in periodicals, 118
  book reviews, 121, 123
  books and pamphlets, 107–08
  collected essays, 112–13
  colloquy, names not given, 123

  congressional documents and reports, 94
  essays in collection, 112–13
  forewords, 113
  institutional, 108–09
  law reviews and journals, 118
  model codes, 87–89
  multiple, books and pamphlets, 107–08
  multivolume works, 108
  newspapers, 120
  news reports and articles, 120
  no author, 119–20, 122–23
  periodical materials, 118
  periodicals, surveys and symposia in, 123
  prefaces, 113
  restatements, 88
  reviewer of book, 121, 123
  standards, 88
  student, 121–23
  symposium, names not given, 123
  U.N. material, 169
Author's mistakes in quoted material, 45
"*Available at,***" 29, *121,* 130, 132, 133, 134
Ballentine's Law Dictionary, *113*
Bankruptcy
  appellate panels, 65, 185
  cases, 58, *63, 147, 148*
  courts, *63,* 65, *147,* 185, 304
  pending or unreported cases, *63*
Bankruptcy Reporter, 185
Bar publications, 124–25
"Baron," abbreviation of, 315
Basic charters, international and world organizations, *157,* 174, 176–77
Bible, 114
Bills
  bills and resolutions, 92–93
  congressional, 92–93
  state, 93
  statutory, 92–93
Black's Law Dictionary, *113*
Blackstone's *Commentaries,* *111*
Block quotations, 43–44
The Bluebook, *108,* 114
Board of Tax Appeals
  citation of cases, 99, 102, 185–86
Book notes, 123
Book reviews
  citation order, 27

Page references in regular type are to INSTRUCTIONS; page references in *Italics* are to EXAMPLES

periodicals, 121, 123
"Book(s)," **abbreviation of,** 349
Books and pamphlets
ABA publications, *89, 124*
abbreviation of title, 109
administrative agency records and
    reports, 98–100, 109
ALI publications, 87–88
author, 107–09
basic form of citation, 107
book reviews, 121, 123
capitalization, 51, 109
citation, components of, 107
citation analyzed, 7–8
citation order, 27
collected documents, 112–13
collected essays, 112–13
congressional materials, 91–96
corporate author, 108–09
date, 110–112
date in title, 109–10
date not given by source, 111
Declaration of Independence, 37
dictionaries, legal, *113*
edition, 110–12
editor, when indicated, 108–09
encyclopedias, legal, *113*
The Federalist, 113–14
footnote typefaces, 107, 109
forewords, *35,* 113
forthcoming publications, 128
generally, 107–17
given names of authors, 107–08
government agencies as authors,
    108–09
government agency reports, 98
institutional authors, 94, 98, 108–09
Internet sources, 139–40
italicization, when referred to in text,
    32
law reviews and journals, 117–20,
    121–24, 317–41
legal dictionaries and encyclopedias,
    113
letters, 112, 127
manuscripts, typed, 127, 128
multiple authors, 107–08
multiple editions, 110–11
multiple printings, 110–11
multivolume works, 108
name of author, 107–09
names and titles, capitalization, 51,
    109
number, serial, 110

offprints, 112
order within signal, 27
page citation, 34–36, 107
paragraph citation, 37–39, 107
periodicals, 317–41
photoduplicated reprints, 111
place of publication not given by
    source, 111
place of publication, when required,
    111
pocket parts, 111–12
pre-1900 works, 111
prefaces, 113
printings, 110
publication number, 110
repagination, 111
repeated citation of, *40–43*
reprints, 111
restatements, 87–88, 113
sections, 107
serial number, 110
series of, 110
short citation forms, 114–17
shorter works in collection, 112–13
special citation forms, 113–14
star pages, 111
subdivisions of, 33–40
subtitles, omitted, 109
supplements, 111–12
theses, unpublished, 127
titles, 109–10
translator, when given, 108
typed manuscripts, *127*
typeface, 107, 109
typeface, authors, 12, 107
typeface in court documents and
    legal memoranda, 12
typeface in law review citations, 31
typeface in law review text, 32–33
unpublished works, 126–29
volume designations, *108, 112*
well-known works, 113–14
writer of, 107–09
year, 110–11
Bound services
abbreviations, 343–48
generally, 147–49
typeface, 147
Brackets
alterations in quotations, 44–45
establishing short citation or transla-
    tion, used in, 43, 151–52, *153,*
    154–55
quotations, used in, 44–45

X

volume designations, 34, 147
years, 34, *147, 152*
Brazil
sources of national law, 252–53
treaty source, 253
Briefs and legal memoranda (see
Court documents and legal
memoranda)
Briefs and records, citation of
citation order, 27
generally, *56,* 71
British Columbia
sources of law, 255–56
British materials (see England)
Broadcasts, 142
"Bros.," in case names, 59, 61, 302
Bureau of National Affairs (BNA)
services, 343
Business firms, in case names, 59,
61
"But cf.," **as signal,** 23–24
"But see," **as signal,** 23–24
"But see, e.g.," **as signal,** *22*
Byline, newspaper articles, 120

California
sources of law, 191–93
Canada
sources of national law, 254–57
treaty source, 255
***Canadian Guide to Uniform Legal
Citation,*** 257
Canal Zone
sources of law, 242
**Canons of Professional
Responsibility,** 89
Canon Law, 257
Cantons, Swiss, 288–89
Capitalization
change in quotation, indication of,
44–45
court documents and legal memoranda, 17–18
courts, 17–18, 52
generally, 51–53
headings, 51
party designations, 17
people or groups, nouns referring to,
51
titles of books and articles, 51, 109,
118
titles of court documents, 17–18
titles of foreign documents, 151

Case comments in law reviews,
121–22
Case history (see History of cases)
Case names
abbreviations, 56–62, 302–03
abbreviations, in citations, 62, 302–03
abbreviations, in textual sentences,
57–62
administrative actions, 98–100
"administrator," omission of, 60
ampersand, use of in text, 59
appeal, when different on, 69
"appellee," omission of, 60
arbitrations, 98–100
arbitrations, international, 167–68
"Ass'n," abbreviation in text, 59
bankruptcy, 58
"Bros.," abbreviation in text, 59
business firms, 59, 61
citations, abbreviations in, 62, 302–03
cite as in official reporter, 57
cite first listed party only, 57–58
"Co.," abbreviation in text, 59
Commissioner of Internal Revenue,
as party, 62
Common Market cases, 164–66
consolidated actions, 57
"Corp.," abbreviation in text, 59
court documents and legal memoranda, 11–12
"d/b/a," omission of, 57
descriptive terms, 58–59, 60
different on appeal, 69
"estate of," 58–59
"et al.," 57
European Court of Justice, 164–66
"executor," omission of, 60
"ex parte," *58–59*
"ex rel.," 58
first word, retention in full, 57
foreign cases, 152–53
generally, 56–62
geographical terms, 60
given names and initials of parties,
60–61
"In re," *58–59*
in rem actions, 58
"Inc.," abbreviation in text, 59
"Inc.," when omitted, 61
Internal Revenue Commissioner, as
party, 62
international arbitrations, 167–68
International Court of Justice, 163
"Judgment of," 57

Page references in regular type are to INSTRUCTIONS; page references in *Italics* are to EXAMPLES

Latin words italicized, 59
lengthy, 57
"licensee," omission of, 60
"Ltd.," abbreviation in text, 59
"Ltd.," when omitted, 61
"No.," abbreviation in text, 59
omissions in, 57–62
omitted in official reporter, 57
parenthetical, 58
parties, only first-listed named, 57–58
partnerships, 57
Permanent Court of International
    Justice, 163
popular names, 59
procedural phrases, 58–59
real property, as party, 58
running heads, words omitted in, 57
short forms, 71–73
state as party in state court decision,
    60
surnames, 60–61
textual references, 11–12, 32, 57–62
"The," omission of, 59
"trustee," omission of, 60
typeface used in court documents,
    11–12
typeface used in law review citations,
    31
typeface used in law review text, 32
unions as parties, 61–62
"Will of," 58–59
World Court, 163
Case notes in law reviews, 121–22
Case number
  administrative cases, 99–100
  appeal or petition for certiorari, *56, 70*
  court documents, 71
  Federal Cases, 184, 185
  pending cases, *56,* 70
  unreported cases, *56,* 70
Case writeups
  citation of, 121–22
  cited with case, 29–30
Cases
  (see also individual jurisdiction or
    court)
  administrative actions, 98–100
  appeal, disposition on, *56*
  appeal docketed, *56*
  arbitrations, 98–100
  bankruptcy, 58, *63, 147, 148*
  basic citation forms, *55–56*
  before decision, *56*
  briefs, citation of, 18–19, *56,* 71

British, 289–96
certiorari, citation of petition for, *56*
citation, basic forms of, *55–56*
citation, components of, 55–56
citation analyzed, 5–6
citation order, 26
citation to particular page, 34–35
civil law, 153
commentary on, cited with case,
    29–30, 153
common law, 152–53
components of citations, 55–56
computerized research services,
    130–31
concurring opinion, 67
country, indication of, 152
court of decision, 64–66
court of decision, abbreviations,
    304–06
court of decision, American, 64–66
court of decision, other jurisdictions,
    152–53
court, when indicated, 64–66
date, civil law, 153
dates, 55, 66–67, 70
denial of rehearing, 68
dictum, 67
different name on appeal, 69
dissenting opinion, 67
docket number, *56,* 70, 99–100
dual citation of sources, 14–15,
    62–63
electronic databases, 72–73, 130–31
England, 289–95
European Communities, 164–66
explanatory phrases, 68–69
federal court, 183–86
filed, *56,* 70
foreign, 152–53
history on remand, 68
history, prior and subsequent, 68
in rem, 58, 59
interim orders, *56*
international and world organization,
    157, 162–67
international arbitrations, 167–68
International Court of Justice,
    163–64
Internet sources, 137–38
italicization of names in court docu-
    ments, 11–12
italicization of names in text, 32
italicization of procedural phrases in
    citations, 31

italicized words in history of, 68–69,
 309
Judge or Justice writing opinion,
 67–68
LEXIS, cited to, *130–31*
medium neutral citation, 64
memoranda in, citations to, 71
memorandum decision, 67
motions, citation to, 71
name cited as in official report, 57
named in text, initial and subsequent
 citation, 40–42
names, 56–62
newspapers, cited in, *56,* 63, 120
no name, citation of, 57
non-common-law, 153
number of case, *56,* 70
official reporters, when cited, 62–64
order within signal, 25–27
page citations, 34–35
parallel citation of sources, 14–15,
 62–64
parenthetical information, 68–69
pending, 56, 66, 70
per curiam decisions, 67
periodicals, when cited, 63
Permanent Court of International
 Justice, 163–64
plurality opinion, 67
prior history, 68–69
procedural phrases, 58–59
public domain format, 64
published decision, *56*
recent, *56, 66*
records, citation of, 18–19, *56,* 71
releases of administrative agencies,
 cited to, 98
repeating citations of, 40–42, 71–73
reporters, 62–64
reporters, defined, 63
reporters, reprinted, 63–64
services, appearing in, *56*
services, when cited, 63
short citation form, 71–73
slip opinions, reported in, *56,* 63, 70
sources, 62–64
state courts, 65–66, 188–241
statutory material, cited with, *30*
subsequent history, *56,* 68–69
transcript of record, citations to,
 18–19, *56,* 71
typeface used in court documents,
 11–13

typeface used in law review citations,
 31
typeface used in law review text, 32
unofficial reporter, when cited, 63
unreported, *56,* 70
weight of authority, 68–69
Westlaw, cited to, *130–31*
World Court, 163–64
year of decision, 66–67
Catholic Church, codes, 257
CD-ROM, 141–42, 144
Certiorari
 applied for, granted, denied, *56,*
  68–69, *309*
 indication in case history, 68–69
 petition, citation of, *56*
 "sub nom." not used, 69
"*Cf.*," as signal, 23
C.F.R., 97–98, *104, 186*
"Chancellor," abbrevation of, 53, 315
Chancery Division, English, 294
Chapters
 codes, statutory, 79
 number, when given for federal
  statute, 79
"Chapter(s)," abbreviation of, 349
**Charters, international organiza-
 tions,** *157,* 174, 178
Chicago Manual of Style, 4
**"Chief Baron," "Justice," "Judge,"
 abbreviation of,** 53, 315
China, People's Republic of
 sources of national law, 257–58
 treaty source, 258
"Circuit," capitalization of, 52
Circuit courts of appeals (see
 Courts)
Circuit courts, old federal, 65,
 183–84
Circuit Justices, 65, 183
**Citation of commentary with case or
 book,** 29–30
Citation order, 25–27
Citation sentences and clauses,
 13–14, 21–22, 24–27
Citations
 (see also specific types of material)
 abbreviations of case names, 56–62
 analogous authority, 23
 authoritativeness, order within citation, 25–27
 authorities, 24–27
 background authority, 23

citations analyzed, 5–9
comparing authorities, 23
contradictory proposition, 23–24
court documents and legal memoranda, 11–19
direct contradiction, 23
direct support, 22–23
footnotes, 35–36
law review text and footnotes, *21–22*
material cited more than once, 40–43
numerous authorities, *40–43*
omission from quotation, indication
of, 45–47
opposing proposition, 23–24
order of, 24–27
pages, 34–35
parenthetical explanations, 28
placement, 24–27
placement after quotation, 43–44
punctuation of, 24, 31, 37–38
quotations, 43–47
related authority, 29–30
repeating citations, 40–43
sampling of authorities, *22*
signals in, 22–24
string citations, *22,* 24–27
subdivisions, 33–34, 349
supplementary material, 24
supporting proposition, 22–23
typeface used, 11–13, 30–32
weight of, 67
Citations analyzed
books, 7–8
cases, 5–6
constitutions, 6
periodical materials, 8
regulations, 7
rules, 7
statutes, 6–7
treaties, 9
United Nations materials, 9
"Cited in," **use of,** 29
City and county ordinances, 85–86
**"City of," when omitted in case
names,** 60
Civil law jurisdictions
cases, 153, 245–89
codes, 154, 245–89
constitutions, 153–54, 245–89
courts, 245–89
session laws, 154, 155, 245–89
statutes, 154, 245–89
Civil Rights Act of 1964, 95

Clark Boardman Callaghan (CBC)
services, 343
(see also Services and topical
reporters)
"Clause(s)," abbreviation of, 349
Clean Air Act, 95
Closing up of abbreviations, 48
C.M.L.R. *(Common Market Law
Reports),* 165–66, 298
"Co.," in case names, 59, 61
"Code," capitalization of, 51
Code, Internal Revenue (see Internal
Revenue Code)
Code of Federal Regulations (C.F.R.),
97–98, 104, 186
Code of Justinian, 280
Code of Theodosius, 281
Codes
(see also Statutes)
abbreviations, 78–79
administrative compilations, 96–98
American, *77,* 78–79
appendices, 80
appendix with reprinted statute, *80*
basic citation forms, *76–77*
Canadian, 254–57
chapters, 79
citation analyzed, 6–7
city ordinances, 85–86
Code of Federal Regulations, 97–98,
104, 186
compilations of, 80
components of citation, 78–79
county ordinances, 85–86
date, 80–81
editors, 80
electronic databases, 131
English, 290–91
ethics, 89
federal, 78–81
foreign, 154, 245–96 (see also name
of individual country)
future location of statutes, 83
Internal Revenue, 16, 85
legislative materials, 91–96
LEXIS, 131
materially different from statute, 78
official and unofficial, 78–80
ordinances, municipal, 85–86
parallel citation to, 81–83
pocket parts, 80
positive law, enacted into, 78
publishers of, 78–80

Page references in regular type are to INSTRUCTIONS; page references in *Italics* are to EXAMPLES

Roman law, 280–81
scattered sections, 78
secondary sources cited to, 77,
    83–84
sections cited, 78–79
state, 79–80, 188–244
statutes, when cited to, 76–77
subject-matter, 79
supplements, 78, 80
tax materials, 16, 85
titles, 79
Treasury materials, 16, 85, 100–02
typeface used, 13, *79*
uncodified laws, 80
uniform acts, 86–87
unofficial, differently numbered, 80
volumes, 79
Westlaw, 131
which to cite, 77–78
year, 80–81
Codification
session laws, parenthetical indication
    of, 81–83
Collected works
citation of works in, 112–13
editor, 108–09, 112
"*id.*" short form, 116–17
"*in,*" used to introduce collection, 29
parallel citation to, using "*reprinted
    in,*" 29
"*supra*" short form, 116–17
Colloquia, in periodicals, 123
Colorado
sources of law, 193–94
"Column(s)," abbreviation of, 349
Comma
citing commentary with case or
    statute, 29–30
citing multiple sections of code, *38*
"compare . . . with" signal, 23
italicization, 32, 33, 309
periodical names, 317
titles ending in dates, 34–35, 109–10
Command number, English, 291–92
Command Papers, English, 291–92
"Comment," abbreviation of, 349
**"Comment," designating student
    work,** *122*
Commentary
citation of, 29–30
foreign cases, on, 153
Comments
model codes, 88–89
periodicals, 117–18

restatements, 88
rules of ethics, 89
sentencing guidelines, 88
standards, 87–88
**Commerce Clearing House (CCH)
    services,** 343
(see also Services and topical
    reporters)
Commerce Court, 184
Commercial electronic databases
(see Electronic databases)
"Commissioner," abbreviation of, 315
**Commissioner of Internal Revenue,
    in case names,** 62
Committee materials, UN, 168–69
Committee prints, *91,* 93–94
Common law jurisdictions
cases, 152–53, 155, 246–96
codes, 154, 246–96
constitutions, 153–54, 246–96
courts, 246–96
session laws, 154, 155, 246–96
statutes, 154, 155, 246–96
Common Market Law Reports
    (C.M.L.R.), 165, 298
Common Market materials, *157–58,*
    165–66, 174–77, 297–98
Common Market Reporter, 165–66,
    297–98
"Commonwealth of,"
capitalization, 52
when omitted in case names, 60
"Compare . . . with . . . ," **as signal,** 23
Compilations
administrative regulations, 97–102
treaties, *157,* 300
Compilations of statutes
(see also Codes, Statutes)
federal, 78–80
foreign, 154, 246–96
state, 79–80, 189–244
Compiler of codes, 80
Computerized research services (see
    Electronic databases)
Concurrent resolutions, 92–93
Concurring opinions, 67
"Congress," capitalization of, *51*
Congressional debates, *91,* 95
Congressional Globe, 95
Congressional materials
bills and resolutions, *91,* 92–93
committee prints, *91,* 93–94
concurrent resolutions, 92–93
debates, *91,* 95

Page references in regular type are to INSTRUCTIONS; page references in *Italics* are to EXAMPLES

documents, *91–92,* 93–94
hearings, *91,* 93
joint resolutions, 92–93
parallel citations, 92, 94, 95
reports, *91,* 93–95
resolutions, *91,* 92–93
secondary authority, 95
unnumbered documents, 94
Congressional Record
daily edition, *91,* 93, 95
debates, 95
permanent edition, 95
resolutions cited to, 92–93
Conjunctions, capitalization of, 51
Connecticut
sources of law, 194–95
Consecutive pages or footnotes,
citation of, 36
Consecutive sections of codes, 38
Consolidated actions, case names,
57
Constitutions
amended provisions, 75
capitalization of parts of, 52
citation analyzed, 6
citation order, 25
European Communities, 176–77
federal and state, 75
foreign, 153–54, 245–96
generally, 75
League of Nations, 174
order within signal, 25
repealed provisions, 75
subdivision, *52,* 75
superseded, 75
typeface in footnotes, 13, 75
U.N. charter, *157,* 174
"*Construed in,*" use of, 29–30
"Construing," use of, 29–30
"Contra," as signal, 23
Conventions, international, *159*
"Corp.," in case names, 59, 61
Corporations
abbreviations, 59, 61
authors, 108–09
case names, 59, 61
Corpus Juris Secundum (C.J.S.), *113*
Council of Europe materials, 177
Countries
(see also name of jurisdiction)
abbreviated in case names, 62
abbreviated in international arbitra-
tions, 167–68
abbreviated treaty citations, *157,* 160

abbreviations of, 311–14
County and city ordinances, 85–86
"Court," capitalization of, 52
Court administrative orders, 103
Court documents and legal memo-
randa
abbreviations of documents in, 18–19
capitalization in, 17–18
citations in, 13–15
federal taxation materials, citations to,
16–17
Internal Revenue Code, citations to,
16
parallel citations in, 14–15
short forms in, 15–16
typeface of citations in, 11–13
Court of Claims, 184
Court of Customs and Patent
Appeals, 184
Court of decision
abbreviations, 64–66, 304–06
American, 64–66
civil law jurisdictions, 153
common law jurisdictions, 152–53
international arbitrations, 167–68
international cases, 162–67
state, 64–66
when indicated, 55, 64–66, 70–71,
152–53
when omitted, 64–66
World Court cases, 163–64
Court of International Trade, 184–85
Court of Justice of the European
Communities, *157,* 164–66,
297–98
Court of Military Appeals, 186
Courts
(see also name of court or jurisdiction)
abbreviations, 64–66, 304–06
administrative orders, 103
Appeals, District of Columbia Circuit,
Court of, 65, 183
Appeals, District of Columbia
Municipal Court of, 196
appeals, United States courts of, 65,
183
Arbitration, Permanent Court of, *168*
bankruptcy, 58, 65, 185
bankruptcy appellate panels, 65, 185
Board of Tax Appeals, 185–86
circuit courts, old federal, 65, 183–84
Circuit Justices, 183
civil law countries, 245–96

Claims Court, 184
Commerce Court, 184
common law countries, 246–96
Customs and Patent Appeals, Court
   of, 184
district, federal, 65, 185
Emergency Court of Appeals, 184
English, 292–95
federal, 183–88
foreign countries, 245–96
foreign, language used in citation of,
   151–52
international, 162–68
International Court of Justice, *157,*
   163–64
International Justice, Permanent
   Court of, 163–64
International Trade, Court of, 184–85
Judicial Panel on Multi-District
   Litigation, 65, 185
Military Appeals, Court of, 186
old circuit, federal, 65, 183–84
Permanent Court of Arbitration, *168*
Permanent Court of International
   Justice, 163–64
Rail Reorganization Court, 185
rules, 86
state, 188–244
Tax Court, 102, 185–86
Temporary Emergency Court of
   Appeals, 184
terms, 53
U.S. Supreme (see U.S. Supreme
   Court)
World Court, *157,* 163–64, 297
Courts of Military Review, 186
Cross-references
court documents and legal memoran-
   da, 13, 39–40
generally, 39–40
groups of authorities previously cited,
   39–40
order of authorities, 27
previous footnotes, 39–40
textual material in same work, 39–40
Cumulative Bulletin, 102
Customs Court, 184
***Cyclopedia of the Law of Private
   Corporations,*** *110*
Czech Republic
sources of national law, 259

**Dash, used in citing sections of
   codes,** 38

Databases (see Electronic databases)
Dates
administrative compilations, 97–98
amended constitutional provisions, 75
amended statutes, 84
bilateral and multilateral treaties,
   158–60
books and pamphlets, 110–12
case history, 66–67, 68
cases, 56, 66–67
cases, cited to U.S.L.W., *56*
cases, foreign, 152–53
cases, in electronic databases,
   130–31
cases, in looseleaf services, *56, 70,*
   148
cases, in newspapers, *56, 63*
cases, in periodicals, *56*
cases, in slip opinions, 70
cases, pending, 66, 70
cases, unreported, *56, 70*
cases, World Court, *157,* 164
Code of Federal Regulations, 96,
   97–98
codifications of statutes, 79, 80–81,
   82
constitutions, when used, 75
enactment, session laws, 82–83
ethical opinions, 89
ethical rules, 89
exact date, administrative cases, 99
exact date, cases, *56,* 66–67, 70, 148
exact date, Congressional debates,
   91
exact date, international agreements,
   160
exact date, letters, speeches, and
   interviews, *19,* 126–28
exact date, ordinances, 85–86
exact date, periodicals, 117–18,
   119–20
exact date, services, 148
exact date, statutes, 82
exact date, treaties, 160
exact date, unpublished works,
   126–28
exact date, unreported cases, 70
exact date, World Court cases, 164
exchange of notes, 160
filing of appeal, *56*
filing of cases, 70
forewords, 113
Internal Revenue Code, 16–17, 85

Page references in regular type are to INSTRUCTIONS; page references in *Italics* are to EXAMPLES

international agreements, *157,* 159–60
Internet sources, 136–37
legislative materials, 83–84, 93–96
looseleaf statutory codifications, 81
model codes, 87, *88*
multilateral treaties, 159–62
multiple decisions in one year, 66–67
multivolume works, *108,* 110–11
newspapers, 120
ordinances, municipal, 85–86
periodicals, 119–20
pocket parts, books, 111–12
prefaces, 113
prior to 1900, books, 111
regnal years, in English statutes, 290–91
repealed constitutional provisions, 75
repealed statutes, 84
restatements, 87
rules of court, 86
rules of procedure, 86
services, 147–48
session laws, 82
standards, 87
statutes, 80–81
statutes, amended, 84
statutes, cited to session laws, 82
statutes, foreign, 154
statutes, in current code, 80–81
statutes, in supplements to code, 81
statutes, not in current code, 82
statutes, repealed, 84
statutes, uniform acts, 86–87
supplements, books, 111–12
supplements, codes, 81
titles ending in, *34–35,* 109–10
treaties, *157,* 159–60
U.N. materials, 168, 171
uniform acts, 86–87
unreported cases, *56,* 70
U.S. Supreme Court cases, *55–56,* 66
year of decision of case, 55–56
"D/b/a," omission in case names, *57*
Debates
congressional, *91,* 95
English parliamentary, 291
European Parliamentary Assembly, 177, 298
legislative, *91,* 95
Republic of Ireland, 268–69
United Kingdom, 291
Decimal point, 49
"Decision(s)," abbreviation of, 349

Declaration of Independence, 37
Delaware
sources of law, *38, 79,* 195–96
Deletions from quotations, 45–47
Denial of certiorari, 68–69, 309
Denial of rehearing, when given, 68
Department of State publications, 161
Department, state court, 66
Descriptive terms, omitted in case names, 60
Development Programme, U.N., 172
"Developments in the Law," *122*
Dictionaries, *113*
Dictum, indication of, 67
Digest of Justinian, 280
Digests, international, *158,* 179–80
Digest of United States Practice in International Law, 179–80
Disciplinary rules, 89
Discussion drafts, 87, *89*
Dismissal of appeal, 68, 309
Dissenting opinions, 67
Dissertations, unpublished, 127
District court, federal
cases in, 65, 185
rules of, 86
District of Columbia
Circuit Court of Appeals for the, 65, 183
sources of law, 196–97
Divided court, parenthetical indication of, 67
Division, federal courts, 65
Docket number
appeal or petition for certiorari, *56*
briefs, records, motions, memoranda, 71
pending cases, 70
renumbering, 70
unreported cases, *56,* 70
Document number
intergovernmental organizations' materials, 178–79
U.N. publications, 168–74
Documents
legislative, *91–92,* 93–95
intergovernmental organizations, 174–79
published, collected, 113
U.N., 168–74
unpublished, collected, 112–13
Dollar amounts
numerals used, 50

Dominion Law Reports, 254
Dual citation, when required, 14–15,
    62–63

East African Court of Appeal, 167,
    299
Ecclesiastical courts, 294
Economic and Social Council, offi-
    cial records, U.N., 171
E.C.R. *(European Community
    Reports),* 164–65
Editions
    abbreviation of, 110, 342
    books and pamphlets, 110–11
    Code of Federal Regulations, 97
    Congressional Record, 95
    The Federalist, 113–14
    first edition, when cited, 110–11
    names of, 342
    newspapers, 120
    when indicated, books and pam-
        phlets, 110–11
    year, 110–11
Editors
    books and pamphlets, 107–09
    codes, 80
    collected works, 112–13
    reporters, 63–64
    shorter works in collection, 112–13
"E.g.," as signal, 22–24
Electronic databases
    cases, 72–73, 130–31
    containing separately published
        works, 129–30
    Dialog, 130, *132*
    generally, 130–32
    LEXIS, *73, 121,* 129–30, *131–32, 143*
    Loislaw.com, *73, 131, 144*
    news reports, 120–21
    secondary materials, 132
    short citation forms, 143–44
    statutes, 131
    VersusLaw, 130, *131*
    Westlaw, *72–73, 121,* 129–30,
        131–32, 143–44
Eleventh Circuit (see Fifth Circuit
    Split)
Ellipsis, 45–47
E-Mail, 141
Emergency Court of Appeals, 184
Emphasis in quotations, 45
Emphasis, italics for, 50
"En banc," parenthetical indication
    of, 67

Encyclopedias, legal, *113*
Endnotes, 36
"Enforced," in case history, *69,* 309
"Enforcing," in case history, 309
England
    administrative materials, 291
    case reports, abbreviations, 292–95
    cases, court of decision, 152–53,
        292–95
    cases, generally, 152–53, 289,
        292–95
    cases, House of Lords and Privy
        Council, appeals to, 289–90
    courts, 292–95
    parliamentary material, 291
    sovereigns, abbreviations, 290
    statutes, 290–91
    treaties, 291–92
English *Law Reports* series, 289,
    292–95
English Reports—Full Reprint,
    289–90
Epilogues, 113
Equal Employment Opportunity Act,
    95
Essays in collection
    (see also Shorter works in collection)
    citation of material in, 112–13
    editor, 112
    parallel citation to, 29
    "supra" short form, 42–43
    typeface, 112
"Estate of," in case names, 58–59
"Et al."
    authors' names, 108
    case names, omitted, 57
    editors' names, 108
"Et seq.," prohibition on use, 38
Ethical considerations, 89
Ethics, codes of, 89
European Commission of Human
    Rights, 166, 298–99
European Community materials,
    157, 158, 164–66, 174–77,
    297–98
European Court of Human Rights,
    157, 166, 298
European Court of Justice (see Court
    of Justice of the European
    Communities)
European Parliament Working
    Document, 176
European Parliamentary Assembly,
    176

Evidence, rules of, 86
"*Ex rel.*," in case names, *57*, 58
Executive Agreement Series (E.A.S.),
    300
Executive materials (see
    Administrative materials)
Executive orders, 103
Explanation of cited authorities, use
    of parentheticals, 28, 67–68,
    84–85
Explanatory phrases
    abbreviations used in case citation,
        309
    amended statutes, 84
    constitutions, amended or repealed,
        75
    italicization of, 68, 309
    repealed statutes, 84
    typeface used in court documents
        and legal memoranda, 13
    typeface used in law review citations,
        31
    weight of authority, 67, 68–69

Family Divisional Court, English, 294
Federal Cases, 183–84, 185
Federal courts
    (see also individual court name)
    courts of appeals, 183–84
    courts of decision, 64–66
    district courts, 185
    generally, 183–86
    Supreme Court, official cite only, 183
Federal government (see United
    States)
Federal Judicial Center
    Manual for Complex Litigation, 114
Federal Practice and Procedure, 108,
    114
Federal Register, 96, 97–98, 101–03,
    186
Federal Regulations, Code of, 96,
    97–98, 104, 186
Federal Reporter, 183–84, 185
Federal Rules Decisions, 185
Federal Rules of Appellate
    Procedure, *86*
Federal Rules of Civil Procedure, *86*
Federal Rules of Criminal Procedure,
    86
Federal Rules of Evidence, *86*
Federal Rules Service, 185
Federal statutes (see Statutes,
    Statutes at Large)

Federal Supplement, 184, 185
Federal taxation materials (see Tax
    materials)
The Federalist, 113–14
Fifth Circuit Split, 71
Films, 142
Financial reports, *108*
First editions, when cited, 110–11
First listed relator, not omitted in
    case names, 57
First names and initials
    authors of books and pamphlets,
        107–08, 115
    authors of articles, 117–18, 125
    case names, 60–61
Florida
    sources of law, *84,* 197–98
"Folio(s)," abbreviation of, 349
Footnotes
    abbreviation of, 35–36, 349
    citation of, 35–36
    consecutive and nonconsecutive, 36
    cross-reference to, 39–40
    material previously cited in, 40–43
    multipage, 35–36
    multiple, 36
    numbers in, 49–50
    omission from quotation, indication
        of, *44,* 45–46
    spanning several pages, 35–36
    textual material, typeface used in,
        32–33
    typeface used for citations in, 30–32
"Footnote(s)," abbreviation of, 35–36,
    349
"For the use of," abbreviated to "*ex
    rel.*," 58
Foreign alphabets, 152
Foreign countries
    (see also name of individual country)
    abbreviation of, 311–14
    World Court cases, 163–64
Foreign derivation, italicization of
    words of, 50
Foreign language
    abbreviation of words, 151–52
    constitutions, 154
    court name and location, give English
        version, 153
    English versions and translations,
        151, 158, 174
    names, 61
    words italicized, 50

Page references in regular type are to INSTRUCTIONS; page references in *Italics* are to EXAMPLES

Foreign materials
(see also name of individual country)
abbreviations, 151–52
alphabet, 152
cases, generally, 152–53
civil law, 153
common law, 152–53
codes, statutory, 154
constitutions, 153–54
English used in naming courts, 153
establishing abbreviations in initial
  citation, 151–52
international (see International agreements, International organization
  materials)
international agreements, *157,* 158–62
jurisdiction, 152, 158
official treaty sources, 300
periodicals, 154–55
short citation forms, 155
statutes, 154
treaty sources, 300
treaties, *157,* 158–62
Forewords, *35,* 113
**Formal opinions on professional
  responsibility,** *89*
Forthcoming publications, 128
France
sources of national law, 259–62
treaty source, 262
**Frequently cited authorities, short
  forms for,** 40–43
"F.S.B.," in case names, 61

Gaius, Institutes of, 280
**General Agreement on Tariffs and
  Trade (GATT),** *158,* 177–78
**General Assembly, official records,
  U.N.,** *157,* 171
**Generally Accepted Accounting
  Principles,** 88
**Generally Accepted Auditing
  Standards,** 88
Geographical terms
abbreviations, 311–14
case names, 60
Georgia
sources of law, 198–99
Germany
sources of national law, 262–65
treaty source, 265
Given names
authors, 107–08

corporation, partnership, and business names, 57, 61, 108–09
individuals, 60–61
Government agencies
annual and regular reports, 98
authors, as, 108–09
books and numbered publications,
  110
capitalization of, 51
subdivisions, 109
***Government Printing Office Style
  Manual,*** 4, 51
Government publications, U.S.,
  97–98, 108–09
Graphical materials, 37
**Groups of authorities previously
  cited, reference to,** 39–43
Guam
sources of law, 242–43

Hague Court Reports, *168*
Hawaii
sources of law, *34,* 199
Headings, capitalization in, 51
Hearings
congressional, 12, *28,* 42, *43,* 93
titles of, printed in italic type, 12, *91,*
  93
typeface used in court documents, 12
**"Hereinafter," used for shortened
  citation forms,** 43
High Court of Justice, English, 293
History of cases
both prior and subsequent, 68–69
dates of decisions, 66–67
different case name on appeal, 69
explanatory words, abbreviations, 309
explanatory words italicized or underscored, 13, 31, 309
"mem.," opinions designated as, 67
multiple decisions within single year,
  66–67
multiple dispositions, 69
ordering within signal unaffected by,
  26
overruled cases, *68,* 69
"per curiam," opinions designated as,
  67
position of parentheticals, 28
prior and subsequent, 55–56, 68–69
prior history indicated for memorandum decision, 67, 68
remand, when given, 68

Page references in regular type are to INSTRUCTIONS; page references in *Italics* are to EXAMPLES

separate decisions of other issues, when cited, 68
significance of disposition, 69
subsequent history, *55–56, 68*
subsequent history, appeal filed, docketed, *56,* 69
subsequent history, certiorari applied for, granted, denied, *56,* 68–69, 309
subsequent history, names of parties, when different on appeal, 69
subsequent history, reason for subsequent disposition, 69
typeface, 13, 31, 309
weight of authority, 67
History of statutes
amended statutes, 78, 84
parenthetically indicated, 84–85
Holdings
alternative, indication of, 67
concurring opinion, 67
contrary to citations, 23
dictum, 67
dissenting opinion, 67
implied, indication of, 67
plurality opinion, 67
unclear, indication of, 67
House of Commons
debates and Journal, 291
House of Lords
court, 290
debates and Journal, 291
House of Representatives
(see Congressional materials)
Human Rights
European Commission of, 166, 298–99
European Court of, *157,* 166, 298
Inter-American Commission of, *157,* 166–67, 299
Hungary
sources of national law, 266

"Id.," **use of,** 40–42, 115
Idaho
sources of law, 200
Illinois
sources of law, 200–01
Implied holdings, indication of, 67
"In re," **in case names,** 58–59
In rem jurisdiction, 58
"In the matter of," **abbreviated to** *"In re,"* 58–59
"In," **use of,** 29–30, 112–13

"Inc.," **in case names,** 59, 61
Inclusive numbers, 35–39
Income tax materials (see Tax materials)
India
sources of national law, 266–68
Indiana
sources of law, *81,* 201–02
Indian Nations (see Navajo Nation)
Informal opinions on professional responsibility, 89
"Infra," **use of,** 39–40
Initials
authors of books and pamphlets, 107–09
authors of periodicals, 107–08, 118
closing up of, 48
commonly abbreviated names, 49
editors, 108–09
parties in case names, 60–62
punctuation of, 48–49
translators, 108
Insertions in quotations, 44–45
Institutes of Gaius, 280
Institutes of Justinian, 280
Institutes, regular publications by, 124–25
Institutional authors, 108–09
Inter-American Commission on Human Rights, *157,* 166–67, 299
Intergovernmental organization materials
(see also U.N. materials)
abbreviated names, 297–99
arbitrations, 167–68
basic citation forms, *157–58,* 180–81
cases, 162–67
Common Market, 165–66, 174–77, 297–98
Council of Europe, *158,* 177
Court of Justice of the European Communities, *157,* 164–66, 297–98
courts, *157,* 162–67
debates, European Parliamentary Assembly, 176, 298
document number of League of Nations materials, 174
document number of U.N. materials, *157–58,* 170
East African Court of Appeal, 167, 299
European Commission of Human Rights, 166, 298–99

Page references in regular type are to INSTRUCTIONS; page references in *Italics* are to EXAMPLES

European Community, *157–58,*
  164–66, 174–77, 297–98
founding documents, U.N., 174
General Agreement on Tariffs and
  Trade, *158,* 177–78
generally, 168–79, *297–99*
Inter-American Commission on
  Human Rights, *157,* 166–67, *299*
International Court of Justice, *157,*
  163–64
League of Nations, 174
League of Nations covenant, 174
League of Nations Official Journal,
  174
League of Nations Treaty Series
  (L.N.T.S.), 300
mimeographed documents, U.N., 173
number, League of Nations documents, 174
number, U.N. document, *157–58,* 170
number, U.N. sales, 172–73
official records, U.N., 168–72
order of citation, 27
pages, U.N. materials, 170
paragraphs, U.N. materials, 170
Permanent Court of International
  Justice, 163–64
Reports of International Arbitral
  Awards, United Nations, 301
sales number of U.N. materials,
  172–73
sources, *297–99*
treaty sources, 300
United Nations Treaty Series
  (U.N.T.S.), 300
World Court, *157,* 163–64, *297*
yearbooks, international, 179
yearbooks, U.N., 173
Interim orders, *56*
Internal Revenue Code
citation to other than current code, 85
court documents and legal memoranda, citations in, 16–17
generally, 16–17, 85
legislative history, 95
supplements, 85
unofficial codes, 85
year, 85
Internal Revenue Commissioner, in
  case names, 62
"Internal Revenue," omitted in case
  names, 62
Internal revenue regulations and rul-
  ings, 16–17, *97,* 100–02

International agreements
American treaties, *157,* 158–62
basic citation forms, *157,* 158–62
bilateral, *157*
citation analyzed, 9
citation, basic form of, *157,* 158–62
citation order, 26
compilations of agreements, 300
components of citation, 159
country names, 160
date, 160
entry into force, 160
Executive Agreement Series (E.A.S.),
  300
foreign language, titles in, 151–52
foreign sources, 245–96
intergovernmental organization materials, 168–79, *297–99*
language of source, 151–52
League of Nations Treaty Series
  (L.N.T.S.), 300
multilateral, *157,* 161–62
name, 159–60
official sources, 300
opening for signature, 160
order within signal, 25–26
parallel citation, 161–62
parties to, 160
popular name, 160
short citation forms, 180–81
sources, intergovernmental, 297–99
sources, official, foreign, 245–96
sources, official, U.S., 300
sources, unofficial, 300
State Department sources, 161
Statutes at Large (Stat.), 300
subdivision, 161
subject matter, 160
title, 159–60
Treaties and Other International Acts
  Series (T.I.A.S.), 300
treaty series, 300
Treaty Series (T.S.), 161, 300
United Nations Treaty Series
  (U.N.T.S.), *162,* 300
United States
U.S. a party, *157,* 161–62
U.S. not a party, *157,* 162
U.S. Treaties and Other International
  Agreements (U.S.T.), 161, 300
year, 160
International Court of Justice, *157,*
  163–64, *297*

Page references in regular type are to INSTRUCTIONS; page references in *Italics* are to EXAMPLES

International law
arbitrations, 167–68
cases, 162–67
Common Market, *157*, 165–66,
297–98
Council of Europe, 177
courts, 162–67
digests, 179–80
European Community, *157–58*,
164–66, 177–79
generally, 157–81
intergovernmental organizations,
168–79, 297–99
international agreements, 158–62
League of Nations, 174
short citation forms, 180–81
treaties, 158–62
U.N., 168–74
yearbooks, international, 179
yearbooks, U.N., 173
International Law Reports, 167
International Legal Materials (I.L.M.),
162
International materials
arbitrations, 167–68
basic citation forms, 157–58
cases, 162–67
Common Market, *157*, 165–66,
297–98
Council of Europe, 177
digests, 179–80
European Community, *157–58,*
164–66, 174–77
generally, 157–81
international agreements, 158–62
jurisdiction, 158
League of Nations, 174
non-English language documents,
151–52, 158
periodicals, 154–55
short citation forms, 180–81
treaties, 158–62
treaty series, 300
U.N., 168–74
yearbooks, international, 179
yearbooks, U.N., 173
International organization materials
(see Intergovernmental organization materials)
Internet sources
administrative and executive materials,
139
basic citation principles, 132–37
books, 139–40

cases, 137–38
constitutions, 138
date, 136–37
directories and subdirectories,
134–35
domain name, 134–35
e-mail, 141
explanatory parentheticals, 137
FTP, 140–41
generally, 132–41
Gopher, 140–41
hypertext markup language (HTML),
135
journals, 139–40
legislative materials, 138–39
listservs, 141
magazines, 139–40
on-line journals, 140
parenthetical information, 137
pinpoint citation, 137
portable document format (pdf), 135,
137
preservation of information, 137
protocol, 134–35, 140–41
secondary sources, 140
short forms, 143–44
statutes, 138
Telnet, 140–41
URL, 134–36
Interviews
citation of, 127–28
typeface of citations to, *128*
Introductions, citation of, 113
Introductory signals (see Signals)
Iowa
sources of law, 202
"I.R.C." replacing "26 U.S.C.," 16, 85,
186
Ireland, Northern, 295
Ireland, Republic of
sources of national law, 268–69
treaty source, 269
Israel
sources of national law, 269–70
treaty source, 270
Italicization
(see also Typeface)
equations, 51
foreign words, 50
hypothetical parties, 51
stylistic purposes, 50–51
Italy
sources of national law, 270–72
treaty source, 272

Japan
sources of national law, 272–76
treaty source, 276
Joining citations
order of citations, 24–27
punctuation, 13–14, 21–22
Joint resolutions, 92–93
Journal
European Communities, Official,
174–75
House of Commons, 291
House of Lords, 291
Internet journals, 139
League of Nations, Official, 174
"Journal," abbreviation of, 328
Judge
indication of, in citation, 53, 65, 315
used as title, 315
"Judge," capitalization of, 52
Judgements of the U.N.
Administrative Tribunal, 172
"Judge(s)," abbreviation of, 53, 315
Judges and Justices
order of listing, 53
titles, use of, 53
"Judgment of," use in citation, 57
Judicial history of cases (see History
of cases)
Judicial Panel on Multidistrict
Litigation, 65, 185
Jump cites (see Pinpoint citations)
Jurisdiction, indication of
American cases, 64–66
American statutes, 78–79, 81–82
civil law cases, 153
civil law statutes, 154
common law cases, 152–53
common law statutes, 154
foreign cases, 152–53
foreign materials, 152
international materials, 158
municipal ordinances, 85–86
session laws, 81–83
Justice
indication of, in citation, 53, 65, 315
"Justice," capitalization of, 52
"Justice(s)," abbreviation of, 53, 315
Justinian, Institutes, Digest, and
Code of, 280

Kansas
sources of law, 203
Kentucky
sources of law, 204–05

King's Bench Division, 293–94

"L" italicized as letter in subdivision,
51
Labor unions, in case names, 61–62
Länder (see Germany)
Large and small capitals (see
Typeface)
Latin words
citation forms, italicization in, 58–59
italicization of, 50
italicization in case names, 11–12,
31, 32, 58–59
procedural phrases in case names,
58–59
shortened citation forms, italicization
in, *40–43*
Law Journal Reports, 292
Law journals and reviews
abbreviations, English-language,
317–41
abbreviations, spacing of, 48
authors' names, 118
basic citation forms, 117–18
book reviews, 121, 123
citation analyzed, 8
citation order, 27
comments, 121–22
commentary cited with case, 29–30
components of citation, 117–18
consecutively paginated, 119
generally, 117–20, 121–24
new series (n.s.), 318
nonconsecutively paginated, 119–20
notes, 121–22
order within signal, 27
projects, 122
short citation forms, 125–26
short commentary, 122
student material, 121–23
typeface in court documents and
legal memoranda, 12
typeface in law review citations, 30–32
typeface in law review text, 32–33
Law Times Reports, 292
Lawyer's Reports Annotated (L.R.A.),
annotations in, 124
Leaflets, *110*
League of Nations materials
(see Intergovernmental organization
materials)
League of Nations Treaty Series
(L.N.T.S.), 300
Legal dictionaries, *113*

Legal encyclopedias, *113*
Legal newspapers (see Newspapers)
Legal services, looseleaf (see
    Services and topical reporters)
Legislation (see Codes, Session laws,
    Statutes)
Legislative histories, 92–95
Legislative materials, 91–96
  basic citation forms, 91–92
  bills and resolutions, 92–93
  citation order, 26
  committee prints, 93–94
  components of citation, 91
  debates, 95
  documents, 93–95
  English, 291
  hearings, 12, *28,* 42, *43,* 93
  Internet sources, 138–39
  legislative histories, 92–95
  order within signal, 26
  parallel citations, 94, 95
  presidential messages, *103*
  reports, 93–95
  secondary authorities, 95
  short forms, 95–96
  state, 93, 94–95
  typeface used in court documents
    and legal memoranda, 12
  United Kingdom, 290–91
  unnumbered documents, 94
Letters and memoranda, 18–19, 127
**Letters of the alphabet, altered in
    quotations,** 44–45
LEXIS, *73, 121,* 129–30, *131–32, 143*
Local court rules, 86
Location, phrases of
  letters, speeches, and interviews,
    127–28
  omitted from case names, 60
  unpublished works, 126–28
Loislaw.com, *73, 131, 144*
Long case names, 56–57
  "hereinafter" form, when used, 43
Looseleaf services (see Services and
    topical reporters)
Looseleaf statutory codifications, 81
"Lord Justice," abbreviation of, 315
Louisiana
  sources of law, 205–06
"Ltd.," in case names, 59, 61

Magazines
  abbreviations, 317–41
  citation analyzed, 8

  citation order, 27
  consecutively paginated, 119
  generally, 117–20
  Internet sources, 139–40
  nonconsecutively paginated, 119–20
"Magistrate," abbreviation of, 315
Maine
  sources of law, 206–07
Manitoba
  sources of national law, 255–57
Manual for Complex Litigation, 114
Manuscripts, typed, 127–29
Maritime provinces
  sources of law, 255–57
Maryland
  sources of law, 207–08
Massachusetts
  sources of law, *80,* 208–10
"Master of the Rolls," abbreviation of,
    315
**Materially different language in code
    and statute,** 78
Mathematical equations, 51
Matthew Bender services (MB), 343
  (see also Services and topical
    reporters)
"Mediator," abbreviation of, 315
Medium neutral citation, *14,* 64
Memoranda, 17–19, 71, 127
Memorandum decision
  indication of, 67
  prior history must be given, 68
Mexico
  sources of national law, 276–77
Michigan
  sources of law, 210–11
  statutes cited to official or unofficial
    code, *80*
Microfiche, 142, 144
Microform, 142, 144
Military cases, 186
Military Justice Reporter, 186
**Mimeographed and other informally
    printed matter,** 126–27, 128
Mimeographed documents, U.N., 173
Minnesota
  sources of law, *82,* 211
Mississippi
  sources of law, 211–12
Missouri
  sources of law, 212–13
**Mistakes in quotations, indicated by
    "[sic],"** 45

X

Page references in regular type are to Instructions; page references in *Italics* are to Examples

Mixed arbitral tribunals, cases before, 167–68
Model Code of Professional Responsibility, 89
Model codes, 87–89
Model Penal Code, *88*
Model Rules of Professional Conduct, 89
"Modified" **and** *"modifying,"* **in case history,** 68–69, 309
Monarchs, English, 290
Montana
  sources of law, *38,* 213
Month used to indicate volume, *148*
Months, abbreviation of, *316*
Moore's Federal Practice, 109
Motions, 17–19, 71
Multinational materials (see International materials)
Multipart articles, 123–24
Multiple authors, 107–08
Multiple decisions within a single year, 66–67
Multiple editions and printings of book, 110–11
Multiple pages, footnotes, and end- notes, 36–37
Multiple parties, words indicating, omitted in case names, 57
Multiple printings of books, 110–11
Municipal ordinances, 85–86
Music, 143
"N.A.," in case names, 61
Name of state, when omitted in case name, 60
Names
  authors, articles, 118
  authors, books and pamphlets, 107–09
  book reviews, 121, 123
  bound services, abbreviated, 343–48
  commonly abbreviated, 49, 59, 62, 302–03
  editions of books and pamphlets, 110–12
  editors, 108–09
  looseleaf services, abbreviated, 343–48
  newspaper sections, 120
  newspapers, abbreviated, 317–41
  parties, when different on appeal, 69
  periodicals, abbreviated, English lan- guage, 317–41

  periodicals, abbreviation and type- face, 117–18
  prepositions in periodical names, 317
  rules and regulations, 97–98
  services, 147–48
  services, abbreviated, 343–48
  session laws, 81
  state, when omitted, 60
  statutes, 78–79
  translators, 108
  treaties, 159–60
Names of cases (see Case names)
National Conference of Commissioners on Uniform State Law, 88
National Labor Relations Act, 95
National Reporter System (see Unofficial reporters)
Navajo Nation
  sources of law, 243
Nebraska
  sources of law, 213–14
Netherlands
  sources of national law, 277–79
  treaty source, 279
Nevada
  sources of law, 214
New Brunswick
  sources of law, 255–56
New Hampshire
  sources of law, 214–15
New Jersey
  sources of law, *38, 81,* 215–16
New Mexico
  sources of law, *38,* 216–17
New series (n.s.) **of periodical,** 317
New York
  sources of law, *39, 80,* 217–22
New Zealand
  sources of national law, 279–80
  treaty source, 280
Newfoundland
  sources of law, 255–57
Newsletters, 125
Newspapers
  abbreviated names, 317–41
  articles, 120–21
  authors, 120
  bylines of articles, 120
  cases cited to, *56,* 63
  citation analyzed, 8
  citation of, 120–21
  citation order, 27
  columns, not indicated, 120

Page references in regular type are to INSTRUCTIONS; page references in *Italics* are to EXAMPLES

consecutively paginated, 120
dates, 120
editions, 120
electronic databases, 120–21, 132
generally, 120–21
pages, 120–21
pinpoint citations, 120–21
sections, 120
statutes cited to, 76, 77, 83
titles of articles, 120
titles of, printed in italic type, 31, 32
typeface, 12, 31, 32, *117,* 118–19, 120–21
typeface in court documents and legal memoranda, 12
typeface in law reviews, 31, 32
when cited, 63, 77
"No.," in case names, 59
"[No signal]" as signal, 22
No-action letters, SEC, *97,* 102
Nonconsecutive pages, citation of, 36
Nonconsecutive sections, citation of, 38
Nonperiodic materials (see Books and pamphlets)
North Carolina
sources of law, *79,* 222–23
North Dakota
sources of law, 223–24
Northern Ireland
sources of law, 295
Northern Mariana Islands
sources of law, 243
Northwest Territories
sources of law, 255–57
"Note," designating student work, 122
"*Noted in,*" use of, 29–30
Notes
(see also Footnotes)
appended material, 39
student-written, 122
Nouns, capitalization of, 51–53
Nova Scotia
sources of law, 255–57
Novels (Roman Law), 280
Number and series
European Community materials, 174–77
League of Nations materials, 174
Permanent Court of International Justice, 163–64
U.N. materials, *157–58,* 170–74

Number of case
administrative cases, 99–100
appeal or petition for certiorari, *56,* 71
court documents, 71
Federal Cases, 184, 185
medium neutral citation, 64
pending cases, *56,* 70
public domain citation, 64
renumbered, 70
service citations, 148
unreported cases, *56,* 70
Numbers
Arabic numerals designating monarchs, 290
Arabic numerals designating volumes, 33
beginning sentence, 49
commas in, 49–50
Congress and session, 92–96
designating subdivision, numerals used, 49
docket (see Number of case)
dollar amounts, numerals used, 49
English monarchs, 290
ethical opinion, 89
five or more digits, 49–50
generally, 49
inclusive pages, 36
inclusive paragraphs, 38–39
inclusive sections of codes, 38
legislature, 92–96
ordinal, 50
ordinance, 85–86
percentages, numerals used, 49
round numbers spelled out, 49
Roman numerals, when not used, 33, 290
serial, of books and pamphlets, 110
serial, of publications, 110
series, consistency in, 49
spacing of, in abbreviations, 48
volumes designated by Arabic numerals, 33
"Number(s)," abbreviation of, 349

Occupational Safety and Health Act, 95
"Of America," omitted in case names, 60
Office of Legal Counsel, opinions, *100*
Official and West reporters
generally, 14–15, 62–64
U.S. Supreme Court, 183

Official codes
American, 78–79
Canadian, 254–55
civil law jurisdictions, 154, 245–96
common law jurisdictions, 154,
 245–96
English, 290–91
*Official Journal of the European
 Communities,* 174–76, 298
Official names of statutes, 78–79
Official public domain citation, 64
Official records (see Records)
Official records, U.N., 168–72
**Official releases of administrative
 agencies,** 99–100
Official reporters
(see also name of individual jurisdiction)
abbreviations used, 183–244
administrative cases, 99, 186–88
foreign cases, 245–96
state cases, 14–15, 62–63, 65–66,
 188–244
U.S. Supreme Court cases, 183
when to cite, 14–15, 62–63
Official sources
international agreements, 300
international arbitrations, 301
public domain citation, 62–64
statutes, foreign, 245–96
treaties, 300
Offprints (see Photoduplicated
 reprints)
Ohio
sources of law, 224–25
Oklahoma
sources of law, *81,* 226
Omissions
book and pamphlet titles, 109
case names, 56–62
quotations, 45–47
**"On the relation of," abbreviated to
 "ex rel.,"** *57,* 58
Ontario
sources of law, 255–57
"Opened for signature," **use of,** *157,* 160
Opinions
administrative, 100
concurring and dissenting, *35,* 67
ethics, 89
formal advisory, *97,* 100
Opinions of Attorney General, *97,* 100
**Opposing citations, introductory
 signals to,** 23–24

Order of citation, 21–22, 24–27
Order of parentheticals, 67–68
**Orders, regulations, and rulings of
 administrative agencies,** 96–100
Ordinal numbers, 50
Ordinances, municipal and county,
 85–86
Oregon
sources of law, 227
**Original edition of books, citation to
 star pages,** 111
Original source
identified after a quotation, *29–30*
"Overruled by," **in case history,** *67–68,*
 309

Pages
administrative compilations, 97–98
annotations, 124
"at," used in citations to particular
 pages, 29, 34–35, 37, 109–10, 170
books and pamphlets, 34–35, 107
bound services, 63, 148–49
Code of Federal Regulations, 97–98,
 103
collected works, 112–13
Common Market cases, 164–66
consecutive and nonconsecutive, 36
electronic databases, 130
Federal Register, 97–99
first page of authority, citation to, 35
generally, 34–37
graphical materials, 37
inclusive, 36
institutes, publications by, 124–25
International Court of Justice cases,
 163–64
law journals and reviews, 117–20
legal newspapers, 120–21
legislative reports and documents,
 93–95
looseleaf services, 148
multipart articles, 123–24
multiple, citation of, 36
newspapers, 120–21
on-line sources, 130, 137
particular, reference to, 34–37, 40
"passim," use of, 36
periodicals, 117–21
Permanent Court of International
 Justice cases, 163–64
reporters, 63–64
reprinted reporters with different pagination, 63–64

services, 148
session laws, 81–82
shorter works in collection, 112–13
slip opinions, 70
star, in books and pamphlets, 111
statutes, 78–79
statutes, secondary sources, 81–82
U.N. materials, 170
unpublished opinion, 70
World Court cases, 164
"Page(s)," abbreviation of, 34, 40, 349
Pamphlets (see Books and pamphlets)
Panama (see Canal Zone)
Paragraph number, in services, *39,*
148
Paragraphed reporters (see Services
and topical reporters)
Paragraphs
ABA section reports, 124–25
ALI proceedings, 124–25
books and pamphlets, 37, 39, 107
citations to, 37–39, 50
consecutive and nonconsecutive,
38–39
indented but unnumbered, 37
institutes, publications by, 124–25
international agreements, 161
Internet journals, 139
multiple, 38–39
omission of, in quotations, 47
proceedings, 124–25
public domain citations, 63
services, 37, 148
treaties, 161
U.N. materials, 170
unnumbered, citation of, 37
"Paragraph(s)," abbreviation of, 37,
50, 349
Parallel citations
articles and collected essays, 29–30
cases, administrative, 99–100
cases, American, 14–15, 62–64
cases, federal, 183–86
cases, international, 167
cases, reprinted reporters, 63–64
cases, state, 14–15, 62
collected essays and articles, 29–30
European Community materials, 165
international agreements, 161–62
international arbitration awards, 168
international law reports, 167
limited circulation, works of, 126–27
medium neutral citation, 64
order of citations, generally, 14–15

public domain citation, 64
repeating citations, 15–16
services, 62–63, 147
speeches, 128
statutes, American, 83–84
statutes, foreign (see name of individual country)
Treasury regulations, 100–01
treaties, 161–62
treaty collections, 161–62
unpublished works, 126–28
**Parenthetical explanations of author-
ities,** 28, 67–68, 84–85
Parenthetical indications
administrative adjudications, 99
alterations in quotations, 45
alternative holding, 67
amended statutes, 84
amendment of statutes, 84
arbitration, international, 168
arbitrator, 99
author of opinion, 67
broadcasts, 142
codification of session laws, 83
commentary, 28
concurring opinions, 67
court of decision, 55, 64–66
court of decision, international cases,
158
dates, 66–67
dictum, 67
dissenting opinions, 67
divided court, 67
docket numbers, *56,* 70
editors of books, 108–09
editors of reports, 63–64
effective date of statute, 80–81,
82–83
en banc decisions, 67
ethical opinions, 89
explanatory phrases, 68–69
films, 142
forthcoming publications, 128
implied holding, 67
International Court of Justice, 163–64
judge writing opinion, *67*
jurisdiction, American cases, 64–66
jurisdiction, international materials,
158
Justice writing opinion, *67*
letters, 127
location of, 67–68
location of letters, speeches, and
interviews, 126–28

Page references in regular type are to INSTRUCTIONS; page references in *Italics* are to EXAMPLES

location of unpublished works,
  126–28
memorandum decisions, 67
microform, 142
model codes, 87–89
multipart articles, 123–24
new series (n.s.), 318
number and series of books and
  pamphlets, 110
order, 28, 67–68
per curiam decision, 67
Permanent Court of International
  Justice, 163–64
plurality opinions, 67
popular name of statute, 79
prior history of statute, 84
proposed drafts, 87
repealed statutes, 84
restatements, 87–89
sentencing guidelines, 87–89
separate opinions, 67
serial number, books and pamphlets,
  110
series and number in series publications, 110
services, later bound form, 147–48
session laws, 81–83
split decisions, 67
standards, 87–89
statutes, 84
statutes, amended, 84
statutes, history of, 84
statutes, prior history, 84
statutes, repealed, 84
tentative draft, 87–89
translators of books, 108
unclear holdings, 67
weight of authority, 67
World Court cases, 163–64
year, English statutes, 291
***Parlement Européen Documents de
  Séance,*** 176, 298
Parliamentary materials, British, 291
Parties
appeal, under different names, 69
arbitrations, international, *157,*
  167–68
citation in case names, 56–62
hypothetical, 51
international agreements, *157,* 160
international arbitrations, *157,*
  167–68
International Court of Justice, *157,*
  163

omitted in case names, 57–58
Permanent Court of International
  Justice, *157,* 163
treaties, *157,* 160
World Court, *157,* 163
Partnership names in cases, 57
"Part(s)," abbreviation of, 349
"Passim," use of, 36
Patents, 103
Pending cases, *56,* 70
Pennsylvania
sources of law, 227–29
"People of," omitted in case names, 60
"Per curiam"
in case history, 67
parenthetical indication of, 67
Percentages, numerals used, 49
Periodicals
ABA section reports, 124
abbreviations, English-language,
  317–41
abstracts in, 122
ALI proceedings, 124
annotations, 124
articles, 117–18
authors, 118
book notes, 123
book reviews, 121, 123
case comments, 121–22
case notes, 121–22
cases, when cited to, 63
citation analyzed, 8
citation order, 27
colloquia, 123
comments, law review, 121–22
components of citation, 8, 117–18
consecutively paginated, 119
date, 118–19
forthcoming materials, 128
"Developments in the Law," *122*
generally, 117–26
institutes, regular publications by,
  124–25
Internet journals, 140
jump cites, 35, 119, 140
multipart articles, 123–24
names, abbreviation of, 151–52,
  154–55, 317–41
names, typeface used, 118
new series (n.s.), 318
newsletters, 125
newspapers, 120–21
noncommercial, 125
nonconsecutively paginated, 119–20

notes, law review, 121–22
on-line journals, 140
order within signal, 27
page citation, 34–37
pages, 119
pinpoint citations, 119
proceedings, 124–25
punctuation in titles, when omitted, 317
recent cases, 121–22
recent developments, 121–22
recent statutes, 121–22
short citation forms, 125–26
special projects, law review, 121–22
statutes cited to, 77, 83
student-written material, 121–23
Supreme Court note, *122*
surveys of law, 123
symposia, 123
titles, 118–19
typeface, in court documents, 12
typeface, in law reviews, 30–33
volume, 33–34
year, 119
Periods, to indicate omissions in quotations, 45–47
Permanent Court of Arbitration, *157,* 168
Permanent Court of International Justice, *157,* 163–64
Permanently bound services
abbreviations of, 343–48
generally, 147–49
Photoduplicated reprints, 111
Phrases of location
letters, speeches, and interviews, 126–28
omitted from case names, 60
unpublished works, 126–28
Pike & Fischer (P & F) services, 343
(see also Services and topical reporters)
Pinpoint citations
Federal Register, 97–98
generally, 34–39
Internet sources, 137, 140
medium neutral citation, 64
multipart articles, 123–24
newspapers, 120–21
opinions, formal advisory, 100
periodicals, 119–20
public domain citation, 64
session laws, 81–82
statutes, 79–82

treaties, *157,* 161
U.N. materials, 170, 172
World Court cases, 164
Pleadings, 17–19, 71
Pleadings, Oral Arguments and Documents, 164
Pleadings, World Court cases, 164
Plenary materials, U.N., 168–72
Plurality opinion, indication of, 67
Pluralization of abbreviations, 302
Pocket parts
books and pamphlets, 111–12
codes, 34, 80
Popular names
cases, 59
international agreements, 160
statutes, 79
treaties, 160
Positive law, codes enacted into, 78
Pre-1900 works, 111
Preamble, constitutional, *75*
Prefaces, 113
Prepositions
capitalization, 51
in periodical names, 317
Presidential papers and executive orders, 103
Press releases, 127
Previously cited authorities
(see also entry under authority cited)
cross-reference to, 40–43
short forms for, *40–43*
Prince Edward Island
sources of law, 255–57
Printing, when indicated, 110–11
Prior history (see History of cases, History of statutes)
Private laws, 78
Private letter rulings, 17, 101
Privy Council, 289–90
***"Probable jurisdiction noted,"* in case history,** 309
Procedural phrases, in case names, 11–12, 30–31, 58–59
Procedure, rules of, 86
Proceedings, 124–25
Professional Responsibility, Code of, 89
Professionally written law review material, 117–18
Projects, in law reviews, 121–22
Proposed administrative rules and regulations, 98

Proposed drafts, restatements and model codes, 87
Provinces, Canadian, 255–57, 311
Provisional editions, U.N. official records, 169, 171
Public domain citation, *14,* 64
Public International Law Cases, Annual Digest and Reports of, 167
Public law number, when given for federal statutes, *78,* 81–82
Public Papers of the Presidents, 103
Publication number
  intergovernmental organizations' materials, 178–79
  League of Nations publications, 174
  series publications, 110
  U.N. publications, 170, 172–74
Publication, place of, 111
Publications
  ABA section reports, 124
  ALI proceedings, 124
  considered periodicals or reporters, 63
  forthcoming, 128
  institutes, regular publications, 124–25
  proceedings, 124–25
  typeface in court documents and legal memoranda, 12
  typeface in law review citations, 30–31
  typeface in law review text, 32
  typeface used for names, 31–32
Publisher
  books, 110–11
  CD-ROM, 141–42
  codes, 80
  foreign codes, 154
  microform collections, 142
  services, 147–48
  session laws, 81–82
  statutes, 80
Puerto Rico
  sources of law, 244
Punctuation
  between case and commentary, 29–30
  between statute and case construing it, 29–30
  citations, separated by semicolons, 13–14, 21–22
  initials, 48–49
  italicization of, 32, 33

periodical titles, 317
  quotations, 43–47
  subdivisions, 38–39
  subsequent history of cases, 68
  with introductory signals, 22, 24–25

Quasi-statutory material, 91–98, 100–01
Quebec
  sources of law, 256–57
Queen's Bench Division, 293–94
"Questioned in," **use of,** 29–30
Quotation marks, 43–47
Quotations
  alteration of, 44–45
  generally, 43–47
  identification of original source, 45
  long and short, 43–44
  mistakes in, indicated by "[sic]," 45
  omissions in, 45–47
"Quoted in," **use of,** 29–30
"Quoting," **use of,** *30*

Radio broadcasts, 142
Recent cases, citation of, *56,* 63, 70
Recent cases, in law reviews, 122
Recent decisions, in law reviews, 122
Recent developments, in law reviews, 122
Recent statutes, 77–78, 81–83
Recent statutes, in law reviews, 122
Recordings, audio 142–43
Records
  cases, 18–19, 71
  U.N., 168–72
"Referee," abbreviation of, 315
References to previously cited authorities, 40–43
Regional Rail Reorganization Court, 185
Regional reporters, 14–15, 62–63
Regnal years, in English statutes, 290
Regulations of administrative agencies
  citation analyzed, 7
  generally, *96–97,* 97–98
  Internal Revenue, 16–17, *97,* 100–02
  short citation forms, 104
  Treasury, 16–17, *97,* 100–02
Rehearing
  denial, when indicated, 68
  "sub nom." not used, 69
"Rehearing granted," **in case history,** 309

Page references in regular type are to INSTRUCTIONS; page references in *Italics* are to EXAMPLES

Related authority, 29–30
"Relation of," abbreviated to *"ex rel.,"* 58
Relator, first listed, not omitted, 57
Releases, SEC, *97,* 102–03
Remand, history of case on, 68
Renumbered and reprinted reports, 63–64
Reorganization plans, 103
Repagination
  books and pamphlets, 110–11
  case reporters, 64
"Repealed by"
  in constitution citation, *75*
  in statute citation, *84*
Repealed constitutions, 75
Repealed statutes, 84
Repeating citations, 40–43
Report of Judgments, Advisory Opinions and Orders, 163
Reporter editor, when given, 63–64
Reporters of cases
  (see also Services and topical reporters)
  abbreviations, 63
  administrative, 99–100, 187–88
  American, 183–244
  annotations of cases, 124
  Common Market cases, 165–66
  computer services, 72–73
  court administrative orders, 103, 187–88
  dual citations, 14–15, 62–63
  early American, 63
  editor named, 63–64
  electronic databases, 72–73
  federal, 183–86
  foreign, 152–53, 245–96
  generally, *55–56,* 62–64
  international arbitrations, 167–68, 301
  jurisdiction named, 64–66
  medium neutral citation, 62–64
  official and West, when cited, 14–15, 63
  page citation, 63
  parallel citation, 14–15, 62–63
  public domain citation, 64
  publications considered as, 63
  renumbered and reprinted, 63–64
  requiring dual citation, 14–15, 62–63
  services, permanently bound, 147
  state, 14–15, 62–63
  typeface, *55–56*
  unofficial, when cited, 14–15, 62–63

  volume citation, 63
  World Court, 163–64
Reports
  (see also Reporters of cases)
  administrative and executive, 98–99
  legislative, *91–92,* 93–95
"Representative," abbreviation of, 315
Reprinted case reporters, 63–64
"Reprinted in," **use of,** 29, *92, 94,* 95, 103
"Reprinted in," **with multiple sources,** *92,* 95, 103
Reprints, photoduplicated, 111
Research Institute of America (RIA) services, 343
  (see also Services and topical reporters)
Resolutions
  congressional, 92–93
  intergovernmental organizations, 178–79
  statutory, *92–93*
  U.N. organs, 168
Restatements, 87–88
  comments, *39*
Revenue Acts, 16–17, 85
Revenue rulings, 101
Revenue procedures, 101
Reversals, in subsequent case history, 68
"Reversed," **in case history,** *68,* 309
Reversed names of parties, citation of on appeal, 69
"Reversing," **in case history,** 309
Review, cited with book reviewed, 29–30, 121, 123
"Reviewed by," **use of,** 29–30
Reviewer of book, 121, 123
"Reviewing," use of in book review citation, 29–30, 121, 123
"Revised by," **use of,** 168–69
Revised Reports, 292
Revision **(Canadian statutes),** 254
Rhode Island
  sources of law, 229
Roman Catholic Church, see Catholic Church
Roman law references, 280–81
Roman numerals, when not used, 33, 290
Roman type (see Typeface)
"R.R.," in case names, 61, *62*
Rules
  administrative, *96,* 97–98
  court, 86

ethics, 89
evidence, 86
procedure, 86
Rules and regulations, proposed, 98
Russian Federation
  sources of national law, 281–83
  treaty sources, 282

Sales number, U.N., 172–73
Saskatchewan
  sources of law, 256–57
Scattered sections of code, 78
"Schedule(s)," abbreviation of, 349
Scotland
  sources of law, 295–96
SEC materials
  releases, *97,* 102–03
  no-action letters, *97,* 102
Secondary authorities
  administrative reporters, 99–100
  books and pamphlets, 107–17
  British materials, 289–96
  citation order, 27
  congressional materials, 93–95
  law journals and reviews, 117–24
  legislative histories, 95
  letters, speeches, interviews, 19,
    127–28
  newsletters, 125
  newspapers, 120–21
  magazines, 317–41
  order within signal, 27
  periodicals, 117–26
  periodicals, English-language, 317–41
  periodicals, foreign-language, 154–55
  services, 147–49, 343–48
  statutes cited to, 76–77, 83–84
  Treasury regulations, 16–17, *97,*
    100–02
  unpublished works, 126–28
Section number
  generally, 37–38, 50, 349
  services, 148
Sections
  ABA section reports, 124–25
  administrative compilations, 98
  ALI proceedings, 124
  amending act, 82
  books and pamphlets, 107
  citation to, 81–82
  Code of Federal Regulations, 97
  codes, consecutive, 38
  codes, statutory, 79
  generally, 37–38, 50, 349

institutes, publications by, 124–25
international agreements, 161
model codes, 87
newspapers, 120
ordinances, municipal, 85–86
proceedings, 124–25
restatements, 87
scattered, 78
sentencing guidelines, 87
services, 148
session laws, 82
standards, 87
statutes, 79
treaties, 161
"Section(s)," abbreviation of, 37–38,
  50, 349
Securities Exchange Act of 1934, 95
Security Council official records,
  U.N., 171
"See also," **as signal,** 23
"See," **as signal,** 22–23
"See, e.g.," **as signal,** *22*
"See generally," **as signal,** 24
Senate materials (see Congressional
  materials)
"Senator," abbreviation of, 315
Sentencing guidelines, 87–88
Separate decisions of other issues,
  in case history, 68
Separate opinions
  indication of, *35,* 67
  slip opinions, 70
Serial numbers
  books and pamphlets, 107, 110
  European Community materials,
    174–75
  intergovernmental organizations'
    materials, 178–79
  executive orders, 103
  leaflets, *110*
  League of Nations documents, 174
  monographs, 110
  pamphlets and books, 107, 110
  proclamations, 103
  publications in series, 110
  reorganization plans, 103
  U.N. documents, 169, 170, 172, 173
  World Court cases, 163–64
"Series" and "Serial(s)," abbreviation
  of, 349
Series, books and pamphlets in, 110
Series, renumbered, 63–64, 318
Services and topical reporters
  abbreviations, 343–48

Page references in regular type are to INSTRUCTIONS; page references in *Italics* are to EXAMPLES

abbreviations of publishers, 343
administrative rules and announcements, 98–100
basic citation form, 147–48
cases, *56*
citation of cases, 63
Common Market materials, 165–66, 297–98
components of citation, 147–48
dates, 148
dates of materials in, 148
European Community materials, 165–66, 297–98
generally, 147–49
looseleaf, citations of, 147
name, 147
pages, 148
paragraphs, 148
parallel citations, for administrative cases, 99–100
parenthetical indications of later bound form, 147
publishers, 147–48, 343
sections, 148
short citation forms, 148–49
statutes, 77, 83
subdivisions, 148
title of service, 147, 343–48
transfer binders, 147
typeface, 13, 147
U.S. Law Week, 56, 183, 348
volumes and editions, 33–34, 147
years, 148
Session laws (see also Codes, Statutes)
abbreviations, 82
"Act of _____", 81
amendments cited to, 78, 82
Canadian, 256–57
chapter numbers, 81, 186
citation, basic forms, *77*
cited by page, 82
civil law countries, 245–96
codification, future, 83
common law countries, 245–96
dates, 82
effective date of statutes, 82
enactment, year or date, 82
English, 291
federal, 81–82
foreign countries, 154, 245–96
former version of statute, 77
historical fact, statutes cited as, 78
jump cites, 82

jurisdiction, abbreviated name of, 82
municipal ordinances, 85–86
name, 81
official and privately published, 77–78
omission of words in title, 81
ordinances, uncodified, 86
pages, when cited to, 82
parallel citation of, 81
pinpoint citations, 82
printed in roman type, 81–82
public law number, 81
recent statutes, 77, 81–84
scattered sections of code, 78
sections and subsections, 37–38, 82
short title of statute, 81–82
signature by executive, year of, 82
state, 81–83, 188–244
statute cited as historical fact, 78
statute, name of, 81
statute not in current code but in force, 77
statute not in force, 77
Statutes at Large, 82, 93, 103, 186, 197
statutes, when cited to, 77
subsections and sections, 37–38, 82
typeface, *81–82*
U.S. Code Congressional & Administrative News, cited to, 83
volume, 81–82
year as volume number, 81–82
Shakespeare, 114
Short citation forms
administrative materials, 103–04
audio recordings, 144
books and pamphlets, 115–17
broadcasts, 144
cases, 71–73
CD-ROM, 144
constitutions, 75
court documents and legal memoranda, 15–16
electronic media, 143–44
films, 144
foreign materials, 155
forthcoming sources, 129
generally, 40–43
international materials, 180–81
Internet sources, 144
legislative materials, 95–96
nonprint resources, 143–44
periodicals, 125–26
practitioners' notes, 15–16, 18–19
regulations, 103–04

X

repeating citations, 40–43
services, 148–49
statutes, 89–90
treaties, 160
unpublished sources, 129
works in collection, 116–17
Short Titles Act, 290
Shorter works in collection
citation form, 112–13
editor, 112
"in," 112
parallel citation, 29
"supra" short form, *42*
"[Sic]," use of, 45
Signals
analogous support, 23
authority from different jurisdiction, 22
authority stating proposition, 22
background material, 24
comparison, 23
contradiction, 23–24
direct contradiction, 23
direct support, 22–23
generally, 22–25
identification, 22
order of citation, 24–25
order within signal, 25–27
sampling of authorities, 22
source of quotation, 22
string citations, 21, *22*
support, 22–23
table of signals, 22–24
typeface used in court documents
and legal memoranda, 12–13
typeface used in law review citations,
31
Slip opinions, *56,* 70, 99
Songs, 143
Sound recordings, 143
South Africa
sources of national law, 283–85
South Carolina
sources of law, 230–31
South Dakota
sources of law, 231–32
Spacing of abbreviations and
initials, 48
Spain
sources of national law, 285–86
Special Fund, U.N., 172
Special projects in periodicals,
121–22
Special reports of government agen-
cies, 98

Speeches, 29, 112, 128
Split decision
indication of, 67
Standards, 87–88
Star pages in books and pamphlets,
111
State administrative agencies
generally, 188–241
reports, 98
State cases
court of decision, abbreviations,
65–66, 188–241
courts of decision, indication of, 65–66
department or division of court, 66
official and unofficial reporters,
14–15, 62–64
parallel citations, 14–15, 62–64,
188–241
reporters (see name of individual
state)
State courts
generally, 188–241
rules of court, *86*
State Department publications, 161
"State of," omitted in case names, 60
States
(see also name of individual jurisdiction)
abbreviated in case names, 62
abbreviation of, 311
omitted in case names, 60
reporters, 188–241
session laws, 81–83, 188–241
statutes, 76–90, 188–241
statutory codes, 188–241
Statute Law Revision Act, 290
Statutes
(see also Codes, Session laws)
administrative rules and regulations,
97–98
amended, 77, 84
amended, uniform acts, 87
amendments, 84
amendments of Canadian, 254
appendices to codes, appearing in,
80
basic forms of citation, 76–77
bills and resolutions, 92–93
Canadian, 254–57
case construing statute, cited with, *30*
citation analyzed, 6–7, 76
citation order, 25
cited by page, 82
city ordinances, 85–86

code appendices, appearing in, 80
commentary on, cited with, *30*
compilations, 80
components of citation, 76–86
concurrent resolutions, 92–93
county ordinances, 85–86
current code, 78–79
date, Internal Revenue Code, 85
dates, 80–81
dates of amendment, 84
effective date, 82, 84
electronic databases, 131
English, 290–91
ethics, rules of, 89
explanatory parenthetical phrases, 84–85
federal and state, *77*
foreign jurisdictions, 154, 245–96
future codification, 83
generally, 76–90
historical fact, cited as, 78
history of, as amended, 78, 84
Internal Revenue Code, 16–17, 85
Internet sources, 138
joint resolutions, 92–93
legislative history, 91–96
legislative materials, 91–96
LEXIS, 131
materially different from code, 78
miscellaneous citation forms, 85–89
multiple sections and subsections, 37–39
municipal ordinances, 85–86
name of, in session laws, 81
names, 79
newspapers, cited to, *77,* 120–21
no longer in force, 77
not in current code, 77, 84
order within signal, 25
ordinances, municipal and county, 85–86
original enactment, indication of, *84*
pages, when cited to, 82
parallel citations to, 80, 81
parenthetical indications, 84–85
parenthetical indications of amendment, 84
periodicals, cited to, *77*
present similar statute, indication of, *84*
prior history, 84
private editor or compiler, 80
private laws, 78

privately published, Internal Revenue Code, 85
publication of, 77
publisher, 80
recent, 81–83
related authority, 29–30
repealed, 77, 84
reprinted in appendix of code, 80
resolutions, 92–93
scattered sections of code, 38, 78
secondary sources, *77,* 83–84
sections, citation to, 37–39, 78
services and topical reporters, *77,* 83–84
short citation forms, 89–90
source to cite, 77–78
special citation forms, 85–89
state, 188–241
state, uniform acts, 86–87
subsequent history, 84
substance, parenthetical indication of, *84–85*
superseded, 77, 84
supplements, 80
Treasury regulations, 100–01
uncodified, 80, 83
uniform acts, 86–87
United States Code (U.S.C.), 78–79, 103, 186
United States Code Annotated (U.S.C.A.), 78–79, 103, 186
United States Code Service (U.S.C.S.), 78–79, 103, 186
very recent, 83–84
Westlaw, 131, *132*
withdrawn, uniform acts, 87
Statutes at Large, 82, 83, 93, 103, 161, 186, 197
(see also Session laws)
Statutes of Canada, 254–55
String citations, 21, *22*
Structure of the *Bluebook,* 3
Student work, in periodicals, 121–23
order within citations, 27
Style
abbreviations, 47–49, 302–49
capitalization, 51–53
Chicago Manual of Style, 4
quotations, 43–47
titles of officials, 53, 315
typeface, 11–13, 30–33
U.S. Government Printing Office Style Manual, 4, 51
"*Sub nom.,*" in case history, 69

Subdivisions in cited material
ABA section reports, 124–25
abbreviations, 349
administrative compilations, 97–98
ALI proceedings, *124*
appended material, 39
"at," used to indicate page citations,
  29, 34–35, 37, 109–10, 170
books and pamphlets, 107
Code of Federal Regulations, 96,
  97–98
codes, statutory, 78–80
constitutions, 75
cross-references, internal, 39–40
endnotes, 36–37
English statutes, 290–91
footnotes, 35–37
generally, 33–40
graphical materials, 37
"*in,*" used to indicate location in an
  entire work, 29, 112
institutes, publications by, 124–25
international agreements, 161
model codes, 87–88
multipart articles, 123–24
multiple pages, 36–37
multiple paragraphs, 39
multiple sections, 38
newspapers, 120–21
ordinances, municipal, 85–86
pages, generally, 34–35
pages or sections, in books, 34–38,
  107
pages or sections, in codes, 37–38,
  79
pages or sections, in services, 148
pages or sections, in session laws,
  82
paragraphs, 37, 39
parts, 34
"*passim,*" use of, 36
proceedings, 124–25
restatements, 87–88
schedules, 290, 349
sections and subsections, 37–38
separately paginated, 34
services, 147–48
session laws, 37, 81–82
standards, 87–88
statutes, 37–39, 79, 82
supplements, 34
treaties, 161
U.N. materials, 170
volumes, 33–34

Subject-matter title of codes, 79–80
Subsections
  multiple, in statutes, 38
  session laws, 82
Subsequent citations, short forms,
  40–43
Subsequent history (see History of
  cases, History of statutes)
Subsidiary organs, U.N., 172, 297
Substitutions in quotations, 44–45
Subtitles of books, 109
Successive citations, short forms,
  40–43
Supplementing citations
  introductory signals to, 22–24
Supplements
  books and pamphlets, 111–12
  codes, 80
  Internal Revenue Code, 85
  separately paginated, 34
  statutory, 80
  U.N., 170
Supporting citation
  introductory signals to, 22–24
"Supra"
  court documents and legal memoran-
    da, use in, 16
  groups of authorities in work, 39–40,
    42–43
  order of authorities, 27
  previously cited authority, 42–43, 115
  textual material in work, 39–40
Supreme Court Justice sitting as
  Circuit Justice, *65,* 183
Supreme Court note, *122*
Supreme Court Foreword, *119*
Supreme Court of Judicature,
  English, 293
Supreme Court Reporter, 183
Supreme Court Review, 119
Supreme Court, U.S. (see United
  States Supreme Court)
Surnames, composed of two words,
  61
Surveys, in periodicals, 123
Switzerland
  sources of national law, 287–89
Symbols, 49–50
Symposia, in periodicals, 123

Tax Court, citation of cases, 99, 102,
  185–86
Tax materials
  cases, 102

codes, 16–17, 85
Cumulative Bulletin, 17, 101
general counsel memoranda, 17, 102
generally, 100–02
Internal Revenue Bulletin, 101
Internal Revenue Code, 16–17, 85
practitioners' citation forms, 16–17
private letter rulings, 17, *97,* 101
revenue procedures, 101
revenue rulings, *97,* 101
technical advice memoranda, 101
Treasury decisions, 101–02
Treasury regulations, 16–17, *97,* 100–01
Telephone interviews, 127–28
Television broadcasts, 142
Temporary Emergency Court of Appeals, 184
Tennessee
sources of law, 232–33
Tentative drafts, restatements, and model codes, 87
"Term," capitalization of, 53
Term of court, 53
Territories
(see also name of individual territory)
abbreviation of, 311
souces of law, 241–44
Texas
sources of law, 233–36
Text
abbreviation of case names in, 56–62
court documents and legal memoranda, typeface in, 11–13
law reviews, typeface in, 32–33
numbers in, 49–50
Textual footnote materials
typeface used in, 30–32
Textual material in same work, cross reference to, 39–40
Textual reference to statutes, 89–90
"The," in case name, 59
Theodosius, Code of, 281
Theses, unpublished, 127
Times Law Reports, 292
Titles
abbreviations, 109
articles in periodicals, 118–19
book reviews, 118–19, 121, 123
books and pamphlets, 109–10
capitalization of, 51–53, 109
codes, statutory, 79
collected documents, 112–13
congressional documents and reports, 93–94

ending with date, 109–10
foreign, 151
hearings, 93
international agreements, *157,* 158–60
multivolume works, 109–10
newspaper articles, 120
pamphlets and books, 109
personal titles, 53, 315
services, 147
student-written materials, 121–23
subtitles of books, 109
Supreme Court Justices, 53, 315
surveys and symposia, 123
treaties, *157,* 158–59
typeface, 11–12, 30–33, 109, 112, 119, 126
U.N. materials, *157–58,* 168–69
unpublished works, 112–13, 126–28
"Title(s)," abbreviation of, 349
"To," used in place of hyphen, 36
"To be codified at," 83, 98
Topical reporters (see Services and topical reporters)
Trade and Development Board official records, U.N., 172
Transcript of record, 18–19, 71
Transfer binders, services, 147
Translations of titles, 151–52
Translators of books, 108
Treasury decisions, 101–02
Treasury Decisions Under Customs and Other Laws, 188
Treasury Decisions Under Internal Revenue Laws, 101, 188
Treasury regulations, 16–17, *97,* 100–01
Treaties (see also International agreements)
citation analyzed, 9, 158–59
generally, 158–62
Treaties and Other International Acts Series (T.I.A.S.), 161, 300
Treatises, *37,* 107–12
(see also Books and pamphlets)
Treaty collections, 300
Treaty Series (T.S.), 300
Trusteeship Council Official Records, U.N., 171–72
Typed manuscripts, 127–29
Typeface
articles, authors of, 118
articles, titles of, 118–19
authors, articles, 118

386   Index

Page references in regular type are to INSTRUCTIONS; page references in *Italics* are to EXAMPLES

authors, books, 107–08
authors, works in collection, 112
bills and resolutions, *91–93*
books and pamphlets, 107, 109, 112
books, cited in court documents and legal memoranda, 12
books, cited in law reviews, 32–33
bound services, 147
case history terms, 13, 309
case names, in court documents and legal memoranda, 11–12
case names, in law review citations, 30–32
case names, in law review text, 32
citations in court documents, 11–13
codes, 79
collected works, 112–13
commentary, indication of, 29–30
constitutions, 75
court documents and legal memoranda, 11–13
documents, legislative, *93–95*
explanatory phrases in court documents and legal memoranda, 13
explanatory phrases in law review footnotes, 31
footnotes, citations in, 30–32
footnotes, text in, 32
generally, 11–13, 30–33
hearings, *93*
international agreements, *157*
interviews, *127–28*
italics, 11–13, 30
italics, in footnote citations, 30–32
italics, in law review text, 32–33
italics represented by underscoring, 11
italics showing style, 50–51
large and small capitals, 30–31, 85, 107–09, 112
large and small capitals, in footnote citations, 30–31
law review citations, 30–32
law review text, 32–33
letters, memoranda and press releases, *127*
looseleaf services, *147*
manuscripts, 127
model codes, 87
newspapers, 120
ordinances, municipal, 85–86
ordinary roman type, 11–13, 30–33
periodicals, names of, 117–19
publications, cited in court documents and legal memoranda, 12

publications, cited in law review footnotes, 31
punctuation, 32, 33
related authority, indication of, 29–30
reporters, *55–56,* 63
reports, legislative, *94–95*
restatements, 87
roman type, in footnote citations, 30–31
roman type, in text, 32–33
rules of court procedure, 86
services, 147
session laws, *81–83*
shortened citation form, *40–43*
signals, 12–13, 31
speeches, citations to, *128*
standards, 87
student-written materials, 121–22
subsequent and prior history of cases, *68,* 309
textual footnote material, 32
textual material in law reviews, 32–33
theses, *127*
titles, 109, 112
treaties and other international agreements, *157*
underscoring, use of to represent italics, 11
uniform acts, *86–87*

Unclear holdings, indication of, 67
Uncodified laws, 80
Understandings, international, 159
Uniform acts, 86–87
Uniform Adoption Act, *87*
Uniform Commercial Code (U.C.C.), *40, 86*
Uniform Laws Annotated (U.L.A.), 87
Uniform State Law, National Conference of Commissioners on, 88
Unions, in case names, 61–62
United Kingdom
   administrative materials, 291
   command numbers, 291–92
   courts and statutes, 289–91
   parliamentary materials, 291
   statutes, 290–91
   treaty source, 291–92
United Nations materials
   Charter, 174
   citation analyzed, 9, 168
   founding documents, 174
   generally, 168–74

Page references in regular type are to INSTRUCTIONS; page references in *Italics* are to EXAMPLES

mimeographed documents, 173
official records, 168–72
periodicals, 173
sales documents, 172–73
yearbook, 173
*United Nations Reports of
International Arbitration
Awards,* 301
United Nations Treaty Series
(U.N.T.S.), *9, 160, 162,* 300
United States
administrative publications, 96–104,
187–88
bankruptcy appellate panels, 65, 185
bankruptcy courts, *63,* 65, *147,* 185
Board of Tax Appeals, 99, 102, 185
circuit courts, old federal, 65, 183–84
Circuit Justices, 65, 183
Claims Court, 184
Commerce Court, 184
Court of Appeals for the Armed
Forces, 186
Court of Appeals for the Federal
Circuit, 184
Court of Appeals for Veterans Claims,
186
Court of Claims, 184
Court of Customs and Patent
Appeals, 184
Court of Customs Appeals, 184
Court of Federal Claims, 184
Court of International Trade, 184
Court of Military Appeals, 186
Court of Military Review, 186
Court of Veterans Appeals, 186
courts of appeals, 65, 183
Customs Court, 184
district courts, 65, 185
Emergency Court of Appeals, 184
international agreements, *157,*
161–62
Judicial Panel on Multidistrict
Litigation, 65, 185
Military Service Courts of Criminal
Appeals, 186
Rail Reorganization Court, 185
session laws, 81–83, 186
statutory compilations, 78–81, 186
Supreme Court (see U.S. Supreme
Court)
Tax Court, 99, 185
Temporary Emergency Court of
Appeals, 184
treaties, *157,* 161

"United States," abbreviation of, 49,
60, 62, 109
United States Code (U.S.C.)
appendix, *39,* 80, *97*
generally, *37–39,* 78, 84–85, *85, 90,*
103, 186
supplement, 80
United States Code Annotated
(U.S.C.A.), 78–79, *80,* 85, 103, 186
*United States Code Congressional &
Administrative News*
(U.S.C.C.A.N.), 77, 83, 103
United States Code Service
(U.S.C.S.), 79, *80,* 103, 186
United States Department of State
official treaty sources, 300
United States Law Week (U.S.L.W.),
65, 183, 348
United States Reports, 183
United States Supreme Court
abbreviation of, 65, 183
administrative orders, 103
capitalization of, 52
Circuit Justices, 65, 183
citation, 55–56, 183
citation in subsequent history, 55–56,
68
cite only to official reporter, 183
date of decision, 66–67
docket numbers, *56, 70*
Justice, sitting as Circuit Justice, 65,
183
Lawyer's Edition, 183
recent decisions, *55–56,* 183
renumbered and reprinted reporters,
63–64, 183
rules, 86
subsequent history, 68–69
Supreme Court Reporter, 183
U.S. Law Week, 65, 183
U.S. Reports, 183
**United States Treasury, decisions
and regulations,** 100–02
*United States Treaties and Other
International Agreements*
(U.S.T.), 161, 300
**Unofficial codes, differently num-
bered,** 80
Unofficial reporters
(see also name of individual jurisdiction)
administrative cases, 99–100
federal courts, 183–86
state courts, 14–15, 62–63

Unofficial sources
English, 292–96
international arbitration awards, 301
statutes, American, 77–79
statutes, foreign, generally, 154
Unpublished materials, 126–29
Unreported cases, *56,* 70
**"Use of," changed to *"ex rel."* in case
names,** 58
Utah
sources of law, 236–37

"Vacated," **in case history,** 309
"Vacating as moot," **in case history,** *56,*
309
Vermont
sources of law, *81,* 237
VersusLaw, 130, *131*
"Vice Chancellor," abbreviation of, 315
Videotapes, noncommercial, 142–43
Virgin Islands
sources of law, 244
Virginia
sources of law, 238
Volume number
administrative reports, 98, 100
ALI proceedings, 124
Arabic numerals, 33
books and pamphlets, 33, 109–10,
112–13
case reports, 63–64
codes, statutory, 34, 79
Common Market cases, 165
Cumulative Bulletin, 102
Federal Register, 97–98
generally, 33–34
institute publications, 124
law journals and reviews, *117,* 119
location in citation, 33–34
looseleaf services, 34, 147
month used to indicate, 148
newspaper, 120
periodicals, 33–34, 119
proceedings, 124
renumbered reports, 63
services, 33, 147
session laws, 81–82
U.N. materials, 170
World Court cases, 163–64
"Volume(s)," abbreviation of, 349

Wales (see England)
Washington
sources of law, *38,* 239

*Weekly Compilation of Presidential
Documents,* 103
Weekly Notes **and** *Weekly Law
Reports,* 292
Weight of authority (see Parenthetical
indications)
West reporters
(see also Unofficial reporters)
generally, 14–15, 62–63
West Virginia
sources of law, 239–40
Western Weekly Reports, 256
Westlaw, *72–73, 121,* 129–30, *131–32,
143–44*
"Will of," in case name, 58–59
Wisconsin
sources of law, 240–41
Working papers, *110*
World Court, *157,* 163–64, 297
World Trade Organization, 177–78
World Wide Web, 129–30, 132
(see also Internet sources)
Writers, (see Authors)
Wyoming
sources of law, 241

Years
(see also Dates)
administrative agency reports, *98*
administrative compilations, 97–98
books and pamphlets, 110–12
Code of Federal Regulations, 96, 97
codes, 80–81
Common Market cases, 164–65
enactment, session laws, 82
English statutes, 290
ethical opinions, 89
ethical rules, 89
Federal Register, 96, 97–98
forewords, 113
Internal Revenue Code, 16–17, 85
international agreements, *157,* 160
Internet, 136–37
League of Nations materials, 174
legislative materials, 91–96
model codes, 87–88
ordinances, municipal, 85–86
periodicals, 117–20
pocket parts, 111–12
prefaces, 113
regnal, in English statutes, 290
restatements, 87–88
rules of court, 86
rules of procedure, 86

Page references in regular type are to INSTRUCTIONS; page references in *Italics* are to EXAMPLES

services, 147–48
session laws, 82–83
standards, 87–88
statutes not in current code, 81–83
statutes, uniform acts, 86–87
supplements, 34, 80–81, 111–12
Treasury regulations, *97,* 100–01
treaties, *157,* 160
U.N. materials, *168,* 171
uniform acts, 86–87
volume numbers, in administrative
    reports, 33–34, 100
volume numbers, in common law
    case reporters, 33–34
volume numbers, in looseleaf ser-
    vices, 34, 147
volume numbers, in periodicals,
    33–34, 119
volume numbers, in session laws,
    81–82
Yearbooks
basic citation forms, 179
generally, *158,* 179
sales number, cited to, 172, *173*
U.N., *157–58,* 173
World Court, *158,* 163, 179
Yukon Territory
sources of national law, 255–57

Quick Reference: Court Documents and Legal Memoranda

This table gives examples of commonly used citation forms printed in the type-faces used in briefs and legal memoranda (as explained in **practitioners' note P.1**). The inside front cover and first page present these same examples in the typefaces used in law review footnotes (as explained in **rule 2**).

cases (rule 10)

reporter (rule 10.3)	Jackson v. Metro. Edison Co., 348 F. Supp. 954, 956-58 (M.D. Pa. 1972), aff'd, 483 F.2d 754 (3d Cir. 1973), aff'd, 419 U.S. 345 (1974).
	Herrick v. Lindley, 59 Ohio St. 2d 22, 23-25, 391 N.E.2d 729, 731 (1979).
service (rule 19)	In re Looney, [1987-1989 Transfer Binder] Bankr. L. Rep. (CCH) ¶ 72,447, at 93,590 (Bankr. W.D. Va. Sept. 9, 1988).
pending and unreported cases (rule 10.8.1)	Albrecht v. Stanczek, No. 87-C9535, 1991 U.S. Dist. LEXIS 5088, at *1 n.1 (N.D. Ill. Apr. 18, 1991).
	Jackson v. Virginia, No. 77-1205, slip op. at 3 (4th Cir. Aug. 3, 1978) (per curiam), aff'd, 44. U.S. 307 (1979).
	Charlesworth v. Mack, No. 90-345 (D. Mass. filed Sept. 18, 1990).
	Charlesworth v. Mack, 925 F.2d 314 (1st Cir. 1991), petition for cert. filed, 60 U.S.L.W. 3422 (U.S. Jan. 14, 1992) (No. 92-212).
constitutions (rule 11)	N.M. Const. art. IV, § 7.

statutes (rule 12)

code (rule 12.3)	Administrative Procedure Act § 6, 5 U.S.C. § 555 (1994).
	22 U.S.C. § 2567 (Supp. I 1983).
session laws (rule 12.4)	Department of Transportation Act, Pub. L. No. 89-670, § 9, 80 Stat. 931, 944-47 (1966).

legislative materials (rule 13)

unenacted bill (rule 13.2)	H.R. 3055, 94th Cong. § 2 (1976).
hearing (rule 13.3)	Toxic Substances Control Act: Hearings on S. 776 Before the Subcomm. on the Env't of the Senate Comm. on Commerce, 94th Cong. 343 (1975).
report (rule 13.4)	S. Rep. No. 89-910, at 4 (1965).
books (rule 15)	Deborah L. Rhode, Justice and Gender 56 (1989).
	Charles Dickens, Bleak House 49-55 (Norman Page ed., Penguin Books 1971) (1853).
	21 Charles Alan Wright & Arthur R. Miller, Federal Practice and Procedure § 1006 (2d ed. 1987).
pamphlets (rule 15)	Women's Bureau, U.S. Dep't of Labor, Leaflet No 55, A Working Woman's Guide to Her Job Rights (1978).
shorter works in collection (rule 15.5)	Urvashi Vaid, Prisons, in AIDS and the Law 235, 237-39 (Harlon L. Dalton et al. eds., 1987).
	Oliver Wendell Holmes, Law in Science and Science in Law, in Collected Legal Papers 210, 210 (1920).
	John Adams, Argument and Report, in 2 Legal Papers of John Adams 285, 322-35 (L. Kinvin Wroth & Hiller B. Zobel eds., 1965).

periodical materials
(rule 16)

consecutively paginated journals (rule 16.3)

Patricia J. Williams, <u>Alchemical Notes: Reconstructed Ideals from Deconstructed Rights</u>, 22 Harv. C.R.-C.L. L. Rev. 401, 407 (1987).

Thomas R. McCoy & Barry Friedman, <u>Conditional Spending: Federalism's Trojan Horse</u>, 1988 Sup. Ct. Rev. 85, 100.

student-written work (rule 16.6.2)

Mei-lan E. Wong, Note, <u>The Implications of School Choice for Children with Disabilities</u>, 103 Yale L.J. 827, 830 n.10 (1993).

Note, <u>The Death of a Lawyer</u>, 56 Colum. L. Rev. 606 (1956).

book review (rule 16.6.1)

Bruce Ackerman, <u>Robert Bork's Grand Inquisition</u>, 99 Yale L.J. 1419, 1422-25 (1990) (book review).

nonconsecutively paginated journals (rule 16.4)

Lynn Hirschberg, <u>The Misfit</u>, Vanity Fair, Apr. 1991, at 158.

newspapers (rule 16.5)

Andrew Rosenthal, <u>White House Tutors Kremlin in How a Presidency Works</u>, N.Y. Times, June 15, 1990, at A1.

<u>Cop Shoots Tire, Halts Stolen Car</u>, S.F. Chron., Oct. 10, 1975, at 43.

unpublished manuscripts (rule 17.1.1)

Adrienne D. Davis, African American Literature and the Law: Revising and Revisiting Freedom 12-15 (Dec. 1989) (unpublished manuscript, on file with The Yale Law Journal).

letters (rule 17.1.3)

Letter from Flaxman to Bertin of 4/7/96, at 2.

interviews (rule 17.1.4)

Telephone Interview with Michael Leiter, President, Harvard Law Review (Oct. 22, 1999).

forthcoming publications (rule 17.2)

Pierre Schlag, <u>Law and Phrenology</u>, 110 Harv. L. Rev. (forthcoming Jan. 1997) (manuscript at 31, on file with author).

Internet sources (rule 18.2)

J.T. Westermeier, <u>Ethical Issues for Lawyers on the Internet and World Wide Web</u>, 6 Rich. J.L. & Tech. 5, ¶ 7 (1999), <u>at</u> http://www.richmond. edu/jolt/v6il/westermeier.html.

foreign cases (rule 20.3)

common law

<u>The King v. Lockwood</u>, 99 Eng. Rep. 379 (K.B. 1782).

civil law

Entscheidungen des Bundesgerichtshofes in Zivilsachen [BGHZ] [Supreme Court] 53, 125 (126) (F.R.G.).

foreign constitutions (rule 20.4)

Grundgesetz [GG] [Constitution] art. 51 (F.R.G.).

foreign statutes (rule 20.5)

common law

Emergency Powers Act, No. 3 (1976) (Ir.).

civil law

Code civil [C. civ.] art. 1112 (Fr.).

treaties (rule 21.4)

Treaty of Friendship, Commerce and Navigation, Apr. 2, 1953, U.S.-Japan, art. X, 4 U.S.T. 2063, 2071.

United Nations official records (rule 21.7.1)

U.N. GAOR, 10th Sess., Supp. No. 6A, at 5, U.N. Doc. A/2905 (1955).

I Introduction

P Practitioners' Notes

R
1–9
General Rules of Citation and Style

R
10
Cases

R
11–14
Constitutions, Statutes, and Legislative, Administrative, and Executive Materials

R
15–18
Books, Periodical Materials, and Other Secondary Sources

R
19
Services

R
20
Foreign Materials

R
21
International Materials

T Tables and Abbreviations

X Index